Touring Euro
Central and South East
Benelux and Scandinavia

Also available:

Published by The Caravan and Motorhome Club Limited
East Grinstead House, East Grinstead
West Sussex RH19 1UA

General Enquiries: 01342 326944
Travel Service Reservations: 01342 316101
Red Pennant Overseas Holiday Insurance: 01342 336633
Website: camc.com

Editor: Kate Walters
Publishing service provided by Fyooz Ltd
Printed by Stephens & George Ltd
Merthyr Tydfil

ISBN 978-0-9932781-7-4

Maps and distance charts generated from Collins Bartholomew Digital Database

Welcome

Caravan and motorhome holidays really capture the spirit of adventure, whether you have a planned itinerary or like to see where the wind takes you there is nothing like travelling in your own home-from-home for giving you the ultimate sense of freedom. We want to make your holidays simple, so these guides are designed to give you the basic information you need while touring and help you find a pitch for the night.

As we get closer to Britain's departure from the European Union, there may be some changes to some of the information given in this book, such as customs details and pet passports. With this uncertainty it is always best to double check important details before you travel, either via official government websites which are provided in the handbook where available, or by checking the overseas advice section of www.camc.com.

As you start another year of touring adventures, I would like to thank you for continuing to buy and contribute to these unique guides. If you can, please spare five minutes to fill in one of the site report forms at the back of this book or visit www.camc.com/europereport to let us know what you think about the sites you've stayed on this year. The more site reports we receive, the more people we can help to enjoy the freedom of independent touring in Europe.

Happy touring in 2018!

Kate Walters

Kate Walters, Editor

Contents

How To Use This Guide

Planning your trip

Motoring advice

During your stay

Continental Campsites

Site Listings

How to use this guide

The Handbook

This includes general information about touring in France and Andorra, such as legal requirements, advice and regulations. The Handbook chapters are at the front of the guide and are separated as follows:

Planning Your Trip	Information you'll need before you travel including information on documents and insurance, advice on money, customs regulations and planning your channel crossings.
Motoring Advice	Advice on motoring overseas, essential equipment and roads in Europe including mountain passes and tunnels.
During Your Stay	Information for while you're away including telephone, internet and TV advice, medical information and advice on staying safe.

Country Introduction

Following on from the Handbook chapters you will find the Country Introductions containing information, regulations and advice specific to each country. You should read the Country Introduction in conjunction with the Handbook chapters before you set off on your holiday.

Campsite Entries

After the country introduction you will find the campsite entries listed alphabetically under their nearest town or village. Where there are several campsites shown in and around the same town they will be listed in clockwise order from the north.

To find a campsite look for the town or village of where you would like to stay, or use the maps at the back of the book to find a town where sites are listed.

In order to provide you with the details of as many site as possible in Touring Europe we use abbreviations in the site entries.

For a full and detailed list of these abbreviations please see the following pages of this section.

We have also included some of the most regularly used abbreviations, as well as an explanation of a campsite entry, on the fold-out on the back cover.

Campsite Fees

Campsite entries show high season fees per night for an outfit plus two adults, as at the year of the last report. Prices given may not include electricity or showers, unless indicated. Outside of the main holiday season many sites offer discounts on the prices shown and some sites may also offer a reduction for longer stays.

Campsite fees may vary to the prices stated in the site entries, especially if the site has not been reported on for a few years. You are advised to always check fees when booking, or at least before pitching, as those shown in site entries should be used as a guide only.

Site Maps

Each town and village listed alphabetically in the site entry pages has a map grid reference number, e.g. 3B4. The map grid reference number is shown on each site entry.

The maps can be found at the end of the book. The reference number will show you where each town or village is located, and the site entry will tell you how far the site is from that town. Place names are shown on the maps in two colours:
Red where we list a site which is open all year (or for at least eleven months of the year)

Black where we only list seasonal sites which close in winter.

These maps are intended for general campsite location purposes only; a detailed road map or atlas is essential for route planning and touring.

Town names in capital letters (RED, BLACK or in *ITALICS*) correspond with towns listed on the Distance Chart.

The scale of the map means that it isn't possible to show every town or village where a campsite is listed, so some sites in small villages may be listed under a nearby larger town instead.

Satellite Navigation

Most campsite entries now show a GPS (sat nav) reference. There are several different formats of writing co-ordinates, and in this guide we use decimal degrees, for example 48.85661 (latitude north) and 2.35222 (longitude east).

Minus readings, shown as -1.23456, indicate that the longitude is west of the Greenwich meridian. This will only apply to sites in the west of France, most of Spain and all of Portugal as the majority of Europe are east of the Greenwich meridian.

Manufacturers of sat navs all use different formats of co-ordinates so you may need to convert the co-ordinates before using them with your device. There are plenty of online conversion tools which enable you to do this quickly and easily - just type 'co-ordinate converter' into your search engine.

Please be aware if you are using a sat nav device some routes may take you on roads that are narrow and/or are not suitable for caravans or large outfits.

The GPS co-ordinates given in this guide are provided by members and checked wherever possible, however we cannot guarantee their accuracy due to the rural nature of most of the sites. The Caravan and Motorhome Club cannot accept responsibility for any inaccuracies, errors or omissions or for their effects.

Site Report Forms

With the exception of campsites in The Club's Overseas Site Booking Service (SBS) network, The Caravan and Motorhome Club does not inspect sites listed in this guide. Virtually all of the sites listed in Touring Europe are from site reports submitted by users of these guides. You can use the forms at the back of the book or visit camc.com/europereport tell us about great sites you have found or update the details of sites already within the books.

Sites which are not reported on for five years are deleted from the guide, so even if you visit a site and find nothing different from the site listing we'd appreciate a update to tell us as much.

You will find site report forms towards the back of this guide which we hope you will complete and return to us by freepost (please post when you are back in the UK). Use the abbreviated site report form if you are reporting no changes, or only minor changes, to a site entry. The full report form should be used for new sites or sites which have changed a lot since the last report.

You can complete both the full and abbreviated versions of the site report forms by visiting camc.com/europereport.

Please submit reports as soon as possible. Information received by mid August 2018 will be used wherever possible in the next edition of Touring Europe. Reports received after that date are still very welcome and will appear in the following edition. The editor is unable to respond individually to site reports submitted due to the large quantity that we receive.

Tips for Completing Site Reports

- If possible fill in a site report form while at the campsite. Once back at home it can be difficult to remember details of individual sites, especially if you visited several during your trip.
- When giving directions to a site, remember to include the direction of travel, e.g. 'from north on D137, turn left onto D794 signposted Combourg' or 'on N83 from Poligny turn right at petrol station in village'. Wherever possible give road numbers, junction numbers and/or kilometre post numbers, where you exit from motorways or main roads. It is also helpful to mention useful landmarks such as bridges, roundabouts, traffic lights or prominent buildings.

We very much appreciate the time and trouble you take submitting reports on campsites that you have visited; without your valuable contributions it would be impossible to update this guide.

Acknowledgements

The Caravan and Motorhome Club's thanks go to the AIT/FIA Information Centre (OTA), the Alliance Internationale de Tourisme (AIT), the Fédération International de Camping et de Caravaning (FICC) and to the national clubs and tourist offices of those countries who have assisted with this publication.

Every effort is made to ensure that information contained in this publication is accurate and that the details given in good faith in the site report forms are accurately reproduced or summarised. The Caravan and Motorhome Club Ltd has not checked these details by inspection or other investigation and cannot accept responsibility for the accuracy of these reports as provided by members and non-members, or for errors, omissions or their effects. In addition The Caravan and Motorhome Club Ltd cannot be held accountable for the quality, safety or operation of the sites concerned, or for the fact that conditions, facilities, management or prices may have changed since the last recorded visit. Any recommendations, additional comments or opinions have been contributed by caravanners and people staying on the site and are not those of The Caravan and Motorhome Club.

The inclusion of advertisements or other inserted material does not imply any form of approval or recognition, nor can The Caravan and Motorhome Club Ltd undertake any responsibility for checking the accuracy of advertising material.

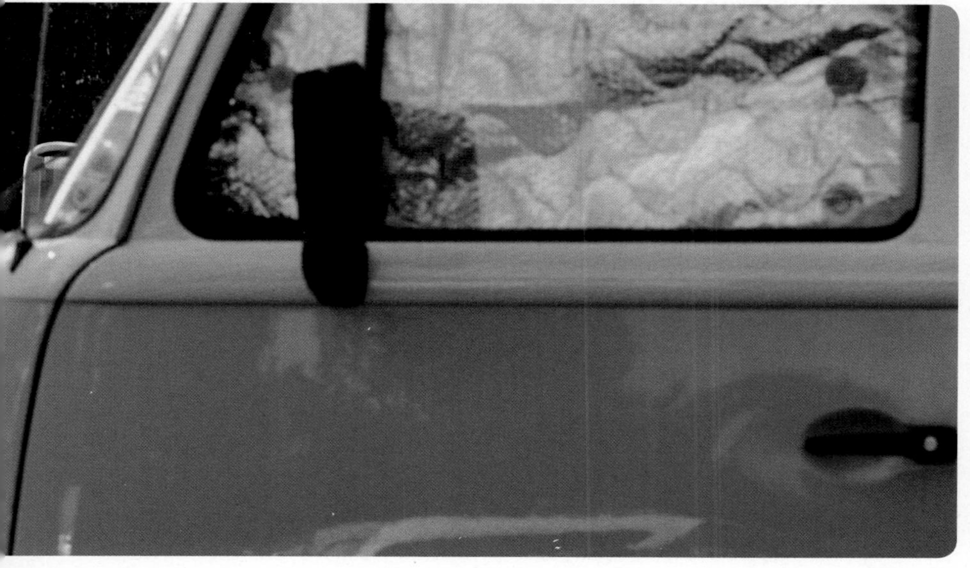

Explanation of a Campsite Entry

The town under which the campsite is listed, as shown on the relevant Sites Location Map at the end of each country's site entry pages

Distance and direction of the site from the centre of the town the site is listed under in kilometres (or metres), together with site's aspect

Site Location Map grid reference

Indicates that the site is open all year

Campsite name

Contact email and website address

Telephone and fax numbers including national code where applicable

Directions to the campsite

Description of the campsite and its facilities

The year in which the site was last reported on by a visitor

Unspecified facilities for disabled guests. If followed by 'ltd' this indicates that the facilities are limited

Charge per night in high season for car, caravan + 2 adults as at year of last report

> ⊞ **MUNSTERTAL 03B4 (1.5km W Rural) 47.85995, 7.76370 Feriencamping Münstertal, Dietzelbachstrasse 6, 79244 Münstertal [(07636) 7080; fax (07636) 7448; info@camping-muenstertal.de;www.camping-muenstertal.de]** Exit A5 junc 64a at Bad Krozingen-Staufen-Münstertal. By-pass Staufen & foll Münstertal sps. Site on L 1.5km past Camping Belchenblick off rd L123. Lge, mkd pitch, shd; wc; chem disp; mv service pnt; serviced pitches; sauna; steam rm; solarium; private bathrms avail; shwrs inc; el pnts (16A) metered; gas; lndtte; shop; rest; snacks; adventure playgrnd; 2 htd pools (1 covrd); fishing; wintersports nr; skilift 10km; tennis; horseriding; games area; games rm; beauty treatments avail; wifi; entmnt; cab TV; some statics; dogs €3.50; phone; rlwy stn 200m; gates clsd 1300-1430 & 2200-0730; m'van o'night area; adv bkg rec school hols; quiet; red long stay. CCI. "Superb, well-managed site; luxurious, clean facs; many activities for all family; gd walking; vg rest; conv Freiburg & Black Forest." ♦ € 31.55 2011*

Campsite address

GPS co-ordinates – latitude and longitude in decimal degrees. Minus figures indicate that the site is west of the Greenwich meridian

Comments and opinions of caravanners who have visited the site (within inverted commas)

Opening dates

The site accepts Camping Cheques, see the Continental Campsites chapter for details

Booking reference for a site the Club's Overseas Travel Service work with, i.e. bookable via The Club

> **BALATONSZEPEZD C1 (4km SW Rural) 46.82960, 17.64014 Balatontourist Camping Napfény, Halász út 5, 8253 Révfülöp [(87) 563031; fax 464309; napfeny@balatontourist.hu; www.balatontourist.hu]** Take m'way E71/M7 & exit junc 90 along N shore of lake, passing Balatonalmádi & Balatonfüred to Révfülöp. Site sp. Lge, mkd pitch, pt shd; wc; chem disp; mv service pnt; baby facs; private san facs avail; shwrs inc; el pnts (6A) inc; lndtte (inc dryer); shop; supmkt 500m; tradsmn; rest; snacks; bar; BBQ; playgrnd; paddling pool; lake sw & beach adj; fishing; watersports; cycle & boat hire; tennis 300m; horseriding 5km; games area; games rm; wifi; entmnt; TV rm; 2% statics; dogs HUF900; twin-axles acc (rec check in adv); phone; adv bkg; quiet; ccard acc; red low ssn. "Warm welcome; excel, well-organised lakeside site; gd pitches; gd for families; fees according to pitch size & location." ♦ 27 Apr-30 Sep. HUF 7150 (CChq acc) SBS - X06 2011*

MOT Certificate

Carry your vehicle's MOT certificate (if applicable) when driving on the Continent. You may need to show it to the authorities if your vehicle is involved in an accident, or in the event of random vehicle checks. If your MOT certificate is due to expire while you are away you should have the vehicle tested before you leave home.

Passport

In many european countries everyone is required to carry photographic ID at all times. Enter next-of-kin details in the back of your passport and keep a separate photocopy. It's also a good idea to leave a photocopy of it with a relative or friend at home.

The following information applies to British passport holders only. For information on passports issued by other countries you should contact the local embassy.

Applying for a Passport

Each person travelling out of the UK (including babies) must hold a valid passport - it is no longer possible to include children on a parent's passport. A standard British passport is valid for ten years, or 5 years for children under 16.

All newly issued UK passports are now biometric, also known as e-passports, which contain a microchip with information which can be used to authenticate the holder's identity.

Full information and application forms are available from main post offices or from the Identity & Passport Service's website, www.gov.uk where you can complete an online application. Allow at least six weeks for first-time passport applications, for which you may need to attend an interview at your nearest Identity and Passport Service (IPS) regional office. Allow three weeks for a renewal application or replacement of a lost, stolen or damaged passport.

Post offices offer a 'Check & Send' service for passport applications which can prevent delays due to errors on your application form. To find your nearest 'Check & Send' post office call 0345 611 2970 or see www.postoffice.co.uk.

Passport Validity

Most countries in the EU only require your passport to be valid for the duration of your stay. However, in case your return home is delayed it is a good idea make sure you have six month's validity remaining. Any time left on a passport (up to a maximum of nine months) will be added to the validity of your new passport on renewal.

Schengen Agreement

The Schengen Agreement allows people and vehicles to pass freely without border checks from country to country within the Schengen area (a total of 26 countries). Where there are no longer any border checks you should still not attempt to cross land borders without a full, valid passport. It is likely that random identity checks will continue to be made for the foreseeable future in areas surrounding land borders. The United Kingdom and Republic of Ireland do not fully participate in the Schengen Agreement.

Regulations for Pets

Some campsites do not accept dogs at all and some have restrictions on the number and breed of dogs allowed. Visit camc.com/overseasadvice for more informaiton and country specific advice.

In popular tourist areas local regulations may ban dogs from beaches during the summer months.

Pet Travel Scheme (PETS)

The Pet Travel Scheme (PETS) allows owners of dogs, cats and ferrets from qualifying European countries, to bring their pets into the UK (up to a limit of five per person) without quarantine. The animal must have an EU pet passport, be microchipped and be vaccinated against rabies. Dogs must also have been treated for tapeworm. It also allows pets to travel from the UK to other EU qualifying countries.

There are country specific regulations regarding certain breeds of dogs. You can't import breeds classed as dangerous dogs to many countries, and other breeds will require additional documentation. For more information or to find out which breeds are banned or restricted visit camc.com/pets or call us on 01342 336766.

Pets resident anywhere in the British Isles (excluding the Republic of Ireland) are able to travel freely within the British Isles and are not subject to PETS rules.

For details of how to obtain a Pet Passport visit www.defra.gov.uk of call 0370 241 1710.

Returning to the UK

On your return to the UK with your pet you will need to visit a vet between 24 and 120 hours prior to your return journey in order for your pet to be treated for tapeworm. The vet will need to sign your pet passport - ensure that they put the correct date against their signature or you may not fall within the correct time range for travel. Ask your campsite to recommend a local vet, or research vets near to the port you will be returning from before you travel.

Travelling with Children

Some countries require evidence of parental responsibility for people travelling alone with children, especially those who have a different surname to them (including lone parents and grandparent). The authorities may want to see a birth certificate, a letter of consent from the child's parent (or other parent if you are travelling alone with your own child) and some evidence as to your responsibility for the child.

For further information on exactly what will be required at immigration contact the Embassy or Consulate of the countries you intend to visit.

Vehicle Tax

While driving abroad you still need to have current UK vehicle tax. If your vehicle's tax is due to expire while you are abroad you may apply to re-license the vehicle at a post office, by post, or in person at a DVLA local office, up to two months in advance.

Since October 2014 the DVLA have no longer issued paper tax discs - EU Authorities are aware of this change.

Vehicle Registration Certificate (V5C)

You must always carry your Vehicle Registration Certificate (V5C) and MOT Certificate (if applicable) when taking your vehicle abroad. If yours has been lost, stolen or destroyed you should apply to a DVLA local office on form V62. Call DVLA Customer Enquiries on 0300 790 6802 for more information.

Caravan – Proof of Ownership (CRIS)

In Britain and Ireland, unlike most other European countries, caravans are not formally registered in the same way as cars. This may not be fully understood by police and other authorities on the Continent. You are strongly advised, therefore, to carry a copy of your Caravan Registration Identification Scheme (CRIS) document.

Hired or Borrowed Vehicles

If using a borrowed vehicle you must obtain a letter of authority to use the vehicle from the registered owner. You should also carry the Vehicle Registration Certificate (V5C).

In the case of hired or leased vehicles, including company cars, when the user does not normally possess the V5C, ask the company which owns the vehicle to supply a Vehicle On Hire Certificate, form VE103, which is the only legal substitute for a V5C. The BVRLA, the trade body for the vehicle rental and leasing sector, provide advice on hired or leased vehicles - see www.bvrla.co.uk or call them on 01494 434747 for more information.

If you are caught driving a hired vehicle abroad without this certificate you may be fined and/or the vehicle impounded.

Visas

British citizens holding a full UK passport do not require a visa for entry into any EU countries, although you may require a permit for stays of more than three months. Contact the relevant country's UK embassy before you travel for information.

British subjects, British overseas citizens, British dependent territories citizens and citizens of other countries may need visas that are not required by British citizens. Again check with the authorities of the country you are due to visit at their UK embassy or consulate. Citizens of other countries should apply to their own embassy, consulate or High Commission.

Insurance

Car, Motorhome and Caravan Insurance

It is important to make sure your outfit is covered whilst you are travelling abroad. Your car or motorhome insurance should cover you for driving in the EU or associated countries, but check what you are covered for before you travel. If you are travelling outside the EU or associated countries you'll need to inform your insurer and may have to pay an additional premium.

Make sure your caravan insurance includes travel outside of the UK, speak to your provider to check this. You may need to notify them of your dates of travel and may be charged an extra premium dependent on your level of cover.

The Caravan and Motorhome Club's Car, Caravan and Motorhome Insurance schemes extend to provide policy cover for travel within the EU free of charge, provided the total period of foreign travel in any one year does not exceed 270 days for Car and Motorhome Insurance and 182 for Caravan Insurance. It may be possible to extend this period, although a charge may apply.

Should you be delayed beyond these limits notify your broker or insurer immediately in order to maintain your cover until you can return to the UK.

If your outfit is damaged during ferry travel (including while loading or unloading) it must be reported to the carrier at the time of the incident. Most insurance policies will cover short sea crossings (up to 65 hours) but check with your insurer before travelling.

Visit camc.com/insurance or call 01342 336610 for full details of our Caravan Insurance or for Car or Motorhome Insurance call 0345 504 0334.

European Accident Statement

Your car or motorhome insurer may provide you with a European Accident Statement form (EAS), or you may be given one if you are involved in an accident abroad. The EAS is a standard form, available in different languages, which gives all parties involved in an accident the opportunity to agree on the facts. Signing the form doesn't mean that you are accepting liability, just that you agree with what has been stated on the form. Only sign an EAS if you are completely sure that

you understand what has been written and always make sure that you take a copy of the completed EAS.

Vehicles Left Behind Abroad

If you are involved in an accident or breakdown abroad which prevents you taking your vehicle home, you must ensure that your normal insurance will cover your vehicle if left overseas while you return home. Also check if you're covered for the cost of recovering it to your home address.

In this event you should remove all items of baggage and personal belongings from your vehicles before leaving them unattended. If this isn't possible you should check with your insurer if extended cover can be provided. In all circumstances, you must remove any valuables and items liable for customs duty, including wine, beer, spirits and cigarettes.

Legal Costs Abroad

If an accident abroad leads to you being taken to court you may find yourself liable for legal costs – even if you are not found to be at fault. Most UK vehicle insurance policies include cover for legal costs or have the option to add cover for a small additional cost – check if you are covered before you travel.

Holiday Travel Insurance

A standard motor insurance policy won't cover you for all eventualities, for example vehicle breakdown, medical expenses or accommodation so it's important to also take out adequate travel insurance. Make sure that the travel insurance you take out is suitable for a caravan or motorhome holiday.

Remember to check exemptions and exclusions, especially those relating to pre-existing medical conditions or the use of alcohol. Be sure to declare any pre-existing medical conditions to your insurer.

The Club's Red Pennant Overseas Holiday Insurance is designed specifically for touring holidays and can cover both motoring and personal use. Depending on the level of cover chosen the policy will cover you for vehicle recovery and repair, holiday continuation, medical expenses and accommodation.

Visit camc.com/redpennant for full details or call us on 01342 336633.

Holiday Insurance for Pets

Taking your pet with you? Make sure they're covered too. Some holiday insurance policies, including The Club's Red Pennant, can be extended to cover pet expenses relating to an incident normally covered under the policy – such as pet repatriation in the event that your vehicle is written off.

However in order to provide cover for pet injury or illness you will need a separate pet insurance policy which covers your pet while out of the UK. For details of The Club's Pet Insurance scheme visit camc.com/petins or call 0345 504 0336.

Home Insurance

Your home insurer may require advance notification if you are leaving your home unoccupied for 30 days or more. There may be specific requirements, such as turning off mains services (except electricity), draining water down and having somebody check your home periodically. Read your policy documents or speak to your provider.

The Club's Home Insurance policy provides full cover for up to 90 days when you are away from home (for instance when touring) and requires only common sense precautions for longer periods of unoccupancy. See camc.com/homeins or call 0345 504 0335 for details.

Personal Belongings

The majority of travellers are able to cover their valuables such as jewellery, watches, cameras, laptops, and bikes under a home insurance policy. This includes the Club's Home Insurance scheme.

Specialist gadget insurance is now commonly available and can provide valuable benefits if you are taking smart phones, tablets, laptops or other gadets on holiday with you. The Club offers a Gadget Insurance policy - visit camc.com/gadget or call 01342 779413 to find out more.

Customs Regulations

Caravans and Vehicles

You can temporarily import a caravan, trailer tent or vehicle from one EU country to another without any Customs formalities. Vehicles and caravans may be temporarily imported into non-EU countries generally for a maximum of six months in any twelve month period, provided they are not hired, sold or otherwise disposed of in that country.

If you intend to stay longer than six months, dispose of a vehicle while in another country or leave your vehicle there in storage you should seek advice well before your departure from the UK.

Borrowed Vehicles

If you are borrowing a vehicle from a friend or relative, or loaning yours to someone, you should be aware of the following:

- The total time the vehicle spends abroad must not exceed the limit for temporary importation (generally six months).
- The owner of the caravan must provide the other person with a letter of authority.
- The owner cannot accept a hire fee or reward.
- The number plate on the caravan must match the number plate on the tow car.
- Both drivers' insurers must be informed if a caravan is being towed and any additional premium must be paid.

Currency

You must declare cash of €10,000 (or equivalent in other currencies) or more when travelling between the UK and a non-EU country. The term 'cash' includes cheques, travellers' cheques, bankers' drafts, notes and coins. You don't need to declare cash when travelling within the EU.

For further information contact HMRC Excise & Customs Helpline on 0300 200 3700.

Customs Allowances

Travelling within the European Union

If you are travelling to the UK from within the EU you can bring an unlimited amount of most goods without being liable for any duty or tax, but certain rules apply. The goods must be for your own personal use, which can include use as

a gift (if the person you are gifting the goods to reimburses you this is not classed as a gift), and you must have paid duty and tax in the country where you purchased the goods. If a customs official suspects that any goods are not for your own personal use they can question you, make further checks and ultimately seize both the goods and the vehicle used to transport them. Although no limits are in place, customs officials are less likely to question you regarding your goods if they are under the following limits:

- 800 cigarettes
- 400 cigarillos
- 200 cigars
- 1kg tobacco
- 10 litres of spirits
- 20 litres of fortified wine (e.g. port or sherry)
- 90 litres of wine
- 110 litres of beer

The same rules and recommended limits apply for travel between other EU countries.

Travelling Outside the EU

There are set limits to the amount of goods you bring back into the UK from countries outside of the EU. All goods must be for your own personal use. Each person aged 17 and over is entitled to the following allowance:

- 200 cigarettes, or 100 cigarillos, or 50 cigars, or 250g tobacco
- 1 litre of spirits or strong liqueurs over 22% volume, or 2 litres of fortified wine, sparkling wine or any other alcoholic drink that's less than 22% volume
- 4 litres of still wine
- 16 litres of beer
- £390 worth of all other goods including perfume, gifts and souvenirs without having to pay tax and/or duty
- For further information contact HMRC National Advice Service on 0300 200 3700.

Medicines

There is no limit to the amount of medicines you can take abroad if they are obtained without prescription (i.e. over the counter medicines). Medicines prescribed by your doctor may contain controlled drugs (e.g. morphine), for which you will need a licence if you're leaving the UK for 3 months or more. Visit www.gov.uk/travelling-controlled-drugs or call 020 7035 0771 for a list of controlled drugs and to apply for a licence.

You don't need a licence if you carry less than 3 months' supply or your medication doesn't contain controlled drugs, but you should carry a letter from your doctor stating your name, a list of your prescribed drugs and dosages for each drug. You may have to show this letter when going through customs.

Personal Possessions

Visitors to countries within the EU are free to carry reasonable quantities of any personal possessions such as jewellery, cameras, and electrical equipment required for the duration of their stay. It is sensible to carry sales receipts for new items in case you need to prove that tax has already been paid.

Prohibited and Restricted Goods

Regardless of where you are travelling from the importation of some goods into the UK is restricted or banned, mainly to protect health and the environment. These include:

- Endangered animals or plants including live animals, birds and plants, ivory, skins, coral, hides, shells and goods made from them such as jewellery, shoes, bags and belts.
- Controlled, unlicensed or dangerous drugs.
- Counterfeit or pirated goods such as watches, CDs and clothes; goods bearing a false indication of their place of manufacture or in breach of UK copyright.
- Offensive weapons such as firearms, flick knives, knuckledusters, push daggers, self-defence sprays and stun guns.
- Pornographic material depicting extreme violence or featuring children

This list is not exhaustive; if in doubt contact HMRC on 0300 200 3700 (+44 2920 501 261 from outside the UK) or go through the red Customs channel and ask a Customs officer when returning to the UK.

Plants and Food

Travellers from within the EU may bring into the UK any fruit, vegetable or plant products without restriction as long as they are grown in the EU, are free from pests or disease and are for your own consumption. For food products Andorra, the Channel Islands, the Isle of Man, San Marino and Switzerland are treated as part of the EU.

From most countries outside the EU you are not allowed to bring into the UK any meat or dairy products. Other animal products may be severely restricted or banned and it is important that you declare any such products on entering the UK.

For up to date information contact the Department for Environment, Food and Rural Affairs (Defra) on 0345 33 55 77 or +44 20 7238 6951 from outside the UK. You can also visit www.defra.gov.uk to find out more.

Money

Being able to safely access your money while you're away is a necessity for you to enjoy your break. It isn't a good idea to rely on one method of payment, so always have a backup plan. A mixture of a small amount of cash plus one or two electronic means of payment are a good idea.

Traveller's cheques have become less popular in recent years as fewer banks and hotels are willing or able to cash them. There are alternative options which offer the same level of security but are easier to use, such as prepaid credit cards.

Local Currency

It is a good idea to take enough foreign currency for your journey and immediate needs on arrival, don't forget you may need change for tolls or parking on your journey. Currency exchange facilities will be available at ports and on ferries but rates offered may not be as good as you would find elsewhere.

The Post Office, banks, exchange offices and travel agents offer foreign exchange. All should stock Euros but during peak holiday times or if you need a large amount it may be sensible to pre-order your currency. You should also pre-order any less common currencies. Shop around and compare commission and exchange rates, together with minimum charges.

Banks and money exchanges in central and eastern Europe won't usually accept Scottish and Northern Irish bank notes and may be reluctant to change any sterling which has been written on or is creased or worn.

Foreign Currency Bank Accounts

Frequent travellers or those who spend long periods abroad may find a Euro bank account useful. Most such accounts impose no currency conversion charges for debit or credit card use and allow fee-free cash withdrawals at ATMs. Some banks may also allow you to spread your account across different currencies, depending on your circumstances. Speak to your bank about the services they offer.

Prepaid Travel Cards

Prepaid travel money cards are issued by various providers including the Post Office, Travelex, Lloyds Bank and American Express.

They are increasingly popular as the PIN protected travel money card offers the security of Traveller's Cheques, with the convenience of paying by card. You load the card with the amount you need before leaving home, and then use cash machines to make withdrawals or use the card to pay for goods and services as you would a credit or debit card. You can top the card up over the telephone or online while you are abroad. However there can be issues with using them with some automated payment systems, such as pay-at-pump petrol stations and toll booths, so you should always have an alternative payment method available.

These cards can be cheaper to use than credit or debit cards for both cash withdrawals and purchases as there are usually no loading or transaction fees to pay. In addition, because they are separate from your bank account, if the card is lost or stolen you bank account will still be secure.

Credit and Debit Cards

Credit and debit cards offer a convenient way of spending abroad. For the use of cards abroad most banks impose a foreign currency conversion charge of up to 3% per transaction. If you use your card to withdraw cash there will be a further commission charge of up to 3% and you will be charged interest (possibly at a higher rate than normal) as soon as you withdraw the money.

There are credit cards available which are specifically designed for spending overseas and will give you the best available rates. However they often have high interest rates so are only economical if you're able to pay them off in full each month.

If you have several cards, take at least two in case you encounter problems. Credit and debit 'Chip and PIN' cards issued by UK banks may not be universally accepted abroad so if check that your card will be accepted if using it in restaurants or other situations where you pay after you have received goods or services

Contact your credit or debit card issuer before you leave home to let them know that you will be travelling abroad. In the battle against card fraud, card issuers frequently query transactions which they regard as unusual or suspicious, causing your card to be declined or temporarily stopped. You should always carry your card issuer's helpline number with you so that you can contact them if this happens. You will also need this number should you need to report the loss or theft of your card.

Dynamic Currency Conversion

When you pay with a credit or debit card, retailers may offer you the choice of currency for payment, e.g. a euro amount will be converted into sterling and then charged to your card account. This is known as a 'Dynamic Currency Conversion' but the exchange rate used is likely to be worse than the rate offered by your card issuer, so will work out more expensive than paying in the local currency.

Emergency Cash

If an emergency or theft means that you need cash in a hurry, then friends or relatives at home can send you emergency cash via money transfer services. The Post Office, MoneyGram and Western Union all offer services which, allows the transfer of money to over 233,000 money transfer agents around the world. Transfers take approximately ten minutes and charges are levied on a sliding scale.

Ferries & the Channel Tunnel

Booking Your Ferry

If travelling at peak times, such as Easter or school holidays, make reservations as early as possible. Each ferry will have limited room for caravans and large vehicles so spaces can fill up quickly, especially on cheaper crossings. If you need any special assistance or arrangements request this at the time of booking.

When booking any ferry crossing, make sure you give the correct measurements for your outfit including bikes, roof boxes or anything which may add to the length or height of your vehicle - if you underestimate your vehicle's size you may be turned away or charged an additional fee.

The Caravan and Motorhome Club is an agent for most major ferry companies operating services. Call The Club's Travel Service on 01342 316 101 or see camc.com/ferries to book.

The table at the end of this section shows ferry routes from the UK to the Continent and Ireland. Some ferry routes may not be operational all year, and during peak periods there may be a limit to the number of caravans or motorhomes accepted. For the most up-to-date information visit camc.com/ferries or call the Club's Travel Services team.

On the Ferry

Arrive at the port with plenty of time before your boarding time. Motorhomes and car/caravan outfits will usually either be the first or last vehicles boarded onto the ferry. Almost all ferries are now 'drive on – drive off' so you won't be required to do any complicated manoeuvres. You may be required to show ferry staff that your gas is switched off before boarding the ferry.

Be careful using the ferry access ramps, as they are often very steep which can mean there is a risk of grounding the tow bar or caravan hitch. Drive slowly and, if your ground clearance is low, consider whether removing your jockey wheel and any stabilising devices would help.

Vehicles are often parked close together on ferries, meaning that if you have towing extension mirrors they could get knocked or damaged by people trying to get past your vehicle. If you leave them attached during the ferry crossing then make sure you check their position on returning to your vehicle.

Channel Tunnel

The Channel Tunnel operator, Eurotunnel, accepts cars, caravans and motorhomes (except those running on LPG) on their service between Folkestone and Calais. You can just turn up and see if there is availability on the day, however prices increase as it gets closer to the departure time so if you know your plans in advance it is best to book as early as possible.

On the Journey

You'll need to open your roof vents prior to travel and apply the caravan brake once you have parked your vehicle on the train. You will not be able to use your caravan until arrival.

Pets

It is possible to transport your pet on a number of ferry routes to the Continent and Ireland, as well as on Eurotunnel services from Folkestone to Calais. Advance booking is essential as restrictions apply to the number of animals allowed on any one crossing. Make sure you understand the carrier's terms and conditions for transporting pets. Brittany Ferries ask for all dogs to be muzzled when out of the vehicle but this varies for other operators so please check at the time of booking.

Once on board pets are normally required to remain in their owner's vehicle or in kennels on the car deck and you won't be able to access your vehicle to check on your pet while the ferry is at sea. On longer crossings you should make arrangements at the on-board information desk for permission to visit your pet in order to check its well-being. You should always make sure that ferry staff know your vehicle has a pet on board.

Information and advice on the welfare of animals before and during a journey is available on the website of the Department for Environment, Food and Rural Affairs (Defra), www.defra.gov.uk.

Gas

UK based ferry companies usually allow up to three gas cylinders per caravan, including the cylinder currently in use, however some may restrict this to a maximum of two cylinders. Some operators may ask you to hand over your gas cylinders to a member of the crew so that they can be safely stored during the crossing. Check that you know the rules of your ferry operator before you travel.

Cylinder valves should be fully closed and covered with a cap, if provided, and should remain closed during the crossing. Cylinders should be fixed securely in or on the caravan in the position specified by the manufacturer.

Gas cylinders must be declared at check-in and the crew may ask to inspect each cylinder for leakage before travel.

The carriage of spare petrol cans, whether full or empty, is not permitted on ferries or through the Channel Tunnel.

LPG Vehicles

Vehicles fully or partially powered by LPG can't be carried through the Channel Tunnel. Gas for domestic use (e.g. heating, lighting or cooking) can be carried, but the maximum limit is 47kg for a single bottle or 50kg in multiple bottles. Tanks must be switched off before boarding and must be less than 80% full; you will be asked to demonstrate this before you travel.

Most ferry companies will accept LPG-powered vehicles but you must let them know at the time of booking. During the crossing the tank must be no more than 75% full and it must be turned off. In the case of vehicles converted to use LPG, some ferry companies also require a certificate showing that the conversion has been carried out by a professional - before you book speak to the ferry company to see what their requirements are.

Club Sites Near Ports

If you've got a long drive to the ferry port, or want to catch an early ferry then an overnight stop near to the port gives you a relaxing start to your holiday. The following table lists Club sites which are close to ports.

Club Members can book online at camc.com or call 01342 327490. Non-members can book by calling the sites directly on the telephone numbers below when the sites are open.

Please note that Commons Wood, Fairlight Wood, Hunter's Moon, Mildenhall and Old Hartley are open to Club members only. Non-members are welcome at all other sites listed below.

Port	Nearest Club Site	Tel No.
Cairnryan	New England Bay	01776 860275
Dover, Folkestone, Channel Tunnel	Bearsted	01622 730018
	Black Horse Farm*	01303 892665
	Daleacres	01303 267679
	Fairlight Wood	01424 812333
Fishguard, Pembroke	Freshwater East	01646 672341
Harwich	Cambridge Cherry Hinton*	01223 244088
	Commons Wood*	01707 260786
	Mildenhall	01638 713089
Holyhead	Penrhos	01248 852617
Hull	York Beechwood Grange*	01904 424637
	York Rowntree Park*	01904 658997
Newcastle upon Tyne	Old Hartley	0191 237 0256
Newhaven	Brighton*	01273 626546
Plymouth	Plymouth Sound	01752 862325
Poole	Hunter's Moon*	01929 556605
Portsmouth	Rookesbury Park	01329 834085
Rosslare	River Valley	00353 (0)404 41647
Weymouth	Crossways	01305 852032

** Site open all year*

Ferry Routes and Operators

Route	Operator	Approximate Crossing Time	Maximum Frequency
Belgium			
Hull – Zeebrugge	P & O Ferries	11-14 hrs	1 daily
France			
Dover – Calais	P & O Ferries	1½ hrs	Up to 23 daily
Dover – Calais	DFDS Seaways	1½ hrs	Up to 30 daily
Dover – Dunkerque	DFDS Seaways	2 hrs	Up to 24 daily
Folkestone – Calais	Eurotunnel	35 mins	Up to 4 per hour
Newhaven – Dieppe	DFDS Seaways	4 hrs	4 daily (6 daily May - Sept)
Plymouth – Roscoff	Brittany Ferries	6-8 hrs	2 daily
Poole – St Malo (via Channel Islands)*	Condor Ferries	5 hrs	1 daily (May-Sep)
Portsmouth – Caen	Brittany Ferries	6 / 7 hrs	Up to 3 daily
Portsmouth – Cherbourg	Brittany Ferries	3 hrs	Up to 2 daily
Portsmouth – Le Havre	Brittany Ferries	3¼ or 8 hrs	1 daily (min)
Portsmouth – St Malo	Brittany Ferries	9 hrs	1 daily
Poole - Cherbourg	Brittany Ferries	4.5 hrs	1 daily
Northern Ireland			
Cairnryan – Larne	P & O Irish Sea	2 hrs	7 daily
Liverpool (Birkenhead) – Belfast	Stena Line	8 hrs	2 daily
Cairnryan – Belfast	Stena Line	2 - 3 hrs	6 daily
Republic of Ireland			
Cork – Roscoff*	Brittany Ferries	13-15 hrs	1 per week
Dublin - Cherbourg*	Irish Ferries	19 hrs	1 per week
Fishguard – Rosslare	Stena Line	3½ - 4½ hrs	2 daily
Holyhead – Dublin	Irish Ferries	2-4 hrs	Up to 6 daily
Holyhead – Dublin	Stena Line	3½ hrs	Up to 4 daily
Liverpool – Dublin	P & O Irish Sea	7½ - 8½ hrs	2 daily
Pembroke – Rosslare	Irish Ferries	4 hrs	2 daily
Rosslare – Cherbourg*	Irish Ferries	19½ hrs	2-4 per week
Rosslare – Cherbourg	Stena Line	16-19 hrs	3 per week
Rosslare – Roscoff*	Irish Ferries	19½ hrs	2-4 per week
Netherlands			
Harwich – Hook of Holland	Stena Line	7-8 hrs	2 daily
Hull – Rotterdam	P & O Ferries	11-12 hrs	1 daily
Newcastle – Ijmuiden (Amsterdam)	DFDS Seaways	15½ hrs	1 daily
Spain			
Portsmouth – Bilbao	Brittany Ferries	24 or 32 hrs	2 per week
Portsmouth or Plymouth – Santander	Brittany Ferries	20 or 32 hrs	4 per week

**Not bookable through the Club's Travel Service.*

Note: Services and routes correct at time of publication but subject to change. Check our website for the most up-to-date routes and times.

Motoring Advice

Preparing for Your Journey

The first priority in preparing your outfit for your journey should be to make sure it has a full service. Make sure that you have a fully equipped spares kit, and a spare wheel and tyre for your caravan - it is easier to get hold of them from your local dealer than to have to spend time searching for spares where you don't know the local area.

Club members should carry their UK Sites Directory & Handbook with them, as it contains a section of technical advice which may be useful when travelling.

The Club also has a free advice service covering a wide range of technical topics - download free information leaflets at www.camc.com/advice or contact the team by calling 01342 336611 or emailing technical@camc.com.

For advice on issues specific to countries other than the UK, Club members can contact the Travel Service Information Officer, email: travelserviceinfo@camc.com or call 01342 336766.

Weight Limits

From both a legal and a safety point of view, it is essential not to exceed vehicle weight limits. It is advisable to carry documentation confirming your vehicle's maximum permitted laden weight - if your Vehicle Registration Certificate (V5C) does not state this, you will need to produce alternative certification, e.g. from a weighbridge.

If you are pulled over by the police and don't have certification you will be taken to a weighbridge. If your vehicle(s) are then found to be overweight you will be liable to a fine and may have to discard items to lower the weight before you can continue on your journey.

Some Final Checks

Before you start any journey make sure you complete the following checks:

- All car and caravan or motorhome lights are working and sets of spare bulbs are packed
- The coupling is correctly seated on the towball and the breakaway cable is attached
- Windows, vents, hatches and doors are shut
- On-board water systems are drained

- Mirrors are adjusted for maximum visibility
- Corner steadies are fully wound up and the brace is handy for your arrival on site
- Any fires or flames are extinguished and the gas cylinder tap is turned off. Fire extinguishers are fully charged and close at hand
- The over-run brake is working correctly
- The jockey wheel is raised and secured, the handbrake is released.

Driving in Europe

Driving abroad for the first time can be a daunting prospect, especially when towing a caravan. Here are a few tips to make the transition easier:

- Remember that Sat Navs may take you on unsuitable roads, so have a map or atlas to hand to help you find an alternative route.
- It can be tempting to try and get to your destination as quickly as possible but we recommend travelling a maximum of 250 miles a day when towing.
- Share the driving if possible, and on long journeys plan an overnight stop.
- Remember that if you need to overtake or pull out around an obstruction you will not be able to see clearly from the driver's seat. If possible, always have a responsible adult in the passenger seat who can advise you when it is clear to pull out. If that is not possible then stay well back to get a better view and pull out slowly.
- If traffic builds up behind you, pull over safely and let it pass.
- Driving on the right should become second nature after a while, but pay particular attention when turning left, after leaving a rest area, petrol station or site or after a one-way system.
- Stop at least every two hours to stretch your legs and take a break.

Fuel

Grades of petrol sold on the Continent are comparable to those sold in the UK; 95 octane is frequently known as 'Essence' and 98 octane as 'Super'. Diesel may be called 'Gasoil' and is widely available across Europe.
E10 petrol (containing 10% Ethanol) can be found in certain countries in Europe. Most modern cars are E10 compatible, but those which aren't could be damaged by filling up with E10. Check your vehicle handbook or visit www.acea.be and search for 'E10' to find the publication 'Vehicle compatibility with new fuel standards'.

Members of The Caravan and Motorhome Club can check current average fuel prices by country at www.camc.com/overseasadvice.

Away from major roads and towns it is a good idea not to let your fuel tank run too low as you may have difficulty finding a petrol station, especially at night or on Sundays. Petrol stations offering a 24-hour service may involve an automated process, in some cases only accepting credit cards issued in the country you are in.

Automotive Liquefied Petroleum Gas (LPG)

The increasing popularity of dual-fuelled vehicles means that the availability of LPG – also known as 'autogas' or GPL – has become an important issue for more drivers.

There are different tank-filling openings in use in different countries. Currently there is no common European filling system, and you might find a variety of systems. Most Continental motorway services will have adaptors but these should be used with care – see www.autogas.ltd.uk for more information.

Low Emission Zones

Many cities in countries around Europe have introduced 'Low Emission Zones' (LEZ's) in order to regulate vehicle pollution levels. Some schemes require you to buy a windscreen sticker, pay a fee or register your vehicle before entering the zone. You may also need to provide proof that your vehicle's emissions meet the required standard.

Before you travel visit www.lowemissionzones.eu for maps and details of LEZ's across Europe. Also see the Country Introductions later in this guide for country specific information.

Motorhomes Towing Cars

If you are towing a car behind a motorhome, our advice would be to use a trailer with all four wheels of the car off the ground. Although most countries don't have specific laws banning A-frames, they may be laws in place which prohibit motor vehicle towing another motor vehicle.

Priority and Roundabouts

When driving on the Continent it can be difficult to work out which vehicles have priority in different situations. Watch out for road signs which indicate priority and read the Country Introductions later in this guide for country specific information.

Take care at intersections – you should never rely on being given right of way, even if you have priority; especially in small towns and villages where local traffic may take right of way. Always give way to public service and military vehicles and to buses and trams.

In some countries in Europe priority at roundabouts is given to vehicles entering the roundabout (i.e. on the right) unless the road signs say otherwise.

Public Transport

In general in built-up areas be prepared to stop to allow a bus to pull out from a bus stop when the driver is signalling his intention to do so.

Take particular care when school buses have stopped and passengers are getting on and off.

Overtaking trams in motion is normally only allowed on the right, unless on a one way street where you can overtake on the left if there is not enough space on the right. Do not overtake a tram near a tram stop. These may be in the centre of the road. When a tram or bus stops to allow passengers on and off, you should stop to allow them to cross to the pavement. Give way to trams which are turning across your carriageway. Don't park or stop across tram lines; trams cannot steer round obstructions!

Pedestrian Crossings

Stopping to allow pedestrians to cross at zebra crossings is not always common practice on the Continent as it is in the UK. Pedestrians expect to wait until the road is clear before crossing, while motorists behind may be taken by surprise by your stopping. The result may be a rear-end shunt or vehicles overtaking you at the crossing and putting pedestrians at risk.

Traffic Lights

Traffic lights may not be as easily visible as they are in the UK, for instance they may be smaller or suspended across the road with a smaller set on a post at the roadside. You may find that lights change directly from red to green, bypassing amber completely. Flashing amber lights generally indicate that you may proceed with caution if it is safe to do so but you must give way to pedestrians and other vehicles.

A green filter light should be treated with caution as you may still have to give way to pedestrians who have a green light to cross the road. If a light turns red as approached, continental drivers will often speed up to get through the light instead of stopping. Be aware that if you brake sharply because a traffic light has turned red as you approached, the driver behind might not be expecting it.

Motoring Equipment

Essential Equipment

The equipment that you legally have to carry differs by country. For a full list see the Essential Equipment table at the end of this chapter. Please note equipment requirements and regulations can change frequently. To keep up to date with the latest equipment information visit camc.com/overseasadvice.

Child Restraint Systems

Children under 10 years of age are not permitted to travel in front seats of vehicles, unless there are no rear seats in the vehicle, the rear seats are already occupied with other children, or there are no seat belts in the rear. In these situations a child must not be placed in the front seats in a rear-facing child seat, unless any airbag is deactivated. Children up to 10 must travel in an approved child seat or restraint system, adapted to their size. A baby up to 13kg in weight must be carried in a rear facing baby seat. A child between 9kg and 18kg in weight must be seated in a child seat. A child from 15kg in weight up to the age of 10 can use a booster seat with a seat belt.

In Andorra children under 10 years of age and under 1.5m in height must always use a restraint system that has been approved by the EU and has been adapted to their size. Children must not travel in the front of a vehicle if there are rear seats available. If they travel in the front the airbag must be deactivated and again they must use an EU approved restraint system adapted to their size.

Fire Extinguisher

As a safety precaution, an approved fire extinguisher should be carried in all vehicles. This is a legal requirement in several countries in Europe.

Lights

When driving in on the continent headlights should be adjusted to deflect to the right if they are likely to dazzle other road users. You can do this by applying beam deflectors, or some newer vehicles have a built-in adjustment system. Some modern high-density discharge (HID), xenon or halogen-type lights, may need to be taken to a dealer to make the necessary adjustment.

Remember also to adjust headlights according to the load being carried and to compensate for

the weight of the caravan on the back of your car. Even if you do not intend to drive at night, it is important to ensure that your headlights are correctly adjusted as you may need to use them in heavy rain, fog or in tunnels. If using tape or a pre-cut adhesive mask remember to remove it on your return home.

All vehicle lights must be in working condition. If your lights are not in working order you may be liable for a fine of up to €450 and confiscation of your vehicle is a possibility in some European countries.

Headlight-Flashing

On the Continent headlight-flashing is used as a warning of approach or as an overtaking signal at night, and not, as is commonly the case in the UK, an indication that you are giving way. Be more cautious with both flashing your headlights and when another driver flashes you. If a driver flashes his headlights they are generally indicating that he has priority and you should give way, contrary to standard practice in the UK.

Hazard Warning Lights

Hazard warning lights should not be used in place of a warning triangle, but should be used in addition to it.

Nationality Plate (GB/IRL)

A nationality plate must be fixed to the rear of both your car or motorhome and caravan. Checks are made and a fine may be imposed for failure to display a nationality plate correctly. If your number plates have the Euro-Symbol on them there is no requirement to display an additional GB sticker within the EU and Switzerland. If your number plate doesn't have the EU symbol or you are planning to travel outside of the EU you will need a GB sticker.

GB is the only national identification code allowed for cars registered in the UK.

Reflective Jackets/ Waistcoats

If you break down outside of a built-up area it is normally a legal requirement that anyone leaving the vehicle must be wearing a reflective jacket or waistcoat. Make sure that your jacket is accessible from inside the car as you will need to put it on before exiting the vehicle. Carry one for each passenger as well as the driver.

Route Planning

It is always a good idea to carry a road atlas or map of the countries you plan to visit, even if you have Satellite Navigation. You can find information on UK roads from Keep Moving – www.keepmoving.co.uk or call 09003 401100. Websites offering a European route mapping service include www.google.co.uk/maps, www.mappy.com or www.viamichelin.com.

Satellite Navigation/GPS

European postcodes don't cover just one street or part of a street in the same way as UK postcodes, they can cover a very large area.
GPS co-ordinates and full addresses are given for site entries in this guide wherever possible, so that you can programme your device as accurately as possible.

It is important to remember that sat nav devices don't usually allow for towing or driving a large motorhome and may try to send you down unsuitable roads. Always use your common sense, and if a road looks unsuitable find an alternative route.

Use your sat nav in conjunction with the directions given in the site entries, which have been provided by members who have actually visited. Please note that directions given in site entries have not been checked by the Caravan and Motorhome Club.

In nearly all European countries it is illegal to use car navigation systems which actively search for mobile speed cameras or interfere with police equipment (laser or radar detection).

Car navigation systems which give a warning of fixed speed camera locations are legal in most countries with the exception of France, Germany, and Switzerland where this function must be de-activated.

Seat Belts

The wearing of seat belts is compulsory throughout Europe. On-the-spot fines will be incurred for failure to wear them and, in the event of an accident failure to wear a seat belt may reduce any claim for injury. See the country introductions for specific regulations on both seat belts and car seats.

Caravan Spares

It will generally be much harder to get hold of spare parts for caravans on the continent, especially for UK manufactured caravans. It is therefore advisable to carry any commonly required spares (such as light bulbs) with you.

Take contact details of your UK dealer or manufacturer with you, as they may be able to assist in getting spares delivered to you in an emergency.

Car Spares Kits

Some car manufacturers produce spares kits; contact your dealer for details. The choice of spares will depend on the vehicle and how long you are away, but the following is a list of basic items which should cover the most common causes of breakdown:

- Radiator top hose
- Fan belt
- Fuses and bulbs
- Windscreen wiper blade
- Length of 12V electrical cable
- Tools, torch and WD40 or equivalent water repellent/ dispersant spray

Spare Wheel

Your local caravan dealer should be able to supply an appropriate spare wheel. If you have any difficulty in obtaining one, the Club's Technical Department can provide Club members with a list of suppliers on request.

Tyre legislation across Europe is more or less consistent and, while the Club has no specific knowledge of laws on the Continent regarding the use of space-saver spare wheels, there should be no problems in using such a wheel provided its use is in accordance with the manufacturer's instructions. Space-saver spare wheels are designed for short journeys to get to a place where it can be repaired and there will usually be restrictions on the distance and speed at which the vehicle should be driven.

Towbar

The vast majority of cars registered after 1 August 1998 are legally required to have a European Type approved towbar (complying with European Directive 94/20) carrying a plate giving its approval number and various technical details, including the maximum noseweight. Your car dealer or specialist towbar fitter will be able to give further advice.

All new motorhomes will need some form of type approval before they can be registered in the UK and as such can only be fitted with a type approved towbar. Older vehicles can continue to be fitted with non-approved towing brackets.

Tyres

Tyre condition has a major effect on the safe handling of your outfit. Caravan tyres must be suitable for the highest speed at which you can legally tow, even if you choose to drive slower.

Most countries require a minimum tread depth of 1.6mm but motoring organisations recommend at least 3mm. If you are planning a long journey, consider if they will still be above the legal minimum by the end of your journey.

Tyre Pressure

Tyre pressure should be checked and adjusted when the tyres are cold; checking warm tyres will result in a higher pressure reading. The correct pressures will be found in your car handbook, but unless it states otherwise to add an extra 4-6 pounds per square inch to the rear tyres of a car when towing to improve handling. Make sure you know what pressure your caravan tyres should be. Some require a pressure much higher than that normally used for cars. Check your caravan handbook for details.

Tyre Sizes

It is worth noting that some sizes of radial tyre to fit the 13" wheels commonly used on older UK caravans are virtually impossible to find in stock at retailers abroad, e.g. 175R13C.

After a Puncture

A lot of new cars now have a liquid sealant puncture repair kit instead of a spare wheel. These sealants should not be used to achieve a permanent repair and in some cases have been known to make repair of the tyre impossible. If you need to use a liquid sealant you should get the tyre repaired or replaced as soon as possible.

Following a caravan tyre puncture, especially on a single-axle caravan, it is advisable to have the opposite side (non-punctured) tyre removed from its wheel and checked inside and out for signs of damage resulting from overloading during the deflation of the punctured tyre.

Winter Driving

Snow chains must be fitted to vehicles using snow-covered roads in compliance with the relevant road signs. Fines may be imposed for non-compliance. Vehicles fitted with chains must not exceed 50 km/h (31mph).

They are not difficult to fit but it's a good idea to carry sturdy gloves to protect your hands when handling the chains in freezing conditions. Polar Automotive Ltd sells and hires out snow chains, contact them on 01892 519933, www.snowchains.com, or email: polar@snowchains.com.

In Andorra winter tyres are recommended. Snow chains must be used when road conditions necessitate their use and/or when road signs indicate.

Warning Triangles

In almost all European countries it is compulsory to carry a warning triangle which, in the event of vehicle breakdown or accident, must be placed (providing it is safe to do so) on the carriageway at least 30 metres from the vehicle. In some instances it is not compulsory to use the triangle but only when this action would endanger the driver.

A warning triangle should be placed on the road approximately 30 metres (100 metres on motorways) behind the broken down vehicle on the same side of the road. Always assemble the triangle before leaving your vehicle and walk with it so that the red, reflective surface is facing oncoming traffic. If a breakdown occurs round a blind corner, place the triangle in advance of the corner. Hazard warning lights may be used in conjunction with the triangle but they do not replace it.

Essential Equipment Table

The table below shows the essential equipment required for each country. Please note that this information was correct at the time of going to print but is subject to change. For up to date information on equipment requirements for countries in Europe visit camc.com/overseasadvice.

Country	Warning Triangle	Spare Bulbs	First Aid Kit	Reflective Jacket	Additional Equipment to be Carried/Used
Andorra	Yes (2)	Yes	Rec	Yes	Dipped headlights in poor daytime visibility. Winter tyres recommended; snow chains when road conditions or signs dictate.
Austria	Yes	Rec	Yes	Yes	Winter tyres from 1 Nov to 15 April.*
Belgium	Yes	Rec	Rec	Yes	Dipped headlights in poor daytime visibility.
Croatia	Yes (2 for vehicle with trailer)	Yes	Yes	Yes	Dipped headlights at all times from last Sunday in Oct - last Sunday in Mar. Spare bulbs compulsory if lights are xenon, neon or LED. Snow chains compulsory in winter in certain regions.*
Czech Rep	Yes	Yes	Yes	Yes	Dipped headlights at all times. Replacement fuses. Winter tyres or snow chains from 1 Nov - 31st March.*
Denmark	Yes	Rec	Rec	Rec	Dipped headlights at all times. On motorways use hazard warning lights when queues or danger ahead.
Finland	Yes	Rec	Rec	Yes	Dipped headlights at all times. Winter tyres Dec - Feb.*
France	Yes	Rec	Rec	Yes	Dipped headlights recommended at all times. Legal requirement to carry a breathalyser, but no penalty for non-compliance.

Country	Warning Triangle	Spare Bulbs	First Aid Kit	Reflective Jacket	Additional Equipment to be Carried/Used
Germany	Rec	Rec	Rec	Rec	Dipped headlights recommended at all times. Winter tyres to be used in winter weather conditions.*
Greece	Yes	Rec	Yes	Rec	Fire extinguisher compulsory. Dipped headlights in towns at night and in poor daytime visibility.
Hungary	Yes	Rec	Yes	Yes	Dipped headlights at all times outside built-up areas and in built-up areas at night. Snow chains compulsory on some roads in winter conditions.*
Italy	Yes	Rec	Rec	Yes	Dipped headlights at all times outside built-up areas and in poor visibility. Snow chains from15 Oct - 15 April.*
Luxembourg	Yes	Rec	Rec	Yes	Dipped headlights at night and daytime in bad weather.
Netherlands	Yes	Rec	Rec	Rec	Dipped headlights at night and in bad weather and recommended during the day.
Norway	Yes	Rec	Rec	Rec	Dipped headlights at all times. Winter tyres compulsory when snow or ice on the roads.*
Poland	Yes	Rec	Rec	Rec	Dipped headlights at all times. Fire extinguisher compulsory.
Portugal	Yes	Rec	Rec	Rec	Dipped headlights in poor daytime visibility, in tunnels and in lanes where traffic flow is reversible.
Slovakia	Yes	Rec	Yes	Yes	Dipped headlights at all times. Winter tyres compulsory when compact snow or ice on the road.*
Slovenia	Yes (2 for vehicle with trailer)	Yes	Rec	Yes	Dipped headlights at all times. Hazard warning lights when reversing. Use winter tyres or carry snow chains 15 Nov - 15 Mar.
Spain	Yes (2 Rec)	Rec	Rec	Yes	Dipped headlights at night, in tunnels and on 'special' roads (roadworks).
Sweden	Yes	Rec	Rec	Rec	Dipped headlights at all times. Winter tyres 1 Dec to 31 March.
Switzerland (inc Liechtenstein)	Yes	Rec	Rec	Rec	Dipped headlights recommended at all times, compulsory in tunnels. Snow chains where indicated by signs.

NOTES:
1) All countries: seat belts (if fitted) must be worn by all passengers.
2) Rec: not compulsory for foreign-registered vehicles, but strongly recommended
3) Headlamp converters, spare bulbs, fire extinguisher, first aid kit and reflective waistcoat are strongly recommended for all countries.
4) In some countries drivers who wear prescription glasses must carry a spare pair.
5) Please check information for any country before you travel. This information is to be used as a guide only and it is your responsibility to make sure you have the correct equipment.

* For more information and regulations on winter driving please see the Country Introduction.

Route Planning – North

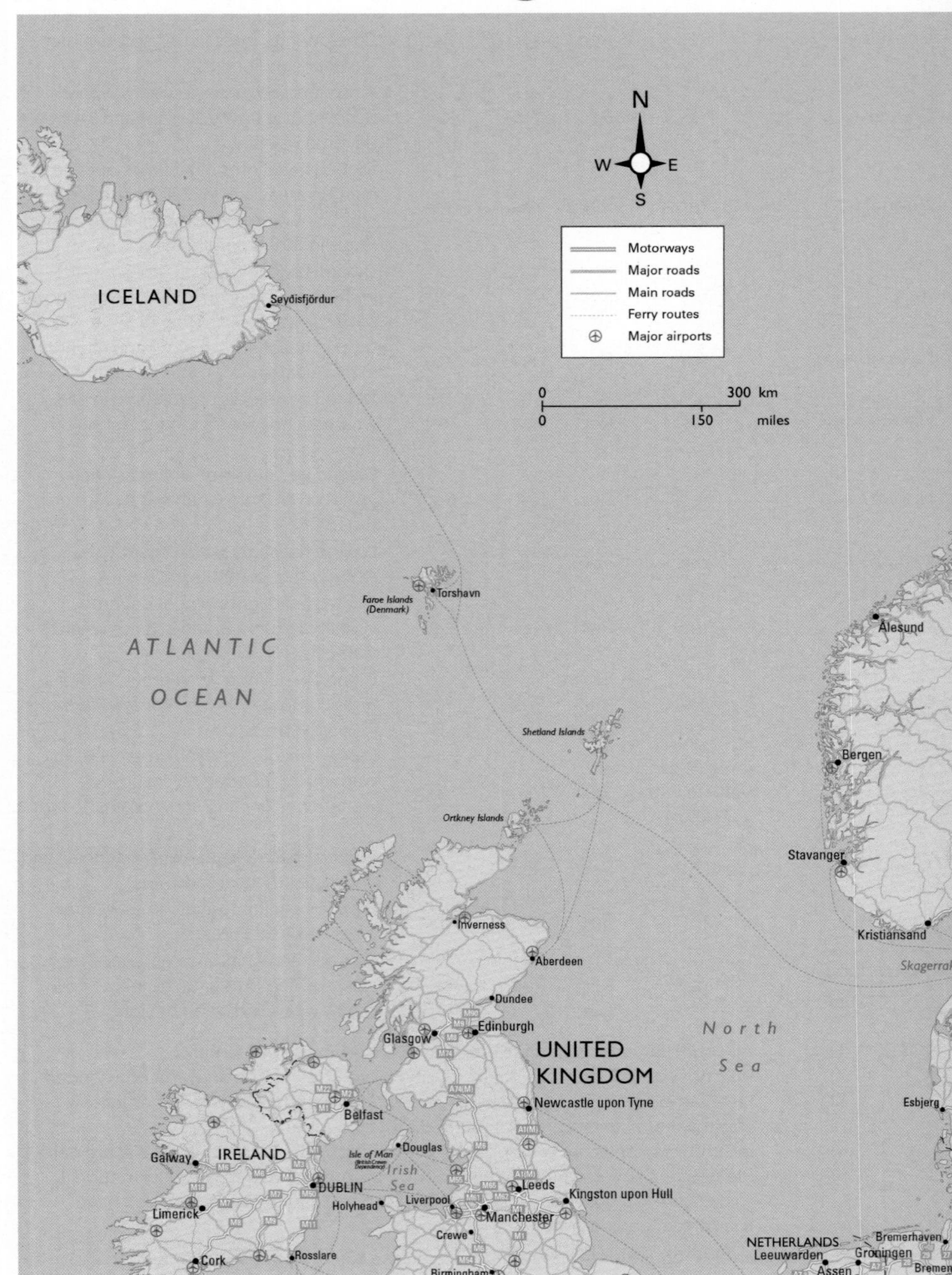

Kirkenes
Murmansk
Tromsø
Ivalo
Narvik
Kiruna
Kemijärvi
Bodø
NORWAY
Luleå
Oulu / Uleåborg
Kajaani
FINLAND
Gulf of Bothnia
SWEDEN
Umeå
Kuopio
Trondheim
Vaasa / Vasa
Petrozavodsk
Östersund
Jyväskylä
RUSSIA
Sundsvall
Tampere
Pori
Ladozhskoye Ozero
Lahti
Sankt Peterburg
Pushkin
Mora
HELSINKI / HELSINGFORS
Hamar
Gävle
Falun
Turku / Åbo
Gulf of Finland
Narva
Vårdö
Novgorod
Uppsala
TALLINN
Drammen
OSLO
Västerås
ESTONIA
Karlstad
Skien
Örebro
STOCKHOLM
Tartu
Pärnu
Pskov
Linköping
Gulf of Riga
Göteborg (Gothenburg)
Jönköping
Gotland
Visby
LATVIA
Velikiye Luki
Hirtshals
Frederikshavn
Oskarshamn
Jūrmala
RĪGA
Jelgava
Aalborg
Kalmar
Öland
Baltic Sea
Liepāja
Daugavpils
Navapolatsk
Vitsyebsk
Halmstad
Šiauliai
Panevėžys
Kattegat
Grenaa
Karlskrona
Klaipėda
LITHUANIA
KØBENHAVN
Malmö
DENMARK
Odense
VILNIUS
Kaunas
Mahilyow
RUSSIA
Kaliningrad
Marijampolė
MINSK
Rønne
Bornholm
Gedser
Sassnitz
Gdańsk
BELARUS
Babruysk
Kiel
Rostock
Hrodna
Olsztyn
Baranavichy
Hamburg
Schwerin
Białystok
Szczecin
POLAND
Bydgoszcz
GERMANY
© Collins Bartholomew Ltd 2018

Route Planning – Central

Baltic Sea
RUSSIA
LITHUANIA
POLAND
BELARUS
GERMANY
CZECHIA (CZECH REPUBLIC)
SLOVAKIA
UKRAINE
AUSTRIA
HUNGARY
ROMANIA
SLOVENIA
CROATIA
BOSNIA AND HERZEGOVINA
SERBIA
BULGARIA
MONTENEGRO
KOSOVO
MACEDONIA
ALBANIA
GREECE
ITALY
SAN MARINO
LIECHTENSTEIN
Adriatic Sea
Tyrrhenian Sea
Motorways
Major roads
Main roads
Ferry routes
Major airports
N
W
E
S
© Collins Bartholomew Ltd 2018

Route Planning – South

HUNGARY
Kecskemét
Békéscsaba
Hódmezővásárhely
Szeged
Subotica
Osijek
Novi Sad
Zrenjanin
Arad
Timișoara
Reșița
Târgu Mureș
Alba Iulia
Deva
Sibiu
Târgu Jiu
Sfântu Gheorghe
Brașov
Focșani
Tulcea
ROMANIA
Buzău
Ploiești
Slobozia
Pitești
Constanța
BUCUREȘTI
Călărași
Silistra
Drobeta-Turnu Severin
Craiova
BEOGRAD
Šabac
Tuzla
SERBIA
Kragujevac
Kraljevo
Kruševac
SARAJEVO
Mostar
Niš
Ruse
Razgrad
Dobrich
Varna
Shumen
Pleven
Vratsa
Veliko Tŭrnovo
Gabrovo
Sliven
Burgas
BULGARIA
Stara Zagora
SOFIYA
Kyustendil
Blagoevgrad
Kŭrdzhali
Kırklareli
Edirne
Tekirdağ
TURKEY
Çanakkale
Mitrovicë
MONTENEGRO
Nikšić
Pejë
PRISHTINË
KOSOVO
Prizren
PODGORICA
Kumanovo
Shkodër
SKOPJE
Veles
MACEDONIA
Prilep
Bitola
Durrës
TIRANË
Elbasan
ALBANIA
Korçë
Vlorë
Thessaloniki
Limnos
Mytilini
Lesvos (Lesbos)
Larisa
Ioannina
Kerkyra (Corfu)
İzmir
Chios
Chios
Evvoia
Aegean Sea
GREECE
ATHINA
Andros
Tinos
Patra
Agios Dimitrios
Keffalonia (Cephalonia)
Zakynthos (Zante)
Naxos
Naxos
Ionian Sea
Gytheio
Kriti (Crete)
Chania
Irakleio (Iraklion)
0 300 km
0 150 miles
© Collins Bartholomew Ltd 2018

Mountain Passes & Tunnels

Mountain Passes

Mountain passes can create difficult driving conditions, especially when towing or driving a large vehicle. You should only use them if you have a good power to weight ratio and in good driving conditions. If in any doubt as to your outfit's suitability or the weather then stick to motorway routes across mountain ranges if possible.

The tables on the following pages show which passes are not suitable for caravans, and those where caravans are not permitted. Motorhomes aren't usually included in these restrictions, but relatively low powered or very large vehicles should find an alternative route. Road signs at the foot of a pass may restrict access or offer advice, especially for heavy vehicles. Warning notices are usually posted at the foot of a pass if it is closed, or if chains or winter tyres must be used.

Caravanners are particularly sensitive to gradients and traffic/road conditions on passes. The maximum gradient is usually on the inside of bends but exercise caution if it is necessary to pull out. Always engage a lower gear before taking a hairpin bend and give priority to vehicles ascending. On mountain roads it is not the gradient which puts strain on your car but the duration of the climb and the loss of power at high altitudes: approximately 10% at 915 metres (3,000 feet) and even more as you get higher. To minimise the risk of the engine overheating, take high passes in the cool part of the day, don't climb any faster than necessary and keep the engine pulling steadily. To prevent a radiator boiling, pull off the road safely, turn the heater and blower full on and switch off air conditioning. Keep an eye on water and oil levels. Never put cold water into a boiling radiator or it may crack. Check that the radiator is not obstructed by debris sucked up during the journey.

A long descent may result in overheating brakes; select the correct gear for the gradient and avoid excessive use of brakes. Even if you are using engine braking to control speed, caravan brakes may activate due to the overrun mechanism, which may cause them to overheat.

Travelling at altitude can cause a pressure build up in tanks and water pipes. You can prevent this by slightly opening the blade valve of your portable toilet and opening a tap a fraction.

Tunnels

Long tunnels are a much more commonly seen feature in Europe than in the UK, especially in mountainous regions. Tolls are usually charged for the use of major tunnels.

Dipped headlights are usually required by law even in well-lit tunnels, so switch them on before you enter. Snow chains, if used, must be removed before entering a tunnel in lay-bys provided for this purpose.

'No overtaking' signs must be strictly observed. Never cross central single or double lines. If overtaking is permitted in twin-tube tunnels, bear in mind that it is very easy to underestimate distances and speed once inside. In order to minimise the effects of exhaust fumes close all car windows and set the ventilator to circulate air, or operate the air conditioning system coupled with the recycled air option.

If you break down, try to reach the next lay-by and call for help from an emergency phone. If you cannot reach a lay-by, place your warning triangle at least 100 metres behind your vehicle. Modern tunnels have video surveillance systems to ensure prompt assistance in an emergency. Some tunnels can extend for miles and a high number of breakdowns are due to running out of fuel so make sure you have enough before entering the tunnel.

Mountain Pass Information

The dates of opening and closing given in the following tables are approximate. Before attempting late afternoon or early morning journeys across borders, check their opening times as some borders close at night.

Gradients listed are the maximum which may be encountered on the pass and may be steeper at the inside of curves, particularly on older roads.

Gravel surfaces (such as dirt and stone chips) vary considerably; they can be dusty when dry and slippery when wet. Where known to exist, this type of surface has been noted.

In fine weather winter tyres or snow chains will only be required on very high passes, or for short periods in early or late summer. In winter conditions you will probably need to use them at altitudes exceeding 600 metres (approximately 2,000 feet).

Converting Gradients

20% = 1 in 5	11% = 1 in 9
16% = 1 in 6	10% = 1 in 8
14% = 1 in 7	8% = 1 in 12
12% = 1 in 8	6% = 1 in 16

Tables and Maps

Much of the information contained in the following tables was originally supplied by The Automobile Association and other motoring and tourist organisations. The Caravan and Motorhome Club haven't checked this information and cannot accept responsibility for the accuracy or for errors or omissions to these tables.

The mountain passes, rail and road tunnels listed in the tables are shown on the following maps. Numbers and letters against each pass or tunnel in the tables correspond with the numbers and letters on the maps.

Abbreviations

MHV	Maximum height of vehicle
MLV	Maximum length of vehicle
MWV	Maximum width of vehicle
MWR	Minimum width of road
OC	Occasionally closed between dates
UC	Usually closed between dates
UO	Usually open between dates, although a fall of snow may obstruct the road for 24-48 hours.

Major Alpine Mountain Passes

Before using any of these passes, please read the advice at the beginning of this chapter.

	Pass Height In Metres (Feet)	From To	Max Gradient	Conditions and Comments
1	**Achenpass** (Austria – Germany) 941 (3087)	Achenwald *Glashütte*	4%	UO. Well-engineered road, B181/307. Gradient not too severe.
2	**Albula** (Switzerland) 2312 (7585)	Tiefencastel *La Punt*	10%	UC Nov-early Jun. MWR 3.5m (11'6") MWV 2.25m (7'6") Inferior alternative to the Julier; fine scenery. **Not recommended for caravans.** Alternative rail tunnel.
3	**Allos** (France) 2250 (7382)	Colmars *Barcelonette*	10%	UC early Nov-early Jun. MWR 4m (13'1") Very winding, narrow, mostly unguarded pass on D908 but not difficult otherwise; passing bays on southern slope; poor surface, MWV 1.8m (5'11"). **Not recommended for caravans**.
4	**Aprica** (Italy) 1176 (3858)	Tresenda *Edolo*	9%	UO. MWR 4m (13'1") Fine scenery; good surface; well-graded on road S39. Narrow in places; watch for protruding rock. Not recommended for caravanners to attempt this pass E or W. Poor road conditions, repairs reduce width drastically.
5	**Aravis** (France) 1498 (4915)	La Clusaz *Flumet*	9%	OC Dec-Mar. MWR 4m (13'1"). Fine scenery; D909, fairly easy road. Poor surface in parts on Chamonix side. Some single-line traffic.
6	**Arlberg** (Austria) 1802 (5912)	Bludenz *Landeck*	13%	OC Dec-Apr. MWR 6m (19'8"). Good modern road B197/E60 with several pull-in places. Steeper fr W easing towards summit; heavy traffic. **Caravans prohibited.** Parallel road tunnel (tolls) available on E60 (poss long queues).
7	**Ballon d'Alsace** (France) 1178 (3865)	Giromagny *St Maurice-sur-Moselle*	11%	OC Dec-Mar. MWR 4m (13'1") Fairly straightforward ascent/descent; narrow in places; numerous bends. On road D465.
8	**Bayard** (France) 1248 (4094)	Chauffayer *Gap*	14%	UO. MWR 6m (19'8") Part of the Route Napoléon N85. Fairly easy, steepest on the S side with several hairpin bends. Negotiable by caravans from N-to-S via D1075 (N75) and Col-de-la-Croix Haute, avoiding Gap.
9	**Bernina** (Switzerland) 2330 (7644)	Pontresina *Poschiavo*	12.50%	OC Dec-Mar. MWR 5m (16'5") MWV 2.25m (7'6") Fine scenery. Good with care on open narrow sections towards summit on S-side; on road no. 29.
10	**Bracco** (Italy) 613 (2011)	Riva Trigoso *Borghetto di Vara*	14%	UO. MWR 5m (16'5") A two-lane road (P1) more severe than height suggests due to hairpins and volume of traffic; passing difficult. Rec cross early to avoid traffic. Alternative toll m'way A12 available.

Before using any of these passes, please read the advice at the beginning of this chapter.

	Pass Height In Metres (Feet)	From To	Max Gradient	Conditions and Comments
53	**Mauria** (Italy) 1298 (4258)	Lozzo di Cadore *Ampezzo*	7%	UO. MWR 5m (16'5") A well-designed road (S52) with easy, winding ascent and descent.
54	**Mendola** (Italy) 1363 (4472)	Appiano/Eppan *Sarnonico*	12.50%	UO. MWR 5m (16'5") A fairly straightforward but winding road (S42), well-guarded, many hairpins. Take care overhanging cliffs if towing. The E side going down to Bolzano is not wide enough for caravans, especially difficult on busy days, not recommended for caravans.
55	**Mont Cenis** (France – Italy) 2083 (6834)	Lanslebourg *Susa*	12.50%	UC Nov-May. MWR 5m (16'5") Approach by industrial valley. An easy highway (D1006/S25) with mostly good surface; spectacular scenery; long descent into Italy with few stopping places. Alternative Fréjus road tunnel available.
56	**Monte Croce-di-Comélico (Kreuzberg)** (Italy) 1636 (5368)	San Candido *Santo-Stefano-di-Cadore*	8.50%	UO. MWR 5m (16'5") A winding road (S52) with moderate gradients, beautiful scenery.
57	**Montgenèvre** (France – Italy) 1850 (6070)	Briançon *Cesana-Torinese*	9%	UO. MWR 5m (16'5") Easy, modern road (N94/S24), some tight hairpin bends, good road surface on French side; road widened & tunnels improved on Italian side, in need of some repair but still easy. Much used by lorries; may need to give way to large vehicles on hairpins.
58	**Monte Giovo (Jaufen)** (Italy) 2094 (6870)	Merano *Vipiteno/Sterzing*	12.50%	UC Nov-May. MWR 4m (13'1") Many well-engineered hairpin bends on S44; good scenery. **Caravans prohibited.**
	Montets (See **Forclaz**)			
59	**Morgins** (France – Switzerland) 1369 (4491)	Abondance *Monthey*	14%	UO. MWR 4m (13'1") A lesser used route (D22) through pleasant, forested countryside crossing French/Swiss border. **Not recommended for caravans.**
60	**Mosses** (Switzerland) 1445 (4740)	Aigle *Château-d'Oex*	8.50%	UO. MWR 4m (13'1") MWV 2.25m (7'6") A modern road (no. 11). Aigle side steeper and narrow in places.
61	**Nassfeld (Pramollo)** (Austria – Italy) 1530 (5020)	Tröpolach *Pontebba*	20%	OC Late Nov-Mar. MWR 4m (13'1") The winding descent on road no. 90 into Italy has been improved. **Not recommended for caravans.**
62	**Nufenen (Novena) (Switzerland)** 2478 (8130)	Ulrichen *Airolo*	10%	UC Mid Oct-mid Jun. MWR 4m (13'1") MWV 2.25m (7'6") The approach roads are narrow, with tight bends, but the road over the pass is good; negotiable with care. Long drag from Ulrichen.
63	**Oberalp** (Switzerland) 2044 (6706)	Andermatt *Disentis*	10%	UC Nov-late May. MWR 5m (16'5") MWV 2.3m (7'6") Much improved and widened road (no.19) with modern surface but narrow in places on E side; many tight hairpin bends, but long level stretch on summit. Alternative rail tunnel during the winter. **Not recommended for caravans.**

Before using any of these passes, please read the advice at the beginning of this chapter.

	Pass Height In Metres (Feet)	From To	Max Gradient	Conditions and Comments
64	**Ofen (Fuorn)** (Switzerland) 2149 (7051)	Zernez *Santa Maria-im-Münstertal*	12.50%	UO. MWR 4m (13'1") MWV 2.25m (7'6") Good road (no. 28) through Swiss National Park.
65	**Petit St Bernard** (France – Italy) 2188 (7178)	Bourg-St Maurice *Pré-St Didier*	8.50%	UC mid Oct-Jun. MWR 5m (16'5") Outstanding scenery, but poor surface and unguarded broken edges near summit. Easiest from France (D1090); sharp hairpins on climb from Italy (S26). **Caravans prohibited**.
66	**Pillon** (Switzerland) 1546 (5072)	Le Sépey *Gsteig*	9%	OC Jan-Feb. MWR 4m (13'1") MWV 2.25m (7'6") A comparatively easy modern road.
67	**Plöcken (Monte Croce-Carnico)** (Austria – Italy) 1362 (4468)	Kötschach *Paluzza*	14%	OC Dec-Apr. MWR 5m (16'5") A modern road (no. 110) with long, reconstructed sections; OC to caravans due to heavy traffic on summer weekends; delay likely at the border. Long, slow, twisty pull from S, easier from N.
68	**Pordoi** (Italy) 2239 (7346)	Arabba *Canazei*	10%	OC Dec-Apr. MWR 5m (16'5") An excellent modern road (S48) with numerous blind hairpin bends; fine scenery; used by tour coaches. Long drag when combined with Falzarego pass.
69	**Pötschen** (Austria) 982 (3222)	Bad Ischl *Bad Aussee*	9%	UO. MWR 7m (23') A modern road (no. 145). Good scenery.
70	**Radstädter-Tauern** (Austria) 1738 (5702)	Radstadt *Mauterndorf*	16%	OC Jan-Mar. MWR 5m (16'5") N ascent steep (road no. 99) but not difficult otherwise; but negotiable by light caravans using parallel toll m'way (A10) through tunnel.
71	**Résia (Reschen)** (Italy – Austria) 1504 (4934)	Spondigna *Pfunds*	10%	UO. MWR 6m (19'8") A good, straight forward alternative to the Brenner Pass. Fine views but no stopping places. On road S40/180.
72	**Restefond (La Bonette)** (France) 2802 (9193)	Barcelonnette *St Etienne-de-Tinée*	16%	UC Oct-Jun. MWR 3m (9'10") The highest pass in the Alps. Rebuilt, resurfaced road (D64) with rest area at summit – top loop narrow and unguarded. Winding with hairpin bends. **Not recommended for caravans.**
73	**Rolle** (Italy) 1970 (6463)	Predazzo *Mezzano*	9%	OC Dec-Mar. MWR 5m (16'5") A well-engineered road (S50) with many hairpin bends on both sides; very beautiful scenery; good surface.
	Rombo (See **Timmelsjoch**)			
74	**St Gotthard (San Gottardo)** (Switzerland) 2108 (6916)	Göschenen *Airolo*	10%	UC mid Oct-early Jun. MWR 6m (19'8") MHV 3.6m (11'9") MWV 2.5m (8'2") Modern, fairly easy two- to three-lane road (A2/E35). Heavy traffic. Alternative road tunnel.

Before using any of these passes, please read the advice at the beginning of this chapter.

	Pass Height In Metres (Feet)	From To	Max Gradient	Conditions and Comments
75	**San Bernardino** (Switzerland) 2066 (6778)	Mesocco *Hinterrhein*	10%	UC Oct-late Jun. MWR 4m (13'1") MWV 2.25m (7'6") Easy modern road (A13/E43) on N and S approaches to tunnel, narrow and winding over summit via tunnel suitable for caravans.
76	**Schlucht** (France) 1139 (3737)	Gérardmer *Munster*	7%	UO. MWR 5m (16'5") An extremely picturesque route (D417) crossing the Vosges mountains, with easy, wide bends on the descent. Good surface.
77	**Seeberg (Jezersko)** (Austria – Slovenia) 1218 (3996)	Eisenkappel *Kranj*	12.50%	UO. MWR 5m (16'5") An alternative to the steeper Loibl and Wurzen passes on B82/210; moderate climb with winding, hairpin ascent and descent. **Not recommended for caravans**.
78	**Sella** (Italy) 2240 (7349)	Selva *Canazei*	11%	OC Dec-Jan. MWR 5m (16'5") A well-engineered, winding road; exceptional views of Dolomites. **Caravans prohibited**.
79	**Sestriere** (Italy) 2033 (6670)	Cesana-Torinese *Pinarolo*	10%	UO MWR 6m (19'8") Mostly bitumen surface on road R23. Fairly easy; fine scenery.
80	**Silvretta (Bielerhöhe)** (Austria) 2032 (6666)	Partenen *Galtur*	11%	UC late Oct-early Jun. MWR 5m (16'5") Mostly reconstructed road (188); 32 easy hairpin bends on W ascent; E side more straightforward. Tolls charged. **Caravans prohibited**.
81	**Simplon** (Switzerland – Italy) 2005 (6578)	Brig *Domodóssola*	11%	OC Nov-Apr. MWR 7m (23') MWV 2.5m (8'2") An easy, reconstructed, modern road (E62/S33), 21km (13 miles) long, continuous ascent to summit; good views, many stopping places. Surface better on Swiss side. Alternative rail tunnel fr Kandersteg in operation from Easter to September.
82	**Splügen** (Switzerland – Italy) 2113 (6932)	Splügen *Chiavenna*	13%	UC Nov-Jun. MWR 3.5m (11'6") MHV 2.8m (9'2") MWV 2.3m (7'6") Mostly narrow, winding road (S36), with extremely tight hairpin bends, not well guarded; care also required at many tunnels/galleries. **Not recommended for caravans**.
83	**Stelvio** (Italy) 2757 (9045)	Bormio *Spondigna*	12.50%	UC Oct-late Jun. MWR 4m (13'1") MLV 10m (32') Third highest pass in Alps on S38; 40-50 acute hairpin bends either side, all well-engineered; good surface, traffic often heavy. Hairpin bends too acute for long vehicles. **Not recommended for caravans**.
84	**Susten** (Switzerland) 2224 (7297)	Innertkirchen *Wassen*	9%	UC Nov-Jun. MWR 6m (19'8") MWV 2.5m (8'2") Scenic, well-guarded road (no. 11); easy gradients and turns; heavy weekend traffic. East side easier than west. Negotiable by caravans (rec small/medium sized only) with care, not for the faint-hearted. Large summit parking area.

Before using any of these passes, please read the advice at the beginning of this chapter.

	Pass Height In Metres (Feet)	From To	Max Gradient	Conditions and Comments
85	**Tenda (Tende)** Italy – France 1321 (4334)	Borgo-San Dalmazzo *Tende*	9%	UO. MWR 6m (19'8") Well-guarded, modern road (S20/ND6204) with several hairpin bends; road tunnel (height 3.8m) at summit narrow with poor road surface. Less steep on Italian side. **Caravans prohibited during winter**.
86	**Thurn** (Austria) 1274 (4180)	Kitzbühel *Mittersill*	8.50%	UO. MWR 5m (16'5") MWV 2.5m (8' 2") A good road (no. 161) with narrow stretches; N approach rebuilt. Several good parking areas.
87	**Timmelsjoch (Rombo)** (Austria – Italy) 2509 (8232)	Obergurgl *Moso*	14%	UC mid Oct-Jun. MWR 3.5m (11'6") Border closed at night 8pm to 7am. On the pass (road no 186/S44b) **caravans are prohibited**. (toll charged), as some tunnels on Italian side too narrow for larger vehicles. Easiest N to S.
88	**Tonale** (Italy) 1883 (6178)	Edolo *Dimaro*	10%	UO. MWR 5m (16'5") A relatively easy road (S42); steepest on W; long drag. Fine views.
89	**Tre Croci** (Italy) 1809 (5935)	Cortina-d'Ampezzo *Auronzo-di-Cadore*	11%	OC Dec-Mar. MWR 6m (19'8") An easy pass on road R48; fine scenery.
90	**Turracher Höhe** (Austria) 1763 (5784)	Predlitz *Ebene-Reichenau*	23%	UO. MWR 4m (13'1") Formerly one of the steepest mountain roads (no. 95) in Austria; now improved. Steep, fairly straightforward ascent followed by a very steep descent; good surface and mainly two-lane; fine scenery. **Not recommended for caravans**.
91	**Umbrail** (Switzerland – Italy) 2501 (8205)	Santa Maria-im-Münstertal *Bormio*	9%	UC Nov-early Jun. MWR 4.3m (14'1") MWV 2.3m (7'6") Highest Swiss pass (road S38); mostly tarmac with some gravel surface. Narrow with 34 hairpin bends. **Not recommended for caravans**.
92	**Vars** (France) 2109 (6919)	St Paul-sur-Ubaye *Guillestre*	9%	OC Dec-Mar. MWR 5m (16'5") Easy winding ascent and descent on D902 with 14 hairpin bends; good surface.
93	**Wurzen (Koren)** (Austria – Slovenia) 1073 (3520)	Riegersdorf *Kranjska Gora*	20%	UO. MWR 4m (13'1") Steep two-lane road (no. 109), otherwise not particularly difficult; better on Austrian side; heavy traffic summer weekends; delays likely at the border. **Caravans prohibited**.
94	**Zirler Berg** (Austria) 1009 (3310)	Seefeld *Zirl*	16.50%	UO. MWR 7m (23') South facing escarpment, good, modern road (no. 171). Heavy tourist traffic and long steep descent with one hairpin bend into Inn Valley. Steepest section from hairpin bend down to Zirl. **Caravans not permitted northbound and not recommended southbound**.

Technical information by courtesy of the Automobile Association. Additional update and amendments supplied by caravanners and tourers who have themselves used the passes and tunnels. The Caravan and Motorhome Club has not checked the information contained in these tables and cannot accept responsibility for their accuracy, or for any errors, omissions, or their effects.

Major Alpine Rail Tunnels

Before using any of these tunnels, please read the advice at the beginning of this chapter.

	Tunnel	Route	Journey Time	General Information and Comments	Contact
A	**Albula** (Switzerland) 5.9 km (3.5 miles)	**Chur – St Moritz** Thusis to Samedan	80 mins	MHV 2.85m + MWV 1.40m or MHV 2.50m + MWV 2.20 This tunnel no longer operates a car transport service, but there are regular passenger transport services.	Thusis (081) 2884716 Samedan (081) 2885511 www.rhb.ch
B	**Furka** (Switzerland) 15.4 km (9.5 miles)	**Andermatt – Brig** Realp to Oberwald	15 mins	Hourly all year from 6am to 9pm weekdays; half-hourly weekends. MHV 3.5m Saturdays in February and March are exceptionally busy.	(027) 9277777 www.mgbahn.ch
C	**Oberalp** (Switzerland) 28 km (17.3 miles)	**Andermatt – Disentis** Andermatt to Sedrun	60 mins	MHV 2.50m 2-6 trains daily when the Oberalp Pass is closed for winter. Advance booking is compulsory.	(027) 9277777 www.mgbahn.ch
D	**Lötschberg** (Switzerland) 14 km (8.7 miles)	**Bern – Brig** Kandersteg to Goppenstein	15 mins	MHV 2.90m Frequent all year half-hourly service. Journey time 15 minutes. Advance booking unnecessary; extension to Hohtenn operates when Goppenstein-Gampel road is closed.	Kandersteg (0)900 553333 www.bls.ch/autoverlad
E	**Simplon** (Switzerland – Italy)	**Brig – Domodossola** Brig to Iselle	20 mins	10 trains daily, all year.	(0)900 300300 http://mct.sbb.ch/mct/autoverlad
	Lötschberg/ Simplon Switzerland – Italy	**Bern – Domodossola** Kandersteg to Iselle	75 mins	Limited service Easter to mid-October up to 3 days a week (up to 10 times a day) and at Christmas for vehicles max height 2.50m, motor caravans up to 5,000 kg. Advance booking compulsory.	(0)900 553333 www.bls.ch
F	**Tauerbahn** (Austria)	**Bad Gastein – Spittal an der Drau** Böckstein to Mallnitz	11 mins	East of and parallel to Grossglockner pass. Half-hourly service all year.	(05) 1717 http://autoschleuse.oebb.at
G	**Vereina** (Switzerland) 19.6 km (11.7 miles)	**Klosters – Susch** Selfranga to Sagliains	18 mins	MLV 12m Half-hourly daytime service all year. Journey time 18 minutes. Restricted capacity for vehicles over 3.30m high during winter w/ends and public holidays. Steep approach to Klosters.	(081) 2883737 www.rhb.ch

NOTES: Information believed to be correct at time of publication. Detailed timetables are available from the appropriate tourist offices. Always check for current information before you travel.

Major Alpine Road Tunnels

Before using any of these tunnels, please read the advice at the beginning of this chapter.

	Tunnel	Route and Height above Sea Level	General Information and Comments
H	**Arlberg** (Austria) 14 km (8.75 miles)	**Langen to St Anton** 1220m (4000')	On B197 parallel and to S of Arlberg Pass which is closed to caravans/trailers. **Motorway vignette required; tolls charged**. www.arlberg.com
I	**Bosruck** (Austria) 5.5 km (3.4 miles)	**Spital am Pyhrn to Selzthal** 742m (2434')	To E of Phyrn pass; with Gleinalm Tunnel (see below) forms part of A9 a'bahn between Linz & Graz. Max speed 80 km/h (50 mph). Use dipped headlights, no overtaking. Occasional emergency lay-bys with telephones. **Motorway vignette required; tolls charged**.
J	**Felbertauern** (Austria) 5.3 km (3.25 miles)	**Mittersill to Matrei** 1525m (5000')	MWR 7m (23'), tunnel height 4.5m (14'9"). On B109 W of and parallel to Grossglockner pass; downwards gradient of 9% S to N with sharp bend before N exit. Wheel chains may be needed on approach Nov-Apr. **Tolls charged**.
K	**Frejus** (France – Italy) 12.8 km (8 miles)	**Modane to Bardonecchia** 1220m (4000')	MWR 9m (29'6"), tunnel height 4.3m (14'). Min/max speed 60/70 km/h (37/44 mph). Return tickets valid until midnight on 7th day after day of issue. Season tickets are available. Approach via A43 and D1006; heavy use by freight vehicles. Good surface on approach roads. **Tolls charged**. www.sftrf.fr
L	**Gleinalm** (Austria) 8.3 km (5 miles)	**St Michael to Fiesach (nr Graz)** 817m (2680')	Part of A9 Pyhrn a'bahn. **Motorway vignette required; tolls charged**.
M	**Grand St Bernard** (Switzerland – Italy) 5.8 km (3.6 miles)	**Bourg-St Pierre to St Rhémy (Italy)** 1925m (7570')	MHV 4m (13'1"), MWV 2.55m (8'2.5"), MLV 18m (60'). Min/max speed 40/80 km/h (24/50 mph). On E27. Passport check, Customs & toll offices at entrance; breakdown bays at each end with telephones; return tickets valid one month. Although approaches are covered, wheel chains may be needed in winter. Season tickets are available. **Motorway vignette required; tolls charged**. For 24-hour information tel: (027) 7884400 (Switzerland) or 0165 780902 (Italy), www.letunnel.com
N	**Karawanken** (Austria – Slovenia) 8 km (5 miles)	**Rosenbach to Jesenice** 610m (2000')	On A11. **Motorway vignette required; tolls charged**.
O	**Mont Blanc** (France – Italy) 11.6 km (7.2 miles)	**Chamonix to Courmayeur** 1381m (4530')	MHV 4.7m (15'5"), MWV 6m (19'6") On N205 France, S26 (Italy). Max speed in tunnel 70 km/h (44 mph) – lower limits when exiting; min speed 50 km/h. Leave 150m between vehicles; ensure enough fuel for 30km. Return tickets valid until midnight on 7th day after issue. Season tickets are available. **Tolls charged**. www.tunnelmb.net

Before using any of these tunnels, please read the advice at the beginning of this chapter.

	Tunnel	Route and Height above Sea Level	General Information and Comments
P	**Munt La Schera** (Switzerland – Italy) 3.5 km (2 miles)	**Zernez to Livigno** 1706m (5597')	MHV 3.6m (11'9"), MWV 2.5m (8'2"). Open 24 hours; single lane traffic controlled by traffic lights; roads from Livogno S to the Bernina Pass and Bormio closed Dec-Apr. On N28 (Switzerland). **Tolls charged.** Tel: (081) 8561888, www.livigno.eu
Q	**St Gotthard** (Switzerland) 16.3 km (10 miles)	**Göschenen to Airolo** 1159m (3800')	Tunnel height 4.5m (14'9"), single carriageway 7.5m (25') wide. Max speed 80 km/h (50 mph). No tolls, but tunnel is part of Swiss motorway network (A2). **Motorway vignette required.** Tunnel closed 8pm to 5am Monday to Friday for periods during June and September. Heavy traffic and delays high season. www.gotthard-strassentunnel.ch
-	**Ste Marie-aux-Mines** 6.8 km (4.25 miles)	**St Dié to Ste-Marie-aux Mines** 772m (2533')	Re-opened October 2008; the longest road tunnel situated entirely in France. Also known as Maurice Lemaire Tunnel, through the Vosges in north-east France from Lusse on N159 to N59. **Tolls charged.** Alternate route via Col-de-Ste Marie on D459.
R	**San Bernardino** (Switzerland) 6.6 km (4 miles)	**Hinterrhein to San Bernadino** 1644m (5396')	Tunnel height 4.8m (15'9"), width 7m (23'). On A13 motorway. No stopping or overtaking; keep 100m between vehicles; breakdown bays with telephones. Max speed 80 km/h (50 mph). **Motorway vignette required.**
S	**Tauern and Katschberg** (Austria) 6.4 km (4 miles) & 5.4km (3.5 miles)	**Salzburg to Villach** 1340m (4396') & 1110m (3642')	The two major tunnels on the A10, height 4.5m (14'9"), width 7.5m (25'). **Motorway vignette required; tolls charged.**

NOTES: *Dipped headlights should be used (unless stated otherwise) when travelling through road tunnels, even when the road appears well lit. In some countries police make spot checks and impose on-the-spot fines. During the winter wheel chains may be required on the approaches to some tunnels. These must not be used in tunnels and lay-bys are available for the removal and refitting of wheel chains. Much of the information contained in the table was originally supplied by The Automobile Association and other motoring and tourist organisations. Updates and amendments are supplied by caravanners and tourers who have themselves used the passes and tunnels.*

The Caravan and Motorhome Club has not checked the information contained in these tables and cannot accept responsibility for their accuracy, or for any errors, omissions, or for their effects.

Alpine Countries – East

AUSTRIA
SLOVENIA
St Pölten
Traun
Wels
Amstetten
Steyr
Salzburg
Zellerrain
Lahnsattel
Hengstpass
Semmering
Pyhrnpass
Pfaffensattel
Pass Gschütt
Schoberpass
Kapfenberg
Leoben
Solker Tauern
Gaberl
Perchauer Sattel
Obdacher Sattel
Graz
Packsattel
Wolfsberg
Villach
Klagenfurt
Radlje ob Dravi
Pesnica
Dravograd
Maribor
Ravne na Koroškem
Slovenj Gradec
Jesenice
Tržič
Mozirje
Velenje
Slovenske Konjice
Slovenska Bistrica
Radovljica
Šmarje pri Jelšah
Žalec
Celje
Kranj
Kamnik
Šentjur pri Celju
Tolmin
Škofja Loka
Trbovlje
Laško
Hrastnik
Zagorje ob Savi
Domžale
LJUBLJANA
Litija
Sevnica
Udine
Idrija
Vrhnika
Krško
Gorizia
Nova Gorica
Logatec
Grosuplje
Trebnje
Brežice
Pordenone
Ajdovščina
Novo Mesto
Cerknica
Monfalcone
Portogruaro
San Donà di Piave
Piran
Izola
Jesolo
Motorway
Motorway (Proposed)
Motorway Road Tunnel
Major/Main Roads
Minor Mountain Passes (suitability for caravans not checked)
Major Mountain Passes Suitable for Caravans
Major Mountain Passes Unsuitable for Caravans
Major Rail Tunnels
Major Road Tunnels
0 10 20 30 40 50 km
These maps should be used in conjunction with the information in the Mountain Passes and Tunnels tables in this chapter.
2000m – +3000m
1000m – 2000m
100m – 1000m
0 – 100m

Alpine Countries – West

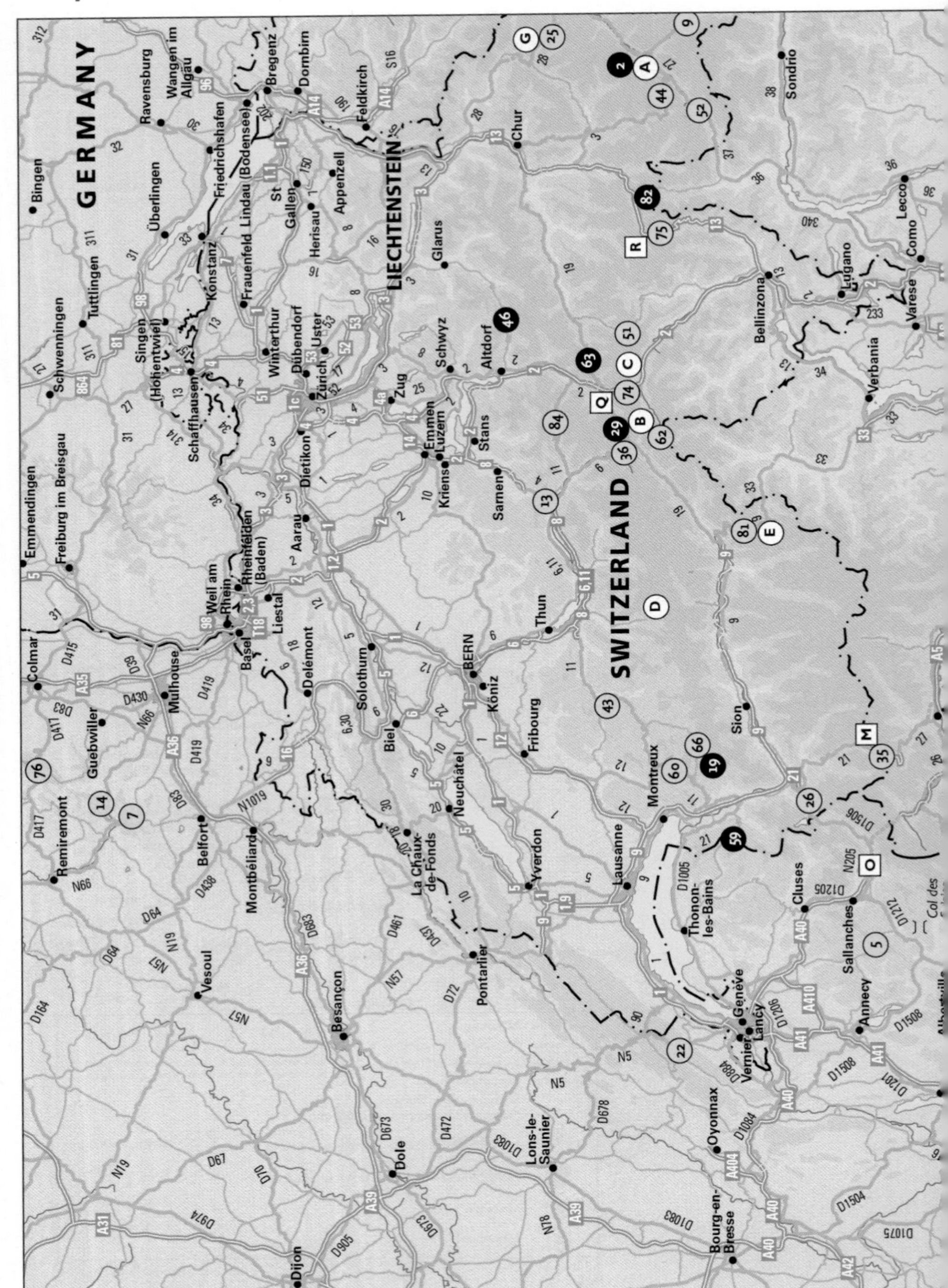

ITALY
FRANCE
MONACO
Torino
Milano
Genova
Savona
Cuneo
Grenoble
Gap
Nice
Cannes
Marseille
Toulon
Aix-en-Provence
Monte-Carlo
Menton
San Remo
Ventimiglia
Imperia
Albenga
La Spezia
Piacenza
Pavia
Alessandria
Asti
Alba
Col Agnel
Col de la Croix
Col de la Traversette
Col des Champs
Col de Maure
Col du Festre
Col de Rousset
Col de la Bataille
Col de la Croix de Fer
Col de la Bigue
Col de Gratteloup
Passo della Cisa
Motorway
Motorway (Proposed)
Motorway Road Tunnel
Major/Main Roads
Minor Mountain Passes (suitability for caravans not checked)
Major Mountain Passes Suitable for Caravans
Major Mountain Passes Unsuitable for Caravans
Major Rail Tunnels
Major Road Tunnels
0 10 20 30 40 50 km
These maps should be used in conjunction with the information in the Mountain Passes and Tunnels tables in this chapter.
2000m – +3000m
1000m – 2000m
100m – 1000m
0 – 100m
© Collins Bartholomew Ltd 2018

Keeping in Touch

Telephones and Calling

Most people need to use a telephone at some point while they're away, whether to keep in touch with family and friends back home or call ahead to sites. Even if you don't plan to use a phone while you're away, it is best to make sure you have access to one in case of emergencies.

International Direct Dial Calls

Each country has a unique dialing code you must use if phoning from outside that country. You can find the international dialing code for any country by visiting www.thephonebook.bt.com. First dial the code then the local number. If the area code starts with a zero this should be omitted.

The international access code to dial the UK from anywhere in the world is 0044.

Ringing Tones

Ringing tones vary from country to country, so may sound very different to UK tones. Some ringing tones sound similar to error or engaged tones that you would hear on a UK line.

Phone Cards

You can buy pre-paid international phone cards which offer much lower rates for international calls than most mobile phone providers. You load the card with your chosen amount (which you can top up at any time) and then dial an access code from any mobile or landline to make your call.

See www.planetphonecards.com or www.thephonecardsite.com for more details.

Using Mobile Phones Abroad

Mobile phones have an international calling option called 'roaming' which will automatically search for a local network when you switch your phone on. You should contact your service provider to ask about their roaming charges as these are partly set by the foreign networks you use and fluctuate with exchange rates. Most network providers offer added extras or 'bolt-ons' to your tariff to make the cost of calling to/from abroad cheaper.

Storing telephone numbers in your phone's contact list in international format (i.e. use the prefix of +44 and omit the initial '0') will mean that your contacts will automatically work abroad as well as in the UK.

Global SIM Cards

If you're planning on travelling to more than one country consider buying a global SIM card. This will mean your mobile phone can operate on foreign mobile networks, which will be more cost effective than your service provider's roaming charges. For details of SIM cards available, speak to your service provider or visit www.0044.co.uk or www.globalsimcard.co.uk.

You may find it simpler to buy a SIM card or cheap 'pay-as-you-go' phone abroad if you plan to make a lot for local calls, e.g. to book campsites or restaurants. This may mean that you still have higher call charges for international calls (such as calling the UK). Before buying a different SIM card, check with you provider whether your phone is locked against use on other networks.

Hands-Free

Legislation in Europe forbids the use of mobile or car phones while driving except when using hands-free equipment. In some European countries it is now also illegal to drive while wearing headphones or a headset - including hands-free kits.

If you are involved in an accident whilst driving and using a hand-held mobile phone, your insurance company may refuse to honour the claim.

Accessing the internet

Accessing the internet via your mobile (data roaming) while outside of the UK can be very expensive. It is recommended that you disable your internet access by switching 'data roaming' off to avoid a large mobile phone bill.

Internet Access

Wi-Fi is available on lots of campsites in Europe, the cost may be an additional charge or included in your pitch fee. Most larger towns may have internet cafés or libraries where you can access the internet, however lots of fast food restaurants and coffee chains now offer free Wi-Fi for customers so you can get access for the price of a coffee or bite to eat.

Many people now use their smartphones for internet access. Another option is a dongle – a device which connects to your laptop to give internet access using a mobile phone network. While these methods are economical in the UK, overseas you will be charged data roaming charges which can run into hundreds or thousands of pounds depending on how much data you use. If you plan on using your smartphone or a dongle abroad speak to your service provider before you leave the UK to make sure you understand the costs or add an overseas data roaming package to your phone contract.

Making Calls from your Laptop

If you download Skype to your laptop you can make free calls to other Skype users anywhere in the world using a Wi-Fi connection. Rates for calls to non-Skype users (landline or mobile phone) are also very competitively-priced. You will need a computer with a microphone and speakers, and a webcam is handy too. It is also possible to download Skype to an internet-enabled mobile phone to take advantage of the same low-cost calls – see www.skype.com.

Club Together

If you want to chat to other members either at home or while you're away, you can do so on The Club's online community Club Together. You can ask questions and gather opinions on the forums at camc.com/together.

Radio and Television

The BBC World Service broadcasts radio programmes 24 hours a day worldwide and you can listen on a number of platforms: online, via satellite or cable, DRM digital radio, internet radio or mobile phone. You can find detailed information and programme schedules at www.bbc.co.uk/worldservice.

Whereas analogue television signals were switched off in the UK during 2012, no date has yet been fixed for the switch off of analogue radio signals.

Digital Terrestrial Television

As in the UK, television transmissions in most of Europe have been converted to digital. The UK's high definition transmission technology may be more advanced than any currently implemented or planned in Europe. This means that digital

televisions intended for use in the UK might not be able to receive HD terrestrial signals in some countries.

Satellite Television

For English-language TV programmes the only realistic option is satellite, and satellite dishes are a common sight on campsites all over Europe. A satellite dish mounted on the caravan roof or clamped to a pole fixed to the drawbar, or one mounted on a foldable free-standing tripod, will provide good reception and minimal interference. Remember however that obstructions to the south east (such as tall trees or even mountains) or heavy rain, can interrupt the signals. A specialist dealer will be able to advise you on the best way of mounting your dish. You will also need a satellite receiver and ideally a satellite-finding meter.

The main entertainment channels such as BBC1, ITV1 and Channel 4 can be difficult to pick up in mainland Europe as they are now being transmitted by new narrow-beam satellites. A 60cm dish should pick up these channels in most of France, Belgium and the Netherlands but as you travel further afield, you'll need a progressively larger dish. See www.satelliteforcaravans.co.uk (created and operated by a Club member) for the latest changes and developments, and for information on how to set up your equipment.

Medical Matters

Before You Travel

You can find country specific medical advice, including any vaccinations you may need, from www.nhs.uk/healthcareabroad, or speak to your GP surgery. For general enquiries about medical care abroad contact NHS England on 0300 311 22 33 or email england.contactus@nhs.uk.

If you have any pre-existing medical conditions you should check with your GP that you are fit to travel. Ask your doctor for a written summary of any medical problems and a list of medications , which is especially imporant for those who use controlled drugs or hypodermic syringes.

Always make sure that you have enough medication for the duration of your holiday and some extra in case your return is delayed. Take details of the generic name of any drugs you use, as brand names may be different abroad, your blood group and details of any allergies (translations may be useful for restaurants).

An emergency dental kit is available from High Street chemists which will allow you temporarily to restore a crown, bridge or filling or to dress a broken tooth until you can get to a dentist.

A good website to check before you travel is www.nathnac.org/travel which gives general health and safety advice, as well as highlighting potential health risks by country.

European Heath Insurance Card (EHIC)

Before leaving home apply for a European Health Insurance Card (EHIC). British residents temporarily visiting another EU country are entitled to receive state-provided emergency treatment during their stay on the same terms as residents of those countries, but you must have a valid EHIC to claim these services.

To apply for your EHIC visit www.ehic.org.uk, call 0300 330 1350 or pick up an application form from a post office. An EHIC is required by each individual family member - children under 16 must be included in a parent or guardian's application.

The EHIC is free of charge, is valid for up to five years and can be renewed up to six months before its expiry date. Before you travel remember to check that your EHIC is still valid.

An EHIC is not a substitute for travel insurance and it is strongly recommended that you arrange

full travel insurance before leaving home regardless of the cover provided by your EHIC. Some insurance companies require you to have an EHIC and some will waive the policy excess if an EHIC has been used.

If your EHIC is stolen or lost while you are abroad contact 0044 191 2127500 for help. If you experience difficulties in getting your EHIC accepted, telephone the Department for Work & Pensions for assistance on the overseas healthcare team line 0044 (0)191 218 1999 between 8am to 5pm Monday to Friday. Residents of the Republic of Ireland, the Isle of Man and Channel Islands, should check with their own health authorities about reciprocal arrangements with other countries.

Holiday Travel Insurance

Despite the fact that you have an EHIC you may incur thousands of pounds of medical costs if you fall ill or have an accident. The cost of bringing a person back to the UK, in the event of illness or death, is never covered by the EHIC. You may also find that you end up with a bill for treatment as not all countries offer free healthcare.

Separate additional travel insurance adequate for your destination is essential, such as the Club's Red Pennant Overseas Holiday Insurance – see camc.com/redpennant.

First Aid

A first aid kit containing at least the basic requirements is an essential item, and in some countries it is compulsory to carry one in your vehicle (see the Essential Equipment Table in the chapter Motoring – Equipment). Kits should contain items such as sterile pads, assorted dressings, bandages and plasters, antiseptic wipes or cream, cotton wool, scissors, eye bath and tweezers. Also make sure you carry something for upset stomachs, painkillers and an antihistamine in case of hay fever or mild allergic reactions.

If you're travelling to remote areas then you may find it useful to carry a good first aid manual. The British Red Cross publishes a comprehensive First Aid Manual in conjunction with St John Ambulance and St Andrew's Ambulance Association.

Accidents and Emergencies

If you are involved in or witness a road accident the police may want to question you about it. If possible take photographs or make sketches of the scene, and write a few notes about what happened as it may be more difficult to remember the details at a later date.

For sports activities such as skiing and mountaineering, travel insurance must include provision for covering the cost of mountain and helicopter rescue. Visitors to the Savoie and Haute-Savoie areas should be aware that an accident or illness may result in a transfer to Switzerland for hospital treatment. There is a reciprocal healthcare agreement for British citizens visiting Switzerland but you will be required to pay the full costs of treatment and afterwards apply for a refund.

Sun Protection

Never under-estimate how ill exposure to the sun can make you. If you are not used to the heat it is very easy to fall victim to heat exhaustion or heat stroke. Avoid sitting in the sun between 11am and 3pm and cover your head if sitting or walking in the sun. Use a good quality sun-cream with high sun protection factor (SPF) and re-apply frequently. Make sure you drink plenty of fluids.

Tick-Borne Encephalitis (TBE) and Lyme Disease

Hikers and outdoor sports enthusiasts planning trips to forested, rural areas should be aware of tick-borne encephalitis, which is transmitted by the bite of an infected tick. If you think you may be at risk, seek medical advice on prevention and immunisation before you leave the UK.

There is no vaccine against Lyme disease, an equally serious tick-borne infection, which, if left untreated, can attack the nervous system and joints. You can minimise the risk by using an insect repellent containing DEET, wearing long sleeves and long trousers, and checking for ticks after outdoor activity. Avoid unpasteurised dairy products in risk areas. See www.tickalert.org or telephone 01943 468010 for more information.

Water and food

Water from mains supplies throughout Europe is generally safe, but may be treated with chemicals which make it taste different to tap water in the UK. If in any doubt, always drink bottled water or boil it before drinking.

Food poisoning is potential anywhere, and a complete change of diet may upset your stomach as well. In hot conditions avoid any food that hasn't been refrigerated or hot food that has been left to cool. Be sensible about the food that you eat – don't eat unpasteurised or undercooked food and if you aren't sure about the freshness of meat or seafood then it is best avoided.

Returning Home

If you become ill on your return home tell your doctor that you have been abroad and which countries you have visited. Even if you have received medical treatment in another country, always consult your doctor if you have been bitten or scratched by an animal while on holiday. If you were given any medicines in another country, it may be illegal to bring them back into the UK. If in doubt, declare them at Customs when you return.

Electricity and Gas

Electricity – General Advice

The voltage for mains electricity is 230V across the EU, but varying degrees of 'acceptable tolerance' mean you may find variations in the actual voltage. Most appliances sold in the UK are 220-240V so should work correctly. However, some high-powered equipment, such as microwave ovens, may not function well – check your instruction manual for any specific instructions. Appliances marked with 'CE' have been designed to meet the requirements of relevant European directives. The table below gives an approximate idea of which appliances can be used based on the amperage which is being supplied (although not all appliances should be used at the same time). You can work it out more accurately by making a note of the wattage of each appliance in your caravan. The wattages given are based on appliances designed for use in caravans and motorhomes. Household kettles, for example, have at least a 2000W element. Each caravan circuit will also have a maximum amp rating which should not be exceeded.

Amps	Wattage (Approx)	Fridge	Battery Charger	Air Conditioning	LCD TV	Water Heater	Kettle (750W)	Heater (1kW)
2	400	✓	✓					
4	900	✓	✓		✓	✓		
6	1300	✓	✓	*	✓	✓	✓	
8	1800	✓	✓	✓**	✓	✓	✓	✓**
10	2300	✓	✓	✓**	✓	✓	✓	✓**
16	3600	✓	✓	✓	✓	✓	✓	✓**

* Usage possible, depending on wattage of appliance in question
** Not to be used at the same time as other high-wattage equipment

Electrical Connections – EN60309-2 (CEE17)

EN60309-2 (formerly known as CEE17) is the European Standard for all newly fitted connectors. Most sites should now have these connectors, however there is no requirement to replace connectors which were installed before this was standardised so you may still find some sites where your UK 3 pin connector doesn't fit. For this reason it is a good idea to carry a 2-pin adapter. If you are already on site and find your connector doesn't fit, ask campsite staff to borrow or hire an adaptor. You may still encounter a poor electrical supply on site even with an EN60309-2 connection.

If the campsite does not have a modern EN60309-2 (CEE17) supply, ask to see the electrical protection for the socket outlet. If there is a device marked with IDn = 30mA, then the risk is minimised.

Hooking Up to the Mains

Connection should always be made in the following order:

- Check your outfit isolating switch is at 'off'.
- Uncoil the connecting cable from the drum. A coiled cable with current flowing through it may overheat. Take your cable and insert the connector (female end) into your outfit inlet.
- Insert the plug (male end) into the site outlet socket.
- Switch outfit isolating switch to 'on'.
- Use a polarity tester in one of the 13A sockets in the outfit to check all connections are correctly wired. Never leave it in the socket. Some caravans have these devices built in as standard.

It is recommended that the supply is not used if the polarity is incorrect (see Reversed Polarity overleaf).

Warnings:

If you are in any doubt of the safety of the system, if you don't receive electricity once connected or if the supply stops then contact the site staff.

If the fault is found to be with your outfit then call a qualified electrician rather than trying to fix the problem yourself.

To ensure your safety you should never use an electrical system which you can't confirm to be safe. Use a mains tester such as the one shown above to test the electrical supply.

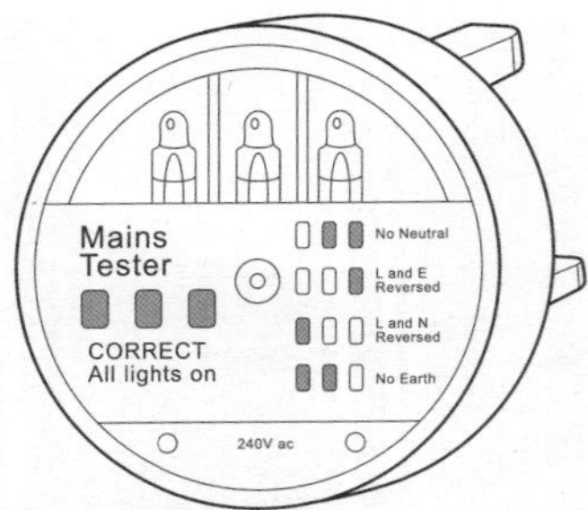

Always check that a proper earth connection exists before using the electrics. Please note that these testers may not pick up all earth faults so if there is any doubt as to the integrity of the earth system do not use the electrical supply.

Disconnection

- Switch your outfit isolating switch to 'off'.
- At the site supply socket withdraw the plug.
- Disconnect the cable from your outfit.

Motorhomes – if leaving your pitch during the day, don't leave your mains cable plugged into the site supply, as this creates a hazard if the exposed live connections in the plug are touched or if the cable is not seen during grass-cutting.

Reversed Polarity

Even if the site connector meets European Standard EN60309-2 (CEE17), British caravanners are still likely to encounter the problem known as reversed polarity. This is where the site supply 'live' line connects to the outfit's 'neutral' and vice versa. You should always check the polarity immediately on connection, using a polarity tester available from caravan accessory shops. If polarity is reversed the caravan mains electricity should not be used. Try using another nearby socket instead. Frequent travellers to the Continent can make up an adaptor themselves, or ask an electrician to make one for you, with the live and neutral wires reversed. Using a reversed polarity socket will probably not affect how an electrical appliance works, however your protection is greatly reduced. For example, a lamp socket may still be live as you touch it while replacing a blown bulb, even if the light switch is turned off.

Shaver Sockets

Most campsites provide shaver sockets with a voltage of 220V or 110V. Using an incorrect voltage may cause the shaver to become hot or break. The 2-pin adaptor available in the UK may not fit Continental sockets so it is advisable to buy 2-pin adaptors on the Continent. Many modern shavers will work on a range of voltages which make them suitable for travelling abroad. Check you instruction manual to see if this is the case.

Gas – General Advice

Gas usage can be difficult to predict as so many factors, such as temperature and how often you eat out, can affect the amount you need. As a rough guide allow 0.45kg of gas a day for normal summer usage.

With the exception of Campingaz, LPG cylinders normally available in the UK cannot be exchanged abroad. If possible, take enough gas with you and bring back the empty cylinders. Always check how many you can take with you as ferry and tunnel operators may restrict the number of cylinders you are permitted to carry for safety reasons.

Site Hooking Up Adaptor

ADAPTATEUR DE PRISE AU SITE (SECTEUR)
CAMPINGPLATZ-ANSCHLUSS (NETZ)

EXTENSION LEAD TO CARAVAN
Câble de rallonge à la caravane
Verlâengerungskabel zum wohnwagen

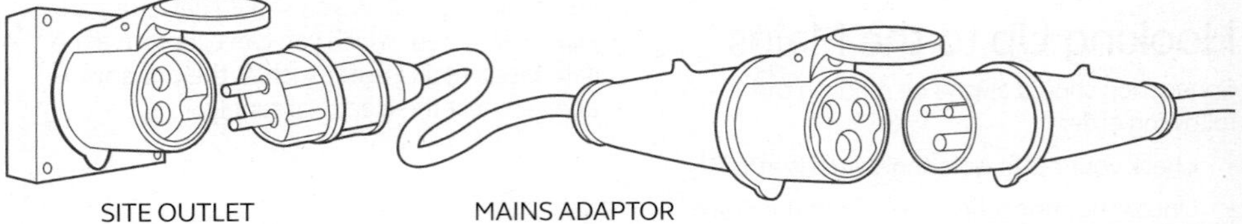

SITE OUTLET
Prise du site
Campingplatz-Steckdose

MAINS ADAPTOR
Adaptateur Secteur
Netzanschlußstacker

16A 230V AC

The full range of Campingaz cylinders is widely available from large supermarkets and hypermarkets, although at the end of the holiday season stocks may be low. Other popular brands of gas are Primagaz, Butagaz, Totalgaz and Le Cube. A loan deposit is required and if you are buying a cylinder for the first time you may also need to buy the appropriate regulator or adaptor hose.

If you are touring in cold weather conditions use propane gas instead of butane. Many other brands of gas are available in different countries and, as long as you have the correct regulator, adaptor and hose and the cylinders fit in your gas locker these local brands can also be used.

Gas cylinders are now standardised with a pressure of 30mbar for both butane and propane within the EU. On UK-specification caravans and motorhomes (2004 models and later) a 30mbar regulator suited to both propane and butane use is fitted to the bulkhead of the gas locker. This is connected to the cylinder with a connecting hose (and sometimes an adaptor) to suit different brands or types of gas. Older outfits and some foreign-built ones may use a cylinder-mounted regulator, which may need to be changed to suit different brands or types of gas.

Warnings:

- Refilling gas cylinders intended to be exchanged is against the law in most countries, however you may still find that some sites and dealers will offer to refill cylinders for you. Never take them up on this service as it can be dangerous; the cylinders haven't been designed for user-refilling and it is possible to overfill them with catastrophic consequences.
- Regular servicing of gas appliances is important as a faulty appliance can emit carbon monoxide, which could prove fatal. Check your vehicle or appliance handbook for service recommendations.
- Never use a hob or oven as a space heater.

The Caravan and Motorhome Club publishes a range of technical leaflets for its members including detailed advice on the use of electricity and gas – you can request copies or see camc.com/advice-and-training.

Safety and Security

EU countries have good legislation in place to protect your safety wherever possible. However accidents and crime will still occur and taking sensible precautions can help to minimise your risk of being involved.

Beaches, Lakes and Rivers

Check for any warning signs or flags before you swim and ensure that you know what they mean. Check the depth of water before diving and avoid diving or jumping into murky water as submerged objects may not be visible. Familiarise yourself with the location of safety apparatus and/or lifeguards.

Use only the designated areas for swimming, watersports and boating and always use life jackets where appropriate. Watch out for tides, undertows, currents and wind strength and direction before swimming in the sea. This applies in particular when using inflatables, windsurfing equipment, body boards, kayaks or sailing boats. Sudden changes of wave and weather conditions combined with fast tides and currents are particularly dangerous.

Campsite Safety

Once you've settled in, take a walk around the site to familiarise yourself with its layout and locate the nearest safety equipment. Ensure that children know their way around and where your pitch is.

Natural disasters are rare, but always think about what could happen. A combination of heavy rain and a riverside pitch could lead to flash flooding, for example, so make yourself aware of site evacuation procedures.

Be aware of sources of electricity and cabling on and around your pitch – electrical safety might not be up to the same standards as in the UK.

Poison for rodent control is sometimes used on sites or surrounding farmland. Warning notices are not always posted and you are strongly advised to check if staying on a rural site with dogs or children.

Incidents of theft on campsites are rare but when leaving your caravan unattended make sure you lock all doors and shut windows. Conceal valuables from sight and lock up any bicycles.

Children

Watch out for children as you drive around the site and don't exceed walking pace.

Children's play areas are generally unsupervised, so check which are suitable for your children's ages and abilities. Read and respect the displayed rules. Remember it is your responsibility to supervise your children at all times.

Be aware of any campsite rules concerning ball games or use of play equipment, such as roller blades and skateboards. When your children attend organised activities, arrange when and where to meet afterwards. You should never leave children alone inside a caravan.

Fire

Fire prevention is important on sites, as fire can spread quickly between outfits. Certain areas of southern Europe experience severe water shortages in summer months leading to an increased fire risk. This may result in some local authorities imposing restrictions at short notice on the use of barbecues and open flames.

Fires can be a regular occurrence in forested areas, especially along the Mediterranean coast during summer months. They are generally extinguished quickly and efficiently but short term evacuations are sometimes necessary. If visiting forested areas familiarise yourself with local emergency procedures in the event of fire. Never use paraffin or gas heaters inside your caravan. Gas heaters should only be fitted when air is taken from outside the caravan. Don't change your gas cylinder inside the caravan. If you smell gas turn off the cylinder immediately, extinguish all naked flames and seek professional help.

Make sure you know where the fire points and telephones are on site and know the site fire drill. Make sure everyone in your party knows how to call the emergency services.

Where site rules permit the use of barbecues, take the following precautions to prevent fire:

- Never locate a barbecue near trees or hedges.
- Have a bucket of water to hand in case of sparks.
- Only use recommended fire-lighting materials.
- Don't leave a barbecue unattended when lit and dispose of hot ash safely.
- Never take a barbecue into an enclosed area or awning – even when cooling they continue to release carbon monoxide which can lead to fatal poisoning.

Swimming Pools

Familiarize yourself with the pool area before you venture in for a swim - check the pool layout and identify shallow and deep ends and the location of safety equipment. Check the gradient of the pool bottom as pools which shelve off sharply can catch weak or non-swimmers unawares.

Never dive or jump into a pool without knowing the depth – if there is a no diving rule it usually means the pool isn't deep enough for safe diving.

For pools with a supervisor or lifeguard, note any times or dates when the pool is not supervised. Read safety notices and rules posted around the pool.

On the Road

Don't leave valuables on view in cars or caravans, even if they are locked. Make sure items on roof racks or cycle carriers are locked securely.

Near to ports British owned cars have been targeted by thieves, both while parked and on the move, e.g. by flagging drivers down or indicating that a vehicle has a flat tyre. If you stop in such circumstances be wary of anyone offering help, ensure that car keys are not left in the ignition and that vehicle doors are locked while you investigate.

Always keep car doors locked and windows closed when driving in populated areas. Beware of a 'snatch' through open car windows at traffic lights, filling stations or in traffic jams. When driving through towns and cities keep your doors locked. Keep handbags, valuables and documents out of sight at all times.

If flagged down by another motorist for whatever reason, take care that your own car is locked and windows closed while you check outside, even if someone is left inside.

Be particularly careful on long, empty stretches of motorway and when you stop for fuel. Even if the people flagging you down appear to be officials (e.g. wearing yellow reflective jackets or dark, 'uniform-type' clothing) lock your vehicle doors. They may appear to be friendly and helpful, but could be opportunistic thieves. Have a mobile phone to hand and, if necessary, be seen to use it.

Road accidents are a increased risk in some countries where traffic laws may be inadequately enforced, roads may be poorly maintained, road signs and lighting inadequate, and driving standards poor. It's a good idea to keep a fully-charged mobile phone with you in your car with the number of your breakdown organisation saved into it.

On your return to the UK there are increasing issues with migrants attempting to stowaway in vehicles, especially if you're travelling through Calais. The UK government have issued the following instructions to prevent people entering the UK illegally:

- Where possible all access to vehicles or storage compartments should be fitted with locks.
- All locks must be engaged when the vehicle is stationary or unattended.
- Immediately before boarding your ferry or train check that the locks on your vehicle haven't been compromised.
- If you have any reason to suspect someone may have accessed your outfit speak to border control staff or call the police. Do not board the ferry or train or you may be liable for a fine of up to £2000.

Overnight Stops

Overnight stops should always be at campsites and not at motorway service areas, ferry terminal car parks, petrol station forecourts or isolated 'aires de services' on motorways where robberies are occasionally reported. If you decide to use these areas for a rest then take appropriate precautions, for example, shutting all windows, securing locks and making a thorough external check of your vehicle(s) before departing. Safeguard your property, e.g. handbags, while out of the caravan and beware of approaches by strangers.

For a safer place to take a break, there is a wide network of 'Aires de Services' in cities, towns and villages across Europe, many specifically for motorhomes with good security and overnight facilities. They are often less isolated and therefore safer than the motorway aires. It is rare that you will be the only vehicle staying on such areas, but take sensible precautions and trust your instincts.

Personal Security

Petty crime happens all over the world, including in the UK; however as a tourist you are more vulnerable to it. This shouldn't stop you from exploring new horizons, but there are a few sensible precautions you can take to minimise the risk.

- Leave valuables and jewellery at home. If you do take them, fit a small safe in your caravan or lock them in the boot of your car. Don't leave money or valuables in a car glovebox or on view. Don't leave bags in full view when sitting outside at cafés or restaurants, or leave valuables unattended on the beach.
- When walking be security-conscious. Avoid unlit streets at night, walk away from the kerb edge and carry handbags or shoulder bags on the side away from the kerb. The less of a tourist you appear, the less of a target you are.
- Keep a note of your holiday insurance details and emergency telephone numbers in more than one place, in case the bag or vehicle containing them is stolen.
- Beware of pickpockets in crowded areas, at tourist attractions and in cities. Be especially aware when using public transport in cities.
- Be cautious of bogus plain-clothes policemen who may ask to see your foreign currency or credit cards and passport. If approached, decline to show your money or to hand over your passport but ask for credentials and offer instead to go to the nearest police station.
- Laws and punishment vary from country to country so make yourself aware of anything which may affect you before you travel. Be especially careful on laws involving alcohol consumption (such as drinking in public areas), and never buy or use illegal drugs abroad.
- Respect customs regulations - smuggling is a serious offence and can carry heavy penalties. Do not carry parcels or luggage through customs for other people and never cross borders with people you do not know in your vehicle, such as hitchhikers.

The Foreign & Commonwealth Office produces a range of material to advise and inform British citizens travelling abroad about issues affecting their safety - www.gov.uk/foreign-travel-advice has country specific guides.

Money security

We would rarely walk around at home carrying large amounts of cash, but as you may not have the usual access to bank accounts and credit cards you are more likely to do so on holiday. You are also less likely to have the same degree of security when online banking as you would in your own home. Take the following precautions to keep your money safe:

- Carry only the minimum amount of cash and don't rely on one person to carry everything. Never carry a wallet in your back pocket. Concealed money belts are the most secure way to carry cash and passports.
- Keep a separate note of bank account and credit/debit card numbers. Carry your credit card issuer/bank's 24-hour UK contact number with you.
- Be careful when using cash machines (ATMs) – try to use a machine in an area with high footfall and don't allow yourself to be distracted. Put your cash away before moving away from the cash machine.
- Always guard your PIN number, both at cash machines and when using your card to pay in shops and restaurants. Never let your card out of your sight while paying.
- If using internet banking do not leave the PC or mobile device unattended and make sure you log out fully at the end of the session.

Winter Sports

If you are planning a skiing or snowboarding holiday you should research the safety advice for your destination before you travel. A good starting point may be the relevant embassy for the country you're visitng. All safety instructions should be followed meticulously given the dangers of avalanches in some areas.

The Ski Club of Great Britain offer a lot of advice for anyone taking to the mountains, visit their website www.skiclub.co.uk to pick up some useful safety tips and advice on which resorts are suitable for different skill levels.

British Consular Services Abroad

British Embassy and Consular staff offer practical advice, assistance and support to British travellers abroad. They can, for example, issue replacement passports, help Britons who have been the victims of crime, contact relatives and friends in the event of an accident, illness or death, provide information about transferring funds and provide details of local lawyers, doctors and interpreters.

But there are limits to their powers and a British Consul cannot, for example, give legal advice, intervene in court proceedings, put up bail, pay for legal or medical bills, or for funerals or the repatriation of bodies, or undertake work more properly done by banks, motoring organisations and travel insurers.

If you are charged with a serious offence, insist on the British Consul being informed. You will be contacted as soon as possible by a Consular Officer who can advise on local procedures, provide access to lawyers and insist that you are treated as well as nationals of the country which is holding you. However, they cannot get you released as a matter of course.

British and Irish embassy contact details can be found in the Country Introduction chapters.

Continental Campsites

The quantity and variety of sites across Europe means you're sure to find one that suits your needs – from full facilities and entertainment to quiet rural retreats. If you haven't previously toured outside of the UK you may notice some differences, such as pitches being smaller or closer together. In hot climates hard ground may make putting up awnings difficult.

In the high season all campsite facilities are usually open, however bear in mind that toilet and shower facilities may be busy. Out of season some facilities such as shops and swimming pools may be closed and office opening hours may be reduced. If the site has very low occupancy the sanitary facilities may be reduced to a few unisex toilet and shower cubicles.

Booking a Campsite

To save the hassle of arriving to find a site full it is best to book in advance, especially in high season. If you don't book ahead arrive no later than 4pm (earlier at popular resorts) to secure a pitch, after this time sites fill up quickly. You also need to allow time to find another campsite if your first choice is fully booked.

You can often book directly via a campsite's website using a credit or debit card to pay a deposit if required.

Please be aware that some sites regard the deposit as a booking or admin fee and will not deduct the amount from your final bill.

Overseas Travel Service

The Club's Overseas Travel Service offers members an site booking service on over 250 campsites in Europe. Full details of these sites plus information on ferry special offers and Red Pennant Overseas Holiday Insurance can be found in the Club's Venture Abroad brochure – call 01342 327410 to request a copy or visit camc.com/overseas.

Overseas Site Booking Service sites are marked 'SBS' in the site listings. Many of them can be booked at camc.com. We can't make advance reservations for any other campsites listed in this guide. Only those sites marked SBS have been inspected by Club staff.

Low season discounts

The Club operates a low season scheme in association with Camping Cheques, offering flexible holidays. The scheme covers approximately 635 sites in 29 countries.

Camping Cheques are supplied as part of a package which includes return ferry fare and a minimum of seven Camping Cheques. Those sites which feature in the Camping Cheques scheme and which are listed in this guide are marked 'CChq' in their site entries. For full details of the Camping Cheque scheme visit camc.com/campingcheques.

Caravan Storage Abroad

Storing your caravan on a site in Europe can be a great way to avoid a long tow and to save on ferry and fuel costs. Before you leave your caravan in storage abroad always check whether your insurance covers this, as many policies don't.

If you aren't covered then look for a specialist policy - Towergate Insurance (tel: 01242 538431 or www.towergateinsurance.co.uk) or Look Insurance (tel: 0333 777 3035 or www.lookinsuranceservices.co.uk) both offer insurance policies for caravans stored abroad.

Facilities and Site Description

All of the site facilities shown in the site listings of this guide have been taken from member reports, as have the comments at the end of each site entry. Please remember that opinions and expectations can differ significantly from one person to the next.

The year of report is shown at the end of each site listing – sites which haven't been reported on for a few years may have had significant changes to their prices, facilities, opening dates and standards. It is always best to check any specific details you need to know before travelling by contacting the site or looking at their website.

Sanitary Facilities

Facilities normally include toilet and shower blocks with shower cubicles, wash basins and razor sockets. In site listings the abbreviation 'wc' indicates that the site has the kind of toilets we are used to in the UK (pedestal style). Some sites have footplate style toilets and, where this is known, you will see the abbreviation 'cont', i.e. continental. European sites do not always provide sink plugs, toilet paper or soap so take them with you.

Waste Disposal

Site entries show (when known) where a campsite has a chemical disposal and/or a motorhome service point, which is assumed to include a waste (grey) water dump station and toilet cassette-emptying point. You may find fewer waste water disposal facilities as on the continent more people use the site sanitary blocks rather than their own facilities.

Chemical disposal points may be fixed at a high level requiring you to lift cassettes in order to empty them. Disposal may simply be down a toilet. Wastemaster-style emptying points are not very common in Europe. Formaldehyde chemical cleaning products are banned in many countries. In Germany the 'Blue Angel' (Blaue Engel) Standard, and in the Netherlands the 'Milieukeur' Standard, indicates that the product has particularly good environmental credentials.

Finding a Campsite

Directions are given for all campsites listed in this guide and most listings also include GPS co-ordinates. Full street addresses are also given where available. The directions have been supplied by member reports and haven't been checked in detail by The Club.

For information about using satellite navigation to find a site see the Motoring Equipment section.

Overnight Stops

Many towns and villages across Europe provide dedicated overnight or short stay areas specifically for motorhomes, usually with security, electricity, water and waste facilities. These are known as 'Aires de Services', 'Stellplatz' or 'Aree di Sosta' and are usually well signposted with a motorhome icon. Facilities and charges for these overnight stopping areas will vary significantly.

Many campsites in popular tourist areas will also have separate overnight areas of hardstanding with facilities often just outside the main campsite area. There are guidebooks available which list just these overnight stops, Vicarious books publish an English guide to the Aires including directions, GPS co-ordinates and photographs. Please contact 0131 208 3333 or visit their website www.vicarious-shop.co.uk.

For security reasons you shouldn't spend the night on petrol station service areas, ferry terminal car parks or isolated 'Aires de Repos' or 'Aires de Services' along motorways.

Municipal Campsites

Municipal sites are found in towns and villages all over Europe, in particular in France. Once very basic, many have been improved in recent years and now offer a wider range of facilities. They can usually be booked in advance through the local town hall or tourism office. When approaching a town you may find that municipal sites are not always named and signposts may simply state 'Camping' or show a tent or caravan symbol. Most municipal sites are clean, well-run and very reasonably priced but security may be basic.

These sites may be used by seasonal workers, market traders and travellers in low season and as a result there may be restrictions or very high charges for some types of outfits (such as twin axles) in order to discourage this. If you may be affected check for any restrictions when you book.

Naturist Campsites

Some naturist sites are included in this guide and are shown with the word 'naturist' after their site name. Those marked 'part naturist' have separate areas for naturists. Visitors to naturist sites aged 16 and over usually require an INF card or Naturist Licence - covered by membership of British Naturism (tel 01604 620361, visit www.british-naturism.org.uk or email headoffice@british-naturism.org.uk) or you can apply for a licence on arrival at any recognised naturist site (a passport-size photograph is required).

Opening Dates and times

Opening dates should always be taken with a pinch of salt - including those given in this guide. Sites may close without notice due to refurbishment work, a lack of visitors or bad weather. Outside the high season it is always best to contact campsites in advance, even if the site advertises itself as open all year.

Most sites will close their gates or barriers overnight – if you are planning to arrive late or are delayed on your journey you should call ahead to make sure you will be able to gain access to the site. There may be a late arrivals area outside of the barriers where you can pitch overnight. Motorhomers should also consider barrier closing times if leaving site in your vehicle for the evening.

Check out time is usually between 10am and 12 noon – speak to the site staff if you need to leave very early to make sure you can check out on departure. Sites may also close for an extended lunch break, so if you're planning to arrive or check out around lunchtime check that the office will be open.

Pets on Campsites

Dogs are welcome on many sites, although you may have to prove that all of their vaccinations are up to date before they are allowed onto the site. Certain breeds of dogs are banned in some countries and other breeds will need to be muzzled and kept on a lead at all times.
A list of breeds with restrictions by country can be found at camc.com/pets.

Sites usually charge for dogs and may limit the number allowed per pitch. On arrival make yourself aware of site rules regarding dogs, such as keeping them on a lead, muzzling them or not leaving them unattended in your outfit.

In popular tourist areas local regulations may ban dogs from beaches during the summer. Some dogs may find it difficult to cope with changes in climate. Also watch out for diseases transmitted by ticks, caterpillars, mosquitoes or sandflies - dogs from the UK will have no natural resistance. Consult your vet about preventative treatment before you travel.

Visitors to southern Spain and Portugal, parts of central France and northern Italy should be aware of the danger of Pine Processionary Caterpillars from mid-winter to late spring. Dogs should be kept away from pine trees if possible or fitted with a muzzle that prevents the nose and mouth from touching the ground. This will also protect against poisoned bait sometimes used by farmers and hunters.

In the event that your pet is taken ill abroad a campsite should have information about local vets.

Most European countries require dogs to wear a collar identifying their owners at all times. If your dog goes missing, report the matter to the local police and the local branch of that country's animal welfare organisation.
See the Documents section of this book for more information about the Pet Travel Scheme.

Prices and Payment

Prices per night (for an outfit and two adults) are shown in the site entries. If you stay on site after midday you may be charged for an extra day. Many campsites have a minimum amount for credit card transactions, meaning they can't be used to pay for overnight or short stays. Check which payment methods are accepted when you check in.

Sites with automatic barriers may ask for a deposit for a swipe card or fob to operate it.

Extra charges may apply for the use of facilities such as swimming pools, showers or laundry rooms. You may also be charged extra for dogs, Wi-Fi, tents and extra cars.

A tourist tax, eco tax and/or rubbish tax may be imposed by local authorities in some European countries. VAT may also be added to your campsite fees.

Registering on Arrival

Local authority requirements mean you will usually have to produce an identity document on arrival, which will be retained by the site until you check out. If you don't want to leave your passport with reception then most sites will accept a camping document such as the Camping Key Europe (CKE) or Camping Card International (CCI) - if this is known site entries are marked CKE/CCI.

CKE are available for Club members to purchase by calling 01342 336633 or are free to members if you take out the 'motoring' level of cover from the Club's Red Pennant Overseas Holiday Insurance.

General Advice

If you've visiting a new site ask to take a look around the site and facilities before booking in. Riverside pitches can be very scenic but keep an eye on the water level; in periods of heavy rain this may rise rapidly.

Speed limits on campsites are usually restricted to 10 km/h (6 mph). You may be asked to park your

car in a separate area away from your caravan, particularly in the high season.

The use of the term 'statics' in the campsite reports in this guide may to any long-term accommodation on site, such as seasonal pitches, chalets, cottages, fixed tents and cabins, as well as static caravans.

Complaints

If you want to make a complaint about a site issue, take it up with site staff or owners at the time in order to give them the opportunity to rectify the problem during your stay.

The Caravan and Motorhome Club has no control or influence over day to day campsite operations or administration of the sites listed in this guide. Therefore we aren't able to intervene in any dispute you should have with a campsite, unless the booking has been made through our Site Booking Service - see listings marked 'SBS' for sites we are able to book for you.

Campsite Groups

Across Europe there are many campsite 'groups' or 'chains' with sites in various locations.

You will generally find that group sites will be consistent in their format and the quality and variety of facilities they offer. If you liked one site you can be fairly confident that you will like other sites within the same group.

If you're looking for a full facility site, with swimming pools, play areas, bars and restaurants on site you're likely to find these on sites which are part of a group. You might even find organised excursions and activities such as archery on site.

Schafberg peak to Mondsee

Welcome to Austria

From bustling, cosmopolitan cities, packed with culture, to stunning natural landscapes that will take your breath away, Austria is a rich and varied country that caters to every taste.

The Alps offer endless appeal for those looking to enjoy an active, outdoor holiday while the picturesque towns and villages that punctuate the landscape are ideal for relaxing and soaking up the local culture.

Country highlights

Austria is an important centre for European culture; in particular music. As the birthplace of many notable composers – Mozart, Strauss and Haydn to name just a few – Austria is a magnet for classical music fans.

When it comes to food, one of Austria's most famous dishes is strudel, and there are many different varieties of flavours and types available. The oldest strudel recipes can be found in a handwritten cookbook from 1696 at the Vienna City Library.

Major towns and cities

- Vienna – enjoy a slice of sachertorte in this historic capital.
- Linz – a city of arts and music on the banks of the Danube.
- Graz – the old town is filled with sights and is on the UNESCO World Heritage List.
- Salzburg – this fairytale city was the birthplace of Mozart.

Attractions

- Schönbrunn Palace – a Baroque palace in the heart of Vienna.
- Hallstatt – this Alpine village has a fascinating history as well as picturesque views.
- Grossglockner Alpine Road – the highest road in Austria with unparalleled mountain views.
- Innsbruck – a renowned winter sports centre packed with historical sights.

Find out more

www.austria.info
Tel: 0043 (0)1 58 86 60 Austrian Tourist Office

BRUCK AN DER MUR *C4* (4km W Urban) *47.40311, 15.22755* **Camping Raddörf'l, Bruckerstrasse 110, 8600 Oberaich [(03862) 51418; fax 59940; info@gasthofpichler.at; www.gasthofpichler.at]** Fr S6 take Oberaich exit 4km W of Bruck, Foll site sp (in opp dir to vill of Oberaich), go under rlwy bdge, turn L at T-junc. Site is 300m on L at Gasthof Pichler, ent thro car park. Sm, pt shd; wc; shwrs inc; EHU (10A) inc; lndry; shop 3km; rest, snacks; bar; playgrnd; dogs €2; poss cr; some rlwy noise; CKE/CCI. "Gd NH; site (10 o'fits max) in orchard at rear of Gasthof; gd rest; cramped." 1 May-1 Oct. € 21.00 2015*

DELLACH IM DRAUTAL *D2* (1km S Rural) *46.73085, 13.07846* **Camping Waldbad, 9772 Dellach-im-Drautal (Kärnten) [(04714) 234-18 or (04714) 288; info@camping-waldbad.at; www.camping-waldbad.at]** Clearly sp on B100 & in vill of Dellach on S side or Rv Drau. Med, hdg/mkd pitch, pt shd; wc; chem disp; mv service pnt; fam bthrm; shwrs inc; EHU (6A) inc; gas; lndry; shop; rest, snacks; bar; playgrnd; htd pool complex adj inc paddling pool, waterslide etc; games area; games rm; entmnt; internet; 5% statics; dogs €2.50; poss cr; adv bkg; quiet; ccard acc. "Peaceful, wooded site; vg leisure facs adj." ♦ 1 May-30 Sep. € 37.50 2013*

⊞ **DOBRIACH** *D3* (2km S Rural) *46.77020, 13.64788* **Komfort Campingpark Burgstaller, Seefeldstrasse 16, A-9873 Döbriach (Kärnten) [04246 7774; fax 7774426; info@burgstaller.co.at; www.burgstaller.co.at]** Fr on A10/E55/E66 take exit Millstätter See. Turn L at traff lts on B98 dir Radenthein. Thro Millstatt & Dellach, turn R into Döbriach, sp Camping See site on L by lake after Döbriach. V lge, hdg/mkd pitch, pt shd; wc; chem disp; mv service pnt; fam bthrm; sauna; private san facs avail; shwrs inc; EHU (6-10A) inc; gas; lndry; shop; rest, snacks, bar adj; playgrnd; htd pool; lake sw; boating; solarium; games area; horseriding; bike hire; cinema; golf 8km; entmnt; internet; TV; 10% statics; dogs €4; poss cr; Eng spkn; adv bkg; quiet; red snr citizens/LS; CKE/CCI. "Organised walks & trips to Italy; excel rest; some pitches tight; fantastic facs." ♦ € 35.00 2013*

⊞ **DOBRIACH** *D3* (2km SW Urban) *46.76811, 13.64809* **Camping Brunner am See, Glanzerstrasse 108, 9873 Döbriach [(04246) 7189 or 7386; fax 718914; office@camping-brunner.at; www.camping-brunner.at]** Fr Salzburg on A10 a'bahn take Seeboden-Millstatt exit bef Spittal. Foll rd 98 N of Millstattersee to camping sp. Med, pt shd; wc; chem disp; mv service pnt; fam bthrm; shwrs inc; EHU (6A) inc; rest, snacks; bar; shop; pool 300m; playgrnd; tennis; watersports; poss cr; dogs €4.50; adv bkg; ccard acc; CKE/CCI. "Great site with excel, clean san facs; gd size pitches; lakeside location; supmkt nrby & rests in vicinity; superb scenery." ♦ € 55.00 2013*

DROBOLLACH see Villach *D3*

⊞ **EBEN IM PONGAU** *C3* (1.5km S Rural) *47.39932, 13.39566* **See-Camping Eben, Familie Schneider, Badeseestraße 54, 5531 Eben I Pg [tel/fax 06458 8231 or 0664 450 2000; info@seecamping-eben.at; www.seecamping-eben.at]** Head E on A10, take exit 60 - Eben. Turn L onto B99. R onto Badeseestr. Campsite 800m on the L. Med, pt shd; htd wc; mv service pnt; fam bthrm; shwrs inc; EHU (16A) inc; lndry (inc dryer); bar; lake adj; games area; wifi; dogs; train 800km; adv bkg; quiet. "Helpful owners; saunas; steam rm; direct access fr mountains; clean & well organise; gd site." € 25.00 2014*

EBERNDORF see Völkermarkt *D3*

⊞ **EHRWALD** *C1* (3km SW Rural) *47.38249, 10.90222* **Camping Biberhof, Schmitte 8, 6633 Biberwier (Tirol) [(05673) 2950; info@biberhof.at; www.biberhof.at]** Fr Reutte, leave B179 sp Lermoos. In Leermoos cent turn R sp Biberwier. At t-junc in Biberwier turn L sp Ehrwald. Site on R in 300mtrs. Med, mkd, hdstg, pt shd; wc; chem disp; mv service pnt; fam bthrm; shwrs; EHU (10A); lndry (inc dryer); café; bar; BBQ; playgrnd; pool at Lermoos 2km; games area; wifi; 80% statics; dogs €1.90; bus adj; twin axles; Eng spkn; adv bkg; quiet; red in LS. "Site under power cables; sometimes noisy; trampoline, volleyball, wall climbing, table tennis, walking/cycle rtes adj; mountain views; 3 scenic vill; outstanding san facs; drying rm." € 29.00 2016*

⊞ **EHRWALD** *C1* (3km W Rural) *47.40250, 10.88893* **Happy Camp Hofherr, Garmischerstrasse 21, 6631 Lermoos [(05673) 2980; fax 29805; info@camping-lermoos.com; www.camping-lermoos.com]** On ent Lermoos on B187 fr Ehrwald site located on R. Med, pt sl, pt shd; htd wc; chem disp; mv service pnt; shwrs inc; EHU (16A) metered; gas (metered); lndry (inc dryer); shops 200m; rest; playgrnd; htd pool 200m; tennis; ski lift 300m; wifi; cab TV; 40% statics; dogs; phone; site clsd 1 Nov-mid Dec; adv bkg; quiet; ccard acc. "Ideal for walks/cycling; v picturesque; adj park; ask for guest card for discount on ski lifts etc; excel san facs; superb rest (clsd Mon & Tue eve); family run site." € 28.00 2014*

EISENSTADT *B4* (16km SE Rural) *47.80132, 16.69185* **Storchencamp Rust, Ruster Bucht, 7071 Rust-am-Neusiedlersee (Burgenland) [tel/fax (02685) 595; office@gmeiner.co.at; www.gmeiner.co.at]** Fr Eisenstadt take rd to Rust & Mörbisch. In Rust foll sps to site & Zee; lakeside rd to ent. Lge, pt shd; wc; chem disp; shwrs inc; EHU (16A) €2.30; lndry; shop; rest, snacks; pool 200m; lake sw 500m; boating; 60% statics; dogs €2.90; poss cr; quiet. "Nr Hungarian border; attractive vill with nesting storks." ♦ 1 Apr-31 Oct. € 20.00 2012*

EMMERSDORF AN DER DONAU see Melk *B4*

ENGELHARTSZELL *B3* (950m NW Rural) *48.51238, 13.72428* **Camp Municipal an der Donau, Nibelungenstrasse 113, 4090 Engelhartszell [(0664) 8708787; tourismus@engelhartszell.ooe.gv.at; www.camping-audonau.at]** Fr Passau (Germany) exit SE on B130 along Rv Danube. Site on L in approx 28km just bef Engelhartszell adj municipal pool complex. Sm, unshd; wc; chem disp; shwrs; EHU (6A) metered; lndry; snacks; bar; playgrnd; pool adj; 50% statics; bus nr; poss cr; quiet. "Excel, clean, friendly site on rvside; Danube cycleway passes site." ♦ 15 Apr-15 Oct. € 22.60 2016*

FAAK/FAAK AM SEE see Villach *D3*

FEICHTEN IM KAUNERTAL see Prutz *C1*

FIEBERBRUNN see St Johann in Tirol *C2*

FURSTENFELD *C4* (2km NW Rural) *47.05631, 16.06255* **Camping Fürstenfeld, Campingweg 1, 8280 Fürstenfeld [(03382) 54940; fax 51671; camping.fuerstenfeld@chello.at; www.camping-fuerstenfeld.at]** Exit A2/E59 sp Fürstenfeld onto B65. Site well sp fr town cent. Med, pt sl, pt shd; wc; chem disp; shwrs inc; EHU (10A) €2.30 (poss long lead req); lndry (inc dryer); shop 500m; rest 1.5km; snacks; bar; pool; paddling pool; waterslide; rv fishing; golf 5km; entmnt; 25% statics; dogs €2; phone; quiet; rec CKE/CCI. "Pleasant rvside site; ltd facs but clean; conv Hungarian border." 15 Apr-15 Oct. € 21.00 2016*

GMUND (KARNTEN) *C3* (6km NW Rural) *46.94950, 13.50940* **Terrassencamping Maltatal, Malta 6, 9854 Malta [(04733) 234; fax 23416; info@maltacamp.at; www.maltacamp.at]** Exit A10/E14 onto B99 to Gmünd. Foll sp Malta & after 6km site sp, on R next to filling stn. Lge, mkd pitch, terr, pt shd; htd wc; chem disp; mv service pnt; 20% serviced pitches; sauna; shwrs inc; EHU (10A) inc; lndry (inc dryer); sm supmkt; rest, snacks; pizzeria; bar; BBQ; playgrnd; htd pool; paddling pool; canoeing; trout-fishing; games area; games rm; tennis; guided walks; children's mini-farm; wifi; 5% statics; dogs €2.90; phone; poss cr; adv bkg; quiet; CKE/CCI. "Gmund & Spittal gd shopping towns; Millstättersee 15km, Grossglocknerstrasse 1hr's drive; magnificant area with rvs, waterfalls, forests & mountains; vg rest; excel site." ♦ 1 Apr-31 Oct. € 30.00 2012*

GNESAU *D3* (1km W Rural) *46.77966, 13.95062* **Camping Hobitsch, Sonnleiten 24, 9563 Gnesau (Kärnten) [(0676) 6032848; office@camping-hobitsch.at; www.camping-hobitsch.at]** Site sp on B95. Sm, pt shd; wc; chem disp; shwrs inc; EHU €3.50; lndry; shop, rest 2km; snacks; bar; playgrnd; pool; tennis; games area; dogs €1.50; Eng spkn; quiet. "Beautiful setting in meadow; excel san facs; adj to cycle path." 1 May-30 Sep. € 16.60 2016*

GRAN *C1* (1km N Rural) *47.51000, 10.55611* **Comfort-Camp Grän, Engetalstrasse 13, 6673 Grän (Tirol) [(05675) 6570; fax 65704; info@comfortcamp.at; www.comfortcamp.at]** Leave A7 (Germany) at Oy exit, foll 310 via Wertach, Oberjoch to Gran. Rtes fr Sonthofen or Reutte only suitable for MH's. Med, mkd pitch, pt sl, pt terr, unshd; htd wc; chem disp; fam bthrm; shwrs; private bthrms avail extra cost; EHU (16A) 0.75 per kWh; gas; lndry (inc dryer); shops 1km; rest, snacks; bar; BBQ; playgrnd; htd, covrd pool; solarium; games rm; wifi; TV; 20% statics; dogs €4; phone; bus; Eng spkn; adv bkg; quiet; CKE/CCI. "Ski-rm facs avail; vg facs; luxurious facs, sauna, massage; beautiful area; cable car nrby; walking/cycle rtes fr site." 10 May-1 Nov & 15 Dec-16 Apr. € 36.00 2017*

GRAZ *C4* (7km SW Urban) *47.02447, 15.39719* **Stadt-Camping Central, Martinhofstrasse 3, 8054 Graz-Strassgang [(0316) 697824 or 0676 3785102 (mob); fax 0318 631112; office@reisemobilstellplatz-graz.at; www.reisemobilstellplatz-graz.at]** Fr A9/E57 exit Graz-Webling, then dir Strassgang onto B70, site sp on R after Billa supmkt & filling stn. Med, mkd pitch, some hdstg, pt shd; wc; chem disp; mv service pnt; shwrs inc; EHU (6A) inc; gas; lndry (inc dryer); supmkt 200m; rest, snacks adj; bar; BBQ; playgrnd; pool, paddling pool adj; tennis; wifi; dogs free; 20% statics; bus to city; poss v cr; quiet. "Pleasant, conv site; reg bus service fr the nrby main rd (no traff noise); free ent superb lido (pt naturist); site manager v helpful; mainly MH." ♦ 1 Apr-31 Oct. € 30.00 2017*

⊞ **GREIFENBURG** *D2* (2km E Rural) *46.74744, 13.19448* **Fliergercamp am See, Seeweg 333, 9761 Greifenburg (Kärnten) [(04712) 8666; info@fliegercamp.at; www.fliegercamp.at]** Leave A10 & J139 onto 100 dir Lienz. Site on L after 15km, mkd & visible fr rd. Med, hdg/mkd pitch, pt shd; htd wc; chem disp; mv service pnt; fam bthrm; shwrs inc; EHU (16A) inc; gas; lndry; shop 3km; rest, snacks, bar adj; pool adj; lake sw adj; games area; 20% statics; dogs; twin axles; poss cr; Eng spkn; quiet; ccard acc; CCI. "Gd cycling; vg site; well run." ♦ ltd. € 24.00 2015*

GREIN *B3* (700m SW Urban) *48.22476, 14.85428* **Campingplatz Grein, Donaulände 1, 4360 Grein [(07268) 21230; fax 2123013; office@camping-grein.at; www.camping-grein.net]** Sp fr A1 & B3 on banks of Danube. Med, pt shd; wc; chem disp; shwrs inc; EHU (6-10A) €3; gas; lndry; shop adj; rest in vill; snacks; bar; playgrnd; htd, covrd pool 200m; open air pool 500m; fishing; canoeing; wifi; 10% statics; dogs €1.50; poss cr; some rd/rlwy noise; red long stay; CKE/CCI. "Friendly, helpful owner lives on site; recep in café/bar; vg, modern san facs; lovely scenery; quaint vill; gd walking; excursions; conv Danube cycle rte & Mauthausen Concentration Camp." 1 Mar-31 Oct. € 32.50 2014*

GRUNDLSEE see Bad Aussee *C3*

HALL IN TIROL *C2* (6km E Rural) *47.28711, 11.57223* **Schlosscamping Aschach, Hochschwarzweg 2, 6111 Volders [tel/fax (05224) 52333; info@schlosscamping.com; www.schlosscamping.com]** Fr A12 leave at either Hall Mitte & foll sp to Volders, or leave at Wattens & travel W to Volders (easiest rte). Site well sp on B171. Narr ent bet lge trees. Lge, mkd pitch, pt sl, pt shd; wc; chem disp; mv service pnt; shwrs inc; EHU (16A) €2.70 (long cable req some pitches; adaptor lead avail); gas; lndry; shop; 2 supmkts 500m; rest, snacks; bar; BBQ; playgrnd; htd pool; horseriding, tennis; wifi; TV rm; dogs €2.50; phone; bus 250m; Eng spkn; adv bkg; quiet but church bells, clock & some rlwy noise at night; red long stay; ccard acc (for 4+ days); CKE/CCI. "Well-run, efficient, clean site with vg, modern facs & helpful management; few water & waste points; grassy pitches; beautiful setting & views; gd walking/touring; arr early to ensure pitch; excel." 1 May-20 Sep. € 29.00 2017*

HALL IN TIROL *C2* (1km NW Urban) *47.28423, 11.49658* **Schwimmbad-Camping, Scheidensteinstrasse 26, 6060 Hall-in-Tirol [(05223) 5855550; h.niedrist@hall.at; www.hall.ag]** Exit A12/E45/E60 at junc 68 at Hall-in-Tirol. Cross rv strt into town & foll camp sp fr 2nd turn L; site on B171. Diff ent. Med, pt shd; wc; chem disp; mv service pnt; shwrs inc; EHU (6A) €2.50; lndry; shop high ssn; supmkt 500m; rest; playgrnd; htd pool adj; tennis, minigolf adj; wifi; 15% statics; dogs; bus; poss cr; Eng spkn; adv bkg; some rd noise & church bells; red long stay/CKE/CCI. "Well-cared for site; friendly welcome; vg, modern facs, poss stretched high ssn; local excursions, walking; pt of sports complex; Hall pretty, interesting medieval town; frequent music festivals; less cr than Innsbruck sites; no twin-axles; walk to town; conv for m'vans; NB m'vans only 1 Oct-30 Apr for €7.50 per night." ♦ 1 May-30 Sep. € 28.00 2015*

HALLEIN *B2* (5km NW Rural) *47.70441, 13.06868* **Camping Auwirt, Salzburgerstrasse 42, 5400 Hallein [(06245) 80417; info@auwirt.com; www.auwirt.com]** Exit A10/E55 junc 8 onto B150 sp Salzburg Süd, then B159 twd Hallein. Site on L in 4km. Med, pt shd; wc; chem disp; mv service pnt; shwrs €2; EHU (10A) €3; lndry; rest, snacks; bar; playgrnd; paddling pool; wifi; dogs €2; bus to Salzburg at site ent; poss cr; Eng spkn; adv bkg; CKE/CCI. "Mountain views; cycle path to Salzburg nr; gd san facs & rest; conv salt mines at Hallein & scenic drive to Eagles' Nest; conv for Berchtesgaden; friendly helpful family owners; flat site; excel." ♦ 26 Mar-8 Oct, 9 Apr-5 Oct & 1 Dec-31 Dec. € 36.00 2017*

HALLSTATT *C3* (1km S Rural) *47.55296, 13.64786* **Camping Klausner-Höll, Lahnstrasse 201, 4830 Hallstatt [(06134) 6134 or 8322; fax 83221; camping@hallstatt.net; http://camping.hallstatt.net/home]** On exit tunnel 500m thro vill, site on R nr lge filling stn. Med, pt shd; wc; chem disp; shwrs inc; EHU (16A) €3; lndry; shop; rest adj; snacks; bar; playgrnd; pool adj; lake sw; boat trips; dogs; poss cr; Eng spkn; ccard acc; red long stay/CKE/CCI. "Excel, level site; gd, clean san facs; chem disp diff to use; conv Salzkammergut region, Hallstatt salt mines, ice caves; pretty town 10 mins walk; family run site; relaxed & friendly; walks; idyllic quiet setting with mountains all around; cycle path around lake; supmkt 300m." 15 Apr-15 Oct. € 27.00 2014*

HEILIGEN GESTADE see Ossiach *D3*

HEITERWANG see Reutte *C1*

"There aren't many sites open at this time of year"

If you're travelling outside peak season remember to call ahead to check site opening dates – even if the entry says 'open all year'.

⊞ **HIRSCHEGG** *C3* (500m N Rural) *47.02300, 14.95325* **Campingplatz Hirschegg, Haus No. 53, 8584 Hirschegg [info@camping-hirschegg.at; www.camping-hirschegg.at]** Exit A2 junc 224 Modriach N. At T-junc foll sp to Hirschegg & in cent of vill turn R at petrol stn. Site in 300m on L by fire stn. Med, hdg/mkd pitch, pt shd; wc; chem disp; shwrs inc; EHU (10A) €2; lndry; shop, rest, bar in vill; playgrnd; pool; lake sw adj; wifi; 30% statics; dogs €1; adv bkg; quiet. "Excel, family-run site." € 18.00 2016*

HOPFGARTEN see Wörgl *C2*

⊞ **IMST** *C1* (1.5km S Rural) *47.22861, 10.74305* **Caravanpark Imst-West, Langgasse 62, 6460 Imst [(05412) 66293; fax 662319; info@imst-west.com; www.imst-west.com]** Fr A12/E60 exit Imst-Pitztal onto B171 N dir Imst. In 1km at rndabt turn L and sweep R round Billa store. Immed turn L & L again to site (sp). Med, mkd pitch, pt sl, pt shd; wc; chem disp; mv service pnt; shwrs inc; EHU (6-10A) €3; gas; lndry; shop 200m; excel rest 400m; snacks; bar; playgrnd; pool 1.5km; ski lift 2km; free skibus; dogs (€1.80-€2); Eng spkn; quiet. "Gd cent for Tirol, trips to Germany & en rte for Innsbruck; lovely views; immac new san facs (2015); gd." € 28.00 2017*

⊞ **INNSBRUCK** *C1* (9.5km SW Rural) *47.23724, 11.33865* **Camping Natterersee, Natterer See 1, 6161 Natters [(0512) 546732; fax 54673216; info@natterersee.com; www.natterersee.com]** App Innsbruck fr E or W on A12 take A13/E45 sp Brenner. Leave at 1st junc sp Innsbruck Süd, Natters. Foll sp Natters - acute R turns & severe gradients (care across unguarded level x-ing), turn sharp R in vill & foll sp to site. Take care on negotiating ent. Narr rds & app. Fr S on A13 Brennerautobahn exit junc 3 & foll dir Mutters & Natters. Med, pt shd, sl, terr; htd wc; chem disp; mv service pnt; fam bthrm; shwrs inc; EHU (10A)€3.75; gas; lndry (inc dryer); shop; rest, snacks; bar; BBQ; playgrnd; lake sw; waterslide; tennis; bike hire; games area; games/TV rm; wifi; entmnt; no dogs Jul/Aug, otherwise €4.50; bus to Innsbruck; train 2.5km; sep car park high ssn; guided hiking; clsd 1 Nov-mid Dec; poss v cr; Eng spkn; adv bkg; ccard acc; red LS; CKE/CCI. "Well-kept site adj local beauty spot; lakeside pitches gd views (extra charge); gd, scenic cent for walking & driving excursions; gd for children; friendly, helpful staff; excel modern san facs; some sm pitches & narr site rds diff lge o'fits; fantastic setting; special shwr for dogs; excel." ♦ € 40.00 SBS - G01 2016*

⊞ **INNSBRUCK** *C1* (7km W Rural) *47.26339, 11.32629* **Camping Kranebittehof, Kranebitter Allee 216, 6020 Innsbruck-Kranebitten [(0512) 281958; info@kranebitterhof.at; www.kranebitterhof.at]** Fr W fork L after Zirl bef main rd rv bdge, sp Innsbruck & foll B171 for 5km. Fr S on A13 fr border foll dir Bregenz on A12 exit Kranebitten & foll sp to site. Sharp ent on R. Med, mkd pitch, some hdstg, terr, pt sl, pt shd; htd wc; chem disp; mv service pnt; shwrs inc; EHU (6-10A) inc; lndry; shop; pizzeria; hiking; ski lift 5km; wifi; 20% statics; dogs; bus; poss cr; Eng spkn; some m'way & airport noise; ccard acc; red LS/long stay/CKE/CCI. "Excel, refurbished site in lovely situation; vg, modern san facs; friendly, helpful staff; site easy to find fr m'way, excel rest on site." ♦ € 25.00 2016*

ITTER BEI HOPFGARTEN see Wörgl *C2*

⊞ **JENBACH** *C2* (6.5km NW Rural) *47.42156, 11.74043* **Camping Karwendel, 6212 Maurach [(05243) 6116; fax 20036; info@karwendel-camping.at; www.karwendel-camping.at]** Exit A12/E45/E50 junc 39 onto B181. Foll sp Pertisau & Maurach. In 8km (climbing fr a'route turn L at Maurach. Foll rd thro vill, turn L at T-junc, then strt across rndabt twd lake. Site sp past recycling cent. Med, unshd; htd wc; chem disp; shwrs €1; EHU (10A) €2; lndry; shop 500m; rest, snacks; bar; playgrnd; lake sw 500m; golf 4km; internet; TV; 80% statics; dogs €2; site clsd Nov; poss cr; quiet. "In open country, glorious views of lake & mountains; diff access lge o'fits; site neglected & rundown." € 35.00 2014*

KALS AM GROßGLOCKNER *C2* (3km N Rural) *47.01912, 12.63680* **National Park Camping, Berg 22, A9981 Kals am Großglockner [(043) 4852 67389; info@nationalpark-camping-kals.at; www.nationalpark-camping-kals.at]** Fr 108 (Leinz - Millersill) take L26 to Kals am Großglockner. Site thro vill in abt 2km well sp. Care needed at 3 way rd junc at end of vill, take ctr rd. Med, mkd pitch, terr, unshd; htd wc; chem disp; mv service pnt; shwrs; EHU 10A; lndry; CKE/CCI. "Excel, brand new purpose built site in Hohe Tauren Nat Park at 1460m; superb san facs." 1 Apr-31 Oct. € 30.00 2015*

⊞ **KITZBUHEL** *C2* (3km NW Rural) *47.45906, 12.3619* **Campingplatz Schwarzsee, Reitherstrasse 24, 6370 Kitzbühel [(05356) 62806 or 64479; fax 6447930; office@bruggerhof-camping.at; www.bruggerhof-camping.at]** Site sp fr Kitzbühel dir Kirchberg-Schwarzsee. Lge, pt sl, pt shd; htd wc; chem disp; mv service pnt; fam bthrm; sauna; shwrs inc; EHU (16A) metered; mains gas conn some pitches; lndry; shop; rest adj; snacks; bar; playgrnd; pool 2km; lake sw 300m; cab TV; 80% statics; dogs €5.50; phone; bus; poss cr; Eng spkn; adv bkg; ccard acc; CKE/CCI. "Gd walks, cable cars & chair lifts; vg, well-maintained site; poss mosquito & vermin prob; some pitches in statics area; friendly owner." ♦ € 46.00 2015*

KLAGENFURT *D3* (5km W Rural) *46.61826, 14.25641* **Camping Wörthersee, Metnitzstrand 5, 9020 Klagenfurt am wörthersee (Kärnten) [(0463) 287810; fax 2878103; info@campingfreund.at; www.camping-woerthersee.at]** Fr A2/E66 take spur to Klagenfurt-West, exit at Klagenfurt-Wörthersee. Turn R at traff lts & immed L at rd fork (traff lts), then foll sp to site. Lge, shd; wc; chem disp; sauna; shwrs inc; EHU (10A) inc; lndry; shop; rest; playgrnd; sand beach adj; bike hire; entmnt; dogs €3.20; 10% statics; bus; quiet; ccard acc. "V clean facs; local tax €3.50 per visit." ♦ 1 May-30 Sep. € 31.00 2013*

KLOSTERNEUBURG *B4* (650m N Rural) *48.31097, 16.32810* **Donaupark Camping Klosterneuburg, In der Au, 3402 Klosterneuburg [(02243) 25877; fax 25878; campklosterneuburg@oeamtc.at; www.campingklosterneuburg.at]** Fr A22/E59 exit junc 7 onto B14, site sp in cent of town behind rlwy stn. After passing Klosterneuburg Abbey on L turn 1st R (sharp turn under rlwy). Site immed ahead. Med, mkd pitch, pt shd; htd wc; chem disp; mv service pnt; shwrs inc; EHU (6-12A) €3; gas; lndry (inc dryer); shop; rest 200m; snacks; BBQ; cooking facs; playgrnd; leisure cent & htd pools adj; bike & boat hire; tennis; wifi; TV rm; 5% statics; dogs free; phone; bus; train to Vienna; poss cr; quiet; ccard acc; red CKE/CCI. "Well-organised, popular site; vg san facs; helpful staff; sm pitches; conv Danube cycle path & Vienna; church & monastery worth visit." ♦ 13 Mar-5 Nov. € 36.00 2017*

⊞ **KOSSEN** *B2* (3km SE Rural) *47.65388, 12.41544* **Eurocamping Wilder Kaiser, Kranebittau 18, 6345 Kössen [(05375) 6444; fax 2113; info@eurocamp-koessen.com; www.eurocamp-koessen.com]** Leave A12 at Oberaudorf/Niederndorf junc, head E on 172 thro Niederndorf & Walchsee to Kössen. Strt across at rndabt, in 1km turn R sp Hinterburg Lift. At next junc turn R & site located after 400m. Lge, mkd pitch, pt shd; htd wc; chem disp; mv service pnt; serviced pitches; sauna; solarium; fam bthrm; shwrs inc; EHU (6A) metered + conn fee; gas; lndry; shop high ssn; rest, snacks high ssn; bar; playgrnd; htd pool adj; tennis; games area; golf 2km; entmnt; internet; cab TV; 50% statics; dogs €4; poss cr; Eng spkn; adv bkg; ccard acc; CKE/CCI. "Lovely site; excel play area & organised activities; rafting, hang-gliding & canoeing 1km; excel." € 23.50 2012*

⊞ **KOTSCHACH** *D2* (1km SW Rural) *46.66946, 12.99153* **Alpencamp, Kötschach 284, 9640 Kötschach-Mauthen [tel/fax (04715) 429; info@alpencamp.at; www.alpencamp.at]** At junc of rds B110 & B111 in Kötschach turn W onto B111, foll camp sps to site in 800m on L. Med, mkd pitch, pt shd; htd wc; chem disp; mv service pnt; sauna; shwrs inc; EHU (16A) inc; lndry (inc dryer); sm shop; supmkt 400m; rest 100m; snacks; playgrnd; 2 pools (1 htd, covrd); waterslide; tennis; games area; games rm; boat & bike hire; tennis 400m; wifi; TV; dogs €2; phone; site clsd 1 Nov-14 Dec; poss cr; Eng spkn; quiet; ccard acc. "Useful for Plöcken Pass; cycle tracks on rv bank nrby; vg san facs; friendly, helpful owner; vg site." ♦ € 19.00 2016*

KRAMSACH AM REINTALERSEE see Rattenberg *C2*

⊞ **LANDECK** *C1* (500m W Urban) *47.14263, 10.56147* **Camping Riffler, Bruggfeldstrasse 2, 6500 Landeck [(05442) 64898; fax 648984; info@camping-riffler.at; www.camping-riffler.at]** Exit E60/A12 at Landeck-West, site in 1.5km, 500m fr cent on L. Sm, pt shd; wc; chem disp; shwrs inc; EHU (10A) €2.70 (poss rev pol); gas; lndry; shop adj; snacks, rest adj; playgrnd; pool 500m; bike hire; dogs free; poss cr; site clsd May; ccard acc; red CKE/CCI. "Well-kept, clean, friendly site; sm pitches; narr rds; recep open 1800-2000 LS - site yourself & pay later; excel NH." € 25.00 2016*

⊞ **LANGENWANG** *C4* (260m N Rural) *47.56875, 15.62008* **Europa Camping, Siglstrasse 5, 8665 Langenwang [(03854) 2950; fax (02143) 380982394; europa.camping.stmk@aon.at; www.campsite.at/europa.camping.langenwang]** Exit S6 sp Langenwang, site sp in town cent. Sm, hdg pitch, pt shd; htd wc; chem disp; shwrs €0.80; EHU (16A) metered; lndry; shop, rest, snacks, bar 100m; playgrnd adj; htd, covrd pool 7km; lake sw 4km; ski facs; 30% statics; dogs; bus; Eng spkn; adv bkg; quiet; red long stay. "Pleasant, friendly site; family atmosphere; excel facs; peaceful site." € 15.00 2013*

LERMOOS see Ehrwald *C1*

LEUTASCH see Seefeld in Tirol *C1*

LIENZ *C2* (6km SE Rural) *46.80730, 12.80350* **Camping Seewiese, Tristachersee 2, 9900 Tristach [tel/fax (04852) 69767; seewiese@hotmail.com; www.campingtirol.com]** On B100 to Lienz dir Tristach, turn sharp L after rlwy underpass & rv bdge to by-pass Trisach. Turn R after 4km opp golf course. Steep (11%) climb to site. Sp. Med, some hdstg, sl, pt shd; wc; chem disp; mv service pnt; shwrs inc; EHU (6-16A) €2.70; gas; lndry (inc dryer); sm shop & 5km; rest & 500m; bar; playgrnd; htd pool 5km; lake sw 200m; tennis; bike hire; wifi; TV rm; dogs €3; bus high ssn to Tristach; phone; poss cr; Eng spkn; quiet; red LS; CKE/CCI. "Fairly secluded, relaxing site; mountain views; gd walks; gd san facs; helpful owner." 15 May-14 Sep. € 36.00 2015*

LIENZ *C2* (2km S Rural) *46.81388, 12.76388* **Dolomiten-Camping Amlacherhof, Lake rd 20, 9908 Amlach Lienz [(04852) 62317 or 69917 62317-1 (mob); fax 62317-12; info@amlacherhof.at; www.amlacherhof.at]** S fr Lienz on B100, foll sp in 1.5km to Amlach. In vill, foll site sp. Med, hdg/mkd pitch, pt shd; htd wc; chem disp; mv service pnt; fam bthrm; shwrs €0.80; EHU (16A) metered inc; lndry (inc dryer); rest 500m; snacks; bar; BBQ; playgrnd; htd pool; tennis; bike hire; games rm; golf 7km; wifi; TV rm; 5% statics; dogs €2.90; bus adj; site clsd 1 Nov-15 Dec; poss cr; Eng spkn; adv bkg; quiet. "Excel touring cent; many mkd walks & cycle rtes; cable cars, ski lifts 3km; attractive, historic town; excel, scenic site; local taxes €5." ♦ 1 Mar-31 Oct. € 35.40 (CChq acc) 2014*

LIEZEN *C3* (11km SW Rural) *47.52061, 14.13080* **Camping Putterersee, Hohenberg 2A, 8943 Aigen [tel/fax (03682) 22859; camping.putterersee@aon.at; www.camping-putterersee.at]** S on A10 fr Salzburg, exit 63 for E651/B320 twds Hohenberg. Foll sp. Med, pt sl, pt shd, htd wc; chem disp; shwrs inc; EHU (13A); gas; lndry (inc dryer); shop 1km; rest; snacks; bar; BBQ; playgrnd; sw lake, beach; fishing; bike hire; boat hire; games rm; wifi; dogs €2.20; twin axles; poss cr; Eng spkn; adv bkg; quiet; red LS; CKE/CCI. "Excel san facs; gd views, walking & cycling; v helpful staff; vg." ♦ ltd. 15 Apr-31 Oct. € 21.00 2015*

LINZ *B3* (14km SE Rural) *48.23527, 14.37888* **Camping-Linz am Pichlingersee, Wienerstrasse 937, 4030 Linz [(0732) 305314; office@camping-linz.at; www.camping-linz.at]** Exit A1/E60 junc 160; take Enns dir; go L on 1st rndabt; do not go under rndabt thro underpass; site is sp on R. Med, mkd pitch, pt shd; htd wc; chem disp; mv service pnt; shwrs inc; EHU (6A) inc; gas; lndry; sm shop & 2km; rest, snacks; bar; cooking facs; lake sw adj; tennis; internet; 40% statics; dogs €1.90; bus; site clsd 1300-1500; poss cr; Eng spkn; adv bkg; some noise fr m'way; red long stay. "Excel modern san facs, well-run, family-run site; friendly staff; gd walks around lake; monastery at St Florian worth visit; conv NH; gd." ♦ ltd. 15 Mar-15 Oct. € 26.50 2017*

LOFER *C2* (2km SE Rural) *47.57500, 12.70804* **Camping Park Grubhof, St Martin 39, 5092 St Martin-bei-Lofer [(06588) 82370; fax 82377; home@grubhof.com; www.grubhof.com]** Clear sps to camp at ent on rd B311 Lofer to Zell-am-See. Site on L after garden cent. Lge, pt shd; htd wc; chem disp; mv service pnt; fam bthrm; serviced pitches; shwrs inc; EHU (10A) €2; lndry (inc dryer); supmkt 700m; rest; bar; pool 1km; fitness cent; playgrnd; wifi; dogs €3; phone; adv bkg; bus to Salzburg; quiet; ccard not acc; CKE/CCI. "Beautiful scenery; roomy, peaceful site; excel san facs; adult only & dog free areas; sh walk to vill; highly rec; mountain views; some meadowside and rvside pitches; delightful rest/bar." ♦
1 Jan-23 Mar, 11 Apr-2 Nov, 6 Dec-31 Dec. € 36.00
SBS - G04 2015*

See advertisement

⊞ **LUNZ AM SEE** *B4* (900m E Urban) *47.86194, 15.03638* **Ötscherland Camping, Zellerhofstrasse 23, 3293 Lunz-am-See [tel/fax (07486) 8413; info@oetscherlandcamping.at; www.oetscherlandcamping.at]** Fr S on B25 turn R into Lunz-am-See. In 300m turn L, cross rv & take 1st L, site on L on edge of vill. Sm, hdstg, pt shd; htd wc; chem disp; mv service pnt; shwrs €1; EHU (16A) inc; lndry; shop, rest in vill; lake sw 500m; winter skiing; 80% statics; dogs €1; Eng spkn; quiet. "Excel walking; immac facs; vg site on Rv Ybbs & Eisenstrasse." € 19.50 2016*

MAISHOFEN see Zell am See *C2*

MALTA see Gmünd (Kärnten) *C3*

MARBACH AN DER DONAU *B4* (1km W Rural) *48.21309, 15.13828* **Campingplatz Marbacher, Granz 51, 3671 Marbach-an-der Donau [tel/fax (07413) 20733; info@marbach-freizeit.at; www.marbach-freizeit.at]** Fr W exit A1 junc 100 at Ybbs onto B25. Cross Rv Danube & turn R onto B3. Site in 7km. Fr E exit A1 junc 90 at Pöchlarn, cross rv & turn L onto B3 to Marbach, site sp. Med, mkd pitch, pt shd; htd wc; chem disp; mv service pnt; shwrs inc; EHU (16A) €2.50; lndry (inc dryer); shop 500m; rest 500m; BBQ; rv sw; watersports; tennis 800m; boat & bike hire; internet; entmnt; 5% statics; Eng spkn; adv bkg; rlwy & rv noise; ccard acc; red CKE/CCI. "Beautiful, well-managed site; sm, narr pitches; excel facs & staff; gd rst & bar; gd cycling & watersports; v clean facs; gd NH fr m'way or longer stay for touring." ♦
1 Apr-31 Oct. € 28.00 (CChq acc) 2014*

MARIAZELL *B4* (4km NW Rural) *47.79009, 15.28221* **Campingplatz am Erlaufsee, Erlaufseestrasse 3, 8630 St Sebastien-bei-Mariazell [(03882) 4937 or (066460) 644400 (mob); gemeinde@st-sebastian.at; www.st-sebastian.at]** On B20 1km N of Mariazell turn W sp Erlaufsee. Site in 3km on app to lake, turn L thro car park ent to site. Med, pt sl, pt shd; wc; chem disp; shwrs €0.50; EHU (12A) metered; lndry; shop 3km; rest, snacks adj; beach nr; bus high ssn; dogs €1.90; quiet. "Cable car in Mariazell; pilgrimage cent; all hot water by token fr owner." 1 May-15 Sep. € 16.30 2016*

MATREI IN OSTTIROL *C2* (500m S Rural) *46.99583, 12.53906* **Camping Edengarten, Edenweg 15a, 9971 Matrei-in-Osttirol [tel/fax (04875) 5111; info@campingedengarten.at; www.campingedengarten.at]** App fr Lienz on B108 turn L bef long ascent (by-passing Matrei) sp Matrei-in-Osttirol & Camping. App fr N thro Felbertauern tunnel, by-pass town, turn R at end of long descent, sps as above. Med, pt shd; wc; chem disp; mv service pnt; shwrs €0.50; EHU (10A); gas; lndry; supmkt, rest, snacks adj; bar; playgrnd; pool 300m; 10% statics; dogs; bus; poss cr. "Gd mountain scenery; helpful owner; beautiful views; pretty town; some rd noise during daytime."
1 Apr-31 Oct. € 29.00 2014*

MATREI IN OSTTIROL *C2* (23km W Rural) *47.01912, 12.63695* **Camping Kals Am Großglockner, Burg 22, 9981 Kals am Großglockner [04852 67389; info@nationalpark-camping-kals.at; www.nationalpark-camping-kals.at]** Fr 108 Matrei in Osttirol to Lienz, exit at Huben onto L26 to Kals. 3km after vill foll sp to Dorfertal. National Park campsite on L. Med, unshd; htd wc; chem disp; mv service pnt; fam bthrm; shwrs inc; lndry (inc dryer); shop; rest; wifi; dogs €2.50; ski bus; twin axles acc; Eng spkn; quiet; ccard acc; CCI. "Excel site; excel walking & climbing." ♦
17 May-13 Oct. € 21.00 2014*

MAURACH see Schwaz *C2*

MAYRHOFEN *C2* (1km N Rural) *47.17617, 11.86969* **Camping Mayrhofen, Laubichl 125, 6290 Mayrhofen [(05285) 6258051; fax 6258060; camping@alpenparadies.com; www.alpenparadies.com]** Site at N end of vill off B169. Lge, mkd pitch, hdstg, pt shd; wc; chem disp; mv service pnt; sauna; shwrs inc; EHU (10A) €2.50 or metered; gas; lndry; shop 1km; rest, snacks; playgrnd; pool; bike hire; wifi; 50% statics; dogs €3; site clsd 1 Nov-15 Dec; adv bkg; poss cr; some factory noise; CKE/CCI. "Modern san facs; diff for lge o'fits, narr rds; gd rest." ♦
1 Jan-31 Oct & 10 Dec-31 Dec. € 25.00 2012*

MELK *B4* (3km N Urban) *48.24298, 15.34040* **Donau Camping Emmersdorf, Bundesstrasse 133, 3644 Emmersdorf-an-der-Donau [(02752) 71707; fax (2752) 7146930; office@emmersdorf.at; www.emmersdorf.at]** Fr A1 take Melk exit. Turn R, foll sp Donaubrücke, cross rv bdge. Turn R, site 200m on L, well sp. Sm, mkd/hdg pitch, pt shd; wc; chem disp; fam bthrm; shwrs inc; EHU (6A) inc; lndry (inc dryer); shops 300m; supmkt 3km; rest 300m; BBQ; pool 13km; fishing; tennis; bike hire; games rm; dogs; phone; noise fr rd & disco w/end; ccard acc; CKE/CCI. "Liable to close if rv in flood; clean facs; attractive vill; vg." ♦
1 May-30 Sep. € 19.00 2014*

MELK *B4* (6km NE Rural) *48.25395, 15.37115* **Campingplatz Stumpfer, 3392 Schönbühel [(02752) 8510; fax 851017; office@stumpfer.com; www.stumpfer.com]** Exit A1 junc 80. Foll sp for Melk on B1 as far as junc with B33. Turn onto B33 (S bank of Danube) for 2km to Schönbühel. Site on L adj gasthof, sp. Sm, pt shd, wc; chem disp; shwrs; EHU (10-16A) €2.40 or metered; gas; lndry; shops 5km; rest, snacks; rv adj; dogs; poss v cr; Eng spkn; adv bkg; ccard acc; red long stay/CKE/CCI. "On beautiful stretch of Danube; arr early for rvside pitch; abbeys in Melk & Krems worth visit; lower end site unrel in wet; helpful staff; vg facs but poss stretched high ssn; cycle path adj." 1 Apr-31 Oct. € 28.50 2017*

MELK *B4* (3.6km NW Rural) *48.23347, 15.32888* **Camping Fährhaus Melk, Kolomaniau 3, 3390 Melk [tel/fax (02752) 53291; info@faehrhaus-melk.at; www.faehrhaus-melk.at]** Skirt Melk on B1, immed after abbey at traff lts, turn N on bdge over rv (sp). Site in 700m. Sm, pt shd; wc; shwrs; EHU (6A) inc; shop & 1km; rest at Gasthaus; snacks; bar; BBQ; playgrnd; fishing. "Basic site but adequate; abbey adj & boating on Danube; NB all sites on banks of Danube liable to close if rv in flood." 1 Apr-31 Oct. € 12.50 2016*

MILLSTATT *D3* (4km SE Rural) *46.78863, 13.61418* **Camping Neubauer, Dellach 3, 9872 Millstatt-am-See [(04766) 2532; fax 25324; info@camping-neubauer.at; www.camping-neubauer.at]** Exit A10/E55 dir Seeboden & Millstatt. Take lakeside rd B98 fr Millstatt to Dellach, R turn & foll sp camping sp. Med, mkd pitch, some hdstg, terr, pt shd; htd wc; chem disp; fam bthrm; shwrs inc; EHU (6A) inc; gas; lndry (inc dryer); shop; rest adj; snacks; bar; BBQ; playgrnd; lake sw; watersports; tennis; bike hire; golf 6km; wifi; entmnt; 10% statics; dogs €2; poss cr; no adv bkg; quiet; ccard acc. "Gd touring base; easy access to Italy; superb scenery with lakes & mountains; gd walks; excel facs; boat trips nr; gd rest; steep narr rd's to pitches, tractor avail to help; pt shd on lake pitches." 1 May-15 Oct. € 33.00 2013*

MITTERSILL *C2* (1km E Rural) *47.27761, 12.49267* **Camping Schmidl, Museumstrasse 6, 5730 Mittersill [(06562) 6158]** Fr Zell-am-See or Kitzbühel, exit to Mittersill, fr town sq foll camping sp past hospital. Sm, pt shd; wc; chem disp; shwrs €0.60; EHU (15A) inc; shop 1km; dogs; poss cr; quiet. "Friendly & welcoming; useful stop bef Felbertauern tunnel; conv Krimml waterfall & Grossglockner; large CL type with pitches for 10 o'fits; gd for NH." 1 May-30 Sep. € 12.00 2015*

MONDSEE *B3* (5km SE Rural) *47.82956, 13.36554* **Austria Camp, Achort 60, 5310 St Lorenz [(06232) 2927; fax 29274; office@austriacamp.at; austriacamp.at]** Exit A1/E55/E60 junc 265 onto B154. In 4km at St Lorenz at km 21.4 turn L onto unclassified rd to site in 600m at lakeside. Fr SW via Bad Ischl, at St Gilgen take Mondsee rd; 500m after Plomberg turn R at St Lorenz; Austria Camp sps clear. Med, shd; wc; chem disp; mv service pnt; sauna; fam bthrm; shwrs inc; EHU (6A) €2.90; lndry (inc dryer); rest, snacks; bar; shop; playgrnd; lake sw; fishing; boat-launch; tennis; bike hire; golf nr; entmnt; 45% statics; dogs €2.90; poss cr (Jul-Aug); adv bkg; quiet; 10% red CKE/CCI. "Gd, clean san facs; gd rest; friendly, family-run site; no arrivals bet 1200 & 1500." ♦ 1 Apr-30 Sep. € 30.00 2015*

⊞ **MURAU** *C3* (3km W Rural) *47.10791, 14.13883* **Camping Olachgut, Kaindorf 90, 8861 St Georgen-ob-Murau [(03532) 2162 or 3233; fax 21624; office@olachgut.at; www.olachgut.at]** Site sp on rd B97 bet Murau & St Georgen. Med, pt shd; wc; chem disp; mv service pnt; fam bthrm; sauna; shwrs inc; EHU (16A) metered; gas conn; lndry (inc dryer); shop 2.5km; rest, snacks; bar; playgrnd; lake sw; games area; bike hire; ski lift 2.5km; horseriding; entmnt; internet; 40% statics; dogs €2.20; adv bkg; quiet."Rural site nr rlwy." ♦ € 25.00 2012*

MURECK *D4* (700m S Rural) *46.70491, 15.77240* **Campingplatz Mureck, Austrasse 10, 8480 Mureck [(03472) 210512; fax 21056; m.rauch@mureck.steiermark.at; www.mureck.gv.at/tourismus-freizeit/campingplatz]** Fr Graz on A9, turn E at junc 226 onto B69 sp Mureck. NB: Low archway in Mureck. Med, mkd pitch, some hdstg, shd; wc; chem disp; shwrs €0.50; EHU (10A) inc; lndry (inc dryer); shops adj; rest, snacks; bar; BBQ; playgrnd; htd pool complex inc waterslide adj; fishing; tennis; bike hire; games area; wifi; 30% statics; dogs €3.50; phone; adv bkg; quiet; red long stay; ccard acc; red CKE/CCI. "Off beaten track in pleasant country town; pt of leisure complex; gd, modern san facs." ♦ 1 May-3 Nov. € 23.00 2016*

⊞ **NASSEREITH** *C1* (2.5km SE Rural) *47.30975, 10.85466* **Camping Rossbach, Rossbach 325, 6465 Nassereith [tel/fax (05265) 5154; rainer.ruepp@gmx.at; www.campingrossbach.com]** On ent vill of Nassereith turn E & foll dir Rossbach/Dormitz, site in 1.5km. Foll sm green sps. Narr app. Med, mkd pitch, pt shd; htd wc; chem disp; mv service pnt; fam bthrm; shwrs inc; EHU (6A); lndry (inc dryer); shop; rest, snacks; bar; BBQ; playgrnd; htd pool; paddling pool; fishing; games rm; ski lift 500m; skibus; TV; 5% statics; dogs €1.50; phone; adv bkg; quiet; CKE/CCI. "Mountain views; friendly welcome; ACSI prices; pitch in various sep areas; vg san facs." ♦ € 23.50 2017*

NATTERS see Innsbruck *C1*

NAUDERS *C1* (4km S Rural) *46.85139, 10.50472* **Alpencamping, Bundestrasse 279, 6543 Nauders [(05473) 87217; fax 8721750; info@camping-nauders.at; www.camping-nauders.com]** On W side of B180 just bef Italian border. Sm, some hdstg, unshd; htd wc; chem disp; fam bthrm; shwrs €0.50; EHU €1.90; gas conn; lndry; shop & 2km; rest, snacks; bar; no statics; dogs €2; phone; poss cr; ccard acc; CKE/CCI. "Conv NH for Reschen pass; gd touring base; excel cycling, walking; excel san facs." 1 Jan-16 Apr, 30 Apr-15 Oct, 20 Dec-31 Dec. € 25.00 2016*

⊞ **NEUSTIFT IM STUBAITAL** *C1* (500m NE Rural) *47.10977, 11.30770* **Camping Stubai, Stubaitalstrasse 94, 6167 Neustift-im-Stubaital [(05226) 2537; fax 29342; info@campingstubai.at; www.campingstubai.at]** S fr Innsbruck on B182 or A13, take B183 dir Fulpmes & Neustift. Site sp, in vill opp church & adj Billa supmkt. If app via A13 & Europabrucke, toll payable on exit junc 10 into Stubaital Valley. Med, some mkd pitch, pt sl, pt terr, pt shd; htd wc; chem disp; mv service pnt; fam bthrm; sauna; shwrs inc; EHU (6A) €2.90; lndry; shops adj; rest, bar adj; playgrnd; htd pool 500m; games rm; 50% statics; dogs €2.60; Eng spkn; adv bkg; quiet but church bells (not o'night) & rd noise fr some pitches; debit cards acc; CKE/CCI. "Friendly, family-run site; pitches nr rv poss flood; recep open 0900-1100 & 1700-1900 - barrier down but can use farm ent & find space; excel mountain walking & skiing; lovely location." € 34.00 2017*

⊞ **NEUSTIFT IM STUBAITAL** *C1* (6km SW Rural) *47.06777, 11.25388* **Camping Edelweiss, Volderau 29, 6167 Neustift-im-Stubaital [tel/fax (05226) 3484; info@camping-edelweiss.at; www.camping-edelweiss.com]** Fr B182 or A13 exit junc 10 take B183 to Neustift, site on R at Volderau vill. Med, hdstg, unshd; htd wc; chem disp; mv waste; shwrs inc; EHU (4A) €2; gas; lndry; shop 6km; rest, snacks; 30% statics; dogs €1.50; phone; bus; quiet. "Excel peaceful site in scenic valley; vg, modern san facs; haphazard mix of statics & tourers; winter skiing." € 20.00 2012*

NUZIDERS see Bludenz *C1*

⊞ **OBERNBERG AM INN** *B3* (1km SW Rural) *48.31506, 13.32313* **Panorama Camping, Saltzburgerstrasse 28, 4982 Obernberg-am-Inn [tel/fax (07758) 30024 or 173 2306 571 (mob); obernberg-panoramacamping@aon.at; http://obernberg-panoramacamping.jimdo.com]** Exit A8/E56 junc 65 to Obernberg. Then take dir Braunau, site well sp. Sm, hdg pitch, pt sl, pt shd; wc; chem disp; serviced pitches; shwrs inc; EHU (10A) metered or €2 (poss rev pol); lndry; shop 200m; rest 400m; pool, tennis 800m; o'night area for m'vans; Eng spkn; adv bkg; quiet. "Friendly, excel sm site; site yourself if office clsd; nr to border; spectacular views; san facs clean; gd walking, birdwatching; network of cycle paths around vills on other side of rv; pleasant walk to town past rv viewpoint." € 29.00 2015*

OBERSAMMELSDORF see Völkermarkt *D3*

OBERTRAUN WINKL see Hallstatt *C3*

Motorways
Major roads
Main roads
All year site(s)
Seasonal site(s)
No sites listed
200m +
0–200m
GERMANY
CZECHIA (CZECH REPUBLIC)
SWITZERLAND
ITALY
SLOVENIA
CROATIA
HUNGARY
N
E
S
W
München
Memmingen
Rosenheim
Passau
Frymburk
GMUND
Waidhofen an der Thaya
Zwettl
Znojmo
Brno
Poysdorf
SCHÄRDING
Engelhartszell
Aschach an der Donau
Krems an der Donau
BRAUNAU AM INN
Obernberg am Inn
LINZ
Grein
Melk
ST PÖLTEN
Klosterneuburg
WIEN
Marbach an der Donau
Sulz im Wienerwald
Steyr
Attersee
GMUNDEN
Mondsee
Scharnstein
Lunz am See
Kaumberg
Purbach am Neusiedlersee
SALZBURG
EISENSTADT
MARIAZELL
Kössen
Hallein
Eben im Pongau
St Wolfgang im Salzkammergut
Abersee
Füssen
Garmisch-Partenkirchen
BREGENZ
Dornbirn
GRAN
REUTTE
St Johann in Tirol
Lofer
Spital am Pyhrn
Bad Aussee
Sopron
Ehrwald
Seefeld in Tirol
Jenbach
Werfen
Hallstatt
Liezen
Langenwang
Nassereith
Rattenberg
KITZBÜHEL
RADSTADT
Imst
Pettnau
Telfs
ZELL AM SEE
BRUCK AN DER MUR
St Anton am Arlberg
INNSBRUCK
Hall in Tirol
BLUDENZ
LANDECK
Oetz
Zell am Ziller
Mittersill
Bruck an der Grossglocknerstrasse
Prutz
Neustift im Stubaital
Mayrhofen
St Peter am Kammersberg
Oberwölz
Ried Im Oberinntal
Murau
JUDENBURG
St Michael im Lungau
Nauders
Sölden
Vipiteno
Matrei in Osttirol
Kals am Großglockner
GRAZ
FÜRSTENFELD
Vasvár
Hirschegg
Gmünd
LIENZ
Malles Venosta
SPITTAL AN DER DRAU
Millstatt
Bad Gleichenberg
Dellach im Drautal
SILLIAN
Döbriach
Gnesau
St Veit an der Glan
LEIBNITZ
Kötschach
Ossiach
Völkermarkt
Mureck
Bolzano
Greifenburg
VILLACH
KLAGENFURT
Cortina d'Ampezzo
Keutschach am See
Lenti
Maribor
Kranjska Gora
Jesenice
Bled
LJUBLJANA
0 30 60 90 120 150 kms
0 30 60 90 mls
© Collins Bartholomew Ltd 2018

Ghent

Welcome to Belgium

Although a country of two halves, with French-speaking Wallonia making up the southern part of the country, and Dutch-speaking Flanders the north, Belgium is very much united when it comes to delicious cuisine, fascinating historic attractions and breathtaking modern architecture.

With several UNESCO world heritage sites, a diverse landscape and a range of museums and art galleries, you will be spoilt for choice when deciding how best to spend your time in this delightful country.

Country highlights

Most people associate Belgium with chocolate, mussels and beer, but there are other products which share an equal amount of tradition. Lace making has been practiced in Belgium for centuries, Bruges still renowned for the intricate designs and delicacy of its product.

Belgium has also played an important role in the development of comics, and can boast Georges Remi (Hergé), the creator of Tintin, and Pierre Culliford (Peyo) the man behind the smurfs amongst its talented celebrities.

Major towns and cities

- Brussels – this historic city is Belgium's capital.
- Ghent – a city filled with beautiful buildings and important museums.
- Antwerp – Belgium's largest city is filled with stunning landmarks.
- Liège – famous for its folk festivals and for hosting a large annual Christmas Market.

Attractions

- Grand-Place, Brussels – this opulent central square is a UNESCO World Heritage site.
- Gravensteen Castle, Ghent – a magnificent 12th century castle that houses a museum.
- Historic Centre, Bruges – the medieval architecture of the city centre is a must-see.
- Ypres – an ancient town filled with historic monuments, including the Menin Gate.

Find out more

www.visitbelgium.com

Tel: 0032 (0) 250 40 211 Bruxelles Tourist Office

Traffic Jams

During periods of fine weather roads to the coast, the Ardennes and around Brussels and Antwerp are very busy on Friday afternoons and Saturday mornings, and again on Sunday evenings.

Other busy routes are the E40 (Brussels to Ostend), the E25 (Liège to Bastogne and Arlon), the E411 (Brussels to Namur and Luxembourg), and the N4 from Bastogne to Arlon around the border town of Martelange caused by motorists queuing for cheap petrol in Luxembourg. Avoid traffic on the E40 by taking the R4 and N49, and on the E411 by taking the N4 Bastogne to Marche-en-Famenne and Namur.

These routes are heavily used and consequently the road surface can be poor.

Traffic Lights

A green light (arrow) showing at the same time as a red or amber light means that you can turn in the direction of the green arrow providing you give way to other traffic and to pedestrians. An amber light, possibly flashing, in the form of an arrow inclined at an angle of 45 degrees to the left or to the right, shows that the number of traffic lanes will be reduced.

Tunnels

Three road tunnels go under the River Scheldt at Antwerp. In the Liefkenhoeks tunnel on road R2 to the north of the city a toll of €17.60-19.00 (2018) for vehicles over 2.75m in height. Vehicles under 2.75m are charged €4.95-6.00. If you're towing your caravan will be included within this height categorisation. The Kennedy Tunnel on road R1 to the south of the city is toll-free but is heavily congested in both directions for much of the day. The smallest tunnel, the Waasland Tunnel is part of the N59a and is also toll-free.

Violation of Traffic Regulations

The police may impose on-the-spot fines on visitors who infringe traffic regulations such as speeding and parking offences. Penalties may be severe and if you are unable to pay on the spot your vehicle(s) may be impounded or your driving licence withdrawn. Fines can be paid in cash or with a debit or credit card. An official receipt must be issued.

In an effort to improve road safety the authorities have increased the number of speed traps throughout the country in the form of cameras and unmarked police vehicles.

Vehicles of 3,500 kg or over are not allowed to use the left lane on roads with more than three lanes except when approaching a fork in a motorway when vehicles have to move to the left or right lane, depending on their destination.

Motorways

Belgium has an extensive network of approximately 1,750km of motorways (A roads). Although Belgian motorways are toll free, the introduction of a motorway toll for vehicles over 3,500kg was introduced in April 2016.

Service areas usually have a petrol station, restaurant, shop, showers and toilets. Rest areas have picnic facilities. For detailed information about the motorway network see www.autosnelwegen.net.

Some motorways are so heavily used by lorries that the inside lane may become heavily rutted and/or potholed. These parallel ruts are potentially dangerous for caravans travelling at high speed. It is understood that parts of the A2/E314 and A3/E40 are particularly prone to this problem.

Touring

Flemish is spoken in the north of Belgium, whilst French is spoken in the south. Brussels is bi-lingual. English is widely spoken.

Prices in restaurants are quoted 'all inclusive' and no additional tipping is necessary. Smoking is severely restricted in public places including restaurants and cafés.

Carrier bags are generally not provided in supermarkets, so take your own.

When visiting Brussels visitors may buy a Brussels Card, valid for 24, 48 or 72 hours, which offers free access to virtually every major museum in the city and unlimited use of public transport, together with discounts at a number of other attractions. The pass is available from the tourist information office in the Hotel de Ville and from many hotels, museums and public transport stations, or visit www.brusselscard.be to buy online.

Public Transport

Anyone under the age of 25 years is entitled to free or reduced price travel on public transport in the Brussels region. During periods of severe air pollution public transport in that region is free to all passengers.

Brussels and Antwerp have metro systems together with extensive networks of trams and buses. Tram and bus stops are identified by a red and white sign and all stops are request stops; hold out your arm to signal an approaching bus or tram to stop. Tickets, including 10-journey and one-day travel cards, are available from vending machines at metro stations and some bus stops, newsagents, supermarkets and tourist information centres.

Most of Belgium is well connected by train and most main routes pass through Antwerp, Brussels or Namur. Trains are modern, comfortable and punctual and fares are reasonably priced. Buy tickets before boarding the train or you may be charged a supplement. Eurostar tickets to Brussels allow free, same day transfers to domestic Belgian stations.

Bikes are allowed on some buses in the Flanders area of the country.

Plans are in hand to introduce a unified smart card ticketing system covering all public transport, irrespective of company or mode of transport. This system will use chip cards, card readers and on-board computers.

Bruges

Sites in Belgium

ADINKERKE see De Panne *A1*

AISCHE EN REFAIL *B3* (350m E Rural) *50.59977, 4.84335* **Camping du Manoir de Là-Bas, Route de Gembloux 180, 5310 Aische-en-Refail [(081) 655353; europa-camping.sa@skynet.be; www.camping-manoirdelabas.be]** Fr E411/A4 exit junc 12 & foll sps to Aische-en-Refail. Site on o'skts of vill. Lge, pt sl, pt shd; wc; chem disp; mv service pnt; fam bthrm; shwrs €1; EHU (6A) inc; gas; lndry; shop 0.5km; rest; snacks; bar; BBQ; playgrnd; htd pool; paddling pool; fishing; tennis; games rm; entmnt; 50% statics; dogs €3; phone; poss cr; Eng spkn; adv bkg; quiet; CKE/CCI. "Friendly staff; site little run down; ltd hot water; poor san facs, dated & long way fr pitches; some site rds are narr; recep far side of chateau; gd rest & bar (clsd in Sep); site needs updating (2014); poor; NH only; sm pitches; rec NH only." ♦ 1 Apr-31 Oct. € 25.00 2017*

AMBERLOUP/STE ODE see Tenneville *C3*

"There aren't many sites open at this time of year"

If you're travelling outside peak season remember to call ahead to check site opening dates – even if the entry says 'open all year'.

⊞ **ANTWERPEN** *A3* (6km NW Urban) *51.23347, 4.39261* **Camping De Molen, Thonelaan - Jachthavenweg 6, St Annastrand, 2050 Antwerpen [tel/fax (03) 2198179; info@camping-de-molen.be; www.camping-de-molen.be]** Clockwise on ring rd, take 1st exit after Kennedy tunnel, exit 6. R at traff lts, 3rd L where cannot go strt on (rv on R), site on R in 1km on bank of Rv Schelde. Or on ent Antwerp foll sp Linkeroever, go strt on at 3 traff lts, then turn L & foll camping sp. Fr A14/E17 exit junc 7 & foll sp for Linkeroever Park & Ride until site sp appear, then foll sp. Med, pt shd; wc; chem disp; shwrs; EHU (10A) €2.50 (poss rev pol) - €30 deposit for adaptor/cable; shops 1km; supmkt by metro; rest adj; pool nr; wifi; bus nrby; metro 1km; poss cr; Eng spkn; adv bkg rec; quiet, but some rv traff noise & poss noise fr local bar; ccard not acc; red LS. "Popular site; max 14 nt stay; pedestrian/cycle tunnel to city cent 1km; gd for rollerblading, cycling; friendly, helpful staff; mosquitoes poss a problem; san facs satisfactory; 30 min walk or bus to city cent; site tired." ♦ € 28.00 2016*

⊞ **ARLON** *D3* (2km N Urban) *49.70215, 5.80678* **Camping Officiel Arlon, 373 Rue de Bastogne, Bonnert, 6700 Arlon [tel/fax (063) 226582; camping officiel@skynet.be; www.campingofficielarlon.be]** Fr E411 exit junc 31 onto N82 Arlon for 4km, turn twd Bastogne on N4. Site sp on R. Med, pt sl, pt shd; wc; chem disp; fam bthrm; shwrs inc; EHU (6A) €2.40 (check earth); gas; lndry (inc dryer); shop 2km; rest, snacks; bar; BBQ; playgrnd; pool; wifi; TV rm; dogs €2; Eng spkn; poss cr; adv bkg; some rd noise; red long stay; CKE/CCI. "Charming, clean, well laid out, pretty site; levelling blocks/ramps req - supplied by site; c'vans tight-packed when site busy; 5km approx to Luxembourg for cheap petrol; Arlon interesting town; vg NH & longer stay; thoroughly rec for stop over; payment cash only; 3 hdstgs for m'van; new pool; san facs updated, v clean; busy but organised." ♦ € 24.50 2017*

ARLON *D3* (7.6km N Rural) *49.74833, 5.78697* **Camping Sud, 75 Voie de la Liberté, 6717 Attert [(063) 223715; fax 221554; info@campingsudattert.com; www.campingsudattert.com]** Off N4 Arlon rd on E side of dual c'way. Sp to site fr N4 (500m). U-turn into site ent. Med, hdg/mkd pitch, some hdstg, pt shd; htd wc; chem disp; shwrs €0.50 (high ssn); EHU (5-10A) €2.50 (check earth); lndry; shop; rest, snacks; bar; BBQ; playgrnd; pool; dogs €2; phone; bus; adv bkg; Eng spkn; quiet, some rd noise; red long stay; CKE/CCI. "Vg, well-organised site; special NH pitches; fishing & walking; peaceful site; v friendly staff; highly rec." 1 Apr-15 Oct. € 25.00 2014*

ATTERT see Arlon *D3*

AVE ET AUFFE see Han sur Lesse *C3*

⊞ **AYWAILLE** *C3* (1km E Urban) *50.47633, 5.68916* **Domaine Chateau de Dieupart, Route de Dieupart 37, 4920 Aywaille [(042) 631238; fax 462690; info@dieupart.be; www.dieupart.be]** Leave E25 at exit 46 Remouchamps/Aywaille. Turn R at traff lts dir Aywaille, and R by church. Immed L and Rt at Delhaise car park, take ave up to the castle. Site SP. Med, pt sh; wc; chem disp; mv service pnt; shwrs; EHU (6A) inc; rest; bar; BBQ; playgrnd; wifi; 50% statics; bus 500m, train 1.5km, Eng spkn, adv bkg acc; CKE/CCI, red LS. "Nice site by rv; gd walking and cycling; supmkt 300m." ♦ € 23.00 2013*

BASTOGNE *C3* (1.6km WNW Urban) *50.00340, 5.69525* **Camping de Renval, 148 Route de Marche, 6600 Bastogne [tel/fax (061) 212985; www.campingderenval.be]** Fr N leave A26 exit 54, foll Bastogne sp. Fr Marche-en-Famenne dir, exit N4 at N84 for Bastogne; site on L in 150m opp petrol stn. Fr E foll Marche, in 1km site on R opp petrol stn. Med, hdstg, pt sl, terr, pt shd; htd wc; chem disp; fam bthrm; shwrs inc; EHU (10A) inc (poss rev pol); lndry (inc); shops 1km; snacks; BBQ; playgrnd; tennis; games area; wifi; entmnt; 95% statics; dogs €3; site clsd Jan; quiet; ccard acc; red LS. "Take care speed bumps; helpful staff; clean san facs but long walk fr tourers' pitches; gd security; facs ltd LS; gd NH." 1 Feb-31 Dec. € 24.00 2014*

"That's changed – Should I let The Club know?"

If you find something on site that's different from the site entry, fill in a report and let us know. See camc.com/europereport.

BERTRIX *D3* (2km S Rural) *49.83942, 5.25360* **Ardennen Camping Bertrix, Route de Mortehan, 6880 Bertrix [(061) 412281; fax 412588; info@campingbertrix.be; www.campingbertrix.be]** Exit A4/E411 junc 25 onto N89 for Bertrix & foll yellow sps to site. Lge, mkd pitch, terr, pt shd; htd wc; chem disp; mv service pnt; fam bthrm; some serviced pitches; sauna; shwrs inc; EHU (10A) €4; gas; lndry (inc dryer); shop high ssn; rest, snacks; bar; playgrnd; htd pool high ssn; paddling pool; tennis; bike hire; internet; TV rm; 35% statics; dogs €5; poss cr; Eng spkn; adv bkg; quiet; ccard acc; red LS/snr citizens; red LS/CKE/CCI. "Excel site; scenic location; friendly, helpful owners; gd for families; excel clean facs; gd rest; lg pitches; big pool." ♦ 26 Mar-11 Nov. € 43.00 (CChq acc) 2013*

BREDENE see Oostende *A1*

BRUGES see Brugge *A2*

⊞ **BRUGGE** *A2* (5km E Urban) *51.20722, 3.26305* **Camping Memling, Veltemweg 109, 8310 Sint Kruis [(050) 355845; fax 357250; info@camping-memling.be or info@brugescamping.be; www.camping-memling.be or www.brugescamping.be]** Exit A10 junc 8 Brugge. In 2km turn R onto N397 dir St Michiels & cont 2km to rlwy stn on R. Turn R under rlwy tunnel & at 1st rndbt take dir Maldegem onto ring rd & in a few kms take N9 sp Maldegem & St Kruis. After 3km at traff lts adj MacDonalds, turn R & immed L sp Camping to site on R in 400m past sw pool. Fr Gent exit E40 sp Oostkamp & foll Brugge sp for 7km to N9 as above. Med, mkd pitch, some hdstg, pt shd; htd wc; chem disp; mv service pnt; shwrs inc; EHU (6A) inc (poss rev pol); lndry; shops 500m; 3 supmkts nrby; rest, snacks, bar 500m; htd pool adj; bike hire; wifi; 13% statics; dogs €2; bus 200m; poss v cr; Eng spkn; adv bkg ess high ssn; poss noisy at w/ends & rd noise; ccard acc; red LS/long stay; CKE/CCI. "Busy site; red LS as no shwrs/rest/bar; friendly, helpful owners; recep open 0800-2200 (all day to 2200 high ssn); arr early high ssn to ensure pitch; LS site yourself & report to recep; conv Zeebrugge ferry (30mins) & allowed to stay to 1500; conv bus svrs every 20 mins to Bruges; adv bkgs taken but no pitch reserved; m'van pitches sm, rec pay extra for standard pitch; clean new san facs (2016); cycle rte or 35 min walk to Bruges; nice site; rec." € 32.00 2016*

⊞ **BRUGGE** *A2* (4km S Urban) *51.19634, 3.22573* **Motorcaravan Park, Off ring rd R30, Buiten Katelijnevest, Brugge** Exit A10 at junc 7 twd Brugge. After going under rlwy bdge, turn R on ring rd immed after marina to dedicated mv parking adj coach parking, nr marina. Sm, hdstg, pt shd; chem disp €0.50; EHU (10A) inc; washrm nr; water €0.50; shop 500m; dogs; noisy; m'vans only; red LS. "In great location - gd view of canal, sh walk to town cent thro park; rec arr early high ssn; if full, take ticket & park in coach park opp; NH only; vg for city ctr; narr spaces; bef leaving pay at machine & leave thro coach pk." € 25.00 2017*

⊞ **BRUGGE** *A2* (13km SW Urban) *51.18448, 3.10445* **Recreatiepark Klein Strand, Varsenareweg 29, 8490 Jabbeke [(050) 811440; fax 814289; info@kleinstrand.be; www.kleinstrand.be]** Fr W leave A10/E40 at Jabbeke exit, junc 6; turn R at rndabt & in 100m turn R into narr rd. Foll site to statics car pk on L & park - walk to check-in at recep bef proceeding to tourer site in 400m. Fr E leave A10/E40 at junc 6 (Jabbeke) turn L at 1st rndabt. Drive over m'way twd vill. Turn L at next rndabt & foll site sp into site car pk as above. Out of ssn carry on along rd to recep by lake. V lge, hdg/mkd pitch, pt shd; wc; chem disp; mv service pnt; fam bthrm; shwrs €0.75; EHU (10A) inc; gas; lndry (inc dryer); shop & 1km; 2 rests (1 open all yr); snacks; 3 bars; BBQ; playgrnd; paddling pool; direct access to lake sw adj; tennis; fishing; watersports; bike hire; games rm; wifi; entmnt; TV; 75% statics; dogs €2; no o'fits over 12m; bus to Brugge; poss cr with day visitors; Eng spkn; quiet but backgrnd m'way noise; ccard acc; red LS/CKE/CCI. "Busy site; vg touring base; lge pitches; wide range of entmnt & excursions; bus to Bruges every 20 mins." ♦ € 39.00 (up to 4 persons) SBS - H15 2017*

See advertisement opposite

BRUSSELS see Bruxelles *B2*

BRUXELLES *B2* (13km N Rural) *50.93548, 4.38226* **Camping Grimbergen, Veldkantstraat 64, 1850 Grimbergen [(0479) 760378 or (02) 2709597; fax (02) 2701215; camping-grimbergen@webs.com]** Fr Ostend on E40/A10 at ringrd turn E & foll sp Leuven/Luik (Liège)/Aachen. Exit junc 7 N sp Antwerpen/Grimbergen N202. At bus stn traff lts turn R twd Vilvourde N211. Turn L at 2nd traff lts (ignore no L turn - lorries only). Site sp 500m on R. Ent via pool car pk. Med, hdg pitch, pt sl, pt shd; wc; chem disp; shwrs inc; EHU (10A) €2.50; lndry; shops 500m; rest adj; pool adj; bike hire; dogs €1; phone; hourly bus to city 200m; Eng spkn; adv bkg; quiet but some aircraft noise & cock crowing; CKE/CCI. "Well-run, popular site - rec arr early; gd, clean, modern san facs; helpful staff; sh walk to town; train to Brussels fr next vill; red facs LS; gates clsd 1130-1400 and 2000 onwards; gd rest by bus stop; conv Brussels; excel san facs; rec; gd NH." ♦ 1 Apr-25 Oct. € 26.00 2014*

BRUXELLES *B2* (13km E Urban) *50.85720, 4.48506* **RCCC de Belgique, Warandeberg 52, 1970 Wezembeek [(02) 7821009; info@campingbrussels.be; www.rcccb.com]** Leave ringrd RO at junc 2 sp Kraainem turning E. In 140m 1st intersection on dual c'way (by pedestrian x-ing) turn L into Wezembeek. Foll orange camping sp taking rd to the R around church. Foll rd to crest of hill. Site on L bet houses. Narr ent, easy to miss. Med, mkd pitch, hdstg, terr, pt sl, pt shd; wc; chem disp; shwrs inc; EHU (6A) inc (poss rev pol & no earth); gas 3km; lndry rm; shop, rest, snacks 1km; bar; playgrnd; 65% statics; dogs €1; metro nr; gates clsd 1200-1400 & 2200-0800; Eng spkn; adv bkg; some rd & aircraft noise; ccard acc; CKE/CCI. "Poss diff for lge o'fits due narr site ent, v tight corners, raised kerbs; updated san facs (2015); gd for metro into Brussels fr Kraainem; welcoming wardens." 1 Apr-30 Sep. € 22.50 2016*

BURE/TELLIN see Tellin *C3*

DAMME see Brugge *A2*

DE HAAN *A1* (2.6km ENE Coastal) *51.28330, 3.05610* **Camping Ter Duinen, Wenduinesteenweg 143, Vlissegem, 8421 De Haan [(050) 413593; fax 416575; lawrence.sansens@scarlet.be; www.campingterduinen.be]** Exit A10/E40 junc 6 Jabbeke onto N377 dir De Haan. Go thro town dir Wenduine, site on R in 4km. Med, mkd pitch, pt shd; pt terr; htd wc; chem disp; mv service pnt; fam bthrm; shwrs €1.20; EHU (6A) inc; lndry (inc dryer); shop; snacks; bar; BBQ; playgrnd; htd pool 200m; water complex 1km; sand/shgl beach 500m; lake sw adj; fishing, bike hire 200m; horseriding 1km; golf 4km; wifi; 85% statics; dogs €5.75; phone; tram nrby; poss cr; Eng spkn; adv bkg ess; fairly quiet; CKE/CCI. "Neat, clean, well-managed site; friendly staff; poss long walk to excel san facs inc novelty wcs!; conv ferries, Bruges; excel; hot dish water req tokens, mkt in nrby towns." ♦ 15 Mar-15 Oct. € 40.00 (CChq acc) 2013*

DE HAAN *A1* (5km SW Urban/Coastal) *51.25698, 2.99150* **Camping 't Rietveld, Driftweg 210, 8420 De Haan [(0475) 669336; camping.rietveld@telenet.be; www.campingrietveld.be]** Fr Ostend on N34; fork R onto Driftweg bef golf club dir Vosseslag & Klemskerke, site sp. Sm, unshd, mkd pitch; htd wc; chem disp; fam bthrm; shwrs €1.20; EHU (16A) €1.95; lndry; shop, rest, snacks, bar in town; playgrnd; sand beach 1km; 80% statics; dogs €1.85; poss cr; Eng spkn; quiet; CKE/CCI. "Friendly, helpful staff; clean san facs." 1 Apr-15 Oct. € 20.50 2013*

⊞ **DE PANNE** *A1* (3km S Rural) *51.08288, 2.59094* **Camping Ter Hoeve, Duinhoekstraat 101, 8660 Adinkerke [(058) 412376; info@campingterhoeve.be; www.camping-terhoeve.be]** Leave Calais-Ostend m'way at junc 1 (ignore junc 1a) dir De Panne. Foll rd past theme park (Plopsaland), L at filling stn, site 1km on L. Lge, hdg pitch, pt shd; wc; chem disp; mv service pnt; shwrs inc; EHU (4A) €2 (poss no earth); lndry (inc dryer); shop; supmkt 1km; snacks; playgrnd; beach 2km; 60% statics; no dogs; tram 1km; poss cr; some daytime noise fr nrby theme park; ccard not acc. "Nice pitches; friendly, helpful owner; lge grassed area for tourers & hdstg area for late arr/early dep; barrier clsd 2200-0800 - go to visitors' car park on R bef booking in; v busy site high ssn, phone to check opening times LS; conv Dunkerque ferries & Plopsaland park; tram tickets avail at filling stn; coin operated dishwash water; san facs dated & clsd LS; Oct-Mar by appointment only." € 16.00 2017*

"I need an on-site restaurant"

We do our best to make sure site information is correct, but it is always best to check any must-have facilities are still available or will be open during your visit.

DE PANNE *A1* (4km S Rural) *51.07666, 2.58663* **Familie Camping Kindervreugde, Langgeleedstraat 1, 8660 Adinkerke [(050) 811440; fax 814289; info@kindervreugde.be; www.familiecamping.net]** Leave Calais-Ostend m'way at junc 1 (ignore junc 1a) dir De Panne. Foll rd past theme park (Plopsaland), L at filling stn, site 1.3km on L. Med, hdg pitch, pt shd; htd wc; chem disp; shwrs inc; EHU (6A) €2.50; lndry; shop, rest, snacks, bar 1km; BBQ; playgrnd; dogs; 50% statics; phone; bus 800m; Ltd Eng spkn; adv bkg; quiet; ccard not acc; red CKE/CCI. "Conv Dunkerque/Calais ferries; final appraoch diff for o'fits over 12ft." ♦ ltd. 1 Apr-30 Sep. € 30.00 (3 persons) 2013*

DEINZE see Ghent *A2*

⊞ **DINANT** *C3* (2km N Urban) *50.27722, 4.89694* **Camping Communal Devant-Bouvignes, 1 Quai de Camping, 5500 Dinant [(082) 224002; fax 224132; camping.communal@dinant.be; www.dinant.be]** Exit E11 junc 20 onto N936; drive to cent of Dinant (steep descent) to T-junc; turn R onto N92; cont along rv for 1.5km; site on L after bend. Med, pt shd; htd wc; chem disp; fam bthrm; shwrs €1; EHU (16A) €3; supmkt 1km; drinks avail; playgrnd; rv sw; 50% statics; dogs free; bus at ent; adv bkg; noisy, rd & rlwy noise; ccard not acc. "Excel situtation on rv bank; scruffy san facs; 25 min walk to interesting town." € 25.00 2017*

DINANT *C3* (14km NE Rural) *50.33557, 4.99534* **Camping de Durnal - Le Pommier Rustique, Rue de Spontin, 5530 Durnal [tel/fax (083) 699963 or (0475) 407827 (mob); info@camping-durnal.net; www.camping-durnal.net]** Leave E411 at junc 19. Turn S dir Spontin onto D946, then N937, foll site sp. Sm, mkd pitch, terr, unshd; wc; chem disp; fam bthrm; sauna; shwrs inc; EHU (10A) inc (check rev pol); lndry (inc dryer); shop; rest, snacks; playgrnd; games area; child entmnt high ssn; cab TV; wifi; mainly statics; dogs free; 4 nights for price of 3; Eng spkn; quiet; ccard acc. "Friendly, helpful owner; well-run, well-maintained site; ltd touring pitches; sm pitches; conv NH fr m'way; v quiet LS; modern san facs." ♦ 1 Mar-31 Dec. € 27.00 2013*

DINANT *C3* (18km SE Rural) *50.19094, 5.00611* **Camping de la Lesse, Rue du Camping 1, 5560 Houyet [(82) 666100; fax 667214; lafamiliale@coolweb.be; www.campingdelalesse.be]** S on N95 fr Dinant for about 13km; turn L onto D929 sp Houyet. Cross rlwy & immed turn L along Rv Lesse. Lge, pt shd; htd wc; chem disp; shwrs; EHU (15A) inc; lndry; shop 500m; rest, snacks; bar; playgrnd; pool adj; tennis; kayaking; fishing; 50% statics; dogs €2; train; poss noisy; CKE/CCI. "Pleasant area for walking/cycling; caves at Han-sur-Lesse worth visit; basic san facs." 1 Apr-31 Oct. € 20.00 2012*

⊞ **DOCHAMPS** *C3* (700m ESE Rural) *50.23080, 5.63180* **Panorama Campsite Petite Suisse, Al Bounire 27, 6960 Dochamps [(084) 444030; fax 444455; info@petitesuisse.be; www.petitesuisse.be]** Fr E25, take N89 (La Roche) at Samrée turn R onto N841 headed twrds Dochamp. Turn R into rd sp Al Bounire and foll sp to site. Lge, various sizes, mkd pitch, some hdstg, pt sl, terr, pt shd; htd wc; chem disp; mv service pnt; shwrs; fam bthrm; EHU (10A) inc; gas; lndry (inc dryer); shop; rest, snacks; bar; BBQ; playgrnd; htd pool; paddling pool; waterslide; tennis; games area; games rm; wifi; TV rm; adv bkg; 50% statics; dogs €5; bus 8km; phone; quiet; poss cr; ccard acc; red LS/snr citizens; CKE/CCI. "Outstanding facs; beautiful spot; busy, popular, excel site." ♦ € 35.50 2017*

⊞ **EEKLO** *A2* (7km E Rural) *51.18093, 3.64180* **Camping Malpertuus, Tragelstraat 12, 9971 Lembeke [(09) 3776178; fax 3270036; camping malpertuus@telenet.be; www.vkt.be]** Exit A10/E40 junc 11 onto N44 dir Aalter & Maldegem. Foll sp Eekloo onto N49 & then foll sp Lembeke, site sp. Med, pt shd; htd wc; chem disp; mv service pnt; shwrs €1; EHU (4A) €3; gas; lndry rm; shop 2km; rest 200m; snacks; bar; 85% statics; dogs; phone; bus 300m; Eng spkn; adv bkg; quiet; 10% red CKE/CCI. "Gd site in lovely area; friendly staff; entmnt/events at w/end; gd size pitches; gd site." ♦ ltd. € 15.50 2016*

⊞ **EUPEN** *B4* (3km SW Rural) *50.61457, 6.01686* **Camping Hertogenwald, Oestraat 78, 4700 Eupen [(087) 743222; fax 743409; info@camping-hertogenwald.be; www.camping-hertogenwald.be]** Fr German border customs on E40 a'bahn for Liège, take 2nd exit for Eupen. In Eupen L at 3rd traff lts & 1st R in 100m. Drive thro Eupen cent, foll sp to Spa. Camping sp immed at bottom of hill, sharp hairpin R turn onto N629, site on L in 2km. Med, unshd; htd wc; chem disp; shwrs inc; EHU (6A) inc (long lead req & poss no earth); lndry; shop 2km; rest, snacks; bar; playgrnd; htd, covrd pool 3km; games area; 90% statics; dogs €1.60; phone; poss cr; Eng spkn; quiet. "Sm tourer area; clean site adj rv & forest; muddy after rain; gd walking & cycling beside rv; conv Aachen." ♦ € 18.00 2016*

FLORENVILLE *D3* (17km E Rural) *49.68499, 5.52058* **Camping Chênefleur, Norulle 16, 6730 Tintigny [(063) 444078; fax 445271; info@chenefleur.be; www.chenefleur.be]** Fr Liège foll E25 dir Luxembourg. Exit junc 29 sp Habay-la-Neuve to Etalle, then N83 to Florenville. Site sp off N83 at E end of Tintigny vill. Med, pt shd; htd wc; chem disp; shwrs inc; fam bthrm; EHU (6-8A) inc; gas; lndry (inc dryer); shop; rest, snacks; bar; playgrnd; htd pool; paddling pool; games area; bike hire; wifi; entmnt; dogs €4; Eng spkn; adv bkg; quiet; ccard acc. "Orval Abbey, Maginot Line worth visit; friendly staff; gd, clean site & modern san facs; well kept site." ♦ 1 Apr-30 Sep. € 32.00 2012*

GEDINNE *C3* (1km SW Rural) *49.97503, 4.92719* **Camping La Croix Scaille, Rue du Petit Rot 10, 5575 Gedinne [(061) 588517; fax 588736; camping.croix-scaille@skynet.be; www.campingcroixscaille.be]** Fr N95 turn W to Gedinne on N935. Site sp S of vill on R after 1km. Lge, mkd pitch, some hdstg, terr, pt shd; htd wc; chem disp; shwrs inc; EHU (16A) €1.60; gas; lndry (inc dryer); snacks; bar; playgrnd; TV; pool; tennis, fishing adj; bike hire; 75% statics; dogs; poss cr; quiet; ccard acc; CKE/CCI. 1 Apr-15 Nov. € 13.40 2013*

⊞ **GEEL** *A3* (8km N Rural) *51.22951, 4.97836* **Camping Houtum, Houtum 51, 2460 Kasterlee [(014) 859216; fax 853803; info@campinghoutum.be; www.campinghoutum.be]** On N19 Geel to Turnhout rd 1km bef Kasterlee site sp on R at windmill opp British WW2 cemetery. Foll sps to site 500m on rd parallel to N19, cross next rd, site in 300m. Lge, mkd pitch, pt shd; htd wc; chem disp; shwrs €1; EHU (4-6A) €2; lndry; shops adj; snacks; lge playgrnd; pool 2km; adj to rv with boating, canoeing, fishing; tennis & mini-golf 300m; bike hire; nature trails adj; 60% statics; phone; poss v cr; adv bkg; v quiet; ccard acc; red long stay/CKE/CCI. "Orderly, attractive site; lots for children all ages." € 20.70 2013*

GHENT *A2* (14km SW Rural) *51.00508, 3.57228* **Camping Groeneveld, Groeneveldreef 14, Bachte-Maria-Leerne, 9800 Deinze [(09) 3801014; fax 3801760; info@campinggroeneveld.be; www.campinggroeneveld.be]** E or W E40/E10 on Brussels to Ostend m'way exit junc 13 at sp Gent W/Drongen. Take N466 sp Dienze. Approx 1km beyond junc with N437, turn L just after 2nd 70 km/h sp down narr side rd - house on corner has advert hoarding. Site on L opp flour mill. Sm sp at turning. Med, some hdg pitch, pt shd; htd wc; chem disp; mv service pnt; shwrs inc; EHU (10A) inc (poss no earth); shops 2km; rest (bkg ess), snacks, bar (w/end only LS); playgrnd; fishing; entmnt; TV; 40% statics; dogs €2; phone; poss cr; Eng spkn; adv bkg; quiet; red LS/long stay; CKE/CCI. "Gd welcome; additional san facs at lower end of site; office open 1900-2000 LS but staff in van adj san facs, or site yourself; barrier clsd until 0800; do not arr bef 1400; 1km fr Ooidonk 16th Castle; OK NH; gd site; bus to vill; some pitches tight." 1 Apr-31 Oct. € 23.00 2015*

GHENT *A2* (4km W Urban) *51.04638, 3.68083* **Camping Blaarmeersen, Zuiderlaan 12, 9000 Gent [(09) 2668160; fax 2668166; camping.blaarmeersen@gent.be; www.blaarmeersen.be]** Exit A10/E40 Brussels-Ostend m'way at junc 13 sp Gent W & Drongen. At T-junc turn onto N466 twd Gent. In 4km cross canal then turn R to site, sp (3 rings) Sport & Recreatiecentrum Blaarmeersen. Fr Gent cent foll N34 twd Tielt for 1km past city boundary & turn L to site; adj lake & De Ossemeersen nature reserve. NB Due to rd layout, rec foll camping sp on app to site rather than sat nav. Lge, hdg/mkd pitch, pt shd; htd wc; chem disp; mv service pnt; serviced pitch; shwrs inc; EHU (10A) metered + conn fee €1.25 (poss rev pol); lndry (inc dryer); shop; rest, snacks; bar; playgrnd; pool & full sports facs adj; lake sw adj; watersports; tennis; frequent bus to Gent; 5% statics; dogs €1.25; phone; bus to town nr; no dep bef 0815 hrs; Eng spkn; rd/rlwy noise; ccard acc; passport req. "Clean, well-organised, busy site; beautiful lake with path around; helpful staff; rest gd value; gd cycle track fr site; cycle into cent avoiding main rd; gd location for walks & activities; poss travellers LS; pitches muddy when wet; some m'van pitches sm & v shd; excel." 1 Mar-3 Nov. € 31.00 2015*

⊞ **GODARVILLE** *B2* (12km E Rural) *50.50501, 4.39928* **Camping Trieu du Bois, Rue Picolome, 63 6238 Luttre (Pont-a-Celles) (Hainaut) Belgique [(071) 845937 or (0477) 200343; trieudubois@hotmail.com; www.trieudobois.be]** Fr J21 Luttre, foll sp twrds Luttre. After 1km at T-junc turn L. Site on R after 1km. Sm, hdg, pt shd; wc; chem disp; shwrs €1; EHU (6A) €2; BBQ; 20% statics; dogs; twin axles; Eng spkn; adv bkg; quiet. "Conv for Waterloo & Brussels; adj canal path dir fr site; fair." € 15.00 2017*

GODARVILLE *B2* (2km S Rural) *50.48794, 4.29318* **Camping Domaine Claire-Fontaine, 11 Ave Clémenceau, 7160 Godarville [(064) 443675; sites. voiesdeau@hainaut.be]** Exit A15/E42 junc 18 onto N59 to Godarville, site sp. Lge, unshd; wc; chem disp; shwrs inc; EHU (6A) inc; lndry rm; shop 1km; snacks; bar; BBQ; playgrnd; lake sw; games area; 85% statics; dogs; phone; ccard acc; CKE/CCI. "Facs better than 1st impression but avoid san facs nr touring area & avoid area outside barrier; helpful warden; NH only."
1 Mar-31 Oct. € 22.00 2016*

GRIMBERGEN see Bruxelles *B2*

⊞ **HAN SUR LESSE** *C3* (280m N Urban) *50.12727, 5.18773* **Camping Aire Gîte d'Etape, Rue du Gîte d'Etape 10, 5580 Han-sur-Lesse [(084) 377441; gite. han@gitesdetape.be; www.gitesdetape.be/han]** Exit A4/E411 junc 23 sp Ave-et-Auffe & Rochefort. Go over 2 rv bdges then immed L & 1st R. Site on L. Sm, hdstg, unshd; wc; mv service pnt; shops, rests etc nr; playgrnd nrby; games area; entmnt; m'van only. "Excel; attendant calls." € 11.00 2016*

HAN SUR LESSE *C3* (260m S Rural) *50.12330, 5.18587* **Camping de la Lesse, Rue du Grand Hy, 5580 Han-sur-Lesse [(084) 377290; fax 377576; han. tourisme@skynet.be; www.valdelesse.be]** Site 500m off Han-sur-Lesse main sq adj Office de Tourisme. If app fr Ave-et-Auffe, turn R at Office du Tourisme, take care over rlwy x-ing to site on R in 150m. Med, mkd pitch, pt shd; htd wc; chem disp; shwrs inc; EHU (3-6A) inc; gas; lndry; shops, rests 200m; playgrnd; canoeing adj; rv adj; 50% statics; dogs; phone; poss cr; adv bkg ess high ssn via TO; phone adj; noisy; ccard not acc; CKE/CCI. "Gd touring base; undergrnd grotto trip; take care on narr rds to site - v high kerbs; excel; san facs immac; pleasant LS." 1 Apr-15 Nov. € 29.00 2013*

⊞ **HAN SUR LESSE** *C3* (5km SW Rural) *50.11178, 5.13308* **Camping Le Roptai, Rue Roptai 34, 5580 Ave-et-Auffe [(084) 388319; fax 387327; info@ leroptai.be; www.leroptai.be]** Fr A4 exit 23 & take N94 dir Dinant. At bottom of hill turn R onto N86. Turn L in vill of Ave, foll sp, 200m to L. Med, mkd pitch, hdstg, pt sl, terr, pt shd; wc; chem disp; mv service pnt; shwrs €0.90; EHU (6A) €1.80; gas; shop & 5km; snacks; bar; playgrnd; htd pool; TV; 80% statics; dogs €1.50; site clsd Jan; poss cr; Eng spkn; adv bkg; quiet; CKE/ CCI. "Some pitches awkwardly sl; generally run down & poor facs; ltd facs LS; NH only." € 25.00 2014*

HAN SUR LESSE *C3* (230m NW Urban) *50.12632, 5.18478* **Camping Le Pirot, Rue Joseph Lamotte 3, 5580 Han-sur-Lesse [(084) 377280; fax 377576; han. tourisme@skynet.be; www.valdelesse.be]** Exit A4/ E411 junc 23 sp Ave-et-Auffe & Rochefort. Go over 1st bdge then L immed bef 2nd bdge in Han cent; sh, steep incline. Sm, unshd; wc; shwrs inc; EHU (10A) inc (poss rev pol); shop nr; rest, snacks, bar 200m; dogs; bus adj; poss cr; adv bkg; quiet; ccard acc; CKE/CCI. "Excel position on raised bank of rv; adj attractions & rests; interesting town; helpful staff; basic, dated san facs; conv NH or sh stay in attractive town."
1 Apr-15 Nov. € 20.00 2015*

HASSELT *B3* (12km NE Rural) *50.99775, 5.42537* **Camping Holsteenbron, Hengelhoefseweg 9, 3520 Zonhoven [tel/fax 011 817140; camping. holsteenbron@telenet.be; www.holsteenbron.be]** Leave A2 junc 29 twd Hasselt; turn L at 1st traff lts in 1km, foll sp thro houses & woods for 3km. Site is NE of Zonhoven. Med, hdg/mkd pitch, hdstg, pt shd; htd wc; chem disp; shwrs €1; EHU (6A) inc; lndry rm; snacks; bar; playgrnd; games area; TV; 30% statics; dogs €1; phone; Eng spkn; quiet; CKE/CCI. "Pleasant, happy site in woodland; gd touring base; friendly owners."
1 Apr-13 Nov. € 22.00 2016*

HOTTON *C3* (900m NW Urban) *50.27085, 5.43833* **Camping Eau Zone, rue des Fonzays 10, 6990 Hotton [(084) 477715; campingeauzone@hotmail. be; www.campingeauzone.be]** E411 exit 18 to Marche then N86 to Hotton, over bdge in Hotton, turn L twds Melreux, foll rv and sp. Sm, pt shd; wc; chem disp; shwrs €2.50; EHU (10A); snacks; bar; BBQ; wifi; 20% statics; dogs; phone; public transport 1km; twin axles; Eng spkn; adv bkgs; CKE/CCI. "Site conv for Hotton caves; easy walk to town; gd NH." ♦ ltd.
1 Mar-30 Nov. € 20.00 2015*

⊞ **HOUTHALEN** *B3* (4km E Rural) *51.03222, 5.41613* **Camping De Binnenvaart (formerly Kelchterhoef), Binnenvaartstraat, 3530 Houthalen-Helchteren [(011) 526720; debinnenvaart@limburgcampings. be; www.limburgcampings.be]** Exit A2/E314 junc 30 N. In 2km at x-rds turn L, in 2km at rndabt turn R into Binnenvaartstraat, then foll site sp. Lge, mkd pitch, pt shd; htd wc; chem disp; shwrs; EHU (16A) inc; lndry; shop; snacks; playgrnd; lake sw adj; entmnt; internet; TV; 40% statics; adv bkg; Eng spkn; quiet. "Press button at ent for access; friendly welcome; lge serviced pitches; excel NH or longer." € 26.00 2017*

HOUYET see Dinant *C3*

JABBEKE see Brugge *A2*

KASTERLEE see Geel *A3*

KEMMEL/HEUVELLAND see Ypres/Ieper *B1*

KNOKKE HEIST *A2* (1.6km S Urban) *51.33530, 3.28959* **Camping Holiday, Natiënlaan 70-72, 8300 Knokke-Heist [(050) 601203; fax 613280; info@camping-holiday.be; www.camping-holiday.be]** On N49/E34 opp Knokke-Heist town boundary sp. Site ent at side of Texaco g'ge. Med, unshd; wc; chem disp; shwrs inc; EHU (6A) €1.90 (poss rev pol); supmkt opp; rest, snacks 500m; playgrnd; beach 1.5km; bike hire; phone; 60% statics; poss cr; quiet but rd noise. "V clean, tidy site but ltd san facs and waste disp pnts; may need to manhandle c'van onto pitch." ♦ ltd. Easter-30 Sep. € 27.00 2012*

⊞ **KOKSIJDE** *A1* (2km W Rural) *51.10287, 2.63066* **Camping Noordduinen, Noordduinen 12, 8670 Koksijde aan Zee [(058) 512546 or 0477 276469 (mob); fax 512618; roos@campingbenelux.be; www.campingnoordduinen.be]** Exit A18/E40 junc 1A onto N8. Foll sp Koksijde to rndabt, strt over into Leopold III Laan, site on L. Do not use SatNav. Sm, hdg pitch, hdstg, pt shd; wc; shwrs €1; EHU €2.50; lndry; supmkt 300m; sand beach 3km; wifi; 80% statics; dogs €2.50; bus 500m; Eng spkn; adv bkg; quiet; CKE/CCI. "Gd site; adj cycle rte to Veurne - attractive, historic town; san facs now closer to pitches." € 30.00 2017*

LEMBEKE see Eeklo *A2*

LILLE-GIERLE see Turnhout *A3*

⊞ **LONDERZEEL** *B2* (3.6km NNE Rural) *51.02041, 4.31936* **Camping Diepvennen, Molenhoek 35, 1840 Londerzeel [(052) 309492; fax 305716; info@camping-diepvennen.be; www.camping-diepvennen.be]** On A12 exit at Londerzeel, foll sp Industrie Zone & Diepvennen. Foll Diepvennen sp to site. Site on W side of A12. Lge, pt shd; wc; shwrs €1; EHU €3; lndry; shop; rest, snacks; playgrnd; pool; fishing pond; tennis; games area; 95% statics; rd noise; red long stay. "Long walk to san facs block; easy access by train to Antwerp & Brussels." ♦ € 18.00 2013*

MALONNE see Namur *C3*

⊞ **MARCHE EN FAMENNE** *C3* (6.5km NW Rural) *50.24911, 5.27978* **Camping Le Relais, 16 Rue de Serinchamps, 5377 Hogne [(0475) 423049; info@campinglerelais.com; www.campinglerelais.com]** Sp fr N4 bet Marche-en-Famenne & Namur. Fr Namur ent immed R under new bdge. Med, pt sl, unshd; htd wc; chem disp; fam bthrm; shwrs inc; EHU (10A) €2.50; lndry; rest, snacks; playgrnd; lake adj; TV; 30% statics; dogs free; adv bkg; some rd noise; CKE/CCI. "V pleasant; gd, clean facs but dated (2015); conv for N4." € 20.50 2015*

MEMBACH-BAELEN see Eupen *B4*

NAMUR *C3* (9km SW Rural) *50.44164, 4.80182* **Camping Les Trieux, 99 Rue Les Tris, 5020 Malonne [tel/fax (081) 445583 or 473 810742 (mob); camping.les.trieux@skynet.be; www.campinglestrieux.be]** Fr Namur take N90 sp Charleroi, after 8km take L fork sp Malonne (camp sp at junc). After 400m turn L at camp sp & site at top of 1 in 7 (13%) hill, approx 200m. To miss steep hill, fr Namur take Dinant (N92) S. In 2km R at camping sp. Take care at hairpin in 200m. Foll site sps. Located up steep, but surfaced rd. Med, mkd pitch, terr, pt shd; htd wc; chem disp; mv service pnt; shwrs €1; EHU (10A) €2; lndry; shop; snacks; playgrnd; TV; 50% statics; phone; Eng spkn; quiet; ccard not acc; red LS; CKE/CCI. "Friendly owners; pretty site, but steep - take care ent pitch; pitches diff for lge o'fits; basic san facs but clean; NH only." 1 Apr-31 Oct. € 21.00 2015*

NEUFCHATEAU *D3* (2km SW Rural) *49.83502, 5.41640* **Camping Val d'Emeraude, Route de Malome 1-3, 6840 Neufchâteau [tel/fax (061) 511952; valdemeraude@skynet.be; www.valdemeraude.be]** Take Florenville rd out of town. In 2km site at lge cream hse on L. Sm, pt sl, unshd, mkd pitch; wc; chem disp; shwrs; EHU €3 (poss rev pol); lndry rm; shop 3km; rest, snacks, bar 1km; BBQ; playgrnd; fishing 500m; pool (child); sw; TV rm; wifi; dogs €1.25; 70% statics; dogs €1.50; phone; bus adj; Eng spkn; adv bkg; quiet but some rd noise; CKE/CCI. "Beautiful setting; gd walks; helpful owner; well-kept, flat pitches; basic, ltd san facs; attractive location; gd NH." ♦ 1 Apr-31 Oct. € 28.00 2013*

⊞ **NEUFCHATEAU** *D3* (2.5km SW Rural) *49.83305, 5.41721* **Camping Spineuse, Rue de Florenville, 6840 Neufchâteau [061 27 73 20; fax 27 71 04; info@camping-spineuse.be; www.camping-spineuse.be]** Fr A4/E411 exit junc 26 or junc 27 fr E25 to Neufchâteau. Take N85 dir Florenville, site is 3rd on L. Ent easy to miss. Med, pt shd; htd wc; chem disp; mv service pnt; shwrs free; EHU (16A) €3; lndry; shops 1km; rest, snacks; bar; playgrnd; sm pool; wifi; TV; 30% statics; dogs €1.25; phone; Eng spkn; quiet; ccard acc; red LS/snr citizens. "Pleasant, pretty site; poss diff lge o'fits if site full; vg san facs; some flooding after heavy rain." € 21.50 2015*

⊞ **NIEUWPOORT** *A1* (1.5km NE Rural) *51.13324, 2.76031* **Parking De Zwerver, Brugsesteenweg 16, 8620 Nieuwpoort [(0474) 669526; de_zwerver@telenet.be]** Nr Kompass Camping - see dirs under Kompass Camping. Site behind De Zwerver nursery. Sm, mkd pitch, all hdstg, unshd; wc; mv service pnt €2.50; shwrs & hot water; lndry; BBQ; playgrnd; m'vans only. "Coin & note operated facs; modern & efficient; walking/cycling dist to town cent & port." ♦ € 0.50 (per hour) 2016*

NIEUWPOORT *A1* (3km E Rural) *51.12960, 2.77220* **Kompascamping Nieuwpoort, Brugsesteenweg 49, 8620 Nieuwpoort [(058) 236037; fax 232682; nieuwpoort@kompascamping.be; www.kompascamping.be]** Exit E40/A18 at junc 3 sp Nieuwpoort; in 500m turn R at full traff lts; after 1km turn R at traff lts; turn R at rndabt & immed turn L over 2 sm canal bdgs. Turn R to Brugsesteenweg, site on L approx 1km. Fr Ostende on N34 (coast rd) turn L at rndabt after canal bdge as above. V lge, hdg/mkd pitch, some hdstg, pt shd; htd wc; chem disp; fam bthrm; shwrs inc; EHU (10A) inc; gas; lndry (inc dryer); shop & 2km; rest, snacks; bar; playgrnd; 2 pools (1 htd, covrd); paddling pool; waterslide; tennis; sports/games area adj; bike hire; golf 10km; wifi; entmnt; 50% statics; dogs €3.20; adv bkg; quiet; red long stay/CKE/CCI. "Well-equipped site; helpful staff; boat-launching facs; sep area for sh stay tourers; very busy w/ends; excel cycle rtes; conv Dunkerque ferry." 23 Mar-6 Nov. € 44.00 (4 persons) SBS - H19 2017*

See advertisement

"There aren't many sites open at this time of year"

If you're travelling outside peak season remember to call ahead to check site opening dates – even if the entry says 'open all year'.

NIEUWPOORT *A1* (16km S Rural) *51.02401, 2.84370* **De Ijzerhoeve, Kapellestraat 4, B-8600 Diksmuide [(51) 439439 or (472) 961220; info@deijzerhoeve.be; www.deijzerhoeve.be]** Fr Ypres take N369 to Diksmuide. Turn L onto N35, L again strt after bdge then R onto Kapellestraat. Site in 1km on R. Sm, unshd; wc; chem disp; shwrs inc; EHU (6A); shop 2km; bar; pool 2km; tv rm; 50% statics; dogs €1; bus; phone; Eng spkn; adv bkg; red long stay. "Site conv & cheap; renovation in progress(2017); gd. ♦ ltd. 1 Apr/31 Oct. € 14.00 2017*

⊞ **OOSTENDE** *A1* (5km NE Coastal) *51.24882, 2.96710* **Camping 17 Duinzicht, Rozenlaan 23, 8450 Bredene [(059) 323871; fax 330467; info@campingduinzicht.be; www.campingduinzicht.be]** Fr Ostend take dual c'way to Blankenberge on N34. Turn R sp Bredene, L into Driftweg which becomes Kappelstraat & turn R into Rozenlaan. Site sp. Lge, mkd pitch, hdstg, unshd; htd wc; chem disp; mv service pnt; serviced pitches; fam bthrm; shwrs €1; EHU (10A) inc (poss no earth); gas; lndry (inc dryer); shop 500m; rest; snacks, bar adj; BBQ; playgrnd; sand beach 500m; wifi; 60% statics; dogs; phone; security barrier; poss cr; Eng spkn; adv bkg; quiet; ccard acc; red LS; CKE/CCI. "Excel site; poss long walk to san facs; take care slippery tiles in shwrs; Bredene lovely, sm seaside town." € 24.00 (4 persons) 2012*

⊞ **OOSTENDE** *A1* (6km NE Rural) *51.24366, 2.98002* **Camping T Minnepark, Zandstraat 105, 8450 Bredene-Dorp [(059) 322458; fax 330495; info@minnepark.be; www.minnepark.be]** Fr Ostend take N34 sp Blankenberge. After tunnel under rlwy turn R sp Brugge. Cross canal & in 300m turn L at filter sp Bredene-Dorp. In 2km immed after blue/white water tower on R, turn L at x-rds. At mini-rndabt turn R passing Aldi supmkt. Site on L after Zanpolder site. Fr A18 exit junc 6 & take N37 sp De Haan. In 5km turn L at rndabt onto N9 sp Oostende. In 5km turn R sp Bredene-Dorp, then R in 2.5km at rndabt into Zandstraat, then as above. V lge, unshd; wc; chem disp; shwrs €1; EHU (16A) €1 (poss rev pol); lndry (inc dryer); shops 1km; playgrnd; sand beach 2km; wifi; cab TV; 75% statics; dogs €3; Eng spkn; adv bkg; quiet. "Lge pitches; friendly, helpful staff; warm welcome; excel, well-run site; vg san facs; conv ferries, Bruges & coast." € 30.00 2013*

⊞ **OOSTENDE** *A1* (5km E Urban/Coastal) *51.24970, 2.96834* **Camping Astrid, Koning Astridlaan 1, 8450 Bredene [(059) 321247; fax 331470; info@camping-astrid.be; www.camping-astrid.be]** Foll tourist sp. Med, unshd; wc; chem disp; serviced pitch; shwrs; EHU (10A) inc; shops 100m; sand beach adj; cab/sat TV; 80% statics; phone; poss cr; Eng spkn; ccard not acc. "Most sites nrby are statics only; friendly, helpful owners; rec NH; barrier for new arr." ♦ € 29.00 2013*

⊞ **OPGLABBEEK** *B3* (2km SE Rural) *51.02825, 5.59745* **Camping Wilhelm Tell, Hoeverweg 87, 3660 Opglabbeek [(089) 854444; fax 810010; receptie@wilhelmtell.com; www.wilhelmtell.com]** Leave A2/E314 at junc 32, take rd N75 then N730 N sp As. In As take Opglabbeek turn, site sp in 1km. Med, mkd pitch, pt shd; wc; chem disp; mv service pnt; shwrs €0.90; EHU (10A) inc; gas; lndry (inc dryer); shop high ssn; rest, snacks; bar; BBQ; playgrnd; 2 htd pools (1 covrd); paddling pool; waterslide; tennis; bike hire; golf 10km; wifi; entmnt; TV rm; 55% statics; dogs €4; phone; adv bkg; red long stay/LS; quiet; CKE/CCI. "Nice site; narr ent; superb pools, wave machine; site in nature reserve; helpful staff; san facs dist; bit expensive; not suitable for lge o'fits." ♦ € 32.00 2012*

OTEPPE *B3* (500m N Rural) *50.58239, 5.12455* **Camping L'Hirondelle Château, Rue de la Burdinale 76A, 4210 Oteppe [(085) 711131; fax 711021; info@lhirondelle.be; www.lhirondelle.be]** App fr E A15/E42 at exit 8; turn W on N643 for 1.5km; turn at sp on R for Oteppe. In vill 3km pass church to x-rds & R by police stn: site 150m on L. Fr W exit A15 at exit 10 onto N80, turn R onto N652 at Burdinne for Oteppe - easier rte. V lge, pt sl, shd; wc; shwrs €1; EHU (6A) inc; gas; lndry; shop; rest, snacks; bar; BBQ; playgrnd; 2 pools; waterslide; tennis; games area; internet; 75% statics; dogs €2.50; poss cr; quiet; ccard acc; red CKE/CCI. "Site in grnds of chateau; excel facs for children; touring pitches at top of site poss diff (steep); gd area for walking, fishing; conv NH; very quiet LS." 1 Apr-31 Oct. € 29.00 2013*

OUDENAARDE *B2* (15km SW Urban) *50.76250, 3.48719* **Panorama Camping, Boskouter 24, Ruien, 9690 Kluisbergen [(032) 55 38 86 68; info@campingpanorama.be; www.campingpanorama.be]** Fr N8 (Oudenaarde - Berchem) foll sp to Kluisbergen, Ruien. Cont thro Ruien, past church on L turn into Wuipelstraat, then R at rndabt, then L into Boskouter foll sp to site. Med, mkd pitch, pt sl, terr, pt shd; wc; chem disp; shwrs, EHU; rest, snacks; bar; playgrnd; 90% statics; adv bkg; Eng spkn; CKE/CCI. "Gd site; very sm touring area; helpful owner; excel cycling and walking fr site." 1 Feb - 30 Nov. € 25.00 2012*

OVERIJSE see Bruxelles *B2*

PHILIPPEVILLE *C2* (11km NW Rural) *50.23920, 4.45927* **Camping Le Chesle, 1 rue d'Yves, 5650 Vogenee [(071) 612632; info.camping.chesle@gmail.com; www.chesle.be]** N5 Charleroi-Philippeville, exit Yves Gomezee. After rlwy, turn R to Vogenee and foll sp. Med, pt sl, unshd; wc; chem disp; shwrs inc; EHU (16A); lndry (inc dryer); shop; snacks; BBQ; playgrnd; wifi; tv; 50% statics; dogs; bus 1km; Eng spkn; adv bkg; quiet; CKE/CCI. "Pleasant walking rtes fr site, ask for map; cycling poss, but v hilly; vg." ♦ ltd. 15 Feb-15 Dec. € 24.60 2017*

PROFONDEVILLE see Namur *C3*

ROCHE EN ARDENNE, LA *C3* (800m S Rural) *50.17465, 5.57774* **Camping Le Vieux Moulin, Rue Petite Strument 62, 6980 La Roche-en-Ardenne [(084) 411507; fax 411080; info@strument.com; www.strument.com]** Off N89 site sp fr La Roche town cent (dir Barrièr-de-Champlon), site in 800m. Med, some hdg pitch, pt sl, shd; htd wc; chem disp; shwrs €2; EHU (6A) €2.50 (poss no earth); gas 800m; lndry; shops 800m; fishing; canoeing; 70% statics in sep area; dogs €2; poss cr; Eng spkn; adv bkg; quiet; CKE/CCI. "Beautiful site; gd pitches; poss unclean san facs & dishwashing (7/09); poss youth groups; poor security; gd walking (map avail)." Easter-Nov. € 14.00 2012*

"That's changed – Should I let The Club know?"

If you find something on site that's different from the site entry, fill in a report and let us know. See camc.com/europereport.

ROCHEFORT *C3* (500m E Rural) *50.15947, 5.22609* **Camping Communal Les Roches, 26 Rue du Hableau, 5580 Rochefort [(084) 211900 or (479) 261759 (mob); fax 312403; campingrochefort@lesroches.be; www.lesroches.be]** Fr Rochefort cent on N86 & turn L at rndabt, then 1st R. Site well sp. Lge, hdg/mkd pitch, hdstg, pt sl, unshd; htd wc; chem disp; mv service pnt; fam bthrm; serviced pitches; shwrs inc; EHU (16A) metered; lndry (inc dryer); shop, rest; bar; BBQ; playgrnd; pool high ssn adj; tennis; games area; games rm; internet; entmnt; TV; 50% statics (in sep area); dogs; phone; bus 250m; train 2km; Eng spkn; quiet; ccard acc. "Vg, well-managed, pleasant, refurbished site; gd walking; sh walk to charming town; gd, modern clean san facs; v popular site." ♦ 1 Apr-11 Nov. € 27.00 2017*

SART LEZ SPA see Spa *C4*

SINT JOB IN'T GOOR see Antwerpen *A3*

SINT KRUIS see Brugge *A2*

SINT MARGRIETE *A2* (2.6km NW Rural) *51.2860, 3.5164* **Camping De Soetelaer, Sint Margrietepolder 2, 9981 Sint Margriete [(09) 3798151; fax 3799795; camping.desoetelaer@telenet.be; www.desoetelaer.be]** Fr E on N49/E34 to Maldegem or fr W on N9 or N49 turn N onto N251 to Aardenburg (N'lands), then turn R twd St Kruis (N'lands) - site situated 1.5km strt on fr St Margriete (back in Belgium). Med, mkd pitch, pt shd; wc; chem disp; all serviced pitches; shwrs inc; EHU (6A) inc; lndry rm; shops 3km; no dogs; Eng spkn; adv bkg; quiet; ccard not acc; CKE/CCI. "Vg, clean site; excel, modern san facs; peace & quiet, privacy & space; highly rec for relaxation; o'fits pitched v close end to end." Easter-15 Oct. € 30.00 2014*

BELGIUM

⊞ **SOUMAGNE** *B3* (3.5km S Rural) *50.61099, 5.73840* **Domaine Provincial de Wégimont, Chaussée de Wégimont 76, 4630 Soumagne [(04) 2372400; fax 2372401; wegimont@prov-liege.be; www.prov-liege.be/wegimont]** Exit A3 at junc 37 onto N3 W twd Fléron & Liège. In 500m at traff lts turn L sp Soumagne. In Soumagne at traff lts form R dir Wégimont, site on top of hill on R directly after bus stop. Med, hdg pitch, pt sl, pt shd; htd wc; chem disp; fam bthrm; shwrs inc; EHU (16A) inc poss rev pol; shop; rest; bar; communal BBQ; playgrnd; pool adj high ssn; tennis; games area; some entmnt; 70% statics; dogs; bus; site clsd Jan; poss cr; some rd noise; CKE/CCI. "Welcoming site in chateau grnds (public access); clean facs; conv sh stay/NH nr m'way." € 13.50 2016*

SPA *C4* (6km NE Rural) *50.50806, 5.91928* **Camping Spa d'Or (TCB), Stockay 17, 4845(B) Sart-lez-Spa [087 47 44 00; fax 47 52 77; info@campingspador.be; www.campingspador.be]** App fr N or S on m'way A27/E42, leave at junc 9, foll sp to Sart & Spa d'Or. Lge, pt sl, pt shd; htd wc; chem disp; fam bthrm; shwrs & bath inc; EHU (10A) €4. (check earth); gas; lndry; shop high ssn; rest, snacks; BBQ; playgrnd; htd pool; bike hire; entmnt; 60% statics; dogs €5; poss cr; quiet; ccard acc; red CKE/CCI. "Conv F1 Grand Prix circuit Francorchamps & historic town Stavelot; vg; gd NH." 1 Apr-14 Nov. € 27.50 (CChq acc) 2013*

SPA *C4* (1.6km SE Rural) *50.48559, 5.88385* **Camping Parc des Sources, Rue de la Sauvenière 141, 4900 Spa [(087) 772311; fax 475965; info@parcdessources.be; www.parcdessources.be]** Bet Spa & Francorchamps on N62, sp on R. Med, mkd pitch, pt sl, pt shd; htd wc; chem disp; mv service pnt; fam bthrm; shwrs; EHU (10A) €2.75; gas; lndry; shops 1.5km; snacks; bar; playgrnd; pool; dogs €1.50; 60% statics; phone; poss cr; quiet. "Excel facs, modern lndry, beautiful location, nr forest; friendly & helpful staff." ♦ ltd. 25 Mar-31 Oct. € 25.00 2016*

⊞ **STAVELOT** *C4* (3km N Rural) *50.41087, 5.95351* **Camping L'Eau Rouge, Cheneux 25, 4970 Stavelot [(080) 863075; fb220447@skynet.be; www.eaurouge.eu]** Exit A27/E42 junc 11 onto N68 twd Stavelot. Turn R at T-junc, then 1st R into sm rd over narr bdge. Med, mkd pitch, pt sl, pt shd; htd wc; chem disp; mv service pnt; fam bthrm; shwrs €0.50; EHU (6-10A) €3 rev polarity; lndry (inc dryer); shop 2km; snacks; bar; BBQ; playgrnd; games area; archery; wifi; TV; 50% statics; dogs €1; poss cr; Eng spkn; quiet. "Vg rvside site; friendly, helpful owners; twin-axles not acc; conv Francorchamps circuit." ♦ € 25.00 2013*

STEKENE *A2* (4km SW Rural) *51.18366, 4.00730* **Camping Vlasaard, Heirweg 143, 9190 Stekene [(03) 7798164; fax 7899170; info@camping-vlasaard.be; www.camping-vlasaard.be]** Fr N49 Antwerp-Knokke rd, exit sp Stekene. In Stekene, take dir Moerbeke, site on L in 4km. V lge, mkd pitch, unshd; htd wc; chem disp; serviced pitches; shwrs €1.25; EHU (16A); lndry; supmkt adj; rest, snacks; bar; playgrnd; pool; games area; 75% statics; poss cr; Eng spkn; poss noisy; ccard acc. ♦ 7 Jan-20 Dec. € 18.00 2016*

⊞ **TELLIN** *C3* (5km NE Rural) *50.09665, 5.28579* **Camping Parc La Clusure, 30 Chemin de la Clusure, 6927 Bure-Tellin [(084) 360050; fax 366777; info@parclaclusure.be; www.parclaclusure.be]** Fr N on A4 use exit 23A onto N899, fr S exit junc 24. Foll sp for Tellin & then take N846 thro Bure dir Grupont vill. At rndabt at junc N803 & N846 take 2nd exit to site, sp. Lge, mkd pitch, pt shd; htd wc; chem disp; mv service pnt; fam bthrm; shwrs inc; EHU (16A) inc (check rev pol); lndry (inc dryer); shop; rest, snacks; bar; playgrnd; htd pool; paddling pool; rv fishing; tennis; bike hire; games area; games rm; wifi; entmnt; TV rm; 35% statics; dogs €5; phone; poss cr; Eng spkn; adv bkg; some rlwy noise; ccard acc; red LS/CKE/CCI. "V pleasant, lovely, popular rvside site; conv m'way; conv for limestone caves at Han-sur-Lesse & gd touring base Ardennes; friendly owners; clean facs; wild beavers in adj rv; excel site." ♦ € 55.00 SBS - H09 2013*

TILFF SUR OURTHE see Liège *B3*

⊞ **TOURINNES LA GOSSE** *B3* (500m SW Rural) *50.77952, 4.73657* **Camping au Val Tourinnes, Rue du Grand Brou 16A, 1320 Tourinnes-la-Grosse [(010) 866642; info@campingauvaltourinnes.com; www.campingauvaltourinnes.com]** Fr N on E40/A3 m'way exit junc 23 onto N25 S dir Hamme-Mille. In Hamme-Mille turn L at traff lts, site on R in 2km. Or fr S on E411/A4 exit junc 8 onto N25 to Hamme-Mille & turn R at traff lts, then as above. Sm, hdg/mkd pitch, shd; htd wc; chem disp; mv service pnt; fam bthrm; shwrs €0.50; EHU (2A) €4, (10A) €8; lndry (inc dryer); rest; bar; playgrnd; lake fishing; wifi; some statics; dogs €4; Eng spkn; quiet. "Pleasant touring pitches on lakeside (take care goose droppings!); friendly owners; vg, modern san facs; access tight for lge o'fits; airshow 1st w/end July." € 19.00 2016*

⊞ **TOURNAI** *B2* (2km SE Urban) *50.59967, 3.41349* **Camp Municipal de l'Orient, Jean-Baptiste Moens 8, 7500 Tournai [(069) 222635; fax 890229; campingorient@tournai.be]** Exit E42 junc 32 R onto N7 twd Tournai. L at 1st traff lts, foll sp Aquapark, L at rndabt, site immed on L (no sp). Med, hdg pitch, some hdstg, pt shd; htd wc; chem disp; some serviced pitches; shwrs inc; EHU (10A) inc (poss rev pol/no earth) or metered; gas; lndry (inc dryer); shops 1km; rest, bar & playgrnd at leisure complex; htd indoor pool adj; leisure cent/lake adj (50% disc to campers); poss cr; Eng spkn; adv bkg ess high ssn; some rd noise daytime & fr leisure cent adj; ccard not acc; CKE/CCI. "Well-kept site in interesting area & old town; facs stretched high ssn, but excel site; take care raised kerbs to pitches; max length of c'van 6.5m due narr site rds & high hdgs; helpful wardens; E side of site quietest; EHU had no earth on a nbr of pitches; handy for Lille and Dunkerque ferries." € 16.00 2015*

Brac

Welcome to Croatia

Croatia's Adriatic coast is a land of sun, beauty and history. Soaked in culture going back thousands of years, there are so many different sights to see, from the 16th century walls of Dubrovnik to the Roman amphitheatre in Pula.
With countless galleries, museums and churches to discover, as well as an exquisite natural landscape to explore, there truly is something for everyone.

Country highlights

Licitars are brightly decorated biscuits made of sweet honey dough. Often given as a gift at celebrations such as Christmas or weddings, they are an integral part of Croatian identity dating from the 16th century.

Croatia is well known for its carnivals, festivals and celebrations, which take place throughout the year. Some of the most important are the Spring Procession of Queens from Gorjani, the Bell Ringer's Pageant from the Kastav Area and the Festivity of St. Blaise, Dubrovnik's patron saint.

Major towns and cities

- Zagreb – the capital of Croatia has a rich history that dates from Roman times.
- Rijeka – Croatia's principal port city overlooking the Adriatic.
- Split – the centre of the city is built around an ancient Roman palace.
- Osijek – a gastronomic centre, and the best place to try a traditional dish.

Attractions

- Dubrovnik – a wonderfully-preserved medieval walled city with plenty to see.
- Plitvice Lakes - a stunning series of lakes and waterfalls set in an enchanting woodland.
- Pula Arena – this ancient Roman amphitheatre is one of the best preserved in the world.
- Diocletian's Palace – an ancient monument that makes up the heart of Split.

Find out more

www.croatia.hr
Tel: 0038 5 14 69 93 33 Croatian Tourist Office

Country Information

Population (approx): 4.4 million

Capital: Zagreb (population approx 690,000)

Area: 56,540 sq km, divided into 20 counties

Bordered by: Bosnia-Herzegovina, Hungary, Serbia, Montenegro and Slovenia

Terrain: Flat plains along border with Hungary; low mountains and highlands near Adriatic coast and islands

Climate: Mediterranean climate along the coast with hot, dry summers and mild, wet winters; continental climate inland with hot summers and cold winters

Coastline: 5,835km (inc 4,058km islands)

Highest Point: Dinara 1,830m

Language: Croatian

Local Time: GMT or BST + 1, i.e. 1 hour ahead of the UK all year

Currency: Kuna (HRK) divided into 100 lipa; £1 = HRK 8.54, HRK 10 = £1.17 (November 2017)

Emergency Numbers: Police 192; Fire brigade 193; Ambulance 194. Or dial 112 and specify the service you need.

Public Holidays in 2018: Jan 1, 6; Apr 2; May 1, 31; Jun 22, 25 (National Day); Aug 5 (Thanksgiving Day), 15; Oct 8 (Independence Day); Nov 1; Dec 25, 26.

Some Christian Orthodox and Muslim festivals are also celebrated locally. School summer holidays take place from the last week in June to the end of August.

Camping and Caravanning

There are more than 150 campsites in Croatia including several well-established naturist sites, mainly along the coast. Sites are licensed according to how many people they can accommodate, rather than by the number of vehicles or tents, and are classed according to a grading system of 1 to 4 stars. There are some very large sites catering for up to 10,000 people at any one time but there are also many small sites, mainly in Dalmatia, situated in gardens, orchards and farms.

Many sites open from April to October; few open all year. They are generally well-equipped.

A tourist tax is levied of between HRK 4 and HRK 7 per person per day according to region and time of year.

Casual/wild camping is illegal and is particularly monitored at beaches, harbours and rural car parks. Most campsites have overnight areas for late arrivals and there are a number of rest areas established along main roads for overnight stays or brief stopovers.

Electricity and Gas

Current on campsites ranges from 10 to 16 amps. Plugs have 2 round pins. There may not be CEE connections and a long cable might be required.

Campingaz cylinders are not available, so take a good supply of gas with you.

Entry Formalities

British and Irish passport holders may visit Croatia for up to three months without a visa.

Unless staying at official tourist accommodation (hotel or campsite) all visitors are obliged to register at the nearest police station or town tourist agency within 24 hours of arrival in the country. Campsites and other tourist accommodation should carry out this function for their guests but make sure you check this with them. If you fail to register you may receive a fine or you may even have to leave Croatia.

British citizens intending to stay for an extended period should seek advice from the Croatian Embassy.

Medical Services

For minor ailments, first of all consult staff in a pharmacy (ljekarna).

Emergency hospital and medical treatment is available at a reduced cost on production of a valid EHIC. You will be expected to pay a proportion of the cost (normally 20%). Only basic health care facilities are available in outlying areas and islands

Opening Hours

Banks: Mon-Fri 7am-7pm; Sat 7am-1pm.

Museums: Tue-Sun 10am-5pm; most close Mon and some close Sun afternoons.

Post Offices: Mon-Fri 7am-7pm (2pm in small villages). In major towns or tourist places, post offices on duty are open until 9pm.

Shops: Mon-Fri 8am-8pm; Sat & Sun 8am-2pm.

Safety and Security

The level of street crime is low, but you should be aware of pickpockets in major cities, coastal areas (pavement cafés are particularly targeted), and on trains, and take sensible precautions when carrying money, credit cards and passports.

Incidents have been reported of gangs robbing car occupants after either indicating that they are in trouble and require assistance, or pulling alongside a car and indicating that something is wrong with the vehicle. Be extremely cautious should something similar occur.

If you are planning to travel outside the normal tourist resorts you should be aware that there are areas affected by the war, which ended in 1995, where unexploded mines remain. These include Eastern Slavonia, Brodsko-Posavska County, Karlovac County, areas around Zadar County and in more remote areas of the Plitvice Lakes National Park. See the Croatian Mine Action Centre's website at www.hcr.hr/en/protuminUvod.asp for more specific information about mine-affected areas.

Croatia shares with the rest of Europe an underlying threat from terrorism. Attacks could be indiscriminate and against civilian targets, including places frequented by tourists.

British Embassy

UL IVANA LUČIĆA 4
HR-10000 ZAGREB
Tel: (01) 6009100
www.british.embassyzagreb@fco.gov.uk

Irish Honorary Consulate

MIRAMARSKA 23 (EUROCENTER)
10000 ZAGREB
Tel: (01) 6310025
irish.consulate.zg@inet.hr

TRUMBICEVA OBALA 3
21000 SPLIT
Tel: (021) 343715
9csain@cpad.hr

Customs Regulations

Customs Posts

Main border crossings are open 24 hours a day.

Foodstuffs

Up to 10kg of meat and meat products and 10kg of dairy products may be imported into Croatia from EU countries. If you are entering from outside the EU, you can bring 2kg of meat products as long as they are in sealed packages.

Documents

Driving Licence

All types of full, valid British driving licence are recognised but if you have an old-style green licence then it is advisable to change it for a photocard licence in order to avoid any local difficulties.

Passport

You must be able to show some form of identification if required by the authorities and, therefore, should carry your passport or photocard driving licence at all times.

Vehicle(s)

Carry your vehicle registration certificate (V5C), insurance details and MOT certificate (if applicable).

Green Card

While an International Motor Insurance Certificate (Green Card) is not necessary, you should ensure that your vehicle insurance includes cover for Croatia.

If you are driving to or through Bosnia and Herzegovina (for example, along the 20 km strip of coastline at Neum on the Dalmatian coastal highway to Dubrovnik) you should ensure that you have obtained Green Card cover for Bosnia and Herzegovina. For Club members insured under the Club's Motor Insurance schemes full policy cover is available for this 20km strip, however you must ask at the time of taking out or renewing your insurance policy for one that specifically covers

Bosnia. If you have difficulties obtaining this cover before departure Club members can contact the Club's Travel Service Information Officer for advice, email travelserviceinfo@camc.com. Alternatively, temporary third-party insurance can be purchased at the country's main border posts, or in Split and other large cities. It is not generally obtainable at the Neum border crossing itself.

As an alternative, you can take the ferry from Ploče to Trpanj on the Pelješac peninsula and avoid the stretch of road in Bosnia and Herzegovina altogether. There are frequent ferries during summer months, but be aware that motorhome drivers are sometimes requested to reverse onto them.

Money

Visitors may exchange money in bureaux de change, banks, post offices, hotels and some travel agencies but you are likely to get the best rates in banks. Exchange slips should be kept in order to convert unspent kuna on leaving the country. Many prices are quoted in both kuna and euros, and euros are widely accepted.

Most shops and restaurants accept credit cards. There are cash machines in all but the smallest resorts.

The police are warning visitors about a recent increase in the number of forged Croatian banknotes in circulation, especially 200 and 500 kuna notes. Take care when purchasing kuna and use only reliable outlets, such as banks and cash points.

Motoring in Croatia

Accidents

Any visible damage to a vehicle entering Croatia must be certified by the authorities at the border and a Certificate of Damage issued, which must be produced when leaving the country. In the event of a minor accident while in Croatia resulting in material damage only, the police must be called and they will assist, if necessary, with the exchange of information between drivers and will issue a Certificate of Damage to the foreign driver. You should not try to leave the country with a damaged vehicle without this Certificate as you may be accused of a 'hit and run' offence.

Confiscation of passport and a court appearance within 24 hours are standard procedures for motoring accidents where a person is injured.

The Croatian Insurance Bureau in Zagreb can assist with Customs and other formalities following road accidents, tel: (01) 4696600, email: huo@huo.hr or see www.huo.hr.

Alcohol

The general legal limit of alcohol is 50 milligrams in 100 millilitres of blood, i.e. less than the level in the UK (80 milligrams). For drivers of vehicles over 3,500 kg and for drivers under 24 years of age the alcohol limit is zero. The general legal limit also applies to cyclists.

It is prohibited to drive after having taken any medicine whose side-effects may affect the ability to drive a motor vehicle.

Breakdown Service

The Hrvatski Auto-Klub (HAK) operates a breakdown service throughout the country, telephone 987 (or 01987 from a mobile phone) for assistance. On motorways use the roadside emergency phones which are placed at 2km intervals. Towing and breakdown services are available 24 hours a day in and around most major cities and along the coast in summer (6am to midnight in Zagreb).

Essential Equipment

First aid kit

All vehicles, including those registered abroad, must carry a first aid kit.

Lights

Dipped headlights are compulsory at all times, regardless of weather conditions, from the end of October to the end of March and in reduced visibility at other times of the year. It is compulsory to carry spare bulbs, however this rule does not apply if your vehicle is fitted with xenon, neon, LED or similar lights.

Reflective Jacket/Waistcoat

It is obligatory to carry a reflective jacket inside your car (not in the boot) and you must wear it if you need to leave your vehicle to attend to a breakdown, e.g. changing a tyre. It is also common sense for any passenger leaving the vehicle to also wear one.

Warning Triangle(s)

All motor vehicles must carry a warning triangle. If you are towing a caravan or trailer you must have two warning triangles.

Child Restraint Systems

Children under the age of 12 are not allowed to travel in the front seats of vehicles, with the exception of children under 2 years of age who can travel in the front if they are placed in a child restraint system adapted to their size. It must be rear-facing and the airbag must be de-activated.

Children up to 5 years old must be placed in a seat adapted to their size on the back seat. Children between the ages of 5 and 12 must travel on the back seat using a 3 point seat belt with a booster seat if necessary for their height.

Winter Driving

It is compulsory to carry snow chains in your vehicle and they must be used if required by the weather conditions (5cm of snow or black ice). The compulsory winter equipment in Croatia consists of a shovel in your vehicle and a set of snow chains on the driving axel.

Fuel

Petrol stations are generally open from 7am to 7 or 8pm, later in summer. Some of those on major stretches of road stay open 24 hours a day. Payment by credit card is widely accepted. LPG (Autogas) is fairly widely available.

Parking

Lines at the roadside indicate parking restrictions. Traffic wardens patrol roads and impose fines for illegal parking. Vehicles, including those registered outside Croatia, may be immobilised by wheel clamps.

Roads

In general road conditions are good in and around the larger towns. The Adriatic Highway or Jadranksa Magistrala (part of European route E65) runs the whole length of the Adriatic coast and is in good condition, despite being mostly single-carriageway. Minor road surfaces may be uneven and, because of the heat-resisting material used to surface them, may be very slippery when wet. Minor roads are usually unlit at night.

Motorists should take care when overtaking and be aware that other drivers may overtake unexpectedly in slow-moving traffic. The standard of driving is generally fair.

Road Signs and Markings

Road signs and markings conform to international standards. Motorway signs have a green background; national road signs have a blue background.

Speed Limits

	Open Road (km/h)	Motorway (km/h)
Car Solo	90-110	130
Car towing caravan/trailer	80	90
Motorhome under 3500kg	90-110	130
Motorhome 3500-7500kg	80	90

In addition to complying with other speed limits, drivers under the age of 25 must not exceed 80 km/h (50 mph) on the open road, 100 km/h (62 mph) on expressways and 120 km/h (74 mph) on motorways.

Traffic Jams

During the summer, tailbacks may occur at the border posts with Slovenia at Buje on the E751 (road 21), at Bregana on the E70 (A3) and at Donji Macelj on the E59 (A1). During July and August there may be heavy congestion, for example at Rupa/Klenovica and at other tourist centres, and on the E65 north-south Adriatic Highway. This is particularly true on Friday evenings, Saturday mornings, Sunday evenings and holidays. Queues form at ferry crossings to the main islands.Road and traffic conditions can be viewed on the HAK website (in English), www.hak.hr or tel: (01) 4640800 (English spoken) or (072) 777777 while in Croatia for round-the-clock recorded information.

Violation of Traffic Regulations

The police may impose on-the-spot fines for parking and driving offences. If you are unable to pay the police may confiscate your passport. Motoring law enforcement, especially for speeding offences, is strictly observed.

Motorways

There is just over 1250km of motorways, with the major stretches being shown in the table below. Tolls (cestarina) are levied according to vehicle category. Electronic display panels above motorways indicate speed limits, road conditions and lane closures. Information on motorways can be found on www.hac.hr.

Motorway Tolls

Class 1	Vehicle with 2 axles, height up to 1.3m (measured from front axle) excluding vans
Class 2	Vehicle with 2 or more axles, height up to 1.3m (measured from front axle), including car + caravan or trailer, motorhomes and vans.
Class 3	Vehicle with 2 or 3 axles, height over 1.3m (measured from front axle), including van with trailer
Class 4	Vehicle with 4 or more axles, height over .3m (measured from front axle)

Tolls can be paid in cash or by credit card. Details of toll prices can be found in English at www.hac.hr.

Touring

There are a number of national parks and nature reserves throughout the country, including the World Heritage site at the Plitvice lakes, the Paklenica mountain massif, and the Kornati archipelago with 140 uninhabited islands, islets and reefs. Dubrovnik, itself a World Heritage site, is one of the world's best-preserved medieval cities, having been extensively restored since recent hostilities.

While Croatia has a long coastline, there are few sandy beaches; instead there are pebbles, shingle and rocks with man-made bathing platforms.

The Croatian National Tourist Board operates 'Croatian Angels', a multi-lingual tourist information and advice service available from the end of March to mid-October, tel: 062 999 999 or 00385 62 999 999 from outside Croatia.

Croatia originated the concept of commercial naturist resorts in Europe and today attracts an estimated 1 million naturist tourists annually. There are approximately 20 official naturist resorts and beaches and numerous other unofficial or naturist-optional 'free' beaches. Smoking is prohibited in restaurants, bars and public places. A service charge is general included in the bill. English is widely spoken.

Public Transport

Rail travel is slow and cab be unreliable. By contrast the bus network offers the cheapest and most extensive means of public transport. Buy bus tickets when you board or from kiosks, which you must validate once on board. Trams operate in Zagreb and you can buy tickets from kiosks.

Coastal towns and cities have regular scheduled passenger and car ferry services. Most ferries are drive-on/drive-off – see www.jadrolinija.hr for schedules and maps.

Car ferries operate from Ancona, Bari, Pescara and Venice in Italy to Dubrovnik, Korèula, Mali Lošinj, Poreè, Pula, Rijecka, Rovinj, Sibenik, Split, Starigrad, Vis and Zadar. Full details from:

VIAMARE LTD
SUITE 108, 582 HONEYPOT LANE
STANMORE
MIDDX HA7 1JS
Tel: 020 8206 3420

Email: ferries@viamare.com
www.viamare.com

Sites in Croatia

BANJOLE see Pula *A3*

⊞ **BIOGRAD NA MORU** *B3* (12km NW Coastal) *44.00532, 15.36748* **Autokamp Filko, Aleksandar Colic 23207 Sveti Petar Na Moru [tel/fax 02 33 91 177; info@autokamp-filko.hr; www.autokamp-filko.hr]** On D8 bet Zadar & Biograd Na Moru at Sv Petar NM. 1st camp on the R by sea. Sm, pt shd; wc; chem disp; mv service pnt; shwrs; lndry; rest; bar; shingle beach; wifi; 30% statics; dogs; poss cr; Eng spkn; some rd noise. "Some pitches by water on hdstg with views across to islands; dir access fr rd; ideal LS; gd." HRK 170 2014*

BRAC ISLAND *C4* **Sites on Brač Island are listed together at the end of the Croatia site entry pages.**

CRES ISLAND *A3* **Sites on Cres Island are listed together at the end of the Croatia site entry pages.**

DRASNICE see Drvenik *C4*

DUBROVNIK *C4* (7km S Coastal) *42.62471, 18.20801* **Autocamp Kate, Tupina 1, 20207 Mlini [(020) 487006; fax 487553; info@campingkate.com; www.campingkate.com]** Fr Dubrovnik on rd 8 foll sp Cavtat or Čilipi or airport into vill of Mlini. Fr S past Cavtat into Mlini. Site well sp fr main rd. Sm, hdstg, pt sl, terr, pt shd; wc; chem disp; shwrs inc; EHU (10-16A) inc; lndry; shop adj; rest, bar adj; BBQ; shgl beach 200m; phone; wifi; bus to Dubrovnik 150m; dogs HRK4; Eng spkn; adv bkg; some rd noise; red long stay/LS; CKE/CCI. "Family-run site in lovely setting; v helpful, hard-working, welcoming owners; vg clean facs; boats fr vill to Dubrovnik; long, steep climb (steps) down to beach." 4 Apr-27 Oct. HRK 173 2017*

"There aren't many sites open at this time of year"

If you're travelling outside peak season remember to call ahead to check site opening dates – even if the entry says 'open all year'.

⊞ **DUBROVNIK** *C4* (10km S Coastal) *42.62444, 18.19301* **Autocamp Matkovica, Srebreno 8, 20207 Dubrovnik [(020) 485867; u.o.matkovica@hotmail.com]** Fr Dubrovnik S on coast rd. At Kupari foll sp to site behind Camping Porto. Sm, mkd pitch, shd; wc; chem disp; shwrs inc; EHU (6A) inc; lndry; supmkt, rest, snacks, bar 200m; shgl beach adj; wifi; dogs; Eng spkn; phone; bus 200m; Eng spkn; no ccard, cash only; poss traff noise; red LS. "Well-kept site; friendly, helpful owners; san facs old but clean; water bus to Dubrovnik 1km." HRK 135 2014*

DUBROVNIK *C4* (5km NW Urban/Coastal) *42.66191, 18.07050* **Autocamp Solitudo, Vatroslava Lisinskog 17, 20000 Dubrovnik [(052) 465010; fax 460199; camping-dubrovnik@valamar.com; www.camping-adriatic.com/solitudo-camp-dubrovnik]** S down Adriatic Highway to Tuđjman Bdge over Dubrovnik Harbour. Turn L immed sp Dubrovnik & in 700m take sharp U-turn sp Dubrovnik & carry on under bdge. Site on Babin Kuk across harbour fr bdge. Lge, mkd pitch, hdstg, pt sl, pt terr, pt shd; htd wc; chem disp; mv service pnt; fam bthrm; shwrs inc; EHU (10A) inc (long lead poss req); lndry (inc dryer); shop; rest, snacks, bar; BBQ; pool, paddling pool 200m; shgl beach 500m; fishing; tennis; bike hire; wifi; dogs HRK46; twin-axles acc (rec check in adv); phone; bus 150m; poss cr; Eng spkn; adv bkg; quiet; ccard acc; red LS/CKE/CCI. "Friendly, clean, well-run, v busy site; sm pitches poss stony &/or boggy; some lge pitches; levelling blocks poss req; san facs poss stretched high ssn & dated; nearest site to city cent; conv Bari ferry; sat nav/map advised as few sp; site in two parts, upper numbered but not mrkd and informal, lower numbered and mkd." ♦ 1 Apr-30 Oct. HRK 366 (CChq acc) SBS - X01 2013*

DUGA RESA see Karlovac *B2*

FAZANA *A3* (1km S Coastal) *44.91717, 13.81105* **Camping Bi-Village, Dragonja 115, 52212 Fažana [(052) 300300; fax 380711; info@bivillage.com; www.bivillage.com]** N fr Pula on rd 21/A9/E751 at Vodnjan turn W sp Fažana. Foll sp for site. V lge, mkd pitch, pt shd; htd wc; chem disp; mv service pnt; shwrs inc; EHU (10A) inc; gas; lndry (inc dryer); supmkt; rest, snacks, bar; BBQ; playgrnd; 3 pools; waterslide; shgl/rocky beach adj; watersports; tennis 1km; games area; bike & boat hire; golf 2km; wifi; entmnt; 30% statics/apartments; dogs HRK37; phone; bus; poss cr; Eng spkn; adv bkg; quiet; ccard acc; red LS/snr citizens; CKE/CCI. "Excel, modern, clean san facs; private bthrms avail; site surrounded by pine trees; some beachside pitches; conv Brijuni Island National Park; excel leisure facs for families; vg cycle paths; no emptying point for Wastermaster; vg; prices vary per ssn." ♦ 20 Apr-14 Oct. HRK 342 (5 persons) (CChq acc) 2017*

FUNTANA see Poreč *A2*

HVAR ISLAND *B4* **Sites on Hvar Island are listed together at the end of the Croatia site entry pages.**

ICICI see Opatija *A2*

KARLOVAC *B2* (12km SW Rural) *45.41962, 15.48338* **Autocamp Slapić, Mrežničke Brig, 47250 Duga Resa [tel/fax (098) 860601; autocamp@inet.hr; www.campslapic.hr]** Exit A1/E65 junc 3 for Karlovac; strt over traff lts immed after toll booth sp Split & Rijecka. Take D23 to Duga Resa; turn L by church in Duga Resa; cont over bdge & turn R; foll rd keeping rv on your R; cont thro vill of Mrnžnički Brig in 3km; site sp in another 1km. NB new bdge at Belavici. Site well sp fr Duga Resa. Sm, mkd pitch, pt shd; wc; chem disp; shwrs inc; EHU (16A) HRK20; lndry (inc dryer); shop 500m; rest, snacks, bar adj; BBQ; playgrnd; rv sw & beach adj; fishing; canoeing; tennis; games area; bike hire; wifi; dogs HRK15; phone; train to Zagreb 500m; Eng spkn; adv bkg; poss noise fr daytrippers; ccard acc. "Friendly, pleasant, family-owned site in gd location on rv; lovely area; gd bar/rest; gd clean facs; lge pitches; long hoses req LS; easy drive into Zagreb; excel; new, superb sans block (2014); rds to site narr." ♦
1 Apr-31 Oct. HRK 220 2014*

KORENICA *B3* (1.5km NW Urban) *44.76527, 15.68833* **Camping Borje, Vranovaca bb, 53230 Korenica [(053) 751790; fax 751791; info@np-plitvicka-jezera.hr; www.np-plitvicka-jezera.hr]** Exit A1/A6 at Karlovac & take rd 1/E71 S dir Split. Site on R approx 15km after Plitvička Jezera National Park, well sp. Med, mkd pitch, sl, pt shd; htd wc; chem disp; mv service pnt; fam bthrm; shwrs inc; EHU (10A) inc; gas (1km); lndry (inc dryer); supmkt 2km; rest, snacks; bar; BBQ; playgrnd; lake sw nr; TV in adj rest; wifi; dogs HRK20; twin axles; poss cr; Eng spkn; adv bkg; ccard acc; quiet; excel; CKE/CCI. "Vg, clean, well-kept, spacious, sl site - levelling poss tricky; gd, modern, immac facs; helpful staff; well run by Plitvicka National Park; excel for visiting the Lakes & waterfalls; free bus runs to park at 1030 and returns at 1730; mountain views." ♦
1 Apr-15 Oct. HRK 255 2014*

KRK ISLAND *A3* **Sites on Krk Island are listed together at the end of the Croatia site entry pages.**

KUCISTE see Orebič *C4*

LABIN *A2* (3km SW Rural) *45.08179, 14.10167* **Mini Camping Romantik, HR-52220 Labin, Kapelica 47b [(911) 396423; mario.braticic@pu.t-com.hr]** Fr Labin on A21/E751, take 5103 twds Koramomacno for 2km. Site sp on this rd. Turn L into sm lane. Foll sp. Sm, mkd pitch, hdstg, unshd; wc; chem disp; shwrs; EHU (10A); lndry; BBQ; cooking facs; playgrnd; sw pool; games area; wifi; 10% statics; dogs; Eng spkn; adv bkgs; quiet; red in LS. "Sm family site; 4 mkd and 4 unmkd pitches; v friendly, helpful, lovely family run site; 2km walk to old Labin." ♦ ltd. 24 Apr-15 Oct. HRK 164 2016*

LANTERNA see Poreč *A2*

LOSINJ ISLAND *A4* **Sites on Lošinj Island are listed together at the end of the Croatia site entry pages.**

LOVRECICA see Umag *A2*

LOZOVAC see Sibenik *B3*

MLINI see Dubrovnik *C4*

⊞ **MOLUNAT** *D4* (500m N Coastal) *42.45298, 18.4276* **Autokamp Monika, Molunat 28, 20219 Molunat [tel/fax (020) 794557; info@camp-monika.hr; www.camp-monika.hr]** Site well sp in Molunat off Adriatic Highway E65. Sm, terr, pt shd; wc (some cont); chem disp; mv service pnt; shwrs inc; EHU (6A) HRK27; lndry; rest, snacks; bar; BBQ; sand beach adj; internet; dogs HRK8; bus; poss cr; Eng spkn; quiet; red LS. "Gd site close to Montenegro border & in quiet cove; sea view fr all pitches; owner's wine & olive oil for sale; beautiful views, v quiet LS; v friendly & helpful owner; highly rec." HRK 248 2014*

MURTER see Jezera (Murter Island) *B3*

MURTER ISLAND *B3* **Sites on Murter Island are listed together at the end of the Croatia site entry pages.**

NOVIGRAD (DALMATIA) *B3* (550m N Coastal) *44.18472, 15.54944* **Camping Adriasol, 23312 Novigrad [(023) 375618; fax 375619; info@adriasol.com or office@adriasol.com; www.adriasol.com]** Exit A1 at Posedarje & foll sp Novigrad. Site sp at end of vill. Med, pt shd; wc; chem disp; mv service pnt; fam bthrm; shwrs inc; EHU (16A) HRK31; lndry; shop 500m; rest, snacks, bar adj; cooking facs; playgrnd; beach adj; watersports; bike hire; games area; internet; some statics; dogs HRK23; TV; adv bkg; quiet; red CKE/CCI. "Well-positioned site - poss windy; gd facs; friendly staff; popular level pitches by beach cost more; freezer avail for camper use; very helpful staff."
♦ 1 May-30 Sep. HRK 234 2013*

⊞ **OMIS** *C4* (8km S Coastal) *43.40611, 16.77777* **Autocamp Sirena, Četvrt Vrilo 10, 21317 Lokva Rogoznica [tel/fax (021) 870266; autocamp-sirena@st.t.hr; www.autocamp-sirena.com]** Thro Omiš S'wards on main coastal rd, site up sm lane on R immed bef sm tunnel. Med, hdstg, sl, terr, pt shd; wc; chem disp; mv service pnt; shwrs inc; EHU (16A) HRK15; gas; lndry; shop; rest, snacks; bar; BBQ; shgl beach adj; watersports; internet; dogs HRK15; phone; bus; poss cr; Eng spkn; adv bkg; quiet; CKE/CCI. "Enthusiastic, welcoming staff; improving site; easy access lge o'fits; stunning location above beautiful beach; excel stop bet Split & Dubrovnik; excel rest."
HRK 206 2014*

⊞ **OMIS** *C4* (1.5km W Coastal) *43.44040, 16.67960* **Autocamp Galeb, Vukovarska bb, 21310 Omiš [tel/ fax (021) 864430; camping@galeb.hr; www.camp. galeb.hr]** Site sp on rd 2/E65 fr Split to Dubrovnik. Lge, mkd pitch, pt shd; wc; chem disp; mv service pnt; fam bthrm; serviced pitches; private bthrms avail; shwrs; EHU (16A) inc; gas; lndry; supmkt adj; rest, snacks; bar; BBQ (gas, elec); playgrnd; sand beach; watersports; white water rafting; sports area; bike hire; tennis; wifi; entmnt; 50% statics; dogs HRK33; bus; poss cr; noisy high ssn; ccard acc; red LS/CKE/CCI. "Excel, well-maintained site in gd position; extra for waterside pitch; clean san facs; suitable young children; easy walk or water taxi to town." ♦ ltd. HRK 289 SBS - X02 2012*

OPATIJA *A2* (5km S Coastal) *45.30633, 14.28354* **Autocamp Opatija, Liburnijska 46, 51414 Ičići [(051) 704387; tz-icici@ri.t-com.hr]** Fr Opatija take Pula rd 66. Site sp on R of rd 5km after Opatija. Sp fr Ičići. Med, terr, pt shd; wc; chem disp; mv service pnt; shwrs inc; EHU (10A); rest, snacks 1km; shgl beach adj; tennis; dogs; Eng spkn; quiet. "Gd site nr coastal promenade; diff for lge o'fits without motor mover." 1 May-30 Sep. HRK 247 2013*

⊞ **OREBIC** *C4* (1km E Coastal) *42.9810, 17.1980* **Nevio Camping, Dubravica bb, 20250 Orebič [(020) 713100; fax 713950; info@nevio-camping.com; www.nevio-camping.com]** Fr N take ferry fr Ploče to Trpanj & take rd 415 then 414 dir Orebič, site sp. Fr S on rd 8/E65 turn W at Zaton Doli onto rd 414 to site. Site ent immed after lge sp - not 100m further on. Sm, terr, pt shd; htd wc; chem disp; mv service pnt; some serviced pitches; fam bthrm; shwrs inc; EHU (16A) inc; lndry (inc dryer); shop 300m; rest, snacks; beach bar; BBQ; cooking facs; pool; dir access to shgl beach; tennis; bike hire; wifi; TV rm; 40% statics; dogs HRK15-38; Eng spkn; adv bkg; quiet; red LS/snr citizens. "Excel new site in gd location; friendly, helpful, welcoming staff; gd views; gd, clean facs; not suitable lge o'fits." ♦ HRK 282 2013*

PAKOSTANE *B3* (4km SE Coastal) *43.88611, 15.53305* **Autocamp Oaza Mira, Ul. Dr. Franje Tudmana 2, 23211 Drage [023 635419; info@oaza-mira.hr; www.oaza-mira.hr]** A1 Karlovac-Split past Zadar, exit Biograd dir Sibenik on coast rd; sp on coastal side of rd; foll sp site after bay. Med, hdstg, terr, pt shd; wc; chem disp; mv serv pnt; fam bthrm; shwr; EHU inc; lndry rm; shop; rest; bar; BBQ; playgrnd; pool; beach adj; games rm; wifi; dogs HRK61; Eng spkn; adv bkg; quiet. "Excel new lovely site in beautiful location; generous pitches; rec using ACSI card; 2 beautiful bays adj to site; highly rec." 1 Apr-31 Oct. HRK 427 2012*

POREC *A2* (10km N Coastal) *45.29728, 13.59425* **Camping Lanterna, Lanterna 1, 52465 Tar [(052) 404 500; fax 404591; lanterna@valamar.com; www. camping-adriatic.com/camp-lanterna]** Site sp 5km S of Novigrad (Istria) & N of Poreč on Umag-Vrsar coast rd. V lge, hdg/mkd pitch, hdstg, pt sl, terr, pt shd; wc; chem disp; mv service pnt; fam bthrm; shwrs inc; EHU (10A); gas; lndry; supmkts; rest, snacks; bar; BBQ; playgrnd; pool; 2 hydro-massage pools; paddling pool; shgl beach adj; watersports; boat launch; tennis; games area; bike hire; wifi; entmnt; 10% statics; dogs €5; phone; adv bkg (fee); noise fr ships loading across bay; ccard acc; red CKE/CCI (cash payments only). "V busy, well-run site; excel san facs & leisure facs; although many san facs they may be a long walk; variety of shops; gd sightseeing; extra for seaside/hdg pitch; vg." ♦ 12 Apr-10 Oct. HRK 298 (CChq acc) SBS - X10 2014*

POREC *A2* (8km NW Coastal) *45.25680, 13.58350* **Naturist-Center Ulika (Naturist), 52440 Poreč (Istra) [(052) 436325; fax 436352; reservations@plava laguna.hr; www.lagunaporec.com]** Site sp on rd fr Poreč to Tar & Novigrad. V lge, pt sl, shd; wc; shwrs; EHU (6A) HRK23; lndry; shop; rest, snacks; bar; playgrnd; pool; shgl & rocky beach; tennis; watersports; entmnt; 9% statics; dogs HRK48; adv bkg; quiet; ccard acc; red INF card/long stay; "Excel site; picturesque shore; vg facs, poss far fr some pitches; lge site, bike useful for getting around." ♦ 8 Apr-1 Oct. HRK 287 2017*

PREMANTURA see Medulin *A3*

PRIMOSTEN *B4* (2km N Coastal) *43.60646, 15.92085* **Auto Kamp Adriatic, Huljerat BB, 22202 Primošten [(022) 571223; fax 571360; camp-adriatiq@adriatiq. com; www.autocamp-adriatiq.com]** Off Adriatic Highway, rd 8/E65, sp. V lge, all hdstg, pt sl, pt terr, unshd; wc; chem disp; mv service pnt; fam bthrm; shwrs inc; EHU (16A) inc; gas; lndry (inc dryer); shop & 2km; rest, snacks; bar; rocky beach adj; boat hire; watersports; diving cent; tennis; games area; wifi; entmnt; dogs HRK32; Eng spkn; quiet; red CKE/CCI. "Gd sea views; excel san facs; some pitches poss diff to get onto; beautiful views fr beach." ♦ 7 Apr-31 Oct. HRK 190 2016*

PULA *A3* (7km S Coastal) *44.82290, 13.85080* **Camping Peškera, Indije 73 52100 Banjole/Pula (Istra) [052 573209; fax 573189; info@camp-peskera. com; www.camp-peskera.com]** Fr N take A9 to Pula. Cont on m'way twd Premantura. Exit at Banjole, cont twd Indije. Campsite is 100m after Indije. Sm, pt sl, pt shd; wc; cont; chem disp; mv service pnt; shwrs; supmkt 2km; rest 1km; snacks; bar; shingle beach adj; wifi; dogs HRK15; bus 0.5km; poss cr; Eng spkn; adv bkg; quiet; ccard acc; red LS; CCI. "Beautiful situation; helpful & friendly owners; gd clean san facs; vg." ♦ ltd. 1 Apr-31 Oct. HRK 212 2014*

CROATIA

PULA *A3* (8km S Rural) *44.82472, 13.85885* **Camping Diana, Castagnes b b, 52100 Banjole [(385) 99 293 1963 or (385) 99 738 0313; kristijan.modrusan@gmail.com; www.camp-diana.com]** Fr Pula ring rd foll sp Premantura & Camping Indije. Site 1km bef Cmp Indije. Sm, pt sl, pt shd; wc; chem disp (wc); shwrs inc; EHU (16A) inc; shop 200m; bar; playgrnd; pool; paddling pool; tennis; games area; wifi; no dogs; adv bkg; quiet. "Pleasant site in garden setting; gd range of facs; immac san facs; welcoming family owners; narr ent poss diff for lge o'fits." 15 May-22 Sep. HRK 254 2016*

PULA *A3* (9km S Coastal) *44.82012, 13.90252* **Autocamp Pomer, Pomer bb, 52100 Pula [052 573746; fax 573062; acpomer@arenaturist.hr; www.arenacamps.com]** Fr N on A9 to Pula, take exit to Pula. At bottom of hill turn L after filling stn & foll dir Medulin/Premantura. In Premantura turn L by Consum supmkt & foll sp to Pomer & site. Med, mkd pitch, terr, shd; wc; chem disp; shwrs; EHU (16A) HRK21 (long lead poss req); lndry rm; shop; rest, snacks; bar; BBQ; playgrnd; rocky beach adj; fishing; watersports; games area; entmnt; some statics; dogs HRK23; phone; Eng spkn; adv bkg; quiet; red CKE/CCI. "Clean san facs poss stretched high ssn; friendly owner; quiet, relaxing site." 21 Apr-15 Oct. HRK 127 2016*

PULA *A3* (10km S Coastal) *44.82393, 13.85069* **Camping Indije, Indije 96, 52203, Banjole, Pula [052 573066; info@arenaturist.hr; arenacamps.com]** Fr Pula ring rd, drive twd Premantura. At Banjole, exit rndbt 1st R and foll site sp. Lge, mkd pitch, pt sl, terr, pt shd; wc; chem disp; mv service pnt; fam bthrm; shwrs; EHU (10A); lndry (inc dryer); shop; rest; café; snacks; bar; BBQ; playgrnd; beach on site; games area; bike hire; entmnt; wifi; TV; 20% statics; dogs €4; phone; bus 2km; twin axles; Eng spkn; adv bkg; red LS/long stay; CKE/CCI. "Watersports/diving; mkd walks & cycle tracks; vg site." ♦ ltd. 21 Apr-25 Sep. HRK 222 2016*

PUNAT see Krk (Krk Island) *A3*

RAB ISLAND *A3* **Sites on Rab Island are listed together at the end of the Croatia site entry pages.**

RABAC *A3* (500m W Coastal) *45.08086, 14.14583* **Camping Oliva, 52221 Rabac [tel/fax (052) 872258; olivakamp@maslinica-rabac.com; www.maslinica-rabac.com]** On ent Rabac fr Labin, turn R at sp Autocamp; site ent in 500m. V lge, mkd pitch, pt shd; wc (mainly cont); fam bthrm; shwrs; EHU (10A) inc (long lead poss req); gas; lndry (inc dryer); shop 100m; rest, snacks; bar; playgrnd; shgl beach; watersports; boat-launching; sports complex; 30% statics; dogs HRK22; phone; poss cr; adv bkg Aug ess; quiet; ccard acc; red CKE/CCI. "Conv historic walled town Labin; walk along beach to shops & rest." ♦ ltd. 21 Apr-6 Oct. HRK 402 (CChq acc) 2013*

RAKOVICA *B3* (7km SW Rural) *44.95020, 15.64160* **Camp Korana, Plitvička Jezera, 47246 Drežnik Grad [(053) 751888; fax 751882; autokamp.korana@np-plitvicka-jezera.hr; www.np-plitvicka-jezera.hr]** On A1/E59 2km S of Grabovac, site on L. Site is 5km N of main ent to Plitvička Nat Park, sp. Lge, some hdstg, pt sl, pt shd; wc; fam bthrm; own san; chem disp; mv service pnt; shwrs inc; EHU (16A) inc (poss long lead req); lndry rm; shop; rest, snacks; bar; BBQ; wifi; 10% statics; dogs HRK23; Eng spkn; no adv bkg; ccard acc; CKE/CCI. "Lovely site, v busy; poss long way fr facs; gd san facs but inadequate for size of site; efficient, friendly site staff; poss muddy in wet; bus to National Park (6km) high ssn; new san facs; gd rest." 1 Apr-31 Oct. HRK 259 2014*

RIJEKA *A2* (9km W Coastal) *45.35638, 14.34222* **Camping Preluk, Preluk 1, 51000 Rijeka [(051) 662185; fax 622381; camp.preluk@gmail.com]** On Rijeka to Opatija coast rd. Sm, shd; wc (some cont); own san; chem disp; shwrs; EHU (10A) inc; shop; snacks; mainly statics; dogs; bus; poss cr; Eng spkn; rd noise. "NH only; Many statics; facs recently renovated (2012); bus to town; sm beach on site; gd windsurfing." 1 May-30 Sep. HRK 158 2012*

RIZVANUSA *B3* (10km W Rural) *44.49580, 15.29165* **Eco Camp Rizvan City, Rizvanuša 1, 53000 Gospić [053 57 33 33; info@adria-velebitica.hr; www.camp-rizvancity.com]** Fr A1 take exit 12 (Gospic). Head 10km E twd Karlobag on highway 25. Turn L off main rd into Vill Rizvanusa. Camp 500m. Sm, pt shd; wc; chem disp; mv service pnt; fam bthrm; shwrs; EHU (16A); lndry (inc dryer); BBQ; playgrnd; beach 30km; games area; wifi; dogs; twin axles; Eng spkn; adv bkg; quiet. "Walks, high rope course; quad & jeep safari; archery; paintball; zip line; wall climbing; giant swing; bike trails; vg." ♦ ltd. 1 Mar-1 Nov. HRK 163 2014*

ROVINJ *A2* (5km N Coastal) *45.10444, 13.62527*
Camping Valdaliso, Monsena b.b, 52210 Rovinj [(052) 805505; fax 811541; ac-valdaliso@maistra.hr; www.campingrovinjvrsar.com] N fr Rovinj dir Valalta for 2km, turn W to coast, site sp. Lge, hdg/mkd pitch, some hdstg, pt sl, pt shd; htd wc; chem disp; mv service pnt; fam bthrm; shwrs; EHU (10A) inc; gas; lndry; shop; rest, snacks; bar; BBQ; playgrnd; shgl beach adj; waterslide; tennis; bike hire; games area; games rm; wifi; entmnt; sat TV; 10% statics; no dogs; phone; bus; water taxi; Eng spkn; adv bkg; quiet; ccard acc; CKE/CCI. "Pretty site in olive trees; use of all amenities in hotel adj; excel modern san facs; poss waterlogged after heavy rain; excel; facs stretched if site full; pitches uneven; closing in Sep 2015 for redevelopment." ♦ 12 Apr-26 Sep. HRK 288 2015*

"We must tell The Club about that great site we found"

Get your site reports in by mid-August and we'll do our best to get your updates into the next edition.

ROVINJ *A2* (7km N Coastal) *45.12287, 13.62970*
Campsite Valalta Naturist (Naturist), Cesta Za Valaltu-Lim 7, 52210 Rovinj (Istra) [052 804800; fax 821004; valalta@valalta.hr; www.valalta.hr] 7km NW fr Rovinj. Foll signs to Valalta. V lge, hdg/mkd pitch, hdstg, pt shd; wc; chem disp; mv service pnt; fam bthrm; shwrs; EHU (16A); lndry (inc dryer); shop; rest; snacks; bar; BBQ; playgrnd; pool; waterslide; paddling pool; beach; games area; games rm; bike hire; entmnt; wifi; TV; phone; twin axles; Eng spkn; adv bkg; quiet. "Excel site." ♦ ltd. 1 May-1 Oct. HRK 408 2014*

ROVINJ *A2* (5km NW Coastal) *45.10909, 13.61974*
Camping Amarin, Monsena bb, 52210 Rovinj [(052) 802000; fax 813354; ac-amarin@maistra.hr; www.campingrovinjvrsar.com] Fr town N in dir Valalta, turn L & foll site sp. V lge, mkd pitch, pt sl, pt shd; wc (some cont), chem disp; mv service pnt; shwrs inc; EHU (10A) inc; lndry; shop; rest, snacks; bar; playgrnd; htd pool; paddling pool; waterslide; shgl beach adj; sports facs; tennis; bike hire; entmnt; internet; TV; wifi (at recep); 30% statics; dogs HRK47; phone; poss cr; Eng spkn; adv bkg; quiet; ccard acc; red LS/CKE/CCI. "Excel site; clean, well-maintained san facs & pool; gd entmnt; views of town & islands; lovely situation in pine & olive trees; water taxi to town." ♦ 13 Apr-1 Oct. HRK 289 2017*

ROVINJ *A2* (700m NW Coastal) *45.09472, 13.64527*
Autocamp Porton Biondi, Aleja Porton Biondi 1, 52210 Rovinj [(052) 813557; fax 811509; portonbiondi@web.de; www.portonbiondi.hr] Site sp on ent Rovinj. Lge, pt sl, terr, shd; wc; shwrs inc; EHU inc; shop adj; rest, snacks; rocky beach nr; watersports; entmnt; dogs HRK24; adv bkg; quiet; ccard acc; red LS/ long stay/CKE/CCI. "Gd site within walking dist Rovinj old town; beautiful views; new san facs; sm pitches not suitable lge o'fits; excel rest; 2nd & subsequent nights at red rate." ♦ ltd. 15 Mar-31 Oct. HRK 170 2012*

SELCE *A2* (1.3km SE Coastal) *45.15361, 14.72488*
Autocamp Selce, Jasenová 19, 51266 Selce [(051) 764038; fax 764066; autokampselce@jadran-crikvenica.hr; www.jadran-crikvenica.hr] Thro Selce town cent, site is 500m SE of town, sp. Lge, hdstg, pt sl, terr, pt shd; wc (some cont) chem disp; mv service pnt; shwrs; EHU (10A) HRK27; lndry; shop; rest, snacks; bar; playgrnd; shgl beach adj; TV; statics; dogs HRK17; phone; poss cr; quiet; ccard acc; red long stay/ CKE/CCI. "Wooded site; seaside location; helpful staff; long stay; blocks & wedges ess; san facs run down & neglected; long lead rec; door security." ♦ 1 Apr-15 Oct. HRK 247 2014*

SENJ *A3* (6km NW Coastal) *45.04403, 14.87817*
Autocamp Sibinj, Sibinj 9, 51252 Klenovica [(051) 796916; milieijko.tomijanovic@ri.hinet.hr] Fr Novi Vinodolski, take rd S. In approx 12km site sp. Med, sl, terr, pt shd; wc (male cont); shwrs inc; EHU (10A); shops, sm bar & rest; private shgl beach adj; some rd noise. "Well-run site; clean facs but in need of modernising; magnificent views; poss open all yr; noisy rd; NH only." 1 May-31 Oct. HRK 152 2016*

"I need an on-site restaurant"

We do our best to make sure site information is correct, but it is always best to check any must-have facilities are still available or will be open during your visit.

SIBENIK *B3* (10km NE Rural) *43.80063, 15.94210*
Camp Krka, Skocici 21, 22221 Lozovac [(022) 778495; goran.skocic@si.t-com.hr; www.camp-krka.hr] Exit A1 at junc 22 Šibenik, turn E at T-junc, thro tunnel & site in approx 4km. Fr main coast rd at Sibenik turn N onto rte 33 twd Drniš. After 15km turn L dir Skradin, site sp on L. Med, hdstg, pt shd; wc; chem disp; shwrs; EHU (16A) HRK23 (poss rev pol; check earth); lndry; shop 4km; bar; some statics & B&B; Eng spkn; quiet; red LS/CKE/CCI. "Pleasant, basic site in orchard; friendly owner; gd modern san facs; conv Krka National Park & Krka gorge; gd; clean new shwr/wc facs (2014); rest, cheap basic food." 1 Apr-30 Oct. HRK 151 2014*

SIBENIK *B3* (4km S Coastal) *43.69925, 15.87942* **Camping Solaris, Hotelsko Naselje Solaris, 22000 Šibenik [(022) 364000; fax 364450; info@solaris.hr; www.solaris.hr]** Sp fr E65 Zadar-Split rd, adj hotel complex. V lge, hdg/mkd pitch, pt shd; htd wc; chem disp; mv service pnt in adj marina; sauna; serviced pitches; shwrs inc; EHU (6A) inc; lndry; shop adj; rest, snacks; bar; BBQ; playgrnd; pool; paddling pool; waterslide; watersports; tennis; bike hire; wifi; entmnt; TV; dogs; bus; poss v cr; some rd noise; ccard acc; red long stay/LS/CKE/CCI. "Well-situated in olive & pine trees; some pitches adj marina; excel, modern san facs." ♦ 15 Apr-31 Oct. HRK 225 2012*

See advertisement

⊞ **SPLIT** *B4* (8km E Coastal) *43.50451, 16.52598* **Camping Stobreč-Split, Sv Lovre 6, 21311 Stobreč [(021) 325426; fax 325452; camping.split@gmail.com; www.campingsplit.com]** Fr N foll E65 & m'way thro Split to sp Stobreč. Site sp R off E65 at traff lts in Stobreč. Lge, mkd pitch, hdstg, pt sl, shd; wc; chem disp; mv service pnt; shwrs; EHU (16A) inc (long lead poss req); lndry (inc dryer); shop; rest, snacks; bar; playgrnd; sand beach; games area; wifi; dogs HRK45; bus to Split; poss cr; Eng spkn; some rd noise. "Superb, well-run site in lovely setting with views; helpful, welcoming staff; gd facs; own sandy beach; public footpath thro site; rec arr early to secure pitch; gd value for money; highly rec; Diocletian's Palace worth a visit; excel; wellness ctr - pool, sauna, gym." ♦ HRK 278 2017*

STARIGRAD PAKLENICA *B3* (300m S Coastal) *44.28694, 15.44666* **Autocamp Paklenica, Dr Franje Tuđjmana 14, 23244 Starigrad-Paklenica [(023) 209050; fax 209073; camping.paklenica@bluesunhotels.com or alan@bluesunhotels.com; www.bluesunhotels.com]** On rd 8/E65 Adriatic H'way at ent to Paklenica National Park in Zidine vill. Hotel Alan is lge, 10-storey block - ent & cont to site. Lge, pt sl, shd; wc; chem disp; shwrs inc; EHU (16A) inc (long lead poss req); lndry; shop; rest; bar; playgrnd; pool adj; paddling pool; beach adj; tennis; games area; bike hire; wifi; entmnt; TV; 5% statics; dogs HRK37; phone; Eng spkn; poss cr nr shore; adv bkg; ccard acc; red long stay/LS/CKE/CCI. "Gd clean facs; conv National Park; excel walking & rockclimbing; use of facs at adj hotel; site muddy when wet; gd res, pleasant helpful staff, san facs being enlarged (2013)." ♦ 1Apr-15 Nov. HRK 329 2013*

"Satellite navigation makes touring much easier"

Remember most sat navs don't know if you're towing or in a larger vehicle – always use yours alongside maps and site directions.

⊞ **STARLGRAD PAKLENICA** *B3* (1km N Coastal) *44.31340, 15.43579* **Auto-Kamp Plantaža, Put Plantaza 2, 23244 Starigrad Paklenica [(038) 23 369131; fax 23 359159; plantaza@hi.t-com.hr; www.plantaza.com]** Fr Rijeka foll M2/E27 coast rd until 1 km N of Steligrad. V Steep pull out of site. Sm, mkd pitch, hdstg, terr, shd; htd wc; chem disp; mv service pnt; fam bthrm; shwrs; EHU 10A; rest; BBQ; beach; Eng spkn; poss cr; quite; ACSI; CKE/CCI. "Vg site; excel new facs; handy for NP; shopping for fresh food v ltd locally." HRK 114 2012*

STOBREC see Split *B4*

SVETI JURAJ see Senj *A3*

CROATIA

TROGIR *B4* (5km W Coastal) *43.51150, 16.19430* **Camping Vranjica-Belvedere, Seget Vranjica bb, 21218 Seget Donji [(021) 798222; fax 894151; info@vranjica-belvedere.hr; www.vranjica-belvedere.hr]** Site clearly sp on coast rd, W of Trogir, 100m bef start of by-pass. Lge, mkd pitch, terr, pt sl, pt shd; wc (some cont); chem disp; mv service pnt; fam bthrm; private san facs avail; shwrs inc; EHU (16A) HRK36; lndry (inc dryer); supmkt; rest, snacks; bar; BBQ; playgrnd; shgl beach adj; watersports; tennis; games area; wifi; entmnt; TV rm; 30% statics; dogs HRK25; phone; bus, water taxi; poss cr; Eng spkn; adv bkg; quiet; ccard acc; red lw ssn/long stay/CKE/CCI. "Beautiful position with views of bay; lovely town; gd facs; vg site; site OK, bit scruffy but clean san facs; v helpful staff." 15 Apr-15 Oct. HRK 303 (CChq acc) 2013*

See advertisement

TUHELJSKE TOPLICE *B2* (Urban) *46.06583, 15.78513* **Camping Terme Tuhelj, Ljudevita Gaja 4, 49215 Tuhelj [(049) 203000; info@terme-tuhelj.hr; www.terme-tuhelj.hr]** N fr Zagreb on A2 for approx 24km, exit junc 5 Zabok & foll rds 24/301/205 to sp Tuheljske Toplice. Check in at Hotel Toplice. Sm, pt shd; wc; chem disp; mv service pnt; shwrs inc; EHU (6A) HRK25; lndry rm; rest, snacks; bar; playgrnd; htd pool; waterslide; paddling pool; thermal spa adj; games area; games rm; wifi; TV; dogs HKR25; phone; bus; Eng spkn; adv bkg; quiet. "Gd, conv Zagreb & gd alt to Zagreb site." ♦ ltd. 1 Apr-31 Oct. HRK 210 2016*

UMAG *A2* (6km S Coastal) *45.39271, 13.54193* **Autocamp Finida, Križine br 55A, 52470 Umag [(052) 756296; fax 756295; camp.finida@instraturist.hr; www.istracamping.com]** Site clearly sp. Lge, mkd pitch, pt sl, pt shd; wc; chem disp; mv service pnt; fam bthrm; shwrs inc; EHU (10A) inc; lndry; shop; rest, snacks; bar; playgrnd; shgl beach adj; bike hire; TV; 50% statics; dogs HRK25; phone; bus; poss cr; Eng spkn; adv bkg; quiet; ccard acc; red long stay/CKE/CCI. "Gd base for touring Istria; gd, clean, modern facs; lovely site amongst oak trees; friendly staff." 23 Apr-30 Sep. HRK 125 2016*

VRSAR *A2* (2km N Coastal) *45.16505, 13.60796* **Camping Valkanela, Petalon 1, 52450 Vrsar [(052) 800200; fax 800215; info@maistra.hr; www.campingrovinjvrsar.com]** Site sp N of town fr coast rd. V lge, pt sl, terr, pt shd; wc (some cont); chem disp; mv service pnt; fam bthrm; shwrs inc; EHU (6A) inc; gas 1km; lndry; supmkt; shops; 2 rests; snacks; bar; playgrnd; rocky beach; watersports; tennis; games area; bike hire; entmnt; TV; 40% statics; dogs HRK50; phone; poss cr; Eng spkn; adv bkg; quiet; ccard acc; red CKE/CCI. "Excel for watersports; vg san facs; vg site for children." ♦ 25 Apr-3 Oct. HRK 275 2013*

VRSAR *A2* (1km SE Coastal) *45.14233, 13.60541* **Naturist-Park Koversada (Naturist), Petalon 1, 52450 Vrsar [(052) 441378; fax 441761; koversada-camp@maistra.hr; www.campingrovinjvrsar.com]** Site sp fr Vrsar in dir Koversada. V lge, hdg/mkd pitch, pt sl, terr, pt shd; wc (some cont); chem disp; mv service pnt; fam bthrm; shwrs inc; EHU (10-16A) inc; gas 500m; lndry; supmkt; shops; rests; snacks; bar; playgrnd; rocky/sandy beach; tennis; games area; diving school; watersports; bike hire; entmnt; internet; TV rm; 50% statics; dogs HRK46; phone; poss cr; Eng spkn; adv bkg; quiet; ccard acc; red long stay/CKE/CCI. "Vg, modern san facs; excel leisure facs; peaceful situation; excel; busy noisy hilly site." ♦ 26 Apr-28 Sep. HRK 214 2013*

ZADAR *B3* (3.5km N Coastal) *44.13408, 15.21115* **Falkensteiner Camping Zadar (formerly Autocamp Borik), Majstora Radovana 7, 23000 Zadar [(023) 206 555 602; reservations.campingzadar@falkensteiner.com; www.falkensteiner.com]** Exit A2 at Zadar 1/West, cont for approx.19 km. In Zadar, turn R at 2nd x-rds with traff lts and take the bypass (dir Nin, Vir). Cont across 2 x-rds (dir Puntamika). In 70m turn R to Falkensteiner Resort Borik. V lge, shd; wc; own san; chem disp; mv service pnt; shwrs; EHU (10A) inc; shop; rest, snacks; bar; playgrnd; 2 pools (1 htd, covrd) nrby; shgl beach; watersports; tennis; no dogs; phone; bus 450m; Eng spkn; no adv bkg; ccard acc; 10% red CKE/CCI. "Pt of resort complex of 6 hotels; facs poor & some cold water only; poor security; gd sw beach; gd rests nrby; site run down; NH only." ♦ 1 May-30 Sep. HRK 229 2016*

ZAGREB *B2* (12km SW Urban) *45.77389, 15.87778* **Camping Motel Plitvice, Lučko, 10090 Zagreb [(01) 6530444; fax 6530445; motel@motel-plitvice.hr; www.motel-plitvice.hr]** Site at motel attached to Plitvice services on A3/E70. Access only fr m'way travelling fr N, otherwise long m'way detour fr S. Lge, pt shd; htd wc; chem disp; shwrs inc; EHU (16A) inc; lndry rm; shop; rest, snacks; bar; tennis; TV; phone; bus to town fr site; m'way noise; ccard acc; red CKE/CCI. "Ask at motel recep (excel Eng) for best way back fr city &/or details minibus to city; Zagreb well worth a visit; site shabby but facs clean & adequate - stretched when site full & in need of update." 1 May-30 Sep. HRK 168 2016*

"There aren't many sites open at this time of year"

If you're travelling outside peak season remember to call ahead to check site opening dates – even if the entry says 'open all year'.

⊞ **ZAGREB** *B2* (16 W Rural) *45.80217, 15.82696* **Camp Zagreb, Jezerska 6, 10437 Rakitje [(01) 3324506; info@campzagreb.com; www.campzagreb.com]** Exit A3 J2 sp Bestovje. After 3km turn R twrds Rakitje. Site on L in 1km. Sm, mkd/hdg pitch, unshd; wc; chem disp; mv service pnt; fam bthrm; shwrs; EHU (16A); lndry (inc dryer); rest; café; bar; playgrnd; lake adj; bike hire; wifi; dogs; train 1km; twin axles; poss cr; Eng spkn; adv bkg; quiet; red LS; CKE/CCI. "Excel site; sauna & massage; kayak hire; horse trail." ♦ HRK 256 2017*

ZAOSTROG *C4* (0.5km SE Coastal) *43.13925, 17.28047* **Camp Viter, Obala A.K. Miosica 1, 21334 Zaostrog (Dalmatija) [098 704018; fax 021 629190; info@camp-viter.com; www.camp-viter.com]** Foll Camp Viter signs 600m on R after Zaostrog sp. Sm, pt shd; hdstg; wv; chem disp; mv service pnt; shwrs inc; EHU (16A) HRK25; lndry (inc dryer); shop, rest, snacks & bar 0.25km; BBQ; beach; wifi; dogs HRK25; twin axles; Eng spkn; adv bkg; Quiet; red LS; CCI. "Very helpful, friendly owners; vg." 1 Apr-31 Oct. HRK 237 2014*

ZAOSTROG *C4* (1km S Coastal) *43.13133, 17.28751* **Campsite Uvala Borova, Lucica 23, 21335 Zaostrog [tel/fax 021 629 111 or 099 253 4229 (mob); camp.uvala.borova@gmail.com; www.uvala-borova.com]** On rte 8 fr Split, 1km after Zaotrog on the R. Med, mkd pitch, hdstg, terr, shd; wc; chem disp; mv service pnt; shwrs; EHU (16A) HRK25; lndry; rest; bar; BBQ; pool; beach adj; games rm; wifi; TV rm; dogs HRK20; phone; bus; twin axles; Eng spkn; adv bkg; CCI. "Peaceful site with beautiful views of the Croatian coast & mountains; easy walk/cycle into Zaotrog along minor rd; friendly, helpful ownersl vg." ♦ 1 Apr-30 Sep. HRK 215 2014*

ZATON *B3* (1.5km N Coastal) *44.23434, 15.16605* **Camping Zaton Holiday Resort, Široka ulica bb, 23232 Zaton [023 280215; fax 280310; camping@zaton.hr; www.zaton.hr]** Site 16km NW of Zadar on Nin rd. Pt of Zaton holiday vill. Wel sp. V lge, pt shd; htd wc; chem disp; mv service pnt; shwrs inc; EHU (10A) inc; gas; lndry; supmkt; 3 rest, snacks; bar; playgrnd; pool; paddling pool; sand beach adj; boat hire; watersports; tennis; games area; entmnt; internet; 15% statics; dogs HRK65; phone; adv bkg; quiet; ccard acc; red LS; CKE/CCI. "Excel, well-run, busy site; own beach; excel, modern san facs; cent of site is 'vill' with gd value shops & rests; gd for all ages; nr ancient sm town of Nin, in walking dist; conv National Parks; v expensive outside ACSI discount period but has first class facs and nrby town well worth a visit; Croatia's best campsite; superbly laid out & equipped." ♦ 1 May-30 Sep. HRK 480 2014*

BRAC ISLAND

⊞ **BOL** *C4* (500m W Urban/Coastal) *43.26373, 16.64799* **Kamp Kito (formerly Konobo Kito), Braćke Ceste bb, 21420 Bol [(021) 635551 or 635091; info@camping-brac.com; www.camping-brac.com]** Take ferry fr Makarska to Brač & take rd 113/115 to Bol (37km). On o'skrts do not turn L into town but cont twd Zlatni Rat. Pass Studenac sup'mkt on R, site on L. Sm, pt shd; wc; chem disp; shwrs inc; EHU (16A) HRK20; gas; lndry; rest; BBQ; beach 500m; TV; some statics; dogs; poss cr; Eng spkn; adv bkg; quiet. "Excel for beaches & boating; gd local food in rest; vg, friendly, family-run site; clean, well-equipped; well worth effort to get there." HRK 141 2016*

CRES ISLAND

CRES *A3* (1km N Coastal) *44.96277, 14.39694* **Camping Kovačine (Part Naturist), Melin 1/20, 51557 Cres [(051) 573150; fax 571086; campkovacine@kovacine.com; www.camp-kovacine.com]** Fr N, foll sp bef Cres on R. Fr S app thro vill of Cres. V lge, pt shd; wc; chem disp; fam bthrm; shwrs inc; EHU (12A) inc; lndry; shop; rest, snacks; playgrnd; beach; watersports; tennis; games area; sep area for naturists; wifi; dogs HRK23; Eng spkn; quiet; ccard acc; red long stay/CKE/CCI. "Site in olive grove; rocky making driving diff, but amenities gd & well-run; welcoming staff; delightful walk/cycle rte to sm vill of Cres; excel site." ♦ 4 Apr-15 Oct. HRK 276 2013*

MARTINSCICA *A3* (1km NW Coastal) *44.82108, 14.34298* **Camping Slatina, 51556 Martinšćica [(051) 574127; fax 574167; info@camp-slatina.com; www.camp-slatina.com]** Fr Cres S on main rd sp Mali Lošinj for 17km. Turn R sp Martinšćica, site in 8km at end of rd. V lge, hdg pitch, hdstg, terr, shd; wc; chem disp; mv service pnt; fam bthrm; shwrs inc; EHU (10A) inc (long lead req); lndry; shop; rest, snacks; bar; playgrnd; shgl beach adj; boat launching; entmnt; internet; 20% statics; dogs HRK23; phone; poss cr; Eng spkn; adv bkg; quiet; cc acc. "Site on steep slope; newest san facs superb; beautiful island; dog & car washing facs; vg supmkt; ATM on site." ♦ 19 Mar-10 Oct. HRK 234 2016*

ZIVOGOSCE see Drvenik *C4*

Vltava river

Welcome to the Czech Republic

Lying in the heart of Europe, the Czech Republic is renowned for its ornate castles, fantastically preserved medieval buildings, and numerous other cultural sights.

Considered to be one of the most beautiful cities in the world, the capital, Prague, is a wonderful mix of traditional and modern with treasures old and new waiting to be discovered around every corner.

Country highlights

Traditions are important in the Czech Republic, one of which takes places on the 30th of April – Walpurgis Night. Known as pálení čarodějnic (the burning of the witches), this is a night of bonfires and celebrations throughout the country.

The Czech Republic is the home of Bohemian glass or crystal, which is international renowned for its beauty, quality and craftsmanship. They are immensely popular as gifts and souvenirs and are one of the best known Czech exports.

Major towns and cities

- Prague – home to an impressive castle and old town.
- Brno – filled with gorgeous architecture and historic sights.
- Plzeň – famous worldwide for Pilsner beer, created here in 1842.
- Olomouc – a quaint city of cobbled streets and historic buildings.

Attractions

- Wenceslas Square, Prague – bursting with monuments, restaurants and shops.
- Český Krumlov – the old town is a UNESCO site and the castle houses a baroque theatre.
- Kutná Hora – Founded in the 12th century, this city houses many spectacular churches.
- Hrad Karlštejn – this imposing gothic castle is one of the most famous in the country.

Find out more

www.czechtourism.com
Tel:0042 (0)22 1580 111 Czech Republic Tourism

Country Information

Population (approx): 10.6 million

Capital: Prague (population approx 1.23 million)

Area: 78,864 sq km

Bordered by: Austria, Germany, Poland, Slovakia

Terrain: Diverse landscape with rolling hills and plains in the west (Bohemia) surrounded by low mountains; higher hills and heavily forested mountains in the east (Moravia)

Climate: Temperate continental with warm, showery summers and cold, cloudy, snowy winters

Highest Point: Snezka 1,602m

Language: Czech

Local Time: GMT or BST + 1, i.e. 1 hour ahead of the UK all year

Currency: Czech crown (CZK)
£1 = CZK 28.84, CZK 100 = £3.47 (November 2017)

Emergency numbers: Police 158; Fire brigade 150; Ambulance 155 (operators speak English) or 112.

Public Holidays 2018: Jan 1; Mar 30; Apr 2; May 1, 8 (National Liberation Day); Jul 5, 6; Sep 28 (St Wenceslas), Oct 28 (Independence Day); Nov 17; Dec 24, 25, 26.

School summer holidays are from the beginning of July to the end of August.

Camping and Caravanning

Campsites are divided into four categories from 1 to 4 stars. Normally campsites are open from May to mid September, although some campsites stay open all year. They usually close at night between 10pm and 6am.

Campsites are generally good value and in recent years many have upgraded their facilities. Privacy in the showers may be a problem due to a shortage of, or lack of, shower curtains and only a communal dressing area.

Some sites have communal kitchen facilities which enable visitors to make great savings on their own gas supply.

Motorhomes are recommended to carry a very long hose with a variety of tap connectors. Refill the onboard tank whenever possible as few sites have easily accessible mains water.

Casual/wild camping is not permitted and fines are imposed for violation of this law, especially in national parks. It is prohibited to sleep in a caravan or motorhome outside a campsite.

Cycling

There are around 2,500km of cycle tracks, known as Greenways, in tourist areas. A long-distance cycle track links Vienna and Prague and there are many tracks linking the Czech Republic to Austria and Poland. Helmets are compulsory for cyclists under the age of 18.

Electricity and Gas

Current on campsites varies between 6 and 16 amps. Plugs have two round pins. A few campsites have CEE connections but not many. Reversed polarity may be encountered.

You may find that Campingaz 907 cylinders are available from large DIY warehouses.

Entry Formalities

British and Irish passport holders may visit the Czech Republic for up to three months without a visa. If intending to stay longer, visitors must register with the police. There are no identity checks at the borders with neighbouring countries and normally it is not necessary for a driver to stop when crossing the border. However, random identity checks may be made at any time at the border or inside the country itself

Medical Services

For minor ailments first consult staff at a pharmacy (lékárna) who are qualified to give advice and are sometimes able to sell drugs which are normally only available on prescription in the UK. Language may be a problem outside Prague; if you need particular drugs or a repeat prescription, take an empty bottle or remaining pills with you. For more serious matters requiring a visit to a doctor go to a medical centre (poliklinika) or hospital (nemocnice).

British nationals may obtain emergency medical and hospital treatment and prescriptions on presentation of a European Health Insurance Card (EHIC). You may have to make a contribution towards costs. Make sure that the doctor or dentist you see is contracted to the public health insurance service, the CMU (most are), otherwise you will have to pay in full for private treatment and for any prescription medicines and the Czech insurance service will not reimburse you. See www.cmu.cz, email info@cmu.cz for advice on healthcare in the Czech Republic.

In parts of the country where few foreign visitors venture, medical staff may not be aware of the rights conferred on you by an EHIC. If you have difficulties contact the British Embassy in Prague.

Outbreaks of hepatitis A occur sporadically, particularly in the Prague and Central Bohemia areas, and immunisation is advised for long-stay visitors to rural areas and those who plan to travel outside tourist areas. Take particular care with food and water hygiene.

Opening Hours

Banks: Mon-Fri 9am-5pm. Some foreign exchange bureaux in Prague are open 24 hours.

Museums: Tue-Sun 10am-6pm; closed Monday

Post Offices: Mon-Fri 8am-6pm, some open on Saturday morning; main post office in Prague (Jindrisska Street 14) is open 2am-12am

Shops: Mon-Fri 9am-6pm, small shops usually close at lunchtime; Sat 9am-1pm; some food shops open on Sundays

Safety and Security

There is a high incidence of petty theft, particularly in major tourist areas in Prague, and pickpocketing is common at popular tourist attractions. Particular care should be taken around the main railway station and on trains and trams, particularly routes to and from Prague Castle where pickpockets may operate.

Beware of fake plain-clothes police officers asking to see your foreign currency and passport. If approached, don't get out your passport. You can call 158 or 112 to check if they are genuine officers, or offer to go to the nearest police station or find a uniformed officer. No police officer has the right to check your money or its authenticity.

If your passport, wallet or other items are lost or stolen you should report the incident immediately to the nearest police station and obtain a police report. A police station that is used to dealing with foreign travellers and is open 24 hours, is at Jungmannovo Nàmìstí 9, Praha 1, 24 hour telephone number 974 851 750; nearest metro: Müstek. Any theft of property must be reported in person to the police within 24 hours in order to obtain a crime number.

Seasonal flooding, usually in spring, occurs occasionally.

The Czech Republic shares with the rest of Europe an underlying threat from terrorism. Attacks could be indiscriminate and against civilian targets, including tourist attractions.

British Embassy
THUNOVSKÁ 14
118 00 PRAGUE 1
Tel: 257402111
www.ukinczechrepublic.fco.gov.uk
Email: ukinczechrepublic@fco.gov.uk

Irish Embassy
VELVYSLANECTVÍ IRSKA
TRŽIŠTĚ 13, 118 00 PRAHA 1
Tel: 257011280
www.embassyofireland.cz
Email: pragueembassy@dfa.ie

Documents

Driving Licence

The Czech Republic authorities require foreign drivers to carry a photocard driving licence. If you still have an old-style driving license you should update it to a photocard before you travel, or obtain an International Driving Permit to accompany your old-style licence. The minimum driving age is 18.

Passport

You must have a valid passport to enter Czech Republic. It is recommended that your passport is valid after your planned departure date in case of an unforeseen emergency, which may prevent you from leaving. British nationals with passports in poor condition have been refused entry so you should ensure that your passport is in an acceptable state.

If you hold a British passport where your nationality is shown as anything other than British Citizen contact the Czech Embassy in London to determine whether you require a visa for entry.

Vehicle(s)

Carry your vehicle registration certificate (V5C), insurance details and MOT certificate (if applicable). If you are not the owner of the vehicle you are advised to carry a letter of authority from the owner permitting you to drive it.

Money

The best place to exchange foreign currency is at banks, where commission rates are generally lower. In Prague some foreign exchange bureaux are open 24 hours. Scottish and Northern Irish bank notes will not be changed. Never exchange money with vendors on the street as notes are often counterfeit.

Credit cards are often accepted in tourist areas. Cash points are widely available but take care using them from a personal security point of view. Many retail outlets accept payment in euros.

Motoring in the Czech Republic

Accidents

If an accident causes injury or damage in excess of CZK 100,000 it must be reported to the police immediately. You should wait at the scene of the accident until the police arrive and then obtain a police report. If your vehicle is only slightly damaged it is still a good idea to report the accident to the police as they will issue a certificate which will facilitate the exportation of the vehicle.

Alcohol

It is prohibited to drink alcohol before or whilst driving. No degree of alcohol is permitted in the blood and driving under the influence of alcohol is considered a criminal offence. This rule also applies to cyclists and horse riders. Frequent random breath-testing takes places and drivers are likely to be breathalysed after an accident, even a minor one.

Breakdown Service

The motoring organisation ÚAMK provides roadside assistance and towing services 24 hours a day, telephone 1230 or 261104123. Emergency operators speak English. Breakdown assistance is provided for all motorists at a basic cost of approximately CZK 400 for 30 minutes + CZK 24 per kilometre travelled, payable in cash (2015). Extra charges apply at night, at weekends and for towing.

The vehicles used for road assistance are yellow Skodas, bearing the ÚAMK and/or ARC Transistance logos or the words 'Silnični Služba', together with the telephone number of the emergency centre. ÚMAK also uses the services of contracted companies who provide assistance and towing. These vehicles are also marked with the ÚAMK logo and the telephone number of the emergency centre.

Essential Equipment

First aid kit

You are required to carry a basic first aid kit in your vehicle.

Lights

Dipped headlights are compulsory at all times, regardless of weather conditions. Bulbs are more likely to fail with constant use and it is recommended that you carry a complete set of spares.

Drivers are required to signal when leaving a roundabout and when overtaking cyclists.

Reflective Jacket/ Waistcoat

If your vehicle has broken down, or in the event of an emergency, you must wear a reflective jacket or waistcoat on all roads, carriageways and motorways when getting out of your vehicle. Passengers who leave the vehicle, for example to assist with a repair, should also wear one. Jackets should, therefore, be kept inside your vehicle, and not in the boot. These must be of an EU standard EN471.

Child Restraint System

Children under 1.5m in height must use a suitable child restraint conforming to ECE standard 44/03 or 44/04. If in the front seat, the restraint must be rear facing with any airbag deactivated. If there are no seatbelts fitted in the vehicle children over the age of 3 may travel in the rear of the vehicle without a child restraint.

Warning Triangles

You must carry a warning triangle, which must be placed at least 100m behind the vehicle on motorways and highways and 50m behind on other roads. Drivers may use Hazard Warning lights in conjunction with the warning triangle.

Winter Driving

Winter tyres are compulsory from 1 November to 31 March on all wheels of vehicles up to 3.5 tonnes when there is compacted snow or ice on the road. They are also compulsory whenever the temperature is lower than 4°C and there is a possibility of snow or ice on the road. On roads where there are winter tyres signs (see below), the regulations apply even if the road surface is free of snow and ice, regardless of the weather.

Sign for winter tyres (if shown with a line through indicates the end of restriction)

Vehicles over 3,500 kg must be fitted with winter tyres on the driving wheels or carry snow chains. A full list of roads where this rule applies can be found on www.uamk.cz.

Fuel

Some petrol stations on main roads, international routes and in main towns are open 24 hours a day. Most accept credit cards.

Diesel pumps are marked 'Nafta'. LPG is called 'Autoplyn' or 'Plyn' and is widely available at many filling stations. A list of these is available from the ÚAMK and a map is available from filling stations, or see www.lpg.cz and click on 'Čerpací stanice'.

Parking

Vehicles may only be parked on the right of the road. In a one-way road, parking is also allowed on the left.

Continuous or broken yellow lines along the carriageway indicate parking prohibitions or restrictions. Visitors are advised to park only in officially controlled and guarded parking areas since cars belonging to tourists may be targeted by thieves. Illegally-parked vehicles may be clamped or towed away.

Prague city centre is divided into three parking zones: the orange and green zones are limited to two and six hours respectively between 8am and 6pm, and the blue zones are for residents only. Parking meters have been introduced in both Prague and Brno.

Priority

At uncontrolled intersections which are not marked by a priority road sign, priority must be given to vehicles coming from the right. Where there are priority signs, these may easily be missed and care is therefore needed at junctions which, according to recent visitors, may have no road markings.

Trams turning right have priority over traffic moving alongside them on the right. Drivers must slow down and, if necessary, stop to allow buses and trams to merge with normal traffic at the end of a bus lane. On pedestrian crossings pedestrians have right of way, except if the vehicle approaching is a tram.

Roads

Czech drivers are sometimes described as reckless (particularly when overtaking). Speeding is common and the law on the wearing of seat belts is sometimes ignored.

In general roads are in a good condition and well-signposted. Roads are being upgraded and many have new numbers. It is essential, therefore, to have an up-to-date road map or atlas.

Care is required where roads follow an old route through a village when there may be sudden bends in an otherwise straight road.

Road Signs and Markings

Road signs and markings conform to international standards. Continuous white lines indicate no overtaking, but are often ignored.

The following road signs may be encountered:

Czech	English Translation
Bez poplatků	Free of charge
Chod'te vlevo	Pedestrians must walk on the left
Dálkový provoz	By-pass
Nebezpečí smyku	Danger of skidding
Nemocnice	Hospital
Objizdka	Diversion
Pozor děti	Attention children
Průjezd zakázán	Closed to all vehicles
Rozsvit' světla	Lights needed
Úsek častých nehod	Accident blackspot
Zákaz zastavení	Stopping prohibited

Traffic Lights

A traffic light signal with a green arrow shows that drivers may turn in that direction. If a yellow walking figure accompanies the signal, pedestrians may cross the road and drivers must give them right of way. A green light lit at the same time as a red or yellow light means that drivers may turn in the direction indicated by the arrow, giving way to other traffic and pedestrians.

An illuminated speed signal indicates the speed at which to travel in order to arrive at the next set of traffic lights when they are green.

Speed Limits

	Open Road (km/h)	Motorway (km/h)
Car Solo	90	130
Car towing caravan/trailer	80	80
Motorhome under 3500kg	90	130
Motorhome 3500-7500kg	80	80

Motorhomes over 3,500 kg and cars towing a caravan or trailer are restricted to 80 km/h (50 mph) on motorways and main roads and lower limits in urban areas. Speed limits are strictly enforced and drivers exceeding them may be fined on the spot. Police with radar guns are much in evidence.

The use of radar detectors is prohibited and GPS systems which indicate the position of fixed speed cameras must have that function deactivated.

Traffic Jams

The volume of traffic has increased considerably in recent years, particularly in and around Prague, including its ring road. Traffic jams may also occur on the E50/D1 (Prague-Mirošovice), the E48/R6 (Prague-Kladno), the E50/D5 (Plzeň-Rozvadov) and on the E50/D1 (Prague-Brno).

Traffic may be heavy at border crossings from Germany, Austria and Slovakia, particularly at weekends, resulting in extended waiting times. Petrol is cheaper than in Germany and you may well find queues at petrol stations near the border. Traffic information can be obtained from the ÚAMK Information Centre, tel 261104333, or from their website www.uamk.cz.

Violation of Traffic Regulations

The police are authorised to impose and collect on-the-spot fines up to CZK 5,000 and to withdraw a driving licence in the case of a serious offence. An official receipt should be obtained. Efforts are under way to improve enforcement of traffic regulations and a points system has been introduced, together with stricter penalties.

Motorways

There are approximately 1240 km of motorways and express roads. New sections of motorways are being built and on some motorways junctions are being renumbered to correspond with kilometre markers.

There is a good network of service areas with petrol stations, restaurants and shops, together with rest areas with picnic facilities. Emergency telephones connected to the motorway police are placed at 2 km intervals.

Emergency corridors are compulsory on motorways and dual carriageways. Drivers are required to create a precautionary emergency corridor at least 3m wide to provide access for emergency vehicles whenever congestion occurs. Drivers in the left-hand lane must move as far over to the left as possible, and drivers in the central and right-hand lanes must move as far over to the right as possible.

Motorway Tolls – Vignette

To use motorways and express roads you must purchase a vignette (windscreen sticker) which must be displayed on the right hand side of your windscreen. This is available from post offices, ÚAMK branch offices, petrol stations and border posts where euros may be used in payment. If you have been to the Czech Republic before, make sure you remove your old sticker.

Charges in 2016 (subject to change) are CZK 1,500 for an annual vignette, CZK 440 for one month and CZK 310 for 10 consecutive days. For more information please visit www.motorway.cz/stickers.

Vehicles over 3,500 kg

Vehicles over 3,500 kg are subject to an electronic toll (mýto) and vehicle owners must register with the toll-collection service to obtain an on-board device called a Premid which must be fixed on your windscreen inside the vehicle and for which a deposit is required.

Tolls vary according to the emissions category and weight of the vehicle and distance driven. You must be able to show your vehicle documentation when obtaining the device but if your vehicle registration certificate (V5C) does not give an emissions category, then your vehicle will be classified in category Euro 2 for the purposes of this system. For more information please visit www.premid.cz before you travel.

Touring

It is not necessary to tip in restaurants but if you have received very good service add 10% to the bill or round it up.

Smoking is not permitted in public places (public transport, places of entertainment, etc) and restaurant owners must provide an area for non-smokers.

A Prague Card offers entrance to over 50 tourist attractions and discounts on excursions and activities. It is available from tourist offices, main metro stations, some travel agents and hotels or order online from www.praguecard.com.

German is the most widely spoken foreign language and a basic understanding is particularly helpful in southern Bohemia. However, many young people speak English.

Public Transport

Prague city centre is very congested, so park outside and use buses, trams or the metro which are efficient and cheap. There are guarded Park and Ride facilities at a number of metro stations around Prague.

Public transport tickets must be purchased before travelling and are available from newspaper stands ('Trafika'), tobacconists, convenience stores and from vending machines at stations. Special tourist tickets are available for one or three days. Tickets must be validated before the start of your journey at the yellow machines at metro stations or on board trams and buses, including before boarding the funicular tram at Petřín. Failure to do so may result in an on-the-spot fine.

Take extra care when in the vicinity of tram tracks and make sure you look both ways. Trams cannot stop quickly nor can they avoid you if you are on the track.

As a pedestrian you may be fined if you attempt to cross the road or cross tram tracks within 50 metres of a designated crossing point or traffic lights. You may also be fined if you cross at a pedestrian crossing if the green pedestrian light is not illuminated.

For reasons of safety and economy use major taxi companies wherever possible. If you telephone to order a taxi these companies are usually able to tell you in advance the type, number and colour of the car allocated to you. If you do pick up a taxi in the street always check the per kilometre price before getting in. The price list must be clearly displayed and the driver must provide a receipt if requested.

Sites in Czech Republic

BEROUN *B2* (10km NE Rural) *50.0115, 14.1505* **Camping Valek, Chrustenice 155, 267 12 Chrustenice [tel/fax 311 672 147; info@campvalek.cz; www.campvalek.cz]** SW fr Prague on E50; take exit 10 twd Loděnice then N to Chrustenice. Foll sp. Lge, pt shd; wc; chem disp; mv service pnt; shwrs inc; EHU (10A) CZK100; lndry; sm shop & 4km; rest, snacks; bar; BBQ; playgrnd; pool; tennis; entmnt at w/end; TV; 10% statics; dogs CZK80; phone; Eng spkn; adv bkg; quiet; red long stay/CKE/CCI. "Vg location; money change on site; excel rest; metro to Prague at Zličín (secure car park adj)." 1 May-30 Sep. CZK 430 2016*

⊞ **BESINY** *C1* (500m SW Rural) *49.29533, 13.32086* **Eurocamp Běšiny, Běšiny 150, 339 01 Běšiny [tel/fax 376 375 011; eurocamp@besiny.cz; www.eurocamp.besiny.cz]** Fr E53/rd 27 take rd 171 twd Sušice. Site just outside vill on L. Med, unshd; htd wc; chem disp; shwrs; EHU (6A) inc; lndry; shop 500m; rest; bar; BBQ; cooking facs; pool; paddling pool; tennis; games area; wifi; 50% statics; dogs; poss cr; adv bkg; quiet; ccard acc; CKE/CCI. "Pleasant setting; nrby vill drab." ♦ CZK 303 2016*

BOJKOVICE see Uherský Brod *C4*

BOSKOVICE *C3* (12km NE Urban) *49.50980, 16.77308* **Camping de Bongerd, Benešov U Boskovic C.P. 104. 67953 [tel 516 467 233; campingbenesov@hetnet.nl; www.camping-benesov.nl]** Foll sp fr 373 at E end of Benešov on L. Sm, med, sl, terr, pt shd; wc; chem disp; shwrs; playgrnd; pool; games area; Eng spkn; quiet; CKE/CCI. "Vg site run by helpful talkative Dutch couple; ent narr, unsuitable for lge o'fits." 1 May-20 Sep. CZK 300 2012*

BOSKOVICE *C3* (15km SE Rural) *49.42296, 16.73585* **Camping Relaxa, 679 13 Sloup [tel 516 435 291; info@staraskola.cz; www.camprelaxa.cz]** Fr Boskovice take dir Valchov; at Ludikov head S & onto rte 373 to Sloup. Site sp up track on R. Sm, pt sl, unshd; htd wc; chem disp; shwrs inc; EHU (6A) inc (poss rev pol); lndry rm; shop, rest 1km; bar; pool 250m; dogs; bus 1km; poss cr; quiet; CKE/CCI. "Conv Moravski Kras karst caves; immed access walking/cycling trails." 1 May-20 Sep. CZK 400 2012*

BRECLAV *D3* (6km NW Rural) *48.78549, 16.82663* **Autocamp Apollo, Charvátská Nová Ves, 691 44 Břeclav [tel 519 340 414; info@atcapollo.cz; www.atcapollo.cz]** Fr Breclav take Lednice rd. Site is 3km S of Lednice vill. Lge, pt sl, pt shd; wc; chem disp; shwrs inc; EHU CZK30; shops 3km; rest adj; lake sw 500m; dogs CZK30; bus; poss cr; noisy; CKE/CCI. "Fair sh stay; site in beautiful area; excel cycling & walking; Lednice Castle worth a visit; poss school parties." 1 May-30 Sep. CZK 280 2016*

BRNO *C3* (21km W Rural) *49.21182, 16.40745* **Camping Oáza, Náměstí Viléma Mrštíka 10, 66481 Ostrovačice [tel 606 457 448 or 546 427 552; info@kempoaza.cz; www.kempoaza.cz]** Leave E65/E50 Prague-Brno at junc 178 for Ostrovačice. At T-junc in vill turn L, site on R 100m. Sm, pt sl, pt shd; wc; chem disp (wc); shwrs inc; EHU (10A) inc; lndry; shop & 500m; rest 500m; sm pool; playgrnd; phone 500m; quiet; CKE/CCI. "Excel CL-type site, v clean facs; friendly, helpful lady owner; narr, uneven ent poss diff lge o'fits; poss unrel opening dates." 1 May-31 Oct. CZK 310 2013*

BRNO *C3* (24km NW Rural) *49.27618, 16.4535* **Camping Hana, Dlouhá ul 135, 664 71 Veverská Bítýška [tel 549 420 331 or 607 905 801 (mob); camping.hana@seznam.cz; www.campinghana.com]** On E50 Prague-Brno m'way, exit junc 178 at Ostrovačice & turn N on 386 for 10km to Veverská Bítýška. Site sp bef & in vill. Med, mkd pitch, pt shd; wc; chem disp; shwrs CZK10; EHU (10A) CZK60; lndry (inc dryer); shop; rest in vill 1km; snacks adj; BBQ; cooking facs; wifi; dogs CZK40; Eng spkn; quiet; twin-axles extra; CKE/CCI. "Peaceful, well-run site; family owned; clean, dated san facs; hot water runs out by evening if site full; gd security; interesting caves N of town; bus/tram/boat to Brno; excel rest in vill; flexible open- closing dates if reserved in adv; helpful, friendly owners; pleasant walk along rv to vill; gd NH; gd site; lg shwrs but communal chnge rm." 1 May-30 Sep. CZK 518 2013*

BUCHLOVICE see Uherské Hradiště *C4*

BUDISOV NAD BUDISOVKOU *B4* (800m SE Urban) *49.79089, 17.63668* **Autokemp Budišov, Nábřeží č. 688, 747 87, Budišov nad Budišovkou [tel 736 767 588; autokemp@budisov.cz; www.autokemp.budisov.cz]** Ent town fr E on rd 443; at T junc turn L sp; foll rd which will take you under rlwy; site on R in 100m. Sm, sl, unshd; wc; shwrs; EHU (6A) CZK80; shop 500m; rest, snacks; bar; BBQ; playgrnd; pool; wifi; 50% statics; dogs CZK30 (valid vaccination card req); quiet; CKE/CCI. "Space for 20 vans only, with 4 elec pnts; mini-golf onsite & bike hire avail." 1 May-30 Sep. CZK 240 2016*

CERNA V POSUMAVI see Horni Plana *C2*

CESKA SKALICE see Náchod *B3*

Copenhagen

Welcome to Denmark

Regularly found high on the list of the happiest nations on earth, Denmark is a friendly country that welcomes everyone. You can enjoy a charming, fairytale atmosphere working together with modern cities at the forefront of design and sustainability,

The landscape, too, is enchanting, and the beautiful sandy beaches, lakes, river and plains are a delight to explore, and ideal for cyclists.

Country highlights

The smørrebrød, a traditional open sandwich made with rye bread, salad and meat or fish, is perhaps one of Denmark's most famous dishes. Equally renowned is the Danish pastry - known locally as Vienna bread or wienerbrød. You'll find these at bakeries throughout the country.

A traditional Scandinavian drink, Akvavit is believed to have originated in Denmark in the 16th century. The spirit takes its distinct flavour from herbs and spices and is often sipped slowly from a small shot glass.

Major towns and cities

- Copenhagen – Denmark's bustling capital city is a perfect mix of old and new.
- Aarhus – this compact city is well known for its musical heritage.
- Odense – one of the country's oldest cities, and home of Hans Christian Anderson.
- Aalborg – a vibrant city with an atmospheric waterfront.

Attractions

- Tivoli Gardens, Copenhagen – one of the oldest amusement parks in the world.
- Kronborg Castle, Helsingør – This renaissance castle is a UNESCO site.
- Frederiksborg Castle, Hillerød – a palatial residence that now houses a museum.
- Skagen Beaches – 60km of white, sandy beaches and stunning, rugged coastline.

Find out more

www.visitdenmark.com
Tel: 0045 (0) 32 88 99 00 Denmark Tourist Office

Country Information

Population (approx): 5.5 million

Capital: Copenhagen

Area: 43,094 sq km (excl Faroe Islands and Greenland)

Bordered by: Germany

Terrain: Mostly fertile lowland, undulating hills, woodland, lakes and moors

Climate: Generally mild, changeable climate without extremes of heat or cold; cold winters but usually not severe; warm, sunny summers; the best time to visit is between May and September

Coastline: 7,400km

Highest Point: Ejer Bavnehøj 173m

Languages: Danish

Local Time: GMT or BST + 1, ie 1 hour ahead of the UK all year

Currency: Krone (DKK) divided into 100 øre; £1 = DKK 8.43, DKK 10 = £1.19 (Novemeber 2017)

Emergency numbers: Police 112 (114 for non-urgent calls); Fire brigade 112; Ambulance 112 (operators speak English).

Public Holidays 2018: Jan 1; Mar 29,30; Apr 1, 2, 27; May 10, 20, 21; Jun 5; Dec 25, 26.

School summer holidays extend from end June to mid August.

Camping and Caravanning

Denmark has approximately 500 approved, well-equipped, annually inspected campsites. A green banner flies at each campsite entrance, making it easy to spot. Campsites are graded from 1 to 5 stars, many having excellent facilities including baby-changing areas, private family bathrooms, self-catering cooking facilities and shops. Prices are regulated and there is very little variation.

All except the most basic 1-star sites have water and waste facilities for motorhomes and at least some electric hook-ups. You may find it useful to take your own flat universal sink plug. During the high season it is advisable to book in advance as many Danish holidaymakers take pitches for the whole season for use at weekends and holidays resulting in minimal space for tourers.

A Camping Key Europe (CKE) or Camping Card International (CCI) is required on all campsites.

Approximately 190 campsites have a 'Quick Stop' amenity which provides safe, secure overnight facilities on or adjoining campsites, including the use of sanitary facilities. Quick Stop rates are about two thirds of the regular camping rate but you must arrive after 8pm and leave by 10am next morning. A list of Quick Stop sites may be obtained from local tourist offices or downloaded from DK-Camp www.dk-camp.dk.

Wild camping is prohibited on common or State land, in stopping bays and parking sites, in the dunes, or on the beaches, unless there is an organised camp site. Farmers or landowners may allow you to pitch on their land, but you must always seek permission from them is advance.

Cycling

Although not as flat as the Netherlands, Denmark is very cyclist-friendly and many major and minor roads, including those in all major towns, have separate cycle lanes or tracks. They have their own traffic lights and signals. Cyclists often have the right of way and, when driving, you should check cycle lanes before turning left or right.

In Åarhus and Copenhagen city centre bicycles are free to use between mid-April and November - you will need to pay a refundable deposit. Simply look for one of the many bicycle racks around the central area; see www.visitcopenhagen.com for more information.

There are many separate cycle routes, including eleven national routes, which may be long distance, local or circular, mainly on quiet roads and tracks. Local tourist offices can provide information. When planning a route, take the (often strong) prevailing westerly winds into account.

Transportation of Bicycles

Bicycles may be carried on the roof of a car as well as at the rear. When carried at the rear, the lights and number plate must remain visible.

Electricity and Gas

Current on campsites varies between 6 and 16 amps, a 10 amp supply being the most common. Plugs have 2 round pins. Some sites have CEE17 electric hook-ups or are in the process of converting. If a CEE17 connection is not available site staff will usually provide an adaptor. Visitors report that reversed polarity is common.

Campingaz 904 and 907 butane cylinders are readily available from campsites, or some Statoil service stations and at camping or hardware shops. If travelling on to Norway, Statoil agencies there will exchange Danish propane cylinders.

Entry Formalities

Visas are not required by British or Irish passport holders for a stay of up to three months. Visitors planning to stay longer should contact the Danish Embassy in London before they travel - find contact details at www.denmark.org.uk.

Regulations for Pets

Between April and September all dogs must be kept on a lead. This applies not only on campsites but throughout the country in general.

Medical Services

The standard of healthcare is high. Citizens of the UK are entitled to the same emergency medical services as the Danish, including free hospital treatment, on production of a European Health Insurance Card (EHIC). Tourist offices and health offices (kommunes social og sundhedforvaltning) have lists of doctors and dentists who are registered with the public health service. For a consultation with a doctor you may have to pay the full fee but you will be refunded if you apply to a local health office if they are registered with the Danish Public Health Service. Partial refunds may be made for dental costs and approved medicines. Prescriptions are dispensed at pharmacies (apotek).

Opening Hours

Banks: Mon-Fri 10am-4pm (Thu to 6pm). In the Provinces opening hours vary from town to town.

Museums: Tue-Sun 9am/10am-5pm; most close Mon.

Post Offices: Mon-Fri 9am/10am-5pm/6pm, Sat 9am/10am-12pm/1pm/2pm or closed all day.

Shops: Mon-Fri 9am-5.30pm (Fri to 7pm); Sat 9am-1pm/2pm; supermarkets open Mon-Fri 9am-7pm & Sat 9am-4pm/5pm; open on first Sunday of the month 10am-5pm. Most shops close on public holidays but you may find some bakers, sandwich shops, confectioners, kiosks and florists open.

Safety and Security

Denmark has relatively low levels of crime and most visits to the country are trouble-free. The majority of public places are well lit and secure, most people are helpful and often speak good English. Visitors should, however, be aware of pickpocketing or bag-snatching in Copenhagen, particularly around the central station and in the Christiania and Nørrebro areas, as well as in other large cities and tourist attractions. Car break-ins have increased in recent years; never leave valuables in your car.

Denmark shares with the rest of Europe a general threat from terrorism. Attacks could be indiscriminate and against civilian targets in public places, including tourist sites.

British Embassy
KASTELSVEJ 36-40
DK-2100 Copenhagen Ø
Tel: 35 44 52 00
www.ukindenmark.fco.gov.uk/en

There are also Honorary Consulates in Aabenraa, Åarhus, Fredericia and Herning

Irish Embassy
ØSTBANEGADE 21
DK-2100 Copenhagen Ø
Tel: 35 47 32 00
www.embassyofireland.dk

Documents

Passport

Your passport must be valid for the proposed duration of your stay, however in case of any unforeseen delays it is strongly recommended to have a period of extra validity on your passport.

Vehicle(s)

Carry your vehicle documentation, including vehicle registration certificate (V5C), certificate of insurance and MOT certificate (if applicable). You may be asked to produce your V5C if driving a motorhome over the Great Belt Bridge between Funen and Zealand in order to verify the weight of your vehicle. For more information see the 'Motorways' section of this introduction.

The minimum age you can drive, with a valid driver's licence, is 17.

Money

Some shops and restaurants, particularly in the larger cities, display prices in both krone and euros and many will accept payment in euros.

Travellers' cheques are no longer recommended as it is increasingly difficult to find somewhere to cash them. A prepaid currency card is an alternative - see camc.com/travelmoney for details of the Moneycorp Explorer card.

The major credit cards are widely, but not always, accepted. Credit cards are not normally accepted in supermarkets. Cash machines are widespread. A 5% surcharge is usually applied to credit card transactions. Some banks and/or cash machines may not accept debit cards issued by non-Danish banks.

It is advisable to carry your passport or photocard driving licence if paying with a credit card as you may well be asked for photographic proof of identity. Carry your credit card issuers'/banks' 24-hour UK contact numbers in case of loss or theft of your cards.

Motoring in Denmark

Alcohol

The level of alcohol cannot exceed 50 milligrams (0.05%) in 100 millilitres of blood which is lower than in the UK. Drivers caught over this limit will be fined and their driving licence withdrawn. Police carry out random breath tests.

Breakdown Service

24 hours assistance is available from SOS Dansk Autohjaelp (Danish Automobile Assistance) call Tel: 70 10 80 90.

The hourly charge between Monday and Friday is DKK 638 + VAT and an administration charge; higher charges apply at night and at weekends and public holidays. On-the-spot repairs and towing must be paid for in cash.

On motorways use the emergency telephones, situated every 2 km, to call the breakdown service. The telephone number to dial in case of an accident is 112.

Essential Equipment

Warning Triangle

An EU approved red warning triangle must be used if the vehicle breaks down, punctures or is involved in an accident.

Reflective Jacket

It is recommended, though not compulsory, to carry a reflectorised jacket on board the vehicle in the event the driver has to step out of the car in an emergency.

Lights and Indicators

Dipped headlights are compulsory at all times, regardless of weather conditions. Bulbs are more likely to fail with constant use and you are recommended to carry spares.

On motorways drivers must use their hazard warning lights to warn other motorists of sudden queues ahead or other dangers such as accidents.

By law indicators must be used when overtaking or changing lanes on a motorway and when pulling out from a parked position at the kerb.

Child Restraint System

Children under three years of age must be seated in an approved child restraint system adapted to their size. Children over three years old and under 1.35 metres in height must be seated in an approved child restraint suitable for both their height and weight. If the vehicle is fitted with an active airbag children must not be placed in the front seat in a rear-facing child seat.

Fuel

Some petrol stations in larger towns stay open 24 hours a day and they are increasingly equipped with self-service pumps which accept DKK 50, 100 and occasionally DKK 200 notes. Few display instructions in English and it is advisable to fill up during normal opening hours when staff are on hand.

Unleaded petrol pumps are marked 'Blyfri Benzine'. Leaded petrol is no longer available and has been replaced by Lead Replacement Petrol, called Millennium, which contains an additive. The major credit cards are normally accepted.

LPG (Autogas or Bilgas) is available from a handful of BP, OK, Q8, Uno-X, YX, Shell and Statoil service stations – the Danish Tourist Board publishes a list of outlets on its website www.visitdenmark.com.

Low Emission Zones

Low Emission zones are in operation in many large cities. The rules affect all diesel powered vehicles over 3,500kg, which must meet European Emission Standard 4 (EURO 4). All vehicles over 3,500kg must display an Environmental Zone sticker (Eco-label) You can order the Eco-label online from www.applusbilsyn.dk for DKK 93 or visit a car inspection station in Denmark where the Eco-label will cost DKK 165.

Vehicles which do not meet European Emission Standard 4 are not allowed into the Low Emission Zone. A fine of DKK 20,000 (Approximately £2300 in 2017) is payable for non-compliance.

Parking

Parking prohibitions and limitations are indicated by signs. Hours during which parking is not allowed are displayed in black for weekdays, with brackets for Saturdays and in red for Sundays and public holidays. Parking meters and discs are used and discs are available free of charge from post offices, banks, petrol stations and tourist offices. The centre of Copenhagen is divided into red, green and blue zones and variable hourly charges apply round the clock Monday to Friday (Saturday to 5pm; Sunday and public holidays free). 'Pay and display' tickets may be bought from machines with cash or a credit card. Cars must be parked on the right-hand side of the road (except in one-way streets). An illegally parked vehicle may be removed by the police.

Priority

At intersections where there are 'give way' or 'stop' signs and/or a transverse line consisting of triangles (shark's teeth) with one point facing towards the driver, drivers must give way to traffic at an intersection. If approaching an intersection of two roads without any signs you must give way to vehicles coming from the right. Give way to cyclists and to buses signalling to pull out. On the Danish islands take care as many people travel by foot, bicycle or on horseback.

Roads

Roads are generally in good condition, well-signposted and largely uncongested and driving standards are fairly high.

Caravanners should beware of strong crosswinds on exposed stretches of road. Distances are short; it is less than 500 km (310 miles) from Copenhagen on the eastern edge of Zealand, to Skagen at the tip of Jutland, and the coast is never more than an hour away.

Road Signs and Markings

Signs directing you onto or along international E-roads are green with white lettering. E-roads, having been integrated into the Danish network, usually have no other national number.

Signs above the carriageway on motorways have white lettering on a blue background. Signs guiding you onto other roads are white with red text and a hexagonal sign with red numbering indicates the number of a motorway exit.

Primary (main roads) connecting large towns and ferry connections have signs with black numbers on a yellow background. Secondary (local) roads connecting small towns and primary routes are indicated by signs with black numbers on a white background. Signs of any colour with a dotted frame refer you to a road further ahead. Road signs themselves may be placed low down and, as a result, may be easy to miss.'Sharks teeth' markings at junctions indicate stop and give way to traffic on the road you are entering.

General roads signs conform to international standards. You may see the following:

Place of interest

Recommended speed limits

Dual Carriage-way ends

The following are some other common signs:

Danish	English Translation
Ensrettet kørsel	One-way street
Fare	Danger
Farligt sving	Dangerous bend
Fodgægerovergang	Pedestrian crossing
Gennemkørsel forbudt	No through road
Hold til hojre	Keep to the right
Hold til venstre	Keep to the left
Omkørsel	Diversion
Parkering forbudt	No parking
Vejen er spærret	Road closed

Speed Limits

	Open Road (km/h)	Motorway (km/h)
Car Solo	80-90	110-130
Car towing caravan/trailer	70	80
Motorhome under 3500kg	80-90	110-130
Motorhome 3500-7500kg	70	70

Vehicles over 3,500 kg are restricted to 70 km/h (44 mph) on the open road and on motorways. It is prohibited to use radar detectors.

Traffic Jams

British drivers will enjoy the relatively low density of traffic. At most, traffic builds up during the evening rush hours around the major cities of Copenhagen, Århus, Aalborg and Odense. During the holiday season traffic jams may be encountered at the Flensburg border crossing into Germany, on the roads to coastal areas, on approach roads to ferry crossings and on routes along the west coast of Jutland.

Violation of Traffic Regulations

The police are authorised to impose and collect on-the-spot fines for traffic offences. Driving offences committed in Denmark are reported to the UK authorities.

Motorways

There are approximately 1,000 km of motorways, mainly two-lane and relatively uncongested. No tolls are levied except on bridges. Lay-bys with picnic areas and occasionally motorhome service points are situated at 25 km intervals. These often also have toilet facilities. Service areas and petrol stations are situated at 50 km intervals and are generally open from 7am to 10pm.

Toll Bridges

The areas of Falster and Zealand are linked by two road bridges, 1.6 km and 1.7 km in length respectively.

The areas of Funen and Zealand are linked by an 18 km suspension road bridge and rail tunnel known as the Great Belt Link (Storebæltsbroen), connecting the towns of Nyborg and Korsør. The toll road is part of the E20 between Odense and Ringsted and tolls for single journeys on the bridge are shown in Table 1 below (2017 prices subject to change).

Table 1 – Great Belt Bridge

Vehicle(s)	Price
Solo Car up to 6 metres	DKK 240
Car + trailer/caravan	DKK 365
Motorhome (under 3,500 kg) under 6 metres	DKK 240
Motorhome (under 3,500kg) over 6 metres	DKK 365
Motorhome (over 3,500 kg) up to 10 metres	DKK 715
Motorhome (over 3,500 kg) over 10 metres	DKK 1,130

You may be asked to produce your Vehicle Registration Certificate (V5C) to verify the weight of your vehicle. Day return and weekend return tickets are also available. For more information see www.storebaelt.dk/english.

The 16 km Øresund Bridge links Copenhagen in Denmark with Malmö in Sweden and means that it is possible to drive all the way from mainland Europe to Sweden by motorway. The crossing is via a 7.8 km bridge to the artificial island of Peberholm, and a 4 km tunnel. Tolls for single journeys (payable in cash, including euros, or by credit card) are levied on the Swedish side, and are shown in Table 2 below (2018 prices subject to change).

Table 2 – Øresund Bridge

Vehicle(s)	Price
Solo Car or motorhome up to 6 metres	€ 50
Car + caravan/trailer or motorhome over 6 metres	€ 100

Speed limits apply, and during periods of high wind the bridge is closed to caravans. Bicycles are not allowed. Information on the Øresund Bridge can be found on www.oeresundsbron.com.

On both the Øresund and Storebælts bridges vehicle length is measured electronically and even a slight overhang over six metres, e.g. towbars, projecting loads and loose items, will result in payment of the higher tariff.

Touring

The peak holiday season and school holidays are slightly earlier than in the UK and by mid-August some attractions close or operate reduced opening hours.

Service charges are automatically added to restaurant bills although you may round up the bill if service has been good, but it is not expected. Tips for taxi drivers are included in the fare. Smoking is not allowed in enclosed public places, including restaurants and bars. The 3,500 km Marguerite Route, marked by brown signs depicting a flower (see below), takes motorists to the best sights and scenic areas in Denmark.

Tourist Route

A route map and guide (in English) are available from bookshops, tourist offices and Statoil service stations all over Denmark. Stretches of the route are not suitable for cars towing caravans as some of the roads are narrow and twisting.

The capital and major port, Copenhagen, is situated on the island of Zealand. Grundtvig Cathedral, Amalienborg Palace and the Viking Museum are well worth a visit, as are the famous Tivoli Gardens open from mid April to the third week in September and again for a few days in October and from mid November to the end of December (excluding Christmas). The statue of the Little Mermaid, the character created by Hans Christian Andersen, can be found at the end of the promenade called Langelinie. Copenhagen is easy to explore and from there visitors may travel to the north of Zealand along the 'Danish Riviera' to Hamlet's castle at Kronborg, or west to Roskilde with its Viking Ship Museum and 12th century cathedral.

A Copenhagen Card (CPH Card) offers unlimited use of public transport throughout Greater Copenhagen and North Zealand, free entry to over 60 museums and attractions and discounts at restaurants and other attractions. Cards are valid for 24 or 72 hours and may be purchased from selected tourist offices, travel agents, hotels and railway stations or online from www.visitcopenhagen.com. Two children up to the age of nine are included free of charge on an adult card. The Copenhagen Card is also available to buy and use via a free mobile app.

National Parks in the country include Thy National Park near Thisted along Jutland's north-west coast, Mols Bjerge National Park in eastern Jutland and Wadden Sea National Park in the south-west of the country.

English is widely spoken throughout the country.

Public Transport

Public transport is excellent and you can buy a variety of bus, train and metro tickets at station kiosks and at some supermarkets. Children under the age of 12 travel free on buses and metro trains in the Greater Copenhagen area when accompanied by an adult. Tickets must be purchased for dogs and bicycles.

Numerous car ferry connections operate daily between different parts of the country. The ferry is a common mode of transport in Denmark and there may be long queues, especially at weekends in summer. The most important routes connect the bigger islands of Zealand and Funen with Jutland using high-speed vessels on day and night services. Vehicle

length and height restrictions apply on routes between Odden (Zealand) and Århus and Æbeltoft (Jutland) and not all sailings transport caravans – check in advance. The Danish Tourist Board can provide general information on car ferry services or contact Scandlines for information on inter-island services including timetables and prices - www.scandlines.dk, email scandlines@scandlines.com or telephone 0045 (0) 33 15 15 15.

International ferry services are particularly busy during July and August and it is advisable to book in advance. Popular routes include Frederikshavn to Gothenburg (Sweden), Helsingør to Helsingborg (Sweden), Copenhagen to Oslo (Norway), and Rødby to Puttgarden in Germany (this route involves a road bridge which is occasionally closed to high-sided vehicles because of high winds). The ferry route from Copenhagen to Hamburg is a good alternative to the busy E45 motorway linking Denmark and Germany.

Ribe

Sites in Denmark

AABENRAA *B3* (2.7km S Coastal) *55.02490, 9.41461* **Fjordlyst Aabenraa City Camping, Sønderskovvej 100, 6200 Aabenraa [tel 45 74 62 26 99; fax 45 74 62 29 39; mail@fjordlyst.dk; www.fjordlyst.dk]** Fr S take E45 & exit at junc 72 to Aabenraa. Foll Rd 42 then turn L onto Rd 24. Site sp on R. Med, mkd pitch, sl, terr, pt shd; wc; chem disp; mv service pnt; fam bthrm; shwrs; EHU (16A) DKK35; lndry (inc dryer); shop; bar; BBQ; playgrnd; beach 500m; games area; wifi; TV; 10% statics; dogs DKK10; bus adj; twin axles; poss cr; Eng spkn; adv bkg; quiet; CCI. "Scenic location with views over the bay; excel facs; friendly, helpful staff; some steep slopes on site rds; vg." ♦ ltd. 19 Mar-23 Sep. DKK 225 2016*

AALBORG *B1* (3km W Urban) *57.05500, 9.88500* **Strandparken Camping, Skydebanevej 20, 9000 Aalborg [tel 98 12 76 29; fax 98 12 76 73; info@strandparken.dk; www.strandparken.dk]** Turn L at start of m'way to Svenstrup & Aalborg W, foll A180 (Hobrovej rd) twd town cent. Turn L bef Limfjorden bdge onto Borgergade for 2km, site on R. Fr N turn R after bdge onto Borgergade. Med, shd; wc; chem disp; mv service pnt; fam bthrm; shwrs DKK13; EHU (10A) DKK30 (poss rev pol); kiosk & shops 500m; cooking facs; playgrnd; pool adj; TV; wifi; some statics; dogs DKK10; phone; bus nr; Eng spkn; adv bkg; poss noisy tent campers high ssn; ccard acc; CKE/CCI. "Gd cent for town & N Jutland; gd security; facs block excel; card for elec." ♦ 24 Marr-11 Sep. DKK 248 2016*

AALESTRUP *B2* (1km E Rural) *56.69166, 9.49991* **Aalestrup Camping, Aalestrup Campingplads, Parkvænget 2, 9620 Aalestrup [tel 22 79 92 64; pouledb@ofir.dk; www.rosenparken.dk]** Fr E45 turn W onto rd 561 to Aalestrup; 500m after junc with rd 13 turn L into Borgergade, cross rlwy line. Site sp. Med, pt shd; wc; shwrs; chem disp; mv service pnt; EHU DKK30; shop nr; rest, snacks; playgrnd; quiet. "Free ent beautiful rose garden; gd touring base; friendly staff." 1 Mar-1 Nov. DKK 125 2016*

⊞ **AARHUS** *C2* (8km N Rural) *56.22660, 10.16260* **Åarhus Camping, Randersvej 400, Lisbjerg, 8200 Åarhus Nord [tel 86 23 11 33; fax 86 23 11 31; info@aarhuscamping.dk; www.aarhuscamping.dk]** Exit E45 junc 46 Århus N, then to Ikea rndabt. Then foll sp Lisbjerg & head for smoking factory chimney. Site 400m N of Lisbjerg. Med, pt sl, pt shd; wc; chem disp; mv service pnt; fam bthrm; shwrs DKK5; EHU (16A) metered; gas; lndry (inc dryer); shop; snacks; BBQ; cooking facs; playgrnd; htd pool; paddling pool; beach 9km; games area; golf 10km; wifi; TV rm; 10% statics; dogs DKK10; phone; poss cr; adv bkg; rd noise; red CKE/CCI. "Conv Århus; gd, tidy site; modern san facs; conv for bus into Aarhus, helpful owner; elec cards for shwrs." ♦ DKK 203 2015*

AARHUS *C2* (8km S Coastal) *56.11030, 10.23209* **Blommehaven Camping, Ørneredevej 35, 8270 Højbjerg [tel 86 27 02 07; fax 86 27 45 22; info@blommenhaven.dk; www.blommehaven.dk]** Fr S on E45 at junc 50 take rd 501 twd Århus. In 10km this becomes 01 ring rd. Take 2nd R Dalgas Ave, at T-junc turn L & immed R into Strandvejen. Site 3km on L in Marselisborg Forest. Lge, hdg/mkd pitch, terr, pt shd; wc; chem disp; mv service pnt; fam bthrm; shwrs; EHU DKK35; lndry; shop; BBQ; cooking facs; playgrnd; sand beach adj; TV rm; 4% statics; dogs DKK10; phone; bus; Quickstop o'night facs; poss cr; Eng spkn; adv bkg; quiet. "Some pitches sm & bare earth; helpful staff; clean facs; easy reach woods, cliffs & beach; conv for open-air museum." ♦ 18 Mar-23 Oct. DKK 251 2016*

AARS *B2* (2km N Rural) *56.81530, 9.50695* **Aars Camping, Tolstrup Byvej 17, 9600 Aars [tel 98 62 36 03; fax 98 62 52 99; aarscampingplads@gmail.com; www.aarscamping.dk]** Fr E45 exit junc 33 W to Aars on rd 535. Turn N onto rd 29 (Aggersundvej), site sp. Med, pt sl, pt shd; htd wc; chem disp; mv service pnt; shwrs DKK5; EHU (16A) DKK30; gas; lndry; shop; rest, snacks; bar & 1km; BBQ; cooking facs; playgrnd; tennis; horseriding; internet; TV; some statics; dogs; poss cr; Eng spkn; adv bkg; quiet; ccard acc; CKE/CCI. "Vg." ♦ 1 Apr-1 Nov. DKK 150 2016*

AERO ISLAND *C3* **Sites on Aerø Island are listed together at the end of the Denmark site entry pages.**

ALBAEK *C1* (9.6km N Coastal) *57.64433, 10.46179* **Bunken Camping, Ålbækvej 288, Bunken Klitplantage, 9982 Ålbæk [tel 98 48 71 80; info@bunkenstrandcamping.dk; www.bunkenstrandcamping.dk]** Site in fir plantation E of A10. V lge, hdg pitch, pt shd; wc; chem disp; mv service pnt; fam bthrm;shwrs DKK5; EHU DKK39 (poss rev pol); gas; lndry; shop; cooking facs; playgrnd; sand beach 150m; fishing; boating; TV; dogs DKK15; phone; adv bkg; some rd noise. "Beautiful site in trees; spacious pitches." ♦ 3 Apr-18 Oct. DKK 215 2016*

ALSGARDE see Helsingør *D2*

ASSENS *B3* (12km N Coastal) *55.33400, 9.89002* **Sandager Naes Camping, Strandgårdsvej 12, DK 5610 Assens [tel 45 64 79 11 56; info@sandagernaes.dk; www.sandagernaes.dk]** Fr E20, take exit 57 dir Assens. R at Sandager & foll sp. Med, hdg/mkd pitch, pt sl, pt shd; wc; chem disp; mv service pnt; fam bthrm; shwrs DKK5; EHU (13A); lndry (inc dryer); shop; snacks; bar; BBQ; cooking facs; playgrnd; htd pool; waterslide; paddling pool; beach 0.5km; games area; games rm; wifi; TV rm; 50% statics; dogs; phone; Eng spkn; adv bkg; CCI. "Excel site." ♦ 23 Mar-15 Sep. DKK 330 2014*

ASSENS *B3* (1.6km W Urban/Coastal) *55.26569, 9.88390* **Camping Assens Strand, Næsvej 15, 5610 Assens [tel (45) 63 60 63 62; assens@campone.dk; www.campone.dk/assens]** Site on beach at neck of land W of town adj marina. Med, pt shd; wc; chem disp; mv service pnt; fam bthrm; shwrs DKK5; EHU (10A) DKK30; gas; lndry; shop; playgrnd; sand beach adj; fishing; watersports; TV; 20% statics; dogs DKK25; phone; adv bkg; red LS. "Pleasant site on beach." ♦ Easter-13 Sep. DKK 215 2016*

AUGUSTENBORG see Sønderborg *B3*

⊞ **BILLUND** *B3* (12km SE Rural) *55.68877, 9.26864* **Randbøldal Camping, Dalen 9, 7183 Randbøl [tel 75 88 35 75; fax 75 88 34 38; info@randboldalcamping.dk; www.randboldalcamping.dk]** Fr Vejle take Billund rd. After approx 18km take L turn to Randbol & Bindebolle. Foll sp, site located approx 5km on L. Med, pt sl, shd; htd wc; chem disp; mv service pnt; fam bthrm; shwrs inc; EHU (10A) DKK35; lndry; shop; snacks; cooking facs; playgrnd; lake sw, waterslide & fishing nr; TV; 15% statics; dogs DKK20; phone; poss cr; Eng spkn; adv bkg; quiet; ccard acc. "Wooded site nr rv & trout hatchery; facs stretched high ssn; conv Legoland & Lion Park." ♦ DKK 234 2016*

BLOKHUS *B1* (8km NE Rural) *57.27855, 9.66133* **Jambo Feriepark, Solvejen 60, 9493, Saltum [tel 98 88 16 66]** Take A17/A11 fr Aalborg, L at Saltum Kirke, approx 1.5km, sp on L. Lge, pt shd; wc; chem disp; snacks; shwrs; gas; shops; EHU; sand beach 1.5km; pool; quiet; lndry; cook facs; playgrnd; sauna; tennis. ♦ May-15 Sep. DKK 110 2013*

BLOMMENSLYST see Odense *C3*

BOESLUNDE see Korsor *C3*

BOGENSE *C3* (2km SW Coastal/Urban) *55.56144, 10.08530* **Bogense Strand Camping, Vestre Engvej 11, 5400 Bogense [tel 64 81 35 08; fax 64 81 27 17; info@bogensecamp.dk; www.bogensecamp.dk]** Fr E20 at junc 57 & take 317 NE to Bogense. At 1st traff lts turn L for harbour, site sp at side of harbour. Lge, pt shd; wc; chem disp; mv service pnt; fam bthrm; shwrs DKK5; EHU (12A) DKK35; lndry; shop on site & 200m; cooking facs; playgrnd; pool; paddling pool; shgl beach adj; TV; some statics; dogs DKK20; phone; adv bkg; quiet; red LS; CKE/CCI. "Well-run site; excel facs; interesting sm town 5 mins walk." ♦ 3 Apr-18 Oct. DKK 325 2016*

⊞ **BOGENSE** *C3* (1.2km W Coastal/Urban) *55.56770, 10.08336* **Kyst Camping Bogense, Østre Havnevej 1, 5400 Bogense [tel 64 81 14 43; info@kystcamping.dk; www.kystcamping.dk]** Fr E20 at junc 57 take 317 NE to Bogonense, foll sp for harbour, site sp. Lge, mkd/hdg pitch, unshd pitch; wc; chem disp; mv service pnt; fam bthrm; shwrs DKK6; EHU (16A) DKK35; lndry; BBQ; cooking facs; playgrnd; pool; beach 200m; games area; games rm; wifi; TV; dogs DKK10; bus 200m. "Vg site; friendly, helpful owners; nice sm town and harbour; ideal cycling." ♦ DKK 285 2012*

BOJDEN see Faaborg *C3*

BORNHOLM ISLAND *A1* **Sites on Aerø Island are listed together at the end of the Denmark site entry pages.**

BORRE *D3* (6km SE Rural) *54.97971, 12.52198* **Camping Møns Klint, Klintevej 544, 4791 Magleby [tel 55 81 20 25; fax 55 81 27 97; camping@klintholm.dk; www.campingmoensklint.dk]** Site nr end of metalled section of rd 287 fr Stege to E of Magleby, site sp. Lge, pt sl, pt shd; wc; chem disp; mv service pnt; shwrs DKK7; EHU (10A) DKK40; lndry; gas; shop; rest, snacks; cooking facs; playgrnd; pool; shgl beach 3km; fishing; boating; tennis; games area; bike hire; wifi; TV; 20% statics; dogs; phone; poss cr; Eng spkn; adv bkg; quiet; ccard acc; red LS; CKE/CCI. "150m chalk cliffs adj - geological interest; much flora, fauna, fossils; gd walks; friendly staff; excel facs." 1 Apr-31 Oct. DKK 292 2016*

BRAEDSTRUP *B2* (6.3km SSE Rural) *55.93552, 9.65314* **Gudenå Camping Brædstrup, Bolundvej 4, 8740 Brædstrup [tel 75763070; info@gudenaacamping.dk; www.gudenaacamping.dk]** Fr Silkeborg take rd 52 twds Horsens; site sp R off rd 52 approx 4km fr Braedstrup. Sm, mkd pitch, unshd; htd wc; chem disp; MV service pnt; fam bthrm; shwrs metered; EHU (10A) metered; lndry; rest, snacks; bar; BBQ; playgrnd; pool; games rm; wifi; TV rm; 25% statics; dogs DKK10; adv bking; quiet; CKE/CCI. "Sm, attractive site beside Rv Gudenå; v well run fam site; fishing fr site; excel san facs." ♦ 29 Apr-27 Sep. DKK 223 2015*

CHARLOTTENLUND see København *D3*

COPENHAGEN see København *D3*

EBELTOFT *C2* (5.2km SE Coastal) *56.16775, 10.73085* **Blushøj Camping, Elsegårdevej 55, 8400 Ebeltoft [tel 86 34 12 38; info@blushoj.com; www.blushoj-camping.dk]** Head Sw on Rte 21 twds Nørrealle. Turn L onto Nørrealle, go thro 1st rndabt, cont ontosteralle, turn L onto Elsegardevej, turn L then R to stay on same rd. Site will be on R. Lge, mkd pitch, ter, pt shd; htd wc; chem disp; mv service pnt; child/fam bthrm; shwrs; EHU (10A) DKK5; gas; lndry (inc dryer); shop on site & 4km; BBQ; playgrnd; pool; beach pebble; fishing; games rm; internet; wifi; TV rm; dogs free; bus 0.1km; twin axles; Eng spkn; adv bkg acc; ccard acc; CKE; red LS. "Fantastic location; number of pitches with magnificent sea view; immac facs; friendly owner; highly rec; easy acc to shore." ♦ ltd. 1 Apr-18 Sep. DKK 306 2013*

ENGESVANG *B2* (3km N Rural) *56.18736, 9.35627* **Bøllingsø Camping, Kragelundvej 5, 7442 Engesvang [tel 86 86 51 44; fax 86 86 41 71; post@bollingso-camping.dk; www.bollingso-camping.dk]** Fr A13 dir Viborg, turn E to N of Engesvang & foll minor rd so Kragelund. Site on L 1km after museum. Med, mkd pitch, pt sl, pt shd; htd wc; chem disp; mv service pnt; fam bthrm; shwrs; EHU (16A) DKK30; lndry (inc dryer); shop; snacks; rest 3km; cooking facs; playgrnd; pool; paddling pool; games area; lake fishing 250m; TV; 2% statics; dogs DKK10; phone; poss cr; adv bkg; red LS; quiet; CKE/CCI. "Conv NH for A13; well-kept family site; clean, dated facs; nr Danish lake district." ♦ 1 Apr-1 Oct. DKK 170 2016*

ERTEBOLLE see Farsø *B2*

"Satellite navigation makes touring much easier"

Remember most sat navs don't know if you're towing or in a larger vehicle – always use yours alongside maps and site directions.

ESBJERG *A3* (13km NW Rural/Coastal) *55.54359, 8.33921* **Sjelborg Camping, Sjelborg Standvej 11, Hjerting, 6710 Esbjerg Vest [tel 75 11 54 32; fax 76 13 11 32; info@sjelborg.dk; www.sjelborg.dk]** Fr Esbjerg take coast rd N twds Hjerting & Sjelborg. At T-junc, Sjelborg Vej, turn L & in 100m turn R onto Sjelborg Kirkevej (camping sp); in 600m turn L into Sjelborg Strandvej (sp); site on R in 600m. Lge, hdg/mkd pitch, pt shd; wc; chem disp; mv service pnt; shwrs inc; fam bthrm; EHU (10A)€4.50; lndry (inc dryer); shop; sand/shgl beach nr; lake adj; fishing; golf 5km; bus to town; phone; adv bkg; quiet. "Excel, well maintained site in a quiet country setting; superb facs & activities all ages; spacious on edge of conservation area; mkd walks & bird sanctuary; v welcoming & friendly." ♦ 11 Apr-20 Sep. DKK 190 2015*

FAABORG *C3* (8.5km W Coastal) *55.10568, 10.10776* **Bøjden Strandcamping, Bøjden Landevej 12, 5600 Bøjden [tel 63 60 63 60; fax 63 60 63 63; info@bojden.dk; www.bojden.dk]** Rd 8 W fr Fåborg dir Bøjden/Fynshav, site sp nr ferry. Lge, some hdg/mkd pitch, pt sl, terr, pt shd; htd wc; chem disp; mv service pnt; serviced pitches; fam bthrm; shwrs DKK5; EHU (16A) DKK31; lndry; shop; rest adj; cooking facs; playgrnd; htd pool & paddling pool; sand beach adj; bike & boat hire; games rm; golf 12km; entmnt; internet; TV rm; 80% statics; dogs DKK15; sep car park; Eng spkn; adv bkg; ccard acc. "Excel family site with activity cent; blue flag beach; sea views fr pitches; interesting area; excel facs." ♦ 9 Apr-22 Oct. DKK 395 2017*

FERRING see Lemvig *A2*

⊞ **FREDERICIA** *B3* (6km NE Coastal) *55.62457, 9.83351* **Trelde Næs Camping, Trelde Næsvej 297, Trelde Næs, 7000 Fredericia [tel 75 95 71 83; fax 75 95 75 78; trelde@mycamp.dk; www.mycamp.dk]** Route 28 (Vejle-Fredericia). Fr Vejle take Egeskov exit, then Trelde and Trelde-Næs. Fr Fredericia to Trelde, then Trelde Næs. Lge, pt sl, unshd; htd wc; chem disp; mv service pnt; fam bthrm; sauna; shwrs DKK4; EHU (10A) DKK32; lndry (inc dryer); shop; snacks; BBQ; cooking facs; playgrnd; htd pool; waterslide; sand beach adj; wifi; TV rm; 10% statics; dogs DKK16; phone; poss cr; adv bkg; quiet; ccard acc; red LS. "Vg; friendly; fine views over fjord; conv Legoland & island of Fyn; swipecard for all services - pay on dep." ♦ DKK 405 2013*

FREDERIKSHAVN *C1* (2km N Coastal) *57.46415, 10.52778* **Nordstrand Camping A/S (Formerly TopCamp), Apholmenvej 40, 9900 Frederikshavn [tel 98 42 93 50; fax 98 43 47 85; info@nordstrand-camping.dk; www.nordstrand-camping.dk]** Fr E45/Rd40 foll rd N twd Skagen to outside town boundary (over rlwy bdge), turn R at rndabt into Apholmenvej; site sp. Lge, mkd pitch, unshd; wc; chem disp; shwrs; fam bthrm; EHU (10A); gas; lndry; shop; snacks; playgrnd; covrd pool; beach 1km; entmnt; excursions; TV; some statics; phone; dogs DKK12; poss cr; Eng spkn; adv bkg; ccard acc; red/snr citizens/long stay/CKE. "Vg NH for ferries; recep open 24hrs peak ssn; well-run, clean site; some pitches sm; cycle track to town." ♦ 14 Mar-24 Sep. DKK 305 2017*

GIVE see Jelling *B3*

GRASTEN *B3* (2km SW Coastal) *54.9007, 9.57121* **Lærkelunden Camping, Nederbyvej 17-25, Rinkenæs, 6300 Gråsten [tel 74 65 02 50; fax 74 65 02 25; info@laerkelunden.dk; www.laerkelunden.dk]** Fr Kruså E on rd 8 twds Gråsten & Sønderborg; on E o'skts of Rinkenæs turn R Nederbyvej (car dealer on corner) & foll sp to site in 400m. Lge, few hdstg, pt sl, unshd; wc; chem disp; mv service pnt; fam bthrm; 4% serviced pitches; sauna; shwrs inc; EHU (10A) DKK30; gas; lndry; shop; cooking facs; BBQ; playgrnd; htd, covrd pool; sm sand beach adj; boat launching; solarium; TV; 10% statics; dogs free; phone; poss v cr; Eng spkn; quiet; ccard acc (5% surcharge); CKE/CCI. "Gd sailing/surfing; views over Flensburg fjord; coastal footpath; gd cent for S Jutland & N Germany; excel; lovely, well run site." ♦ 21 Mar-22 Oct. DKK 317 2017*

GRENAA *C2* (4km S Coastal) *56.38957, 10.91213* **Grenaa Strand Camping, Fuglsangsvej 58, 8500 Grenå [tel 86 32 17 18; info@722.dk; www.grenaastrandcamping.dk]** Fr Grenå harbour foll coast rd due S foll sp. V lge, unshd; wc; chem disp; mv service pnt; fam bthrm; shwrs; EHU (10A) DKK35; gas; lndry; shop; snacks; playgrnd; pool; solarium; sand beach 250m; entmnt; TV; some statics; dogs DKK30; phone; poss cr; adv bkg; red LS; poss noisy high ssn. "Conv for ferries to Sweden; busy site." ♦ 1 Apr-16 Sep. DKK 264 2016*

⊞ **GREVE** *D3* (9km E Urban/Coastal) *55.59434, 12.34315* **Hundige Strand Familiecamping, Hundige Strandvej 72, 2670 Greve [tel 43 90 31 85; info@hsfc.dk; www.hsfc.dk]** Leave E20/47/55 at junc 27 & foll sp Hundige, cont strt ahead until T-junc with rd 151. Turn L, ent 200m on L. Or leave at junc 22 & foll rd 151 down coast to site on R in 8km. Med, some mkd pitch, terr, pt shd; wc; chem disp; mv service pnt; shwrs; EHU inc; gas; lndry; shop, hypmkt 1km; rest, snacks; bar adj; BBQ; cooking facs; playgrnd; sand beach 1km; lge sw stadium 5km; TV; 25% statics (sep area); dogs free; phone; site clsd Xmas & New Year; poss cr; Eng spkn; adv bkg; quiet but some rd noise; ccard acc (surcharge); CKE. "Sh walk to rlwy stn & 15 mins to Copenhagen; friendly, helpful staff; office open morning & eves only LS; site in two parts; v scenic; excel, clean facs." DKK 339 2013*

HADERSLEV *B3* (13.6km S Coastal) *55.15313, 9.49424* **Vikaer Strand Camping, Dundelum 29, Djernaes, 6100 Haderslev [tel 74 57 54 64; info@vikaercamp.dk; www.vikaercamp.dk]** S on Katsund twd Lille Klingbjerg, turn R onto Lille Klingbjerg, L onto Højgade, R onto Møllepladsen, L to stay on Møllepladsen then take rte 170 to Diernæs Strandvej for 10.9km, then take 1st R onto Ny Erlevvej for 450m, turn L onto Omkørselsvejen/Rte 170, cont to foll Rte 170 for 8.1km, go thro 1 rndbt, turn L onto Diernæsvej Strandvej for 2.3km foll Diernæs Strandvej to Dundelum, L onto Diernæs Strandvej, R to stay on same rd, R onto Dundelum, L to stay on Dundelum and site on R. Lge, mkd pitch, pt sl, unshd; wc; chem disp; mv service pnt; shwrs; EHU (10-16 A); lndry facs; shop; snacks; playgrnd; dogs 12DKK; Eng spkn; quiet; CCI. "Super site, many outlets for children; lovely beach; immac san facs." ♦ ltd. Easter-31 Oct. DKK 300 2014*

HADERSLEV *B3* (1km W Urban) *55.24431, 9.47701* **Haderslev Camping, Erlevvej 34, 6100 Haderslev [tel 74 52 13 47; fax 74 52 13 64; info@haderslev-camping.dk; www.haderslev-camping.dk]** Turn of E45 at junc 68 sp Haderslev Cent; turn R onto rd 170. On ent town, cross lake & turn R at traff lts. Site on R at rndabt in 500m. Med, mkd pitch, hdstg, pt sl, pt shd; htd wc; chem disp; mv service pnt; fam bthrm; shwrs; EHU (16A) DKK25; lndry (inc dryer); shop 1km; rest, snacks; bar; BBQ; cooking facs; playgrnd; pool 1km; lake sw 1km; games rm; internet; TV; some statics; phone; bus 1km; Eng spkn; adv bkg; quiet; ccard acc (surcharge); CKE/CCI. "Gd, well-kept site conv E45; all facs to high standard; attractive old town." 15 Mar-31 Oct. DKK 34 2013*

⊞ **HANSTHOLM** *B1* (4km E Coastal) *57.10913, 8.66731* **Hanstholm Camping, Hamborgvej 95, 7730 Hanstholm [tel 97 96 51 98; fax 97 96 54 70; info@hanstholm-camping.de; www.hanstholm-camping.dk]** Ent town fr S on rte 26. At rndabt turn R onto coast rd sp Vigsø. Site on L in about 4km. Lge, hdg/mkd pitch, pt sl, pt shd; htd wc; chem disp; mv service pnt; fam bthrm; sauna; shwrs DKK5; EHU (10A) DKK40; gas; lndry (inc dryer); shop; snacks; BBQ; playgrnd; htd pool; paddling pool; sand beach 1km; fishing; horseriding; wifi; TV rm; 30% statics; dogs DKK10; phone; Eng spkn; adv bkg; ccard acc; CKE/CCI. "Fine view of North Sea coast; nr wildlife area; gd cycling/walking on coast path; excel, busy, well-maintained site; generous pitches; gd rest; excel childrens facs." ♦ DKK 230 2016*

HEJLSMINDE *B3* (9km N Coastal) *55.41109, 9.59228* **Gronninghoved Strand Camping, Mosvigvej 21, 6093 Sjolund [tel 75 57 40 45; info@gronninghoved.dk; www.gronninghoved.dk]** Fr E45 at exit 65 take 25 twds Kolding. At lights turn R onto 170. After 3.4km turn L sp Sjolund. On entry Sjolund take 1st L sp Gronninghoved. Take 2nd R in Gronninghoved, then 1st L, foll sp to site. Lge, hdg/mkd pitch, pt sl, pt shd; wc; chem disp; mv service pnt; fam bthrm; shwrs; EHU (10A) DKK37; lndry (inc dryer); shop; cooking facs; playgrnd; htd pool; paddling pool; sand/shingle beach 0.2km; games area; games rm; wifi; TV rm; 75% statics; dogs free; twin axles; poss cr hg ssn; Eng spkn; adv bkg; quiet; red LS; CKE/CCI. "Excel site; tennis, mini golf, billards & waterslide." ♦ 18 Mar-15 Sep. DKK 270 2016*

"There aren't many sites open at this time of year"

If you're travelling outside peak season remember to call ahead to check site opening dates – even if the entry says 'open all year'.

⊞ **HELSINGOR** *D2* (3km NE Urban/Coastal) *56.04393, 12.60433* **Helsingør Camping Grønnehave, Strandalleen 2, 3000 Helsingør [tel 49 28 49 50 or 25 31 12 12; fax 49 28 49 40; campingpladsen@helsingor.dk; www.helsingorcamping.dk]** Site in NE o'skts of town, twd Hornbæk. Site nr beach o'looking channel to Sweden on E side of rd. Foll sps on app or in town (beware: sp are sm & low down). Med, pt shd; wc; chem disp; mv service pnt; shwrs DKK5; EHU (10A) DKK30; lndry; shop; cooking facs; playgrnd; htd pool nr; beach; 25% statics; phone; poss v cr. "10 min walk to Hamlet's castle; 20 min walk to town & stn; gd train service to Copenhagen; max stay 14 days 15 Jun-15 Aug; Baltic ships w/end mid-Aug; v busy/cr high ssn." ♦ DKK 217 2014*

HELSINGOR *D2* (13km SSW Coastal) *55.93949, 12.51643* **Niva Camping, Sølyst Allé 14, 2290 Nivå [tel 49 14 52 26; fax 49 14 52 40; nivaacamping@post8.tele.dk; www.nivaacamping.dk]** Take coast rd bet Copenhagen & Helsingør. Fr N foll sp to Nivå, & site 500m fr main rd, sp. Fr S site 2km after vill. Lge, mkd pitch, hdstg, pt sl, pt shd; htd wc; chem disp; mv service pnt; fam bthrm; shwrs; EHU (16A); lndry (inc dryer); shop; rest 500m, snacks 500m; BBQ; cooking facs; playgrnd; sw beach 800m; fishing adj; games rm; wifi; TV rm; 10% statics; dogs; twin axles; poss cr; Eng spkn; adv bkg; quiet but nr busy rlwy; red snr citizens; ccard acc; CKE/CCI. "Conv Helsingborg ferry, Copenhagen, Kronborg Castle (Hamlet); excel san facs; vg location; v quiet; best site in Zealand; excel help; upper level pitches quietest & coolest if hot." 31 Mar-30 Sep. DKK 240 2014*

HELSINGOR *D2* (10km NW Urban) *56.08104, 12.51348* **Skibstrup Camping, Stormlugen 20, 3140 Ålsgårde [tel 49 70 99 71; fax 49 70 99 61; info@skibstrup-camping.dk; www.skibstrup-camping.dk]** Fr Helsingør take N coast rd to Ålsgårde; then foll site sp. Lge, shd; wc; chem disp; mv service pnt; fam bthrm; shwrs; EHU (10A) DKK35; lndry (inc dryer); shop 1km; cooking facs; playgrnd; pool; paddling pool; beach 500m; wifi; TV; some statics; dogs free; phone; adv bkg; ccard acc; quiet. "Pleasant site amongst trees; conv for ferry & Copenhagen." ♦ 1 Apr-31 Oct. DKK 150 2015*

HENNE *A3* (2.7km NNW Rural) *55.73258, 8.22189* **Henneby Camping, Hennebysvej 20, 6854 Henne [tel 75 25 51 63; fax 75 25 65 01; info@hennebycamping.dk; www.hennebycamping.dk]** Fr Varde on rd 181 & 465 foll sp Henne Strand. Turn R after Kirkeby. Site sp. Lge, hdg pitch, pt shd; htd wc; chem disp; mv service pnt; fam bthrm; shwrs DKK2; EHU (10A) DKK32; gas; lndry; shop; rest; cooking facs; playgrnd; pool 2.5km; beach 2km; bike hire; TV rm; some statics; dogs DKK15; poss cr; Eng spkn; quiet; ccard acc; CKE/CCI. "Superb facs; gd, clean site." ♦ 22 Mar-20 Oct. DKK 349 2013*

HILLEROD *D2* (1km SW Urban) *55.9246, 12.2941* **Hillerød Camping, Blytækkervej 18, 3400 Hillerød [tel 48 26 48 54; info@hillerodcamping.dk; www.hillerodcamping.dk]** Fr Roskilde or Copenhagen on A16 twd Hillerød, take 1st L at traff lts sp Hillerød & Frederiksborg Slot Rv233. Site in town cent, not well sp. Med, pt sl, pt shd; wc; chem disp; mv service pnt; fam bthrm; shwrs inc; EHU (10A) DKK35 (long lead poss req); gas; lndry; shop, rest nrby; snacks; cooking facs; common/dining rm; playgrnd; bike hire; TV; phone; bus, train nr; poss cr; Eng spkn; adv bkg; quiet; ccard acc; CCI. "Frederiksborg castle in town cent; gd base for N Seeland; 30 min by train to Copenhagen; v helpful, charming owner; pleasant, well-run site; excel, new san facs 2010; no mkd pitch, but owner positions o'fits carefully; many personal touches - eg courtyard with herbs, fruit trees, candles & torches; best site." 12 Apr-19 Oct. DKK 340 2014*

⊞ **HIRTSHALS** *C1* (5km SW Coastal) *57.55507, 9.93254* **Tornby Strand Camping, Strandvejen 13, 9850 Tornby [tel 98 97 78 77; fax 98 97 78 81; mail@tornbystrand.dk; www.tornbystrand.dk]** Take rd 55 fr Hjørring twd Hirtshals. In 12km turn L sp Tornby Strand & Camping, site on L in 200m. Lge, pt shd; wc; chem disp; mv service pnt; fam bthrm; shwrs; EHU (16A) DKK30; gas; lndry; shops adj; snacks; playgrnd; pool 2km; sand beach 1km; TV; dogs DKK5; phone; 75% statics; Eng spkn; poss cr; adv bkg; quiet; CKE/CCI. "Useful for ferries to Kristiansand, Arendal, Faroe & Iceland; helpful owner." ♦ DKK 254 2016*

HIRTSHALS *C1* (1.5km W Urban) *57.58650, 9.94583* **Hirtshals Camping, Kystvejen 6, 9850 Hirtshals [tel 98 94 25 35; fax 98 94 33 43; info@hirtshals-camping.dk; www.dk-camp.dk/hirtshals]** Located 16km N of Hjørring. Turn L off rd 14 3km SW of Hirtshals & site on L. Fr ferry foll sp town cent, then site sp. Med, terr, unshd; wc; chem disp; mv service pnt; fam bthrm; shwrs DKK5; EHU (10A) DKK30; kiosk; rest 500m; snacks 300m; playgrnd; beach 200m; fishing & sw 200m; bike hire; TV; dogs DKK10; phone; quiet; red LS. "Open site on cliff top; san facs dated; friendly staff; conv ferries; on coastal cycle path; late arr area; busy but efficient; conv for NH." ♦ 25 Mar-31 Oct. DKK 225 2016*

HJORRING *C1* (14km W Urban) *57.47375, 9.80100* **Lønstrup Camping, Møllebakkevej 20, Lonstrup, 9800 Hjørring [tel 45 21 44 56 37; loenstrupcamping@mail.dk; www.campingloenstrup.dk]** Fr E39 take Exit 3 dir Hjørring for Rte 35 twd Rte 55. Turn R onto Lonstrupvej. Foll sp to site. Med, mkd pitch, pt shd; htd wc; chem disp; mv service pnt; fam bthrm; shwrs inc; EHU (10A) 25DKK; lndry (inc dryer); BBQ; cooking facs; playgrnd; beach 500m; wifi; 30% statics; dogs 15DKK; bus 200m; twin axles; Eng spkn; adv bkg; quiet; CCI. "Vg site; friendly, helpful family owned; lge units may be tight access; close to sm vill & coast." ♦ ltd. 28 Mar-29 Sep. DKK 225 2014*

HOJBJERG **see Åarhus** *C2*

⊞ **HOLBAEK** *D3* (4km E Coastal) *55.71799, 11.76020* **FDM Holbæk Fjord Camping, Sofiesminde Allé 1, 4300 Holbæk [tel 59 43 50 64; fax 59 43 50 14; c-holbaek@fdm.dk]** Fr Rv21 exit junc 20 (fr N) or junc 18 (fr S) & foll sp to harbour. Turn R (E) at harbour - Munkholmvej. Approx 1.5km along Munkholmvej, after traff lts, turn L into Sofiesminde Allé dir marina. Site on R, close to marina. Lge, hdg/mkd pitch, pt shd; htd wc; chem disp; mv service pnt; fam bthrm; sauna; shwrs inc; EHU (10A) inc; gas; lndry (inc dryer); shop; rest, snacks; cooking facs; BBQ; playgrnd; htd pool; paddling pool; whirlpool; spa; watersports, fishing, golf nr; bike hire; games area; games rm; wifi; TV rm; 80% statics; dogs DKK15; no o'fits over 10m high ssn; phone; adv bkg; quiet; ccard acc; red LS. "Well-run site in attractive position; helpful staff; pitches poss tight lge o'fits; clean san facs; gd walks & cycle tracks." ♦ DKK 328 SBS - H17 2015*

*Last year of report

⊞ **HORSENS** *B2* (6km W Rural/Coastal) *55.85928, 9.91747* **Husodde Strand Camping, Husoddevej 85, 8700 Horsens [tel 75 65 70 60; fax 75 65 50 72; camping@husodde.dk; www.husodde-camping.dk]** Site sp to R of Horsens-Odder rd (451), foll rd to fjord, site sp. Med, mkd pitch, pt sl, pt shd; wc; chem disp; mv service pnt; fam bthrm; shwrs DKK5; EHU (10A) DKK35; lndry; kiosk & shops 500m; rest, snacks, bar 5km; cooking facs; BBQ; playgrnd; pool 3km; sand beach & fishing adj; TV; 10% statics; dogs DKK10; phone; Eng spkn; quiet; CKE/CCI. "Lovely location; lge pitches; well-maintained, well-managed site; friendly welcome; cycle tracks." ♦ DKK 238 2015*

"That's changed – Should I let The Club know?"

If you find something on site that's different from the site entry, fill in a report and let us know. See camc.com/europereport.

⊞ **HOVBORG** *B3* (700m NW Rural) *55.60900, 8.93267* **Holme A Camping, Torpet 6, 6682 Hovborg [tel 75 39 67 77 or 60 91 86 65 (mob); holmeaa camping@mail.dk; www.holmeaacamping.dk]** Campsite located besides the 425 Grindsted-Ribe. Well sp after Hovborg. Med, mkd pitch, pt shd; htd wc; chem disp; mv service pnt; child/fam bthrm; shwrs inc; EHU DKK32; gas; lndry (inc dryer); shop 0.5km; rest, snacks, bar 300m; playgrnd; pool; entmnt; wifi; TV rm; dog DKK10; bus 0.5km; twin axles; Eng spkn; ccard acc; CKE; red LS. "Gd cycling; walking; fishing lakes; 20 min fr Legoland; lovely quiet site; immac facs; friendly helpful owner." DKK 165 2013*

HVIDE SANDE *A2* (7.6km S Coastal) *55.94975, 8.15030* **Nordsø Camping & Badeland, Tingodden 3, Årgab, 6960 Hvide Sande [tel 75 52 14 82; info@ dancamps.dk; www.dancamps.dk]** Fr E20 take exit 73 onto rd 11 to Varde. Then take rd 181 twd Nymindegab & Hvide Sande. Lge, some hdstg, unshd; htd wc; chem disp; mv service pnt; fam bthrm; serviced pitches; sauna; private san facs avail; shwrs inc; EHU (10A) DKK30; lndry (inc dryer); shop; rest, snacks; bar; playgrnd; 2 pools (1 htd, covrd); paddling pool; waterslides; sand beach 200m; fishing; tennis; wifi; entmnt; TV rm; 10% statics; dogs DKK20; phone; adv bkg; quiet. "Well-maintained facs; extra charge seaview pitches; vg." ♦ 15 Apr-31 Oct. DKK 199 2016*

IDESTRUP see Nykøbing (Falster) *D3*

ISHOJ HAVN see København *D3*

JELLING *B3* (13km NW Rural) *55.83138, 9.29944* **Topcamp Riis & Feriecenter, Østerhovedvej 43, Riis 7323 Give [tel 75 73 14 33; fax 75 73 58 66; info@ riisferiepark.dk; www.riisferiepark.dk]** Fr S exit E45 at junc 61, turn L & foll rd 28 for approx 8km. Turn R onto rd 441 for 15km, then turn R into Østerhovedvej for 2km & turn L into site. Or fr N on E45 exit junc 57, turn R & foll rd for 25km; turn L & foll 442 for 500m; turn R into Østerhovedvej & cont for 1.5km; turn R into site. Med, pt shd; hdg; mkd; hdstg; wc; chem disp; mv service pnt; serviced pitch; fam bthrm; jacuzzi; sauna; shwrs DKK5; EHU (13A) inc; gas; lndry (ind dryer); shop; rest; bar; BBQ; playgrnd; htd pool; waterslide; paddling pool; jaccuzi; fitness cent; fishing 3.5km; bike hire; games rm; child entmnt high ssn; golf 4km; wifi; TV rm; 60% statics; dogs DKK20; no o'fits over 15m high ssn; phone; recep 0800-2200; poss cr; adv bkg; quiet; ccard acc; red LS; CKE/CCI. "Attractive, well laid-out, well-run site in beautiful countryside; vg san facs; conv for Legoland, Safari Park, Center Mobilium museum in Billund, lakes & E coast; excel; friendly & relaxed; spacious pitches." ♦ 19 Mar-25 Sep. DKK 430 SBS - H11 2014*

⊞ **KARISE** *D3* (5km S Rural) *55.27086, 12.22281* **Lægårdens Camping, Vemmetoftevej 2A, Store Spjellerup, 4653 Karise [tel 56 71 00 67; fax 56 71 00 68; info@laegaardenscamping.dk; www. laegaardenscamping.dk]** Turn S off rd 209 in Karise, site sp. Med, hdg/mkd pitch, pt shd; htd wc; chem disp; mv service pnt; shwrs DKK5; EHU DKK30; lndry; rest, snacks 1km; playgrnd; beach 3km; TV; 60% statics; dogs DKK10; Eng spkn; adv bkg; CKE/CCI. DKK 150 2016*

KARREBAEKSMINDE see Næstved *D3*

"I like to fill in the reports as I travel from site to site"

You'll find report forms at the back of this guide, or you can fill them in online at camc.com/europereport.

KOBENHAVN *D3* (10km N Coastal) *55.74536, 12.58331* **Camping Charlottenlund Fort, Strandvejen 144B, 2290 Charlottenlund [tel 39 62 36 88; fax 39 61 08 16; camping@gentofte.dk; www. campingcopenhagen.dk]** Take København-Helsingør coast rd O2/152, site on seaside 2km N of Tuborg factory. Sm, mkd pitch, few hdstg, shd; wc; chem disp; mv service pnt; shwrs DKK5; EHU (10A) metered; lndry (inc dryer); shops 500m; rest, bar adj; cooking facs; sand beach; bus; poss v cr; wifi; Eng spkn; adv bkg rec; quiet but noisy during mid-summer festivities; ccard acc; CKE/CCI. "Experimentarium Science Park at Tuborg brewery; in grnds of old moated fort; conv Copenhagen & Sweden; gd facs but inadequate high ssn; friendly staff." ♦ 30 Apr-6 Sep. DKK 260 2014*

KOBENHAVN *D3* (20km N Rural) *55.80896, 12.53062* **Nærum Camping, Langebjerg 5, Ravnebakken, 2850 Nærum [tel 42 80 19 57; fax 45 80 11 78; naerum@dcu.dk; www.camping-naerum.dk]** Fr Copenhagen take E47/E55/rd 19 N for 16km, turn W to Nærum at junc 14, over bdge x-ing m'way & sharp L. Lge, pt sl, pt shd; wc; chem disp; mv service pnt; shwrs inc; EHU (10A); gas; lndry; shop; playgrnd; pool 10km; TV rm; train/bus 500m; poss cr; Eng spkn; adv bkg; some rlwy & m'way noise; ccard acc; CKE/CCI. "Popular nr woods; conv Copenhagen & Helsingor; shopping cent nrby over m'way bdge; gd cycle paths; path fr site for suburban rlwy to Copenhagen; if arr bet 1200 & 1400 select pitch & report to office after 1400; facs stretched in high ssn; excel bus service to Copenhagen." ♦ 21 Mar-19 Oct. DKK 331 2014*

⊞ **KOBENHAVN** *D3* (9km W Urban) *55.67055, 12.43353* **DCU Absalon Camping, Korsdalsvej 132, 2610 Rødovre [tel 36 41 06 00; fax 36 41 02 93; absalon@dcu.dk; www.camping-absalon.dk]** Fr E55/E20/E47 exit junc 24 dir København, site on L in 1km, sp. Or fr København foll A156 W for 9km. Sp Rødovre then Brøndbyøster, shortly after this site sp to R at traff lts; ent on L after 100m down side rd, sp. V lge, mkd pitch, pt shd; htd wc; chem disp; mv service pnt; fam bthrm; shwrs inc; EHU (10-16A) DKK30 or metered + conn fee; gas; lndry (inc dryer); shop & 500m; rest 2km; BBQ; cooking facs; playgrnd; htd pool 300m; golf 10km; wifi; TV rm; 10% statics; dogs DKK21; bus/train nr; poss cr; ccard acc (surcharge). "Well located nr Brøndbyøster rlwy stn & bus Copenhagen (rail tickets fr recep); some pitches unrel in wet & dusty when dry; vg, modern san facs; office clsd 1200-1400 LS; sep area for c'vans & m'vans; helpful staff; cycle rte to city; excel site; gd cooking facs; well run." ♦ DKK 260 2016*

⊞ **KOGE** *D3* (14km SE Coastal) *55.39793, 12.29022* **Stevns Camping, Strandvejen 29, 4671 Strøby [tel 60 14 41 54; info@stevnscamping.dk; www.stevnscamping.dk]** Exit E20/E55 junc 33 twd Køge. In Køge take rd 209 & 260 to Strøby. In Strøby turn L onto Strandvejen. Lge, mkd pitch, unshd; htd wc; chem disp; mv service pnt; fam bthrm; shwrs inc; EHU (10A) inc; lndry (inc dryer); shop; rest, bar 400m; BBQ; cooking facs; playgrnd; htd pool; paddling pool; shgl beach 400m; wifi; some statics; dogs DKK10; phone; Eng spkn; quiet; CKE/CCI. "Gd site nr coast & Koge; access to Copenhagen by public transport." ♦ DKK 240 2013*

⊞ **KOLDING** *B3* (16km E Coastal) *55.46777, 9.67972* **Gammel Ålbo Camping, Gammel Aalbovej 30, 6092 Sønder Stenderup [tel 75 57 11 16; camping@gl-aalbo.dk; www.gl-aalbo.dk]** Foll rd SE fr Kolding to Agtrup then on to Sønder Bjert & Sønder Stenderup. Foll site sp thro vill twd coast, site at end of rd. Med, hdg pitch, some hdstg, terr, pt shd; htd wc; chem disp; mv service pnt; fam bthrm; shwrs inc; EHU (16A) DKK38.50; lndry rm; shop; cooking facs; shgl beach adj; fishing; boat hire; skindiving; dogs free; 10% statics; poss cr; Eng spkn; quiet; CKE/CCI. "Well-kept, relaxing site o'looking Lillebælt; v cr in high ssn." DKK 224 2015*

⊞ **KOLDING** *B3* (5km S Urban) *55.46290, 9.47290* **Kolding City Camp, Vonsildvej 19, 6000 Kolding [tel 75 52 13 88; fax 75 52 45 29; info@koldingcitycamp.dk; www.koldingcitycamp.dk]** E45 (Flensbury-Frederikshavn) take exit 65 at Kolding Syd twrds Kolding; at 1st traff lts turn R site 800m on L. Lge, pt sl, pt shd; htd wc; chem disp; mv service pnt; fam bthrm; private san facs avail; shwrs inc; EHU (10A) DKK30; gas; lndry (inc dryer); shop high ssn; supmkt 800m; rest 3km; BBQ; cooking facs; playgrnd; htd, covrd pool 3km; lake beach & fishing 5km; tennis; wifi; TV rm; dogs DKK10; phone; bus to town; poss cr; Eng spkn; adv bkg; some rd noise; ccard acc; 10% red CKE/CCI. "Friendly & v quiet; conv NH Legoland; vg san facs; gd site; level pitches; full kitchen facs." ♦ ltd. DKK 294 2014*

KOLLUND see Kruså *B3*

⊞ **KRUSA** *B3* (600m N Rural) *54.85370, 9.40220* **Kruså Camping, Åbenråvej 7, 6340 Kruså [tel 74 67 12 06; fax 74 67 12 05; info@krusaacamping.dk; www.krusaacamping.dk]** S on E45, exit junc 75 twd Kruså. Turn L onto rd 170, site on L. Lge, pt shd, pt sl; wc; chem disp; mv service pnt; fam bthrm; shwrs DKK5; EHU (10A) DKK30; gas; lndry (inc dryer); shop; rest, snacks; bar; cooking facs; playgrnd; htd pool; TV; dogs; phone; rd noise; CKE/CCI. "Gd NH; bus to Flensburg (Germany) 1km fr site; new san facs 2010." ♦ DKK 338 2013*

LANGELAND ISLAND *C3* **Sites on Langeland Island are listed together at the end of the Denmark site entry pages.**

LAVEN see Ry *B2*

LEMVIG *A2* (4km NW Coastal) *56.56733, 8.29399* **Lemvig Strand Camping, Vinkelhagevej 6, 7620 Lemvig [tel 97 82 00 42; fax 97 81 04 56; lemvig@dk-camp.dk; www.lemvigstrandcamping.dk]** Foll camping sps in Lemvig to site. Med, mkd pitch, unshd; wc; chem disp; mv service pnt; fam bthrm; sauna; shwrs DKK2; EHU (10A) DKK35; lndry; shop; rest adj; cooking facs; playgrnd; htd, covrd pool; beach 300m; games area; games rm; internet; TV rm; 30% statics; dogs DKK10; phone; adv bkg; ccard acc. "Vg sailing cent; pretty area." ♦ 30 Mar-16 Sep. DKK 359 2013*

DENMARK

LOKKEN *B1* (2km N Rural) *57.38580, 9.72580* **Løkken Strandcamping, Furreby Kirkevej 97, 9480 Løkken [tel 45 98 99 18 04; info@loekkencamping.dk]** Head NE on Lokkensvej/Rte 55. At rndabt take 3rd exit onto Harald Fischers Vej. Turn R onto Furreby Kirkevej. Site 1.3km on the L. Med, pt shd; htd wc; chem disp; mv service pnt; fam bthrm; shwrs; lndry (inc dryer); shops 2km; cooking facs; sand beach adj; TV rm; dogs DKK11; twin axles; Eng spkn; adv bkg; quiet; ccard acc. "Vg site; pitches sep by fences; direct access to sand dunes." 1 May-7 Sep. DKK 312 2014*

MIDDELFART *B3* (11km NE Coastal) *55.51948, 9.85025* **Vejlby Fed Camping, Rigelvej 1, 5500 Vejlby Fed [tel 64 40 24 20; fax 64 40 24 38; mail@vejlbyfed.dk; www.vejlbyfed.dk]** Exit E20 junc 57 or 58. Site sp in Vejlby Fed, NE fr Middelfart dir Bogense, on coast. Lge, mkd pitch, pt shd; wc; chem disp; mv service pnt; fam bthrm; sauna; shwrs DKK6; EHU (10A) DKK28; lndry; shop; snacks; bar; cooking facs; playgrnd; htd pool; paddling pool; sand beach adj; boating; fishing; tennis; wifi; 30% statics; dogs DKK15; phone; Eng spkn; adv bkg; CKE/CCI. ♦ 15 Mar-14 Sep. DKK 430 2014*

MIDDELFART *B3* (5km NW Rural) *55.51694, 9.68225* **Gals Klint Camping, Galsklintvej 11, 5500 Middelfart [tel 64 41 20 59; fax 64 41 81 59; mail@galsklint.dk; www.galsklint.dk]** Fr W on E20 take rd 161. At 2 traff lts turn L & cross Little Belt Bdge. In 300m turn R into Galsklintvej & foll sp. Lge, hdg/mkd pitch, pt shd; htd wc; chem disp; mv service pnt; fam bthrm; shwrs DKK3; EHU (16A) DKK28; lndry; shop; rest, snacks; BBQ; cooking facs; playgrnd; shgl beach adj; fishing; boat hire; 10% statics; dogs; Eng spkn; adv bkg; quiet; ccard acc (surcharge); CKE/CCI. "Site surrounded by forest; gd cycling/walking; vg; well run mod facs shoreside next woodland." ♦ 18 Mar-3 Oct. DKK 208 2016*

NAERUM see København *D3*

NORRE AABY see Middelfart *B3*

NYBORG *C3* (4km N Coastal) *55.35853, 10.78660* **Gronnehave Strand, Regstrupvej 83, 5800 Nyborg [tel 65 36 15 50; info@gronnehave.dk; www.gronnehave.dk]** 10 mins N fr E20 on Skaboeshusevej. Med, mkd pitch, terr, unshd; htd wc; chem disp; mv service pnt; fam bthrm; shwrs; EHU (10A) DKK36; lndry (inc dryer); shop 3km; playgrnd; beach adj; games area; wifi; TV rm; dogs; bus 2km; Eng spkn; quiet. "Friendly owner; gd views; bdge to Zeeland; vg." 12 Apr-19 Oct. DKK 244 2015*

NYBORG *C3* (3km SE Coastal) *55.30457, 10.82453* **Nyborg Strandcamping, Hjejlevej 99, 5800 Nyborg [tel 65 31 02 56; mail@strandcamping.dk; www.strandcamping.dk]** Exit E20 at junc 44. Turn N, site sp in 1km. Lge, mkd pitch, pt shd; wc; chem disp; mv service pnt; fam bthrm; shwrs DKK9; EHU (10A) metered; gas; lndry; shop; rest 500m; snacks; playgrnd; sand beach adj; fishing; golf 1km; internet; TV; 50% statics; dogs; phone; Eng spkn; adv bkg; CKE/CCI. "Conv m'way, rlwy & ferry; excel views of bdge; gd facs; gd site; well difined pitches next to beach." ♦ 13 Apr-21 Sep. DKK 256 2014*

NYBORG *C3* (13km S Rural) *55.23693, 10.8080* **Tårup Stand Camping, Lersey Allé 25, Tårup Strand, 5871 Frørup [tel 65 37 11 99; fax 65 37 11 79; mail@taarupstrandcamping.dk; www.taarupstrandcamping.dk]** S fr Nyborg take 163 twds Svendborg; after 6.5km turn L sp Tårup. In 2.7km turn L sp Tårup Strand. Site 1.5km on R. Med, mkd pitch, terr; htd wc; chem disp; mv service pnt; fam bthrm; shwrs DKK5; EHU (6-10A) DKK26; lndry; kiosk; playgrnd; shgl beach; lake; TV; 70% statics; games rm; wifi; phone; dogs; adv bkg; quiet; poss cr high ssn; Ccard acc; CKE/CCI. "Quiet family site; excel views of bdge; fishing; excel site." 4 Apr-21 Sep. DKK 222 2014*

⊞ **ODENSE** *C3* (5km S Rural) *55.36966, 10.39316* **DCU Camping Odense, Odensevej 102, 5260 Odense [tel 66 11 47 02; fax 65 91 73 43; odense@dcu.dk; www.camping-odense.dk]** Exit E20 junc 50 foll sp 'centrum' (Stenlosevej). After rndabt site on L just after 3rd set traff lts. Ent to R of petrol stn. Lge, pt shd; mkd pitch; htd wc; chem disp; mv service pnt; fam bthrm; shwrs inc; EHU (10A) DKK30; gas; lndry; shop; rest 1.5km; playgrnd; pool; TV rm; dogs DKK15; phone; bus; Eng spkn; adv bkg; quiet; ccard acc (surcharge); CKE/CCI. "Hans Christian Andersen's hse; many attractions; excel, friendly, family-run site; busy high ssn & facs stretched; easy bus access to town cent; lovely, easy cycle rte into town cent; gd san fac; pitches tight for larger units; excel." ♦ DKK 380 2016*

ODENSE *C3* (11km W Rural) *55.3894, 10.2475* **Campingpladsen Blommenslyst, Middelfartvej 494, 5491 Blommenslyst [tel/fax 65 96 76 41; info@blommelyst-camping.dk; www.blommenslyst-camping.dk]** Exit E20 onto 161 (junc 53); sp 'Odense/Blommenslyst', site on R after 2km; lge pink Camping sp on side of house. Sm, pt sl, shd; htd wc; chem disp; mv service pnt; shwrs DKK5; EHU (4A) DKK30; lndry; shop; café 500m; playgrnd; sm lake; some statics; dogs DKK10; bus; Eng spkn; adv bkg hg ssn; some rd noise; CKE/CCI. "Picturesque setting round sm lake; gd, clean facs; welcoming owners; frequent bus to town outside site; excel." ♦ 5 Jan-20 Dec. DKK 168 2017*

RAGELEJE see Gilleleje *D2*

⊞ **RANDERS** *B2* (8km SW Rural) *56.44984, 9.95287* **Randers City Camp, Hedevej 9, Fladbro, 8920 Randers [tel/fax 45 29 47 36 55; info@randerscitycamp.dk; www.randerscitycamp.dk]** Take exit 40 fr E45 & turn twd Randers. Approx 100m fr m'way turn R at traff lts dir Langå. Site clearly sp in 3km & also sp fr rd 16. Lge, mkd pitch, terr, pt shd; htd wc; chem disp; mv service pnt; fam bthrm; shwrs inc; EHU (10A) DKK35; lndry (inc dryer); shop; BBQ; cooking facs; playgrnd; htd covrd pool; fishing; games rm; golf adj; wifi; TV; 50% statics; dogs DKK10; phone; bus 0.5km; twin axles; poss cr; Eng spkn; adv bkg; quiet; ccard acc; red LS; CKE/CCI. "On heather hills with view of Nørreå valley; rec arr early for pitch with view; golf course; Randers tropical zoo; ideal for walkers, cyclist & runners; fishing; gd." ♦ DKK 239 2017*

⊞ **RIBE** *B3* (2km SE Rural) *55.31725, 8.75952* **Parking Storkesøen, Haulundvej 164, 6760 Ribe [tel 75 41 04 11; fax 41 08 57; info@storkesoen.dk; www.storkesoen.dk]** Fr S on rte 11, turn R at 1st rndabt onto rte 24 & R at next rndabt. Site 100m on R, sp fishing. Fr S on rte 24, at 1st rndabt after rlwy turn L, site 200m on R. M'vans only - check in at fishing shop on R. Sm, all hdstg, unshd; wc; own san; chem disp; shwrs (2K); EHU (5A/16A) inc; fishing shop; snacks; lake fishing. "Picturesque, quiet site o'looking fishing lakes; walking dist Denmark's oldest city; m'vans & c'vans acc, ideal NH; vg facs." DKK 140 2016*

⊞ **RIBE** *B3* (2.4km NNW Rural) *55.34115, 8.76506* **Ribe Camping, Farupvej 2, 6760 Ribe [tel 75 41 07 77; fax 75 41 00 01; info@ribecamping.dk; www.ribecamping.dk]** Fr S foll A11 by-pass W of Ribe to traff lts N of town; turn W off A11 at traff lts; site 500m on R. Fr N (Esbjerg ferry) to Ribe, turn R at traff lts sp Farup. Site on R, sp. Lge, pt shd; htd wc; chem disp; mv service pnt; fam bthrm; some serviced pitches; shwrs DKK8; EHU (10A) DKK35; gas; lndry; shop; snacks; cooking facs; playgrnd; htd pool; games rm; internet; TV; 10% statics; dogs DKK15; phone; Quickstop o'night facs; poss cr; adv bkg; quiet; ccard acc (transaction charge); CKE/CCI. "Ribe oldest town in Denmark; much historical interest; helpful, friendly staff; well-run; excel, modern san facs; conv Esbjerg ferry." ♦ DKK 271 2016*

RINGKOBING *A2* (5km E Rural) *56.08856, 8.31659* **Ringkøbing Camping, Herningvej 105, 6950 Ringkøbing [tel/fax 97 32 04 20; info@ringkobingcamping.dk; www.ringkøbingcamping.dk]** Take rd 15 fr Ringkøbing dir Herning, site on L. Med, hdg/mkd pitch, pt shd; wc; chem disp; mv service pnt; shwrs DKK2; EHU (10A) DKK29; gas; lndry; shop; sand beach 3km; playgrnd; TV; phone; dogs DKK10; Quickstop o'night facs; poss cr; adv bkg; quiet. "Beautiful site in mixed forest; friendly welcome; excel facs; gd walks; 3km to fjord; 14km to sea." ♦ 1 Apr-30 Sep. DKK 226 2016*

RODOVRE see København *D3*

ROMO ISLAND *A3* **Sites on Rømø Island are listed together at the end of the Denmark site entry pages.**

ROSKILDE *D3* (4km N Rural) *55.67411, 12.07955* **Roskilde Camping, Baunehøjvej 7-9, 4000 Veddelev [tel 46 75 79 96; fax 46 75 44 26; mail@roskildecamping.dk; www.roskildecamping.dk]** Leave rd 21/23 at junc 11 & turn N on rd 6 sp Hillerød. Turn R onto rd 02 (E ring rd); then rejoin 6; (watch for camping sp). At traff lts with camping sp turn L twds city & foll site sp. Lge, mkd pitch, pt sl, pt shd; htd wc; own san; chem disp; fam bthrm; shwrs DKK6; EHU (10A) DKK30; gas; lndry; shop; rest; playgrnd; shgl beach; watersports; games rm; TV; wifi; poss cr high ssn; Eng spkn; adv bkg; quiet; ccard acc (surcharge); CKE/CCI. "Beautiful views over fjord; nr Viking Ship Museum (a must) - easy parking; beautiful Cathedral; excel rest & shop open 0800-2000; bus service to stn, frequent trains to Copenhagen; ltd flat pitches; lovely site; immac, new state of the art san facs block with card for ent (2014); v welcoming & helpful staff." 31 Mar-23 Sep. DKK 225 2014*

RY *B2* (4km NW Rural) *56.10388, 9.74555* **Birkede Camping, Lyngvej 14, 8680 Ry [tel 86 89 13 55; fax 86 89 03 13; info@birkhede.dk; www.birkhede.dk]** Fr S on rd 52 exit onto rd 445 to Ry, then foll sp N on rd dir Laven. Turn R in 1km to site on lakeside. Clearly sp in cent of Ry. Lge, mkd pitch, pt sl, pt shd; wc; chem disp; mv service pnt; fam bthrm; shwrs DKK6; EHU (10A) metered + conn fee; gas; lndry (inc dryer); shop; rest; bar; cooking facs; playgrnd; htd pool; bike & boat hire; fishing; games rm; golf 10km; wifi; TV rm; dogs; phone; poss cr; Eng spkn; adv bkg; CKE/CCI. "Gd site." ♦ 11 Apr-21 Sep. DKK 260 2014*

RY *B2* (7km NW Rural) *56.12421, 9.71055* **Terrassen Camping, Himmelbjergvej 9a, 8600 Laven [tel 86 84 13 01; fax 86 84 16 55; info@terrassen.dk; www.terrassen.dk]** In Silkeborg take Åarhus rd 15 to Linå. In Linå turn R for Laven. In Laven turn R parallel to lake; site up hill on R in 300m. Sharp turn R into ent. Lge, terr, pt shd; wc; chem disp; mv service pnt; fam bthrm; sauna; shwrs DKK7; EHU (10A) DKK32; gas; lndry (inc dryer); rest adj; snacks 1.5km; shops adj; playgrnd; htd pool; fishing; lake sw; games area; pet zoo; wifi; entmnt; TV rm; 15% statics; dogs DKK15; phone; poss cr; adv bkg; ccard acc; quiet. "Excel views of lake & woods; British owner; Jutland's lake district." ♦ 11 Apr-14 Sep. DKK 268 2014*

SAEBY *C1* (3km N Coastal) *57.35498, 10.51026* **Hedebo Strandcamping, Frederikshavnsvej 108, 9300 Sæby [tel 98 46 14 49; fax 98 40 13 13; info@hedebocamping.dk; www.hedebocamping.dk]** Sp on rd 180. Lge, hdg/mkd pitch, unshd; htd wc; chem disp; mv service pnt; fam bthrm; shwrs DKK5; EHU (10A) DKK40; lndry (inc dryer); shop; rest, snacks; bar; BBQ; cooking facs; playgrnd; htd pool; beach adj; wifi; 60% statics; dogs; phone; bus adj; poss cr; Eng spkn; adv bkg; quiet; CKE/CCI. 31 Mar-7 Sep. DKK 250 2016*

DENMARK

⊞ **SAEBY** *C1* (3.7km N Coastal) *57.36000, 10.50861* **Svalereden Camping And Hytteby, Frederikshavnsvej 112b, 9900 Frederikshavn [tel 98 46 19 37; info@svaleredencamping.dk; svaleredencamping.dk]** Take coastal rte 180, exit 13 and 12. Site bet Frederikshavn & Saeby. Med; htd wc; fam bthrm; shwrs inc; EHU (16A); lndry (inc dryer); shop; BBQ; playgrnd; beach; games area; wifi; tv rm; dogs; bus; twin axles; Eng spkn; adv bkg; quiet; ccard acc; red LS; CKE/CCI. "Conv for Fredrerikshavn-Gothenburg ferry; outstanding san facs; excel." ♦ DKK 280 2017*

SAKSKOBING *C3* (750m W Urban) *54.79840, 11.64070* **Sakskøbing Camping, Saxes Allé 15, 4990 Sakskøbing [tel 45 54 70 45 66 or 45 54 70 47 57; fax 54 70 70 90; sax@sport.dk; www.saxcamping.dk]** N fr Rødby exit E47 at Sakskøbing junc 46, turn L twd town: at x-rds turn R. In 300m turn R into Saxes Allé, site sp. Med, hdg/mkd pitch, pt shd; wc; mv service pnt; fam bthrm; shwrs; EHU (6A) DKK30; gas; lndry; shop; rest adj; cooking facs; sand beach 15km; pool 100m; fishing; phone; adv bkg; quiet. "Conv for Rødby-Puttgarden ferry; gd touring base; excel site in pretty area; v welcoming & friendly." 15 Mar-28 Sep. DKK 194 2014*

⊞ **SILKEBORG** *B2* (12km W Rural) *56.14869, 9.39697* **DCU Hesselhus Camping, Moselundsvej 28, Funder, 8600 Silkeborg [tel 86 86 50 66; fax 86 86 59 49; hesselhus@dcu.dk; www.camping-hesselhus.dk]** Take rd 15 W fr Silkeborg twd Herning; after 6km bear R, sp Funder Kirkeby, foll camping sps for several km to site. Lge, mkd pitch, pt shd; wc; chem disp; mv service pnt; shwrs inc; fam bthrm; shwrs; EHU DKK35; gas; lndry; supmkt; snacks; playgrnd; htd pool; TV; 40% statics; dogs DKK20; phone; adv bkg; quiet; 10% red CKE/CCI. "Great family site; beautiful natural surroundings; 1 hr fr Legoland; busy at w'ends." ♦ DKK 144 2016*

"I need an on-site restaurant"

We do our best to make sure site information is correct, but it is always best to check any must-have facilities are still available or will be open during your visit.

⊞ **SINDAL** *C1* (2km W Rural) *57.46785, 10.17851* **Sindal Camping, Hjørringvej 125, 9870 Sindal [tel 98 93 65 30; fax 98 93 69 30; info@sindal-camping.dk; www.sindal-camping.dk]** On rte 35 due W of Frederikshavn on S side of rd. Lge, hdg/mkd pitch, pt shd; wc; chem disp; mv service pnt; fam bthrm; shwrs; EHU (16A) metered; gas; lndry (inc dryer); shop; BBQ; playgrnd; pool; paddling pool; sand beach 11km; games area; golf 3km; bike hire; wifi; TV; 50% statics; dogs DKK10; phone; poss cr; twin axles; Eng spkn; adv bkg; quiet; red for LS, long stay & snrs; CKE/CCI. "Train & bus v conv; lovely beaches 30 mins; excel modern san facs; helpful owners; hg rec; excel." ♦ DKK 220 2017*

SKAGEN *C1* (13km SW Rural) *57.65546, 10.45008* **Råbjerg Mile Camping, Kandestedvej 55, 9990 Skagen [tel 98 48 75 00; fax 98 48 75 88; info@raabjergmilecamping.dk; www.990.dk]** Fr rd 40 Frederiskshavn-Skagen, foll sp Hulsig-Råbjerg Mile, site sp. Lge, hdg/mkd pitch, unshd; wc; chem disp; fam bthrm; shwrs DKK2; EHU (10A) DKK30; lndry; shop; rest 1km; snacks; bar; cooking facs; playgrnd; htd pool; paddling pool; beach 1.5km; tennis; bike hire; golf 1.5km; TV; 25% statics; dogs DKK10; phone; poss cr; Eng spkn; adv bkg; ccard acc; CKE/CCI. "Gd touring base N tip of Denmark; gd cycling." ♦ 24 Mar-30 Sep. DKK 354 (CChq acc) 2013*

SONDER STENDERUP **see Kolding** *B3*

SORO *C3* (2km NW Urban) *55.44673, 11.54628* **Sorø Camping, Udbyhøjvej 10, 4180 Sorø [tel 57 83 02 02; fax 57 82 11 02; info@soroecamping.dk; www.soroecamping.dk]** On rd 150 fr Korsør, 300m bef town name board turn L at camping sp, site in 100m on lakeside. Med, pt sl, pt shd; wc; chem disp; mv service pnt; fam bthrm; shwrs DKK2 per min; EHU (10A) DKK30; lndry; shop; rest 500m; snacks 1km; cooking facs; playgrnd; lake sw adj; fishing; boating; TV; some statics; dogs free; phone; Eng spkn; adv bkg; quiet; ccard acc; CKE or CCI ess. "Conv Copenhagen, friendly owners; busy site; clean facs - up to CC standands." ♦ 1 Mar-31 Oct. DKK 180 2013*

STROBY **see Koge** *D3*

SVENDBORG *C3* (7km SE Coastal) *55.0537, 10.6304* **Svendborg Sund Camping (formerly Vindebyøre), Vindebyørevej 52, Tåsinge, 5700 Svendborg [tel 21 72 09 13 or 62 22 54 25; fax 62 22 54 26; maria@svendborgsund-camping.dk; www.svendborgsund-camping.dk]** Cross bdge fr Svendborg (dir Spodsbjerg) to island of Tåsinge on rd 9; at traff lts over bdge turn L, then immed 1st L to Vindeby, thro vill, L at sp to site. Med, pt sl, pt shd; htd wc; chem disp; mv service pnt; fam bthrm; shwrs; EHU DKK30; lndry; shop; snacks; cooking facs; BBQ; playgrnd; sand beach; bike & boat hire; entmnt; internet; TV; some statics; dogs DKK10; phone; o'night area; poss cr; adv bkg; quiet; ccard acc; CKE/CCI. "V helpful owners; swipe card for facs; excel touring base & conv ferries to islands; beautiful views; immac, excel site; narr sandy beach." ♦ 18 Mar-27 Sep. DKK 225 2015*

TARM *A2* (1.5km S Rural) *55.89309, 8.51278* **Tarm Camping, Vardevej 79, 6880 Tarm [tel 30 12 66 35; fax 97 37 30 15; tarm.camping@pc.dk; www.tarm-camping.dk]** Fr rd 11 S of Tarm take exit twds Tarm; immed turn R, site on L in 500m, sp. Med, mkd pitch, pt shd; wc; chem disp; mv service pnt; fam bthrm; shwrs DKK2; EHU (10A) DKK30; gas; lndry; snacks; cooking facs; playgrnd; pool; some statics; dogs; phone; Eng spkn; adv bkg; some rd noise; CKE/CCI. "Friendly & helpul staff; vg." ♦ 27 Mar-4 Oct. DKK 168 2015*

⊞ **THISTED** *B2* (1km SE Coastal) *56.95226, 8.71286* **Thisted Camping, Iversensvej 3, 7700 Thisted [tel 97 92 16 35; fax 97 92 52 34; mail@thisted-camping.dk; www.thisted-camping.dk]** On side of fjord on o'skts of Thisted, sp fr rd 11. Med, pt sl, unshd; wc; chem disp; mv service pnt; fam bthrm; shwrs DKK5; EHU (16A) DKK30; gas; lndry; shop; bar; cooking facs; BBQ; playgrnd; pool; fishing; games rm; TV; wifi; dogs; Eng spkn; adv bkg; quiet; CKE/CCI. "Attractive views fr some pitches; nice, friendly, helpful, well run site; grnd soft aft heavy rain; easy walk to town; gd facs." ♦ DKK 240 2016*

THORSMINDE *A2* (500m N Coastal) *56.37626, 8.12251* **Thorsminde Camping, Klitrosevej 4, 6990 Thorsminde [tel 20 45 19 76; mail@thorsmindecamping.dk; www.thorsmindecamping.dk]** On rd 16/28 to Ulfborg, turn W twd coast & Husby Klitplantage. Turn N onto rd 181 to Thorsminde, 1st turn R past shops, site sp. Lge, unshd; wc; chem disp; mv service pnt; fam bthrm; sauna; shwrs; EHU (10A) DKK30; lndry; shop; rest; cooking facs; playgrnd; covrd pool; beach 300m; TV; few statics; phone; poss cr; adv bkg; quiet. "Pleasant site; helpful staff; excel sea fishing." ♦ 8 Apr-23 Oct. DKK 200 2016*

⊞ **TONDER** *B3* (5km W Rural) *54.93746, 8.80008* **Møgeltønder Camping, Sønderstrengvej 2, Møgeltonder, 6270 Tønder [tel 74 73 84 60; fax 74 73 80 43; www.mogeltondercamping.dk]** N fr Tønder thro Møgeltønder (avoid cobbled main rd by taking 2nd turning sp Møgeltønder) site sp on L in 200m outside vill. Lge, mkd pitch; pt shd; htd wc; chem disp; mv service pnt; fam bthrm; shwrs DKK2 (per 2 mins); EHU (10A) DKK25; lndry (inc dryer); shop; snacks; BBQ; cooking facs; playgrnd; htd pool; sand beach 10km; internet; TV rm; 25% statics; dogs DKK10; phone; poss v cr; Eng spkn; adv bkg; quiet; ccard not acc; CKE/CCI. "Gd cycle paths; beautiful & romantic little vill adj; Ribe worth visit (43km); friendly owner." ♦ DKK 219 2014*

VAMMEN see Viborg *B2*

VEJERS STRAND *A3* (12km S Coastal) *55.54403, 8.13386* **Hvidbjerg Strand Feriepark, Hvidbjerg Strandvej 27, 6857 Blåvand [tel 75 27 90 40; fax 75 27 80 28; info@hvidbjerg.dk; www.hvidbjerg.dk]** Exit rd 11 at Varde on minor rd, sp Blåvand, turn L at sp to Hvidbjerg Strand 2km; site 1km on L. V lge, hdg pitch, pt shd; wc; chem disp; mv service pnt; fam bthrm; serviced pitches; shwrs inc; EHU (6A) inc; gas; lndry; supmkt; rest, snacks; bar; cooking facs; playgrnd; htd, covrd pool; sand beach; tennis; games area; entmnt; TV; 10% statics; dogs DKK30; phone; adv bkg; quiet; ccard acc. "Superb facs; excel family site; young groups not acc." ♦ 7 Apr-22 Oct. DKK 453 2014*

VEJLE *B3* (2km ENE Urban) *55.7151, 9.5611* **Vejle City Camping, Helligkildevej 5, 7100 Vejle [tel 75 82 33 35; fax 75 82 33 54; info@vejlecitycamping.dk; www.vejlecitycamping.dk]** Exit E45 m'way at Vejle N. Turn L twd town. In 250m turn L at camping sp & 'stadion' sp. Med, pt sl, pt shd; wc; chem disp; mv service pnt; fam bthrm; shwrs; EHU (6-10A) DKK30; lndry; shop on site & 1km; snacks; cooking facs; playgrnd; sand beach 2km; TV; dogs DKK5; phone; poss cr; Eng spkn; adv bkg; quiet; 25% red long stays; ccard acc; red snr citizens. "Site adj woods & deer enclosure; quickstop o'night facs; walk to town; conv Legoland (26km); lovely well kept site; helpful friendly staff." ♦ 19 Mar-25 Sep. DKK 255 2016*

⊞ **VIBORG** *B2* (15km N Rural/Coastal) *56.53452, 9.33117* **Hjarbæk Fjord Camping, Hulager 2, Hjarbæk, 8831 Løgstrup [tel 86 64 23 09; fax 86 64 25 91; info@hjarbaek.dk; www.hjarbaek.dk]** Take A26 (Viborg to Skive) to Løgstrup, turn R (N) to Hjarbæk, keep R thro vill, site sp. Lge, mkd pitch, terr, pt shd; htd wc; chem disp; fam bthrm; shwrs inc; EHU metered; gas; lndry (inc dryer); shop; rest; bar; cooking facs; BBQ; playgrnd; pool; sand beach adj; lake fishing; wifi; TV; 3% statics; phone; dogs DKK10; quiet; Eng spkn; adv bkg; ccard acc; red snr citizens; CKE/CCI. "Friendly & well-run; gd views; close to attractive vill & harbour." ♦ DKK 299 (CChq acc) 2014*

⊞ **VINDERUP** *B2* (6.7km ESE Rural) *56.45901, 8.86918* **Sevel Camping, Halallé 6, Sevel, 7830 Vinderup [tel 97 44 85 50; fax 97 44 85 51; mail@sevelcamping.dk; www.sevelcamping.dk]** Fr Struer on rd 513. In Vinderup L nr church then R past Vinderup Camping. Site sp on R on edge of vill. Sm, hdg pitch, pt sl, pt shd; htd wc; chem disp; mv service pnt; fam bthrm; shwrs DKK5; EHU (16A) DKK30; lndry; shop 100m; cooking facs; rest 1km; snacks; playgrnd; 10% statics; dogs DKK6; Eng spkn; adv bkg; quiet; ccard acc; CKE/CCI. "Family-run site; pleasant, helpful owners; picturesque, historic area." ♦ DKK 182 2016*

VIPPEROD see Holbæk *D3*

⊞ **VORDINGBORG** *D3* (3.6km W Urban/Coastal) *55.00688, 11.87509* **Ore Strand Camping, Orevej 145, 4760 Vordingborg [tel 55 77 8822; mail@orestrandcamping.dk; www.orestrandcamping.dk]** Fr E55/47 exit junc 41 onto rd 59 to Vordingborg 7km. Rd conts as 153 sp Sakskøbing alongside rlwy. Turn R at site sp into Ore, site on L. Med, pt shd; wc; chem disp; mv service pnt; fam bthrm; shwrs; EHU (6A) DKK30; lndry; shop; cooking facs; playgrnd; shgl beach adj; phone; adv bkg; poss cr; quiet; Eng spkn; ccard acc. "Gd touring cent; fine views if nr water; interesting old town." DKK 140 2015*

*Last year of report

AERO ISLAND

⊞ **MARSTAL** *C3* (2km S Urban/Coastal) *54.84666, 10.51823* **Marstal Camping, Eghovedvej 1, 5960 Marstal [tel 63 52 63 69; fax 62 53 36 40; mail@marstalcamping.dk; www.marstalcamping.dk]** Fr Ærøskobing ferry to E end of Ærø Island, thro town of Marstal & turn R at harbour twd sailing club; site adj to club. Med, mkd pitch, pt shd; wc; chem disp; mv service pnt; fam bthrm; shwrs DKK5; EHU (16A) DKK48; lndry (inc dryer); shop; rest, snacks, bar 500m; BBQ; playgrnd; TV; 10% statics; dogs DKK15, phone; poss cr; adv bkg; poss noisy; ccard acc; red LS/CKE/CCI. ♦ DKK 160 2016*

BORNHOLM ISLAND

GUDHJEM *A1* (2km S Coastal) *55.19566, 14.98602* **Sannes Familiecamping, Melstedvej 39, 3760 Melsted [tel 56 48 52 11; fax 56 48 52 52; sannes@familiecamping.dk; www.familiecamping.dk]** SW fr Gudhjem on rd 158, in 2km site on L. Pass other sites. NB: Bornholm Is can be reached by ferry fr Sassnitz in Germany or Ystad in Sweden. Med, mkd pitch, hdstg, terr, pt shd; wc; chem disp; mv service pnt; sauna; shwrs; EHU (6A) DKK30; gas; lndry; shop & supmkt 1km; rest 500m; playgrnd; htd pool; paddling pool; sand beach adj; fishing; fitness rm; bike hire; wifi; TV rm; 10% statics; dogs; phone; Eng spkn; adv bkg; quiet; ccard acc; CKE/CCI. "Friendly & helpful staff; gd cycle paths in area; bus service fr site." ♦ 1 Apr-18 Sep. DKK 270 2016*

NEXO *A1* (5.5km S Coastal) *55.02895, 15.11130* **FDM Camping Balka Strand, Klynevej 6, Snogebæk, 3730 Nexø [tel 56 48 80 74; fax 56 48 86 75; c-balka@fdm.dk; www.balka.fdmcamping.dk]** Fr ferry at Rønne on rd 38 to Nexø, foll sp to site N of Snogebæk. Lge, mkd pitch, pt shd; htd wc; chem disp; mv service pnt; fam bthrm; shwrs inc; EHU (6A) DKK49; lndry; shop; supmkt 500m; rest, snacks 500m; BBQ; cooking facs; playgrnd; sand beach 200m; fishing 500m; windsurfing 1km; bike hire; games area; golf 5km; internet; TV; some statics; dogs DKK15; adv bkg; quiet; ccard acc. "Superb beach; vg touring base Bornholm Is." ♦ 25 Apr-13 Sep. DKK 217 2016*

RONNE *A1* (1km S Coastal) *55.08978, 14.70565* **Galløkken Camping, Strandvejen 4, 3700 Rønne [tel 56 95 23 20; info@gallokken.dk; www.gallokken.dk]** Fr Rønne cent foll dir airport, site well sp. Med, hdg/mkd pitch, pt shd; htd wc; chem disp; mv service pnt; fam bthrm; private san facs avail; shwrs; EHU (13A) DKK31; lndry (inc dryer); shop; supmkt 500m; rest 600m; BBQ; cooking facs; playgrnd; sand beach 200m; tennis 1km; bike hire; games rm; wifi; TV; some statics; dogs; adv bkg; quiet. "Lovely location; gd, modern san facs." ♦ 1 May-31 Aug. DKK 200 2016*

LANGELAND ISLAND

⊞ **LOHALS** *C3* (400m W Urban) *55.13383, 10.90578* **Lohals Camping, Birkevej 11, 5953 Lohals [tel 62 55 14 60; mail@lohalscamping.dk; www.lohalscamping.dk]** On island of Langeland. Cross to Rudkøbing, fr island of Tåsinge, then 28km to N of island (only 1 main rd); site in middle of vill nr ferry to Sjælland Island. Med, shd; wc; chem disp; mv service pnt; fam bthrm; shwrs; EHU (10A) DKK35; gas in vill; lndry; shop; rest, snacks 200m; playgrnd; htd pool; paddling pool; sand beach 1km; boat & bike hire; fishing; tennis; games area; TV; some statics; dogs free; phone; adv bkg; quiet. "Conv ferry (Lohals-Korsor) 500m." ♦ DKK 210 2016*

"Satellite navigation makes touring much easier"

Remember most sat navs don't know if you're towing or in a larger vehicle – always use yours alongside maps and site directions.

ROMO ISLAND

⊞ **HAVNEBY** *A3* (2km N Coastal) *55.09883, 8.54395* **Kommandørgårdens Camping, Havnebyvej 201, 6792 Rømø [tel 74 75 51 22; fax 74 75 59 22; info@kommandoergaarden.dk; www.kommandoergaarden.dk]** Turn S after exit causeway fr mainland onto rd 175 sp Havneby. Site on L in 8km. V lge, mkd pitch, pt shd; htd wc; chem disp; mv service pnt; fam bthrm; shwrs DKK7 (5 mins); EHU (10A) DKK35; gas; lndry; shop; rest, snacks; playgrnd; htd pool; paddling pool; sand beach 1km; tennis; wellness & beauty cent on site; TV; 30% statics; dogs DKK20; phone; poss cr; adv bkg; quiet. "Family-owned site; ferry to German island of Sylt." ♦ DKK 240 2016*

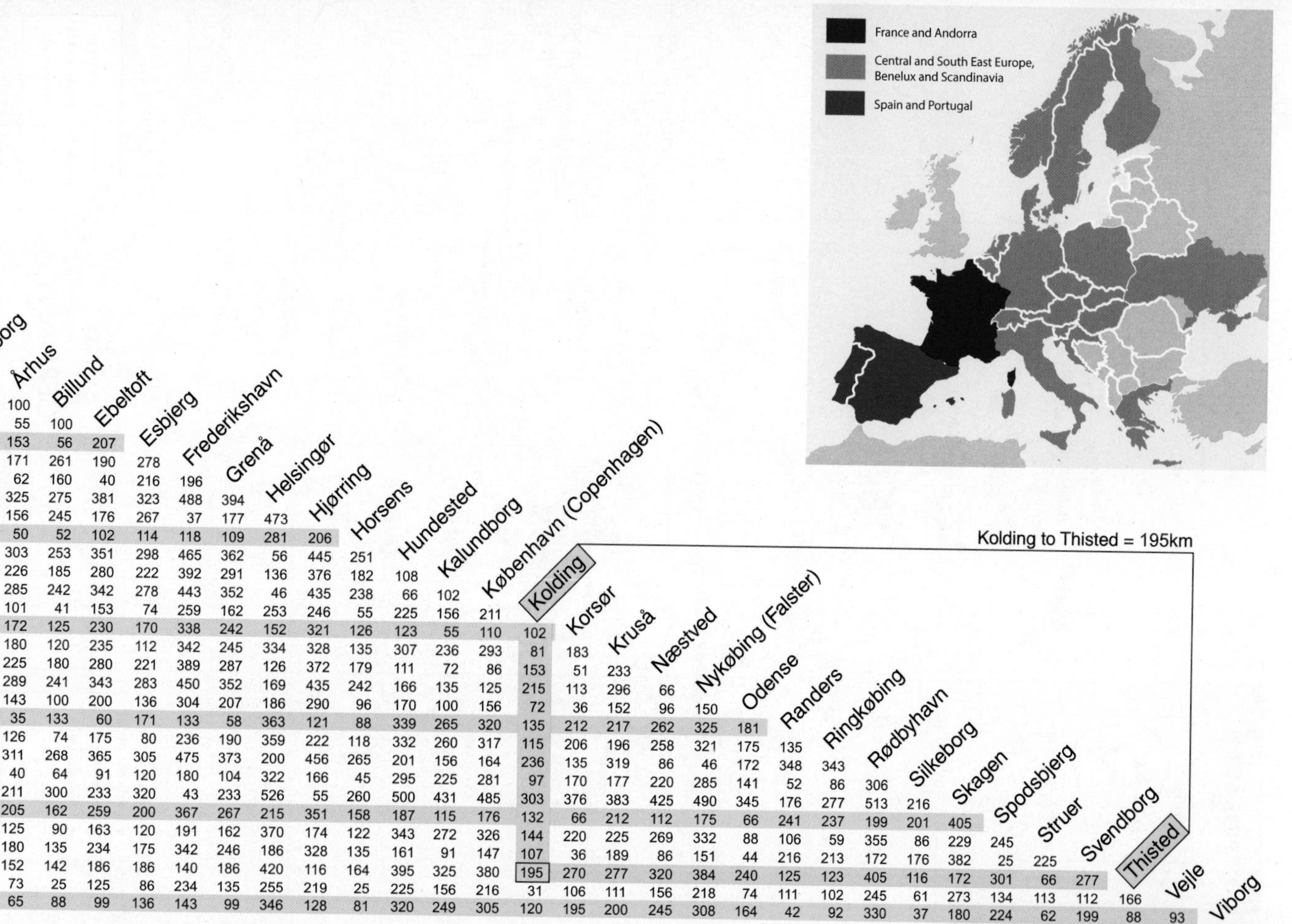

	Aalborg	Århus	Billund	Ebeltoft	Esbjerg	Frederikshavn	Grenå	Helsingør	Hjørring	Horsens	Hundested	Kalundborg	København (Copenhagen)	Kolding	Korsør	Kruså	Næstved	Nykøbing (Falster)	Odense	Randers	Ringkøbing	Rødbyhavn	Silkeborg	Skagen	Spodsbjerg	Struer	Svendborg	Thisted	Vejle
Århus	112
Billund	193	100
Ebeltoft	137	55	100
Esbjerg	216	153	56	207
Frederikshavn	66	171	261	190	278
Grenå	137	62	160	40	216	196
Helsingør	422	325	275	381	323	488	394
Hjørring	51	156	245	176	267	37	177	473
Horsens	162	50	52	102	114	118	109	281	206
Hundested	396	303	253	351	298	465	362	56	445	251
Kalundborg	325	226	185	280	222	392	291	136	376	182	108
København (Copenhagen)	383	285	242	342	278	443	352	46	435	238	66	102
Kolding	200	101	41	153	74	259	162	253	246	55	225	156	211
Korsør	270	172	125	230	170	338	242	152	321	126	123	55	110	102
Kruså	283	180	120	235	112	342	245	334	328	135	307	236	293	81	183
Næstved	320	225	180	280	221	389	287	126	372	179	111	72	86	153	51	233
Nykøbing (Falster)	387	289	241	343	283	450	352	169	435	242	166	135	125	215	113	296	66
Odense	241	143	100	200	136	304	207	186	290	96	170	100	156	72	36	152	96	150
Randers	76	35	133	60	171	133	58	363	121	88	339	265	320	135	212	217	262	325	181
Ringkøbing	170	126	74	175	80	236	190	359	222	118	332	260	317	115	206	196	258	321	175	135
Rødbyhavn	410	311	268	365	305	475	373	200	456	265	201	156	164	236	135	319	86	46	172	348	343
Silkeborg	114	40	64	91	120	180	104	322	166	45	295	225	281	97	170	177	220	285	141	52	86	306
Skagen	103	211	300	233	320	43	233	526	55	260	500	431	485	303	376	383	425	490	345	176	277	513	216
Spodsbjerg	301	205	162	259	200	367	267	215	351	158	187	115	176	132	66	212	112	175	66	241	237	199	201	405
Struer	126	125	90	163	120	191	162	370	174	122	343	272	326	144	220	225	269	332	88	106	59	355	86	229	245
Svendborg	280	180	135	234	175	342	246	186	328	135	161	91	147	107	36	189	86	151	44	216	213	172	176	382	25	225
Thisted	91	152	142	186	186	140	186	420	116	164	395	325	380	195	270	277	320	384	240	125	123	405	116	172	301	66	277
Vejle	171	73	25	125	86	234	135	255	219	25	225	156	216	31	106	111	156	218	74	111	102	245	61	273	134	113	112	166
Viborg	83	65	88	99	136	143	99	346	128	81	320	249	305	120	195	200	245	308	164	42	92	330	37	180	224	62	199	88	93

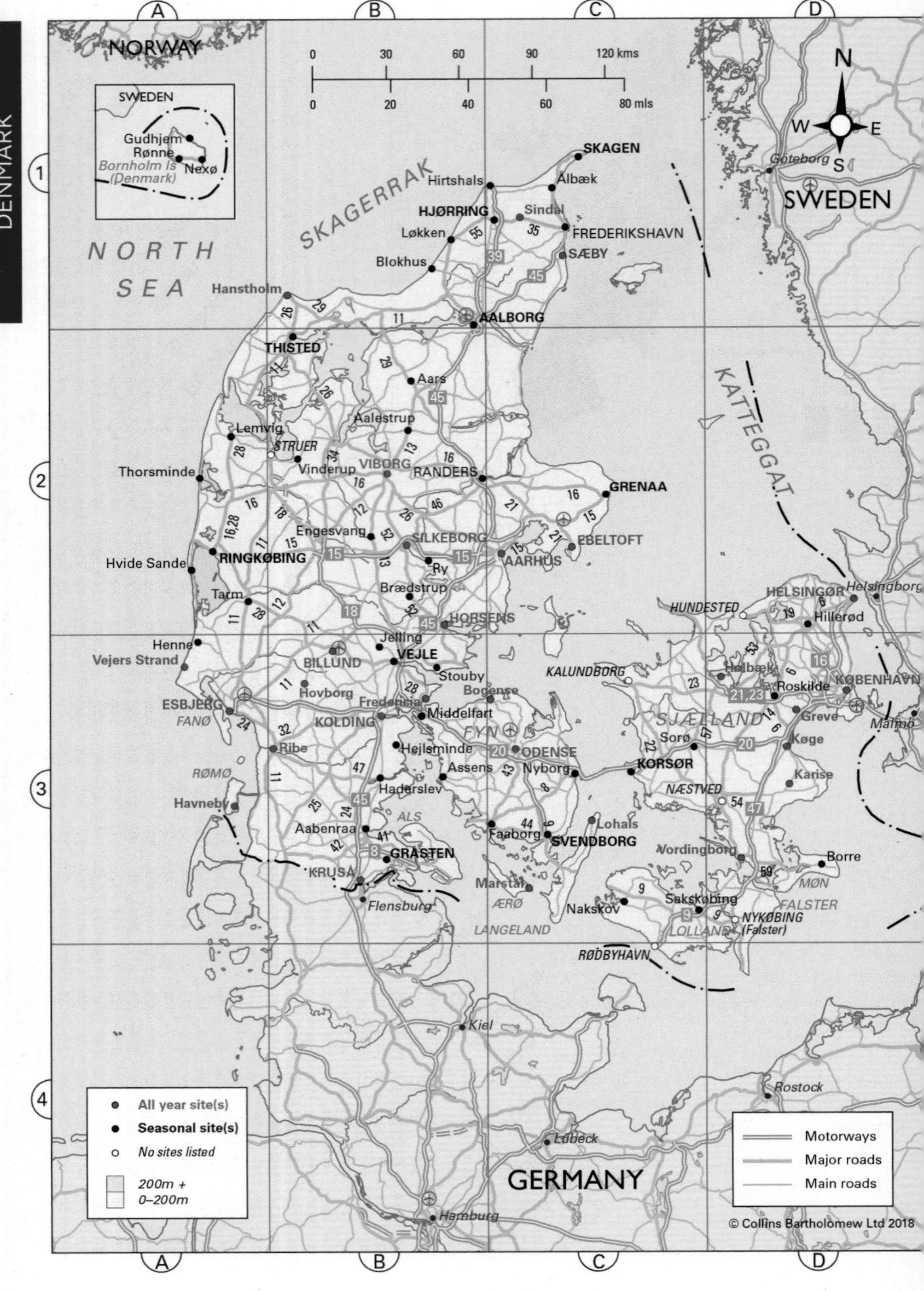
A
B
C
D
1
2
3
4
NORWAY
SWEDEN
Gudhjem
Rønne
Nexø
Bornholm Is
(Denmark)
0
30
60
90
120 kms
0
20
40
60
80 mls
N
W
E
S
Göteborg
SWEDEN
NORTH
SEA
SKAGERRAK
KATTEGAT
SKAGEN
Ålbæk
Hirtshals
HJØRRING
Sindal
FREDERIKSHAVN
Løkken
SÆBY
Blokhus
Hanstholm
AALBORG
THISTED
Aars
Aalestrup
Lemvig
STRUER
Vinderup
VIBORG
RANDERS
Thorsminde
GRENAA
Engesvang
SILKEBORG
EBELTOFT
RINGKØBING
Hvide Sande
Ry
AARHUS
Brædstrup
Tarm
HORSENS
HUNDESTED
HELSINGØR
Helsingborg
Hillerød
Henne
Jelling
Vejers Strand
VEJLE
BILLUND
Stouby
KALUNDBORG
Holbæk
Hovborg
Bogense
Roskilde
KØBENHAVN
ESBJERG
Fredericia
Middelfart
KOLDING
FANØ
FYN
SJÆLLAND
Greve
Malmö
Ribe
Sorø
Køge
Hejlsminde
ODENSE
RØMØ
Assens
Nyborg
KORSØR
Haderslev
Karise
NÆSTVED
Havneby
ALS
Aabenraa
Lohals
Faaborg
SVENDBORG
GRÅSTEN
Vordingborg
Borre
KRUSÅ
Marstal
MØN
Flensburg
ÆRØ
Nakskov
Sakskøbing
FALSTER
NYKØBING
(Falster)
LANGELAND
LOLLAND
RØDBYHAVN
Kiel
Rostock
Lübeck
GERMANY
Hamburg
All year site(s)
Seasonal site(s)
No sites listed
200m +
0–200m
Motorways
Major roads
Main roads
© Collins Bartholomew Ltd 2018

Koli National Park

Welcome to Finland

Finland is a country filled with vast forests, crystal clear lakes and a diverse range of flora and fauna. With the Northern Lights visible from Lapland, the outstanding natural world is one of Finland's finest assets, with a vast, pristine wilderness that captures the imagination.

The cities of Finland are not to be missed, with vibrant atmospheres, museums, galleries, delicious restaurants and gorgeous architecture in spades.

Country highlights

Saunas are an important part of life in Finland, and have been for hundreds of years. They are used as a place to relax with friends and family and are generally sociable spaces.

Design and fashion have always been popular in Finland, with one of its most famous companies, Marimekko, a huge contributor to fashion in the 20th century.

Visit Svalbard to witness the unique spectacle of the Midnight Sun. This natural phenomenon occurs each year around the summer solstice.

Major towns and cities

- Helsinki – this capital city is a hub of shopping and architecture.
- Tempere – Finland's cultural home with theatrical, musical and literary traditions.
- Turku – Finland's oldest city and a former European City of Culture.
- Oulu – a quirky city where many technology companies, including Nokia, are based.

Attractions

- Olavinlinna Castle, Savolinna – a medieval stone fortress that houses several exhibitions.
- Lapland– This region is famous for the midnight sun and the Northern Lights.
- Repovesi National Park – a stunning natural area with plenty of walking and hiking trails.
- Temppeliaukio Kirkko, Helsinki – This church is built directly into solid rock.

Find out more

www.visitfinland.com
Tel: 0035 (0) 82 95 05 80 00 Finnish Tourism

FINLAND

Country Information

Population (approx): 5.4 million

Capital: Helsinki (population approx 620,000)

Area: 338,145 sq km

Bordered by: Norway, Sweden, Russia

Terrain: Flat, rolling, heavily forested plains interspersed with low hills and more than 60,000 lakes; one third lies within the Arctic Circle

Climate: Short, warm summers; long, very cold, dry winters; the best time to visit is between May and September

Coastline: 1,250km (excluding islands)

Highest Point: Haltiatunturi 1,328m

Languages: Finnish, Swedish

Local Time: GMT or BST + 2, ie 2 hours ahead of the UK all year

Currency: Euros divided into 100 cents; £1 = €1.13, €1 = £0.88 (November 2017)

Emergency numbers: Police 112; Fire brigade 112; Ambulance 112 (operators speak English).
Public Holidays 2018: Jan 1, 6; Mar 30; Apr 1,2; May 1, 10, 20; Jun 23; Nov 3; Dec 6, 25, 26.

School summer holidays from early June to mid-August.

Camping and Caravanning

There are around 150 campsites in Finland. Campsites are graded from 1 to 5 stars according to facilities available. Most have cabins for hire in addition to tent and caravan pitches, and most have saunas.

At some sites visitors who do not already have one must purchase a Camping Key Europe, which replaced the Camping Card Scandinavia (CCS) in 2012. The Camping Key is valid across Europe and you may purchase it for €16 (2017) on arrival at your first campsite or from local tourist offices - for more information visit www.camping.fi.

During the peak camping season from June to mid August it is advisable to make advance reservations. Prices at many campsites may double (or treble) over the midsummer holiday long weekend in June and advance booking is essential for this period. Approximately 70 campsites stay open all year.

Casual or wild camping may be allowed for a short period - one or 2 days. For longer periods, permission must be obtained from the landowner. Camping may be prohibited on public beaches and in public recreation areas where campers are often directed to special areas, many of which have facilities provided free of charge.

Cycling

Finland is good for cyclists as it is relatively flat. Most towns have a good network of cycle lanes which are indicated by traffic signs. In built up areas pavements are sometimes divided into two sections, one for cyclists and one for pedestrians. It is compulsory to wear a safety helmet.

Electricity and Gas

Current on campsites is usually between 10 and 16 amps. Plugs are round with two pins. Some sites have CEE connections.

Butane gas is not generally available and campsites and service stations do not have facilities for replacing empty foreign gas cylinders. You will need to travel with sufficient supplies to cover your needs while in Finland or purchase propane cylinders locally, plus an adaptor.
The Club does not recommend the refilling of cylinders.

Entry Formalities

Holders of British and Irish passports are permitted to stay up to three months in any six month period in Finland before a visa is required. Campsites and hotels register foreign guests with the police within 24 hours of arrival.

Medical Services

The local health system is good and Finland generally has a high level of health and hygiene. British citizens are entitled to obtain emergency health care at municipal health centres on presentation of a European Health Insurance Card (EHIC). Treatment will either be given free or for a standard fee. Dental care is provided mainly by private practitioners.

There is a fixed non-refundable charge for hospital treatment, whether for inpatient or outpatient visits. Refunds for the cost of private medical treatment may be obtained from local offices of the Sickness Insurance Department, KELA, (www.kela.fi – English option) up to six months from the date of treatment.

⊞ **JYVASKYLA** *C3* (4km N Urban) *62.25536, 25.6983* **Laajis Camping, Laajavuorentie 15, 40740 Jyväskylä [207 436 436; fax (014) 624888; laajis@laajis.fi; www.laajis.fi]** Well sp fr N on E75 & E63 fr S, site sp adj youth hostel. Med, mkd pitch, hdstg, unshd; htd wc; chem disp; mv service pnt; sauna; shwrs inc; EHU (16A) inc; lndry; shop 500m; rest, snacks; cooking facs; htd pool 3km; lake 2km; ski lift/jumps adj; wifi; entmnt; cab TV; dogs; Eng spkn; quiet; red long stay; CKE/CCI. "Facs stretched if site full; c'vans only." ♦ € 29.00 2016*

KAMMENNIEMI *B4* (7km NW Rural) *61.65423, 23.77748* **Camping Taulaniemi, Taulaniementie 357, 34240 Kämmenniemi [(03) 3785753; taulaniemi@yritys.soon.fi; www.taulaniemi.fi]** Fr Tampere take rte 9/E63 dir Jyvaskyla. In 10km take rte 338 thro Kämmenniemi. Foll sp Taulaniemi on unmade rd to lakeside site. Sm, pt sl, terr, unshd; htd wc; chem disp; mv service pnt; sauna; shwrs inc; EHU (16A) €3; lndry; shop; rest, snacks; cooking facs; playgrnd; sandy beach/lake on site; boat hire; TV; adv bkg; v quiet; CKE/CCI. "Beautiful site." 1 Jun-31 Sep. € 30.50 2017*

KARIGASNIEMI *B1* (850m NW Rural) *69.39975, 25.84278* **Camping Tenorinne, Ylätenontie 55, 99950 Karigasniemi [040 832 8487; camping@tenorinne.com; www.tenorinne.com]** N of town cent on rd 970 Karigasniemi to Utsjoki. Sm, pt shd; htd wc; chem disp; sauna; shwrs inc; EHU (16A) €4; lndry; shop, rest 200m; playgrnd; TV; some statics; no adv bkg; quiet; ccard acc; red CKE/CCI. 5 Jun-20 Sep. € 26.00 2016*

⊞ **KILPISJARVI** *A1* (4.6km SSE Rural) *69.01413, 20.88235* **Kilpisjärvi Holiday Village, Käsivarrentie 14188, 99490 Kilpisjärvi [(0400) 396684; fax (016) 537803; www.tundrea.com]** On main rd 21 almost opp g'ge, in middle of vill, sp. Lge, hdstg, unshd; htd wc; chem disp; fam bthrm; shwrs €2; EHU (10A) inc; lndry; supmkt 100m; rest, snacks; bar; BBQ; cooking facs; bus adj; Eng spkn; quiet. "Gd NH to/fr N Norwegian fjords; access to Saana Fells for gd walking/trekking; winter sports cent." ♦ € 20.00 2016*

KOKKOLA *B3* (2.5km N Coastal) *63.85500, 23.11305* **Kokkola Camping, Vanhansatamanlahti, 67100 Kokkola [tel/fax (06) 8314006; info@kokkola-camping.fi; www.kokkola-camping.fi]** Exit A8 at Kokkola onto rte 749. Site on R, sp fr town. Med, pt shd; wc; chem disp; mv service pnt; sauna; fam bthrm; shwrs inc; EHU inc; shop; snacks; cooking facs; playgrnd; sand beach adj; games area; poss cr; quiet; red CKE. "Lovely site, no adv bkg; call ahead in winter for pitching instructions." 1 Jun-31 Aug. € 30.00 2016*

⊞ **KUHMO** *C3* (3km SE Rural) *64.11898, 29.57771* **Kalevala Caravan Parking, Vainamoinen 2, 88900 Kuhmo [(086) 557111; kalevalan.kuntoutuskoti@kalevalankk.fi; www.hyvinvointisampo.fi]** Fr Kajaani on 76 turn R in ctr of town to 912 Kalevala (brown sp). After 1.6km turn L onto 912. Site on R. Obtain key fr Hyvinvoiti Sampo (old peoples home) on R as you enter. Site at bottom of hill. Hdstg (8); wc; shwr; EHU (10A). "Clean modern san facs; waste water & chem disp in town (ask recep)." € 10.00 2016*

⊞ **KUOPIO** *C3* (9km SW Rural) *62.86432, 27.64165* **Rauhalahti Holiday Centre, Kiviniementie, 70700 Kuopio [(017) 473000; fax 473099; sales@visitrauhalahti.fi; www.visitrauhalahti.fi]** Well sp fr rte 5 (E63). Site 1.5km fr E63 dir Levänen, on Lake Kallavesi. Lge, hdstg, pt sl, pt shd; htd wc; chem disp; mv service pnt; fam bthrm; sauna; shwrs inc; EHU (16A) inc; gas; lndry; shop; rest, snacks; bar; cooking facs; playgrnd; lake sw; boat trips; watersports; TV rm; ccard acc; red CKE/CCI. "Hdstg for cars, grass for van & awning; ltd services Sept-May; adv bkg rec winter." ♦ € 35.00 2016*

⊞ **KUUSAMO** *C2* (5km N Rural) *66.00143, 29.16713* **Camping Rantatropiikki, Kylpyläntie, 93600 Kuusamo/Petäjälampi [(08) 8596000; fax 8521909; myyntipalvelu.tropiikki@holidayclub.fi]** Three sites in same sm area on rd 5/E63, sp. Med, pt shd; htd wc; chem disp; mv service pnt; sauna; shwrs inc; EHU (10A) inc; lndry; pool in hotel adj; sand beach; lake sw; tennis; bike hire; internet; dogs; no adv bkg; quiet; ccard acc; CKE/CCI. "Conv falls area; LS site recep at hotel 500m past site ent." 2016*

⊞ **LAHTI** *C4* (5km N Rural) *61.01599, 25.64855* **Camping Mukkula, Ritaniemenkatu 10, 15240 Lahti [(03) 7535380; fax 7535381; tiedustelut@mukkulacamping.fi; www.mukkulacamping.fi]** Fr S on rte 4/E75 foll camping sps fr town cent. Med, pt shd; htd wc; chem disp; mv service pnt; fam bthrm; sauna; shwrs inc; EHU (10A) inc; lndry; shop 1km; rest, snacks, bar 1km; cooking facs; playgrnd; lake sw; fishing; tennis; bike hire; internet; TV; no dogs; no adv bkg; quiet; ccard acc; red CKE. "Beautiful lakeside views." ♦ 2016*

⊞ **LAHTI** *C4* (8km NW Rural) *61.01872, 25.56387* **Camping Messila, Rantatie 5, 15980 Hollola [3876290; messila@campingmessila.fi; www.campingmessila.fi]** Off A12 onto Messilantie (N), foll rd to lakeshore. Lge, hdg/mkd pitch, hdstg, pt shd; htd wc; shwrs inc; EHU (16A) €5; rest; bar; BBQ (sep area); playgrnd; sandy beach; sw adj; wifi; twin axles; poss cr; Eng spkn; quiet; CKE/CCI. "Gd sized pitches; barrier; v welcoming; well kept; next to marina; golf nrby; conv for Lahti; vg." € 26.00 2017*

LIEKSA *D3* (3km SW Rural) *63.30666, 30.00532* **Timitranniemi Camping, Timitra, 81720 Lieksa [(04) 51237166; loma@timitra.com; www.timitra.com]** Rte 73, well sp fr town on Lake Pielinen. Med, pt sl, pt shd; wc; chem disp; sauna; shwrs inc; EHU (16A) €4; lndry; shop; rest 2km; snacks; cooking facs; playgrnd; lake sw; fishing; boat & bike hire; internet; TV; ccard acc; red CKE/CCI. "Pt of recreational complex; Pielinen outdoor museum worth visit." 20 May-10 Sep. € 28.00 2016*

MERIKARVIA *B4* (3km SW Coastal) *61.84777, 21.47138* **Mericamping, Palosaarentie 67, 29900 Merikarvia [tel/fax (04) 00 719589; info@mericamping.fi; www.mericamping.fi]** Fr E8 foll sp to Merikarvia, site sp 2km W beyond main housing area. Med, mkd pitch, unshd; wc; chem disp; mv service pnt; shwrs inc; EHU €5; rest, snacks; beach adj; wifi; some cottages; Eng spkn; quiet; ccard acc; red CKE. "Vg site on water's edge; friendly, helpful staff." 1 Jun-31 Aug. € 22.00 2016*

⊞ **MUONIO** *B1* (3km S Rural) *67.93333, 23.6575* **Harrinivan Lomakeskus, Harrinivantie 35, 99300 Muonio [016 5300 300; fax 532 750; info@harriniva.fi; www.harriniva.fi]** On E8 5km S of Muonio, well sp on R going S. Sm, some hdstg, pt sl, pt shd; htd wc; chem disp; shwrs inc; en pnts (16A) €4; shop 5km; rest; bar; BBQ; playgrnd; shingle rv; wifi; twin axles; Eng spkn; adv bkg; quiet; ccard acc; CCI. "Canoe hire for white water rafting; huskies; san facs stretch in high ssn; fair." € 22.00 2014*

⊞ **NOKIA** *B4* (5km S Rural) *61.44798, 23.49247* **Camping Viinikanniemi, Viinikanniemenkatu, 37120 Nokia [(400) 420772; info@viinikanniemi.com; www.viinikanniemi.com]** SW fr Tampere on rd 12, site well sp. Med, mkd pitch, hdstg, pt sl, pt shd; htd wc; chem disp; mv service pnt; fam bathrm; shwrs inc; EHU (16A) €5.90-10; gas; lndry; shop; rest, snacks; bar; BBQ; playgrnd; sand beach & lake sw adj; boat hire; fishing; bike hire; games area; entmnt; internet; some statics; dogs; Eng spkn; adv bkg; quiet; ccard acc; CKE/CCI. "Excel site; conv Tampere." ♦ € 21.00 2016*

NURMES *C3* (4km SE Rural) *63.53274, 29.19889* **Hyvärilä Camping, Lomatie 12, 75500 Nurmes [(013) 6872500; fax 6872510; hyvarila@nurmes.fi; www.hyvarila.com]** On rte 73 to Lieksa, turn R 4km fr rte 6/73 junc. Well sp on Lake Pielinen. Check in at hotel. Lge, unshd; wc; chem disp; mv service pnt; sauna; shwrs inc; EHU (16A) €5; lndry; shop 2km; rest, snacks; playgrnd; lake sw; tennis; games area; some statics; dogs; quiet; ccard acc; red long stay/CKE/CCI. "Gd base for N Karelia; pt of recreational complex." 1 Jun-15 Sep. € 24.00 2016*

⊞ **OULU/ULEABORG** *B2* (6km NW Coastal) *65.0317, 25.4159* **Camping Nallikari, Leiritie 10, Hietasaari, 90500 Oulu/Uleäborg [(08) 55861350; fax 55861713; nallikari.camping@ouka.fi; www.nallikari.fi]** Off Kemi rd. Sp fr town & rte 4/E75 fr Kemi. (Do not take Oulu by-pass app fr S). Lge, pt shd; htd wc; chem disp; mv service pnt; sauna; shwrs inc; EHU (16A) €4.50; lndry; shop; rest 300m; snacks; bar; BBQ; cooking facs; playgrnd; pool & spa adj; sw 500m; bike hire; games area; child entmnt high ssn; wifi; TV; 20% statics; dogs; poss cr; no adv bkg; quiet; ccard acc; red CKE/CCI. "Gd cycling; excel modern services block." ♦ € 23.00 2016*

PELLO *B2* (1km NW Rural) *66.78413, 23.94540* **Camping Pello, Nivanpääntie 58, 95700 Pello [050 3606611; pello.camping@gmail.com; www.travelpello.fi/palvelu/camping-pello]** Foll site sp fr town cent. Med, hdstg, pt shd; htd wc; chem disp; mv service pnt; sauna; shwrs; EHU (16A) inc; lndry; shop, rest 1km; snacks; playgrnd; rv adj; fishing; boat hire; 30% statics; Eng spkn; quiet; ccard acc. "Rvside pitches avail - insects!" 1 Jun-20 Sep. € 21.00 2016*

"That's changed – Should I let The Club know?"

If you find something on site that's different from the site entry, fill in a report and let us know. See camc.com/europereport.

PERANKA *C2* (2km E Rural) *65.39583, 29.07094* **Camping Piispansaunat, Selkoskyläntie 19, 89770 Peranka [(040) 5916784 or (0400) 387615; piispansaunat@elisanet.fi; piispansaunat@elisanet.fi]** Take rte 5/63 N or S; at Peranka turn E on rd 9190 for 2km; site on R in trees. Sm, hdstg, pt sl, shd; wc; chem disp; sauna; shwrs inc; EHU (10A) €4; lndry; shop 2km; snacks; BBQ; cooking facs; playgrnd; lake sw & sand beach adj; fishing; dogs; Eng spkn; quiet; red CKE/CCI. 1 Jun-31 Aug. € 25.00 2016*

PORVOO/BORGA *C4* (2km S Rural) *60.3798, 25.66673* **Camping Kokonniemi, Uddaksentie 17, 06100 Porvoo [(452) 550074; myynti@suncamping.fi]** Fr E on rte 7/E18 m'way ignore 1st exit Porvoo, site sp fr 2nd exit. Med, some hdstg, sl, pt sh; wc; chem disp; mv service pnt; sauna; shwrs inc; EHU (16A) €5; lndry rm; shop, rest 2km; snacks; playgrnd; poss cr; Eng spkn; no adv bkg; quiet; ccard acc; red CKE. "Access to old town & rv walk; conv Helsinki & ferry; nice welcome; v clean; ideal NH or longer; Porvoo interesting." 1 Jun-26 Aug. € 33.00 2017*

⊞ **PUNKAHARJU** *D4* (9km NW Rural) *61.80032, 29.29088* **Punkaharjun Camping, Tuunaansaarentie 4, 58540 Punkaharju [29 007 4050; info@punkaharjuresort.fi; www.punkaharjuresort.fi]** 27km SE of Savonlinna on rte 14 to Imatra, sp on R. Med, pt shd; wc; chem disp; mv service pnt; sauna; shwrs inc; EHU (16A) €7; lndry; shop; rest, snacks; bar; playgrnd; lake sw; waterslide; fishing; tennis; games area; TV; poss cr; no adv bkg; quiet but noise fr bar; ccard acc; red CKE/CCI. "Theme park nrby (closes 15/8); Kerimäki, world's largest wooden church; Retretti Art Cent adj." € 24.00 2016*

⊞ **RAUMA** *B4* (3km NW Coastal) *61.13501, 21.47085* **Poroholma Camping, Poroholmanti 8, 26100 Rauma [(02)533 5522; fax (02) 83882400; info@poroholma.fi; www.poroholma.fi]** Enter town fr coast rd (8) or Huittinen (42). Foll campsite sp around N pt of town to site on coast. Site well sp. Lge, pt sl, shd; wc; chem disp; sauna; shwrs inc; EHU (16A) €5; lndry; shop; snacks; bar; playgrnd; pool 250m; sand beach; dogs; no adv bkg; quiet; ccard acc; red CKE/CCI. "Attractive, peaceful location on sm peninsula in yacht marina & jetty for ferry (foot passengers only) to outlying islands; excel beach; warm welcome fr helpful staff; clean facs." € 25.00 2016*

ROVANIEMI *B2* (7km E Rural) *66.51706, 25.84678* **Camping Napapiirin Saarituvat, Kuusamontie 96, 96900 Saarenkylä [tel/fax (016) 3560045; reception@saarituvat.fi; www.saarituvat.fi]** Fr town cent take rd 81, site on R at side of rd on lakeside. NB ignore 1st campsite sp after 2km. Sm, terr, pt shd; htd wc; chem disp; sauna; shwrs inc; EHU (16A) €5.50; lndry; shop 4km; rest; bar; BBQ; playgrnd; dogs; Eng spkn; adv bkg; quiet; red CKE/CCI. "Excel; friendly staff; vg base for Santa Park & Vill." 20 May-9 Sep. € 32.50 2014*

ROVANIEMI *B2* (1km SE Urban) *66.49743, 25.74340* **Ounaskoski Camping, Jäämerentie 1, 96200 Rovaniemi [tel/fax (016) 345304; ounaskoski-camping@windowslive.com]** Exit rte 4 onto rte 78 & cross rv. Over bdge turn S on rvside along Jäämerentie. Site on R in approx 500m immed bef old rd & rail bdge, sp. Med, mkd pitch, unshd, some hdstg; htd wc; chem disp; mv service pnt; fam bthrm; sauna; shwrs inc; EHU (16A) inc; lndry (inc dryer); shop; rest 400m; snacks; BBQ; cooking facs; playgrnd; pool 1km; rv sw & sand beach; bike hire; wifi; TV rm; 10% statics; dogs; bus 500m; twin axles; poss v cr; Eng spkn; adv bkg; quiet; ccard acc; red CKE/CCI. "Helpful staff; excel site beside rv in parkland; gd facs; suitable RVs & twin-axles; 9km fr Arctic Circle; 6km to Santa Park, 'official' home of Santa; Artikum Museum worth visit; easy walk to town cent; gd flea mkts; excel san facs." ♦ 21 May-24 Sep. € 38.50 2017*

SAVONLINNA *C4* (7km W Rural) *61.86216, 28.80513* **Camping Vuohimäki, Vuohimäentie 60, 57600 Savonlinna [(015) 537353 or (045) 2550073; savonlinna@suncamping.fi; www.suncamping.fi]** On rte 14, 4km W of Savonlinna turn L immed after bdge twd Pihlajaniemi; site sp for approx 4km on R. Med; wc; chem disp; shwrs inc; EHU (16A) €5; lndry (inc dryer); supmkt 3km; rest, snacks; bar; playgrnd; sauna; sand beach & lake sw; watersports; bike hire; some statics; bus; wifi; dogs; Eng skpn; adv bkg; quiet; ccard acc; red CKE. "Gd area for touring; lake trips; views over lake; gd san facs." ♦ 10 Jun-22 Aug. € 31.00 2016*

TORNIO *B2* (3km SE Rural) *65.83211, 24.19953* **Camping Tornio, Matkailijantie, 95420 Tornio [(016) 445945; fax 445030; camping.tornio@co.inet.fi; www.campingtornio.com]** App Tornio on E4 coast rd fr Kemi sp on L of dual c/way; turn L at traff lts then immed R. Site well sp. Lge, pt shd; wc; sauna; shwrs inc; EHU (16A) €4; lndry (inc dryer) hg ssn only; shop 3km; snacks; cooking facs; playgrnd; tennis; bike hire; TV; quiet; ccard acc; red CKE/CCI. "Poss boggy in wet." ♦ ltd. 5 May-30 Sep. € 28.00 2016*

⊞ **TURKU/ABO** *B4* (12km SW Rural) *60.42531, 22.10258* **Ruissalo Camping (Part Naturist), Saaronniemi, 20100 Turku [(02) 2625100; fax 2625101; ruissalocamping@turku.fi]** Well sp fr m'way & fr Turku docks; recep immed after sharp bend in a layby. Med, pt shd, some hdstg; htd wc; chem disp; mv service pnt; sauna; shwrs inc; EHU (16A) inc; lndry; shop; rest 200m; snacks; playgrnd; sand beach adj; watersports; games area; wifi; TV; some statics; sep area for naturists; bus; Eng spkn; quiet; ccard acc; red CKE/CCI. "Conv for ferry; modern, clean san facs; ltd EHU some parts." ♦ ltd. € 32.00 2016*

⊞ **UUKUNIEMI** *D4* (3km NW Coastal) *61.80222, 29.96538* **Papinniemi Camping, Papinniementie 178, Uukuniemi Parikkala 59730, Suomi [(40) 7369852; info@papinniemicamping.net; www.papinniemicamping.net]** Fr Karelia rd foll sp. Fr S take R Niukkalantie. Fr N take L Uukuniementie. Sm, pt shd; wc; shwrs; EHU (16A) €4; games area; sauna €15; rest, snacks; BBQ; wifi; bicycles; rowing boats & canoes; "Amazing nature; peaceful beautiful place; lake water so clean." € 33.00 2013*

VAASA/VASA *B3* (3km NW Coastal) *63.1008, 21.57618* **Top Camping Vaasa, Niemeläntie 1, 65170 Vaasa [(0)20 7961 255; fax 7961 254; vaasa@topcamping.fi; www.topcamping.fi/vaasa]** Fr town cent foll sp to harbour (Satama), site sp. Lge, pt shd; htd wc; chem disp; mv service pnt; fam bthrm; sauna; shwrs inc; EHU (10A) €7; lndry; shop; snacks; bar; playgrnd; bike hire; TV; 10% statics; dogs; no adv bkg; ccard acc; red long stay/CKE/CCI. ♦ 25 May-10 Aug. € 29.50 2016*

FINLAND

VIRRAT *B4* (6km SE Rural) *62.20883, 23.83501* **Camping Lakarin Leirintä, Lakarintie 405, 34800 Virrat [(03) 4758639; fax 4758667; lakari@virtainmatkailu.fi; www.virtainmatkailu.fi]** Fr Virrat on rte 66 twd Ruovesi. Fr Virrat pass info/park & take 2nd L, then 1st L. Site 1.7km on R (poor surface), sp. Med, pt sl, pt shd; htd wc; chem disp; sauna; shwrs inc; EHU (16A) €3.40; lndry rm; shop in Virrat; snacks; playgrnd; lake sw adj; boating; fishing; 50% statics; Eng spkn; quiet; red CKE. "Beautiful lakeside pitches." 1 May-30 Sep. € 20.00 2016*

"I like to fill in the reports as I travel from site to site"

You'll find report forms at the back of this guide, or you can fill them in online at camc.com/europereport.

⊞ **VUOSTIMO** *C2* (2km SW Rural) *66.95783, 27.50350* **Camping Kuukiurun, Sodankyläntie, 98360 Vuostimo [(0) 400 199 184; office@kuukiuru.fi; www.kuukiuru.fi]** N fr Kemijarvi on rd 5, site on R of rd leaving Vuostimo adj rv. Sm, mkd pitch, pt sl, unshd; wc; chem disp; sauna; shwrs; EHU inc; snacks; fishing; boat hire; x-country skiing; TV; many statics; dogs; quiet. "Beautiful, peaceful site; friendly owners." 2016*

ALAND ISLANDS

SUND *A4* (12km SE Coastal) *60.21252, 20.23508* **Puttes Camping, Bryggvägen 40, Bomarsund, 22530 Sund [(018) 44040; fax 44047; puttes.camping@aland.net; www.visitaland.com/puttescamping]** N fr Mariehamn on rd 2 for 40+ km, site at Bomarsund fortress ruins. Med, pt sl, pt shd; wc; chem disp; mv service pnt; shwrs €1; EHU (10A) inc; lndry; shop; rest, snacks; bar; BBQ; cooking facs; shgl beach adj; bike hire; games area; 5% statics; dogs; phone; bus adj; Eng spkn; adv bkg; quiet; CKE/CCI. "Basic, but clean & welcoming; vg." ♦ ltd. 15 May-11 Sep. € 12.00 2016*

VARDO *A4* (4km N Coastal) *60.27073, 20.38819* **Sandösunds Camping, Sandösundsvägen, 22550 Vårdö [tel/fax (018) 47750; info@sandocamping.aland.fi; www.sandocamping.aland.fi]** Site sp fr ferry at Hummelvik & fr rd 2. Med, pt sl, pt shd; htd wc; chem disp; mv service pnt; fam bthrm; shwrs inc; EHU (10A) €4 (long lead poss req); lndry; shop; rest, snacks; bar; BBQ; cooking facs; playgrnd; sand beach adj; bike & kayak hire; games area; wifi; 5% statics; dogs; phone; Eng spkn; adv bkg; quiet; CKE/CCI. "Well-run site in beautiful location; excel facs." ♦ ltd. 15 Apr-31 Oct. € 14.00 2016*

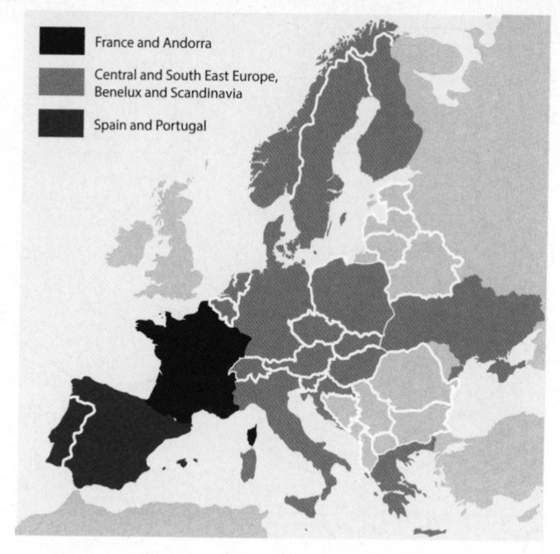

Kuusamo to Turku = 848km

	Forssa	Hanko	Helsinki	Hämeenlinna	Ivalo	Joensuu	Jyväskylä	Kajaani	Kemijärvi	Kokkola	Kouvola	Kuopio	Kurikka	Kuusamo	Kyyjärvi	Lahti	Lappeenranta	Mikkeli	Muonio	Nurmes	Oulu	Pori	Rovaniemi	Savonlinna	Sodankylä	Tampere	Tornio	Turku	Vaasa
Hanko	150																												
Helsinki	114	129																											
Hämeenlinna	56	195	100																										
Ivalo	1091	1238	1122	1041																									
Joensuu	464	546	439	410	839																								
Jyväskylä	238	380	271	187	848	244																							
Kajaani	555	664	556	500	623	229	313																						
Kemijärvi	889	1031	920	835	268	600	646	384																					
Kokkola	417	544	493	391	709	428	241	244	505																				
Kouvola	192	271	143	134	1037	310	192	436	821	432																			
Kuopio	383	493	382	332	800	135	145	170	557	314	264																		
Kurikka	263	390	345	245	882	449	230	385	679	174	356	335																	
Kuusamo	792	910	803	740	406	460	552	245	140	411	680	415	585																
Kyyjärvi	318	474	389	278	802	332	118	293	599	120	310	215	137	503															
Lahti	127	219	107	73	1017	336	170	450	813	409	61	282	294	704	288														
Lappeenranta	275	354	220	221	1062	236	220	437	820	459	82	266	424	682	338	147													
Mikkeli	258	341	231	204	957	208	114	330	718	356	99	162	345	579	233	129	105												
Muonio	975	1121	1004	918	325	782	732	568	275	590	922	670	764	420	686	901	945	840											
Nurmes	514	624	512	459	720	130	272	110	479	342	393	127	434	339	296	414	363	290	660										
Oulu	580	723	612	529	510	392	340	180	308	197	531	286	370	212	290	508	551	447	390	278									
Pori	127	257	242	180	1019	507	273	555	817	310	302	405	177	725	292	236	387	369	900	535	510								
Rovaniemi	807	941	831	747	287	550	561	339	85	420	750	510	593	192	513	730	774	669	230	429	221	730							
Savonlinna	362	449	333	310	958	142	207	332	717	440	207	162	444	578	325	232	155	106	839	272	447	471	671						
Sodankylä	929	1070	960	876	160	680	691	466	108	548	879	640	722	248	643	858	904	798	166	560	352	862	131	798					
Tampere	92	242	173	74	1002	395	152	463	796	324	192	294	171	702	228	128	275	256	882	420	493	115	710	355	841				
Tornio	711	851	742	659	413	523	469	309	210	329	660	416	501	315	423	637	682	578	262	406	129	640	123	576	252	621			
Turku	88	140	165	148	1144	549	304	615	943	434	274	448	283	848	384	217	364	349	1027	577	632	138	855	444	986	153	764		
Vaasa	317	453	418	316	827	494	282	365	626	120	430	379	79	530	164	363	502	398	711	461	317	194	540	489	668	245	448	346	
Varkaus	344	429	320	288	875	118	125	250	634	355	190	75	353	496	242	217	191	87	756	206	362	390	586	88	714	276	494	428	396

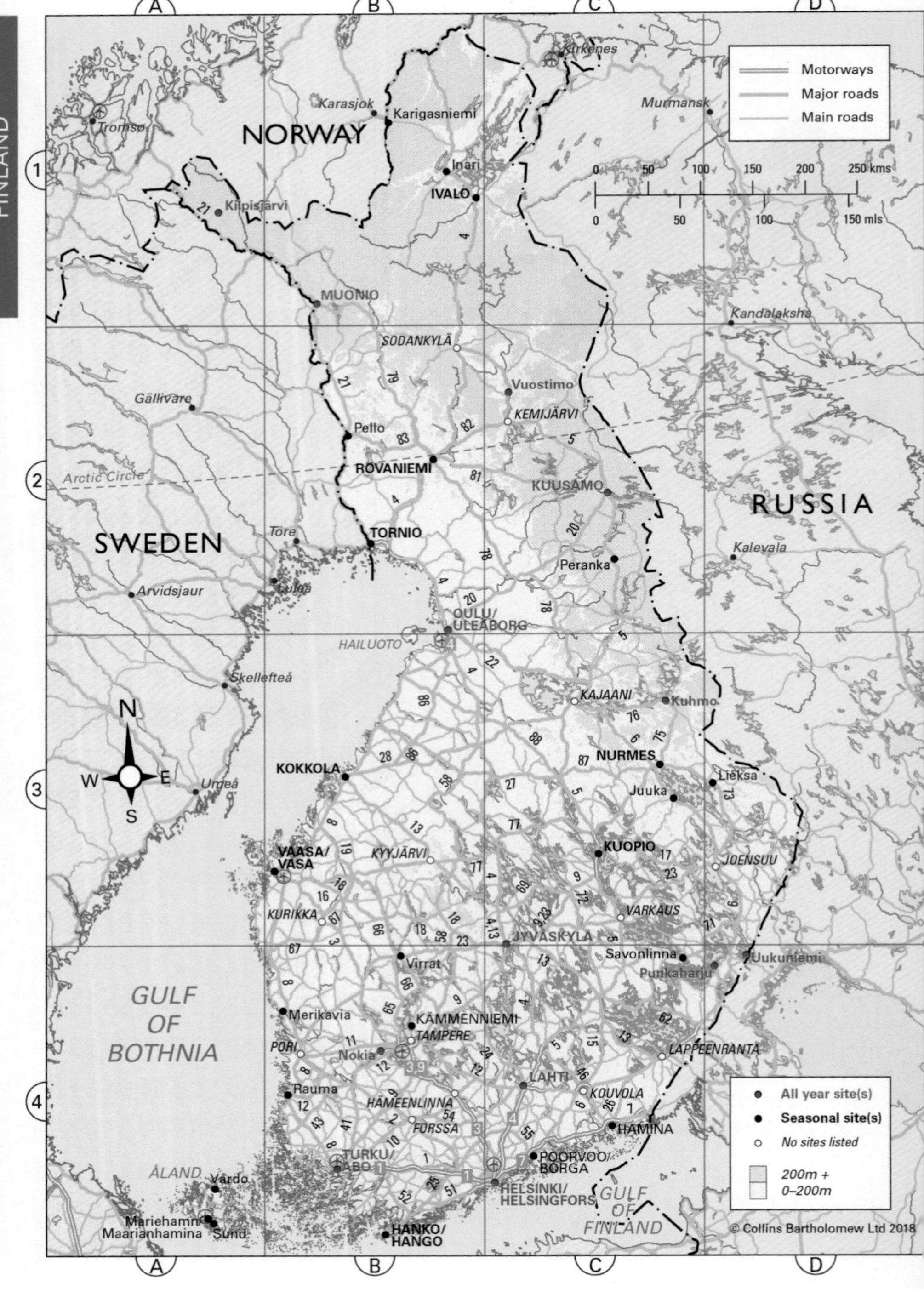
NORWAY
SWEDEN
RUSSIA
GULF OF BOTHNIA
GULF OF FINLAND
Motorways
Major roads
Main roads
0 50 100 150 200 250 kms
0 50 100 150 mls
All year site(s)
Seasonal site(s)
No sites listed
200m +
0–200m
Arctic Circle
Kirkenes
Karasjok
Karigasniemi
Tromsø
Murmansk
Inari
IVALO
Kilpisjärvi
MUONIO
Kandalaksha
SODANKYLÄ
Vuostimo
Gällivare
KEMIJÄRVI
Pello
ROVANIEMI
KUUSAMO
Töre
TORNIO
Kalevala
Peranka
Luleå
Arvidsjaur
OULU/ ULEÅBORG
HAILUOTO
Skellefteå
KAJAANI
Kuhmo
NURMES
KOKKOLA
Lieksa
Umeå
Juuka
VAASA/ VASA
KYYJÄRVI
KUOPIO
JOENSUU
KURIKKA
VARKAUS
JYVÄSKYLÄ
Savonlinna
Uukuniemi
Punkaharju
Virrat
Merikavia
KÄMMENNIEMI
TAMPERE
PORI
Nokia
LAPPEENRANTA
Rauma
LAHTI
KOUVOLA
HÄMEENLINNA
FORSSA
HAMINA
TURKU/ ÅBO
POORVOO/ BORGÅ
ÅLAND
Vårdö
HELSINKI/ HELSINGFORS
Mariehamn/ Maarianhamina
Sund
HANKO/ HANGO
© Collins Bartholomew Ltd 2018

Rothenburg ob der Tauber

Welcome to Germany

Home to beautiful landscapes, architectural delights and diverse cities, Germany has a rich culture and history for you to discover. Berlin is undoubtedly one of the culture and arts capitals of the world, while the picturesque timbered villages and castles have inspired countless works of literature, film and art.

Often thought of as the home of beer and bratwurst, Germany has much more to offer on a gastronomic level, with Riesling wine, Black Forest Gateaux and Stollen just some of the treats that are waiting to be discovered and enjoyed.

Country highlights

Germany is the home of the modern car, and its automobile industry is one of the most innovative in the world. BMW, Audi, Porsche and Mercedes all have interesting museums to visit.

Oktoberfest, the largest beer festival in the world, is held annually in Munich and attracts people from around the globe. This 17-day festival only serves traditional beers that are brewed within Munich city limits.

Major towns and cities

- Berlin – this capital is an exciting city of culture and science.
- Hamburg – enjoy stunning and varied architecture in this gorgeous city.
- Munich – a magnificent city of culture and technology.
- Cologne – this city is brimming with bars, restaurants and pubs.

Attractions

- Neuschwanstein, Füssen – this fairytale castle inspired the palace from Sleeping Beauty.
- Holstentor, Lübeck – a relic of the medieval city fortifications, this gate has UNESCO status.
- Cologne Cathedral – This grand, gothic cathedral is Germany's most visited landmark.
- Lindau – an enchanting island town boasting beautiful architecture and wonderful gardens.

Find out more

www.germany.travel
Tel: 0049 (0) 69 97 46 40 German Tourism Board

Country Information

Population (approx): 81million

Capital: Berlin (population approx 3.4 million)

Area: 357,050 sq km

Bordered by: Austria, Belgium, Czech Republic, Denmark, France, Luxembourg, Netherlands, Poland, Switzerland

Terrain: Lowlands in north; uplands/industrialised belt in the centre; highlands, forests and Bavarian alps in the south

Climate: Temperate throughout the year; warm summers and cold winters; rain throughout the year

Coastline: 2,389km

Highest Point: Zugspitze 2,962m

Language: German

Local Time: GMT or BST + 1, i.e. 1 hour ahead of the UK all year

Currency: Euros divided into 100 cents; £1 = €1.13, €1 = £0.88 (November 2017)

Emergency numbers: Police 112; Fire brigade 112; Ambulance 112. Operators speak English

Public Holidays 2018: Jan 1, 6; Apr 14, 16, 17; May 1, 25; June 4, 5, 15; Aug 15; Oct 3, 31; Nov 1, 22; Dec 25, 26.

Public holidays vary according to region. The dates shown here may not be celebrated throughout the country. School summer holidays also vary by region but are roughly July to mid/end Aug or Aug to mid Sept.

Camping and Caravanning

There are approximately 3,500 campsites in Germany, which are generally open from April to October. Many (mostly in winter sports areas) stay open in winter and have all the necessary facilities for winter sports enthusiasts. Sites may have a very high proportion of statics, usually in a separate area. In the high summer season visitors should either start looking for a pitch early in the afternoon or book in advance.

Campsites are usually well equipped with modern sanitary facilities, shops and leisure amenities, etc. Some sites impose a charge for handling rubbish, commonly €1 to €2 a day. Separate containers for recycling glass, plastic, etc, are now the norm.

A daily tourist tax may also be payable of up to €2 or €3 per person per night.

Naturism is popular, particularly in eastern Germany, and sites which accept naturists will generally display a sign 'FKK'.

Many sites close for a two hour period between noon and 3pm (known as Mittagsruhe) and you may find barriers down so that vehicles cannot be moved on or off the site during this period. Some sites provide a waiting area but where a site entrance is off a busy road parking or turning may be difficult.

For a list of small sites (up to 150 pitches) see www.kleincamp.de.

Casual/wild camping is discouraged and is not allowed in forests and nature reserves. In the case of private property permission to pitch a tent or park a caravan should be obtained in advance from the owners, or on common land or state property, from the local town hall or police station.

Cycling

There is an extensive network of over 70,000 km of cycle routes across all regions. Children under eight years are not allowed to cycle on the road. Up to the age of 10 years they may ride on the pavement but must give way to pedestrians and dismount to cross the road. Bicycles must have front and rear lights and a bell.

Cyclists can be fined €25 for using a mobile phone while cycling and €10 for using earphones.

Electricity and Gas

Current on campsites varies between 2 and 16 amps, 6 to 10 amps being the most common. Plugs have two round pins. Most campsites have CEE connections.

Many sites make a one-off charge – usually €1 or €2 however long your stay – for connection to the electricity supply, which is then metered at a rate per kilowatt hour (kwh) of approximately €0.50-€0.70, with or without an additional daily charge. This connection charge can make one night stays expensive. During the summer you may find only a flat, daily charge for electricity of €2-€5, the supply being metered during the rest of the year.

Campingaz is available and the blue cylinders in general used throughout Europe may be exchanged for German cylinders which are green-grey. At some campsites in winter sports areas a direct connection with the gas mains ring is available and the supply is metered.

Entry Formalities

British and Irish passport holders may stay in Germany for up to three months without a visa. While there are no Customs controls at Germany's borders into other EU countries, when you enter or leave the Czech Republic and Poland you may still have to show your passport.

Regulations for Pets

Certain breeds of dogs, such as pit bull terriers and American Staffordshire terriers, are prohibited from entering Germany. There is an exception to this rule, whereby these dogs can be imported for up to 4 weeks with a Certificate of Personality Test, which must be given by a vet on entering Germany. Other large dogs and breeds such as Dobermann, Mastiff and Rottweiler may need to be kept on a lead and muzzled in public, which also means in your car. You are advised to contact the German embassy in London before making travel arrangements for your dog and check the latest available information from your vet or from the PETS Helpline on 0370 241 1710

Medical Services

Local state health insurance fund offices offer assistance round-the-clock and telephone numbers can be found in the local telephone directory. EU citizens are entitled to free or subsidised emergency care from doctors contracted to the state health care system on presentation of a European Health Insurance Card (EHIC). Private treatment by doctors or dentists is not refundable under the German health service. You will be liable for a percentage of prescribed medication charges at pharmacies and this is also non-refundable. Pharmacies offer an all-night and Sunday service and the address of the nearest out-of-hours branch will be displayed on the door of every pharmacy.

There is a fixed daily charge for a stay in hospital (treatment is free for anyone under 18 years of age) which is not refundable. If you are required to pay an additional patient contribution for treatment then reduced charges apply to holders of an EHIC. For refunds of these additional charges you should apply with original receipts to a local state health insurance fund office.

Opening Hours

Banks: Mon-Fri 8.30am-12.30pm & 1.30pm-3.30pm (to 5pm or 6pm on Thurs).

Museums: Check locally as times vary.

Post Offices: Mon-Fri 7/8am-6/8pm; Sat 8am-12pm.

Shops: Mon-Fri 8/9am-6pm/8pm. Sat 8/9am-12/4pm; in some places bakers are open Sun mornings.

Safety and Security

Most visits to Germany are trouble free but visitors should take the usual commonsense precautions against mugging, pickpocketing and bag snatching, particularly in areas around railway stations, airports in large cities and at Christmas markets. Do not leave valuables unattended.

Germany shares with the rest of Europe a general threat from terrorism. Attacks could be indiscriminate and against civilian targets in public places, including tourist sites. You should maintain a high level of vigilance at all times.

British Embassy

WILHELMSTRASSE 70, D-10117 BERLIN
Tel: (030) 204570,
www.ukingermany.fco.gov.uk/en/

British Consulates-General

OststraBe 86, 40210
DÜSSELDORF
Tel: (0211) 94480
MÖHLSTRASSE 5, 81675 MÜNCHEN
Tel: (089) 211090

Irish Embassy

JÄGERSTRASSE 51, 10117 BERLIN
Tel: (030) 220720
www.embassyofireland.de
There are also Irish Honorary Consulates in Frankfurt, Hamburg, Köln (Cologne) and München (Munich).

Documents

Passport

It is a legal requirement to carry your passport at all times. German police have the right to ask to see identification and for British citizens the only acceptable form of ID is a valid passport.

Vehicle(s)

Carry your valid driving licence, insurance and vehicle documents with you in your vehicle at all times. It is particularly important to carry your vehicle registration document V5C, as you will need it if entering a low emission zone (see later in this chapter for more information).

If you are driving a hired or borrowed vehicle, you must be in possession of a letter of authorisation from the owner or a hire agreement.

Money

The major debit and credit cards, including American Express, are widely accepted by shops, hotels, restaurants and petrol stations. However, you may find that credit cards are not as widely accepted in smaller establishments as they are in the UK, including many shops and campsites, due to the high charges imposed on retailers, and debit cards are preferred. Cash machines are widespread and have instructions in English.

British visitors have been arrested for possession of counterfeit currency and the authorities advise against changing money anywhere other than at banks or legitimate bureaux de change.

Carry your credit card issuers'/banks' 24-hour UK contact numbers in case of loss or theft of your cards.

Motoring in Germany

Roads in Germany are of an excellent standard but speed limits are higher than in the UK and the accident rate is greater. Drivers undertaking long journeys in or through Germany should plan their journeys carefully and take frequent breaks.

Accidents

In the event of a road accident the police must always be called even if there are no injuries.

Alcohol

The maximum permitted level of alcohol is 50 milligrams per 100 millilitres of blood, i.e. lower than that in the UK (80 milligrams). For novice drivers who have held a driving licence for less than two years, and for drivers under the age of 21, no alcohol is permitted in the bloodstream. Penalties for driving under the influence of alcohol or drugs are severe.

Breakdown Service

The motoring organisation Allgemeiner Deutscher Automobil-Club (ADAC) operates road patrols on motorways and in the event of a breakdown, assistance can be obtained by calling from emergency phones placed every 2 km. Members of clubs affiliated to the AIT or FIA, such as The Caravan and Motorhome Club, must ask specifically for roadside assistance to be provided by ADAC as they should be able to receive assistance free of charge. You must pay for replacement parts and towing. ADAC breakdown vehicles are yellow and marked 'ADAC Strassenwacht'.

If ADAC Strassenwacht vehicles are not available, firms under contract to ADAC provide towing and roadside assistance, against payment. Vehicles used by firms under contract to ADAC are marked 'Strassendienst im Auftrag des ADAC'.

On other roads the ADAC breakdown service can be reached 24 hours a day by telephoning 01802-22 22 22 (local call rates) or 22 22 22 from a mobile phone.

Essential Equipment

First Aid Kit

Drivers of German registered vehicles must carry a first aid kit but this is not a legal requirement for foreign visitors.

Lights

Dipped headlights are recommended at all times and must always be used in tunnels, as well as when visibility is poor and during periods of bad weather. Bulbs are more likely to fail with constant use and you are recommended to carry spares.

Child Restraint Systems

Children under three years of age must be placed in an approved child restraint and cannot be transported in a vehicle otherwise. Children of three years and over must travel in the rear of vehicles. Children under 12 years old and 1.5 metres in height must be seated in an approved child restraint. If a child restraint won't fit into the vehicle because other children are using a child restraint, then children of three years and over must use a seat belt or other safety device attached to the seat.

Winter Driving

All vehicles, including those registered outside Germany, must be fitted with winter tyres (or all season tyres) during winter conditions, bearing the mark 'M+S' (Mud + Snow) or the snowflake symbol. Failure to use them can result in a fine and penalty points. There must also be anti-freeze in the windscreen cleaning fluid.

The use of snow chains is permitted and for vehicles fitted with them there is a maximum speed limit of 50 km/h (31 mph). In mountainous areas the requirement for chains is indicated by signs. The use of spiked tyres is not authorised.

Fuel

Most petrol stations are open from 8am to 8pm. In large cities many are open 24 hours. In the east there are fewer petrol stations than in the south and west. Some have automatic pumps operated using credit cards.

LPG (autogas or flussiggas) is widely available. You can view a list of approximately 800 outlets throughout the country, including those near motorways, from the website www.autogastanken.de (follow the links under 'Tanken' and 'Tankstellan-Karte). On some stretches of motorway petrol stations may be few and far between, e.g. the A45, A42 and A3 to the Dutch border, and it is advisable not to let your fuel tank run low.

Low Emission Zones

A large number of German cities and towns now require motorists to purchase a 'Pollution Badge' (Umwelt Plakette) in the form of a windscreen sticker in order to enter city centre 'Umwelt' or green zones. The areas where restrictions apply are indicated by signs showing coloured vignettes, the colour of the vignette issued (red, yellow or green) depending on your vehicle's engine type and its Euro emission rating.

You must present your vehicle registration document, V5C, at an 'Umwelt Plakette' sales outlet, which can be found at vehicle repair centres, car dealers, MOT (Tüv) stations and vehicle licensing offices and it is understood that badges are also available from ATU motoring supplies shops. The cost varies between €5 and €10 + VAT and postage.

Failure to display a badge could result in a fine of €40. Enforcement is managed by the police, local authorities and traffic wardens. Older vehicles without a catalytic converter or a particulate filter (generally emission-rated Euro 1) will not be issued with a badge and will not be permitted to enter the centres of those cities and towns participating in the scheme.

Visit www.lowemissionzones.eu or www.umwelt-plakette.de (you may also be able to purchase your badge here before you travel to Germany). Alternatively contact The Club's Travel Service Information Officer (Club members only), email: travelserviceinfo@camc.com.

Parking

Zigzag lines on the carriageway indicate a stopping (waiting) and parking prohibition, e.g. at bus stops, narrow roads and places with poor visibility, but double or single yellow lines are not used. Instead look out for 'no stopping', 'parking prohibited' or 'no parking' signs.

Except for one-way streets, parking is only permitted on the right-hand side. Do not park in the opposite direction to traffic flow. Parking meters and parking disc schemes are in operation and discs may be bought in local shops or service stations.

Priority

At crossroads and junctions, where no priority is indicated, traffic coming from the right has priority. Trams do not have absolute priority over other vehicles but priority must be given to passengers getting on or off stationary trams. Trams in two-way streets must be overtaken on the right. Drivers must give way to a bus whose driver has indicated his intention to pull away from the kerb. Do not overtake a stationary school bus which has stopped to let passengers on or off. This may be indicated by a red flashing light on the bus.

Traffic already on a roundabout has right of way, except when signs show otherwise. Drivers must use their indicators when leaving a roundabout, not when entering.

Always stop to allow pedestrians to cross at marked pedestrian crossings. In residential areas where traffic-calming zones exist, pedestrians are allowed to use the whole street, so drive with great care.

Road Signs and Markings

Most German road signs and markings conform to the international pattern. Other road signs that may be encountered are:

Keep distance shown

Street lights not on all night

Lower speed limit applies in the wet

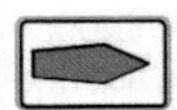
Recommended route on motorways

One way street

Tram or bus stop

German	English Translation
Einsatzfahrzeuge Fre	Emergency vehicles only
Fahrbahnwechsel	Change traffic lane
Freie Fahrt	Road clear
Frostchaden	Frost damage
Gefährlich	Danger
Glatteisgefahr	Ice on the road
Notruf	Emergency roadside telephone
Radweg Kreuzt	Cycle-track crossing
Rollsplitt	Loose grit
Stau	Traffic jam
Strassenschaden	Road damage
Umleitung	Diversion
Vorsicht	Caution

Road signs on motorways are blue and white, whereas on B roads (Bundesstrasse) they are orange and black. If you are planning a route through Germany using E road numbers, be aware that E roads may be poorly signposted and you may have to navigate using national A or B road numbers.

Speed Limits

	Open Road (kmph)	Motorway (kmph)
Solo Car	100	130
Car towing caravan/trailer	80*	80
Motorhome under 3500kg	100	130
Motorhome 3500-7500kg	80	100

* 100 km/h (62 mph) if your car and caravan passes a TUV test in Germany (test costs €70 and takes 2 hours to complete)

There is a speed limit of 50 km/h (31 mph) in built-up areas for all types of motor vehicles, unless otherwise indicated by road signs. A built-up area starts from the town name sign at the beginning of a town or village.

The number of sections of autobahn with de-restricted zones, i.e. no upper speed limit, is diminishing and the volume of traffic makes high speed motoring virtually impossible. Regulations on many stretches of two-lane motorway restrict lorries, together with cars towing caravans, from overtaking.

Speed cameras are frequently in use but they may be deliberately hidden behind crash barriers or in mobile units. A GPS navigation system which indicates the location of fixed speed cameras must have the function deactivated. The use of radar detectors is prohibited.

A car towing a caravan or trailer is prohibited to 80km/h (50 mph) on motorways and other main roads. You may occasionally see car/caravan combinations displaying a sign indicating that their maximum permitted speed is 100 km/h (62 mph). This is only permitted for vehicles that have passed a TUV test in Germany, who will then need to apply for a sticker at a Zulassungsstelle. The application process can be complicated as some Zulassungsstelles will insist they see a registration certificate for your caravan. Obtaining a 100km/h sticker without a registration certificate is best done in Aachen as they are the only Zulassungsstelle familiar with this process. If you are having difficulty at a different Zulassungsstelle ask them to call the Zulassungsstelle in Aachen to confirm that a registration document is not required.

In bad weather when visibility is below 50 metres, the maximum speed limit is 50 km/h (31 mph) on all roads.

Towing

Drivers of cars towing caravans and other slow-moving vehicles must leave enough space in front of them for an overtaking vehicle to get into that space, or they must pull over from time to time to let other vehicles pass.

If you are towing a car behind a motorhome, our advice would be to use a trailer with all four wheels of the car off the ground. Although Germany doesn't have a specific law banning A-frames, they do have a law which prohibits a motor vehicle towing another motor vehicle. Outside built-up areas the speed limit for such vehicle combinations is 80 km/h (50 mph) or 60 km/h (37 mph) for vehicles over 3,500 kg.

Traffic Jams

Roads leading to popular destinations in Denmark, the Alps and Adriatic Coast become very congested during the busy holiday period of July and August and on public holidays. In those periods traffic jams of up to 60 km are not unheard of.

Congestion is likely on the A3 and A5 north-south routes. Traffic jams are also likely to occur on the A7 Kassel-Denmark, the A8 Stuttgart-Munich-Salzburg and on the A2 and A9 to Berlin. Other cities where congestion may occur are Würzburg, Nürnberg (Nuremberg), Munich and Hamburg. Alternative routes, known as U routes, have been devised; those leading to the south or west have even numbers and those leading to the north or east have odd numbers. These U routes often detour over secondary roads to the following motorway junction and the acquisition of a good road map or atlas is recommended.

ADAC employs 'Stauberater' (traffic jam advisors) who are recognisable by their bright yellow motorbikes. They assist motorists stuck in traffic and will advise on alternative routes.

Upgrading of motorways to Berlin from the west and improvements to many roads in the old east German suburbs may result in diversions and delays, and worsened traffic congestion.

Violation of Traffic Regulations

Police are empowered to impose and collect small on-the-spot fines for contravention of traffic regulations. Fines vary according to the gravity of the offence and have in recent years been increased dramatically for motorists caught speeding in a built-up area (over 50 km/h – 31 mph). A deposit may be required against higher fines and failure to pay may cause the vehicle to be confiscated.

It is an offence to use abusive language, or make rude gestures in Germany, including to other drivers while driving. It is also an offence to stop on the hard shoulder of a motorway except in the case of mechanical failure - please note that running out of fuel is not classed as a mechanical failure so you may be liable for a fine of up to €20 if you do run out of fuel and stop on the hard shoulder.

It is illegal for pedestrians to cross a road when the red pedestrian light is displayed, even if there is no traffic approaching the crossing. Offenders could be fined and will find themselves liable to all costs in the event of an accident.

Motorways

With around 12,845 toll free kilometres, Germany's motorways (autobahns) constitute one of the world's most advanced and efficient systems. For a complete list of autobahns, including the location of all junctions and roadworks in progress, see www.autobahn-online.de.

Some motorways are so heavily used by lorries that the inside lane has become heavily rutted. These parallel ruts are potentially dangerous for caravans travelling at high speed and vigilance is necessary. It is understood that the A44 and A7 are particularly prone to this problem. Caution also needs to be exercised when driving on the concrete surfaces of major roads.

On motorways emergency telephones are placed at 2 km intervals; some have one button to request breakdown assistance and another to summon an ambulance. Other telephones connect the caller to a rescue control centre. A vehicle that has broken down on a motorway must be towed away to the nearest exit.

There are hundreds of motorway service areas offering, at the very least, a petrol station and a restaurant or cafeteria. Tourist information boards are posted in all the modern motorway service areas. Recent visitors have reported an increase in service facilities just off Autobahn exit ramps, in particular with 'Autohof' (truck stops). The facilities at Autohofs are reported to be comparable to service areas, but usually with considerably lower prices.

Touring

German food is generally of high quality and offers great regional range and diversity. In the country there is at least one inn – 'gasthof' or 'gasthaus' – in virtually every village. A service charge is usually included in restaurant bills but it is usual to leave some small change or round up the bill by 5-10% if satisfied with the service.

Smoking is generally banned on public transport and in restaurants and bars, but regulations vary from state to state.

The German National Tourist Board (GNTB) produces guides to walking and cycle paths throughout the country, as well an extensive range of other brochures and guides. The individual tourist offices for the 16 federal states can also supply a wealth of information about events, attractions and tourist opportunities within their local regions. Obtain contact details from the GNTO.

Christmas markets are an essential part of the run-up to the festive season and they range in size from a few booths in small towns and villages, to hundreds of stalls and booths in large cities. The markets generally run from mid November to 22 or 23 December.

There are 32 UNESCO World Heritage sites in Germany, including the cities of Lübeck, Potsdam and Weimar, the cathedrals of Aachen, Cologne and Speyer, together with numerous other venues of great architectural and archaeological interest.

The Berlin Welcome Card is valid for 2, 3 or 5 days and includes free bus and train travel (including free travel for three accompanying children up to the age of 14), as well as discounted or free entrance to museums, and discounts on tours, boat trips, restaurants and theatres. It can be extended to include Potsdam and the Museuminsel and is available from tourist information centres, hotels and public transport centres or from www.visitberlin.de. A 3 day museum card – SchauLUST-MuseenBERLIN – is also available, valid in more than 60 national museums in and around the city.

Other cities, groups of cities or regions also offer Welcome Cards, including Bonn, Cologne, Dresden, Düsseldorf, Frankfurt, Hamburg, Heidelberg and Munich. These give discounts on public transport, museums, shopping, dining and attractions. Enquire at a local tourist office or at the German National Tourist Office in London.

Public Transport

Most major German cities boast excellent underground (U-bahn), urban railway (S-bahn), bus and tram systems whose convenience and punctuality are renowned. On public transport services, pay your fare prior to boarding the vehicle using the automated ticketing machines. Your ticket must then be date stamped separately using the machines onboard the vehicle or at the entry gates at major stops. Daily tickets permit the use of trains, buses and trams. Berlin's integrated transport system extends as far as Potsdam.

A number of car ferries operate across the Weser and Elbe rivers which allow easy touring north of Bremen and Hamburg. Routes across the Weser include Blexen to Bremerhavn, Brake to Sandstedt and Berne to Farge. The Weser Tunnel (B437) connects the villages of Rodenkirchen and Dedesdorf, offering an easy connection between the cities of Bremerhaven and Nordenham. Across the Elbe there is a car ferry route between Wischhafen and Glückstadt. An international ferry route operates all year across Lake Constance (Bodensee) between Konstanz and Meersburg. There is also a route between Friedrichshafen and Romanshorn in Switzerland.

Neuschwanstein castle in Bavarian alps

Sites in Germany

⊞ **AACHEN** *1A4* (3.5km SE Urban) *50.76140, 6.10285* **Aachen Platz für Camping, Branderhoferweg 11, 52066 Aachen-Burtscheid [(0241) 6088057; fax 6088058; mail@aachen-camping.de; www.aachen-camping.de]** Exit A44 junc 2 onto L233 Monschauerstrasse dir Aachen. In 3.8km at outer ring rd Adenauer Allee L260 turn R, then in 800m L at 2nd traff lts onto Branderhoferweg twd Beverau. Site on R at bottom of hill. Sm, mkd pitch, hdstg, pt shd; htd wc; chem disp; mv service pnt; EHU (16A) inc; shwr; dogs; bus 500m; poss cr; Eng spkn; no adv bkg; quiet, but poss noise fr bar. "Nice, clean, well-run municipal site; gd, modern san facs; max stay 5 nights; excel o'night stop; rec arr bef 1600 high ssn; ideal Xmas mkts; gd conv site; close to city cent; open access site; fair." ♦ ltd. € 15.00 2015*

⊞ **AACHEN** *1A4* (18km SE Rural) *50.69944, 6.22194* **Camping Vichtbachtal, Vichtbachstrasse 10, 52159 Roetgen-Mulartshütte [tel/fax (02408) 5131; camping@vichtbachtal.de; www.vichtbachtal.de]** On E40/A44 exit junc 3 Aachen/Brand onto B258 dir Kornelimünster. In 5km at R-hand bend turn L sp Mulartshütte. Thro Venwegen. Site ent on L 50m bef T-junc app Mulartshütte, site sp. Med, pt sl, shd; wc; chem disp; mv service pnt; shwrs inc; EHU (16A) €1.50 or metered (rev pol); lndry; shop; rest 150m; playgrnd; 80% statics; site clsd Nov; poss cr; quiet; CKE/CCI. "Sm area for tourers; v friendly Eng spkn owners; gd site for visiting Aachen; gd walks adj; gd bus service to Aachen; v pretty wooded area." € 21.50 2016*

⊞ **ACHERN** *3C3* (5km NW Rural) *48.64578, 8.03728* **Camping am Achernsee, Oberacherner Strasse 19, 77855 Achern [(07841) 25253; fax 508835; camping@achern.de; www.achern.de]** Exit A5/E35/E52 junc 53 to Achern, site sp in 1km. Med, mkd pitch, shd; wc; shwrs €0.50; chem disp; mv service pnt; EHU (10A) €2.50; lndry (inc dryer); shop 2km; rest adj; BBQ; playgrnd; fishing; lake sw; 80% statics; dogs €3.50; quiet, but noise nr m'way. "Useful stop for Strasbourg' gd NH." ♦ € 30.00 2014*

ADELBERG see Göppingen *3D3*

AEGIDIENBERG see Bad Honnef *1B4*

AICHELBERG see Göppingen *3D3*

AITRACH see Memmingen *3D4*

AITRANG see Marktoberdorf *4E4*

ALLENSBACH see Radolfzell am Bodensee *3C4*

⊞ **ALPIRSBACH** *3C3* (2km N Rural) *48.35576, 8.41224* **Camping Alpirsbach, Grezenbühler Weg 18-20, 72275 Alpirsbach [(07444) 6313; fax 917815; info@camping-alpirsbach.de; www.camping-alpirsbach.de]** On B294 leave Alpirsbach twds Freudenstadt. 1st site sp on L. Med, pt shd, serviced pitch; wc; chem disp; mv service pnt; shwrs inc; EHU (16A) metered; gas; lndry; shop; rest, snacks; bar; playgrnd; tennis; golf 5km; 10% statics; dogs €1; o'night area for m'vans €10; poss cr; Eng spkn; quiet; ccard not acc; red long stay/CKE/CCI. "Excel site; helpful, informative & friendly owner; vg welcome, free bottle of local beer per person; immac san facs; gd rest; gd walking; guest card for free transport on some local transport; some rvside pitches (v shd)." ♦ € 30.00 2014*

ALSFELD *1D4* (11km W Rural) *50.73638, 9.15222* **Camping Heimertshausen, Ehringshäuserstrasse, 36320 Kirtorf-Heimertshausen [(06635) 206; fax 918359; info@campingplatz-heimertshausen.de; campingplatz-heimertshausen.de]** Exit A5 junc 3 Alsfeld West onto B49 dir Frankfurt. Turn R in vill of Romrod to Heimertshausen & L to site. Site also sp fr B62. Med, shd; wc; chem disp; shwrs €0.55; EHU (10-16A) €2 or metered; lndry; shop; rest, snacks; playgrnd; htd pool adj; dogs €1; 65% statics; clsd 1300-1500 & 2200-0800; o'night area for m'vans; Eng spkn; adv bkg; quiet; red CKE/CCI. "Beautiful, wooded area; lovely 'hunting lodge' type cosy rest; bar/food open Jul/Aug; site run down (2015); facs dated but clean & adequate." 1 Apr-30 Sep. € 27.50 2015*

ALTENAU see Goslar *1D3*

⊞ **ALTENBERG** *4G1* (1km W Rural) *50.76666, 13.74666* **Camping Kleiner Galgenteich (Naturist), Galgenteich 3, 01773 Altenberg [(035056) 31995; fax 31993; mail@camping-erzgebirge.de; www.camping-erzgebirge.de]** Leave A4 at Dresden-Nord onto B170 sp Zinnwald then Altenberg. On SW side of B170; clearly sp. Lge, pt sl, pt shd; wc; chem disp; mv service pnt; shwrs €0.50; EHU (10A) metered + conn fee; lndry; shop; rest; snacks adj; playgrnd; lake sw & sailing adj; ski lift 500m; wifi; 50% statics; dogs €1; poss cr; quiet. "Sep area for naturists; site clsd in Nov." € 21.00 2016*

ALTENKIRCHEN *2F1* (9km W Coastal) *54.62905, 13.22281* **Caravancamp Ostseeblick, Seestr. 39a, 18556 Dranske [(03839) 18196; www.caravancamp-ostseeblick.de]** Clearly sp fr main rd bet Kuhle & Dranske. Sm, open, grassy, hdg/mkd pitches, hdstg, pt shd; wc; chem disp; mv service pnt; shwrs €1; EHU €2.50; lndry (inc dryer); sea adj; wifi; 20% statics; dogs; twin axles; poss cr; Eng spkn; adv bkg. "Excel." ♦ ltd. 1 Apr-31 Oct. € 23.00 2017*

⊞ **ALTENSTEIG** *3C3* (3km W Rural) *48.58456, 8.57866* **Schwarzwald Camping Altensteig, Im Oberen Tal 3-5, 72213 Altensteig [(07453) 8415; fax 930476; info@schwarzwaldcamping.de; www.schwarzwaldcamping.de]** Take Obere Talstrasse (L362) due W fr town ctr. Aft 2km site on L. Easy access. Sm, open, grassy, pt shd; wc; chem disp; shwrs; EHU; rest; bar; BBQ; lake; games area; 75% statics; dogs €2; bus 2km; twin axles; Eng spkn; quiet. "Gd; table tennis, beach volleyball, boating, walking fr site; Black Forest; cross country skiing." ♦ ltd. € 23.00 2017*

ALVERN see Celle *1D3*

ANNWEILER AM TRIFELS see Landau in der Pfalz *3C3*

ASBACHERHUTTE see Idar Oberstein *3B2*

⊞ **AUGSBURG** *4E3* (7km N Rural) *48.41168, 10.92371* **Camping Bella Augusta, Mühlhauserstrasse 54B, 86169 Augsburg-Ost [(0821) 707575; fax 705883; info@caravaningpark.de; www.caravaningpark.de]** Exit A8/E52 junc 73 dir Neuburg to N, site sp. Lge, pt shd; wc; chem disp; mv service pnt; shwrs inc; EHU (10A) inc; lndry rm; shop; supmkt 4km; rest; snacks & bar adj; playgrnd adj; lake sw & shgl beach adj; boating; 80% statics; dogs €2.55; noise fr a'bahn; ccard acc. "V busy NH; excel rest; camping equipment shop on site; vg san facs but site looking a little run down; cycle track to town (map fr recep); vg; nice lake." € 31.00 2014*

AUGSBURG *4E3* (8km N Rural) *48.43194, 10.92388* **Camping Ludwigshof am See, Augsburgerstrasse 36, 86444 Mühlhausen-Affing [(08207) 961724; fax 961770; info@campingludwigshof.de; www.campingludwigshof.de]** Exit A8/E52 junc 73at Augsburg Ost/Pöttmes exit; foll sp Pöttmes; site sp on L on lakeside. Lge, unshd; wc; chem disp; mv service pnt; shwrs inc; EHU (16A) €3.50 (long cable req); lndry; supmkt 500m; bar; rest; snacks; BBQ; playgrnd; tennis; lake sw; wifi; 70% statics sep area; dogs €2; bus; clsd 1300-1500; poss cr; twin axles; Eng spkn; quiet; 10% red 3+ days; ccard acc; CKE/CCI. "Pleasant site; lge unmkd field for tourers, close to san facs but long walk to recep; both 6A panel & 16A panels for EHU -16A only accepts German type of plug; beautiful clean, modern facs; nr A8 m'way; conv NH on way to E Italy; gd for long stay, special rates can be negotiated; poss need long cable as EHU in corner of field."
1 Apr-31 Oct. € 26.50 2016*

AUGSBURG *4E3* (9km NE Rural) *48.4375, 10.92916* **Lech Camping, Seeweg 6, 86444 Affing-Mühlhausen [(08207) 2200; fax 2202; info@lech-camping.de; www.lech-camping.de]** Exit A8/E52 at junc 73 Augsburg-Ost; take rd N sp Pöttmes; site 3km on R. Sm, mkd pitch, hdstg, pt shd; htd wc; chem disp; mv service pnt; shwrs; EHU (16A); lndry; shop 300m; supmkt 1km; rest; bar; BBQ; lake sw adj; boating; wifi; adv bkg rec; statics sep area; poss cr; dogs €3; bus to Augsburg; train Munich; Eng spkn; some rd noise; ccard acc. "Lovely, well-ordered site; friendly, helpful owners; excel san facs; gd play area; deposit for san facs key; camping accessory shop on site; cycle rte to Augsburg; excel NH for A8; excel site espec lakeside pitch; c'vans close together; constant rd noise." ♦
15 Apr-4 Oct. € 34.90 SBS - G19 2017*

BACHARACH see Oberwesel *3B2*

BAD ABBACH *4F3* (6km W Rural) *48.93686, 12.01992* **Campingplatz Freizeitinsel, Inselstraße 1a, D93077 Bad Abbach [(09405) 9570401 or (0176) 96631729; fax 9570402; info@campingplatz-freizeitinsel.de; www.campingplatz-freizeitinsel.de]** A93 Regensburg, exit Pentling B16 dir twrds Kelheim. Cont on B16 past Bad Abbach and take next exit R to Poikam/Inselbad. Over rv and foll rd round to R past Poikam sp. At junc turn R sp Inselbad. Site on R. Med, mkd pitches, terr; wc; chem disp; mv service pnt; fam bthrm; shwrs; EHU; lndry (inc dryer); snacks; bar; BBQ; cooking facs; playgrnd; sw 400m; bike hire; wifi; 20% statics; twin axles; Eng spkn; adv bkg; quiet; CKE/CCI. "New (2014) family run developing site; vg, modern, clean facs; some deluxe serviced pitches avail with supp; gd area for touring, cycling & walking; nrby lake, sw & thermal baths; gd rest in vill 1km; train to Regensburg 1km; excel site." ♦
25 Mar-31 Oct & 27 Nov-18 Dec. € 28.00 2017*

⊞ **BAD BEDERKESA** *1C2* (1km S Rural) *53.62059, 8.84879* **Regenbogen-Camp Bad Bederkesa, Ankeloherstrasse 14, 27624 Bad Bederkesa [(04745) 6487 or (0431) 2372370; fax 8033; badbederkesa@regenbogen-camp.de; www.regenbogen-camp.de]** Exit A27 junc 5 Debstedt, dir Bederkesa, site sp. V lge, pt shd; wc; chem disp; mv service pnt; shwrs inc; EHU (16A) metered + conn fee; lndry (inc dryer); shop 800m; rest, snacks; bar; playgrnd; games area; golf 4km; wifi; TV; 60% statics; dogs €4; clsd 1300-1500; o'night area for m'vans; adv bkg; quiet; ccard acc; red long stay/CKE/CCI. ♦ € 27.00 2013*

BAD BELLINGEN see Lörrach *3B4*

GERMANY

BAD BENTHEIM *1B3* (3km E Rural) *52.29945, 7.19361* **Campingplatz am Berg, Suddendorferstrasse 37, 48455 Bad Bentheim [(05922) 990461; fax 990460; info@campingplatz amberg.de; www.campingplatzamberg.de]** Exit A30 ad junc 3 onto B403, foll sp to Bad Bentheim. After sh incline, passing g'ge on R at traff lts, at next junc turn R round town to hospital (sp Orthopäde). Turn L & cont past hospital to rndabt, strt over then 1.5km on L. Sm, mkd pitch, pt shd; htd wc; chem disp; shwrs inc; EHU (16A) €2.50; gas; lndry; shop 2.5km; rest; bar; cooking facs; playgrnd; 50% statics in sep area; dogs; phone; site clsd 24 Dec-26 Jan; poss v cr; Eng spkn; adv bkg; quiet; CKE/CCI. "Friendly, helpful owners; easy drive to Europort & ferries; rlwy museum on Dutch side of border." ♦ 4 Mar-24 Dec. € 24.50 2013*

BAD BRAMSTEDT *1D2* (1km N Rural) *53.9283, 9.8901* **Kur-Camping Roland, Kielerstrasse 52, 24576 Bad Bramstedt [(04192) 6723; fax 2783]** Exit A7 junc 17 dir Bad Bremstedt; site sp, ent immed at Nissan g'ge at top of hill at start of dual c'way. Fr N exit A7 junc 16 dir Bad Bremstedt; site on L in 4km. Sm, shd; wc; chem disp; shwrs inc; EHU (6-16A) €2 & metered; lndry; shop; rest 300m; snacks; dogs €2; Eng spkn; some rd noise; CKE/CCI. "Excel CL-type site; friendly owner; EHU not rec if site v full; gd sh stay/NH." ♦ 1 Apr-31 Oct. € 24.00 2017*

"Satellite navigation makes touring much easier"

Remember most sat navs don't know if you're towing or in a larger vehicle – always use yours alongside maps and site directions.

BAD BREISIG see Remagen *3B1*

BAD DOBERAN *2F1* (10km N Coastal) *54.15250, 11.89972* **Ferien-Camp Borgerende (Part Naturist), Deichstrasse 16, 18211 Börgerende [(038203) 81126; fax 81284; info@ostseeferiencamp.de; www.ostseeferiencamp.de]** In Bad Doberan, turn L off B105 sp Warnemunde. In 4km in Rethwisch, turn L sp Börgerende. In 3km turn R at site sp. V lge, hdg pitch, unshd; wc; chem disp; mv service pnt; fam bthrm; sauna; shwrs inc; EHU (10-16A) €3; lndry (inc dryer) shop; rest, snacks; bar; cooking facs; playgrnd; shgl beach adj; sep naturist beach; bike hire; games area; internet; child entmnt; 10% statics; dogs €4; bus 500m; phone; o'night area for m'vans; Eng spkn; quiet; red LS/snr citizens; CKE/CCI. "Excel beaches; cycle paths; excel site." ♦ 21 Mar-30 Oct. € 35.00 2016*

⊞ **BAD DURKHEIM** *3C2* (3km NE Rural) *49.47361, 8.19166* **Knaus Campingplatz Bad Dürkheim, In den Almen 3, 67098 Bad Dürkheim [(06322) 61356; fax 8161; badduerkheim@knauscamp.de; www.knauscamp.de]** Fr S on A61/E31 exit junc 60 onto A650/B37 twds Bad Dürkheim. At 2nd traff lts turn R, site sp nr local airfield. Fr N on A6 exit junc 19 onto B271 to Bad Dürkheim. At traff lts after Ungstein turn L dir Lugwigshafen, at next traff lts turn L, then 1st R. Site at end of rd. Ent strictly controlled. Site well sp fr all dir on town o'skts. V lge, mkd pitch, pt shd; htd wc; chem disp; mv service pnt; child/fam bthrm; sauna; shwrs inc; EHU (16A) €2.50; gas; lndry (inc dryer); shop; BBQ; rest; playgrnd; sand beach adj; lake sw adj; tennis; games area; solarium; TV rm; bike hire; golf 8km; 45% statics; phone; bus; m'van o'night facs; poss v cr; quiet but some daytime noise fr adj sports airfield; poss cr; Eng spkn; no ccard acc; red long stay; CKE/CCI. "Well-equipped, busy site in vineyards; sm, well-worn pitches; some modern san facs - all clean; no access 1300-1500; gd pool in Bad Dürkheim; wine-fest & wurst-fest Sep excel; conv NH Bavaria & Austria." ♦ € 36.50 2015*

BAD DURKHEIM *3C2* (3km S Rural) *49.43741, 8.17036* **Campingplatz im Burgtal, Waldstrasse 105, 67157 Wachenheim [(06322) 9580-801; fax 9580-899; touristinfo@vg-wachenheim.de; www.wachenheim.de]** Fr Bad Dürkheim, take B271 S dir Neustadt for approx 2km. After passing Villa Rustica rest area, turn L for Wachenheim, then R. Go strt at traff lts, up hill thro vill (narr). Site on L. Med, hdg/mkd pitch, hdstg, pt shd; wc; chem disp; mv service pnt; serviced pitches; shwrs inc; EHU (16A) inc; lndry (inc dryer); shop & 1.5km; rest; bar; playgrnd; tennis; golf 12km; 50% statics; dogs €1; poss cr; quiet; CKE/CCI. "Forest walks in Pfalz National Park; in heart of wine-tasting country; v busy during wine festival - adv bkg rec; helpful owners; gd facs; site bit shabby (2017)." ♦ ltd. 1 Mar-30 Nov. € 21.50 (3 persons) 2017*

BAD EMS *3B2* (7km E Rural) *50.32773, 7.75483* **Camping Lahn-Beach, Hallgarten 16, 56132 Dausenau [(02603) 13964; fax 919935; info@canutours.de; www.campingplatz-dausenau.de]** Foll rv E fr Bad Ems twd Nassau on B260/417. At ent to vill of Dausenau turn R over bdge, site visible on S bank of Lahn Rv. Med, pt shd; wc; chem disp; mv service pnt; shwrs €1; EHU (6-16A) metered + conn fee; lndry; shop 400m; rest, snacks; playgrnd; boat-launching; bike hire; wifi; 40% statics; dogs; sep car park; poss cr; adv bkg; rd noise. "Pleasant situation; interesting rv traff & sightseeing around Lahn Valley; liable to flood at v high water; gd san facs." 1 Apr-31 Oct. € 23.50 2015*

⊞ **BAD FALLINGBOSTEL** *1D2* (3km NE Rural) *52.87686, 9.73147* **DCC Camping Bohmeschlucht, Vierde 22, D 29683 Fallingbostel-Vierde [(05162) 5604; fax 5160; campingplatz-hoehmeschlucht@t-online.de; www.boehmeschlucht.de]** A7 junc 47 Bad Fallingbostel. Foll sp Dorfmark/Soltau. On leaving Fallingbostel, go strt at rndabt and cont for approx 1 km. Site sp on R. Med, mkd, pt shd; wc; chem disp; mv service pnt; fam bthrm; shwrs; EHU (16A) - €2; lndry (inc dryer); shops 3km; rest; bar; BBQ; playgrnd; rvside sw; games rm; internet; 60% statics; dogs; Eng spkn; acc adv bkg; quiet. "Excel walking, cycling & boat/canoe tours fr site; vg rest; library; helpful staff; excel for exploring Luneburger Heide, Hamburg or Walsrode Bird Park; excel site." € 21.00 2014*

BAD FEILNBACH see Rosenheim *4F4*

⊞ **BAD FUSSING** *4G3* (3km S Urban) *48.33236, 13.31577* **Fuchs Kur Camping, Falkenstraße 14, 94072 Bad Fussing [(0853) 7356; fax (08537) 912083; info@kurcamping-fuchs.de; www.kurcamping-fuchs.de]** Fr A3 Nurnberg-Passau, take exit 118 dir Egglfing. Foll sp. Med, mkd pitch, hdstg; wc; chem disp, dedicated pnt; shwrs inc; EHU inc; lndry; rest; playgrnd; 10% statics; dogs €2; poss cr; Eng spkn; adv bkg; quiet; ccard acc; CKE/CCI. "Gd NH; gd value; vg." € 23.00 2015*

⊞ **BAD FUSSING** *4G3* (3km S Rural) *48.33255, 13.31440* **Kur & Feriencamping Max I, Falkenstrasse 12, 94072 Egglfing-Bad Füssing [(08537) 96170; fax 961710; info@campingmax.de; www.campingmax.de]** Across frontier & bdge fr Obernberg in Austria. Site sp in Egglfing. On B12 Schärding to Simbach turn L immed bef vill of Tutting sp Obernberg. Site on R after 7km, sp. Med, pt shd; htd wc; chem disp; mv service pnt; private san facs avail; shwrs inc; EHU (16A) metered + conn fee; lndry (inc dryer); shop; rest 300m; snacks; bar; cooking facs; playgrnd; pool 3km; lake sw; fishing; thermal facs in Bad Füssing; tennis 2km; bike hire; wellness cent; golf 2km; wifi; entmnt; TV; 20% statics; dogs €2; quiet; red CKE/CCI "Gd rest for snacks & meals on site; well managed site; excel clean facs; new indoor thermal bath & outdoor sw pool (2014)." ♦ € 22.60 2014*

⊞ **BAD GANDERSHEIM** *1D3* (2km E Rural) *51.86694, 10.04972* **DCC-Kur-Campingpark, 37581 Bad Gandersheim [(05382) 1595; fax 1599; info@camping-bad-gandersheim.de; www.camping-bad-gandersheim.de]** Exit A7/E45 at junc 67 onto B64 dir Holzminden & Bad Gandersheim. Site on R shortly after Seboldshausen. Lge, pt shd; wc; chem disp; mv service pnt; shwrs €0.50; EHU (10A) metered + conn fee; lndry; shop; rest, snacks; playgrnd; pool 1.5km; bike hire; 40% statics; dogs €1; sep o'night area; poss cr; quiet. "Excel; always plenty of space." ♦ € 28.00 2014*

BAD HERRENALB see Bad Wildbad im Schwarzwald *3C3*

⊞ **BAD HONNEF** *1B4* (9km E Rural) *50.65027, 7.30166* **Camping Jillieshof, Ginsterbergweg 6, 53604 Bad Honnef-Aegidienberg [(02224) 972066; fax 972067; information@camping-jillieshof.de; www.camping-jillieshof.de]** Exit E35/A3 junc 34 & foll sp Bad Honnef. In Himburg bef pedestrian traff lts turn L, then R. Site in 300m. Lge, mkd pitch, sl, pt shd; wc; chem disp; mv service pnt; shwrs inc; EHU (16A) €2 or metered; shop; playgrnd; pool 9km; fishing; 85% statics; dogs €2; Eng spkn; quiet; red LS. "Excel facs; gated." € 17.50 2012*

BAD KOSEN *2E4* (1.5km S Rural) *51.12285, 11.71743* **Camping an der Rudelsburg, 06628 Bad Kösen [(034463) 28705; fax 28706; campkoesen@aol.com; www.campingbadkoesen.de]** Site sp fr town. Med, pt shd; wc; chem disp; fam bthrm; shwrs €1; EHU (16A) metered + conn fee; gas; lndry; shop 1.5km; rest 1.5km; snacks; bar; playgrnd; 10% statics; dogs €2; o'night area for m'vans; quiet; CKE/CCI. ♦ 23 Mar-1 Nov. € 24.40 2016*

BAD KREUZNACH *3C2* (8km N Rural) *49.88383, 7.85712* **Campingplatz Lindelgrund, Im Lindelgrund 1, 55452 Guldental [(06707) 633; fax 8468; info@lindelgrund.de; www.lindelgrund.de]** Fr A61 exit junc 47 for Windesheim. In cent immed after level x-ing, turn L & pass thro Guldental. Site sp on R in 500m. Sm, some hdstg, terr, pt shd; wc; chem disp; shwrs €0.50; EHU (10-16A) €2 or metered; rest, snacks; playgrnd; htd, covrd pool 2km; tennis; golf 12km; 60% statics in sep area; dogs €1.50; poss cr; no adv bkg; quiet; red long stay. "Lovely, peaceful site; friendly, helpful staff; wine sold on site; narr gauge rlwy & museum adj; gd NH; san facs nr touring pitches; conv base for Rhine & Mosel Valleys." 1 Mar-15 Dec. € 22.00 2016*

BAD LIEBENZELL see Calw *3C3*

⊞ **BAD MERGENTHEIM** *3D2* (3km SE Rural) *49.46481, 9.77673* **Campingplatz Bad Mergentheim, Willinger Tal 1, 97980 Bad Mergentheim [(07931) 2177; fax 5636543; info@camping-mgh.de; www.camping-mgh.de]** Fr Bad Mergentheim foll B19 S, sp Ulm. After 1km take rd to L (sps). Ent 2.7m. Med, sl, pt shd; wc; chem disp; shwrs inc; EHU (10A) metered + conn fee or €1.90; gas; lndry; shop; snacks; playgrnd; htd, covrd pool; paddling pool; tennis; 20% statics; dogs €2.50; bus nr; sep o'night area; quiet; ccard not acc; CKE/CCI. "Nice site; friendly, helpful owner." € 17.00 2013*

BAD NEUENAHR AHRWEILER *3B1* (8km W Rural) *50.53400, 7.04800* **Camping Dernau, Ahrweg 2, 53507 Dernau [(02643) 8517; www.camping-dernau.de]** Exit A61 junc 30 for Ahrweiler. Fr Ahrweiler on B267 W to Dernau, cross rv bef Dernau & turn L into Ahrweg, site sp. Sm, some hdstg, shd; htd wc; chem disp; mv service pnt; shwrs €1; EHU (16A) €2; shops 500m; playgrnd; dogs €1; bus; train; some rlwy noise. "In beautiful Ahr valley - gd wine area; train to Ahrweiler Markt rec; immac, modern san facs; v nice." ♦ 1 Apr-31 Oct. € 17.40 2014*

⊞ **BAD RIPPOLDSAU** *3C3* (7km S Rural) *48.38396, 8.30168* **Schwarzwaldcamping Alisehof, Rippold sauerstrasse 8, 77776 Bad Rippoldsau-Schapbach [(07839) 203; fax 1263; camping@alisehof.de; www. alisehof.de]** Exit A5/E35 junc 55 Offenburg onto B33 dir Gengenbach & Hausach to Wolfach. At end of Wolfach vill turn N dir Bad Rippoldsau. Site on R over wooden bdge after vill of Schapbach. 2 steep passes fr other dir. Med, mkd pitch, pt sl, pt shd; htd wc; chem disp; mv service pnt; 30% serviced pitches; fam bthrm; shwrs inc; EHU (16A) metered + conn fee; gas; lndry; shop; rest, snacks; bar; playgrnd; pool 2km; entmnt; 20% statics; dogs €2.30; phone; site clsd 1230-1430; poss cr; Eng spkn; adv bkg; quiet; red 7+ nts/CKE/CCI. "Highly rec; clean, friendly site; many gd walks in area; not a NH." ♦ € 35.70 2014*

"There aren't many sites open at this time of year"

If you're travelling outside peak season remember to call ahead to check site opening dates – even if the entry says 'open all year'.

⊞ **BAD SCHANDAU** *2G4* (3km E Rural) *50.92996, 14.19301* **Campingplatz Ostrauer Mühle, Im Kirnitzschtal, 01814 Bad Schandau [(035022) 42742; fax 50352; info@ostrauer-muehle.de; www. ostrauer-muehle.de]** SE fr Dresden on B172 for 40km (Pirna-Schmilka). In Bad Schandau turn E twds Hinterhermsdorf; site in approx 3km. Med, terr, pt shd; wc; chem disp; mv service pnt; shwrs €0.50; EHU (10A) €1.75 + conn fee; lndry; shop; supmkt 4km; rest; sm playgrnd; dogs €2; sep car park; quiet; CKE/CCI. "In National Park; superb walking area; rec arr early high ssn; site yourself if office clsd on arr." ♦ ltd. € 18.50 2012*

BAD SEGEBERG *1D2* (5km NE Rural) *53.96131, 10.33685* **Klüthseecamp Seeblick, Stripdorfer Weg, Klüthseehof 2, 23795 Klein Rönnau [(04551) 82368; fax 840638; info@kluethseecamp.de; www. kluethseecamp.de]** Exit A21 junc 13 at Bad Sedgeberg Süd onto B432; turn L sp Bad Sedgeberg; cont on B432 dir Scharbeutz & Puttgarden thro Klein Rönnau, then turn R for site. V lge, pt shd; wc; chem disp; mv service pnt; some serviced pitches; fam bthrm; sauna; steam rm; shwrs inc; EHU (16A) inc; gas; lndry (inc dryer); shop; rest, snacks; BBQ; playgrnd; htd pool; lake sw 200m; fishing; horseriding; tennis; bike hire; spa; golf 6km; internet; games/TV rm; bus adj; wifi; 75% statics (sep area); dogs €2; twin-axles acc (rec check in adv); train to Hamburg, Lübeck; site clsd Feb; poss cr; Eng spkn; adv bkg; quiet; ccard acc; red LS/CKE/CCI. "Spacious, well-kept nr lakeside site; relaxing atmophere; lge pitches; helpful staff; gd facs & pool; wide range of activities; gd cycling, walking; conv Hamburg, Lübeck; excel; peaceful 50 min lakeside walk to town; excel." ♦ 1 Jan-31 Jan & 1 Mar-31 Dec. € 24.00 SBS - G12 2017*

⊞ **BAD TOLZ** *4E4* (7km S Rural) *47.70721, 11.55023* **Alpen-Camping Arzbach, Alpenbadstrasse 20, 83646 Arzbach [(08042) 8408; fax 8570; campingplatz-arbach@web.de; www.arzbach.de]** S fr Bad Tölz on B13. Exit Lenggries, turn R to cross rv & R on Wackers burgerstrasse twds Arzbach; in 5km on ent Arzbach turn L. Site ent past sw pool. Med, pt shd; wc; chem disp; shwrs €1; EHU (16A) inc; gas; lndry; shop 4km; rest; snacks 300m; playgrnd; covrd pool; tennis 100m; 60% statics; no dogs €1; bus 300m; poss cr; no adv bkg; quiet; CKE/CCI. "Gd walking, touring Bavarian lakes, excel facs & rest; care needed with lge c'vans due trees & hedges." ♦ € 20.00 2012*

⊞ **BAD URACH** *3D3* (11km E Rural) *48.48598, 9.50761* **Camping Lauberg, Hinter Lau 3, 72587 Römerstein-Böhringen [(07382) 1509; fax 1074; info@lauberg.de; www.lauberg.de]** Fr Bad Urach, take rd twd Grabenstetten & foll sp to Böhringen, then sp to site. NB Rd to Grabenstetten avoids long, steep climb on B28. Med, mkd pitch, terr, unshd; htd wc; chem disp; 90% serviced pitch; shwrs inc; EHU (16A) metered + conn fee; lndry; shop, rest high ssn; supmkt 1.5km; bar; BBQ; playgrnd; htd pool 9km; wintersports; ski lift 5km; 80% statics; dogs €1.50; poss cr; quiet; adv bkg; 10% red 10+ days. "Ideal walking area, castles, caves, Bad Urach baths." ♦ ltd. € 16.50 2015*

⊞ **BAD WILDBAD IM SCHWARZWALD** *3C3* (9km E Rural) *48.73745, 8.57623* **Camping Kleinenzhof, Kleinenzhof 1, 75323 Bad Wildbad [(07081) 3435; fax 3770; info@kleinenzhof.de; www.kleinenzhof. de]** Fr Calmbach foll B294 5km S. Site sp on R, in rv valley. Fr Bad Wildbad site is on L. Lge, pt sl, pt shd; wc; chem disp; mv service pnt; serviced pitches; sauna; shwrs inc; EHU (16A) metered + conn fee; gas; lndry; shop; rest, snacks; playgrnd; 2 pools (1 htd & covrd); bike hire; ski lift 8km; entmnt; 80% statics; dogs €2.10; o'night area for m'vans; clsd 1300-1500; poss cr; adv bkg; quiet; red long stay. "Nature trails fr site; mountain views; distillery on site; modern san facs; sm pitches." ♦ € 26.40 2012*

See advertisement opposite

⊞ **BAD WILDBAD IM SCHWARZWALD** *3C3* (7km S Rural) *48.69777, 8.52027* **Camping Kälbermühle, Kälbermühlenweg 57, 75323 Bad Wildbad [(07085) 7322 or 7353; fax 1043; information@kaelber muehle.de]** Take Enzklösterle rd S fr Bad Wildbad, site sp on rv bank. Med, pt shd; wc; chem disp (wc); shwrs €0.50; EHU (16A) metered + conn fee; lndry (inc dryer); playgrnd; 60% statics; dogs €0.80; bus; adv bkg; quiet. "Friendly owners; beautifully kept, peaceful site; superb rest; mkd forest walks; gd; no cc/debit cards." € 23.00 2015*

BAD WILDBAD IM SCHWARZWALD *3C3* (20km NW Urban) *48.79268, 8.42908* **Campingplatz Jungbrunnen, Schwimmbadstrasse 29, 76332 Bad Herrenalb [(07083) 932970; fax 932971; info@camping-jungbrunnen.de; www.camping-jungbrunnen.de]** On S o'skirts Bad Herrenalb on L564 to Gernsbach & Baden-Baden. Foll sp on L down slope. NB: Rd dist fr Bad Wildbad is much more than crow flies due to no direct rds & inclines. If app fr Gernsbach, pass site & proceed into Bad Herrenalb to rndabt, then return. This avoids diff turn. Med, terr, pt shd; wc; chem disp; shwrs €0.50; EHU (16A) metered; gas; lndry; shop; snacks; bar; cooking facs; pool; paddling pool; 60% statics; dogs €1.50; bus; Eng spkn; adv bkg; quiet; "Friendly owner; easy walk into interesting sm town; san facs tired but clean." 1 Apr-31 Oct. € 22.30 2013*

BADENWEILER see Neuenburg am Rhein *3B4*

⊞ **BAMBERG** *4E2* (5km S Rural) *49.86138, 10.91583* **Camping Insel, Am Campingplatz 1, 96049 Bamberg-Bug [(0951) 56320; fax 56321; buero@campinginsel.de; www.campinginsel.de]** Exit A70/E48 junc 16 or A73 exit Bamberg-Süd onto B22 dir Würzburg. Site on L of rd along Rv Regnitz. Bug sm vill suburb of Bamburg to S of rv. Fr S on A3 exit junc 79 dir Bamberg. In 12km turn L dir Pettstadt; turn R at rndabt, site in 2km. Lge, pt shd; htd wc; fam bthrm; shwrs inc; chem disp; mv service pnt; EHU (16A) metered (long lead poss req); gas; lndry; supmkt 4km; shop; snacks; playgrnd; TV; 20% statics; dogs €1.10; clsd 1300-1500 & 2300-0700; bus to Bamburg; Eng spkn; quiet; cash only; red long stay/CKE/CCI. "Lovely historic town, Unesco; rvside site; excel cycle facs to town; bus to town €1.50; excel, modern san facs; family run site; gd rest; beautiful walk thro park by rvside; UNESCO World Heritage town; new lgr san facs for 2015." ♦ € 29.50 2015*

BENSERSIEL *1B2* (W Coastal) *53.67531, 7.57001* **Familien & Kurcampingplatz Bensersiel, 26427 Esens-Bensersiel [(04971) 917121; fax 4988; info@bensersiel.de; www.bensersiel.de]** Fr B210 turn N at Ogenbargen; thro Esens to Bensersiel. Site adj to harbour in cent of vill - clearly sp. V lge, unshd; wc; chem disp; mv service pnt; shwrs €0.50; EHU (16A) €2.50; gas; lndry; shop; rest, snacks; playgrnd; htd pool; beach adj; spa complex nr; tennis; games area; bike hire; entmnt; TV; 70% statics; no dogs; poss cr; adv bkg; debit card acc. "Cycling country; gd boat trips; gd san facs; open site adj sea; gd access vill, rests & island ferries; elec metered after 3 days - if staying longer, check meter on arr." ♦ Easter-15 Oct. € 17.00 2017*

"That's changed – Should I let The Club know?"

If you find something on site that's different from the site entry, fill in a report and let us know. See camc.com/europereport.

⊞ **BERCHTESGADEN** *4G4* (5km NE Rural) *47.64742, 13.03993* **Camping Allweglehen, Allweggasse 4, 83471 Berchtesgaden-Untersalzberg [(08652) 2396; camping@allweglehen.de; www.allweglehen.de]** On R of rd B305 Berchtesgaden dir Salzburg, immed after ent Unterau; sp. App v steep in places with hairpin bend; gd power/weight ratio needed. Lge, pt sl, terr, pt shd, some hdstg; htd wc; serviced pitches; chem disp; mv service pnt; fam bthrm; shwrs inc; EHU (16A) metered + conn fee; lndry (inc dryer); shop; rest; bar; playgrnd; htd pool; cycles; wifi; entmnt; 20% statics; dogs €2.95; bus 500m; ski lift; phone; poss cr; adv bkg rec high ssn; quiet; ccard acc; 10% red CKE/CCI. "Gd touring/walking cent; wonderful views some pitches; beautiful scenery; Hitler's Eagles' Nest worth visit (rd opens mid-May) - bus fr Obersalzburg; site rds poss o'grown & uneven; steep app some pitches - risk of grounding for long o'fits; friendly, family-run site; excel rest." ♦ € 45.50 2014*

GERMANY

⊞ **BERGEN** *1D3* (9km E Rural) *52.80443, 10.10376* **Camping am Örtzetal, Dicksbarg 46, 29320 Oldendorf [(05052) 3072; www.campingplatz-oldendorf.de]** Fr S, exit A7/E45 junc 52 dir Celle, in 5km turn L sp Winsen, Belsen & Bergen. Fr N exit A7/E45 at junc 45 onto B3 to Bergen. Foll rd to Bergen. In Bergen foll sp Hermannsburg. In about 7km at T-junc turn R, then 1st L sp Eschede & Oldendorf. In Oldendorf turn L at 2nd x-rds. Site on R in 1km. Lge, pt shd; wc; chem disp; shwrs €0.80; EHU (6A) metered + conn fee; lndry (inc dryer); shop 4km; rest 500m; snacks; bar; htd pool 4km; lake 4km; playgrnd; bike hire; 40% statics; dogs €1.50; phone; quiet; CKE/CCI. "Ideal for walking & cycling on Lüneburg Heath; conv Belsen memorial; welcoming, friendly owner; peaceful site; barrier clsd 1300-1500." € 17.00 2016*

BERGWITZ see Lutherstadt Wittenberg *2F3*

⊞ **BERLIN** *2G3* (23km SW Rural) *52.4650, 13.16638* **DCC Campingplatz Gatow, Kladower Damm 207-213, 14089 Berlin-Gatow [(030) 3654340; fax 36808492; gatow@dccberlin.de; www.dccberlin.de]** Fr A10 to W of Berlin turn E on rd 5 sp Spandau/ Centrum. Go twd city cent & after 14km turn R onto Gatowerstrasse (Esso g'ge) sp Kladow/Gatow. Site 6.5km on L almost opp Kaserne (barracks). Med, pt shd; htd wc; chem disp; mv service pnt; shwrs inc; fam bthrm; EHU (10-16A) metered + conn fee; gas; lndry (inc dryer); supmkt 2km; snacks; bar; playgrnd; sand beach 1km; 60% statics; dogs €2; bus at gate; poss cr; Eng spkn; rd noise; red CKE/CCI. "Excel site; bus tickets fr friendly recep; frequent bus to Berlin cent at gate; highly rec; excel, clean san facs; bicycles can be taken on nrby Kladow ferry to Wannsee S. Bahn; gates close bet 1300 & 1500 and at 2200; rec." ♦ € 26.50 2016*

⊞ **BERLIN** *2G3* (26km SW Rural) *52.40027, 13.18055* **City Campingplatz Hettler & Lange, Bäkehang 9a, 14532 Kleinmachnow-Dreilinden [(033203) 79684; fax 77913; kleinmachnow@city-camping-berlin.de; www.city-camping-berlin.de]** Fr S exit A115/E51 junc 5 sp Kleinmachnow, turn L at T-junc & cont to rndabt. Turn L & foll site sp in 800m. Lge, pt sl, pt shd; htd wc; chem disp; mv service pnt; fam bthrm; shwrs inc; EHU (6A) €2.50; gas; lndry (inc dryer); sm shop & 5km; rest, snacks; playgrnd; lake sw 2km; boats for hire; dogs €2; phone; bus nr; poss v cr; some Eng spkn; adv bkg; quiet but some barge & rd noise; CKE/CCI. "Excel location on canal side; immac, modern san facs; twin-axles by arrangement; gd walking in woods; gd public transport conv Berlin 45 mins - parking at Wannsee S-bahn (family ticket avail for bus & train); vg." € 23.00 2013*

⊞ **BERLIN** *2G3* (13km NW Urban) *52.54861, 13.25694* **City-Camping Hettler & Lange, Gartenfelderstrasse 1, 13599 Berlin-Spandau [(030) 33503633; fax 33503635; spandau@city-camping-berlin.de; www.hettler-lange.de]** Fr N on A111/A115/E26 exit junc 10 sp Tegel Airport & head W on Saatwinkler Damm. Fr S on A100 exit junc 11 onto Saatwinkler Damm. Cont 3.2km to traff lts, turn R, then R again immed bef 2nd bdge. Site on island in rv. Med, pt sl, shd; wc; chem disp; shwrs €1; EHU (16A) €2; lndry; shop 2km; rest; bar; dogs €2; Eng spkn; no adv bkg; aircraft noise; ccard acc; CKE/CCI. "Conv Berlin; 15 min walk to bus stn; gd location beside a canal but aircraft noise; gd san facs; NH/sh stay only; poss to cycle along canal to Potsdam." € 22.50 2014*

BERNKASTEL KUES *3B2* (20km NE Rural) *49.96556, 7.10475* **Camping Rissbach, Rissbacherstrasse 155, 56841 Traben-Trarbach [(06541) 3111; info@moselcampings.de; www.moselcampings.de]** Fr Bernkastel on B53, after Kröv do not cross Mosel bdge but cont strt on twd Traben, site on R in 1km. NB 20km by rd fr Bernkastel to site. Med, mkd pitch, pt sl, shd; htd wc; chem disp; mv service pnt; shwrs €0.25/min; EHU (16A) €2.50; gas 500m; lndry; shop & 2km; rest 1km; snacks; BBQ; playgrnd; htd pool adj; boat-launch; wifi; 30% statics; dogs €3.50; phone; quiet. "In lovely position nr rv; extra for pitches nr rv; well-run site; excel san facs; vg sw pools in town; poss flooding at high water; Sept wine fest." ♦ 1 Apr-31 Oct. € 16.00 2012*

"I like to fill in the reports as I travel from site to site"

You'll find report forms at the back of this guide, or you can fill them in online at camc.com/europereport.

BERNKASTEL KUES *3B2* (2km SW Rural) *49.90883, 7.05600* **Knaus Campingpark (formerly Kueser Werth Camping), Am Hafen 2, 54470 Bernkastel-Kues [(06531) 8200; fax 8282; www.knauscamp.de]** A'bahn A1/48 (E44) exit Salmtal; join rd sp Bernkastel. Bef rv bdge turn L sp Lieser, thro Lieser cont by rv to ent on R for boat harbour, foll camping sp to marina. Diff access via narr single-track rd. Lge, mkd pitch, pt shd; htd wc; chem disp; mv service pnt; shwrs inc; EHU(16A); lndry (inc dryer); sm shop; rest, snacks, bar 1km; BBQ; playgrnd; covrd pool 2km; 10% statics; dogs; bus 1km; poss cr; Eng spkn; adv bkg; quiet, some rd noise & rv barges; 5% red CKE/CCI. "Excel cent for touring Mosel Valley; Bernkastel delightful sm town with gd parking, sailing, boat excursions, wine cent; cycle lanes; site low on rv bank - poss flooding in bad weather; efficient staff; gd site; not rec for NH/sh stay high ssn as pitches & position poor; san facs old but gd condition; newly taken over by Knaus." ♦ 1 Apr-31 Oct. € 22.00 2017*

BERNKASTEL KUES *3B2* (3km NW Rural) *49.93736, 7.04853* **Camping Schenk, Hauptstrasse 165, 54470 Bernkastel-Wehlen [(06531) 8176; fax 7681; info@camping-schenk.de; www.camping-schenk.com]** On Trier/Koblenz rd B53, exit Kues heading N on L bank of rv & site on R in 4km at Wehlen, sp. Steep exit. Med, mkd pitch, some hdstg, pt sl, some terr, pt shd; htd wc; chem disp; mv service pnt; some serviced pitches; shwrs €0.50; EHU (16A) metered + conn fee; gas; lndry; shops 1km; rest adj; snacks; bar; playgrnd; pool; 40% statics; dogs; phone; bus; poss cr; Eng spkn; adv bkg; quiet; CKE/CCI. "In apple orchard on Rv Mosel; price according to pitch size; friendly helpful owners; debit cards acc; pool deep - not suitable non-swimmers; poorly ventilated san facs; rv walks & cycle path to town." ♦ ltd. 19 Mar-31 Oct. € 21.00 2016*

BERNKASTEL KUES *3B2* (4km NW Rural) *49.94122, 7.04653* **Weingut Studert-Prum, Uferallee 22, 54470 Bernkastel Kues [(06531) 2487; info@studert-pruem.de; www.studert-pruem.com]** Fr Bernkastel-Kues, co N on W Bank of Rv Mosel, site on R in 4km at ent to Wehlen. Adj to Camp Schenk. Sm, mkd pitch, hdstg, terr, unshd; own san rec; chem disp; mv service pnt; supmkt 3km; rest, bar 200m; cvrd pool 2km; dogs; adv bkg; quiet. "M'homes only; no san facs; terr site with lovely views of Rv Mosel; vineyards; sh walk to pretty vill; walk/cycle path by rv; boat trips; wineries; excel." 1 Apr-31 Oct. € 10.00 2016*

BERNKASTEL KUES *3B2* (10km NW Rural) *49.97972, 7.0200* **Camping Erden, Moselufer 1, 54492 Erden [(06532) 4060; fax 5294; schmitt@campingplatz-erden.de; www.campingplatz-erden.de]** Exit A1/48 junc 125 onto B50 to Zeltingen. Cross bdge over Mosel, turn L to Erden, site sp. Med, pt sl, shd; htd wc; chem disp; mv service pnt; shwrs; EHU (16A) metered + conn fee; gas; lndry; shop nr; rest, snacks; bar; playgrnd; pool 5km; TV; 90% statics in sep area; dogs €2; phone; bus; poss cr; adv bkg; rd noise; ccard acc; red long stay. "Pleasant, less cr site on opp side of rv to main rd; wonderful setting in scenic area; water point & san facs long way fr tourer pitches; barrier locked 1300-1500 & o'night." ♦ 1 Apr-31 Oct. € 18.00 2013*

BERNRIED see Deggendorf *4G3*

BIELEFELD *1C3* (8km SW Rural) *52.00624, 8.45681* **Campingpark Meyer Zu Bentrup, Vogelweide 9, 33649 Bielefeld [(0521) 4592233; fax 459017; bielefeld@meyer-zu-bentrup.de; www.camping-bielefeld.de]** Fr N or S on A2 - At interchange 21 take A33 Osnabruck. Cont till m'way ends, cont onto A61 dir Bielefeld. After 2km take A68 exit, dir Osnabruck/Halle West. Site on L after 3km. Lge, pt sl, unshd; wc; chem disp; mv service pnt; shwrs €0.30/min; EHU (10-16A) €1.50; lndry (inc dryer); farm shop; bar; cooking facs; playgrnd; games area; games rm; wifi; 70% statics; dogs €2; quiet; red CKE/CCI. "Vg; immac but dated san facs (2015); conv for Bielefeld; well maintained; warm welcome; excel shop at adj fruit farm." ♦ 1 Mar-30 Nov. € 25.00 2015*

BINGEN *3C2* (3km E Urban) *49.97029, 7.93916* **Camping Hindenburgbrucke, Bornstrasse 22, 55411 Kempton-Bingen [(06721) 17160; fax 16998; bauer@bauer-schorsch.de; www.bauer-schorsch.de]** Foll rd on Rhine twd Mainz, site on L bef traff lts. Turn into tarmac rd, bear R, L under rlwy bdge, strt to site ent by Rhine. Lge, some hdg, unshd; wc; chem disp; shwrs; EHU (watch rev pol); rest; snacks; bar; BBQ; playgrnd; 40% statics (adj area); bus/train adj; twin axles; poss cr; quiet (apart fr barges). "Open site on W bank of Rhein; staff conn elec pnts; lovely position for sh stay; mosquitoes abound; close to R⊠desheim-Bingen ferry, vineyards, castles, cruising." ♦ ltd. 1 May-31 Oct. € 19.00 2014*

BINZ *2G1* (6km NW Coastal) *54.44817, 13.56152* **Wohnmobil-Oase Rügen, Proraer Chaussee 60, 18609 Ostseebad Binz OT Prora [(01577) 428 3715; info@.wohnmobilstellplatz-ruegen.de; www.wohnmobilstellplatz-ruegen.de]** Fr Binz foll coast rd to Prora, site on L past traff lts. Med, hdstg, pt shd; htd wc; chem disp; mv service pnt; shwrs, EHU (16A); lndry; gas; snacks; dogs; bus/tram adj; Eng spkn; m'vans only. "Vg site; track to beach." 23 Mar-20 Oct. € 15.00 2012*

⊞ **BITBURG** *3B2* (10km W Rural) *49.95895, 6.42454* **Prümtal Camping, In der Klaus 5, 54636 Oberweis [(06527) 92920; fax 929232; info@pruemtal.de; www.pruemtal.de]** On B50 Bitburg-Vianden rd. On ent Oberweis sharp RH bend immed L bef rv bdge - sp recreational facs or sp Köhler Stuben Restaurant-Bierstube. V lge, pt shd; htd wc; chem disp; shwrs inc; EHU (16A) €2.75 or metered; lndry; shop; rest, snacks; bar; playgrnd; pool; bike hire; internet; entmnt; 60% statics; dogs €2.10; Eng spkn; poss v cr high ssn; adv bkg; ccard acc; CKE/CCI. "Excel facs; san facs stretched high ssn; vg rest." ♦ € 26.00 2012*

⊞ **BONN** *1B4* (13km SE Rural) *50.65388, 7.20111* **Camping Genienau, Im Frankenkeller 49, 53179 Bonn-Mehlem [(0228) 344949; fax 3294989; genienau@freenet.de]** Fr B9 dir Mehlem, site sp on Rv Rhine, S of Mehlem. Med, pt shd; wc; chem disp; shwrs €1; EHU (6A) €3 or metered; lndry; rest & shop 600m; rest, snacks 1km; 60% statics; dogs €2; bus; Eng spkn; no adv bkg; some rv & rlwy noise; CKE/CCI. "Excel site on rv bank; liable to flood when rv v high; nr ferry to cross Rhine; late arr no problem; san facs up steps but disabled facs at grnd level; lots to see & do." ♦ € 20.00 2016*

GERMANY

BOPPARD *3B2* (6km NE Rural) *50.24888, 7.62638* **Camping Sonneneck, 56154 Boppard [(06742) 2121; fax 2076; kontakt@camping-sonneneck.de; www.campingpark-sonneneck.de]** On Koblenz-Mainz rd B9, on W bank of Rhine, in vill of Spay. Lge, mkd pitch, pt shd; wc; chem disp; mv service pnt; serviced pitches; sauna; shwrs inc; EHU (4A) €2.50; gas; lndry; shop; rest, snacks; bar; playgrnd; pool high ssn; shgl beach nr; fishing; crazy-golf; 18-hole golf 2km; 10% statics; dogs €2.40; phone; night watchman; poss cr; Eng spkn; rlwy & barge noise; CKE/CCI. "V pleasant staff; clean san facs, poss long way fr pitches; ltd waste water points; extra for rvside pitch; site poss liable to flood; gd cycle path along Rhine; gd NH." ♦ 1 Apr-31 Oct. € 25.00 2015*

BORGERENDE see Bad Doberan *2F1*

⊞ **BRANDENBURG AN DER HAVEL** *2F3* (9km E Rural) *52.39833, 12.43665* **Camping und Ferienpark am Plauer See, Plauer Landstrasse 200, 14774 Brandenburg [33 81 80 45 44; fax 81 80 46 44; info@camping-plauersee.de; www.camping-plauersee.de]** Fr A2 take 102 to Brandenburg. L onto 1, cont 4km. Just after sp for Plauerhof is a campsite sp. Turn L & foll rd for 1.5km to site on the side of lake. Med, mkd pitch, pt sl, pt shd; wc; chem disp; mv service pnt; fam bthrm; shwrs €1.40; EHU (10A) €1.90; lndry (inc dryer); rest; snacks; bar; BBQ; playgrnd; games area; bike hire; 75% statics; dogs; bus 1.5km; Eng spkn; adv bkg; quiet; CCI. "Next to sm lake; boat, cycles & BBQ hire; nr historic town of Brandenburg; vg site." € 18.00 2014*

BRAUBACH see Lahnstein *3B2*

⊞ **BRAUNEBERG** *3B2* (900m W Rural) *49.90564, 6.97603* **Wohnmobilstellplatz Brauneberger Juffer, Moselweinstraße 101, 54472 Brauneberg [6534 933 333; mfrollison@yahoo.co.uk or info@brauneberg.de]** Fr NE of A1 take exit 127-Klausen onto L47 twds Mulheim. Cont onto L158, then turn L onto B53. Supermkt 20m fr site ent which is down side rd twds rv. Sm, hdg/mkd pitch, hdstg, pt shd; chem disp; mv service pnt; EHU (16A); BBQ; sw 500m; dogs; bus 100m; Eng spkn; quiet. "Gd cycle paths along rv; vg site." € 8.00 2014*

⊞ **BRAUNLAGE** *2E4* (8.6km NE Rural) *51.75713, 10.68345* **Campingplatz am Schierker Stern, Hagenstrasse, 38879 Schierke [(039455) 58817; fax 58818; info@harz-camping.com; www.harz-camping.com]** Fr W on B27 fr Braunlage for 4km to Elend. Turn L & cross rlwy line. Site on L in 2km at x-rds. Med, hdstg, pt sl, pt shd; htd wc; chem disp; mv service pnt; shwrs inc; EHU (6A) €2.60; lndry; sm shop & 8km; rest 200m; snacks 1km; BBQ; cooking facs; TV rm; dogs €1.60; bus at site ent; train 1km; adv bkg; quiet. "Conv & pleasant site in Harz mountains; excel san facs; friendly, helpful owners live on site; sm pitches; vg." € 24.00 2013*

⊞ **BRAUNLAGE** *2E4* (12km SE Rural) *51.65697, 10.66786* **Campingplatz am Bärenbache, Bärenbachweg 10, 38700 Hohegeiss [(05583) 1306; fax 1300; campingplatz-hohegeiss@t-online.de; www.campingplatz-hohegeiss.de]** Fr Braunlage S on B4 thro Hohegeiss; site sp on L downhill (15%) on edge of town. Med, hdg/mkd pitch, terr, pt shd; htd wc; chem disp; mv service pnt; fam bthrm; shwrs inc; EHU (10A); lndry (inc dryer); shops 500m; rest, snacks; bar; cooking facs; BBQ; playgrnd; htd pool; paddling pool; bike hire; some statics; wifi; dogs €1.50; Eng spkn; adv bkg; quiet; red snr citizens. "Gd walking; friendly; walking dist to vill; vg." ♦ ltd. € 22.50 2014*

BREISACH AM RHEIN *3B4* (7km E Rural) *48.03104, 7.65781* **Kaiserstuhl Camping, Nachwaid 5, 79241 Ihringen [(07668) 950065; fax 950071; info@kaiserstuhlcamping.de; www.kaiserstuhlcamping.de]** Fr S exit A5/E35 junc 64a, foll sp twds Breisach, then camping sp to Ihringen. At Ihringen site sp dir Merdingen. Fr N exit junc 60 & foll sp. Med, unshd; wc; chem disp; mv service pnt; fam bthrm; shwrs €0.50; EHU (16A) metered + conn fee; lndry; shop 800m; rest adj; snacks; bar; playgrnd; htd pool, tennis adj; golf 8km; 10% statics; dogs €2.50; poss cr; quiet; 10% red long stay/CKE/CCI."Can get cr in high ssn." ♦ 15 Mar-31 Oct. € 32.00 2014*

⊞ **BREMEN** *1C2* (16km SW Rural) *53.01055, 8.68972* **Camping Wienberg, Zum Steller See 83, 28816 Stuhr-Gross Mackenstedt [(04206) 9191; fax 9293; info@camping-wienburg.de; www.camping-wienberg.de]** Exit A1/E37 junc 58a onto B322 sp Stuhr/Delmenhorst. Foll Camping Steller See sp. Sp also call site Marchen Camping. Lge, mkd pitch, pt sl, hdstg, pt shd; htd wc; chem disp; mv service pnt; fam bthrm; shwrs €1; EHU (16A) metered or €3; lndry (inc dryer); shop; rest, snacks; bar; playgrnd; pool; bike hire; entmnt; TV; 50% statics; dogs €2; some Eng spkn; adv bkg; rd noise; ccard acc; CKE/CCI. "Helpful staff; basic facs; gd." € 17.00 2016*

BREMEN *1C2* (17km SW Rural) *53.00694, 8.69277* **Campingplatz Steller See, Zum Stellersee 15, 28817 Stuhr-Gross Mackenstedt [(04206) 6490; fax 6668; steller.see@t-online.de; www.steller-see.de]** Exit A1/E37 junc 58a onto B322 sp Stuhr/Delmenhorst. Foll site sp. Lge, unshd; htd wc; chem disp; mv service pnt; fam bthrm; shwrs €0.50; EHU (10-16A) metered or €2.50; gas; lndry (inc dryer); rest, snacks; bar; BBQ; playgrnd; lake sw adj; games area; entmnt; 80% statics in sep area; phone; wifi; poss cr at w/end; adv bkg; poss noisy; no ccard acc; red long stay/CKE/CCI. "Site officially clsd but owner may accommodate you; well-appointed, clean, lakeside site; immac san facs; friendly owners; conv NH fr m'way & for trams to Bremen; some m'way noise; gd space, easy to position; vg." ♦ 1 Apr-30 Sep. € 25.50 2014*

⊞ **BREMEN** *1C2* (5km NW Rural) *53.11483, 8.83263* **Camping Hanse (formerly Camping am Stadtwaldsee), Hochschulring 1, 28359 Bremen [(0421)30746825; fax (0421) 30746826]** Fr A27 take exit 19 for Universitat, foll sp for Universitat and camping. Site on L in 1km after leaving University area. Lge, mkd pitch, hdstg, pt shd; htd wc; chem disp; mv service pnt; fam bthrm; shwrs inc; EHU (16A) metered; gas; lndry (inc dryer); shop; rest, snacks; bar; cooking facs; BBQ; playgrnd; lake sw adj; wifi; some statics; dogs €4; phone; bus 100m; poss cr; Eng spkn; adv bkg; some rd noise; ltd ccard acc; red long stay; CKE/CCI. "Excel, spacious lakeside site; superb san facs; cycle path to beautiful city; gd bus service; v gd rest adj; spacious pitches but unkept & poorly maintained." ♦ € 35.50 2017*

⊞ **BRIESELANG** *2F3* (5km W Rural) *52.57138, 12.96583* **Campingplatz Zeestow im Havelland, 11 Brieselangerstrasse, 14665 Brieselang [(033234) 88634; fax 22863; info@campingplatz-zeestow.de; www.campingplatz-zeestow.de]** Exit A10/E55 junc 27; turn W dir Wustermark; site on L after canal bdge in 500m. Lge, pt sl, unshd; wc; chem disp; shwrs €1; EHU (16A) metered; gas; lndry; shop; rest; bar; 75% statics; dogs €2; bus; poss cr; CKE/CCI. "Gd NH nr a'bahn; facs dated but clean; 13km fr Berlin & 25km fr Potsdam; fair." ♦ ltd. € 14.00 2016*

"I need an on-site restaurant"

We do our best to make sure site information is correct, but it is always best to check any must-have facilities are still available or will be open during your visit.

⊞ **BRUGGEN** *1A4* (2km SE Rural) *51.23416, 6.19815* **Camping-Forst Laarer See, Brüggenerstrasse 27, 41372 Niederkrüchten [(02163) 8461 or 0172 7630591 (mob); info@campingforst-laarersee.com; www.campingforst-laarersee.com]** Fr A52 junc 3 or A61 junc 3 - take B221 to Brüggen, turn R at 1st traff lts into site. Lge, pt sl, pt shd; htd wc; chem disp; mv service pnt; fam bthrm; shwrs €1; EHU (16A) inc; lndry; shop, rest 1km; snacks; bar; BBQ; playgrnd; games area; 80% statics; dogs €1; Eng spkn; adv bkg; quiet; CKE/CCI. "Unspoilt area nr pretty town; many leisure amenities nr site - gd for children; vg site; ltd touring pitches; pleasant site with lake; walking/bike paths." ♦ € 21.00 2016*

BRUNNEN see Füssen *4E4*

⊞ **BUHL** *3C3* (7km NW Rural) *48.72719, 8.08074* **Ferienpark & Campingplatz Adam, Campingstrasse 1, 77815 Bühl-Oberbruch [(07223) 23194; fax 8982; info@campingplatz-adam.de; www.campingplatz-adam.de]** Exit A5 at Bühl take sp Lichtenau & foll sp thro Oberbruch, then L twd Moos to site in 500m. If app on rd 3 take rd sp W to Rheinmünster N of Bühl. Site sp to S at W end of Oberbruch. Lge, mkd pitch, hdstg, pt shd; serviced pitches; wc; chem disp; mv service pnt; shwrs €0.50; EHU (10A) €3; lndry; shop; supmkt 1km; rest, snacks; bar; playgrnd; tennis; lake sw; boating; sailing; fishing; entmnt; wifi; 60% statics; dogs €2.50; o'night area tarmac car park; extra for lakeside pitches; poss cr; Eng spkn; adv bkg; quiet; ccard acc; red long stay/LS; CKE/CCI. "Excel, clean san facs; conv for Strasbourg, Baden-Baden & Black Forest visits; if recep clsd use area outside gate; vg; excel camp with own lake; gd rest; friendly staff; handy for m'way but still quiet; o'night tarmac area excel for NH but worth a longer stay; highly rec; 45 mins to Europe Pk." ♦ € 28.00 2017*

BULLAY see Zell *3B2*

BURGEN *3B2* (600m N Rural) *50.21457, 7.38976* **Camping Burgen, 56332 Burgen [(02605) 2396; fax 4919; info@camping-burgen.de; www.camping-burgen.de]** Leave A61 at J39; foll B411 twds Dieblich to reach S bank of Mosel; turn L and foll B49 for approx 12km; site on L bet rd and rv bef vill. Sat nav uses rte thro vill, not suitable. Med, mkd pitch, unshd; wc; mv service pnt; shwrs inc; EHU (10A) metered + conn fee (poss rev pol); lndry; gas; shop; rest 200m; snacks adj; playgrnd; pool; boat-launching; entmnt; 30% statics; dogs €2; Eng spkn; some rd, rlwy & rv noise; red CKE/CCI. "Scenic area; ideal for touring Mosel, Rhine & Koblenz areas; gd shop; poss liable to flood; lovely, clean site; gd san facs; rec." 11 Apr-19 Oct. € 30.00 (CChq acc) 2014*

⊞ **CALW** *3C3* (12km SW Rural) *48.67766, 8.68990* **Camping Erbenwald, 75387 Neubulach-Liebelsberg [(07053) 7382; fax 3274; info@camping-erbenwald.de; www.camping-erbenwald.de]** On B463 S fr Calw, take R slip rd sp Neubulach to go over main rd. Foll Neubulach sp until camping sp at R junc. Site well sp. Lge, hdg/mkd pitch, pt shd; wc; chem disp; mv service pnt; fam bthrm; shwrs €0.50; EHU (10A) metered; lndry; shop; rest, snacks; bar; playgrnd; htd pool; paddling pool; games area; internet; 60% statics; dogs €2; phone; Eng spkn; adv bkg; quiet. "Gd size pitches; child-friendly site; no vehicles in or out fr 1300-1500; excel; cash only." ♦ € 22.00 2014*

⊞ **CANOW** *2F2* (2km E Rural) *53.19636, 12.93116* **Camping Pälitzsee, Am Canower See 165, 17255 Canow [(039828) 20220; fax 26963; info@mecklenburg-tourist.de; www.mecklenburg-tourist.de]** Fr N on B198 turn S dir Rheinsberg to Canow vill, site sp. Lge, pt shd; wc; chem disp; shwrs €1; EHU (16A) metered or €3; lndry; shop high ssn; supmkt 2km; rest 2m; snacks; bar; playgrnd; lake sw & boating; 50% statics; dogs €2; adv bkg; quiet. "Canow charming vill; vg touring base for lakes." ♦ € 20.00 2016*

⊞ **CHEMNITZ** *2F4* (10km SW Rural) *50.76583, 13.01444* **Waldcampingplatz Erzgebirgsblick, An der Dittersdorfer Höhe 1, 09439 Amtsberg [(0371) 7750833; fax 7750834; info@waldcamping-erzgebirge.de; www.waldcamping-erzgebirge.de]** Fr A4 take A72 S & exit junc 15. Foll sp 'Centrum' & join 'Südring' ring rd. Turn onto B174 & foll sp Marienberg twd junc with B180. Site sp 500m fr junc. Med, mkd pitch, pt shd; htd wc; chem disp; mv service pnt; fam bthrm; shwrs €0.50; EHU (16A) metered; gas; lndry; shop; supmkt 4km; playgrnd; games area; TV rm; dogs free; bus 800m; site clsd 6-27 Nov; Eng spkn; red long stay; ccard not acc; red long stay/snr citizens/ CKE/CCI. "Gd san facs; relaxing site; gd walking; vg standard of site." € 17.00 2016*

⊞ **COBURG** *4E2* (15km SW Rural) *50.19433, 10.83809* **Campingplatz Sonnland, Bahnhofstrasse 154, 96145 Sesslach [(09569) 220; fax 1593; info@camping-sonnland.de; www.camping-sonnland.de]** Exit A73 junc 10 Ebersdorf onto B303 W. Then at Niederfüllbach turn S onto B4, then turn W dir Sesslach. Site sp N of Sesslach dir Hattersdorf; turn R at sp opp filling stn, site in 150m. Med, mkd pitch, some hdstg, terr, pt shd; htd wc; chem disp; mv service pnt; serviced pitches; shwrs €1.50; EHU (16A) metered; lndry (inc dryer); shop 300m; rest 400m; BBQ; playgrnd; lake sw; 70% statics; dogs €1.50; adv bkg; CKE/CCI. "Sesslach unspoilt, medieval, walled town; site well laid-out." € 21.50 2016*

"Satellite navigation makes touring much easier"

Remember most sat navs don't know if you're towing or in a larger vehicle – always use yours alongside maps and site directions.

COCHEM *3B2* (1.5km N Rural) *50.15731, 7.17360* **Campingplatz am Freizeitzentrum, Moritzburgerstrasse 1, 56812 Cochem [(02671) 4409; fax 910719; info@campingplatz-cochem.de; www.campingplatz-cochem.de]** On rd B49 fr Koblenz, on ent town go under 1st rv bdge then turn R over same bdge. Foll site sp. Lge, mkd pitch, pt sl, pt shd; wc; chem disp; mv service pnt; shwrs €0.90; EHU (10-16A) €2.50 + conn fee (some rev pol); gas; lndry (inc dryer); snacks; shops/supmkt nrby, rest nrby; playgrnd; 10% statics; bike hire; dogs €3; poss cr; some rd/rlwy/rv noise; red LS; CKE/CCI. "Gd, clean site adj Rv Mosel; pitches tight & poss diff access fr site rds; gd for children; easy walk along rv to town; train to Koblenz, Trier, Mainz." 1 Apr-31 Oct. € 23.00 2016*

COCHEM *3B2* (10km E Rural) *50.17056, 7.29285* **Camping & Watersports Mosel-Islands, Yachthafen, 56253 Treis-Karden/Mosel [(02672) 2613; fax 912102; campingplatz@mosel-islands.de; www.mosel-islands.de]** Fr Cochem take B49 to Treis-Karden (11km), cross Mosel bdge bear L then 1st sharp L back under Mosel bdge & parallel with rv. After 300m at bdge over stream turn R then thro allotments. Site over bdge by boating cent. Fr A61 Koblenz/Bingen a'bahn descend to rv level by Winningen Valley Bdge, turn L onto B49 (Moselweinstrasse). Do not descend thro Dieblich as c'vans are prohibited. After 25km; turn R immed bef Mosel bdge & then as above. Avoid Treis vill (narr with thro traff priorities). Med, mkd pitch, pt shd; wc; serviced pitches; shwrs €0.80; EHU (6A) metered & conn fee; gas; lndry; shops 200m; rest; BBQ; pool 1km; tennis 300m; 50% statics; dogs €4; adv bkg; some rv & rlwy noise. "Ideal for touring Mosel valley; rv cruising & historical sites; vg san facs 1st floor; poss midges; gd site." ♦ 1 Apr-31 Oct. € 20.00 2013*

COCHEM *3B2* (6km SE Rural) *50.10999, 7.23542* **Campingplatz Happy-Holiday, Moselweinstrasse, 56821 Ellenz-Poltersdorf [(02673) 1272; fax 962367; www.camping-happy-holiday.de]** Fr Cochem, take B49 S to Ellenz; site sp on bank of Rv Mosel. Med, pt sl, shd; htd wc; chem disp; shwrs €1; EHU (6A) metered; gas; lndry (inc dryer); sm shop; rest, snacks; bar; pool 300m; fishing; watersports; wifi; 70% statics; dogs €1; poss cr; Eng spkn; quiet but rd & rv noise. "Pleasant situation; gd value rest; clean facs; conv touring base." 1 Apr-31 Oct. € 15.00 2014*

COCHEM *3B2* (7km SE Rural) *50.08231, 7.20796* **Camping Holländischer Hof, Am Campingplatz 1, 56820 Senheim [(02673) 4660; fax 4100; holl.hof@t-online.de; www.moselcamping.com]** Fr Cochem take B49 twd Traben-Trarbach; after approx 15km turn L over rv bdge sp Senheim; site on rv island. Med, mkd pitch, pt shd; wc; chem disp; mv service pnt; fam bthrm; shwrs €0.85; EHU (6-10A) metered; lndry; gas; shop & 1km; rest, snacks; bar; playgrnd; rv sw adj; tennis; wifi at office; 20% statics; no dogs; phone; poss cr; Eng spkn; adv bkg; quiet; debit card acc; red long stay; CKE/CCI. "Pleasant, well-run site; beautiful location; helpful staff; sm pitches on loose pebbles; excel cycle paths; poss flooding when wet weather/high water; poss overcr." ♦ 15 Apr-1 Nov. € 16.00 2012*

COCHEM *3B2* (7km SE Rural) *50.13253, 7.23029* **Campingplatz Bruttig, Am Moselufer, 56814 Bruttig-Fankel [(02671) 915429; www.camping platz-bruttig.de]** Leave Cochem on B49 twd Trier. In 8km turn L over bdge to Bruttig-Fankel. Thro vill, site on R on banks Rv Mosel. Sm, mkd pitch, pt shd; htd wc; chem disp; shwrs €0.50; EHU (16A) metered; lndry; snacks; bar; playgrnd; rv sw adj; 50% statics; phone; Eng spkn; quiet. "Pleasant site in pretty vill; gd walking, cycling; Mosel boat trips fr Bruttig." Easter-31 Oct. € 16.00 2016*

ERLANGEN *4E2* (7km NW Rural) *49.63194, 10.9425* **Camping Rangau, Campingstrasse 44, 91056 Erlangen-Dechsendorf [(09135) 8866; fax 724743; infos@camping-rangau.de; www.camping-rangau.de]** Fr A3/E45 exit junc 81 & foll camp sp. At 1st traff lts turn L, strt on at next traff lts, then L at next traff lts, site sp. Med, pt shd; htd wc; shwrs inc; chem disp; EHU (6A) €3 (long lead poss req); lndry; shop 2km; rest, snacks; playgrnd; pool; lake sw; boat hire; dogs €2.50; gates clsd 1300-1500 & 2200 hrs; poss cr; Eng spkn; adv bkg; quiet; ccard acc; red long stay/CKE/CCI. "Gd site, espec for families; clean facs; welcoming & well-run; some sm pitches; popular NH - overflow onto adj sports field; vg, busy NH; arrive early; dog wash facs." ♦ ltd. 1 Apr-15 Oct. € 28.50 2014*

⊞ **ESSEN** *1B4* (8km S Urban) *51.38444, 6.99388* **DCC Campingpark Stadtcamping, Im Löwental 67, 45239 Essen-Werden [(0201) 492978; fax 8496132; essen@knauscamp.de; www.dcc-stadtcamping-essen-werden.de]** Exit A52 junc 28 onto B224 S dir Solingen. Turn R bef bdge over Rv Ruhr at traff lts & immed sharp R into Löwental, site sp. Med, mkd pitch, hdstg, pt shd; wc; chem disp; mv service pnt; shwrs; EHU (16A) metered; gas; lndry; shop; rest; bar; playgrnd; games area; games rm; 95% statics; no dogs; phone; poss cr; Eng spkn; adv bkg; site clsd 1300-1500 & 2130-0700; car park adj; quiet; no ccard acc. "Rv trips; poss ssn workers; gd." € 27.30 2016*

ETTENHEIM see Lahr (Schwarzwald) *3B3*

⊞ **ETTLINGEN** *3C3* (5km SE Rural) *48.91465, 8.45567* **Campingplatz Albgau, Kochmühle 1, 76337 Waldbronn-Neurod [tel/fax 07243 61849; erwilux@gmx.de; www.campingplatzstueble-albgau-waldbronn.de]** Exit A8/E52 at junc 42 & foll sp Bad Herrenalb. When rlwy on R, site sp in 4km on R. Lge, pt shd; wc; own san rec; chem disp; shwrs €0.50; EHU (16A) €2.30; gas; lndry (inc dryer); shop; snacks; bar; playgrnd; 90% statics; dogs €3; gates locked 1300-1500 & 2200-0700; quiet but poss noisy at w/end & fr rlwy; ccard not acc. "On edge of Black Forest; footpath walks in vicinity; adj field for NH; modern san facs; helpful owner; ltd facs in high ssn." ♦ € 33.60 2014*

⊞ **EXTERTAL** *1C3* (3km SW Rural) *52.05118, 9.10223* **Camping Extertal, Eimke 4, 32699 Extertal-Eimke [(05262) 3307; info@campingpark-extertal.de; www.campingpark-extertal.de]** Fr Rinteln on B238 S twd Barntrup; about 1.5km S Bösingfeld turn L at sp to site over level x-ing. Med, hdg/mkd pitch, pt sl, pt shd; htd wc; chem disp; mv service pnt; serviced pitches; fam bthrm; shwrs inc; EHU (16A) €1.50 or metered; gas; lndry (inc dryer); shop; rest 500m; snacks high ssn; bar; cooking facs; playgrnd; pool; lake sw; games rm; wifi; entmnt; 90% statics in sep area; dogs €1.50; bus adj; some Eng spkn; quiet; red long stay; CKE/CCI. "Gd site; dry & well-drained in v wet weather; all facs clean; forest walks & cycle paths fr site; 80 touring pitches; gd facs; some rd noise in day; clsd 1300-1500." ♦ € 15.50 2015*

⊞ **FASSBERG** *1D2* (6km E Rural) *52.87593, 10.22718* **Ferienpark Heidesee (Part Naturist), Lüneburger-Heidesee, 29328 Fassberg-Oberohe [(05827) 970546; fax 970547; heidesee@ferienpark.de; www.campingheidesee.com]** Leave A7/E45 at exit 44 onto B71. Turn S to Müden, then dir Unterlüss. Foll site sp. V lge, terr, pt shd; htd wc; chem disp; mv service pnt; sauna; private bthrms avail; fam bthrm; shwrs inc; EHU (10A) €3; lndry (inc dryer); gas; shop; rest, snacks; playgrnd; pool 250m; lake sw; fishing; tennis; bike hire; horseriding; games rm; entmnt; 65% statics; dogs €2; ccard acc; Eng spkn; quiet; CKE/CCI. "Naturist camping in sep area; long leads maybe req; friendly helpful staff; places of interest nrby; gd mkd cycling and walking rtes fr site." ♦ € 21.00 2014*

FEHMARN ISLAND *2E1* **Sites on Fehmarn Island are listed together at the end of the Germany site entry pages.**

⊞ **FELDBERG** *2G2* (2km NE Rural) *53.34548, 13.45626* **Camping am Bauernhof, Hof Eichholz 1-8, 17258 Feldberg [(039831) 21084; fax 21534; info@campingplatz-feldberg.de; www.campingplatz-am-bauernhof.de]** Fr B198 at Möllenbeck turn dir Feldburg, thro Feldburg dir Prenzlau, site sp. Med, mkd pitch, pt sl, unshd; wc; chem disp; shwrs inc; EHU (16A) metered + conn fee; lndry; shop; rest 800m; snacks; playgrnd; lake sw; fishing; 30% statics; dogs €3; quiet; CKE/CCI. "Well-situated, vg site among lakes; many cycle paths in area." ♦ € 18.00 2016*

⊞ **FINSTERAU** *4G3* (1km N Rural) *48.94091, 13.57180* **Camping Nationalpark-Ost, Buchwaldstrasse 52, 94151 Finsterau [(08557) 768; fax 1062; berghof-frank@berghof-frank.de; www.camping-nationalpark-ost.de]** Fr B12 turn N dir Mauth. Cont to Finsterau & site 1km adj parking for National Park. Sm, pt shd; wc; chem disp; shwrs €1; EHU (6-16A) metered + conn fee or €2.50; gas; lndry (inc dryer); shop 1km; wifi; TV rm; dogs €2; quiet; red CKE/CCI. "Gd walking & mountain biking; site in beautiful Bavarian forest." ♦ € 17.60 2016*

FRANKFURT AM MAIN *3C2* (8km NE Rural) *50.81700, 8.46550* **Campingplatz Mainkur, Frankfurter Landstraße 107, 63477 Maintal [(069)-412193; campingplatz-mainkur@t-online.de; www.campingplatz-mainkur.de]** Fr Frankfurt head NE B4 and Hanua cross over A661 and cont over 8 sets of traff lts pass car showrooms and Bauhaus on L. 100m aft flyover bear R into single track tarmac rd to site. Sp on B8/B4. Med, mkd pitch, pt shd; wc; shwrs; lndry; mv waste disp; basic shop; bar; BBQ; 35% statics; dogs; bus 3km; adv bkg; Eng spkn; boating; playgrnd. "Family run site o'looking rv; conv for Frankfurt; vg, rec." ♦ ltd. 1 Apr-30 Sept. € 28.00 2012*

⊞ **FRANKFURT AM MAIN** *3C2* (9km NW Urban) *50.16373, 8.65055* **City-Camp Frankfurt, An der Sandelmühle 35b, 60439 Frankfurt Am Main [(069) 570332; fax 57003604; info@city-camp-frankfurt.de; www.city-camp-frankfurt.de]** Exit A661 junc 6 dir Heddernheim, site in park, sp. Med, hdstg, pt shd; wc; chem disp; mv service pnt; shwrs €1.10; EHU (10A) €3; gas; lndry; shop 800m; snacks 800m; rest 500m; 30% statics; dogs €2.50; poss cr; Eng spkn; poss noisy; CKE/CCI. "Conv for city via adj U-Bahn (20 min to cent); clean but dated; v busy when trade fair on; vg for visiting Frankfurt." ♦ ltd. € 28.50 2013*

FREIBURG IM BREISGAU *3B4* (21km NE Rural) *48.02318, 8.03253* **Camping Steingrubenhof, Haldenweg 3, 79271 St Peter [(07660) 210; fax 1604; info@camping-steingrubenhof.de; www.camping-steingrubenhof.de]** Exit A5 junc 61 onto B294. Turn R sp St Peter. Steep hill to site on L at top of hill. Or fr B31 dir Donaueschingen, after 4km outside Freiburg turn N sp St Peter; by-pass vill on main rd, turn L under bdge 1st R. Fr other dir by-pass St Peter heading for Glottertal; site on R 200m after rd bdge on by-pass. Med, hdg/mkd pitch, hdstg, pt terr, unshd; wc; chem disp; mv service pnt; serviced pitches; shwrs €0.50; EHU (16A); lndry (inc dryer); shop & 1km; rest & bar adj; BBQ; playgrnd; wifi; 70% statics; dogs €2; phone; Eng spkn; adv bkg; quiet; ccard acc; 10% red long stay; CKE/CCI. "Peaceful site in heart of Black Forest; wonderful location; pleasant staff; immac facs; gate clsd 1200-1400 & 2200-0800; v diff to manoeuvre twin-axle vans onto pitches as narr access paths; pitches are sm & few for tourers; great site." ♦ ltd. 1 Jan-10 Nov & 15 Dec-31 Dec. € 25.00 2014*

⊞ **FREIBURG IM BREISGAU** *3B4* (4km E Rural) *47.99250, 7.87330* **Camping Hirzberg, Kartäuserstrasse 99, 79104 Freiburg-im-Breisgau [(0761) 35054; fax 289212; hirzburg@freiburg-camping.de; www.freiburg-camping.de]** Exit A5 at Freiburg-Mitte & foll B31 past town cent sp Freiburg, Titisee. Foll camping sp twd Freiburg-Ebnet, nr rocky slopes on R. Then approx 2.5km on narr, winding rd. Site on R just after start of blocks of flats on L. Med, pt sl, terr, pt shd; htd wc; chem disp; mv service pnt; shwrs inc; EHU (10A) €2.50; gas; lndry; sm shop; rest, snacks; bar; BBQ; playgrnd; pool 500m; bike hire; wifi; 40% statics; dogs €1; bus 300m/tram; clsd 1300-1500; poss v cr; Eng spkn; adv bkg; quiet; CKE/CCI. "Pleasant, v helpful owner; site clsd 2000 - ltd outside parking; gd cycle path & easy walk to town; busy in high ssn; excel, v clean & modern san facs; gd value rest." € 27.00 2016*

FREIBURG IM BREISGAU *3B4* (5km SE Urban) *47.98126, 7.88127* **Camping Möslepark, Waldseestrasse 77, 79117 Freiburg-im-Breisgau [(0761) 7679333; fax 7679336; information@camping-freiburg.com; www.camping-freiburg.com]** Fr A5 exit junc 62 onto B31 & foll sp Freiburg strt thro city sp Donauschingen. Bef ent to tunnel take L lane & foll site sp (do not go thro tunnel). Site nr Möselpark Sports Stadium. When sps run out, cross level x-ing and turn L. Med, pt sl, shd; wc; chem disp; mv service pnt; sauna; shwrs inc; EHU (16A) €2.50; lndry (inc dryer); shop 100m; supmkts 500m; rest adj; playgrnd; htd, covrd pool nr; tennis 1km; bike hire; wifi; dogs €1.90; tram to city nr; o'night m'van area; Eng spkn; no adv bkg; noise fr stadium adj; ccard acc; red CKE/CCI. "Conv Freiburg & Black Forest (footpath adj); wooded site easily reached fr a'bahn; clsd 1200-1430 & 2200-0800 - waiting area in front of site; excel, modern san facs; public transport tickets fr recep; parking nr tram stop; v helpful staff; red CC Members." 26 Mar-24 Oct. € 30.00 2013*

⊞ **FREIBURG IM BREISGAU** *3B4* (11km SE Rural) *47.96015, 7.95001* **Camping Kirchzarten, Dietenbacherstrasse 17, 79199 Kirchzarten [(07661) 9040910; fax 61624; info@camping-kirchzarten.de; www.camping-kirchzarten.de]** Sp fr Freiburg-Titisee rd 31; into Kirchzarten; site sp fr town cent. Lge, mkd pitch, pt shd; htd wc; chem disp; mv service pnt; serviced pitches; fam bthrm; shwrs inc; EHU (16A) €2.50 or metered; lndry; shops 500m; rest adj; snacks; bar; BBQ; playgrnd; 3 htd pools adj; tennis adj; wintersports area; entmnt; 20% statics; dogs €2.50 (not acc Jul/Aug); train 500m; office clsd 1300-1430; Quickstop o'night area; poss cr; Eng spkn; adv bkg (ess Jul/Aug); quiet; ccard acc; red long stay/red LS; CKE/CCI. "Gd size pitches; choose pitch then register at office (clse fr 1200-1400); spacious, well-kept site; excel san facs; gd rest; site fees inc free bus & train travel in Black Forest region; helpful staff; call to inq about dogs late Aug." ♦ € 35.00 2016*

See advertisement opposite

⊞ **FREUDENSTADT** *3C3* (8km ENE Rural) *48.48011, 8.5005* **Höhencamping Königskanzel, Freizeitweg 1, 72280 Dornstetten-Hallwangen [(07443) 6730; fax 4574; info@camping-koenigskanzel.de; www.camping-koenigskanzel.de]** Fr Freudenstadt head E on rte 28 foll sp Stuttgart for 7km. Camping sp on R, sharp R turn foll sp, sharp L on narr, winding track to site in 200m. Fr Nagold on R28, 7km fr Freudenstadt fork L; sp as bef. NB: 1st sharp R turn is v sharp - take care. Med, some hdg pitch, pt sl, terr, pt shd; wc; chem disp; mv service pnt; serviced pitch; sauna; shwrs inc; EHU (10A) metered; gas; lndry (inc dryer); shop; sm rest, snacks; bar; BBQ; playgrnd; htd pool; bike hire; golf 7km; ski lift 7km; wifi; 60% statics sep area; dogs €2; phone; site clsd 3 Nov-15 Dec; Eng spkn; adv bkg (bkg fee); quiet; ccard not acc; red long stay/CKE/CCI. "Pleasant owners; friendly welcome; excel shwr facs, inc for dogs; well run family site; hill top location with gd views of Black Forest; recep clsd 1300-1400; excel value rest." ♦ € 25.00 2014*

FREUDENSTADT *3C3* (5km W Rural) *48.45840, 8.37255* **Camping Langenwald, Strassburgerstrasse 167, 72250 Freudenstadt-Langenwald [(07441) 2862; fax 2891; info@camping-langenwald.de; www.camping-langenwald.de]** Foll sp fr town on B28 dir Strassburg. Med, terr, pt shd; htd wc; chem disp; mv service pnt; fam bthrm; serviced pitch; shwrs inc; EHU (16A) metered; gas; lndry; shop; rest, snacks; playgrnd; htd pool; bike hire; golf 4km; 10% statics; dogs €2; Eng spkn; noisy nr rd; ccard acc (not VISA); red long stay/LS/CKE/CCI. "Gd, clean san facs & site; woodland walks fr site; gd rest; friendly owners." ♦ 26 Mar-1 Nov. € 30.00 2016*

FRICKENHAUSEN AM MAIN *3D2* (1km W Rural) *49.66916, 10.07444* **Knaus Campingpark Frickenhausen, Ochsenfurterstrasse 49, 97252 Frickenhausen/Ochsenfurt [(09331) 3171; fax 5784; info@knauscamp.de; www.knauscamp.de]** Turn off B13 at N end of bdge over Rv Main in Ochsenfurt & foll camping sp. Lge, hdg/mkd pitch, pt shd; wc; serviced pitches; chem disp; mv service pnt; fam bthrm; shwrs inc; EHU (16A) €2.40 or metered; gas; lndry; shop; rest high ssn; bar; playgrnd; htd pool; bike hire; TV; wifi; 40% statics; dogs €3; site clsd 1300-1500; Eng spkn; adv bkg; quiet; red long stay/snr citizens. "Vg, well-managed site on rv island; excel facs; located on Romantischestrasse with many medieval vills; v clean, cared for site; gd rest; friendly staff." 31 Mar-5 Nov. € 35.00 2013*

FRIEDRICHSHAFEN *3D4* (8km W Rural) *47.66896, 9.40253* **Camping Fischbach, Grenzösch 3, 88048 Friedrichschafen-Fischbach [(07541) 42059; fax 401113; info@camping-fischbach.de; www.camping-fischbach.de]** Take B31 fr Friedrichshafen to Meersburg. Site sp on L at end of vill. Turning lane avail for easy access off busy rd. Med, mkd pitch, some hdstg, pt shd; wc; chem disp; mv service pnt; shwrs; EHU (10-16A) €2 (poss rev pol); lndry (inc dryer); shop; rest, snacks; bar; lake sw adj; sand beach adj; 40% statics; no dogs; phone; poss v cr; Eng spkn; no adv bkg; rd noise; CKE/CCI. "Tranquil, relaxing site; some lake view pitches, worth the extra; excel, clean, modern san facs; ferries to Konstanz nrby; Zeppelin/Dornier museums nrby; cr; on Lake Constance cycle rte." 14 Apr-8 Oct. € 27.00 2017*

FRIEDRICHSHAFEN *3D4* (10km W Coastal) *47.66583, 9.37694* **Campingplatz Schloss Helmsdorf, Friedrichshafenerstrasse, 88090 Immenstaad-am-Bodensee [(07545) 6252; fax 3956; info@schloss-helmsdorf.org; www.schloss-helmsdorf.org]** Site sp fr B31 bet Meersburg & Friedrichshafen at Immenstaad. Lge, pt sl, pt shd; htd wc; chem disp; mv service pnt; shwrs €0.04 per 10sec; EHU (6A) €2.50; lndry; shop; rest, snacks; lake beach & sw; boating; windsurfing; 80% statics; no dogs high ssn; poss cr; quiet. "Vg, well-run site; gd position on lakeside; gd, clean san facs; helpful owners; sh walk to lake ferry; gd but expensive; Zeppelin & Dornier museums 8km level bike rte." ♦ 25 Mar-9 Oct. € 32.00 2016*

⊞ **FRIESOYTHE** *1C2* (13km SE Rural) *52.93703, 7.92923* **Campingplatz Wilken, Thülsfelder Str. 3, 26169 Friesoythe [04 49 52 61; info@camping-wilken.de; www.camping-wilken.de]** Fr B72 Cloppenburg-Friesoythe. After 13km turn L onto Thülsfelder Straße. Site next to Thülsfeld Reservoir on L. Lge, mkd pitch, hdstg, unshd; htd wc; chem disp; mv service pnt; shwrs inc; EHU (16A) inc; lndry rm; shop; playgrnd; dogs; quiet. "Excel site for long stay; spacious pitches; v clean san facs; would rec." € 13.50 2014*

*Last year of report

GERMANY

FUSSEN *4E4* (6km N Rural) *47.61553, 10.7230* **Camping Magdalena am Forggensee, Bachtalstrasse 10, 87669 Osterreinen [(08362) 4931; fax 941333; campingplatz.magdalena@t-online.de; www.sonnenhof-am-forggensee.de]** Fr Füssen take rd 16 sp Kaufbeuren & Forggensee for 5km; R sp Osterreinen for 500m; L at T-junc foll site sp; site on R in 50m; app rd steep with sharp bends. Site well sp. Med, mkd/hdg pitch, terr, pt shd; wc; chem disp; shwrs €0.50; EHU (10A) metered + conn fee (poss rev pol); gas; lndry (inc dryer); shop; rest; bar; playgrnd; beach on lake; sailing; watersports; 40% statics; dogs €3; poss cr; Eng spkn; adv bkg rec; v quiet; CKE/CCI. "Ltd touring pitches; superb views over lake; peaceful; gd site; sm pitches; conv for Zugspitze, Royal Castles, Oberammergau; lakeside cycle track to Füssen & to Neuschwanstein Castle." 1 Apr-31 Oct. € 22.00 2014*

⊞ **FUSSEN** *4E4* (6km NE Rural) *47.59638, 10.73861* **Camping Brunnen, Seestrasse 81, 87645 Brunnen [(08362) 8273; fax 8630; info@camping-brunnen.de; www.camping-brunnen.de]** S on rte 17 twd Füssen turn R in vill of Schwangau N to Brunnen; turn R at ent to vill at Spar shop, site clearly sp. Fr Füssen N on B17; turn L in Schwangau; well sp on lakeside. Lge, mkd pitch, hdstg, pt sl, pt shd; wc; chem disp; mv service pnt; serviced pitches; shwrs inc; EHU (10-16A) metered + conn fee; gas; lndry rm; sm shop; rest/bar adj; playgrnd; sw & yachting in Lake Forggensee adj; beach adj; bike hire; golf 3km; dogs €4; bus; site clsd 5 Nov-20 Dec; poss cr; Eng spkn; adv bkg; ccard acc; CKE/CCI. "Lovely location, next to lake; o'fits poss tightly packed; steel pegs ess; excel san facs; some pitches cramped; gd for Royal castles; gd cycle rtes; 10% red visits to Neuschwanstein Castle nrby; gates clsd 2200-0700; excel, busy, vg site; handy rest, supmkt & g'ge." ♦ € 32.00 2014*

FUSSEN *4E4* (5km NW Rural) *47.60198, 10.68333* **Camping Hopfensee, Fischerbichl 17/Uferstrasse, 87629 Hopfen-am-See [(08362) 917710; fax 917720; info@camping-hopfensee.de; www.camping-hopfensee.com]** Fr Füssen N on B16 twd Kaufbeuren in 2km L on rd sp Hopfen-am-See, site at ent to vill on L thro c'van car park. Lge, mkd pitch, hdstg, pt shd; wc; chem disp; mv service pnt; fam bthrm; all serviced pitches; sauna; shwrs inc; EHU (16A) metered; gas; lndry; shop; rest, snacks; bar; playgrnd; htd covrd pool; shgl beach & lake sw adj; boating & fishing; fitness cent; solarium; wintersports area; entmnt; dogs €4.15; internet; poss cr; Eng spkn; adv bkg rec high ssn; quiet; ccard not acc; red LS; CKE/CCI. "Gd location; excel facs; helpful staff; gd rest on site; no tents allowed except for awnings; tight squeeze in high ssn; vans need manhandling; gd walking & cycling; lakeside pitches rec; excel; highly rec; 5 star facs." ♦ 1 Jan-3 Nov & 17 Dec-31 Dec. € 38.00 2014*

FUSSEN *4E4* (6km NW Rural) *47.60883, 10.66918* **Haus Guggemos, Uferstrasse 42, 87629 Hopfen-am-See [(08362) 3334; fax 6765; haus.guggemos@t-online.de; www.haus-guggemos.de]** Fr Füssen take B16 N dir Kaufbeuren; in 2km turn L sp Hopfen-am-See. Drive thro vill; site on R opp lake. Sm, some hdstg, pt shd; terr; wc; chem disp; shwrs inc; EHU (10A) metered; lndry; shop 500m; rest, snack & bar 200m; playgrnd; lake sw adj; dogs €2; bus adj; Eng spkn; adv bkg; quiet; CKE/CCI. "Excel, family-run, farm site in beautiful area; views across lake to Alps." 1 Apr-31 Oct. € 16.00 2013*

GAIENHOFEN HORN see Radolfzell am Bodensee *3C4*

⊞ **GANDERKESEE** *1C2* (7km W Rural) *53.04666, 8.46388* **Ferienpark Falkensteinsee, Am Falkensteinsee 1, 27777 Ganderkesee-Steinkimmen [(04222) 9470077; fax 9470079; camping@falkensteinsee.de; www.falkensteinsee.de]** Exit A28/E22 junc 18 dir Habbrügge. Site on R in 2km. Lge, pt shd; wc; sauna; shwrs inc; EHU (16A) €3.50 or metered; lndry; shop; rest 1km; snacks; playgrnd; lake sw adj; sep naturist beach; golf 8km; 70% statics; dogs €1.50; o'night m'van area; Eng spkn; quiet; ccard not acc; 5% red CKE/CCI. "Conv Oldenburg & Bremen; new owners; completely refurb (2015); sw lake with 2 sandy beaches; pleasant holiday park; well organised; friendly staff; new facs & v high quality; excel; sep sw area for dogs." ♦ ltd. € 21.50 2016*

GARBSEN see Hannover *1D3*

GARTOW *2E2* (4km NW Rural) *53.03972, 11.41583* **Camping Laascher See, Ortsteil Laasche 13, 29471 Gartow [(05846) 342; pewsdorf@campingplatz-laascher-see.de; www.elbtalaue-camping.de]** Fr S on B493 to Gartow, turn N on L256 (Rondelerstrasse) dir Gartower See & Laasche See, site sp on R. Or E fr Dennenberg on L256 dir Gorleben & Gartow, site sp approx 5km after Gorleben. Med, hdg pitch, pt sl, pt shd; wc; chem disp; mv service pnt; shwrs €0.80; EHU (6A) inc; lndry (inc dryer); shop, rest 2.5km; bar; playgrnd; lake sw 300m; 60% statics; dogs €1.50; adv bkg; quiet; CKE/CCI. "Pleasant owners; clean, modern san facs; vg." ♦ 1 Apr-31 Oct. € 19.50 2016*

⊞ **GEESTHACHT** *1D2* (9km SW Rural) *53.42465, 10.29470* **Campingplatz Stover Strand International, Stover Strand 10, 21423 Drage [(04177) 430; info@stover-strand.de; www.camping-stover-strand.de]** Fr N on A25 to Geesthacht, then B404 dir Winsen to Stove. Site at end Stover Strand on banks of Rv Elbe. Fr S on A7 to Maschen, then A250 to Winsen then B404, as above. V lge, mkd pitch, pt shd; htd wc; chem disp; mv service pnt; fam bthrm; shwrs €0.50; EHU (6-16A) €2 or metered; lndry (inc dryer); shop; rest, snacks; bar; BBQ; cooking facs; playgrnd; rv sw & beach; fishing; watersports; marina; bike hire; games area; wifi; entmnt; 80% statics; dogs €2; poss cr; adv bkg; quiet; ccard acc; CKE/CCI. "Excel rvside site; poss cr even LS; site clsd 1300-1500; Hamburg Card avail." ♦ € 20.00 2012*

GEMUNDEN AM MAIN *3D2* (5km W Rural) *50.05260, 9.65656* **Spessart-Camping Schönrain, Schönrain strasse 4-18, 97737 Gemünden-Hofstetten [(09351) 8645; fax 8721; info@spessart-camping.de; www.spessart-camping.de]** Rd B26 to Gemünden, cross Rv Main & turn R dir Hofstetten, site sp. Lge, hdg/mkd pitch, some hdstg, terr, pt shd; htd wc; chem disp; mv service pnt; sauna; shwrs €0.50; EHU (10A) metered + conn fee €2.15; lndry (inc dryer); shop & 2km; rest, snacks; bar; playgrnd; children's pool; games area; bike hire; fitness rm; solarium; TV; 50% statics (sep area); dogs €2.80; phone; variable pitch sizes/prices; poss cr; Eng spkn; quiet; CKE/CCI. "Clean, well-kept, wooded site; interesting towns nrby; excel." ♦ 1 Apr-30 Sep. € 25.00 2016*

GEORGENTHAL see Ohrdruf *2E4*

GERBACH see Rockenhausen *3C2*

⊞ **GERSFELD (RHON)** *3D2* (2.5km N Rural) *50.46223, 9.91953* **Camping Hochrhön, Schachen 13, 36129 Gersfeld-Schachen [tel/fax (06654) 7836; camping hochrhoen@aol.com; www.rhoenline.de/camping-hochrhoen]** Exit A7 exit Fulda-Süd S onto B27/B279 to Gersfeld, then B284 sp Ehrenberg, Turn L dir Schachen, foll sp to site. Med, hdg/mkd pitch, hdstg, pt shd; wc; chem disp; mv service pnt; shwrs €0.60; EHU (16A) metered; lndry; shops 1.5km; rest 500m; playgrnd; ski lift 3km; some statics (sep area); dogs free; poss cr; red CKE/CCI. "Conv for gliding & air sports at Wasswerkuppe; friendly." € 18.00 2012*

GIROD see Montabaur *3C2*

GLUCKSBURG (OSTSEE) *1D1* (6km NE Coastal) *54.85901, 9.59109* **Ostseecamp, An der Promenade 1, 24960 Glücksburg-Holnis [(04631) 622071; fax 622072; info@ostseecamp-holnis.de; www.ostseecamp-holnis.de]** Fr Flensburg on rd 199 turn off thro Glücksburg & further 6km to Holnis. Med, mkd pitch, some hdstg, pt shd; htd wc; chem disp; mv service pnt; fam bthrm; shwrs inc; EHU (16A) €3; lndry (inc dryer); shop; rest 200m; snacks; BBQ; cooking facs; playgrnd; pool; sand beach adj; fishing; windsurfing 1km; bike hire; wifi; entmnt; 30% statics; dogs €2.50; adv bkg; quiet; CKE/CCI. "Lovely coastal loc; v friendly staff; clean facs. ♦ 28 Mar-16 Oct. € 29.00 (CChq acc) 2016*

GOPPINGEN *3D3* (13.5km SW Rural) *48.63946, 9.55508* **Campingplatz Aichelberg, Bunzenberg 1, 73101 Aichelberg [(07164) 2700; fax 903029]** Exit E52/A8 junc 58 sp Aichelberg-Goppingen & foll sp to camp site in 1km. Med, pt shd; wc; chem disp; shwrs inc; EHU (10A) €2; shop; rest 500m; bar; poss cr; adv bkg; 80% statics; dogs €2; poss cr; quiet. "Fills up after 1600 hrs but gd overflow field with EHU for NH; family-run site; new excel facs; owner helpful; nr A8; gd conv NH." 7 Apr-8 Oct. € 20.00 2017*

⊞ **GOSLAR** *1D3* (4km SW Rural) *51.88958, 10.39889* **Campingplatz Sennhütte, Clausthalerstrasse 28, 38644 Goslar [(05321) 22498; sennhuette@campingplatz-goslar.de; www.campingplatz-goslar.de]** Fr Goslar on B241 twd Clausthal, Zellerfeld site on R in 2km. Ent thro car pk of Hotel Sennhütte. Med, pt shd; wc; chem disp; shwrs €0.50; EHU (16A) metered + €2 conn fee (poss long lead req); lndry (inc dryer); shop; rest; 30% statics; dogs; bus at ent to town; no adv bkg; noisy nr rd; ccard acc. "Gd NH/sh stay nr beautiful town." € 17.00 2016*

⊞ **GRAFENDORF** *3D2* (11km SE Rural) *50.10678, 9.78241* **Camping Rossmühle, 97782 Gräfendorf-Weickersgrüben [(09357) 1210; fax 832; www.campingplatz-rossmuehle.de]** Exit A7 junc 96 onto B27 sp Karlstadt. At Hammelburg foll sps to Gräfendorf & site in 8km on rvside, beyond Weickersgrüben. Lge, mkd pitch, terr, pt shd; wc; chem disp; mv service pnt; shwrs €1; EHU (6-10A) €2; lndry; shop, rest high ssn; bar; playgrnd; watersports; fitness rm; bike & canoe hire; solarium; entmnt; TV; 50% statics; dogs €2; o'night area for m'vans; adv bkg; quiet. "Poss liable to flooding after heavy rain; clean san facs; excel; cycle rte tourers sep fr statics." ♦ € 18.00 2012*

⊞ **GREFRATH** *1A4* (4km N Rural) *51.36492, 6.32328* **Campingplatz Waldfrieden, An der Paas 13, 47929 Grefrath [(02158) 3855; fax 3685; ferienpark@waldfrieden@t-online.de; www.ferienpark-waldfrieden.de]** Fr A40-E34 S to Duisburg; turn S at exit 3 sp Grefrath; site sp on L in 3km. Lge, hdg pitch, hdstg, pt shd; htd wc; chem disp; mv service pnt; shwrs; EHU (10A) metered + conn fee; gas; lndry; shop 1.2km; playgrnd; lake sw adj; sw pools 1.5km; 80% statics; dogs €2; poss cr; Eng spkn; quiet; CKE/CCI. "Conv NH North Sea ports; WWII cemetaries at Reichswald; site over-used & weary." € 17.50 2013*

⊞ **GREVEN** *1B3* (6km SW Rural) *52.08328, 7.55806* **Campingplatz Westheide, Altenbergerstrasse 23, 48268 Greven [(02571) 560701; kontakt@campingplatz-westheide.de; www.campingplatz-westheide.de]** Exit A1 junc 76 onto B481 around E side of Greven, then turn L onto B219 for 2km. Turn R onto L555 Nordwalderstrasse & in 2km at Westerode turn L into Altenbergerstrasse, site on L in 1km. Med, hdg pitch, pt shd; htd wc; chem disp; fam bthrm; shwrs €0.50; EHU (16A) metered; lndry; snacks; bar; playgrnd; lake & sand beach adj; fishing; games rm; 80% statics; dogs €1; quiet; ccard acc; CKE/CCI. "Gd for sh stay; walks around lake." € 18.00 2016*

GROSS QUASSOW see Neustrelitz *2F2*

GERMANY

⊞ **GYHUM** *1D2* (4km SE Rural) *53.19308, 9.33638* **Waldcamping Hesedorf, Zum Waldbad 3, 27404 Gyhum-Hesedorf [(04286) 2252; fax 924509; info@waldcamping-hesedorf.de; www.waldcamping-hesedorf.de]** Exit A1/E22 junc 49 in dir Zeven. In 1km turn R sp Gyhum & foll site sp to Hesedorf. Med, unshd; htd wc; chem disp; mv service pnt; shwrs; EHU (16A) inc; lndry; shop 1km; rest; playgrnd; htd pool 150m inc; wifi; 70% statics (sep area); dogs €0.50; barrier clsd 1300-1500; Eng spkn; quiet; CKE/CCI. "Clean, well-kept site; attractive area; gd rest; lge sep area for tourers; dated san facs but clean; gd NH." € 22.50 2017*

⊞ **HALBERSTADT** *2E3* (3km NE Rural) *51.90981, 11.0827* **Camping am See (Part Naturist), Warmholzberg 70, 38820 Halberstadt [(03941) 609308; fax 570791; info@camping-am-see.de; www.camping-am-see.de]** Sp on B81 (Halberstadt-Magdeburg). Med, terr, unshd; wc; chem disp; shwrs inc; EHU (10A) metered + conn fee €2.50 (poss rev pol); lndry; shop; snacks; pool adj; lake beach & sw adj (sep naturist beach); 75% statics; dogs €2; sep car park; quiet; red CKE/CCI. "Conv Harz mountains & Quedlinburg (770 houses classified as historic monuments by UNESCO); quiet, green site; some individual shwrs; clsd 1300-1500." € 34.00 2013*

⊞ **HAMBURG** *1D2* (7km NW Urban) *53.5900, 9.93083* **Campingplatz Buchholz, Keilerstrasse 374, 22525 Hamburg-Stellingen [(040) 5404532; fax 5402536; info@camping-buchholz.de; www.camping-buchholz.de]** Exit A7/E45 junc 26 & foll dir 'Innenstadt' - city cent. Site sp in 600m on L. Sm, hdg/mkd pitch, all hdstg, pt shd; wc; shwrs €1; chem disp; EHU (16A) €3; lndry; shop, rest, snacks 200m; bar; 10% statics; dogs €3.80; bus, train nr; poss v cr; adv bkg; rd noise; no ccard acc. "Fair NH nr a'bahn & Hamburg cent; conv transport to city - tickets fr recep; friendly management; sm pitches; busy site, rec arr early; diff access for lge o'fits." ♦ € 34.00 2014*

⊞ **HAMBURG** *1D2* (9km NW Urban) *53.64916, 9.92970* **Knaus Campingpark Hamburg (formerly Camping Schnelsen-Nord), Wunderbrunnen 2, 22457 Hamburg [(040) 5594225; fax 5507334; service@campingplatz-hamburg.de; www.campingplatz-hamburg.de]** Heading N on A7 exit junc 23 to Schnelsen Nord; L at traff lts, foll sp Ikea & site behind Ikea. Med, pt shd, mkd pitch; wc; chem disp; mv service pnt; shwrs inc; EHU (6A) €2.50; lndry rm; shop; rest adj (in Ikea); snacks; bar; playgrnd; TV rm; no dogs; phone; bus to city; stn adj; deposit for key to san facs & el box; Eng spkn; quiet but some rd noise; ccard acc; CKE/CCI. "Useful NH; helpful staff; gates clsd 2200 hrs & 1300-1600 LS; elec pylons & cables cross site; 3-day Hamburg card excel value." ♦ € 40.00 2014*

⊞ **HAMELN** *1D3* (2km W Urban) *52.10916, 9.3475* **Campingplatz zum Fährhaus, Uferstrasse 80, 31785 Hameln [(05151) 67489; fax 61167; info@campingplatz-hameln.de; www.campingplatz-hameln.de]** Fr A2/E30 at Bad Eilsen junc 35 onto B83 to Hameln on NE side of Rv Weser; in town foll sp Detmold/Paderborn; cross bdge to SW side (use Thiewall Brücke); turn R on minor rd twd Rinteln; foll site sp. Med, unshd; htd wc; chem disp; mv service pnt; shwrs inc; EHU (10-16A); lndry; supmkt 500m; rest; bar; 20% statics; dogs €1; phone; clsd 1300-1430; quiet; red CKE/CCI. "Picturesque & historic district; open-air performance of Pied Piper in town on Sun to mid-Sep; sm pitches & poss uneven; helpful, lovely owner; san facs refurb, best in Europe!(2017); gd cycle paths by rv to town; site beautifully kept." ♦ ltd. € 18.50 2017*

HAMELN *1D3* (8km W Rural) *52.10725, 9.29588* **Camping am Waldbad, Pferdeweg 2, 31787 Halvestorf [tel/fax (05158) 2774; info@camping amwaldbad.de; www.campingamwaldbad.de]** Fr Hameln on B83 dir Rinteln. In approx 10km turn L, cross rv & foll sp Halvestorf & site. Med, pt sl, unshd; wc; chem disp; shwrs €0.50; EHU (16A) €2; lndry (inc dryer); shops 2km; snacks; playgrnd; htd pool; paddling pool; 80% statics; dogs free; adv bkg; quiet. "Pleasant site - better than site in Hameln." ♦ 1 Apr-31 Oct. € 15.00 2013*

⊞ **HAMM** *1B3* (13km E Rural) *51.6939, 7.9710* **Camping Uentrop, Dolbergerstrasse 80, 59510 Lippetal-Lippborg [(02388) 437 or (0172) 2300747; fax 1637; info@camping-helbach.de; www.camping-helbach.de]** Exit A2/E34 junc 19, site sp; behind Hotel Helbach 1km fr a'bahn. Lge, pt sl, pt shd; htd wc; chem disp; shwrs inc; EHU (16A) €2; gas; lndry; shops adj; rest adj; playgrnd; 90% statics; dogs €2; poss cr; Eng spkn; rd noise; ccard acc. "Friendly; gd security; barrier clsd 1300-1500 & 2200-0500; fair NH." € 18.00 2016*

HAMMELBACH *3C2* (600m S Rural) *49.63277, 8.83000* **Camping Park Hammelbach, Gasse 17, 64689 Grasellenbach/Hammelbach [(06253) 3831; info@camping-hammelbach.de; www.camping-hammelbach.de]** Exit A5/E35 exit junc 31 onto B460 E. Turn S in Weschnitz to Hammelbach & foll site sp. Med, hdg pitch, pt shd; htd wc; chem disp; mv service pnt; fam bthrm; sauna adj; shwrs inc; EHU (16A) metered; gas; lndry (inc dryer); shop 300m; rest, snacks, bar 300m; BBQ; htd pool 300m; wifi; 70% statics; dogs €1.50; bus 300m; poss cr; Eng spkn; adv bkg; quiet; ccard acc; red LS; CKE/CCI. "Excel family run site with views; v pleasant, helpful staff; red for snrs; conv Heidelberg; immac hotel like san facs; well up to CC standards." ♦ 1 Apr-31 Oct. € 20.00 2014*

HANNOVER *1D3* (14km NE Urban) *52.45383, 9.85611* **Campingplatz Parksee Lohne, Alter Postweg 12, 30916 Isernhagen [05139 88260; fax 891665; parksee-lohne@t-online.de; www.parksee-lohne.de]** Fr A2 take exit 46 to Altwarmbüchen. Cont onto K114, turn R onto Alter Postweg & foll sp to campsite. V lge, pt shd; htd wc; chem disp; mv service pnt; fam bthrm; shwrs inc; lndry (inc dryer); rest; snacks; bar; cooking facs; 95% statics; dogs; Eng spkn; quiet. "Vg site; next to golf course; excel san facs; narr cobbled rd 1/2 m; under flight path, but quiet at night." ♦ 1 Apr-15 Oct. € 29.60 2014*

⊞ **HANNOVER** *1D3* (16km SE Rural) *52.30447, 9.86216* **Camping Birkensee, 30880 Laatzen [(0511) 529962; fax 5293053; birkensee@camping-laatzen.de; www.camping-laatzen.de]** Fr N leave A7 junc 59 dir Laatzen, turn R, then turn L & site well sp on L after traff lts. Fr S exit junc 60 twd Laatzen, site sp on L on lakeside. Lge, pt shd; wc; chem disp; mv service pnt; sauna; shwrs inc; EHU (10A) €2.50 (poss rev pol); lndry; snacks; bar; playgrnd; covrd pool; lake sw & fishing; games area; 60% statics; dogs €2.50; Eng spkn; rd noise; CKE/CCI. "Gd, clean facs; sm touring area; site needs TLC; v helpful staff." ♦ ltd. € 27.00 2014*

⊞ **HANNOVER** *1D3* (10km S Rural) *52.30133, 9.74716* **Campingplatz Arnumer See, Osterbruchweg 5, 30966 Hemmingen-Arnum [(05101) 3534; fax 85514999; info@camping-hannover.de; www.camping-hannover.de]** Leave A7 junc 59 onto B443 dir Pattensen, then B3 dir Hannover. Site sp in Hemmingen dir Wilkenburg. Lge, hdg/mkd pitch, pt shd; htd wc; chem disp; mv service pnt; fam bthrm; shwrs €0.50; EHU (16A) €2.50; gas; lndry (inc dryer); shop 500m; rest, snacks; bar; cooking facs; playgrnd; lake sw; fishing; tennis; bike hire; wifi; 95% statics; dogs €1.50; bus to Hannover 1.5km; quiet; CKE/CCI. "Friendly staff; excel, modern, clean san facs; sm area for tourers - gd size open pitches; gd lake sw & boating; insect repellent ess!" € 31.00 2014*

⊞ **HANNOVER** *1D3* (16km NW Rural) *52.42083, 9.54638* **Camping Blauer See, Am Blauen See 119, 30823 Garbsen [(05137) 89960; fax 899677; info@camping-blauer-see.de; www.camping-blauer-see.de]** Fr W exit A2 at junc 41 onto Garbsen rest area. Thro service area, at exit turn R, at T-junc turn R (Alt Garbson). All sp with int'l camp sp. Fr E exit junc 40, cross a'bahn & go back to junc 41, then as above. Lge, some hdstg, pt shd; htd wc; chem disp; mv service pnt; some serviced pitches; fam bthrm; shwrs €1; EHU (16A) €2.70; gas; lndry (inc dryer); shop; rest, snacks; bar; BBQ; lge playgrnd; lake sw & watersports adj; 90% statics; dogs €2.50; phone; bus to Hannover 1.5km; barrier clsd 2300-0500 & 1300-1500; poss cr; Eng spkn; rd noise; ccard acc; CKE/CCI. "Excel san facs; well-organised site; helpful staff; conv bus/train to Hannover; rec pitch by lake." ♦ ltd. € 29.00 2014*

HANNOVERSCH MUNDEN *1D4* (900m W Rural) *51.41666, 9.64750* **Campingplatz Grüne Insel Tanzwerder, Tanzwerder 1, 34346 Hannoversch-Münden [(05541) 12257; fax 660778; info@busch-freizeit.de; www.busch-freizeit.de]** A7/E45 exit junc 76 onto B496 to Hann-Münden. Cross bdge & site sp on an island on Rv Fulda next to town cent. App over narr swing bdge. Fr junc 75 foll sp to Hann-Münden. At Aral g'ge in town take next L & foll sp to site (sp Weserstein). Med, mkd pitch, pt shd; wc; chem disp; mv service pnt; shwrs €1; EHU (16A) metered + conn fee; lndry; shops, rest, snacks, bar 1km; playgrnd; htd pool 1km; wifi; dogs €2; poss cr; Eng spkn; adv bkg; noisy bdge traff; red long stay; CKE/CCI. "Pleasant, well looked after site on island bordered by rv both sides; easy stroll to historic old town." 1 Apr-16 Oct. € 21.00 2016*

⊞ **HARZGERODE** *2E4* (8km SW Rural) *51.60833, 11.08444* **Ferienpark Birnbaumteich, Birnbaumteich 1, 06493 Neudorf Harzgerode [(03948) 46243; info@ferienpark-birnbaumteich.de; www.ferienpark-birnbaumteich.de]** Fr Harzgerode on B242 dir Halle, after 1km turn R, dir Stolberg. In 4.3km after Neudorf turn R at camping sp. Site 1km on R. Med, pt sl, pt shd; wc; chem disp; mv service pnt; fam bthrm; sauna; shwrs; EHU (16A) €3; lndry (inc dryer); shop; rest; café; snacks; bar; BBQ; playgrnd; lake sw; games area; games rm; entmnt; wifi; 50% statics; dogs €4; phone; bus 1km, train 3km; twin axles; Eng spkn; adv bkg; CKE/CCI. "Forest walk & bike trails; steam rlwy 3km; interesting towns nrby; vg." ♦ ltd. € 24.00 2015*

"I need an on-site restaurant"

We do our best to make sure site information is correct, but it is always best to check any must-have facilities are still available or will be open during your visit.

HASSENDORF see Rotenburg (Wümme) *1D2*

HATTINGEN *1B4* (3km NW Urban) *51.40611, 7.17027* **Camping Ruhrbrücke, Ruhrstrasse 6, 45529 Hattingen [(02324) 80038; info@camping-hattingen.de; www.camping-hattingen.de]** Fr A40 bet Essen & Bochum exit junc 29 dir Höntrop & Hattingen. Foll sp Hattingen on L651 & B1, site sp bef rv bdge. Med, pt sl, unshd; htd wc; chem disp; shwrs €1; EHU (16A) €3; shop 1km; rest, snacks 1km; bar 800m; BBQ; rv sw adj; canoeing, windsurfing adj; dogs €2; phone; bus, train adj; Eng spkn; adv bkg; quiet; CKE/CCI. "Beautiful rvside setting; plentiful, clean facs; friendly owner; excel cycle tracks." ♦ ltd. 1 Apr-20 Oct. € 18.00 2016*

HAUSBAY see Lingerhahn *3B2*

HAUSEN IM TAL *3C4* (100m E Rural) *48.08365, 9.04290* **Camping Wagenburg, Kirchstr. 24, 88631 Beuron / i Tal Hausen [(07579) 559; fax 1525; info@camping-wagenburg.de; www.camping-wagenburg.de]** Fr E on B32 stay on Sigmaringen bypass and take minor rd L227 sp Gutenstein/Beuron to Hausen, site in vill beside Rv Donau. Med, hdstg, pt shd; wc; chem disp; mv service pnt; shwrs €0.50; EHU (16A) metered + conn fee; lndry; shop 50m; rest adj; bar; playgrnd; rv sw adj; tennis 300m; TV; dogs €1.50; poss cr; Eng spkn; adv bkg; red long stay. "Beautiful location in Danube Gorge; friendly, helpful owner; clsd 1230-1430; poss flooding in wet weather/high rv level; gd walking/cycling; vg; excel site gd for walking cycling; rv canoeing." ♦ ltd. 10 Apr-3 Oct. € 26.00 2012*

"Satellite navigation makes touring much easier"

Remember most sat navs don't know if you're towing or in a larger vehicle – always use yours alongside maps and site directions.

⊞ **HECHTHAUSEN** *1D2* (4km SW Rural) *53.62525, 9.20298* **Ferienpark & Campingpark Geesthof, Am Ferienpark 1, 21755 Hechthausen-Klint [(04774) 512; fax 9178; info@geesthof.de; www.geesthof.de]** Site sp on B73 rd to Lamstedt. Med, hdg/mkd pitch, pt shd; wc; chem disp; mv service pnt; sauna; fam bthrm; shwrs inc; EHU (10A) €2; lndry (inc dryer); shop; rest, snacks; playgrnd; 2 pools (1 htd, covrd); paddling pool; waterslide; watersports; fishing; boat & bike hire; wifi; entmnt; 60% statics; dogs €2; Eng spkn; quiet; red 7+ nts. "Superb site with mature trees around pitches; peaceful surroundings adj to rv, lake & woods; friendly staff." ♦ € 22.50 (CChq acc) 2015*

HEIDELBERG *3C2* (10km E Rural) *49.40175, 8.77916* **Campingplatz Haide, Ziegelhäuser Landstrasse 91, 69151 Neckargemünd [(06223) 2111; fax 71959; info@camping-haide.de; www.camping-haide.de]** Take B37 fr Heidelberg, cross Rv Neckar by Ziegelhausen bdge by slip rd on R (avoid vill narr rd); foll site sp. Site on R bet rv & rd 1km W of Neckergemünd on rvside. Lge, hdstg; unshd; wc; chem disp; mv service pnt; shwrs €1; EHU (6A) €2.50 (long lead req); lndry (inc dryer); shop 2km; rest, snacks; BBQ; playgrnd; bike hire; wifi; 5% statics; dogs €2; bus 1.5km; Eng spkn; some rd, rlwy (daytime) & rv noise; red CKE/CCI. "Conv Neckar Valley & Heidelberg; NH/sh stay only; long attractive site along rv." ♦ 1 Apr-31 Oct. € 20.30 2016*

HEIDELBERG *3C2* (12km E Urban) *49.39638, 8.79472* **Campingplatz an der Friedensbrücke, Falltorstrasse 4, 69151 Neckargemünd [tel/fax (06223) 2178; nfo@campingplatz-am-neckar.de; www.campingplatz-am-neckar.de]** Exit Heidelberg on S side of rv on B37; on ent Neckargemünd site sp to L (grey sp) mkd Poststrasse; site adj rv bdge. Fr S on B45 turn L sp Heidelberg, then R at camping sp. Fr A6 exit junc 33 onto B45 sp Neckargemünd, then as above. Foll sp - do not foll sat nav. Lge, unshd; htd wc; chem disp; mv service pnt; fam bthrm; shwrs €0.75; EHU (6-16A) €5 or metered (poss rev pol); gas; lndry; shop, ltd; rest adj; snacks; bar; playgrnd nr; pool adj; kayaking 500m; tennis; wifi; TV rm; dogs €1.50; phone; transport to Heidelberg by boat, bus & train 10 mins walk fr site; poss cr; Eng spkn; adv bkg; rd & rv noise; ccard not acc. "Gd location by busy rv, poss liable to flood; immac, well-run, relaxing site; ask for rvside pitch (sm) - extra charge; owner will site o'fits; warm welcome; helpful staff; no plastic grndsheets; 26 steps up to main san facs; gd rvside walks & cycling; TO 500m; gd NH facs, nr ent." ♦ 1 Apr-22 Oct. € 28.00 2017*

⊞ **HEIDENAU** *1D2* (2.6km W Rural) *53.30851, 9.62038* **Ferienzentrum Heidenau, Minkens Fuhren, 21258 Heidenau [(04182) 4272 or 4861; fax 401130; info@ferienzentrum-heidenau.de; www.ferienzentrum-heidenau.de]** Exit A1 Hamburg-Bremen m'way junc 46 to Heidenau; foll sp. Lge, pt shd; htd wc; chem disp; mv service pnt; sauna; shwrs inc; EHU (16A) €2.50 (poss long lead req); lndry; shop; rest, snacks; bar; BBQ (sep area); playgrnd; htd pool; fishing lakes; gd cycling; tennis; games area; internet; 75% statics; no dogs; phone; Eng spkn; quiet; CKE/CCI. "Pleasant, wooded site; tourers on grass areas by lakes; clean, modern facs; ltd shop; gd; visa ccards not acc; pitches maybe unusable in v wet weather." € 26.00 2016*

"There aren't many sites open at this time of year"

If you're travelling outside peak season remember to call ahead to check site opening dates – even if the entry says 'open all year'.

HEIDENBURG see Trittenheim *3B2*

HEINSEN see Holzminden *1D3*

HELLENTHAL see Schleiden *3B1*

HEMMINGEN ARNUM see Hannover *1D3*

HEMSBACH see Weinheim *3C2*

HERBOLZHEIM *3B3* (2km E Rural) *48.21625, 7.78796* **Terrassen-Campingplatz Herbolzheim, Laue-Dietweg 1, 79336 Herbolzheim [(07643) 1460; fax 913382; s.hugoschmidt@t-online.de; www.laue-camp.de]** Fr E35/A5 exit 58 to Herbolzheim. Turn R in vill. Turn L on o'skts of vill. Site in 1km next to sw pool, sp. Med, terr, pt shd; wc; chem disp; mv service pnt; shwrs inc; EHU (10A) €2; lndry; shop; rest; playgrnd; pool & tennis nrby; 30% statics; dogs €2 (not acc mid-Jul to mid-Aug); o'nights facs for m'vans; clsd 1300-1500; adv bkg; quiet; ccard acc; red long stay; ACSI; CKE/CCI. "Excel friendly, well-maintained site; conv Vosges, Black Forest & Europapark; gd simple rest, spotless and supmkt nrby, excel staff; immac grass on firm base." 23 Mar-3 Oct. € 30.00 2013*

HERSBRUCK *4E2* (6km E Rural) *49.51884, 11.49200* **Pegnitz Camping, Eschenbacherweg 4, 91224 Hohenstadt [(09154) 1500; fax 91200]** Exit A9 junc 49 onto B14 dir Hersbruck & Sulzbach-Rosenberg. By-pass Hersbruck & after 8km turn L sp Hohenstadt. Bef vill, cross rv bdge & immed turn R at site sp. Med, pt shd; wc; chem disp; mv service pnt; shwrs inc; EHU (10A) inc; gas; lndry; shop & rest 1km; bike hire; 10% statics; trains nrby; Eng spkn; adv bkg; quiet; CKE/CCI. "Lovely, peaceful, friendly site; gd walking & cycling area; helpful owner; vg san facs; train to Nuremberg; gd; stn 200m." 1 Mar-31 Oct. € 16.00 2014*

HIRSCHAU *4F2* (6km E Rural) *49.55608, 12.00634* **Campingplatz am Naturbad, Badstrasse 13, 92253 Schnaittenbach [tel/fax (09622) 1722; info@campingplatz.schnaittenbach.de; www.schnaittenbach.de]** On B14 bet Rosenberg & Wernberg, clearly sp in vill. Med, sl, unshd; wc; chem disp; shwrs inc; EHU (16A) €1.50 or metered + conn fee; lndry (inc dryer); shop 1.5km; rest adj; playgrnd; pool; games area; 80% statics; quiet; red CKE/CCI. "Gd NH; scenic area; v pleasant site." ♦ ltd. 1 Apr-30 Sep. € 17.50 2013*

HIRSCHHORN see Eberbach *3C2*

HOCHDONN *1D1* (1.5km East Rural) *54.02395, 9.29381* **Campingplatz Klein Westerland, Zur Holstenau 1, 25712 Hochdonn [04948 252345; info@campingplatz-klein-westerland.de; www.campingplatz-klein-westerland.de]** Fr A23, take exit 5 to Süderhastedt. Turn L on 431 to Hochdonn. Site sp. Canal ferry maybe diff for trailer c'vans, steep ramps. Med, pt shd; wc; shwrs; EHU; rest, snacks, bar, 70% statics; dogs €1.50; poss cr; noisy, passing ships; gd. "Interesting canal traff & lge locks at Brunsbüttel, 20km S; only site on the Northsea-Baltic sea canal." 1 Apr-31 Oct. € 18.00 2016*

⊞ **HOF** *4F2* (10km NW Rural) *50.37494, 11.83804* **Camping Auensee, 95189 Joditz-Köditz [(09295) 381; rathaus@gemeinde-koeditz.de; www.gemeinde-koeditz.de]** Exit A9 at junc 31 Berg/Bad Steben. Turn R fr m'way & in 200m L to Joditz, foll site sp in vill (1-way ent/exit to site). Med, terr, unshd; wc; mv service pnt; shwrs; EHU (16A) €1.80 or metered; lndry; shops adj; rest high ssn; playgrnd; lake sw; fishing; tennis; wifi; 75% statics; dogs €1.50; clsd 1230-1500; quiet; red CKE/CCI. € 16.00 2016*

HOFHEIM AM RIEGSEE see Murnau am Staffelsee *4E4*

HOHENFELDEN see Kranichfeld *2E4*

HOHENSTADT see Hersbruck *4E2*

HOHENSTADT *3D3* (500m NE Rural) *48.54693, 9.66794* **Camping Waldpark Hohenstadt, Waldpark 1, 73345 Hohenstadt [(07335) 6754; fax (7335) 184574; camping@waldpark-hohenstadt.de; www.waldpark-hohenstadt.de]** Exit A8/E52 junc 60 Behelfs & foll sp to Hohenstadt & site in approx 5km. Med, some hdstg, pt sl, pt shd; htd wc; chem disp; mv service pnt; fam bthrm; shwrs €0.50; EHU (16a) €2.50; lndry (inc dryer); rest, snacks; bar; BBQ; playgrnd; htd pool; wifi; 75% statics; dogs €1; Eng spkn; quiet; red LS; CKE/CCI. "Gd, peaceful NH to/fr Austria; handy off A8 - conv for mway; helpful & friendly staff; gd facs; long walk to shwrs fr tourer parking; lovely site; area ideal for walking, cycling, climbing, skiing and cross country skiing; excel." 1 Mar-31 Oct. € 27.50 2013*

HOLZMINDEN *1D3* (10km N Rural) *51.88618, 9.44335* **Weserbergland Camping, Weserstrasse 66, 37649 Heinsen [(05535) 8733; fax 911264; info@weserbergland-camping.de; www.weserbergland-camping.de]** Fr Holzminden on B83 twd Hameln, site sp in Heinsen cent twd rv bank. Med, pt sl, pt shd; htd wc; chem disp; mv service pnt; fam bthrm; sauna; shwrs €0.50; EHU (10A) €1.90; gas; lndry (inc dryer); shop 600m; rest; bar; playgrnd; htd pool; bike hire; games area; entmnt in high ssn; wifi; 50% statics; dogs €3; twin axles; Eng spkn; adv bkg; quiet; ccard acc; 10% red long stay/CKE/CCI. "Beautiful site on rv bank; gd modern san facs (2015); gd area for walking/cycling; gd local bus service; accomodating owner; excel." 1 Apr-31 Oct. € 23.00 2015*

HOOKSIEL *1C2* (2km N Coastal) *53.64100, 8.03400* **Nordsee Camping Hooksiel (Part Naturist), Bäderstrasse, 26434 Wangerland [(04425) 958080; fax 991475; info@wangerland.de; www.wangerland.de]** Exit A29 at junc 4 sp Fedderwarden to N. Thro Hooksiel, site sp 1.5km. V lge, some hdstg, unshd; wc; chem disp; mv service pnt; fam bthrm; shwrs inc; EHU (6-10A) inc; gas; lndry (inc dryer); shop; rest, snacks; playgrnd; muddy beach; fishing; sailing; watersports; games area; bike hire; wifi; entmnt; 50% statics; dogs €3.10; naturist site adj with same facs; poss cr; quiet. "Main san facs excel but up 2 flights steps - otherwise facs in Portakabin." ♦ 25 Mar-17 Oct. € 24.00 2016*

GERMANY

⊞ **HORB AM NECKAR** *3C3* (4km W Rural) *48.44513, 8.67300* **Camping Schüttehof, Schütteberg 7-9, 72160 Horb-am-Neckar [(07451) 3951; fax 623215; camping-schuettehof@t-online.de; www.camping-schuettehof.de]** Fr A81/E41 exit junc 30; take Freudenstadt rd out of Horb site sp. Med, mkd pitch, pt sl, pt shd; wc; chem disp; shwrs €0.50; EHU (16A) metered + conn fee; gas; lndry; shop; rest; playgrnd; htd pool; paddling pool; internet; entmnt; 75% statics; dogs €2; poss cr; adv bkg; quiet. "Horb delightful Black Forest town; site close to saw mill & could be noisy; steep path to town; site clsd 1230-1430; superb, new, state of the art facs; peaceful; v pleasant helpful staff." € 18.50 2017*

HORSTEL *1B3* (5km N Rural) *52.32751, 7.60061* **Campingplatz Herthasee, Herthaseestrasse 70, 48477 Hörstel [(05459) 1008; fax 971875; contact@hertha-see.de; www.hertha-see.de]** Exit A30/E30 junc 10 to Hörstel, then foll sp Hopsten. Site well sp fr a'bahn. V lge, pt sl, shd; wc; chem disp; mv service pnt; fam bthrm; shwrs €0.50; EHU (16A) €2.40 or metered + conn fee (poss long lead req); gas; lndry; shop; rest 2km; snacks; bar; BBQ; playgrnd; lake sw & beach adj; tennis; bike hire; TV; wifi; 70% statics; no dogs; Eng spkn; quiet; CKE/CCI. "Excel site." ♦ 22 Mar-29 Sep. € 31.00 2013*

"That's changed – Should I let The Club know?"

If you find something on site that's different from the site entry, fill in a report and let us know. See camc.com/europereport.

HOXTER *1D3* (2km S Rural) *51.76658, 9.38308* **Wesercamping Höxter, Sportzentrum 4, 37671 Höxter [tel/fax (05271) 2589; info@campingplatz-hoexter.de; www.campingplatz-hoexter.de]** Fr B83/64 turn E over rv sp Boffzen, turn R & site sp almost on rv bank. Turn R in 300m at green sp, turn L in car park. Med, pt shd; wc; chem disp; fam bthrm; shwrs €0.50; EHU (10-16A) €2; lndry (inc dryer); shop; rest; playgrnd; internet; child entmnt; 60% statics; dogs €1.50; quiet; red CKE/CCI. "Lge open area for tourers; clsd 1300-1500; spaces beside rv; easy walk along rv to town." 15 Mar-15 Oct. € 14.50 2014*

⊞ **HUCKESWAGEN** *1B4* (4km NE Rural) *51.15269, 7.36557* **Campingplatz Beverblick, Grossberghausen 29, Mickenhagen, 42499 Hückeswagen [(02192) 83389; info@beverblick.de; www.beverblick.de]** Fr B237 in Hückeswagen at traff lts take B483 sp Radevormwald. Over rv & in 500m turn R sp Mickenhagen. In 3km strt on (no thro rd), turn R after 1km, site on R. Steep app. Med, hdstg, pt sl, unshd; htd wc; chem disp (wc); shwrs €1.10; EHU (10A) metered; shop & 5km; rest; bar; 90% statics; dogs; quiet. "Few touring pitches; helpful owners; gd rest & bar; gd touring base; vg." € 15.00 2012*

⊞ **HUNFELD** *1D4* (5km SW Rural) *50.65333, 9.72388* **Knaus Campingpark Praforst, Dr Detlev-Rudelsdorff Allee 6, 36088 Hünfeld [(06652) 749090; fax 7490901; huenfeld@knauscamp.de; www.knauscamp.de/huenfeld-praforst]** Exit A7 junc 90 dir Hünfeld, foll sp thro golf complex. Med, mkd pitch, pt sl, pt shd; wc; shwrs; chem disp; mv service pnt; EHU (16A) metered or €3.50; lndry; shop; playgrnd; pool; fishing; games rm; games area; golf adj; wifi; 40% statics; dogs €2; quiet. "Excel san facs; gd walking/cycling." ♦ € 26.80 2016*

⊞ **IDAR OBERSTEIN** *3B2* (15km N Rural) *49.80455, 7.26986* **Camping Harfenmühle, 55758 Asbacherhütte [(06786) 7076; fax 7570; mail@harfenmuehle.de; www.camping-harfenmuehle.de]** Fr rte 41 fr Idar twd Kirn, turn L at traff lts at Fischbach by-pass sp Herrstein/Morbach, site 3km past Herrstein vill. Sharp turn to site. Med, pt shd; wc; chem disp; mv service pnt; sauna; shwrs €0.50; EHU (16A) metered; lndry; gas; shop; rest, snacks; bar; playgrnd; lake sw adj; fishing; tennis; games area; games rm; golf 10km; internet; TV rm; 50% statics; dogs €2; phone; o'night area for m'vans; adv bkg; Eng spkn; no ccard acc; 10% red CKE/CCI. "Vg rest; gd san facs but poss inadequate in high ssn; sep area late arr; barrier clsd 2200; gd site." ♦ ltd. € 25.00 2014*

IHRINGEN see Breisach am Rhein *3B4*

⊞ **ILLERTISSEN** *3D4* (11km S Rural) *48.14138, 10.10665* **Camping Christophorus Illertal, Werte 6, 88486 Kirchberg-Sinningen [(07354) 663; fax 91314; info@camping-christophorus.de; www.camping-christophorus.de]** Exit A7/E43 junc 125 at Altenstadt. In cent of town turn L, then R immed after level x-ing. Foll site sp. Lge, pt shd; htd wc; chem disp; sauna; shwrs; EHU (16A) €2.50 or metered; lndry; shop high ssn; rest, snacks; playgrnd; covrd pool; lake sw adj; fishing; bike hire; 80% statics; dogs €3.50; Eng spkn; adv bkg; red CKE/CCI. "Gd site; sm sep area for tourers; excel san facs." € 26.00 2017*

ILLERTISSEN *3D4* (2km SW Rural) *48.21221, 10.08773* **Camping Illertissen, Dietenheimerstrasse 91, 89257 Illertissen [(07303) 7888; fax 2848; campingplatz-illertissen@t-online.de; www.camping-illertissen.de]** Leave A7 at junc 124, twd Illertissen/Dietenheim; after rlwy x-ing turn R then L foll site sp. Off main rd B19 fr Neu Ulm-Memmingen fr N, turn R in Illertissen, foll sp. Sm, mkd pitch, terr, pt shd; wc; chem disp; mv service pnt; shwrs inc; EHU (16A) €2 or metered; gas; lndry; shop & 1.5km; snacks; rest in hotel adj; playgrnd; pool; 65% statics; dogs €2; poss cr; quiet; ccard acc; 10% red CKE/CCI. "Trains to Ulm & Kempten; 20 mins walk to town or cycle track; some pitches poss unrel in wet; site clsd bet 1300-1500 & 2200-0700; obliging owner; conv a'bahn; vg." ♦ 1 Apr-30 Oct. € 20.00 2015*

IMMENSTAAD AM BODENSEE see Friedrichshafen *3D4*

⊞ **IMMENSTADT IM ALLGAU** *3D4* (3km NW Rural) *47.57255, 10.19358* **Buchers Alpsee Camping, Seestrasse 25, 87509 Bühl-am-Alpsee [(08323) 7726; fax 2956; mail@alpsee-camping.de; www.alpsee-camping.de]** Fr Immenstadt, W on B308; turn R dir Isny & Missen. In 1.3km turn L sp Bühl & site sp. Lge, unshd; wc; shwrs inc; EHU (16A) €2.50 (poss rev pol); gas; lndry; shop; rest; playgrnd; pool 2km; lake sw adj; ski lift 3km; dogs €3; poss cr; Eng spkn; adv bkg; quiet. "Lake sm but pleasant; gd mountain walks; friendly welcome; excel site, first class facs." € 45.00 2014*

"I like to fill in the reports as I travel from site to site"

You'll find report forms at the back of this guide, or you can fill them in online at camc.com/europereport.

⊞ **INGOLSTADT** *4E3* (4.5km E Rural) *48.75416, 11.46277* **Campingpark Am Auwaldsee, 85053 Ingolstadt [(0841) 9611616; fax 9611617; ingolstadt@azur-camping.de; www.azur-camping.de]** Exit A9/E45 junc 62 Ingolstadt Süd, foll sp for camp site & Auwaldsee. Lge, pt shd; wc; shwrs inc; chem disp; mv service pnt; EHU (10A) inc; gas; lndry (inc dryer); shop 1.5km; rest, snacks; bar; playgrnd; pool 1km; rv beach & sw; fishing & boating; wifi; 50% statics; dogs €3.50; bus; adv bkg. "Wooded site by lake; useful NH nr m'way." € 27.00 SBS - G07 2017*

⊞ **INZELL** *4F4* (800m SW Rural) *47.76722, 12.75341* **Camping Lindlbauer, Kreuzfeldstraße 44, 83334 Inzell [08665 928 99 88; fax 928 99 86; info@camping-inzell.de]** Fr A8 exit 112 Traunstein-Siegsdorf. Take B306 twds Inzell. Foll sp in vill to campsite. Med, mkd pitch, hdstg, terr, unshd; htd wc; chem disp; mv service pnt; fam bthrm; shwrs inc; EHU (16A); lndry (inc dryer); shop; rest; snacks; bar; playgrnd; htd covrd pool; games area; wifi; dogs €4; phone adj; bus adj; twin axles; Eng spkn; adv bkg; quiet; red LS; CCI. "Excel site; beautiful views; friendly, family run site; excel location for walking & cycling." ♦ € 44.70 2014*

⊞ **JENA** *2E4* (2km NE Rural) *50.93583, 11.60833* **Campingplatz Unter dem Jenzig, Am Erlkönig 3, 07749 Jena [(03641) 666688; post@camping-jena.com; www.camping-jena.com]** Exit A4/E40 junc 54 to Jena, then B88 for 4m N dir Naumberg. Turn R just outside Jena at campsite sp, R over blue bdge; site nr sports stadium/sw pool on L, sp. Med, unshd; wc; chem disp; mv service pnt; shwrs inc; EHU (10A) €2.50 or metered; lndry; rest 500m; snacks; bar; playgrnd; pool adj; dogs €1; phone; bus 1km; shop 1.5km; some Eng spkn; adv bkg; quiet. "Gd san facs in Portakabin; sh walk to interesting town; gd cycle paths." ♦ ltd. € 23.50 2014*

JESTETTEN *3C4* (750m SW Urban) *47.64802, 8.56648* **Campingplatz & Schwimmbad, Waldshuterstrasse 13, 79798 Jestetten [(07745) 1220; info@jestetten.de; www.jestetten.de]** Site in town on B27 main rd, sp. Sm, pt sl, pt shd; htd wc; chem disp (wc); shwrs inc; EHU (10A) metered; lndry; shop, rest in town; snacks; playgrnd; htd pool; wifi; no dogs; bus at gate; train 500m; Eng spkn; adv bkg; quiet. "Gd for walk or train Rhine Falls & Switzerland; shwr token inc; friendly; site in Schwimmbad grnds." ♦ ltd. Mid May-Mid Sep. € 22.00 2015*

JODITZ KODITZ see Hof *4F2*

⊞ **KALKAR** *1A3* (5km N Rural) *51.76100, 6.28483* **Freitzeitpark Wisseler See, Zum Wisseler-See 15, 47546 Kalkar-Wissel [(02824) 96310; fax 963131; info@wisseler-see.de; www.wisseler-see.de]** Fr A3 take junc 4 onto B67 dir Kalkar & Wissel. Fr Kleve take B57 SE for 8km twd Kalkar, E to Wissel & foll camp sp. V lge, hdg/mkd pitch, pt shd; serviced pitches; wc; chem disp; mv service pnt; shwrs inc; EHU (16A) inc; lndry; shop; rest, snacks; pool; playgrnd; beach; watersports; tennis; bike hire; games area; wifi; entmnt; 75% statics; dogs €3; Eng spkn; adv bkg. "Commercialised & regimented but conv NH Rotterdam ferry; gd facs; gd for children & teenagers." ♦ € 25.00 2016*

KAMENZ *2G4* (7km NE Rural) *51.30465, 14.15272* **Campingplatz Deutschbaselitz, Grossteichstrasse 30, 01917 Kamenz [(03578) 301489; fax 308098; info@campingplatz-deutschbaselitz.com; www.campingplatz-deutschbaselitz.com]** Fr Kamenz N on rd S95 dir Wittichenau; at Schiedel turn R twd lake, site sp. Med, pt shd; htd wc; chem disp; mv service pnt; fam bthrm; shwrs inc; EHU (16A) €3; lndry (inc dryer); shop; snacks; BBQ; cooking facs; playgrnd; lake sw & beach adj; watersports; bike hire; games area; games rm; wifi; 10% statics; dogs; adv bkg; quiet; CKE/CCI. ♦ 1 Mar-31 Oct. € 23.00 (CChq acc) 2016*

⊞ **KARLSHAGEN** *2G1* (2km E Coastal) *54.11769, 13.84477* **Dünencamp, Zeltplatzstraße; 17449 Ostseebad; Karlshagen [038371 20291; fax 20310; camping@karlshagen.de; www.duenencamp.de]** Site sp fr Karlshagen along Zeltplatzstrasse. Lge, mkd pitch, pt sl, shd; htd wc; chem disp; mv service pnt; fam bthrm; shwrs (metered); elec pnt (16A) €2 (or metered); lndry; playgrnd; beach adj; dogs €4; phone; Eng spkn; quiet. "Site has direct access to long clean sandy beach; long mains lead may be needed for some pitches; conv for visiting Peenemünde; gd site." € 26.00 2016*

GERMANY

KARLSRUHE *3C3* (7km E Rural) *49.00788, 8.48303* **Azur Campingpark Turmbergblick, Tiengenerstrasse 40, 76227 Karlsruhe-Durlach [(0721) 497236; fax 497237; karlsruhe@azur-camping.de; www.azur-camping.de]** Exit A5/E35 junc 44 dir Durlach/Grötzingen onto B10 & foll sp to site 3km. Lge, mkd pitch, pt shd; htd wc; chem disp; mv service pnt; fam bthrm; shwrs inc; EHU (10A) €3 (long lead poss req); gas; lndry; shop; supmkt 500m; rest, snacks; bar; playgrnd; 2 pools nr; tennis; entmnt; internet; 20% statics; dogs €3.50; Eng spkn; adv bkg; some rd & rlwy noise; ccard acc; CKE/CCI. "NH conv to a'bahn; adequate, clean san facs; clsd 1230-1400; expensive for average site; Karlsruhe worth a visit." ♦
1 Apr-31 Oct. € 32.00 2016*

⊞ **KASSEL** *1D4* (4km S Urban) *51.29055, 9.48777* **Wohnmobilstellplatz Kassel, Giesenallee, 34121 Kassel [(0561) 707707; strassenverkehrsamt@stadt-kassel.de]** Exit A49 junc 5; strt on at traff lts; 1st R sp camping. Site 80m beyond Fulda Camp. Sm, hdstg, unshd; chem disp; mv service pnt; EHU (10A) metered; dogs; bus adj; m'vans only. "Max stay 3 nights; excel stopover; nice walk along rv & lge park nrby." € 12.50 2014*

KASSEL *1D4* (22km S Rural) *51.17757, 9.47781* **Camping Fuldaschleife, zum Bruch 6, 34302 Guxhagen-Büchenwerra [(0566) 5961044; info@fuldaschleife.de; www.fuldaschleife.de]** Exit A7 at J81 twrds Guxhagen. Foll sp. Site in 4km. Sm, mkd pitch, pt shd; htd wc; chem disp; mv service pnt; fam bthrm; shwrs €0.50; lndry (inc dryer); shops 3km; rest; snacks; bar; BBQ; playgrnd; pool; games area; wifi; 60% statics; dogs €1.50; bus adj; twin axles; Eng spkn; adv bkg; ccard acc (fee of €2); CKE/CCI. "Pleasant site adj rv; helpful staff; boating, canoeing & cycling rtes fr site; Hann Munden & Gottingen worth visiting; conv for N, S, E & W Germany; excel." ♦ ltd. 1 Mar-31 Oct. € 22.00 2016*

⊞ **KASTELLAUN** *3B2* (800m SE Rural) *50.06846, 7.45382* **Burgstadt Camping Park, Südstrasse 34, 56288 Kastellaun [(06762) 40800; fax 4080100; info@burgstadt.de; www.burgstadt.de]** Exit A61 junc 42 dir Emmelshausen onto L206/L213 for 1.2km; turn L onto B327; cont for 13.5km to Kastellaun. Site adj hotel on B237. Med, mkd pitch, hdstg, terr, unshd; htd wc; chem disp; mv waste; fam bthrm; sauna; solarium; shwrs inc; EHU (16A) metered; lndry; shop; rest, snacks; bar; BBQ; playgrnd; htd, covrd pool 300m; tennis, bike hire, riding & kayaking nrby; wifi; dogs €2; o'night m'van area; Eng spkn; adv bkg; quiet; ccard acc; CKE/CCI. "Lge pitches; clean site; excel, clean san facs; helpful staff; conv touring base; fitness & beauty cent in hotel adj; excel; v peaceful." ♦ € 24.00 2015*

KEHL *3B3* (12km ESE Rural) *48.54375, 7.93518* **Europa-Camping, Waldstrasse 32, 77731 Willstätt-Sand [tel/fax (07852) 2311; europa.camping@t-online.de; www.europa-camping-sand.de]** Exit A5/E35/E52 at junc 54 almost immed turn R at Int'l Camping sp; foll site sp. Med, some hdstg, pt shd; htd wc; shwrs inc; EHU (16A) €2.50 (long lead poss req); lndry (inc dryer); shop & 5km; rest; cooking facs; playgrnd; 30% statics; dogs €2; poss cr; Eng spkn; quiet but some rd noise; ccard acc; red long stay/CKE/CCI. "Easy reach Black Forest & Strasbourg; 1km fr a'bahn exit; well-managed, clean, tidy site; gd san facs; friendly helpful owner; cycle tracks fr site."
1 Feb-30 Nov. € 26.00 2013*

KEHL *3B3* (3km S Urban) *48.5615, 7.80861* **DCC Campingpark Kehl-Strassburg, Rheindammstrasse 1, 77694 Kehl-Kronenhof [(07851) 2603; fax 73076; CampingparkKehl@aol.com; www.campingplatz-kehl.de]** Fr A5/E35, take exit 54 onto B28 at Appenweier twd Kehl & foll site sp. Lge, pt shd; htd wc; chem disp; mv service pnt; shwrs €0.50; EHU (16A) metered + conn fee (long lead poss req); gas; lndry; shop & 1km; rest, snacks; bar; playgrnd; sw pool adj; wifi; 15% statics; dogs €1; bus 1km; poss cr; Eng spkn; adv bkg; quiet but noise fr adj stadium w/end; ccard acc; red CKE/CCI. "Peaceful site adj Rv Rhine; excel rest & modern san facs; sm pitches; pleasant rv walk & cycle paths to town; barrier clsd 1300-1500." ♦
15 Mar-31 Oct. € 23.50 2014*

⊞ **KELBRA** *2E4* (2km W Rural) *51.42551, 11.00307* **Seecamping Kelbra, Langestrasse 150, 06537 Kelbra [(034651) 45290; fax 45292; info@seecamping kelbra.de]** Exit A38 at Berga (bet junc 12 & 14); on app to town turn L at traff lts onto B85 to Kelbra; go thro chicane in vill, then R onto L234/L1040 dir Sonderhausen; site sp. L234 is Langestrasse. Lge, pt sl, unshd; htd wc; chem disp; mv service pnt; shwrs €0.50; EHU (16A) €2; lndry; shop; rest, snacks; bar; BBQ (gas/elec); playgrnd; lake sw adj; sand beach 1km; games area; internet; TV; dogs €2; phone; bus adj; poss cr; Eng spkn; adv bkg; quiet; CKE/CCI. "Gd touring base & walking area; boat hire on site; vg; 2 toilet blocks now (2015); NH outside main gates." € 18.50 2015*

⊞ **KEMPTEN (ALLGAU)** *3D4* (25km E Rural) *47.80283, 10.55377* **Camping Platz Elbsee, Am Elbsee 3, 87648 Aitrang [08 34 32 48; fax 34 31 406; info@elbsee.de; www.elbsee.de]** S on A7. Take J134 dir Marktobedorf on B12. Take exit twd Unterthingau on OAL10. Turn L on OAL3, cont onto OAL 5. Turn R on Am Elbsee. Foll sp. Lge, hdg/mkd pitch, hdstg, pt shd; htd wc; chem disp; mv service pnt; fam bthrm; shwrs; EHU (16A); lndry (inc dryer); shop; rest; snacks; BBQ; cooking facs; playgrnd; lake adj; games rm; entmnt; wifi; dogs €4.50; bus 0.75km; twin axles; poss cr; Eng spkn; adv bkg; quiet; ccard acc; CCI. "Excel site; gd base; many local historical places & amazing architecture; camp has much to offer - peace & quiet, spa art, yoga." ♦ € 34.50 2014*

⊞ **KINDING** *4E3* (5km E Rural) *49.00328, 11.45200* **Camping Kratzmühle, Mühlweg 2, 85125 Kinding-Pfraundorf [(08461) 64170; fax 641717; info@kratzmuehle.de; www.kratzmuehle.de]** Exit A9/E45 junc 58, dir Beilngries. Site sp. Lge, pt shd; wc; chem disp; mv service pnt; fam bthrm; some serviced pitches; sauna; shwrs inc; EHU (16A) €2.50; gas; lndry; shop; rest; cooking facs; playgrnd; lake sw adj & shgl beach; games area; wifi; 40% statics; dogs €2; clsd 1300-1500; poss cr; adv bkg; 10% red 2+ days; quiet; ccard acc; CKE/CCI. "Beautiful situation; conv NH for a'bahn; ideal boating & bathing, public access to lake; poss mosquito prob; helpful staff." ♦ € 26.00
2016*

KIRCHBERG SINNINGEN see Illertissen *3D4*

⊞ **KIRCHHEIM** *1D4* (5km SW Rural) *50.81435, 9.51805* **Camping Seepark, Reimboldshäuserstraße, 36275 Kirchheim [(06628) 1525; fax 8664; info@campseepark.de; www.campseepark.de]** Exit A7 at Kirchheim junc 87, site clearly sp. Lge, mkd pitch, pt sl, terr, mkd pitch, pt shd; htd wc; chem disp; mv service pnt; sauna; shwrs €1; EHU (16A) €3; metered; gas; lndry; dishwashers; shop; rest, snacks; bar; playgrnd; covrd pool; lake sw & sand beach; tennis; games area; golf 3km; entmnt; 50% statics; dogs €2; bus 500m; phone; o'night area for m'vans; adv bkg; quiet but poss noisy high ssn; ccard acc; red long stay/CKE/CCI. "Gd walking; helpful owner; excel site - leisure facs pt of lge hotel complex; NH only." ♦ € 26.00 (6 people)
2017*

"We must tell The Club about that great site we found"

Get your site reports in by mid-August and we'll do our best to get your updates into the next edition.

KIRCHZARTEN see Freiburg im Breisgau *3B4*

KIRCHZELL see Amorbach *3D2*

⊞ **KIRKEL** *3B3* (1km S Urban) *49.28175, 7.22860* **Caravanplatz Mühlenweiher, Unnerweg 5c, 66459 Kirkel-Neuhäusel [(06849) 1810555; fax 1810556; info@camping-kirkel.de; www.caravanplatz-kirkel.de]** Fr A6 junc 7 & fr A8 junc 28, take dir into town & foll sp for 'schwimmbad'. Site on L past pool, well sp. Med, mkd pitch, hdstg, pt shd; htd wc; chem disp; mv service pnt; fam bthrm; shwrs inc; EHU (10A) €3 or metered + conn fee (poss rev pol); gas; lndry (inc dryer); shop 1km; rest; bar; pool adj; wifi; TV cab/sat; 60% statics; dogs €1.15; phone; noise fr pool & church bells all night; CKE/CCI. "Gd welcome; excel area for cycling; site/office clsd 1230-1500." ♦ € 15.00
2016*

KIRTORF HEIMERTSHAUSEN see Alsfeld *1D4*

KITZINGEN *3D2* (3km E Urban) *49.73233, 10.16833* **Camping Schiefer Turm, Marktbreiterstrasse 20, 97318 Kitzingen-Hohenfeld [(09321) 33125; fax 384795; info@camping-kitzingen.de; www.camping-kitzingen.de]** Fr A3 take exit junc 74 sp Kitzingen/Schwarzach or exit 72 Würzburg-Ost, or fr A7 exit junc 103 Kitzingen. Site sp in town 'Schwimmbad'. Med, mkd pitch, pt shd; wc; chem disp; mv service pnt; shwrs €0.50; EHU (16A) €2 or metered; gas; lndry; shop; supmkt 200m; rest, snacks; pool adj; dogs €1.50; bus; poss cr w/end & high sn; ccard acc. "Bird reserve; pleasant town in evening; gd cycling; busy NH high ssn; san facs up steps; excel Lido adj." 1 Apr-15 Oct. € 18.00
2012*

KLAIS KRUN see Mittenwald *4E4*

KLEIN RONNAU see Bad Segeberg *1D2*

KLEINROHRSDORF see Dresden *2G4*

KOBLENZ *3B2* (4km NE Urban) *50.36611, 7.60361* **Camping Rhein-Mosel, Schartwiesenweg 6, 56070 Koblenz-Lützel [(0261) 82719; fax 802489; info@camping-rhein-mosel.de; www.camping-rhein-mosel.de]** Fr Koblenz heading N on B9 turn off dual c'way at sp for Neuendorf just bef Mosel rv bdge; foll sp to Neuendorf vill. Or heading S on B9 exit dual c'way at camping sp (2nd sp) bef Koblenz; fr Koblenz cent foll sp for 'Altstadt' until Baldwinbrücke (bdge); N over bdge instead of foll sp along S bank of Rv Mosel; R after bdge, then foll sp; site on N side of junc Rhine/Mosel rvs. Lge, some hdstg, pt sl, pt shd; wc; chem disp; mv service pnt; shwrs inc; EHU (6-16A) €2.05 or metered (long lead poss req); lndry (inc dryer); shop; supmkt 500m; cooking facs; rest, snacks; bar; dogs; poss v cr; Eng spkn; adv bkg rec; heavy rv & rlwy noise; no ccard acc; CKE/CCI. "Pleasant, informal site in beautiful location; muddy in wet; staff helpful; no veh acc after 2200; adj ferry to city & easy cycle rte; mkt Sat; sep dog shwr; flea mkt Sun; 'Rhine in Flames' fireworks 2nd Sat in Aug - watch fr site; MH stopover called Knaus Campingpark just outside main gates, basic price €12.50, both sites under same owner." ♦ 1 May-20 Oct. € 33.00
2016*

⊞ **KOBLENZ** *3B2* (8km SW Rural) *50.33194, 7.55277* **Camping Gülser Moselbogen, Am Gülser Moselbogen 20, 56072 Koblenz-Güls [(0261) 44474; fax 44494; info@moselbogen.de; www.moselbogen.de]** Fr A61/E31 exit 38 dir Koblenz/Metternich. After 400m turn R at rndabt dir Winningen. Stay on this rd to T-junc in Winningen, turn L dir Koblenz-Güls, site sp on R in 3km. Med, hdg/mkd pitch, pt shd; htd wc; chem disp; mv service pnt; fam bthrm; shwrs €0.50; EHU (16A) €1.50 + conn fee; gas; lndry (inc dryer); shop 2km; rest 200m; playgrnd; bike hire - €5; cab/sat TV; 50% statics; dogs €2; phone; poss cr; Eng spkn; adv bkg; rd & rlwy noise; ccard acc; CKE/CCI. "High quality, high-tech san facs; no vehicles 1200-1400; poss subject to flooding; excel." ♦ € 27.00 2014*

KOBLENZ *3B2* (12km SW Urban) *50.30972, 7.50166* **Campinginsel Winningen (previously Campingplatz Ziehfurt), Inselweg 10, 56333 Winningen [(02606) 357 or 1800; fax 2566; ferieninsel-winningen@t-online.de; www.mosel-camping.com]** Exit A61/E31 junc 38 to Winningen. In Winningen turn R twds Cochem B416, then L at sw pool. In approx 100m turn R and then in 700m turn L over bdge to site recep. Lge, pt shd; wc; chem disp; mv service pnt; shwrs €0.90; EHU (16A) €2.50; lndry; shop; rest, snacks; playgrnd; pool 300m; rv adj; 50% statics; dogs €3; poss v cr; Eng spkn; no adv bkg; some noise fr rd & rlwy. "Cent of wine-growing country; boat trips avail fr Koblenz; cycle rtes; scenic area; poss flooding if v high water; lively site when busy; gd, modern san facs up steep steps but poss stretched when busy; excel rest; excel site." 1 May-1 Oct. € 25.00 2017*

KOCHEL AM SEE *4E4* (3km SW Rural) *47.63642, 11.34827* **Camping Kesselberg, Altjoch 2 ½, 82431 Kochel-am-See [(08851) 464; mailto@campingplatz-kesselberg.de; www.campingplatz-kesselberg.de]** S fr Kochel on Bundestrasse 11. After 3km fork R for Walchensee Kraftwerk, many hairpins, site 150m on R. Med, mkd pitch, pt sl, pt shd; wc; chem disp; mv service pnt; child/fam bthrm; shwrs €0.50; EHU (10A) metered; gas; lndry; shop; rest, snacks; bar; BBQ; lake sw adj; sailing; wifi; 40% statics; dogs €3; poss cr; Eng spkn; adv bkg; quiet; red 10+ days; CKE/CCI. "Friendly site; beautifully situated by Kochelsee; attractive peaceful lakeside site; clean san facs; friendly & helpful staff; vg." 22 Mar-15 Oct. € 29.50 2013*

⊞ **KOLN** *1B4* (4km NE Urban) *50.96305, 6.98361* **Reisemobilhafen Köln, An der Schanz, 50735 Köln [017 84674591 (mob); info@reisemobilhafen-koeln.de]** Fr A1 Köln ring rd exit junc 100 dir Köln 'Zentrum' until reach rv. Turn L & foll sp to site. M'vans only. Sm, mkd pitch, hdstg; own san; mv service pnt; EHU (10A) €1 for 12 hrs; shop, rest, snacks, bar 500m; dogs; bus, train nr. "Adj Rv Rhine; must have change for elec & water (metered) - €0.50, parking (€10 note) etc; easy access to city cent; site is unmanned; cycle rte to city, zoo & botanic gdns." € 10.00 2017*

⊞ **KOLN** *1B4* (12km NE Rural) *50.99551, 7.06021* **Camping Waldbad, Peter Baum Weg, 51069 Köln-Dünnwald [(0221) 603315; fax 608831; info@waldbad-camping.de; www.waldbad-camping.de]** Exit A3/E35 at junc 24. E for 2km on Willy Brandt ringrd, turn R onto B51 (Mülheimstrasse). In 2.7km turn L into Odenthalerstrasse then foll site sp. Med, pt sl, pt shd; wc; chem disp; mv service pnt; fam bthrm; shwrs inc; EHU (10-16A) metered & conn fee; lndry; shop; rest adj; pool adj; 75% statics; dogs €2; phone; metro to city 10 mins drive; no adv bkg; v quiet. "Close to wildpark, pool & sauna; no ent/exit for cars 1300-1500 & 2200-0700; friendly warden." ♦ € 16.00 2012*

⊞ **KOLN** *1B4* (8km SE Rural) *50.8909, 7.02306* **Campingplatz Berger, Uferstrasse 71, 50996 Köln-Rodenkirchen [(0221) 9355240; fax 9355246; camping.berger@t-online.de; www.camping-berger-koeln.de]** Fr A4 turn S onto A555 at Köln-Sud exit 12. Leave A555 at Rodenkirchen exit 3. At 1st junc foll site sp to R. Fr A3 Frankfurt/Köln a'bahn, take A4 twd Aachen (Köln ring rd); exit at Köln Sud; foll sp Bayenthal; at lge rndabt turn R sp Rheinufer & R again at camp sp, under a'bahn. App rd narr & lined with parked cars. Lge, pt shd; htd wc; chem disp; mv service pnt; shwrs inc; EHU (4-10A) €1.50; gas; lndry; shop; supmkt 1km; rest, snacks; bar; cooking facs; playgrnd; bike hire; wifi; 80% statics; dogs €1; phone; bus 500m; poss v cr; Eng spkn; no adv bkg; quiet but some noise fr Rhine barges; ccard acc; red long stay; CKE/CCI. "Pleasant, popular, wooded site on banks of Rhine; rvside pitches best; excel rest; helpful staff; gd dog walking; cycle path to city cent; conv cathedral, zoo & museums; don't arr early eve at w/end as narr app rd v busy; pitches poss muddy after rain; san facs up steps - poss clsd 2300-0600; gd site; vr gd facs." ♦ € 30.40 2014*

KOLN *1B4* (6km S Urban) *50.90263, 6.99070* **Campingplatz der Stadt Köln, Weidenweg 35, 51105 Köln-Poll [(0221) 831966; fax 4602221; info@camping-koeln.de; www.camping-koeln.de]** Exit fr A4 (E40) at junc 13 for Köln-Poll-Porz at E end of bdge over Rv Rhine, 3km S of city. At end of slip rd, turn L twd Poll & Köln. Cont about 1000m turn L at sp just bef level x-ing, then foll site sp. Narr lane to ent. Lge, pt shd; wc; chem disp; mv service pnt; shwrs €0.50; EHU (10A) €3.50 (some rev pol & long lead poss req); gas; lndry; basic shop; snacks; rest 200m; cooking facs; dogs €2.50; phone; trams 1.5km; clsd 1230-1430; poss cr at w/ends; Eng spkn; no adv bkg; some rd & aircraft noise; CKE/CCI. "Tram to city over rv bdge; rural site in urban setting on bank of Rv Rhine & subject to flooding; gd undercover cooking facs; gd refurbished san facs on 1st floor; friendly site; v busy at w/end; rvside cycle track to city; cycle theft a problem (store in caged kitchen o'night); friendly owner; site in green zone." ♦ 1 Apr-15 Oct. € 29.40 2016*

KOLPIN see Storkow *2G3*

⊞ **KONIGSSEE** *4G4* (1km N Rural) *47.5992, 12.98933* **Camping Mühlleiten, Königsseerstrasse 70, 83471 Königssee [(08652) 4584; fax 69194; info@muehlleiten.eu; www.camping-muehlleiten.de]** On on R of B20 Berchtesgaden-Königssee. Med, unshd; wc; chem disp; shwrs inc; EHU (16A) €3 or metered; gas; lndry; shop & 1km; rest adj; snacks; bar; beach 1km; ski lift 500m; golf 6km; entmnt; dogs €2.50; poss cr; quiet; red CKE/CCI. "Beautiful area; friendly staff; excel san facs; excel site with mixed MH's, c'van and camping; walking trails; free/red bus fares with visitor card; off clsd 1200-1500 daily." € 30.00 2016*

KONIGSSEE *4G4* (2km N Rural) *47.59445, 12.98583* **Camping Grafenlehen, Königsseer Fussweg 71, 83471 Königssee [(08652) 6554488; fax 690768; camping-grafenlehen@t-online.de; www.camping-grafenlehen.de]** On B20 fr Berchtesgaden 5km to Königssee. Where car park with traff lts is ahead, turn R sp Schönau, site on R. Lge, terr, pt shd; htd wc; chem disp; mv service pnt; shwrs inc; EHU (16A) metered; lndry; shop; rest, snacks; playgrnd; 10% statics; dogs €2; site clsd Nov to mid-Dec; quiet; red CKE/CCI. "Pleasant site; spectacular views; gd san facs; superb walking; cycle path by rv; gd value rest; 30 mins drive Salzburg Park & Ride; conv Berchtesgaden." 1 Jan-1 Nov & 15 Dec-31 Dec. € 31.00 2015*

KONIGSTEIN *2G4* (1km E Rural) *50.92222, 14.08833* **Camping Königstein, Schandauerstrasse 25e, 01824 Königstein [(035021) 68224; fax 60725; info@camping-koenigstein.de; www.camping-koenigstein.de]** Foll B172 SE fr Dresden/Pirna. Site 500m past Königstein rlwy stn. Turn L over rlwy x-ing & R into site ent on Rv Elbe. Med, pt sl, unshd; wc; chem disp; mv service pnt; shwrs €0.80; EHU (16A) €2.60; gas; lndry; shop 1km; rest; playgrnd; 15% statics; dogs €3 (not acc Jul/Aug); sep car park; adv bkg; rlwy noise; red 5+ days. "Gd san facs; lovely location nr national parks & Czech border; on Elbe cycle path; frequent trains to Dresden; boat trips; gates clsd 1300-1500; red for 7+ days." ♦ 1 Apr-31 Oct. € 32.00 2013*

⊞ **KONIGSTEIN** *2G4* (3km E Rural) *50.91500, 14.10730* **Caravan Camping Sächsische Schweiz, Dorfplatz 181d, 01824 Kurort-Gohrisch [350 21 59107; caravan-camping@web.de; www.caravan-camping-saechsischeschweiz.de]** Fr Königstein foll B172 E dir Bad Schandau. Fork R dir Gohrisch for 2.5km, turn L into Dorfplatz & foll site sp. Med, hdg/mkd pitch, hdstg, pt sl, pt shd; wc; chem disp; mv service pnt; fam bthrm; fam bathrm; sauna; shwrs €0.50; EHU (16A) metered; lndry (inc dryer); shop; rest; bar; BBQ; cooking facs; playgrnd; htd, covrd pool 4km; padding pool; games area; bike hire; wifi; sat/cable TV; 5% statics; dogs €2; bus 500m; Eng spkn; adv bkg; quiet; red LS/long stay. "Excel site; gd touring base; interesting area; guided walks." ♦ € 22.00 2012*

KONIGSWALDE see Annaberg Buchholz *4G1*

KONSTANZ *3D4* (13km N Rural) *47.74596, 9.14701* **Camping Klausenhorn, Hornwiesenstrasse, 78465 Dingelsdorf [(07533) 6372; fax 7541; info@camping-klausenhorn.de; www.camping-klausenhorn.de]** Site sp N of Dingelsdorf on lakeside. Lge, mkd pitch, hdstg, pt shd; htd wc; chem disp; fam bthrm; shwrs €0.50; EHU (10A) inc; lndry; shop & 1.5km; rest 800m; snacks; bar; BBQ; playgrnd; shgl beach & lake adj; boating; games area; wifi; entmnt; 50% statics; no dogs; bus 500m; sep car park; poss cr; Eng spkn; adv bkg; v quiet; ccard acc; CKE/CCI. "Excel site; 1st class san facs; v helpful recep; free bus svrs fr site." ♦ 27 Mar-5 Oct. € 30.00 2016*

KONSTANZ *3D4* (12km W Rural) *47.69871, 9.04603* **Camping Sandseele, Bradlengasse 24, 78479 Niederzell [(07534) 7384; fax 98976; info@sandseele.de; www.sandseele.de]** Clearly sp off B33 Konstanz-Radolfzell rd. Foll sp on island & sm multiple sp. Lge, pt shd; wc; chem disp; mv service pnt; shwrs; EHU (16A) €3.50; gas; lndry; shop; rest, snacks; playgrnd; lake sw & beach; watersports; 30% statics; no dogs; sep car park high ssn; poss v cr; poss noisy. "Insect repellent rec, excel san facs; excel walking & cycling all over island; poor layout." ♦ 18 Mar-9 Oct. € 33.00 2016*

KONZ see Trier *3B2*

KRESSBRONN AM BODENSEE *3D4* (9km NE Rural) *47.63395, 9.6477* **Gutshof-Camping, Badhütten 1, 88069 Laimnau [(07543) 96330; fax 963315; gutshof.camping@t-online.de; www.gutshof-camping.de]** Fr Kressbronn take B467 to Tettnang & Ravensburg. In 3km immed after x-ing Rv Argen turn R & site sp for approx 3km. Take care on final app rd. Dark, steep and twisty, great care needed. V lge, hdg/mkd pitch, pt shd; wc; chem disp; mv service pnt; serviced pitches; fam bthrm; shwrs inc; EHU (16A) metered; gas; lndry; shop; rest, snacks; bar; playgrnd; pool; lake 7km; entmnt; 40% statics; dogs €2; adv bkg; quiet; red long stay; CKE/CCI. "Sep area for naturists; gd facs; v rural site; clean, quiet & pleasant; excel." ♦ 7 Apr-3 Oct. € 29.00 SBS - G15 2016*

KRESSBRONN AM BODENSEE *3D4* (2km SW Rural) *47.58718, 9.58281* **Campingplatz Irisweise, Tunau 16, 88079 Kressbronn [(07543) 8010; fax 8032; info@campingplatz-irisweise.de; www.camping platz-iriswiese.de]** Fr E or W take exit off B31 bypass for Kressbronn, site well sp. Lge, hdg/mkd pitch, pt shd; htd wc; chem disp; mv service pnt; fam bthrm; shwrs inc; EHU (10A) metered + conn fee; gas; lndry; shop; rest; bar; BBQ; playgrnd; beach, lake sw adj (sep naturist beach); sailing; watersports; internet; 10% statics; dogs €2; phone; poss v cr; Eng spkn; no adv bkg; quiet; CKE/CCI. "Steamer trips on lake; no car access 2100-0700, park outside site; excel san facs but some dist fr touring pitches; gd." ♦ 22 Mar-21 Oct. € 30.00 2014*

KROV see Wittlich *3B2*

KRUMBACH *4E4* (7km SW Rural) *48.22720, 10.29280* **See Camping Günztal, Oberrieder Weiherstrasse 5, 86488 Breitenthal [(08282) 881870; info@see-camping-guenztal.de; www.see-camping-guenztal.de]** W fr Krumbach on rd 2018, in Breitenthal turn S twd Oberried & Oberrieder Weiher, site sp on lakeside. Med, mkd pitch, some hdstg; pt shd; htd wc; chem disp; mv service pnt; fam bthrm; shwrs inc; EHU (10A) inc; lndry (inc dryer); shop 800m; rest 1.5km; snacks; bar; BBQ; playgrnd; lake sw; watersports; fishing; games area; wifi; TV; 30% statics; dogs €2; adv bkg; quiet. ♦ 15 Apr-30 Oct. € 21.00 (CChq acc) 2016*

KULMBACH *4E2* (11km NE Rural) *50.16050, 11.51605* **Campingplatz Stadtsteinach, Badstrasse 5, 95346 Stadtsteinach [(09225) 800394; fax 800395; info@campingplatz-stadtsteinach.de; www.campingplatz-stadtsteinach.de]** Fr Kulmbach take B289 to Untersteinach (8km); turn L to Stadtsteinach; turn R at camping sp & foll rd for 1km. Site also sp fr N side of town on B303. Or fr A9/E51 exit junc 39 onto B303 NW to Stadtsteinach. Med, pt shd; htd wc; chem disp; mv service pnt; shwrs inc; EHU (16A) €2.10; lndry; shop 600m; rest, snacks; bar; cooking facs; playgrnd; htd pool adj; paddling pool; rv fishing; tennis; bike hire; games area; 75% statics; dogs €2; Eng spkn; adv bkg; ccard acc; CKE/CCI. "Excel site in beautiful countryside; excel, modern facs; highly rec." ♦ 1 Mar-30 Nov. € 29.50 2014*

LAHNSTEIN *3B2* (3km E Urban) *50.30565, 7.61313* **Kur-Campingplatz Burg Lahneck, Am Burgweg, 56112 Lahnstein-Oberlahnstein [(02621) 2765; fax 18290]** Take B42 fr Koblenz over Lahn Rv, if fr low bdge turn L immed after church & sp fr there; if fr high level bdge thro sh tunnel turn L at 1st rd on L sp to Burg-Lahneck - site sp on L. Med, pt sl, pt shd; wc; chem disp; mv service pnt; shwrs €0.50; EHU (16A) metered + conn fee; lndry; shop; rest; playgrnd; pool adj; 10% statics; dogs €1; poss cr; Eng spkn; quiet but distant rlwy noise at night; ccard not acc. "Gd views over Rhine; scenic area; delightful, helpful owner v particular about pitching; gd size pitches; immac, well-run site." 1 Apr-31 Oct. € 21.50 2012*

LAHNSTEIN *3B2* (6km SE Urban) *50.27393, 7.64098* **Campingplatz Uferwiese, Am Campingplatz 1, 56338 Braubach [tel/fax (02627) 8762; uferwiese@web.de; www.campingplatz-braubach.de]** Take B42 S twd Rüdesheim. Site behind hotel opp church. Med, shd; wc; chem disp; shwrs €1; EHU (16A) €2 (poss rev pol); lndry; shop 300m; rest 200m; snacks; bar; wifi; 50% statics; dogs €1; bus; rd & rlwy noise; no ccard acc; CKE/CCI. "Scenic on Rv Rhine; poss flooding after heavy rain; gd san facs; no shd on rvside pitches." 15 Apr-25 Oct. € 21.50 2015*

⊞ **LAHR (SCHWARZWALD)** *3B3* (9km SE Rural) *48.29999, 7.94395* **Ferienparadies Schwarzwälder Hof, Tretenhofstrasse 76, 77960 Seelbach [(07823) 960950; fax 9609522; info@spacamping.de; www.campingplatz-schwarzwaelder-hof.de]** Fr A5 take exit 56 to Lahr. In 5km turn R twd Seelbach & Schuttertal. Thro town & site on S o'skts of Seelbach just after town boundary. Med, mkd pitch, some hdstg, pt sl, terr, pt shd; serviced pitches (extra charge); wc; chem disp; mv service pnt; shwrs inc; EHU (10A) metered + conn fee; gas; lndry; shop; rest; snacks 1km; bar; playgrnd; htd pool adj; lake adj; 10% statics; dogs €3.50; o'night area for m'vans; poss v cr; Eng spkn; adv bkg ess high ssn; quiet; ccard acc; red CKE/CCI. "Vg touring base; well-laid out pitches & excel facs; many gd mkd walks; gd programme of events in Seelbach; within easy reach of Strasbourg." ♦ € 37.00 2015*

⊞ **LAICHINGEN** *3D3* (6km SE Rural) *48.47560, 9.7458* **Camping & Freizeitzentrum Heidehof, Heidehofstrasse 50, 89150 Laichingen-Machtolsheim [(07333) 6408; fax 21463; info@heidenhof.info; www.camping-heidehof.de]** Exit A8 junc 61 dir Merklingen. At T-junc turn R sp Laichingen. In 3km site sp to L. V lge, hdg/mkd pitch, hdstg, pt sl, pt shd, some hdstg; wc; chem disp; mv service pnt; fam bthrm; sauna; shwrs inc; EHU (10-16A) €2 or metered; gas; lndry; shop; rest; playgrnd; htd pool; bike hire; 95% statics; adv bkg; red long stay/CKE/CCI. "Blaubeuren Abbey & Blautopf (blue pool of glacial origin) worth visit; sep area for o'nighters immed bef main camp ent - poss unrel when wet; hdstg pitches sm & sl; vg rest; gd NH; clean modern facs; lack of elec boxes; no water taps excep at facs; whole site on uneven sl; arr early to get nr elec." ♦ € 33.00 2014*

LAIMNAU see Kressbronn am Bodensee *3D4*

LANDAU IN DER PFALZ *3C3* (13km W Rural) *49.20138, 7.97222* **Camping der Naturfreunde, Victor von Scheffelstrasse 18, 76855 Annweiler-am-Trifels [(06346) 3870; fax 302945; info@naturfreunde-annweiler.de; www.naturfreunde-annweiler.de]** Fr Landau take B10 dir Pirmasens, take 1st exit to Annweiler then turn L into vill along Landauerstrasse. Turn L immed after VW/Audi g'ge, site sp. Tight access at ent. Sm, hdstg, pt shd; htd wc; chem disp; mv service pnt; shwrs inc; EHU (10A) €2; lndry; shops 500m; rest adj; playgrnd; 80% statics; dogs €2; poss cr; quiet; CKE/CCI. "Friendly, helpful owner poss on site evenings only; immac, modern san facs; ltd space for tourers but adequate facs; vg views across valley & forest; Ent is up steep hill with acute L turn; advise use campingplatz on R." ♦ 1 Apr-31 Oct. € 16.00 2012*

⊞ **LANDSBERG AM LECH** *4E4* (4km SE Rural) *48.03195, 10.88526* **DCC Campingpark Romantik am Lech, Pössinger Au 1, 86899 Landsberg-am-Lech [(08191) 47505; fax 21406; campingparkgmbh@aol.com; www.campingplatz-landsberg.de]** Not rec to tow thro Landsberg. If app fr S, get onto rd fr Weilheim & foll sp on app to Landsberg. Fr other dir, exit junc 26 fr a'bahn A96 Landsberg Ost, then app town via Muchenstrasse. Foll sp dir Weilheim, after 400m turn R & foll site sp. Lge, hdg/mkd pitch, pt sl, pt shd; wc; chem disp; mv service pnt; shwrs inc; EHU (16A) metered (some rev pol); gas; lndry; shop; rest 2km; snacks; bar; playgrnd; pool 3km; tennis; bike hire; 50% statics; dogs €1; adv bkg; Eng spkn; quiet; red CKE/CCI. "V pleasant site; excel, clean facs; nature reserve on 2 sides; gd walking & cycling; attractive old town; site clsd 1300-1500 & 2200-0700." ♦ € 19.00 2015*

LANDSHUT *4F3* (3km NE Urban) *48.55455, 12.1795* **Camping Landshut, Breslauerstrasse 122, 84028 Landshut [tel/fax (0871) 53366; www.landshut.de]** Fr A92/E53 exit junc 14 onto B299 dir Landshut N. After approx 5km turn L at int'l camping sp & foll site sp. Med, pt shd; wc; chem disp; mv service pnt; shwrs inc; EHU (16A) €2.50; lndry; shop 500m; rest 200m; snacks; bar; BBQ; htd pool 3km; 10% statics; dogs €1.50; poss cr; quiet; CKE/CCI. "Well-run, friendly site; gd san facs; beautiful medieval town & castle - easy cycle rte." ♦ 1 Apr-30 Sep. € 17.00 2016*

LANGELSHEIM see Goslar *1D3*

LANGSUR METZDORF see Trier *3B2*

"I need an on-site restaurant"

We do our best to make sure site information is correct, but it is always best to check any must-have facilities are still available or will be open during your visit.

⊞ **LANGWEDEL** *1D1* (1km W Rural) *54.21465, 9.91825* **Caravanpark am Brahmsee, Mühlenstrasse 30a, 24631 Langwedel [(04329) 1567; info@caravanpark-am-brahmsee.de; www.caravanpark-sh.de]** Exit A7 at junc 10 dir Tierpark Warder (animal park) & foll site sp to lakeside. Or exit A215 at Blumenthal onto L298 thro Langwedel dir Tierpark Warder, site sp. Med, hdg/mkd pitch, some hdstg, pt shd; htd wc; chem disp; mv service pnt; shwrs inc; EHU (16A) €2.50; lndry (inc dryer); shop 1km; rest 1km; cooking facs; BBQ; playgrnd; lake sw 100m; fishing; wifi; 80% statics; dogs; adv bkg; quiet. "Peaceful site in nature park; gd; diff access to some pitches for lge o'fits; excel san facs; dedicated hdstg area for campers; v cramped." ♦ ltd. € 15.00 (CChq acc) 2013*

LEEDEN see Osnabrück *1C3*

⊞ **LEER (OSTFRIESLAND)** *1B2* (7km W Rural) *53.22416, 7.41891* **Camping Ems-Marina Bingum, Marinastrasse 14-16, 26789 Leer-Bingum [(0491) 64447; fax 66405; into-camping-bingum@t-online.de; www.ems-marina-bingum.de]** Leave A32/E12 junc 12; site 500m S of Bingum; well sp. Lge, pt shd; wc; chem disp; mv service pnt; fam bthrm; shwrs €1; EHU (16A) €2.50 or metered; gas; lndry (inc dryer); shop 500m; rest, snacks; playgrnd; bike hire; 65% statics; dogs €3.50; gate clsd 1230-1500; adv bkg; quiet; red long stay/CKE/CCI. ♦ € 23.00 2016*

LEINATEL see Ohrdruf *2E4*

⊞ **LEIPHEIM** *3D3* (3.5km NNW Rural) *48.46566, 10.2035* **Camping Schwarzfelder Hof, Schwarzfelderweg 3, Riedheim, 89340 Leipheim [(08221) 72628; fax 71134; info@schwarzfelder-hof.de; www.schwarzfelder-hof.de]** Fr A8 exit junc 66 Leipheim onto B10. In Leipheim foll sp Langenau & Riedheim, site sp. Do not confuse with Laupheim 25km S of Ulm on B30. Sm, hdstg, pt shd; htd wc; chem disp (wc); serviced pitches; shwrs inc; EHU (16A) €2.10 or metered; lndry; shop 2km; rest 1.5km; snacks; bar; BBQ; playgrnd; 50% statics; dogs €3.20; train 1km; poss cr; Eng spkn; quiet. "Peaceful, delightful, farm-based site on site of old quarry; ideal for children & adults; welcoming, helpful owner; lge pitches; vg san facs but ltd; farm animals & riding for children; conv Ulm; recep open 0800-1000 & 1730-2000; poss noisy youth groups; conv NH for m'way." € 25.00 2014*

LEIPZIG *2F4* (21km W Rural) *51.38946, 12.15727* **Campingplatz Elsteraue, Delitscherstrasse 68, 06184 Ermlitz [tel/fax (0341) 9121874; ccl-camping@web.de; www.campingplatzleipzig.de]** Exit A9/E51 junc 16 Grosskugel dir Leipzig. Foll sp W to Erlmitz. Site sp (blue sp) at end of single track, unsurfaced but gd rd. Sm, pt shd; wc; chem disp; shwrs €0.50; EHU (16A) €1.50; lndry; shop 500m; dogs €1.50; Eng spkn; adv bkg; quiet; CKE/CCI. "Peaceful; v clean facs; charge for refilling water tanks & water/waste removal; gd security; cycle rte into Leipzig; pleasant site nr rv; conv to town." 15 May-15 Sep. € 17.00 2013*

⊞ **LEIPZIG** *2F4* (7km NW Urban) *51.37030, 12.31375* **Campingplatz Auensee, Gustav-Esche Strasse 5, 04159 Leipzig [(0341) 4651600; fax 4651617; leipzig@knauscamp.de; www.camping-auensee.de]** Fr A9/E51 exit junc 16 onto B6 two Leipzig. In Leipzig-Wahren turn R at 'Rathaus' sp Leutzsch (camping symbol), site on R in 1.5km, sp. Lge, mkd pitch, some hdstg, pt shd; htd wc; chem disp; mv service pnt; shwrs inc; EHU (16A) €3; lndry (inc dryer); supmkt 1.5km; rest, snacks; bar; BBQ; cooking facs; playgrnd; Lake Auensee 500m; TV; dogs €2; phone; bus; tram 1.5km; poss cr; Eng spkn; adv bkg; ccard acc; CKE/CCI. "Roomy, well-run, clean site; plentiful, excel, modern san facs; gd size pitches; vg rest; friendly, helpful staff; 10 mins walk to tram for city cent or bus stop at site ent; excel." ♦ € 29.00 2017*

⊞ **LEMGO** *1C3* (600m E Urban) *52.02503, 8.90874* **Campingpark Lemgo, Regenstorstrasse 10, 32657 Lemgo [(05261) 14858; fax 188324; info@camping-lemgo.de; www.camping-lemgo.de]** Exit A2 junc 28 onto L712N to Lemgo; at traff lts turn L following L712; at rndbt take Bismarckstrasse exit; at traff lts turn R into Regenstorstrasse. Site sp. Med, pt shd; wc; shwrs €0.50; EHU (6A) metered + conn fee; lndry (inc dryer); shop 500m; rest 300m; snacks 500m; playgrnd; pool 200m; wifi; 25% statics; dogs €2; adv bkg. "Pleasant site in cent of lovely medieval town; o'night area for m'vans; sm, modern, clean san facs." € 25.60 2016*

LIETZOW *2G1* (150m N Coastal) *54.48358, 13.50846* **Störtebecker Camp, Gästehaus Lietzow, Waldstraße 59a, 18528 Lietzow [038302 2166; info@lietzow.net; www.lietzow.net]** On rd 96, E22 fr Stralsund to ferry harbour at Sassnitz; when you arr at Lietzow site sp 'Gästehaus Lietzow' on RH side of rd; sh, steep incline fr main rd. Med, hdg pitch, pt shd; wc; chem disp; MV waste; shwrs inc; EHU inc; gas; lndry; rest, snacks; bar; playgrnd; beach 250m; dogs €2.50; adv bking; CKE/ CCI. "Pleasant, beautifully kept sm site in woodland; cent for the island, sightseeing & useful stopover nr ferry point; many mkd cycle rtes around island; charming owners; excel san facs; sh walk to delightful coast." 29 Mar-15 Oct. € 33.50 2015*

LIMBURG AN DER LAHN *3C2* (2km SSW Urban) *50.38916, 8.07333* **Lahn Camping, Schleusenweg 16, 65549 Limburg-an-der-Lahn [(06431) 22610; fax 92013; info@lahncamping.de; www.lahncamping.de]** Exit A3/E35 junc 42 Limburg Nord, site sp. By Rv Lahn in town, easy access. Lge, pt shd; wc; chem disp; mv service pnt; fam bthrm; shwrs €1; EHU (6A) €2.60 (long lead poss req); gas; lndry; shop; rest; playgrnd; htd pool 100m; rv sw & fishing; 20% statics; dogs €1.50; bus; poss v cr; Eng spkn; rd & rlwy noise; red CKE/CCI. "Busy, well-organised site; delightful location by rv; sm pitches - some poss diff to manoeuvre; gd views; friendly staff; poss flooding in wet weather; sh walk to interesting town; gates clsd 1300-1500; useful NH." ♦ 28 Mar-27 Oct. € 25.00 2014*

LIMBURG AN DER LAHN *3C2* (9km SW Rural) *50.38151, 8.00046* **Camping Oranienstein, Strandbadweg, 65582 Diez [(06432) 2122; fax 924193; info@camping-diez.de; www.camping-diez.de]** In Diez on L bank of Lahn. Exit A3 junc 41 Diez or junc 43 Limburg-Süd. Site sp 1km bef Diez, 8km fr a'bahn. Lge, pt shd; wc; chem disp; mv service pnt; shwrs; EHU (6A) inc; gas; lndry; shop; rest; playgrnd; children's pool; watersports; bike hire; 60% statics; dogs; adv bkg; ccard acc; CKE/CCI. "Pleasant vill; gd rests; hot water metered; gd NH." ♦ 1 Apr-31 Oct. € 20.00 2015*

⊞ **LINDAU (BODENSEE)** *3D4* (5km NE Rural) *47.58509, 9.70667* **Campingpark Gitzenweiler Hof, Gitzenweiler 88, 88131 Lindau-Gitzenweiler [(08382) 94940; fax 949415; info@gitzenweiler-hof.de; www.gitzenweiler-hof.de]** Exit A96/E43/E54 junc 4 onto B12 sp Lindau. Turn off immed after vill of Oberreitnau twd Rehlings. Site well sp fr all dirs. Lge, mkd pitch, pt sl, pt shd; wc; chem disp; mv service pnt; serviced pitches; fam bthrm; shwrs inc; EHU (6A) €2.50; gas; lndry; shop; rest, snacks; playgrnd; pool; sm boating/fishing lake; lake sw 6km; entmnt high ssn; TV; 50% statics; dogs €2.50; bus 1km; o'night facs for m'vans; Eng spkn; adv bkg; poss noisy high ssn; red long stay; CKE/CCI. "Well-run, busy site in scenic area; gd facs; friendly staff; excel site for children; gd cycling; poss prone to flooding after v heavy rain; pitches poorly maintained; poss cr." ♦ € 33.00 SBS - G18 2014*

LINDAU (BODENSEE) *3D4* (9km SE Coastal) *47.53758, 9.73143* **Park-Camping Lindau am See, Fraunhoferstrasse 20, 88131 Lindau-Zech [(08382) 72236; fax 976106; info@park-camping.de; www.park-camping.de]** On B31 fr Bregenz to Lindau, 200m after customs turn L to site in 150m; ent could be missed; mini-mkt on corner; ent rd crosses main rlwy line with auto barriers. B31 fr Friedrichshafen, site well sp fr o'skts of Lindau. Lge, mkd pitch, hdstg, pt shd; wc; chem disp; mv service pnt; shwrs inc; EHU (10A) €1 (long lead poss req); lndry (inc dryer); sm shop; mini-mkt nr; rest, snacks; playgrnd; shgl beach; lake sw; bike hire; golf 3km; wifi; entmnt high ssn; 20% statics; dogs €3; m'van o'night area €10; poss cr; Eng spkn; rd & rlwy noise. "Busy site; immac san facs; sh stay pitches poss diff to manoeuvre as v cramped; office/gate clsd 1300-1400; helpful staff; shwr rm for dogs; excel walking in Pfänder area; excel." ♦ 25 Mar-10 Nov. € 33.50 2016*

LINDAUNIS *1D1* (1km SSW Rural) *54.58626, 9.8173* **Camping Lindaunis, Schleistrasse 1, 24392 Lindaunis [(04641) 7317; fax 7187; info@camping-lindaunis.de; www.camping-lindaunis.de]** Exit A7/E45 junc 5 onto B201 sp Brebel & Süderbrarup. At Brebel turn R & foll dir Lindaunis, site approx 12km on R beside Schlei Fjord. Lge, mkd/hdg pitch, terr, pt shd; htd wc; chem disp; fam bthrm; shwrs; EHU (16A); lndry (inc dryer); shop; café; bar; BBQ; playgrnd; lakeside setting; boating; canoing; fishing; boat & bike hire; games area; games rm; bike hire; entmnt; wifi; TV; 80% statics; dogs €2; twin axles; Eng spkn; adv bkg rec; quiet; red CKE/CCI. "Vg, family-run site ideally placed for exploring Schlei fjord & conv Danish border; boat & canoe rentals; gd walks & cycle rtes; attractive area; vg." ♦ 28 Mar-15 Oct. € 23.00 2016*

"Satellite navigation makes touring much easier"

Remember most sat navs don't know if you're towing or in a larger vehicle – always use yours alongside maps and site directions.

⊞ **LINGERHAHN** *3B2* (1km NE Rural) *50.09980, 7.57330* **Campingpark am Mühlenteich, Am Mühlenteich 1, 56291 Lingerhahn [(06746) 533; fax 1566; info@muehlenteich.de; www.muehlenteich.de]** Exit A61/E31 exit junc 44 to Laudert & Lingerhahn. In Lingerhahn foll sp Pfalzfeld, site sp. Lge, unshd; wc; chem disp; mv service pnt; serviced pitches; fam bthrm; shwrs inc; EHU (6A) €2; lndry; shop; rest, snacks; playgrnd; pool; tennis; entmnt; golf 12km; 75% statics; dogs €3.50; ent clsd 1300-1500 & 2200; poss cr; adv bkg; quiet; 10% red CKE/CCI. "Delightful rest & beer garden; excel site." € 22.50 2012*

LIPPETAL LIPPBORG see Hamm *1B3*

LIPPSTADT *1C4* (8km NE Rural) *51.70095, 8.40808* **Campingparadies Lippstadter Seenplatte, Seeufer Straße 16, 59558 Lippstadt [02 948 22 53; fax 02948 28 94 14; info@camping-lippstadt.de; www.camping-lippstadt.de]** Turn R off B55 to Lipperode. In town turn R onto Niederdedinghauser. After 2.5km turn L onto Seeuferstraße. Site 200m on R. Sm, mkd pitch, pt shd; wc; chem disp; mv service pnt; fam bthrm; shwr; EHU (16A); lndry (inc dryer); playgrnd; bike hire; 25% statics; dogs €2.50; bus 200m; twin axles; adv bkg; quiet; CCI. " Vg site; fishing in adj lake; excel modern facs; lge pitches; friendly owners; Paderborn lovely city." ♦ 1 Mar-31 Oct. € 22.00 2016*

LOISSIN see Greifswald *2G1*

"There aren't many sites open at this time of year"

If you're travelling outside peak season remember to call ahead to check site opening dates – even if the entry says 'open all year'.

LORCH *3C2* (6km SE Rural) *50.01820, 7.85493* **Naturpark Camping Suleika, Im Bodenthal 2, 65391 Lorch-bei-Rüdesheim [(06726) 839402; fax 9440; info@suleika-camping.de; www.suleika-camping.de]** Site off B42 on E bank of Rv Rhine, 3km NW of Assmannshausen. 3km SE of Lorch foll sp over rlwy x-ing on narr winding, steep rd thro vineyards to site. App poss diff & dangerous for lge o'fits. Sm, pt sl, terr, pt shd; wc; mv service pnt; serviced pitches; shwrs inc; EHU (16A) metered + conn fee; lndry; shop; rest, snacks; playgrnd; bike hire; dogs €2; poss cr; quiet; sep car park; red CKE/CCI. "Vg site in magnificent setting; excursions by Rhine steamer, local places of interest, wine district; access & exit 1-way system; helpful staff; excel rest; environmentally friendly." 15 Mar-1 Nov. € 23.00 2015*

⊞ **LOWENSTEIN** *3D3* (4km N Rural) *49.11697, 9.38321* **Camping Heilbronn Breitenauer See, 74245 Löwenstein [(07130) 8558; fax 3622; info@breitenauer-see.de; www.breitenauer-see.de]** Exit m'way A81 (E41) at J10, Weinsberg/Ellhofen & on B39 twd Löwenstein/Schwäbisch Hall; site in approx 8km. V lge, mkd pitch, pt shd; htd wc; chem disp; mv service pnt; fam bthrm; shwrs inc; EHU (16A) €2 or metered + conn fee; gas; lndry; shop; rest, snacks; bar; playgrnd; lake sw adj; boating; watersports; golf 15km; dog-washing facs; child entmnt high ssn; 50% statics; dogs €5; poss cr; Eng spkn; adv bkg; quiet; ccard acc; 10% red long stay/LS; red CKE/CCI. "Lake walks; beautiful location; pleasant site close to A6 & A81; all facs highest quality & superb; some fully serviced pitches; excel." ♦ € 25.00 2015*

LUBBEN *2G3* (1km S Urban) *51.93641, 13.89490* **Spreewald Camping, Am Burglehn 218, 15907 Lübben [(03546) 7053 or 3335 or 8874; fax 181815; info@spreewald-camping-luebben.de; www.spreewald-camping-luebben.de]** Fr N on A13 exit junc 7 at Freiwalde onto B115 twd Lübben. In town cent turn R to stay on B115 sp Lübbenau. Site on L - well sp. Or fr S exit junc 8 onto B87 to Lübben. Cross rlwy, cont along Luckauerstrasse. Turn R at traff lts into Puschkinstrasse, sp Cottbus. Site on L, well sp. Lge, pt shd; wc; chem disp; mv service pnt; shwrs €0.50; EHU (10A) metered; gas; lndry (inc dryer); shop 400m; rest; playgrnd; wifi; 20% statics; dogs free; adv bkg; quiet; CKE/CCI. "Excel location; modern, clean facs; excel cycle rtes; adj rv for boating; conv for Berlin." ♦ 15 Mar-31 Oct. € 27.00 2015*

⊞ **LUBECK** *2E2* (6km W Rural) *53.86943, 10.63086* **Campingplatz Lübeck-Schönböcken, Steinrader Damm 12, 23556 Lübeck-Schönböcken [tel/fax (0451) 893090; info@camping-luebeck.de; www.camping-luebeck.de]** Fr A1 exit junc 23 on sh slip rd, stay in L lane, foll sp to Schönböcken & then camp sp (not v obvious); turn R at traff lts bef Dornbreite, site in 1km on L. Med, pt sl, unshd; wc; chem disp; mv service pnt; shwrs €0.50; EHU (6A) inc; gas; lndry; shop; BBQ; playgrnd; dogs €1; bus to town; games rm; wifi; Eng spkn; quiet; ccard acc; CKE/CCI. "Helpful owners; busy site; gd san facs but poss stretched if site full; conv Travemünde ferries; Lübeck interesting town; cycle path to town; vg; some rd noise; nice place; gd hypermkt nrby; gd site; gd bus service to fascinating town." € 22.00 2017*

⊞ **LUNEBURG** *1D2* (6km S Rural) *53.20303, 10.40976* **Camping Rote Schleuse, Rote Schleuse 4, 21335 Lüneburg [(04131) 791500; fax 791695; kontakt@camp-rote-schleuse.de; www.camprote schleuse.de]** Exit A250 junc 4 onto Neu Häcklingen twd Lüneburg. Site sp to R in 300m. Med, pt shd; wc; chem disp; fam bthrm; shwrs; EHU (16A) €2.50 or metered; lndry; shop; rest adj; snacks; bar; BBQ; playgrnd; pool; bike hire; games rm; wifi; 60% statics; dogs €1; bus fr site ent; clsd 1300-1500; poss cr; Eng spkn; adv bkg; quiet; ccard acc. "Pleasant, friendly owners; interesting town; gd rest." ♦ € 25.80 2016*

⊞ **LUTHERSTADT WITTENBERG** *2F3* (5km S Rural) *51.85465, 12.64563* **Marina-Camp Elbe, Brückenkopf 1, 06888 Lutherstadt-Wittenberg [(03491) 4540; fax 454199; info@marina-camp-elbe.de; www.marina-camp-elbe.de]** Site on S side of Elbe bdge on B2 dir Leipzig; well sp. Med, pt shd; wc; chem disp; mv service pnt; serviced pitches; fam bthrm; sauna; shwrs; EHU (16A)€2.50; gas; lndry (inc dryer); shop 1.5km; BBQ; cooking facs; snacks; marina adj; bike hire; wifi; TV; dogs €1.50; bus at gate; quiet; ccard acc; CKE/CCI. "Delightful rvside site; excel, modern san facs." ♦ € 27.00 2017*

GERMANY

⊞ **LUTHERSTADT WITTENBERG** *2F3* (14km S Rural) *51.79135, 12.56995* **Camping Bergwitzsee, Zeltplatz, 06773 Bergwitz [(034921) 28228; fax 28778; info@bergwitzee.de; www.bergwitzsee.de]** S fr Berlin on B2 thro Wittenberg, then thro Eutzsch, bear R onto B100 into Bergwitz; at cent site is sp, foll to lake, turn R & site ahead. Fr main rd to site thro vill 1.5km, cobbled. Site on lakeside. Lge, shd; wc; chem disp; mv service pnt; shwrs €0.50; EHU (10-16A) €2; lndry; shop; rest, snacks; bar; playgrnd; lake sw & sand beach; fishing; watersports; games area; bike hire; TV; 90% statics; dogs €3; adv bkg rec; red CKE/CCI. "Interesting town - Martin Luther Haus; gd cycling/walking area; quiet, restful site; Lakeside site nr Ferropolis, popular with families." ♦ € 16.00 2012*

MAGDEBURG *2E3* (15km N Rural) *52.21888, 11.65944* **Campingplatz Barleber See, Wiedersdorferstrasse, 39126 Magdeburg [(0391) 503244; fax 2449692; campingplatz@cvbs.de; www.cvbs.de]** Exit A2/E30 junc 71 sp Rothensee-Barleber See; site 1km N of a'bahn. Lge, mkd pitch, pt shd; wc; chem disp; mv service pnt; shwrs inc; EHU (10A) €2; gas; lndry; shop; rest, snacks; bar; playgrnd; pool; sand beach adj; lake sw; bike hire; wifi; 80% statics; dogs €2; poss cr; some Eng spkn; no adv bkg; poss noisy w/end; fairly quiet; red long stay/CKE/CCI. "Gd beach & watersports; pleasant site; gd sports facs; gd touring base; v noisy due to adj gravel quarry; unhelpful staff; v busy at w/end; crowded beach." ♦ ltd. 15 Apr-1 Oct. € 24.00 2016*

⊞ **MALLISS** *2E2* (2km SE Rural) *53.19596, 11.34046* **Camping am Wiesengrund, Am Kanal 4, 19294 Malliss [tel/fax (038750) 21060; sielaff-camping@t-online.de; www.camping-malliss.m-vp.de]** Sp in Malliss on rd 191 fr Ludwigslust to Uelzen. Sm, pt shd; wc; chem disp; mv service pnt; shwrs €0.75; EHU (16A) €2; gas; lndry; shop & 2km; rest 2km; snacks; bar; playgrnd; rv sw adj; watersports; bike hire; 30% statics; dogs €2.50; phone; m'van o'night facs; quiet; red CKE/CCI. "Well-run, pleasant, family site; beautiful surroundings; barrier clsd 1200-1400; visit Ludwigslust Palace & Dömitz Fortress; vg; lovely site and v friendly staff." € 16.50 2012*

⊞ **MALSCH** *3C3* (4km S Rural) *48.86165, 8.33789* **Campingpark Bergwiesen, Waldenfelsstrasse 1, 76316 Malsch [(07246) 1467; fax 5762; email@campingpark-bergwiesen.eu; www.campingpark-bergwiesen.eu]** Fr Karlsruhe on B3 thro Malsch vill over level x-ing to Waldprechtsweier. Foll site sp, take care tight L turn & steep app thro residential area. Lge, hdg/mkd pitch, hdstg, terr, pt shd; wc; chem disp; serviced pitches; shwrs inc; EHU (16A); gas; lndry; supmkt 3km; shop 200m; rest; bar; playgrnd; pool 1km; sw adj; 80% statics; dogs €2; Eng skn; adv bkg (no fee); quiet; red CKE/CCI. "1st class facs; well-run site in beautiful forest setting; v friendly site & owner; not rec for long o'fits or lge m'vans; gd walks fr site; no wifi." € 19.00 2016*

MANDERSCHEID see Wittlich *3B2*

MANNHEIM *3C2* (8km S Urban) *49.44841, 8.44806* **Camping am Strandbad, Strandbadweg 1, 68199 Mannheim-Neckarau [(0176) 55422268; fax (0621) 8619968; cfsm.mannheim@googlemail.com; www.campingplatz-mannheim-strandbad.de]** Exit A6 Karlsruhe-Frankfurt at AB Kreuz Mannheim (junc 27) L onto A656 Mannheim-Neckarau. Exit junc 2 onto B36 dir Neckarau, site sp. Med, pt shd; wc; mv service pnt; shwrs €1; EHU (16A) metered; gas; lndry; shop 2km; rest 300m; snacks; shgl beach & rv sw; wifi; 60% statics; dogs €1.50; poss cr; quiet; CKE/CCI. "Some noise fr barges on Rhine & factories opp; poss flooding at high water; interesting area; barrier down & recep clsd 1200-1500." 1 Apr-31 Oct. € 20.00 2014*

MARBURG AN DER LAHN *1C4* (2km S Urban) *50.80000, 8.76861* **Camping Lahnaue, Trojedamm 47, 35037 Marburg-an-der-Lahn [tel/fax (06421) 21331; info@lahnaue.de; www.lahnaue.de]** Site by Rv Lahn, app fr sports cent. Exit a'bahn at Marburg Mitte & sp fr a'bahn. Med, mkd pitch, pt shd; wc; chem disp; shwrs inc; EHU (10A) €2; lndry (inc dryer); shops 1km; rest 1.5km; snacks; bar; pool adj; rv canoeing; tennis, sw & boating nrby; 10% statics; dogs €2.50; clsd 1300-1500; poss cr; Eng spkn; quiet but m'way & rlwy noise; ccard acc; CKE/CCI. "Busy site; some pitches v narr; cycle & footpath to interesting town; excel pool adj; gd." ♦ 1 Apr-30 Oct. € 27.00 2013*

⊞ **MARKTHEIDENFELD** *3D2* (5km S Rural) *49.81885, 9.58851* **Camping Main-Spessart-Park, Spessartstrasse 30, 97855 Triefenstein-Lengfurt [(09395) 1079; fax 8295; info@camping-main-spessart.de; www.camping-main-spessart.de]** Exit A3/E41 junc 65 or 66 sp Lengfurt. In Lengfurt foll sp Marktheidenfeld; site in 1km. Lge, pt sl, terr, pt shd; wc; chem disp; mv service pnt; serviced pitches; shwrs inc; EHU (6-10A) €3; lndry; shop; rest; playgrnd; pool adj; watersports; 50% statics; dogs €2.50; Eng spkn; adv bkg; ccard acc; red CKE/CCI. "Excel, high quality site; vg rest; vg san facs; easy access A4; sep NH area; helpful owners; access diff parts of site due steep terrs; busy site; gd facs." ♦ € 24.00 2016*

⊞ **MEDELBY** *1D1* (700m W Rural) *54.81490, 9.16361* **Camping Kawan Mitte, Sonnenhügel 1, 24994 Medelby [(04605) 189391; info@camping-mitte.de; www.camping-mitte.de]** Exit A7 junc 2 onto B199 dir Niebüll to Wallsbüll, turn N dir Medelby, site sp. Lge, mkd pitch, pt shd; htd wc; chem disp; mv service pnt; fam bthrm; sauna; shwrs inc; EHU (16A) metered; lndry (inc dryer); shop; supmkt 600m; rest 600m; snacks; BBQ; cooking facs; playgrnd; 2 htd pool; games area; fitness rm; bike hire; horseriding 600m; golf 12km; wifi; TV rm; 20% statics; dogs free; adv bkg; quiet; CKE/CCI. "Conv m'way & Danish border; vg." ♦ € 29.00 2017*

MEERBUSCH see Düsseldorf *1B4*

MEISSEN *2G4* (5km S Rural) *51.13942, 13.49883* **Camping Rehbocktal, Rehbocktal 4, 01665 Scharfenberg-bei-Meissen [(03521) 404827; fax 404828; info@camping-rehbocktal.de; www.camping-rehbocktal.de]** Exit E40/A4 at Dresden Altstadt; foll sp Meissen on B6 to Scharfenberg; site on L opp Rv Elbe. Med, pt sl, pt shd; wc; chem disp; shwrs inc; EHU (16A) €3; lndry; shop & 3km; rest adj; snacks; bar; playgrnd; 10% statics; dogs €2; bus; poss cr; no adv bkg; v quiet; CKE/CCI. "In wooded valley opp vineyard; friendly staff; conv Colditz; Meissen factory & museum worth visit; cycle path to Meissen nr." 15 Mar-31 Oct. € 26.00 2013*

MEISSENDORF see Winsen (Aller) *1D3*

⊞ **MELLE** *1C3* (8km NW Rural) *52.22428, 8.2661* **Campingplatz Grönegau-Park Ludwigsee, Nemdenerstrasse 12, 49326 Melle [(05402) 2132; fax 2112; info@ludwigsee.de; www.ludwigsee.de]** Exit A30/E30 junc 22 twd Bad Essen, site sp on lakeside. Lge, hdg/mkd pitch, pt shd; wc; chem disp; mv service pnt; shwrs €1; EHU (10A) inc; lndry; shop 1.5km; rest, snacks; bar; playgrnd; lake sw; games area; bike hire; internet; entmnt; 80% statics; dogs €2; sep car park; barrier clsd 1300-1500; adv bkg; quiet; ccard acc; red CKE/CCI. "Beautiful & pleasant site; helpful owners; sep area for tourers." € 30.00 2014*

MENDIG *3B2* (7km N Rural) *50.42151, 7.26448* **Camping Laacher See, Am Laacher See, 56653 Wassenach [(02636) 2485; fax 929750; info@camping-laacher-see.de; www.camping-laacher-see.de]** Fr A61, exit junc 34 Mendig. Foll tents sp to Maria Laach. Site on Laacher See. Lge, hdg/mkd pitch, hdstg, pt sl, pt terr, pt shd; htd wc; chem disp; mv service pnt; fam bthrm; shwrs €0.50; EHU (16A) metered + conn fee; gas; lndry (inc dryer); shop; rest, snacks; bar; playgrnd; lake sw; sailing; fishing; wifi; 50% statics; dogs €4; bus 500m; Eng spkn; quiet; adv bkg; ccard acc; CKE/CCI. "Neat, clean, relaxing site; all pitches lake views; busy at w/end; modern, outstanding san facs; gd woodland walks, cycling & sw; excel sailing facs; excel site & rest; close to m'way; rec; helpful staff." ♦ ltd. 24 Mar-20 Sep. € 27.00 2016*

⊞ **MENDIG** *3B2* (2km NNW Rural) *50.38646, 7.27237* **Camping Siesta, Laacherseestrasse 6, 56743 Mendig [(02652) 1432; fax 520424; service@campingsiesta.de; www.campingsiesta.de]** Fr A61 exit junc 34 for Mendig dir Maria Laach; foll camp sps; site on R in 300m by ent to car park. Med, some hdg pitch, sl, pt shd; wc; chem disp; shwrs inc; EHU (16A) €1.80; gas; lndry; rest; bar; playgrnd; sm pool; sw pool 500m; 60% statics; dogs €1.30; poss v cr; Eng spkn; noise fr nrby a'bahn; CKE/CCI. "Useful NH; easy access fr A61; owner helpful in siting NH o'fits; longest waterslide in Europe; gd base for region's castles & wines; friendly owners; spotless site; gd rest; site has so much more to offer than only a NH; v welcoming; vg refurbished; new san facs (2014)." € 24.00 (CChq acc) 2014*

⊞ **MESCHEDE** *1C4* (10km S Rural) *51.29835, 8.26425* **Knaus Campingpark Hennesee, Mielinghausen 7, 59872 Meschede [(0291) 952720; fax 9527229; hennesee@knauscamp.de; www.knauscamp.de]** S fr Meschede on B55 for 7km; at sp for Erholungszentrum & Remblinghausen turn L over Lake Hennesee, site on L in 500m, sp. Lge, mkd pitch, terr, pt shd; wc; chem disp ltd; mv service pnt; sauna; serviced pitches; shwrs inc; EHU (6A) conn fee; gas; lndry; supmkt; rest, snacks; bar; playgrnd; lake sw 200m; bike hire; entmnt high ssn; internet; 60% statics; dogs €3.80; poss cr; adv bkg; Eng spkn; quiet; red CKE/CCI. "Conv Sauerland mountains & lakes; 50m elec cable advisable; vg." € 28.70 (CChq acc) 2012*

MESENICH see Trier *3B2*

"That's changed – Should I let The Club know?"

If you find something on site that's different from the site entry, fill in a report and let us know. See camc.com/europereport.

⊞ **METTINGEN** *1B3* (2km SW Rural) *52.31251, 7.76202* **Camping Zur Schönen Aussicht, Schwarzestrasse 73, 49497 Mettingen [(05452) 606; fax 4751; info@camping-schoene-aussicht.de; www.camping-schoene-aussicht.de]** Exit A30 junc 12 dir Mettingen. Go thro town cent, uphill turn L at traff lts, site sp. Med, hdg/mkd pitch, pt sl, pt shd; wc; chem disp; mv service pnt; shwrs €1.30; EHU (10A) €3 or metered; lndry; shop; rest; bar; playgrnd; htd, covrd pool; internet; 50% statics; no dogs; Eng spkn; adv bkg; quiet; CKE/CCI. "Nice, friendly site; gd walking, cycling; easy walk to town; gd facs." € 27.50 2015*

⊞ **MITTENWALD** *4E4* (4km N Rural) *47.47290, 11.27729* **Naturcamping Isarhorn, Am Horn 4, 82481 Mittenwald [(08823) 5216; fax 8091; camping@mittenwald.de; www.camping-isarhorn.de]** E fr Garmisch-Partenkirchen on rd 2; at Krün turn S on D2/E533 dir Mittenwald. Site on R in approx 2km at int'l camping sp. Ent on R fr main rd. NB: Rd thro to Innsbruck via Zirlerberg improved & no longer clsd to c'vans descending S; long & steep; low gear; not to be attempted N. Lge, pt shd, unmkd, some hdstg; wc; chem disp; mv service pnt; shwrs €0.50; EHU (16A) €2.80 or metered; lndry; shop; snacks; rest; BBQ; htd, covrd pool 4km; canoeing (white water); ski lift; tennis; wifi; dogs €2.90; bus adj; site clsd 1300-1500 & 2200-0700; site clsd 1 Nov-mid Dec; Eng spkn; quiet but some rd noise; ccard acc; red LS; "Relaxed, secluded site in pines; mountain views; excel base for walking; cycle track to attractive town; poss some noise fr nrby military base; owner v keen on recycling waste; facs gd but insufficient for size of site; highly rec." € 27.50 2015*

GERMANY

MITTENWALD *4E4* (8km N Rural) *47.49040, 11.25438* **Alpen-Caravanpark Tennsee, Am Tennsee 1, 82493 Klais-Krün [(08825) 170; fax 17236; info@camping-tennsee.de; www.camping-tennsee.de]** N fr Mittenwald on main Innsbruck-Garmisch rd turn off for Krun, foll Tennsee & site sp. 2km SE of Klais, not well sp. Lge, mkd pitch, hdstg, pt terr, pt shd; htd wc; chem disp; mv service pnt; 50% serviced pitches; family & fam bthrm; shwrs inc; EHU (16A) metered; gas; lndry; shop & 2km; rest, snacks; bar; playgrnd; ski lift 2.5km; bike hire; entmnt; dogs €3.30; phone; poss cr; Eng spkn; adv bkg; ccard acc; CKE/CCI. "Excel area for Bavarian Alps, Tirol; barrier clsd 1200-1500; gd size pitches; red snr citizens; vg, clean, friendly, family-run site; price inc use of tourist buses; some rd noise." ♦ 1 Jan-2 Nov, 18 Dec-31 Dec. € 35.00 2016*

⊞ **MITTERTEICH** *4F2* (3km NW Rural) *49.97311, 12.22497* **Campingplatz Großbüchlberg, Großbüchlberg 32, 95666 Mitterteich [09633 40 06 73; fax 40 06 77; camping@freizeithugl.de; www.freizeithugl.de]** Fr A93 Marktredwitz-Mitterteich take exit 16 Mitterteich. At xrds in town cent foll Freizeithugl signs. Turn L after 200m twds Grossbuchberg. Foll sp. Med, hdg/mkd pitch, hdstg, pt sl, terr, pt shd; htd wc; chem disp; mv service pnt; fam bthrm; shwrs inc; EHU (16A); lndry (inc dryer); shop; rest; snacks; bar; playgrnd; wifi; TV rm; dogs €1.50; phone adj; bus adj; twin axles; poss cr; Eng spkn; adv bkg; quiet; ccard acc; CCI. "Excel site; superb htd san facs; close to mini-golf, toboggan run, etc; extensive views; v friendly." ♦ € 25.00 2014*

"I like to fill in the reports as I travel from site to site"

You'll find report forms at the back of this guide, or you can fill them in online at camc.com/europereport.

MOHNESEE see Soest *1C4*

MONSCHAU *3A1* (3km SW Rural) *50.54305, 6.23694* **Camping Perlenau, 52156 Monschau [(02472) 4136; fax 4493; familie.rasch@monschau-perlenau.de; www.monschau-perlenau.de]** Fr N (Aachen) foll B258 past Monschau dir Schleiden. Site on L just bef junc with B399 to Kalterherberg. Steep & narr app. Fr Belgium, exit A3 junc 38 for Eupen & foll rd thro Eupen to Monschau. Site on rvside. Med, hdg/mkd pitch, hdstg, pt sl, terr, pt shd; htd wc; chem disp; mv service pnt; fam bthrm; shwrs; EHU (10-16A) €2.60 or metered; gas; lndry; shop; rest, snacks; bar; BBQ; cooking facs; playgrnd; 20% statics; dogs €2.60; phone; bus 500m; poss cr; Eng spkn; adv bkg; quiet; red long stay; CKE/CCI. "Gd touring base for Eifel region; attractive site beside stream; historic town in walking dist." ♦ 20 Mar-31 Oct. € 27.60 2013*

⊞ **MONTABAUR** *3C2* (8km E Rural) *50.43761, 7.90498* **Camping Eisenbachtal, 56412 Girod [(06485) 766; fax 4938]** S on A3/E35 exit junc 41 dir Montabaur; at Girod turn L to site, well sp. Med, hdg/mkd pitch, some hdstg, pt sl, pt shd; htd wc; chem disp; mv service pnt; some serviced pitches; shwrs €0.50; EHU (10A) inc; (poss rev pol); gas; lndry; 2 x rest adj; playgrnd; sw 5km; 75% statics; dogs €2; poss cr; Eng spkn; adv bkg; quiet; red long stay; CKE/CCI. "Beautiful, well-equipped site in Naturpark Nassau; conv NH fr a'bahn & worth longer stay; friendly, welcoming staff; gd for nature lovers & children; gd walking & cycling; adj rest excel; site clsd 1300-1500 but car park opp; conv Rhine & Mosel valleys." ♦ € 18.00 2017*

⊞ **MORFELDEN** *3C2* (3km E Rural) *49.97986, 8.59461* **Campingplatz Mörfelden, Am Zeltzplatz 5-15, 64546 Mörfelden-Walldorf [(06105) 22289; fax 277459; info@campingplatz-moerfelden.de; www.campingplatz-moerfelden.de]** Fr A5 exit 24, turn W on 486 twds Morfelden. In 200m turn L, opp Holiday Inn. Site on R in 100m. Med, pt shd; wc; chem disp; mv service pnt; shwrs €1; EHU (16A) metered or €2.50; gas; lndry (inc dryer); rest; snacks 1km; playgrnd; internet; dogs €1.50; phone; poss cr; Eng spkn; quiet but some aircraft noise; no adv bkg. "Conv NH/sh stay for Frankfurt; excel, modern san facs; helpful owner; vg." € 26.50 2016*

MORFELDEN *3C2* (9km S Rural) *49.94461, 8.60544* **Campingplatz Am Steinrodsee, Triftweg 33, 64331 Weiterstadt [06150 53593; fax 591345; rezeption.koehres@t-online.de; www.camping-steinrodsee.de]** Leave A5 twds Darmstadt at exit 25. L at 2nd traff lts onto L3113. Turn R in 5km & foll signs. Lge, hdg/mkd pitch, pt shd; htd wc; chem disp; mv service pnt; fam bthrm; shwrs inc; EHU (16A); lndry (inc dryer); rest; bar; BBQ; playgrnd; wifi; 60% statics; dogs; bus 2km; twin axles; quiet; CCI. "Vg site; quiet with some aircraft & m'way noise; clean, tidy, well regulated site; immac san facs; conv for Darmstadt." ♦ 1 Jan-31 Oct. € 23.00 2015*

MORITZBURG *4G1* (3km S Rural) *51.1450, 13.67444* **Campingplatz Bad Sonnenland, Dresdnerstrasse 115, 01468 Moritzburg [(0351) 8305495; fax 8305494; bad-sonnenland@t-online.de; www.bad-sonnenland.de]** Leave A4/E40 exit 80. Turn R sp Moritzburg, foll site sp thro Reichenberg. Site on L 3km bef Moritzburg. Lge, pt shd; wc; chem disp; mv service pnt; shwrs (inc); EHU (16A) €2.50; gas; lndry; shop; supmkt 2km; rest, snacks; bar; playgrnd; lake sw adj; games rm; games area; statics in sep area; dogs €3; bus to Dresden; Eng spkn; quiet; ccard acc; CKE/CCI. "Scenic area; friendly staff; excel, immac facs; site clsd 1300-1500 & 2200-0700; also holiday vill with many huts; conv Dresden, Meissen; narr gauge steam train Dresden-Moritzburg; day trip to Prague; many mkd walking & cycling rtes in area; Schloss Moritzburg in vill; vg site; poss cr high ssn." 1 Apr-31 Oct. € 22.00 2015*

MOSCHWITZ see Plauen *4F1*

MUDEN AN DER ORTZE see Fassberg *1D2*

⊞ **MUHLBERG** *2E4* (1.6km NW Rural) *50.87516, 10.80843* **Campingplatz Drei Gleichen, Am Gut Ringhofen, 99869 Mühlberg [(036256) 22715; fax 86801; service@campingplatz-muehlberg.de; www. campingplatz-muehlberg.de]** Leave A4/E40 at junc 43 (Wandersleben) S twds Mühlberg; site well sp in 2km on rd to Wechmar. Med, hdg/mkd pitch, pt sl, unshd; wc; chem disp; mv service pnt; shwrs €1; EHU (16A) €1.80 + conn fee; lndry; shop 3km; rest adj; bar; playgrnd; sw adj; 50% statics; dogs €2.20; site clsd 1300-1500; adv bkg; quiet; CKE/CCI. "Gd facs; helpful staff; conv a'bahn." ♦ € 16.00 2015*

MUHLHAUSEN see Augsburg *4E3*

MUNCHEN *4E4* (7km S Urban) *48.09165, 11.54516* **Camping München-Thalkirchen, Zentralländstrasse 49, 81379 München [(089) 7231707; fax 7243177; campingplatz.muenchen@web.de; www.muenchen. de]** Fr S on A95/E533 at end of a'bahn keep strt on (ignore zoo sp). After tunnel exit R at sp Thalkirchen. Turn L at traff lts & foll sp to camp. If app fr S on A8/ E45 turn L at traff lts at end twd Garmish & strt on to tunnel, site sp. Fr NW at end of A8 in 200m turn R & foll sp to zoo (Tierpark). Cont to foll zoo sp until in approx 10km pick up sp to site. (Zoo on E side of Rv Isar, site on W side.) App fr N not rec due v heavy traff. V lge, mkd pitch, pt shd; htd wc; chem disp; mv service pnt; many serviced pitches; shwrs €1; EHU (10A) €2 (long lead req); lndry (inc dryer); shop; rest 500m; snacks; playgrnd; pool & rv 500m; internet; dogs inc; phone; bus 100m; poss cr esp Oktoberfest; Eng spkn; quiet; ccard not acc; CKE/CCI. "Busy site; some m'van/o'night pitches v sm; bus/U-bahn tickets avail fr recep; cycle track/walk along rv to town cent, avoiding traff; helpful staff; san facs clean, stretched when site full; gd site when visiting Munich." ♦ 15 Mar-31 Oct. € 28.00 2013*

⊞ **MUNCHEN** *4E4* (12km NW Urban) *48.19888, 11.49694* **Campingplatz Nord-West, Auf den Schrederwiesen 3, 80995 München-Moosach [(089) 1506936; info@campingplatz-nord-west.de; www. campingplatz-nord-west.de]** Fr N exit A99 junc 10 Lugwigsfeld onto B304 S - Dachauerstrasse, sp München. Turn L in approx 800m at traff lts. Turn R at T-junc to site on R. Med, hdstg, shd; htd wc; chem disp; mv service pnt; shwrs €1.50; EHU (10-16A) €5 or metered; lndry (inc dryer); shop & 1km; rest 3km; snacks; bar; entmnt; 50% statics; dogs €2; phone; bus to city; poss cr; Eng spkn; adv bkg; quiet; ccard acc; CKE/CCI. "Friendly, helpful welcome; enquire about public transport tickets; ltd facs LS; Dachau - pretty town 10km; gd; Dachau Concentration Camp Memorial worth a visit." ♦ € 23.20 2017*

⊞ **MUNCHEN** *4E4* (17km NW Rural) *48.19821, 11.41161* **Campingplatz am Langwieder See, Eschenriederstrasse 119, 81249 München-Langwied [(089) 8641566; fax 8632342; info@camping-langwieder-see.de; www.camping-langwieder-see. de]** Exit A8 junc 80 at Langwieder See & foll sp Dachau; site within 200m. Fr ring rd A99 junc 8 join A8 to N, then as above. Med, hdstg, pt shd; htd wc; chem disp; shwrs €0.50; EHU (10A) metered + conn fee €1; gas; lndry; shop; snacks; rest; bar; lake sw adj; 95% statics; dogs €1.70; poss v cr; Eng spkn; no adv bkg; m'way noise; CKE/CCI. "Pleasant owners; tourers in a row outside recep area parked v close together; v sm pitches, mostly on gravel; gd san facs; site used by workers; easy access to Munich by train fr Dachau; lge free car park at stn; NH/sh stay only." € 21.50 2016*

"We must tell The Club about that great site we found"

Get your site reports in by mid-August and we'll do our best to get your updates into the next edition.

MUNCHSTEINACH see Neustadt an der Aisch *4E2*

MUNICH see München *4E4*

⊞ **MUNSTER** *1B3* (9km SE Rural) *51.94638, 7.69027* **Camping Münster, Laerer Wersuefer 7, 48157 Münster [(0251) 311982; fax 3833985; mail@ campingplatz-muenster.de; www.campingplatz-muenster.de]** Fr A43 exit junc 2 or A1/E37 exit junc 78 onto B51 dir Münster then Bielefeld. On leaving built-up area, turn R after TV mast on R. Cross Rv Werse & turn L at 1st traff lts, site sp. (Site is also sp fr Münster S by-pass). Lge, mkd pitch, some hdstg, pt shd; htd wc; chem disp; mv service pnt; serviced pitches; fam bthrm; shwrs €0.50; EHU (16A) inc; lndry; shop; rest, snacks; BBQ; playgrnd; htd pool adj; fishing; tennis; bike hire; wifi; 50% statics; dogs €3; bus 150m; o'night m'van area; barrier clsd 1300-1500; poss very cr w/e; twin axles; Eng spkn; adv bkg; quiet; ccard acc; red CKE/CCI. "Excel; quiet mid wk; Münster very interesting; radio/TV mast useful landmark fr S; gd cycle rtes; vg site, tokens for shwrs; sep motor parking outside camp; excel for bus to Munster; helpful staff; clean facs & plentiful; well organised; pitches cramped; gd rest." ♦ € 24.00 2016*

⊞ **MUNSTERTAL** *3B4* (2km WNW Rural) *47.85995, 7.76370* **Feriencamping Münstertal, Dietzelbachstrasse 6, 79244 Münstertal [(07636) 7080; fax 7448; info@camping-muenstertal.de; www.camping-muenstertal.de]** Exit A5 junc 64a at Bad Krozingen-Staufen-Münstertal. By-pass Stauffen & foll Münstertal sps. Site on L 1.5km past Camping Belchenblick off rd L123. Lge, mkd pitch, shd; wc; chem disp; mv service pnt; serviced pitches; sauna; steam rm; solarium; private bathrms avail; shwrs inc; EHU (16A) metered; gas; lndry; shop; rest, snacks; adventure playgrnd; 2 htd pools (1 covrd); fishing; wintersports nr; ski lift 10km; tennis; horseriding; games area; games rm; beauty treatments avail; wifi; entmnt; cab TV; some statics; dogs €3.50; phone; rlwy stn 200m; gates clsd 1300-1430 & 2200-0730; m'van o'night area; adv bkg rec school hols; quiet; red long stay/CKE/CCI. "Superb, well-managed site; luxurious, clean facs; many activities for all family; gd walking; vg rest; conv Freiburg & Black Forest; new premium pitches (2016); friendly staff; organised activities;." ♦ € 36.50 2017*

See advertisement

"I need an on-site restaurant"

We do our best to make sure site information is correct, but it is always best to check any must-have facilities are still available or will be open during your visit.

MURNAU AM STAFFELSEE *4E4* (3.5km NW Rural) *47.68493, 11.17918* **Camping Halbinsel Burg, Burgweg 41, 82418 Murnau-Seehausen [(08841) 9870; fax 626071; info@camping-staffelsee.de; www.camping-staffelsee.de]** Exit A95 junc 9 Sindelsdorf/Peissenberg to Murnau. Site sp at traff lts in cent of Murnau, dir Seehausen. Med, pt shd; wc; chem disp; mv service pnt; shwrs inc; EHU (16A) €1.80; lndry; shop; rest; playgrnd; lake sw & beach; watersports; entmnt high ssn; 20% statics; no dogs; no adv bkg; red CKE/CCI. "Wonderful sw & boating; pleasant, lovely, well-equipped site in superb location for alps, lakes & local amenities." ♦ 6 Jan-25 Oct. € 26.00 2014*

⊞ **NAUMBURG (HESSEN)** *1C4* (800m NW Rural) *51.25070, 9.16060* **Camping in Naumburg (formerly Kneipp Kur Camping), Am Schwimmbad 12, 34311 Naumburg [(05625) 9239670 or 0170 4418621 (mob); info@camping-naumburg.de; www.camping-naumburg.de]** Exit A44 junc 67 onto B251 thro Istha. At Bründersen foll sp Altenstadt & Naumburg. Foll int'l camping sp, well sp. Med, mkd pitch, terr, unshd; htd wc; chem disp; mv service pnt; fam bthrm; shwrs; EHU (16A) €2 or metered (poss rev pol); lndry; bar; BBQ; cooking facs; playgrnd; games area; pool adj; tennis; horseriding 5km; golf 15km; spa treatments; 30% statics; dogs €2.50; bus 500m; clsd 1300-1500; twin axles; Eng spkn; adv bkg; quiet; red LS; CKE/CCI. "Charming site; excel, modern san facs; spacious pitches; friendly, helpful staff; interesting town; gd walks fr site; rec; nr pool, smkt, Dambusters Dam; new management." ♦ € 22.00 2015*

NECKARGEMUND see Heidelberg *3C2*

NEEF *3B2* (500m N Rural) *50.09500, 7.13694* **Wohnmobilplatz Am Frauenberg, Am Moselufer, 56858 Neef [(06542) 21575]** Exit A1/E44 junc 125 onto B49 to Neef. In Neef cross rv bdge, site sp on L beside rv. M'vans only. Med, pt shd; chem disp; mv service pnt; EHU (10A) inc; shop 400m; rest 100m; some rlwy & rv noise. "Gd; owner calls am & pm for payment; beautiful location." 1 Mar-30 Oct. € 5.00 2013*

NEEF *3B2* (4km S Urban) *50.05294, 7.13115* **Bären Camp Bullay, Am Moselufer 1+3, D-56859 Bullay (Mosel) [06542 900097; info@baeren-camp.de; www.baeren-camp.de]** Foll B49 to Alf, cross Moselle bdge to Bullay. Turn L and drive under the rlwy bdge, foll the rd. At the vill sq turn into Fährstrasse, drive across Moselle car park past the football grnd foll sp to site. Sm, mkd pitch, pt shd; htd wc; chem disp; shwrs; fam bthrm; lndry; playgrnd; shop; rest, bar; BBQ; dogs; Eng spk; poss noisy; CKE/CCI. "Fair site; handy for Mosel Cycle Rte; diff ent, barrier down rest time." 18 Apr-27 Aug. € 21.00 2012*

NEHREN see Cochem *3B2*

NENNIG *3A2* (1.6km N Rural) *49.54195, 6.37126* **Mosel-Camping Dreiländereck, Am Moselufer, 66706 Perl-Nennig [(06866) 322; fax 1005; info@mosel-camping.de; www.mosel-camping.de]** Site on bank of Mosel opp Remich (Luxembourg), access on R just bef bdge (fr German side). Fr Luxembourg cross rv bdge, turn L after former border post cont to rv & turn L under bldg; site is ahead. Med, unshd; htd wc; chem disp; mv service pnt; shwrs €1.40; EHU (16A) inc; lndry; shops 400m; rest, snacks; bar; BBQ; playgrnd; fishing; cycling; golf 15km; 65% statics; dogs €1; phone; poss cr; adv bkg; quiet; no ccard acc; Eng spkn; 10% red long stay; 5% red CKE/CCI. "Nice, lovely site; dishwashing & chem disp adj; ltd, tired facs; conv vineyards, Roman mosaic floor in Nennig; cycle track along rv; sh walk to Remich; friendly welcome." 1 Apr-15 Oct. € 18.60 2016*

NENNIG *3A2* (1.8km N Rural) *49.54331, 6.37207* **Camping Mosella am Rothaus (formerly Moselplatz), Zur Moselbrücke 15, 66706 Perl-Nennig [(06866) 510 or 26660222 (Lux'bourg); fax 1486; info@mosel-camping.de]** Site on bank of Mosel opp Remich (Luxembourg), access on R just bef bdge. Fr Luxembourg cross rv bdge, turn L after former border post, site is ahead, opp Mosel-Camping Dreiländereck. Med, hdg pitch, pt shd; htd wc; chem disp; mv service pnt; shwrs inc; EHU (10A) inc; gas 1km; shop 500m; rest, snacks; bar; BBQ; 50% statics; dogs; bus 100m; poss cr; Eng spkn; quiet, some rd noise; CKE/CCI. "Lovely, well placed site by rv for sh or long stay; helpful, friendly owner; ltd facs, a bit tired; rest adj; rvside pitch sm extra charge; gd touring base; frequent bus to Luxembourg City." ♦ ltd. 1 Apr-15 Oct. € 22.60 2017*

"Satellite navigation makes touring much easier"

Remember most sat navs don't know if you're towing or in a larger vehicle – always use yours alongside maps and site directions.

⊞ **NESSLBACH** *4G3* (700m W Rural) *48.69400, 13.11638* **Donautal Camping, Schillerstrasse 14, 94577 Nesslbach-Winzer [(08545) 1233 or 0121 or 8225; fax 911562; info@camping-donautal.de; www.camping-donautal.de]** Exit A3/E56 junc 112 to Nesslbach. Site adj sports stadium, sp. Sm, mkd pitch, unshd; htd wc; chem disp; mv service pnt; shwrs inc; EHU (6A) inc; lndry; shop 100m; rest 300m; snacks 100m; games area; 20% statics; dogs free; quiet. "Adj Danube cycleway; lovely, open site; friendly staff; lge pitches - easy access lge o'fits; ltd san facs but clean; site yourself instructions if site not manned; vg." € 15.00 2013*

NEUHAUSEN SCHELLBRONN see Pforzheim *3C3*

NEUMAGEN DHRON see Trittenheim *3B2*

⊞ **NEUMARKT IN DER OBERPFALZ** *4E3* (10km N Rural) *49.32944, 11.42876* **Campingplatz Berg, Hausheimerstrasse 31, 92348 Berg [tel/fax (09189) 1581; campingplatz-herteis@t-online.de; www.camping-in-berg.de]** Exit A3 junc 91 & foll sp Berg bei Neumarkt. In cent of Berg, turn R, site on R in 800m, sp. On ent turn R to tourers area & walk to recep. Med, pt sl, unshd; wc; chem disp; mv service pnt; fam bthrm; shwrs €0.60; EHU (20A) €2.50; lndry (inc dryer); shop, rest 400m; snacks; golf 8km; 60% statics (sep area); dogs €2; Eng spkn; quiet. "Well-run, friendly, family-owned site; excel san facs; sh walk to Berg cent; excel touring base; gd NH fr m'way; pleasant views of countryside; canal walk." € 20.00 2016*

GERMANY

⊞ **NEUMUNSTER** *1D1* (6km SW Rural) *54.04636, 9.92306* **Familien-Camping Forellensee, Humboldredder 5, 24634 Padenstedt [(04321) 82697; fax 84341; info@familien-campingplatz.de; www.familien-campingplatz.de]** Exit A7 junc 14 for Padenstedt, join dual c'way for 1km & turn L sp Centrum. In 1km turn L at traff lts sp Padenstedt for 3km, under m'way. Site on L in vill. Lge, mkd pitch, pt shd; wc; chem disp; mv service pnt; shwrs inc; EHU (16A) €3 or metered; lndry; rest 500m; snacks; bar; playgrnd; lake sw; trout-fishing; tennis; games area; 75% statics; phone; poss cr; Eng spkn; some rd noise; CKE/CCI. "Gd NH; conv for trains to Hamburg/ Lübeck." ♦ € 26.50 2014*

⊞ **NEUREICHENAU** *4G3* (8km E Urban) *48.74861, 13.81694* **Knaus Campingpark Lackenhäuser, Lackenhäuser 127, 94089 Neureichenau [(08583) 311; fax 91079; lackenhaeuser@knauscamp.de; www.knauscamp.de]** Leave A3/E56 at junc 14 (Aicha-vorm Wald) & go E for 50km via Waldkirchen, Jandelsbrunn, Gsenget & Klafferstrasse to Lackenhäuser. Lge, some hdg/mkd pitch, pt sl, terr, pt shd; wc; chem disp; mv service pnt; some serviced pitches; fam bthrm; sauna; shwrs inc; EHU (16A) €2.60 or metered; gas; lndry; shop; rest, snacks; bar; BBQ; playgrnd; 2 pools (1 htd); paddling pool; tennis 500m; bike hire; fishing; horseriding adj; games rm; entmnt; solarium; hairdresser; internet; games/TV rm; wifi; 40% statics; dogs €2.50; adv bkg; quiet; ccard acc; red LS/long stay. "Lge site with little waterfalls & walkways; ski lift on site - equipment for hire; mv service pnt diff to access; excel shop; 2km to 3 point border with Austria & Czech Republic; excursions booked; recep clsd 1200-1500 & after 1800." ♦ € 34.00 2016*

NEUSTADT *3C2* (10km SW Rural) *49.30083, 8.09027* **Campingplatz Wappenschmiede, Talstrasse 60, 67487 St Martin [(06323) 6435; cpwappenschmiede@ hotmail.de; www.campingplatz-wappenschmiede. beep.de]** Exit A65 at junc 13 or 14 to Maikammer, then foll sp St Martin & site (blue/white or yellow/ brown sp). At end houses take 1st L into touring area (do not go up hill to statics area). Sm, shd; wc; chem disp; shwrs €1; EHU €2; lndry; supmkt 5km; rest; bar; playgrnd; 50% statics; dogs; Eng spkn; adv bkg; quiet; red long stay; CKE/CCI. "Poss long walk to facs; friendly site; St Martin very picturesque; gd rests; gd walking area; gd site." 1 Apr-1 Nov. € 20.00 2015*

⊞ **NEUSTADT AN DER AISCH** *4E2* (9km N Rural) *49.64058, 10.59975* **Campingplatz Münchsteinach, Badstrasse 10, 91481 Münchsteinach [(09166) 750; fax 278; gemeinde@muenchsteinach.de; www. muenchsteinach.de]** Turn NW fr rd 470 Neustadt-Höchstadt at camp sp 8km fr Neustadt & thro Gutenstetten. Int'l camping sp in 5km turn R, foll camp sp. Lge, unshd; wc; mv service pnt; chem disp; shwrs inc; EHU (16A) metered; lndry (inc dryer); shop, snacks 500m; pool adj; 60% statics; dogs €2; quiet; red long stay; CKE/CCI. "Sm touring area; clean facs; site muddy when wet." ♦ € 11.00 2016*

⊞ **NEUSTADT AN DER WALDNAAB** *4F2* (1km NW Urban) *49.73750, 12.17222* **Waldnaab Camping, Gramaustrasse 64, 92660 Neustadt-an-der-Waldnaab [(09602) 3608; fax 943466; pfoster@ neustadt-waldnaab.de; www.neustadt-waldnaab. de]** Exit A93 junc 21a onto B15 for 4km S into Neustadt. Site sp fr N side of vill. Sm, hdg pitch, pt shd; htd wc; chem disp; mv service pnt; shwrs €0.50; EHU (16A)inc; lndry; supmkt 500m; rest 1km; snacks; bar; playgrnd; pool; games area; dogs €1.50; quiet. "Helpful owners; clean facs; excel value for money." € 17.00 2013*

⊞ **NEUSTADT/HARZ** *2E4* (2km NW Rural) *51.56897, 10.82836* **Campingplatz am Waldbad, An der Burg 3, 99762 Neustadt/Harz [036331 479891; fax 479892; info@neustadt-harz-camping.de]** Fr A38, exit J10 for B243 to Nordhausen. Turn L onto B4 dir Niedersachswerfen. Turn R onto L1037, L onto Osteroder Straße and R onto Klostergasse. Foll sp to campsite. Med, hdg pitch, pt sl, pt shd; htd wc; chem disp; mv service pnt; shwrs inc; EHU (10A); lndry (inc dryer); snacks; bar; playgrnd; games area; 50% statics; bus/train 4km; twin axles; adv bkg; quiet; CCI. "Gd site; conv for Harz; helpful owners; vg san facs." ♦ € 31.00 2014*

NEUSTRELITZ *2F2* (10km SW Rural) *53.30895, 13.00305* **Camping- und Ferienpark Havelberge, An der Havelbergen 1, 17237 Gross Quassow [(03981) 24790; fax 247999; info@haveltourist.de; www. haveltourist.de]** Fr Neustrelitz foll sp to Userin on L25 & bef Userin turn L sp Gross Quassow. Turn S in vill at camping sp, cross rlwy line & rv, sm ent in 1.5km. Site 1.7km S of Gross Quassow twd lake, sp. Lge, pt sl, pt shd; wc; chem disp; mv service pnt; sauna; shwrs €0.90; EHU (16A) €2.90; lndry (inc dryer); shop adj; rest high ssn; snacks; bar; playgrnd; lake sw; watersports; bike hire; wifi; entmnt & 30% statics; dogs - free; quiet. "Lovely wooded area; poss diff lge o'fits; not rec as NH." ♦ ltd. 01 Apr- 03 Nov. € 33.40 SBS - G11 2016*

NIEDERAU see Meissen *2G4*

NIEDERZELL see Konstanz *3D4*

NIESKY *2H4* (3km W Rural) *51.30156, 14.80302* **Campingplatz Tonschächte (Part Naturist), Raschkestrasse, 02906 Niesky [(03588) 205771; info@campingplatz-tonschacht.de; campingplatz-tonschacht.de]** Leave A4/E40 at junc 93 onto B115 sp Niesky; cont on B115 site sp on L; do not go into Niesky but stay on B115. Lge, shd; wc; shwrs €0.75; EHU (10A); lndry; shop; rest 1km; snacks; playgrnd; games area; 50% statics; dogs; poss cr. "Conv Polish border x-ing & a'bahn; sep naturist area." ♦ 15 Apr-15 Oct. € 12.50 2016*

⊞ **NOHFELDEN** *3B2* (10km SW Rural) *49.56072, 7.06105* **Campingplatz Bostalsee, 66625 Nohfelden-Bosen [(06852) 92333; fax 92393; campingplatz@bostalsee.de; www.bostalsee.de]** Fr A62 exit junc 3 sp Nohfelden/Türkismühle & Bostalsee. Turn R & foll camp sp. Site on R in 1.6km after passing thro vill of Bosen. V lge, mkd pitch, pt sl, unshd; htd wc; chem disp; mv service pnt; fam bthrm; sauna; shwrs inc; EHU (16A) €2; lndry (inc dryer); shop 1km; rest; snacks adj; playgrnd; lake sw 800m; watersports; golf 7km; wifi; entmnt; 75% statics; dogs €2; clsd to vehicles 1300-1500 & 2200-0700; adv bkg; quiet. "Vg san facs; pleasant lakeside site but poss unrel in wet; spacious, hdstg pitches; conv NH." ♦ € 20.00 2012*

NORDEN *1B2* (5km W Coastal) *53.60471, 7.13863* **Nordsee-Camp Norddeich, Deichstrasse 21, 26506 Norden-Norddeich [(04931) 8073; fax 8074; info@nordsee-camp.de; www.Nordsee-Camp.de]** Off B70 N of Norden. Well sp. V lge, mkd pitch, pt shd; wc; chem disp; mv service pnt; fam bthrm; shwrs inc; EHU (6A) €2.20; lndry; shop; rest, snacks; playgrnd; beach 200m; fishing; bike hire; internet; entmnt; 25% statics; dogs; €3.80; ccard acc; red CKE/CCI. "Immac san facs; friendly atmosphere; day trips to Frisian Islands; excel rest; vg site." ♦ 8 Mar-25 Oct. € 20.80 2016*

⊞ **NORDLINGEN** *4E3* (1.6km NW Urban) *48.85529, 10.48162* **Nördlingen Wohnmobil Stellplatz, Würtzburger Strasse, Nördlingen** Fr Donauwörth foll B25 round Nördlingen. Site on R, NW of town. Sm, hdstg, unshd; chem disp; mv service pnt; EHU €2; dogs; bus/train adj; noisy. " Along main rd; mvs only, pt of car & coach park; grassy area alongside; services fr coin operated machines; notice in Eng; easy walk to cent of lovely town, built on site of ancient meteorite hit; NH only." 2014*

NUREMBERG see Nürnberg *4E2*

⊞ **NURNBERG** *4E2* (8km SE Urban) *49.42305, 11.12138* **Knaus Campingpark Nürnberg, Hans-Kalb-Strasse 56, 90471 Nürnberg [(0911) 9812717; fax 9812718; nuernberg@knauscamp.de; www.knauscamp.de]** Exit E45/A9 junc 52 or E50/A6 junc 59 dir Nürnberg-Langwasser heading N, or Nürnberg-Fischbach exit travelling S; foll sp to 'Stadion', turn L. Site ent off wide rd opp Nürnberg Conference Cent. Lge, pt mkd pitch, pt shd; htd wc; chem disp; mv service pnt; shwrs inc; EHU (6-16A) €3 (long cable rec); gas; lndry (inc dryer); shop; rest 1km; playgrnd; htd, pool adj; tennis; wifi; TV; 25% statics; dogs €5 (on request); tram/metro 1.2km; poss cr; Eng spkn; adv bkg; noise fr rd & poss fr stadium; red long stay; ccard acc; CKE/CCI. "Friendly, helpful staff; peaceful, surrounded by trees; san facs poss stretched high ssn; very quiet midwk LS; gd security; office & access clsd 1300-1500 & 2200-0700; gd cycle rte to town; national rlwy museum in town worth visit; 1.2km to metro to town cent; red squirrels on site." ♦ € 40.00 2013*

NURNBERG *4E2* (12km W Rural) *49.43174, 10.92541* **Camping Zur Mühle, Seewaldstraße 75, 90513 Zirndorf/Leichendorf [(0911) 693801; fax 9694601; camping.walther@t-online.de; www.camping-zur-muehle.de]** Head W on Adlerstraße twd Stangengäßchen, cont onto Josephspl, then Vordere Lederg. Cont onto Schlotfegerg then onto Further Tor; Cont onto Dennerstraße then slight R onto Am Plärrer. Cont onto Rothenburger Str, turn L to stay on Rothenburger. Turn R twd Seewaldstraße, keep R. Site on L. Med, mkd pitch, pt shd; htd wc; chem disp; fam bthrm; shwrs €0.50; EHU metered; lndry (inc dryer); rest; snacks; bar; BBQ; playgrnd; wifi; dogs €2; quiet; ccard acc; CKE/CCI. "Mastercard acc not Visa; local style rest in traditional building on site; conv for visiting Nurnberg; vg site." 1 Apr-31 Dec. € 24.00 2014*

⊞ **OBERAMMERGAU** *4E4* (1km S Rural) *47.58988, 11.0696* **Campingpark Oberammergau, Ettalerstrasse 56B, 82487 Oberammergau [(08822) 94105; fax 94197; info@camping-oberammergau.de; www.campingpark-oberammergau.de]** Fr S turn R off B23, site on L in 1km. Fr N turn L at 2nd Oberammergau sp. Do not ent vill fr N - keep to bypass. Med, plenty hdstg, hdg/mkd pitch, pt shd; wc; chem disp; mv service pnt; fam bthrm; shwrs inc; EHU (16A) metered + conn fee; gas; lndry (inc dryer); shop in vill; rest adj; playgrnd; bike hire; wifi; entmnt; 25% statics; dogs €2; sep car park; bus; poss cr; Eng spkn; adv bkg ess high ssn; red long stay/LS; CKE/CCI. "Plenty of space; helpful recep; excel san facs; excel rest adj; easy walk to vill; well run site, visitor tax does not apply to one night stays." ♦ € 29.00 2017*

⊞ **OBERSTDORF** *3D4* (2km N Rural) *47.42370, 10.27843* **Rubi-Camp, Rubingerstrasse 34, 87561 Oberstdorf [(08322) 959202; fax 959203; info@rubi-camp.de; www.rubi-camp.de]** Fr Sonthofen on B19, just bef Oberstdorf at rndabt take exit sp Reichenbach, Rubi. Site in 1km over level x-ing, 2nd site on R. Med, hdstg, unshd; htd wc; chem disp; mv service pnt; fam bthrm; serviced pitches; shwrs inc; EHU (8A) metered; lndry; shop 1km; rest, snacks; bar; BBQ; playgrnd; skiift 1km; TV; 10% statics; dogs €2.70; phone; bus; site clsd Nov; Eng spkn; adv bkg; quiet; CKE/CCI. "Well-run, well-maintained site; immac facs; block paved paths to pitches; block hdstg with grass growing thro; excel scenery; excel facs; easy 20 min level walk to town." ♦ € 32.00 2014*

OBERSTDORF *3D4* (3km N Rural) *47.42300, 10.27720* **Campingplatz Oberstdorf, Rubingerstrasse 16, 87561 Oberstdorf [(08322) 6525; fax 809760; camping-oberstdorf@t-online.de; www.camping-oberstdorf.de]** Fr B19 dir Oberstdorf, foll site sp. Med, hdstg, wc; chem disp; mv service pnt; serviced pitches; shwrs inc; EHU (10A) metered; lndry (inc dryer); shops 1.5km; rest, snacks; golf 5km; ski lift 3km; skibus; wifi; 45% statics (sep area); dogs €0.50; rd & rlwy noise. "Cable cars to Nebelhorn & Fellhorn in town; Oberstdorf pedestrianised with elec buses fr o'skirts; vg." 1 Jan-31 Oct, 15 Dec-31 Dec. € 32.00 2017*

OBERWEIS see Bitburg *3B2*

⊞ **OBERWESEL** *3B2* (5km N Rural) *50.14188, 7.72101* **Camping Loreleyblick, An der Loreley 29-33, 56329 St Goar-am-Rhein [(06741) 2066; fax 7233; info@camping-loreleyblick.de; www.camping-loreleyblick.de]** Exit A61/E31sp Emmelshausen junc 42 & foll sp for St Goar; site adj B9 1km S of St Goar opp Loreley rock on rv bank. Or exit A48 junc 10 dir Koblenz, then B9 St Goar. Lge, pt sl, unshd; htd wc; chem disp; mv service pnt; shwrs inc; EHU (6A) €2.50; gas; lndry; shop & 500m; rest, snacks, bar adj (hotel opp); pool 3km; 10% statics; dogs €1.70; phone adj; poss very cr; wifi; Eng spkn; no adv bkg; much noise fr rlwy 24 hrs, plus noise fr rd & rv barges; red long stay; CKE/CCI. "Lovely setting in scenic area; friendly, helpful owner; excel modern san facs, stretched when site full; pool complex in hills behind; conv boat trips & car ferry across Rhine 500m; if office clsd site self & report later; site clsd if rv in flood Dec-Feb; el voltage drops when site very cr; easy walk to town; castles & museums; wine cents; chair lift at Boppard; gd range of shops in St Goar." ♦ € 19.00 2012*

OBERWESEL *3B2* (8km N Urban) *50.15995, 7.70875* **Camping Loreleystadt, Wellmicher Str 55, 56346 St Goarshausen [(06771) 2592; info@camping-loreleyblick.de; www.camping-loreleystadt.de]** Site on B42, E side of Rhine on N o'skts of St Goarshausen, sp, but take care not to overshoot. Med, unshd; wc; chem disp; mv service pnt; shwrs €0.75; EHU (10A) metered + conn fee €1.28; rest 200m; snacks 100m; gas; shop; entmnt; sw in rv; poss cr; adv bkg; few statics; quiet. "Poss flooding in heavy rain." ♦ 20 Mar-31 Oct. € 24.00 2013*

OBERWESEL *3B2* (7.6km SE Rural) *50.05111, 7.7750* **Camping Sonnenstrand, Strandbadweg 9, 55422 Bacharach [(06743) 1752; fax 3192; info@camping-sonnenstrand.de; www.camping-rhein.de]** S on A61. Exit 44 Laudert via Oberwesel to Bacharach (B9). Turn Sat Nav off after Laudert. Foll sp to Oberwesel-Bacharach. Med, mkd pitch, hdstg, pt shd; wc; chem disp; mv service pnt; fam bthrm; shwrs €1; EHU (6A); lndry (inc dryer); shop; rest; bar; BBQ; playgrnd; beach adj; boating; golf 6km; games area & rm; bike hire; wifi; 25% statics; dogs €1; twin axles; Eng spkn; rv, rd & rlwy noise; red LS/long stay/CKE/CCI. "Helpful, knowledgeable owner; poss lge groups m'cyclists; scenic area; busy, noisy rvside site; sm pitches; wine cellar visits; shwrs/san facs ltd & poss stretched high ssn; plenty of rv activities; excel rest; sh walk to sm medieval town; sh stay/NH; gd." ♦ ltd. 25 Mar-31 Oct. € 19.50 2016*

OBERWESEL *3B2* (900m S Urban) *50.10251, 7.73664* **Camping Schönburgblick, Am Hafendamm 1, 55430 Oberwesel [(06744) 714501; fax 714413; camping-oberwesel@t-online.de; www.camping-oberwesel.de]** Fr A61/E31 exit sp Oberwesel, site sp on L at ent to sports stadium, on rvside. Sm, pt shd; wc; chem disp; mv service pnt; shwrs inc; EHU (6A) €4.20; supmkt 200m; rest 200m; snacks; bar; tennis adj; o'night area for m'vans; poss cr; adv bkg; some rlwy/rv noise; red long stay; CKE/CCI. "Clean, modern san facs in Portacabins - stretched when site full; rv trips, cycling, walking." 17 Mar-1 Nov. € 23.40 2017*

⊞ **OBERWESEL** *3B2* (9km NW Rural) *50.14976, 7.69478* **Camping Friedenau, Gründelbach 103, 56329 St Goar-am-Rhein [tel/fax (06741) 368; info@camping-friedenau.de; www.camping-friedenau.de]** App on B9 fr Boppard or Bingen; turn under rlwy bdge 1km N of St Goar; keep L; site on L in 1km. NB - do not app fr J43 off m'way. Sm, pt sl, shd; wc; chem disp; mv service pnt; shwrs inc; EHU (16A) €2.50; gas; lndry; shops 1.5km; rest; bar; playgrnd; pool 1.5km; wifi; dogs €2; bus; poss cr; Eng spkn; quiet; red CKE/CCI. "Quieter than other sites in area - uphill fr busy Rhine & resorts; some pitches uneven & poss diff after heavy rain; vg welcome; easy walk or cycle to rv town; country walks fr site; relaxed atmosphere; friendly staff; gd bar/rest; san fac gd; great views fr Rheinfels Castle; in very pleasant valley; washing up and lndry facs in female toilet block." ♦ € 21.50 2016*

OHNINGEN WANGEN see Radolfzell am Bodensee *3C4*

⊞ **OHRDRUF** *2E4* (10km W Rural) *50.82452, 10.61060* **Campingplatz Paulfeld, Catterfeld, 99894 Leinatal [(036253) 25171; fax 25165; info@paulfeld-camping.de; www.paulfeld-camping.de]** Fr E exit A4 junc 42 onto B88 sp Friedrichroda & foll sp Catterfeld & site on R. Or fr W exit junc 41a at Gotha. Take B247 S twd Ohrdruf. After 6km bear R sp Georgenthal. In Georgenthal vill, bear R onto B88. After 2km site sp L on app Catterfeld vill. Foll rd 2km thro forest to site, sp. Site approx 12km fr A4. Lge, some hdg, pt shd; chem disp; mv service pnt; wc; sauna; shwrs €0.80; EHU (16A) inc; gas; lndry (inc dryer); shop; rest, snacks; bar; BBQ; playgrnd; sm pets corner; lake sw & fishing; solarium; games area; bike hire; games rm; internet; 40% statics in sep area; dogs €2; twin-axles acc (rec check in adv); poss cr w/end; quiet; ccard not acc; red LS/long stay; CKE/CCI. "Excel, well-kept site; gd access to pitches; clean san facs; gd for families with young children; woodland walks; conv stop en rte eastern Europe; happy family site; helpful friendly owners." ♦ € 26.50 2013*

OLDENDORF see Bergen *1D3*

SCHLESWIG *1D1* (6km S Rural) *54.50111, 9.57027* **Wikinger Camping Haithabu, 24866 Haddeby [(04621) 32450; fax 33122; info@campingplatz-haithabu.de; www.campingplatz-haithabu.de]** Leave A7/45 N & S junc 6. Travel E two Schleswig & turn R onto B76 sp Kiel & Eckernförde. Site on L in 2km sp. Med, pt shd; wc; chem disp; mv service pnt; fam bthrm; shwrs €0.50; EHU (16A) €2; lndry; supmkt 1.5km; rest, snacks; BBQ; playgrnd; lake sw adj; boating facs; fishing; bike hire; wifi; 10% statics; dogs €2; bus; poss cr; Eng spkn; adv bkg; some rd noise; CKE/CCI. "Lovely site on rv with lovely views; foot & cycle paths to Schleswig (4.5km) & ferry; gd area for children; Schloss Gottorf worth visit; vg Viking museum adj; shwrs newly refurb (2015); boating; gd." ♦ ltd. 1 Mar-31 Oct. € 23.00 2017*

⊞ **SCHOMBERG** *3C3* (2km N Rural) *48.79820, 8.63623* **Höhen-Camping, Schömbergstrasse 32, 75328 Langenbrand [(07084) 6131; fax 931435; info@hoehencamping.de; www.hoehencamping.de]** Fr N exit A8 junc 43 Pforzheim, take B463 dir Calw. Turn R sp Schömberg & foll sp Langenbrand. Med, hdg/mkd pitch, pt sl, pt shd; htd wc; chem disp; fam bthrm; shwrs €0.50; EHU (10-16A) €3; lndry; shop 200m; playgrnd; TV; 70% statics; dogs €2; phone; adv bkg; quiet; CKE/CCI. "Clean, well-maintained site in N of Black Forest; vg san facs; no recep - ring bell on house adj site ent; blocks req for sl pitches." € 19.00 2013*

⊞ **SCHONAU IM SCHWARZWALD** *3B4* (1km N Rural) *47.79127, 7.90076* **Camping Schönenbuchen, Friedrichstrasse 58, 79677 Schönau [(07673) 7610; fax 234327; info@camping-schoenau.de; www.camping-schoenau.de]** Fr Lörrach on B317 dir Todtnau for approx 23km. Site thro Schönau main rd on R on rvside, ent thro car park. Narr access diff for l'ge o'fits. Med, hdg pitch, pt shd; wc; chem disp; mv service pnt; fam bthrm; sauna; shwrs; EHU inc (16A) (poss rev pol); lndry; shop 400m; rest; bar; playgrnd; htd pool; sw & watersports adj; tennis; horseriding; bike hire; 70% statics; dogs €1; adv bkg; quiet; red long stay; CKE/CCI. "Friendly staff; site poss not well-kept; gd walking & cycling; lovely old town." ♦ € 28.00 2014*

SCHUTTORF *1B3* (2km N Rural) *52.33960, 7.22617* **Camping Quendorfer See, Weiße Riete 3, 48465 Schüttorf [05923 90 29 39; fax 90 29 40; info@camping-schuettorf.de; www.camping-schuettorf.de]** A1/A30, exit J4 Schüttorf-Nord. Or A31 exit J28 Schüttorf-Ost twds town cent. Foll sp to site. Sm, hdg/mkd pitch, unshd; htd wc; chem disp; mv service pnt; fam bthrm; shwrs inc; EHU (16A); lndry (inc dryer); shop 2km; snacks; bar; playgrnd; sw adj; games area; dogs €2; bus 2km; twin axles; adv bkg; quiet; ccard acc; CCI. "Excel site; immac san facs; mostly fully serviced pitches; conv NH for ferries fr Holland; flat cycling & walking." ♦ 1 Apr-31 Oct. € 25.00 2014*

SCHWAAN *2F2* (3.6km S Rural) *53.92346, 12.10688* **Camping Schwaan, Güstrowerstrasse 54/ Sandgarten 17, 18258 Schwaan [(03844) 813716; fax 814051; info@campingplatz-schwaan.de; www.campingplatz-schwaan.de]** Fr A20 exit junc 13 to Schwaan, site sp. Fr A19 exit junc 11 dir Bad Doberan & Schwaan. Site adj Rv Warnow. Lge, mkd pitch, pt shd; htd wc; mv service pnt; sauna; fam bthrm; shwrs inc; EHU (16A) €2.20 or metered; lndry (inc dryer); shop high ssn; supmkt 800m; rest, snacks; bar; cooking facs; playgrnd; canoeing; boat & bike hire; tennis 700m; games area; wifi; entmnt; TV; 30% statics; dogs €2; site clsd 21 Dec-4 Jan; adv bkg; quiet. "Pleasant rvside site; gd touring base; tight app thro Schwaan town (esp fr N)." ♦ 1 Mar-31 Oct. € 26.50 2014*

SCHWABISCH HALL *3D3* (2km S Urban) *49.09868, 9.74288* **Camping am Steinbacher See, Mühlsteige 26, 74523 Schwäbisch Hall-Steinbach [(0791) 2984; fax 9462758; thomas.seitel@t-online.de; www.camping-schwaebisch-hall.de]** Fr A6/E50 exit junc 43 fr W or junc 42 fr E & foll permanent diversion via new B19 rd. At x-rds at lge Lidl store, turn L twds town and foll sp S to Comburg & site. Med, mkd pitch, pt shd; htd wc; chem disp; mv service pnt; shwrs €0.50; EHU (10A) metered + conn fee; lndry; shop 3km; rest 200m; snacks; bar; BBQ; playgrnd; bike hire; 50% statics; dogs €2; clsd 1300-1500; poss cr; Eng spkn; adv bkg; red CKE/CCI. "Lovely well kept idiosyncratic site; friendly; walking dist to interesting medieval town; cycle track to town." ♦ 15 Mar-15 Oct. € 22.00 2015*

SCHWANGAU see Füssen *4E4*

SCHWEDENECK see Gettorf *1D1*

SCHWEICH *3B2* (1.6km S Urban) *49.81459, 6.75019* **Campingplatz zum Fährturm, Am Yachthafen, 54338 Schweich [(06502) 91300; fax 913050; camping@kreusch.de; www.kreusch.de]** Fr exit 129 or 130 fr A1/E44. Site by rv bank by bdge into town, sp. Lge, mkd pitch, pt shd; wc; chem disp; mv service pnt; fam bthrm; shwrs inc; EHU (16A) €1.60; gas; lndry (inc dryer); supmkt 0.5km; rest; snacks; bar; BBQ; playgrnd; sports cent with pool adj; watersports; bike hire; dogs; bus to Trier nr; twin axles; Eng spkn; adv bkg; quiet; red LS; CKE/CCI. "Poss long wait for conn to EHU; poss long walk to san facs - dated; m'van o'night area outside site - no EHU; on banks of Mosel with cycle rte; yacht/boating harbour adj; gd rest/bar; vg." ♦ ltd. 8 Apr-21 Oct. € 20.00 2017*

GERMANY

SCHWEPPENHAUSEN *3B2* (1km N Rural) *49.93392, 7.79194* **Campingplatz Aumühle, Naheweinstraße 65, 55444 Schweppenhausen [06724 602392; fax 601610; info@camping-aumuehle.de]** Fr A61 take exit 47 - Waldlaubersheim. Foll signs to Schweppenhausen. Sp to camp site. Med, mkd pitch, pt shd; htd wc; chem disp; fam bthrm; shwrs inc; EHU (10A); lndry; rest; snacks; bar; playgrnd; 50% statics; dogs; twin axles; Eng spkn; adv bkg; poss cr; quiet; CKE/CCI. "V gd site; cycle rtes fr site; v helpful Dutch owners; gd san facs; touring vans in sep area nr m'way; gd NH." 1 Apr-31 Oct. € 20.50 2017*

⊞ **SCHWERIN** *2E2* (10km N Rural) *53.69725, 11.43715* **Ferienpark Seehof, Am Zeltzplatz 1, 19069 Seehof [(0385) 512540; fax 5814170; info@ferienparkseehof.de; www.ferienparkseehof.de]** Take B106 N fr Schwerin for approx 5km: turn R at city boundary & site within 5km at end of vill, sp. Lge, pt sl, pt shd; wc; chem disp; mv service pnt; serviced pitches; shwrs €1; EHU (4A) inc (poss rev pol); gas; lndry; shop; rest, snacks; bar; playgrnd, lake sw & sand beach; windsurfing; sailing school; bike hire; entmnt; 30% statics; dogs €1; poss cr; adv bkg; quiet; ccard acc. "Lge pitches; vg." € 33.00 2015*

⊞ **SEEBURG** *2E4* (1km NW Rural) *51.49400, 11.69400* **Camping Seeburg am Süsser See, Nordstrand 1, 06317 Seeburg [(034774) 28281; fax 41757; info@campingplatz-seeburg.de; www.campingplatz-seeburg.de]** W fr Halle on B80 twd Eisleben, sp fr Seeburg. Site on N shore of Lake Süsser See. Lge, pt shd; wc; chem disp; shwrs €1; EHU (16A) €1.10; rest 500m; playgrnd; lake sw; fishing; 95% statics; dogs €1.20. "Attractive, busy site by lake; excel base for medieval towns nr & 'Martin Luther country'; gd; nice site by lake; not many pitches; new immac facs (2015)." ♦ € 19.60 2015*

⊞ **SEESHAUPT** *4E4* (4km E Rural) *47.82651, 11.33906* **Camping beim Fischer, Buchscharnstrasse 10, 82541 St Heinrich [(08801) 802; fax 913461; info@camping-beim-fischer.de; www.camping-beim-fischer.de]** Exit A95 junc 7 & foll sp Seeshaupt for 1.6km to T-junc. Turn R, site in 200m on R. Med, mkd pitch, unshd; htd wc; chem disp; fam bthrm; shwrs inc; EHU (16A) metered; gas; lndry; rest, snacks, bar 200m; playgrnd; lake sw adj; games area; TV; 45% statics; dogs free; bus adj; Eng spkn; adv bkg; quiet; CKE/CCI. "Well-maintained, friendly, lovely, honest family-run site; immac facs; conv Munich & Bavarian castles." ♦ € 23.50 2014*

SENHEIM see Cochem *3B2*

SESSLACH see Coburg *4E2*

⊞ **SIGMARINGEN** *3D4* (2km SW Urban) *48.08366, 9.20794* **Erlebnis-Camp Sigmaringen, Georg-Zimmererstrasse 6, 72488 Sigmaringen [(07571) 50411; fax 50412; info@outandback.de; www.erlebnis-camp.de]** App town fr N or SW, ent town over Danube bdge, turn R into car pk (camp sp). To far end of car park, turn R in front of supmkt. Ent camp fr far end. Site adj to stadium by rv, sp fr town. Med, pt shd; wc; chem disp; mv service pnt; shwrs €0.50; EHU (6-16A) €3; lndry; shop 300m; rest; snacks 300m; playgrnd; htd pool 300m; bike hire; internet; 10% statics; dogs €1; CKE/CCI. "On Danube cycle way; gd outdoor activities; lovely site; clsd 12-1400; new facs; new ent." ♦ € 26.50 2015*

SIMMERATH *1A4* (8km E Rural) *50.61777, 6.37690* **Camping Rursee, Seerandweg 26, D 52152 Simmerath/Rurberg [(02473) 2365; info@camping-rursee.de; http://camping-rursee.de]** Fr Simmerath L166 to Kesternich; R on 266 for 1 km; then L on L166 twds Rurberg. L on L128 twds Woffelsbach then sp R to site. Sm, grassy, mkd pitch, unshd; wc; chem disp; shwr; EHU; lndry; shop; snacks; bar; games area. 1 Apr-Nov. € 21.00 2014*

SIMONSBERG see Husum *1D1*

SIMONSWALD see Waldkirch *3C4*

⊞ **SOEST** *1C4* (12km S Rural) *51.47722, 8.10055* **Camping Delecke-Südufer, Arnsbergerstrasse 8, 59519 Möhnesee-Delecke [(02924) 8784210; fax 1771; info@campingplatz-moehnesee.de; www.campingplatz-moehnesee.de]** Exit A44/E331 at junc 56 onto B229 sp Arnsberg/Mohnesee. Cont to lake, cross bdge. At next junc turn L & site immed on L, sp. Med, hdg pitch, pt sl, unshd; wc; chem disp; mv service pnt; shwrs (inc); EHU (16A); snacks; bar; rest 800m; lndry; shop; playgrnd; lake sw & beach adj; boating; 50% statics; phone; no dogs; poss cr; quiet; clsd 1300-1500 & 2000-0800; Eng spkn; adv bkg; CKE/CCI. "Excel site on boating lake; san facs locked o'night; gd walking & sailing; v busy at w/ends; gd disable facs." ♦ € 25.00 2016*

⊞ **SOLINGEN** *1B4* (6km S Rural) *51.13388, 7.11861* **Waldcamping Glüder, Balkhauserweg 240, 42659 Solingen-Glüder [(0212) 242120; fax 2421234; info@camping-solingen.de; www.camping-solingen.de]** Exit A1 junc 97 Burscheid onto B91 N dir Hilgen. In Hilgen turn L onto L294 to Witzhelden then R on L359 dir Solingen. Site sp in Glüder by Rv Wupper. Med, hdg/mkd pitch, some hdstg, unshd; htd wc; chem disp; shwrs inc; chem disp; EHU (6-10A) €3; gas; lndry; shop 3km; rest adj; snacks; bar; playgrnd; TV; 80% statics; dogs €2.30; bus; Eng spkn; quiet; CKE/CCI. "Beautiful location in wooded valley; clsd 1300-1500; resident owner; excel san facs; easy walk to Burg-an-der-Wupper Schloss - worth visit." € 27.40 2013*

SOMMERACH see Dettelbach *3D2*

⊞ **SOTTRUM** *1D2* (5km SW Rural) *53.08335, 9.17697* **Camping-Paradies Grüner Jäger, Everinghauser Dorfstrsse 17, 27367 Sottrum/Everinghausen [(04205) 319113; fax 319115; info@camping-paradies.de; www.camping-paradies.de]** Exit A1 junc 50 at Stuckenborstel onto B75 dir Rotenburg. In approx 500m turn R & foll sp Everinghausen. Site in 4km. Med, mkd pitch, unshd; htd wc; chem disp; mv service pnt; fam bthrm; shwrs inc; EHU (16A) inc; lndry; shop 6km; rest; bar; playgrnd; pool; paddling pool; 30% statics; dogs free; Eng spkn; some rd noise; CKE/CCI. "Excel NH; new superb facs block (2016)." € 22.50 2017*

"We must tell The Club about that great site we found"

Get your site reports in by mid-August and we'll do our best to get your updates into the next edition.

SPEYER *3C3* (3km N Rural) *49.33600, 8.44300* **Camping Speyer, Am Rübsamenwühl 31, 67346 Speyer [(06232) 42228; fax 815174; info@camping-speyer.de; www.camping-speyer.de]** Fr Mannheim or Karlsruhe take rd 9 to exit Speyer Nord dir Speyer. At 3rd traff lts turn L into Auestrasse, then at 2nd rndabt L into Am Rübsamenwühl. Site in 500m. Sm, some mkd pitch; shwrs €1; EHU €3; supmkt 500m; rest, snacks; bar; playgrnd; lake sw & sand beach; 90% statics; dogs €2; no adv bkg; quiet; red long stay. "Speyer pleasant town, cathedral & Technik Museum worth visit; v basic site; scruffy & not well-kept; fair NH/sh stay." 15 Mar-15 Oct. € 29.00 2014*

⊞ **SPEYER** *3C3* (1km SE Urban) *49.31250, 8.44916* **Camping Technik Museum, Am Technik Museum 1, Geibstrasse, 67346 Speyer [(06232) 67100; fax 6710 20; info@hotel-speyer.de; www.hotel-speyer.de]** Exit A61/E34 at junc 64, foll sp to museum. Med, unshd; htd wc; chem disp; mv service pnt; shwrs inc; EHU inc (10A); shop 1km; rest, snacks, bar adj; dogs free; phone (hotel); bus; poss cr; Eng spkn; adv bkg; ccard acc; 3 nights max stay. "Book in at hotel adj; excel museum & IMAX cinema on site; conv Speyer cent and cathedral; site unkept; excel san facs; 24hr CCTV controlled ent gate." ♦ ltd. € 22.00 2016*

STADTSTEINACH see Kulmbach *4E2*

⊞ **STAUFEN IM BREISGAU** *3B4* (1.4km SE Rural) *47.87194, 7.73583* **Ferien-Campingplatz Belchenblick, Münstertälerstrasse 43, 79219 Staufen-im-Breisgau [(07633) 7045; fax 7908; info@camping-belchenblick.de; www.camping-belchenblick.de]** Exit A5/E35 junc 64a dir Bad Krozingen-Staufen-Münstertal. Avoid Staufen cent, foll Münstertal sp. Camp on L 500m past Staufen. Visibility restricted fr Münstertal dir. Lge, pt shd; wc; chem disp; mv service pnt; fam bthrm; sauna; shwrs inc; EHU (16A) metered; gas; lndry (inc dryer); shop; rest 500m; snacks; bar; BBQ area; sm htd indoor pool; playgrnd, public pool & tennis nrby over unfenced rv via footbdge; bike hire; horseriding 500m; wifi; entmnt; games/TV rm; 60% statics; dogs €2.50; no o'fits over 8m high ssn; phone; no veh access 1230-1500 & night time - parking area avail; poss cr; Eng spkn; adv bkg rec high ssn; some rd & rlwy noise in day; no ccard acc; red LS/CKE/CCI. "Well-run, family-owned site; some pitches sm; strict pitching rules; beautiful area & Staufen pleasant town; beware train app round blind corner at x-ing; gd walking, cycling, horseriding; san facs tired, need refurbishing (2013); better cheaper sites close by." ♦ € 30.00 SBS - G02 2015*

STEINENSTADT *3B4* (200m W Urban) *47.76895, 7.55115* **Camping Vogesenblick, Eichwaldstrasse 7, 79395 Steinenstadt [(07635) 1846]** Exit A5/E35 junc 65 Neuenburg-am-Rhein. Turn S at traff lts for Steinenstadt, site sp. Sm, pt shd; wc; chem disp; mv service pnt; shwrs €0.50; EHU (16A) metered; lndry; shop, rest adj; bar; htd, covrd pool 5km; 20% statics; dogs €1.50; bus nr; poss cr; adv bkg; quiet. "Peaceful, friendly site; gd cycling beside Rv Rhine; easy access Black Forest, Freiburg etc; v quiet site and vill; petrol 2km." 15 Mar-31 Oct. € 20.50 2012*

"I need an on-site restaurant"

We do our best to make sure site information is correct, but it is always best to check any must-have facilities are still available or will be open during your visit.

STOCKACH *3C4* (7.5km SSW Rural) *47.80860, 8.97000* **Campinggarten Wahlwies, Stahringerstrasse 50, 78333 Stockach-Wahlwies [(07771) 3511; fax 4236; info@camping-wahlwies.de; www.camping-wahlwies.de]** Exit A98 junc 12 Stockach West onto B313 to Wahlwies. In vill turn L immed after level x-ing, site on R bef next level x-ing, sp. Med, pt shd; wc; chem disp; mv service pnt; shwrs inc; EHU (16A) €2; lndry; shop 1km; rest 1km; snacks; bar; lake sw 5km; 50% statics; dogs; phone; poss cr; Eng spkn; adv bkg rec bank hols; quiet; CKE/CCI. "Pleasantly situated, orchard site 6km fr Bodensee; friendly, helpful staff; female san facs inadequate; gd touring cent; gd local train service; excel cycle tracks." 1 Jan-15 Nov & 15 Dec-31 Dec. € 23.00 2016*

STOCKACH *3C4* (2.5km SW Urban) *47.84194, 8.99500* **Camping Papiermühle, Johann Glatt Strasse 3, 78333 Stockach [(07771) 9190490; fax 9190492; campingpark-stockach@web.de; www.campingpark-stockach-de.webnode.com]** Fr Stockach at junc rndabt of B31 & B313, turn L (E) to Caramobil C'van Sales Depot. Site adj under same management. Med, mkd pitch, some hdstg, pt sl, terr, pt shd; htd wc; chem disp; mv service pnt; shwrs inc; EHU (6A) €2; lndry (inc dryer); shop; rest adj; snacks; bar; BBQ; playgrnd; 50% statics; dogs €2.20; phone; bus 200m; poss cr; Eng spkn; adv bkg; quiet; ccard acc; CKE/CCI. "Sep m'van area adj; v clean facs; helpful staff; conv location for town; gd walking & cycling; vg site." ♦ 1 Mar-30 Nov. € 21.50 2016*

⊞ **STORKOW** *2G3* (6km NE Rural) *52.29194, 13.98638* **Campingplatz Waldsee, 15526 Reichenwalde-Kolpin [(033631) 5037; fax 59891; mail@campingplatz-waldsee.de; www.camping platz-waldsee.de]** Fr A12/E30, exit junc 3 Storkow. Just bef ent Storkow, turn N twd Fürstenwalde. In 6km turn R leaving Kolpin, site sp. Med, pt sl, pt shd; wc; chem disp; sauna; shwrs €0.50; EHU (16A) €2; lndry; shops 2km; rest 6km; rest 6km; snacks; bar; playgrnd; lake sw adj; bike hire; 60% statics; dogs €1; Eng spkn; adv bkg; quiet; ccard acc; red CKE/CCI. "Gd san facs; haphazard pitching; conv NH en rte to/fr Poland; gd cycling area; Bad Saarow lakeside worth visit; facs dated (2012); staff friendly." € 16.00 2012*

STUHR see Bremen *1C2*

⊞ **STUTTGART** *3D3* (5km E Urban) *48.79395, 9.21911* **Campingplatz Cannstatter Wasen, Mercedesstrasse 40, 70372 Stuttgart [(0711) 556696; fax 557454; info@campingplatz-stuttgart.de; www.campingplatz-stuttgart.de]** Fr B10 foll sp for stadium & Mercedes museum & then foll camping sp. Access poss diff when major events in park adj. Lge, all hdstg, pt shd; htd wc; chem disp; mv service pnt; serviced pitches; shwrs inc; EHU (16A) metered + conn fee; lndry; shop 1.5km; rest; BBQ; playgrnd; pool 2km; dogs €3; bus nr; stn 1.5km; poss v cr; Eng spkn; adv bkg; poss noise fr local stadium; ccard acc; CKE/CCI. "Helpful staff; clean san facs (2015); town cent best by train, tickets fr recep; cycle ride to town thro park; Mercedes museum 15 mins walk; fr Sep site/office open 0800-1000 & 1700-1900 only; site within low emission zone; camping field for tents." ♦ € 22.00 2016*

SULZBERG see Kempten (Allgäu) *3D4*

⊞ **SULZBURG** *3B4* (1.5km SE Rural) *47.83583, 7.72333* **Terrassen-Camping Alte Sägemühle, Badstrasse 57, 79295 Sulzburg [(07634) 551181; fax 551182; info@camping-alte-saegemuehle.de; www.camping-alte-saegemuehle.de]** Exit A5 junc 64a to Heitersheim & Sulzburg. Fr cent of Sulzburg, foll camp sps SE past timber yard on rd to Bad Sulzburg hotel. Sm, mkd pitch, terr, pt shd; htd wc; chem disp; mv service pnt; shwrs inc; EHU (16A) metered + conn fee; gas 1km; lndry; shop; rest, snacks, bar 1.5km; BBQ; lake sw adj; 10% statics; dogs €2; Eng spkn; quiet; 10% red CKE/CCI. "Excel san facs, poss long walk; v friendly, helpful owners site van with tractor; restful site in beautiful hilly countryside; gd walks, cycling." € 26.00 2016*

⊞ **SULZBURG** *3B4* (1km NW Rural) *47.84778, 7.69848* **Camping Sulzbachtal, Sonnmatt 4, 79295 Sulzburg [(07634) 592568; fax 592569; a-z@camping-sulzbachtal.de; www.camping-sulzbachtal.de]** Fr A5/E35 exit junc 64a Bad Krozingen onto L120/L123 dir Staufen-in-Breisgau. Cont on L125, site sp on L. Med, mkd pitch, hdstg, terr, pt shd; htd wc; chem disp; mv service pnt; 65% serviced pitches; fam bthrm; shwrs inc; EHU (16A) metered; lndry (inc dryer); shop 1km; snacks; rest 1km; playgrnd; pool; tennis; wifi; 10% statics; dogs €2.60; phone; m'van o'night facs; Eng spkn; adv bkg; quiet; ccard acc; red long stay/CKE/CCI. "Gd base for S Black Forest & Vosges; well laid-out site; clean facs; conv m'way; 45 mins to Basel; helpful, pleasant owners; ask about bus/train pass; high standards; well maintained; excel san facs; lge pitches; in wine growing area; excel walks." ♦ € 38.00 2014*

SYLT ISLAND *1C1* **Sites on Sylt Island are listed together at the end of the Germany site entry pages.**

⊞ **TENGEN** *3C4* (1km NW Rural) *47.82365, 8.65296* **Hegau Familien-Camping, An der Sonnenhalde 1, 78250 Tengen [(07736) 92470; fax 9247124; info@hegau-camping.de; www.hegau-camping.de]** Exit A81 junc 39 thro Engen dir Tengen, site sp. Lge, mkd pitch, hdstg, pt sl, pt shd; htd wc; chem disp; mv service pnt; serviced pitches; fam bthrm; sauna; shwrs inc; EHU (16A) metered or €2; gas; lndry (inc dryer); shop; supmkt 500m; rest, snacks; bar; playgrnd; htd, covrd pool; paddling pool; lake sw; canoeing; tennis adj; games area; games rm; bike hire; horseriding 2km; wifi; entmnt; 40% statics; dogs €4 inc dog shwr; bus 500m; clsd 1230-1430; o'night area for m'vans; Eng spkn; adv bkg; quiet; ccard acc; red long stay/LS/CKE/CCI. "Site of high standard; fairly isolated; gd family facs; excel; same price in hg ssn; beautifully maintained; well run; 1st rate pool complex; wonderful children's play facs; rec." ♦ € 42.00 2016*

⊞ **TIEFENSEE** *2G3* (1km E Rural) *52.68019, 13.85063* **Country-Camping Tiefensee, Schmiedeweg 1, 16259 Tiefensee [(033398) 90514; fax 86736; info@country-camping.de; www.country-camping.de]** Site sp fr B158 on lakeside. Lge, hdg/mkd pitch, pt shd; htd wc; chem disp; mv service pnt; sauna; fam bthrm; shwrs €0.50; EHU (16A) metered or €2.50; lndry (inc dryer); shop; rest, snacks; bar; BBQ; playgrnd; lake sw & beach adj (sep naturist area); fishing; games area; internet; TV; 75% statics; dogs €1.50; sep car park; o'night area for m'vans; clsd 1300-1500; poss cr; Eng spkn; adv bkg; quiet; ccard acc; red long stay. "Family-owned site; sep m'van pitches; gd cycling & walking; train to Berlin fr Arensfeldt; working ship lift at Niederfinow; vg." ♦ € 20.00 (CChq acc) 2012*

TITISEE NEUSTADT *3C4* (7km SW Rural) *47.88693, 8.13776* **Terrassencamping Sandbank, Seerundweg 9, 79822 Titisee-Neustadt [(07651) 8243 or 8166; fax 8286 or 88444; info@camping-sandbank.de; www.camping-sandbank.de]** Fr rte 31 Freiberg-Donauschingen turn S into Titisee. Fork R after car park on R, foll sp for Bruderhalde thro town. After youth hostel fork L & foll sp at T junc. Lge, mkd pitch, terr, mainly hdstg by lake; wc (htd); chem disp; mv service pnt; fam bthrm; shwrs €0.50; EHU (16A) €1.40; lndry; shop; rest, snacks; bar; playgrnd; lake sw; boating; bike hire; 50% statics; dogs €1.50; poss cr; Eng spkn; no adv bkg; quiet but some rlwy noise; ccard acc; red long stay/CKE/CCI. "Ltd touring pitches; steel pegs ess; clean, well-run, well laid-out site in gd position; terr gives gd lake views; helpful owner; gd welcome; larger pitches avail at extra cost; gd touring base for Black Forest; gd walks round lake; lakeside walk into town thru woods (approx 30 mins); ask for Konus card for free travel on local buses; clsd 1200-1400; excel; rd to site tarmaced." ♦ 1 Apr-18 Oct. € 25.50 2016*

⊞ **TITISEE NEUSTADT** *3C4* (7.6km SW Rural) *47.89516, 8.13789* **Camping Bühlhof, Bühlhofweg 13, 79822 Titisee-Neustadt [(07652) 1606 or (01713) 634160 (mob); fax 1827; info@camping-buehlhof.de; www.camping-buehlhof.de]** Take rd 31 out of Freiburg to Titisee; R fork on ent Titisee; bear R to side of lake, site on R after end of Titisee, up steep but surfaced hill, sharp bends. Lge, mkd pitch, pt sl, terr, pt shd; wc; chem disp; mv service pnt; serviced pitch; fam bthrm; shwrs €0.50; EHU (16A) €1.80; gas; lndry (inc dryer); rest 300m; BBQ; playgrnd; htd pool 1km; tennis; 300m fr Lake Titisee (but no access); watersports; wintersports area - ski lift 6km; boats for hire; horseriding; wifi; 30% statics; dogs €2.30; recep 0700-2200; site clsd Nov to mid-Dec; Eng spkn; quiet; ccard not acc; CKE/CCI. "Beautiful situation on hillside above Lake Titisee; lower terr gravel & 50% statics; top terr for tents & vans without elec; pitches sm; woodland walks; pleasant walk to town; gd san facs." € 25.50 2017*

TITISEE NEUSTADT *3C4* (8km SW Rural) *47.88996, 8.13273* **Natur-Campingplatz Weiherhof, Bruderhalde 26, 79822 Titisee-Neustadt [(07652) 1468; fax 1478; info@camping-titisee.de; www.camping-titisee.de]** Fr B31 Frieberg-Donaueschingen, turn S into Titisee & fork R after car park on R, foll sp Bruderhalde thro town. Site on L on lakeside. Lge, shd; htd wc; chem disp; shwrs inc; EHU (10A) €2.50; lndry; shop; rest, snacks; bar; playgrnd; pool 1km; lake sw adj; bike hire; golf 2km; 20% statics; dogs €2; phone; poss cr; quiet; CKE/CCI. "Site in woodland next to the lake; no mkd pitches but ample rm; vg; trip to town along lakeside well worth a visit." ♦ 1 May-15 Oct. € 23.00 2012*

⊞ **TITISEE NEUSTADT** *3C4* (8.6km SW Rural) *47.88633, 8.13055* **Camping Bankenhof, Bruderhalde 31a, 79822 Titisee-Neustadt [(07652) 1351; fax 5907; info@camping-bankenhof.de; www.camping-bankenhof.de]** Fr B31 Frieberg-Donaueschingen, turn S into Tittisee & fork R after car park on R, foll sp Bruderhalde thro town. In 2.5km fork L after youth hostel; foll sp to site in 200m. If app Titisee fr Donausechingen (B31) do not take Titisee P sp exit but exit with int'l camping sp only, then as above. Lge, mkd pitch, hdstg, pt shd; wc; chem disp; mv service pnt; fam bthrm; shwrs inc; EHU (10A) metered (poss rev pol); gas; lndry (inc dryer); shop; rest; bar; playgrnd; lake sw adj; bike hire; wifi; entmnt high ssn; boat-launching 200m; 20% statics; dogs €2.80 (free in m'van area); shwr inc; o'night area for m'vans €12; poss cr; Eng spkn; adv bkg; quiet; ccard acc; red CKE/CCI. "Gd walk to town & in forest; lovely scenery; helpful staff; vg san facs; excel rest; most pitches gravel; ask at recep for red/free tickets on public transport; excel, well-run, clean site, some pitches narr." ♦ € 28.00 2015*

TRABEN TRARBACH see Bernkastel Kues *3B2*

⊞ **TRAUNSTEIN** *4F4* (8km SW Rural) *47.81116, 12.5890* **Camping Wagnerhof, Campingstrasse 11, 83346 Bergen [(08662) 8557; fax 5924; info@camping-bergen.de; www.camping-bergen.de]** Exit A8/E52/E60 junc 110. On ent Bergen take 2nd R turn (sp). Med, mkd pitch, pt shd; wc; chem disp; mv service pnt; shwrs €0.50; EHU (16A) metered; lndry; shop on site & 500m; rest 400m; playgrnd; htd pool adj; shgl beach 10km; tennis; 30% statics; dogs €2; site clsd 1230-1500; some Eng spkn; adv bkg; quiet; debit & euro card acc; red long stay; CKE/CCI. "Excel, v clean, pleasant site in beautiful location; helpful owner; when not full owner tries to offer pitches with empty pitches adjoining; conv a'bahn; cable car to Hockfelln." € 22.00 2014*

GERMANY

⊞ **TRAVEMUNDE** *2E2* (4km SW Rural) *53.94196, 10.84417* **Camping Ivendorf, Frankenkrogweg 2, 23570 Ivendorf [(04502) 4865; fax 75516; mail@camping-travemuende.de; www.camping-travemuende.de]** Fr A1 exit junc 19 take B226 to Ivendorf, then B75 dir Travemünde, site well sp. Med, mkd pitch, pt shd; wc; chem disp; fam bthrm; shwrs inc; EHU €3.50 or metered; lndry (inc dryer); shop; rest 200m; playgrnd; pool 4km; 10% statics; dogs €2; train 2km; poss cr; CKE/CCI. "Sep disabled pitches; conv ferries to/fr Sweden; easy access to Lübeck, a beautiful city." ♦ € 23.00 2016*

TREIS KARDEN see Cochem *3B2*

TRIER *3B2* (2km SW Urban) *49.74385, 6.62523* **Camping Treviris, Luxemburgerstrasse 81, 54290 Trier [(0651) 8200911; fax 8200567; info@camping-treviris.de; www.camping-treviris.de]** On E side of Rv Mosel on A1/A603/B49/B51 cross to W side of rv on Konrad Adenauerbrücke. Cont in R lane & foll sp Koln/Aachen - Luxemburgerstrasse. In 500m turn R to site, site on R. Well sp fr W bank of rv. Med, mkd pitch, pt shd; wc; chem disp; mv service pnt; fam bthrm; shwrs (€1); EHU (10A) metered; lndry (inc dryer); shop 500m; rest, snacks; bar; BBQ; playgrnd; wifi; dogs €1.70; bus 200m; poss cr; site clsd 1-10 Jan; quiet; ccard acc; CKE/CCI. "Cycle/walk to town cent; m'van park adj open all yr - ltd facs; clean, modern, clean san facs; swipe card for all facs; elec pylon in cent of site; gd touring base; gd sh stay/NH; well placed." ♦ ltd. 18 Mar-30 Oct. € 24.00 2017*

TRIER *3B2* (8.4km SW Rural) *49.70460, 6.57398* **Camping Konz, Saarmünding, 54329 Konz [(06501) 2577; fax 947790; camping@campingplatz-konz.de; www.campingplatz-konz.de]** On B51 S of rv at rndabt just bef rv x-ing, go L & foll sp Camping Konz (not Konz-Könen). Do not go into Konz. Med, mkd pitch, pt shd; wc; mv service pnt; shwrs €1; EHU metered + conn fee; lndry rm; shops 500m; rest, snacks; playgrnd; watersports; dogs €0.70; Eng spkn; some rd noise. "Conv NH/sh stay for Trier - cycle rte or public transport; facs clean; poss flooding; sm pitches." 15 Mar-15 Oct. € 15.00 2014*

TRIER *3B2* (9km SW Rural) *49.70555, 6.55333* **Campingplatz Igel, Moselstrasse, 54298 Igel [(06501) 12944; fax 601931; info@camping-igel.de; www.camping-igel.de]** SW on A49 Luxembourg rd fr Trier; in cent of Ige vill, turn L by Sparkasse Bank, thro narr tunnel (3.6m max height); in 200m turn L along rv bank; site 300m on L; café serves as recep. Med, pt shd; htd wc; chem disp; mv service pnt; shwrs €1; EHU (6A) €2 (poss rev pol); lndry; shop in vill; rest; bar; playgrnd; fishing lakes adj; 90% statics (sep area); dogs €2; bus/train to Trier & Roman amphitheatre; poss cr; quiet but some noise fr rlwy & rv barges; CKE/CCI. "Excel, friendly, well-run site; immac san facs; gd rest; ltd touring pitches; rv bank foot & cycle path to Trier; conv Roman amphitheatre in Trier; close to Luxembourg border for cheap petrol; conv for bus into Trier." 1 Apr-31 Oct. € 24.50 2014*

⊞ **TRIER** *3B2* (15km W Rural) *49.75416, 6.50333* **Campingplatz Alter Bahnhof-Metzdorf, Uferstrasse 42, 54308 Langsur-Metzdorf [(06501) 12626; fax 13796; info@camping-metzdorf.de; www.camping-metzdorf.de]** Fr W leave A64/E44 junc 15 & foll sp Wasserbillig; at T-junc in Wasserbillig turn L onto B49 sp Trier. Ignore campsite in 500m. On ent Germany at end of bdge turn sharp L onto B418 sp Ralingen/Metternich. In 3km turn L sp Metzdorf; in 750m turn L, site in 750m. Fr N (Bitburg) join A64 at junc 3 sp Luxembourg, then as above. Fr SE on A1/E422 join A602 (Trier) & approx 1km past end of a'bahn turn R over Kaiser Wilhelm Bdge sp A64 Lux'bourg) & immed L at end of bdge. In 9km in Wasserbillig turn R under rlwy bdge & keep R on B418 sp Ralingen/Mesenich. In 3km turn L sp Melzdorf, in 750m turn L, site in 750m. Do not use sat nav if app fr the E. Med, pt sl, pt shd; htd wc; chem disp; mv service pnt; shwrs €0.50; EHU (6-16A) €2 or metered (10A); lndry; rest; bar; playgrnd; wifi; 75% statics; dogs €1; phone; bus 500m; m'van o'night €9; poss cr; Eng spkn; adv bkg; quiet; ccard not acc; red long stay/LS; CKE/CCI. "Rvside location; gd san facs but poss long walk & steep climb; cycle rte to Trier; vg NH." ♦ ltd. € 17.50 2015*

TRITTENHEIM *3B2* (4km N Urban) *49.84933, 6.89283* **Camping Neumagen-Dhron, Moselstrasse 100, 54347 Neumagen-Dhron [(06507) 5249; camping-neumagen@t-online.de; www.campingneumagen.de]** On B53 fr Trittenheim twd Piesport. Immed after x-ing rv turn R, then R again sp Neumagen. Site sp in vill on rvside. Med, mkd pitch, pt shd; wc; chem disp; fam bthrm; shwrs inc (timed); EHU (6A) metered + conn fee; lndry (inc dryer); shop; rest, snacks; bar; BBQ; playgrnd; fishing; boating; wifi; 40% statics; dogs free; phone adj; poss cr; adv bkg; quiet; CKE/CCI. "Gd; site clsd if rv in flood; marina adj; rvside park; excel site; interesting Roman town; poss noise fr adj rest; main san facs up 25 steps; Hot water 7am-9pm." ♦ ltd. 1 Apr-31 Oct. € 22.00 2017*

"Satellite navigation makes touring much easier"

Remember most sat navs don't know if you're towing or in a larger vehicle – always use yours alongside maps and site directions.

TRITTENHEIM *3B2* (400m E Urban) *49.82472, 6.90305* **Reisemobil/Wohnmobilstellplatz (Motorhome Camping), Am Moselufer, 54349 Trittenheim [(06507) 5331; info@trittenheim.de; www.trittenheim.de]** Fr Trier foll B53 dir Bernkastel Kues. Site sp in Trittenheim dir Neumagen-Dhron, on rvside. Sm, hdstg, pt sl, unshd; own san req; chem disp; mv service pnt; EHU (16A) €2.50; shop, rest, snacks nr; dogs; poss cr; quiet. "M'vans only; pleasant site poss clsd if rv floods; warden calls for payment." 1 Apr-31 Oct. € 5.00 2013*

Motorways
Major roads
Main roads
BALTIC
SEA
POLAND
CZECHIA
(CZECH REPUBLIC)
Spodsbjerg
Tårs
Rødbyhavn
FEHMARN
Wulfen
Dahme
Rerik
Bad Doberan
ROSTOCK
Travemünde
LÜBECK
Wismar
Schwaan
Retgendorf
SCHWERIN
Zingst am Darss
Pruchten
Altefähr
STRALSUND
Ribnitz-Damgarten
Altenkirchen
Lietzow
RÜGEN
Binz
Karlshagen
Swinoujście
NEUBRANDENBURG
Szczecin
Zislow
Neustrelitz
Feldberg
Malliss
Warnitz
Canow
Gartow
Gorzów Wielkopolski
Tiefensee
Brieselang
Kostrzyn
BERLIN
Wolfsburg
Potsdam
Brandenburg an der Havel
Colbitz
FRANKFURT AN DER ODER
Storkow
Swiebodzin
MAGDEBURG
Plötzky
Halberstadt
Wernigerode
Quedlinburg
Lutherstadt Wittenberg
LÜBBEN
Harzgerode
Neustadt
Seeburg
Kelbra
LEIPZIG
Ortrand
Kamenz
Niesky
Bolesławiec
Meissen
Moritzburg
Coswig
DRESDEN
Pirna
Zgorzelec
Bad Kösen
Colditz
Weimar
Jena
Mühlberg
Reinsberg
Bad Schandau
Zittau
Königstein
Chemnitz
Altenberg
Ústí nad Labem
Annaberg-Buchholz
N
W
E
S
© Collins Bartholomew Ltd 2018

Map 2

A
B
1
C
D
NETHERLANDS
Eindhoven
Dortmund
ESSEN
Hattingen
Grefrath
Brüggen
DÜSSELDORF
Solingen
Radevormwald
Hückeswagen
Meschede
Hannoversch Münden
Dransfeld
KASSEL
Witzenhausen
Naumburg (Hessen)
Eschwege
Spangenberg
Olpe
KÖLN
Maastricht
AACHEN
Liège
Nideggen
BONN
Bad Honnef
Simmerath
Monschau
Schleiden
Remagen
Bad Neuenahr-Ahrweiler
Waldbreitbach
Wissen
Marburg an der Lahn
Rotenburg an der Fulda
Alsfeld
KIRCHHEIM
Urnshausen
Hünfeld
Wetzlar
Grünberg
Weilburg
FULDA
Ehrenberg
BELGIUM
Mendig
Montabaur
Limburg an der Lahn
Gersfeld (Rhön)
KOBLENZ
BAD EMS
Lahnstein
Boppard
Prüm
Burgen
Daun
Cochem
Pfalzfeld
Waxweiler
Lingerhahn
Oberwesel
Lorch
Gräfendorf
Gemünden am Main
FRANKFURT AM MAIN
Neef
Zell
Kastellaun
Bitburg
Rüdesheim
Bingen
Schweppenhausen
Mörfelden
Brauneberg
Wintrich
Bernkastel-Kues
Trittenheim
Echternacherbrück
LUXEMBOURG
Schweich
TRIER
Bad Kreuznach
Marktheidenfeld
Wertheim
WÜRZBURG
Kitzingen
Frickenhausen am Main
Idar-Oberstein
LUXEMBOURG
Nennig
Saarburg
Nohfelden
Rockenhausen
Weinheim
Hammelbach
Mannheim
Bad Mergentheim
Uffenheim
Creglingen
Weikersheim
Saarlouis
Bad Dürkheim
Neustadt
HEIDELBERG
SAARBRÜCKEN
Kirkel
Zweibrücken
Speyer
Rothenburg ob der Tauber
Schillingsfürst
Pirmasens
Dahn
Landau in der Pfalz
Metz
Schwäbisch
Dinkelsbühl
KARLSRUHE
Löwenstein
Ettlingen
Malsch
Pforzheim
Schömberg
STUTTGART
Nancy
Rheinmünster
Bad Wildbad im Schwarzwald
Calw
Göppingen
Bühl
Strasbourg
Achern
ALTENSTEIG
Wildberg
Kehl
Tübingen
Hohenstadt
Freudenstadt
Bad Rippoldsau
Horb am Neckar
Bad Urach
Leipheim
Laichingen
Alpirsbach
Lahr (Schwarzwald)
Wolfach
Schiltach
Herbolzheim
FRANCE
Riegel am Kaiserstuhl
Illertissen
Breisach am Rhein
Hausen im Tal
Sigmaringen
FREIBURG IM BREISGAU
Titisee-Neustadt
Staufen im Breisgau
Münstertal
Donaueschingen
Sulzburg
Tengen
Stockach
Steinenstadt
Schönau im Schwarzwald
Überlingen
Ravensburg
Mulhouse
Radolfzell am Bodensee
Konstanz
Waldshut
Jestetten
Friedrichshafen
Basel
Kressbronn am Bodensee
Immenstadt im Allgäu
Lindau (Bodensee)
OBERSTDORF
Zürich
SWITZERLAND
Bludenz
0 20 40 60 80 100 kms
0 10 20 30 40 50 60 mls
N
W
E
S
All year site(s)
Seasonal site(s)
No sites listed
200m +
0–200m
© Collins Bartholomew Ltd 2018

Map 3

POLAND
CZECHIA
(CZECH REPUBLIC)
AUSTRIA
Neustadt
Seeburg
Torgau
Kelbra
LEIPZIG
Ortrand
Kamenz
Bautzen
Niesky
Boleslawiec
Weissensee
Colditz
Meissen
Moritzburg
Coswig
DRESDEN
Zgorzelec
Bad Kösen
ERFURT
Weimar
Jena
Reinsberg
Pirna
Bad Schandau
Zittau
Ohrdruf
Kranichfeld
Chemnitz
Königstein
Altenberg
Usti nad Labem
Plauen
Coburg
Hof
Karlovy Vary
Kulmbach
PRAHA
Mitterteich
Bamberg
BAYREUTH
Pottenstein
Plzen
Neustadt an der Waldnaab
Erlangen
Hersbruck
Hirschau
NÜRNBERG
Waldmünchen
Klatovy
Neumarkt in der Oberpfalz
Pielenhofen
REGENSBURG
Kinding
Finsterau
Bad Abbach
Ingolstadt
Neureichenau
Donauwörth
Eging am See
Nessibach
PASSAU
Landshut
Linz
Bad Füssing
MÜNCHEN
Diessen
Waging am See
Prien am Chiemsee
Seeshaupt
Traunstein
Rosenheim
Übersee
Salzburg
Murnau am Staffelsee
Bad Tölz
Inzell
Kochal am See
Reit im Winkl
Berchtesgaden
Oberammergau
Königssee
Füssen
Kufstein
Mittenwald
Innsbruck
Motorways
Major roads
Main roads
© Collins Bartholomew Ltd 2018

Map 4

Federal States of Germany

Balos bay Crete

Welcome to Greece

Whether you want to marvel at ancient ruins, lay on an idyllic sandy beach or sample local dishes, Greece is undoubtedly the place to be.

From rugged hillsides to the sparkling blue waters of the Mediterranean, this is a country steeped in myths of gods and heroes. The country is also famed for the friendly and hospitable nature of its people, so you're sure to receive a warm welcome.

Country highlights

Music is an integral part of Greek society and laïkó is a modern folk music genre that boomed in the 1960s and 70s. There are now many different forms of this music and often generally refers to Greek popular music, but it still retains a sense of being a song of the people.

Greece can be considered the birthplace of wine, and the origins of wine-making in Greece go back well over 6000 years. Although not as well-known as other European nations for its wine, Greece has a thriving industry and the local varieties pair up well with food dishes from the same area.

Major towns and cities

- Athens – the cradle of Western civilization and one of the world's oldest cities.
- Thessalonika – a charming city filled with museums to explore.
- Patras – this amazing city is home to fascinating sites from ancient times.
- Larissa – surrounded by mountains and home to several ancient sites.

Attractions

- The Acropolis, Athens – an ancient citadel containing the Parthenon and other ruins.
- Meteora – stunning monasteries built on natural sandstone pillars.
- Delphi – this site boasts some of Greece's most important ancient ruins.
- Cape Sounion – fantastic views over the Aegean and the ruins of an ancient temple.

Find out more

www.visitgreece.gr
Tel: 0030 (0) 21 03 31 05 29 Greece Tourist Board

GREECE

Country Information

Population (approx): 10.8 million

Capital: Athens

Area: 131,957 sq km

Bordered by: Albania, Bulgaria, Macedonia, Turkey

Coastline: 13,676km

Terrain: Mainly mountain ranges extending into the sea as peninsulas and chains of islands

Climate: Warm Mediterranean climate; hot, dry summers; mild, wet winters in the south, colder in the north; rainy season November to March; winter temperatures can be severe in the mountains

Highest Point: Mount Olympus 2,919m

Language: Greek

Local Time: GMT or BST + 2, i.e. 2 hours ahead of the UK all year

Currency: Euros divided into 100 cents; £1 = €1.13, €1 = £0.88 (November 2017)

Emergency numbers: Police 100; Fire brigade 199; Ambulance 166. Operators speak English. Dial 171 for emergency tourist police.

Public Holidays 2018: Jan 1, 6; Feb 19; Mar 25; Apr 6, 8, 9; May 1, 27, 28; Aug 15; Oct 28; Dec 25, 26.

School summer holidays run from the beginning of July to the first week in September.

Camping and Caravanning

There are over 340 campsites licensed by the Greek National Tourist Office. These can be recognised by a sign displaying the organisation's blue emblem. Most are open from April until the end of October, but those near popular tourist areas stay open all year. There are other unlicensed sites but visitors to them cannot be assured of safe water treatment, fire prevention measures or swimming pool inspection.

Casual/wild camping is not allowed outside official sites in Greece.

Electricity and Gas

Usually current on campsites varies between 4 and 16 amps. Plugs have two round pins. There are few CEE connections.

The full range of Campingaz cylinders are available from hypermarkets and other shops, but when purchasing a cylinder you may not be given a refundable deposit receipt.

Entry Formalities

Visas are not required by British or Irish passport holders for a stay of up to three months. Visitors planning to stay longer should contact the Greek Embassy in London before they travel www.greekembassy.org.uk.

Medical Services

For minor complaints seek help at a pharmacy (farmakio). Staff are generally well trained and in major cities there is usually one member of staff in a pharmacy who speaks English. You should have no difficulty finding an English speaking doctor in large towns and resorts.

Medications containing codeine are restricted. If you are taking any medication containing it, you should carry a letter from your doctor and take no more than one month's supply into the country.

There are numerous public and private hospitals and medical centres of varying standards. Wards may be crowded and the standards of nursing and after care, particularly in the public health sector, are generally below what is normally acceptable in Britain. Doctors and facilities are generally good on the mainland, but may be limited on the islands. The public ambulance service will normally respond to any accident but there are severe shortages of ambulances on some islands.

Emergency treatment at public medical clinics (yiatria) and in state hospitals registered by the Greek Social Security Institute, IKA-ETAM, is free on presentation of a European Health Insurance Card (EHIC) but you may face a long wait. You will be charged for prescriptions so keep the adhesive labels from the medicines packages in order to claim a refund at an IKA-ETAM office. See www.ika.gr for a list of local offices.

You may consult a doctor or dentist privately but you will have to present your EHIC and pay all charges up front. You can then claim back the charges later from the IKA-ETAM.

If staying near a beach, ensure that you have plenty of insect repellent as sand flies are prevalent. Do not be tempted to befriend stray dogs as they often harbour diseases which may be passed to humans.

Opening Hours

Banks: Mon-Fri 8am-2pm (1.30pm on Friday); 8am-6pm in tourist areas.

Museums: Check locally for opening hours. Normally closed on Mon or Tues and some bank holidays.

Post Offices: Mon-Fri 8am-2pm; 8am-7pm in tourist areas; many in Athens open Sat mornings in summer.

Shops: Mon-Fri 8am/8.30am/9am-2pm/4.30pm & on some days 5pm-8.30pm; Sat 8.30am-3pm; check locally as hours vary according to season.

Safety and Security

Normally visits to Greece are trouble-free, but the tourist season results in an increase in incidents of theft of passports, wallets, handbags, etc, particularly in areas or at events where crowds gather.

Take care when visiting well-known historical sites; they are the favoured haunts of pickpockets, bag-snatchers and muggers. Women should not walk alone at night and lone visitors are strongly advised never to accept lifts from strangers or passing acquaintances at any time.

Since banking services were restricted in 2015, the FCO has recommended that you take enough cash to cover your needs while you are in Greece. If you are carrying large amounts of cash, make sure you take safety precautions. Be aware that tourists are expected to be carrying larger amounts of money, making them potential targets for thieves.

Multi-lingual tourist police are available in most resorts offering information and help; they can be recognised by a 'Tourist Police' badge, together with a white cap band. There is also a 24-hour emergency helpline for tourists; dial 171 from anywhere in Greece.

Certain areas near the Greek borders are militarily sensitive and you should not take photographs or take notes near military or official installations. Seek permission before photographing individuals.

There is a general threat from domestic terrorism. Attacks could be indiscriminate and against civilian targets in public places. Public protests are a standard feature of Greek politics and it is wise to avoid public gatherings and demonstrations. Domestic anarchist groups remain active but their actions are primarily directed against the Greek state.

During especially hot and dry periods there is a danger of forest fires. Take care when visiting or driving through woodland areas. Ensure that cigarette ends are properly extinguished, do not light barbecues and do not leave rubbish or empty bottles behind.

Some motorists have encountered stowaway attempts while waiting to board ferries to Italy from Patras. Keep a watch on your vehicle(s).

In order to comply with the law, always ensure that you obtain a receipt for goods purchased. If you buy pirate CDs or DVDs you could be penalised heavily.

British Embassy

1 PLOUTARCHOU STREET
106 75 ATHENS
Tel: (210) 7272600
www.ukingreece.fco.gov.uk
There are also British Consulates/Vice-Consulates/Honorary Consulates in Corfu, Heraklion (Crete), Rhodes and Zakynthos.

Irish Embassy

7 LEOF.VAS
KONSTANTINOU, 106 74 ATHENA
Tel: (210) 7232771
www.embassyofireland.gr
There are also Honorary Consulates in Corfu, Crete, Rhodes and Thessaloniki.

Border Posts

Borders may be crossed only on official routes where a Customs office is situated. These are usually open day and night. Customs offices at ports are open from 7.30am to 3pm Monday to Friday.

Documents

Passport

Carry your passport at all times as a means of identification.

Vehicle(s)

Carry your vehicle registration certificate (V5C), insurance certificate and MOT certificate (if applicable) at all times.

Money

Major credit cards are accepted in hotels, restaurants and shops and at some petrol stations. They may not be accepted at shops in small towns or villages. There is an extensive network of cash machines in major cities.

Carry your credit card issuers'/banks' 24-hour UK contact numbers in case of loss or theft.

Motoring in Greece

Accidents

It is not essential to call the police in the case of an accident causing material damage only, however motorists are advised to call at the nearest police station to give a description of the incident to the authorities.

Whenever an accident causes physical injury, drivers are required to stop immediately to give assistance to the injured and to call the police. Drivers who fail to meet these requirements are liable to imprisonment for up to three years.

If a visiting motorist has an accident, especially one causing injuries, they should inform the motoring organisation, ELPA, preferably at its head office in Athens, on (210) 6068800, email: info@elpa.gr, as they should be able to offer you assistance.

Alcohol

The maximum permitted level of alcohol is 50 milligrams in 100 millilitres of blood, i.e. lower than that permitted in the UK (80 milligrams). A level of 20 milligrams in 100 millilitres of blood applies to drivers who have held a driving licence for less than two years and to motorcyclists. Police carry out random breath tests and refusal to take a test when asked by the police, and/or driving while over the legal limit, can incur high fines, withdrawal of your driving licence and even imprisonment.

Breakdown Service

The Automobile & Touring Club of Greece (ELPA) operates a roadside assistance service (OVELPA) 24 hours a day on all mainland Greek roads as well as on most islands. The number to dial from most towns in Greece is 10400.

Members of AIT/FIA affiliated clubs, such as The Caravan and Motorhome Club, should present their valid membership card in order to qualify for reduced charges for on-the-spot assistance and towing. Payment by credit card is accepted.

Essential Equipment

First Aid Kit

All vehicles must carry a first aid kit.

Fire Extinguisher

All vehicles must carry a fire extinguisher.

Warning Triangles

The placing of a warning triangle is compulsory in the event of an accident or a breakdown. It must be placed 100 metres behind the vehicle.

Child Restraint System

Children under three years of age must be seated in a suitable and approved child restraint. Children between the ages of 3 and 11 years old that are less than 1.35 metres in height must be seated in an appropriate child restraint for their size. From 12 years old children that are over 1.35 metres in height can wear an adult seat belt.

A rear facing child restraint can be placed in the front seat but only if the airbag is deactivated.

Fuel

Petrol stations are usually open from 7am to 7pm; a few are open 24 hours. Some will accept credit cards but those offering cut-price fuel are unlikely to do so. In rural areas petrol stations may close in the evening and at weekends, so keep your tank topped up. There are no automatic petrol pumps operated with either credit cards or bank notes.

LPG (autogas) is available from a limited number of outlets.

Parking

Parking is only permitted in the Athens 'Green Zone' where there are parking meters. Special parking sites in other areas are reserved for short-term parking for tourists.

There may be signs on the side of the road indicating where vehicles should be parked. Parking restrictions are indicated by yellow lines at the side of the road. The police are entitled to remove vehicles. They can also confiscate the number plates of vehicles parked illegally and, while this usually applies only to Greek-registered vehicles, drivers of foreign registered vehicles should nevertheless avoid illegal parking.

Parking is not permitted within three metres of a fire hydrant, five metres of an intersection, stop sign or traffic light, and fifteen metres of a bus stop, tram stop and level crossings.

Roads

The surfaces of all major roads and of the majority of other roads are in good condition. Some mountain roads, however, may be in poor condition and drivers must beware of unexpected potholes (especially on corners), precipitous, unguarded drops and single-carriageway bridges. Even on narrow mountain roads you may well encounter buses and coaches.

British motorists visiting Greece should be extra vigilant in view of the high incidence of road accidents. Driving standards are generally poorer than in the UK and you may well have to contend with dangerous overtaking, tailgating, weaving motorcycles and scooters, constant use of the horn, roaming pedestrians and generally erratic driving. Greece has one of the highest rate of road fatalities in Europe and overtaking and speeding are common causes of accidents, particularly on single lane carriageways. Drive carefully and be aware of other drivers at all times.

August is the busiest month of the year for traffic and the A1/E75 between Athens and Thessalonika is recognised as one of the most dangerous routes, together with the road running through the Erimanthos mountains south of Kalavrita. Mountain roads in general can be dangerous owing to narrow carriageways, blind bends and unprotected embankments, so keep your speed down.

You are strongly advised against hiring motorcycles, scooters and mopeds, as drivers of these modes of transport are particularly at risk. The wearing of crash helmets is a legal requirement. Never hand over your passport when hiring a vehicle.

Greece has a high level of pedestrian fatalities. Where there is a shortage of parking spaces drivers park on pavements so that pedestrians are forced to walk in the road. Collisions between pedestrians and motorcycles are common.

Road Signs and Markings

Road signs conform to international conventions. Motorway signs have white lettering on a green background, signs on other roads are on a blue background. All motorways, major and secondary roads are signposted in Greek and English.

Some open roads have a white line on the nearside, and slower-moving vehicles are expected to pull across it to allow vehicles to overtake.

Traffic Jams

There is heavy rush hour traffic in and around the major cities and traffic jams are the norm in central Athens any time of day. During the summer months traffic to the coast may be heavy, particularly at weekends. Traffic jams may be encountered on the A1/E75 Athens to Thessalonika road and on the A8/E65 Athens to Patras road. Traffic may also be heavy near the ferry terminals to Italy and you should allow plenty of time when travelling to catch a ferry. Delays can be expected at border crossings to Turkey and Bulgaria.

Speed Limits

	Open Road (km/h)	Motorway (km/h)
Car Solo	90-110	130
Car towing caravan/trailer	80	80
Motorhome under 3500kg	80	90
Motorhome 3500-7500kg	80	80

Violation of Traffic Regulations

The Greek police are authorised to impose fines in cases of violation of traffic regulations, but they are not allowed to collect fines on the spot. Motorists must pay fines within ten days, otherwise legal proceedings will be started.

Motorways

There are over 2,000 km of motorways in Greece. Service areas provide petrol, a cafeteria and shops. The main motorways are A1 Agean, A2 Egnatia, A6 Attiki, A7 Peloponissos, A8 Pathe, A29 Kastorias. For further information visit www.greek-motorway.net.

Motorway Tolls

Tolls are charged according to vehicle classification and distance travelled. By European standards the tolls are generally quite low. Cash is the preferred means of payment.

The Egnatia Highway

The 804 km Egnatia Highway (the A2), part of European route E90 linking the port of Igoumenitsa with the Turkish border at Kipoi, has undergone extensive upgrade and improvement in recent years. The route includes many bridges and tunnels with frequent emergency telephones for which the number to call from a landline or mobile phone is 1077. The road provides a continuous high speed link from west to east and will eventually connect with Istanbul. An electronic toll collection system is planned for the future.

Patras – Antirrio Bridge

A 2.8 km long toll suspension bridge between Rio (near Patras) and Antirrio links the Peloponnese with western central Greece and is part of the A8/E55 motorway. It has cut the journey time across the Gulf of Corinth – formerly only possible by ferry – to just five minutes. Tolls are charged.

Preveza – Aktio Tunnel

This undersea toll tunnel links Preveza with Aktio near Agios Nikolaos on the E55 along the west coast of mainland Greece and is part of a relatively fast, scenic route south from Igoumenitsa to central and southern regions.

Touring

Mainland Greece and most of the Greek islands that are popular with British tourists are in seismically active zones, and small earth tremors are common. Serious earthquakes are less frequent but can, and do, occur.

Smoking is prohibited in bars and restaurants. In restaurants, if the bill does not include a service charge, it is usual to leave a 10 to 20% tip. Taxi drivers do not normally expect a tip but it is customary to round up the fare.

The best known local wine is retsina but there is also a wide range of non-resinated wines. Beer is brewed under licence from German and Danish breweries; Ouzo is a popular and strong aniseed-flavoured aperitif.

The major Greek ports are Corfu, Igoumenitsa, Patras, Piraeus and Rhodes. Ferry services link these ports with Cyprus, Israel, Italy and Turkey. The routes from Ancona and Venice in Italy to Patras and Igoumenitsa are very popular and advance booking is recommended.

For further information contact:

VIAMARE LTD
SUITE 108
582 Honeypot Lane
STANMORE
MIDDX
HA7 1JY
Tel: 020 8206 3420,
www.viamare.com
Email: ferries@viamare.com

Some ferries on routes from Italy to Greece have 'camping on board' facilities whereby passengers are able to sleep in their caravan or motorhome. Mains hook-ups are available, together with showers and toilets.

There are several World Heritage Sites in Greece (with more under consideration), including such famous sites as the Acropolis in Athens, the archaeological sites at Olympia and Mistras, and the old towns of Corfu and Rhodes.
See www.worldheritagesite.org for more information. When visiting churches and monasteries dress conservatively, i.e. long trousers for men and no shorts, sleeveless T-shirts or short skirts for women.

Public Transport

Greece has a modern, integrated public transport system, including an extensive metro, bus, tram and suburban railway network in and around Athens – see www.ametro.gr for a metro map.

A metro system is under construction in Thessaloniki that is not due for completion until 2018.

Buy bus/tram tickets from special booths at bus stops, newspaper kiosks or from metro stations. A ticket is valid for a travel time of 90 minutes.

Taxis are relatively cheap. All licensed taxis are yellow and are equipped with meters (the fare is charged per kilometre) and display a card detailing tariffs and surcharges. In certain tourist areas, you may be asked to pay a predetermined (standard) amount for a ride to a specific destination.

Taxis run on a share basis, so they often pick up other passengers on the journey.

There are many ferry and hydrofoil services from Piraeus to the Greek islands and between islands.

Amphitheater of the Acropolis of Athens

Sites in Greece

AGIOS KONSTANTINOS see Kamena Vourla *B2*

⊞ **ALEXANDROUPOLI** *C1* (2km W Coastal) *40.84679, 25.85614* **Camping Alexandroupolis Beach, Makris Ave, 68100 Alexandroupolis [tel/fax (25510) 28735; camping@ditea.gr; www.ditea.gr]** Site on coast - after drainage channel, at 2nd set traff lts close together. Lge, hdg/mkd pitch, pt hdstg, shd; wc (some cont); chem disp; shwrs inc; EHU (8A) €3.60; gas; shop; snacks; bar; playgrnd; sand beach adj; watersports; tennis; games area; wifi; 20% statics; phone; Eng spkn; quiet but cr & noisy high ssn; red CKE/CCI. "Spacious, secure, well-run site; clean, hot shwrs; easy walk to pleasant town cent." € 18.50 2016*

ALISSOS see Patra *A2*

ANTIRRIO see Nafpaktos *B2*

ASSINI see Nafplio *B3*

ATHENS see Athina *B3*

⊞ **ATHINA** *B3* (17km NE Urban) *38.09944, 23.79166* **Camping Nea Kifissia, Potamou 60, Adames, 14564 Athina [tel/fax (210) 8075579 or 6205646; camping@hol.gr; www.camping-neakifissia.gr]** Sp both dirs on E75 Athens-Lamia rd. Heading twd Athens exit at sp, to U-turn onto service rd then take 1st L & foll sp. Sm, hdg pitch, hdstg, terr, shd; wc; chem disp; shwrs inc; EHU (10A) €4; lndry rm; shop 800m; pool high ssn; TV; 50% statics; dogs; phone; bus to metro stn 200m; poss cr; Eng spkn; aircraft, rlwy & rd noise; red CCI. "Conv base for Athens - metro at Kifissia; pleasant, quiet, well-run site; excel pool; clean san facs but tired; helpful recep staff; san facs down 30+ steps." € 33.00 2015*

⊞ **ATHINA** *B3* (7km NW Urban) *38.00916, 23.67236* **Camping Athens, 198-200 Athinon Ave, 12136 Athens [(210) 5814114 or 5814101 winter; fax 5820353; info@campingathens.com.gr; www.campingathens.com.gr]** Fr Corinth on E94 m'way/highway, stay on this rd to Athens o'skts; site is approx 4km past Dafni Monastery, set back on L of multi-lane rd, sh dist beyond end of underpass. Go past site to next traff lts where U-turn permitted. Fr N use old national rd (junc 8 if on toll m'way). Med, pt shd; wc (some cont); chem disp; mv service pnt; shwrs inc; EHU (16A) €4; lndry; shop, rest high ssn; snacks; bar; internet; TV; dogs; frequent bus to Athens; poss v cr; rd noise; ccard acc; red LS. "V dusty but well-managed site; gd san facs but poss insufficient high ssn; helpful staff; bus tickets to Athens sold; visitors rec not to use sat nav to find site, as it misdirects!" € 42.00 2013*

CHRISSA see Delfi *B2*

CORINTH see Korinthos *B3*

⊞ **DELFI** *B2* (2km W Rural) *38.4836, 22.4755* **Camping Apollon, 33054 Delfi [(22650) 82762 or 82750; fax 82888; apollon4@otenet.gr; www.apolloncamping.gr]** Site on N48 fr Delfi twd Itea & 1st of number of campsites on this rd. Site 25km fr Parnassus ski cent. Med, mkd pitch, pt sl, pt terr, pt shd; wc; chem disp; mv service pnt; shwrs inc; EHU (16A) €3; gas; lndry; shop; rest; bar; playgrnd; pool; TV; bike hire; 30% statics; dogs free; phone; Harmonie Group site; poss cr; adv bkg; ccard acc; red CKE/CCI. "Magnificent views over mountains & Gulf of Corinth; site cooler than some other sites due to its elevation; vg site; popular with groups of students; vg campsite." ♦ € 30.00 2015*

DELFI *B2* (5km W Rural) *38.47868, 22.47461* **Camping Delphi, Itea Road, 33054 Delfi [(22650) 82209; fax 82363; info@delphicamping.com; www.delphicamping.com]** App fr Itea-Amfissa rd or Levadia; well sp. Med, terr, shd; wc; chem disp; mv service pnt; shwrs inc; EHU (16A) €3.90; gas; lndry; shop, rest, snacks high ssn; bar; pool; tennis; wifi; TV; dogs free; phone; bus to Delfi; Sunshine Group site; poss cr; adv bkg; ccard acc; red CKE/CCI. "Visit grotto, refuge of Parnassus; Delfi archaeological sites 3km; friendly, helpful staff; magnificent views; gd pool; tired facs; 20% discount for Minoan Line ticketholders; delightful site; san facs bit tired but clean & tidy; excel site." 1 Apr-31 Oct. € 25.00 2014*

⊞ **DELFI** *B2* (8.5km W Rural) *38.47305, 22.45926* **Chrissa Camping, 33055 Chrissa [(22650) 82050; fax 83148; info@chrissacamping.gr; www.chrissacamping.gr]** 1st site on Itea to Delfi rd, sp. Med, pt sl, terr, shd; wc; chem disp; shwrs inc; EHU (10A) €4 first 4KWh/day then metered; gas; lndry; shop; rest, snacks; bar; playgrnd; pools; paddling pool; shgl beach 10km; tennis 300m; games area; wifi; TV rm; adv bkg; quiet; ccard acc; red CKE/CCI. "Excel, scenic site." € 21.50 (CChq acc) 2017*

DREPANO see Nafplio *B3*

⊞ **DREPANO** *B3* (12km E Coastal) *37.49710, 22.99028* **Iria Beach Camping, Iria Beach 21100, Nafplio [tel/fax 02 75 20 94 253; iriabeach@naf.forthnet.gr; www.iriabeach.com]** Fr Drepano head E on Epar. Od. Drepanou-Kantias. Cont onto Kantias-Irion. 800m after Iria Beach Hotel turn R. Site on L after 1.5km. Med, hdstg, shd; wc; chem disp; mv service pnt; fam bthrm; shwrs; EHU (16A); lndry; shop; snacks; bar; BBQ; cooking facs; pool; beach adj; wifi; TV; 5% statics; dogs; twin axles; Eng spkn; adv bkg; quiet; CCI. "Opp beach; gd sw; site quiet & relaxing; helpful staff; vg site." ♦ ltd. € 33.50 2014*

EGIO *B2* (13km NW Coastal) *38.32078, 21.97195* **soli's Camping, Lambíri Egion, 25100 Lambiri (26910) 31469 or 31621; fax 32473]** Fr Athens: A8/ 65 exit Kamaras, site clearly sp 1km W of Lambiri. r Patras: Leave A8/E65 at exit Longos, take the Old Nat. On L in 1.5km after Lampiri. Med, hdstg, shd; wc; hem disp; shwrs inc; EHU (16A) inc; gas; lndry; shop; est high ssn; snacks; bar; BBQ; playgrnd; shgl beach dj; watersports; fishing; boat-launching; entmnt; TV; 0% statics; dogs; phone; bus; sep car park; Eng spkn; dv bkg; some rd & rlwy noise & noise fr bar; ccard acc; ed LS; CKE/CCI. "Bus & train service to Athens & atras; gd site with gd facs in delightful position; few hd pitches for tourers & poss diff for high o'fits." 24.00 2015*

FINIKOUNDAS *A3* (1km W Coastal) *36.80555, 1.79583* **Camping Thines, 24006 Finikoundas (27230) 71200; fax 71027; thines@otenet.gr; www. inikounda.com]** Fr Methoni dir Finikoundas, turn R km bef vill, site on L. Sm, hdg/mkd pitch, hdstg, pt hd; wc; chem disp; shwrs inc; EHU (6-10A); gas; lndry; hop & 1km; snacks; bar; BBQ; cooking facs; sand each adj; boat-launching; wifi; TV; dogs; poss cr; Eng pkn; quiet; ccard acc; red winter long stay; CKE/CCI. Excel facs; helpful, friendly management; wonderful cenery & beach; lovely vill in walking dist; beautiful ite." ♦ € 26.50 (CChq acc) 2015*

ERAKINI *B2* (3km SE Coastal) *40.26464, 23.46338* **amping Kouyoni, 63100 Gerakini [tel/fax (23710) 2226; info@kouyoni.gr; www.kouyoni.gr]** ake main rd S fr Thessaloniki to Nea Moudania, then urn E twd Sithonia. Site is 18km on that rd past erakini on R, past filling stn. Well sp. Med, hdg/mkd itch, pt sl, shd; wc; chem disp; shwrs inc; EHU (16A) 3.30; lndry; shop & 1km; rest, snacks; bar; BBQ; laygrnd; pool; paddling pool; sand beach adj; games rea; boat-launching; TV rm; wifi; 30% statics; dogs; hone; adv bkg; quiet; red long stay/CKE/CCI. "Gd ouring base set in olive grove; friendly owner; gd facs; d beach; influx of w/enders high ssn." 1 May-30 Sep. 29.00 2016*

IALOVA see Pylos *A3*

IANNITSOCHORI see Kyparissia *A3*

ITHIO *B3* (5km SSW Coastal) *36.73055, 22.55305* **amping Meltemi, Mavrovouni Gytheio Lakonias 3200 [(02733) 023260; fax 023833; info@ ampingmeltemi.gr; www.campingmeltemi.gr]** ite is approx 3km S of Githio on the L of the rd to reopoli. Lge, mkd pitch, shd; wc; chem disp; mv ervice pnt; shwrs; EHU (16A); lndry; shop; rest; nacks; BBQ; cooking facs; playgrnd; pool, waterslide; each 20m; games area; wifi; TV; dogs; phone; twin xles; Eng spkn; adv bkg; red LS; CKE/CCI. "Beach olleyball, tennis, table tennis & basketball court; vg." Apr-31 Oct. € 26.00 2015*

REEK ISLANDS Campsites in towns on Greek slands are listed together at the end of the Greek ite entries.

IGOUMENITSA *A2* (10km S Coastal) *39.46346, 20.26037* **Camping Elena's Beach, 46100 Plataria [(26650) 71031; fax 71414; bteo@altecnet.gr or info@campingelena.gr; www.epirus.com/ campingelena]** Sp on Igoumenitsa-Preveza rd, 2km NW of Plataria. Med, hdstg, pt terr, pt shd; wc; chem disp; shwrs inc; EHU (5A) inc; gas; lndry; shop; rest, snacks; bar; BBQ; playgrnd; shgl beach adj; a few statics; dogs; phone; bus; adv bkg; quiet; red long stay; CKE/CCI. "Well-maintained, family-run, friendly site; clean, modern san facs; beautiful location with pitches next to sea; excel rest; conv ferries Corfu, Paxos." ♦ 1 Apr-31 Oct. € 33.50 2014*

IGOUMENITSA *A2* (5km W Coastal) *39.51014, 20.22133* **Camping Drepanos, Beach Drepanos, 46100 Igoumenitsa [tel/fax (26650) 26980; camping@drepano.gr; www.drepano.gr]** Fr Igoumenitsa take coast rd N. Foll sp for Drepanos Beach. Fr either port turn L and head N up coast. Med, hdstg, pl sl, pt shd; wc, some cont; chem disp; mv service pnt; shwrs inc; gas 4km; lndry; shop 2km; rest; snacks; bar; BBQ; playgrnd; sandy beach; wifi; 10% statics; dogs; bus adj; twin axles; poss cr; Eng spkn; adv bkg; CKE/CCI. "Beside nature reserve; amazing sunsets; friendly; dated san facs; attractive walks/cycle; vg." € 26.50 2016*

"There aren't many sites open at this time of year"

If you're travelling outside peak season remember to call ahead to check site opening dates – even if the entry says 'open all year'.

IOANINA *A2* (2km NW Urban) *39.67799, 20.84279* **Camping Limnopoula, Kanari 10, 45000 Ioanina [(26510) 25265; fax 38060]** At Ioanina Nautical Club on Igoumenitsa rd at W o'skts of town on rd that runs along lake fr citadel; site well sp fr all dirs. Med, pt shd; wc; chem disp; shwrs inc; EHU (10A) inc; gas; lndry; shop; rest, snacks, bar adj; BBQ; playgrnd; watersports; dogs free; phone; Eng spkn; quiet. "Beautiful situation on lake, mountain views; excel touring base; helpful staff; gd facs; clean; may close earlier; adv bkg acc 1-2 days ahead only LS; popular with groups LS; vg." 1 Apr-15 Oct. € 27.00 2015*

KALAMBAKA *A2* (4km SE Rural) *39.68250, 21.65510* **Camping Philoxenia, 42200 Kalambaka [(24320) 24466; fax 24944; philoxeniacamp@ath.forthnet.gr]** Site on N side of E92 Trikala rd, behind barrier. Med, some hdstg, shd; htd wc; chem disp; mv service pnt; shwrs inc; EHU (6A) inc; gas; lndry; shop; rest 1km; snacks; bar; BBQ; cooking facs; playgrnd; pool; paddling pool; waterslide; bike hire; TV; 30% statics; dogs free; poss cr; Eng spkn; adv bkg; quiet; ccard acc; red CKE/ CCI. "Interesting area esp during Easter religious festivals; Still open 2016 but call bef travelling" ♦ ltd. 1 Mar-30 Nov. € 20.00 (CChq acc) 2017*

⊞ **KALAMBAKA** *A2* (2km NW Rural) *39.71315, 21.61588* **Camping Vrachos, Meteoron Street, 42200 Kastraki [(24320) 22293; fax 23134; tsourvaka@yahoo.gr; www.campingkastraki.com]** Fr cent of Kalambaka take rd at app to vill of Kastraki. Site is 2km N of E92. Med, hdg/mkd pitch, hdstg, pt sl, terr, pt shd; wc; chem disp; mv service pnt; fam bthrm; shwrs inc; EHU (16A) inc; gas; lndry; shop; rest, snacks; bar; BBQ; cooking facs; playgrnd; htd pool; TV; internet (ltd); wifi; dogs free; phone; bus adj, train 1km; twin axles; poss cr; Eng spkn; adv bkg; quiet; Harmonie Group site; red CKE/CCI. "V friendly management; clean san facs; vg views fr some pitches; ltd facs open in winter; conv for monasteries, tour bus fr camp." ♦ € 19.00 2017*

KALIVIA VARIKOU see Plaka Litohorou *B2*

KARDAMILI see Stoupa *B3*

KASTRAKI see Kalambaka *A2*

KATO ALISSOS see Patra *A2*

KATO GATZEA see Volos *B2*

⊞ **KAVALA** *C1* (4km SW Urban/Coastal) *40.91573, 24.37851* **Camping Multiplex Batis, 65000 Kavala [(2510) 245918; nfo@batis-sa.gr; www.batis-sa.gr]** On W app to town on old coast rd, ent on a curving hill. Med, hdg/mkd pitch, pt sl, shd; htd wc; chem disp; shwrs inc; EHU (6A) €4; lndry rm; shop; rest, snacks; bar; pool; paddling pool; sand beach adj; entmnt; phone; bus; poss cr; Eng spkn; adv bkg; ccard acc; red CKE/CCI. "Beautiful location but v developed; conv ferry to Thassos & archaeological sites; clean facs but site poss unkempt LS; vg." ♦ € 26.00 2016*

KORINTHOS *B3* (7km W Coastal/Urban) *37.93470, 22.86543* **Blue Dolphin Camping, 20011 Lecheon Korinth [(27410) 25766 or 25767; fax 85959; info@camping-blue-dolphin.gr; www.camping-blue-dolphin.gr]** Best app fr E to avoid town; Fr A8 exit sp Ancient Corinth, then N (R) to T-junc end of rd, W (R) past pipe factory, sp 400m N (R) at bottom of bdge sl. Fr W take exit sp Ancient Corinth after toll point. Fr Old National rd turn N (L) immed over rlwy bdge bef pipe factory. Fr Corinth foll old National rd twd Patras, past pipe factory. Med, mkd pitch, hdstg, pt shd; wc; chem disp; shwrs inc; EHU (6A) €3.50; gas; lndry; shop; rest, snacks; bar; BBQ; playgrnd; shgl beach; games area; wifi; TV; dogs; Sunshine Group site; Eng spkn; quiet; ccard acc; red CKE/CCI. "V obliging, friendly owners; pleasant site; sm pitches; lovely site by sea." ♦ 1 Apr-31 Oct. € 23.00 2015*

KYLLINI *A3* (10km S Coastal) *37.88539, 21.11175* **Campsite Melissa, 27050 Kastro Kyllinis Ilia [02 62 30 95 213; fax 62 30 95 453; camping_melissa@yahoo.gr]** S fr Patras twd Pygros on E55. Turn R twds Lehena after 58km marker. Foll signs to Kastro Kyllinis. Med, hdg pitch, shd; wc; chem disp; mv service pnt; shwrs; EHU (10A); lndry; shop; rest; bar; BBQ; cooking facs; playgrnd; beach; wifi; TV; 2% statics; dogs; twin axles; Eng spkn; adv bkg; quiet; CCI. "Great campsite to chill; excel rest, bar & shop; lovely sandy beach; excel sw; fabulous views across the bay." ♦ ltd. 1 Apr-31 Oct. € 31.00 2014*

⊞ **KYLLINI** *A3* (17km S Coastal) *37.83828, 21.12972* **Camping Aginara Beach, Lygia, 27050 Loutra Kyllinis [(26230) 96211; fax 96271; info@camping-aginara.gr; www.camping-aginara.gr]** S fr Patras on E55 twds Pyrgos; exit Gastouni & turn W thro Vartholomio twd Loutra Kyllinis; turn L about 3km bef Kyllinis then foll sps. Lge, hdg pitch, hdstg, pt sl, shd; wc; chem disp; mv service pnt; shwrs inc; EHU (10A); gas; lndry; shop; rest, snacks; bar; BBQ; playgrnd; sand/shgl beach adj; watersports; wifi; TV; 25% statics; dogs; phone; Eng spkn; adv bkg; quiet; ccard acc; red CKE/CCI. "Friendly proprietor; excel, modern facs; site on lovely beach; beautiful views." ♦ € 36.00 2014*

LECHEON see Korinthos *B3*

METHONI *A3* (1km ESE Coastal) *36.81736, 21.71515* **Camp Methoni, 24006 Methoni [(27230) 31228 or 0728 31455]** Fr Pylos on rd 9, strt thro Methoni to beach, turn E along beach, site sp. Med, hdstg, pt shd; wc (some cont); shwrs inc; EHU (10A) inc; lndry rm; rest, snacks; bar; BBQ; playgrnd; sand beach; dogs; phone; Eng spkn; adv bkg; some rd noise; ccard not acc; CKE/CCI. "Superb Venetian castle; close to pleasant vill; park away fr taverna & rd to avoid noise; excel sw; v dusty site; clean san facs; new owner & undergoing renovations (2013); quiet & gd site." 1 Jun-30 Sep. € 19.00 2014*

⊞ **MIKINES** *B3* (95m E Urban) *37.71922, 22.74676* **Camping Mikines/Mykenae, 21200 Mikines [(27510) 76247; fax 76850; dars@arg.forthnet.gr; www.ecogriek.nl]** In town of Mikines (Mycenae) nr bus stop On R as heading to archeological site, sp. Sm, mkd pitch, hdstg, pt shd; wc; chem disp (wc); shwrs inc; EHU (10A) €4.50; lndry; shops 500m; meals served; dogs; Eng spkn; quiet; CKE/CCI. "Quaint family-run site; v warm welcome; conv ancient Mycenae; friendly staff; vg." ♦ ltd. € 21.00 2014*

NAFPLIO *B3* (12km SE Coastal) *37.5287, 22.87553* **Kastraki Camping, Kastraki Assinis, 21100 Assini [(27520) 59386 or 59387; fax 59572; sgkarmaniola@kastrakicamping.gr; www.kastrakicamping.gr]** Fr Nafplio take rd to Tolon. Immed after Assini, take L fork sp Ancient Assini. Site 3km on L. Lge, shd; wc; chem disp; mv service pnt; fam bthrm; shwrs €0.20; EHU (16A) shared €4; lndry; shop; rest, snacks; bar; playgrnd; sand beach; tennis; games area; TV; dogs; quiet; red facs LS; ccard acc. "Vg location with own private beach & excel facs; day trips to several islands fr Tolón harbour; many pitches too sm for lge m'vans." ♦ 1 Apr-30 Sep. € 35.00 2013*

NEOS PANTELEIMONAS see Platamonas *B2*

OLIMBIA *A3* (1km W Rural) *37.64337, 21.61943* **Camping Alphios, 27065 Olimbia [(26240) 22951; fax 22950; alphios@otenet.gr; www.camping alphios.gr]** Fr E55 Pyrgos to Tripoli rd take exit sp 'Ancient Olympia' & foll site sp. Med, hdg/mkd pitch, hdstg, terr, pt sl, pt shd; wc; chem disp; mv service pnt; shwrs inc; EHU (16A) inc; gas; lndry; shop; rest, snacks; bar; BBQ; cooking facs; playgrnd; pool; wifi; TV; quiet; ccard acc. "Superb views fr some pitches; excel pool; very friendly; walking dist to ancient Olympic site." 1 Apr-15 Oct. € 30.00 2013*

OLYMPIA see Olimbia *A3*

PARGA *A2* (2km W Coastal) *39.28550, 20.38997* **Camping Valtos, Valtos Beach, 48060 Parga [(26840) 31287; fax 31131; info@campingvaltos.gr; www.campingvaltos.gr]** Foll sp fr Parga twd Valtos Beach, site sp. Site at far end of beach behind bar/club. Med, mkd pitch, pt sl, shd; wc; chem disp; shwrs inc; EHU (10A); lndry; shop; rest, snacks; bar; sand beach adj; wifi; no statics; dogs; poss cr; Eng spkn; poss noise fr tents; CKE/CCI. "Helpful owners; gd walking area; steep walk to town; poor san facs." 1 May-30 Sep. € 28.50 2016*

PATRA *A2* (21km SW Coastal) *38.14986, 21.57740* **Camping Kato Alissos, 25002 Kato Alissos [(26930) 71249 or 71914; fax 71150; demiris-cmp@otenet.gr; www.camping-kato-alissos.gr]** W of Patra on old national rd turn R at Kato Alissos & foll site sp for 500m. Med, shd; wc; chem disp; shwrs inc; EHU (10A) €4; lndry; shop; rest, snacks; bar; cooking facs; playgrnd; shgl beach adj (down 50 steps); watersports; wifi; 10% statics; dogs; phone; bus 1km; Sunshine Camping Group site; poss cr; Eng spkn; adv bkg; quiet; ccard acc; red snr citizens; CKE/CCI. "Clean ltd facs; gd NH." 1 Apr-25 Oct. € 19.00 2013*

⊞ **PLAKA LITOHOROU** *B2* (10km N Coastal) *40.18230, 22.55885* **Camping Stani, 60200 Kalivia Varikou [(23520) 61277]** Leave E75 (Athens-Thessaloniki) at N Efesos/Variko, foll sp Varikou & site. Lge, mkd pitch, shd; wc; chem disp; shwrs inc; EHU; lndry; shop; rest, snacks; bar; TV rm; dogs; phone; poss cr; CKE/CCI. "Ltd facs LS; conv Dion; fair site." € 22.00 2014*

PLATARIA see Igoumenitsa *A2*

POSSIDI see Kassandria *B2*

⊞ **PYLOS** *A3* (7km N Coastal) *36.94784, 21.70635* **Camping Navarino Beach, 24001 Gialova [(27230) 22973; fax 23512; info@navarino-beach.gr; www.navarino-beach.gr]** Fr Pylos N twds Kiparissia for 5km around Navarino Bay, site at S end of Gialova vill; sp. Med, some hdstg, pt shd, wc; chem disp; mv service pnt; shwrs inc; EHU (16A) €4; gas; lndry; shop 300m; rest, snacks; BBQ; cooking facs; playgrnd; beach; windsurfing, boat-launch; internet; dogs; bus; Eng spkn; adv bkg; quiet; ccard acc; red long stay; CKE/CCI. "Management v helpful; gd, clean, modern facs; several rest & shops in easy walking dist; some pitches on beach; vg." € 32.50 2014*

SPARTI *B3* (5km W Rural) *37.06941, 22.38163* **Camping Castle View, 23100 Mistras [(27310) 83303; fax 20028; info@castleview.gr; www.castleview.gr]** Fr Kalamata take 1st turning to Mistras, past castle then thro vill dir Sparti. Site in approx 1km on L, well sp. Med, pt shd; wc; chem disp; shwrs inc; EHU (16A) inc; gas; lndry; shop; rest, snacks; bar; playgrnd; pool; wifi; TV; some statics; dogs; phone; Eng spkn; quiet; red CKE/CCI. "Gd clean facs; gd rest; close to archaeological remains; helpful owner." 1 Apr-20 Oct. € 26.00 2016*

⊞ **STYLIDA** *B2* (4km SE Coastal) *38.89638, 22.65555* **Camping Interstation, Rd Athens-Thessalonika, Km 230, 35300 Stylida [tel/fax (22380) 23828; www.campinginterstation.com]** Fr Lamia take rd E to Stylis; cont for further 3km & site situated to side of dual-c'way opp petrol stn. Med, shd; wc; chem disp; shwrs; EHU (16A); gas; lndry; shop, rest high ssn; playgrnd; beach adj; tennis; watersports; TV; entmnt; some statics; dogs; Eng spkn; adv bkg; quiet but some rd noise; red CKE/CCI. "Day visitors have access to beach via site; do not confuse with Cmp Paras adj - not rec; Sunshine Camping Group site; poss poor san facs LS; NH only." ♦ € 27.40 2017*

TIROS see Leonidi *B3*

TOLON see Nafplio *B3*

⊞ **VARTHOLOMIO** *A3* (10km SW Coastal) *37.83555, 21.13333* **Camping Ionion Beach, 27050 Glifa [(26230) 96828; fax 96138; ioniongr@otenet.gr; www.ionion-beach.gr]** Fr E55 Patras-Pirgos rd turn W to Gastouni, Ligia & Glifa, then Glifa Beach. Site is 1km SW of Glifa. Med, hdg pitch, hdstg, pt shd; htd wc; chem disp; mv service pnt; serviced pitch; shwrs; EHU (16A); gas; lndry (inc dryer); shop in vill; rest, snacks; bar; BBQ; playgrnd; pool; paddling pool; beach adj; watersports; games area; wifi; TV; statics; dogs; Eng spkn; adv bkg; poss noisy; ccard acc; red LS; CKE/CCI. "Excel, well-run site; superb facs." ♦ € 30.60 2016*

GREECE

VIVARI *B3* (1km E Coastal) *37.53421, 22.93179* **Camping Lefka Beach, 21100 Drepanon Vivari [tel/fax (27520) 92334; info@camping-lefka.gr; www.camping-lefka.gr]** On the Nafplio-Drepanon-Iria rd. About 1km on the R after vill of Vivari. Foll sp. Med, mkd pitch, hdstg, terr, shd; wc; chem disp; shwrs; EHU (16A); lndry; shop; rest; snacks; bar; BBQ; beach 20m; wifi; TV; dogs; twin axles; Eng spkn; adv bkg; CKE/CCI. "Beautiful views of bay fr site; close to antiquities; vg." ♦ ltd. 1 Apr-10 Nov. € 28.00 2015*

VLYCHO see Lefkada (Lefkas Island) *A2*

⊞ **VOLOS** *B2* (18km SE Coastal) *39.31027, 23.10972* **Camping Sikia, 37300 Kato Gatzea [(24230) 22279 or 22081; fax 22720; info@camping-sikia.gr; www.camping-sikia.gr]** Fr Volos take coast rd S to Kato Gatzea site on R, sp immed next to Camping Hellas. Med, terr, shd; wc; chem disp; mv service pnt; shwrs inc; EHU (16A) €3; gas; lndry; shop; rest, snacks; shgl beach; internet; entmnt; 20% statics; dogs; phone; poss cr; Eng spkn; adv bkg; quiet; Sunshine Group site; ccard acc; red long stay/CKE/CCI. "Highly rec; some beautiful, but sm, pitches with sea views; excel, friendly family-run site; v clean; v helpful staff; take care o'hanging trees." ♦ € 24.00 2016*

"I like to fill in the reports as I travel from site to site"

You'll find report forms at the back of this guide, or you can fill them in online at camc.com/europereport.

ZACHARO *A3* (8km S Coastal) *37.41068, 21.66850* **Camping Tholo Beach, Tholo, 27054 Zacharo [(26250) 61345 or 33454 (winter); campingtholo@hotmail.com]** S fr Pyrgos on E55 dir Kyparissia, 8km S of Zacharo turn R to Tholo. Site sp in 500m on L. Med, shd; wc; chem disp; mv service pnt; shwrs inc; EHU €4; lndry rm; shop; rest; bar; BBQ; playgrnd; sand beach adj; wifi; TV; dogs; Eng spkn; adv bkg; quiet; CKE/CCI. "Excel, quiet, clean site; gd, clean san facs; friendly staff; excel sandy beach where loggerhead turtles lay eggs; dolphins off shore; san facs need updating; great location; excel mkt on Tuesdays; Ancient Olympia about an hr's drive." 1 May-30 Oct. € 24.50 2015*

GREEK ISLANDS

⊞ **AGIA GALINI (CRETE)** *C4* (2km E Rural/Coastal) *35.10004, 24.69514* **Camping No Problem!, 74056 Agia Galini [(28320) 91386; www.agia-galini.com]** Site sp on Tympaki rd. Sm, mkd pitch, pt shd; wc; chem disp; mv service pnt; shwrs; EHU (6A) €4; lndry; shop; rest, snacks; bar; BBQ; pool; paddling pool; sand/shgl beach 500m; wifi; some statics; dogs free; bus 500m; poss cr; Eng spkn; adv bkg; quiet. "Vg, family-run site; gd walks." ♦ € 22.00 2016*

ERETRIA (EVIA) *B2* (11km NE Coastal) *38.39148, 23.77562* **Milos Camping, 34008 Eretria [(22290) 60420; fax 60360; info@camping-in-evia.gr; www.camping-in-evia.gr]** Fr Chalkida for 20km; ignore any previous sp for Milos Camping. Med, mkd pitch, terr, pt shd; wc; chem disp; mv service pnt; shwrs inc; EHU (16A) inc; gas; lndry; shop; rest, snacks; bar; BBQ; playgrnd; shgl beach adj; internet; TV; 70% statics; dogs; phone; Eng spkn; quiet but some rd noise; red CKE/CCI. "Friendly site; excel rest; rather scruffy (5/09) but gd san facs." ♦ 15 Apr-30 Sep. € 25.00 2015*

LEFKADA (LEFKAS) *A2* (26km SE Coastal) *38.67511, 20.71475* **Camping Santa Maura, Dessimi, 31100 Vlycho [(26450) 95007, (00306) 976085621, (00306) 932902309; fax 95493; campingsantamavra@yahoo.gr; www.campingsantamaura.com]** Take coast rd S fr Lefkada to Vlycho, turn L for Dessimi, site in 2.5km (after Camping Dessimi). Access via v steep hill - severe gradients both sides. Med, mkd pitch, terr, pt shd; wc; chem disp; mv service pnt; shwrs inc; EHU (6A) inc; gas; lndry; shop; rest, snacks; bar; BBQ; sand/shgl beach adj; TV rm; dogs; phone; quiet; CKE/CCI. "Excel site & beach; gd, clean san facs; friendly owners; pls call for prices." 1 Apr-31 Oct. 2016*

PEFKARI (THASSOS) *C2* (250m W Coastal) *40.61630, 24.60021* **Camping Pefkari Beach, 64002 Pefkari [tel/fax (25930) 51190; info@camping-pefkari.gr; www.camping-pefkari.gr]** SW fr Thassos port approx 43km to Limenaria, Pefkari is next sm vill. Site well sp in vill. Med, hdstg, pt shd; own san; chem disp; shwrs inc; EHU (6A) €2.90; lndry rm; shop; rest, snacks; bar; BBQ; sand beach adj; 5% statics; bus 1km; Eng spkn; quiet; CKE/CCI. "Lovely spot; worth putting up with poor, dated san facs; gd local rest; vg; improving site; beautiful; easy walk to Pefkari and Potos; excel on site rest; lovely spot." 1 May-30 Sep. € 27.50 2014*

⊞ **RETHYMNO (CRETE)** *C4* (3km E Coastal) *35.36795, 24.51487* **Camping Elizabeth, Ionias 84 Terma, 74100 Missiria [tel/fax (28310) 28694; wallydewever@yahoo.gr; www.camping-elizabeth.com]** W fr Iraklio/Heraklion exit Platanes/Arkadi. Site 1km bef Platanes, on R on sh unsurfaced rd. Lge, hdg pitch, shd; wc; chem disp; mv service pnt; shwrs; EHU (12A) inc; lndry (inc dryer); shop; rest, snacks; bar; BBQ; cooking facs; beach adj; wifi; 3% statics; dogs; phone; bus 500m; poss cr; Eng spkn; adv bkg; quiet; red LS; CKE/CCI. "Gd walking on mkd rtes; gd cycling; excursion programme; vg." ♦ ltd. € 29.50 2016*

"We must tell The Club about that great site we found"

Get your site reports in by mid-August and we'll do our best to get your updates into the next edition.

TINOS (TINOS) *C3* (500m E Coastal) *37.53994, 25.16377* **Tinos Camping Bungalows, Louizas Sohou 5, 84200 Tinos [(22830) 22344 or 23548; fax 24551; tinoscamping@thn.forthnet.gr; tinoscamping.gr]** Clearly sp fr port. Sm, hdg/mkd pitch, hdstg; shd; wc; chem disp (wc); shwrs inc; EHU €4.50; lndry rm; shop; rest, snacks; BBQ; cooking facs; sand/shgl beach 500m; dogs; phone; Eng spkn; adv bkg; ccard acc; red long stay/CKE/CCI. "1,600 Venetian dovecots & 600 churches on island; monastery with healing icon." ♦ 1 May-31 Oct. € 21.50 2016*

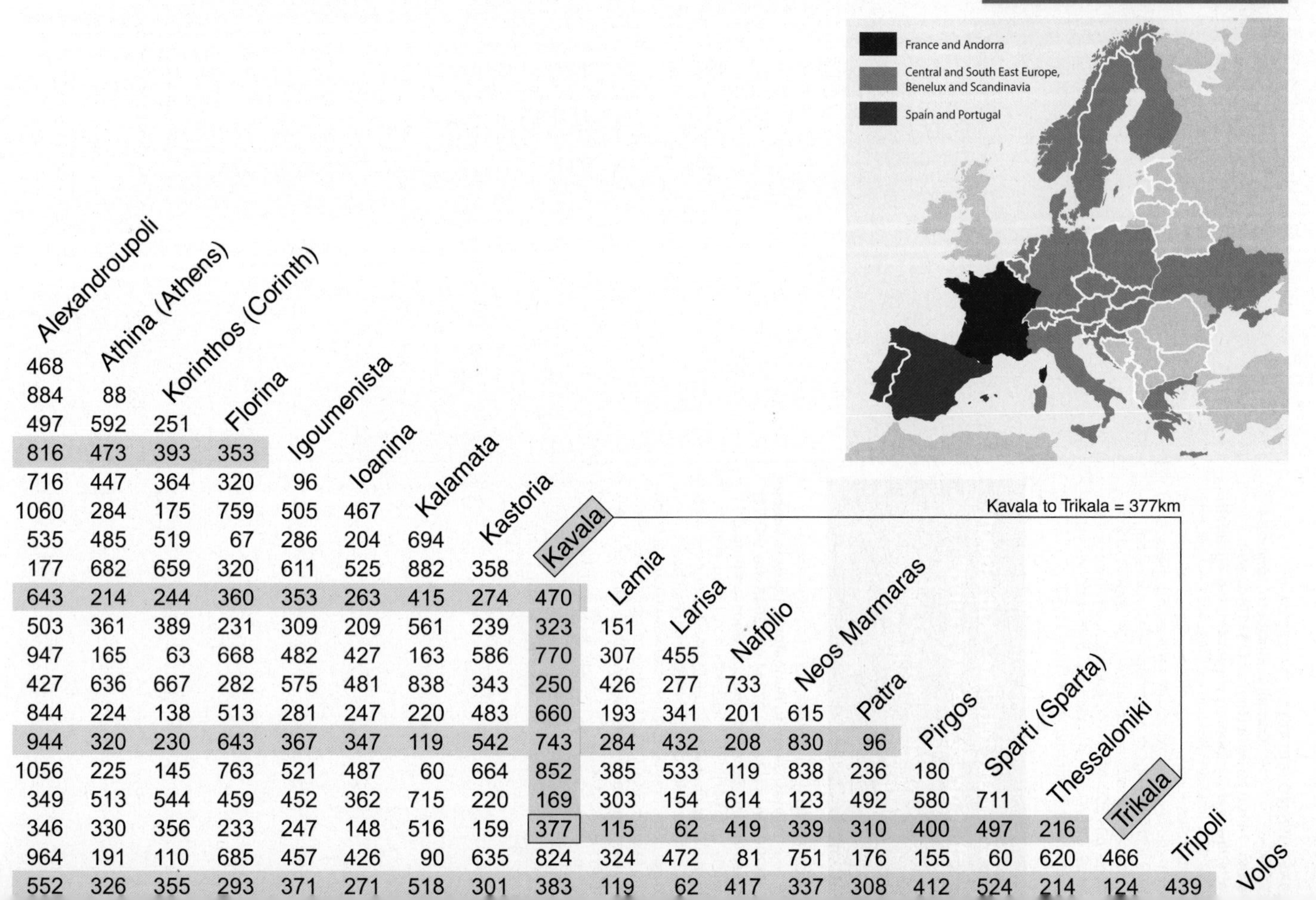

	Alexandroupoli	Athina (Athens)	Korinthos (Corinth)	Florina	Igoumenista	Ioanina	Kalamata	Kastoria	Kavala	Lamia	Larisa	Nafplio	Neos Marmaras	Patra	Pirgos	Sparti (Sparta)	Thessaloniki	Trikala	Tripoli
Athina (Athens)	468																		
Korinthos (Corinth)	884	88																	
Florina	497	592	251																
Igoumenista	816	473	393	353															
Ioanina	716	447	364	320	96														
Kalamata	1060	284	175	759	505	467													
Kastoria	535	485	519	67	286	204	694												
Kavala	177	682	659	320	611	525	882	358											
Lamia	643	214	244	360	353	263	415	274	470										
Larisa	503	361	389	231	309	209	561	239	323	151									
Nafplio	947	165	63	668	482	427	163	586	770	307	455								
Neos Marmaras	427	636	667	282	575	481	838	343	250	426	277	733							
Patra	844	224	138	513	281	247	220	483	660	193	341	201	615						
Pirgos	944	320	230	643	367	347	119	542	743	284	432	208	830	96					
Sparti (Sparta)	1056	225	145	763	521	487	60	664	852	385	533	119	838	236	180				
Thessaloniki	349	513	544	459	452	362	715	220	169	303	154	614	123	492	580	711			
Trikala	346	330	356	233	247	148	516	159	377	115	62	419	339	310	400	497	216		
Tripoli	964	191	110	685	457	426	90	635	824	324	472	81	751	176	155	60	620	466	
Volos	552	326	355	293	371	271	518	301	383	119	62	417	337	308	412	524	214	124	439

SERBIA
KOSOVO
MONTENEGRO
MACEDONIA
ALBANIA
BULGARIA
TURKEY
AEGEAN SEA
MEDITERRANEAN SEA
SOFIYA
SKOPJE
TIRANË
Bitola
Blagoevgrad
Plovdiv
Burgas
Edirne
KAVALA
ALEXANDROUPOLI
FLORINA
THESSALONIKI
KASTORIA
Gjirokastër
Pefkári
THASSOS
Gerakini
NEOS MARMARAS
LEMNOS
Plaka Litohorou
IOANINA
Kalambaka
LARISA
IGOUMENITSA
TRIKALA
VOLOS
CORFU KERKIRA
Parga
LESBOS
Lefkada
LEVKAS
LAMIA
Stylida
EUBOEA/ EVIA
Delfi
Eretria
CHIOS
İzmir
PATRA
Egio
CEPHALONIA
Kyllini
Vartholomio
ZANTE
KORINTHOS
ATHINA
Mikines
Olimbia
PYRGOS
NAFPLIO
Drepano
Vivari
TINOS
Tinos
Zacharo
TRIPOLI
CYCLADES
KALAMATA
SPARTI
Pylos
Methoni
Finikoundas
Githio
Bodrum
KOS
RHODES
Rethymno
Sisi
Agia Galini
CRETE
N
W
E
S
All year site(s)
Seasonal site(s)
No sites listed
200m +
0–200m
0 50 100 150 200 250 kms
0 50 100 150 mls
Motorways
Major roads
Main roads
© Collins Bartholomew Ltd 2018

Fisherman's Bastioin, Budapest

Welcome to Hungary

Hungary is home to some of the most dramatic and exotic architecture found in Europe, with buildings spanning from the Art Nouveau era to Ancient Rome. Turkish, Slavic, Magyar and Roman influences entwine with its own unique culture to make Hungary a fascinating place.

There are more medicinal spas in Hungary than anywhere else in Europe and the spa culture is an important part both of the tourist industry and everyday life. You can enjoy spas that range from traditional bathhouses to modern wellness centres that cater for the whole family.

Country highlights

Many folk festivals are celebrated in Hungary throughout the year, the biggest of which is the Festival of Folk Arts/Crafts held every August in Buda Castle. Thousands of visitors attend to view the fantastic traditional crafts on offer.

One of the most renowned crafts is pottery making, with Hungary having a long tradition of creating both fine porcelain, such as Herend, and tiling and stoneware, such as Zsolnay produces.

Major towns and cities

- Budapest – an enchanting city full of galleries, theatres and museums.
- Debrecen – this former capital is one of Hungary's most important cultural centres.
- Pécs – an ancient city with countless things to see and do.
- Eger – a city famous for its fine red wines.

Attractions

- Fisherman's Bastion, Budapest – enjoy unmatched views over the city.
- Hungarian Parliament Building, Budapest – a magnificent building on the banks of the Danube.
- Lake Hévíz – one of the largest thermal lakes in the world with its own unique ecosystem.
- Esztergom Basilica – a spectacularly enormous cathedral with Renaissance art.

Find out more

www.gotohungary.com
Tel: 0036 (0) 14 88 87 00 Tourist Information

Country Information

Population (approx): 9.9 million

Capital: Budapest (population approx 1.7 million)

Area: 93,000 sq km

Bordered by: Austria, Croatia, Romania, Serbia, Slovakia, Slovenia, Ukraine

Terrain: Mostly flat and rolling plains; hills and low mountains to the north

Climate: Temperate, continental climate; cold, cloudy winters; warm, sunny summers; changeable in spring and early summer with heavy rain and storms. The best times to visit are spring and autumn

Highest Point: Kekes 1,014m

Language: Hungarian

Local Time: GMT or BST + 1, i.e. 1 hour ahead of the UK all year

Currency: Forint (HUF); £1 = HUF 360, HUF 1000 = £2.78 (January 2017)

Emergency numbers: Police 107; Fire brigade 105; Ambulance 104. Operators speak English.

Public Holidays 2018: Jan 1; Mar 15, 16, 30; Apr 2,30; May 1, 21; Aug 20; Oct 22, 23; Nov 1, 2; Dec 24, 25, 26, 31.

School summer holidays are from mid-June to the end of August.

Camping and Caravanning

There are approximately 100 organised campsites in Hungary rated from 1 to 4 stars. These are generally well signposted off main routes, with the site name shown below a blue camping sign. Most campsites open from May to September and the most popular sites are situated by Lake Balaton and the Danube. A Camping Key Europe (CKE) or Camping Card International (CCI) is essential.

Facilities vary from site to site, but visitors will find it useful to carry their own flat universal sink plug. There has been much improvement in recent years in the general standard of campsites, but communal changing areas for showers are not uncommon. Many sites have communal kitchen facilities which enable visitors to make great savings on their own gas supply.

Many campsites require payment in cash. Prices have risen sharply in recent years. Therefore, prices in this guide for sites not reported on for some time might not reflect the current prices.

Casual/wild camping is prohibited.

Cycling

There are approximately 2,000km of cycle tracks, 100km of which are in Budapest and 200km around Lake Balaton. Tourinform offices in Hungary provide maps of cycling routes.

Children under 14 years are not allowed to ride on the road and all cyclists must wear a reflective jacket at night and in poor daytime visibility.

Electricity and Gas

Current on campsites varies between 6 and 16 amps.
Plugs have two round pins. There are some sites that do not have CEE connections.

Only non-returnable and/or non-exchangeable Campingaz cylinders are available.

Entry Formalities

British and Irish passport holders may stay for a period of three months without a visa. Your passport needs to be valid for the duration of your stay and it is always recommended when visiting a foreign country to have an additional period of validity on your passport in case of any unforeseen delays. Anyone planning to stay longer than three months should contact the Hungarian Embassy for further information

There are no immigration or Customs checks at borders with other EU countries, i.e. Slovakia, Slovenia and Austria. Border crossings with other countries are generally open 24 hours.

Medical Services

British nationals may obtain emergency medical and dental treatment from practitioners contracted to the national health insurance scheme, Országos Egészségbiztosítási (OEP), together with emergency hospital treatment, on presentation of a European Health Insurance Card (EHIC) and a British passport.

Fees are payable for treatment and prescribed medicines, and are not refundable in Hungary. You may be able to apply for reimbursement when back in the UK.

Pharmacies (gyógyszertár) are well stocked. The location of the nearest all-night pharmacy is displayed on the door of every pharmacy.

Opening Hours

Banks: Mon-Thurs 8am-3pm. Fri 8am - 1pm. Hours may vary slightly.

Museums: Tue-Sun 10am-6pm; closed Mon.

Post Offices: Mon-Fri 8am-6pm; post office at Budapest open Mon-Sat 7am-9pm.

Shops: Mon-Fri 10am-6pm (supermarkets from 7am-7pm with some grocery stores open 24 hours); open half day Saturdays.

Safety and Security

Petty theft in Budapest is common in areas frequented by tourists, particularly on busy public transport, at markets and at popular tourist sites. Beware of pickpockets and bag snatchers.

Do not carry large amounts of cash. Take care when receiving bank notes and change as some that are no longer valid are still in circulation, e.g. HUF 200 notes were withdrawn in 2009. There has been a small number of instances of taxi drivers deliberately passing these notes to tourists. Be aware especially when paying with a HUF 10,000 or 20,000 bank note.

Theft of and from vehicles is common. Do not leave your belongings, car registration documents or mobile phones in your car and ensure that it is properly locked with the alarm on, even if leaving it for just a moment. Beware of contrived 'incidents', particularly on the Vienna-Budapest motorway, designed to stop motorists and expose them to robbery.

Visitors have reported in the past that motorists may be pestered at service areas on the Vienna to Budapest motorway by people insisting on washing windscreens and demanding money.

During the summer season in Budapest, uniformed tourist police patrol the most frequently visited areas of the city. Criminals sometimes pose as tourist police and ask for visitors' money, credit cards or travel documents in order to check them. Always ensure that a uniformed police officer is wearing a badge displaying the word 'Rendörség' and a five-digit identification number, together with a separate name badge. Plain clothes police carry a badge and an ID card with picture, hologram and rank. If in doubt, insist on going to the nearest police station.

There are still occasional incidents of exorbitant overcharging in certain restaurants, bars and clubs in Budapest, accompanied by threats of violence. Individuals who have been unable to settle their bill have frequently been accompanied by the establishment's security guards to a cash machine and made to withdraw funds. Visitors are advised to ask for a menu and only order items which are priced realistically. A five digit price for one dish is too high. Never accept menus which do not display prices and check your bill carefully.

Taxi drivers are sometimes accomplices to these frauds, receiving 'commission' for recommending restaurants and bars which charge extortionate prices to visitors. Never ask a taxi driver to recommend a bar, club or restaurant. If a driver takes you to one or you are approached on the street with an invitation to an unfamiliar bar or restaurant, you should treat such advice with extreme caution.

Do not change money or get involved in gambling in the street; these activities are illegal.

If you need help, go to the nearest police station or the Tourist Information Point open 8am - 8pm, Deák Ferenc Square, 1052 Budapest, Sütő Street 2 (1) 438 8080

There is a low threat from terrorism.

British Embassy

HARMINCAD UTCA 6, BUDAPEST 1051
Tel: (1) 2662888
www.ukinhungary.fco.gov.uk

Irish Embassy

SZABADSÁG TÉR 7,
BANK CENTRE, GRANIT TOWER, V. FLOOR
1054 BUDAPEST
Tel: (1) 3014960
www.embassyofireland.hu

Documents

Passport

Carry your passport at all times. A photocopy is not acceptable.

Vehicle(s)

Carry your vehicle registration certificate (V5C), vehicle insurance certificate and MOT certificate (if applicable) with you when driving.

Money

Hungarian currency is available from banks in Austria before crossing the border. For emergency cash reserves, it is advisable to have euros, rather than sterling. Foreign currency is best exchanged at banks as, by law, this is at the rate shown on the banks' currency boards and they are not permitted to charge commission. Private bureaux de change, however, do charge commission, but the rate of exchange may be better.

Credit cards are accepted at many outlets in large towns and cities and cash dispensers, 'bankomats', are widespread even in small towns. There is a high incidence of credit card fraud and payment in cash wherever possible is advisable. Carry your credit card issuers'/banks' 24 hour UK contact numbers separately in case of loss or theft of your cards.

Recent visitors report that some newer types of debit and credit cards issued in the UK do not work in certain cash machines in Hungary. The banks are working on a solution but, in the meantime, if you encounter this problem you should try a cash machine at a different bank. It is possible to obtain cash from post offices with a debit or credit card.

Euros are widely accepted in shops and restaurants frequented by tourists, but check the exchange rate.

When leaving Hungary on the MI motorway (Budapest-Vienna), it is important to change back your forints on the Hungarian side of the border by crossing the carriageway to the left at the designated crossing-point, as visitors report that there are no facilities on the right hand side and none on the other side in Austria.

Motoring in Hungary

Accidents

Accidents causing damage to vehicles or injury to persons must be reported to the nearest police station and to the Hungarian State Insurance Company (Hungária Biztositó) within 24 hours. The police will issue a statement which you may be asked to show when leaving the country.

If entering Hungary with a conspicuously damaged vehicle, it is recommended that you obtain a report confirming the damage from the police in the country where the damage occurred, otherwise difficulties may arise when leaving Hungary.

Alcohol

It is illegal to drive after consuming any alcohol whatsoever.

Breakdown Service

The motoring organisation, Magyar Autóklub (MAK), operates a breakdown service 24 hours a day on all roads. Drivers in need of assistance should telephone 188 or (1) 3451680. The number (1) is the area code for Budapest. On motorways emergency phones are placed at 2km intervals.

MAK road patrol cars are yellow and marked 'Segélyszolgálat'. Their registration numbers begin with the letters MAK.

The roadside breakdown service is chargeable, higher charges applying at night. There is a scale of charges by vehicle weight and distance for towing vehicles to a garage. Payment is required in cash.

Essential Equipment

First Aid Kit

It is a legal requirement that all vehicles should carry a first aid kit.

Lights

Outside built-up areas dipped headlights are compulsory at all times, regardless of weather conditions. Bulbs are more likely to fail with constant use and you are recommended to carry spares. At night in built-up areas dipped headlights must be used as full beam is prohibited.

Headlight flashing often means that a driver is giving way, but do not carry out a manoeuvre unless you are sure that this is the case.

Reflective Jackets/ Waistcoats

If your vehicle is immobilised on the carriageway outside a built-up area, or if visibility is poor, you must wear a reflective jacket or waistcoat when getting out of your vehicle. Passengers who leave the vehicle, for example, to assist with a repair, should also wear one. Keep the jackets inside your vehicle, not in the boot.

In addition, pedestrians and cyclists walking or cycling at night or in poor visibility along unlit roads outside a built-up area must also wear a reflective jacket.

Warning Triangles

In the event of accident, it is compulsory to place a warning triangle 100 metres behind the vehicle on motorways and 50 metres on other roads.

Child Restraint System

Children under the height of 1.5m must be seated in a suitable child restraint system appropriate for their size in the rear of the vehicle.

If no child restraint is available a child over 3 who is over 1.35m in height may travel in the rear seat with a seatbelt. Children younger or shorter than this may not ever travel without a suitable restraint system in the vehicle.

Winter Driving

The use of snow chains can be made compulsory on some roads when there is severe winter weather.

Fuel

Leaded petrol is no longer available. The sign 'Ólommentes üzemanyag' or 'Bleifrei 95' indicates unleaded petrol. LPG is widely available.

Most petrol stations are open from 6am to 8pm. Along motorways and in large towns they are often open 24 hours. Some petrol stations accept credit and debit cards but cash is the most usual means of payment.

Parking

Zigzag lines on the carriageway and road signs indicate a stopping/parking prohibition. Illegally-parked vehicles will be towed away or clamped. On two-way roads, vehicles must park in the direction of traffic; they may park on either side in one-way streets. In certain circumstances, parking on the pavement is allowed.

Budapest is divided into various time restricted parking zones (maximum three hours) where tickets must be purchased from Monday to Friday from a machine. For longer periods you are advised to use 'Park and Ride' car parks located near major metro stations and bus terminals.

Priority

Pedestrians have priority over traffic at pedestrian crossings and at intersections. They do not have priority on the roadway between central tram loading islands and pavements, and drivers must exercise care on these sections. Major roads are indicated by a priority road ahead sign. At the intersection of two roads of equal importance, where there is no sign, vehicles coming from the right have priority. Trams and buses have priority at any intersection on any road and buses have right of way when leaving bus stops after the driver has signalled his intention to pull out.

Roads

Hungary has a good system of well surfaced main roads and driving standards are higher than in many other parts of Europe. There are few dual carriageways and care is required, therefore, when overtaking with a right-hand drive vehicle. Extra care is required on provincial roads which may be badly lit, poorly maintained and narrow. In the countryside at night be on the alert for unlit cycles and horse drawn vehicles

Road Signs and Markings

Road signs and markings conform to international conventions. Square green road signs indicate the number of km to the next town. At traffic lights a flashing amber light indicates a dangerous intersection. Destination signs feature road numbers rather than the names of towns, so it is essential to equip yourself with an up-to-date road map or atlas. Signs for motorways have white lettering on a blue background; on other roads signs are white and green.

Speed Limits

	Open Road (km/h)	Motorway (km/h)
Car Solo	90-110	130
Car towing caravan/trailer	70	80
Motorhome under 3500kg	90-110	130
Motorhome 3500-7500kg	70	80

A speed limit of 30 km/h (18 mph) is in force in many residential, city centre and tourist resort areas.

Traffic Jams

Roads around Budapest are busy on Friday and Sunday afternoons. In the holiday season roads to Lake Balaton (M7) and around the lake (N7 and N71) may be congested. There are regular traffic hold ups at weekends at the border crossings to Austria, the Czech Republic and Serbia. Motorway traffic information (in English) is available on www.motorway.hu

Violation of Traffic Regulations

The police make spot vehicle document checks and are keen to enforce speed limits. They are permitted to impose on-the-spot fines of up to HUF300,000. Credit cards are accepted for the payment of fines in some circumstances.

Motorways

All motorways (autópálya) and main connecting roads run to or from Budapest. In recent years the road network has been extended and improved and there are now approximately 900 kilometres of motorway and dual carriageways or semi-motorways. However, most roads are still single carriageway, single lane and care is recommended. The M0 motorway is a 75km ringroad around Budapest which links the M1, M7, M6, M5 and Highway 11. The recently built Megyeri Bridge on the Danube is part of the M0 and its opening has considerably reduced traffic congestion to the north of Budapest.

Emergency corridors are compulsory on motorways and dual carriageways. Drivers are required to create a precautionary emergency corridor to provide access for emergency vehicles whenever congestion occurs. Drivers in the left-hand lane must move as far over to the left as possible, and drivers in the central and right-hand lanes must move as far over to the right as possible.

Motorway Vignettes

Approximately 30% of motorways are toll-free; otherwise you must purchase an electronic vignette (matrica) or e-vignette (sticker) before entering the motorway.

They are available online, from motorway customer service offices and at large petrol stations near the motorways.
You can pay in forints or by credit card.

Leaflets are distributed to motorists at the border and a telephone information centre is available in Hungary – tel 36 58 75 00. Vignettes should only be purchased from outlets where the prices are clearly displayed at the set rates. For full details (in English), including how to buy online and toll-free sections, see www.motorway.hu

When purchasing an e-vignette a confirmation message will be sent or a coupon issued and this must be kept for a year after its expiry date. There is no need to display the vignette in your windscreen as the motorway authorities check all vehicles electronically (without the need for you to stop your vehicle) and verify registration number, category of toll paid and validity of an e-vignette. Charges in forints (2017 charges, subject to change) are shown below:

Category of Vehicle	Period of Validity	
	10 Days	1 month
Vehicle up to 3,500kg with or without caravan or trailer	2,975	4,780
Motorhome	5,950	9,560

Since the beginning of 2013 Hungary's State Motorway Management company (AAK) have been imposing on-the-spot fines for motorists who do not have a vignette. Fines amount to HUF 14,875 (around £40) for vehicles under 3,500kg or HUF 66,925 (around £178) for vehicles between 3,500kg and 7,500kg if paid within

30 days. 78% of the motorists fined so far have been foreign nationals, so ensure you have a vignette before travelling on motorways.

Touring

Hungary boasts eight World Heritage sites including the national park at Aggtelek which contains Europe's largest cave network, the Christian cemetery at Pécs and the monastery at Pannonhalma. Lake Balaton, the largest lake in Central Europe, attracts lovers of bathing, sailing, fishing and windsurfing. With 200km of sandy shoreline and shallow warm waters, it is very popular with families and easily Hungary's favourite tourist area.

A Budapest Card is available, allowing unlimited travel on public transport for two or three consecutive days, free city walking tours, discounted entry to museums and other attractions, plus discounts on many guided tours, events, shops and restaurants. Cards are available from metro stations, tourist information offices, many travel agencies, hotels, museums and main Budapest transport ticket offices, as well as from the Hungarian National Tourist Office in London. A child under 14 travelling with the cardholder is included free of charge. You may also order online from www.budapest-card.com

A tip of 10-15% of the bill is expected in restaurants. Check your bill first to ensure that a service charge has not already been added.

Take your own supply of plastic carrier bags to supermarkets, as generally they are not supplied.

Hungarian is a notoriously difficult language for native English speakers to decipher and pronounce. English is not widely spoken in rural areas, but it is becoming increasingly widespread elsewhere as it is now taught in schools. German is widely spoken and a dictionary may be helpful.

Public Transport & Local Travel

Cars are not permitted within the Castle District and on Margaret Island in Budapest. It is advisable to use public transport when travelling into the city and there is an excellent network of bus, tram and metro routes (BKV). All public transport in Hungary is free for over 65s, and this also applies to foreign visitors with proof of age (passport).

There are a number of ticket options, including family tickets, 1, 3 and 7 day tickets, and they can be bought at metro stations, ticket machines, tobacconists and newsagents. Validate your bus and metro tickets before use at each stage of your journey and every time you change metro lines at the red machines provided. Tickets are often checked on vehicles or at metro station exits by controllers wearing arm bands and carrying photo ID. For further information on public transport in Budapest see www.bkv.hu

As a general rule, it is better to phone for taxis operated by reputable local companies, rather than flag them down in the street, and always ensure that fares are metered. A tip of approximately 10% of the fare is customary.

Mahart, the Hungarian Shipping Company, operates a regular hydrofoil service from April to October along the Danube between Budapest and Vienna. The journey lasts six hours and covers 288km.

Local companies Legenda (www.legenda.hu) and Mahart also offer city cruises between May and October, as well as regular trips to tourist attractions outside Budapest, such as Szentendre, Visegrád and Esztergom.

A ferry service takes cars across Lake Balaton from Szántód to Tihany. There are crossings every 10 minutes from June to September and every hour during the low season. Regular bus and train services link the towns and villages along the lakeside.

Sites in Hungary

AGGTELEK *A3* (1km NW Rural) *48.47094, 20.49446* **Baradla Camping, Baradla Oldal 1, 3759 Aggtelek [tel/fax (06) 308619427; szallas@anp.hu]** Fr Slovakia turn off E571/A50 at Plesivec onto rd 587 S via Dlha Ves to border x-ing. Cont S for approx 800m & hotel/campsite complex is on L. Fr Miskolc 45km N on rte 26, turn onto rte 27 sp Perkupa then foll sp Nemzeti National Park & Aggtelek. Site sp in vill. Med, pt sl, pt shd; wc; shwrs; EHU (16A) inc; rest, snacks, bar at motel; BBQ; cooking facs; playgrnd; some statics; quiet. "Gd NH to/fr Slovakia; ent to lge Barlang Caves system adj; facs poss stretched high ssn."
15 Apr-15 Oct. HUF 4366 2016*

ALSOORS see Balatonfüred *C2*

BALATONAKALI *C1* (1km SW Rural) *46.87939, 17.74190* **Balatontourist Camping Levendula (Naturist), Hókuli u 25, 8243 Balatonakali [36 30 309 7797; info@levendulacamp.com; levendulacamp.com]** NE on rte 71 on N shore of Lake Balaton twds Tihany. Site sp on W app to Balatonakali. Turn R twds lake; go over level x-ing, site ent on R. Med, mkd pitch, pt shd; wc; chem disp; mv service pnt; sauna; shwrs inc; EHU (4A) inc; gas; lndry (inc dryer); shop; supmkt 1km; rest, snacks; bar; playgrnd; sand beach & lake sw; fishing; windsurf school; games area; bike hire; wifi; TV rm; dogs HUF950; adv bkg; Eng spkn; quiet at night, train noise fr early morning; ccard acc; CKE/CCI. "Superb site." ♦ 7 May-12 Sep. HUF 7500 2016*

BALATONALMADI *C2* (2km SW Rural) *47.0205, 18.00828* **Balatontourist Camping Yacht, Véghely Dezsö út 18, 8220 Balatonalmádi [(88) 584101; fax 584102; yacht@balatontourist.hu; www.balatontourist.hu]** Fr rd 71, km post 25.5, site sp at lakeside. Lge, hdg/mkd pitch, pt shd; wc; chem disp; mv service pnt; shwrs inc; EHU (4A) inc (rev pol); lndry; shop; rest, snacks; bar; playgrnd; beach adj; watersports; bike hire; entmnt; TV; 10% statics; dogs HUF990; Eng spkn; adv bkg; ccard acc; CKE/CCI. "Excel san facs; excel rest; several sites in close proximity; great site with friendly owners." ♦ 1 May-15 Sep. HUF 9980 2013*

BALATONBERENY *C1* (1km NW Rural) *46.71340, 17.31080* **FKK Naturista Camping (Naturist), Hetvezer u.2, 8649 Balatonberény [tel/fax (85) 377299; bereny@balatontourist.hu]** Fr Keszthely foll rte 71 & rte 76 round SW end of lake. Lge sp indicates Balatonberény & site. Sps change fr Naturista Camping to FKK at turn off main rd. Med, hdg/mkd pitch, pt shd; wc; chem disp; shwrs inc; EHU (12-16A) inc; lndry; shop; rest, snacks; bar; BBQ; direct access lake sw adj; playgrnd; windsurfing; watersports; games area; wifi; entmnt; TV; few statics; dogs €2.60; phone; quiet; poss cr; adv bkg; red INF. "Vg site; gd sized pitches; excel san facs." 15 May-15 Sep. HUF 8695 2013*

⊞ **BALATONFURED** *C2* (9km NE Rural) *46.99184, 17.98698* **Présház Camping, Présház út 1, 8226 Alsóörs [(87) 447736]** Rd 71 fr Balatonfüred, site just past vill of Alsóörs on L. Sm, pt sl, pt shd; wc; chem disp; shwrs inc; EHU (10A) inc; lake sw 1km; games area; dogs; quiet. "Vg, lovely, CL-type site in orchard of wine shop; friendly owner; wine-tasting; paid in Euros but Forint preferred; sighting of wild boar nrby!"
HUF 4360 2015*

BALATONSZEPEZD *C1* (4km SW Rural) *48.82950, 17.64000* **Balatontourist Camping Napfény, Halász út 5, 8253 Révfülöp [(87) 563031 or (88) 544444 (LS); fax 464309 or (88) 544455 (LS); napfenyj@balatontourist.hu; www.balatontourist.hu]** Take m'way E71/M7 & exit junc 90 along N shore of lake, passing Balatonalmádi & Balatonfüred to Révfülöp. Site sp. Lge, mkd pitch, pt shd; wc; chem disp; mv service pnt; fam bthrm; private san facs avail; shwrs inc; EHU (6A) inc; lndry (inc dryer); shop; supmkt 500m; rest, snacks; bar; BBQ; playgrnd; paddling pool; lake sw & beach adj; fishing; watersports; bike & boat hire; spa; tennis 300m; horseriding 5km; games area; games rm; wifi; entmnt; TV rm; 2% statics; dogs HUF900; twin-axles acc (rec check in adv); phone; adv bkg; quiet; ccard acc; red LS. "Warm welcome; excel, well-organised lakeside site; gd pitches; gd for families; fees according to pitch size & location." ♦
25 Apr-27 Sep. HUF 9449 SBS - X06 2012*

BOLDOGASSZONYFA *D2* (1km S Rural) *46.17807, 17.83812* **Camping Horgásztanya, Petőfi út 53, 7937 Boldogasszonyfa [(73) 702003; csukabeno@ciromail.hu; www.horgasztanya.hu]** Take rte 67 S fr Kaposvár. Immed after vill of Boldogasszonyfa turn L, site sp on rvside. Sm, hdg pitch, pt sl, shd; wc; chem disp (wc); shwrs inc; EHU (10A); rest; bar; fishing; quiet; CKE/CCI. "Simple, rural site; conv Pécs & border area; rec use own facs." ♦ ltd. 1 May-30 Sep. 2012*

BOZSOK see Köszeg *B1*

⊞ **BUDAPEST** *B2* (10km N Urban) *47.57434, 19.05179* **Római Camping, Szentendrei útca 189, 1031 Budapest [(1) 3887167; fax 2500426; info@romaicamping.hu; www.romaicamping.hu]** Fr Gyor/Budapest m'way M1/E50 foll rte 11 twd Szentendre/Esztergom for approx 9km. Turn R at site sp. Site adj Római Fürdő rlwy stn. Med, mkd pitch, shd; wc; chem disp; shwrs inc; EHU (16A) HUF600; lndry (inc dryer); shop 500m; rest, snacks; BBQ; playgrnd; htd pool; playgrnd; waterslide; TV; dogs HUG590; train 300m; phone; Eng spkn; poss noisy; ccard not acc; CKE/CCI. "V conv for city." HUF 10613 2013*

HUNGARY

BUDAPEST *B2* (14km N Rural) *47.6013, 19.0191* **Jumbo Camping, Budakalászi út 23, 2096 Üröm [tel/fax (26) 351251; jumbo@campingbudapest.com; www.jumbocamping.hu]** Best app fr N on rd 10 or 11. Fr M1 take Zsámbék exit thro Perbál to join rd 10 & turn W twd Budapest. After Pilisvörösvar turn L in 8km sp Üröm Site well sp. Med, hdg pitch, hdstg, pt sl, terr, pt shd; wc; chem disp; shwrs inc; EHU (6-10A) inc; lndry; shop 500m; rest 300m; snacks; bar; playgrnd; htd pool high ssn; TV; 10% statics; dogs; bus to Budapest fr vill; Eng spkn; adv bkg; quiet. "Highly rec; clean, modern facs; immac, family-run site, v helpful." 1 Apr-31 Oct. HUF 6495 2017*

⊞ **BUDAPEST** *B2* (10km E Urban) *47.50421, 19.15834* **Camping Arena, Pilisi Str 7, 1106 Budapest [06 30 29 691 29; info@budapestcamping.hu; www.budapestcamping.hu]** Leave M0 at exit 60 Kistarcsa & foll Rd 3 twd city cent for 7.5km. Turn L just bef rlwy bdge. Site 200m on R. Sm, hdg pitch, pt shd; wc; chem disp; mv service pnt; shwrs; EHU (16A); lndry (inc dryer); cooking facs; wifi; 10% statics; dogs; bus 400m; metro 1km; Eng spkn; adv bkg; CCI. "Some rlwy & aircraft noise; supermkt 400m; shopping arcade 1km; rec all day travel card for metro, trams & busses; vg." ♦ ltd. HUF 5800 2014*

BUDAPEST *B2* (5km SE Urban) *47.47583, 19.08305* **Haller Camping, 27 Haller útca, 1096 Budapest [(20) 3674274; info@hallercamping.hu; www.hallercamping.hu]** Fr S on M5 twd Budapest cent. At ring rd foll dir Lagnymanyosi Hid (bdge). Bef bdge by lge shopping cent (Lurdy-Ház) turn R. Site sp. Or fr SE on rd 4 sp airport/Cegléd, turn R 100m bef new church steeple on L, foll sp Haller Piac. Med, hdstg, pt shd; wc; chem disp; mv service pnt; shwrs inc; EHU (16A) inc; lndry; lge shoping cent 500m; rest adj; snacks; BBQ; wifi; dogs free; phone; tram & bus 100m; poss cr; Eng spkn; adv bkg; quiet; red long stay/CKE/CCI. "V friendly; vg security; gd, clean san facs; tram stop opp site; conv for city cent; v helpful staff." ♦ ltd. 10 May-30 Sep. HUF 8985 2013*

⊞ **BUK** *B1* (4km E Rural) *47.38433, 16.79051* **Romantik Camping, Thermál Krt 12, 9740 Bükfürdõ [(94) 558050; fax 558051; info@romantikcamping.com; www.romantikcamping.com]** Fr Sopron on rte 84 twd Lake Balaton for approx 45km, foll sp & exit Bükfürdõ. After service stn turn R then cont for 5km sp Thermalbad & site. Lge, pt shd; htd wc; chem disp; mv service pnt; shwrs inc; EHU (10-16A) metered; lndry; shop; rest; bar 100m; playgrnd; pool high ssn; thermal cent 500m; tennis 500m; bike hire; entmnt; 10% statics; dogs €2; adv bkg; quiet; ccard acc; red long stay/CKE/CCI. "Quiet and peaceful an ideal place to unwind." ♦ HUF 5604 2015*

⊞ **CSERKESZOLO** *C3* (800m S Urban) *46.86386, 20.2019* **Thermal Camping Cserkeszölö, Beton út 5, 5465 Cserkeszölö [(6) 56568450; fax 56568464; hotelcamping@cserkeszolo.hu; www.touring-hotel.hu/en]** On rte 44 bet Kecksemet & Kunszentmárton. Site sp in Cserkeszölö. Lge, pt shd; htd wc; chem disp; mv service pnt; sauna; shwrs inc; EHU (10A) inc; lndry; shop 200m; rest, snacks; BBQ; cooking facs; 2 pools (1 htd, covrd); paddling pool; waterslide; tennis; games area; 10% statics; dogs; phone; bus 200m; poss cr; quiet; CKE/CCI. "Use of sw pools & thermal pools inc in site fee; gd." HUF 6226 2016*

"I need an on-site restaurant"

We do our best to make sure site information is correct, but it is always best to check any must-have facilities are still available or will be open during your visit.

DOMOS *B2* (500m E Rural) *47.7661, 18.91495* **Dömös Camping, Dömös Dunapart, 2027 Dömös [(33) 482319; fax 414800; info@domoscamping.hu; www.domoscamping.hu]** On rd 11 fr Budapest, site on R on ent Dömös, adj Rv Danube. Med, hdg pitch, pt shd; wc; chem disp; shwrs inc; EHU (10A) HUF950; lndry (inc dryer); rest, snacks; bar; cooking facs; playgrnd; pool; paddling pool; wifi; TV rm; dogs HUF500; phone; bus to Budapest; poss cr; Eng spkn; adv bkg; some rd & rlwy noise; red long stay/CKE/CCI. "Delightful site with views Danube bend; spacious pitches - lower ones poss subject to flooding; excel, clean facs & rest." ♦ 1 May-30 Sep. HUF 6150 2017*

⊞ **DUNAFOLDVAR** *C2* (2km NE Rural) *46.81227, 18.92664* **Kék-Duna Camping, Hösök Tere 23, 7020 Dunafoldvár [tel/fax (75) 541107; ddifzrt@freemail.hu]** Fr rndabt S of Dunafoldvár turn twd town cent. At traff lts turn R down to rv, then turn L, under green bdge & foll towpath 300m to site. Sm, shd; wc; shwrs inc; EHU (16A) inc; lndry; shop high ssn & 500m; rest; BBQ; 2 pools adj (1 covrd); paddling pool; watersports; fishing; tennis; bike hire; adv bkg; quiet; 10% red CKE/CCI. "Pleasant position o'looking Danube; adequate, clean san facs but dated; gd touring base Transdanubia." HUF 4100 2016*

GYENESDIAS see Keszthely *C1*

GYOR *B1* (7km NE Rural) *47.72547, 17.71446* **Piheno Camping, Weg 10, 9011 Gyor [tel/fax (96) 523008; piheno@piheno.hu; www.piheno.hu]** E fr Gyor on rte 1 twds Budapest, stay on rte 1 for Komarom. Site on L 3km past m'way (M1) junc. Sm, hdg/mkd pitch, pt sl, pt shd; htd wc; chem disp; shwrs HUF10 per min; EHU (16A); gas; lndry; rest; bar; BBQ; cooking facs; playgrnd; pool; paddling pool; wifi; TV; 10% statics; dogs HUF1000; phone; bus; Eng spkn; noise fr adj arms range; adv bkg; ccard acc; 10% red CKE/CCI. "Gd facs; fair." 1 May-30 Sep. HUF 4593 2017*

⊞ **HAJDUSZOBOSZLO** *B4* (2km N Urban) *47.45756, 21.39396* **Thermál Camping, Böszörményi út 35A, 4200 Hajdúszoboszló [tel/fax (52) 558552; thermal camping@hungarospa.hu; www.hungarospa.hu]** Fr W on rte 4/E573 thro town, site sp on L. Fr Debrecen, turn R 500m past Camping Hadjdútourist on lakeside. Lge, hdg pitch, pt shd; wc; chem disp; mv service pnt; shwrs inc; EHU (12A) inc; gas 1km; lndry; shop, rest high ssn; snacks; BBQ; cooking facs; playgrnd; htd, covrd pool & thermal baths adj; paddling pool; waterslide; TV rm; dogs HUF440; phone; poss cr; Eng spkn; no adv bkg; quiet; ccard acc; red CKE/CCI. "Pleasant site; sm naturist island in lake." HUF 9136 2016*

HEGYKO see Fertöd *B1*

HEVIZ see Keszthely *C1*

JASZAPATI *B3* (1.5km S Urban) *47.50537, 20.14012* **Tölgyes Strand Camping, Gyöngyvirág u 11, 5130 Jászapáti [(57) 441187; fax 441008; info@tolgyes strand.hu; www.tolgyesstrand.hu]** Fr Budapest E on M3, exit at Hatvan & take rd 32 to Jászberény then foll rd 31 to Jászapáti. Site sp fr town cent. Med, mkd pitch, pt shd; wc; chem disp; mv service pnt; shwrs; EHU (10A); lndry (inc dryer); rest, snacks; bar; playgrnd; 2 pools (1 htd, covrd); tennis 200m; games area; bike hire; internet; TV rm; some statics; dogs; site clsd 1 Nov to mid-Dec; adv bkg; quiet. "Gd, modern facs." 1 Apr-30 Nov. 2016*

KESZTHELY *C1* (8.5km N Rural) *46.80803, 17.21248* **Camping Panoráma, Köz 1, 8372 Cserszegtomaj [(83) 314412; fax 330215; matuska78@freemail.hu; www.panoramacamping.com]** Exit Keszthely by direct rd to Sümeg. After turn to Hévíz (Thermal Spa). Clearly sp on R of side rd. Med, terr, pt shd; htd wc; chem disp; shwrs €0.90; EHU (16A) €2.50; lndry; shops 200m; rest; lake sw 2km; TV; 30% statics; dogs €1; phone; quiet; red CKE/CCI. "Conv Lake Balaton area; v friendly & clean; remedial massage avail; gd views." 1 Apr-31 Oct. HUF 4000 2015*

⊞ **KESZTHELY** *C1* (18km N Rural) *46.89442, 17.23166* **Camping St Vendal, Fö út Hrsz 192/3, 8353 Zalaszántó [tel/fax (83) 370147; camping. stvendel@freemail.hu; www.szallas.net/st. vendel-camping]** Fr N on rd 84 turn dir Bazsi/Hévíz at Sümeg. Site at ent to town. Fr S take Sümeg/Hévíz off rd 71 bef Keszthely & foll sp Sümeg & Zalaszántó. Sm, pt shd; htd wc; chem disp; shwrs inc; EHU (6A) HUF540 long lead poss req'd; lndry; rest, snacks; bar; BBQ; cooking facs; internet; TV rm; dogs HUF250; quiet; CKE/CCI. "Friendly welcome; gd walking/cycling; conv for thermal lake at Heviz & Lake Balaton but without crowds, noise of lakeside sites; delightful site in orchard - awkward for lge o'fits; spotless facs; lovely peaceful site." HUF 9293 2013*

KESZTHELY *C1* (8km NW Rural) *46.78393, 17.19575* **Kurcamping Castrum, Tópart, 8380 Héviz [(83) 343198; fax 540263; heviz@castrum.eu; www. castrum-group.hu]** Fr Keszthely foll sp to Héviz & site 700m to E, opp Héviz thermal lake. Lge, mkd pitch, pt shd; htd wc; chem disp; mv service pnt; 20% serviced pitches; shwrs inc; EHU (6-16A) €3; lndry; shop; rest; bar; htd pool adj; lake sw adj; sat TV; dogs €4; poss cr; Eng spkn; adv bkg; quiet; CKE/CCI. "Lake fed by hot springs so gd for sw; casino adj; easy cycle ride/walk into lovely spa town & cycle path to Keszthely; excel san facs; excursions Budapest fr gate; v nice site; gd location to explore by foot or bike." 1 Mar-31 Dec. HUF 3113 2013*

MANFA *D2* (18km NE Rural) *46.23372, 18.30844* **Campsite Mare Vara, Varvolgyi utca 2, 7332 Magyaregregy [tel/fax (72) 420126; info@camping-marevara.com; www.camping-marevara.com]** Fr Pecs head N on 6. Turn L onto Cseresznyes ut, which then becomes Komlo-Zobakpuszta. In 6.8km turn R onto Varvolgyi u. Site in 120m. Sm, pt sl, pt shd; htd wc; chem disp; fam bthrm; shwrs inc; EHU (10A) inc; lndry (inc dryer); snacks; bar; BBQ; pool; games area; wifi; 1% statics; dogs; Eng spkn; adv bkg; quiet; CKE/CCI. "Dutch owners, warm welcome; ample space to pitch; almost an orchard setting; vg." ♦ ltd. 15 Apr-30 Sep. HUF 5499 2015*

MATRAFURED *B3* (4km N Rural) *47.84416, 19.95725* **Mátra Camping Sástó, Farkas út 4, 3232 Mátrafüred [tel/fax (37) 374025; www.matrakemping.hu]** Take rte 24 N fr Gyöngyös. Site on L 2km after Mátrafüred. Med, some hdstg, pt sl, pt shd; wc; shwrs inc; EHU (10A) inc; shop, rest, snacks, bar adj; cooking facs; TV; wifi; some statics; dogs; phone adj; poss cr; ccard acc. "Site pt of controlled sports complex; vg secure site." 1 Apr-31 Oct. HUF 5543 2016*

MOSONMAGYAROVAR *B1* (1km E Urban) *47.87718, 17.27874* **Termál Aqua Camping, Kigyó út 1, 9200 Mosonmagyaróvár [tel/fax (96) 579168; aquahotel@t-online.hu; www.tha.hu]** Foll sp fr town cent to Termál Hotel Aqua; site in grnds, just behind lge thermal baths. Sm, hdg/mkd pitch, shd; htd wc; chem disp; mv service pnt; shwrs inc; EHU €3; lndry; shop 1km; rest, snacks; bar; BBQ; cooking facs; htd, covrd thermal & sw pool adj; dogs €2; bus, train 1km; phone; Eng spkn; quiet. "Vg site; price inc ent to thermals & sauna." 1 Apr-30 Oct. HUF 9028 2016*

⊞ **MOSONMAGYAROVAR** *B1* (3km SE Urban) *47.84224, 17.28591* **Camping Kis-Duna, Gabonarakpart 6, 9200 Mosonmagyaróvár [tel/fax (96) 216433]** Site on L of M1 Mosonmagyaróvár-Győr in grnds of motel & rest, 15km fr border. Sm, some hdstg, unshd; wc; chem disp; shwrs inc; EHU (16A) HUF500; lndry; shop 1km; rest; thermal pool 2.5km; TV; dogs HUF500. "Gd, clean, facs; rest gd but busy; gd alt to Bratislava site (Slovakia); ideal NH." HUF 5616 2016*

HUNGARY

⊞ **PAPA** *B1* (2km N Urban) *47.33797, 17.47367* **Termál Camping Pápa, Várkert út 7, 8500 Pápa [tel/fax 36 89 320 735; info@thermalkemping.hu; www.thermalkemping.hu]** Fr 83 exit at Gyori Way. Foll sp. Lge, hdg/mkd pitch, hdstg, pt shd; htd wc; chem disp; mv service pnt; fam bthrm; shwrs; EHU (16A); gas; lndry rm (inc dryer); shop 1km; rest; snacks; bar; BBQ; cooking facs; playgrnd; htd pool adj; paddling pool; sw thermal adj; games area; games rm; entmnt; wifi; 20% statics; dogs €2; phone; bus 500m; twin axles; Eng spkn; quiet; adv bkg; red LS; CCI. "Onsite kids club; boccia; basketball; archery; disco adj; thermal baths with indoor & outdoor pools, slides; excel; well managed site; gd area for long stay & touring; very helpful staff." ♦ HUF 7390 2014*

REVFULOP see Balatonszepezd *C1*

SAROSPATAK *A4* (2km NE Rural) *48.33274, 21.58245* **Tengerszem Camping, Herceg Ferenc ut 2, 3950 Sárospatak [(47) 312744; fax 323527; info@tengerszem-camping.hu; www.tengerszem-camping.hu]** NW fr Tokaj on R38; then NE on R37 to Sárospatak; foll camp sp. Med, hdg pitch, pt shd; wc; mv service pnt; shwrs; EHU (10A) inc; shop; rest, snacks; playgrnd; pool; tennis; games area; TV; rlwy noise; CKE/CCI. "Refurbished thermal sw baths next door; gd site for mountains." 30 Apr-15 Oct. HUF 6441 2016*

⊞ **SARVAR** *B1* (2km SE Urban) *47.24671, 16.9473* **Sárvár Thermal Camping, Vadkert út 1, 9600 Sárvár [(95) 523610; fax 523612; info@thermalcamping.com; www.thermalcamping.com]** E fr Szombathely via rtes 86 & 88. Site on Sopron-Lake Balaton rte 84. Med, some hdstg, pt shd; htd wc; chem disp; mv service pnt; sauna; fam bthrm; private san facs avail; shwrs; EHU (16A) €3; lndry; shop; rest, snacks adj; BBQ; cooking facs; playgrnd; htd thermal pools adj; paddling pool; waterslide; lake fishing; tennis 500m; wifi; dogs €2; poss cr; 10% statics; ccard acc; quiet; red long stay; CKE/CCI. "Barrier clsd 1330-1500; free ent to spa & fitness cent adj." ♦ HUF 13007 2016*

SOPRON *B1* (8km SE Rural) *47.6525, 16.6575* **Kurcamping Castrum Balf-Sopron, Fürdö Sor 59-61, 9494 Balf [tel/fax (99) 339124; balfcamping@gmail.com; sopron-balf-camping.hu]** On rte 84 S of Sopron turn E sp Balf. In 2km turn N sp Sopron & foll sps. Site at W end Balf vill. Med, hdg/mkd pitch, pt shd; htd wc (cont); chem disp; sauna; shwrs inc; EHU (6A) HUF800; lndry (inc dryer); shops 350m; rest 250m; pool & 250m; bike hire; TV; wifi; dogs €2.50; phone; Eng spkn; rd noise; ccard acc; CKE/CCI. "Thermal baths avail; Tesco hypmkt on app to Sopron 6km, with ATM; pitches uneven; ltd facs LS & poss unkempt; poss cold shwrs; site in need of maintenance; overpriced NH." 1 Apr-31 Oct. HUF 4770 2016*

TAMASI *C2* (1km S Urban) *46.62577, 18.28734* **Thermál Camping, Hársfa út 1, 7090 Tamási [tel/fax (74) 471738; camping@tamasistrand.hu; www.tamasikemping.hu]** Site & thermal baths sp on rd 65 adj motel. Med, pt shd; wc; shwrs inc; EHU (10A) HUF575 (long lead req); lndry; shop 500m; rest 200m; htd pool; dogs HUF67; 10% statics; phone; CKE/CCI. "Security gate; free access to lge thermal pool complex; vg; perfect location for spa next door; nice town and surrounding area." 1 May-15 Oct. HUF 5099 2013*

TATABANYA *B2* (14km N Rural) *47.6679, 18.3090* **Fényes Camping, Környei út 24, 2890 Tata [(34) 481208; fax 588144; fenyesfurdo@tata.hu; www.fenyesfurdo.hu]** Exit junc 67 fr M1 to Tata town cent; foll sp for 3km E to site. Lge, shd; wc; own san rec; shwrs inc; EHU; shop; rest; playgrnd; 3 pools; games area; dogs HUF500; Eng spkn; CKE/CCI. "Tata interesting town; fair site set in lge park." 1 May-15 Sep. HUF 1800 2016*

TOKAJ *A4* (1km NE Rural) *48.12306, 21.41806* **Tiszavirág Camping, Horgász út 11a, 3910 Tokaj [tel/fax (06) 709344175; tiszavir@axelero.hu; www.tokaj.hu]** Fr town cent turn E over rv on rte 38 sp Nyiregyháza. Camp ent 100m over bdge on L. Med, shd; wc; chem disp; shwrs inc; EHU (10A) HUF450; lndry; shops 300m; bar; fishing; dogs HUF400; poss cr; quiet. "On rv bank; wine cellars in walking dist; ltd facs on Sun." 1 Apr-30 Oct. HUF 4200 2015*

TURISTVANDI *A4* (1km SW Rural) *48.04710, 22.64300* **Vizimalom Camping, Malom út 3, 4944 Túristvándi [(30) 289 9808; turvizimalom@freemail.hu; www.turvizimalom.hu]** Fr Fehérgyarmat foll rd 491 NE for 4km to Penyige, turn L to Túristvándi. After approx 12km site on R adj 18thC water mill on Rv Túr. Sm, some hdstg, pt shd; wc; shwrs; EHU (10A); shop 500m; rest, snacks; bar; BBQ; playgrnd; canoeing; games area; games rm; TV; internet; dogs; quiet. "Excel location; no hdstg." 1 Mar-1 Nov. HUF 5853 2016*

UROM see Budapest *B2*

ZALAKAROS *C1* (3km S Rural) *46.53165, 17.12443* **Kurcamping Castrum, Ady Endre út, 8754 Galambok [tel/fax (93) 358610; zalakaros@castrum.eu; www.castrum-group.hu]** Fr rte 7 N dir Zalakaros, site sp. Med, hdg/mkd pitch, pt shd; htd wc; chem disp; sauna; shwrs inc; EHU (6A) inc; lndry; shop, rest 1km; snacks; bar; BBQ; htd, covrd pool; thermal complex 2km; wifi; some statics; dogs; bus; quiet; ccard acc; CKE/CCI. ♦ 1 Mar-31 Oct. HUF 8000 (CChq acc) 2016*

ZALASZANTO see Keszthely *C1*

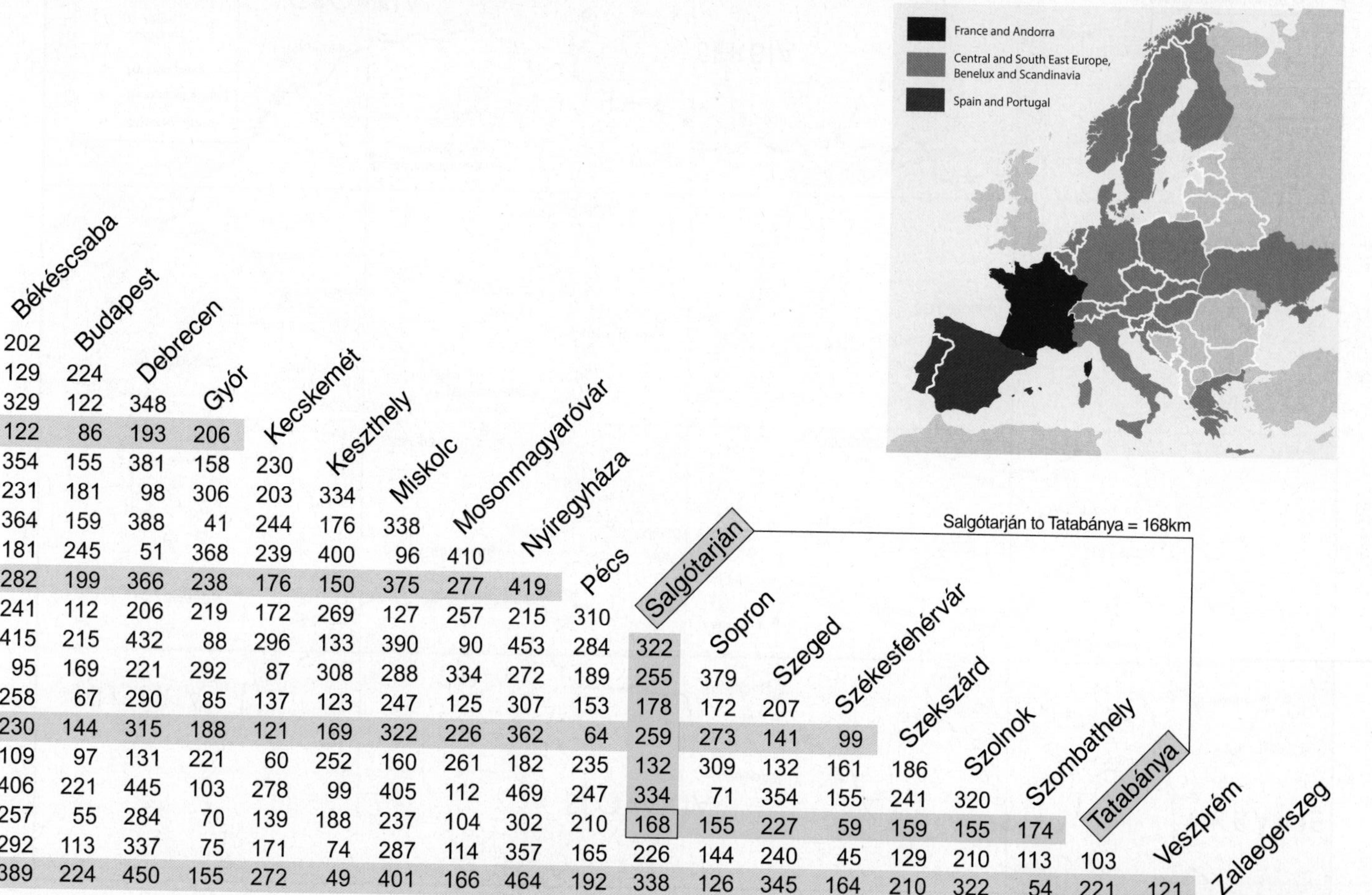

Salgótarján to Tatabánya = 168km

	Békéscsaba	Budapest	Debrecen	Győr	Kecskemét	Keszthely	Miskolc	Mosonmagyaróvár	Nyíregyháza	Pécs	Salgótarján	Sopron	Szeged	Székesfehérvár	Szekszárd	Szolnok	Szombathely	Tatabánya	Veszprém
Budapest	202																		
Debrecen	129	224																	
Győr	329	122	348																
Kecskemét	122	86	193	206															
Keszthely	354	155	381	158	230														
Miskolc	231	181	98	306	203	334													
Mosonmagyaróvár	364	159	388	41	244	176	338												
Nyíregyháza	181	245	51	368	239	400	96	410											
Pécs	282	199	366	238	176	150	375	277	419										
Salgótarján	241	112	206	219	172	269	127	257	215	310									
Sopron	415	215	432	88	296	133	390	90	453	284	322								
Szeged	95	169	221	292	87	308	288	334	272	189	255	379							
Székesfehérvár	258	67	290	85	137	123	247	125	307	153	178	172	207						
Szekszárd	230	144	315	188	121	169	322	226	362	64	259	273	141	99					
Szolnok	109	97	131	221	60	252	160	261	182	235	132	309	132	161	186				
Szombathely	406	221	445	103	278	99	405	112	469	247	334	71	354	155	241	320			
Tatabánya	257	55	284	70	139	188	237	104	302	210	168	155	227	59	159	155	174		
Veszprém	292	113	337	75	171	74	287	114	357	165	226	144	240	45	129	210	113	103	
Zalaegerszeg	389	224	450	155	272	49	401	166	464	192	338	126	345	164	210	322	54	221	121

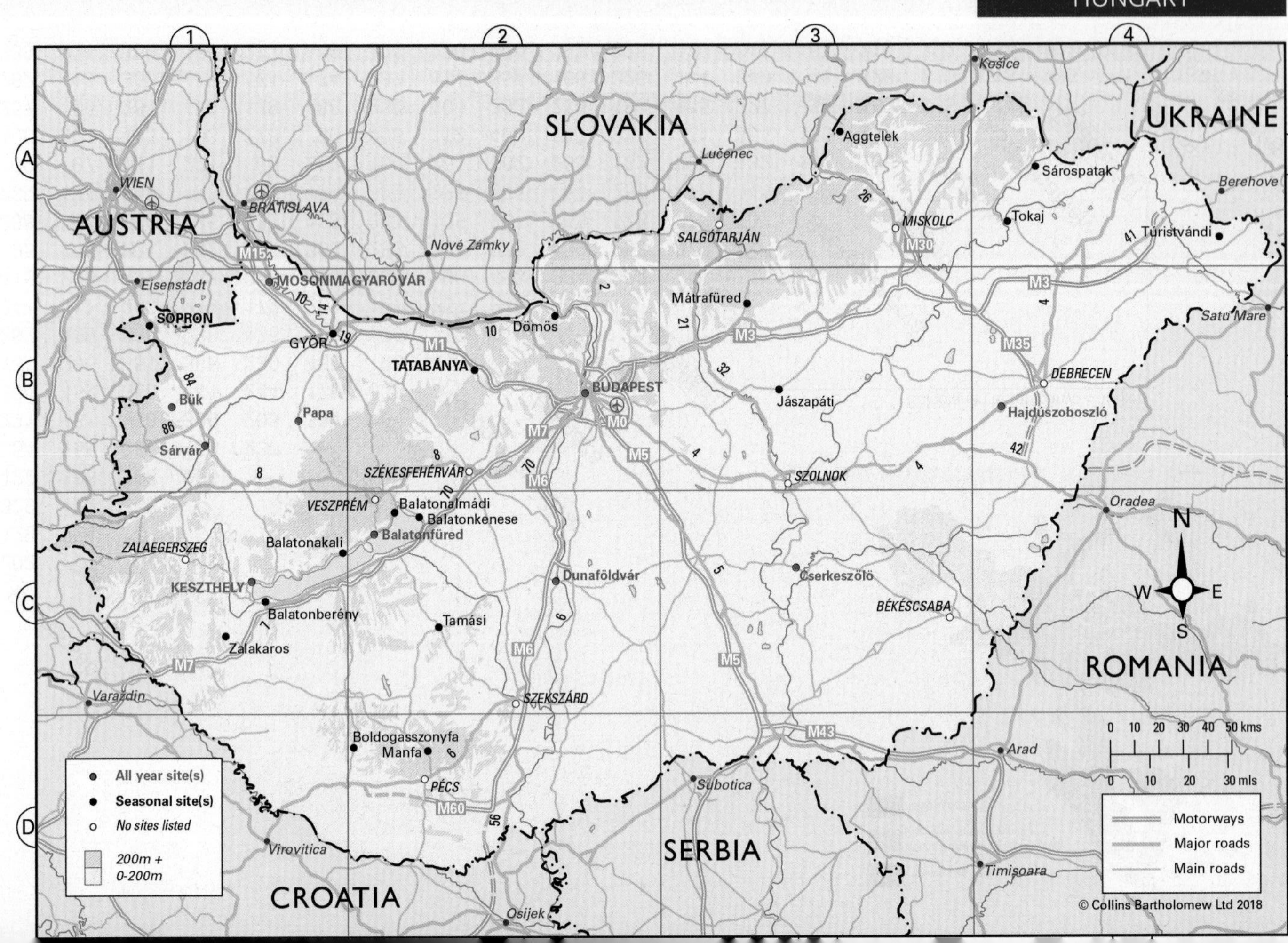
1
2
3
4
A
B
C
D
SLOVAKIA
UKRAINE
AUSTRIA
ROMANIA
SERBIA
CROATIA
Košice
Aggtelek
Lučenec
Sárospatak
Berehove
WIEN
BRATISLAVA
SALGÓTARJÁN
MISKOLC
Tokaj
Túristvándi
Nové Zámky
Eisenstadt
MOSONMAGYARÓVÁR
Mátrafüred
Satu Mare
SOPRON
Dömös
GYŐR
TATABÁNYA
DEBRECEN
BUDAPEST
Jászapáti
Bük
Papa
Hajdúszoboszló
Sárvár
SZÉKESFEHÉRVÁR
SZOLNOK
VESZPRÉM
Balatonalmádi
Balatonkenese
Oradea
Balatonfüred
Balatonakali
ZALAEGERSZEG
Dunaföldvár
Cserkeszölö
KESZTHELY
Balatonberény
BÉKÉSCSABA
Tamási
Zalakaros
Varaždin
SZEKSZÁRD
Boldogasszonyfa
Manfa
Arad
PÉCS
Subotica
Virovitica
Timişoara
Osijek
N
W
E
S
0 10 20 30 40 50 kms
0 10 20 30 mls
All year site(s)
Seasonal site(s)
No sites listed
200m +
0-200m
Motorways
Major roads
Main roads
© Collins Bartholomew Ltd 2018

Manarola town, Cinque Terre, Liguria

Welcome to Italy

One of the greatest cultural jewels in Europe's crown has to be Italy. It is a country alive with art and fashion that is envied across the world, and boasts some of the most extraordinary architectural masterpieces in existence. Alongside the grandeur is a country with great natural diversity, from the snow-capped Alps in the north to the stunning Mediterranean coastline. The variety of local customs and traditions encountered through the different regions are always captivating.

Country highlights

Italy is often considered the fashion capital of the world, and leather working has often been at the forefront of its fashion industry. The Italian tanning industry is considered a world leader and there are many products available from bags to belts which showcase this skill.

Italy is also a country of celebration, with hundreds of festivals and carnivals taking place. One of the most famous is the Carnival of Venice, where traditional masks and costumes are worn by attendees.

Major towns and cities

- Rome – this remarkable city is known as the "Capital of the World".
- Milan – a global centre of fashion and known for its exquisite galleries.
- Turin – famous for its baroque architecture and monuments.
- Naples – boasting a wealth of historical buildings from a variety of periods.

Attractions

- Venice – one of the world's most beautiful cities and boasting a wealth of historic sites.
- Santa Maria del Fiore, Florence – one of the most recognisable cathedrals that houses several important works of art.
- Pompeii – the remains of an ancient Roman town in the shadow of Mount Vesuvius.
- Cinque Terre – five beautiful and traditional villages that lie on the Italian Riviera.

Find out more

www.enit.it
Tel: 0039 (0) 06 49 711 Italian Tourist Board

Country Information

Population (approx): 61.8 million

Capital: Rome

Area: 301,318 sq km (inc Sardinia & Sicily)

Bordered by: France, Switzerland, Austria, Slovenia

Terrain: Mountainous in the north descending to rolling hills in the centre; some plains and coastal lowlands

Climate: Predominantly Mediterranean climate, alpine in the far north, hot and dry in the south

Coastline: 7,600km

Highest Point: Monte Bianco (Mont Blanc) 4,810m

Language: Italian, German (in the northern Alps)

Local Time: GMT or BST + 1, i.e. 1 hour ahead of the UK all year

Currency: Euros divided into 100 cents; £1 = €1.13, €1 = £0.88 (November 2017)

Emergency numbers: Police 113; Fire brigade 115; Ambulance 118

Public Holidays 2018: Jan 1, 6; Apr 1,2, 25; May 1; Jun 2; Aug 15; Nov 1; Dec 8, 25, 26.

Each locality also celebrates its patron saint's day. School summer holidays run from mid June to mid September.

Camping and Caravanning

There are approximately 2,000 organised and supervised campsites in Italy. They are usually well signposted and are open from April to September. Advance booking is recommended in high season, especially by the lakes and along the Adriatic coast. About 20% of campsites are open all year including some in the mountains and around large towns. Campsites organised by the Touring Club Italiano (TCI) and the Federcampeggio are particularly well equipped.

In general pitch sizes are small at about 80 square metres and it may be difficult to fit a large outfit plus an awning onto a pitch. You will frequently find that hot water is supplied to showers only, for which you will be charged. Published opening and closing dates may be unreliable - phone ahead if travelling during the low season.

It is not compulsory to have a Camping Key Europe (CKE) or Camping Card International (CCI), but it is recommended as a means of identification. If for any reason details are missing from the CKE or CCI a site will insist on holding a visitor's passport instead.

Casual camping is not recommended and is not permitted in national parks or in state forests.

Motorhomes

Many local authorities permit motorhomes to park overnight in specially designated places known as 'Camper Stops' or 'Aree di Sosta' and a list of their locations and the services provided are contained in a number of publications and on a number of websites including the French 'Guide Officiel Aires de Service Camping-Car' published by the Fédération Française de Camping et de Caravaning, www.ffcc.fr. You will also find a list of 'Camper Stops' on www.turismoitinerante.com

Transportation of bicycles

An overhanging load must be indicated by an aluminium square panel (panello) measuring 50cm x 50cm with reflective red and white diagonal stripes. The load must not exceed 30% of the length of the vehicle, may only overhang at the rear and the regulation applies to a car or caravan carrying bicycles at the rear or windsurf boards on the roof. A fine may be imposed for failure to display the approved sign which is made by Fiamma and in the UK may be purchased from or ordered through motorhome or caravan dealers/ accessory shops. For a list of Fiamma stockists please see www.fiamma.com.

At night, outside built up areas, cyclists must wear a reflective jacket and must ride in single file.

Electricity and Gas

Current at campsites varies between 2 and 16 amps and often it is very low, offering a maximum of only 4 amps across the whole site. Many sites have CEE connections. Plugs have three round pins in line.

Campingaz cylinders are generally available, except in the south of Italy, Sardinia and Sicily where exchange may be difficult outside of marinas and holiday resorts.

Entry Formalities

British and Irish passport holders may stay in Italy for up to three months without a visa.

Regulations for Pets

All dogs, including those temporarily imported, must be on a leash at all times. It is advisable to carry a muzzle as the police/authorities can insist on your dog wearing one if they consider your dog to be dangerous. Some sites and some public transport operators insist that all dogs are muzzled at all times - check local requirements on arrival.

A domestic animal may be transported in a car provided it does not distract the driver. More than one animal may be transported provided they are kept in the rear of the car, separated from the driver by bars, or kept in special cages.

Medical Services

Ask at a pharmacy (farmacia) for the nearest doctor registered with the state health care scheme (SSN) or look in the telephone directory under 'Unita Sanitaria Locale'. The services of a national health service doctor are normally free of charge.

A European Health Insurance Card (EHIC) entitles you to emergency treatment and medication at local rates and to hospital treatment under the state healthcare scheme. Any charges you do incur are non-refundable in Italy but you may be able to make a claim on your return to the UK. Dental treatment is expensive and you will be charged the full fee.

Emergency services (Guardia Medica) are available at weekends and at night and there are first aid posts at major train stations and airports. Staff at pharmacies can advise on minor ailments and at least one pharmacy remains open 24 hours in major towns.

Opening Hours

Banks: Mon-Fri 8.30am-1.30pm & 3pm-4pm.

Museums: Check locally as may vary. The Vatican museums and Sistine Chapel are not open to visitors Sun. Visitors under 18 or over 60 are admitted free to State museums on production of a passport.

Post Offices: Mon-Fri 8.30am-2pm/5.30pm, Sat 8.30am-12 noon.

Shops: Mon-Sat 8.30am/9am-1pm & 3.30pm/4pm-7.30pm/8pm. In southern Italy and tourist areas shops may stay open later. There is no lunch time closing in large cities. Shops are closed half a day each week (variable by region).

Safety and Security

Most visits to Italy are trouble free and, in general, levels of crime are low, but visitors should take care on public transport and in crowded areas where pickpockets and bag snatchers may operate. In Rome take particular care around the main railway station, Roma Termini, and on the bus to and from St Peter's Square. Also take care in and around railway stations in large cities. Be particularly wary of groups of children who may try to distract your attention while attempting to steal from you. Do not carry your passport, credit cards and cash all together in one bag or pocket and only carry what you need for the day. Do not wear expensive jewellery, particularly in the south of Italy.

Take care in bars and don't leave drinks unattended. Recently there have been cases of drinks being spiked. Check prices before ordering food and insist on seeing a priced menu. Be particularly careful when ordering items, such as lobster, which are charged by weight.

When driving in towns keep your car windows shut and doors locked and never leave valuables on display. Around Rome and Naples moped riders may attempt to snatch bags from stationary cars at traffic lights. Always lock your vehicle and never leave valuables in it, even if you will only be away for a short time or are nearby. Avoid leaving luggage in cars for any length of time or overnight.

Increasingly robberies are taking place from cars at rest stops and service stations on motorways. Treat offers of help with caution, for example with a flat tyre, particularly on the motorway from Naples to Salerno, as sometimes the tyre will have been punctured deliberately.

Do not be tempted to enter or bathe in Italy's many fountains – there are heavy fines if you do. Dress conservatively when visiting places of worship, i.e. cover shoulders and upper arms and do not wear shorts. Avoid queues in the peak season by visiting early in the morning.

The authorities are making strenuous efforts to stamp out the illegal production and sale of counterfeit goods. Illegal traders operate on the streets of all major cities, particularly tourist cities such as Florence and Rome. You are advised not to buy from them at the risk of incurring a fine.

Italy shares with the rest of Europe a general threat from terrorism. Attacks could be indiscriminate and against civilian targets in public places, including tourist sites. There continue to be isolated cases of domestic terrorism by extreme left wing and secessionist groups, aimed primarily at official Italian targets.

British Embassy
VIA XX SETTEMBRE 80A, I-00187 ROMA RM
Tel: 06 4220 0001 (24 hour emergency number)
www.ukinitaly.fco.gov.uk/en

British Consulate-General
VIA SAN PAOLO 7, I-20121 MILANO MI
Tel: 02 7230 01
There is also a British Consulates in Naples.

Irish Embassy
VILLA SPADA, VIA GIACOMO MEDICI
1 - 00153 ROMA
Tel: 06 5852 381
www.embassyofireland.it
There is also an Irish Honorary Consulate in Milan.

Documents

Driving Licence

The standard pink UK paper driving licence is recognised in Italy but holders of the old-style green UK licence are recommended to change it for a photocard licence. Alternatively an International Driving Permit may be purchased from the AA, the RAC or selected Post Offices.

Vehicle(s)

You must be able to present to the police on demand your vehicle and insurance documents, i.e. vehicle registration certificate (V5C), insurance certificate and MOT certificate (if applicable) and, if you are not the owner of your vehicle(s), authorisation for its use from the owner.

Money

There are few bureaux de change, so change cash at a bank.

Major credit cards are widely accepted including at petrol stations, but not as widely as in some other European countries. Automatic cash machines (Bancomat) are widespread. Carry your credit card issuers'/banks' 24-hour UK contact numbers in case of loss or theft of your cards.

Motoring in Italy

Alcohol

The maximum permitted level of alcohol is 50 milligrams in 100 millilitres of blood, i.e. less than in the UK (80 milligrams). For drivers with less than three years' driving experience, the limit is zero. It is advisable to adopt the 'no drink and drive' rule at all times as penalties are severe.

Breakdown Service

The motoring organisation, Automobile Club d'Italia (ACI) operates a breakdown service 24 hours a day throughout Italy, including San Marino and Vatican City. Telephone 803116 from a landline or mobile phone. ACI staff speak English. This number also gives access to the ACI emergency information service, operated by multi-lingual staff, for urgent medical or legal advice. You may also use the emergency phones placed every 2km on motorways.

On all roads, including motorways, standard charges are made for assistance and/or recovering a vehicle weighing up to 2,500kg to the nearest ACI garage. Higher charges apply at night, over weekends and public holidays and for towing to anywhere other than the nearest ACI garage. Vehicles over 2,500kg also incur higher charges. Payment is required in cash.

Road police, 'Polizia Stradale', constantly patrol all roads and motorways and can assist when vehicles break down.

Congestion Charge in Milan

In January 2012 a new congestion charge scheme in Milan was introduced to replace the old Pollution Charge (Ecopass). The new scheme is more restrictive than the old Ecopass scheme. To access the historical centre (Area C) from 7.30am – 7.30pm on Monday, Tuesday, Wednesday and Friday and from 7.30am- 6pm on Thursday you must pay a fee of €5 a day.

You can buy a ticket for entrance from parking meters, newsagents and some ATM points or online at www.areac.it – tickets must then be activated on the day before you plan to drive into the area. You can activate the ticket via text message or telephone. Visit the above website address to find out more. Petrol vehicles classed as Euro 0 and diesel vehicles in classes Euro 0 - 3 are not allowed to enter Area C at all during the above times.

Essential Equipment

Lights

It is compulsory for all vehicles to have dipped headlights at all times when driving outside built-up areas, on motorways and major roads, when driving in tunnels and when visibility is poor, e.g. in rain or snow. Bulbs are more likely to fail with constant use so you are advised to carry spares.

Reflective Jackets/ Waistcoats

If your vehicle is immobilised on the carriageway outside a built-up area at night, or in poor visibility, you must wear a reflective jacket or waistcoat when getting out of your vehicle. This rule also applies to passengers who may leave the vehicle, for example, to assist with a repair. Keep the jackets to hand inside your vehicle, not in the boot.

Warning Triangle

At night a warning triangle must be used to give advance warning of any vehicle parked outside a built-up area near a bend, or on a hill if rear side lights have failed, or in fog. Place the triangle at least 50 metres behind the vehicle (100 metres on motorways). Failure to use a triangle may result in a fine.

Child Restraint System

Children travelling in UK registered vehicles must be secured according to UK legislation.

Winter Driving

In the area of Val d'Aosta vehicles must be equipped with winter tyres or snow chains must be carried between 15 October and 15 April. This rule may apply in other areas and over other periods as conditions dictate.

Fuel

Unleaded petrol is sold from pumps marked 'Super Unleaded' or 'Super Sensa Piombo'. Diesel is called 'gasolio' and LPG is known as 'gas auto' or 'GPL'.

Fuel is sold 24 hours a day on motorways but elsewhere petrol stations may close for an extended lunch break and overnight from approximately 7pm. Opening hours are clearly displayed, as are the addresses of the nearest garages which are open.

Major credit cards are accepted, but possibly not in rural areas, so always carry some cash. Look for the 'Carta Si' sign. Recent visitors report that many petrol stations in rural areas and on major routes between towns are now unmanned and automated. Payment may be made with bank notes but the machines will usually only accept credit cards issued by Italian banks.

Low Emission Zones

Many Italian cities and towns operate low emission zones. They often affect all vehicles, but rules vary from city to city. For more information visit www.lowemissionzones.eu.

Overtaking

On roads with three traffic lanes, the middle lane is reserved for overtaking, but overtaking is only allowed if a vehicle travelling in the opposite direction is not already in the middle lane.

When pulling out to overtake on motorways check for cars travelling at well over the maximum speed limit of 130km/h (81 mph).

Parking

In major towns there are parking zones where payment is required and these are indicated by blue road signs. Pay either at a machine with coins or buy a card from local tobacconists or newspaper shops and display it inside your vehicle. Some cities also have green zones where parking is prohibited on working days during the morning and afternoon rush hours.

Parking against the traffic flow and parking on the pavement are not allowed. Illegally parked vehicles may be clamped or towed away.

Priority

In general, priority must be given to traffic coming from the right except if indicated by road signs. At traffic lights a flashing amber light indicates that traffic must slow down and proceed with caution, respecting the priority rules.

ITALY

Roads

The road network is of a high standard and main and secondary roads are generally good. Many main roads are winding and hilly but provide a more interesting route than the motorways. Stopping places for refreshments may be few and far between in some areas.

Standards of driving may be erratic, especially overtaking, and lane discipline poor; some roads have a particularly bad reputation for accidents. Those where special vigilance is called for include the Via Aurelia between Rome and Pisa, which is mostly two lane and is extremely busy at weekends, the A12 to the north with its series of tunnels and curves, the A1 between Florence and Bologna, the Rome ring road, roads around Naples and Palermo, and mountain roads in the south and in Sicily.

Road Signs and Markings

Road signs conform to international standards. White lettering on a green background indicates motorways (autostrada), whereas state and provincial roads outside built-up areas have white lettering on a blue background.

Other frequently encountered signs include the following:

Snow chains required

Horizontal traffic light

Carabinieri (police)

Ecopass zone (Milan)

Italian	English Translation
Attenzione	Caution
Autocarro	Lorries
Coda	Traffic jam
Curva pericolosa	Dangerous bend
Destra	Right
Deviazione	Diversion
Divieto di accesso	No entry
Divieto di sorpasso	No overtaking
Divieto di sosta	No parking
Ghiaia	Gravel
Incidente	Accident
Incrocio	Crossroads
Lavori in corso	Roadworks ahead
Pericoloso	Danger
Rallentare	Slow down
Restringimento	Narrow lane
Senso unico	One-way street
Senso vietato	No entry
Sinistra	Left
Sosta autorizzata	Parking permitted (times shown)
Sosta aietata	No parking
Svolta	Bend
Uscita	Exit
Vietato ingresso veicili	No entry for vehicles

A single or double unbroken line in the centre of the carriageway must not be crossed.

Speed Limits

	Open Road (km/h)	Motorway (km/h)
Car Solo	90-110	130
Car towing caravan/trailer	70	80
Motorhome under 3500kg	90-110	130
Motorhome 3500-7500kg	80	100

Motorhomes over 3,500kg are restricted to 80 km/h (50 mph) outside built-up areas and 100 km/h (62 mph) on motorways.

Speed on some sections of Italian motorways is electronically controlled. When you leave a motorway the toll booth calculates the distance a vehicle has travelled and the journey time. The police are automatically informed if speeding has taken place, and fines are imposed.

In bad weather the maximum speed is 90 km/h (56 mph) on roads outside built-up areas and 110 km/h (68 mph) on motorways.

The transportation or use of radar detectors is prohibited.

Traffic Jams

During the summer months, particularly at weekends, the roads to the Ligurian and Adriatic coasts and to the Italian lakes are particularly busy, as are the narrow roads around the lakes. Travelling mid week may help a little. Bottlenecks are likely to occur on the A1 north-south motorway at stretches between Milan and Bologna, Rioveggio and Incisa and on the ring road around Rome. Other traffic jams occur on the A14 to the Adriatic coast; on the A4 between Milan and Brescia caused by heavy traffic to Lakes Iseo and Garda; the A11 Florence to Pisa (before the A12 junction); the A12 Rome to Civitavecchia; the A23 Udine to Tarvisio and before the tunnels on the A26 between Alessandria and Voltri.

Italians traditionally go on holiday during the first weekend of August when traffic density is at its worst. Rush hour traffic jams regularly occur on the ring roads for Milan, Rome and Naples.

Violation of Traffic Regulations

The police may impose on the spot fines, which are particularly heavy for speeding and drink and/or drug related driving offences. Payment is required in cash and a receipt must be given. It can take up to a year for notice of a traffic violation and resulting fine to reach the owner of a foreign registered vehicle.

Motorways

There are approximately 6,500km of motorway (autostrade) in Italy. Tolls (pedaggio) are levied on most of them.

On some motorways, tolls are payable at intermediate toll booths for each section of the motorway used. On a few others the toll must be paid on entering the motorway.

Motorway Tolls

Category A Cars with height from front axle less than 1.30m.

Category B Motor vehicles with 2 axles with height from front axle over 1.30m including motorhomes.

Category C Motor vehicles with 3 axles, e.g. car plus caravan.

Category D Motor vehicles with 4 axles, e.g. car plus twin-axle caravan.

To calculate the tolls payable and find traffic and motorway services information see www.autostrade.it which allows you to enter your route and class of vehicle.

Tolls can prove to be expensive especially over long distances.

Toll Payment

Cash (euro only), debit and credit cards are accepted. Credit cards are also accepted for payment in the Fréjus, Mont-Blanc and Grand St Bernard tunnels. However, visitors advise that on some stretches of motorway automated pay desks which accept credit cards will only do so for solo vehicles. If you are towing a caravan it is advisable to have cash available as you may need to pass through the manned white channel for cash payments.

The prepaid Viacard, available in values of €25, €50 and €75, is also accepted on the majority of motorways and is obtainable from motorway toll booths, service areas and PuntoBlu points of sale along the motorways. The card may be used for any vehicle. When leaving a motorway on which the Viacard is accepted (use the blue or white lanes – do not use the yellow 'Telepass' lanes), insert your entry ticket and card into the machine or give them to the attendant who will deduct the amount due. A Viacard is valid until the credit expires and may be used on a subsequent visit to Italy but cannot be refunded. Viacards are not accepted on Sicilian motorways.

Touring

Italy's great cities, with their religious, artistic and historic treasures, are high on the short break list and are worthy destinations in their own right. Visitors over 65 often qualify for reduced or free entrance to museums and other attractions, so carry your passport as proof of age.

In Rome an Archaeological Card is available, valid for up to seven days, offering entry (ahead of any queues) to many of the most famous sites, together with discounts on guided tours. The cards are available from participating sites and museums.

Smoking is not permitted in public places including restaurants and bars.

In bars prices shown are for drinks taken standing at the bar. Prices are higher if you are seated at a table. In restaurants a service or cover charge is usually added to the bill but it is customary to add 50 cents or €1 per person if you are happy with the service provided. Not all restaurants accept credit cards; check before ordering.

The east coast of Italy has many holiday resorts with fine, sandy beaches, from Ravenna, to Pescara and beyond. However, most beaches in Italy are commercially managed and unless a campsite or hotel has its own private beach, be prepared to pay to enjoy a day by the sea. By law a part of every beach must have free access, but usually it is the least attractive part.

Many parts of Italy lie on a major seismic fault line and tremors and minor earthquakes are common. Visitors climbing Mount Etna should follow the marked routes and heed the advice of guides. There is also ongoing low-intensity volcanic activity on the island of Stromboli.

Visitors to Venice should note that parts of the city are liable to flood in late autumn and early spring.

There are more than 40 World Heritage Sites in Italy (more than any other country) including the historic centres of Florence, Siena, Naples, Pienza, Urbino and the Vatican City.

The Vatican museums and Sistine Chapel are closed on Sundays, except on the last Sunday of the month. When visiting art galleries in Florence, in particular the Uffizi and Accademia, you are advised to buy timed tickets in advance, either online or in person. Otherwise you will encounter very long queues.

There are numerous ferry services transporting passengers and vehicles between Italy and neighbouring countries. Major ports of departure for Croatia, Greece and Turkey are Ancona, Bari, Brindisi, Trieste and Venice. Services also operate to Corsica from Citavecchia, Genoa, Livorno, Porto Torres (Sardinia), Santa Teresa di Gallura (Sardinia) and Savona.

For further information contact:

VIAMARE LTD
SUITE 108, 582 HONEYPOT LANE
STANMORE
MIDDX HA7 1JS
Tel: 020 8206 3420, Fax: 020 8206 1332
www.viamare.com
Email: ferries@viamare.com

If you are planning a skiing holiday contact the Italian State Tourist Board for advice on safety and weather conditions before travelling. Off-piste skiing is highly dangerous and all safety instructions should be followed meticulously in view of the dangers of avalanches in some areas. Italy has introduced a law requiring skiers and snowboarders to carry tracking equipment if going off-piste. The law also obliges children up to 14 years of age to wear a helmet. There are plans for snowboarders to be banned from certain slopes, check local news for updates.

Public Transport & Local Travel

Traffic is restricted or prohibited at certain times in the historical centre of most Italian cities in order to reduce congestion and pollution levels, and you are advised to use out of centre car parks and public transport. The boundaries of historic centres are usually marked with signs displaying the letters ZTL (zona traffico limitato). A crossed hammer on the sign means the restriction does not apply on Sundays and public holidays. Do not pass the ZTL sign as your registration number is likely to be caught on camera and notice of a fine - or fines if you cross more than one ZTL zone – will probably be sent to your home address. Fines are around €100 each time you enter a ZTL.

In addition many northern Italian regions have banned traffic in town and city centres on Sundays. Buses and taxis are permitted to operate.

Public transport is usually cheap and efficient. All the major cities have extensive bus networks and Messina, Milan, Padova, Rome and Turin also have trams. At present only Rome and Milan have an extensive underground network and Perugia has recently inaugurated a 'minimetro'. Bus and metro tickets cannot be purchased on board and must be obtained prior to boarding from newsagents, tobacconists, ticket kiosks or bars. Books of tickets and daily, weekly and monthly passes are also available for purchase.

Validate your ticket when using public transport at the yellow machines positioned at the entrance to platforms in railway stations, in the entrance hall of metro stations and on board buses and trams. Officials patrol all means of public transport and will issue an on the spot fine if you do not hold a validated ticket. Tickets for buses and the metro tend to be time limited (75 minutes) and it is therefore necessary to complete your journey within the allotted time and purchase a new ticket for any additional travel.

Only use taxis which are officially licensed. They will have a neon taxi sign on the roof and are generally white or yellow. Also ensure that the meter in the taxi has been reset before starting your journey. Fares are quite high and there are additional charges for luggage and pets, at night and on public holidays. A tip is expected (up to 10%) and this is sometimes already added to the fares for foreigners.

Car ferry services operate between Venice and the Lido, the Italian mainland and the Aeolian Islands, Sardinia, Sicily, Elba and Capri, Corsica (France) and on Lakes Maggiore, Como and Garda. Parking in Venice is very difficult; instead park at a mainland car park and use a bus or ferry to the city. However, be aware that thieves may operate in car parks in Mestre. Driving and parking in Naples are not recommended in any circumstances.

Cars towing caravans are prohibited at all times from using the S163 south of Naples because it is narrow and has many bends. Motorhomes are prohibited in summer between Positano and Vietri-a-Mare.

Venice

Sites in Italy

⊞ **AGEROLA** *3A3* (3.5km SE Urban) *40.62537, 14.56761* **Camping Beata Solitudo, Piazza Generale Avitabile 4, San Lazzaro, 80051 Agerola (NA) [tel/ fax 081 8025048; beatasol@gmail.com; www. beatasolitudo.it]** Exit A3/S145 at Castellammare-di-Stabia & foll dirs S on S366 to Agerola. Turn L sp San Lazzaro, site in vill sq - narr access rds. Do not app via Amalfi coast rd. Sm, terr, shd; wc (cont); chem disp; mv service pnt; shwrs inc; EHU (3A) inc; lndry rm; shop, rest, snacks, bar in vill; sm playgrnd; shgl beach 16km; wifi; 70% statics; dogs free; bus adj; poss cr; Eng spkn; adv bkg; quiet; red CKE/CCI. "Vg access to Amalfi coast via bus; site at 650m - sea views; v helpful owner; bungalows & hostel accomm avail in restored castle building on site; vg but suitable m'vans only; facs tired." € 20.00 2016*

⊞ **ALBA** *1B2* (1km SW Urban) *44.68507, 8.01019* **Camping Village Alba, Corso Piave 219, San Cassiano, 12051 Alba (CN) [0173 280972; fax 288621; info@ albavillagehotel.it; www.albavillagehotel.it]** Fr A21 exit Asti Est onto S231 to Alba ring rd. Take Corso Piave dir Roddi & Castiglione Falletto, site sp (Campo Sportivo) on L - red block. Or fr A6 exit at SP662 & foll sp Cherasco & Marene, then at rndabt foll sp Pollenza, then Roddi. Fr Roddi site sp dir Alba. Med, hdg/mkd pitch, pt shd; htd wc; chem disp; mv service pnt outside site; shwrs inc; EHU (16A) €2.50; lndry; shop 150m; rest; bar; BBQ; htd pool adj; paddling pool; sports cent adj; bike hire; games area; internet; some statics/apartmnts; dogs free; bus; Eng spkn; adv bkg; quiet; ccard acc; red-stays over 2 nights; red CKE/CCI. "Excel, friendly, clean site; open country to rear; vg facs; conv Barolo vineyards; attractive town & area; camper van stop adj €5." ♦ € 30.00 2017*

ALBENGA *1B2* (2km E Rural/Coastal) *44.08277, 8.21611* **Camping Baciccia, Via Torino 19, 17023 Ceriale (SV) [0182 990743; fax 993839; info@ campingbaciccia.it; www.campingbaciccia.it]** Exit A10 for Albenga, turn L onto SS1 Via Aurelia dir Savona for 3km. Turn L inland at traff lts bef Famiglia Supmkt in Ceriale, site in 200m on L, sp. Med, mkd pitch, pt sl, pt shd; htd wc (some cont); chem disp; mv service pnt; serviced pitches; fam bthrm; shwrs inc; EHU (6A) inc; gas; lndry; shop; supmkt nr; rest, snacks; bar; BBQ; playgrnd; pool high ssn; paddling pool; public shgl beach 600m, private beach nrby; tennis 500m; bike hire; horseriding 2km; golf 10km; wifi; entmnt; TV rm; 5% statics; dogs €4; bus to private beach; sep car park; poss cr; Eng spkn; adv bkg; quiet; ccard acc; red long stay/LS/CKE/CCI. "Family-run site; ltd touring pitches; narr site rds & ent & sm pitches; friendly owners; gd san facs & pool; busy w/ends; lovely pool & café; conv many historical attractions." 1 Apr-3 Nov & 1 Dec-10 Jan. € 50.00 (3 persons) 2013*

ALBEROBELLO *3A4* (1.5km N Rural) *40.80194, 17.25055* **Camping Dei Trulli, Via Castellana Grotte, Km 1.5, 70011 Alberobello (BA) [0804 323699; fax 322145; info@campingdeitrulli.it; www.campingdei trulli.com]** Fr Alberobello, site sp on R. Lift barrier to ent if clsd. Med, mkd pitch, hdstg, pt shd; wc; mv service pnt opp; shwrs €0.50; EHU (6A) €2.50; shop &1.5km; rest, snacks; bar; 2 pools high ssn; bike hire; wifi; entmnt; phone; Eng spkn; ccard acc; red long stay/CKE/CCI. "Gd touring base; some pitches sm due to trees; ltd, basic facs LS; hot water to shwrs only; site run-down." 1 Apr-30 Sep. € 42.50 2014*

⊞ **ALBEROBELLO** *3A4* (1km S Rural) *40.77507, 17.24040* **Camping Bosco Selva, 27 Via Bosco Selva, 70011 Alberobello (BA) [080 4323726; fax 4323863; info@campingboscoselva.it; www.campingbosco selva.it]** Sp fr S172/S239 Alberobello ring rd. Med, some hdstg, pt sl, shd; wc; chem disp; mv service pnt; shwrs inc; EHU (2A) inc; lndry; shop 1km; rest; bar; wifi; Eng spkn; quiet; red LS; CKE/CCI. "In heart of 'Trulli' region of sm beehive-shaped houses; wooded site; friendly owner; vg facs; v nice site; tennis courts; walks in forest adj." € 37.00 2014*

ALBINIA see Orbetello *1D4*

AMEGLIA see Sarzana *1C2*

⊞ **ANGHIARI** *1D3* (600m S Urban) *43.53666, 12.05204* **Agrturism Vel della Pieve, Via della Fossa, 8 - 52031(AR) [tel/fax 0575 788593; info@agriturism ovaldellapieve.it; www.agriturismovaldellapieve.it]** Fr N on the SP47 turn L on to Via della Fossa rd to the site. Sm, hdstg, pt shd; htd wc; chem disp; mv service pnt; shwrs; fam bthrm; EHU (6A) inc; gas 1km; lndry (inc dryer); shop, rest, snacks 0.5km; playgrnd; htd pool; wifi; dogs; twin axles; Eng spkn; adv bkg; CKE/ CCI. € 25.00 2013*

AOSTA *1B1* (1km N Rural) *45.74666, 7.31897* **Camping Ville d'Aoste, Viale Gran San Bernardo 67, Loc Les Fourches, 11100 Aosta (AO) [0165 361360]** 1st site on L off old rd fr Aosta to Grand St Bernard tunnel rte S27. Nr Hotel Rayon du Soleil. Sm, pt shd; wc (some cont); chem disp; mv service pnt; shwrs inc; EHU (4-10A) inc; gas; lndry; shop; snacks; bar; playgrnd; TV; phone; train at Saraillon; some rd noise; ccard acc; CKE/CCI. "Interesting town with many Roman historic remains; excel mountain views; uncr, even in high ssn; clean & friendly site; unrel opening dates." 9 Jul-31 Oct. € 17.40 2014*

AOSTA *1B1* (4km E Rural) *45.74088, 7.39355*
Camping Aosta, Villaggio Clou 29, 11020 Quart (AO) [tel/fax 0165 765602; info@campingaosta.com]
Site 1km fr Villefranche at Quart on SS26. Med, pt sl, terr, shd; wc (some cont); chem disp; shwrs inc; mv service pnt; EHU (6A) inc; lndry; sm shop; supmkt 2km; rest; bar; playgrnd; pool 5km; bike hire; mainly statics; phone; rlwy noise. "Ltd touring pitches; poorly-maintained site; NH only." 15 May-15 Sep. € 21.00 2012*

AOSTA *1B1* (5km SW Rural) *45.71706, 7.26161*
Camping Monte Bianco, St Maurice 15, 11010 Sarre (AO) [tel/fax 0165 258514; info@campingmonte bianco.it; www.campingmontebianco.it]
Fr A5/E25 exit Aosta W twd Aosta, site on R, well sp. Fr Mont Blanc tunnel on S26 site on R at Sarre 500m past St Maurice sp. W fr Aosta, site on L 100m past boundary sp St Maurice/Sarre, yellow sp. Turn into site poss tight for lge o'fits. Sm, terr, pt shd; wc (some cont); chem disp; mv service pnt; shwrs €0.50; EHU (6-10A) €2.80; gas; lndry rm; shop adj; supmkt 800m; rest 200m; bar 100m; playgrnd; pool 4km; phone; Eng spkn; adv bkg; quiet; red long stay LS; CKE/CCI. "Sm, gd, family-run site set in orchard on rv; friendly, helpful; excel tourist info; beautiful alpine scenery & walks; last tunnel is close to exit when coming fr Mont Blanc do not rely on sat nav to restart in time; pleasant site." 15 May-30 Sep. € 25.00 2017*

AQUILEIA *2E1* (300m NE Rural) *45.77786, 13.36943*
Camping Aquileia, Via Gemina 10, 33051 Aquileia (UD) [0431 91042; fax 30804; info@campingaquileia.it; www.campingaquileia.it] Fr A4/E70 take Grado/Palmanova exit & foll sp Grado on SS352. Turn L at traff lts at ent to Aquileia. Site in 400m on R. Fr SS14 turn onto SS352, site sp. Med, shd; wc (some cont); chem disp; mv service pnt; shwrs inc; EHU (6A) inc; lndry rm; supmkt adj; rest, snacks; playgrnd; pool; paddling pool; some statics; dogs €3; bus 300m; quiet; red long stay; ccard acc; CKE/CCI. "Excel site; lge pitches; 10 mins walk thro Roman ruins to magnificent, unique basilica & mosaics; poss noisy concerts July festival week; gd, friendly site; great site." 1 May-30 Sep. € 30.50 2013*

AQUILEIA *2E1* (3km S Coastal) *45.72640, 13.39860*
Camping Village Belvedere Pineta, Via Martin Luther King, 33051 Belvedere-di-Grado (UD) [0431 91007; fax 918641; info@belvederepineta.it; www.belvederepineta.it] Fr Venezia/Trieste a'strada, exit for Palmanova & foll Grado sp on S352 to Aquileia. Drive thro Belvedere, & site is nr lagoon. Slow app to site due to uneven surface. V lge, mkd pitch, shd; wc; chem disp; mv service pnt; fam bthrm; shwrs inc; EHU (3-6A) inc; gas; lndry (inc dryer); supmkt; rest, snacks; bar; BBQ; playgrnd; pool; paddling pool; waterslide; sand beach adj; watersports; tennis; games area; games rm; bike hire; excursions; entmnt; golf 5km; 50% statics; dogs €7.50; rlwy stn 10km at Cervignano; adv bkg; quiet; red long stay/snr citizens; CKE/CCI. "Wooded site - poss mosquitoes; steamer trips fr Grado; gd touring base, inc Venice; red for Seniors; excel site with v clean san facs." ♦ 1 May-30 Sep. € 59.00 (CChq acc) 2013*

ARCO *2D1* (6km SSW Coastal) *45.87614, 10.86779*
Camping Bellavista, Via Gardesana, 31 - Arco [0464 505644; fax 505166; www.camping-bellavista.it]
Fr A22 take exit for Roveretto Sud-Lago di Garda; at rndabt take 4th exit twrds Riva Del Garda; in 3km turn L onto SS240. After town cent in 8km take L into site bef lakeside tunnel, just after Lidl supmkt on L. Med, mkd pitch, shd; wc; chem disp; mv service pnt; fam bthrm; shwrs; EHU (3A) inc; lndry (inc dryer); shop; rest; snacks; takeaway; bar; BBQ; pool; lakeside beach; bike hire; wifi; dogs €3.50; phone; public transport 100m; twin axles; poss cr; Eng spkn; noisy (fr deliveries at adj supmkt & busy rd); "V busy but v pleasant site; direct access to beach; excel, immac san facs; vg & reasonable rest; next to supmkt; town cent 5 min walk along lakeside path; vg touring area for northern towns of lake Garda; excel site." ♦ 1 Apr-30 Oct. € 33.50 2014*

ARENZANO see Genova *1C2*

⊞ **AREZZO** *1D3* (10km SW Rural) *43.44982, 11.78990*
Camping Villaggio Le Ginestre, Loc Ruscello 100, 52100 Arezzo [0575 363566; fax 366949; info@campingleginestre.it; www.campingleginestre.it]
Onto A1 sp Arezzo. Foll sp to Battifolle & Ruscello, proceed for 2km to rndabt, turn L to Ruscello and foll sp to site which is on the L. Med, some hdstg, terr, pt sl, pt shd; htd wc; chem disp; mv service pnt; shwrs inc; EHU (5-10A) inc; lndry; shop 500m; rest, snacks; bar; playgrnd; pool; tennis; games area; games rm; 5% statics; dogs; bus; site clsd Jan; poss cr; adv bkg; ccard acc; CKE/CCI. "Pleasant, grassy site with views; friendly owner; gd rest; trains fr Arezzo to Florence, Rome etc; gd touring base." ♦ € 41.00 2013*

"Satellite navigation makes touring much easier"

Remember most sat navs don't know if you're towing or in a larger vehicle – always use yours alongside maps and site directions.

ARONA *1B1* (8km N Rural) *45.81583, 8.54992*
Camping Solcio, Via al Campeggio, 28040 Solcio-de-Lesa (NO) [0322 7497; fax 7566; info@campingsolcio.com; www.campingsolcio.com] Foll S33 N fr Arona, thro Meina campsite on R of rd app Solcio; well sp, adj boatyard. Med, mkd pitch, pt shd; htd wc (some cont); chem disp; mv service pnt; fam bthrm; shwrs inc; EHU (6A) inc; gas; lndry (inc dryer); shop & 1km; rest, snacks; bar; BBQ; lake sw & shgl beach adj; fishing; watersports (boat hire €4.50); wifi; entmnt; 40% statics; dogs €3.80; phone; rlwy noise; poss cr; Eng spkn; adv bkg; red LS/long stay; CKE/CCI. "Gd site adj lake; some sm pitches; premium for lakeside pitches; gd rest; gd cent for area; conv Stresa and Borromeo Islands; friendly; highly rec; beach has permanent wooden parasols; immac san facs; lovely site." 4 Mar-22 Oct. € 45.00 (CChq acc) 2017*

ITALY

ARSIE *1D1* (3km S Rural) *45.96333, 11.76027* **Camping Al Lago, Via Campagna 14, 32030 Rocca di Arsie (BL) [0439 58540; fax 58471; info@camping allago.bl.it; www.campingallago.bl.it]** Fr Trento on S47, turn E dir Feltre/Belluno rd SS50B, take 1st exit after long tunnel. Fr Belluno on S50 & S50B take Arsié exit & foll site sp. Med, pt shd; wc; chem disp (wc); shwrs inc; EHU (4A) inc; gas 2.5km; shop 3km; rest high ssn; bar; playgrnd; lake sw adj; 15% statics; dogs; phone; poss cr; adv bkg; quiet; ccard acc; CKE/CCI. "Excel, well-run, clean, tidy site in unspoilt area of historical & cultural interest; simple facs, basic but clean; boat hire locally; ent clsd 1400-1530 & 0000-0800; passport req to register." 20 Apr-18 Sep. € 26.00 2016*

⊞ **ASCOLI PICENO** *2E3* (200m Urban) *42.85274, 13.58182* **Parking De Gasperc, Viale A De Gasperi, Ascoli Piceno** Foll signs in town ctr. Sm, hdstg, unshd; own san rec; shops 200m; train 500. "C'van parking only; NH; historic town." € 1.00 2014*

⊞ **ASSISI** *2E3* (1km SE Rural) *43.06605, 12.63056* **Camping Fontemaggio, Via Eremo delle Carceri, 24 Assisi 06081 (PG) [075 813636 or 812317; fax 813749; info@fontemaggio.it; www.fontemaggio.it]** Fr Perugia on S75, turn L onto rd SS147 twd Assisi; keeping Assisi walls on L past coach car park & foll sp to Porta Nuova. In sq at front of gate turn R & foll sp to Eremo delle Carceri, Foligno & Cmp Fontemaggio. Foll sp 1km to sq in front of next gate, turn R (sharp hairpin), site sp 800m on R at gate with narr arch, site 800m on R. Diff long, winding uphill app; recep in hotel. Pls do not use sat nav. Lge, terr, hdstg, pt shd; htd wc (some cont); chem disp; mv service pnt; some serviced pitches; shwrs inc; EHU (6A) inc (long lead rec); gas; lndry rm; shop (high ssn) & 1km; rest; snacks (high ssn); bar; htd pool 3km; TV cab/sat; some statics; dogs; phone; poss cr; Eng spkn; adv bkg; quiet; ccard acc; CKE/CCI. "Lovely, spacious site in olive grove; views; footpath to attractive town; steep site rds diff when wet; order bread at hotel recep; firefly displays on site; facs tired; great rest." ♦ € 25.50 2015*

ASSISI *2E3* (3km W Rural) *43.07611, 12.57361* **Camping Assisi (Formaly Internazionale), Via San Giovanni Campiglione 110, 06081 Assisi (PG) [075 816813; fax 812335; info@campingassisi.it; www.campingassisi.com]** Fr Perugia SS75 to Ospedalicchio, then SS147 twd Assisi. Site well sp on R bef Assisi. Fr Assisi take SS147 to Perugia. Site on L in 3km adj Hotel Green. Lge, mkd pitch, shd; wc (mainly cont); chem disp; mv service pnt; shwrs inc; EHU (3A) €2 (rev pol), 6A avail; gas; lndry (inc dryer); shop & supmkt 3km; rest; pizzeria; bar; playgrnd; pool high ssn; tennis; 40% statics; dogs €2; phone; bus; car wash; poss cr; Eng spkn; adv bkg rec high ssn; quiet; ccard acc; red LS; CKE/CCI. "Helpful staff; minibus to Assisi; lovely, tidy, clean site; busy even in LS; immac san facs; gd rest; sm pitches; caves at Genga worth visit; excel; 10% red on next site if pt of same chain." ♦ ltd. 20 Mar-2 Nov. € 42.00 2014*

ASTI *1B2* (15km S Rural) *44.79688, 8.24183* **International Camping Le Fonti, Via Alle Fontane 54, 14041 Agliano Terme [tel/fax 0141 954820; info@campinglefonti.eu; www.campinglefonti.eu]** Fr A21 Torino to Alessandria exit Asti Est, dir Alba. Then Isola d'Asti exit, rd 456. Camp sp at the end of Montegrosso d'Asti vill, R twds Agliano Terme. Med, mkd pitch, terr, shd; wc; chem disp; mv service pnt; fam bthrm; shwrs; EHU (6A); lndry; rest; snacks; bar; BBQ; playgrnd; htd sw pool; paddling pool; games area; wifi; TV; 10% statics; dogs; twin axles; Eng spkn; red LS. "Beautiful (if challenging) area for cycling; v friendly & helpful staff; some pitches small & diff to access; v gd." ♦ ltd. 25 Mar-30 Oct. € 28.50 2016*

ASTI *1B2* (2km NW Rural) *44.94087, 8.18726* **Camping Umberto Cagni, Loc Valmanera 152, 14100 Asti [0141 271238; info@campingcagniasti.it; www.campingcagniasti.it]** Leave A21 at Asti E. Foll sp to Asti. At beg of town cntre with Asti Service Stn on L; turn R foll sp to camping site. Med, pt sl, shd; wc (mainly cont); shwrs; EHU €3; shop; rest, snacks; bar; games area; entmnt; 50% statics; dogs €2; poss cr & noisy; 10% red CKE/CCI. "Fair NH/sh stay; friendly staff; not suitable lge o'fits; poss travellers; gates clsd 1300-1500." 1 Apr-30 Sep. € 23.50 2012*

"There aren't many sites open at this time of year"

If you're travelling outside peak season remember to call ahead to check site opening dates – even if the entry says 'open all year'.

BAIA DOMIZIA see Marina di Minturno *2F4*

BALISIO DI BALLABIO see Lecco *1C1*

BARBERINO VAL D'ELSA see Poggibonsi *1D3*

BARDOLINO *1D2* (1.2km N Rural) *45.56388, 10.71416* **Camping La Rocca, Loc San Pietro, Via Gardensana 37, 37011 Bardolino (VR) [045 7211111; fax 7211300; info@campinglarocca.com; www.campinglarocca.com]** Exit A22/E45 Affi/Lago di Garda Sud & foll SR249 sp Bardolino. Camp 1st site on both sides of rd exit town at km 53/IV. V lge, shd; wc (some cont); chem disp; mv service pnt; shwrs inc; EHU (10A) inc; lndry; shop; rest, snacks; bar; BBQ; playgrnd; pool; paddling pool; shgl beach adj; lake sw; fishing; bike hire; TV rm; 15% statics; dogs €5.90; phone; poss cr; Eng spkn; no adv bkg; some rd noise (rd thro site); ccard acc; red CKE/CCI. "Pleasant, popular site; gd views; avoid field nr lake; lakeside walk to Garda or Bardolino 20mins; mkt Thurs Bardolino, Fri Garda; red snr citizens." ♦ Easter-6 Oct. € 52.00 2013*

BARDOLINO *1D2* (2km S Rural) *45.52525, 10.72977* **Camping Cisano/San Vito, Via Peschiera 48, 37011 Cisano (VR) [045 6229098; fax 6229059; cisano@camping-cisano.it; www.camping-cisano.it]** Sites on S boundary of Cisano, on SE shore of Lake Garda. V lge, mkd pitch, terr, sl, shd; wc; chem disp; mv service pnt; shwrs inc; EHU (4A) inc; gas; lndry (inc dryer); supmkt; rest, snacks; bar; pool; paddling pool; waterslide; private beach & lake sw adj; waterskiing; windsurfing; canoeing; tennis; games area; bike hire; entmnt; TV rm; statics; no dogs; Eng spkn; quiet; red LS. "Two lovely, clean, lakeside sites run as one - San Vito smaller/quieter; helpful staff; san facs in need of refurb; some pitches diff access & chocks req; passport req at site check-in; Verona Opera excursions arranged high ssn; gd; v popular; helpful staff; gd walking/cycling; gd rest." ♦ 29 Mar-12 Oct. € 66.00 (CChq acc) 2014*

⊞ **BARDONECCHIA** *1A2* (5km SW Rural) *45.04954, 6.66510* **Camping Bokki, Loc Pian del Colle, 10052 Bardonecchia (TO) [tel/fax 0122 99893; info@bokki.it; www.bokki.it]** Fr A32 ent Bardonecchia & foll sp Melezet. After Melezet foll rd uphill for 1.5km. Bokki is 2nd site on R. Med, mkd pitch, pt sl, pt shd; htd wc; chem disp; mv service pnt; fam bthrm; shwrs inc; EHU (2A) inc; lndry; shop 3km; rest, snacks; bar; playgrnd; lake sw adj; TV rm; 95% statics; dogs €1; phone; Eng spkn; adv bkg; quiet; CKE/CCI. "Helpful owners; beautiful location; conv Fréjus tunnel; diff ent to v sm sl, uneven pitch; no red in LS." € 31.00 2014*

BAROLO *1B2* (1km W Rural) *44.61246, 7.92106* **Camping Sole Langhe, Piazza della Vite e Del Vino, Frazione Vergne, 12060 Barolo (CN) [0173 560510; fax 386819; info@solelanghe.com; www.campingsolelanghe.it]** Fr S exit A6 E sp Carru. At Carru turn N onto SP12 & foll sp Barolo. Site sp on ent Barolo. Sm, hdg pitch, pt shd; wc; chem disp; mv service pnt; shwrs inc; EHU (6A) inc; lndry; shop; rest; snacks, bar 1km; BBQ; playgrnd; games area; dogs; Eng spkn; quiet. "Lovely orchard site in cent Barolo wine region; v helpful owner; highly rec." 1 Mar-30 Nov. € 26.00 2017*

BARREA *2F4* (2km S Rural) *41.74978, 13.99128* **Camping La Genziana, Loc Tre Croci 1, 67030 Barrea (AQ) [tel/fax 0864 88101; pasettanet@tiscalinet.it; www.campinglagenzianapasetta.it]** Fr S83 to S end Lago di Barrea, thro Barrea S, site immed on L on uphill L-hand bend. Med, mkd pitch, terr, pt shd; wc; chem disp; mv service pnt; shwrs; EHU (3A) €2.60; lndry; sm shop; rest 300m; bar; BBQ; playgrnd; sand beach & lake sw 3km; dogs €3; bus; Eng spkn; adv bkg; quiet. "Knowledgeable owner; delightful site; excel area cycling; trekking, skiing; ltd shops Barrea 10 mins walk; conv Abruzzi National Park; updated facs (2015)." 5 Apr-20 Oct. € 33.50 2016*

BASTIA MONDOVI *1B2* (1km N Rural) *44.44871, 7.89417* **Camping La Cascina, Loc Pieve 3, 12060 Bastia-Mondovi (CN) [tel/fax 0174 60181; info@campinglacascina.it; www.campinglacascina.it]** Fr Cuneo on S564 turn R at rndabt adj to Rv Tanaro sp to Bastìa Mondovi, site on R in 500m. Lge, pt shd; wc; chem disp; mv service pnt; shwrs inc; EHU (6A) €2.50; lndry; shop; rest 1km; bar; playgrnd; pool; games area; 90% statics; phone; site clsd Sep; poss cr; Eng spkn; ccard acc; CKE/CCI. "Touring vans on edge of sports field; conv wine vills; hot water poss erratic; v busy w/end high ssn." ♦ 2 Jan-24 Dec. € 35.50 2013*

BAVENO see Stresa *1B1*

"That's changed – Should I let The Club know?"

If you find something on site that's different from the site entry, fill in a report and let us know. See camc.com/europereport.

BELLAGIO *1C1* (1.8km S Rural) *45.97093, 9.25381* **Clarke Camping, Via Valassina 170/C, 22021 Bellagio, Como [031 951325; elizabethclarke54@icloud.com; www.bellagio-camping.com]** Fr Como, on arr in Bellagio foll sp Lecco to R, foll site sps uphill. Narr rds & site ent. Med, terr, pt shd; wc (some cont); chem disp; mv service pnt; shwrs inc; EHU (16A) €2; shop 500m; rest, snacks, bar 1.5km; lake sw 1.5km; no dogs; ferries, water taxis 1.5km; quiet; wifi; ccards & chq's not acc. "Friendly British owner; views over lake; uphill walk fr town to campsite; town is on lakeside; site & ent not suitable for o'fits over 7m; no twin-axles; beautiful, peaceful site; basic san facs but clean; use vehicle ferry fr Cadenabbis or Varenne €20 for m'van & 2 people, then foll dirs." 1 May-20 Sep. € 34.00 2016*

⊞ **BELLARIA** *2E2* (2km NE Coastal) *44.16076, 12.44836* **Happy Camping Village, Via Panzini 228, San Mauro a Mare, 47814 Bellaria (RN) [0541 346102; fax 346408; info@happycamping.it; www.happycamping.it]** Fr A14 exit Rimini Nord onto S16 N. Turn off dir San Mauro Mare & Bellaria Cagnona, foll sp Aquabell Waterpark. Over rlwy x-ing, turn R, site on L. Lge, mkd pitch, hdstg, pt sl, pt shd; wc (some cont); chem disp; mv service pnt; fam bthrm; shwrs inc; EHU (8-10A) €3.50; gas; lndry (inc dryer); shop; rest, snacks; bar; playgrnd; pool; paddling pool; sand beach adj; tennis; games area; games rm; wifi; TV; 40% statics; dogs €6; phone; poss cr & noisy; ltd Eng spkn; adv bkg; red LS; CKE/CCI. "Conv Rimini, San Marino; variable size pitches; clean, private beach; pool clsd 1300-1530 & after 1900; lge shopping cent & cinema complex 2km; Bellaria pleasant resort with port & marina." € 39.00 2012*

BELVEDERE DI GRADO see Aquileia *2E1*

ITALY

ITALY

BERGAMO *2C1* (25km N Rural) *45.78866, 9.94705* **Camping La Tartufaia, Via Nazionale 2519, 24060 Ranzanico al Lago di Endine [tel/fax 39 035 819 259; info@latartufaia.com; www.latartufaia.com]** Fr A4 Milan-Venice, exit at Seriate. Take SS42 dir Lovere. Campsite on L past Ranzanico exit. Med, mkd pitch, hdstg, terr, pt shd; wc; chem disp; mv service pnt; shwr; EHU (6A) inc; gas; lndry (inc dryer); shop 50m; rest; snacks; bar; BBQ; pool; beach adj; sw adj; games rm; wifi; dogs; bus adj; twin axles; Eng spkn; ccard acc; red LS; CCI. "Excel site; beautiful views over lake & mountains; gd bus conns; foothpath around lake; v friendly & helpful owners." ♦ 25 Apr-21 Sep. € 42.50 2014*

BEVAGNA *2E3* (4.5km SW Rural) *42.91236, 12.58622* **Camping Pian di Boccio, Via Pian de Boccio 10, 06031 Bevagna [0742 360 164; fax 360 391; info@piandiboccio.com; www.piandiboccio.com]** Fr Foligno to Bevagna in c'van strt on S316 & turn R after 3km, foll signs. In car - just past Bevagna 1st rd on the R past the bdge. Med, hdg pitch, pt sl, hdstg, terr, shd; wc; chem disp; mv service pnt; shwrs; EHU (6A); lndry; rest; bar; playgrnd; htd pool; paddling pool; games area; games rm; wifi; dogs; phone; bus 2km; Eng spkn; adv bkg; quiet. "Excel site; beautiful location; conv for Assis and historic hill towns; dated san facs." ♦ ltd. 1 Apr-30 Sep. € 26.50 2015*

BIBIONE *2E1* (6km W Coastal) *45.63055, 12.99444* **Camping Village Capalonga, Viale della Laguna 16, 30020 Bibione-Pineda (VE) [0431 438351 or 0431 447190 LS; fax 438370 or 0431 438986 LS; capalonga@bibionemare.com; www.capalonga.com]** Well sp approx 6km fr Bibione dir Bibione Pineda. V lge, shd; wc (some cont); chem disp; mv service pnt; fam bthrm (on request); shwrs inc; EHU (10A) inc; gas; lndry; shop; rest, snacks; bar; BBQ; playgrnd; pool; private Blue Flag sand beach adj; watersports; fishing; tennis; archery; bike hire nrby; horseriding 6km; golf 10km; games rm; excursions; various activities; wifi; entmnt; TV; 25% statics; no dogs; no o'fits over 10m high ssn; phone; adv bkg; quiet; ccard acc; red LS. "Well-organised site; gd for families; extra for pitches on beach; spacious, clean san facs; rest o'looking lagoon; voracious mosquitoes!" ♦ 24 Apr-21 Sep. € 52.00 SBS - Y15 2016*

⊞ **BIELLA** *1B1* (88km NNW Rural) *45.84781, 7.93980* **Campeggio Alagna, Localita Miniere, 3, 13020 Riva Valdobbia VC [0163 922947; info@campeggioalagna.it; www.campeggioalagna.it]** Site on R hand side up valley on the S299 at Riva Valdobbia, just bef Alagna Valsesia. Sm, shd; chem disp; shwrs; EHU; lndry (inc dryer); shop; rest; bar; playgrnd; games area; dogs; phone; bus adj; twin axles; Eng spkn; adv bkg; quiet; ccard acc. "Excel site." € 20.00 2016*

⊞ **BOBBIO** *1C2* (1.5km S Rural) *44.75340, 9.38456* **Camping PonteGobbo Terme, Via San Martino 4, 29022 Bobbio (PC) [0523 936927 or 0523 936068; fax 960610; camping.pontegobbe@iol.it; www.campingpontegobbo.com]** Heading twd Genova on S45 turn L on long bdge & immed R. Site sp. Lge, pt sl, shd; htd wc (some cont); chem disp; shwrs €0.50; EHU (4A) €2; gas; shop & 1km; bar; playgrnd; games area; entmnt; TV; 40% statics; phone; sep car park; No dogs; Eng spkn; no adv bkg; quiet; ccard acc; red LS/CKE/CCI. "Trout-fishing in rv; gd scenery; lovely town; hot water to shwrs only; rvside walks and cycling." ♦ € 21.50 2013*

BOGLIASCO see Genova *1C2*

BOLOGNA *1D2* (2km NE Rural) *44.52333, 11.37388* **Centro Turistico Campeggio Città di Bologna, Via Romita 12/4a, 40127 Bologna [051 325016; fax 325318; info@hotelcamping.com; www.hotelcamping.com]** Access is fr A14 Bologna to Ancona. Leave at junc 7 sp Fiera & Via Stalingrado. Can be accessed fr the parallel 'Tangenziale' at same junc. Sp at 1st junc after toll. Med, mkd pitch, pt shd; htd wc; chem disp; mv service pnt; shwrs inc; EHU (6A) inc; lndry (inc dryer); shop; supmkt nrby; rest, snacks; bar; BBQ (charcoal/gas); playgrnd; pool; fitness cent; games rm; wifi; TV rm; dogs €2; no o'fits over 15m on hdstg & over 9m on grass; bus to city; site clsd 20 Dec-9 Jan; Eng spkn; adv bkg; some rd & aircraft noise; ccard acc; red LS/long stay/CKE/CCI. "Conv Bologna Trade Fair & Exhibition cent; friendly, helpful staff; excel, clean san facs; excel pool; tourist pitches at rear nr san facs block; gd bus service fr ent into city; access to pitches poss diff lge o'fits; sat nav dir may take you down narr rds; poss lots mosquitoes; excel site." ♦ 26 Jan-19 Dec. € 44.00 SBS - Y14 2014*

BOLSENA *1D3* (2km S Rural) *42.62722, 11.99444* **Camping Village Lido di Bolsena, Via Cassia, Km 111, 01023 Bolsena (VT) [0761 799258; fax 796105; info@bolsenacamping.it; www.bolsenacamping.it]** Fr S on a'strada A1 foll sp Viterbo & Lago di Bolsena, then take SR2 N to site; sp. Fr N exit A1 at Orvieto onto SS71 to Bolsena. At traff lts in cent of town turn L, site on R in approx 2km. V lge, pt shd; wc; chem disp; mv service pnt; private bthrms avail; shwrs €0.50; EHU (3A) inc (poss rev pol); gas; lndry (inc dryer); shop; rest, snacks; bar; playgrnd; pool; private sand beach adj; lake sw; watersports; tennis; bike hire; games area; entmnt; some statics; phone; sep car park; Eng spkn; adv bkg; quiet; ccard not acc. "Beautiful lakeside location; gd size pitches; all facs excel; cycle path around lake to town; sm dogs acc; charge for pool." 20 Apr-30 Sep. € 44.50 2014*

BOLSENA *1D3* (1.8km SW Rural) *42.63039, 11.99802* **Camping Le Calle, Via Cassia, Km 111.2, 01023 Bolsena (VT) [0761 797041]** On S2 bet Lido Camping Vill & Camping Blu, ent by Fornacella rest. Sm, mkd pitch, pt shd; wc; chem disp; mv service pnt; shwrs inc; EHU (6A) inc; lndry rm; rest adj; lake sw & beach adj; dogs €2; adv bkg; quiet; CKE/CCI. "Family-run CL-type 'Agrituristico' site; friendly, helpful owners offer own produce inc wine & olive oil; vg san facs; foot/cycle path to Bolsena; excel sm site." ♦ 1 Mar-31 Oct. € 17.00 2015*

BOLZANO/BOZEN *1D1* (10km S Rural) *46.42982, 11.34357* **Camping-Park Steiner, Kennedystrasse 32, 39055 Laives/Leifers (BZ) [0471 950105; fax 593141; info@campingsteiner.com; www.campingsteiner.com]** Fr N take Bolzano/Bozen-Sud exit fr A22/E45 & pick up rd S12 twd Trento to site; site on R on ent Laives at N edge of vill. Fr S leave A22 at junc for Egna onto rd S12 dir Bolzano. Poorly sp. Lge, hdg/mkd pitch, pt sl, shd; htd wc; (some cont) chem disp; mv service pnt; fam bthrm; shwrs inc; EHU (6A) inc; gas; lndry; shop; rest, snacks; pizzeria; bar; playgrnd; 2 pools (1 covrd); bike hire; wifi; TV; some statics; dogs €5, no dogs hg ssn; phone; Eng spkn; adv bkg rec; some rd & rlwy noise; CKE/CCI. "Pleasant, well-run, excel site on edge of Dolomites; attractive pitches; helpful staff; gd, clean, modern san facs; gates clsd 1300-1500 & 2200-0700; beautiful area; vg walking; well stocked shop; highly rec; easy 5 min walk into town; excel rest; busy in high ssn; excel value transport passes fr TO." ♦ 12 Mar-31 Oct. € 40.00 2016*

"I like to fill in the reports as I travel from site to site"

You'll find report forms at the back of this guide, or you can fill them in online at camc.com/europereport.

⊞ **BOLZANO/BOZEN** *1D1* (2km NW Rural) *46.50333, 11.3000* **Camping Moosbauer, Via San Maurizio 83, 39100 Bolzano [0471 918492; fax 204894; info@moosbauer.com; www.moosbauer.com]** Exit A22/E45 at Bolzano Sud exit & take S38 N dir Merano (keep L after toll booths). After tunnel take 1st exit sp Eppan & hospital, & turn L at top of feeder rd sp Bolzano. After approx 2km at island past 08 G'ge turn L & foll site sp. Site on R in 1km by bus stop on S38, sp. Med, hdg/mkd pitch, hdstg, pt sl, pt shd; htd wc; chem disp; mv service pnt; serviced pitches; fam bthrm; shwrs inc; EHU (5A) inc; lndry; shop; rest, snacks; bar; playgrnd; htd pool; games rm; cab/sat TV; entmnt; dogs €4; bus; poss cr; Eng spkn; adv bkg; quiet but some rd noise; CKE/CCI. "Popular, well-maintained, attractive site; gd welcome fr friendly owners; pitches narr; excel, modern san facs; gate shut 1300-1500; bus service adj for archaeological museum (unique ice man); gd cent for walks in Dolomites." ♦ ltd. € 34.00 2012*

BORGO SAN LORENZO *1D3* (7km SE Rural) *43.93087, 11.46426* **Camping Vicchio Ponte, Via Costoli 16, 50039 Vicchio [055 8448306; fax 579405; info@campingvecchioponte.it; www.campingvecchioponte.it]** On SP551 adj to sw pool in Vicchio. Med, pt shd; wc (cont); chem disp; mv service pnt; shwrs inc; EHU (4A) inc; lndry rm; shop, rest, bar in vill; htd pool adj inc in price; dogs; train to Florence 1km; poss cr; Eng spkn; quiet; CKE/CCI. "Simple, municipal site; v clean san facs; v helpful staff." 1 Jun-15 Sep. € 24.00 2016*

BORGO SAN LORENZO *1D3* (5km W Rural) *43.96144, 11.30918* **Camping Mugello Verde, Via Massorondinaio 39, 50037 San Piero-a-Sieve (FI) [055 848511; fax 8486910; mugelloverde@florencecamping.com; www.florencecamping.com]** Exit A1 at Barberino exit & foll Barberino sp twd San Piero-a-Sieve & Borgo San Lorenzo. Turn S on S65 twd Florence. Site sp immed after Cafaggiolo. Lge, sl, terr, pt shd; htd wc (some cont); chem disp; mv service pnt; shwrs inc; EHU (6A) inc; gas; lndry (inc dryer); shop; rest, snacks; bar; playgrnd; pool (bathing caps req); tennis; bike hire; wifi; entmnt; 50% statics; bus/train; no adv bkg; quiet; ccard acc; red LS; CKE/CCI. "Hillside site; bus to Florence high ssn (fr vill LS) or 20 mins drive; hard grnd diff for awnings; poss long walk to recep & shop; helpful, friendly staff; refurbed, gd, clean san facs; avoid early Jun - Italian Grand Prix!." ♦ 15 Mar-30 Oct. € 42.00 2014*

BORGO SAN LORENZO *1D3* (28km NW Rural) *44.09810, 011.26836* **Camping La Futa, Via Bruscoli Futa, 889/h, Firenzuola [3289248746; info@campinglafuta.it; www.campinglafuta.it]** A1 Bologna to Firenze - exit Roncobiaccio SS65 to Passo Della Futa. Site close to pass. Med, mkd pitch, terr, pt shd; wc; chem disp; fam bthrm; shwrs; EHU(10A); lndry (inc dryer); shop; rest; bar; BBQ; playgrnd; htd pool; games area; games rm; entmnt; wifi; TV; 25% statics; dogs €2; phone; twin axles; Eng spkn; adv bkg; CKE/CCI. "Excel site." 15 Apr-30 Sep. € 28.00 2016*

BOTTAI see Firenze *1D3*

BRACCIANO *2E4* (3km N Rural) *42.1300, 12.17333* **Kwan Village Roma Flash Sporting, Via Settevene Palo 42, 00062 Bracciano [tel/fax 0699 805458 or 3389 951738 LS; info@romaflash.it; www.romaflash.it]** Fr A1 exit at Magliano Sabina dir Civita Castellana. Then foll sp Nepi, Sutri, Trevignano & Bracciano. Sp on lakeside rd N of Bracciano. Lge, mkd pitch, pt shd; wc (some cont); chem disp; mv service pnt; fam bthrm; sauna; shwrs inc; EHU (6A) inc; lndry (inc dryer); shop high ssn; rest, snacks; bar; BBQ (charcoal, gas); playgrnd; pool; lake sw & free beach; fitness cent; watersports; fishing; horseriding 4km; tennis; bike hire; games rm; wifi; entmnt; TV; 5% statics; dogs €5.50; no o'fits over 12m; shuttle bus to Bracciano; bus/train to Rome; sep car park; Eng spkn; quiet; ccard acc; red LS. "Attractive, well-kept lakeside site; clean, modern san facs; conv Rome." ♦ 1 Apr-29 Sep. € 42.00 (CChq acc) SBS - Y16 2012*

ITALY

BRUNICO/BRUNECK *1D1* (10km E Rural) *46.77600, 12.03688* **Camping Residence Corones, Niederrasen 124, 39030 Rasun-di-Sotto/Niederrasen (BZ) [0474 496490; fax 498250; info@corones.com; www.corones.com]** On SS49 dir Rasun, turn N to site to Antholz, bear L in front of Gasthof, over bdge turn L, site in 400m. Med, pt shd; wc; chem disp; mv service pnt; serviced pitches; sauna; shwrs inc; private bthrms avail; EHU (3A) metered; gas; lndry; shop; rest, snacks; bar; playgrnd; htd pool; paddling pool; tennis; games area; bike hire; solarium; some statics; dogs €4.20; phone; Eng spkn; adv bkg; quiet; ccard acc (poss not in rest); red LS. "Gd cent for walking & skiing - outings arranged; superb facs, inc in winter; conv day visit to Dolomites; helpful owner & staff; excel." ♦
1 Dec-19 Apr & 20 May-25 Oct. € 33.00 2013*

CALCERANICA AL LAGO see Levico Terme *1D1*

CANAZEI *1D1* (2km W Rural) *46.47479, 11.74067* **Camping Miravalle, Strèda de Greva 39, 38031 Campitello-di-Fassa (TN) [0462 750502; fax 751563; info@campingmiravalle.it; www.campingmiravalle.it]** In vill cent on rte 48 site sp down side rd. Lge, sl, unshd; wc; chem disp; mv service pnt; fam bthrm; shwrs inc; EHU (6A) inc (poss rev pol), extra €2 for 6A; lndry; shop 100m; rest, snacks; 100m; bar; dogs €4; poss cr; Eng spkn; adv bkg; quiet; ccard acc; CKE/CCI. "Excel new san facs 2015; conv cable car." ♦
1 Jan-30 Mar, 1 Jun-30 Sep & 1 Dec-31 Dec. € 37.00 2015*

CANNIGIONE see Arzachena (Sardinia) *1C4*

CANNOBIO *1C1* (1km N Rural) *46.07791, 8.69345* **Villaggio Camping Bosco, Punta Bragone, 28822 Cannobio (VB) [0323 71597; fax 739647; bosco@boschettoholiday.it; www.boschettoholiday.it/bosco]** On W side of lakeshore rd bet Cannobio & Swiss frontier. Sh steep app to site & hairpin bend fr narr rd, unsuitable for car/c'van o'fits & diff for m'vans. Med, terr, pt shd; wc; chem disp; shwrs; EHU (3A) €3.90; gas; lndry; shop; BBQ; bar; playgrnd; private shgl beach; lake sw; dogs €4; Eng spkn; adv bkg - ess in high ssn; quiet; CKE/CCI. "All pitches with magnificent lake view; beautiful town; hot water to shwrs only." ♦ 1 Apr-22 Oct. € 32.30 2017*

CANNOBIO *1C1* (1.5km N Urban) *46.07136, 8.69366* **Camping Campagna, Via Casali Darbedo, 20-22 - 28822 Cannobio (VB) [0323 70100; fax 72398 or 0323 71190; info@campingcampagna.it; www.campingcampagna.it]** Brissago-Cannobio rd, site on L on ent town. Med, shd; wc; mv service pnt; shwrs inc; EHU (6-10A) €4; gas; lndry; shop; rest, snacks; bar; shgl beach; some statics; dogs €5; poss cr; Eng spkn; adv bkg; quiet. "Steamer trips on Lake Maggiore; vg Sunday mkt in Cannobio; vg, modern facs; friendly staff; clean; friendly staff; fabulous views of lake." ♦
15 Mar-15 Nov. € 47.00 2013*

CANNOBIO *1C1* (200m N Rural) *46.06515, 8.6905* **Camping Riviera, Via Casali Darbedo 2, 28822 Cannobio (VB) [tel/fax 0323 71360; riviera@riviera-valleromantica.com; www.riviera-valleromantica.com]** N of Cannobio twd Switzerland on main rd. Over rv at o'skts of town, site ent on R in 30m; sp. Lge, hdg/mkd pitch, shd; wc; chem disp; mv service pnt; private san facs some pitches; shwrs inc; EHU (4A) €4; gas; lndry; shop; rest, snacks; bar; playgrnd; private shgl beach & lake sw adj; boat hire; windsurfing; some statics; dogs €4.50; poss cr; adv bkg. "Popular, peaceful, well-maintained site bet rv & lake; extra for lakeside pitch; gd sailing; v helpful staff." ♦
1 Apr-18 Oct. € 47.00 2013*

CANNOBIO *1C1* (500m N Urban) *46.06678, 8.69507* **Camping Del Sole, Via Sotto i Chiosi 81/A, 28822 Cannobio (VB) [0323 70732; fax 72387; info@campingsole.it; www.campingsole.it]** Fr S fr A26 foll Verbania sp then sp Cannobio or Locarno. Ent vill, over cobbles, 2nd R in 750m. Bef rv bdge immed sharp R under main rd, site on L after quick R turn. Fr N ent Cannobio, 1st L after x-ing rv, then as above. Lge, hdg/mkd pitch, hdstg, pt shd; wc; chem disp; mv service pnt; shwrs inc; EHU (4A) €3; gas; lndry; supmkt 150m; rest; snacks; bar; playgrnd; pool; shgl beach & lake sw 250m; wifi; 60% statics; dogs €3; poss cr; Eng spkn; poss noisy; red long stay/LS; CKE/CCI. "Attractive vill & lake frontage; friendly, family-run site; poss tight access some pitches; lovely pool area; cramped pitches; diff to park m'van; dated clean san facs; close to town; fair." 1 Mar-2 Nov. € 31.00 2014*

CANNOBIO *1C1* (1.5km SW Rural) *46.05756, 8.67831* **Camping Valle Romantica, Via Valle Cannobina, 28822 Cannobio (VB) [tel/fax 0323 71249; valleromantica@riviera-valleromantica.com; www.riviera-valleromantica.com]** Turn W on S o'skirts of Cannobio, sp Valle Cannobina. In 1.5km at fork keep L. Site immed on R. On ent site cont to bottom of hill to park & walk back to recep. Lge, hdg/mkd pitch, pt sl, terr, pt shd; wc; chem disp; mv service pnt; shwrs inc; EHU (4-6A) €4.50; lndry; shop; rest, snacks; bar; playgrnd; pool; golf 12km; 25% statics; dogs €4; adv bkg; quiet. "Vg; some sm pitches; particularly helpful& friendly staff; narr site rds poss diff m'vans; masses of flowers; beautiful situation; footpath to town, poss cr high ssn; v well kept; req to show passport." ♦
1 Apr-11 Sep. € 41.50 2017*

CA'NOGHERA see Mestre *2E2*

CAORLE *2E2* (5km SW Coastal) *45.56694, 12.79416* **Camping Villaggio San Francesco, Via Selva Rosata 1, Duna Verde, 30020 Porto-Santa-Margherita (VE) [0421 299333; fax 299284; info@villaggiostrancesco.com; www.villaggiosfrancesco.com]** Fr A4/E70 exit Santo Stino di Livenza, then dir Caorle. By-pass town & cont on coast rd, site sp on L. V lge, shd; wc (some cont); chem disp; mv service pnt; fam bthrm; shwrs inc; EHU (6A) inc; gas; lndry (inc dryer); shop; 3 rests; snacks; bar; 5 pools; waterslide; private beach adj; boat hire; windsurfing; waterskiing; tennis; games area; games rm; bike hire; solarium; internet; entmnt; TV; 60% statics; dogs €3; phone; min 2 nights' stay; poss cr; quiet; ccard not acc; red snr citizens/CKE/CCI. "Excel family facs." ♦
24 Apr-25 Sep. € 44.60 (CChq acc) 2016*

CAPANNOLE see Montevarchi *1D3*

CAPRAROLA *2E4* (6km NW Rural) *42.33504, 12.20488* **Camping Natura, Loc Sciente Le Coste, 01032 Caprarola (VT) [tel/fax 0761 612347; info@camping-natura.com; www.camping-natura.com]** Fr Viterbo take Via Cimina sp Ronciglione. After approx 19km bef Ronciglione turn R sp Nature Reserve Lago di Vico, in 200m turn R, site sp on R in 3km. Med, mkd pitch, pt shd; wc; chem disp; mv service pnt; shwrs; EHU (4A) €3; shop; rest, snacks; bar; lake sw adj; dogs €3; quiet; red LS; ccard acc. "Friendly site; guided walks in nature reserve; run down LS & ltd facs." Easter-30 Sep.
€ 18.00 2012*

CARLAZZO see Porlezza *1C1*

CASAL BORSETTI see Marina di Ravenna *2E2*

CASALBORDINO *2F4* (7km NE Coastal) *42.20018, 14.60897* **Camping Village Santo Stefano, S16, Km 498, 66020 Marina-di-Casalbordino (CH) [0873 918118; fax 918193; info@campingsantostefano.com; www.campingsantostefano.com]** Exit A14 Vasto N onto S16 dir Pescara, site at km 498 on R. Med, mkd pitch, shd; wc; chem disp; shwrs inc; EHU (6A) inc; shop; rest, snacks; bar; playgrnd; pool; paddling pool; beach adj; entmnt; 10% statics; no dogs; Eng spkn; adv bkg; quiet but some rlwy noise; CKE/CCI. "Pleasant, well-maintained, family-run site; sm pitches; beautiful private beach & pool area; gd rest." 24 Apr-12 Sep.
€ 41.00 2014*

CA'SAVIO see Punta Sabbioni *2E2*

CASSONE see Malcesine *1D1*

CASTELDIMEZZO see Pesaro *2E3*

CASTELLETTO SOPRA TICINO see Sesto Calende *1B1*

CASTELLINA IN CHIANTI see Poggibonsi *1D3*

CASTELSANTANGELO SUL NERA *2E3* (4km S Rural) *42.88223, 13.18181* **Camping Monte Prata, Loc. Schianceto, 62030 Castel S Angelo Sul Nera [07 37 97 00 62 or 33 32 95 18 60 (mob); sostare@campingmonteprata.it; www.campingmonteprata.it]** Fr SP209 Muccia-Visso. Thro Visso on the Strada Provinciale 134 twds Castelsantangelo Sur Nera. Aft vill slight R onto SP 136. Campsite on L after vill of Gualdo. Med, mkd pitch, hdstg, terr, pt shd; htd wc; chem disp; mv service pnt; shwrs inc; EHU; lndry (inc dryer); shop; rest; snacks; bar; BBQ; playgrnd; games area; 0% statics; dogs; Eng spkn; quiet; ccard acc. "Gd site; excel position nr top of Monte Prata; guided walks & other excursions fr site in Nat Park." ♦
15 Jun-15 Sep. € 29.50 2014*

CASTIGLIONE DEL LAGO *2E3* (1km N Rural) *43.13460, 12.04383* **Camping Listro, Via Lungolago, Lido Arezzo, 06061 Castiglione-del-Lago (PG) [tel/fax 075 951193; listro@listro.it; www.listro.it]** Fr N A1 Val di Chiana exit 75 bis Perugia, site clearly sp on N edge of town on lakeside. Med, mkd pitch, pt shd; wc; chem disp; mv service pnt; shwrs inc; EHU (3A) inc (poss rev pol); gas; lndry; shop & 500m; rest 200m; snacks; bar; playgrnd; pool nr; private sand beach & lake sw adj; tennis nr; bike hire; poss cr; Eng spkn; adv bkg; rd noise; ccard acc; red long stay/LS; CKE/CCI. "On W shore of Lake Trasimeno; facs stretched when site full; v helpful staff; bus to Perugia; rlwy stn 1km for train to Rome; 'tree fluff' a problem in spring; new san facs (2016); poor elecs." ♦ ltd. 1 Apr-30 Sep.
€ 22.30 2016*

CAVALLINO *2E2* (2.5km S Coastal) *45.46726, 12.53006* **Union Lido Park & Resort, Via Fausta 258, 30013 Cavallino (VE) [041 968080 or 2575111; fax 5370355; info@unionlido.com; www.unionlido.com]** Exit a'strada A4 (Mestre-Trieste) at exit for airport or Quarto d'Altino & foll sp for Jesolo & then Punta Sabbiono; site on L 2.5km after Cavallino. V lge, mkd pitch, shd; htd wc; chem disp; mv service pnt; 60% serviced pitches; fam bthrm; sauna; shwrs inc; EHU (6A) inc; gas; lndry (inc dryer); 30 shops & supmkt; 7 rests; snacks; bars; playgrnd; pools & children's lagoon with slides; dir access private beach; tennis; gym; golf; fishing; boating; horseriding; watersports; bike hire; skating rink; hairdressers; babysitting; wifi; entmnt; sat TV some pitches; late arr (after 2100) area with EHU; church; banking facs; Italian lessons; wellness cent; 50% statics; no dogs; Eng spkn; adv bkg; ccard acc. "Variable pitch size; min stay 7 days high ssn; some pitches soft sand (a spade useful!); many long-stay campers; no admissions 1230-1500 (poss busy w/end); excursions; varied entmnt programme high ssn; well-organised, well-run; clean facs; worth every penny! excel." ♦ 21 Apr-10 Oct.
€ 66.00 (CChq acc) 2017*

CAVALLINO *2E2* (5km SW Coastal) *45.45638, 12.4960* **Camping Enzo Stella Maris, Via delle Batterie 100, 30013 Cavallino-Treporti (VE) [041 966030; fax 5300943; info@enzostellamaris.com; www.enzostellamaris.com]** Exit A4 at sp for airport. Foll sp Jesolo, Cavallino, Punta Sabbioni rd SW. Site sp after Ca'Ballarin. Lge, mkd pitch, pt shd; wc; chem disp; mv service pnt; fam bthrm; serviced pitches; shwrs inc; EHU (10A) inc; gas; lndry; shop; rest, snacks; bar; no BBQ; playgrnd; htd pool; sand beach adj; fitness rm; games area; wifi; entmnt; TV rm; 25% statics; no dogs; phone; clsd 1230-1600 & 2300-0700; poss cr; Eng spkn; no adv bkg; quiet; ccard acc; red snr citizens/long stay; CKE/CCI. "Well-run, friendly, family-owned site; excel facs; beware mosquitoes; indoor htd pool; wellness cent; €30 in LS." ♦ 29 Apr-22 Oct. € 60.00 2017*

CAVALLINO *2E2* (6km SW Coastal) *45.44872, 12.47116* **Camping Dei Fiori, Via Vettor Pisani 52, 30010 Cavallino-Treporti (VE) [041 966448; fax 966724; fiori@vacanze-natura.it; www.deifiori.it]** Fr Lido di Jesolo foll sp to Cavallino; site on L approx 6km past Cavallino & bef Ca'Vio. Lge, mkd pitch, shd; wc; chem disp; mv service pnt; serviced pitch; shwrs inc; EHU (5A) inc (poss rev pol); gas; lndry; shop; supmkt; rest, snacks; bar; playgrnd; pool; sand beach adj; hydro massage; games area; entmnt; internet; no dogs; Eng spkn; adv bkg ess Jul/Aug; quiet; ccard acc; red snr citizens/long stay. "V clean & quiet even in Aug; excel facs & amenities; conv water bus stop at Port Sabbioni; 3/5 day min stay med/high ssn; highly rec; excel." ♦ 19 Apr-30 Sep. € 22.50 2016*

CA'VIO see Cavallino *2E2*

CAVRIGLIA see Montevarchi *1D3*

CECINA *1D3* (3km NW Coastal) *43.31850, 10.47440* **Camping Mareblu, Via dei Campilunghi, Mazzanta, 57023 Cecina Mare (Li) [0586 629191; fax 629192; info@campingmareblu.com; www.campingmareblu.com]** Fr S on SS1 exit sp Cecina Nord & foll dir Mazzanta, site sp. Fr N exit sp Vada then Mazzanta. Lge, hdg/mkd pitch, pt shd; wc (some cont); chem disp; mv service pnt; shwrs inc; EHU (3A) inc; gas; lndry (inc dryer); shop; rest, snacks; bar; BBQ (gas only); playgrnd; pool; paddling pool; sand beach adj; wifi; 10% statics; dogs free (not acc Jul & Aug); phone; sep car park; ATM; poss cr; Eng spkn; adv bkg; red LS; ccard acc; red CKE/CCI. "Lge pitches; gd facs & pool area; car must be parked in sep car park; well-organised, friendly site." ♦ 1 Apr-21 Oct. € 42.50 (CChq acc) 2017*

CERIALE see Albenga *1B2*

CERVIA *2E2* (3.6km S Coastal) *44.24760, 12.35901* **Camping Adriatico, Via Pinarella 90, 48015 Cervia (RA) [0544 71537; fax 72346; info@campingadriatico.net; www.campingadriatico.net]** On SS16 S fr Cervia twd Pinarella, turn L at km post 175, over rlwy line & take 1st R, site sp. Lge, shd; wc (some cont); chem disp; mv service pnt; fam bthrm; shwrs inc; EHU (6A) inc; lndry; shop; rest, snacks; bar; playgrnd; htd pool; paddling pool; sand beach 600m; fishing; tennis 900m; golf 5km; entmnt; TV rm; 40% statics; dogs €6; Eng spkn; adv bkg; ccard acc; red CKE/CCI. "V pleasant site; friendly staff; gd san facs; excel pizza at rest; ACSI acc." ♦ 14 Apr-19 Sep. € 33.70 (CChq acc) 2016*

CERVO see Diano Marina *1B3*

⊞ **CESENATICO** *2E2* (1.5km N Coastal) *44.21545, 12.37983* **Camping Cesenatico, Via Mazzini 182, 47042 Cesenatico (FC) [0547 81344; fax 672452; info@campingcesenatico.it; www.campingcesenatico.com]** Travelling S on S16 look for Esso g'ge on R on app Cesenatico. Take 2nd L after Erg g'ge, over rlwy x-ing, site on L, sp. V lge, mkd pitch, hdstg, pt shd; htd wc (some cont); chem disp; mv service pnt; shwrs inc; EHU (4A) €3.60; gas; lndry; shop; snacks; rest; bar; playgrnd; htd pool; private sand beach adj; tennis; games area; entmnt; hairdresser; medical cent; wifi; entmnt; TV; 80% statics; dogs €8.70; phone; poss cr; Eng spkn; adv bkg; ccard acc; red long stay/LS/CKE/CCI. "Many long stay winter visitors; gd touring base; unspoilt seaside resort with canal (designed by Da Vinci), port & marina; excel; in easy walking/cycling dist fr Cesenatico." ♦ € 55.00 2014*

CESENATICO *2E2* (2km N Coastal) *44.21584, 12.37798* **Camping Zadina, Via Mazzini 184, 42047 Cesenatico (FC) [0547 82310; fax 702381; info@campingzadina.it; www.campingzadina.it]** Leave A14 at Cesena Sud; foll sp Cesenático; after 10.5km turn R at T-junc onto SS16; after 2km fork L over level x-ing; site on L. Lge, mkd pitch, pt terr, pt shd; wc; chem disp; mv service pnt; shwrs inc; EHU (6A) inc; gas; lndry; shop; rest, BBQ; snacks; bar; playgrnd; private sand beach; entmnt; wifi; fishing; 80% statics; dogs €7; train 1.5km; Eng spkn; sep car park; poss cr; adv bkg; noisy in high ssn; ccard not acc; red LS. "Sea water canal runs thro site; pitches poss tight lge o'fits; gd." ♦ ltd. 20 Apr-21 Sep. € 56.00 2014*

CHATILLON see St Vincent *1B1*

CHIENES/KIENS see Brunico/Bruneck *1D1*

CHIOGGIA *2E2* (2km E Urban/Coastal) *45.19027, 12.30361* **Camping Miramare, Via A. Barbarigo 103, 30015 Sottomarina (VE) [tel/fax 041 490610; campmir@tin.it; www.miramarecamping.com]** Fr SS309 foll sp Sottomarina. In town foll brown sp to site. Lge, mkd pitch, pt shd; wc; chem disp; mv service pnt; shwrs inc; EHU (6A) inc; gas; lndry; shop; rest, snacks; bar; playgrnd; pool; private sand beach; games area; wifi; entmnt; 75% statics; dog €3.50; poss cr; adv bkg; ccard acc; CKE/CCI. "Busy site - field across rd quieter; friendly staff; gd entmnt facs for children; cycle tracks to picturesque Chioggia; site 10 min walk fr ferry point and beach or free shuttle bus service until mid Sept; free sun umbrella for the beach fr rec." ♦ 18 Apr-23 Sep. € 35.00 2015*

"I need an on-site restaurant"

We do our best to make sure site information is correct, but it is always best to check any must-have facilities are still available or will be open during your visit.

⊞ **CHIUSA/KLAUSEN** *1D1* (650m E Rural) *46.64119, 11.57332* **Camping Gamp, Via Griesbruck 10, 39043 Chiusa/Klausen (BZ) [0472 847425; fax 845067; info@camping-gamp.com; www.camping-gamp.com]** Exit A22 Chiusa/Klausen & bear L at end of slip rd (sp Val Gardena). Site on L at rd fork 800m, sp. Sm, mkd pitch, pt shd; htd wc; chem disp; shwrs inc; mv service pnt; fam bthrm; EHU (6A) €2.60; lndry; shop & 500m; rest, snacks; bar; playgrnd; pool; table tennis; htd ski & boot rm; internet; sat TV; dogs €3.50; phone; sep m'van o'night facs; Eng spkn; some rd & rlwy noise; CKE/CCI. "Excel cent for mountain walks; Chiusa attractive town; immac facs, sep m'van o'night area; busy site; some pitches sm for lge o'fits; discount with Camping Euro card." ♦ € 34.00 2014*

CISANO see Bardolino *1D2*

COLTANO see Pisa *1C3*

COMO *1C1* (5km S Urban) *45.78385, 9.06034* **International Camping-Sud, Breccia, Via Cecilio, 22100 Como [tel/fax 031 521435; campingint@hotmail.com; www.camping-internazionale.it]** Fr E to Como, on SS35 Milano rd foll sp a'strada Milano; site on Como side of rndabt at junc S35 & S432; ent/exit diff unless turn R. Or take 2nd exit off m'way after border (Como S), site sp. Med, pt sl, pt shd; wc; shwrs inc; EHU (4-6A) €2.50 (rev pol); gas; lndry; shop; supmkt nr; rest, snacks; bar; playgrnd; pool; bike hire; golf 5km; dogs €2; poss cr; no adv bkg; rd noise; red LS; ccard acc. "Conv NH for m'way." 1 Apr-31 Oct. € 24.00 2014*

⊞ **CORIGLIANO CALABRO** *3A4* (7km N Coastal) *39.70333, 16.52583* **Camping Onda Azzurra, Contrada Foggia, 87064 Corigliano-Calabro (CS) [tel/fax 0983 851157; info@onda-azzurra.it; www.onda-azzurra.it]** On SS106-bis Taranto to Crotone rd, after turn off for Sibari, cont S for 6km. Turn L at 4 lge sp on 1 notice board by lge sep building, 2km to site on beach. Lge, mkd pitch, shd; htd wc; chem disp; mv service pnt; shwrs inc; EHU (6-10A) €3-4; lndry; shop; rest (all year); snacks; bar; playgrnd; sand beach adj; tennis; bike hire; 10% statics; dogs €3; adv bkg; ccard acc; red long stay/CKE/CCI. "Excel, well-run site all ssns - facs open all yr; popular long stay; clean facs; lge pitches; water not drinkable; v friendly helpful owner; popular in winter; special meals Xmas/New Year; site conv Sybaris & Rossano; high standard site; excel friendly welcome; free acitivities LS." ♦ € 45.00 2014*

⊞ **CORIGLIANO CALABRO** *3A4* (8km N Coastal) *39.68141, 16.52160* **Camping Il Salice, Contrada da Ricota Grande, 87060 Corigliano-Calabro (CS) [0983 851169; fax 851147; info@salicevacanze.it; www.salicevacanze.it]** Exit A3 dir Sibari onto SS106 bis coast rd dir Crotone. At 19km marker after water tower on L, turn L sp Il Salice - 1.5km to new access rd to site on L. Site sp easily missed. Lge, mkd pitch, hdstg, pt sl, pt shd; htd wc (cont); chem disp; mv service pnt; serviced pitches; fam bthrm; shwrs inc; EHU (3-6A) inc; gas; lndry; shop & 2km; rest, snacks; bar; BBQ; playgrnd; pool; sand beach adj; watersports; tennis; games area; games rm; bike hire; TV; 70% statics; dogs €4; phone; poss cr; Eng spkn; red LS; CKE/CCI. "Narr rds thro vill to site - care needed when busy; v popular, well-run winter destination; haphazard siting in pine trees; clean, private beach; modern san facs; ltd facs LS; big price red LS; scenic area." ♦ € 48.00 2012*

⊞ **CORIGLIANO CALABRO** *3A4* (10km N Coastal) *39.69130, 16.52233* **Camping Thurium, Contrada Ricota Grande, 87060 Ricota Grande (CS) [tel/fax 0983 851101; info@campingthurium.com; www.campingthurium.com]** Exit SS106 at km stone 21. Site sp on gd app rd for 2km. Rd narr and bumpy in places. Do not foll sat nav. Lge, mkd pitches, pt shd; wc; chem disp; mv service pnt; shwrs (€0.35); EHU inc (3-6A); lndry (inc dryer); shop; snacks; rest; bar; gas; playgrnd; pool; paddling pool; sand beach adj; tennis; games area; bike hire; windsurfing lessons; entmnt; wifi; 20% statics; dogs (€4.80); twin axles; Eng spkn; CKE/CCI. "Vg well-run site; site rdways narr on corner, tight for lge o'fits; fair." ♦ ltd. € 65.00 2014*

CORTENO GOLGI see Edolo *1D1*

ITALY

CORTINA D'AMPEZZO *2E1* (3.5km S Rural) *46.51858, 12.1370* **Camping Dolomiti, Via Campo di Sotto, 32043 Cortina-d'Ampezzo (BL) [0436 2485; fax 5403; campeggiodolomiti@tin.it; www.campeggiodolomiti.it]** 2km S of Cortina turn R off S51. Site beyond Camping Cortina & Rocchetta. Lge, mkd pitch, pt shd; htd wc; shwrs inc; chem disp; EHU (4A) inc (check earth); gas; lndry; shop; rest 1km; bar; playgrnd; htd pool; games area; games rm; wifi; 10% statics; dogs; phone; bus; poss cr; Eng spkn; no adv bkg; quiet; red LS; ccard acc. "Superb scenery in mountains, gd walks; cycle rte into Cortina; helpful owner; beautiful setting; choice of open meadow or shd woodland pitches." ♦ 1 Jun-20 Sep. € 24.00 2014*

COURMAYEUR *1A1* (6.2km NE) *45.83293, 6.99095* **Campsite Grandes Jorasses, Via per la Val Ferret 53, 11013 Courmayeur (Valle d'Aosta) [0165 869708; info@grandesjorasses.com; www.grandesjorasses.com]** Foll the brown 'Val Ferret' signs bet Courmayeur and the Mont Blanc tunnel, and the campsite is located a few km on the L of the rd. Med, hdstg, pt shd; wc; chem disp; mv service pnt; shwrs (50c); lndry; shop on site; rest; snacks; bar; games rm; wifi; CKE/CCI. "Beautiful site at the foot of Mt Blanc; nature trails thro forest; trekking expeditions arranged; gd rest." ♦ ltd. 20 Jun-15 Sep. € 30.00 2014*

DEIVA MARINA *1C2* (3km E Coastal) *44.22476, 9.55146* **Villaggio Camping Valdeiva, Loc Ronco, 19013 Deiva-Marina (SP) [0187 824174; fax 825352; camping@valdeiva.it; www.valdeiva.it]** Fr A12 exit Deiva Marina, site sp on L in approx 4km by town sp. Med, mkd pitch, hdstg, pt sl, pt shd; wc (some cont); chem disp; shwrs inc; EHU (3-6A) inc; lndry; shop; rest, snacks; bar; BBQ; playgrnd; pool; shgl beach 3km; wifi; entmnt; sat TV; 90% statics; dogs; phone; bus to stn; sep car park high ssn; poss cr; Eng spkn; adv bkg ess high ssn; ccard acc; red LS; CKE/CCI. "Free minibus to stn - conv Cinque Terre or Portofino; helpful, friendly staff; gd rest; excel walking; v quiet LS & shwrs ltd." 1 Jan-8 Jan, 5 Feb-6 Nov & 1 Dec-31 Dec. € 36.00 (3 persons) 2017*

⊞ **DEMONTE** *1B2* (1.5km N Rural) *44.32260, 7.29222* **Campeggio Il Sole, Frazione Perosa 3/B, 12014 Demonte (CN) [0334 1132724; fax 0171 955630; erikamelchio@virgilio.it; www.ghironda.com]** Fr lge town sq on S21 go E for 100m, fork L & in 100m turn L. Pass 2 churches on L, turn L, then R over rv into Via Colle dell'Urtica to N. Foll this rd uphill for 1.2km, turn L at T-junc & in 300m L at T-junc again. Site on R. Town cent side rds v narr with arches & app rd narr & steep in places. Sm, mkd pitch, unshd; wc; chem disp; mv service pnt; shwrs €1; EHU €2; lndry rm; rest; bar; BBQ; playgrnd; dogs; quiet. "Lovely, peaceful site in mountains; vg value rest." ♦ ltd. € 17.00 2013*

DEMONTE *1B2* (1.5km W Rural) *44.31357, 7.27275* **Camping Piscina Demonte, Loc Bagnolin, 12014 Demonte (CN) [338 2464353; fax 011 2274301; info@campingdemonte.com; www.campingdemonte.com]** App only fr Borgo on S21, 500m after Demonte turn L, foll sp. Med, pt shd; wc; chem disp; shwrs €0.60; EHU (6A) €1.50; gas; lndry; shop, rest 1.5km; bar; pool; 90% statics; dogs €1.60; poss cr; adv bkg; quiet; ccard acc; CKE/CCI. "Gd NH bef Col d'Larche; helpful, friendly owner; gd mountain scenery." 15 Jun-15 Sep. € 16.50 2013*

DESENZANO DEL GARDA *1D2* (5km SE Rural) *45.46565, 10.59443* **Camping San Francesco, Strada V San Francesco, 25015 Desenzano-del-Garda (BS) [030 9110245; fax 9902558; booking@campingsanfrancesco.com; www.campingsanfrancesco.com]** E fr Milan on A4 a'strada take exit Sirmione & foll sp twd Sirmione town; join S11 twd Desenzano & after Garden Center Flowers site 1st campsite on R after rndabt; site sp twd lake bet Sirmione & Desanzano. Or fr Desenzano, site just after Rivoltella. Lge, mkd pitch, pt sl, shd; wc; chem disp; fam bthrm; shwrs inc; EHU (6A) inc; gas; lndry (inc dryer); shop; rest, snacks; bar; BBQ (charcoal/gas); playgrnd; pool; lake sw & shgl beach; boat hire; windsurfing; sailing; canoe hire; fishing; tennis; games area; bike hire; golf 10km; wifi; entmnt; TV rm; 50% statics; dogs free; no o'fits over 6m high ssn; phone; recep clsd 1300-1500 & no vehicle movement; poss cr; Eng spkn; adv bkg; noisy entmnt high ssn; ccard acc; red LS; CKE/CCI. "Lovely lakeside pitches for tourers (extra); muddy if wet; poss diff lge o'fits due trees; helpful staff; well managed site; gd position on edge of lake; handy for local bus; excel site; v clean facs; gd rest." ♦ 1 Apr-30 Sep. € 51.00 (CChq acc) 2014*

DIANO MARINA *1B3* (4km NE Coastal) *43.92177, 8.10831* **Camping del Mare, Via alla Foce 29, 18010 Cervo (IM) [0183 400130 or 0183 405556; fax 402771; info@campingdelmare-cervo.com; www.campingdelmare-cervo.com]** Exit A10/E80 at San Bartolomeo/Cervo onto Via Aurelia. Turn L at traff lts twd Cervo. Sp adj rv bdge. R turn acute - long o'fits app fr NE. Med, hdg/mkd pitch, hdstg, shd; wc; chem disp; fam bthrm; shwrs; EHU (6A) €2; gas; lndry; shop; snacks; shgl beach adj; internet; TV; 40% statics; dogs; phone; Eng spkn; adv bkg rec Jun-Aug; quiet; ccard acc. "Immac site; spacious pitches; friendly, helpful staff; picturesque beach & perched vill (Cervo); easy walk San Bartolomeo; gd mkts; highly rec site; pitches close together; office closes 1200-1500." ♦ 23 Mar-15 Oct. € 50.00 2014*

⊞ **EDOLO** *1D1* (1.5km W Rural) *46.17648, 10.31333* **Camping Adamello, Via Campeggio 10, Loc Nembra, 25048 Edolo (BS) [tel/fax 0364 71694 or 0333 8275354; info@campingadamello.it; www.campingadamello.it]** On rd 39 fr Edolo to Aprica; after 1.5km turn sharp L down narr lane by rest; camping sp on rd; diff app. Med, pt sl, terr, pt shd; wc; chem disp; shwrs inc; EHU (6A) €1.50; lndry; shop; rest, snacks 1km; bar; 50% statics; dogs €3; poss cr; quiet; no ccard acc. "Useful NH; beautiful mountain site; steep rds all round; v diff app fr W; quiet for couples; nothing for children." ♦ € 27.00 2016*

"Satellite navigation makes touring much easier"

Remember most sat navs don't know if you're towing or in a larger vehicle – always use yours alongside maps and site directions.

ELBA ISLAND *1C3* **Sites on Elba Island are listed together at the end of the Italy site entry pages.**

ERACLEA MARE see Lido di Jesolo *2E2*

⊞ **FALZE DI PIAVE** *2E1* (700m S Rural) *45.85674, 12.16565* **Parking Le Grave, Via Passo Barca, 31020 Falze-di-Piave (TV) [tel/fax 0390 43886896; belleluigi@libero.it; www.legrave.it]** Fr A27 exit Conegliano & turn R onto SP15 then SS13 to Susegana. At Ponte-della-Priula turn onto SP34 to Falze-di-Piave. Fr town cent turn L just past war memorial into Via Passo Barca, site on R. Sm, unshd; no wc or shwrs; chem disp; mv service pnt; EHU(4A) inc; BBQ; playgrnd; quiet. "CL-type site in delightful area; friendly, helpful owner; gd walking/cycling; wine tasting last w/end May." € 10.00 2016*

FERIOLO see Verbania *1B1*

⊞ **FERRARA** *1D2* (3km NE Rural) *44.85303, 11.63328* **Campeggio Comunale Estense, Via Gramicia 76, 44100 Ferrara [tel/fax 0532 752396; campeggio.estense@freeinternet.it or idem@libero.it]** Exit A13 Ferrara N. After Motel Nord Ovest on L turn L at next traff lts into Via Porta Catena. Rd is 500m fr city wall around town; foll brown/yellow sps - well sp fr all dirs. Med, pt shd; htd wc (some cont); chem disp; mv service pnt; shwrs inc; EHU (6A) €3.50; lndry; shops, rest 200m; pool in park nrby; bike hire; golf adj; some stored c'vans; dogs €1.50; site clsd early-Jan to end-Feb; Eng spkn; quiet; ccard acc €50+; 10% red CKE/CCI. "Peaceful, well-kept, clean site; helpful staff; lge pitches; ltd privacy in shwrs; interesting, beautiful town; gd cycle tracks round town; rlwy stn in town for trains to Venice; gd NH; watch out for low branches when driving thro site." ♦
1 Jan-11 Jan & 1 Mar-31 Dec. € 24.50 2016*

FIANO ROMANO *2E4* (2km W Rural) *42.15167, 12.57670* **Camping I Pini, Via delle Sassete 1/A, 00065 Fiano-Romano [0765 453349; fax 1890941; ipini@camping.it; www.camping.it/roma/ipini]** Fr A1/E35 exit sp Roma Nord/Fiano Romano (use R-hand lane for cash toll), foll sp Fiano at rndabt. Take 1st exit at next rndabt sp I Pini & stay on this rd for approx 2km. Take 2nd exit at next rndabt, L at T-junc under bdge, site sp on R. Med, hdg/mkd pitch, pt sl, terr, pt shd; htd wc; chem disp; mv service pnt; shwrs inc; EHU (6A) inc (poss rev pol); lndry (inc dryer); shop; rest, snacks; bar; BBQ; playgrnd; pool; paddling pool; tennis; bike hire; horseriding nrby; fishing; wifi; entmnt; games rm; TV; 60% statics (tour ops); dogs €2; no o'fits over 10m high ssn; phone; bus; poss cr; Eng spkn; adv bkg rec high ssn; quiet, but noisy nr bar; ccard acc; red LS/CKE/CCI. "Well-run, clean, excel san facs; helpful, friendly staff; excel rest; access poss diff lge o'fits; kerbs to all pitches; most pitches slope badly side to side req double height ramps; excursions by coach inc daily to Rome or gd train service; super site."
♦ 18 Apr-21 Sep. € 56.00 SBS - Y13 2014*

FIE/VOLS *1D1* (3km N Rural) *46.53334, 11.53335* **Camping Alpe di Siusi/Seiser Alm, Loc San Constantino 16, 39050 Fiè-allo-Sciliar/Völs-am-Schlern (BZ) [0471 706459; fax 707382; info@camping-seiseralm.com; www.camping-seiseralm.com]** Leave Bolzano on SS12 (not A22) sp Brixen & Brenner. After approx 7km take L fork in tunnel mouth sp Tiers, Fiè. Foll rd thro Fiè, site in 3km dir Castelrotto, sp on L. Lge, mkd pitch, hdstg, terr, unshd; htd wc; chem disp; mv service pnt; fam bthrm; sauna; shwrs inc; EHU (16A) metered; lndry (inc dryer); shop; rest, snacks; bar; playgrnd; golf 1km; sat TV; wifi; 20% statics; dogs €4.50; bus; phone; site clsd 5 Nov to 20 Dec; poss cr; Eng spkn; adv bkg; quiet; CKE/CCI. "Well-organised site with gd views; impressive, luxury undergrnd san facs block; private san facs avail; vg walking/skiing; an amazing experience; v popular site; efficiently run!"
1 Jan-2 Nov & 20 Dec-31 Dec. € 47.00 2014*

⊞ **FIESOLE** *1D3* (1km NE Rural) *43.80666, 11.30638* **Camping Panoramico, Via Peramonda 1, 50014 Fiesole (FI) [055 599069; fax 59186; panoramico@florencecamping.com; www.florencecamping.com]** Foll sp for Fiesole & Camping Panoramico fr Florence; site on R. Rd to Fiesole v hilly & narr thro busy tourist area. Lge, terr, pt shd; wc; chem disp; shwrs inc; EHU (3A) inc; gas; lndry; shop; bar; rest in high ssn; playgrnd; pool; internet; 20% statics; dogs free; poss cr; Eng spkn; quiet; ccard acc. "Access v diff - more suitable tenters; site soggy in wet; ltd water points; Florence 20 mins bus but 1.5km steep walk to stop; excel views; excel site." ♦ € 39.00 2012*

FIGLINE VALDARNO *1D3* (20km SW Rural) *43.53847, 11.41380* **Camping Orlando in Chianti, Localita Caffggiolo, 52022 Cavriglia [tel/fax 055 967 422; info@campingorlandoinchianti.it; www.campingorlandoinchianti.it]** Fr A1 Firenze-Roma, exit Incisa. Foll Figline Val d'Arno. Dir Greve in Chianti, exit at Lucolena, then foll signs to 'Piano Orlando Parco Cavriglia'. Med, mkd pitch, hdstg, pt sl, shd; wc; chem disp; mv service pnt; shwrs inc; EHU (16A); lndry; BBQ; shop; rest; snacks; bar; pool; 10% statics; poss cr; Eng spkn; adv bkg; quiet; CCI. "Vg site; excel priced rest; rural; v friendly staff." ♦ 12 Apr-19 Oct. € 48.50 2014*

FIGLINE VALDARNO *1D3* (2.5km W Rural) *43.61111, 11.44940* **Camping Norcenni Girasole Club, Via Norcenni 7, 50063 Figline-Valdarno (FI) [055 915141; fax 9151402; girasole@ecvacanze.it; www.ecvacanze.it]** Fr a'strada A1, dir Rome, take exit 24 (sp Incisa SS69) to Figline-Valdarno; turn R in vill & foll sp to Greve; site sp Girasole; steep app rd to site with some twists for 3km. V lge, some hdg pitch, terr, pt shd; wc (some cont); chem disp; mv service pnt; fam bthrm; private bthrm extra; sauna; shwrs inc; EHU (6A) inc; gas; lndry (inc dryer); shop; rest, snacks; bar; BBQ; playgrnd; 2 pools (1 covrd); paddling pool; jacuzzi; tennis; games area; horseriding; bike hire; fitness cent; games rm; wifi; entmnt; TV; dogs free; twin-axles acc (rec check in adv); stn 1.5km; bus to Florence; excursions; Eng spkn; adv bkg; ccard acc. "Excel, well-run site; some pitches sm; steep site rds poss diff lge o'fits; steel pegs rec; upper level pool area excel for children; site clsd 1330-1530; site hilly; gd touring base." ♦ ltd. 19 Apr-13 Oct. € 50.00 SBS - Y07 2017*

"There aren't many sites open at this time of year"

If you're travelling outside peak season remember to call ahead to check site opening dates – even if the entry says 'open all year'.

FINALE LIGURE *1B2* (1.5km N Rural) *44.18395, 8.35349* **Eurocamping Calvisio, Via Calvisio 37, 17024 Finale-Ligure (SV) [019 601240; info@eurocampingcalvisio.it; www.eurocampingcalvisio.it]** On SS1 Savona-Imperia, turn R at ent to Finale-Ligure; sp to site in Calvisio vill. Med, hdg/mkd pitch, shd; wc (some cont); chem disp; shwrs €0.50; EHU (6A) inc; lndry (inc dryer); shop; rest, snacks; bar; playgrnd; pool high ssn; paddling pool; sand beach 2km; solarium; wifi; entmnt; 80% statics; dogs; sep car park high ssn; poss cr; adv bkg; quiet; ccard acc; red LS. "Security guard at night; clean, well-maintained san facs." ♦ Easter-5 Nov. € 54.50 2016*

FIRENZE *1D3* (24km SE Rural) *43.70138, 11.40527* **Camping Village Il Poggetto, Strada Provinciale Nr1 Aretina Km14, 50067 Troghi [tel/fax 055 8307323; info@campingilpoggetto.com; www.campingilpoggetto.com]** Fr S on E35/A1 a'strada take Incisa exit & turn L dir Incisa. After 400m turn R dir Firenze, site in 5km on L. Fr N on A1 exit Firenze-Sud dir Bagno a Ripoli/S. Donato; go thro S. Donato to Troghi, site on R, well sp. Narr, hilly app rd & sharp turn - app fr S easier. Lge, hdg/mkd pitch, pt sl, pt terr, pt shd; wc (some cont); chem disp; mv service pnt; fam bthrm; private san facs avail; shwrs inc; EHU (7A) inc (poss rev pol); gas; lndry; shop; rest, snacks; bar; playgrnd; 2 pools; bike hire; table tennis; internet; 5% statics; dogs €2.20; phone; bus adj; money change; poss cr; Eng spkn; adv bkg ess high ssn; quiet but some m'way noise; red long stay; ccard acc over €200; 10% red CKE/CCI (LS). "Superb, picturesque, family-run site in attractive location inc vineyard; clean, modern facs; lovely pool; bus to Florence 45mins - tickets fr recep; trains fr Incisa Valdarno (free parking at stn); excursions; gd rest; LS offers for long stay (7+ days); vg site; helpful staff; lge o'fits come fr S; highly rec." ♦ 1 Apr-15 Oct. € 37.00 2017*

FLORENCE see Firenze *1D3*

FOCE DI VARANO see Rodi Garganico *2G4*

FONDOTOCE see Verbania *1B1*

⊞ **FORNI DI SOPRA** *2E1* (2km E Rural) *46.42564, 12.56928* **Camping Tornerai, Stinsans. Via Nazionale, 33024 Forni-di-Sopra (UD) [0433 88035; www.campingtornerai.it]** Site sp on SS52 Tolmezzo-Pieve di Cadore rd, 2km E of Forni-di-Sopra (approx 35km by rd fr Pieve-di-Cadore). Sm, pt sl, pt shd; wc (cont); chem disp (wc); EHU (2A) €1 (extra for 6A) (long lead poss req); 50% statics; dogs €2; poss cr; Eng spkn; quiet; ccard acc. "Conv CL-type site for Forni-di-Sopra chairlift & Passo-della-Mauria; gd san facs." € 20.00 2016*

FUCINE DI OSSANA see Dimaro *1D1*

FUSINA see Venezia *2E2*

GALLIPOLI *3A4* (4km SE Coastal) *39.99870, 18.02590* **Camping Baia di Gallipoli, Litoranea per Santa Maria di Leuca, 73014 Gallipoli (LE) [0833 273210 or 338 8322910 LS; fax 275405; info@baiadigallipoli.com; www.baiadigallipoli.com]** Fr Brindisi/Lecce take S101 to Gallipoli. Exit at sp Matino-Lido Pizzo & foll sp to site, on coast rd bet Gallipoli & Sta Maria di Leuca. V lge, pt shd; htd wc; chem disp; mv service pnt; shwrs inc; EHU (6A) inc; lndry (inc dryer); shop; rest, snacks; bar; BBQ; playgrnd; pool; paddling pool; sand beach 800m (free shuttle bus); tennis; games area; wifi; entmnt; excursions; TV rm; statics; dogs (sm only) €3; sep car park; quiet; ccard acc. ♦ 1 Apr-15 Sep. € 64.00 2014*

GENOA see Genova *1C2*

⊞ **GENOVA** *1C2* (15km W Coastal) *44.41437, 8.70475* **Caravan Park La Vesima, Via Aurelia, Km 547, 16100 Arenzano (GE) [010 6199672; fax 6199686; info@caravanparklavesima.it; www.caravanparklavesima.it]** E of Arenzano on coast rd, clearly sp. Or leave A10 at Arenzano & go E on coast rd. Med, mkd pitch, hdstg, unshd; htd wc (cont); chem disp; fam bthrm; shwrs €0.50; EHU (3A) inc (poss rev pol); gas; lndry; shop high ssn & 3km; rest, snacks, bar high ssn; private shgl beach adj; 90% statics; no dogs; poss cr; Eng spkn; adv bkg; rd, rlwy noise; CKE/CCI. "Useful LS NH/sh stay; gd security; gd, clean san facs; v cr, noisy high ssn; some pitches sm; vg site." € 32.60 2012*

GIANO DELL'UMBRIA *2E3* (1km SW Rural) *42.82932, 12.57178* **Camping Pineta Di Giano, Via Monte Cerreto, 25 06030 Giano Dell'Umbria [39 07 42 93 00 40 or 39 34 03 76 23 43; fax 34 92 43 69 72; info@pinetadigiano.com; www.pinetadigiano.com]** N fr Spoleto on S418 twds Montefalco. Turn L after Mercatello. Site well sp (brown) to Griano dell'Umbria. Site just outside vill. Sm, mkd pitch, hdstg, terr, shd; htd wc; shwr inc; EHU (3A); shop 1km; rest; snacks; bar; htd pool; 60% statics; dogs; quiet. "Gd site; off beaten track, v quiet in pine forest surrounded by long dist trails; v conv for Spoleto." 1 Apr-30 Sep. € 18.00 2014*

GIGNOD see Aosta *1B1*

GLURNS/GLORENZA see Mals/Malles Venosta *1D1*

GOLDRAIN *1D1* (1km SW Urban) *46.61762, 10.81859* **Camping Cevedale, Via Val Venosta 59, 39021 Goldrain [0473 742132; info@camping-cevedale.com; www.camping-cevedale.com]** SS38 Merano-Silandro, pass Latsch/Laces to rndabt sp Goldrain/Martelltal, sp on R (do not confuse vill of Lasa/Laas). Med, hdg pitch, pt shd; wc; chem disp; mv service pnt; fam bthrm; shwrs; EHU (6A); lndry (inc dryer); shop; BBQ; htd & cov pool; wifi; dogs €4; phone; bus/train 50m; Eng spkn; adv bkg; quiet. "Excel site." ♦ ltd. 15 Mar-7 Nov. € 35.50 2015*

GOREGLIA ANTELMINELLI *1D2* (750m N Rural) *44.06642, 10.52879* **Camping Pian d'Amora, Via Crocifisso, Loc. Pian d'Amora, 55025 Coreglia Antelminelli [0583 78334; info@campingpiandamora.nl; www.campingpiandamora.nl]** Fr A11 at Lucca foll sp Val Gaifagnama SS12. After 30km at Piano di Coreglia turn N on minor rd 7km to Coreglia Antelminelli. Site top of town. Sm, terr, shd; wc; chem disp; mv service pnt; shwrs; EHU (10A); lndry; rest; bar; playgrnd; htd/covrd pool; wifi; Eng spkn; adv bkg; quiet. "Beautiful historic hill top town, 5 min walk; gd walking area; conv Lucca; sm c'vans rec; excel." ♦ ltd. 15 Apr-1 Oct. € 35.50 2015*

GRAVEDONA *1C1* (3km SW Rural) *46.13268, 9.28954* **Camping Magic Lake, Via Vigna del Lago 60, 22014 Dongo (CO) [tel/fax 034 480282; camping@magiclake.it; www.magiclake.it]** Site sp on S340d adj Lake Como. Sm, pt sl, pt shd; htd wc; chem disp; mv service pnt; fam bthrm; shwrs inc; EHU (6A) inc; lndry; shop adj; snacks; bar; BBQ; playgrnd; lake sw adj; TV; 40% statics; dogs €3; bus 100m; poss cr; Eng spkn; adv bkg; quiet; red long stay; CKE/CCI. "Excel, friendly, family-run site; walk, cycle to adj vills along lake; excel facs; v clean mod facs; bike/kayak hire on site; bike repairs on site; helpful staff." ♦ 1 Apr-10 Oct. € 30.00 2016*

GROTTAMMARE see Martinsicuro *2F3*

⊞ **GUBBIO** *2E3* (1.2km W) *43.35213, 12.56704* **Camping Parking Gubbio, Via Bottagnone 06024 Area Communale P4 [07 59 22 06 93]** Head NW on SR298 twd Via Bruno Buozzi, at rndbt take 2nd exit onto Viale Parruccini cont for 500m, take 1st exit at rndabt onto Viale Leonardo da Vinci, after 250m turn L onto Via Botagore. Sm; pt shd; no san facs; chem disp; mv service pnt; gd NH. "Only campervan parking allowed; historical town worth a visit." € 5.00 2014*

IDRO *1D1* (2km NE Rural) *45.7540, 457540* **Rio Vantone, Via Vantone 45, 25074 Idro (BS) [0365 83125; fax 823663; idro@azur-camping.de; www.idrosee.eu]** Fr Brescia, take S237 N. At S tip of Lago d'Idro, turn E to Idro. thro Crone, on E shore of lake, thro sh tunnel, site 1km on L, last of 3 sites. Lge, shd; wc; chem disp; mv service pnt; fam bthrm; serviced pitches; shwrs; EHU (6A) inc; lndry; gas; shop; rest, snacks; bar; playgrnd; paddling pool; tennis; lake adj; boat hire; windsurfing; games area; bike hire; internet; entmnt; TV rm; dogs €5; phone; poss cr; adv bkg; quiet; ccard acc; 5% red CKE/CCI. "Idyllic on lakeside with beautiful scenery; superb san facs; excel." ♦ 20 Apr-30 Sept. € 45.00 SBS - Y08 2017*

⊞ **IMPERIA** *1B3* (1km SW Coastal) *43.86952, 7.99810* **Camping de Wijnstok, Via Poggi 2, 18100 Porto-Maurizio (IM) [tel/fax 0183 64986; info@campingdewijnstok.com; www.campingdewijnstok.com]** Exit A10/E80 Imperia W twds sea, take coast rd SS1 Via Aurelia dir San Remo. At km 651/1 turn dir Poggi, site sp. Med, shd; wc (some cont); chem disp; shwrs €0.70; EHU (3A) €2; gas; lndry; shop 200m; snacks; bar; shgl beach 500m; wifi; TV; 80% statics; dogs; phone; sep car park; site clsd mid-Dec to mid-Jan; quiet but some rd noise; ccard acc. "Shabby facs ltd LS; sm pitches diff for lge o'fits; sh walk to town; NH only." ♦ € 31.00 2016*

ITALY

ISEO *1C1* (1km NE Rural) *45.66527, 10.06277* **Camping Quai, Via Antonioli 73, 25049 Iseo (BS) [tel/fax 030 9821610; info@campingquai.it; www.campingquai.it]** Fr Brescia-Boario Terme rd by-passing Iseo, take NE exit; look for 'Camping d'Iseo' sp on corner. After 200m cross rlwy, site sp (sps obscured - go slow). Site adj Punta d'Oro on lakeside. Med, mkd pitch, shd; wc (some cont); chem disp; mv service pnt; shwrs inc; EHU (4A) inc (poss rev pol); lndry; shop, rest 1km; snacks; bar; BBQ; playgrnd; shgl beach & lake sw adj; watersports; games area; boat-launching; 25% statics; dogs; phone; bus, train 1km; sep car park; poss cr; Eng spkn; adv bkg; some rd noise; ccard acc; red long stay/snr citizens. "Well-kept; lake views fr some pitches; helpful manager; some noise fr nrby rlwy." ♦ ltd. 18 Apr-21 Sep. € 41.00 2014*

ISEO *1C1* (500m NE Rural) *45.66416, 10.05722* **Camping Iseo, Via Antonioli 57, 25049 Iseo (BS) [tel/fax 030 980213; info@campingiseo.it; www.campingiseo.com]** Fr A4 exit sp Rovato & immed foll brown sp Lago d'Iseo. Site well sp in vill. Med, some hdg pitch, pt shd; wc (some cont); chem disp; mv service pnt; fam bthrm; some serviced pitches; shwrs inc; EHU (6-10A) €2; gas; lndry; shop; rest 300m; snacks; bar; playgrnd; beach adj; windsurfing; games area; bike hire; golf 3km (red for campers); wifi; entmnt; some statics; dogs €3.50; phone; poss v cr; Eng spkn; adv bkg; quiet; red CKE/CCI. "V scenic; friendly, welcoming owner; well-organised, smart site; sm pitches; extra for lakeside pitches; well-maintained, clean facs but ltd; cruises on lake; many rests nr; excel; site next to a rlwy line, poss sm noise; sm pitches." ♦ 1 Apr-1 Nov. € 37.00 2017*

ISEO *1C1* (500m NE Rural) *45.66388, 10.05638* **Camping Punta d'Oro, Via Antonioli 51-53, 25049 Iseo (BS) [tel/fax 030 980084; info@camping-puntadoro.com; www.puntadoro.com]** Fr Brescia-Boario Terme into Iseo, look for `Camping d'Iseo' sp on corner; after 200m cross rlwy, 1st R to site in 400m on lakeside. Med, pt sl, pt shd; wc; chem disp; mv service pnt; shwrs inc; EHU (4A) inc; lndry; shop 500m; rest 500m; snacks; bar; playgrnd; shgl beach; lake sw; boating; golf 6km; wifi; dogs €5; poss v cr high ssn; Eng spkn; some rlwy noise; red snr citizens; CKE/CCI. "Gd security; beautiful area; friendly family run site, eager to help." ♦ 1 Apr - 15 Oct. € 35.50 2017*

ISEO *2F2* (1km E Urban) *45.66700, 10.06766* **Camping Covelo, Via Covelo 18, 25049 Iseo [tel/fax 030 982 13 05; info@campingcovelo.it; www.campingcovelo.it]** Fr A4 Bergamo-Brescia, take exit Palazzolo/SP469. Cont Onto SP12. At rndabt take 2nd exit SPxi. Take 3rd exit at next rndabt and foll sp to camp. Med, pt shd; wc; chem disp; shwrs; EHU (6A); lndry (inc dryer); shops; rest; snacks; bar; playgrnd; sw adj; games area; wifi; dogs €3.50; poss cr; Eng spkn; adv bkg; ccard acc. "Excel site; v well run; adj to lake; beautiful views; range of watersports; v helpful staff." 17 Apr-2 Nov. € 40.00 2014*

ISEO *1C1* (1.5km W Rural) *45.65689, 10.03739* **Camping Del Sole, Via per Rovato 26, 25049 Iseo (BS) [030 980288; fax 9821721; info@campingdelsole.it; www.campingdelsole.it]** Exit Brescia-Milan a'strada at Rivato-Lago d'Iseo exit & foll sp to Iseo. At complex rd junc with rndabts on Iseo o'skirts, site ent on L (lge sp). Site bet lakeside & rd, bef API petrol stn on R. Lge, mkd pitch, shd; wc; chem disp; mv service pnt; htd private bthrms avail; shwrs; EHU (6A) inc; lndry (inc dryer); supmkt; rest, snacks; bar; playgrnd; htd pool; paddling pool; shgl beach & lake sw; tennis; waterskiing; bike hire; games area; wifi; entmnt; TV rm; 75% statics; dogs €3.5 (not acc high ssn); sep car park; poss cr; Eng spkn; adv bkg; quiet; ccard acc. "Glorious views; excel facs; well-run, pleasant, popular lakeside site; pitches poss closely packed; ltd waste/water disposal; narr site rds." ♦ 15 Apr-25 Sep. € 46.00 (CChq acc) 2017*

ISEO *1C1* (1.5km W Rural) *45.65690, 10.03429* **Camping Sassabanek, Via Colombera 2, 25049 Iseo (BS) [030 980300; fax 9821360; sassabanek@sassabanek.it; www.sassabanek.it]** On periphery of Iseo by lakeside. Lge, pt shd; wc (some cont); chem disp; mv service pnt; sauna; shwrs inc; EHU (6A) inc; gas; lndry; shop; rest, snacks; bar; BBQ; playgrnd; pool; paddling pool; boating; windsurfing; tennis; bike hire; TV; 50% statics; no dogs; phone; sep car park; adv bkg; quiet; ccard acc. "Clean facs; sh walk to pretty lakeside & vill; helpful staff; gd NH/sh stay; nice location; cramped pitches; vg." ♦ 1 Apr-30 Sep. € 39.00 2017*

"That's changed – Should I let The Club know?"

If you find something on site that's different from the site entry, fill in a report and let us know. See camc.com/europereport.

ISPRA see Sesto Calende *1B1*

LAIVES/LEIFERS see Bolzano/Bozen *1D1*

⊞ **LAVENA** *1C1* (9km SW Rural) *45.95960, 8.86340* **International Camping di Rimoldi Claudio, Via Marconi 18, 21037 Lavena-Ponte-Tresa (VA) [0332 550117; fax 551600; info@internationalcamping.com; www.internationalcamping.com]** On rte S233 going SW into Italy fr Switzerland, turn SE after border twd Lavena-Ponte-Tresa. Going twd Switzerland fr Italy on same rte turn R twd vill. Site sp in vill. Med, pt sl, hdg pitch; pt shd; wc (some cont); shwrs; EHU (2-6A) €1.50; lndry; supmkt opp; rest, snacks; bar; playgrnd; sand beach on lake; mainly statics; poss cr; adv bkg; quiet; ACSI card acc; CKE/CCI. "On smallest, most W bay of Lake Lugano; excel facs; friendly, helpful staff; wall around site so no lake views." € 40.50 2013*

LAZISE *1D2* (1.5km N Urban) *45.50807, 10.73166* **Camp Municipale, Via Roma 1,37017 Lazise (VR) [045 7580020; fax 7580549; camping.municipale@comune.lazise.vr.it; www.comune.lazise.vr.it]** N on S249 fr Peschiera, thro Pacengo & Lazise, at rndabt cont on S249 then turn L into Via Roma. Site sp at end of rd. Care req in 100m, sharp R turn; site ent pt hidden. Med, hdg/mkd pitch, pt shd; wc; chem disp; mv service pnt; shwrs inc; EHU (10A) inc; lndry; shop 250m; rest, snacks, bar adj; lake sw & beach adj; 5% statics; dogs €3; Eng spkn; quiet; ccard acc. "Gd touring cent; some pitches v muddy; gd, clean facs; friendly staff; avoid arr bef 1500 Wed (mkt on app rd); easy walk along lake to interesting sm town." ♦ ltd. 22 Mar-2 Nov. € 32.00 2012*

"I like to fill in the reports as I travel from site to site"

You'll find report forms at the back of this guide, or you can fill them in online at camc.com/europereport.

LAZISE *1D2* (1.5km S Rural) *45.49277, 10.73305* **Camping La Quercia, Loc Bottona, 37017 Lazise (VR) [045 6470577; fax 6470243; laquercia@laquercia.it; www.laquercia.it]** Exit A22/E45 at Affi/Lago di Garda Sud or exit A4/E70 at Peschiera-del-Garda. Site on SR249, on SE shore of lake. V lge, hdg/mkd pitch, pt sl, shd; htd wc; chem disp; mv service pnt; fam bthrm; fam bathrm; shwrs inc; EHU (6A) inc; gas; lndry (inc dryer); shops; rest, snacks; bar; playgrnd; pool; paddling pool; waterslide; jacuzzi; private sand beach; watersports; tennis; games area; gym; wifi; entmnt; 15% statics; dogs €6.90; phone; vehicle safety checks for cars/m'vans; poss cr; adv bkg. "Superb site for family holidays; many excel sports & leisure facs; some pitches on lakeside; easy walk to town along beach; highly rec." ♦ 1 Apr-4 Oct. € 61.00 2012*

⊞ **LAZISE** *1D2* (3.5km S Urban) *45.47912, 10.72635* **Camping Amici di Lazise, Loc Fossalta Nuova, Strada del Roccolo 8, 37017 Lazise (VR) [045 6490146; fax 6499448; info@campingamicidilazise.it; www.campingamicidilazise.it]** S fr Lazise, immed bef high rest with Greek columns (bef Gardaland) take side rd on R, site on R. Med, pt shd; wc (some cont); chem disp; mv service pnt; some serviced pitches; shwrs inc; EHU (6A) inc; lndry; shop; rest; bar; playgrnd; pool; paddling pool; shgl beach 300m; entmnt; 40% statics; dogs €4.50; poss cr; Eng spkn; adv bkg; quiet; poss noisy; red LS. "Gd; nice friendly site; gd pool; noise fr theme pk next door." ♦ € 34.00 2016*

LAZISE *1D2* (900m S Rural) *45.49861, 10.7375* **Camping Du Parc, Via Gardesana, 110 I, 37017 Lazise (VR) [045 7580127; fax 6470150; duparc@campingduparc.com; www.campingduparc.com]** Site on W side of lakeside rd SR249. Lge, pt sl, hdg pitch, pt shd; wc; chem disp; mv service pnt; shwrs; EHU (5A) inc (rev pol); lndry; shop; rest, snacks; bar; playgrnd; pool; waterslides; sand beach & lake sw; watersports; boat & bike hire; gym; entmnt; wifi; 15% statics; dogs €5.70; poss cr at w/end; Eng spkn; adv bkg; red LS; ccard acc; red LS. "Sh walk to old town & ferry terminal; lovely lakeside position; excel, well-maintained site; vg san facs; gd size pitches, some on lake - long walk to water point; vg pizzeria & pool; quiet LS; ideal for families; gd security; Magic of Europe discount; vg; site improved every year; most pitches have water & drain." ♦ 15 Mar-4 Nov. € 50.00 2017*

⊞ **LECCE** *3A4* (10km W Rural) *40.36417, 18.09889* **Camping Lecce Namaste, 73100 Lecce [0832 329647; info@camping-lecce.it; www.camping-lecce.it]** Fr Lecce ring rd exit junc 15 W dir Novoli, in 5km immed after (abandoned) sm petrol stn turn R at sp Namaste. App rd to site potholed/gravelled. Site may appear clsd - sound horn for attention. Sm, some hdstg, pt shd; wc; shwrs inc; EHU (10A) inc; shop 2km; beach 16km; bus to Lecce; quiet. "Gd, clean site but dated facs; conv for Baroque city of Lecce & coast around heel of Italy." € 21.00 2015*

LECCO *1C1* (5.8km S) *45.81555, 9.39969* **Camping Village Riviera, Via Foppaola 113, 23852, Garlate [0341 680346; info@campingvillageriviera.com; www.campingvillageriviera.com]** Head S on SS36, take exit Pescate/Lecco, cont strt, at rndbt take 3rd exit onto Via Roma, over rndbt, cont onto Via Statale, turn L onto Via Foppaola, site on L. Sm, hdg pitch, pt shd; wc; shwrs; chem disp; EHU (10A); lndry; playgrnd; games rm; wifi; TV in bar; bus; Eng spkn. "Lake location with free kayak, pedalo, gym, playgrnd & pool." ♦ ltd. € 26.00 2014*

LECCO *1C1* (4km W Rural) *45.81730, 9.34307* **Camping Due Laghi, Via Isella 34, 23862 Civate (LC) [tel/fax 0341 550101; erealin@tin.it; www.duelaghicamping.com]** S side of Lecco-Como rd on lake. Use slip rd mkd Isella/Civate. Turn L at T-junc, then L over bdge; foll v narr app rd to site, sp. Med, pt sl, shd; wc (cont); shwrs inc; EHU (4A) inc; gas; lndry; shop; rest, snacks; bar; pool; paddling pool; games area; mainly statics; dogs €3; quiet; Eng spkn. "Unkempt site; gd, modern san facs; app to site is v narr." 1 Apr-30 Sep. € 36.00 2014*

LECCO *1C1* (9km NW Rural) *45.92138, 9.28777* **Camping La Fornace, Via Giuseppe Garibaldi, 52 23865 Oliveto-Lario (LC) [tel/fax 031 969553; lafornace@libero.it; www.lafornace.it]** Fr Lecco SP583 twd Bellagio. Site on R at '37km' sp. Fr Bellagio on SP583 site on L 100m after Onno boundary sp. V sharp L turn at yellow sp. App diff for lge o'fits, narr app rd. Sm, mkd pitch, hdstg, pt sl, pt shd; wc (male cont); chem disp; mv service pnt; shwrs inc; EHU (5A) inc; shop; rest, snacks; bar; beach & lake sw adj; games rm; dogs; poss cr; adv bkg; quiet; red LS; CKE/CCI. "Peaceful, lakeside site but poss loud music fr bar until sm hrs; delightful setting; simple, clean facs." 1 Apr-30 Sep. € 22.00 2013*

LENNO see Menaggio *1C1*

LEVANTO *1C2* (1km NE Coastal) *44.17364, 9.62550* **Camping Cinque Terre, Sella Mereti, 19015 Levanto (SP) [tel/fax 0187 801252; info@campingcinqueterre.it; www.campingcinqueterre.it]** Clearly sp fr cent of Lèvanto. Fr E turn L off SS1 to Lèvanto, sp Carradano, site on R bef town. Sm, hdg/mkd pitch, terr, shd; htd wc (mainly cont); chem disp; mv service pnt; shwrs €2; EHU (3A) inc; gas; lndry; shop 500m; rest 500m; snacks; bar; sm playgrnd; shgl/sand beach 1km; games rm; wifi; TV; no dogs high ssn; sep car park; bus to beach high ssn; poss cr; adv bkg; quiet; ccard not acc; red LS; CKE/CCI. "Excel, friendly, family-run site; gd, modern san facs; steep ent, but site level; quiet and secluded; helpful staff; some rd noise; sm pitches." ♦ ltd. Easter-30 Sep. € 35.00 2013*

⊞ **LEVANTO** *1C2* (4km NE Rural) *44.17561, 9.63665* **Camping San Michele, Localita' Busco, 19015 Levanto (SP) [tel/fax 0187 800 449; info@campingsanmichele.net; www.campingsanmichele.net]** Head S on SS566 dir Carrodano Inferiore-Levanto. At 2nd rndabt take 3rd exit, then turn L onto Localita Albero D'Oro. Campsite on the R after 2.3km. Lge, hdstg, terr, pt shd, wc (cont), chem disp; shwrs; snacks; bar; scooter hire; poss cr; Eng spkn. "Helpful staff; fair site; clean but tired facs." € 29.00 2014*

⊞ **LEVANTO** *1C2* (400m SE Coastal/Urban) *44.16656, 9.61366* **Camping Acqua Dolce, Via Guido Semenza 5, 19015 Levanto (SP) [0187 808465; fax 807365; mail@campingacquadolce.com; www.campingacquadolce.com]** Site sp fr town cent, app rd to Levanto steep & winding. Site ent steep. Pls do not use sat nav fr town. Med, mkd pitch, hdstg, terr, shd; wc (some cont); chem disp; mv service pnt; serviced pitches; shwrs inc; EHU (6A) €2.50 (rev pol); lndry; shops adj; rest, snacks; bar; playgrnd; pool 250m; sand beach 300m; dogs; phone; sep car park; site clsd mid-Jan to end Feb; poss cr; Eng spkn; adv bkg; ccard acc; red LS. "Site ent poss diff; sm pitches; vg, modern san facs but unisex; o'fits parked v close high ssn; not rec c'vans over 6m; gd touring base Cinque Terre vills; gd walks fr site; lovely, clean beach; easy walk to boat terminal & rlwy stn." ♦ € 38.50 2015*

LEVICO TERME *1D1* (1km S Rural) *46.00638, 11.28944* **Camping Lago Levico (Formerly Camping Jolly), Via Pleina 5, 38056 Levico-Terme (TN) [0461 706934; fax 700227; info@campinglevico.com; www.campinglevico.com]** Foll sp to Levico fr A22 or SS12 onto SS27; site sp. Lge, mkd pitch, shd; wc; chem disp; mv service pnt; serviced pitches; fam bthrm; shwrs inc; EHU (6A) inc; gas; lndry (inc dryer); shop & 150m; rest; snacks; bar; BBQ; playgrnd; pool high ssn; paddling pool; shgl beach 200m; golf 7km; internet; entmnt; 30% statics; dogs €2-6 (not allowed on lakeside pitches); poss cr; adv bkg; quiet; red snr citizens. "Health spa nr; vg; supp for lakeside pitch;" ♦ 1 Apr-10 Oct. € 38.00 2017*

LEVICO TERME *1D1* (5km SW Rural) *46.00392, 11.25838* **Camping Spiaggia, Viale Venezia 12, 38050 Calceranica al Lago (TN) [tel/fax 0461 723037; info@campingspiaggia.net; www.campingspiaggia.net]** Foll sp to Levico fr Trento; after exit rd turn L & in 400m turn L foll sp to site. Site after Camping Jolly on S side of lake. Med, hdg/mkd pitch, pt shd; wc; chem disp; mv service pnt; private san facs avail; shwrs inc; EHU inc; playgrnd; private shgl beach & lake sw (across rd); some statics; dogs €3; poss cr; Eng spkn; quiet. "Gd site; new san facs (2015) & private bthrms." 10 Apr-27 Sep. € 22.50 2015*

LEVICO TERME *1D1* (6km SW Urban) *46.00574, 11.24698* **Camping Penisola Verde, Via Penisola Verde, 5 38050 Galceranica Al Lago [0461 723272; fax 1820746; info@penisolaverde.it; www.penisolaverde.it]** Exit Trento-Padova SS47 either end of lake for Calceranica. Turn W in vill at camping sp, over rlwy x-ing and immed L to lakeside site. Med, mkd pitch, hdstg, pt shd; wc; chem disp; mv service pnt; shwrs inc; EHU (6A); lndry (inc dryer); rest; café; snacks; bar; BBQ; playgrnd; beach, lake sw; games area; wifi; 10% statics; dogs €3; train 200m; bus 100m; twin axles; poss cr; Eng spkn; adv bkg; quiet; red in LS. "Mountain views across lake; beach has sep area for sw, fishing & boating; excel." 9 May-13 Sep. € 36.00 2015*

LIDO DELLE NAZIONI see Comacchio *2E2*

LIDO DI JESOLO *2E2* (5.8km NE Coastal) *45.52862, 12.69693* **Campsite Parco Capraro, Via Corer 2 ramo, 4 30016 Lido di Jesolo [0421 961073; fax 362994; info@parcocapraro.it; www.parcocapraro.it]** Fr Jesolo head NE on Via Roma Destra twrds Via Giotto da Bondone. Cont onto Via Loghetto, then onto Via Cà Gamba, L onto Via Corer. Site on L. Lge, pt shd, wc, chem disp, mv service pnt; fam bthrm; shwrs; EHU (16A); lndry (inc dryer); shop; rest; café; bar; takeaway; bar; BBQ; playgrnd; htd pool; games rm; bike hire; entmnt; wifi; TV in bar; dogs; public transport 1km; twin axles; Eng spkn; quiet. "Vg; v well kept family site; path thro sm pine forest leads to beach & bus stop to cent of town; vg rest/bar; superb sw pool." 1 Mar-28 Sep. € 44.50 2014*

LIDO DI SAVIO see Cervia *2E2*

LIMONE SUL GARDA *1D1* (650m S Rural) *45.80555, 10.7875* **Camping Garda, Via 4 Novembre, 25010 Limone-sul-Garda (TN) [tel/fax 0365 954550; horstmann.hotel@tin.it]** Site sp fr SS45b. Sm, mkd pitch, hdstg, pt sl, terr, pt shd; wc (cont); chem disp; shwrs €0.25; EHU (3A) €1; lndry; shop 250m; rest, snacks high ssn; pool; paddling pool; shgl beach & lake sw; bike hire; 10% statics; dogs €4; poss cr; Eng spkn; adv bkg; quiet; CKE/CCI. "Splendid views; v friendly owner; clean, well-kept site adj to lake; excel pool; tired facs but OK (2014)." ♦ 1 Apr-31 Oct. € 38.00 (CChq acc) 2015*

⊞ **LUCCA** *1D3* (800m NW Urban) *43.85000, 10.48583* **Camper Il Serchio, Via del Tiro a Segno 704, Santa Anna, 55100 Lucca (LU) [tel/fax 0583 317385; info@camperilserchio.it; www.camperilserchio.it]** Sp fr main rds to Lucca & fr town. Gd access rds. Med, hdg/mkd pitch, hdstg, pt shd; wc; chem disp; mv service pnt; shwrs inc; EHU (5A) inc; lndry (inc dryer); rest nr; BBQ; playgrnd; pool €5; tennis, games area opp; bike hire; wifi; dogs; bus; poss cr; adv bkg; quiet but disco noise nrby; "Attractive pitches; mainly for m'vans - not suitable lge car/c'van o'fits or lge tents; vg site." ♦ € 25.00 2012*

LUINO *1C1* (6km N Rural) *46.04189, 8.73279* **Camping Lido Boschetto Holiday, Via Pietraperzia 13, 21010 Maccagno (VA) [tel/fax 0332 560250; lido@boschettoholiday.it; www.boschettoholiday.it/lido]** On E shore of Lake Maggiore on SS394 bet Bellinzona & Laveno. Fr Luino pass under 2 rlwy bdges & foll sp L twd lake, site clearly sp. Med, pt shd; wc; shwrs inc; chem disp; shwrs inc; EHU (3-4A) €3.50; (poss rev pol); lndry; shop; snacks adj; playgrnd; lake sw & beach adj; watersports; 4 statics; dogs €3; adv bkg; quiet; ccard acc; CKE/CCI. "Hydrofoil/ferries fr vill to all parts of lake; trains to Locarno; barrier clsd 1300-1500, no place to pk outside; well kept." 31 Mar-22 Oct. € 31.00 2017*

MACCAGNO see Luino *1C1*

MAGIONE *2E3* (10km S Rural) *43.08140, 12.14340* **Camping Polvese, Via Montivalle, 06060 Sant' Arcangelo-sul-Trasimeno (PG) [075 848078; fax 848050; polvese@polvese.com; www.polvese.com]** Fr A1 exit dir Lake Trasimeno to Castiglione-del-Lago, then S599 to San Arcangelo. Med, mkd pitch, pt shd; wc (cont); chem disp; mv service pnt; shwrs inc; EHU (10A) inc; gas; lndry; shop; snacks; bar; playgrnd; 2 pools; paddling pool; sand beach adj; watersports; lake fishing; bike hire; games area; wifi; entmnt; 40% statics; dogs €2; phone; poss cr; adv bkg; quiet; red long stay; CKE/CCI. "Gd touring base for Umbria; lakeside pitches avail; helpful staff." ♦ 1 Apr-30 Sep. € 22.00 (CChq acc) 2012*

MALCESINE *1D1* (Urban) *45.76583, 10.81096* **Camping Villaggio Turistico Priori, Via Navene 31, 37018 Malcesine (VR) [045 7400503; fax 6583098; info@appartement-prioriantonio.it; www.appartement-prioriantonio.it]** Well sp in town cent. Take care if app fr N. Sm, mkd pitch, hdstg, pt sl, terr, pt shd; wc; chem disp; shwrs inc; EHU (3A) inc; lndry; shop adj; rest, snacks, bar adj; lake sw & shgl beach 200m; no dogs; phone; poss cr; some rd noise; adv bkg; Eng spkn; CKE/CCI. "Vg; conv all amenities & Monte Baldo funicular." 15 Apr-16 Oct. € 24.00 2016*

MALCESINE *1D1* (3km N Rural) *45.78971, 10.82609* **Camping Martora, Campagnola, Martora 2, 37018 Malcesine (VR) [045 4856733 or 338 1453795; fax 4851278; martora@martora.it; www.martora.it]** On E side of lake on rd SS249 at km 86/11. Ent up concrete rd bet iron gates at 'Prinz Blau' sp. Med, mkd pitch, pt sl, pt shd; wc; chem disp; shwrs; EHU (4A) inc; gas 200m; rest 100m; lake sw, windsurfing adj; wifi; 10% statics; poss cr; adv bkg; quiet. "Lakeside cycle path to town." 1 Apr-3 Oct. € 27.00 2016*

MALS/MALLES VENOSTA *1D1* (3km S Rural) *46.67305, 10.5700* **Campingpark Gloria Vallis, Wiesenweg 5, 39020 Glurns/Glorenza (BZ) [0473 835160; fax 835767; info@gloriavallis.it; www.gloriavallis.it]** Sp on rd S41 E of Glorenza. Med, mkd pitch, terr, unshd; htd wc; chem disp; mv service pnt; fam bthrm; shwrs inc; EHU (10A) inc; gas; lndry; shop; snacks; bar; playgrnd; pool 1km; tennis; games area; entmnt; 5% statics; dogs €4; phone; o'night parking place for m'vans; Eng spkn; adv bkg; quiet; ccard acc; CKE/CCI. "Excel mountain views; dog shwr rm; higher prices in winter; excel well run site; serviced pitches; 7 day travel pass in 'all inc' package." ♦ 23 Mar-31 Oct. € 37.00 2016*

MANERBA DEL GARDA *1D2* (2km N Rural) *45.56138, 10.55944* **Camping Rio Ferienglück, Via del Rio 37 Pianarolli, 25080 Manerba-del-Garda (BS) [0365 551450 summer 0365 551075 winter; fax 551044; info@campingrioferiengluck.com; www.gardalake.it/rioferiengluck]** Fr S572 rd turn E at traff lts sp Manerba Centro. At TO turn L down hill & at petrol stn turn R into Viale Degli Alpini. At next rndabt turn L & foll site sp. Site 1.5km N of Manerba opp Hotel Zodiaco. Lge, mkd pitch, pt shd; wc (some cont); chem disp; mv service pnt; shwrs inc; EHU (6A) €3; gas; lndry (inc dryer); shop; rest nr; snacks; bar; BBQ; playgrnd; htd pool; paddling pool; shgl beach & lake sw adj; watersports; wifi; some statics; dogs €2; Eng spkn; no adv bkg; quiet; CKE/CCI. "Excel, family-run lakeside site with lge, level, grass pitches; welcoming vill nr; cent for Garda sightseeing; conv for train to Venice & Milan; beautiful area; cr but delightful situation." ♦ 23 Mar-20 Oct. € 40.50 2013*

MANERBA DEL GARDA *1D2* (2.5km N Rural) *45.56333, 10.56611* **Camping San Biagio, Via Cavalle 19, 25080 Manerba-del-Garda (BS) [0365 551549; fax 551046; info@campingsanbiagio.net; www.campingsanbiagio.net]** Fr S572 rd turn E at sp Manerba, site sp 1.5km N fr Manerba. Lge, mkd pitch, hdstg, terr, shd; htd wc; fam bthrm; shwrs inc; EHU (16A) metered; lndry (inc dryer); shop; rest, snacks; bar; BBQ; playgrnd; shgl beach & lake sw; wifi; dogs €5; poss cr; Eng spkn; adv bkg; quiet; ccard acc. "Terr pitches with views over Lake Garda; v clean, modern san facs; easily got twin axle into lge pitch (reserved); beautiful site; extra for lakeside pitches; gd cent for touring area - Verona, Mantua, Sigurta, Torri." ♦ ltd. 23 Mar-30 Sep. € 31.00 2016*

MANERBA DEL GARDA *1D2* (3km S Rural) *45.52555, 10.54333* **Camping Fontanelle, Via del Magone 13, 25080 Moniga-del-Garda (BS) [0365 502079; fax 503324; info@campingfontanelle.it; www.campingfontanelle.it]** Exit A4 m'way dir Desenzano del Garda & foll sp Salo. In 10km arr at Moniga del Garda take 2nd exit off 1st rndabt twd Salo, then 1st R into Via Roma sp Moniga Centro. Immed after 'Api' g'ge on L turn R into into Via Caccinelli; at end of this narr rd turn R into Via del Magone; site on L by lake. Access poss diff lge o'fits due narr vill rds. Lge, mkd pitch, sl, terr, pt shd; wc; chem disp; mv service pnt; fam bthrm; shwrs inc; EHU (6A) inc; gas; lndry (inc dryer); shop; supmkt; rest, snacks; bar; BBQ (gas/charcoal only); playgrnd; pool; paddling pool; lake sw & shgl beach; watersports; boat trips; fishing; tennis; golf 5km; horseriding 8km; bike hire 2km; wifi; entmnt; games/TV rm; 20% statics; dogs €7; no o'fits over 6.5m high ssn; phone; poss cr nr lake; Eng spkn; adv bkg; ccard acc; red LS/snr citizens; extra for lakeside pitches; CKE/CCI. "Vg site; excursions to Venice, Florence, Verona; friendly, helpful staff; excel san facs; levellers needed all pitches; pitches poss tight lge o'fits due trees; mkt Mon; lovely site." ♦ 18 Apr-26 Sep. € 45.00 SBS - Y01 2017*

⊞ **MANFREDONIA** *2G4* (10.5km SSW Coastal) *41.55477, 15.88794* **Camping Lido Salpi, SS159 delle Saline Km 6,200, 71043 Manfredonia [tel/fax 0884 571160; lidosalpi@alice.it; www.lidosalpi.it]** Head S on A14, exit at Foggia dir Manfredonia/SS89. Take ramp to Manfredonia Sud and cont strt. Turn R onto SS159, site on the R. Sm, mkd pitch, pt shd; wc; chem disp; mv service pnt; shwrs €0.50; EHU (6A) €2; lndry (inc dryer); shop; rest; café; bar; BBQ; beach; wifi; 10% statics; dogs; ltd bus 0.5km; twin axles; Eng spkn; red LS. "V well located for San Giovanni Rotondo & Gargano; gd o'night stop fr A14; some pitches awkward for lge o'fits due to trees & site furniture; gd site." ♦ ltd. € 31.00 (CChq acc) 2014*

MARCIALLA CERTALDO see Poggibonsi *1D3*

MARINA DI BIBBONA see Cecina *1D3*

MARINA DI CAULONIA *3B4* (1km NE Coastal) *38.35480, 16.48375* **Camping Calypso, Contrada Precariti, 89040 Marina-di-Caulonia (RC) [tel/fax 0964 82028; info@villaggiocalypso.com; www.villaggiocalypso.com]** On o'skts of Marina-di-Caulonia on S106. Med, mkd pitch, shd; wc (mainly cont); mv service pnt; chem disp; fam bthrm; shwrs €0.50; EHU (2A) €3.50; lndry; shop; rest, snacks; bar; playgrnd; sand beach adj; games area; tennis 500m; games area; entmnt; TV rm; wifi; 5% statics; dogs €2.50; phone; sep car park high ssn; Eng spkn; ccard acc; CKE/CCI. "Superb sandy beach; gd (if dated) facs; close to early Byzantine church at Stilo & medieval hill vill of Gerace." 1 Apr-30 Sep. € 28.50 2013*

MARINA DI EBOLI see Paestum *3A3*

MARINA DI GROSSETO see Grosseto *1D3*

MARINA DI MINTURNO *2F4* (6km SE Coastal) *41.20731, 13.79138* **Camping Villlagio Baia Domizia, Via Pietre Bianche, 81030 Baia-Domizia (CE) [0823 930164; fax 930375; info@baiadomizia.it; www.baiadomizia.it]** Exit A1 at Cassino onto S630, twd Minturno on S7 & S7quater, turn off at km 2, then foll sp Baia Domizia, site in 1.5km N of Baia-Domizia. V lge, hdg pitch, shd; wc (some cont); chem disp; mv service pnt; fam bthrm; shwrs inc; EHU (10A) inc (poss rev pol); gas; lndry; shop; rest, snacks; bar; 2 pools; sand beach adj; boat hire; windsurfing; tennis; games area; bike hire; entmnt; TV; no dogs; poss cr; quiet; ccard acc; red LS. "Excel facs; 30/7-16/8 min 7 night stay; site clsd 1400-1600 but adequate parking area; top class site with all facs; gd security." ♦ 19 Apr-23 Sep. € 56.00 SBS - Y10 2017*

MARINA DI MONTENERO *2F4* (1km NW Coastal) *42.06500, 14.77700* **Centro Vacanze Molise, SS Adriatica, Km 525, 86036 Montenero di Bisaccia [tel/fax 0873 803570 or 3385 408323 (mob); info@campingmolise.it; www.campingmolise.it]** Exit A14 at Vasto Sud to SS16 dir S. On R Centro Commerciale Costa Verde, site opp on L. Med, mkd pitch, pt shd; wc (some cont); chem disp; mv service pnt; shwrs inc; EHU (3A) inc; gas; lndry; shop opp; rest, snacks; bar; private sand beach adj; tennis; games area; dogs €1; phone; bus; poss cr; Eng spkn; adv bkg; poss noisy high ssn; CKE/CCI. "Excel site; helpful staff; vg beach; Aqualand Water Park nr; Tremiti Isands rec; gd touring base; conv for m'way A14." ♦ 1 Jun-8 Sep. € 33.00 2015*

MARTINSICURO *2F3* (1km S Coastal/Urban) *42.88027, 13.92055* **Camping Riva Nuova, Via dei Pioppi 6, 64014 Martinsicuro (TE) [0861 797515; fax 797516; info@rivanuova.it; www.rivanuova.it]** Fr N exit A14/E55 sp San Benedetto-del-Tronto onto S16 dir Pescara to Martinsicuro, site sp. Lge, shd; wc (some cont); chem disp; mv service pnt; fam bthrm; shwrs inc; EHU inc; lndry; shop; rest, snacks; bar; playgrnd; pool; paddling pool; sand beach adj; watersports; games area; gym; bike hire; entmnt; TV rm; excursions; adv bkg; ccard acc. "San facs were exceptionally gd & spotless; quiet." ♦ 14 May-18 Sep. € 43.00 2016*

MASSA LUBRENSE see Sorrento *3A3*

⊞ **MATERA** *3A4* (2km S Rural) *40.65305, 16.60694* **Azienda Agrituristica Masseria del Pantaleone, Contrada Chiancalata 27, 75100 Matera (MT) [0835 335239; fax 240021; info@agriturismopantaleone matera.it; www.agriturismopantaleonematera.it]** Do not use sat nav. Fr S on SS7 take Matera Sud exit, site 2km on L, not well sp. Opp Ospedale Madonna delle Grazie. Sm, all hdstg, terr, pt shd; wc; chem disp; mv service pnt; shwrs €1; EHU (16A) inc; rest; bar; BBQ; dogs; Eng spkn; quiet; CKE/CCI. "Conv Matera - World Heritage site; helpful owners provide transport to/fr Matera cent." € 12.00 2013*

MENAGGIO *1C1* (500m N Rural) *46.02516, 9.23996* **Camping Europa, Loc Leray, Via dei Cipressi 12, 22017 Menaggio (CO) [344 31187; europamenaggio@ hotmail.it]** On ent Menaggio fr S (Como) on S240 turn R & foll 'Campeggio' sp along lakeside prom. On ent fr N turn L at 'Campeggio' sp, pass site ent & turn in boatyard. Sm, mkd pitch, terr, pt shd; wc; shwrs €70 for 5 mins; EHU; shop; rest 300m; snacks; bar; lake sw; boat hire; bike hire; 80% statics; dogs; poss v cr; Eng spkn; adv bkg; rd noise; CKE/CCI. "V sm pitches cramped high ssn; narr site rds diff for lge o'fits; old-fashioned facs but clean; poor security; helpful owner; m'vans rec to arr full of water & empty of waste; hardly any rd noise, Menaggio delightful place; v friendly." 25 Mar-30 Sep. € 26.50 2016*

MENAGGIO *1C1* (6km S Urban) *45.96937, 9.19298* **Camping La'vedo, Via degli Artigiani 1, 22016 Lenno (CO) [0344 56288; www.campinglavedo.it]** Fr Como foll S340 along W shore of lake, site SE of Lenno 200m fr lake, adj to supmkt. Sm, pt sl, pt shd; wc (cont); chem disp; mv service pnt; shwrs €0.50; EHU (3A) inc; lndry; shop adj; rest opp; bar; BBQ; games area; entmnt; 25% statics; dogs; rd noise; CKE/CCI. "Picturesque, friendly site in sm town; basic facs; 15 mins to boat stn for other towns on lake; great care needed on S340 - v narr & busy rd." ♦ 1 Apr-30 Sep. € 20.00 2013*

MERANO/MERAN *1D1* (5km E Rural) *46.67144, 11.20091* **Camping Hermitage, Via Val di Nova 29, 39012 Meran [0473 232191; fax 256407; info@ einsiedler.com; www.einsiedler.com]** Exit SS38 at Meran Süd & foll sp twds Merano to Meran 2000 past Trautmannsdorf. Site sp. Med, mkd pitch, hdstg, terr, pt shd; wc; chem disp; mv service pnt; fam bthrm; sauna; shwrs; EHU (10-16A); lndry (inc dryer); rest; café; snacks; bar; BBQ; pool; bike hire; wifi; dogs €3; phone; public transport 100m; twin axles; adv bkg; quiet, some daytime traff noise. "Tennis; all serviced pitches; mountain views; hotel facs avail to campers; forest walk; ACSI site; excel." 8 Apr-5 Nov. € 41.00 2017*

⊞ **MERANO/MERAN** *1D1* (1km S Urban) *46.66361, 11.15638* **Camping Merano, Via Piave/Piavestrasse 44, 39012 Merano/Meran (BZ) [0473 231249; fax 235524; info@meran.eu]** Exit S38 at Merano Sud & foll rd into town. Brown site sps to Camping & Tennis (no name at main juncs in town cent). Site ent mkd 'Camping Tennis'. Site also sp fr N. Med, hdstg, pt shd; wc; chem disp; mv service pnt; shwrs inc; EHU (6A) €2.40; shop opp; supmkt 500m; rest, snacks, bar adj; htd pool; tennis adj; dogs €3.30; phone; poss cr; some rd noise; red long stay days; CKE/CCI. "Sh walk to town cent; fine site surrounded by spectacular mountain scenery; helpful staff; pitches soft after rain; gd clean san facs; helpful staff; 10% surcharge for 1 night; excel thermal baths." € 36.00 2015*

MERANO/MERAN *1D1* (15km S Rural) *46.59861, 11.14527* **Camping Völlan, Zehentweg 6, 39011 Völlan/Foiana [0473 568056; fax 557249; info@ camping-voellan.com; www.camping-voellan.com]** Leave S38 dual c'way (Merano-Bolzano) S of Merano sp Lana. Drive thro Lana, turn uphill sp Gampenpass. Turn R sp Foliana/Völlan & foll sp to site. Sm, mkd pitch, terr, pt shd; wc; chem disp; mv service pnt; some serviced pitches; shwrs €0.50; EHU (4A) €2.50; lndry (inc dryer); shop; rest 800m; playgrnd; pool; golf 6km; 10% statics; dogs €3; phone; Eng spkn; quiet; CKE/CCI. "Long drag up to site fr Lana, but worth it; beautiful situation o'looking Adige Valley; excel facs & pool; barriers clsd 1300-1500 & 2200-0700; v helpful owners; some pitches with steep acc & tight for lge units." 19 Mar-7 Nov. € 34.00 2014*

"We must tell The Club about that great site we found"

Get your site reports in by mid-August and we'll do our best to get your updates into the next edition.

MESTRE *2E2* (3km E Urban) *45.48098, 12.27516* **Venezia Camping Village, Via Orlanda 8/C, 30170 Mestre/Venezia (VE) [041 5312828; fax 5327618; info@veneziavillage.it; www.veneziavillage.it]** On A4 fr Milan/Padova take exit SS11 dir Venice. Exit SS11 for SS14 dir Trieste & airport. 200m after Agip g'ge on R watch for sp and take 1st exit R fr rdbt bet two major dealerships. Keep in R lane all way to site. Med, mkd pitch, pt shd; wc; chem disp; mv service pnt; shwrs inc; EHU (6A) inc (poss rev pol); gas; lndry (inc dryer); shop high ssn; rest, snacks; bar; playgrnd; pool 3km; sand beach 6km; rv sw 2km; wifi; TV; 20% statics; dogs €2; phone; buses to Venice; poss cr & noisy high ssn; Eng spkn; adv bkg; red long stay/CKE/CCI. "V conv Venice - tickets/maps fr recep; clean, well-run site; popular with m'vans; friendly, helpful owners; pitches poss cramped when site full; mosquitoes; new recep, bar/rest, shop, wellness area & toilet block (2011); excel." 22 Feb-9 Nov & 26 Dec-31 Dec. € 44.70 2014*

MESTRE *2E2* (4km E Urban) *45.48425, 12.28227* **Camping Rialto, 16 Via Orlanda, Loc Campalto, 30175 Mestre (VE) [tel/fax 041 5420295; rialto@camping.it; www.campingrialto.com]** Fr A4 take Marco Polo Airport exit, then fork R onto SS14 dir Venice. Site on L 1km past Campalto opp lge car sales area, well sp. Do not enter Mestre. Med, pt shd; wc (mainly cont); chem disp; mv service pnt; shwrs inc; EHU (15A) €1.50; lndry; shop; dogs €3; phone; wifi; bus to Venice; poss cr; Eng spkn; adv bkg; some rd noise; red CKE/CCI. "Site in need of refurb but v conv Venice; bus tickets fr recep; friendly, helpful staff; vg san facs, vg rest; rec." 20 Feb-6 Mar & 1 Apr-20 Oct. € 39.60 2014*

"I need an on-site restaurant"

We do our best to make sure site information is correct, but it is always best to check any must-have facilities are still available or will be open during your visit.

⊞ **MESTRE** *2E2* (5.5km SW Urban) *45.47138, 12.21166* **Camping Jolly delle Querce, Via G De Marchi 7, 30175 Marghera (VE) [tel/fax 041 920312; campingjolly@ecvacanze.it; www.ecvacanze.it]** App fr Milan, exit A4/E70 immed after toll, sp Mestre/Ferrovia/Marghera, then onto SS309 at rndabt sp Chioggia, then 1st R, site sp on R. Med, hdg/mkd pitch, hdstg, unshd; wc; chem disp; mv service pnt; shwrs; EHU (4-16A) inc (rev pol); gas; lndry (inc dryer); shop; rest; snacks; bar; BBQ; pool; entmnt; wifi; 50% statics; dogs; twin axles; poss cr; Eng spkn; adv bkg; v noisy fr adj airport & m'way. "Bus to Venice 15 min walk; excel modern facs block; beach volleyball court; hydromassage tub; gd." ♦ € 38.00 2016*

⊞ **MILANO** *1C2* (8km W Urban) *45.47390, 9.08233* **Camping Citta di Milano, Via Gaetano Airaghi 61, 20153 Milano [0248 207017; fax 202999; info@campingmilano.it; www.campingmilano.it]** Fr E35/E62/A50 Tangentiale Ovest ring rd take Settimo-Milanese exit & foll sp San Siro along Via Novara (SS11). Turn R in 2km at Shell petrol stn, then R at traff lts in 500m & L to site in 600m. Site ent at Gardaland Waterpark, poorly sp. Lge, hdstg, mkd pitch, pt shd; wc; chem disp; mv service pnt; shwrs inc; EHU (6A) inc; lndry; shop 500m; rest, snacks; bar; waterspark adj; dogs €3.50; phone; bus 500m; poss cr; Eng spkn; no adv bkg; rd, aircraft noise, disco at w/end & waterpark adj; ccard acc; red LS/CKE/CCI. "Gd san facs; noise fr adj concerts high ssn; conv bus/metro Milan; penned animals for kid to enjoy; gd security; peacocks roaming site." ♦ € 44.00 2013*

MISURINA see Cortina d'Ampezzo *2E1*

MOLINA DI LEDRO see Pieve di Ledro *1D1*

MONIGA DEL GARDA see Manerba del Garda *1D2*

⊞ **MONOPOLI** *2H4* (5km S Coastal) *40.91333, 17.34387* **Camping Atlantide, Contrada Lamandia 13E, 70043 Capitolo Monopoli (BA) [080 801212; fax 4120238; demattia@residenceatlantide.it; www.residenceatlantide.it]** On SS379 (Bari-Brindisi coast rd), 3km S of Monopoli, fr SS16 (Adriatica) take exit Capitolo. Lge, mkd hdstg pitch, pt sl, terr, pt shd; wc; chem disp; mv service pnt; serviced pitches; shwrs; EHU (6A) inc (poss rev pol); lndry; shop 2km; rest; bar; pool; tennis; games area; rocky waterfront adj; golf 5km; entmnt; 40% statics; dogs €4 on leash (not acc Aug); bus adj; adv bkg; Eng spkn; poss noisy; ccard acc; red LS/CKE/CCI. "Friendly owner; gd, clean site; basic facs LS; hot water to shwrs only; gd size pitches; disco every Sat high ssn until v late; Conv Roman ruins & UNESCO site; excel seafood rest 1km; site & area highly rec; conv Bari ferries; gd rest." € 41.00 2013*

MONTEFORTINO *2E3* (0.8km W Rural) *42.94495, 13.34017* **Camping Sibilla, Via Tenna, 63858 Montefortino FM [3387695040; info@campingsibilla.it; www.campingsibilla.it]** A14 exit Civitanova Marche. M'way Macerata take Sarnano exit and on to Amondola. Foll sp for Montefortino. In about 5km, fork R after IP g'ge. Site 200m on L. Med, mkd pitches, hdstg, terr, pt shd; wc; chem disp; mv service pnt; fam bthrm; shwrs; EHU (6A) inc; lndry (inc dryer); BBQ; pool 2km, beach 45km; wifi; TV; dogs; bus 0.8km; twin axles; Eng spkn; adv bkg; red LS; CKE/CCI. "New site opened June 2016; great mountain views; family owned; excel site." ♦ 1 May-10 Nov. € 25.00 2016*

"Satellite navigation makes touring much easier"

Remember most sat navs don't know if you're towing or in a larger vehicle – always use yours alongside maps and site directions.

⊞ **MONTOPOLI IN VAL D'ARNO** *1D3* (1km N Rural) *43.67611, 10.75333* **Kawan Toscana Village, Via Fornoli 9, 56020 Montópoli (PI) [0571 449032; fax 449449; info@toscanavillage.com; www.toscanavillage.com]** Bet Pisa & Florence; exit Fi-Pi-Li dual c'way at Montópoli, foll site sps. Turn L bef Montópoli vill - site well sp. Med, mkd pitch, terr, pt shd; htd wc (some cont); chem disp; mv service pnt; some serviced pitches; fam bthrm; shwrs inc; EHU (10A) €2.50; gas; lndry (inc dryer); shop; supmkt 4km; rest, snacks; bar; BBQ; playgrnd; pool high ssn; bike hire; golf 7km; wifi; TV rm; 15% statics; dogs; phone; train 3km; poss cr; Eng spkn; adv bkg req; some rd noise; ccard acc; red long stay; CKE/CCI. "Helpful staff; gravel site rds, steep in places; some v sm pitches; spotless facs; gd food in rest; gd pool; well organised; excel for Florence, Pisa & Tuscany; walking dist to Montopoli; beautiful surroundings; reasonably priced rest." ♦ € 43.50 (CChq acc) 2013*

MONZA *1C2* (4km N Urban) *45.62305, 9.28027* **Camping Autodromo, Autodromo Nazionale Monza 20900 [tel/fax 039 339 2665523; segreteria@campeggiomonza.it; www.monzanet.it/eng/campeggi.aspx]** Fr E exit A4 at Agrate-Brianza; fr W A4 exit Sesto San Giovanni onto S36. Foll sp to Autodromo/Biassono, then to site in Parco Reale complex. NB: Do not go to Monza Centro or exit main rd to Autodromo as no access to site; site clearly sp by g'ge. Lge, shd; wc (cont); own san rec; mv service pnt; shwrs €0.50; EHU (5A) €6; lndry (inc dryer); shop; rest adj; snacks; bar; playgrnd; pool adj; games area; 10% statics; dogs; phone; bus to Milan nr; poss cr; Eng spkn; no adv bkg; quiet except during racing. "Day ticket for all transport; bus 200m fr gate to Sesto FC (rlwy stn, bus terminal & metro line 1) - fr there take metro to Duomo; poor facs; NH/sh stay only for racing." ♦ 31 Aug - 9 Sep. € 60.00 2013*

MORGEX see Courmayeur *1A1*

MUGGIA see Trieste *2F1*

NATURNO/NATURNS *1D1* (500m S Rural) *46.6475, 11.00722* **Camping Adler, Via Lido 14, 39025 Naturno (BZ) [0473 667242; fax 668346; info@campingadler.com; www.campingadler.com]** Fr E on SS38 turn L at rndabt into Naturno, L at traff lts & foll sp to site. Fr W after passing thro tunnel bypass, turn R at rndabt then as above. Med, mkd pitches, pt shd; htd wc; chem disp; mv service pnt; fam bthrm; shwrs inc; EHU (4-6A) €3.90; lndry (inc dryer); shop, rest 200m; snacks; htd pool 300m; wifi; TV; 10% statics; dogs €2.50; bus/train 500m; twin axles; poss cr; Eng spkn; adv bkg; quiet; ccard acc; CKE/CCI. "Well-kept site; conv town cent; gd hill walks; friendly staff; off clsd 1230-1500; cable car nrby; excel." ♦ 15 Mar-15 Nov. € 33.00 2015*

⊞ **NICOTERA** *3B4* (3km S Coastal) *38.50755, 15.92666* **Camping Villaggio Mimosa, Mortelletto, 89844 Nicotera Marina (VV) [tel/fax 0963 81397; info@villaggiomimosa.com]** Exit A3/E45 at Rosarno exit. Cross S18 & site sp dir San Ferdinando Porto. Foll sp on SP50 for approx 7km. Sm, mkd pitch, pt shd (reed matting); wc; chem disp; mv service pnt; hot shwrs; EHU (12A); lndry; gas; shop; rest, snacks; bar; BBQ; playgrnd; pool; paddling pool; sand beach adj; boat hire; windsurfing; tennis; games area; bike hire; entmnt; wifi; 40% statics; dogs; twin axles; Eng spkn; CKE/CCI. "Some pitches have tight corners for lge o'fits; gd site." ♦ ltd. € 54.00 2014*

OLIVETO LARIO see Lecco *1C1*

OLMO, L' see Perugia *2E3*

ORBETELLO *1D4* (5.5km N Coastal) *42.46341, 11.18597* **Camping Village Obertello, Strada Gianella 166, 58015 Orbetello [0564 820 201; fax 821 198; info@orbetellocampingvillage.com; www.orbetellocampingvillage.it]** Fr SS1 Aurelia take exit Albinia. Cont twds Porto Santo Stefano. Campsite on L after 5km. V lge, mkd pitch, hdstg, pt shd; wc; chem disp; mv service pnt; fam bthrm; shwrs; EHU (6A); lndry (inc dryer); shop; rest; snacks; bar; BBQ; cooking facs; playgrnd; htd pool; paddling pool; beach adj; games area; bike hire; entmnt; wifi; TV; quiet; Eng spkn; adv bkg; CCI. ♦ 19 Apr-27 Sep. € 62.00 2014*

ORBETELLO *1D4* (7km N Coastal) *42.49611, 11.19416* **Argentario Camping Village, Torre Saline, 58010 Albinia (GR) [0564 870302; fax 871380; info@argentariocampingvillage.com; www.argentariocampingvillage.com]** Turn W off Via Aurelia at 150km mark, sp Porto S. Stefano, site on R, clearly sp in 500m. Ignore sps Zona Camping. Lge, mkd pitch; shd; wc; mv service pnt; shwrs inc; EHU (6A) inc; lndry; rest, snacks; bar; shop; playgrnd; pool & paddling pool; sand/shgl beach; boat hire; games area; 90% statics; no dogs; phone; sep car park; poss cr; adv bkg; quiet. "Better suited for campervans and tent; san facs due for upgrade; excel rest; easy access to beach." ♦ 1 Apr-30 Sep. € 42.00 2012*

ORIAGO see Venezia *2E2*

ORTA SAN GIULIO *1B1* (2km N Rural) *45.81212, 8.41076* **Camping Verde Lago, Corso Roma 76, 28028 Pettenasco (NO) [0323 89257; fax 888654; campingverdelago@campingverdelago.it; www.campingverdelago.it]** Site bet SS229 & lake at km 46, 500m S of Pettenasco on Orta Lake. Gd access. Sm, pt sl, pt shd; wc (some cont); chem disp; shwrs inc; EHU (6A) €2.50; lndry rm; shop, rest, snacks; bar; BBQ; playgrnd; lake sw & sand beach adj; games rm; TV; 60% statics; no dogs; poss cr at w/end; Eng spkn; quiet, some rlwy noise; ccard acc. "Vg family-run site; friendly, helpful; clean facs but dated; dir access private beach & boat mooring; recep 0930-1200 & 1630-1900; excel rest; beautiful setting by lake; if visiting Orta by car take lots of €1 coins for parking; excel." 25 Mar-16 Oct. € 38.00 2016*

ORTA SAN GIULIO *1B1* (500m N Rural) *45.80125, 8.42093* **Camping Orta, Via Domodossola 28, Loc Bagnera, 28016 Orta San Giulio (NO) [tel/fax 0322 90267; info@campingorta.it; www.campingorta.it]** Fr Omegna take rd on SS229 for 10km to km 44.5 sp Novara. Site both sides of rd 500m bef rndabt at Orta x-rds. Recep on L if heading S; poor access immed off rd. Med, pt sl, pt terr, pt shd; htd wc (some cont); chem disp; shwrs €0.20; EHU (3-6A) €2.50; gas; lndry (inc dryer); shop; rest 500m; bar; playgrnd; lake sw adj; waterskiing; wifi; dogs €4; Eng spkn; adv bkg; rd noise; ccard not acc; red LS. "Popular site in beautiful location; sm pitches; narr site rds & tight corners; arr early for lakeside pitch (extra charge); slipway to lake; friendly, helpful owner; Orta a gem; noise fr Beach Club at night; €4.50 for lakeside pitches." ♦ 1 Mar-31 Dec. € 45.50 2013*

⊞ **ORVIETO** *2E3* (500m S Urban) *42.72379, 12.13162* **Aree di Sosta Parcheggio Funicolare, Via della Direttissima, 05018 Orvieto (TR) [0763 300161 or 338 6843153 or 328 0644317; renzo.battistelli@hotmail.com; www.orvietoonline.com]** At Orvieto foll sp rlwy stn & funicular parking. Site on L just beyond funicular parking & behind rlwy stn. Foll sp 'Parcheggio Camper'. Sm, mkd pitch, hdstg, unshd; htd wc; chem disp; shwrs inc; EHU (10A) inc; lndry (inc dryer); shops 500m; rest, snacks, bar 200m; dogs; phone; bus, train 200m; rlwy noise; CKE/CCI. "M'vans only but c'vans poss acc LS; conv A1; gd san facs." ♦ € 15.00 2013*

OSTRA *2E3* (200m SW Rural) *43.61032, 13.15351* **Camping 'L Prè, Viale Matteotti 45, 60010 Ostra (AN) [tel/fax 071 68045; info@lpre.it; www.lpre.it]** Exit A14 at Senigallia onto S360. After approx 10km turn R to Ostra. Sp in vill. Sm, terr, pt shd; wc (some cont); chem disp; shwrs inc; EHU (3A) €2.50; shop 300m; rest 100m; sand beach 10km; games rm; dogs; red long stay. "Gd san facs; very friendly owners; lovely, quiet, simple site with easy access Ancona, Esini Valley; beautiful views over valley; gd for cyclists; gd place to relax after Venice." 1 Apr-30 Sep. € 24.50 2014*

PACENGO see Peschiera del Garda *1D2*

PADENGHE SUL GARDA see Desenzano del Garda *1D2*

PAESTUM *3A3* (4km N Coastal) *40.42780, 14.98244* **Camping Villaggio Ulisse, Via Ponte di Ferro, 84063 Paestum (SA) [tel/fax 0828 851095; info@campingulisse.com; www.campingulisse.com]** Foll site sp in cent Paestum, well sp. Lge, unmkd pitch, shd; wc (some cont); chem disp; shwrs inc; EHU (3A) inc; lndry; shop; rest, snacks; bar; playgrnd; sand beach adj; games area; 80% statics; dogs; poss cr; quiet; CKE/CCI. "Direct access to beach; gd, clean, friendly site; cash only." ♦ 1 Apr-30 Sep. € 36.00 2017*

PAESTUM *3A3* (5km WNW Coastal) *40.42896, 14.98214* **Campsite Athena, Via Ponte di Ferro, 84063 Paestum [0828 851105; fax 724809; vathena@tiscali.it; www.campingathena.com]** Site 50km S of Salerno. Foll a'strada to Battipaglia onto main rd to Paestum. Head S on SS18. At rndabt take 1st exit onto SP276, then at next rndabt take 1st exit onto Via della Repubblica. Go thro 1 rndabt, turn L onto SP175, at rndabt take 1st exit onto Via Marittima, L onto Via Poseidonia and 1st L onto Via Ponte di Ferro. Site on R. Med, pt shd; wc; chem disp; mv service pnt; shwrs; EHU (5A); lndry; shop; rest; snacks; takeaway; bar; wifi; dogs; train 2.5km; twin axles; Eng spkn; red LS; CKE/CCI. "Gd site, direct access to beach." ♦ ltd. 1 Apr-30 Oct. € 51.00 2014*

⊞ **PAESTUM** *3A3* (5km NW Coastal) *40.41330, 14.99140* **Camping Villaggio Dei Pini, Via Torre, 84063 Paestum (SA) [0828 811030; fax 811025; info@campingvillaggiodeipini.com; www.campingvillaggiodeipini.com]** Site 50km S of Salerno in vill of Torre-de-Paestum. Foll a'strada to Battipaglia onto main rd to Paestum, site sp bef Paestum on rd S18, foll to beach. Med, hdg/mkd pitch, shd; wc (mainly cont); chem disp; mv service pnt; shwrs inc; EHU (6A) inc; lndry; shop; rest, snacks; bar; BBQ; playgrnd; private sand beach adj; games area; internet; entmnt; 30% statics; no dogs Jul/Aug; phone; adv bkg; quiet LS; red LS; ccard acc; CKE/CCI. "Historical ruins nr; narr access rd fr vill due parked cars; lge o'fits may grnd at ent; some sm pitches - c'vans manhandled onto pitches; pleasant site by beach; gd rest; helpful owner; rec." ♦ ltd. € 51.00 (4 persons) 2014*

⊞ **PALMI** *3B4* (7km N Coastal) *38.39317, 15.86280* **Sosta Camper Prajola, Lungomare Costa Viola, 4, 89015 Palmi RC [03662 529692; sostacamper.praiola@gmail.com]** Sp fr camp site San Fantino (Palmi), on beach front, down the hill in 2km. Sm, hdstg, pt shd; wc; chem disp; mv service pnt; shwrs €0.50; EHU (6A); BBQ; beach opp; wifi; dogs; twin axles. "Gd basic NH to & fr Sicily; fair." 2016*

PALMI *3B4* (9.5km N Coastal) *38.40676, 15.86912* **Villaggio Camping La Quiete, Contrada Scinà, 89015 Palmi (RC) [0966 479400; fax 479649; info@villaggiolaquiete.it; www.villaggiolaquiete.it]** N fr Lido-di-Palmi on Contrada Pietrenere coast rd dir Gioia Tauro, site sp. Lge, all hdstg, pt shd; wc; chem disp; shwrs inc; EHU (10A) €3; gas; lndry service; rest, snacks; bar; sand beach 200m; 5% statics; dogs; phone; Eng spkn; adv bkg; ccard acc; red LS/long stay; CKE/CCI. "Sm pitches; fair sh stay/NH." ♦ ltd. 1 May-31 Oct. € 30.00 2016*

PASSIGNANO SUL TRASIMENO *2E3* (1km E Rural) *43.18338, 12.15085* **Camping Kursaal, Viale Europa 24, 06065 Passignano-sul-Trasimeno (PG) [075 828085; fax 827182; info@campingkursaal.it; www.campingkursaal.it]** Fr Perugia on S75 to Lake Trasimeno. Exit at Passignano-Est twd lake; site on L past level x-ing adj hotel, well sp. Med, hdg/mkd pitch, pt sl, pt shd; wc; chem disp; mv service pnt; fam bthrm; shwrs inc; EHU (6A) €2 (poss rev pol); lndry (inc dryer); shop; rest, snacks; bar; playgrnd; pool; private shgl lake beach; bike hire; wifi; TV; dogs €1.50; phone; poss v cr; Eng spkn; adv bkg ess; some rlwy noise; red LS; ccard acc; red CKE/CCI. "Pleasant site in gd position; vg rest; some pitches have lake view; ltd space & pitches tight; gd clean site." ♦ 10 Apr-31 Oct. € 43.00 2014*

PASSIGNANO SUL TRASIMENO *2E3* (800m E Rural) *43.18397, 12.15089* **Camping La Spiaggia, Via Europe 22, 06065 Passignano-sul-Trasimeno (PG) [tel/fax 075 827246; info@campinglaspiaggia.it; www.campinglaspiaggia.it]** Exit A1 at Bettolle-Valdichiana & foll sp Perugia for 30km. Exit at Passignano Est & foll sp to site. Sm, mkd pitch, shd; htd wc (some cont); chem disp; mv service pnt; fam bthrm; shwrs inc; EHU (6A/10A) inc; lndry; shop 800m; rest, snacks; bar; BBQ; playgrnd; pool; lake & sand beach adj; slip for boats; beach for dogs; nursery; table tennis; games area; bike hire; wifi; sat TV; dogs €2; phone; bus/train 800m; poss cr; Eng spkn; adv bkg; quiet; ccard acc; red long stay/LS. "Lovely lakeside site; friendly owner; lge pitches; excel san facs but hot water variable; gd rest; interesting lakeside town; 800m fr the historic cent of Passignano; excel touring base for hill towns." ♦ 27 Mar-13 Oct. € 29.00 2013*

PEGLI see Genova *1C2*

"There aren't many sites open at this time of year"

If you're travelling outside peak season remember to call ahead to check site opening dates – even if the entry says 'open all year'.

PERTICARA *2E3* (2km N Rural) *43.89608, 12.24302* **Camping Perticara, Via Serra Masini 10/d, 47863 Perticara (PS) [0335 7062260; info@campingperticara.com; www.campingperticara.com]** Fr A14 at Rimini take S258 to Novafeltria. Foll sp Perticara & site. Steep, hairpins on pt of rte. Med, hdg/mkd pitch, hdstg, terr, unshd; htd wc; chem disp; mv service pnt; fam bthrm; serviced pitches; shwrs inc; EHU (10A) inc; gas; lndry; shop & 2km; snacks; bar; playgrnd; pool; paddling pool; wifi; entmnt; TV rm; 5% statics; dogs; phone; bus; poss cr; Eng spkn; adv bkg; quiet; ccard acc; red LS; CKE/CCI. "Clean, well-maintained, scenic site; hospitable Dutch owners; many activities arranged; immac san facs; poss diff egress to SW (hairpins with passing places) - staff help with 4x4 if necessary; rough terrain; excel; well run." 13 May-20 Sep. € 38.00 2016*

⊞ **PESCASSEROLI** *2F4* (500m S Rural) *41.79888, 13.79222* **Camping Sant' Andrea, Via San Donato, 67032 Pescasseroli (AQ) [tel/fax 0863 912725 or 335 5956029 (mob); info@campingsantandrea.com; www.campingsantandrea.com]** Site sp on R bet Pescasseroli & Opi. If gate clsd ent thro side gate & turn key to open main gate. Sm, mkd pitch, pt shd; htd wc (some cont); chem disp; mv service pnt; shwrs inc; EHU (10A) inc; shop, rest, snacks, bar in town; playgrnd; statics in sep area; dogs; phone; CKE/CCI. "Beautiful, open pitches in lovely area; clean facs but ltd high ssn." € 15.00 2013*

PESCHIERA DEL GARDA *1D2* (1km N Urban) *45.44780, 10.70195* **Camping del Garda, Via Marzan 6, 37019 Castelnuovo-del-Garda (VR) [045 7551682; fax 6402023; info@camping-delgarda.com; www.campingdelgarda.it]** Exit A4/E70 dir Peschiera onto SR249 dir Lazise. Turn L in 500m dir Lido Campanello, site in 1km on L on lakeside. V lge, shd; wc (some cont); chem disp; mv service pnt; shwrs inc; EHU (4A) inc; gas; lndry; shop; rest, snacks; bar; playgrnd; 3 pools; shgl beach; lake sw; tennis; games area; entmnt; 60% statics; no dogs; phone; adv bkg; quiet. "Busy, well-organised site; helpful staff, discount snr citizens; gd rest; walking & cycling rtes adj; conv Verona." ♦ 1 Apr-5 Nov. € 60.00 2017*

PESCHIERA DEL GARDA *1D2* (1km N Rural) *45.46722, 10.71638* **Eurocamping Pacengo, Via del Porto 13, 37010 Pacengo (VR) [tel/fax 045 7590012; info@eurocampingpacengo.it; www.eurocampingpacengo.it]** On SS249 fr Peschiera foll sp to Gardaland, Pacengo in 1km. Turn L at traff lts in cent of vill, site on L. Lge, mkd pitch, sl, pt shd; wc (some cont); chem disp (wc); mv service pnt; shwrs €0.30; EHU (4A) inc; lndry; shop & 500m; rest, snacks; bar; playgrnd; pool adj; lake sw, boat-launching adj; entmnt; 25% statics; dogs €2.40; phone; poss cr; Eng spkn; adv bkg; quiet; CKE/CCI. "Well-equipped site on shore Lake Garda; helpful staff; some sm pitches; espec gd end of ssn; excel rest; conv Verona." ♦ 10 Apr-22 Sep. € 41.60 2014*

PESCHIERA DEL GARDA *1D2* (2.5km N Rural) *45.45480, 10.70200* **Camping Gasparina, Loc Cavalcaselle, 37014 Castelnuovo-del-Garda (VR) [045 7550775; fax 7552815; info@gasparina.com; www.gasparina.com]** On SS249 dir Lazise, turn L at site sp. Lge, mkd pitch, sl, pt shd; wc; chem disp; mv service pnt; shwrs inc; EHU (3A) inc; gas; lndry; shop; rest, snacks; bar; playgrnd; pool; lake adj; games area; entmnt; some statics; dogs; poss cr; adv bkg; poss noisy; ccard acc; "Popular, busy site; variable pitch sizes; lake views some pitches; long lead req." 1 Apr-30 Sep. € 35.00 2013*

PESCHIERA DEL GARDA *1D2* (6km NE Rural) *45.46472, 10.71416* **Camping Le Palme, Via del Tronchetto 2, 37017 Pacengo (VR) [045 7590019; fax 7590554; info@lepalmecamping.it; www.lepalmecamping.it]** A4/E70 exit at Peschiera onto SS249, sp Lazise. Site sp bef Pacengo in approx 5km. Lge, mkd pitch, terr, pt shd; wc; chem disp; serviced pitches; fam bthrm; shwrs inc; EHU (6A) inc; lndry (inc dryer); shop; rest 300m; snacks; bar; playgrnd; htd pool; paddling pool; waterslide; lake sw & shgl beach adj; wifi; 40% statics; dogs €4.60; Eng spkn; adv bkg; ccard acc; red LS. "Well-maintained site; excel, clean facs; extra for lakeside pitches; helpful staff; sh walk to vill; 4 theme parks nr; excel." ♦ 27 Mar-26 Oct. € 37.00 2015*

ITALY

PESCHIERA DEL GARDA *1D2* (1km W Urban) *45.44222, 10.67805* **Camping Bella Italia, Via Bella Italia 2, 37019 Peschiera del Garda (VR) [045 6400688; fax 6401410; info@camping-bellaitalia.it; www.camping-bellaitalia.it]** Fr Brescia or Verona on SP11 to Peschiera del Garda, site sp on lakeside. Fr Brescia or Verona on A4/E70 exit at Peschiera on to SP11 in dir of Brescia, site on R in about 2km. V lge, slight sl, shd; wc; chem disp; mv service pnt; fam bthrm; shwrs inc; EHU (16A); gas; lndry (inc dryer); shop; 2 rests; snacks; bar; BBQ; playgrnd; pool; paddling pool; waterslides; lake sw adj; windsurfing; tennis; games area; bike hire; archery; wifi; entmnt; many static tents; no dogs; bus to Verona; poss cr; Eng spkn; adv bkg rec; poss noisy high ssn; red LS; CKE/CCI. "Busy, popular site, nr theme park, Aqua World, Verona; suits all ages; v clean; rests gd & gd price; gd recep for satellite & wifi." ♦ 16 Mar-26 Oct. € 56.50 (CChq acc) 2013*

PESCHIERA DEL GARDA *1D2* (6km W Coastal) *45.45120, 10.66557* **Camping Wien, Loc. Fornaci, 37019 Peschiera (VR) [045 7550379; fax 7553366; info@campingwien.it]** On Verona-Brescia rd (not a'strada) W of Peschiera, turn R at San Benedetto, turn R 400m after traff lts, site has 2 ents 100m apart. Med, mkd pitch, hdstg, pt sl, shd; wc; chem disp; mv service pnt; shwrs inc; EHU inc (3A); gas; lndry; ice; shop; rest; snacks; bar; playgrnd; pool; shgl beach adj; games area; entmnt; boating; fishing; 50% statics; dogs; phone; bus adj; Eng spkn; adv bkg; poss cr; quiet; ccard not acc; red long stay; CKE/CCI. "Wonderful pool o'looking Lake Garda; walking/cycle path into town; vg site; busy hg ssn." ♦ 9 Apr-30 Sep. € 40.00 2017*

"That's changed – Should I let The Club know?"

If you find something on site that's different from the site entry, fill in a report and let us know. See camc.com/europereport.

PESCHIERA DEL GARDA *1D2* (700m W Rural) *45.44555, 10.69472* **Camping Butterfly, Lungo Lago Garibaldi 11, 37019 Peschiera (VR) [045 6401466; fax 7552184; info@campingbutterfly.it; www.campingbutterfly.it]** Fr A4/E70 exit twd Peschiera for 2km. At x-rds with bdge on L, strt over & foll rv to last site after RH bend at bottom. Lge, shd; wc (some cont); shwrs; EHU inc; gas; lndry; shop; rest, snacks; bar; playgrnd; pool; paddling pool; lake sw; entmnt; 75% statics; dogs €5; poss cr; adv bkg; quiet except w/end; ccard acc. "Busy holiday site; conv town & lake steamers; sm pitches; clean san facs; adv bkg rec." ♦ 9 Mar-10 Nov. € 50.00 (4 persons) (CChq acc) 2013*

PESCHIERA DEL GARDA *1D2* (2km NW Urban) *45.44825, 10.66978* **Camping San Benedetto, Strada Bergamini 14, 37019 San Benedetto (VR) [045 7550544; fax 7551512; info@campingsanbenedetto.it; www.campingsanbenedetto.it]** Exit A4/E70 dir Peschiera-del-Garda, turn N at traff lts in cent of vill, site on lake at km 274/V111 on rd S11. Lge, pt sl, shd; wc; mv service pnt; shwrs inc; EHU (3A) inc; lndry; shop; rest, snacks; bar; playgrnd; pool; paddling pool; lakeside shgl beach nr; boat hire; windsurfing; canoeing; bike hire; games area; entmnt; 30% statics; dogs €1.50-2; poss cr; adv bkg; quiet; red snr citizens. "Pleasant, well-run; sm harbour; site clsd 1300-1500; excel modern rest beside lake; excel new san facs (2017)." 1 Apr-8 Oct. € 44.60 2017*

"I like to fill in the reports as I travel from site to site"

You'll find report forms at the back of this guide, or you can fill them in online at camc.com/europereport.

PETTENASCO see Orta San Giulio *1B1*

PEVERAGNO see Cuneo *1B2*

⊞ **PIENZA** *1D3* (7km E Rural) *43.08089, 11.71159* **Camping Il Casale, 64 53026 Pienza (SI) [tel/fax 0578 755109, 333 4250705 (mob); info@podereilcasale.it; www.podereilcasale.com]** Fr Pienza dir Montepulciano on S146, turn R in 4km onto sm, gritted track sp Monticchiello. Site in 3km on L sp Podereilcasale. Sm, pt shd; pt sl; wc; shwrs inc; EHU (16A) inc; lndry; shop; rest; bar; playgrnd; lake adj; wifi; dogs; phone; poss cr; Eng spkn; adv bkg; quiet; ccard acc. "8 pitches only for c'vans/mvans; simple farm site; panoramic views; rec phone to check availability; v friendly owners, site fees inc breakfast." ♦ € 26.00 2013*

⊞ **PIEVE TESINO** *1D1* (6km N Rural) *46.11361, 11.61944* **Villaggio Camping Valmalene, Loc Valmalene, 38050 Pieve-Tesino (TN) [0461 594214; fax 592654; info@valmalene.com; www.valmalene.com]** Fr Trento E for 50km on S47. Turn N at Strigno to Pieve-Tesino, site sp. Med, mkd pitch, pt shd; htd wc; mv service pnt; sauna; private bthrms avail; fam bthrm; shwrs; EHU inc; lndry; shop; supmkt 6km; rest, snacks; bar; playgrnd; htd pool; padding pool; tennis; bike hire; games area; fitness rm; internet; some statics; dogs €5; site clsd Nov; adv bkg rec; quiet; ccard acc. "Gd base for summer & winter hols." ♦ € 32.00 2016*

PISA *1C3* (1km N Urban) *43.72416, 10.3830* **Camp Torre Pendente, Viale delle Cascine 86, 56122 Pisa [050 561704; fax 561734; info@campingtorrependente.com; www.campingtorrependente.com]** Exit A12/E80 Pisa Nord onto Via Aurelia (SS1). After 8km & after x-ing rlwy bdge, turn L after passing Pisa sp at traff lts. Site on L, sp. Lge, mkd pitch, pt shd; wc; mv service pnt; chem disp; fam bthrm; shwrs inc; EHU (5A) inc (poss rev pol); gas; lndry (inc dryer); shop; supmkt 400m; rest; pizzeria; snacks; bar; BBQ; playgrnd; pool; sand beach 10km; bike hire; wifi; TV rm; dogs €1.60; phone; poss cr; Eng spkn; no adv bkg; ccard acc over €100; red long stay; CKE/CCI. "Gd base Pisa; leaning tower 15 mins walk; immac, modern, well-maintained san facs; private san facs avail; pitches typically 50sqm; poss tight lge o'fits due narr site rds & corners; many pitches shd by netting; site rds muddy after rain; friendly staff; excel, well-run site; 300m fr Pisa San Rossore rlwy stn, trains to Lucca etc." ♦ 1 Apr-2 Nov. € 37.00 2015*

⊞ **PISA** *1C3* (500m N Urban) **Camper Parking, Via Pietrasantina, 56100 Pisa** On Via Aurelia SS1 fork R app Pisa, then turn E approx 1km N of Arno Rv, sp camping. After 1km turn L into Via Pietrasantina. Site on R behind lge Tamoil petrol stn, sp coach parking. Max height under rlwy bdge 3.30m. C'vans acc. Lge, hdstg, unshd; own san ess; mv service pnt; no EHU; shop; rest, snacks, bar 100m; dogs; bus adj; quiet. "Excel NH; parking within walking dist of leaning tower; water & waste inc; plenty of space; san facs open at café opp during day." ♦ € 12.00 2012*

PISTOIA *1D3* (10km S Rural) *43.84174, 10.91049* **Camping Barco Reale, Via Nardini 11, 51030 San Baronto-Lamporecchio (PT) [0573 88332; fax 856003; info@barcoreale.com; www.barcoreale.com]** Leave A11 at Pistoia junc onto P9 & foll sp to Vinci, Empoli & Lamporecchio to San Baronto. In vill turn into rd by Monti Hotel & Rest, site sp. Last 3km steep climb. Lge, mkd pitch, pt sl, terr, shd; wc; chem disp; mv service pnt; 30% serviced pitch; fam bthrm; shwrs inc; EHU (3-6A) inc (poss rev pol); gas; lndry; shop; rest, snacks; bar; playgrnd; pool; games area; bike hire; internet; wifi; entmnt; dogs; phone; Eng spkn; adv bkg ess; quiet; red long stay/LS; ccard acc; red long stay; CKE/CCI. "Excel site in Tuscan hills; helpful staff; gd touring base; excel mother & fam bthrm; vg rest; poss diff access some pitches but towing help provided on request; unsuitable lge o'fits; well-organised walking & bus trips; excel pool." ♦ 1 Apr-30 Sep. € 57.40 2014*

POGGIBONSI *1D3* (12km N Rural) *43.58198, 11.13801* **Camping Panorama Del Chianti, Via Marcialla 349, 50020 Marcialla-Certaldo (FI) [tel/fax 0571 669334; info@campingchianti.it; www.campingchianti.it]** Fr Florence-Siena a'strada exit sp Tavarnelle. On reaching Tavernelle turn R sp Tutti Direzione/Certaldo & foll by-pass to far end of town. Turn R sp to Marcialla, in Marcialla turn R to Fiano, site in 1km. NB Some steep hairpins app site fr E. Med, mkd pitch, hdstg, terr, pt shd; wc (some cont); chem disp; mv service pnt; shwrs inc; EHU (3A) inc; shop, rest, snacks, bar 800m; sm pool; bike hire; dogs €2; phone; adv bkg; Eng spkn; quiet; red long stay; ccard not acc; CKE/CCI. "Gd tourist info (in Eng); sports facs in area; cultural sites; helpful staff; friendly owner; san facs clean - hot water to shwrs only; 4 excel rests nr; panaromic views; midway bet Siena & Florence; popular site - arr early to get pitch; facs need updating." 21 Mar-31 Oct. € 36.00 (CChq acc) 2014*

⊞ **POMPEI** *3A3* (1km S Urban) *40.74638, 14.48388* **Camping Spartacus, Loc Pompei Scavi, Via Plinio 127, 80045 Pompei (NA) [tel/fax 081 8624078; staff@campingspartacus.it; www.campingspartacus.it]** Fr N on A3 exit Pompei Ovest. At T-junc turn L & site on R just after passing under rlwy bdge. Fr S exit Pompei Est & foll sp Pompei Scavi (ruins). Sat nav may lead to low bdge. Sm, mkd pitch, shd; wc; chem disp; mv service pnt; shwrs inc; EHU (5A) €2.3.(poss rev pol); gas; lndry; supmkt 400m; rest, snacks, bar in high ssn; internet; TV rm; poss v cr; Eng spkn; adv bkg; some rd/rlwy noise; ccard acc; red LS/ CKE/CCI. "Nice, family-run, welcoming site, 50m fr historical ruins; conv train to Naples, boats to Capri; stray dogs poss roam site & ruins; v popular with students high ssn; best of 3 town sites; gd site for exploring area; friendly owners; clean san facs; poss cr high ssn; steep access rd. " ♦ € 34.00 2015*

PORLEZZA *1C1* (4km E Rural) *46.04074, 9.16827* **Camping Ranocchio, Via Al Lago 7,22010 Loc Piano di Porlezza, Carlazzo (CO) [tel/fax 0344 70385 or 61505; info@campingranocchio.com; www.campingranocchio.com]** On main rd bet Menaggio & Porlezza. Ent in vill of Piano on S side. Sp. Steep app in Lugano with hairpin bends; 15% gradient. V narr rd fr Lugano - clsd to c'vans at peak times. Lge, terr, shd, pt sl; wc; chem disp; mv service pnt; fam bthrm; shwrs €0.50; EHU inc; gas; lndry (inc dryer); shop adj; rest 50m; snacks; bar; playgrnd; pool; paddling pool; lake sw & fishing; horseriding 2km; wifi; TV rm; dogs €2; Eng spkn; quiet; CKE/CCI. "Friendly recep; gd for exploring Como & Lugano; steamer trips on both lakes; lovely, v attractive site; helpful recep; excel corner shop & rest." ♦ 1 Apr-30 Sep. € 25.00 2016*

PORTESE see San Felice Del Benaco *1D2*

PORTO RECANATI *2F3* (4km N Coastal) *43.47123, 13.64150* **Camping Bellamare, Lungomare Scarfiotti 13, 62017 Porto-Recanati (MC) [071 976628; fax 977586; info@bellamare.it; www.bellamare.it]** Exit A14/E55 Loreto/Porto-Recanati; foll sp Numana & Sirolo; camp on R in 4km on coast rd. Lge, unshd; wc; chem disp; shwrs; EHU (6A) €3; gas; lndry; shop; rest, snacks; bar; playgrnd; pool; paddling pool; sand & shgl beach (shelves steeply); bike hire; games area; games rm; entmnt; internet; some statics; no dogs; phone; Eng spkn; ccard acc; red LS; CKE/CCI. "V well-run site; NH tariff of €17-28 (inc elec) for a pitch at the edge of the site but OK; beach access." ♦ 23 Apr-30 Sep. € 46.00 2017*

⊞ **PORTO RECANATI** *2F3* (7.7km NW Urban) *43.44155, 13.61446* **Area Attrezzata Camper Loreto, Via Maccari, 60025 Loreto [07 19 77 748; info@prolocoloreto.com]** Fr A14 S of Ancona, exit at Loreto. Fr town ctr foll sp to campsite. Med, mkd pitch, hdstg, unshd; wc; mv service pnt; shwrs inc; EHU inc; dogs; quiet. "M'van NH; conv for Basilica, beach & Ancona ferries; clean & well run; occasional c'vans allowed if not busy; vg site." € 12.00 2014*

PORTO SANTA MARGHERITA see Caorle *2E2*

PORTOFERRAIO *1C3* (9km E Rural) *42.80072, 10.36452* **Rosselba Le Palme, Loc. Ottone 3, 57037 Elba Portoferraio [0565 933 101; fax 933 041; info@rosselbalepalme.it; www.rosselbalepalme.it]** Fr ferry terminal foll signs 'tutti direzioni'. At 3rd rndabt head twds Porto Azzurro. Take L fork to Bagnaia. Site sp. Sm, hdg pitch, terr, pt shd; wc; chem disp; mv service pnt; shwrs inc; EHU (6A); lndry rm; shop; rest; snacks; bar; playgrnd; pool; sand beach 0.5km; entmnt; wifi; 80% statics; bus adj; twin axles; Eng spkn; adv bkg; quiet; CCI. "Ferry service fr Piombino every 1/2 hr; statics enhance site facs." 20 Apr-6 Oct. € 49.00 2014*

POZZA DI FASSA *1D1* (500m SW Rural) *46.42638, 11.68527* **Camping Rosengarten, Via Avisio 15, 38036 Pozza-di-Fassa (TN) [0462 763305; fax 762247; info@catinacciorosengarten.com; www.catinacciorosengarten.com]** Fr S SS48 site sp just after San Giovanni. Lge, hdstg, pt shd; wc; chem disp; mv service pnt; shwrs inc; EHU (2A) inc (extra for higher amperage); lndry; shop 500m; rest, snacks adj; bar; pool 300m; ski lift 1km; ski bus; wifi; 30% statics; dogs €4; site clsd Oct; poss cr; Eng spkn; adv bkg ess; quiet; 10% red 14+ days; ccard acc; CKE/CCI. "Superb scenery; helpful staff; luxury san facs; free taxi (2010) to Vigo di Fassa cable car; excel site; v convly sited for access to vill & public transport; 20 min walk to Buffaure cable car; off clsd 1230-1500." 1 Jan-30 Apr, 1 Jun-15 Oct, 1 Dec-31 Dec. € 32.00 2015*

PRATO ALLO STELVIO *1D1* (500m E Rural) *46.61777, 10.59555* **Camping Sägemühle, Dornweg 12, 39026 Prato-allo-Stélvio (BZ) [0473 616078; fax 617120; info@campingsaegumuehle.com; www.campingsaegemuehle.com]** Fr rd S40 turn E at Spondigna onto rd S38 dir Stélvio, site sp in vill. Med, hdg/mkd pitch, hdstg, pt sl, pt shd; htd wc; chem disp; mv service pnt; fam bthrm; sauna; shwrs inc; EHU (16A) inc; lndry (inc dryer); shop 200m; rest; bar; playgrnd; 2 pools (1 htd, covrd); paddling pool; games area; ski lift 10km; skibus; wifi; TV; phone; dogs €4; adv bkg; quiet; 10% red LS; ccard acc; CKE/CCI. "Excel, well-run site; gd, clean facs; helpful staff; gd walking area in National Park; conv for the reschen pass Austria Italy; all pitches fully serviced." 1 Jan-9 Nov & 16 Dec-31 Dec. € 55.00 2014*

"I need an on-site restaurant"

We do our best to make sure site information is correct, but it is always best to check any must-have facilities are still available or will be open during your visit.

PRATO ALLO STELVIO *1D1* (500m NW Rural) *46.62472, 10.59388* **Camping Kiefernhain, Via Pineta 37, 39026 Prato-allo-Stélvio (BZ) [0473 616422; fax 617277; kiefernhain@rolmail.net; www.camping-kiefernhain.it]** Fr rd S40 turn SW at Spondigna onto rd S38 dir Stélvio, site sp in vill. Lge, mkd pitch, pt shd; wc; chem disp; mv service pnt; fam bthrm; private bthrms avail; shwrs inc; EHU (6A) €2.50; lndry; shop; rest 300m; snacks; bar; BBQ; playgrnd; htd pool; waterslide; sports cent adj; dogs €4; phone; dog shwr; wifi; Eng spkn; adv bkg rec high ssn; quiet; red long stay. "V modern, clean san facs; superb views; facs stretched high ssn; vg value." ♦ 1 May-4 Oct. € 52.50 2014*

PRECI *2E3* (3km NW Rural) *42.88808, 13.01483* **Camping Il Collaccio, 06047 Castelvecchio-di-Preci (PG) [0743 665108; fax 939094; info@ilcollaccio.com; www.ilcollaccio.com]** S fr Assisi on S75 & S3, turn off E sp Norcia, Cascia. Then foll sp for Visso on S209. In approx 30km turn R for Preci, then L, site sp. Rte is hilly. Med, mkd pitch, terr, pt shd; htd wc (some cont); chem disp; mv service pnt; fam bthrm; shwrs inc; EHU (6A) inc (long lead poss req); lndry; shop & 2km; rest, snacks; bar; playgrnd; 2 pools; tennis; games area; horseriding; paragliding; bike hire; TV rm; 20% statics; dogs; phone; Eng spkn; adv bkg; quiet; ccard acc; red CKE/CCI. "Beautiful views; well-maintained, clean site; pleasant rest; maganificent pool area; sm pitches; gd walking in Monti Sibillini National Park; conv Assisi & historic hill towns; excel; well run." ♦ 1 Apr-30 Sep. € 35.00 2015*

PREDAZZO *1D1* (2.5km E Rural) *46.31027, 11.63138* **Camping Valle Verde, Loc Ischia 2, Sotto Sassa, 38037 Predazzo (TN) [tel/fax 0462 502394; info@campingvalleverde.it; www.campingvalleverde.it]** Exit A22 dir Ora onto rd S48 dir Cavalese/Predazzo. Fr Predazzo take SS50 W, turn R in 1.5km, site on L in 500m. Med, mkd pitch, pt sl, pt shd; htd wc (some cont); chem disp; mv service pnt; shwrs inc; EHU (6A) €2; lndry (inc dryer); rest, snacks; bar; BBQ; playgrnd; rv sw 1km; games area; wifi; 5% statics; dogs €3.50; mini train adj; bus 0.5km; twin axles; poss cr; Eng spkn; adv bkg; quiet; red low stay/snr citizens; ccard acc. "Excel; bus & cable car rides; walks, cycle tracks & mountain climbs nrby; beautiful site." ♦ 1 May-1 Oct. € 32.00 2015*

PUNTA MARINA TERME see Ravenna *2E2*

PUNTA SABBIONI *2E2* (2km NE Coastal) *45.44560, 12.46100* **Campéole Camping Ca'Savio, Via di Ca'Savio 77 - 30013 Cavallino Treporti Ca'Savio (VE) [041 966017 or 041 966 570 (mob); fax 5300707; info@casavio.it; www.casavio.it or www.campeole.com]** Fr Lido di Jesolo head twd Punta-Sabbioni; at x-rds/rndabt in cent of Ca'Savio turn L twd beach (La Spiaggia) for 800m; turn L into site just bef beach. Or at L turn at rndabt - rd poss clsd at night - cont to Punta-Sabbioni, turn L at sp to beach; L at T-junc, then R at x-rds. V lge, hdg/mkd pitch, shd; wc (some cont); chem disp; mv service pnt; fam bthrm; shwrs; EHU (5A) inc (check pol); gas; lndry (inc dryer); supmkt; rest; pizzeria; snacks; bar; playgrnd; pool; paddling pool; direct access to adj sandy beach; water sports; canoeing/kayaking; fishing; games area; archery; bike hire; wifi; entmnt; games rm; TV; 50% statics; no dogs; no o'fits over 7m high ssn; phone; bus to Venice ferry; ccard acc; red LS; CKE/CCI. "Well laid-out, well-run, busy site - noisy high ssn; helpful staff; conv Venice by ferry fr Punta Sabbioni; excel, clean san facs; facs ltd LS; long, narr pitches; access poss diff lge o'fits; gd supmkt; min 3 nights stay high ssn; barriers clsd 1300-1500." ♦ 26 Apr-27 Sep. € 38.50 (CChq acc) SBS - Y02 2013*

PUNTA SABBIONI *2E2* (700m S Coastal) *45.44141, 12.42127* **Parking Dante Alighieri, Lungomare Dante Alighieri 26, 30010 Punta-Sabbioni (VE)** Take rd Jesolo to Punta-Sabbioni, pass all camps & go to end of peninsula. Turn L at boat piers & foll rd alongside beach; site on L just bef Camping Miramare. Sm, pt shd; wc; chem disp; mv service pnt; shwrs inc; EHU (8A) inc; shop, rest, snacks, bar 500m; bus 500m; dogs; poss cr; Eng spkn; quiet. "M'vans only; friendly, helpful owner; 10 min walk for boats to Venice; vg." € 23.00 2012*

PUNTA SABBIONI *2E2* (1.6km SSW Coastal) *45.44035, 12.4211* **Camping Miramare, Lungomare Dante Alighieri 29, 30013 Punta-Sabbioni (VE) [041 966150; fax 5301150; info@camping-miramare.it; www.camping-miramare.it]** Take rd Jesolo to Punta-Sabbioni, pass all camps & go to end of peninsula. Turn L at boat piers & foll rd alongside beach; site 500m on L. Med, hdg/mkd pitch, pt shd; htd wc; chem disp; mv service pnt; shwrs inc; EHU (6A) inc (rev pol); gas; lndry; shop; rest & pizzeria adj; playgrnd; internet; statics; dogs €4 (only sm dogs allowed); phone; bus to beach 2km & ferry; min 3 nights stay high ssn; Eng spkn; quiet; ccard acc (min €100); red LS/snr citizens. "Excel, well-organised, helpful, friendly family-owned site - 10 mins walk for Venice (tickets fr recep) - can leave bikes at terminal; gd security; new pt of site v pleasant wooded area; clean facs; poss mosquito problem; superior to many other sites in area; min stay 2 nights Jul/Aug; don't miss camping supmkt on way in - an Aladdin's cave; avoid dep on Sat due traff; Magic of Italy site; highly rec, reasonable mob home rentals; excel staff." ♦ 19 Mar- 6 Nov. € 37.00 2015*

⊞ **PUNTA SABBIONI** *2E2* (1km Rural) *44.44278, 12.42260* **Al Batèo, via Lungomare Dante Alighieri 19/A, 30013 Cavallino Treporti Venice [040 5301 455 or 041 5301 564; info@albateo.it; www.albateo.it]** Take rd Jesolo to Punta Sabbioni and go to end of the peninsula. Turn L at boat piers and foll rd along side beach. Site 300 on L. Sm, hdg pitch, shd; htd wc; chem disp; mv service pnt; shwrs inc; lndry; shop; dogs; bus; Eng spkn; adv bkg; quiet. "M'vans only; gd value; Vapporetti to Venice 300m." € 25.00 2014*

QUART see Aosta *1B1*

RAPALLO *1C2* (2.5km W Urban) *44.35691, 9.1992* **Camping Rapallo, Via San Lazzaro 4, 16035 Rapallo (GE) [tel/fax 0185 262018; campingrapallo@libero.it; www.campingrapallo.it]** Exit A12/E80 dir Rapallo, turn immed R on leaving tolls. Site sp in 500m on L at bend (care), over bdge then R. Narr app rd. Site sp. Med, hdg/mkd pitch, pt shd; wc (some cont); chem disp; mv service pnt; shwrs inc; EHU (3A) €2.20; gas; lndry; supmkt 500m; rest 200m; bar; htd pool; shgl beach 2.5km; bike hire; 10% statics; dogs; bus (tickets fr recep); poss cr; Eng spkn; adv bkg; some daytime rd noise; ccard acc; CKE/CCI. "Clean, family-run site; conv Portofino (boat trip) & train to Cinque Terre; beautiful coastlline; shwrs clsd during day but hot shwrs at pool; v busy public hols - adv bkg rec; awkward exit, not suitable for lge o'fits; NH only." 13 Mar-15 Nov. € 32.50 2014*

RASUN DI SOTTO/NIEDERRASEN see Brunico/Bruneck *1D1*

RAVENNA *2E2* (10.6km E Coastal) *44.43335, 12.29680* **Camping Park Adriano, Via dei Campeggi 7, 48122 Punta-Marina-Terme (RN) [0544 437230; fax 438510; info@adrianocampingvillage.com; www.campingadriano.com]** Fr S309 Ravenna-Venezia rd foll sp to Lido Adriano. Site at N end of Lido. Lge, shd; wc; chem disp; mv service pnt; shwrs inc; EHU (5A) inc (poss rev pol/no earth); lndry (inc dryer); shop; rest, snacks; bar; BBQ; playgrnd; pool; paddling pool; beach 300m; bike hire; golf 10km; wifi; entmnt; TV rm; 70% statics; dogs €3; bus to Ravenna; ATM; Eng spkn; adv bkg; poss noisy disco; ccard acc; red snr citizens/CKE/CCI. "Site in pine forest; excel san facs; sh walk to beach." ♦ 20 Apr-18 Sep. € 43.00 (CChq acc) 2015*

RHEMES ST GEORGE *1B1* (Rural) *45.64966, 7.15150* **Camping Val di Rhemes, Loc Voix 1, 11010 Rhêmes-St George (AO) [tel/fax 0165 907648; info@camping valdirhemes.com; www.campingvaldirhemes.com]** Fr S26 or A54/E25 turn S at Introd dir Rhêmes-St George & Rhêmes-Notre-Dame; site on R in 10km past PO; app is diff climb with hairpins. Med, pt sl, pt shd; htd wc (some cont); chem disp; mv service pnt; shwrs; EHU (2-6A) €2; lndry dryer; shop; bar; wifi; Eng spkn; ccard acc; playgrnd; 10% statics; dogs €2.50; adv bkg; quiet; CCI. "Peaceful, family-run site; nr Gran Paradiso National Park; gd walking; excel." ♦ 1 Jun-10 Sep. € 35.60 2014*

RIVA DEL GARDA *1D1* (2.5km E Rural) *45.88111, 10.86194* **Camping Monte Brione, Via Brione 32, 38066 Riva-del-Garda (TN) [0464 520885; fax 520890; info@campingbrione.com; www.campingbrione.com]** Exit A22 Garda Nord onto SS240 to Torbole & Riva; on app to Riva thro open-sided tunnel; immed R after enclosed tunnel opp Marina; site ent 700m on R. Med, mkd pitch, terr, pt shd; wc (some cont); chem disp; mv service pnt; shwrs inc; EHU (6A) inc; gas; lndry; shop; rest 200m; snacks; bar; BBQ; playgrnd; htd pool; shgl beach & lake sw 500m; watersports; bike hire; solarium; wifi; dogs €4; barriers clsd 1300-1500 & 2300-0700; Eng spkn; adv bkg; quiet; ccard acc; CKE/CCI. "Olive groves adj; pleasant site with lge pitches; gd, modern san facs." ♦ 15 Apr-16 Oct. € 31.50 2016*

⊞ **ROCCARASO** *2F4* (2km NE Rural) *41.84194, 14.10277* **Camping Del Sole, Piana del Leone, Via Pietransieri, 67037 Roccaraso (AQ) [0864 62532 or 0864 62571; fax 619329; albergodelsole@libero.it; www.villaggiodelsole.com]** Turn E fr S17 at sp Petransieri & site on R in 2km. Med, pt sl, pt shd; wc; chem disp; shwrs inc; EHU inc (poss no earth - long lead rec); gas; lndry; shop 2km; rest; bar; playgrnd; sw 2km; ski school; 50% statics; dogs (sm only); bus; quiet; ccard acc; CKE/CCI. "Excel & conv National Park; ltd facs LS; unrel opening, suggest phone to confirm." ♦ € 26.00 2013*

⊞ **ROMA** *2E4* (8km N Urban) *41.95618, 12.48240* **Camping Village Flaminio, Via Flaminia Nuova 821, 00189 Roma [06 3332604 or 3331429; fax 3330653; info@villageflaminio.com; www.villageflaminio.com]** Exit GRA ring rd at exit 6 & proceed S along Via Flaminia twd Roma Centrale. In 3km where lanes divide keep to L-hand lane (R-hand land goes into underpass). Cross underpass, then immed back to R-hand lane & slow down. Site on R 150m, sp as Flaminio Bungalow Village. No vehicular access to site fr S or exit to N. Lge, pt sl, pt shd; htd wc; chem disp; mv service pnt; shwrs inc; EHU (3-12A) inc; gas; lndry (inc dryer); shop; supmkt 200m; rest, snacks; bar; playgrnd; pool (sw caps req); bike hire; wifi; TV rm; some statics; phone; bus (cross v busy rd); train nr; site clsd mid-Jan to end Feb; poss cr; no adv bkg; red long stay/LS; ccard acc (min €155). "Well-run site; excel, clean san facs; poss long walk fr far end of site to ent (site transport avail); poss dusty pitches; take care sap fr lime trees; cycle/walking track to city cent nrby; train 10 mins walk (buy tickets on site); local excursions pick-up fr site (tickets fr recep)." ♦ € 57.00 (CChq acc) 2013*

ROMA *2E4* (9km N) *42.00353, 12.45283* **Happy Village & Camping, Via Prato della Corte 1915, 00123 Roma [06 33626401 or 06 33614596; fax 33613800; info@happycamping.net; www.happycamping.net]** Take exit 5 fr Rome ring rd sp Viterbo. Site sp on ring rd, fr N & S on dual c'way Rome/Viterbo at 1st exit N of ring rd. Lge, pt terr, pt shd; wc; chem disp; mv service pnt; shwrs inc; EHU (6A) inc; gas; lndry; shop; rest, snacks; bar; BBQ; playgrnd; pool high ssn; some statics; dogs free; train into Rome; poss cr; adv bkg; poss noisy; ccard acc; red CKE/CCI. "Friendly, busy site in hills; sm pitches; vg rest; mini bus shuttle to train stn; gd site; v nice well kept site; steep access rd." ♦ 1 Mar-6 Jan. € 25.00 2015*

ROMA *2E4* (19km N Urban) *43.00976, 12.50566* **Camping Tiber, Via Tiberina, Km 1.4, 00188 Roma [06 33610733; fax 33612314; info@campingtiber.com; www.campingtiber.com]** Fr Florence, exit at Rome Nord-Fiano on A1 & immed after tolls turn S on Via Tibernia, site sp. Fr any dir on Rome ring rd take exit 6 N'bound on S3 Via Flaminia. Site 1km S of Prima Porta. Lge, pt shd; wc; mv service pnt; shwrs inc; EHU (4-6A) inc (long lead req & poss rev pol); gas; lndry (inc dryer); shop; rest, snacks; bar; pool high ssn; games area; wifi; some statics; dogs; free bus to metro stn; Eng spkn; quiet; ccard acc; red long stay/CKE/CCI. "Ideal for city by metro (20 mins) & bus; helpful staff; recep 0700-2300; modern san facs; some lge pitches; poss ant/mosquito prob; Magic of Europe discount; perfectly comfortable; excel, well-run site; quiet on outer edges, but no wifi; discount fr 'We love camping'." ♦ 1 Apr-31 Oct. € 37.00 2014*

ROMA *2E4* (10km SW Rural) *41.77730, 12.39605* **Camping Fabulous, Via Cristoforo Colombo, Km 18, 00125 Acilia (RM) [06 5259354; fabulous@ecvacanze.it; www.ecvacanze.it]** Exit junc 27 fr Rome ring rd into Via C Colombo. At 18km marker turn R at traff lts, site 200m on R. V lge, mkd pitch, pt sl, shd; htd wc; fam bthrm; shwrs inc; EHU (6-10A) inc; lndry; shop; rest, snacks; bar; BBQ; playgrnd; pool; paddling pool; waterslide; sand beach 12km; tennis; games area; entmnt; quiet at night; 80% statics; dogs €1.50; phone; bus on main rd; Eng spkn; adv bkg; ccard acc; CKE/CCI. "Set in pinewoods; gd sh stay; ltd facs in LS; helpful staff." ♦ ltd. 14 Apr-31 Oct. € 40.00 (CChq acc) 2017*

⊞ **ROMA** *2E4* (4km W Urban) *41.88741, 12.40468* **Roma Camping, Via Aurelia 831, Km 8.2, 00165 Roma [06 6623018; fax 66418147; campingroma@ecvacenze.it]** Site is on Via Aurelia approx 8km fr Rome cent on spur rd on S side of main dual c'way opp lge Panorama Hypmkt. Fr GRA ring rd exit junc 1 Aurelio & head E sp Roma Cent & Citta del Vaticano. In approx 3km take spur rd on R 50m bef covrd pedestrian footbdge x-ing dual c'way & 250m bef flyover, sp camping; site gates on R (S) in 100m. W fr Rome take spur rd 8km fr cent sp camping just after Holiday Inn & just bef Panorama Hypmkt. At top turn L (S) over flyover & immed R sp camping; site gates on L in 200m. V lge, hdstg, terr, pt shd; wc (some cont); fam bthrm; shwrs inc; EHU (4-6A) inc; lndry; supmkt opp; rest, snacks; bar; playgrnd; pool high ssn; games area; wifi; 75% statics; dogs €1.50; bus to city; poss cr; Eng spkn; rd noise; ccard acc; red LS/CKE/CCI. "Gd, clean site; excel san facs & pool; friendly staff; popular site - rec arr early; rec not leave site on foot after dark; rest open all year; conv walk to hypermkt." ♦ € 55.00 2013*

ROME see Roma *2E4*

ROSETO DEGLI ABRUZZI *2F3* (3km S Coastal) *42.65748, 14.03568* **Eurcamping Roseto, Lungomare Trieste Sud 90, 64026 Roseto-degli-Abruzzi (TE) [085 8993179; fax 8930552; info@eurcamping.it; www.eurcamping.it]** Fr A14 exit dir Roseto-degli-Abruzzi to SS16. At rndabt turn R, next L & under rlwy bdge to promenade. Turn R at sea front, site at end of promenade. Med, shd, hdg/mkd pitch; wc; chem disp; mv service pnt; shwrs inc; EHU (3A) inc; lndry (inc dryer); shop; rest, snacks; bar; playgrnd; pool; paddling pool; private sand & shgl beach adj; tennis; bike hire; games area; wifi; entmnt; 20% statics; dogs €5; poss cr; Eng spkn; adv bkg; quiet but some rlwy noise; red LS; CKE/CCI. "Phone to check if open LS; gates close 2300; pitches poss flood after heavy rainfall; Roseto excel resort." ♦ 1 May-24 Oct. € 43.50 2015*

⊞ **SALBERTRAND** *1A2* (1km SW Rural) *45.06200, 6.86821* **Camping Gran Bosco, SS24, Km 75, Monginevro, 10050 Salbertrand (TO) [0122 854653; fax 854693; info@campinggranbosco.it; www.campinggranbosco.it]** Leave A32/E70 (Torino-Fréjus Tunnel) at Oulx Ouest junc & foll SS24/SS335 sp Salbertrand. Site sp 1.5km twd Salbertrand at km 75. Fr S (Briançon in France) on N94/SS24 to Oulx cent, foll SS24 thro town & foll sp Salbertrand, then as above. Lge, pt shd; htd wc (mainly cont); chem disp; mv service pnt; shwrs; EHU (3-6A) inc; gas; lndry; shop; rest 1km; snacks; bar; playgrnd; tennis; games area; entmnt; 80% statics (sep area); some rd & rlwy noise; ccard acc. "Beautiful setting; excel NH bef/after Fréjus Tunnel or pass to/fr Briançon; gates open 0830-2300; excel, modern, clean san facs; sm pitches; grnd soft in wet - no hdstg; conv for m'way; popular with m'cyclists but quiet at night." € 29.00 2016*

SALSOMAGGIORE TERME *1C2* (3km E Rural) *44.80635, 10.00931* **Camping Arizona, Via Tabiano 42, 43039 Tabiano-Salsomaggiore Terme (PR) [0524 565648; fax 567589; info@camping-arizona.it; www.camping-arizona.it]** Exit A1 for Fidenza & foll sps for Salsomaggiore fr Co-op supmkt, to Tabiano; sp on S side of rd. Not rec to attempt to find site fr S9 fr Piacenza. Lge, pt sl, shd; wc (some cont); chem disp (wc); mv service pnt; shwrs inc; EHU (3A) inc (rev pol); lndry (inc dryer); shop; rest, snacks; bar; playgrnd; 4 pools high ssn; 2 waterslides; jacuzzi; fishing; tennis; games rm; games area; bike hire; golf 7km; wifi; entmnt; 30% statics; dogs €3; phone; sep car park; bus to Salsomaggiore; phone; quiet; red LS; ccard not acc. "Vg site; friendly, helpful staff; interesting, smart spa town; excel touring base; gd for families; san facs vg; best campsite shop; vg rest." ♦ 1 Apr-7 Oct. € 47.00 2014*

"Satellite navigation makes touring much easier"

Remember most sat navs don't know if you're towing or in a larger vehicle – always use yours alongside maps and site directions.

SALTO DI FONDI see Terracina *2E4*

SAN BARONTO LAMPORECCHIO see Pistoia *1D3*

SAN CANDIDO/INNICHEN see Dobbiaco/Toblach *2E1*

ITALY

SAN FELICE DEL BENACO *1D2* (1km E Rural) *45.58500, 10.56583* **Camping Fornella, Via Fornella 1, 25010 San Felice-del-Benaco (BS) [0365 62294; fax 559418; fornella@fornella.it; www.fornella.it]** N fr Desenzano on S572 twd Salo. Turn R to San Felice-del-Benaco, over x-rds & take 2nd R turn at sp to site. R into app rd, L into site. Rd narr but accessible. Avoid vill cent, site sp (with several others) fr vill by-pass just bef g'ge. Lge, pt sl, terr, pt shd; htd wc (some cont); chem disp; mv service pnt; fam bthrm; shwrs inc; EHU (6A) inc; gas; lndry (inc dryer); shop; rest, snacks; bar; BBQ (charcoal); playgrnds; pool; paddling pool; sw & shgl beach on lake; fishing; boat hire & windsurfing; bike hire; tennis; games area; entmnt; games rm; wifi; entmnt; TV (in bar); 20% statics; dogs €7; no o'fits over 7m high ssn; sep car park; recep 0800-1200 & 1400-2000; poss v cr; Eng spkn; adv bkg; quiet; ccard acc; extra for lge pitches & lakeside pitches; red LS & snr citizens LS; CKE/CCI. "Family-run site in vg location by Lake Garda; park outside until checked in; excel pool; excursions to Venice, Florence & Verona opera; excel rest; gd san facs." ♦ 1 May-20 Sep. € 49.50 SBS - Y11 2014*

SAN LORENZO DI SEBATO see Brunico/Bruneck *1D1*

⊞ **SAN MARINO** *2E3* (7km N Rural) *43.95990, 12.46090* **Centro Vacanze San Marino, Strada San Michele 50, 47893 Cailungo, Repubblica di San Marino [0549 903964; fax 907120; info@centrovacanzesanmarino.com; www.centrovacanzesanmarino.com]** Exit A14 at Rimini Sud, foll rd S72 to San Marino. Pass under 2 curved footbdges, then 800m after 2nd & 13km after leaving a'strada, fork R. Cont uphill for 1.5km then turn R at Brico building, site sp. Steep long-haul climb. Lge, hdg pitch, hdstg, terr, pt shd; htd wc; chem disp; mv service pnt; serviced pitch; shwrs inc; EHU (6A) inc (poss rev pol); lndry; sm shop, rest high ssn; snacks; bar; BBQ; cooking facs; playgrnd; htd pool; paddling pool; tennis; games area; bike hire; solarium; mini-zoo; wifi; sat TV; some statics; dogs €5; bus; poss v cr; Eng spkn; adv bkg; quiet; red 7+ days; ccard acc; CKE/CCI. "V busy at w/end - rec arr early; superb hill fort town; excel rest & pool; sm pitches; conv Rimini 24km; excel, clean site; bus calls at site ent for San Marino." ♦ € 37.00 SBS - Y04 2016*

SAN MENAIO see Rodi Garganico *2G4*

SAN MICHELE ALL'ADIGE *1D1* (3km SW Rural) *46.16789, 11.11452* **Camping Moser, Via Nazionale 64, 38015 Nave San Felice (TN) [0461 870248]** 12km N of Trento on SS12. Sm, mkd pitch, shd; wc; chem disp; shwrs; EHU inc; shop in vill; rest; bar; dogs; bus 500m; poss cr; Eng spkn; adv bkg; rd & rlwy noise; ccard acc. "Gd, friendly NH; site run by Hotel Moser (well sp on S12); scruffy & run down but busy; new san facs block almost completed (2014)." 1 May-31 Oct. € 18.00 2015*

SAN PIERO A SIEVE see Borgo San Lorenzo *1D3*

⊞ **SAN REMO** *1B3* (2.5km W Coastal) *43.80244, 7.74506* **Camping Villaggio Dei Fiori, Via Tiro a Volo 3, 18038 San Remo (IM) [0184 660635; fax 662377; info@villaggiodeifiori.it; www.villaggiodeifiori.it]** Fr A10/E80 take Arma-di-Taggia exit & foll sp San Remo Centro. At SS1 coast rd turn R sp Ventimiglia. At 2.5km look for red/yellow Billa supmkt sp on R; 50m past sp take L fork, site on L in 50m. Fr W on A10 take 1st exit dir San Remo - winding rd. Turn R & site on L after Stands supmkt. Fr Ventimiglia on SS1, 150m past San Remo boundary sp turn sharp R (poss diff lge o'fits) to site. Lge, some hdg/mkd pitch, all hdstg, pt terr, pt shd; htd wc (some cont); chem disp; mv service pnt; fam bthrm; shwrs inc; EHU (3-6A) €4-7; lndry (inc dryer); supmkt 200m; rest, snacks; bar; BBQ; playgrnd; htd pool; shgl beach adj; tennis; games area; bike hire; wifi; entmnt; 60% statics; no dogs; train to Monaco & bus San Remo nr; poss cr; Eng spkn; adv bkg rec high ssn; rd & fairgrnd noise; red long stay/LS; ccard acc; CKE/CCI "Gd location; well-kept, tidy, paved site; vg, clean facs; beach not suitable for sw; some pitches superb sea views (extra charge), some sm; lge o'fits not acc high ssn as sm pitches; vg rest; conv Monaco; gates locked at night." ♦ ltd. € 67.00 (4 persons) 2013*

SAN ROCCO CASTAGNARETTA see Cuneo *1B2*

⊞ **SAN VALENTINO ALLA MUTA** *1D1* (700m N Rural) *46.7700, 10.5325* **Camping Thöni, Landstrasse 83, 39020 St Valentin-an-der-Haide, Graun [0473 634020; thoeni.h@rolmail.net; www.camping-thoeni.it]** N twd Austrian border site on L on edge of vill on S edge of Lago di Resia. Sm, pt sl, unshd; htd wc; chem disp; shwrs inc; EHU (6A) €1.50; shop, rest, snacks, bar 300m; pool 7km; wifi; dogs; site clsd Nov; quiet. "Conv sh stay/NH en rte Austria; cycle rte around lake; scenic area; off open 0900-1000 & 1700-1800; numbered pitches; views; walking rte rnd Haidensee below vill; cable car opens late June." € 25.50 2017*

SANT' ANTONIO DI MAVIGNOLA see Pinzolo *1D1*

SANT' ARCANGELO SUL TRASIMENO see Magione *2E3*

SANTA MARIA DI MERINO see Vieste *2G4*

SANTA TERESA GALLURA *1C4* (1km W Urban) *41.21938, 9.18372* **Camping Gallura Village, Loc Li Lucianeddi, 07028 Santa Teresa Gallura [078 975 55 80; fax 974 19 32; info@galluravillage.it]** Fr Santa Teresa Gallura on SP90. Site 1km on L. Med, mkd pitch, unshd; wc; chem disp; shwrs inc; shop 0.5km; snacks; rest; bar; playgrnd; pool; paddling pool; games area; entmnt; wifi; bike hire; 50% statics; dogs; Eng spkn; ccard acc. "Fair site; power point at each plot; gd NH for ferry to Corsica." 1 Mar-30 Oct. € 52.00 2014*

SARDINIA Campsites in towns in Sardinia are listed together at the end of the Italian site entry pages.

⊞ **SARNANO** *2E3* (3km SSW Rural) *43.01743, 13.28358* **Quattro Stagioni, Contrada Brilli, 62028 Sarnano [0733 651147; fax 651104; quattro stagioni@camping.it; www.camping4stagioni.it]** A14 exit Civitanova Marche. M'way to Macerata as far as Sarnano exit. In Sarnano turn R at sq, foll main rd. Site approx 3km outside Sarnano to the W. Sm, mkd pitch, pt sl, pt shd; wc; chem disp; mv service pnt; shwrs; EHU; lndry; shop; rest; café; snacks; bar; BBQ; playgrnd; pool; paddling pool; games area; wifi; 60% statics; dogs; twin axles; Eng spkn; adv bkg; red LS; CKE/CCI. "Fair site." ♦ ltd. € 41.00 2014*

SARRE see Aosta *1B1*

SARTEANO *1D3* (W Rural) *42.9875, 11.86444* **Camping Parco Delle Piscine, Via del Bagno Santo, 53047 Sarteano (SI) [0578 26971; fax 265889; info@ parcodellepiscine.it; www.parcodellepiscine.it]** Exit A1/E35 onto S478 at Chiusi & foll sp to Sarteano. Site at W end of vill, sp. Lge, pt shd; wc (some cont); chem disp; mv service pnt; serviced pitches; shwrs inc; EHU (6A) inc; lndry; shops 100m; rest, snacks; bar; playgrnd; 3 pools; tennis; solarium; wifi; entmnt; 50% statics; no dogs; Eng spkn; quiet; ccard acc. "Clean, well-run; security guard 24 hrs; no vehicles during quiet periods 1400-1600 & 2300-0700; poss long walk to wc/shwrs; Florence 90 mins on m'way, Siena 1 hr; site at 600m, so cool at night; excel." ♦ 14 Apr-30 Sep. € 70.00 SBS - Y17 2017*

SARZANA *1C2* (8km S Rural/Coastal) *44.07638, 9.97027* **Camping River, Loc Armezzone, 19031 Ameglia (SP) [0187 65920; fax 65183; info@ campingriver.com; www.campingriver.com]** Exit A12 at Sarzana & foll sp Ameglia & Bocca di Magra on SP432. In 7km turn L into Via Crociata to site (blue sp). Narr app rd with few passing places. Lge, mkd pitch; pt shd; wc (mainly cont); chem disp; mv service pnt; sauna; shwrs inc; EHU (3-6A) inc; lndry (inc dryer); supmkt 700m; rest, snacks; pizzeria; bar; playgrnd; 2 pools; paddling pool; beach 2km; rv fishing; tennis 200m; games area; boat & bike hire; horseriding 200m; golf driving range; wifi; entmnt; TV rm; 50% statics; dogs €3; bus to beach; poss cr; adv bkg; red LS. "Gd touring base Cinque Terre; pleasant, helpful staff; vg, well-situated site; gd shop & rest; nice location by rv; dated facs; gd pools." ♦ 12 Apr-4 Oct. € 43.00 (CChq acc) 2014*

SAVONA *1B2* (2km SW Coastal) *44.29079, 8.45331* **Camping Vittoria, Via Nizza 111/113, Zinola, 17100 Savona (SV) [019 881439; www.campingvittoria. com]** Exit Savona heading SW, site on L on seashore immed bef Shell petrol stn behind bar Vittoria. Med, unshd; wc (some cont); shwrs; EHU €2; shops adj; rest adj; bar; private sand beach adj; 90% statics; poss v cr; Eng spkn; adv bkg; quiet; CKE/CCI. "Excel location with views; busy site; helpful, friendly owner; pitches adj beach; clean, simple facs; ltd sm touring pitches." 1 Apr-30 Sep. € 35.00 2013*

SAVONA *1B2* (13km SW Coastal) *44.22731, 8.40795* **Camping Rustia, Via La Torre 4, 17028 Spotorno (SV) [019 745042 or 019 741446; info@camping rustia.it; www.campingrustia.it]** Exit A10/E80 for Spotorno, site sp on app rd to m'way. V steep app rd. C'vans returning to m'way use ent at Albissola Marina. Lge, shd; wc; shwrs €1; EHU (3A) €3; shop; bar; rest, snacks 300m; sand beach 600m; 30% statics; dogs; poss cr; no adv bkg; rd & rlwy noise; Eng spkn; ccard acc. "Site diff for lge o'fits due narr paths & many trees - manhandling necessary onto pitches; gd san facs; gates locked at night; busy, well laid out site; helpful staff." ♦ 1 Mar-30 Sep. € 32.00 2015*

SCARLINO see Follonica *1D3*

SENIGALLIA *2E3* (1km S Coastal) *43.70416, 13.23805* **Villaggio Turistico Camping Summerland, Via Podesti 236, 60019 Senigallia (AN) [tel/fax 071 7926816; info@campingsummerland.it; www. campingsummerland.it]** Exit A14/E55 onto SS16 to Senigallia S. Site on R after lge car park at side of rd. Lge, shd; wc (cont); mv service pnt; fam bthrm; shwrs; EHU (5A) €2.50; gas; lndry; shop; rest, snacks; bar; playgrnd; 2 pools & paddling pool; beach 200m; tennis; games area; entmnt; TV rm; some statics; no dogs Jul/ Aug; sep car park; poss cr; adv bkg. ♦ 1 Jun-15 Sep. € 42.00 2012*

SESTO CALENDE *1B1* (1km N Rural) *45.72988, 8.61989* **Camping La Sfinge, Via Angera 1, 21018 Sesto-Calende (VA) [0331 924531; fax 922050; info@campeggiolasfinge.it; www.campeg giolasfinge.it]** Take rd fr Sesto-Calende to Angera. Site 1km on L bef junc for Sant' Anna. Med, mkd pitch, shd; wc (mainly cont); shwrs; EHU; gas; lndry; shop 1km; snacks; bar; playgrnd; pool; boating; games area; 90% statics; dogs €4; poss cr; quiet; ccard acc. "Friendly owners; gd lakeside location; poss mosquitoes; poor facs; lovely pool; excel position for lake Maggiore; within reach of gd shops and rest." ♦ 1 Jan-30 Oct. € 39.00 2014*

SESTO CALENDE *1B1* (4km N Rural) *45.74892, 8.59698* **Camping Okay Lido, Via per Angera 115, Loc Lisanza, 21018 Sesto Calende (VA) [tel/fax 0331 974235; campingokay@camping-okay.com; www. camping-okay.com]** Exit A8 at Sesto Calende onto SP69 N dir Angera, site sp. Med, mkd pitch, terr, pt shd; wc; chem disp; mv service pnt; private san facs avail; fam bthrm; shwrs €0.60; EHU (6A) €3; lndry; supmkt 3km; rest, snacks; bar; playgrnd; htd pool; paddling pool; lake sw; watersports; games area; games rm; wifi; entmnt; TV rm; some statics; dogs €5; Eng spkn; adv bkg; quiet. "Friendly, welcoming site; NH pitches by lakeside; gd NH for Amsterdam ferry." ♦ 21 Mar-11 Oct. € 36.00 2014*

SESTO CALENDE *1B1* (7.5km N Rural) *45.82712, 8.62722* **International Camping Ispra, Via Carducci, 21027 Ispra (VA) [0332 780458; fax 784882; info@internationalcampingispra.it; www.internationalcampingispra.it]** Site 1km NE of Ispra on E side of lake. Med, pt terr, shd; wc (cont); own san; shwrs €0.20; EHU (6A) €3; lndry; shop; rest, snacks; bar; BBQ; playgrnd; pool (sw caps req); beach & lake sw; boating; fishing; games area; TV rm; 90% statics; dogs €6; poss cr; Eng spkn; adv bkg; quiet; red LS; CKE/CCI. "Gd views of lake; muddy beach; vg rest; nice, peaceful site; friendly, helpful staff; lovely situation on banks of Lake Maggiore; well run; loud music fr bar till midnight." 18 Mar-2 Nov. € 32.00 2016*

⊞ **SESTO/SEXTEN** *2E1* (3km SE Rural) *46.66806, 12.39935* **Caravan Park Sexten, St. Josefstr. 54, 39030 Sexten / Moos [0474 710444; fax 710053; info@caravanparksexten.it; www.caravanparksexten.it]** Fr S49 take S52 SE fr San Candido thro Sexten & Moos. After sh, steep climb site on W of S52 midway bet Moos & Kreuzberg pass. Lge, mkd pitch, pt sl, pt shd; wc; chem disp; mv service pnt; serviced pitches; sauna; private bthrms avail; shwrs inc; EHU (16A) metered; gas; lndry; shop; rest; bar; playgrnd; pool; paddling pool; solarium; tennis; wintersports; internet; entmnt; beauty & wellness treatments; TV; dogs €6; poss cr; Eng spkn; adv bkg ess high ssn; quiet; CKE/CCI. "Excel, clean facs; Waldbad worth visit; rock climbing wall; lovely scenery; mountain walks; v popular & busy site; v well managed & equipped; rest worth a visit." ♦ € 57.00 SBS - Y03 2014*

"There aren't many sites open at this time of year"

If you're travelling outside peak season remember to call ahead to check site opening dates – even if the entry says 'open all year'.

⊞ **SETTIMO VITTONE** *1B1* (2.5km N Rural) *45.56474, 7.81668* **Camping Mombarone, Torre Daniele, 10010 Settimo-Vittone (TO) [0125 757907; fax 757396; info@campingmombarone.it; www.campingmombarone.it]** On E side of Ivrea-Aosta rd (SS26), 100m S of Pont-St Martin. Exit A5 at Quincinetto, turn R onto SP69 across bdge, R at end onto SP26 & site on L in 150m. (App fr S, sp at ent but if overshoot go on 100m to rndabt to turn). Tight ent off busy rd. Med, pt sl, pt shd; wc; chem disp; shwrs inc; EHU (6A) €2.50; lndry; shop 400m; rest adj; snacks; bar; sm pool; games area; wifi; 80% statics; poss v cr & noisy high ssn; ccard not acc; red CKE/CCI. "Gd base Aosta valley; superb views; Quincinetto medieval vill walking dist; lovely, grassy, well-kept site; ltd space for tourers; v pleasant, helpful owner who speaks gd Eng, friendly welcome; san facs immac; gd NH; rlwy stn nrby." ♦ € 29.50 2014*

SIBARI *3A4* (4km E Coastal) *39.77944, 16.47889* **Camping Villaggio Pineta di Sibari, 87070 Sibari (CS) [0981 74135; fax 74302; info@pinetadisibari.it; www.pinetadisibari.it]** Exit A3 at Frascineto onto SS106, then exit at Villapiana-Scalo. Site sp on beach. Lge, pt shd; wc; mv service pnt; shwrs inc; EHU (4A) inc; lndry; shop; rest, snacks; bar; playgrnd; sand beach adj; tennis; bike hire; internet; entmnt; TV rm; 20% statics; dogs €5; poss cr; poss noisy; ccard acc. "Vg beach; site in pine forest; noisy bar/music; gd touring base; watch out for low bdge on app." ♦ 17 Apr-22 Sep. € 56.50 2014*

"That's changed – Should I let The Club know?"

If you find something on site that's different from the site entry, fill in a report and let us know. See camc.com/europereport.

SICILY Campsites in towns in Sicily are listed together at the end of the Italian site entry pages.

SIENA *1D3* (7.4km N Urban) *43.33750, 11.33055* **Camping Siena Colleverde, Via Scacciapensieri 47, 53100 Siena [0577 334080; fax 334005; info@sienacamping.com; www.sienacamping.com]** Site sp ('Camping' or symbol) on all app to Siena, foll sp for 'Ospedale' (hospital). Use exit Siena Nord & foll site sp, but take care as some sp misleadingly positioned. Lge, hdg/mkd pitch, hdstg, pt sl, terr, pt shd; htd wc; chem disp; mv service pnt; shwrs inc; EHU (10A) inc; gas; lndry; shop; rest, snacks; bar; playgrnd; pool high ssn; wifi; TV rm; dogs; phone; bus; poss cr; Eng spkn; adv bkg; some rd noise; CKE/CCI. "Attractive location; gd views old town wall fr upper pitches (no shd); excel touring base; upgraded, well-run site - gd, well kept; modern san facs; easy access by bus to town fr site ent; excel; pt of 'We Love Camping' group; some lge unmkd pitches." ♦ 1 Mar-31 Dec. € 37.00 2015*

SIENA *1D3* (21km W Rural) *43.2815, 11.21905* **Camping La Montagnola, Strada della Montagnola 139, 53100 Sovicille (SI) [tel/fax 0577 314473; info@campinglamontagnola.it; www.campinglamontagnola.it]** Fr N on S2 or S on S223 site well sp fr junc with S73. Avoid Siena town cent. Med, mkd pitch, hdstg, terr, pt shd; wc; chem disp; mv service pnt; shwrs inc; EHU (6A) inc; gas; lndry; shop & 5km; rest 800m; snacks; bar; playgrnd; games area; wifi; 7% statics; dogs free; phone; bus to Siena; sep car park; poss cr; adv bkg rec; Eng spkn; quiet; ccard acc (over €50); red CKE/CCI. "Super site; sm pitches; sharp stone chippings on hdstg pitches; v clean facs; vg refuge fr summer heat in wooded hills; facs poss stretched high ssn & rubbish bins o'flowing; gd walks fr site (booklet fr recep); Magic of Italy disc, conv bus service to Siena fr site." 1 Apr-30 Sep. € 29.00 2015*

SILVI MARINA see Pineto *2F3*

SIRMIONE *2G2* (3km E Coastal) *45.45738, 10.64025* **Tiglio, Loc. Punta Grò, 25019 Sirmione [tel/fax 030 990 4009; info@campingtiglio.it]** A4 Milan-Verona, exit Sirmione. 1st exit at rndabt onto SP13. 1st exit at next rndabt. Turn L twds Via San Martino. 1st exit at rndabt onto Via Verona. Foll sp to camp. Lge, mkd pitch, shd; wc; mv service pnt; shwrs inc; EHU inc (4A); rest; snacks; bar; BBQ; playgrnd; 50% statics; bus adj; twin axles; poss cr; Eng spkn; adv bkg; ccard acc; CKE/CCI. "Gd site; noisy & busy but friendly; on bus rte to Verona." 16 Apr-30 Sep. € 39.00 2014*

SIRMIONE *1D2* (3km S Rural) *45.46845, 10.61028* **Camping Sirmione, Via Sirmioncino 9, 25010 Colombare-di-Sirmione (BS) [030 99 04 665; fax 91 90 45; info@camping-sirmione.it; www.camping-sirmione.it]** Exit S11 at traff lts sp Sirmione, in 500m R at site sp. Lge, mkd pitch, pt sl, some hdstg, pt shd; wc (cont); mv service pnt; shwrs; EHU (6A) inc; lndry; shop; rest, snacks; bar; pool; paddling pool; lake sw; private beach; watersports; games area; 30% statics; dogs; poss cr; adv bkg; quiet; ccard acc. "Excel lakeside site; facs poss stretched when site busy; excel rest, bar, pool & san facs; lovely walk to Sirmione; highly rec." ♦ 25 Mar-5 Oct. € 54.00 2014*

SISTIANA see Monfalcone *2E1*

SOLCIO DE LESA see Arona *1B1*

SORICO *1C1* (500m E Rural) *46.17152, 9.39302* **Camping La Riva, Via Poncione 3, 22010 Sorico (CO) [tel/fax 0344 94571; info@campinglariva.com; www.campinglariva.com]** Fr Lecco take SS36 twd Colico & Sondrio. At end of tunnels fork L sp Como & Menaggio. At end of dual c'way turn L onto S340 to Sorico sp Como & Menaggio. Cross bdge & site 500m down lane on L bef cent Sorico, sp Cmp Poncione & La Riva. Easiest app on SS36 on E side of lake (pt dual c'way). Rd on W side narr & congested. Med, mkd pitch, pt shd; wc (some cont); chem disp; mv service pnt; shwrs €0.80; EHU (6A) inc; gas 50m; lndry; sm shop; rest nr; snacks; bar; BBQ; playgrnd; pool; sw & rv/lakeside beach adj; canoeing; waterskiing; fishing; bike & boat hire; games/TV rm; dogs €4 (must be kept on lead); no o'fits over 7.5m high ssn; phone; Eng spkn; quiet; wifi; 50% statics; red LS; CKE/CCI. "Excel, family-run site; gd views of lake & mountains; clean, well-kept & tidy; immac san facs; v warm welcome; less commercialised than some other sites in area; cycle track to vill; poss mosquito problem in Jun; v tidy clean site; friendly helpful owners; rd fr Lugano to Como not adv for c'vans." ♦ 1 Apr-2 Nov. € 54.00 SBS - Y12 2013*

⊞ **SORRENTO** *3A3* (3km N Coastal) *40.63541, 14.41758* **Camping I Pini, Corso Italia 242, 80063 Piano-di-Sorrento (NA) [081 8786891; fax 8788770; info@campingipini.com; www.campingipini.com]** S fr Naples on A3; Exit A3 sp Castellammare di Stabia & take SS145 sp to Sorrento; pass thro vill of Meta; site on R immed over bdge; lge sp on main rd. Med, hdg/mkd pitch, pt sl, pt shd; wc; chem disp; mv service pnt; shwrs inc; EHU (4A) inc; shops 500m; rest, snacks; bar; pool (in winter htd & open fr 0830-1500); beach 1km; 50% statics; dogs; bus 50m; Eng spkn; adv bkg; quiet; ccard acc; red long stay/LS; CKE/CCI. "Spacious site in mountains bet 2 vills; pool restricted to campers; sh walk to public transport to sites of interest; best site in Sorrento to avoid narr gridlocked rds; old, tired facs (2013); tight narr pitches." ♦ € 47.50 2014*

SORRENTO *3A3* (5km NE Coastal) *40.65953, 14.41835* **Camping Sant Antonio, Via Marina d'Equa 20/21, Seiano, 80069 Vico-Equense (NA) [tel/fax 081 8028570 or 081 8028576; info@campingsantantonio.it; www.campingsantantonio.it]** Fr A3 exit at Castellamare-di-Stabia. Foll sp for Sorrento; app Vico-Equense take L fork thro tunnel, at end of viaduct R to Seiano-Spaggia. Last site of 3 on L down narr twisting rd after 1km (poss v congested). Access to pitches poss diff due to trees. Med, pt sl, shd; wc; chem disp; shwrs €0.50; EHU (5A) inc; gas; lndry rm; shop; rest, snacks; bar; shgl beach 100m; boat hire; excursions; solarium; some statics; dogs €3 (not allowed Aug); phone; bus adj, train 800m; poss cr; Eng spkn; adv bkg; quiet; ccard acc; 10% red CKE/CCI. "Ideal base Amalfi coast, Capri, Naples; lovely harbour adj; v helpful, friendly staff; bus & train tickets avail fr site; gd rest." ♦ ltd. 15 Mar-31 Oct. € 32.50 2013*

SORRENTO *3A3* (2km W Coastal) *40.62818, 14.35816* **Camping Villaggio Santa Fortunata, Via Capo 39, 80067 Capo-de-Sorrento (NA) [081 8073579 or 081 8073574; fax 8073590; info@santafortunata.com; www.santafortunata.com]** Only app fr a'strada, exit Castellamare. Foll sp into Sorrento then sp Massa-Lubrense. Site poorly sp fr Sorrento on R, gd wide ent. V lge, mkd/hdg pitch, pt sl, terr, shd; wc (some cont); chem disp; mv service pnt; shwrs inc; EHU (6A) inc; gas; lndry; shop; rest, snacks; bar; playgrnd; rocky beach; pool high ssn; internet; entmnt; TV; 50% statics; dogs free; phone; bus adj; sep car park; poss cr; Eng spkn; red long stay/CKE/CCI. "Gd, clean facs; pitches sm for lge o'fits (7m+) & poss dusty; bus fr gate, ticket fr recep; boat trips to Capri fr site beach; noisy nr gd rest, disco & 18-30 tours; many scruffy statics; facs dated; steep access & tight hairpins to some pitches; friendly, vg site." ♦ ltd. 1 Apr-15 Oct. € 42.00 2014*

SORSO see Porto Torres (SARDINIA) *3A1*

SOTTOMARINA see Chioggia *2E2*

SOVICILLE see Siena *1D3*

ITALY

SPERLONGA *2E4* (1km SE Coastal) *41.25514, 13.44625* **Camping Villaggio Nord-Sud, Via Flacca, Km 15.5, 04029 Sperlonga (LT) [0771 548255; fax 557240; info@campingnordsud.it; www.campingnordsud.it]** Site on seaward side of S213 at km post 15.9. Lge sp visible fr both dirs. Lge, mkd pitch, hdstg, shd; wc (mainly cont); chem disp; shwrs inc; EHU (4A) inc; lndry; shop, rest high ssn; snacks; bar; private sand beach; windsurfing; tennis; fitness rm; games area; entmnt; some statics; no dogs; adv bkg; quiet; red LS. "Mostly statics but great location; pleasant site; picturesque beach." ♦ 1 Apr-31 Oct. € 48.00 2016*

⊞ **SPOLETO** *2E3* (2km NE Urban) *47.73820, 12.74312* **Parcheggio a Pagamento "Ponzianina", Via del Tiro a Segno 12622 [07 43 21 81]** N on Viale Giacomo Matteotti twd Viale Martiri della Resistenza, take 1st L onto Viale Martiri della Resistenza, over rndbt, turn R onto SS418, turn L onto Piazza Vittoria/SS418 and cont for 80m; turn R onto Via Cacciatore delle Alpi cont 350m; L onto Viale Trento e Trieste, then R onto Via del Tiro a Segno, site in 230m. Sm; no facs; paid parking site only. "200m escalator to the top of historic town and Cathedral; gd NH; m'vans only." € 5.00 2014*

"I like to fill in the reports as I travel from site to site"

You'll find report forms at the back of this guide, or you can fill them in online at camc.com/europereport.

SPOTORNO see Savona *1B2*

STELLA SAN GIOVANNI see Savona *1B2*

STRESA *1B1* (3.4km NW Urban) *45.91246, 8.50410* **Camping Parisi, Via Piave 50, 28831 Baveno (VB) [tel/fax 0323 924160; campingparisi@tiscalinet.it; www.campingparisi.it]** Exit A26 at Baveno, after x-ing bdge on o'skirts Baveno, turn L off main rd bet Hotel Simplon & Agip g'ge & foll sp. Fr Stresa drive thro Baveno. At end of prom, take R fork at Dino Hotel up a minor 1-way rd (poss congested by parked cars); foll Parisi sp. Med, pt sl, pt shd; wc; chem disp; mv service pnt; shwrs inc; EHU (6A) €3.50; lndry; shop, supmkt 500m; rest, snacks 500m; bar adj, playgrnd; lake sw; sm shgl beach adj; boat-launching; fishing; wifi; 10% statics; dogs €4; bus; phone; poss cr; Eng spkn; adv bkg; quiet but w/end evening noise fr adj lido; red CKE/CCI. "Well-managed site on Lake Maggiore; fine views; extra for lakeside pitches; frequent lake steamers nr site; gd rests adj; long hose rec for m'van fill up; sm pitches; busy at w/end; sw in lake - supervise children; many repeat visitors; clean facs; welcoming recep; conv base for visiting Borromeo Islands." ♦ ltd. 25 Mar-30 Sep. € 34.00 2015*

STRESA *1B1* (4km NW Rural) *45.91185, 8.48913* **Camping Tranquilla, Via Cave 2, Oltrefuime, 28831 Baveno (VB) [tel/fax 0323 923452; info@tranquilla.com; www.tranquilla.com]** Fr N go into Baveno & turn R 200m past Hotel Splendide; fr S turn L immed after x-ing bdge. Foll brown sp to site up steep hill 1km. Med, hdg/mkd pitch, some hdstg, pt sl, terr, pt shd; wc (some cont); chem disp; mv service pnt; serviced pitch; shwrs inc; EHU (6A) €2.60; lndry (inc dryer); shops 1km; bar; shgl lake beach 800m; pool; watersports; bike hire; entmnt at w/end; 25% statics; dogs €2.50; train to Milan 2km; car wash; Eng spkn; adv bkg; quiet; red long stay/snr citizens/CKE/CCI. "Clean, comfortable, well-managed, pleasant, family-owned site; v helpful staff; sm pitches; conv Lake Maggiore; day trip by train to Milan." 19 Mar-16 Oct. € 33.50 2016*

STRESA *1B1* (6km NW Urban) *45.90323, 8.50807* **Camping Calaverde, Sempione 24, 28831 Baveno (VB) [0323 922721; info@calaverde.it]** Fr Stresa N on S33, site ent on R 100m after 87km post. Tight, concealed ent. Sm, pt shd; wc, chem disp; shwrs inc; EHU inc; lndry rm; shop opp; bar; lake & private shgl beach adj; quiet but some rd/rlwy noise; Eng spkn; dogs; phone; quiet. "Helpful, friendly owner; clean site; boat-launching; gd size pitches; lake steamer 2km." € 26.00 2014*

TERLAGO see Trento *1D1*

TERNI *2E3* (7km E Rural) *42.54801, 12.71878* **Camping Marmore, Loc Campacci, 05100 Cascata-delle-Marmore (TN) [tel/fax 0744 67198; camping.marmore@hotmail.it; www.campinglemarmore.com]** E fr Terni on S79 dir Marmore & Rieti. Foll site sp. Med, hdstg, pt sl, shd; htd wc (some cont); chem disp; shwrs inc; EHU inc; water free; shop on site & 1km; rest; bar; rv sw adj; watersports on lake nrby; games rm; 90% statics; dogs €4; phone; poss cr; Eng spkn; quiet. "Spectacular waterfalls adj & mountain scenery; gd; Casacata Hydro elec, well worth visiting." ♦ 1 Apr-30 Sep. € 25.00 2013*

TORBOLE *1D1* (350m N Urban) *45.8725, 10.87361* **Camping Al Porto, Via Al Cor, 38069 Tórbole (TN) [tel/fax 0464 505891; info@campingalporto.it; www.campingalporto.it]** On ent Tórbole fr S take rd twd Riva-del-Garda for approx 600m. Petrol stn & car park on R, turn L into narr lane after shops; site sp. Med, mkd pitch, pt shd; wc (some cont); chem disp; mv service pnt; shwrs inc; EHU (5A) inc; lndry; shops 300m; rest 100m; snacks; bar; BBQ; playgrnd; lake sw & shgl beach 100m; watersports; dogs €2.50; poss cr; quiet; red long stay/LS; CKE/CCI. "Excel san facs; excel site; secure; helpful staff; vill has many rest & sportling locations." ♦ 14 Mar-2 Nov. € 33.00 2014*

TORRE DEL LAGO PUCCINI see Viareggio *1C3*

TRAFOI *1D1* (900m S Rural) *46.54332, 10.50750* **Camping Trafoi, Drei Brunnen Weg 1, 39020 Trafoi [tel/fax 0473 611533; info@camping-trafoi.com; www.camping-trafoi.com]** Fr SS40 turn SW at Spondigna onto SS38 dir Stelvio to Trafoi. Site thro vill sp on L. Sm, pt sl, pt shd; wc; chem disp; mv service pnt; shwrs; EHU (4A); lndry; shop; BBQ; dogs €3; bus 500m; Eng spkn; quiet. "Excel cycle rtes, mountaineering; chair lift for skiing; excel." ♦ ltd. 15 Jun-15 Sep. € 30.00 2015*

TRASAGHIS see Gemona del Friuli *2E1*

TRENTO *1D1* (12km NW Rural) *46.11111, 11.04805* **Camping Laghi di Lamar, Via alla Selva Faeda 15, 38070 Terlago (TN) [0461 860423; campeggio@laghidilamar.com; www.laghidilamar.com]** Head W fr Trento for 10km on SS45b dir Riva-del-Garda/Brescia. Turn R twd Monte-Terlago; site sp on R. Last section via SS45 v steep. Med, terr, pt shd; wc; chem disp; mv service pnt; shwrs inc; EHU (10A) inc; gas; lndry (inc dryer); shop; rest 100m; rest, snacks; bar; BBQ; playgrnd; pool; lake sw 700m; games area; games rm; bike hire; wifi; TV; 30% statics; dogs €2.50; phone; Eng spkn; quiet; ccard acc; red snr citizens/CKE/CCI. "Excel site; excel new san facs." ♦ 1 Apr-30 Oct. € 35.00 2017*

TREPORTI see Cavallino *2E2*

⊞ **TRIESTE** *2F1* (5.5km N Rural) *45.67974, 13.78387* **Camping Obelisco, Strada Nuova Opicina 37, 34016 Opicina (TS) [tel/fax 040 212744; campeggioobelisco@gmail.com; www.campeggiobelisco.it]** Sp fr S58. Med, hdstg, pt sl, terr, shd; wc (cont); own san; mv service pnt; shwrs inc; EHU €2.50; rest, snacks; bar 1km; playgrnd; 95% statics; dogs €2.50; Eng spkn; quiet; CKE/CCI. "V steep, narr, twisting ent/exit to site - suitable sm c'vans only & diff in wet; excel views Trieste harbour; interesting tram ride into city fr obelisk; demanding up hill walk to top of site, both Turkish & European wcs." € 18.00 2016*

TROGHI see Firenze *1D3*

TROPEA *3B4* (7km NE Coastal) *38.70610, 15.97024* **Villaggio Camping Sambalon, Via del Mare, 89868 Marina-di-Zambrone (VV) [0963 392828; fax 45385; info@sambalon.com; www.sambalon.com]** Fr N exit A3 at Pizzo Calabro onto S522 dir Tropea for 20km. Foll sp Marina di Zambrone & site. Med, mkd pitch, some hdstg, pt shd; wc; mv service pnt; shwrs; EHU; lndry; shop on site & 1km; rest, snacks; bar; playgrnd; sand beach adj; wifi; entmnt; TV; some statics; dogs; adv bkg; quiet. 20 May-23 Sep. € 46.50 2012*

⊞ **URBISAGLIA** *2E3* (5km NE Rural) *43.21136, 13.41544* **Centro Agrituristico La Fontana, Via Selva 8, Abbadia-di-Fiastra, 62010 La Fontana (MC) [tel/fax 0733 514002]** Fr SP77 turn S to Abbadia-di-Fiastra onto SP78. On reaching Abbadia turn L & immed R, then uphill above Monastery for 2km & foll sp to site on R just after sharp RH bend. Sm, terr, pt shd; wc; chem disp; mv service pnt; shwrs inc; EHU (6A) inc; rest, snacks; bar; BBQ; playgrnd; sand beach 35km; TV cab/sat; quiet. "Fair sh stay/NH; CL-type site on farm; not suitable lge o'fits; attactive countryside; v helpful owners." ♦ € 21.00 2012*

VADA see Cecina *1D3*

VARIGOTTI see Finale Ligure *1B2*

⊞ **VENEZIA** *2E2* (18km SW Coastal) *45.41916, 12.25666* **Camping Fusina, Via Moranzani 79, 30030 Fusina (VE) [041 5470055; fax 5470050; info@campingfusina.com; www.campingfusina.com]** Exit A4 at sp Ravenna/Chiogga onto SS309 S, & foll sp to site. Take care when turning into rd leading to Fusina as L-hand turning lane used by locals for o'taking. Lge, pt shd; htd wc; chem disp; mv service pnt; shwrs inc; EHU (6A) inc (poss rev pol); gas; lndry; shop; rest, snacks; bar; playgrnd; boat hire; games area; wifi; entmnt; TV rm; 50% statics; dogs free; poss cr; no adv bkg; some ship & aircraft noise + noise fr bar & adj indus complex; ccard acc; red CKE/CCI. "Pleasant, busy site; some pitches o'looking lagoon; many backpackers, educational groups & 18-30s; gd san facs; gd public transport/boat dir to Venice; ferry to Greece adj; helpful staff; poss mosquitoes; some pitches diff due trees & soft when wet; ltd facs LS & poss travellers; refurb in progress (2017)." € 35.00 2017*

VENEZIA *2E2* (16km W Rural) *45.45222, 12.18305* **Camping Serenissima, Via Padana 334/A, 30176 Malcontenta [041 5386498 or 041 921850; fax 920286; info@campingserenissima.it; www.campingserenissima.com]** Exit A4 at Oriago/Mira exit. At 1st rndabt foll sp Ravenna/Venezia; at next rndabt take 1st exit sp Padova/Riviera del Brenta (SR11) twd Oriago. Rv on L, site on R in approx 2km. Med, mkd pitch, pt shd; htd wc (some cont); chem disp; mv service pnt; shwrs inc; EHU (10/16A) inc; gas; lndry; shop; supmkt 3km; rest, snacks; bar; playgrnd; pool 3km; sand beach 10km; bike & boat hire; wifi; 25% statics; dogs free; phone; poss cr; gd Eng spkn; adv bkg; quiet; ccard acc; red snr citizens; CKE/CCI. "Bus to Venice/Padua - buy tickets on site; friendly, helpful owners; efficient recep; some sm pitches; excel, v clean san facs; poss mosquitoes; conv Padova; highly rec for Venice; supmkt 3km; vg." ♦ 21 Mar-5 Nov. € 34.00 2016*

VENEZIA (VENICE) See also sites listed under Cavallino, Lido di Jesolo, Mestre and Punta Sabbioni.

VERBANIA *1B1* (6km NE Rural) *45.97659, 8.63385* **Camping La Sierra, Corso Belvedere, 337 - 28823 Ghiffa (VB) [0333 7815534; info@campinglasierra.it; www.campinglasierra.it]** Fr Verbania N on SS34 dir Cannobio, site on L just after exit fr Ghiffa. Sm, mkd pitch, hdstg, terr, pt shd; wc; chem disp; shwrs inc; EHU (6A) inc; lndry; shop 1km; rest, snacks; bar; BBQ; playgrnd; shgl beach adj; fishing; watersports; 8% statics; dogs €3; bus; phone; poss cr; Eng spkn; adv bkg; rd noise; CKE/CCI. "Vg site; views of lake; steep walk to sans facs fr upper terraces." 1 Mar-1 Nov. € 33.00 2013*

VERBANIA *1B1* (6km W Rural) *45.93731, 8.48615* **Camping Conca d'Oro, Via 42 Martiri 26, 28835 Feriolo di Baveno (VB) [0323 28116; fax 28538; info@concadoro.it; www.concadoro.it]** Foll S33 NW fr Stresa, thro Bavena to Feriolo. At traff lts in Feriolo fork R, sp Verbania & in 800m immed over rv bdge, turn R into site. Clearly sp. Lge, mkd pitch, pt sl, shd; wc; chem disp; mv service pnt; shwrs inc; EHU (6A) inc; lndry; supmkt; rest, snacks; bar; playgrnd; private sand beach adj; windsurfing; games area; bike hire; internet; entmnt; 10% statics; dogs €5 (not acc Jul/Aug); Eng spkn; adv bkg; quiet; ccard acc; CKE/CCI. "Helpful staff; gd, clean, modern san facs; discount for local services; extra for lakeside pitches; excel site." ♦ 29 Mar-29 Sep. € 48.00 2013*

VERBANIA *1B1* (9km NW Urban) *45.96111, 8.45694* **Camping Lago delle Fate, La Quartina, Via Pallanza 22, 28802 Mergozzo (VB) [0323 80326; fax 800916; info@lagodellefate.com; www.lagodellefate.com]** 1km E of vill of Mergozzo which is 2nd L after exit Gravellona on S34 to Verbania. Med, hdstg, pt shd; wc (cont); chem disp; shwrs; EHU (6A); gas; lndry; shop 1km; rest 100m; snacks; bar; BBQ; shgl beach; lake sw; boat hire; wifi; 10% statics; twin axles; poss cr; Eng spkn; adv bkg; CKE/CCI. "Extra charge for lakeside pitches, slightly bigger with superb views; gd sh stay; town, 5 min walk; gd walking & cycling." ♦ ltd. 2 Apr-4 Oct. € 43.00 2015*

VERONA *1D2* (1.5km N Rural) *45.44985, 11.00415* **Camping San Pietro, Via Castel San Pietro 2, 37100 Verona [tel/fax 045 592037; info@campingcastelsanpietro.com; www.campingcastelsanpietro.com]** Exit A4/E70 to San Martino-Buon-Albergo & foll S11 dir Verona cent, site sp adj Castel San Pietro. Sm, mkd pitch, hdstg, shd; wc (cont); chem disp (wc); shwrs inc; no EHU; lndry; shop; rest 500m; snacks; bar; BBQ; wifi; no dogs; some statics; bus 1km; no vehicles/o'fits over 7m; adv bkg ess; some rd noise. "Basic site in park, more suited to tents or sm m'vans only - no EHU; beautiful views over city; easy walk to town cent, but many steps; poor & ltd san facs." ♦ 2 May-30 Sep. € 41.00 2014*

⊞ **VERONA** *1D2* (15km W Rural) *45.44557, 10.83447* **Camping El Bacàn, Via Verona 11, 37010 Palazzolo di Sona (VR) [348 9317204; fax 045 6080708; info@el-bacan.it; www.el-bacan.it]** Exit A4 onto A22 N & foll sp for Brescia (W) on SR11. Site in 7km on R, sp 150m bef site ent. Sm, hdg/mkd pitch, pt shd; wc (cont); chem disp; shwrs; EHU (16A) inc; lndry; shop (farm produce); rest, snacks, bar 2km; BBQ; playgrnd; internet; TV; dogs; bus 1km; Eng spkn; adv bkg; quiet, some rd noise; cc acc; CKE/CCI. "Charming, pleasant site on wkg farm; conv Verona, Lake Garda; friendly owner & staff; excel farm shop; highly rec; easy access; vg; gd san facs." ♦ € 23.00 2017*

VIAREGGIO *1C3* (2km S Coastal) *43.85133, 10.25963* **Camping Viareggio, Via Comparini 1, 55049 Viareggio (LU) [0584 391012; fax 395462; info@campingviareggio.it; www.campingviareggio.it]** Fr sea front at Viareggio, take rd on canal sp Livorno; after x-ing canal bdge turn L (but not immed on canal) & 2nd R to site in 2km. Lge, shd; wc (some cont); chem disp; mv service pnt; fam bthrm; shwrs €0.50; EHU (4A) (poss rev pol); gas; lndry; shop; rest; bar; playgrnd; pool €3; beach 800m; games area; TV; internet; phone; dogs €4 (not permitted Aug); adv bkg; quiet; red LS/CKE/CCI. "Gd site & facs; hot water to shwrs only; cycle rte/footpath to town." ♦ 1 Apr-4 Oct. € 32.00 2014*

"We must tell The Club about that great site we found"

Get your site reports in by mid-August and we'll do our best to get your updates into the next edition.

VIAREGGIO *1C3* (5km S Coastal) *43.82920, 10.2727* **Camping Italia, Viale dei Tigli 52, 55048 Torre-del-Lago Puccini (LU) [0584 359828; fax 341504; info@campingitalia.net; www.campingitalia.net]** Fr A12 N exit sp Viareggio, fr S exit Pisa N onto SS1 & turn twd Torre del Lago at S junc, site well sp thro vill. Do not turn L at vill cent but cont for 2km N, then L at rlwy bdge. At rndabt turn L, site on R in 250m. Avoid Viareggio town cent. Med, shd; wc (some cont); chem disp; mv service pnt; shwrs €0.50; EHU (6A) €1.30; gas; lndry (inc dryer); shop; rest, snacks; bar; lge playgrnd; pool; sand beach 1.5km; tennis; bike hire; wifi; entmnt; TV rm; some statics (sep area); no dogs Jun-Aug; sep car park; Eng spkn; adv bkg; noisy w/ends high ssn; ccard acc; red LS; "Vg for Lucca - Puccini's birthplace; bus tickets fr site for Pisa & Lucca; some pitches diff for lge o'fits due trees & low branches; gd clean facs; poss problem with mosquitoes." ♦ 16 Apr-25 Sep. € 42.50 2014*

VICCHIO see Borgo San Lorenzo *1D3*

VICENZA *1D2* (9km SE Urban) *45.5175, 11.60222* **Camping Vicenza, Strada Pelosa 239, 36100 Vicenza [0444 582311; fax 582434; info@campingvicenza.it; www.campingvicenza.it]** Exit A4 Vicenza Est dir Torri di Quartesole; turn R immed after toll; site on L 300m fr Vicenza exit, hidden behind Viest Quality Inn. Fr city foll sp Padua & a'strada; sp. Med, pt sl, pt shd; wc (some cont); chem disp; mv service pnt; fam bthrm; shwrs inc; EHU (3A) inc (rev pol); lndry; shops 1km; rest, snacks 500m; bar; BBQ; playgrnd; tennis; bike hire; internet; entmnt; TV rm; bus; Eng spkn; adv bkg; some rd noise; 10% red long stay; ccard acc; red CKE/CCI. "Cycle path to interesting town; functional site; clean san facs; friendly, helpful staff; pleasant site." ♦ ltd. 1 Apr-18 Oct. € 38.00 2016*

VICO EQUENSE see Sorrento *3A3*

VIESTE *2G4* (2km N Coastal) *41.89901, 16.14964* **Camping Punta Lunga, Loc Defensola, 71019 Vieste (FG) [0884 706031 or 0884 706032; fax 706910; puntalunga@puntalonga.com; www.puntalunga.it]** N fr Vieste 1.5km fr end of long beach, turn R at traff lts down narr lane. Site sp. Lge, mkd pitch, pt terr, pt shd; htd wc (some cont); chem disp; mv service pnt; fam bthrm; shwrs inc; EHU (3-5A) inc; gas; lndry; shop; rest, snacks; playgrnd; beach adj; windsurfing; canoeing; bike hire; wifi; entmnt; TV; 15% statics (sep area); no dogs; phone; bus; sep car park; poss cr; Eng spkn; adv bkg; quiet; ccard acc; red LS/CKE/CCI. "Friendly, helpful staff; well-run site on lovely cove; tight pitches - beware pitch marker posts; v clean facs; rec use bottled water; beautiful coastal area; gd rest; lovely cove; excel beaches." 30 May-15 Sep. € 49.00 2014*

VIESTE *2G4* (2km S Coastal) *41.85914, 16.17405* **Camping Adriatico, Lungomare. Enrico Mattei 110, 71019 Vieste (FG) [tel/fax 0884 700954; info@campingadriatico.it; www.campingadriatico.it]** S fr Vieste on coast rd SP53, site on both sides of rd. Med, mkd pitch, pt shd; wc (cont); chem disp; mv service pnt; shwrs inc; EHU (6A) inc; lndry; shop; rest, snacks; bar; BBQ; playgrnd; sand beach adj; windsurfing; games area; wifi; some statics; phone; bus; poss cr; Eng spkn; adv bkg; red LS. "Vg family-run site." ♦ ltd. 1 Apr-31 Oct. € 33.50 2014*

VIGNALE RIOTORTO see Follonica *1D3*

VILLANOVA D'ALBENGA see Albenga *1B2*

⊞ **VIPITENO/STERZING** *1D1* (1km S Urban) *46.88737, 11.43098* **Autoporto, 00098 Vipiteno [0472 760620; info@hotel-brenner.com]** S fr Brenner Pass approx 17km, take exit immed bef toll booths Vipiteno & foll sp 'Autoporto'. Site well sp fr toll booth - 500m. Can also be accessed fr SS12. Push button on site barrier if office clsd. Med, hdstg, pt shd; wc; mv service pnt; shwrs; EHU inc; shop, rest adj. "Excel NH for c'vans or m'vans; conv Austrian border; all facs in services." € 15.00 2015*

VOLLAN/FOIANA see Merano/Meran *1D1*

VOLTERRA *1D3* (1km NW Rural) *43.41271, 10.8509* **Camping Le Balze, Via di Mandringa 15, 56048 Volterra (PI) [tel/fax 0588 87880; campinglebalze@hotmail.it; www.campinglebalze.com]** Take Pisa rd (S68) fr town; site clearly sp ('Camping' or symbol) after 1km. Watch out for R turn at sharp L corner. Med, pt sl, terr, pt shd; wc (some cont); chem disp; shwrs inc; EHU (6A) inc; gas; lndry; shop; supmkt 300m; rest 150m; bar; pool; paddling pool; dogs free; bus adj; poss cr; Eng spkn; no adv bkg; quiet; ccard acc; CKE/CCI. "Beautifully situated with views of Volterra & hills; gd, modern san facs; select own pitch; Etruscan walls just outside site; excel site; helpful staff." ♦ 1 Apr-15 Oct. € 36.00 2017*

ZAMBRONE see Tropea *1B4*

SARDINIA

ALGHERO *3A1* (1.5km N Coastal) *40.57916, 8.31222* **Camping La Mariposa, Via Lido 22, 07041 Alghero (SS) [079 9950480; fax 984489; info@lamariposa.it; www.lamariposa.it]** N fr Alghero on coast rd dir Fertilia. Site on L just beyond pool. Lge, pt sl, hdstg, terr, pt shd; wc; chem disp; mv service pnt; shwrs €0.50; EHU (6-10A) €3; gas; lndry; shop; rest, snacks; bar; BBQ; private sand beach adj; watersports; bike hire; games rm; wifi; entmnt; TV; dogs; 20% statics; dogs; bus nr; sep car park; Eng spkn; ccard acc; red CKE/CCI. "Lovely wooded site; gd clean facs; gd security; friendly staff; boat fr Alghero to caves at Cape Caccia or by rd + 625 steps." 1 Apr-15 Oct. € 41.00 2016*

⊞ **CAGLIARI** *3B1* (1km SE Urban) *39.21129, 9.12883* **Camper Cagliari Park, 13 Via Stanislao Caboni, 09125 Cagliari [329 6713141 or 070 303147 or 0328 3348847 (mob); info@campercagliaripark.it; www.campercagliaripark.it]** Well sp on main rds into Cagliari. Sm, unshd; wc; chem disp; mv service pnt; EHU (10A) €4; lndry nr; bus 200m; Eng spkn; CKE/CCI. "Gd secure site; v helpful owner; walking dist historical cent, rests etc; c'vans enquire 1st." € 21.00 2014*

DORGALI *3A2* (7km W Coastal) *40.28486, 9.63370* **Camping Villaggio Calagonone, Via Collodi 1, 08022 Cala-Gonone (NU) [0784 93165; fax 93255; info@campingcalagonone.it; www.campingcalagonone.it]** Fr S125 turn E twd Cala Gonone, thro tunnel. Site sp on L of main rd. Med, terr, shd; wc; chem disp; mv service pnt; EHU (6A) €5; shop; rest, snacks; bar; BBQ; playgrnd; pool; sand/shgl beach 400m; tennis; games area; 30% statics; dogs €5; phone; poss cr; adv bkg; ccard acc. "Beautiful situation in pine forest on edge of pretty town; nrby coves & grottoes accessible by boat or on foot." ♦ 1 Apr-3 Nov. € 63.00 2014*

ITALY

⊞ **NARBOLIA** *3A1* (6km W Coastal) *40.06956, 8.48375* **Camping Nurapolis, Loc Is Arenas, 09070 Narbolia (OR) [0783 52283 or 348 8080839(mob); fax 52255; info@nurapolis.it; www.nurapolis.it]** Fr Oristano take sp to Cuglier on rd SS292i. Site sp fr rd approx 5km fr S. Caterina-di-Pittinura. Lge, pt shd; wc; shwrs; EHU (3A) €3; gas; shop; rest, snacks; bar; sand beach adj; tennis; entmnt; watersports; dogs; poss cr; adv bkg; ccard acc; red CKE/CCI. "Site in pine forest; many sports, guided walks Easter to Oct; very pleasant owners." ♦ € 26.50 2014*

PORTO SAN PAOLO *3A2* (2km S Coastal) *40.85870, 9.64296* **Camping Tavolara, Loc Porto Taverna, 07020 Loiri-Porta San Paolo (SS) [0789 40166; fax 480778; info@camping-tavolara.it; www.camping-tavolara.it]** On SS125, sp. Med, hdg/mkd pitch, shd; wc (mainly cont); mv service pnt; shwrs inc; EHU (3-6A) €3.50; lndry; shop & 2km; rest, snacks; bar; playgrnd; sand beach 500m; tennis; bike hire; entmnt; 50% statics; dogs €3; phone; site clsd Dec & early Jan; Eng spkn; adv bkg; ccard acc; red CKE/CCI. "Friendly staff; conv ferries & boat trips." 20 Apr-15 Oct. € 59.50 2014*

PORTO TORRES *3A1* (7km E Coastal) *40.81607, 8.48541* **Camping Golfo dell'Asinara-Cristina, Loc Platamona, 07037 Sorso (SS) [079 310230; fax 310589; info@campingasinara.it; www.camping asinara.it]** Foll coast rd SP81 E fr Porto-Torres to site. Sp. Lge, pt shd; wc; mv service pnt; shwrs; EHU (4A) €4; gas; lndry; shop; rest, snacks; bar; playgrnd; pool; sand beach adj; tennis; games area; bike hire; 40% statics; no dogs; sep car park; poss cr; quiet; ccard acc; red long stay/CKE/CCI. "Gd position." ♦ 15 May-30 Sep. € 35.00 2016*

PULA *3B1* (4km Coastal) *38.95778, 8.96930* **Camping Cala d'Ostia, Localita Cala d'Ostia, 09010 Pula [39 070 921470; fax 070 921471; info@campingcaladostia.com; www.campingcaladostia.com]** Fr Cagliari, take SS195 past Pula. Foll the rd along the seafront about 1km, sp to site. Lge, pt shd; wc; mv service pnt; fam bthrm; shwrs; EHU (13A); bar; BBQ; beach; games rm; wifi; dogs; bus adj; twin axles; poss cr; Eng spkn; CCI. "Fair site; busy in high ssn; beautiful coastline; lovely area." ♦ ltd. Apr-Sep. € 35.00 2014*

⊞ **TONARA** *3A1* (900m NE Rural) *40.02812, 9.17647* **Camping Sa Colonia, Via Muggianeddu 4, 08039 Tonara (NU) [03921 282340; info@camping sacolonia.it]** Fr S fr Cagliari on SS128/SS295, site sp. Sp rte unsuitable lge car + c'van o'fits or v lge m'vans. Avoid town cent rds - v narr & steep. Med, mkd pitch, terr, shd; wc; chem disp (wc); shwrs; EHU (5A) inc; shop in town; rest; bar; playgrnd; Eng spkn; quiet. CKE/CCI. "Mountain scenery; rds gd but steep, twisty & slow; welcoming owners." € 20.00 2016*

SICILY

⊞ **ACIREALE** *3C4* (1.5km NE Coastal) *37.62015, 15.17320* **La Timpa International Camping, Via Santa Maria La Scala, 25 -Cap 95024 Acireale (CT) [095 7648155; fax 7640049; info@campinglatimpa.com; www.campinglatimpa.com]** Exit A18/E45 onto rd S114 dir Acireale. Foll sp for Santa Maria La Scala; site on L after 1.5km; steep & diff access rds. Med, pt shd; wc; shwrs free; EHU (6A) €3.50; lndry; shop high ssn; rest, snacks; bar; playgrnd; beach adj; 60% statics; dogs €4 (not acc Jul/Aug); sep car park; poss noisy; ccard acc; red CKE/CCI. "Site in orchard, surfaced in black volcanic ash; hot & cold shwrs; chem displ; trips to Etna; lift down to rocky beach; sh, steep walk to vill & harbour." ♦ € 25.50 2013*

⊞ **AGRIGENTO** *3C3* (4km SE Coastal) *37.24395, 13.61423* **Camping Internazionale Nettuno, Via Lacco Ameno 3, San Leone, 92100 Agrigento [tel/fax 0922 416268 or 0922 416983; info@campingnettuno.com; www.campingnettuno.com]** Fr Agrigento to San Leone on SS115, foll rd SE out of San Leone alongside beach until sharp L away fr beach. Turn immed R into lane, site on R. Med, hdg pitch, hdstg, terr, pt shd; wc (some cont); chem disp; mv service pnt; shwrs inc; EHU (6A) €2.50 (rev pol); gas; lndry; shop; rest, snacks; bar; BBQ; sand beach adj; wifi; entmnt; TV rm; 15% statics; dogs free; phone; poss cr; adv bkg; ccard acc; red long stay/CKE/CCI. "Bus to temples at Agrigento; peaceful, unspoilt beach; steep slope to pitches - towed c'vans rec to keep to upper levels if poss; gd rest; take care low branches." ♦ ltd. € 27.00 2013*

⊞ **AVOLA** *3C4* (4km N Coastal) *36.93631, 15.17462* **Camping Sabbiadoro, Via Chiusa di Carlo 45, 96012 Avola (SR) [tel/fax 0931 822415; info@campeggio sabbiadoro.com; www.campeggiosabbiadoro.com]** Fr N exit A18/E45 at Cassibile onto S115 dir Avola, site sp in 4km. Last 500m on narr, winding rd. Med, mkd pitch, terr, pt sl, shd; wc; chem disp; mv service pnt; shwrs €0.50; EHU (2A) €4; lndry; shop & 2km; snacks; bar; dir access to sand beach; horseriding; wifi; 20% statics; dogs; phone; sep car park Jul-Aug; adv bkg; quiet; ccard acc. "V attractive site with clean, ltd facs; rec visit Noto; well run; poss muddy pitches after heavy rain." € 59.00 2014*

CASTELLAMMARE DEL GOLFO *3C3* (4.5km NW Coastal) *38.05596, 12.83868* **Camping Baia di Guidaloca, Corso Garibaldi, 91014 Scopello (TP) [tel/fax 0924 541262 or 0924 32359 or 339 1581927 LS; giovannitod@libero.it; www.campinguidaloca.com]** Fr SS187 foll sp bet km 34 & 33 dir Scopello, site sp on L. Med, pt shd; wc; chem disp; shwrs inc; EHU (3A) €2.50; shop 2km; rest 2km; snacks; bar; sand beach adj; 10% statics; phone; dogs leashed; bus; sep car park high ssn; poss cr; adv bkg; quiet; CKE/CCI. "Conv Zingaro nature reserve - v beautiful; vg." 1 Apr-30 Sep. € 27.00 2013*

⊞ **CASTELVETRANO** *3C3* (13km SE Coastal) *37.59571, 12.84139* **Camping Athena, Loc Marinella, Contrada Garraffo, 91022 Castelvetrano (TP) [tel/ fax 0924 46132; info@campingathenaselinunte.it; www.campingathenaselinunte.it]** Exit SS115 (Castelvetrano-Sciacca) at sp to Selinunte, site on L bef Selinunte. Sm, some hdstg, pt shd; wc; mv service pnt; shwrs inc; EHU (10A) inc; lndry; shop 1km; rest, snacks; bar; BBQ; sand beach 800m; dogs; phone; ccard acc; red CKE/CCI. "Can take lger o'fits than Maggiolino site; conv temples at Selinunte; excel facs; gd rest adj." € 18.00 2012*

"I need an on-site restaurant"

We do our best to make sure site information is correct, but it is always best to check any must-have facilities are still available or will be open during your visit.

⊞ **CATANIA** *3C4* (6km NE Coastal) *37.53279, 15.12012* **Camping Jonio, Loc Ognina, Via Villini a Mare 2, 95126 Catania [095 491139; fax 492277; info@campingjonio.com; www.campingjonio.com]** SS114 N of Catania, exit Ognina. Fr the Catania ring rd, take exit Catania Centro (San Gregorio) and then Catania E. Foll sp to site. Med, hdstg, terr, pt shd; wc; chem disp; mv service pnt; fam bthrm; shwrs; EHU (6A) €4; gas; lndry; shop, supmkt nrby; rest, snacks; bar; BBQ; rocky beach; waterskiing; games area; wifi; 20% statics; dogs; bus to Catania; twin axles; sep car park; Eng spkn; adv bkg; ccard acc; red LS/CKE/CCI. "Mt Etna 45 mins drive N; owner v helpful; some pitches sm; subways, scubadiving; gd." ♦ € 39.00 (CChq acc) 2016*

CEFALU *3B3* (3km W Coastal) *38.02703, 13.98283* **Camping Costa Ponente, C de Ogliastrillo, 90015 Cefalù (PA) [0921 420085; fax 424492]** Fr Palermo E twd Cefalù, on rd SS113 at km stone 190.3, site sp. Lge, hdstg, terr, shd; wc (some cont); chem disp; shwrs; EHU rev pol (3A) €5; gas; lndry rm; shop & 4km; rest high ssn; snacks; bar; pool; paddling pool; sand beach (down steep steps); tennis; 10% statics; dogs €3.50 (not acc Aug); bus nr; sep car park (high ssn); poss cr; no adv bkg; poss noisy; ccard acc; 5% red CKE/ CCI. ♦ 1 Apr-31 Oct. € 30.00 2012*

CEFALU *3B3* (5km W Rural) *38.02700, 13.98247* **Camping Sanfilippo, Ogliastrillo SS113, 90015 Cefalù [tel/fax 0921 420 184; info@campingsanfilippo.com; www.campingsanfilippo.com]** Fr Palermo E twds Cafalu on rd SS113. Med, mkd pitch, hdstg, terr, shd; wc; chem disp; mv service pnt; shwrs; EHU (4A) inc; lndry; shop; snacks; BBQ; playgrnd; beach 150m; games area; games rm; wifi; 50% statics; dogs €3.50; bus 300m; twin axles; poss cr; Eng spkn; adv bkg; quiet; no ccard acc; CCI. "Vg, beautiful site; sea views fr some pitches; newly renovated (2016)." ♦ 1 Apr-31 Oct. € 28.50 2016*

⊞ **DONNALUCATA** *3C3* (3km SE Rural/Coastal) *36.74767, 14.66314* **Camping Club Piccadilly, Via Mare Adriatico, Contrada da Spinasanta, 97010 Donnalucata (RG) [tel/fax 0932 938704; info@club-piccadilly.it; www.club-piccadilly.it]** Site sp fr coast rd bet Donnalucata & Cava d'Aliga. Med, mkd pitch, hdstg, pt shd; wc; chem disp; mv service pnt; shwrs €1; EHU (6A) €4; gas 2km; lndry; shop 2km; rest, snacks, 2km bar; playgrnd; htd, covrd pool 15km; sand beach adj; internet; TV rm; dogs €2; poss cr; Eng spkn; adv bkg; red long stay; CKE/CCI. "Gd touring base; excursions to Malta high ssn; v friendly owner sells own wine; lovely quiet seaside site; strongly rec; poss cr in Aug." ♦ € 33.00 2014*

⊞ **FINALE** *3B3* (500m W Coastal) *38.02305, 14.15388* **Camping Rais Gerbi, di Triscele Tu.Rist Srl - Finale di Pollina (PA) S.S.113 Km. 172,9 [0921 426570; fax 426577; camping@raisgerbi.it; www.raisgerbi.it]** Direct access fr SS113 immed after bdge W of Finale. Lge, hdg/mkd pitch, mainly hdstg, terr, pt shd; wc; chem disp; mv service pnt; shwrs inc; EHU (6A) €5; lndry; shop; rest, snacks; bar; BBQ; playgrnd; pool; private shgl beach 600m; tennis; games area; bike hire; horseriding 200m; entmnt; internet; TV rm; 13% statics; dogs free; phone; bus; poss cr; Eng spkn; adv bkg (min 10 day stay); quiet but some rlwy noise; ccard acc; red long stay/CKE/CCI. "Gd touring base Cefalu & N coast; friendly, helpful staff; excel, clean site & facs." ♦ € 41.00 2013*

⊞ **MENFI** *3C3* (6km S Coastal) *37.56500, 12.96416* **Camping La Palma, Contrada Fiore, Via delle Palme 29, 92013 Menfi (AG) [tel/fax 0925 78392; camping lapalma@libero.it; www.campinglapalma.com]** Foll sp fr SS115 past Menfi to coast. In abt 3-4km look for campsite sp. Med, shd; hdstg; wc; some cont; chem disp; shwrs; EHU 16A; gas; lndry; shop; rest, snacks; bar; BBQ; playgrnd; sand beach adj; games area; quiet; entmnt; wifi; TV; 5% statics; dogs; bus 6km; twin axles; poss cr; Eng spkn; adv bkg; red LS; CKE/CCI. "Lovely, unspoilt quiet beach (blue flag) with dunes; v helpful owner & staff; family run site; excel." ♦ ltd. € 37.00 2017*

⊞ **MILAZZO** *3B4* (2km N Coastal) *38.26090, 15.24335* **Camping Villaggio Riva Smeralda, Strada Panoramica 64, 98057 Milazzo (ME) [090 9282980; fax 9287791; info@rivasmeralda.it; www.riva smeralda.it]** Clearly sp in Milazzo; foll sp Capo-di-Milazzo. Diff app. Med, hdstg, pt sl, terr, shd; wc; chem disp; mv service pnt; shwrs; EHU (6A) €3; lndry rm; shop; gd rest, snacks; bar; BBQ; playgrnd; paddling pool; rocky beach adj; entmnt; 5% statics; poss cr; Eng spkn; adv bkg; twin axles acc; poss noisy; CKE/CCI. "Gd base for trips to adj isles; site a bit run down; 1 in 5 sl access to pitches, ltd turning space; best for sm m'vans; diving cent on site; excel; v nice site with beautiful views of sea; pitches tight; extremely helpful owners; €3 a night to leave camper to go to Aeolian Islands; vg." ♦ € 33.50 2017*

⊞ **OLIVERI** *3B4* (1.5km N Coastal) *38.12913, 15.05813* **Camping Villaggio Marinello, Via del Sole, 17 Contrada Marinello, 98060 Oliveri (ME) [0941 313000 or 0941 526038; fax 313702; marinello@camping.it or villaggiomarinell@gmail.com; www.camping.it/sicilia/marinello or www.villaggiomarinello.it]** Exit A20 Falcone dir Oliveri, site well sp. Lge, hdg/mkd pitch, hdstg, pt shd; wc; chem disp; mv service pnt; shwrs inc; EHU (6A) inc; lndry; shop; rest high ssn; snacks bar; playgrnd; sand/shgl beach adj; watersports; tennis; excursions; 20% statics; dogs free (not acc Jul/Aug); phone; train; poss cr; Eng spkn; quiet but some rlwy noise; red CKE/CCI. "Basic, clean, well-managed site; excel but shelving beach; helpful staff." ♦ € 46.00 2013*

PALERMO *3B3* (12km NW Coastal) *38.19686, 13.24455* **Camping La Playa, Viale Marino 55 - 90040 Isola delle Femmine (PA) [tel/fax 091 8677001; campinglaplaya@virgilio.it; www.laplayacamping.it]** On Palermo-Trapani rd take A29 exit Isola-delle-Femmine & foll sp. Med, hdstg, pt shd; wc; chem disp; mv service pnt; shwrs €0.50; EHU (6A) inc; gas; lndry (inc dryer); shop; rest, snacks; bar; BBQ; playgrnd; sand beach adj; dogs; Eng spkn; adv bkg; quiet; ccard acc; red CKE/CCI. "V helpful staff; bus into Palermo hourly; barrier clsd 1400-1600; very clean, well-managed, busy site; manager well versed on local info." 21 Mar-15 Oct. € 47.00 2013*

⊞ **PIAZZA ARMERINA** *3C3* (4km SE Rural) *37.20239, 14.23155* **Camping Agriturismo Agricasale, C da Ciavarini, 94015 Piazza-Armerina (EN) [tel/fax 0935 686034; www.agricasale.it]** In Piazza-Armerina town foll sp twd Mirabella but at rndabt with stone cross bear R (red fox sign) & foll red fox down nar rd to wooded site. Park with care. Sm, pt sl, pt shd; wc; chem disp; mv service pnt; shwrs inc; EHU (4A) inc; lndry; shop 4km; rest; bar; BBQ; playgrnd; pool; TV rm; dogs; poss cr; Eng spkn; adv bkg; quiet; CKE/CCI. "Excel site close Palazzo Romana mosaics; pony-trekking, archery & other activities high ssn; all inc rate of €50 avail per day inc excel banquet; site run down." ♦ € 15.00 2014*

⊞ **PUNTA BRACCETTO** *3C3* (Coastal/Urban) *36.81722, 14.46583* **Camping Luminoso, Viale dei Canalotti, 97017 Punta Braccetto - Santa Croce Camerina (RG) [0932 918401; fax 918455; info@campingluminoso.com; www.campingluminoso.com]** W fr Marina di Ragusa on SP80/SC25 coast rd. Site sp. Med, mkd pitch, hdstg, shd; wc; chem disp; mv service pnt; private bathrms avail; shwrs; EHU (6A) €5; lndry; shop & 400m; rest, snacks; bar; direct access to private sand beach adj; bike hire; wifi; child entmnt; TV; dogs free; adv bkg rec high ssn; ccard acc; red LS/CKE/CCI. "Well-run site in gd location; easy access to pitches - suitable lge o'fits/m'vans; excel; modern, immac facs; spacious level hdstg pitches; reliable wifi; helpful English manager; direct access to sandy beach; mob shops call daily; ideal long stay in winter." ♦ ltd. € 61.00 (CChq acc) 2014*

⊞ **PUNTA BRACCETTO** *3C3* (Coastal/Urban) *36.81713, 14.46736* **Camping Scarabeo, Via dei Canaletti 120, Punta-Braccetto, 97017 Santa Croce Camerina (RG) [0932 918096; fax 918391; info@scarabeocamping.it; www.scarabeocamping.it]** W fr Marina di Ragusa on SP80/SC25 coast rd. Site sp Sm, hdg pitch, hdstg, pt sl, pt shd; wc; chem disp; mv service pnt; private bthrm €4; fam bthrm; shwrs €0.60 EHU (3-6A); lndry (inc dryer); shop & 4km; rest, snacks 600m, bar nr; BBQ; direct access to sand beach adj; wifi; child entmnt; 5% statics; dogs €2.50; phone; bus 6km; twinaxles; poss cr; excel Eng spkn; adv bkg; quiet ccard acc; red long stay; CKE/CCI. "Beautiful situation well-maintained, friendly, family-run site; gd, clean, modern facs; vg security; friendly, helpful staff; cars parked sep across rd; excel." ♦ € 41.50 2017*

⊞ **PUNTA BRACCETTO** *3C3* (4km SW Coastal) *36.81661, 14.46895* **Camping Baia Dei Coralli, Punta Braccetto, 97017 Santa Croce Camerina [0932 91 81 92; fax 91 82 82; info@baiadeicoralli.it; www.baiadeicoralli.it]** Fr Agrigento take SS115 twds Sircusa to Gela. Turn L onto SP14, cont onto SP13. At rndabt take 3rd exit onto SP20, R onto SP85, L twd Strada Regionale 25. R onto Strada Regionale 24. Campsite on L. Lge, hdg pitch, hdstg, unshd; wc; chem disp; mv service pnt; shwrs inc; EHU (6A); lndry; rest; snacks; bar; BBQ; playgrnd; pool; sand beach; entmnt; wifi; TV rm; dogs; bus; twin axles; Eng spkn; adv bkg; quiet; ccard acc; red LS; CCI. "Excel site; v busy in summer." ♦ € 30.00 2014*

⊞ **SAN VITO LO CAPO** *3B3* (3km S Coastal) *38.15067, 12.73184* **El Bahira Camping Village, Contrada Salinella, 91010 San Vito-lo-Capo (TP) [0923 972577; fax 972552; info@elbahira.it; www.elbahira.it]** W fr Palermo on A29 dir Trapani. Exit at Castellammare del Golfo onto SS187, then turn N onto SP16 sp San Vito-lo-Capo. At Isolidda foll site sp. Lge, mkd pitch, shd; wc (some cont); chem disp; EHU (6A) inc; lndry; shops; rest, snacks; bar; pizzeria; BBQ; playgrnd; pool (sw caps req); paddling pool; sand/shgl beach adj; watersports; tennis; games area; games rm; entmnt; excursions; TV; some statics; phone; bus nr; sep car park; Eng spkn; ccard acc; quiet; CKE/CCI. "Excel, secure site in vg location; gd facs for families; san facs tired need updating (2014)." ♦ € 55.40 2014*

⊞ **SECCAGRANDE** *3C3* (Coastal) *37.43833, 13.2450* **Kamemi Camping Village, Contrada Camemi Superiore, 92016 Seccagrande-di-Ribera (AG) [tel/fax 0925 69212; info@kamemicamping.it; www.kamemicamping.it]** Foll sp fr S115 to Seccagrande & site. Med, hdstg, pt shd; wc; shwrs inc; EHU (6A) €5; lndry; rest, snacks; bar; playgrnd; 2 pools; sand beach 1km; tennis; games area; entmnt; 40% statics; dogs free; sep car park high ssn; Eng spkn; adv bkg. ♦ € 57.00 (CChq acc) 2014*

SFERRACAVALLO see Palermo *3B3*

⊞ **SIRACUSA** *3C4* (4km SW Rural) *37.03841, 15.25063* **Camping Agritourist Rinaura, Strada Laganelli, Loc Rinaura, SS115, 96100 Siracusa [tel/ fax 0931 721224; marinas@sistenia.it]** S fr Siracusa on S115 twd Avola. Turn R 300m past Hotel Albatros then immed R after rlwy x-ing. Narr lane to site in 300m. Lge, pt shd; wc; chem disp (wc); shwrs €0.60; EHU (16A) €3; shop high ssn; rest 2km; bar; playgrnd; sand beach 2km; bike hire; phone; bus 1km; poss cr; Eng spkn; adv bkg; noise fr nrby hol camp; red long stay/CKE/CCI. "CL-type site in lge orchard; basic but adequate san facs; rather neglected LS; helpful owners." ♦ € 27.00 2014*

⊞ **TAORMINA** *3C4* (10km NE Coastal) *37.93159, 15.35560* **Camping La Focetta Sicula, Via Torrente Agro, 98030 Sant' Alessio Siculo (ME) [0942 751657; fax 756708; info@lafocetta.it; www.lafocetta.it]** A'strada fr Messina to Catania, exit Roccalumera. SS114 thro Sta Teresa-di-Riva to vill of Sant' Alessio-Siculo. Sp at beg of vill. NB Many towns poorly sp. Med, mkd pitch, pt shd; wc; mv service pnt; chem disp; shwrs €0.50; EHU (3A) €3 gas; lndry; shop; rest, snacks; bar; playgrnd; sand beach; games area; bike hire; wifi; entmnt; dogs free; sep car park; poss cr; quiet; red long stay/LS/CKE/CCI. "Popular winter site; v helpful owner." € 36.50 2014*

TAORMINA *3C4* (12km S Coastal) *37.74928, 15.20616* **Camping Mokambo, Via Spiaggia 211, Fondachello, 95016 Máscali (CT) [095 938731; fax 934369; info@campingmokambo.it; www.camping mokambo.it]** Exit A18/E45 at Fiumefreddo & take S114 sp Catania. In Máscali turn L twd Fondachello. At Fondachello turn R & foll site sp, site 1km on R. Med, hdstg, pt shd; wc; chem disp; shwrs €0.50; EHU (3A) €4; shop 2km; rest, snacks 1km; BBQ; playgrnd; beach adj; games area; wifi; 10% statics; no dogs Jul/Aug; train 5km; poss cr; Eng spkn; adv bkg; noisy (bar at ent); ccard acc; red CKE/CCI. "Gd views Etna; conv beach & Taormina; wifi unreliable; staff disinterested; poor." ♦ ltd. 1 Apr-30 Sep. € 43.20 2017*

⊞ **TAORMINA** *3C4* (7km SW Coastal) *37.8047, 15.2444* **Camping Internazionale Almoetia, Via San Marco 19, 95011 Calatabiano (CT) [tel/fax 095 641936; info@campingalmoetia.it; www.camping almoetia.it]** Exit a'strada dir Giardini Naxos. Turn S onto S114 dir Catania, foll sp L onto Via San Marco, site clearly sp. Med, pt shd; wc (some cont); chem disp; shwrs inc; EHU (6A) €2.50; gas; lndry; shop & 1.5km; rest, snacks; bar; BBQ; shgl beach 500m; bike hire; tennis; canoeing; TV rm; dogs; phone; poss cr; adv bkg; quiet but noise fr bar in eve; red LS/long stay; CKE/ CCI. "Conv Etna, Taormina; surrounded by orchards; used by tour groups in motor hotels; site well kept; excel facs; lovely beach nrby." ♦ ltd. € 27.00 2012*

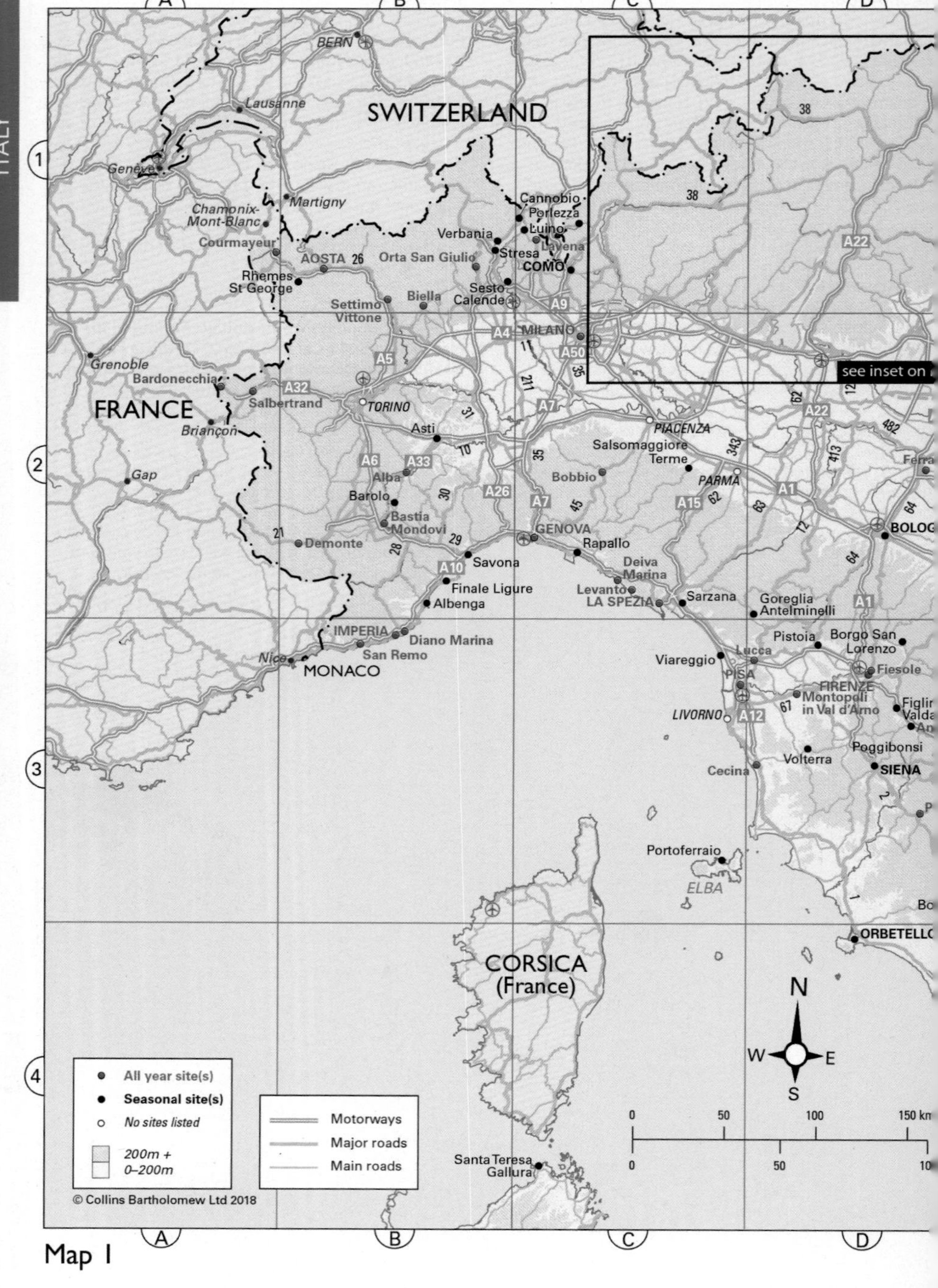

SWITZERLAND
FRANCE
CORSICA (France)
BERN
Lausanne
Genève
Martigny
Chamonix-Mont-Blanc
Courmayeur
AOSTA
Rhemes St George
Settimo Vittone
Biella
Orta San Giulio
Cannobio
Porlezza
Luino
Verbania
Stresa
Lavena
COMO
Sesto Calende
MILANO
Grenoble
Bardonecchia
Salbertrand
TORINO
Briançon
Gap
Asti
Alba
Barolo
Bastia Mondovi
Demonte
Savona
GENOVA
Rapallo
Finale Ligure
Albenga
IMPERIA
Diano Marina
San Remo
Nice
MONACO
PIACENZA
Salsomaggiore Terme
Bobbio
PARMA
Deiva Marina
Levanto
LA SPEZIA
Sarzana
Goreglia Antelminelli
Pistoia
Borgo San Lorenzo
Lucca
Viareggio
PISA
Fiesole
FIRENZE
Montopoli in Val d'Arno
LIVORNO
Volterra
Poggibonsi
SIENA
Cecina
Portoferraio
ELBA
ORBETELLO
BOLOG
Santa Teresa Gallura
see inset on
N
W
E
S
All year site(s)
Seasonal site(s)
No sites listed
200m +
0–200m
Motorways
Major roads
Main roads
0 50 100 150 km
© Collins Bartholomew Ltd 2018

Map 1

AUSTRIA
SLOVENIA
CROATIA
BOSNIA AND HERZEGOVINA
SAN MARINO
ADRIATIC SEA
Sesto/Sexten
CORTINA D'AMPEZZO
Forni di Sopra
TRIESTE
Aquileia
Bibione
Lido di Jesolo
Cavallino
Punta Sabbioni
Chioggia
Pula
Cervia
Cesenatico
Bellaria
Senigallia
ANCONA
Ostra
Porto Recanati
Magione
PERUGIA
Assisi
Bevagna
Urbisaglia
Sarnano
Montefortino
Martinsicuro
Ascolo Piceni
Preci
Castelsantangelo sul Nera
Roseto degli Abruzzi
Terni
PESCARA
L'AQUILA
Fiano Romano
Casalbordino
ROMA
Pescasseroli
Roccaraso
Barrea
Vieste
Manfredonia
FOGGIA
Sperlonga
BARI
Monopoli
SARAJEVO
Split
Vipiteno/Sterzing
Brunico/Bruneck
San Valentino alla Muta
Mals/Malles Venosta
Goldrain
Merano/Meran
Naturno/Naturns
Chiusa/Klausen
Prato allo Stelvio
Trafoi
St Moritz
Fie/Vols
BOLZANO/BOZEN
Canazei
Pozza di Fassa
Predazzo
San Michele All'Adige
Pieve Tesino
TRENTO
Levico Terme
Arsie
Sorico
Gravedona
Menaggio
Bellagio
Edolo
Lecco
Riva del Garda
Arco
Limone sul Garda
Torbole
Idro
Malcesine
Bergamo
Iseo
Monza
San Felice del Benaco
Manerba del Garda
Bardolino
Sirmione
Lazise
DESENZANO DEL GARDA
Peschiera del Garda
VERONA
VICENZA
50 kms
25 mls
ITALY

Map 2

Map 3

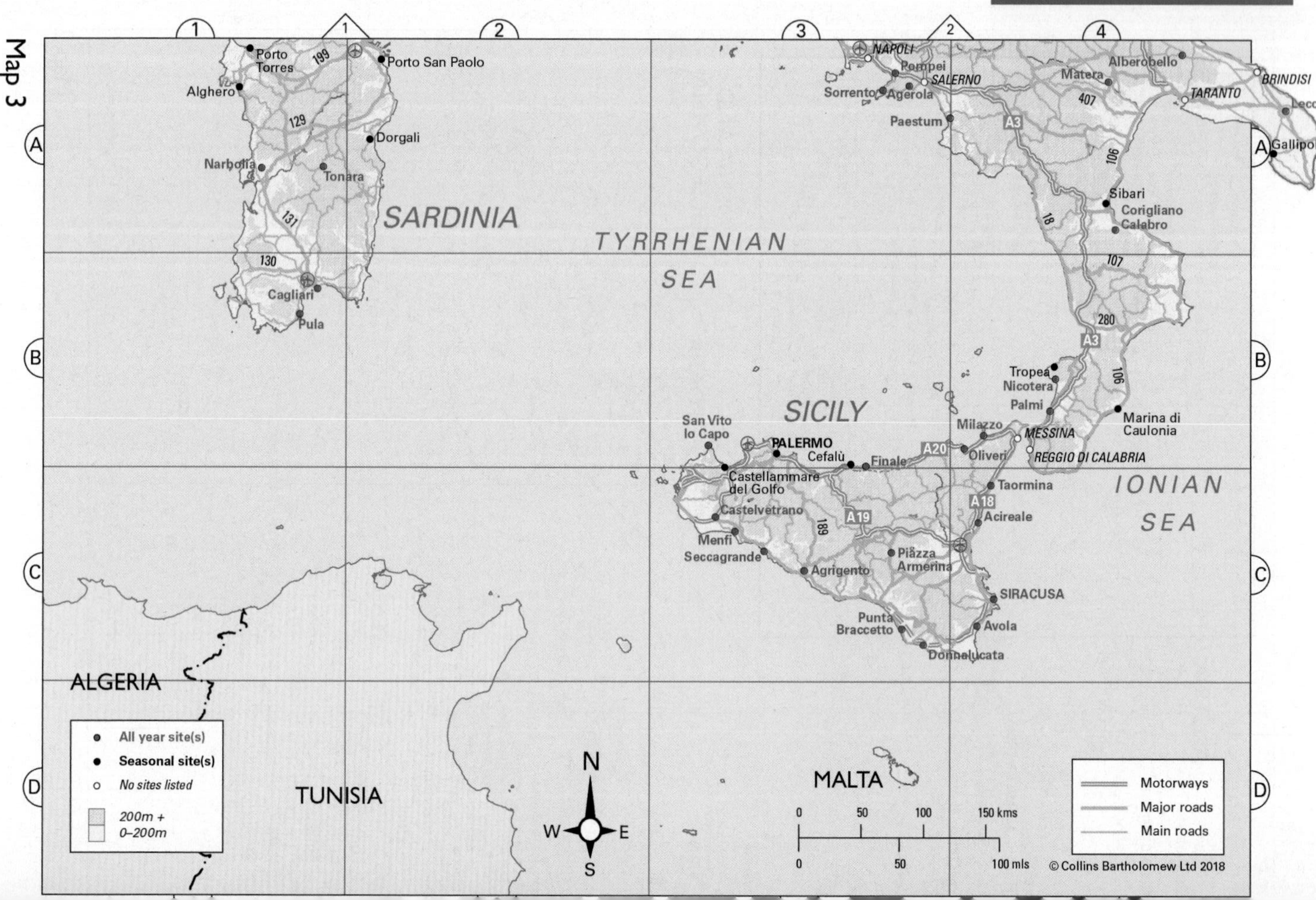

SARDINIA
TYRRHENIAN SEA
SICILY
IONIAN SEA
ALGERIA
TUNISIA
MALTA
Porto Torres
Porto San Paolo
Alghero
Dorgali
Narbolia
Tonara
Cagliari
Pula
199
129
131
130
NAPOLI
Pompei
SALERNO
Sorrento
Agerola
Paestum
Matera
Alberobello
BRINDISI
TARANTO
Lecce
Gallipoli
Sibari
Corigliano Calabro
Tropea
Nicotera
Palmi
Marina di Caulonia
MESSINA
REGGIO DI CALABRIA
Milazzo
Oliveri
San Vito lo Capo
PALERMO
Cefalù
Finale
Castellammare del Golfo
Castelvetrano
Menfi
Seccagrande
Agrigento
Piazza Armerina
Taormina
Acireale
SIRACUSA
Avola
Punta Braccetto
Donnalucata
A3
407
106
18
107
280
A20
A19
A18
189
All year site(s)
Seasonal site(s)
No sites listed
200m +
0–200m
N
S
E
W
0
50
100
150 kms
100 mls
Motorways
Major roads
Main roads
© Collins Bartholomew Ltd 2018

Regions and Provinces of Italy

ABRUZZO
Chieti
L'Aquila
Pescara
Teramo

BASILICATA
Matera
Potenza

CALABRIA
Catanzaro
Cosenza
Crotone
Reggio di Calabria
Vibo Valentia

CAMPANIA
Avellino
Benevento
Caserta
Napoli
Salerno

EMILIA-ROMAGNA
Bologna
Ferrara
Forli
Modena
Parma
Piacenza
Ravenna
Reggio Emilia
Rimini

FRIULI-VENEZIA GIULIA
Gorizia
Pordenone
Trieste
Udine

LAZIO
Frosinone
Latina
Rieti
Roma
Viterbo

LIGURIA
Genova
Imperia
La Spezia
Savona

LOMBARDIA
Bergamo
Brescia
Como
Cremona
Lecco
Lodi
Mantova
Milano
Pavia
Sondrio
Varese

MARCHE
Ancona
Ascoli Piceno
Macerata
Pesaro e Urbino

MOLISE
Campobasso
Isernia

PIEMONTE
Alessandria
Asti
Biella
Cuneo
Novara
Torino
Verbano-Cusio-Ossola
Vercelli

PUGLIA
Bari
Brindisi
Foggia
Lecce
Taranto

SARDEGNA
Cagliari
Nuoro
Oristano
Sassari

SICILIA
Agrigento
Caltanissetta
Catania
Enna
Messina
Palermo
Ragusa
Siracusa
Trapani

TOSCANA
Arezzo
Firenze
Grosseto
Livorno
Lucca
Massa Carrara
Pisa
Pistoia
Prato
Siena

TRENTINO-ALTO ADIGE
Bolzano
Trento

UMBRIA
Perugia
Terni

VALLE D'AOSTA
Aosta/Aoste

VENETO
Belluno
Padova
Rovigo
Treviso
Venezia
Verona
Vicenza

	Ancona	Aosta	Bari	Bologna	Bolzano	Brindisi	Como	Cortina d'Ampezzo	Desanzano del Garda	Firenze (Florence)	Foggia	Genova (Genoa)	Grosseto	Imperia	L'Aquila	La Spezia	Livorno	Messina	Milano (Milan)	Napoli (Naples)	Orbetello	Palermo	Parma	Perugia	Pescara	Piacenza	Pisa	Ravenna	Reggio di Calabria	Roma (Rome)	Salerno	Siena	Siracusa (Syracuse)	Taranto	Torino (Turin)	Trento	Trieste	Venezia (Venice)	Verona
Aosta	619																																						
Bari	467	1075																																					
Bologna	220	404	677																																				
Bolzano	498	447	944	278																																			
Brindisi	573	1188	113	786	1062																																		
Como	475	207	929	258	290	1037																																	
Cortina d'Ampezzo	529	543	981	317	102	1090	381																																
Desanzano del Garda	385	296	839	170	188	937	134	243																															
Firenze (Florence)	262	472	724	104	369	836	355	419	261																														
Foggia	343	947	138	552	825	249	803	864	718	635																													
Genova (Genoa)	508	245	948	299	422	1062	186	497	255	225	842																												
Grosseto	324	556	634	242	512	745	497	561	463	142	552	303																											
Imperia	622	322	1066	403	529	1170	292	602	363	343	946	122	358																										
L'Aquila	203	794	392	411	697	512	675	730	586	372	272	562	305	722																									
La Spezia	428	348	872	212	370	984	274	432	247	146	773	101	232	220	498																								
Livorno	415	419	768	203	446	882	353	506	321	119	678	174	135	295	437	95																							
Messina	910	1445	455	1088	1342	457	525	1367	1469	975	556	1210	893	1317	731	1124	1022																						
Milano (Milan)	426	178	881	212	290	990	50	376	127	301	760	149	438	244	625	223	296	1272																					
Napoli (Naples)	411	962	263	596	858	374	845	1064	746	487	177	718	410	832	247	841	534	731	788																				
Orbetello	308	585	595	275	540	708	525	602	444	170	508	336	41	455	260	260	176	852	471	364																			
Palermo	147	1682	692	1325	1579	694	1565	427	1604	1212	793	1447	1130	1554	968	1361	1265	237	1584	708	1089																		
Parma	314	315	767	98	243	879	170	315	78	185	644	205	329	310	513	122	194	1398	120	675	358	1127																	
Perugia	141	626	636	264	521	745	511	575	417	155	550	379	180	501	179	301	272	1127	457	434	169	1127	340																
Pescara	153	766	299	363	643	415	623	676	531	406	191	655	396	762	100	574	526	980	574	388	352	980	458	262															
Piacenza	365	252	815	150	261	933	115	356	115	242	703	145	379	247	565	162	236	1452	66	725	411	1452	63	399	508														
Pisa	358	401	787	182	446	902	329	487	302	100	700	162	150	270	419	77	19	1279	279	554	179	1279	172	253	499	214													
Ravenna	149	477	605	78	355	716	334	306	245	137	488	374	279	478	353	292	255	1317	285	636	306	1317	173	196	295	229	235												
Reggio di Calabria	910	1441	452	1093	1346	459	1333	1367	1232	975	557	1205	890	1315	728	1128	1018	237	1268	499	576	237	1166	890	741	1219	1035	1086											
Roma (Rome)	286	748	450	379	645	563	632	697	535	276	362	503	192	618	113	427	322	947	571	226	145	942	463	188	206	515	342	382	707										
Salerno	450	1000	240	634	898	355	885	924	787	532	152	763	448	869	286	881	578	684	830	220	405	684	715	442	295	772	599	636	446	260									
Siena	247	535	677	172	435	785	422	486	328	68	590	291	75	411	281	173	121	1165	366	534	105	1165	252	110	379	304	108	205	929	231	480								
Siracusa (Syracuse)	1064	1599	609	1242	1496	611	1482	1521	1386	1129	710	1364	1047	1471	885	1278	1136	154	135	638	1004	259	1315	1044	897	1369	1196	1234	155	859	601	1082							
Taranto	549	1156	98	760	1031	70	1009	1062	922	805	217	1028	722	1149	479	948	850	627	965	305	660	627	852	713	386	906	865	688	392	517	256	755	544						
Torino (Turin)	547	110	1006	333	412	1116	165	503	257	393	883	172	477	208	715	275	345	1607	142	885	502	1607	245	548	699	178	326	405	1375	674	927	463	1524	1089					
Trento	442	394	893	297	60	998	233	135	100	312	773	365	452	475	642	342	413	1525	242	799	485	1525	192	472	582	210	392	296	1286	593	845	381	1442	974	353				
Trieste	506	582	958	295	347	1072	421	236	286	396	839	537	538	643	706	502	492	1607	415	884	567	1607	361	550	652	395	468	288	1374	670	923	465	1524	1045	540	292			
Venezia (Venice)	364	441	816	154	214	931	279	165	147	255	694	399	399	505	566	364	348	1464	274	741	427	1464	218	413	508	255	332	143	1229	533	781	322	1381	899	403	158	159		
Verona	354	331	811	140	155	917	172	236	30	234	689	289	374	388	555	220	295	1439	167	716	403	1439	105	389	503	142	279	215	1206	505	761	295	1356	889	289	103	253	115	
Vicenza	360	376	814	150	183	925	216	167	81	252	693	334	394	439	562	374	347	1464	209	746	424	1464	155	410	505	191	327	166	1223	528	785	322	1381	901	342	144	213	73	52

Milano (Milan) to Venezia (Venice) = 274km

View from Ville Haute, Luxembourg City

Welcome to Luxembourg

Although a tiny country just over 50 miles long, Luxembourg is one of the world's economic powerhouses. Luxembourg City is famous for its stunning, medieval old town and for the number of notable museums and galleries that it boasts.

Most of the country is rural, and the landscape varies from the micro-gorges of Müllerthal to the vineyards of the Moselle wine region. It is a beautiful country with plenty packed in to its borders.

Country highlights

Luxembourg cuisine is heavily influenced by its neighbours and in particular has many Germanic flavourings. Judd mat Gaardebounen, which is a smoked collar of pork with broad beans, is a particularly popular meal and is widely recognised as one of the country's national dishes.

The Festival of Wiltz is an annual affair that celebrates some of the most talented international musicians. With its open air setting and castle backdrop, it attracts large audiences each year and is considered to be a cultural highlight.

Major towns and cities

- Luxembourg City – this fascinating capital lies in the heart of Europe.
- Esch-sur-Alzette – this city has the longest shopping street in the country.
- Diekirck – a city with charming old streets.
- Dudelange – a cultural centre with lots to see.

Attractions

- Mullerthal Trail – explore 112km of varied landscape, from forests to rock formations.
- Vianden Castle, Vianden – a grand building that originates from the 10th century.
- National Museum of Art and History, Luxembourg City – enjoy a fascinating range of exhibitions from archaeology to fine arts.
- Holy Ghost Citadel, Luxembourg City – a majestic fortress with stunning views.

Find out more

www.visitluxembourg.lu
Tel: +352 (0) 42 82 82 10 Luxembourg Tourist Office

Country Information

Population (approx): 570,000

Capital: Luxembourg City (population approx 107,000)

Area: 2,586 sq km

Bordered by: Belgium, France, Germany

Terrain: Rolling hills to north with broad, shallow valleys; steep slope to Moselle valley in south-east

Climate: Temperate climate without extremes of heat or cold; mild winters; warm, wet summers; July and August are the hottest months; May and June have the most hours of sunshine.

Highest Point: Kneiff 560m

Languages: French, German, Lëtzebuergesch (Luxembourgish)

Local Time: GMT or BST + 1, i.e. 1 hour ahead of the UK all year

Currency: Euros divided into 100 cents; £1 = €1.13, €1 = £0.88 (November 2017)

Emergency numbers: Police 113; Fire brigade 112; Ambulance 112. Operators speak English

Public Holidays 2018: Jan 1; Apr 2; May 1, 10,21; Jun 23; Aug 15; Nov 1; Dec 25, 26.

There are other dates such as Luxembourg City Fete and 2 Nov which are not official holidays but many businesses, banks and shops may close. School summer holidays run from mid-July to mid-September.

Camping and Caravanning

There are approximately 120 campsites in Luxembourg; most are open from April to October. Apart from in the industrial south, campsites are found all over the country. The Ardennes, the river banks along the Moselle and the Sûre and the immediate surroundings of Luxembourg City are particularly popular.

Casual/wild camping is only permitted with a tent, not a caravan, but permission must first be sought from the landowner.

Motorhomes

Many campsites have motorhome amenities and some offer Quick Stop overnight facilities at reduced rates.

Electricity and Gas

Most campsites have a supply of between 6 and 16 amps and many have CEE connections. Plugs have two round pins. The full range of Campingaz cylinders is widely available.

Entry Formalities

British and Irish passport holders may stay for up to three months without a visa.

Medical Services

Emergency medical treatment is available on presentation of a European Health Insurance Card (EHIC) but you will be charged both for treatment and prescriptions. Refunds can be obtained from a local sickness insurance fund office, Caisse de Maladie des Ouvriers (CMO). Emergency hospital treatment is normally free apart from a non-refundable standard daily fee.

Opening Hours

Banks: Mon-Fri 8.30am-12 noon & 1.30pm-4.30pm.Some stay open to 6pm and open Sat 9am-12 noon.

Museums: Tue-Sun 10am-6pm, Thurs late opening 5pm-8pm (check locally); most close Mon.

Post Offices: Mon-Fri 8am-12 noon & 1.30pm-4.30pm/5pm; the central post office in Luxembourg City is open 7am-7pm Mon to Fri & 7am-5pm Sat.

Shops: Mon-Sat 9am/10am-6pm/6.30pm. Some close for lunch and Mon mornings. Large malls may be open to 8pm or 9pm.

Safety and Security

There are few reports of crime but visitors should take the usual commonsense precautions against pickpockets. Do not leave valuables in your car.

Luxembourg shares with the rest of Europe an underlying threat from terrorism. Attacks could be indiscriminate and against civilian targets in public places, including tourist sites.

British Embassy

BOULEVARD JOSEPH II, L-1840 LUXEMBOURG
Tel: 22 98 64
www.ukinluxembourg.fco.gov.uk

Irish Embassy
Résidence Christina (2nd floor)

28 ROUTE D'ARLON, L-1140 LUXEMBOURG
Tel: 450 6101
www.embassyofireland.lu

Documents

Passport

When driving it is easy to cross into neighbouring countries without realising it. Although you are unlikely to be asked for it, you must have your valid passport with you.

Vehicle(s)

Drivers of foreign-registered vehicles must be able to produce on demand a current driving licence, vehicle registration document (V5C) insurance certificate, insurance certificate and MOT certificate (if applicable).

Money

Major credit cards are widely accepted although there are often minimum amount requirements. Cash machines are widespread. Carry your credit card issuers'/banks' 24-hour UK contact numbers in case of loss or theft of your cards.

Motoring in Luxembourg

Alcohol

The maximum permitted level of alcohol is 50 milligrams in 100 millilitres of blood, i.e. lower than that permitted in the UK (80 milligrams). For drivers who have held a driving licence for less than two years the permitted level is 20 milligrams i.e. virtually nil. Breath tests are compulsory following serious road accidents and road offences.

Breakdown Service

A 24-hour breakdown service 'Service Routier' is operated by the Automobile Club De Grand-Duche de Luxembourg (ACL) on all roads, telephone 26000. Operators speak English. Payment by credit card is accepted.

Essential Equipment

Warning Triangle

A warning triangle must be used if the vehicle is immobilised on the roadway.

Lights

The use of dipped headlights in the daytime is recommended for all vehicles.

Reflective Jacket/ Waistcoat

It is compulsory to wear a reflective jacket when getting out of your vehicle on a motorway or main road. Pedestrians walking at night or in bad visibility outside built-up areas must also wear one.

Child Restraint System

Children under the age of 3 years old must be seated in an approved child restraint system.

Children from the ages of 3 to 17 and/or under the height of 1.5m must be seated in an appropriate restraint system. If they are over 36kg in weight they can use a seat belt but only if they are in the rear of the vehicle.

Rear-facing child restraint systems are not allowed on seats with front airbags unless the airbag has been deactivated.

Tyres

Vehicles are required to have M&S (Mud and Snow) marked tyres fitted when driving in wintery conditions (frost, snow, ice etc.). This regulation applies to all drivers, regardless of where the vehicle is registered.

Fuel

Petrol stations are generally open from 8am to 8pm with 24 hour service on motorways. Most accept credit cards and many have automatic pumps operated with a credit card.

It is illegal to carry petrol in a can.

LPG is available at a handful of petrol stations – see www.mylpg.eu and use the drop down menu listed under LPG stations.

Overtaking

When overtaking at night outside built-up areas it is compulsory to flash headlights.

Parking

Parking is prohibited where there are yellow lines or zigzag white lines. Blue zone parking areas exist in Luxembourg City, Esch-sur-Elzette, Dudelange and Wiltz. Parking discs are obtainable from the ACL, police stations, tourist offices and shops. Parking meters operate in Luxembourg City. Police will clamp or remove illegally parked vehicles.

There are free car parks two to three kilometres outside Luxembourg City and Esch-sur-Elzette from which regular buses leave for the city.

If there is no public lighting when parking on a public road sidelights must be switched on.

Priority

Where two roads of the same category intersect, traffic from the right has priority. In towns give priority to traffic coming from the right, unless there is a 'priority road' sign (yellow diamond with white border) indicating that the driver using that road has right of way.

Road Signs and Markings

Road signs and markings conform to international standards and are shown in French and German. Traffic lights pass from red immediately to green (no red and amber phase). A flashing amber light allows traffic to turn in the direction indicated, traffic permitting. In Luxembourg City some bus lanes and cycle lanes are marked in red.

Speed Limits

	Open Road (km/h)	Motorway (km/h)
Car Solo	90	130
Car towing caravan/trailer	75	90
Motorhome under 3500kg	90	130
Motorhome 3500-7500kg	90	130

The top speed of 130 km/h (80 mph) for solo cars is reduced to 110 km/h (68 mph) in wet weather. The speed limit for drivers who have held a licence for less than a year is 90 km/h (56 mph) on motorways and 75 km/h (47 mph) outside built-up areas. In some residential areas called 'Zones de Rencontre' the maximum permitted speed is 20 km/h (13 mph).

Traffic Jams

Many holidaymakers travel through Luxembourg in order to take advantage of its cheaper fuel. Queues at petrol stations often cause traffic congestion, in particular along the 'petrol route' past Martelange (N4 in Belgium), at Dudelange on the A3/E25 at the Belgium-Luxembourg border, and at the motorway junction near Steinfort on the A6.

Other bottlenecks occur, particularly during weekends in July and August, at the junctions on the A1/E44 near Gasperich to the south of Luxembourg City, and the exit from the A3/E25 at Dudelange. To avoid traffic jams between Luxembourg City and Thionville (France), leave the western ring road around Luxembourg and take the A4 to Esch-sur-Alzette and then the D16. When past Aumetz join the N52 which then connects to the A30 to Metz.

The website www.cita.lu provides webcam views of all motorways and information on traffic flow.

Violation of Traffic Regulations

Police officers may impose on the spot fines for infringement of regulations. These must be settled in cash and a receipt given. Non-residents of Luxembourg are liable to receive penalty points for serious infringements of traffic law.

Motorways

There are approximately 152km of motorways, all of which are toll-free for private vehicles. Motorway service areas are situated at Capellen on the A6 near Mamer, at Pontpierre on the A4, and at Berchem near Bettenbourg on the A3.

Emergency telephones are situated every 1.5km along main roads and motorways and link motorists to the 'Protection Civile'.

Touring

Luxembourg is the only Grand Duchy in the world and measures a maximum of 81km (51 miles) from north to south and 51km (32 miles) from east to west. The fortifications and old town of Luxembourg City have been designated as a UNESCO World Heritage site.

Smoking is not allowed in bars and restaurants. A service charge is usually added to restaurant bills and it is normal practice to leave a little extra if the service is good.

The Luxembourg Card is valid for one, two or three days, and entitles the holder to free public transport, admission to numerous museums and tourist attractions, and discounts on sightseeing trips. It is available from tourist offices, campsites, hotels, information and public transport offices as well as from participating attractions. You can also buy it online at www.ont.lu.

There are many marked walking trails throughout the country – see www.hiking-in-luxembourg.co.uk for full details. A Christmas market is held in the pedestrianised Place d'Armes in Luxembourg City. Others are held in towns and villages throughout the country.

French is the official language, but Luxembourgish is the language most commonly used. English is widely spoken in Luxembourg City, but less so elsewhere.

Public Transport & Local Travel

A transport network ticket (billet réseau) is available at railway stations throughout the country and at the airport. It allows unlimited travel on city buses, trains and country coaches for one day (until 8am the next morning) throughout Luxembourg. Public transport maps can be downloaded from the Luxembourg Tourist Office website, www.luxembourg.co.uk.

Luxembourg is a compact city and walking around it is easy and pleasant. It is served by an efficient network of buses. You can buy bus tickets valid either for two hours (billet de courte durée) or one day (billet de longue durée). A discount is offered on a block of 10 tickets. Tickets must be validated at the machines on buses and train platforms. Dogs are allowed free of charge on city buses. People over 65 years of age may qualify for travel concessions; show your passport as proof of age.

View over remich, wine capital of luxembourg

Sites in Luxembourg

ALZINGEN see Luxembourg City *C3*

BERDORF see Echternach *C3*

BETTENDORF *C2* (1km SE Rural) *49.87262, 6.22137* **Camping Um Wirt, 12 Rue de la Gare, L-9353 Bettendorf [tel 808386; fax 26804792; info@campingumwirt.lu; campingumwirt.lu]** Foll the N17/N19 Diekirch/Echternach. Turn R and foll camping signs in Bettendorf. Med, pt shd or shd; wc; chem disp; shwrs; EHU (10A); lndry; rest/café; bar; playgrnd; rv adj; games area; games rm; entmnt; wifi; 70% statics; dogs €2.50; Eng spkn; adv bkg; red LS; bowling green; trampoline; tennis court; sports field; "Vg site; gd walking & cycling; open plan, grassy site."
1 Apr-15 Oct. € 25.00 2013*

BORN SUR SURE *C3* (500m NE Rural) *49.76081, 6.51672* **Camping Officiel Born-Sûre, 9 Rue du Camping, 6660 Born-sur-Sûre [tel/fax 730144; syndicat@gmx.lu; www.camping-born.lu]** E along E44 sp Trier; leave immed bef ent Germany. On N10 go N sp Echternach; ignore sat nav & drive to end of vill, site sp. Med, mkd pitch, pt shd; wc; chem disp; shwrs inc; EHU (6A); lndry; supmkt 8km; rest, snacks; bar; BBQ; htd pool 8km; fishing; boating; 70% statics; dogs €2.50; wifi; phone; Eng spkn; adv bkg; some rd noise; ccard acc; CKE/CCI. "Gd, clean site; all tourers on rvside; if barrier clsd find contact in bar; excel." ♦
1 Apr-1 Oct. € 16.00 2014*

CLERVAUX *B2* (16km SW Rural) *49.97045, 5.93450* **Camping Kaul, Rue Joseph Simon, 9550 Wiltz [tel 950359; fax 957770; icamping@campingkaul.lu; www.campingkaul.lu]** Turn N off rd 15 (Bastogne-Ettelbruck) to Wiltz, foll sp N to Ville Basse & Camping. Lge, mkd pitch, unshd; htd wc; chem disp; mv service pnt; fam bthrm; shwrs €0.50; EHU (6-10A) €2.50-2.75; gas; lndry; shop high ssn & 500m; snacks; playgrnd; pool adj; waterslides; tennis; dogs €1.50; poss cr; quiet; adv bkg. "Gd site; pitches tight for awnings if site full; excel san facs & take-away; local children use playgrnd." ♦ 1 Apr-31 Oct. € 28.00
2014*

DIEKIRCH *C2* (10km E Rural) *49.86852, 6.26430* **Camping de la Rivière, 21 Rue de la Sûre, 9390 Reisdorf [tel/fax 836398; campingreisdorf@pt.lu; www.campingreisdorf.com]** Fr Diekirch take N19 (sp Echternach) for 10km to where rd crosses Rv Sûre. Site on L after bdge. Med, mkd pitch, pt shd; htd wc; chem disp; shwrs €1.10; EHU (6-10A) metered; gas; lndry (inc dryer); shop adj; rest, snacks; bar; playgrnd; internet; 20% statics; dogs €1.50; bus; poss cr; Eng spkn; quiet; red CKE/CCI. "Lovely site in beautiful countryside; excel for walking/cycling; helpful, friendly owners; gd touring base." ♦ ltd. Feb-Nov. € 15.00
2013*

DIEKIRCH *C2* (500m SE Urban) *49.86635, 6.16513* **Camping de la Sûre, 34 Route de Gilsdorf, 9234 Diekirch [tel 809425; fax 802786; tourisme@diekirch.lu; www.diekirch.lu]** Fr town cent take N14 twds Larochette, then 1st L after x-ing rv bdge. Well sp. Lge, mkd pitch, pt shd; htd wc; chem disp; fam bthrm; shwrs €1; EHU (10A) €2.50; lndry; shop 500m; bar; playgrnd; pool 200m; 50% statics; dogs €2; m'van o'night area outside gates; Eng spkn; adv bkg; quiet; ccard acc; red CKE/CCI. "Nice welcome; excel, clean facs; pleasant rvside site 5 mins walk fr town cent; vg touring base, Battle of Bulge Museum nrby." ♦
1 Apr-30 Sep. € 20.50 2012*

DIEKIRCH *C2* (900m S Rural) *49.86768, 6.16984* **Camping op der Sauer, Route de Gilsdorf, L 9234 Diekirch [tel 808590; fax 809470; info@campsauer.lu; www.campsauer.lu]** On rd 14 to Larochette, on S o'skts of Diekirch. 1st L after x-ing rv bdge, site well sp on L past Camping de la Sûre and behind sports facs. Lge, mkd pitch, pt shd; htd wc; chem disp; shwrs inc; EHU (6A) €3; gas; lndry; shop & 400m; rest, snacks; bar; playgrnd; pool 400m; dogs €2.50; bus 800m; Eng spkn; adv bkg; CKE/CCI. "On banks Rv Sûre; sh walk/cycle to town; spacious site; friendly owners; ltd facs LS; gd, basic site; helpful recep; clean san facs with plenty of hot water; vet is 20 mins walk."
1 Mar-31 Oct. € 21.00 2015*

ECHTERNACH *C3* (2km SE Rural) *49.79681, 6.43122* **Camping Alferweiher, Alferweiher 1, 6412 Echternach [tel/fax 720271; info@camping-alferweiher.lu; www.camping-alferweiher.lu]** Fr S on N10 turn R at traff lts & pictogram fishing/camping. Then L at sp to Alferweiher. Lge, mkd pitch, pt shd; htd wc; chem disp; mv service pnt; fam bthrm; shwrs inc; EHU (10A) €2.75; gas; lndry; shop; snacks; bar; playgrnd; bike hire; TV rm; entmnt; dogs €2; poss cr; Eng spkn; adv bkg; quiet; CKE/CCI. "Gd walking; office open 0900-1300 & 1400-1800; if shut site yourself - elec boxes not locked; hot water in individ cubicles in san facs block only, other basins cold water; popular site but in need of some tlc (2017)." ♦
21 Apr-17 Sep. € 24.00 2017*

⊞ **ECHTERNACH** *C3* (6km NW Rural) *49.81958, 6.34737* **Camping Belle-Vue 2000, 29 Rue de Consdorf, 6551 Berdorf [tel 790635 or 808149; fax 799349; campbv2000@gmail.com]** Nr cent of vill on rd to Consdorf. 2nd of 3 adj sites with facs on L on way out of vill. Lge, hdg pitch, terr, pt shd; htd wc; chem disp; fam bthrm; shwrs inc; EHU (6A) €2.5; gas; lndry; shop; snacks; BBQ; playgrnd; pool 500m; games rm; 50% statics; dogs; phone; adv bkg; quiet; CKE/CCI. "Gd walking; attractive vill with gd rests; open in Jan only if no snow; pitches poss soft after rain; owner's son now running & improving site (2017)." € 19.00 2017*

ECHTERNACH *C3* (6km NW Rural) *49.81904, 6.34694* **Camping Bon Repos, 39 Rue de Consdorf, 6551 Berdorf [tel 790631; fax 799571; irma@bonrepos.lu; www.bonrepos.lu]** In cent Echternach at x-rds take Vianden rd, then in 2km turn L to Berdorf thro vill twds Consdorf. Site nr cent vill on L adj Camping Belle-Vue. Fr Luxembourg thro Consdorf to Berdorf, site on R on ent to vill, clearly sp. Med, hdg/mkd pitch, terr, pt sl, pt shd; htd wc; chem disp; fam bthrm; shwrs inc; EHU (16A) €2.80 (poss rev pol); gas; lndry; shop adj; rest & bar 100m; playgrnd; pool 5km; games rm; wifi; TV; no dogs; bus 100m; Eng spkn; adv bkg; quiet; red long stay; CKE/CCI. "Clean, tidy site - best in area; clean facs; helpful, friendly owners; some pitches sm; forest walks fr site; conv for trips to Germany; pleasant site but v small pitches." 1 Apr-4 Nov. € 18.00 2017*

⊞ **ESCH SUR ALZETTE** *B3* (2km E Rural) *49.48761, 5.98554* **Camping Gaalgebierg, 4001 Esch-sur-Alzette [tel 541069; fax 549630; gaalcamp@pt.lu; www.gaalgebierg.lu]** Sp in cent of town, turn L dir Kayl. Under rlwy bdge sharp R, up steep hill. Lge, hdstg, terr, shd; htd wc; fam bthrm; shwrs inc; EHU (16A) €1.50 but elec for heating metered & restricted in bad weather; lndry; shop; snacks; bar; playgrnd; pool 2km; TV conn all pitches; mainly statics; bus 1km; train to Luxembourg city; Eng spkn; quiet; ccard acc; CKE/CCI. "V clean san facs; gd walks; park & sm zoo adj site; well-kept site; poss boggy when wet." ♦ € 20.70 2013*

"Satellite navigation makes touring much easier"

Remember most sat navs don't know if you're towing or in a larger vehicle – always use yours alongside maps and site directions.

ESCH SUR SURE *B2* (1km SE Rural) *49.90693, 5.94220* **Camping Im Aal, 7 Rue du Moulin, 9650 Esch-sur-Sûre [tel 839514; fax 899117; info@camping-im-aal.lu; www.campingaal.lu]** Fr N turn R off N15 onto N27 sp Esch-sur-Sûre. Pass thro sh tunnel, site on L in 500m on banks of Rv Sûre. Lge, hdg/mkd pitch, pt sl, pt shd; htd wc; chem disp; shwrs inc; EHU (6A) €2; lndry (inc dryer); shop & 500m; bar; playgrnd adj; fishing; 50% statics; dogs €2; site clsd 1 Jan-14 Feb; Eng spkn; quiet; cash only; red CKE/CCI. "Well-kept, clean site; gd welcome; gd, modern facs; some rvside pitches; walks along towpath & in woods; gd for wheelchair users; gd fishing, walking; gd NH & longer." ♦ 12 Feb-11 Dec. € 24.00 2016*

ETTELBRUCK *B2* (4km E Rural) *49.85043, 6.13461* **Camping Gritt, 2 Rue Gritt, 9161 Ingeldorf [tel 802018; fax 802019; apeeters@pt.lu; www.campinggritt.lu]** On N15 fr Bastogne turn R at rndabt in Ettelbrück sp Diekirch, go under A7 sp Diekirch. In 3km at end of elevated section foll slip rd sp Diekirch, Ettelbrück, Ingeldorf. At rndabt take 2nd exit sp Ingledorf, site on R over narr rv bdge. Fr Diekirch on N7 fork L twd Ingeldorf. Site on L over rv bdge. Lge, mkd pitch, pt shd; htd wc; chem disp; fam bthrm; mv service pnt; shwrs inc; EHU (6A) €2.80; gas; lndry; supmkt 1.5km; snacks; bar; BBQ; rv sw 1.5km; playgrnd; fishing, canoe hire, tennis nrby; ltd wifi; entmnt; games/TV rm; 30% statics; dogs €2; twin-axles acc (rec check in adv); bus/train to Luxembourg City; recep 0900-1800 high ssn; poss cr; Eng spkn; adv bkg; quiet; red for groups; red LS/CKE/CCI. "Peaceful site; helpful, welcoming Dutch owners; lge pitches with open aspect; gd, modern san facs; pitching still OK after heavy rain; on banks of Rv Sûre (swift-flowing & unfenced); gd walking & sightseeing; rest vg; vg site." ♦ 1 Apr-30 Oct. € 28.40 2014*

ETTELBRUCK *B2* (1.5km W Rural) *49.84600, 6.08193* **Camping Ettelbruck (formerly Kalkesdelt), 88 Chemin du Camping, 9022 Ettelbrück [tel 00 352 81 21 85; fax 00 352 81 98 39; ellen.ringelberg@gmx.de; www.campingettelbruck.com]** Exit Ettelbrück on Bastogne rd N15. Site visible as app town; approx 200m fr town cent fork L into lane, turn R at sp at foot of hill, steep & narr rd. Site sp fr town. Lge, mkd pitch, terr, pt shd; htd wc; chem disp; mv service pnt; fam bthrm; shwrs (€0.5); EHU (16A) €2.90; lndry; shop; rest, snacks; bar; playgrnd; pool 3km; TV; 15% statics; dogs €2.50; phone; poss cr; Eng spkn; adv bkg; quiet; CKE/CCI. "Gd, well-maintained, friendly, family-run site in woods; excel san facs; lge pitches; gd walks; train to Luxumbourg city fr town; vg rest." ♦ 1 Apr-1 Oct. € 30.00 2016*

GREVENMACHER *C3* (800m N Urban) *49.68302, 6.44891* **Camping La Route du Vin, 10 route du Vin, L 6794 Grevenmacher [tel 750234 or 758275; fax 758666; campvin@pt.lu; grevenmacher-tourist.lu/unterkuenfte/camping]** Fr E44/A1 exit junc 14 onto N1 to Grevenmacher. After 1km turn R at T-junc opp Esso g'ge. Site sp in town, ent off rndabt. Med, mkd pitch, pt sl, pt shd; wc; chem disp; shwrs inc; EHU (16A) €2.50; lndry; shop, rest, snacks 500m; bar; pool adj; games area; games rm; tennis; child entmnt; wifi; 60% statics; dogs €1; Eng spkn; adv bkg; quiet, some rlwy noise; CKE/CCI. "Easy walk to town cent; wine festival in Sep; pleasant, well kept site; excel new san facs (2015); boat trips; rvside walks; excel base for touring Moselle & Luxembourg; views; helpful staff; excel." ♦ 1 Apr-30 Sep. € 19.40 2017*

HEIDERSCHEID see Ettelbrück *B2*

INGELDORF see Ettelbrück *B2*

⊞ **KAUTENBACH** *B2* (1km E Rural) *49.95387, 6.02730* **Camping Kautenbach, An der Weierbaach, 9663 Kautenbach [tel 950303; fax 950093; campkaut@pt.lu; www.campingkautenbach.lu]** Travelling E fr Bastogne on N84, approx 5km after Luxembourg border take N26 to Wiltz & foll sp to Kautenbach/Kiischpelt. In 10km turn L over bdge into vill, site sp 800m. Lge, mkd pitch, pt shd; htd wc; chem disp; shwrs inc; fam bthrm; EHU (6A) inc; gas; lndry; shop; rest, snacks; bar; BBQ; playgrnd; entmnt; bike hire; wifi; TV rm; 20% statics; phone; dogs; site clsd 21 Dec-14 Jan; Eng spkn; adv bkg; quiet but some rlwy noise; ccard acc. "Gd for walking & mountain biking; long site along beautiful, secluded rv valley." ♦
€ 26.00 2016*

KOCKELSCHEUER see Luxembourg City *C3*

LAROCHETTE *C3* (2km W Rural) *49.78525, 6.21010* **Iris Parc Camping Birkelt, 1 Um Birkelt, 7633 Larochette [tel 879040; fax 879041; info@camping-birkelt.lu; www.camping-birkelt.lu]** Fr Diekirch take N14 to Larochette; turn R in town on CR118 (N8), foll sp for Mersch. At top of hill foll site sp. Fr Luxembourg take N7 foll sp for Mersch & Ettelbruck (ignore Larochette sp bef Mersch). Turn R bef rv bdge at Mersch onto CR118 & foll rd to o'skts of town. Site on R beyond municipal sports cent - fairly steep, winding app rd. Lge, hdg/mkd pitch, pt sl, pt shd; htd wc; chem disp; mv service pnt; serviced pitch; fam bthrm; sauna; shwrs inc; EHU (16A) inc; gas; lndry (inc dryer); shop; rest, snacks; bar; BBQ (gas/charcoal only); playgrnd; 2 pools (1 htd, covrd); paddling pool; tennis; fitness rm; horseriding; fishing, canoeing, golf 5km; bike hire; games rm; games area; games rm; wifi; entmnt; TV rm; 50% statics; dogs €2.50; no o'fits over 9m; poss cr; Eng spkn; ccard acc; red LS; CKE/CCI. "Excel, well-kept, busy site in pleasant wooded hilltop location; friendly, helpful staff; ideal for families; gd san facs, poss stretched high ssn; access poss diff lge o'fits, care req; late arr report to rest/bar; gd bar & rest, open in LS." ♦
25 Mar-6 Nov. € 38.50 SBS - H08 2014*

LAROCHETTE *C3* (7km W Rural) *49.78521, 6.16596* **Camping Nommerlayen, Rue Nommerlayen, 7465 Nommern [tel 878078; fax 879678; info@nommerlayen-ec.lu; www.nommerlayen-ec.lu]** N7 Luxembourg to Diekirch. At Mersch N8 E dir Larochette & Nommern. Site is 1km S of Nommern. Lge, hdg/mkd pitch, terr, pt shd; htd wc; mv service pnt; chem disp; fam bthrm; sauna; shwrs inc; private bthrms avail; EHU (10A) inc; gas; lndry (inc dryer); shop; rest, snacks; bar; playgrnd; htd pool; paddling pool; tennis, games area; games rm; bike hire; wifi; entmnt; TV; 40% statics; dogs €3; Eng spkn; adv bkg; quiet; red LS/snr citizens. "Superb site & facs." ♦ Ltd
1 Mar-5 Nov. € 40.00 SBS - H20 2017*

See advertisement

LAROCHETTE *C3* (3km NW Rural) *49.79991, 6.19816* **Camping auf Kengert, Kengert, 7633 Larochette [tel 837186; fax 878323; info@kengert.lu; www.kengert.lu]** N8 dir Mersch, CR19 dir Schrondweiler. Site sp fr cent Larochette. Lge, mkd pitch, sl, shd; htd wc; chem disp; mv service pnt; fam bthrm; sauna; shwrs inc; EHU (4-16A) €2; gas; lndry; shop; rest, snacks; bar; 2 playgrnds (1 indoor); solar htd pool; solarium; wifi; some statics; dogs €2; poss cr; Eng spkn; adv bkg; quiet; CKE/CCI. "Vg facs; Luxembourg Card (red on attractions & public transport) avail at recep; peaceful, friendly site; excel rest; gd local walks/cycle rtes; ltd hdstdg for MH's." ♦ 1 Mar-8 Nov. € 34.50 2017*

⊞ **LIELER** *B2* (500m SW Rural) *50.12365, 6.10509* **Camping Trois Frontières, Hauptstroos 12, 9972 Lieler [tel 998608; fax 979184; info@troisfrontieres.lu; www.troisfrontieres.lu]** Fr N7/E421 turn E sp Lieler, site sp. Med, mkd pitch, pt shd; htd wc; chem disp; mv service pnt; fam bthrm; shwrs; EHU (6A) €2.75; lndry (inc dryer); rest, snacks; bar; playgrnd; pool; paddling pool; bike hire; games rm; games area; wifi; entmnt; TV; some statics; dogs €2.20; adv bkg; quiet. "V pleasant site; gd touring base; site under new ownership (2014); ACSI registered; discount in LS."
€ 32.00 2014*

LUXEMBOURG CITY *C3* (7km S Rural) *49.57220, 6.10857* **Camping Kockelscheuer, 22 Route de Bettembourg, 1899 Kockelscheuer [tel 471815; fax 401243; caravani@pt.lu; www.ccclv.lu/site/index.php/en]** Fr N on A6 then A4 exit junc 1 sp Leudelange/Kockelscheuer, at top of slip rd turn L N4. After about 1.5km turn R N186 sp Bettemburg/Kockelscheuer & foll camp sp. Foll sp 'Park & Ride', site is 1st R. Fr S exit A3 junc 2 sp Bettembourg & Kockelscheuer. In 700m turn R dir Kockelscheuer & in 3km turn L & foll site sp, rd numberd CR196. Lge, some hdg/mkd pitch, pt terr, pt shd; htd wc; chem disp; mv service pnt; shwrs inc; EHU (10-16A) metered (check pol); gas; lndry (inc dryer); shop; rest adj; snacks; bar; playgrnd; pool 4km; sports complex adj; internet; sat TV; dogs free; bus to city 400m (tickets fr site recep); office & gates clsd 1200-1400 & 2230-0700; Eng spkn; adv bkg; some rd & aircraft noise during day; ccard not acc; LS weekly rate for snr citizens; 10% red CKE/CCI. "Rec arr early afternoon as popular; well-run, clean, pretty site; helpful, pleasant staff; gd san facs; pitch access on lower level needs care; gd size pitches on terr; poss boggy after rain; gd dog walks nrby; useful NH for Zeebrugge; excel site." ♦ 12 Apr-31 Oct. € 19.50 2014*

LUXEMBOURG CITY *C3* (9km S Rural) *49.56907, 6.16010* **Camping Bon Accueil, 2 Rue du Camping, 5815 Alzingen [tel/fax 367069; www.camping-alzingen.lu]** Fr Luxembourg city take A3/E25 S, exit junc 1 sp Hespérange. Cont thro town to Alzingen, site sp on R after Mairie, well sp. Med, hdg/mkd pitch, some hdstg, pt shd; htd wc; chem disp; mv service pnt; fam bthrm; shwrs inc; EHU (16A) inc (poss rev pol); gas; lndry; shop, rest; snacks; bar; BBQ; playgrnd; pool 3km; games area; wifi; dogs €3; phone; bus to city adj; twin axles; Eng spkn; adv bkg; poss cr; quiet; ccard acc; CCI/ACSI. "Pleasant, open, clean, tidy site; gd size pitches; friendly staff; vg, clean, modern san facs; hot water metered; lovely gardens adj; clsd 1200-1400 - ltd waiting space; excel base for city; spotlessly clean; vg site; rec arrive early." ♦ 1 Apr-15 Oct. € 16.00 2015*

MAMER see Luxembourg City *C3*

MERSCH *B3* (2km SW Urban) *49.74339, 6.08963* **Camping Um Krounebierg, Rue du Camping, 7572 Mersch [tel 352329756; fax 327987; contact@campingkrounebierg.lu; www.campingkrounebierg.lu]** In Mersch town cent fr main N7 foll site ss. Fr A7, exit Kopstal dir Mersch, then foll site sps. Lge, hdg/mkd pitch, some hdstg, pt sl, terr, pt shd; htd wc; chem disp; mv service pnt; fam bthrm; shwrs inc; EHU (10A) inc; gas; lndry; shop; rest, snacks; bar; BBQ; playgrnd; htd, covrd pool adj; paddling pool; tennis; skate park; wifi; TV; 20% statics; dogs €2.50; phone; quiet; twin axles; Eng spkn; adv bkg; red LS. "Gd touring & walking cent; conv for trains to Luxembourg City; warden v helpful - only on site 2 hrs morning & 2 hrs evening LS; site guarded; excel clean facs; nice site close to a pleasant town; well laid out; beautiful location; san facs clean." ♦ 25 Mar-31 Oct. € 35.00 (3 persons) 2017*

NOMMERN see Larochette *C3*

REISDORF *C2* (50m W Urban) *49.86958, 6.26746* **Camping De La Sure, 23 Route de la Sure, L-9391 Reisdorf [tel 836509 or 661-151358; reisdorfcamp@gmail.com; www.reisdorf-camp.lu]** Reisdorf is bet Diekirch & Echternach. Site sp off the N10 in Reisdorf. NB-2nd site on L after the bdge driving fr Diekirch. Med, pt shd; wc; chem disp; mv service pnt; fam bthrm; shwrs inc; EHU (10A); lndry rm; shops 2km; rest; snacks; bar; BBQ (charcoal & gas); playgrnd; games area; games rm; wifi; TV rm; 10% statics; dogs; bus adj; poss cr; Eng spkn; adv bkg; quiet; red LS/ACSI; CKE/CCI. "V friendly & helpful; gd cycle paths; site being upgraded to a hg standard (2015); vg." ♦ 30 Mar-31 Oct. € 23.00 2016*

"There aren't many sites open at this time of year"

If you're travelling outside peak season remember to call ahead to check site opening dates – even if the entry says 'open all year'.

REMICH See also sites listed under Nennig in Germany, map ref 3A2.

REMICH *C3* (4km S Rural) *49.5106, 6.36302* **Camping Le Port, 5447 Schwebsange [tel 23664460; fax 26 66 53 05; commune@wellenstein.lu or info@camping-port.lu]** Fr Remich take N10 S on W bank of Moselle. Site 1km E of Schwebsange. Or fr S leave A13 at junc 13 onto N10. Site sp. Lge, mkd pitch, pt shd; wc; chem disp; mv service pnt; serviced pitch; shwrs inc; EHU (10A) inc; gas; lndry; shop 4km; bar; playgrnd; pool 4km; marina & rv activities; 80% statics; dogs; Eng spkn; poss cr; adv bkg rec high ssn; rd, rv & port noise; debit cards acc (no ccards); CKE/CCI. "Busy transit site for Austria/Italy; clean facs; helpful staff; office open 1830-2030; sep area for m'vans on far side of port; red facs LS; gd cycle rtes fr site." ♦ 1 Apr-31 Oct. € 16.50 2016*

SCHWEBSANGE see Remich *C3*

⊞ **SEPTFONTAINES** *B3* (2.5km NE Rural) *49.69274, 5.98514* **Camping Simmerschmelz, Rue de Simmerschmelz 1, 8363 Septfontaines [tel 307072; fax 308210; info@simmerschmelz.com; simmerschmelz.com]** Head NE fr Arlon sp Mersch. In 4km at Gaichel (Bel/Lux frontier) foll valley of Rv Eisch thro Hobscheid, Septfontaines & in 2km at rd junc turn R. Site on L in 100m. Or fr E25 m'way exit at Windhof. Head N to Koerich & onto Septfontaines, as above. Med, pt sl, pt shd; htd wc; chem disp; shwrs inc; EHU (6A) €2.50; gas; lndry; shop high ssn; snacks; pool high ssn; wifi; TV; 40% statics; dogs €3; phone; Eng spkn; adv bkg; quiet. "Pleasant site in valley, wet in winter; 1 hdstg pitch; helpful owner." € 25.80 2017*

TROISVIERGES *B2* (400m S Urban) *50.11908, 6.00251* **Camping Walensbongert, Rue de Binsfeld, 9912 Troisvierges [tel 997141; fax 26957799; wbongert@pt.lu; www.walensbongert.lu]** Fr Belgium on E42/A27 exit at junc 15 St Vith on N62 sp Troisvierges. Site sp. Med, hdg/mkd pitch, pt shd; htd wc; chem disp; mv service pnt; fam bthrm; shwrs inc; EHU (16A) €2.50; lndry (inc dryer); shop 500m; rest 500m; snacks; bar; pools adj; paddling pool; tennis; games rm; 10% statics; dogs €2; phone; train 1km; Eng spkn; adv bkg; quiet; ccard acc; red LS; CKE/CCI. "Pretty town; gd hiking; charming, helpful owners." ♦ ltd. 1 Apr-30 Sep. € 19.50 2014*

VIANDEN *C2* (2km SE Rural) *49.92673, 6.21990* **Camping du Moulin, Rue de Bettel, 9415 Vianden [tel/fax 834501; campingdumoulin@vianden-info.lu; www.campingdumoulin-vianden.lu]** Fr Diekirch take N17 dir Vianden. In 8km at Fouhren take rd N17B sp Bettel then sp Vianden. Site on R behind yellow Vianden sp. Lge, mkd pitch, pt shd; htd wc; chem disp; mv service pnt; fam bthrm; shwrs; EHU (10-16A) €2.20; lndry; shop; rest, bar; playgrnd; pool 2km; rv adj; wifi; cab TV; dogs €1.50; phone; Eng spkn; quiet; CKE/CCI. "Lovely location; spacious pitches, some on rv bank; gd, modern san facs; superb children's san facs; interesting area; rec." 14 Apr-3 Apr. € 24.00 2017*

WASSERBILLIG *C3* (2km SW Rural) *49.70241, 6.47717* **Camping Mertert, Rue du Parc, 6684 Mertert [tel/fax 748174]** On E of rte 1 (Wasserbillig-Luxembourg), clearly sp in both dir. Immed R after rlwy x-ing. Site on rv. Med, some mkd pitch, shd; htd wc; chem disp; fam bthrm; shwrs; EHU (10A) inc; lndry; shops 250m; playgrnd; pool 4km; sm boating pond; 70% statics; buses & trains nr; adv bkg; quiet; ccard not acc. "Grassed tourer area open fr Apr, but owner allows pitching on tarmac rd adj office; excel, clean facs; scruffy statics area; recep clsd 1300-1500; vg." ♦ ltd. 15 Apr-15 Oct. € 12.50 2013*

WILTZ see Clervaux *B2*

"That's changed – Should I let The Club know?"

If you find something on site that's different from the site entry, fill in a report and let us know. See camc.com/europereport.

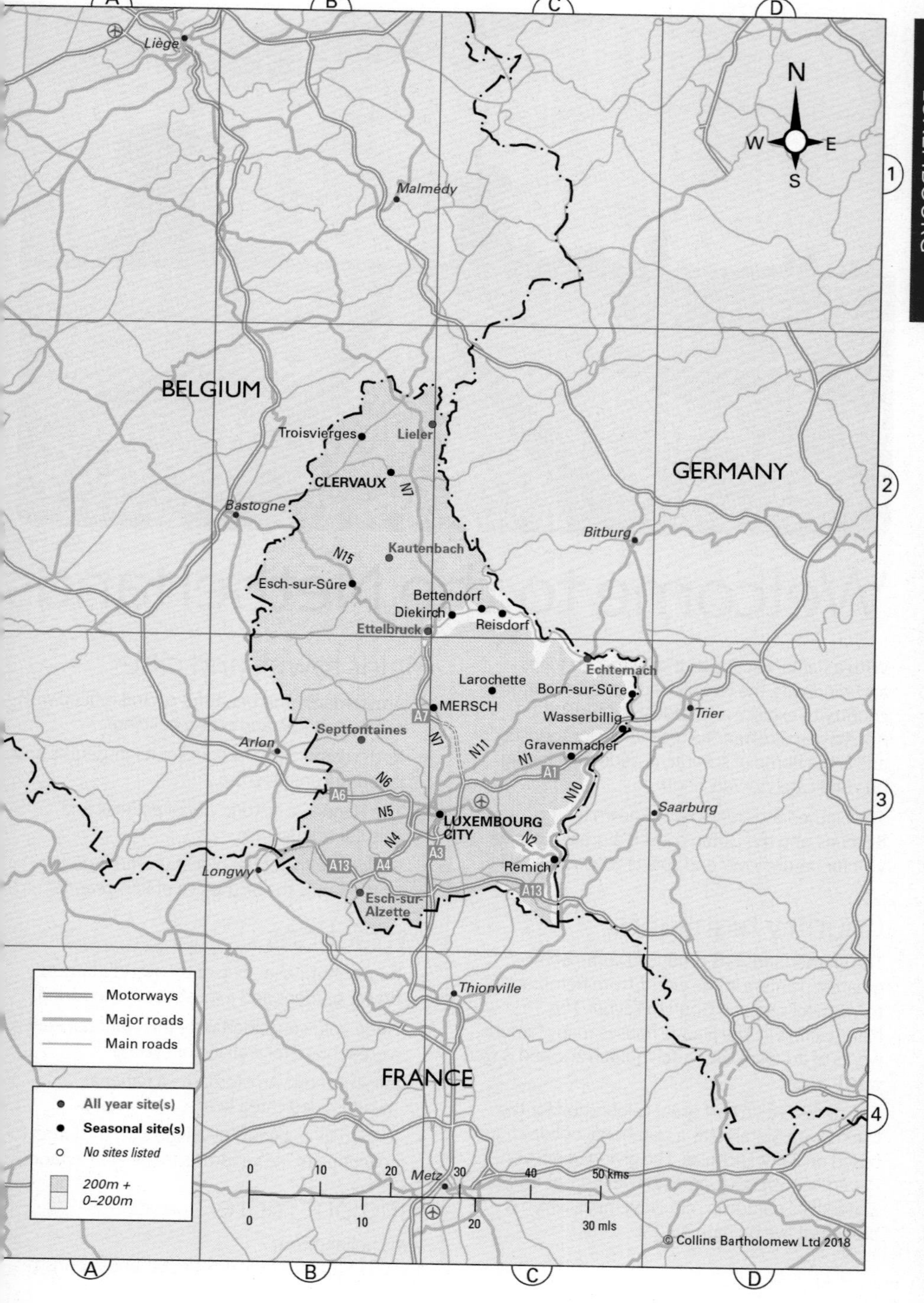

A
B
C
D
1
2
3
4
N
W
E
S
Liège
Malmedy
BELGIUM
GERMANY
FRANCE
Troisvierges
Lieler
CLERVAUX
N7
Bastogne
Kautenbach
N15
Esch-sur-Sûre
Bettendorf
Diekirch
Reisdorf
Ettelbruck
Bitburg
Echternach
Larochette
Born-sur-Sûre
MERSCH
A7
Trier
Wasserbillig
Septfontaines
N11
Arlon
Gravenmacher
N1
A1
N6
N10
A6
N5
LUXEMBOURG CITY
Saarburg
N4
N2
A3
A13
A4
Longwy
Remich
Esch-sur-Alzette
Thionville
Motorways
Major roads
Main roads
All year site(s)
Seasonal site(s)
No sites listed
200m +
0–200m
0
10
20
30
40
50 kms
Metz
30 mls
© Collins Bartholomew Ltd 2018

Tulip Field

Welcome to the Netherlands

With a flat landscape that's covered in tulips and windmills, the Netherlands is an enchanting country to explore and is ideal for cyclists. Amsterdam is often the main draw for tourists, and is the home of several museums, including one dedicated to Van Gogh.

The Netherlands is also well known for its beaches, and the Dutch coast is a great place to visit for nature lover and sports enthusiasts alike.

Country highlights

The Netherlands has produced some of the greatest painters in the world, from Rembrandt to Vermeer and Van Gogh to Escher. The Mauritschuis in The Hague houses many famous works of art from the Dutch golden age and is well worth a visit.

Christmas is a time of great celebration for the Dutch, with Sinterklaas a traditional holiday figure based on Saint Nicholas. The giving of gifts on December 5th is a long-held tradition, as is the Sinterklaas parade in mid-November, which is broadcast live on national TV.

Major towns and cities

- Amsterdam – this beautiful capital is filled with canals, galleries and pretty buildings.
- Rotterdam – a city famous for its museums and landmark architecture.
- The Hague – a historic city of political and cultural significance.
- Leiden – home of the oldest university in the Netherlands the birthplace of Rembrandt.

Attractions

- Keukenhof, Lisse – one of the world's largest flower gardens and a must-see in the spring.
- Hoge Veluwe, Gelderland – this National Park is a great place for walking or cycling.
- Rijksmuseum, Amsterdam – a national museum dedicated to arts and history.
- Kinderdijk - a beautiful village with the largest collection of old windmills in the Netherlands.

Find out more

www.holland.com
Tel: 0031 (0) 70 37 05 705 Netherlands Tourism

Country Information

Population (approx): 16.9million

Capital: Amsterdam (population approx 825,000)

Area: 33,939 sqkm

Bordered by: Belgium, Germany

Terrain: Mostly coastal lowland and reclaimed land (polders) dissected by rivers and canals; hills in the south-east

Climate: Temperate maritime climate; warm, changeable summers; cold/mild winters; spring is the driest season

Coastline: 451km

Highest Point: Vaalserberg 322m

Language: Dutch

Local Time: GMT or BST + 1, i.e. 1 hour ahead of the UK all year

Currency: Euros divided into 100 cents; £1 = €1.13, €1 = £0.88 (November 2017)

Emergency numbers: Police 112; Fire brigade 112; Ambulance 112. Operators speak English

Public Holidays 2018: Jan 1; Mar 30; Apr 1,2, 27; May 5,10,20,21; Dec 25, 26.

School summer holidays vary by region, but are roughly early/mid July to end August/early September.

Camping and Caravanning

There are approximately 2,500 officially classified campsites which offer a wide variety of facilities. Most are well equipped with modern sanitary facilities and they generally have a bar, shop and leisure facilities.

A number of sites require cars to be parked on a separate area away from pitches and this can present a problem for motorhomes. Some sites allow motorhomes to park on pitches without restrictions, but others will only accept them on pitches if they are not moved during the duration of your stay. Check before booking in.

A tourist tax is levied at campsites of approximately €1.00 per person per night. It is not generally included in the prices quoted in the Site Entry listings which follow this chapter.

The periods over, and immediately after, the Ascension Day holiday and the Whitsun weekend are very busy for Dutch sites and you can expect to find many of them full. Advance booking is highly recommended.

Casual/wild camping is prohibited as is overnight camping by the roadside or in car parks. There are overnight parking places specifically for motorhomes all over the country – see the website of the Camper Club Nederland, www.campervriendelijk.nl and look under 'camperplaatsen NL' or write to CCN at Postbus 115, 7480 AC Haaksbergen, tel:(0)634 492 913. Alternatively see www.campercontact.nl or email cnn@camperclubnetherland.nl

Many campsites also have motorhome amenities and some offer Quick Stop overnight facilities at reduced rates.

Cycling

There are twice as many bicycles as cars in the Netherlands and as a result cyclists are catered for better than in any other country. There are 15,000 km of well-maintained cycle tracks in both town and country, all marked with red and white road signs and mushroom-shaped posts indicating the quickest and/or most scenic routes. Local tourist information centres (VVV) sell maps of a wide range of cycling tours and cycling fact sheets and maps are available from the Netherlands Board of Tourism in London. Motorists should expect to encounter heavy cycle traffic, particularly during rush hours.

Obligatory separate bicycle lanes for cyclists are indicated by circular blue signs displaying a white bicycle. Small oblong signs with the word 'fietspad' or 'rijwielpad' indicate optional bicycle lanes. White bicycles and dotted white lines painted on the road surface indicate cycle lanes which may be used by motor vehicles providing they do not obstruct cyclists. Cycle lanes marked by continuous white lines are prohibited for use by motor vehicles.

Cyclists must obey traffic light signals at crossroads and junctions; elsewhere, where no traffic lights are in operation, they must give way to traffic from the right.

Cycle tracks are also used by mobility scooters and mopeds. Pedestrians should be especially cautious when crossing roads, especially on zebra crossings. Look out for both cyclists and riders of mopeds, who often ignore traffic rules as well as red lights. In Amsterdam in particular, many cyclists do not use lights at night.

Transportation of Bicycles

Bicycles may be carried on the roof of a car providing the total height does not exceed 4 metres. They may also be carried at the rear providing the width does not extend more than 20cm beyond the width of the vehicle.

Electricity and Gas

Most campsites have a supply ranging from 4 to 10 amps and almost all have CEE connections. Plugs have two round pins.

The full range of Campingaz cylinders is available.

Entry Formalities

British and Irish passport holders may stay in the Netherlands for up to three months without a visa.

Medical Services

Pharmacies (apotheek) dispense prescriptions whereas drugstores (drogisterij) sell only over-the-counter remedies. Pharmacies may require a photocopy of the details on your European Health Insurance Card (EHIC). You will need to show your EHIC to obtain treatment by a doctor contracted to the state health care system (AGIS Zorgverzekeringen) and you will probably have to pay a fee. You will be charged for emergency dental treatment. Charges for prescriptions vary. Treatment refunds are obtained from AGIS.

Inpatient hospital treatment is free provided it is authorised by AGIS. Local state health insurance fund offices can give advice on obtaining emergency medical services and provide names and addresses of doctors, health centres and hospitals. Tourist Information offices also keep lists of local doctors.

Opening Hours

Banks: Mon-Fri 9am-4pm/5pm (some open Sat).

Museums: Tue-Fri 10am-5pm; Sat & Sun 11am/1pm-5pm.

Post Offices: Mon-Fri 9am-5pm; some Sat 9am-12 noon/1.30pm.

Shops: Mon-Fri 8am/8.30am-6pm/8pm; Sat 8am/8.30am-4pm/5pm; late night shopping in many towns on Thursday or Friday to 9pm. Shops close one day or half day in the week in addition to Sunday.

Safety and Security

In relative terms there is little crime but visitors should take the usual precautions in central Amsterdam (particularly in and around Central Station), in Rotterdam and The Hague. As in many large cities, pickpocketing and bag snatching are more common. Pickpockets operate on trams, especially on numbers 2 and 5 in Amsterdam.

Ensure you keep your valuables safely with you at all times and do not leave them unattended or hanging on the back of a chair. Bicycle theft is a common occurrence in the major cities.

Fake, plain clothes policemen carrying badges are in action pretending to be investigating counterfeit money and false credit cards. Dutch police do not have badges and plain clothes police will rarely carry out this kind of inspection. Always ask for identity, check it thoroughly and do not allow yourself to be intimidated. Call 0900 8844 to contact the nearest police station if you are concerned or suspicious.

Several deaths occur each year due to drowning in canals. Take particular care when driving, cycling or walking alongside canals.

Avoid confrontation with anyone offering to sell you drugs and stay away from quiet or dark alleys, particularly late at night.

There have been incidences of drinks being spiked in city centre locations. Always be aware of your drink and do not leave it unattended. Young women and lone travellers need to be especially vigilant in these situations.

The Netherlands shares with the rest of Europe a general threat from terrorism. Attacks could be indiscriminate and against civilian targets in public places, including tourist sites.

British Embassy

LANGE VOORHOUT 10, 2514 ED THE HAAG
Tel: (070) 4270427
www.ukinnl.fco.gov.uk

British Consulate-General

KONINGSLAAN 44,1075 AE AMSTERDAM
Tel: (020) 6764343

Irish Embassy

SCHEVENINGSEWEG 112, 2584 AE THE HAGUE
Tel: (070) 3630993
www.embassyofireland.nl

Documents

Passport

Everyone from the age of 14 is required to show a valid identity document to police officers on request and you should, therefore, carry your passport at all times.

Vehicle(s)

When driving carry your driving licence, vehicle registration certificate (V5C), insurance certificate and MOT certificate, if applicable. If driving a vehicle that does not belong to you, carry a letter of authority from the owner.

Money

Money may be exchanged at main border crossing posts, major post offices, banks, VVV tourist information offices and some ANWB offices. Other bureaux de change may not give such favourable rates.

The major credit and debit cards are widely accepted but supermarkets will not generally accept credit cards. As a precaution carry enough cash to cover your purchases as you may find that debit cards issued by banks outside the Netherlands are not accepted. Cash machines are widespread.

Motoring in the Netherlands

The Dutch drive assertively and are not renowned for their road courtesy. Pedestrians should be very careful when crossing roads, including on zebra crossings.

Accidents

All accidents which cause injuries or major damage must be reported to the police. Drivers involved in an accident must exchange their identity details and their insurance company contact information.

Alcohol

The maximum permitted level of alcohol is 50 milligrams in 100 millilitres of blood, i.e. lower than that permitted in the UK (80 milligrams). Penalties for driving under the influence of alcohol can be severe. A lower level of 20 milligrams applies to drivers who have held a driving licence for less than five years. It is wisest to adopt a 'no drinking and driving' rule.

Breakdown Service

There are emergency telephones every 2km on all motorways and they are directly linked to the nearest breakdown centre.

ANWB, the motoring and leisure organisation, has a road patrol service which operates 24 hours a day on all roads. Drivers requiring assistance may call the 'Wegenwacht' road patrol centre by telephoning 088 2692888. Alternatively call the ANWB Emergency Centre on (070) 3141414. Operators speak English.

Charges apply for breakdown assistance and towing is charged according to distance and time of day. Members of clubs affiliated to the AIT/FIA, such as The Caravan and Motorhome Club, incur lower charges. Payment by credit card is accepted. In some areas the ANWB Wegenwacht has contracts with local garages to provide assistance to its members and affiliates.

Essential Equipment

Lights

The use of dipped headlights during the day is recommended.

Child Restraint System

Children under the age of 18 years, measuring less than 1.35m, must be seated in an approved child restraint adapted to their size (ECE 44/03 or 44/04 safety approved). Children under 3 years old are able to travel in the front if they are seated in a rear facing child seat with the airbag deactivated, and under no circumstances are they allowed to travel in a car with no child restraint system fitted.

Fuel

Unleaded petrol is available from green pumps marked 'Loodvrije Benzine'. LPG (autogas) is widely available along main roads and motorways.

Petrol stations along motorways and main roads and in main towns are open 24 hours, except in parts of the north of the country where they close at 11pm. Credit cards are accepted but some all night petrol stations only have automatic pumps which may operate with bank notes only.

Low Emission Zones

Low Emission Zones are in operation in 16 cities in the Netherlands. Restrictions only apply to freight vehicles over 3500kg, however currently all foreign vehicles are able to enter the Low Emission Zone without any restrictions. Check www.urbanaccessregulations.eu before you travel.

Parking

Parking meters or discs are in use in many towns allowing parking for between 30 minutes and two or three hours; discs can be obtained from local shops. A sign 'parkeerschijf' indicates times when a disc is compulsory. Paid parking is expensive and there are insufficient parking spaces to meet demand. Clamping and towing away of vehicles are commonplace and fines are high. Check signs for the precise times you are allowed to park, particularly on main roads in Amsterdam.

Priority

Yellow diamond shaped signs with a white border indicate priority roads. In the absence of such signs drivers must give way to all traffic approaching from the right. At the intersection of two roads of the same class where there are no signs, traffic from the right has priority.

At junctions marked with a 'priority road ahead' sign, a stop sign or a line of white painted triangles ('shark's teeth') across the road, drivers must give way to all vehicles on the priority road, including bicycles and mopeds.

Be particularly careful when using roundabouts as on some you have the right of way when on them, but on others you must give way to vehicles entering the roundabout, i.e. on your right.

Trams have priority at the intersection of roads of equal importance, but they must give way to traffic on priority roads. If a tram or bus stops in the middle of the road to allow passengers on and off, you must stop. Buses have right of way over all other vehicles when leaving bus stops in built-up areas.

Roads

Roads are generally good and well maintained, but are overcrowded and are frequently subject to strong winds. Most cities have a policy of reducing the amount of nonessential traffic within their boundaries. Narrowing roads, obstacles, traffic lights and speed cameras are often in place to achieve this.

Road Signs and Markings

National motorways are distinguished by red signs, and prefixed with the letter A, whereas European motorways have green signs and are prefixed E. Dual carriageways and other main roads have yellow signs with the letter N and secondary roads are prefixed B.

In general road signs and markings conform to international standards. The following are some road signs which may also be seen:

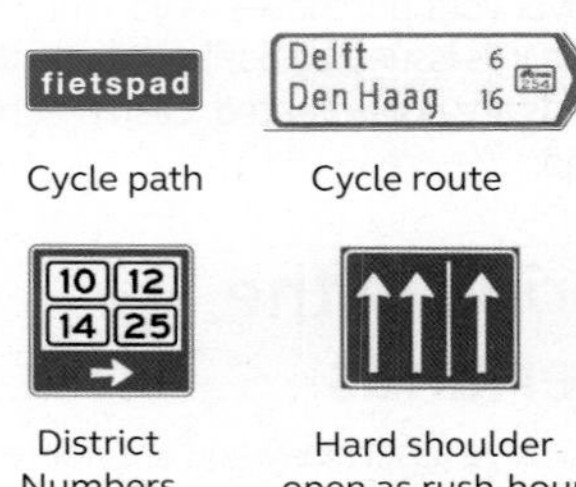

Cycle path | Cycle route

District Numbers | Hard shoulder open as rush-hour lane

Dutch	English Translation
Afrit	Exit
Doorgaand verkeer gestremd	No throughway
Drempels	Humps
Langzaam rijden	Slow down
Omleiding	Detour
Oprit	Entrance
Ousteek u lichten	Switch on lights
Parkeerplaats	Parking

Dutch	English Translation
Pas op!	Attention
Stop-verbod	No parking
Wegomlegging	Detour
Werk in uitvoering	Road works
Woonerven	Slow down (in built-up area)

A continuous central white line should not be crossed even to make a left turn.

Speed Limits

	Open Road (km/h)	Motorway (km/h)
Car Solo	80-100	130*
Car towing caravan/trailer	80-90	90
Motorhome under 3500kg	80-100	130*
Motorhome 3500-7500kg	80	80

*Unless otherwise indicated.

Be vigilant and observe the overhead illuminated lane indicators when they are in use, as speed limits on motorways are variable. Speed cameras, speed traps and unmarked police vehicles are widely used. Radar detectors are illegal, with use resulting in a heavy fine.

Motorhomes over 3,500kg are restricted to 50 km/h (31 mph) in built-up areas and to 80 km/h (50 mph) on all other roads. The beginning of a built up area is indicated by a rectangular blue sign with the name of the locality in white. The end of a built up area is indicated by the same sign with a white diagonal lines across it.

Traffic Jams

The greatest traffic congestion occurs on weekdays at rush hours around the major cities of Amsterdam, Den Bosch, Eindhoven, Rotterdam, Utrecht, The Hague and Eindhoven.

Summer holidays in the Netherlands are staggered and, as a result, traffic congestion is not too severe. However during the Christmas, Easter and Whitsun holiday periods, traffic jams are common and bottlenecks regularly occur on the A2 (Maastricht to Amsterdam), the A12 (Utrecht to the German border) and on the A50 (Arnhem to Apeldoorn). Roads to the Zeeland coast, e.g. the A58, N57 and N59, may become congested during periods of fine weather.

Many Germans head for the Netherlands on their own public holidays and the roads are particularly busy during these periods.

Violation of Traffic Regulations

Police are empowered to impose on-the-spot fines (or confiscate vehicles) for violation of traffic regulations and fines for speeding can be severe. If you are fined always ask for a receipt.

Motorways

There are over 2,750 kilometres of toll-free motorway. There are rest areas along the motorways, most of which have a petrol station and a small shop. Tolls are charged on some bridges and tunnels, notably the Westerschelde Toll Tunnel. This road tunnel links Terneuzen (north of Gent) and Ellewoutsdijk (south of Goes) across the Westerschelde. It provides a short, fast route between Channel ports and the road network in the west of the country. The tunnel is 6.6km long (just over 4 miles) and the toll for a car + caravan (maximum height 3m measured from front axle) is €7.45 and for a motorhome €7.45 height under 2.5m) or €18.20 (height over 3m) (all prices for 2017). Credit cards are accepted. For more information go to www.westerscheldetunnel.nl.

Touring

The southern Netherlands is the most densely populated part of the country but, despite the modern sprawl, ancient towns such as Dordrecht, Gouda, Delft and Leiden have retained their individuality and charm. Rotterdam is a modern, commercial centre and a tour of its harbour – the busiest in Europe – makes a fascinating excursion. The scenery in the north of the country is the most typically Dutch – vast, flat landscapes, largely reclaimed from the sea, dotted with windmills. Some of the most charming towns and villages are Marken, Volendam and Alkmaar (famous for its cheese market). Aalsmeer, situated south of Amsterdam, stages the world's largest daily flower auction.

It is worth spending time to visit the hilly provinces in the east such as Gelderland, known for its castles, country houses and its major city, Arnhem, which has many links with the Second World War. Overijssel is a region of great variety and the old Hanseatic towns of Zwolle and Kampen have splendid quays and historic buildings. Friesland is the Netherland's lake district.

An Amsterdam Card entitles you to free admission to many of the city's famous museums, including the Rijksmuseum and Van Gogh Museum, and to discounts in many restaurants, shops, attractions and at Park & Ride car parks. It also entitles you to discounts on tours as well as free travel on public transport and a free canal cruise. The Card is valid for one, two or three days and is available from tourist information offices, some Shell petrol stations, Canal Bus kiosks, Park & Ride car parks and some hotels. Alternatively purchase online from www.iamsterdamcard.com.

Service charges are included in restaurant bills and tips are not necessary. Smoking is not permitted in bars or restaurants.

Spring is one of the most popular times to visit the Netherlands, in particular the famous Keukenhof Gardens near Lisse, open from 24 March to 16 May in 2016, see www.keukenhof.nl. Visitors enjoy a display of over seven million flowering bulbs, trees and shrubs. Special events take place here at other times of the year, including a National Bulb Market in October.

Public Transport

There is an excellent network of buses and trams, together with metro systems in Amsterdam (called the GVB), Rotterdam and The Hague. An electronic card 'OV Chipkaart' is gradually replacing the previous system of 'Strippenkaart' which were strips of 15 or 45 tickets valid throughout the country.

OV-Chip cards can be bought at vending machines at stations or ticket offices and on board buses and trams and are available for periods from one hour to seven days allowing unlimited travel on trams, buses and the metro. Children under 12 and people over the age of 65 qualify for reduced fares (show your passport as proof of age). See www.gvb.nl for more information.

Tickets must be validated before travel either at the yellow machines on trams and at metro stations or by your bus driver or conductor.

In Amsterdam canal transport includes a regular canal shuttle between Centraal Station and the Rijksmuseum. A 'circle tram' travels from Centraal Station through the centre of Amsterdam past a number of local visitor attractions, such as Anne Frank's house, the Rijksmuseum, Van Gogh museum and Rembrandthuis.

There are Park & Ride facilities at most railway stations. Secure parking is also offered at 'transferiums', a scheme offering reasonably priced guarded parking in secure areas on the outskirts of major towns with easy access by road and close to public transport hubs. Transferiums have heated waiting rooms and rest rooms as well as information for travellers, and some even have a shop.

Frequent car ferry services operate on routes to the Frisian (or Wadden) Islands off the north west coast, for example, from Den Helder to Texel Island, Harlingen to Terschelling Island and Holwerd to Ameland Island. Other islands in the group do not allow cars but there are passenger ferry services. In the summer island-hopping round tickets are available to foot passengers and cyclists and are popular for exploring the country.

Sites in Netherlands

AARDENBURG see Sluis *A4*

AERDT see Zevenaar *C3*

ALKMAAR *B2* (7km W Rural) *52.63100, 4.69500* **Camping Hoeve Engeland, Egmondermeer 9, 1934 PN Egmond aan den Hoef [(072) 5116370; rus.jan@tiscali.nl]** Take A9 to Alkmaar & take N9 ring rd W. Take 1st L turn after rlwy viaduct at traff lts opp ING bank. Foll sm rd past garden cent, site in approx 250m - sp on gate. Sm, pt shd; htd wc; shwrs inc; EHU (16A) inc (poss rev pol); beach 8km; bus 1km; poss cr; Eng spkn; adv bkg; quiet. "CL-type farm site; clean (ltd) facs; mosquitoes; gd cycling to historic Alkmaar & coastal dunes; gd cycling area; friendly, helpful owner." 15 Mar-15 Oct. € 15.00 2013*

⊞ **ALKMAAR** *B2* (2.6km NW Rural) *52.64205, 4.72407* **Camping Alkmaar, Bergerweg 201, 1817 ML Alkmaar [(072) 5116924; info@campingalkmaar.nl; www.campingalkmaar.nl]** Fr W ring rd (Martin Luther Kingweg) foll Bergen sp, bear R at T-junc & site 150m on L. Site well sp. Med, mkd pitch, hdstg, pt shd; htd wc; chem disp; mv service pnt; fam bthrm; shwrs €0.50; EHU (4-10A) inc; lndry; shop 1km; BBQ; playgrnd; pool adj; sand beach 6km; golf 2km; cab TV; some statics; dogs €3; bus at gate; poss cr; Eng spkn; adv bkg; quiet; ccard acc; red CKE/CCI. "Clean, friendly site; sm pitches; buses to town; 10 mins walk to cent; cheese mkt on Friday in ssn; vg cycling." ♦ ltd. € 29.00 2017*

ALMERE *C3* (7km W Rural) *52.35688, 5.22505* **Camping Waterhout, Archerpad 6, 1324 ZZ Almere [(036) 5470632; fax 5470634; info@waterhout.nl; www.waterhout.nl]** Exit A6 junc 4, site sp fr slip rd on S edge Weerwater. Med, mkd pitch, shd; wc; chem disp; fam bthrm; shwrs €0.50; EHU (10A) inc; lndry (inc dryer); shop; rest, snacks; bar; playgrnd; sand beach & lake sw adj; entmnt; TV rm; 30% statics; dogs €2.50; phone; bus 200m; poss cr; Eng spkn; adv bkg; quiet; red CKE/CCI. "Well laid-out site; conv Amsterdam by bus or train - 30 mins; Almere ultra-modern city." 4 Apr-19 Oct. € 25.00 2014*

AMELAND ISLAND *C1* **Sites on Ameland Island are listed together at the end of the Netherlands site entry pages.**

AMERSFOORT *C3* (11km S Rural) *52.07975, 5.38151* **Vakantiepark De Heigraaf, De Haygraeff 9, 3931 ML Woudenberg [(033) 2865066; info@heigraaf.nl; www.heigraaf.nl]** Exit A12 at Maarn junc 21 or junc 22 & foll sp to site on N224, 2km W of Woudenberg. V lge, mkd pitch, pt shd; htd wc; chem disp; mv service pnt; fam bthrm; shwrs €0.50; EHU (4-6A) inc; lndry (inc dryer); shop; rest, snacks; bar; playgrnd; lake sw 150m; wifi; entmnt; 50% statics; no dogs; phone; bus 500m; Eng spkn; adv bkg; quiet. "Vg, well-managed site; modern san facs; well run site, does not accept Visa."♦ 1 Apr-31 Oct. € 20.00 2012*

AMSTELVEEN see Amsterdam *B3*

⊞ **AMSTERDAM** *B3* (12km N Rural) *52.43649, 4.91445* **Camping Het Rietveen, Noordeinde 130, 1121 AL Landsmeer [(020) 4821468; fax 4820214; info@campinghetrietveen.nl; www.campinghetrietveen.nl]** Fr A10 ring rd exit junc 117. At junc off slip rd turn L dir Landsmeer, site sp. Sm, mkd pitch; wc; chem disp; mv service pnt; shwrs inc; EHU (10A) inc; shop, rest, bar 500m; lake sw & fishing; tennis; bike hire; dogs free; phone adj; bus to Amsterdam 200m; poss cr; Eng spkn; adv bkg; quiet; CKE/CCI. "Vg, pretty lakeside site, like lge CL, in well-kept vill; no recep - site yourself & owner will call; sep field avail for rallies; excel touring base; city 30 mins by bus; san facs inadequate." € 27.00 2016*

AMSTERDAM *B3* (5km NE Urban) *52.38907, 4.92532* **Camping Vliegenbos, Meeuwenlaan 138, 1022 AM Amsterdam [(020) 6368855; fax 6322723; vliegenbos@noord.amsterdam.nl; www.vliegenbos.com]** Fr A10 Amsterdam ring rd, take exit S116 Amsterdam Noord, at 2nd slip rd turn R sp Noord over rndabt, turn L at next rndabt, then immed sharp R, L onto service rd, site sp. Lge, hdstg, pt sl, pt shd; htd wc; chem disp; mv service pnt; fam bthrm; shwrs inc; EHU (6A) inc; gas; lndry; shop; rest 2km; snacks; bar; pool 1.5km; no dogs; phone; bus to city nr; poss cr; Eng spkn; poss noisy tent campers; ccard acc. "Sm pitches mainly for tents; ltd EHU; m'vans & c'vans park outside barrier; friendly staff; bus tickets to city cent fr recep; cycle path to city cent via free ferry; clean, modern san facs; v well set up." ♦ 1 Apr-1 Oct. € 30.00 2016*

"I like to fill in the reports as I travel from site to site"

You'll find report forms at the back of this guide, or you can fill them in online at camc.com/europereport.

⊞ **AMSTERDAM** *B3* (6km E Urban) *52.36555, 4.95829* **Camping Zeeburg, Zuider Ijdijk 20, 1095 KN Amsterdam [(020) 6944430; fax 6946238; info@campingzeeburg.nl; www.campingzeeburg.nl]** Fr A10 ring rd exit at S114 & foll site sps. Lge, unshd; wc; chem disp; mv service pnt; shwrs €0.80; EHU (6-16A) inc; gas; lndry; shop; snacks; bike hire; internet; some statics; dogs €3; bus/tram to city nr; poss cr; adv bkg. "Used mainly by tents in summer, but rest of year suitable for c'vans; conv city cent." € 29.00 2016*

AMSTERDAM *B3* (12km SE Urban) *52.31258, 4.99035* **Gaasper Camping, Loosdrechtdreef 7, 1108 AZ Amsterdam-Zuidoost [(020) 6967326; fax 6969369; info@gaaspercamping.nl; www.gaaspercamping.nl]** Fr A2 take A9 E sp Amersfoort. After about 5km take 3rd exit sp Gaasperplas/Weesp S113. Cross S113 into site, sp. Lge, hdg/mkd pitch, some hdstg, pt shd; htd wc; chem disp; mv service pnt; serviced pitches; shwrs metered; EHU (10A) €3.50 (care needed); gas; lndry; shop; rest, snacks; bar; playgrnd; 20% statics; dogs €2.50; metro 5 mins walk (tickets fr site recep); poss cr; Eng spkn; quiet but some rd & air traff noise; CKE/CCI. "Immac site set in beautiful parkland; well-run with strict rules; night guard at barrier (high ssn); vans must be manhandled onto pitch (help avail); high ssn arr early to ensure pitch - no adv bkg for fewer than 7 nights; poss cold shwrs & ltd shop LS; gd security; well run site; conv for metro; adv bkg rec in high ssn." 1 Jan-4 Jan, 15 Mar-1 Nov, 28 Dec-31 Dec. € 30.00 2017*

AMSTERDAM *B3* (15km SW Rural) *52.29366, 4.82316* **Camping Het Amsterdamse Bos, Kleine Noorddijk 1, 1187 NZ Amstelveen [(020) 6416868; fax 6402378; info@campingamsterdam.com; www.camping amsterdamsebos.com]** Foll A10 & A4 twd Schiphol Airport. Fr junc on A4 & A9 m'way, take A9 E twd Amstelveen; at next exit (junc 6) exit sp Aalsmeer. Foll Aalsmeer sp for 1km bearing R at traff lts then at next traff lts turn L over canal bdge onto N231. In 1.5km turn L at 2nd traff lts into site. Fr S exit A4 junc 3 onto N201 dir Hilversum (ignore other camp sps). Turn L onto N231 dir Amstelveen, at rd junc Bovenkirk take N231 dir Schiphol, site on R in 200m, sp. V lge, pt shd; htd wc; chem disp; mv service pnt; shwrs €0.80; EHU (10A) €4.50; gas; lndry; shop; supmkt nr; rest, snacks; bar; waterpark nr; wifi; 20% statics; dogs €3; bus to city; poss cr; Eng spkn; adv bkg; some aircraft noise; ccard acc; CKE/CCI. "Conv Amsterdam by bus - tickets sold on site; poss migrant workers resident on site; san facs stretched high ssn; gd walking & cycling paths; spectacular daily flower auctions at Aalsmeer; conv bulbfields." ♦ 15 Mar-31 Oct. € 30.50 2014*

⊞ **ANNEN** *D2* (3.7km S Rural) *53.03017, 6.73912* **De Baldwin Hoeve, Annerweg 9, 9463 TB Eext [05 92 27 16 29; baldwinhoeve@hetnet.nl; www.baldwin hoeve.nl]** Fr N34 take Annen exit. Turn R onto Anlooerweg. At rndabt take R dir Eext. Bef underpass take sm service rd on L to campsite. Sm, mkd pitch, unshd; wc; chem disp; shwrs; EHU (10A); BBQ; dogs; bus adj; twin axles; Eng spkn; adv bkg; quiet; CCI. "CL type farm site with excel san facs; friendly owners; some rd noise; horses & other livestock; lg group accomodation avail; vg." € 51.00 2014*

APELDOORN *C3* (10km N Rural) *52.29066, 5.94520* **Camping De Helfterkamp, Gortelseweg 24, 8171 RA Vaassen [(0578) 571839; fax 570378; info@ helfterkamp.nl; www.helfterkamp.nl]** Leave A50 junc 26; foll sp to Vaassen; site sp on ent to town - 2.5km W of Vaassen. Med, mkd pitch, pt shd; htd wc; chem disp; fam bthrm; shwrs €0.50; EHU (16A) metered (poss rev pol); gas; lndry; shop; playgrnd; lake sw 1.5km; bike hire; 40% statics; dogs €1.75; phone; Eng spkn; adv bkg ess high ssn; quiet; wifi; ccard acc; 10% red long stay; CKE/CCI. "Excel, immac, well-maintained, busy site in beautiful woodland area; key for shwrs & hot water; v friendly owners; conv for Apeldoorn/Arnhem areas & De Hooge Veluwe National Park; gd walking/cycling." 1 Mar-31 Oct. € 25.00 2017*

⊞ **APELDOORN** *C3* (10km S Rural) *52.11771, 5.90641* **Camping De Pampel, Woeste Hoefweg 35, 7351 TN Hoenderloo [(055) 3781760; fax 3781992; info@pampel.nl; www.pampel.nl]** Exit A1 Amersfoort-Apeldoorn m'way at junc 19 Hoenderloo. Fr Hoenderloo dir Loenen, site sp. Lge, hdg/mkd pitch, pt shd; htd wc; chem disp; mv service pnt; serviced pitches; fam bthrm; private bthrms avail; shwrs inc; EHU (16A) €3; lndry; shop & 1km; rest in ssn; snacks; bar; playgrnd; 2 pools; bike hire; go-kart hire; dogs €3 (not acc high ssn); poss cr; adv bkg ess high ssn & Bank Hols; quiet but rd noise some pitches; red LS. "V pleasant setting 2km fr National Park; excel facs; free 1-day bus ticket; private bthrms avail; some site rds diff for lge o'fits; vg for children; many mkd walks/cycle paths; friendly staff." € 19.60 2017*

APPELSCHA *D2* (4.5km S Rural) *52.92134, 6.34447* **Boscamping Appelscha, Oude Willem 3, 8426 SM Appelscha [(0516) 431391; info@boscamping appelscha.nl; www.campingalkenhaer.nl]** A28 junc 31 sp Drachten. Turn L onto N381. About 13km turn L onto Oude Willem then take 3rd R, site on L. Lge, mkd pitch, pt shd; wc; chem disp; mv service pnt; fam bthrm; shwrs; EHU (16A); lndry (inc dryer); snacks; takeaway; playgrnd; paddling pool; wifi; 60% statics; Eng spkn; quiet; CKE/CCI. "Neat, friendly, well run site; many walking, cycling & riding trails in nrby national park; vg site." 1 Apr-1 Oct. € 33.50 2014*

ARNHEM *C3* (6km W Rural) *51.99365, 5.82203* **Camping Aan Veluwe (formerly De Bilderberg), Sportlaan 1, 6861 AG Oosterbeek [(0224) 563109; fax 563093; info@aannoordzee.nl; www.aanveluwe.nl]** Fr S fr Nijmegen, cross new bdge at Arnhem. Foll Oosterbeek sp for 5km, cont past memorial in Oosterbeek, in 1km turn R at rndabt, 500m L to site. Or fr A50 exit junc 19 onto N225 twd Osterbeek/ Arnhem. In 3km at rndabt turn L, site on L in 500m. Med, pt sl, pt shd; htd wc; chem disp; shwrs inc; EHU (16A) inc; gas; shop; bar; playgrnd; pool 3km; adv bkg; few statics; dogs €1.80; sep car park; quiet; red for long stays. "Conv Airborne Museum & Cemetery & Dutch Open Air Museum; sports club bar open to site guests; shwr facs for each pitch; lovely walks." 29 Mar-13 Oct. € 28.00 2014*

ARNHEM *C3* (5km NW Rural) *52.0072, 5.8714* **Camping Warnsborn, Bakenbergseweg 257, 6816 PB Arnhem [(026) 4423469; fax 4421095; info@campingwarnsborn.nl; www.campingwarnsborn.nl]** Fr Utrecht on E35/A12, exit junc 25 Ede (if coming fr opp dir, beware unnumbered m'way junc 200m prior to junc 25). Take N224 dual c'way twd Arnhem & foll sp Burgers Zoo, site sp. Beware oncoming traff & sleeping policeman nr site ent. Med, pt shd; htd wc; chem disp, mv service pnt; fam bthrm; shwrs €0.60; EHU (6A) inc; gas; lndry; sm shop & 3km; rest 1km; BBQ; playgrnd; internet; 5% statics; dogs €3; phone; bus 100m; poss cr; Eng spkn; adv bkg; quiet; ccard acc; red long stay/CKE/CCI. "Excel, spacious, clean, well-maintained, wooded site; san facs clean; friendly, helpful family owners & staff; airborne museum & cemetery; cycle rtes direct fr site; conv Hooge Veluwe National Park & Kröller-Müller museum (Van Gogh paintings); super site but busy; bus into Arnhem." ♦ ltd. 24 Mar-30 Oct. € 19.50 2016*

ARNHEM *C3* (9km NW Rural) *52.03192, 5.86652* **Droompark Hooge Veluwe, Koningsweg 14, Schaarsbergen, 6816 TC Arnhem [(026) 4432272 or (088) 0551500; fax 4436809; hoogeveluwe@droomparken.nl; www.hoogeveluwe.nl]** Fr Utrecht A12/E35, Oosterbeck exit 25 & foll sp for Hooge Veluwe to site in 4km on R. Lge, pt shd; htd wc; chem disp; mv service pnt; fam bthrm; serviced pitches; shwrs inc; EHU (6-16A) inc; gas; lndry; shop; rest, snacks; bar; playgrnd; 2 pools (1 htd, covrd); paddling pool; games area; entmnt; dogs €3.50; 50% statics in sep area; sep car park; some rd noise; poss cr; adv bkg; Eng spkn; ccard acc. "Vg, espec for children; excel site; lots of facs; helpful staff; care needed turning into site area; great value; vg clean san facs; gd rest; conv for Arnhem area, m'way & Ijmuiden ferry port." ♦ 28 Mar-26 Oct. € 39.00 2014*

ASSEN *D2* (16km NW Rural) *53.07783, 6.44870* **Camping de Norgerberg, Langeloërweg 63. 9331 VA Norg [(0592) 612281; info@norgerberg.nl; www.norgerberg.nl]** Fr Leeuwarden, N31 S to junc 30(20km). Then N381 sp Emmen for 10km, L twrds Waskemeer/Norg on N917. Turn L at Norg onto N373. Site on L in 1km. Med, hdg/mkd pitch, pt shd; htd wc; chem disp; mv service pnt; fam bthrm; shwrs inc; EHU (10A); gas; lndry (inc dryer); supmkt; rest; snacks; bar; BBQ; playgrnd; pool 1km; games area & rm; entmnt; internet; wifi; TV rm; dogs €2.30; bus adj; Eng spkn; adv bkg; quiet; red LS; CCI. "Vg cycling trails including forest; easy access to town, rest & shops; excel." ♦ 27 Mar-1 Nov. € 28.00 2015*

BARENDRECHT see Rotterdam *B3*

BEERZE see Ommen *D2*

BELT SCHUTSLOOT see Meppel *C2*

BERG EN TERBLIJT see Valkenburg aan de Geul *C4*

BERGEIJK see Eersel *C4*

BERGEN OP ZOOM *B4* (5km SE Rural) *51.46913, 4.32236* **Camping Uit en Thuis, Heimolen 56, 4625 DD Bergen op Zoom [(0164) 233391; fax 238328; info@campinguitenthuis.nl; www.campinguitenthuis.nl]** Exit A4/E312 at junc 29 sp Huijbergen & foll site sp. Lge, hdg pitch, pt shd; htd wc; chem disp; mv service pnt; fam bthrm; shwrs €0.50; EHU (4-6A) €2; lndry; rest, snacks; bar; playgrnd; tennis; games area; TV; 75% statics; dogs €2.80; poss cr; Eng spkn; adv bkg; quiet; red long stay; red CKE/CCI. "Spacious site in woodland; gd cycle paths to pleasant town; sep mv places; excel site, v pretty; lge pitches." ♦ 1 Apr-1 Oct. € 22.00 2017*

BERLICUM see 'S-Hertogenbosch *C3*

BIDDINGHUIZEN see Harderwijk *C3*

BILTHOVEN see Utrecht *B3*

BLADEL *C4* (1.6km S Rural) *51.35388, 5.22254* **Mini-Camping De Hooiberg, Bredasebaan 20, 5531 NB Bladel [(0497) 369619 or 06 54341822 (mob); info@minicampingdehooiberg.nl; www.minicampingdehooiberg.nl]** Exit A67 junc 32 onto N284 to Bladel, turn L at traff lts to Bladel-Zuid, site on L in 2km. Sm, pt shd; htd wc; chem disp; shwrs inc; EHU (6A) inc; lndry (inc dryer); dogs free; bus adj; sep car park; Eng spkn; adv bkg; quiet. "Gd, quiet site; clean san fac; v friendly owner; farm shop selling local produce adj; 10 mins fr A67; conv NH & for Eindhoven & Efteling theme park." ♦ ltd. 15 Mar-31 Oct. € 15.00 2014*

BLADEL *C4* (3km S Rural) *51.34325, 5.22740* **Camping De Achterste Hoef, Troprijt 10, 5531 NA Bladel [(0497) 381579; fax 387776; info@achterstehoef.nl; www.achterstehoef.nl]** Fr A67 exit junc 32 onto N284 to Bladel, then Bladel-Zuid, site sp. V lge, pt shd; htd wc; chem disp; mv service pnt; fam bthrm; private san facs avail; shwrs; EHU (6A) inc; lndry (inc dryer); supmkt; rest, snacks; bar; playgrnd; 2 pools (1 htd, covrd); paddling pool; waterslide; tennis; games area; games rm; bike hire; wifi; entmnt; 70% statics; dogs; adv bkg; ccard acc. ♦ 4 Apr-26 Oct. € 48.40 (CChq acc) 2014*

BRIELLE *B3* (1km E Urban) *51.90666, 4.17527* **Camping de Meeuw, Batterijweg 1, 3231 AA Brielle [(0181) 412777; fax 418127; info@demeeuw.nl; www.demeeuw.nl]** On A15/N57 foll sp to Brielle. Turn R after passing thro town gates & foll sp to site. Lge, pt shd; wc; chem disp; mv service pnt; fam bthrm; shwrs inc; EHU (10A) €2 (poss rev pol); gas; lndry; shop; rest, snacks; bar; playgrnd; pool 2km; sand beach; bike hire; entmnt; 70% statics; dogs €3.75; phone; Eng spkn; red CKE/CCI. "Historic fortified town; attractive area for tourers; conv Europoort ferry terminal; gd NH/sh stay; phone warden fr recep when arr after 5pm." 31 Mar-30 Oct. € 28.00 2017*

BROEKHUIZENVORST see Horst *C4*

BURGH HAAMSTEDE *A3* (3km NW Coastal) *51.71478, 3.72219* **Camping Ginsterveld, Maireweg 10, 4328 GR Burgh-Haamstede (Zeeland) [(0111) 651590; fax 653040; info@ginsterveld.nl or ginsterveld@ardoer.com; www.ardoer.com/en/camping/ginsterveld]** SP fr Burgh-Haamstede. Foll R107. Lge, pt shd, wc, chem disp, child/fam bthrm, shwrs; EHU (6A) inc; lndry, shop, rest, snack bar, take away, BBQ; playgrnd, paddling pool, sandy beach 2km, games area, bicycles, entmnt ssn, wifi, 50% statics, Eng spkn, adv bkg acc, red LS, "Excel cycling & walking fr site, vg." ♦ 22 Mar-27 Oct. € 46.00 2013*

CADZAND *A4* (2km SE Rural) *51.36099, 3.42503* **Camping De Wielewaal, Zuidzandseweg 20, 4506 HC Cadzand [(0117) 391216; info@campingwielewaal.nl; www.campingwielewaal.nl]** Head to Cadzand. Travel 1km SE, site ent on L, 3km NW of Zuidzande. Med, hdg/mkd pitch, pt shd; wc; chem disp; mv service pnt; fam bthrm; shwrs; EHU; lndry (inc dryer); shop 3km; rest, snacks, bar 1.5km; BBQ; playgrnd; beach 3km; games rm; entmnt; wifi; dogs €2; bus 3km; Eng spkn; adv bkg; quiet; ccard acc; red LS. "Many cycle tracks; walks fr site; friendly, helpful owners; windmill 1km; highly rec; excel." 19 Mar-31 Oct. € 18.70 2016*

⊞ **CALLANTSOOG** *B2* (2.5km NE Coastal) *52.84627, 4.71549* **Camping Tempelhof, Westerweg 2, 1759 JD Callantsoog [(0224) 581522; fax 582133; info@tempelhof.nl; www.tempelhof.nl]** Fr A9 Alkmaar-Den Helder exit Callantsoog, site sp to NE of vill. Lge, mkd pitch, pt shd; htd wc; mv service pnt; chem disp; mv service pnt; serviced pitches; fam bthrm; sauna; private bthrms avail; shwrs inc; EHU (10A) inc; gas; lndry; rest, snacks, bar high ssn; playgrnd; htd, covrd pool; paddling pool; sand beach 1km; tennis; games area; gym; bike hire; wifi; entmnt; sat TV; 50% statics; dogs €3.50; phone; adv bkg. "Superb, well-run site & facs; ACSI acc." ♦ € 43.00 2017*

CALLANTSOOG *B2* (3km NE Coastal) *52.84143, 4.71909* **NCC Camping De Ooster Nollen, Westerweg 8, 1759 JD Callantsoog [(0224) 581281 or 561351; fax 582098; info@denollen.nl; www.denollen.nl]** N fr Alkmaar on A9; turn L sp Callantsoog. Site sp 1km E of Callantsoog. Lge, mkd pitch, pt shd; htd wc; chem disp; mv service pnt; fam bthrm; shwrs inc; EHU (10A) inc; gas; lndry (inc dryer); shop; rest, snacks; bar; playgrnd; pool 400m; sand beach 1.5km; bike hire; games area; wifi; entmnt; TV; 40% statics; dogs €3; phone; Eng spkn; adv bkg; quiet; ccard acc; 10% red long stay; CKE/CCI. "Nature area nr; cheese mkt; clean & superb san facs; supmkt 3km." 1 Apr-29 Oct. € 34.00 2017*

CHAAM see Breda *B3*

DE VEENHOOP see Drachten *C2*

DELFT *B3* (4km NE Urban) *52.01769, 4.37945* **Camping Delftse Hout, Korftlaan 5, 2616 LJ Delft [(015) 2130040; fax 2131293; info@delftsehout.nl; www.delftsehout.co.uk]** Fr Hook of Holland take N220 twd Rotterdam; after Maasdijk turn R onto A20 m'way. Take A13 twd Den Haag at v lge Kleinpolderplein interchange. Take exit 9 sp Delft (Ikea on R). Turn R twrds Ikea then L at rndabt. Foll sp. Do not use Sat Nav. Lge, hdg/mkd pitch, some hdstg, pt shd; htd wc; chem disp; mv service pnt; fam bthrm; shwrs inc; EHU (10A) inc; gas; lndry (inc dryer); shop; rest, snacks; bar; BBQ; playgrnd; htd pool; paddling pool; watersports, fishing nrby; bike hire; golf 5km; wifi; entmnt; games/TV rm; 50% statics; dogs €3.25; no o'fits over 7.5m; phone; bus to Delft; Holland Tulip Parcs site; Eng spkn; some rd noise; ccard acc; red LS/long stay/snr citizens/CKE/CCI. "Located by pleasant park; gd quality, secure, busy site with excel facs; helpful, friendly staff; little shd; sm pitches poss diff lge o'fits; excursions by bike & on foot; easy access Delft cent; sm m'van o'night area outside site; mkt Thur; excel; site clean & well maintained; gd rest; vg play areas for kids; flea mkt on Sat; gd tram and train svcs to the Hague, Leiden and Gouda fr Delft stn." ♦ 25 Mar-1 Nov. € 34.00 SBS - H06 2016*

"We must tell The Club about that great site we found"

Get your site reports in by mid-August and we'll do our best to get your updates into the next edition.

DELFT *B3* (9.4km SW Rural) *51.95450, 4.28833* **Hoeve Bouwlust, Oostgaag 31, 3155 CE Maasland [(0105) 912775; info@hoevebouwlust.nl; www.hoevebouwlust.nl]** Fr Hofh on A20 turn N at junc 7. Go thro Maasland on N468. Site on L in 3km. Sm, hdg pitch, pt shd; wc; chem disp; mv service pnt; shwrs; EHU; lndry (inc dryer); rest; café; BBQ; playgrnd; wifi; 10% statics; bus adj; twin axles; Eng spkn; adv bkg; CKE/CCI. "Lots of outdoor activities inc tandem, boating & scotters; v friendly & helpful owners; vg site." 1 Apr-31 Oct. € 17.50 2014*

DEN HELDER *B2* (3.5km SW Coastal) *52.93672, 4.73377* **Camping de Donkere Duinen, Jan Verfailleweg 616, 1783 BW Den Helder [(0223) 614731; fax 615077; info@donkereduinen.nl; www.donkereduinen.nl]** Fr S turn L off N9 sp Julianadorp (Schoolweg), strt over at x-rds in Julianadorp (Van Foreestweg). Turn R at t-junc onto N502, site on L in approx 4km. Lge, pt shd; wc; chem disp; mv service pnt; fam bthrm; shwr inc; EHU (4-16A) inc; gas; lndry; shops 3km; playgrnd; sand beach 800m; tennis; bike hire; wifi; 10% statics; dogs €2.75; poss cr; Eng spkn; adv bkg (fee); quiet; ccard acc (matercard only); CKE/CCI. "V helpful owner; excel walking/cycling; ferry to Texel Is; lge naval museum & submarine; opp Heldersee Valley Adventure (treetop) Pk." 13 Apr-12 Sep. € 25.50 2017*

DENEKAMP *D3* (4km NE Rural) *52.39190, 7.04890* **Camping De Papillon, Kanaalweg 30, 7591 NH Denekamp [(0541) 351670; fax 355217; info@depapillon.nl; www.depapillon.nl]** Fr A1 take exit 32 onto N342 Oldenzaal-Denekamp, dir Nordhorn, site sp just bef German border. Lge, pt shd; htd wc; chem disp; mv service pnt; fam bthrm; shwrs €0.20; EHU (6-10A) inc; gas; lndry; shop; rest, snacks; bar; playgrnd; 2 pools (1 htd & covrd); lake sw; tennis; bike hire; TV; 5% statics; dogs €4.50; phone; quiet; red long stay/LS. "Super, clean site; friendly site; helpful owners; man-made lake." ♦ 29 Mar-31 Dec. € 33.00 SBS - H18 2017*

DEVENTER *C3* (11km E Rural) *52.25591, 6.29205* **Camping De Flierweide, Traasterdijk 16, 7437 Bathmen [31 570 541478; info@flierweide.nl; www.flierweide.nl]** Fr A1 junc 25 dir Bathmen. After 1km turn R sp De Flierweide, 800m L onto Laurensweg, thro vill. Cross rlwy, 1st R ontp Traasterdijk. Site on R after 500m at fm buildings. Med, hdg/mkd pitch, hdstg, pt shd; wc; chem disp; mv service pnt; fam bthrm; shwrs; EHU(4-16A) €2.50; lndry (inc dryer); BBQ; playgrnd; games area; bike hire; wifi; 1% statics; dogs; Eng spkn; adv bkg; quiet; red LS/long stay; CKE/CCI. "Walking & cycle rtes; golf nr; boules onsite; excel." ♦ 15 Mar-1 Nov. € 23.00 2016*

⊞ **DIEREN** *C3* (2.5km NW Rural) *52.06908, 6.07705* **De Jutberg Vakantiedorp, Jutberg 78, 6957 DP Laag-Soeren [03 13 61 92 20; jutberg@ardoer.com; www.ardoer.com/jutberg]** Fr A12 take exit 27 onto the A348. Turn L on the N348 into Dieren. Turn L at petrol stn, cont for 2.7km. Foll sp to site. V lge, mkd pitch, pt sl, shd; htd wc; chem disp; fam bthrm; shwrs inc; EHU (6A); lndry; shop; rest; snacks; bar; BBQ; playgrnd; htd covrd pool; games area; games rm; entmnt; wifi; dogs; Eng spkn; adv bkg; quiet; CCI. "Hugh pitches, fully serviced; v lively but not noisy; excursions for adults & kids in summer; wet weather diversions; excel san facs; extensive cycle paths thro countryside & forest; excel site." € 42.50 2014*

DIFFELEN see Hardenberg *D2*

DOKKUM *C2* (400m E Urban) *53.32611, 6.00468* **Camping Harddraverspark, Harddraversdijk 1a, 9101 XA Dokkum [(0519) 294445; fax 571402; info@campingdokkum.nl; www.campingdokkum.nl]** Best app fr E fr ring rd N361 onto Harddraversdijk alongside rv, site sp. Do not app thro town - narr rds. Med, hdg/mkd pitch, some hdstg, pt shd; wc; chem disp; mv service pnt; shwrs €0.50; EHU (6A) €2.50; gas; lndry; shop, rest, snacks, bar 400m; playgrnd; tennis; dogs €2; wifi; Eng spkn; quiet. "Excel location in cent of pleasant town; conv for ferry to Ameland Island (12km)." 1 Apr-31 Oct. € 19.00 2015*

DORDRECHT *B3* (13km N Rural) *51.89530, 4.72209* **Camping en Feestzall Landhoeve, Lekdijk 15, 2957 CA Nieuw-Lekkerland [(3184) 684137 or (316) 40487201; info@landhoeve.info; www.landhoeve.com]** Fr A15 take exit 23. Take 2nd exit at rndabt and then 3rd exit at next rndabt twrds New Lekkerland. Turn R onto the N480 twrds Streefkerk. Then L onto Zijdeweg & L again at the end of rd. Site in 400mtrs. Sm, unshd; htd wc; chem disp; shwrs inc; EHU; BBQ; wifi; dogs; Eng spkn; adv bkg; quiet. "New htd toilet block (2017); views; 19 windmills at Kinderdijk nrby, Unesco site; like lge CL; vg." ♦ ltd. 1 Apr-1 Oct. € 22.00 2017*

DORDRECHT *B3* (3km SE Rural) *51.80738, 4.71862* **Camping Het Loze Vissertje, Loswalweg 3, 3315 LB Dordrecht [(078) 6162751; info@campinghetvissertje.nl; www.campinghetvissertje.nl]** Fr Rotterdam across Brienenoord Bdge foll sp Gorinchem & Nijmegen A15. Exit junc 23 Papendrecht & turn R onto N3 until exit Werkendam. Turn R & foll sp 'Het Vissertje'. Sm, pt shd; wc; chem disp; shwrs €0.50; EHU (6A) inc; wifi; 20% statics; dogs €1; Eng spkn; quiet; red long stay. "Lovely, delightful site; friendly, helpful manager; modern, clean san facs; gd cycle rtes nr; vg; easy acc to town on local train." 1 Apr-30 Sep. € 21.00 2016*

DRACHTEN *C2* (10km W Rural) *53.09696, 5.94695* **Camping De Veenhoop Watersport & Recreatie, Eijzengapaed 8, 9215 VV De Veenhoop [(0512) 462289; fax 461057; info@de-veenhoop.nl; www.de-veenhoop.nl]** Exit A7 junc 28 dir Nij Beets, foll De Veenhoop sp to site. Or exit A32 junc 13 & turn W for approx 6km via Aldeboarn. Turn L at Pieter's Rest to De Veenhoop, site on L bef sm bdge. Med, pt shd; htd wc; chem disp; shwrs €0.50; EHU (6-10A) €3; lndry; shops 5km; rest 200m; BBQ; sm playgrnd; lake sw; boat hire; 50% statics; dogs; bus adj; Eng spkn; adv bkg; quiet. "Excel, peaceful, friendly site; clean & well-maintained; excel sailing, cycling, walking; well situated for lakes & N N'lands; gd NH & longer stays." 1 Apr-1 Oct. € 24.00 2016*

DROONENBURGH *C3* (3km NNW Rural) *51.90416, 5.98529* **Camping de Waay, Rijndijk 67A, 6686 MC Doornenburg [(048) 1421256; info@de-waay.nl; www.de-waay.nl]** A325 S fr Arnhem for 12km turn R onto A15 twrds Tiel, take exit N839 Bemmel. At t-junc foll sp to Gendt. In Gendt take N838. Foll ANWB de Waay sp twrds Angeren. Turn R onto the dyke and site on R. Sm, pt shd; wc; chem disp; fam bthrm; shwrs; EHU 6A; lndry (inc dryer); shop; rest; café; snacks; takeaway; bar; BBQ; playgrnd; htd pool; waterslide; paddling pool; lake; games area; games rm; bike hire; wifi; TV rm; 60% statics; dogs; Eng spkn; adv bkg acc; red in LS; CKE/CCI. "V helpful staff; gd for Arnhem & Nijmegen; ACSI acc; vg." ♦ ltd. 25 Mar-1 Oct. € 33.50 2016*

⊞ **DWINGELOO** *D2* (2km SE Rural) *52.82216, 6.39258* **Camping De Olde Bârgen, Oude Hoogeveensedijk 1, 7991 PD Dwingeloo [(0521) 597261; fax 597069; info@oldebargen.nl; www.oldebargen.nl]** Exit A28 Zwolle/Assen rd at Spier, turn W sp Dwingeloo, site clearly sp, in wooded area. Sm, mkd pitch, pt shd; wc; chem disp; fam bthrm; shwrs inc; EHU (4-6A) inc; lndry; shop 800m; playgrnd; pool 1.5km; few statics; wifi; dogs €2; adv bkg; Eng spkn; quiet; CKE/CCI. "Excel, v clean, well-run site on N side Dwingelderveld National Park; gd for walkers & cyclists; v friendly, helpful owners; delightful, quiet sitewarden avail 1 hr each morning LS, pitch & pay next day." ♦ € 21.00 2017*

EERSEL *C4* (4km SE Rural) *51.33635, 5.35552* **Camping De Paal, De Paaldreef 14, 5571 TN Bergeijk [(0497) 571977; fax 577164; info@depaal.nl; www.depaal.nl]** Fr A67/E34 Antwerp/Eindoven exit junc 32 sp Eersel & bear R onto N284 & stay in R-hand lane. At rndabt take 1st exit onto Eijkereind. In 500m after rndbt turn L at traff lts & foll rd around R & L bend. Take R turn sp Bergeijk after lge church (sm sp on sharp L bend). After approx 5km turn L into site rd. V lge, pt shd, htd wc (some cont); chem disp; mv service pnt; fam bthrm; sauna; fam bthrm; shwrs inc; EHU (6A) inc; gas; BBQ (gas/charcoal); lndry (inc dryer); shop; rest & snacks (high ssn); bar; playgrnds; 2 htd pools (1 covrd); paddling pool; fitness cent; sand beach, lake sw 7km; watersports 10km; fishing; excursions; sm children's zoo; tennis; bike hire; horseriding 500m; wifi; entmnt; games rm/TV rm (sat TV); recep 0900-1800; 10% statics; dogs €5; no o'fits over 8m high ssn; no twin-axles; phone; sep cark park; poss cr; ccard not acc; red LS. "Excel, family-run site set in woodland; espec gd for young children; lge pitches in groups with sep sm play areas; cent play areas; conv Efteling theme park, Hilvarenbeek safari park, Oisterwijk bird park; mkt Mon & Tue pm; 1st class facs." ♦ 25 Mar-30 Oct. € 25.00 SBS - H04 2016*

EINDHOVEN *C4* (16km S Rural) *51.32887, 5.46160* **Recreatiepark Brugse Heide, Maastrichterweg 183, 5556 VB Valkenswaard [(040) 2018304; fax 2049312; info@vakantieparkbrugseheide.nl; www.vakantieparkbrugseheide.nl]** S fr Eindhoven, exit Waalre; take N69 Valkenswaard; drive thro to rndabt, turn L. At next rndabt strt ahead, at next rndabt turn R, foll sp Achel. Site on L in 1km. Lge, mkd pitch, shd; htd wc; all serviced pitches; chem disp; mv service pnt; fam bthrm; shwrs inc; EHU (6A) inc (rev pol); gas; lndry (inc dryer); shop 2km; snacks; bar; BBQ; playgrnd; htd pool; paddling pool; bike hire; wifi; entmnt; TV; 40% statics; dogs; phone; Eng spkn; adv bkg (no dep); quiet (can be v noisy w/end); ccard acc; red LS. "Excel, friendly site; gd NH en rte Germany; excel san facs." ♦ 18 Mar-31 Oct. € 34.00 (4 persons) 2016*

EMMEN *D2* (6km N Rural) *52.82861, 6.85714* **Vakantiecentrum De Fruithof, Melkweg 2, 7871 PE Klijndijk [(0591) 512427; fax (0591 513572; info@fruithof.nl; www.fruithof.nl]** On N34 N fr Emmen dir Borger, turn R sp Klijndijk, foll site sp. Lge, hdg/mkd pitch, pt shd; htd wc; chem disp; mv service pnt; serviced pitches; fam bthrm; shwrs inc; EHU (6A) inc; gas; lndry; shop & 5km; rest, snacks; bar; BBQ; playgrnd; htd pool; paddling pool; lake sw & beach adj; tennis; games area; bike hire; entmnt; wifi; TV; 50% statics; dogs; Eng spkn; adv bkg; red LS/long stay; CKE/CCI. "Excel." 25 Mar-26 Sep. € 33.00 2016*

EMST see Apeldoorn *C3*

⊞ **ENSCHEDE** *D3* (6km E Urban) *52.21034, 6.95127* **Euregio Camping de Twentse Es, Keppelerdijk 200, 7534 PA Enschede [(053) 4611372; fax 4618558; info@twentse-es.nl; www.twentse-es.nl]** Fr Germany, cross border at Gronau on B54/N35; twd Enschede. In 2.5km turn R into Oostweg, then in 2km turn R into Gronausestraat, then in 800m turn R into Esmarkelaan. Foll rd thro residential area, turn L at end, site on R. Not rec to foll sat nav due rd building, rec foll rd signs. Lge, pt shd; htd wc; chem disp; shwrs inc; EHU (10A) inc; gas; lndry; shop; rest, snacks; bar; playgrnd; pool; paddling pool; games area; bike hire; wifi; entmnt; TV rm; 70% statics; dogs free; adv bkg; quiet; ccard acc; red CKE/CCI. "Excel site; modern facs." ♦ ltd. € 27.00 2013*

ERICHEM see Tiel *C3*

⊞ **EXLOO** *D2* (2km SE Rural) *52.86841, 6.88496* **Camping Exloo, Valtherweg 37, 7875 TA Exloo [05 91 54 91 47 or 05 91 56 40 14; info@campingexloo.nl; www.campingexloo.nl]** N34 fr Groningen, exit Exloo. Turn R after vill twd Valthe. Site 2km on L. Sm, pt shd; wc; chem disp; mv service pnt; fam bthrm; shwrs; EHU (6A); lndry; BBQ; wifi; TV rm; dogs €1; twin axles; Eng spkn; adv bkg; quiet; CCI. "Friendly recreation rm; vg site." € 14.00 2014*

GENDT *C3* (1km E Rural) *51.87599, 5.98900* **Waalstrand Camping, Waaldijk 23, 6691 MB Gendt [(0481) 421604; fax 422053; info@waalstrand.nl; www.waalstrand.nl]** Exit A15 to Bemmel, then Gendt. In Gendt foll sp to site on Rv Waal. Med, mkd pitch, terr, unshd; wc; chem disp; fam bthrm; EHU (6A) inc; gas; lndry; snacks, bar adj; playgrnd; pool; rv beach adj; tennis; bike hire; wifi; cab TV inc; 50% statics; dogs €3; poss cr; Eng spkn; adv bkg; quiet but some noise fr rv traff. "Excel, well-kept site; clean, modern san facs; interesting rv traff; v friendly owners; lovely position; gd walks." 1 Apr-30 Sep. € 28.50 2016*

GIETHOORN see Meppel *C2*

GOES *A3* (12km NW Rural) *51.54200, 3.78000* **De Heerlijkheid van Wolphaartsdijk, Muidenweg 10, 4471 NM Wolphaartsdijk [(0113) 581584 or 06 12612728 (mob); fax 581111; info@heerlijkheidwolphaartsdijk.nl; www.heerlijkheidwolphaartsdijk.nl]** Off N256 Zierikzee to Goes rd foll sp Jachthaven Wolphaartsdijk. Shortly after vill turn L twd windmill. Turn R at mini rndabt (ignore camping sp by L turn) sp Arnemuiden, strt on at next rndabt, then L at next rndabt; site on L in 1km on lakeside - ent thro farm gate. Sm, hdg pitch, pt shd; wc; chem disp; shwrs inc; EHU (6-16A) €2.50; lndry; playgrnd; lake sw & beach adj; windsurfing; sailing; dogs €0.50; bus 1km; Eng spkn; quiet; CKE/CCI. "CL-type, farm site; modern san facs; friendly owners; bird reserve opp; excel cycling; rec." 15 Mar-31 Oct. € 19.00 2013*

"I need an on-site restaurant"

We do our best to make sure site information is correct, but it is always best to check any must-have facilities are still available or will be open during your visit.

GORINCHEM *B3* (13km E Rural) *51.81845, 5.12563* **Camping De Zwaan, Waaldijk 56, 4171 CG Herwijnen [(0418) 582354]** Exit A15 at junc 29 dir Herwijnen. In Herwijnen turn R at T-junc sp Brakel. Turn L in 500m (Molenstraat). At T-junc turn R (Waaldijk), site on L in 150m on Rv Waal. Sm, pt shd; wc; chem disp; shwrs €0.50; EHU (4A) inc; shop 1km; playgrnd; rv adj; 75% statics; poss cr; adv bkg rec; Eng spkn; quiet but some boat noise; CKE/CCI. "Helpful owners; ltd but clean facs; 66 m fr Amsterdam ferry." 15 Apr-15 Oct. € 13.00 2012*

⊞ **GOUDA** *B3* (2km E Urban) *52.01226, 4.71544* **Klein Amerika Parking, 2806 Gouda** 500m fr Gouda town cent, sp off Blekerssingel/Fluwelensingel. EHU (16A); wc (sm fee); chem disp; water, rubbish bins. "30 spaces in car pk at Klein Amerika supervised by Gouda City Council; 12 EHU sockets; max stay 3 days; normal car parking fees applicable; poorly maintained. € 8.00 2016*

⊞ **GOUDA** *B3* (10km E Rural) *52.01719, 4.82943* **Camping De Mulderije, Hekendorpsebuurt 33, 3467 PA Hekendorp [(0348) 563233 or 06 20680521 (mob); info@demulderije.nl; demulderije.nl]** Exit A12 junc 14 Woerden onto N204 S. In 5km turn R to Oudewater N228. Cont dir Hekendorp & in approx 2km site sp on R. Narr rd to site. Sm, hdstg, pt shd; wc; chem disp; shwrs inc; EHU (6A) inc; lndry rm; shop, rest, snacks, bar 2km; dogs free; Eng spkn; quiet. "Vg, clean, friendly site in nature reserve; cycle or boat to Gouda; facs clean attractive position; gd base; narr rd to site not suitable for lge o'fits; no passing places; do not use sat nav." ♦ ltd. € 17.00 2017*

GROEDE see Breskens *A4*

GRONINGEN *D2* (6km SW Urban) *53.20128, 6.53577* **Camping Stadspark, Campinglaan 6, 9727 KH Groningen [(050) 5251624; fax 5250099; info@campingstadspark.nl; www.campingstadspark.nl]** Take exit 36-A (dir Drachten) and foll 'Stadspark'. In the park go to the L and foll the sp. Fr Drachten/Winsum, take exit 36. Med, shd; wc; chem disp; mv service pnt; fam bthrm; shwrs; EHU (6A) €2.50 (poss rev pol); gas; shop in ssn; snacks; bar; playgrnd; pool 3km; bike hire; wifi (rest); TV; 20% statics; dogs €2; phone; sep car park; poss cr; Eng spkn; adv bkg; quiet; ccard not acc. "Municipal site adj parkland with gd sports facs; park & ride into town; plenty of space, tents & vans mixed; extensive cycle paths; car park adj to each set of pitches; gd san facs; well run site; interesting town; friendly helpful staff." 15 Mar-15 Oct. € 24.00 2017*

GULPEN *C4* (1.5km S Rural) *50.80720, 5.89430* **Panorama Camping Gulperberg, Berghem 1, 6271 NP Gulpen [(043) 4502330; fax 4504609; info@gulperberg.nl; www.gulperberg.nl]** Fr Maastricht on N278 twd Aachen. At 1st traff lts in Gulpen turn sharp R & foll site sp for 2km (past sports complex). Narr final app. Lge, mkd pitch, some hdstg, terr, pt shd; htd wc; chem disp; fam bthrm; shwrs inc; EHU (10A) inc; gas; lndry (inc dryer); shop; rest, snacks; bar; BBQ; playgrnd; pool; paddling pool; bike hire; games area; wifi; cab/sat TV; 10% statics; dogs €4.50; phone; Eng spkn; adv bkg; quiet; red snr citizens; CKE/CCI. "Nr Maastricht with gd walking/views; mkd cycle rtes & footpaths; modern, clean facs - poss long walk; beautiful views; v popular site, busy even in LS; excel." 17 Mar-3 Nov. € 37.00 (CChq acc) SBS - H12 2017*

HALFWEG see Amsterdam *B3*

HARDERWIJK *C3* (12km NE Rural) *52.39470, 5.73230* **Camping De Hooghe Bijsschel, Randmeerweg 8, 8071 SH Nunspeet [(0341) 252406; fax 262565; info@hooghebijsschel.nl; www.molecaten.nl/nl/de-hooghe-bijsschel]** Fr A28/E232 exit junc 14 & turn L at rndabt. Go strt over next 3 rndbts foll sp Nunspeet then turn L at 4th rndabt sp Hulshorst, then R at next rndabt sp Veluwemeer. Site on R after 3km (after sharp L-hand bend). Lge, mkd pitch, pt sl, pt shd; htd wc (some cont); chem disp; mv service pnt; serviced pitches; fam bthrm; shwrs; EHU (6A) inc; gas; lndry (inc dryer); sm shop; supmkt nr; rest, snacks; bar; BBQ; playgrnd; htd pool; lake sw & sand beach adj; gd watersports; fishing; tennis; bike hire; horseriding 2km; wifi; entmnt; games/TV rm; 60% statics; dogs €3.90 (1 only per pitch); no o'fits over 7.5m; phone; sep car park; recep 0900-2100 high ssn 0900-1700 LS; adv bkg; quiet; ccard acc; red LS. "Excel, spacious pitches; shop at w/end only LS with ltd stock; rec use new san facs block nr rest/pool; gd walking/cycling." ♦ 28 Mar-29 Sep. € 34.50 2014*

HARICH see Lemmer *C2*

HARLINGEN *C2* (2km SW Coastal) *53.16253, 5.41653* **Camping De Zeehoeve, Westerzeedijk 45, 8862 PK Harlingen [(0517) 413465; fax 416971; info@zeehoeve.nl; www.zeehoeve.nl]** Leave N31 N'bound at sp Kimswerd. At rndabt turn L under N31 & foll site sp. Site on R in 1.6km. Lge, pt shd; htd wc; chem disp; mv service pnt; fam bthrm; shwrs €0.50; EHU (6A) inc; gas; lndry (inc dryer); shop 1km; rest, snacks; bar; playgrnd; beach adj; fishing; watersports; bike hire; games area; wifi; entmnt; TV; 30% statics; dogs €3.50; phone; Eng spkn; ccard acc (surcharge). "Roomy, well-maintained, open site; clean facs; easy walk to town & harbour; interesting area; vg; ACSI acc." ♦
1 Apr-31 Oct. € 26.00 2017*

HATTEM see Zwolle *C2*

HAVELTE *D2* (1km SE Rural) *52.76820, 6.24987* **Campsite Jelly's Hoeve, Raadhuislaan 2, 7971 CT Havelte [(052) 1342808; fax 1340475; info@jellyshoeve.nl; www.jellyshoeve.nl]** Take exit 4 on A32. Then N371 twrds Havelte/Diever. After 4km cross the bdge and take immed R, foll rd for 1km. Turn L at canal bdge, bear R & after 75m turn R. Site on R after 100m. Sm, hdg/mkd pitch, pt shd; wc; chem disp; shwrs €0.60; EHU (10A) €2; lndry (inc dryer); BBQ; games area; wifi; dogs €2; bus 5km; twin axles; Eng spkn; quiet. "Plenty of walks & cycle tracks; excel."
♦ ltd. 1 Apr-30 Sep. € 21.00 2015*

HEEZE see Eindhoven *C4*

HEILOO see Alkmaar *B2*

HELDEN *C4* (2km E Rural) *51.31813, 6.0235* **Camping De Heldense Bossen, De Heldense Bossen 6, 5988 NH Helden [tel/fax 07 73 07 24 76; heldensebossen@ardoer.com; www.deheldensebossen.nl]** Fr A67 Eindhoven-Venlo, take exit 38 (Helden). Turn R onto N277 twds Maasbreeseweg. Cont onto N562. Fr Helden dir Kessel. Turn L after 1km. Campsite 1km further on. V lge, mkd pitch, pt shd; wc; chem disp; mv service pnt; fam bthrm; shwrs; EHU (10A); lndry (inc dryer); shop; rest; snacks; bar; BBQ; playgrnd; htd covrd pool; waterslide; paddling pool; games area; bike hire; wifi; 65% statics; dogs 26DKK; twin axles; poss cr; Eng spkn; adv bkg; CCI. "Excel site." ♦ ltd. 29 Mar-26 Oct.
€ 45.00 2014*

HELLEVOETSLUIS *B3* (2km W Coastal) *51.82918, 4.11606* **Camping 't Weergors, Zuiddijk 2, 3221 LJ Hellevoetsluis [(0181) 312430; fax 311010; weergors@pn.nl; www.weergors.nl]** Via m'way A20/A4 or A16/A15 dir Rotterdam-Europoort-Hellevoetsluis; take N15 to N57, exit Hellevoetsluis, site sp. Lge, hdg/mkd pitch, some hdstg, unshd; htd wc; chem disp; mv service pnt; fam bthrm; shwrs €0.15/min; EHU (16A) €2.80; gas; lndry (inc dryer); shop; rest; bar; BBQ; playgrnd; paddling pool; lake fishing; tennis; games area; bike hire; wifi; TV rm; 60% statics; dogs €1.60; sep car park; Holland Tulip Parcs site; poss cr; Eng spkn; quiet; ccard acc. "Delta works 6km worth visit; bird sanctuary adj; flat site; gd san facs; v friendly, helpful staff; excel rest; gd walking/cycling; excel site; charming owners." ♦
1 Apr-31 Oct. € 19.50 (CChq acc) 2013*

HENGELO *D3* (7km W Rural) *52.25451, 6.72704* **Park Camping Mooi Delden, De Mors 6, 7491 DZ Delden [(074) 3761922; fax 3767539; info@parkcamping.nl; www.parkcamping.nl]** Exit A35 junc 28 onto N346 dir Delden. Fr Delden-Oost, site sp. Site ent is R-hand of 2 via barrier (use intercom on arr.) If you have a high vehicle take the turning after Delden-Oost to avoid low rail bdge (3.2m); turn L immed aft lge rv bdge & foll site sp. Med, mkd pitch, pt shd; htd wc; chem disp; fam bthrm; shwrs; EHU (6-10A) €3.40 (poss rev pol); lndry; shop & 1km; snacks; bar; playgrnd; pool; tennis; 50% statics; dogs €3.15; poss cr; Eng spkn; adv bkg; quiet. "Ideal for touring beautiful pt of Holland; sports complex adj; pleasant, well-kept site; clean facs." ♦
25 Mar-1 Oct. € 28.00 2016*

HERKENBOSCH see Roermond *C4*

⊞ **HEUMEN** *C3* (2km NW Rural) *51.76890, 5.82140* **Camping Heumens Bos, Vosseneindseweg 46, 6582 BR Heumen [(024) 3581481; fax 3583862; info@heumensbos.nl; www.heumensbos.nl]** Take A73/E31 Nijmegen-Venlo m'way, leave at exit 3 sp Heumen/Overasselt. Do not re-cross m'way. After 500m turn R at camp sp. Site on R in approx 1.5km, 1km S of Heumen. V lge, hdg/mkd pitch, shd; htd wc (some cont); chem disp; mv service pnt; fam bthrm; shwrs €0.50; EHU (6A) inc; gas; lndry (inc dryer); sm supmkt; rest, snacks; bar; BBQ; playgrnd; 2 pools (1 htd); paddling pool; jacuzzi; lake sw, sandy beach 2km; fishing 2km; watersports 6km; tennis; games area; bike hire; horseriding 100m; activities/entmnt in ssn; wifi; games/TV rm; 60% statics in sep area; dogs €4; no o'fits over 14m; Eng spkn; adv bkg; quiet; phone; sep car park; extra €3 for m'vans; adv bkg; noise fr bar high ssn; ccard acc; red LS; CCI. "Excel, busy, family-run site; modern san facs; lots to do on site & in area - info fr recep; ideal for Arnhem; WW2 museums nr; mkt Sat & Mon in Nijmegen." ♦ € 36.00 SBS - H01 2014*

HOEK *A4* (7km W Rural) *51.31464, 3.72618* **Oostappen Vakantiepark Marina Beach (formerly Braakman), Middenweg 1, 4542 PN Hoek [(0115) 481730; fax 482077; info@vakantieparkmarina beach.nl; www.vakantieparkmarinabeach.nl]** Sp fr N61. V lge, mkd pitch, pt shd; htd wc; chem disp; mv service pnt; shwrs €0.50; fam bthrm; serviced pitches; EHU (4A) inc; gas; lndry; shop; rest, snacks; bar; playgrnd; sub-tropical pool; lake beach; sailing; tennis; squash; entmnt; cab TV; 50% statics; dogs €5; phone; poss cr; Eng spkn; adv bkg; ccard acc. "Excel for families; extensive recreation facs; conv Bruges/ Antwerp; extra for lake view pitches." 18 Mar-31 Oct. € 46.00 2016*

"There aren't many sites open at this time of year"

If you're travelling outside peak season remember to call ahead to check site opening dates – even if the entry says 'open all year'.

HOEK VAN HOLLAND *B3* (1.5km N Urban) *51.98953, 4.12767* **Camping Hoek van Holland, Wierstraat 100, 3151 VP Hoek van Holland [(0174) 382550; fax 310210; info@campinghoekvanholland.nl; www.campinghoekvanholland.nl]** Fr ferry foll N211/220 Rotterdam. After 2.4km turn L, 50m bef petrol stn on R, sp 'Camping Strand', site 400m on R. Lge, mkd pitch, hdstg, pt shd; htd wc; chem disp; fam bthrm; shwrs inc; EHU (6A) inc; gas; lndry; shop; rest, snacks; bar; playgrnd; pool; sand beach nr; tennis; bike hire; entmnt; TV; 60% statics; no dogs; phone; bus; sep car park; poss v cr; Eng spkn; quiet; CKE/CCI. "Open 0800-2300; modern san facs but poss inadequate when site full & long walk fr m'van area; conv ferry." ♦ 19 Mar-16 Oct. € 34.00 (4 persons) 2016*

HOEK VAN HOLLAND *B3* (3km N Coastal) *51.99685, 4.13347* **Camping Jagtveld, Nieuwlandsedijk 41, KV 2691 'S-Gravenzande [(0174) 413479; fax 422127; info@jagtveld.nl; www.jagtveld.nl]** Fr ferry foll N211/220 sp Rotterdam. After 3.2km, turn L at junc with traff lts gantry into cul-de-sac. Site 200m on L. Med, unshd; wc; chem disp; shwrs inc; shop; EHU (16A) poss rev pol €2; gas; lndry; shop; snacks; playgrnd; sand beach 400m; entmnt; mostly statics; no dogs; phone; sep car park; poss cr; Eng spkn; quiet. "Ideal for ferry port; conv Den Haag & Delft; gd, clean, level, family-run site; diff when wet; helpful owners; excel 8km long beach." 1 Apr-1 Oct. € 33.50 2014*

HOENDERLOO see Apeldoorn *C3*

IJHORST see Meppel *C2*

KATWIJK AAN ZEE *B3* (6km E Rural) *52.19990, 4.45625* **Camping Koningshof, Elsgeesterweg 8, 2331 NW Rijnsburg [(071) 4026051; fax 4021336; info@koningshofholland.nl; www.koningshof holland.nl]** Fr A44 (Den Haag/Wassenaar-Amsterdam) exit junc 7 (Rijnsburg-Oegstgeest). In Rijnsburg cont twd Noordwijk. Foll blue & white sps thro Rijnsburg, across a bdge & then R twd Voorhout. Site in 2km. Lge, hdg/mkd pitch, hdstg, pt shd; htd wc (some cont); chem disp; mv service pnt; fam bthrm; shwrs inc; EHU (16A) inc; gas; lndry (inc dryer); shop; rest, snacks; bar; BBQ; playgrnd; 2 pools (1 htd, covrd); paddling pool; sand beach 5km; fishing; bike hire; tennis; games rm; wifi; entmnt; TV cab/sat; 35% statics; dogs €3.25; o'fits over 8m by request; phone; sep car park for some pitches; recep 0900-1230 & 1330-2000 high ssn; Holland Tulip Parcs site; Eng spkn; adv bkg; quiet; red long stay LS/snr citizens; CKE/CCI. "Vg, well-run, busy, friendly site; gd for families; excel rest; excel facs & pool; useful tour base for bulb fields; mkt Tues; well maintained; close to beaches and town; rec cash as few cards acc." ♦ 17 Apr-3 Nov. € 35.00 SBS - H03 2017*

KLIJNDIJK see Emmen *D2*

KOOTWIJK see Apeldoorn *C3*

KORTGENE *A3* (500m S Rural) *51.55446, 3.80483* **Camping Villa Park de Pardakreek, Havenweg 1, NL 4484, N Beevland [0113-302051; fax 0113-3302280; paardekreek@ardoer.com; www.ardoer.com/nl/camping/paardekreek]** Take the N256 to Zierikzee, exit Kortgene foll sps to camp. Med, mkd/hdg pitch, pt shd; wc; chem disp; mv service pnt; fam bthrm; shwrs; EHU (16A); lndry; shop; rest; snacks, bar; BBQ; playgrnd; sw pool; water playgrnd; sauna; adj lake; games rm; wifi; 40% statics; dogs; bus 0.5km; Eng spkn; quiet; CKE/CCI. "Excel site; boat slipway & storage; adj Lake Veerse Meer; many places to visit." ♦ 27 Mar-1 Nov. € 43.00 2015*

⊞ **KOUDUM** *C2* (2km S Rural) *52.90290, 5.46625* **Kawan Village De Kuilart, De Kuilart 1, 8723 CG Koudum [(0514) 522221; fax 523010; info@kuilart.nl; www.kuilart.nl]** Fr A50 exit sp Lemmer/Balk. Foll N359 over Galamadammen bdge, site sp. Lge, mkd pitch, pt shd; htd wc; mv service pnt; fam bthrm; private bthrms some pitches; 90% serviced pitches; sauna; shwrs €0.35; EHU (6-16A) €1.50-3.60; gas; lndry (with dryer); supmkt; rest, snacks; bar; playgrnd; 2 pools (1 htd, covrd); waterslide; sailing; watersports; marina; games area; wifi; entmnt; TV & cinema rm; 50% statics; ltd dogs €3.35 (adv bkg rec); phone; sep car park; poss cr; Eng spkn; adv bkg; Holland Tulip Parcs site; CKE/CCI. ♦ € 26.00 (CChq acc) 2016*

LANDSMEER see Amsterdam *B3*

NETHERLANDS

⊞ **LAUWERSOOG** *D1* (500m SE Coastal) *53.40250, 6.21740* **Camping Beleef Lauwersoog, Strandweg 5, 9976 VS Lauwersoog [(0519) 349133; fax 349195; info@lauwersoog.nl; www.lauwersoog.nl]** Fr N355 Leeuwarden-Groningen rd, take N361 Dokkum exit. Foll rd to Lauwersoog, site sp. V lge, unshd; htd wc; chem disp; mv service pnt; serviced pitches; fam bthrm; shwrs; EHU (10A) inc; gas; lndry (inc dryer); shop; rest, snacks; bar; playgrnd; pool; tennis; bike hire; wifi; entmnt; TV; 50% statics; dogs €4.75; phone; sep car park; Holland Tulip Parcs site; poss v cr; Eng spkn; adv bkg; quiet; ccard acc; CKE/CCI. "Excel, well-maintained site; vg rest; gd facs; next to historic boat harbour." ♦ € 28.50 (CChq acc) 2017*

LEEUWARDEN *C2* (7km W Rural) *53.19484, 5.73785* **Minicamping Van Harinxma, Marssummerdyk 7, 9033 WD Deinnum [0031 (0) 58 215 04 98; Info@minicamping-van-Harinxma.nl; www.minicamping-van-harinxma.nl]** Fr S: take N31/N32 twrds Leeuwarden. Turn L on N31 sp Harlingen, turn R to Masum-Harlingen, and imm R sp Ritsumazijl. Foll rd turn L at T- junc, then fork L into no thro rd. Site on L. Sm, med, hdg pitch, pt shd; wc; chem disp; shwrs; EHU (6A); lndry; snacks; playgrnd; billiards; TV; dogs; twin-axle; Eng spkn; adv bkgs; CKE/CCI. "Vg; fishing fr site." 15 Mar-15 Oct. € 12.00 2012*

LEIDEN *B3* (8km N Rural) *52.20984, 4.51370* **Camping De Wasbeek, Wasbeeklaan 5b, 2361 HG Warmond [(071) 3011380; dewasbeek@hetnet.nl]** Exit A44 junc 4 dir Warmond; in 200m turn L into Wasbeeklaan, then R in 50m. Site sp. Sm, pt shd; wc; chem disp; shwrs €0.70; lndry; shop, rest, snacks, bar 1km; BBQ; pool 2km; sand beach 8km; 40% statics; dogs free; bus 500m; sep car park; Eng spkn; adv bkg; quiet but some aircraft noise. "Attractive, lawned site close to bulb fields; m'vans by arrangement; twin-axles not acc; friendly, helpful staff; gd cycling (track to Leiden); fishing; boating; birdwatching; lovely sm tidy site; nice area." 1 Apr-1 Oct. € 26.00 2014*

LIEREN see Apeldoorn *C3*

LISSE *B3* (6km S Rural) *52.22175, 4.55418* **Camping De Hof van Eeden, Hellegatspolder 2, 2160 AZ Lisse [(0252) 212573; fax 235200; info@dehofvaneeden.nl; www.dehofvaneeden.nl]** Exit A44 junc 3 & turn N onto N208 dir Lisse. Turn R at rest on R bef 1st set traff lts into narr rd, foll rd to end (under A44) to site. Sm, unshd; wc; chem disp (wc); shwrs €0.50; EHU (16A) inc; rest; playgrnd; wifi; 90% statics; Eng spkn; rlwy noise. "Gd CL-type site, space for 10 tourers (sep area) - rec phone or email bef arr; interesting location by waterway & lifting rlwy bdge; conv Keukenhof; helpful owners." 15 Apr-15 Oct. € 17.50 2017*

LUTTENBERG see Nijverdal *D3*

LUYKSGESTEL see Eersel *C4*

MAASDAM see Dordrecht *B3*

⊞ **MAASTRICHT** *C4* (10km E Rural) *50.84468, 5.77994* **Boerderijcamping Gasthoes, Gasthuis 1, 6268 NN Bemelen [(043) 4071346 or (06) 54717951; info@boerderijcamping-gasthoes.nl; www.boerderijcamping-gasthoes.nl]** Head for Bemelen, site is sp. Sm, pt shd; wc; chem disp; fam bthrm; shwrs; EHU (10A); BBQ; dogs inc; public trans; twin axles; Eng spkn; adv bkg; quiet; red LS; CKE/CCI. "Excel." ♦ € 18.00 2017*

MAURIK *C3* (2km NE Rural) *51.97605, 5.43020* **Recreatiepark Eiland van Maurik, Rijnbandijk 20, 4021 GH Maurik [(0344) 691502; fax 692248; receptie@eilandvanmaurik.nl; www.eilandvanmaurik.nl]** Exit A15 junc 33 at Tiel onto B835 N & foll sp to Maurik & site on rvside. Or exit A2 junc 13 at Culembourg onto N320 to Maurik. Lge, pt shd; htd wc; chem disp; mv service pnt; fam bthrm; shwrs €0.50; EHU (10A) inc; gas; lndry; shop; rest, snacks; bar; playgrnd; tennis; fishing; watersports; games area; covrd play area; horseriding; entmnt; wifi; TV; 50% statics; dogs €4; Holland Tulip Parcs site; Eng spkn; adv bkg; quiet. ♦ 1 Apr-1 Oct. € 43.00 (CChq acc) 2014*

"That's changed – Should I let The Club know?"

If you find something on site that's different from the site entry, fill in a report and let us know. See camc.com/europereport.

MEERSSEN *C4* (1.6km ESE Rural) *50.87851, 5.77112* **Camping Meerssen, Houthemerweg 95, 6231 KT Meerssen [(0433) 654743; fax 654745; info@campingmeerssen.nl; www.campingmeerssen.nl]** Fr Eindhoven A2, take exit 51, foll Valkenburg sp. Take A79 to Hellen exit 2 Meerssen. L at junc after 400m, site on R. Sm, mkd, pt shd; wc; chem disp; mv service pnt; shwrs inc; EHU (6A); gas; lndry (inc dryer); shop 1km; rest 1km; snacks 1km; bar 1km; BBQ; wifi; 2% statics; dogs; twin axles; poss cr; Eng spkn; quiet; no ccard acc; red LS. "Nice, peaceful & relaxing site; v popular with Dutch people; cent for touring the area; excel site." 1 Apr-30 Sep. € 34.50 2014*

MIDDELBURG *A4* (8km N Rural) *51.55005, 3.64022* **Mini Camping Hoekvliet, Meiwerfweg 3, 4352 SC Gapinge [(0118) 501615 or (0621) 957185; copgapinge@zeelandnet.nl; www.hoekvliet.nl]** Fr Middleburg turn R off N57 at traff lts sp Veere & Gapinge, site sp after Gapinge vill. Sm, mkd pitch, some hdstg, pt shd; wc; chem disp; mv service pnt; shwrs inc; EHU (10A) inc; lndry (inc dryer); BBQ; rest, snacks, bar 2km; playgrnd; sand beach 5km; TV cab; bike hire; wifi; 20% statics; dogs €1; sep car park; Eng spkn; quiet; CKE/CCI. "Superb little (25 o'fits) farm site; excel, modern san facs; helpful owner; immac san facs; fully serviced pitches; great value." ♦ ltd. 1 Apr-31 Oct. € 23.00 2017*

MIDWOLDA *D2* (2km W Urban) *53.18900, 6.99053* **Camping de Bouwte, Hoofdweg 20A, 9681 AH Midwolda [05 97 59 17 06; fax 97 59 19 63; info@campingdebouwte.nl; www.campingdebouwte.nl]** Via A7 dir Groningen-Winschoten or via N33 Assen-Delfzil, then onto A7. Exit 45 Scheemda-Midwolda. Foll camping signs. Turn R at traff lts, site on R in 500m. Med, pt shd; wc; chem disp; fam bthrm; shwrs; EHU (10A); lndry (inc dryer); shop; rest; bar; BBQ; playgrnd; sw lake; games area; games rm; bike hire; entmnt; wifi; TV rm; 50% statics; dogs €1.75; phone; bus adj; twin axles; poss cr; Eng spkn; adv bkg; CCI. "Vg walking/cycling area with mkd rtes; horse riding 1km; WWll Museum in vill; watersports on Oldambtmeer 2km; vg site." ♦ 6 Jan-20 Dec. € 24.00 2014*

MIERLO *C4* (1.5km S Rural) *51.43250, 5.61694* **Camping De Sprink, Kasteelweg 21, 5731 PK Mierlo [(0492) 661503; info@campingdesprink.nl; www.campingdesprink.nl]** Take A67 and exit at Geldrop/Mierlo. Foll sp for Mierlo. Turn R at rndabt onto Santheuvel West fr Geldropseweg. R onto Heer de Heuschweg, R onto Kasteelweg. Site on the L. Med, mkd pitch, hdstg, unshd; wc; chem disp; mv service pnt; fam bthrm; shwers inc; EHU (6A); lndry; shop 1.5km; rest; snacks; bar; BBQ; playgrnd; wifi; dogs €0.75; Eng spkn; adv bkg; quiet. "Friendly, helpful staff; all facs immac; excel." 31 Mar-30 Oct. € 20.00 2017*

MONTFORT see Echt *C4*

NOORD SLEEN see Emmen *D2*

NOORDWIJK AAN ZEE *B3* (5km N Rural/Coastal) *52.26817, 4.46981* **Camping De Duinpan, Duindamseweg 6, 2204 AS Noordwijk aan Zee [(0252) 371726; fax 344112; contact@campingdeduinpan.nl; www.campingdeduinpan.com]** Exit A44 at junc 3 dir Sassenheim then foll sp Noordwijkerhout. At 5th rndabt (Leeuwenhorst Congress building) turn R then L. Site sp. Med, mkd pitch, unshd; htd wc; chem disp; mv service pnt; shwrs €0.50; EHU (10A) inc; gas; lndry; rest, snacks, bar adj; playgrnd; pool 2.5km; bike hire; wifi; 60% statics; phone; sep car park; ccard acc; CKE/CCI. "Conv for tulip fields in ssn." 15 Mar-31 Oct. € 29.50 2013*

⊞ **NOORDWIJK AAN ZEE** *B3* (2km NE Rural) *52.24874, 4.46358* **Camping op Hoop van Zegen, Westeinde 76, 2211 XR Noordwijkerhout [(0252) 375491; info@campingophoopvanzegen.nl; www.campingophoopvanzegen.nl]** Exit A44 junc 6 dir Noordwijk aan Zee. Cross N206 & turn R in 1km into Gooweg dir Leeuwenhorst. In 1km turn L into Hoogweg & foll sp to site. Med, hdg/mkd pitch, unshd; htd wc; chem disp; mv service pnt; fam bthrm; shwrs; EHU (6A) €2.25; lndry (inc dryer); shop 2km; playgrnd; sand beach 2.5km; bike hire; games area; dogs €3; phone; poss cr; adv bkg rec when Keukenhof open; Eng spkn; quiet; ccard acc; CKE/CCI. "Gd site; modern san facs; conv bulb fields, beaches." € 18.00 2013*

⊞ **NOORDWIJK AAN ZEE** *B3* (5km NE Urban) *52.26580, 4.47376* **De Wijde Blick, Schulpweg 60, 2211 XM Noordwijkerhout [(0252) 372246; info@bungalowparkdewijdeblick.nl; www.bungalowparkdewijdeblick.nl]** Fr Hague exit L fr N206 at Noordwijkerhout Zuid. Shortly turn R at rndabt 1.3km, turn L at rndabt. Site on Rin 1km (1st bldg after felds). Med, mkd pitch, unshd; wc; chem disp; mv service pnt; shwrs €0.50; EHU; lndry (inc dryer); playgrnd; beach 2km; wifi; 90% statics; train 10km; Eng spkn; CKE/CCI. "Site with bungalows + statics; very clean facs; friendly, helpful staff; excel wifi; conv for Keukenhof; Flora Holland at Aalsmeer nrby; train to Amsterdam; excel. € 25.00 2017*

NOORDWIJKERHOUT see Noordwijk aan Zee *B3*

NUNSPEET see Harderwijk *C3*

⊞ **OMMEN** *D2* (6km W Rural) *52.51911, 6.36461* **Resort de Arendshorst, Arendshorsterweg 3A, 7731 RC Ommen [(0529) 453248; fax (0059) 453045; info@resort-de-arendshorst.nl; www.resort-de-arendshorst.nl]** W fr Ommen on N34/N340 turn L at site sp, then 500m along lane past farm, site on rvside. Lge, mkd pitch, pt shd; htd wc; chem disp; serviced pitches; fam bthrm; shwrs €0.20; EHU (10A) inc; gas; lndry; shop; rest, snacks; bar; no BBQ; playgrnd; pool 3km; paddling pool; sw in canal; games area; bike hire; TV rm; wifi; 50% statics; dogs €4; phone; Eng spkn; adv bkg (fee); quiet; red 7+ days/snr citizens; CKE/CCI. "Beautiful area; many cycle rtes; gd children's facs." ♦ € 39.00 SBS - H02 2017*

OOSTERBEEK see Arnhem *C3*

OOSTERHOUT *B3* (6km W Rural) *51.64658, 4.80818* **Koeckers Camping 't Kopske, Ruiterspoor 75, 4911 BA Den Hout [(0613) 142151; info@campingtkopske.nl; www.campingtkopske.nl]** Leave A59 at junc 32 to Oosterhout W. At rndabt take R for Den Hout. In Den Hout R opp Church. 1st site on L after 1km. Sm, mkd pitch, unshd; wc chem disp; shwrs; rest; bar; poss cr; Eng spkn; quiet. "Gd cycling area; activity ctr; rest adj; gd." 26 Mar-2 Oct. € 19.00 2016*

OOSTWOUD see Enkhuizen *C2*

OOTMARSUM *D3* (2.5km S Rural) *52.38959, 6.90016* **Camping De Haer, Rossummerstraat 22, 7636 PL Agelo [0541 291847; info@dehaer.nl; www.dehaer.nl]** Site sp 3km S of Ootmarsum. Lge, hdg/mkd pitch, pt shd; wc; chem disp; fam bthrm; shwrs; EHU(6-10A); lndry (inc dryer); rest; bar; BBQ; playgrnd; pool; games area; games rm; bike hire; entmnt; wifi; TV rm; 30% statics; dogs €1.50; bus adj; twin axles; Eng spkn; adv bkg; red LS; CKE/CCI. "Many cycle paths fr site; vg." ♦ 1 Apr-1 Nov. € 21.00 2016*

NETHERLANDS

OPENDE *D2* (3km SE Rural) *53.16465, 6.22275* **NCC Camping de Watermolen, Openderweg 26, 9865 XE Opende [tel/fax (0594) 659144; info@campingde watermolen.nl; www.campingdewatermolen.nl]** Exit A7 junc 32 dir Kornhorn. In Noordwijk turn L at church & in 2 km turn R into Openderweg. Site in 700m on L. Med, mkd pitch, hdstg, pt shd; htd wc; chem disp; mv service pnt; fam bthrm; shwrs; EHU (16A); lndry (inc dryer); shops 4km; rest; snacks; bar; BBQ; playgrnd; pool; lake sw; internet; wifi (€1 for 24h); TV rm; some statics; dogs (LS) €2.50; phone; Eng spkn; adv bkg; twin axles; ccard acc; quiet; CKE/CCI. "Friendly owners; pt of site for NCC members - CMC members welcome but must book ahead; brilliant site with lakes to walk around & woods; hide for bird watching; excel; fishing on site; bike hire; €10 dep for key; car free pitches." 1 Apr-1 Oct. € 25.30 2017*

⊞ **OTTERLO** *C3* (2km S Rural) *52.08657, 5.76934* **Camping De Wije Werelt, Arnhemseweg 100-102, 6731 BV Otterlo [(0318) 591201; fax 592101; info@ wijewerelt.nl; www.ardoer.com/wije-werelt]** Exit A50 junc 22 dir Hoenderlo & N304 to Otterlo. Site on R after Camping de Zanding. Lge, mkd pitch, unshd; htd wc; chem disp; mv service pnt; fam bthrm; shwrs inc; EHU (6-10A) inc; lndry; shop; rest, snacks; bar; playgrnd; pool; paddling pool; games area; 40% statics; dogs €4; phone; Eng spkn; adv bkg; quiet; ccard acc. "Excel, well-run site; immac san facs; vg for families; conv Arnhem; gd access to Kroller-Muller Museum." € 31.00 2016*

⊞ **OTTERLO** *C3* (2km NW Rural) *52.10878, 5.76040* **Camping 't Kikkergat, Lange Heideweg 7, 6731 EG Otterlo [(0318) 591794; contact@kikkergat.nl; www.kikkergat.nl]** Exit A1/E30 at J17 dir Harskamp. Site on R in 12km, unmade rd. Sm, pt shd; wc; chem disp; mv service pnt; fam bthrm; shwrs; EHU (10A); lndry (inc dryer); snack bar; wifi; dogs; twin axles; Eng spkn; adv bkg; red LS; CKE/CCI. "Excel site". ♦ ltd. € 18.00 2017*

OUDEGA see Drachten *C2*

PANNINGEN *C4* (4km NW Rural) *51.34894, 5.96111* **Beringerzand Camping, Heide 5, 5981 NX Panningen [07 73 07 20 95; fax 73 07 49 80; info@ beringerzand.nl; www.beringerzand.nl]** Fr A67 exit at junc 38 twd S, dir Koningslust/Panningen. Site is 3km NW Panningen, down narr lane thro asparagus fields. Med, mkd pitch, pt shd; wc; chem disp; mv service pnt; shwrs; EHU (10A); lndry (inc dryer); shop; snacks; bar; BBQ; playgrnd; htd pool; covrd pool; waterslide; paddling pool; games area & rm; bike hire; wifi; dogs €4.85 max 2 per pitch; twin axles acc; Eng spkn; adv bkg. ♦ 28 Mar-7 Nov. € 45.00 2014*

REEUWIJK see Gouda *B3*

RENSWOUDE *C3* (2km NE Rural) *52.08435, 5.55069* **Camping de Grebbelinie, Ubbeschoterweg 12, 3927 CJ Renswoude [(0318) 591073; info@campingde grebbelinie.nl; www.campingdegrebbelinie.nl]** Head NW on Dorpsstraat/N224, at rndabt take 1st exit onto Barneveldsestraat, turn R onto Bekerweg, R onto Ubbeschoterweg then turn L. Site on the R. Med, unshd; htd wc; chem disp; fam bthrm; shwrs inc; EHU; lndry; shops 2km; rest 2km; snacks 2km; bar 2km; playgrnd; games area; internet; wifi; dogs €1.75; bus 2km; Eng spkn; adv bkg; quiet; CKE/CCI. "Friendly owners; excel cycling with cycle rte adj; conv for Arnhem & Utrecht; peaceful site on former farm; in open countryside; excel value for money." 19 Mar-15 Oct. € 22.60 2016*

RETRANCHEMENT see Sluis *A4*

RIJEN see Breda *B3*

RIJNSBURG see Katwijk aan Zee *B3*

ROCKANJE *A3* (2km NW Coastal) *51.88000, 4.05422* **Molecaten Park Waterbos, Duinrand 11, 3235 CC Rockanje [(0181) 401900; fax 404233; info@ waterboscamping.nl; www.waterboscamping.nl]** Site clearly sp fr Rockanje vill. Lge, hdg pitch, pt shd; htd wc; chem disp; mv service pnt; fam bthrm; private san facs avail; shwrs €0.50; EHU (6A) inc; lndry; shop; rest, snacks; bar; playgrnd; sand beach/dunes 1km; entmnt; wifi; cab/sat TV; 80% statics; phone; no dogs; phone; poss cr; adv bkg; quiet; CKE/CCI. "Lovely base for Voorne area." ♦ 25 Mar-31 Oct. € 33.00 2016*

ROERMOND *C4* (15km W Rural) *51.20947, 5.83008* **Camping Geelenhoof, Grathemerweg 16, 6037 NR Kelpen-Oler (Limburg) [(0495) 651858; info@ geelenhoof.nl; www.geelenhoof.nl]** 1km S of Kelpen-Oler; bet Roermond & Weert; exit N280 foll sp; well mkd. Med, hdg/mkd pitch, pt shd; htd wc; chem disp; mv service pnt; fam bthrm; shwrs inc; EHU (6A) €3; rest, snacks; bar; playgrnd; games area; games rm; wifi; dogs (on request) €2.50; Eng spkn; adv bkg; quiet; CKE/CCI. "Cars not to be parked with c'van; vg site; semi serviced pitches; sep NH; keycard barrier; no twin axles; lake fishing; warm welcome; excel site." 1 Mar-31 Oct. € 25.00 2017*

ROOSENDAAL *B3* (7km S Rural) *51.49430, 4.48536* **Camping Zonneland, Turfvaartsestraat 6, 4709 PB Nispen [(0165) 365429; info@zonneland.nl; www. zonneland.nl]** Take A58 exit 24 onto N262 dir Nispen. Foll site sps. Lge, some hdstg, shd; wc; chem disp; mv service pnt; shwrs €0.50; EHU (4-10A) €2; lndry; shop; supmkt 4km; snacks; bar; pool; playgrnd; entmnt; 80% statics; no dogs; phone; Eng spkn; adv bkg; quiet; ccard acc. 1 Mar-15 Oct. € 19.00 2012*

⊞ **ROTTERDAM** *B3* (17km SE Rural) *51.83454, 4.54673* **Camping De Oude Maas, Achterzeedijk 1A, 2991 SB Barendrecht [(078) 6772445; fax 6773013; www.campingdeoudemaas.nl]** Leave A29 (Rotterdam-Bergen op Zoom) junc 20 Barendrecht, foll sp for Heerjansdam, site sp. Fr A16 (Breda-Dordrecht) foll Europort sp, then Zierikzee, Barendrecht, site sp. Lge, pt shd; htd wc; chem disp; mv service pnt; fam bthrm; shwrs inc; EHU (10A) inc; lndry; shop; snacks; playgrnd; TV; 80% statics in sep area; dogs; phone; quiet; ccard acc. "Excel site on Rv Maas inc sm marina & joins rec park; excel facs; some pitches rough & long way fr facs; ferry fr site in ssn; check recep opening time if planning dep bef midday (espec Sun) for return of deposit & barrier key (€35); entry via new ent past old." ♦ € 22.00 2016*

⊞ **ROTTERDAM** *B3* (3km W Urban) *51.93100, 4.44200* **Stadscamping Rotterdam, Kanaalweg 84, 3041 JE Rotterdam [(010) 4153440; fax 4373215; info@stadscamping-rotterdam.nl; www.stadscamping-rotterdam.nl]** Adj to junc of A13 & A20, take slip rd sp Rotterdam Centrum & Camping Kanaalweg sp to site. Dist fr m'way 2.5km with 3 L turns. Lge, pt shd; wc; chem disp; fam bthrm; shwrs inc; EHU (6A) €3.75; gas; lndry; shop; snacks; bar; internet; pool 500m; dogs €2; bus; poss cr; adv bkg; quiet but rds, rlwy adj; ccard acc. "Gd bus service to city cent; few water taps; friendly staff." ♦ € 25.00 2016*

SCHIMMERT *C4* (600m E Rural) *50.90746, 5.83122* **Camping Mareveld, Mareweg 23, 6333 BR Schimmert South Limburg [(045) 4041269; fax 4042148; info@mareveld.nl; www.campingmareveld.nl]** A76 exit Spaubeek, turn R twd Schimmert. 2nd on the L in Schimmert. Campsite sp. Sm, pt shd; wc; chem disp; fam bthrm; shwrs, EHU (6A) €2.10; rest/café; bar; playgrnd; htd pool; games area; wifi; TV in bar; 80% statics; dog €1.75; poss cr; Eng spkn; adv bkg; popular with families; red LS. "Gd cycling/walking fr site; gd site; open plan, grassy site." 1 Apr-31 Dec. € 30.00 2014*

⊞ **SEVENUM** *C4* (5km SW Rural) *51.38310, 5.97590* **Camping De Schatberg, Midden Peelweg 1, 5975 MZ Sevenum [(077) 4677777; fax 4677799; receptie@schatberg.nl; www.schatberg.nl]** Fr A2/A67 exit junc 38 for Helden; foll sp Sevenum & site by sm lake. V lge, shd; htd wc; chem disp; mv service pnt; fam bthrm; private san facs some pitches; sauna; shwrs inc; EHU (6-10A) inc; gas; lndry (inc dryer); shop; rest, snacks; bar; playgrnd; 2 pools (1 htd, covrd); paddling pool; waterslide; jacuzzi; lake sw & sand beach; watersports; fishing; tennis; games area; bike hire; entmnt; TV; 60% statics; dogs (in sep area); phone; Holland Tulip Parcs site; Eng spkn; adv bkg; quiet; CKE/CCI. "Excel leisure facs, espec for children; vg site but impersonal; tourers pitched amongst statics; Venlo Sat mkt worth visit." ♦ € 41.00 (4 persons) (CChq acc) 2017*

See advertisement

"I like to fill in the reports as I travel from site to site"

You'll find report forms at the back of this guide, or you can fill them in online at camc.com/europereport.

'S-HEERENBERG *D3* (3km W Rural) *51.87795, 6.21125* **Camping Brockhausen, Eltenseweg 20, 7039 CV Stokkum [(0314) 661212; fax 668563; info@brockhausen.nl; www.brockhausen.nl]** Fr A12 exit junc sp 's-Heerenberg, cont past 's-Heerenberg sp & pick up sp to Stokkum & site on L. Med, mkd pitch, pt shd; htd wc; chem disp; mv service pnt; fam bthrm; shwrs metered; EHU (4-6A) inc; lndry (inc dryer); shop 3km; playgrnd; cab TV; 40% statics; dogs €3.45; Eng spkn; adv bkg; quiet. "V clean, eco-friendly site; facs charged on electronic key; friendly, helpful staff; lovely area walking, cycling; excel." ♦ 1 Apr-31 Oct. € 24.00 2012*

'S-HERTOGENBOSCH *C3* (10km E Rural) *51.6938, 5.4148* **Camping de Hooghe Heide, Werstkant 17, 5258 TC Berlicum [(073) 5031522; fax 5037351; info@hoogheheide.nl; www.hoogheheide.nl]** Fr A59/A2 circular rd around 's-Hertogenbosch exit junc 21 dir Berlicum. Foll sp Berlicum & site. Site is NE of Berlicum. Med, mkd pitch, pt shd; wc; chem disp; fam bthrm; shwrs inc; EHU (10A) €3; lndry; shop; snacks; playgrnd; pool; paddling pool; games area; wifi; TV; 70% statics; dogs €4.25; phone; poss cr/noisy high ssn; Eng spkn; adv bkg ess; quiet; CKE/CCI. "Nice, peaceful wooded site; narr site rds for lge o'fits; tourers on open field; excel." ♦ 26 Mar-1 Nov. € 32.40 2016*

'S-HERTOGENBOSCH *C3* (10km SW Rural) *51.65507, 5.23520* **Topparken Résidence de Leuvert, Loverensestraat 11, 5266 Cromvoirt [088 5002473; info@deleuvert.nl; www.deleuvert.nl]** Exit for Cromvoirt fr A59 or A65. Med, mkd pitch, pt shd; wc; chem disp; mv service pnt; fam bthrm; shwrs €0.75; EHU(10A) inc; lndry (inc dryer); café; snacks; bar; BBQ; playgrnd; htd pool; paddling pool; games area; games rm; entmnt; wifi; TV rm; 75% statics; dogs; bus 0.5km; twin axles; Eng spkn; adv bkg; quiet; red LS; CKE/CCI. "Gd bus access to 's-Hertogenbosch; vg site." ♦ ltd. 1 Jan-31 Oct. € 28.40 2016*

"We must tell The Club about that great site we found"

Get your site reports in by mid-August and we'll do our best to get your updates into the next edition.

⊞ **SINT OEDENRODE** *C3* (3km N Rural) *51.57800, 5.4400* **NCC Camping 't Roois Klumpke, Vliegden 1, 5491 VS Sint Oedenrode [(0413) 474702; www.ncc.nl]** Exit A2 junc 26 to Sint Oedenrode; site sp on Schijndel rd - 100m bef Camping Kienehoef turn R onto Vliegden, site 400m on L. Med, mkd pitch, pt shd; htd wc; chem disp; shwrs inc; EHU (10A); lndry; BBQ; Eng spkn; poss cr; Eng spkn; adv bkg; quiet; CKE/CCI. "Members only - CC members welcome but must pre-book; shop, rest, snacks avail at Camping de Kienehoef; run by volunteers; spacious; woodland." ♦ ltd. € 11.00 2017*

SINT OEDENRODE *C3* (3.7km SE Urban) *51.54780, 5.48703* **Camping De Graspol, Bakkerpad 17, 5492 TL Sint Oedenrode [(0413) 474133 or (0653) 224220; info@campingdegraspol.nl; www.campingdegraspol.nl]** Fr A50 take exit St Oedenrode, dir Nijnsel. Foll sp to site. Med, mkd pitch, pt shd; htd wc; chem disp; mv service pnt; fam bthrm; shwrs; EHU (16A) gas; lndry (inc dryer); BBQ; bike hire; fishing; games rm; wifi; TV; dogs; Eng spkn; quiet; ACSI. "Well kept; gd for NH or longer; warm welcome." 1 Mar-1 Oct. € 25.00 2015*

SLUIS *A4* (800m N Rural) *51.31395, 3.38863* **Camping De Meidoorn, Hoogstraat 68, 4524 LA Sluis [tel/fax (0117) 461662; info@campingdemeidoorn.eu; www.campingdemeidoorn.eu]** Fr Zeebrugge, ignore 1st turn L to Sluis, cont to rndabt sp Sluis 1km. At windmill keep R (do not go to town cent). After LH bend turn R, foll sps. Lge, pt shd; htd wc; chem disp; mv service pnt; fam bthrm; shwrs €0.50; EHU (6A) €3; gas; shop; rest, snacks; bar; playgrnd; tennis; TV; 80% statics; dogs €1.75; phone; Eng spkn; red CKE/CCI. "Bus to Bruges and Breskens fr rear site ent." ♦ 1 Apr-1 Nov. € 33.40 2013*

SNEEK *C2* (2km E Urban) *53.03557, 5.67630* **Jachthaven Camping De Domp, De Domp 4, 8605 CP Sneek [(0515) 412559; fax 439846; www.dedomp.nl]** Fr cent of Sneek on Leeuwarden rd, turn R sp De Domp. Med, pt shd; htd wc; chem disp; mv service pnt; serviced pitches; fam bthrm; shwrs €0.50; EHU (16A) inc; gas; lndry; rest, snacks; bar; supmkt nr; playgrnd; boating; sep car park; wifi; dogs; adv bkg; Eng spkn. "Many canals in Sneek; marina on site; easy walk to pleasant town; gd cycling cent." ♦ 25 Mar-1 Nov. € 18.00 (CChq acc) 2016*

STEENBERGEN *B3* (5km NW Rural) *51.60887, 4.27303* **Camping De Uitwijk, Dorpsweg 136, 4655 AH De Heen [(0167) 560000; fax 560010; info@de-uitwijk.nl; www.de-uitwijk.nl]** Fr N259 at Steenbergen turn W onto N257 dir Zierikzee. In 2km turn N thro De Heen & turn R at T-junc. Site recep on R, site on L. Do not take c'van to recep, but ent site, park on R & walk back. Med, mkd pitch, pt shd; htd wc; chem disp; mv service pnt; fam bthrm; shwrs inc; EHU (4-10A) inc; lndry (inc dryer); shop 4km; rest, snacks; bar; playgrnd; games rm; wifi; entmnt; sat TV; 60% statics; dogs €3.20; bus 750m; poss cr; Eng spkn; adv bkg; CKE/CCI. "Pleasant, well run, quiet site adj marina; friendly staff; excel; excel cycle rtes; conv for ferry." 23 Mar-28 Sep. € 26.00 2014*

TERSCHELLING ISLAND *C1* **Sites on Terschelling Island are listed together at the end of the Netherlands site entry pages.**

TEXEL ISLAND *B2* **Sites on Texel Island are listed together at the end of the Netherlands site entry pages.**

TUITJENHORN *B2* (4km SE Rural) *52.73495, 4.77612* **Campingpark de Bongerd, Bongerdlaan 3, 1747 CA Tuitjenhorn [(0226) 391481; fax 394658; info@bongerd.nl; www.bongerd.nl]** N fr Alkmaar on N245, exit at Dirkshorn & foll sp to site. V lge, mkd pitch, pt shd; htd wc; chem disp; fam bthrm; shwrs inc; EHU (10A) inc; gas; lndry (inc dryer); shop; rest, snacks; bar; BBQ; playgrnd; 2 htd pools (1 covrd); paddling pool; waterslide; lake fishing; tennis; games area; bike hire; wifi; entmnt; 60% statics; dogs €1.90; Eng spkn; adv bkg; ccard acc; quiet. "Excel, attractive family site; vg facs." ♦ 8 Apr-30 Sep. € 43.00 2014*

UDEN *C3* (14km E Rural) *51.66309, 5.77641* **Mini Camping Boszicht, Tipweg 10, 5455 RC Wilbertoord [(0485) 451565 or (06) 12957217; fax (0845) 471522; boszicht-wilbertoord@planet.nl; www.boszichtcamping.nl]** Fr 's-Hertogenbosch on N279 dir Helmond. At Veghel turn L onto N265. Bef Uden turn R onto N264 to Wilbertoord in 11km. Sm, hdg/mkd pitch, unshd; wc; shwrs; EHU (6A) metered; lndry; shops; rest in vill; playgrnd; games area; wifi; dogs €2; Eng spoken; quiet. "Family-run farm site in woodland; conv Arnhem, Nijmegen; delightful site." 20 Mar-19 Oct. € 17.00 2016*

UITDAM see Edam *B2*

UTRECHT *B3* (10km NE Rural) *52.13123, 5.22024* **Camping Bospark Bilthoven, Burg van der Borchlaan 7, 3722 GZ Bilthoven [(030) 2286777; fax 2293888; info@bosparkbilthoven.nl; www.bosparkbilthoven.nl]** Exit A28/E30 Utrecht-Amersfoort at exit sp De Bilt & strt to Bilthoven. Approx 3km after leaving m'way (400m S of level x-ing) turn R sp De Bospark Bilthoven. At edge of town foll sps twd lge brown tower & golf course. Site on L. V lge, pt shd; htd wc; chem disp; mv service pnt; fam bthrm; serviced pitches; shwrs inc; EHU (4-6A) inc (poss rev pol); gas; lndry; shop 1km; snacks; bar; playgrnd; htd pool; TV; 60% statics; dogs €3.50; phone; poss cr; Eng spkn; adv bkg; quiet but some noise fr air base. "Helpful management; 20 mins walk to stn for trains to Utrecht cent." ♦ 1 Apr-31 Oct. € 25.70 2012*

UTRECHT *B3* (14km E Rural) *52.09272, 5.28287* **Camping de Krakeling, Woudensbergseweg 17, 3707 HW Zeist [(030) 6915374; fax 6920707; allurepark@dekrakeling.nl; www.dekrakeling.nl]** Fr A12 exit junc 20 Driebergen/Zeist. In Zeist foll dir Woudenberg, site sp. V lge, hdg/mkd pitch, pt shd; htd wc; chem disp; mv service pnt; fam bthrm; shwrs €0.50; EHU (6-10A) €2.50; lndry; shop; rest, snacks, bar w/end only LS; playgrnd; pool 3km; lake sw 5km; tennis; internet free; cab TV; 90% statics; dogs free; phone; adj nature reserve; bus; adv bkg. "Gd touring base Amsterdam/Utrecht; friendly; excel, clean facs; recep open 0900-1700, clsd for lunch." ♦ 28 Mar-29 Sep. € 28.40 2013*

VAALS *C4* (1.5km N Rural) *50.78159, 6.00694* **Camping Hoeve de Gastmolen, Lemierserberg 23, 6291 NM Vaals [(043) 3065755; fax 3066015; info@gastmolen.nl; www.gastmolen.nl]** Fr A76 exit at Knooppunt Bocholtz onto N281 SW to join N278, turn L twd Aachen. Site on L just bef 1st rndabt as ent Vaals. Med, hdg/mkd pitch, pt sl, pt shd; wc; chem disp; shwrs €0.50; EHU (6A) €2.70; lndry; shops 500m; rest 500m; snacks; playgrnd; 10% statics; dogs €2.70; bus 500m; sep car park; poss cr; Eng spkn; adv bkg rec; quiet; CKE/CCI. "Sm rural site; conv Aachen; vg san facs; diff in wet - tractor avail; mosquitoes; Drielandenpunt 4km, in walking dist (where Netherlands, Germany & Belgium meet); excel." 25 Mar-31 Oct. € 20.50 2016*

VAASSEN see Apeldoorn *C3*

VALKENBURG *C4* (13km N Rural) *50.94973, 5.87883* **De Botkoel, Kerkpad 2, 6155 KJ Puth [(0464) 432374; camping@botkoel.nl; www.botkoel.nl]** Fr W on A2 exit at J4 sp Schinnen. At end of rd turn L, cross x-rds and turn R again on the R until you cross rlwy x-ing, then R on the R. Cont on Stn Street until T-junc, turn L twrds Puth. Uphill to Puth then turn R. At S-turn, turn R into narr rd. Site 200m on L. Sm, pt sl, terr, unshd; wc; chem disp; fam bthrm; shwr inc; lndry (inc dryer); shop, rest, snacks, bar 1km; BBQ; playgrnd; wifi; dogs; train 1km; twin axles; Eng spkn; adv bkg; quiet; CKE/CCI. "Site on fruit fm; views; bike hire; clean facs, rebuilt 2017; excel; conv for Sittard, Maastricht & Aachen; vg." 15 Mar-31 Oct. € 20.00 2017*

"I need an on-site restaurant"

We do our best to make sure site information is correct, but it is always best to check any must-have facilities are still available or will be open during your visit.

VALKENBURG AAN DE GEUL *C4* (2km N Rural) *50.88013, 5.83466* **Familie Camping De Bron, Stoepertweg 5, 6301 WP Valkenburg [(045) 4059292; fax 4054281; info@camping-debron.nl; www.camping-debron.nl]** Fr A79 exit junc 4 dir Hulsberg. Take 3rd exit fr rndabt onto N298, across next rndabt, then L onto N584, site sp. Fr A76 exit junc 3 dir Schimmert, foll sp Valkenburg & site. Lge, mkd pitch, pt shd; htd wc; chem disp; mv service pnt; fam bthrm; shwrs inc; EHU (4-6A) €3-4.50; lndry; shop; rest, snacks; bar; playgrnd; pool; games area; bike hire; entmnt; internet; TV; 30% statics; dogs €3.50; phone; adv bkg; CKE/CCI. "Vg, well laid-out site; gd facs; muddy in wet weather; 2 pools with lots of equipment for kids; statics hidden away in the greenery; helpful staff." ♦ 1 Apr-20 Dec. € 42.50 2014*

VALKENBURG AAN DE GEUL *C4* (3km S Urban) *50.85972, 5.83138* **Stadscamping Den Driesch, Heunsbergerweg 1, 6301 BN Valkenburg [(043) 6012025; fax 6016139; info@campingdendriesch.nl; www.campingdendriesch.nl]** Fr A2 dir Maastricht exit sp Valkenburg-Cauberg. Foll sp Valkenburg N590 & take turning sp Sibbe-Margraten. At rndabt foll sp Valkenburg, pass coal mine & turn R in 250m into sm, sl, unmkd ent. Steep turn off main rd into ent. NB L turn into site diff - proceed to rndabt at top of hill & return downhill to site. Med, mkd pitch, hdstg, pt sl, terr, pt shd; htd wc; chem disp; mv service pnt; shwrs €0.70; EHU (10A) inc; lndry; shop on site & 500m; rest 500m; snacks; no BBQs; htd, covrd pool 1km; bike hire; 10% statics; dogs €3; phone; Eng spkn; adv bkg; quiet; ccard acc; CKE/CCI. "Castle & caves adj; other attractions nr; gd Xmas mkts in caves; easy access Maastricht by bus/train; vg." 23 Mar - 31 Dec. € 42.00 SBS - H10 2017*

VALKENBURG AAN DE GEUL *C4* (1km SW Rural) *50.85672, 5.81891* **Camping De Cauberg, Rijksweg 171, 6325 AD Valkenburg [(043) 6012344; info@campingdecauberg.nl; www.campingdecauberg.nl]** Exit A79 sp Valkenburg, foll Sibbe & Margraten sp to town cent. Take R fork in town sp De Cauberg, site on R at top of hill just past end Valkenburg sp. Med, mkd pitch, pt sl, shd; htd wc; chem disp; fam bthrm; shwrs inc; EHU (10A) inc; lndry; shop, rest, snacks; playgrnd; htd pool 1km; internet; 10% statics; dogs €3.10; bus; phone; site clsd 1-15 Nov; Eng spkn; adv bkg; quiet; red long stay; CKE/CCI. "Excel pool 1km; excel, modern, clean san facs; friendly, helpful owner; conv Maastricht; many rests, cafes in Valkenburg." 1 Jan-5 Jan 14 Mar-31 Oct & 14 Nov-31 Dec. € 34.00 2014*

VALKENBURG AAN DE GEUL *C4* (7km W Rural) *50.86057, 5.77237* **Camping Oriëntal, Rijksweg 6, 6325 PE Berg en Terblijt [(043) 6040075; info@campingoriental.nl; www.campingoriental.nl]** Fr A2/E25 exit onto N278 E & in 1km turn L onto N590 sp Berg en Terblijt & Valkenburg. Cont on N590, site on R in 4km at start of vill. Lge, mkd pitch, pt shd; htd wc; chem disp; mv service pnt; serviced pitch inc TV at extra cost; fam bthrm; serviced pitches (inc cab TV); shwrs; EHU (6A) inc (poss rev pol); gas; lndry; shop; rest 500m; snacks; bar; supmkt; playgrnd; htd, covrd pool; paddling pool; games area; wifi; 10% statics; dogs €3.50; phone; bus to Maastricht adj; Eng spkn; adv bkg; quiet; red LS; red LS; CKE/CCI. "Immac, well-run site; some areas flood in heavy rain; gd entmnt for young children; conv Maastricht." ♦ Easter-30 Oct. € 27.00 2013*

VALKENSWAARD see Eindhoven *C4*

VEERE see Middelburg *A4*

VENLO *C4* (22km N Rural) *51.45989, 6.17120* **Camping Landhuis De Maashof, Veerweg 9, 5973 NS Lottum [07 74 63 19 24; fax 74 63 24 72; info@demaashof.nl; www.demaashof.nl]** Fr A67 Eindhoven - Venlo, take exit 12 onto A73. Then exit 11 twd Horst/Melderslo. Foll sp to Lottum. Foll sp to campsite. Med, pt shd; wc; chem disp; shwr; lndry; snacks; BBQ; playgrnd; wifi; dogs €1.20; bus 800m; twin axles; poss cr; Eng spkn; adv bkg; quiet; CCI. "Cycling, rv bank walks; rose gdn exhibition in vill; lots of rv traff & ferries; working windmill & castle nrby." 1 Apr-30 Sep. € 20.00 2014*

VENLO *D4* (10km NW Rural) *51.42029, 6.10675* **Camping Californië, Horsterweg 23, 5971 ND Grubbenvorst [(077) 3662049; fax 3662997; info@limburgsecamping.nl; www.limburgsecamping.nl]** Exit A73 at Grubbenvorst junc 12 dir Sevenum, site sp. Med, pt shd; htd wc; chem disp; mv service pnt; shwrs inc; EHU (4-10A); lndry; playgrnd; Eng spkn; quiet. "Pleasant, peaceful, warm welcome; unisex shwrs; CL style site with grass cut reg." 15 Mar-15 Oct. € 26.60 2014*

VIERHUIZEN *D1* (300m E Rural) *53.36011, 6.29505* **Camping Lauwerszee, Hoofdstraat 49, 9975 VR Vierhuizen [05 95 40 16 57; info@camping-lauwerszee.nl; www.camping-lauwerszee.nl]** Fr A7/E22 Amsterdam-Groningen take exit 33 Oude Riet onto N388 Grijpskerk. Turn L on N355 then R onto N388. 2.5km after Zoutcamp turn L to Vierhuizen. Site on R in 1km. Med, hdg/mkd pitch, pt shd; wc; chem disp; mv service pnt; shwrs; EHU (6A); lndry (inc dryer); rest; bar; BBQ; playgrnd; bike hire; wifi; dogs; bus 0.5km; twin axles; Eng spkn; adv bkg; quiet; CCI. "Sep field with lge pitches avail for CC memb at red price; helpful owner; vg." ♦ ltd. 1 Apr-1 Nov. € 24.00 2014*

VORDEN *D3* (5km SE Rural) *52.08379, 6.35510* **'t Lebbink, Lindense Enkweg 1, 7251 NH Vorden [(0575) 556680; harmsen@tlebbink.nl; www.tlebbink.nl]** Fr Vordon N316 S for 1.6km. L onto Lindeseweg for 3km to Linde. L just bef windmill along access rd to campsite on R. Med, hdg/mkd pitch, pt shd; wc; chem disp; shwrs; EHC (6-16A); lndry; BBQ; bike hire; wifi; dogs; twin axles; adv bkg; quiet; CKE/CCI. "On numbered cycle rte & walking rte; vg." ♦ ltd. 15 Mar-1 Nov. € 16.00 2015*

"Satellite navigation makes touring much easier"

Remember most sat navs don't know if you're towing or in a larger vehicle – always use yours alongside maps and site directions.

VUREN see Gorinchem *B3*

⊞ **WASSENAAR** *B3* (1km NW Rural) *52.14638, 4.38750* **Camping Duinrell, Duinrell 1, 2242 JP Wassenaar [tel/fax (070) 5155147 or (070) 5155255; touroperator@duinrell.nl; www.duinrell.nl]** Fr Rotterdam in dir Den Haag on A13/E19, then on A4/E19 foll sp for Amsterdam. On A4 keep R onto A12 in dir Voorburg/Den Haag. At end m'way turn R onto N44 sp Wassenaar. In 8km turn L at traff lts immed bef Mercedes g'ge, foll site sp. On arr at site foll sp to campsite not coach park. Not rec to arrive mid-afternoon/early evening due to heavy traff leaving amusement park. V lge, hdg/mkd pitch, pt shd; htd wc; chem disp; mv service pnt; fam bthrm; serviced pitches; sauna; private san facs avail; shwrs inc; EHU (6A) inc; gas; lndry (inc dryer); shop; rest, snacks; bar; BBQ; playgrnd; 2 pools (1 covrd); paddling pool; waterslide; sand beach 3km; fishing, horseriding nrby; tennis; bike hire; free ent adj amusement park; golf 1km; games rm; internet; wifi; entmnt; TV; 30% statics; dogs €6; no o'fits over 7.75m high ssn; phone; sep car park for some pitches; poss cr; Eng spkn; adv bkg; quiet; red LS/snr citizens; ccard acc. "Popular, busy site; some pitches poss diff access, check bef siting; superb, modern facs; tropical indoor pool; vg security; excel." ♦ € 33.50 (CChq acc) SBS - H13 2016*

WEERSELO *D3* (2km N Rural) *52.36530, 6.84285* **Camping De Molenhof, Kleijsenweg 7, 7667 RS Reutum [(0541) 661165 or 661201; fax 662032; info@demolenhof.nl; www.demolenhof.nl]** Exit A1 junc 33 dir Oldenzaal then Tubbergen. At Weerselo, foll site sp. Lge, pt shd; htd wc; chem disp; mv service pnt; fam bthrm; shwrs inc; EHU (10A) inc; gas; lndry (inc dryer); shop; rest, snacks; bar; BBQ; playgrnd; 2 pools (1 htd, covrd); waterslide; fishing; tennis; covrd play area; bike hire; golf 10km; wifi; entmnt; TV rm & cab TV to pitches; 25% statics; dogs €3; Holland Tulip Parcs site; Eng spkn; adv bkg; quiet; ccard acc. "Spacious pitches; spotlessly clean." ♦ 16 Apr-2 Oct. € 39.00 (CChq acc) 2013*

WEERT *C4* (9km SE Rural) *51.22480, 5.79916* **Camping Landgoed Lemmenhof, Kampstraat 10, 6011 RV Ell Limburg [(0495) 551277; fax 551797; info@lemmenhof.nl; www.lemmenhof.nl]** Exit A2 junc 40 dir Kelpen. In 2km at traff lts turn R; in 50m turn R dir Ell. In 2km immed bef vill sp & De Prairie Cafe turn R into Kempstraat, site in 200m. Sm, hdg/mkd pitch, unshd; htd wc; chem disp; shwrs inc; EHU (10A) inc; lndry; shop 500m; rest, bar 200m; playgrnd; dogs €0.70; Eng spkn; adv bkg; quiet; CKE/CCI. "Vg; B&B & apartments avail; v friendly helpful owners and friendly local caravaners on site." ♦ 15 Mar-31 Oct. € 18.60 2013*

WEIDUM see Leeuwarden *C2*

WESTERBORK see Beilen *D2*

⊞ **WEZUPERBRUG** *D2* (300m E Rural) *52.84030, 6.72370* **Rekreatiepark 't Kuierpadtien, Oranjekanaal Noordzijde 10, 7853 TA Wezuperbrug [(0591) 381415; fax 382235; info@kuierpad.nl; www.kuierpad.nl]** Fr A28 m'way exit 31 dir Emmen onto N381. Take exit Zweeloo & turn L immed. Go under viaduct twd Wezuperbrug via Wezup. In Wezuperbrug go over bdge, turn R, site sp. V lge, pt shd; htd wc; chem disp; mv service pnt; fam bthrm; shwrs inc; EHU (6A) inc; gas; lndry (inc dryer); shop; rest, snacks; bar; playgrnd; htd, covrd pool; paddling pool; waterslide; lake sw & boating; tennis; games rm; bike hire; wifi; entmnt; TV; 30% statics; dogs €5; phone; sep car park; Holland Tulip Parcs site; quiet. "Excel site; great for kids; vg pool & extensive sports facs; can get busy; some pitches diff to access, narr & steep ent to pitch espec nr the water." ♦ € 53.00 2014*

WEZUPERBRUG *D2* (9km SW Rural) *52.77911, 6.68607* **Camping De Bronzen Emmer, Mepperstraat 41, 7855 TA Meppen [(0591) 371543; info@de-bronzen-emmer.nl; www.bronzenemmer.nl]** Exit the A37 at Oosterhesselen (N854) twrds Meppen. Foll sp to site. Lge, mkd pitch, pt shd; htd wc; chem disp; fam bthrm; shwrs inc; EHU (10A) €0.40/Kwh; gas; lndry rm; shop 4km; rest; snacks; bar; playgrnd; pool htd/cvrd; games area; games rm; tennis; wifi; tv rm; 10% statics; dogs; Eng spkn; adv bkg; quiet; red LS. "Cycling off-rd to supmkt; friendly, family site; excel facs; sauna; excel." ♦ 1 Apr-28 Oct. € 34.00 2017*

WIJCKEL see Lemmer *C2*

WIJSTER see Beilen *D2*

WILBERTOORD see Uden *C3*

WINTERSWIJK *D3* (5km N Rural) *52.00878, 6.73850* **Poelhuis Boerderijcamping, Poolserweg 3, 7104 DC Winterswijk [(0543) 569246; info@poelhuis.nl; www.poelhuis.nl]** N on Meddosweg to Meddo, R on Wandersweg to x-rds, Poolseweg, L and site on R in 500m. Sm, mkd pitch, hdstg, pt shd; wc; chem disp; shwrs; EHU (6A); lndry; BBQ; games rm; bike hire; wifi; TV rm; Eng spkn; adv bkg; quiet; CKE/CCI. "Numbered cycle rte; close to German border; flamingo nature park with walking rtes; vg." ♦ ltd. 15 Mar-31 Oct. € 18.00 2015*

WOERDEN *B3* (4km NE Rural) *52.09280, 4.88530* **Camping Batenstein, Van Helvoortlaan 37, 3443 AP Woerden [(0348) 421320; fax 409691; camping batenstein@planet.nl; www.camping-batenstein.nl]** Fr A12 exit junc 14 sp Woerden. Twd cent of town, L at rndabt, R at next rndabt, thro rlwy tunnel. L at traff lts, L again at next traff lts, R at camping sp. Ent narr & sm sp. Med, pt shd; wc; chem disp; mv service pnt; fam bthrm; sauna; shwrs €0.60; EHU (6-10A) inc; gas; lndry (inc dryer); shops 1km; snacks; playgrnd; htd, covrd pool; paddling pool; waterslide; games area; wifi; 75% statics; dogs €1.50; phone; bus 750m; Eng spkn; sep car park; poss cr; adv bkg; quiet but some noise fr pool during day; ccard acc; red long stay; CKE/CCI. "Gd touring base; el conn by site staff only (locked boxes); san facs cramped but gd quality & clean; conv for ferries." 28 Mar-26 Oct. € 30.50 2014*

WOLPHAARTSDIJK see Goes *A3*

WOUDENBERG see Amersfoort *C3*

AMELAND ISLAND

⊞ **BUREN** *C1* (1km N Coastal) *53.45355, 5.80460* **Camping Klein Vaarwater, Klein Vaarwaterweg 114, 9164 ME Buren [(0519) 542156; fax 542655; info@kleinvaarwater.nl; www.kleinvaarwater.nl]** Take ferry fr Holwerd to Nes on Ameland Island. Turn R at rndabt twd Buren & strt on to supmkt. At 3-lane intersection turn L twd beach rd & site. Med, mkd pitch, pt shd; htd wc; chem disp; mv service pnt; fam bthrm; shwrs; EHU (16A); gas; lndry (inc dryer); supmkt; ATM; rest, snacks; bar; BBQ; playgrnd; htd, covrd pool; paddling pool; waterslide; sand beach 800m; tennis; 10-pin bowling; games area; fitness rm; wifi; entmnt; TV; 75% statics; no dogs; Holland Tulip Parcs site; poss cr; adv bkg; red LS. "Nature park adj; site in dunes & forest." ♦ € 20.00 2016*

ZANDVOORT *B3* (5km N Coastal) *52.40415, 4.55180* **Kennemer Duincamping De Lakens, Zeeweg 60, 2051 EC Bloemendaal aan Zee [(023) 5411570; fax 5411579; delakens@kennemerduincampings.nl; www.kennemerduincampings.nl]** Site sp N of Zaandvoort on coast rd, site in sand dunes. V lge, unshd; htd wc; chem disp; mv service pnt; fam bthrm; shwrs inc; EHU (4-10A) inc; gas; lndry; shop; rest, snacks; playgrnd; pool 4km; sand beach 200m; windsuring 2km; games area; horseriding 300m; internet; TV rm; 50% statics; no dogs; poss cr; Eng spkn; adv bkg rec high ssn; ccard acc; quiet. "V busy May/June public holidays; gd facs; excel walking, cycling fr site; welcoming helpful staff; excel spar shop; gd position in National Park; gd for sightseeing in Amsterdam, Haarlem, Aalsmeer flower mkt as well as outdoor pursuits." ♦ 28 Mar-26 Oct. € 53.00 2014*

ZEELAND see Uden *C3*

ZEIST see Utrecht *B3*

ZEVENAAR *C3* (8km S Rural) *51.89666, 6.07041* **Camping De Rijnstrangen, Beuningsestraat 4, 6913 KH Aerdt [(0316) 371941 or (0612) 559464; info@derijnstrangen.nl; www.derijnstrangen.nl]** Exit A12 junc 29 onto N 336 Elten & Lobith. At sp Aerdt turn R onto dyke (narr) & cont approx 1.5km to church. Turn L in 100m, site on R (500m W of Aerdt). Sm, hdg/mkd pitch, pt shd, hdstg; htd wc; chem disp; mv service pnt; fam bthrm; shwrs; EHU (6A); lndry; shop 2km; BBQ; cooking facs; games rm; bike hire; wifi; twin axles; poss cr; Eng spkn; adv bkg; quiet; CKE/CCI. "Friendly, welcoming owners; gd cycling area with numbered rte; excel htd facs; excel." ♦ ltd. 1 Mar-1 Nov. € 21.00 2015*

ZEVENHUIZEN see Gouda *B3*

ZIERIKZEE *A3* (2km N Rural) *51.65683, 3.91242* **Camping 't Uulof, Zandweg 37, 4301 TA Zierikzee [(0111) 414614; info@tuulof.nl; www.campingtuulof.nl]** SE fr Serooskerke on N59. In 9km just bef traff lts turn L. Site 300m on R; sp fr N59. Sm, pt shd; wc; chem disp; serviced pitches; shwrs €2; EHU (6A) inc; shop 1km; gas 1km; lndry; pool 2km; sand beach 13km; 25% statics; dogs €1; Eng spkn; some rd noise; CKE/CCI. "Lovely site on farm - produce avail; excel san facs, pt unisex; helpful, friendly owner; interesting town, steamer trips; easy cycling to town; peaceful site, friendly & welcoming, lovely home-grown veg." 1 Apr-1 Oct. € 15.50 2013*

ZIERIKZEE *A3* (5km N Rural) *51.68048, 3.89847* **Mini-Camping Appelgaerd, Zandweg 6, 4321 TA Kerkwerve [(0614) 489332; info@appelgaerd.nl; www.appelgaerd.nl]** Fr Zierikzee take N59 dir Serooskerke. Immed turn R onto Zandwek. Cont for 3km, site on L bef vill of Kerkwerve. Sm, lge, hdg pitch, pt shd; wc; chem disp; mv service pnt; shwrs; EHU (6A) inc; BBQ; playgrnd; beach 4km; wifi; dogs; bus 250m; twin axles; Eng spkn; adv bkg; quiet. "Gd cycling, walking & bird watching area; excel site." ♦ ltd. 1 Apr-30 Oct. € 20.00 2014*

ZOETERMEER *B3* (4km W Rural) *52.06716, 4.44862* **Camping De Drie Morgen, Voorweg 155, 2716 NJ Zoetermeer [(079) 3515107; fax 3512084; mail@dedriemorgen.nl; www.dedriemorgen.nl]** Fr Den Haag take A12/E30 sp Zoetermeer. Exit junc 6 sp Zoetermeer cent. In 1.5km turn L onto Amertaweg. In 2km foll sp to Mini-Camping. At rndabt turn R onto Voorweg, site on R. Sm, unshd; wc; chem disp; mv service pnt; shwrs inc; EHU (6A) €1.75; farm shop; playgrnd; dogs; sep car park; Eng spkn; adv bkg; quiet. "A working farm; gd touring base; pleasant staff; peaceful; busy in ssn." 1 Apr-31 Oct. € 14.50 2013*

"There aren't many sites open at this time of year"

If you're travelling outside peak season remember to call ahead to check site opening dates – even if the entry says 'open all year'.

TERSCHELLING ISLAND

⊞ **OOSTEREND** *C1* (200m N Rural) *53.40562, 5.37947* **Camping 't Wantij, Oosterend 41, 8897 HX Oosterend [(0562) 448522 or (06) 20396345 (mob); info@wantij-terschelling.nl; www.wantij-terschelling.nl]** Fr Harlingen to Terschelling by ferry. Take rd to Oosterend, site ent on L 250m after vill sp, past bus stop & phone box. Sm, mkd pitch, pt shd; htd wc; chem disp; shwrs €0.50; EHU (6A) €3 (poss rev pol); lndry; shop 3km; rest, snacks, bar 100m; cooking facs; playgrnd; sand beach 2km; wifi; TV; dogs €1.75; bus adj; Eng spkn; adv bkg; quiet; CKE/CCI. "Gd area for birdwatching; many cycle/foot paths across dunes; horsedrawn vehicles for conducted tours; Elvis memorabilia 2km at Heartbreak Hotel - rest on stilts; excel site." ♦ ltd. € 18.00 2016*

TEXEL ISLAND

DE KOOG *B2* (500m E Rural) *53.09610, 4.76500* **De Luwe Boshoek, Kamperfoelieweg 3, 1796 MT De Koog [02 22 31 73 90]** Fr ferry take 501 to De Koog. Sp after ref point 17. R at De Zwaluw Hotel. Site on L after 100m. Med, mkd pitch, unshd; htd wc; chem disp; fam bthrm; shwr inc; EHU (16A); lndry (inc dryer); shop 0.5km; BBQ; sandy beach 1km; 10% statics; dogs; quiet. "Excel; gd base to stay; bike hire 0.5 km." ♦ 15 Mar-1 Nov. € 28.00 2014*

DEN BURG *B2* (16km N Rural) *53.16987, 4.86072* **Camping de Hoek, Vuurtorenweg 83, 1795 LK De Cocksdorp [(0222) 316236; saaldehoek@tele2.nl; www.campingdehoek.nl]** Take the main rd fr ferry to top of island, past exit 35, site on L nr end of rd. Sm, pt shd; htd wc; chem disp; mv service pnt; shwrs inc; EHU (16A); lndry (inc dryer); shop, rest, snacks, bar 3km; BBQ; sandy beach 1km; wifi; dogs; poss cr; Eng spkn; adv bkg; quiet. "Farm site; beatifully kept; lovely fam; by rd but v quiet; cycle path; excel." 1 Apr-1 Oct. € 25.00 2017*

ZUIDWOLDE *D2* (2km S Rural) *52.65822, 6.42726* **NCC Camping De Krententerp, Ekelenbergweg 2, 7921 RH Zuidwolde DR [(0528) 372847; zuidwolde@ncc.nl; www.ncc.nl]** Fr S fr Zwolle exit A28 junc 22 dir Dedemsvaart. Turn L at Balkbrug onto N48, then L at junc Alteveer-Linde to site. Sm, mkd pitch, shd; htd wc; chem disp; shwrs inc; EHU (4A) €2.75 (long lead poss req); lndry; shop, rest, snacks, bar 2km, playgrnd; htd, covrd pool 2km; dogs; bus 200m; poss cr; adv bkg; quiet. "Peaceful site; friendly, helpful staff; CC members welcome; phone ahead bet 1700 & 1800; excel cycling, walking; Zuidwolde beautiful town." 1 Apr-31 Oct. € 12.50 2016*

ZWOLLE *C2* (5km NE Urban) *52.53690, 6.12954* **Camping De Agnietenberg, Haersterveerweg 27, 8034 PJ Zwolle [(038) 4531530; fax 4542084; info@campingagnietenberg.nl; www.campingagnietenberg.nl]** N fr Zwolle on A28 exit junc 20 Zwolle Oost & turn R at end of slip rd then immed L. In 400m turn L at traff lts into Haersterveerweg & foll site sp. Lge, mkd pitch, pt shd; htd wc; chem disp; mv service pnt; fam bthrm; shwrs €0.50; EHU (10A); lndry; shop; rest, snacks; bar; BBQ; playgrnd; pool; lake beach & sw adj; fishing; tennis; wifi; entmnt; TV; 60% statics; dogs €3.50; Eng spkn; quiet; ccard acc (Mastercard only). "Excel, family site in pleasant area; gd walking, cycling, water recreation; cars parked in sep areas; single track rd to site." 1 Apr-31 Oct. € 26.00 2014*

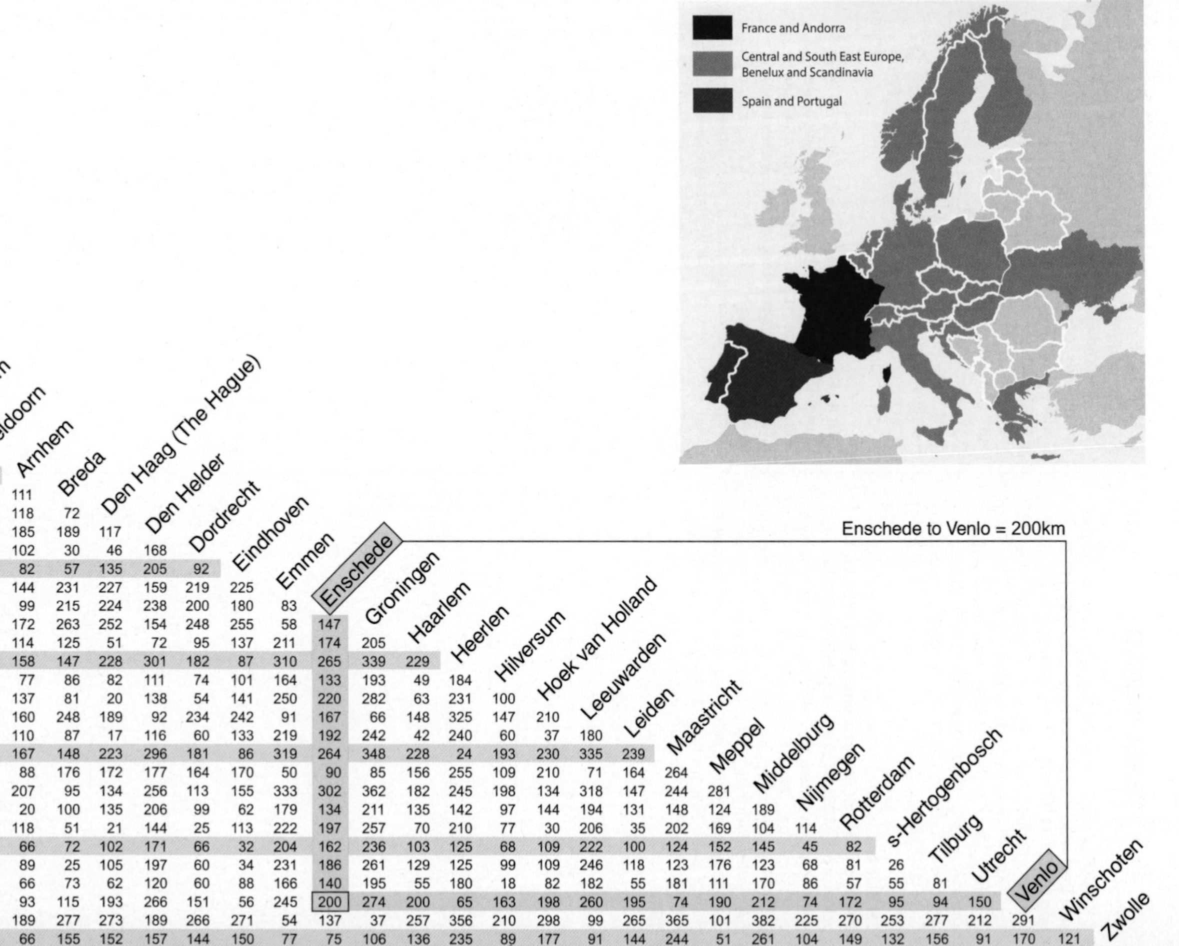

	Alkmaar	Amersfoort	Amsterdam	Apeldoorn	Arnhem	Breda	Den Haag (The Hague)	Den Helder	Dordrecht	Eindhoven	Emmen	Enschede	Groningen	Haarlem	Heerlen	Hilversum	Hoek van Holland	Leeuwarden	Leiden	Maastricht	Meppel	Middelburg	Nijmegen	Rotterdam	s-Hertogenbosch	Tilburg	Utrecht	Venlo	Winschoten
Amersfoort	83																												
Amsterdam	40	47																											
Apeldoorn	120	44	87																										
Arnhem	141	51	99	25																									
Breda	145	89	101	141	111																								
Den Haag (The Hague)	85	85	55	133	118	72																							
Den Helder	42	125	82	166	185	189	117																						
Dordrecht	125	76	99	130	102	30	46	168																					
Eindhoven	162	105	120	110	82	57	135	205	92																				
Emmen	179	145	188	120	144	231	227	159	219	225																			
Enschede	194	120	161	76	99	215	224	238	200	180	83																		
Groningen	105	175	203	147	172	263	252	154	248	255	58	147																	
Haarlem	30	67	19	118	114	125	51	72	95	137	211	174	205																
Heerlen	256	195	210	192	158	147	228	301	182	87	310	265	339	229															
Hilversum	69	17	34	72	77	86	82	111	74	101	164	133	193	49	184														
Hoek van Holland	103	105	78	149	137	81	20	138	54	141	250	220	282	63	231	100													
Leeuwarden	111	161	139	130	160	248	189	92	234	242	91	167	66	148	325	147	210												
Leiden	75	75	46	126	110	87	17	116	60	133	219	192	242	42	240	60	37	180											
Maastricht	255	196	214	201	167	148	223	296	181	86	319	264	348	228	24	193	230	335	239										
Meppel	156	91	133	53	88	176	172	177	164	170	50	90	85	156	255	109	210	71	164	264									
Middelburg	201	190	186	233	207	95	134	256	113	155	333	302	362	182	245	198	134	318	147	244	281								
Nijmegen	164	72	120	66	20	100	135	206	99	62	179	134	211	135	142	97	144	194	131	148	124	189							
Rotterdam	102	80	73	129	118	51	21	144	25	113	222	197	257	70	210	77	30	206	35	202	169	104	114						
s-Hertogenbosch	125	71	88	92	66	72	102	171	66	32	204	162	236	103	125	68	109	222	100	124	152	145	45	82					
Tilburg	156	95	114	116	89	25	105	197	60	34	231	186	261	129	125	99	109	246	118	123	176	123	68	81	26				
Utrecht	80	23	37	73	66	73	62	120	60	88	166	140	195	55	180	18	82	182	55	181	111	170	86	57	55	81			
Venlo	225	137	180	125	93	115	193	266	151	56	245	200	274	200	65	163	198	260	195	74	190	212	74	172	95	94	150		
Winschoten	231	191	234	155	189	277	273	189	266	271	54	137	37	257	356	210	298	99	265	365	101	382	225	270	253	277	212	291	
Zwolle	134	70	113	44	66	155	152	157	144	150	77	75	106	136	235	89	177	91	144	244	51	261	104	149	132	156	91	170	121

A
B
C
D
1
2
3
4
All year site(s)
Seasonal site(s)
No sites listed
200m +
0–200m
0
50
100 kms
0
25
50 mls
Motorways
Major roads
Main roads
© Collins Bartholomew Ltd 2018
N
W
E
S
NORTH
SEA
AMELAND
Buren
TERSCHELLING
Oosterend
Lauwersoog
Vierhuizen
Emden
VLIELAND
Dokkum
GRONINGEN
Midwolda
LEEUWARDEN
Harlingen
TEXEL
De Koog
DEN BURG
DEN HELDER
Drachten
Sneek
Annen
Assen
WINSCHOTEN
Koudum
Appelscha
Exloo
Wezuperbrug
Dwingeloo
Havelte
EMMEN
Newcastle upon Tyne
Callantsoog
Tuitjenhorn
ALKMAAR
MEPPEL
Zuidwolde
ZWOLLE
Nordhorn
Ootmarsum
Denekamp
Weerselo
Hengelo
ENSCHEDE
Zandvoort
AMSTERDAM
Almere
Harderwijk
Noordwijk aan Zee
Lisse
Katwijk aan Zee
Wassenaar
LEIDEN
HILVERSUM
APELDOORN
AMERSFOORT
UTRECHT
DEN HAAG
Zoetermeer
Delft
Gouda
Woerden
Otterlo
Renswoude
Dieren
Harwich
HOEK VAN HOLLAND
ARNHEM
Maurik
Zevenaar
Winterswijk
Rockanje
ROTTERDAM
Gendt
's-Heerenberg
NIJMEGEN
Droonenburgh
Hellevoetsluis
Gorinchem
DORDRECHT
Heumen
Burgh-Hammstede
Zierikzee
'S-HERTOGENBOSCH
Uden
Wesel
Oosterhout
Steenbergen
Kortgene
BREDA
TILBURG
Sint Oedenrode
GERMANY
Goes
Roosendaal
MIDDELBURG
Bergen op Zoom
EINDHOVEN
Cadzand
Sluis
Hoek
Bladel
MIERLO
Eersel
Panningen
VENLO
Helden
Weert
Antwerpen
Roermond
Düsseldorf
Echt
Gent
BELGIUM
Schimmert
HEERLEN
Meerssen
Valkenburg aan de Geul
MAASTRICHT
Köln
BRUSSEL/
BRUXELLES
Vaals
Aachen
Liège
A7
A9
A6
A28
A32
A37
A50
A1
A30
A2
A18
A15
A29
A16
A27
A58
A67
A73
N31
N46
N34
N371
N50
N59

Welcome to Norway

Home to soaring fjords, glaciers and polar bears juxtaposed with cosmopolitan cities and vibrant festivals, Norway truly is a remarkable country. The natural landscape must rank as one of the most beautiful in the world, it is easy to see why people become entranced.

With a rich culture spanning centuries from the ancient Vikings to the present day, and plenty of legends, folklore and fairytales in between, Norway is a magical place that invariably delights and inspires its visitors.

Country highlights

The Nobel Peace Prize has, since its inception, been awarded in Oslo by the Norwegian Nobel Committee. Oslo City Hall, where the ceremony is held, is now one of Norway's most famous buildings.

As a country steeped in myths and legends, Norway has a vibrant heritage of story-telling. Trolls are some of the most talked about fairytale creatures, and statues, books and pictures of them can be found all over the country.

Major towns and cities

- Oslo – Norway's capital city hosts numerous festivals throughout the year.
- Bergen – a colourful and peaceful city surrounded by mountains.
- Trondheim – home to the world's most northerly medieval cathedral.
- Drammen – a city with plenty of attractions such as the oldest brewery in Norway.

Attractions

- Heddal Stave Church, Notodden – Norway's largest medieval wooden church.
- Geirangerfjord, Sunnmøre – one of Norway's most breathtaking fjords and a UNESCO site.
- Jostedal Glacier – Europe's largest glacier and an outstanding natural environment.
- The Royal Palace, Oslo - take a tour through some of the most beautiful state rooms.

Find out more

www.visitnorway.com
Tel: 0047 (0) 22 00 25 00 Norway Tourist Office

Country Information

Population (approx): 5.1 million

Capital: Oslo

Area: 328,878 sqkm

Bordered by: Finland, Russia, Sweden

Terrain: Mostly high plateaux and mountain ranges broken by fertile valleys; deeply indented coastline; arctic tundra in the north

Climate: Moderate climate along coastal areas thanks to the Gulf Stream; more extreme inland with snowy/rainy winters; arctic conditions in the northern highlands; summers can be unpredictable and May and June can be cool

Coastline: 25,148km (including islands and fjords)

Highest Point: Galdhøpiggen 2,469m

Language: Norwegian; Sami in some areas

Local Time: GMT or BST + 1, i.e. 1 hour ahead of the UK all year

Currency: Krone (NOK) divided into 100 øre; £1 = NOK 11.04, NOK 10 = £0.91 (November 2017)

Emergency numbers: Police 112, with mobile phone 911; Fire brigade 110; Ambulance 113. From a mobile phone dial 112 for any service.

Public Holidays 2018: Jan 1; Mar 29, 30; Apr 1, 2; May 1, 10,17,20, 21; Dec 25, 26.

School summer holidays run from mid-June to mid-August.

Camping and Caravanning

There are more than 1,000 campsites in Norway which are classified 1 to 5 stars and which are generally open between June and mid August. A camping guide listing 300 sites is available from the Norwegian Automobile Association, Norges Automobilforbund (NAF), see www.nafcamp.no. The Norwegian Tourist Board also distributes a camping guide free of charge – see www.camping.no. Most 3 star sites and all 4 and 5 star sites have sanitary facilities for the disabled and all classified sites have cooking facilities.

Many sites do not open until mid-June and do not fully function until the beginning of July, particularly if the winter has been prolonged. Sites with published opening dates earlier than June may not open on time if the weather has been particularly bad and if, for example, there has been heavy rain and flooding near rivers or lakes where campsites are situated. Campsites which are open all year will usually have very limited facilities for most of the year outside the short holiday season.

Facilities vary; in main tourist centres there are large, well-equipped sites with good sanitary facilities, grocery shops, leisure facilities and attendants permanently on duty. Sites are generally maintained to a high standard of cleanliness. In more remote areas, sites are small and facilities can be very simple.

Many small campsites have no chemical disposal point. Roadside notice boards at the entrance to each local area (kommune) indicate campsites, chemical disposal points (normally sited at petrol stations) and other local amenities. These disposal facilities are usually coin-operated and have instructions in English. In some areas in the north, there may be no adequate arrangements for the disposal of waste water, either on site or in the immediate area, and you are advised enquire when arriving at a campsite.

The Camping Key Europe, which replaced the Camping Card Scandinavia (CCS) in 2012, may be required at some sites. You can buy the Camping Key Europe on arrival at your first site and will be issued with a temporary card. Alternatively, you can order the card before you travel from www.camping.no/en/cke and click on 'Bestillig av Kort' where you can then select to view the order form in English. If ordering in advance allow at least three weeks for the card to arrive.

There are many sites on the E6 to the North Cape, seldom more than 30km apart. These sites may be subject to road noise. Caravans are allowed to stay at the North Cape but no facilities are available – see Nordkapp later in this chapter and in the Site Entry listing.

In the short summer season campsites can be crowded and facilities stretched and you are recommended to arrive before 3pm (many sites have a latest arrival time of 4pm) in order to have a better choice of pitches and have the opportunity to erect an awning.

Casual/wild camping is not actively encouraged but the Norwegian 'Right of Access' allows visitors to explore the countryside freely, except for cultivated land, farmland, gardens, nurseries, etc. Off-road driving is not allowed. Visitors must respect nature and take their rubbish away with them when they leave. Open fires (which include Primus stoves) are prohibited in forests or on open land between 15 April and 15 September.

Motorhomes

Many towns provide parking places for motorhomes close to city centres, known as Bobil Parks, which are open in June, July and August. In general these parking areas provide limited facilities and car and caravan outfits are not permitted. Details, where known, are listed in the Site Entry pages.

Apart from at campsites, motorhome service points are reported to be few and far between and are generally to be found at petrol stations, where water refill may also be available.

Cycling

Cyclists are fairly well catered for and some areas, such as Vestfold, Rogaland and the Lillehammer area, have a well-developed network of cycle paths. Some old roads have been converted into cycle paths in the mountains and along western fjords. Paths run through magnificent scenery in the Lofoten and Vesterålen Islands in particular, and from Haugastøl in the Hardangervidda National Park to Flåm. A number of tunnels are prohibited to cyclists, but local detours are generally signposted. Information is available at www.cyclingnorway.no

Electricity and Gas

Campsites usually have a minimum 10 amp supply. Plugs are the continental type and have two round pins plus two earth strips. Some sites do not yet have CEE connections. It is recommended that you take an extension cable of at least 50 metres.

There are often problems with both polarity and the earthing of the electrical supply on some sites. Due to its geology and mountainous nature, Norway's electricity supply network is quite different from that found elsewhere in Europe. There is no national grid and electricity systems vary from place to place throughout the country. Any polarity testing system is likely to give false readings. It is understood that progress is being made to improve and standardise the electrical supply throughout the country but you should exercise caution and, if in any doubt, ask site staff to demonstrate the integrity of the earthing system before connecting.

Propane gas cylinders are generally widely available from Esso and Statoil petrol stations. You will need to buy an appropriate adaptor, available from camping shops or Statoil garages. AGA AS dealers will allow you to sell back propane cylinders within six months of purchase prior to leaving Norway at approximately 80% of the purchase price. It is understood that Statoil garages no longer buy them back. Some Statoil garages and AGA AS dealers will exchange Swedish Primus propane cylinders for their Norwegian version but will not accept other foreign propane cylinders. There is no refund for the adaptor.

Gas supplies can be conserved by taking advantage of the kitchens and/or cooking facilities available at classified campsites, and using electrical hook-ups at every opportunity.

Entry Formalities

Holders of British and Irish passports may visit Norway for up to three months without a visa.

Regulations for Pets

For details of the regulations regarding the import of pets into Norway, see website www.mattilsynet.no (English option) or contact the Norwegian Embassy in London.

Medical Services

British visitors are entitled to the same basic emergency medical and dental treatment as Norwegian citizens, on production of a UK passport or European Health Insurance Card (EHIC), but you will have to pay the standard fees. Ensure you consult a doctor who has a reimbursement arrangement with the NAV (Norwegian Employment and Welfare Organisation). Hotels and tourist offices have lists of local doctors and dentists.

You will have to pay in full for most prescribed medicines which are available from pharmacies (apotek). Emergency in-patient hospital treatment at public hospitals, including necessary medication, is free of charge but you will have to pay for out-patient treatment. NAV Health Service Agencies will reimburse any payments that are refundable.

It is recommended to have insect repellent devices as mosquitos and midges may be a nuisance at certain times of the year, especially near lakes.

Opening Hours

Banks: Mon-Fri 8am-3.30pm and some open until 5pm on Thurs.

Museums: 9am/10am-4pm/5pm; no regular closing day.

Post Offices: Mon-Fri 8am/8.30am-4pm/5pm; Sat 8am-1pm.

Shops: Mon-Fri 9am-4pm/5pm (Thurs until 6pm/8pm); Sat 9am/10am-1pm/3pm. Some supermarkets and shopping centres are open longer and some open Sun.

Safety and Security

Norway is considered to have lower crime rates than some other European countries, even in the large cities, however you should always take the usual precautions against pickpockets and petty theft, especially in crowded areas. Do not leave valuables in your car.

Following some recent incidents of robbery, the police are warning motorists with caravans, motorhomes and trailers not to stop in lay-bys overnight. The Norwegian Automobile Association, Norges Automobilforbund (NAF), has also sent out warnings to campsites urging campers to be careful.

If you plan to go off the beaten track or out to sea you should take local advice about weather conditions, have suitable specialist equipment and respect warning signs. Because of Norway's northerly latitude the weather can change rapidly, producing sudden arctic conditions on exposed mountains – even in summer. The winter is long (it can last well into April) and temperatures can drop to minus 25º celcius and below, plus any wind chill factor.

Norway shares with the rest of Europe an underlying threat from terrorism. Attacks could be indiscriminate and against civilian targets in public places, including tourist sites.

British Embassy
THOMAS HEFTYES GATE 8, OSLO
Tel: 23 13 27 00
www.ukinnorway.fco.gov.uk/en/

Irish Embassy
HAAKON VIIS GATE 1, N-0244 OSLO
Tel: 22 01 72 00
www.embassyofireland.no

Customs Regulations

Border Posts

Borders with Sweden and Finland may be crossed on all main roads and Customs posts are usually open day and night.

Storskog on the E105, east of Kirkenes, is the only border crossing for tourist traffic from Norway into Russia (visa required).

Duty-Free Import Allowances

Norway is not a member of the EU and therefore it is possible to import goods duty-free into the country from the EU. Duty-free allowances are not particularly generous and are strictly enforced. Visitors may import the following:

200 cigarettes or 250gm tobacco

1 litre spirits and 1½ litres wine

or 1 litre spirits and 3.5 litres beer
or 3 litres wine and 2 litres beer

or 5 litres beer

Goods to the value of NOK 6,000 (including alcohol and tobacco products)

Visitors must be aged 20 years and over to import spirits and 18 years and over for wine, beer and cigarettes.

Food and Medicines

Up to 10kg (combined weight) of meat, meat products and cheese can be imported into Norway from EU countries for personal consumption. The import of potatoes is not permitted but you can take in up to 10kg of fruit, berries and other vegetables. Visitors may only take in medicines for their own personal use with a covering letter from a doctor stating their requirements.

Money

Travellers may import or export currency up to the equivalent of NOK 25,000 in Norwegian and/ or foreign notes and coins. Any amount above this must be declared to Customs.

Refund of VAT on Export

Some shops have a blue and red sign in their window indicating that visitors may, on presentation of a passport, purchase goods free of VAT. For visitors from the UK the purchase price of individual items (exclusive of VAT) must be at least NOK 250. Shop assistants will issue a voucher and on departure from Norway visitors must present goods and vouchers at a tax-free counter situated on ferries, at airports and at main border crossings where a refund of 11-18% will be made.

Documents

Vehicle(s)

Carry your vehicle registration document (V5C), insurance certificate and MOT certificate (if applicable). If driving a borrowed vehicle carry a letter of authority from the owner.

Money

Norway is expensive; bring or have electronic access to plenty of money, especially if you are intending to eat and drink in restaurants and bars.

Bank opening hours are shorter than in the UK, especially in summer, but cash machines are widespread. Bureaux de change are found in banks, post offices, airports, stations, hotels and some tourist offices.

The major credit cards are widely accepted (although some supermarkets and petrol stations do not accept credit cards) and may be used at cash machines (minibanks) throughout the country. In remote areas banks and cash machines may be few and far between.

It is advisable to carry your passport or photocard driving licence if paying with a credit card as you may well be asked for photographic proof of your identity.

Carry your credit card issuers'/banks' 24-hour UK contact numbers in case of loss or theft of your cards.

Motoring in Norway

Alcohol

Norwegian law is very strict: do not drink and drive. Fines and imprisonment await those who exceed the legal limit of 20 milligrams of alcohol in 100 millilitres of blood, which is considerably lower than that permitted in the UK (80 milligrams), and equates to virtually zero for at least 12 hours before driving. Random roadside breath tests are frequent.

If you are involved in a road accident which causes damage to property or vehicles or injuries you should not drink any alcohol for six hours following the accident as the police may wish to carry out blood alcohol tests.

If purchasing medicines in Norway you should be aware that some containing alcohol should be avoided if you intend to drive. These are marked with a red triangle.

Breakdown Service

Norges Automobilforbund (NAF) operates a 24-hour breakdown service nationwide. Call 08505 from a landline or 0926 08505 from a mobile phone. Emergency yellow telephones have been installed on difficult stretches of road.

NAF Veipatrulje (road patrols) operates from mid-June to mid-August on difficult mountain passes and in remote areas but in Oslo, Stavanger and Bergen, they operate all year round.

If you're a member of The Caravan and Motorhome Club show your membership card in order to benefit from special NAF rates for breakdown assistance. Some breakdown vehicles have credit card payment terminals; otherwise payment for services is required in cash.

Essential Equipment

Warning Triangle

An warning triangle must be used if the vehicle has broken down, punctures or is involved in an accident, and could cause danger to other road users.

Lights

The use of dipped headlights is compulsory at all times, regardless of weather conditions. Bulbs are more likely to fail with constant use and it is recommended that you carry spares.

Reflective Jacket/ Waistcoat

Owners of vehicles registered in Norway are required to carry a reflective jacket to be worn if their vehicle is immobilised on the carriageway following a breakdown or accident. This legislation does not yet apply to foreign registered vehicles but you are strongly advised to carry at least one such jacket. Passengers who leave the vehicle, for example to assist with a repair, should also wear one.

Child Restraint System

Children of four years and under 135cm must be seated in a special child restraint system. If in a rear facing system on the front seat, the airbag must be deactivated. A child between 135-150cm should use a booster seat with an adult seatbelt.

All child restraints must conform to ECE R44-03 or 04 regulations.

Winter Driving

Vehicles with a total weight of 3,500kg or more must carry chains during the winter season, regardless of road conditions. Checks are often carried out.

Generally spiked tyres can be used from 1st November to the first Sunday after Easter. In an effort to discourage the use of spiked tyres in Bergen, Oslo and Trondheim a tax is levied on vehicles equipped with them. For vehicles up to 3,500kg the tax is NOK 30 for one day and NOK 400 for a month. For vehicles over 3,500kg the fee is doubled. Daily permits are available from vending machines along major roads into the city marked 'Frisk luft i byen'. Vehicles over 3,500 kg must be equipped with winter tyres on all axles between 15th November and 31st March.

Fuel

Prices vary not only according to region (they are slightly higher in the north and in mountainous areas) but also according to the manner in which fuel is sold. Prices can also vary on different days and fuel tends to be cheaper on Sunday and Monday. There are automatic petrol pumps where payment is made by credit card or bank notes.

Petrol stations are generally open from 7am to 10pm on weekdays, but may close early. Petrol stations maybe scarce, particularly in the north. In cities some petrol stations remain open 24 hours.

Unleaded petrol is dispensed from pumps marked 'Blyfri'. Not all petrol stations stock diesel. If you fill up with it, ensure that you use the correct pump and do not inadvertently fill with 'Afgift Diesel' (red diesel for agricultural vehicles). LPG is available at a limited number of outlets – see www.visitnorway.com for a list.

Mountain Passes

If you're visiting in the autumn, winter or spring you should check that any mountain passes you intend to use are open. Some high mountain roads close during the winter, the duration of the closure depending on weather conditions, but many others remain open all year. Other passes may close at short notice, at night or during periods of bad weather.

The Norwegian Tourist Board can provide a list, for guidance purposes, of roads which usually close in winter, or contact the Road User Information Centre (Vegtrafikksentralen) which will provide information about roads, road conditions, mountain passes, tunnels, border crossings, etc. The Centre is open round the clock all year, telephone 02030 within Norway or (0047) 91 50 20 30 from abroad. Alternatively a list of roads that are closed in winter or which have limited accessibility can be found at www.vegvesen.no/en/Traffic and click on Truckers' Guide, or email firmapost@vegvesen.no.

Yellow emergency telephones are installed on mountain passes.

Parking

A white line on the edge of the carriageway indicates a parking restriction. Do not park on main roads if visibility is restricted or where there is a sign 'All Stans Førbudt' (no stopping allowed). If you do so you may have your vehicle towed away. Parking regulations in towns are very strict and offences are invariably subject to fines. Pay and display car parks are in use in the main towns.

Priority

Priority roads (main roads) are indicated by a road sign bearing a yellow diamond on a white background. A black diagonal bar through the sign indicates the end of the priority rule. If you are not travelling on a priority road then vehicles coming from the right have priority. Traffic already on a roundabout has priority and trams always have priority.

Narrow roads have passing places (møteplass) to allow vehicles to pass. The driver on the side of the road where there is a passing place must stop for an oncoming vehicle. However heavy goods vehicles tend to take right of way on narrow roads, especially if travelling uphill, and it may be necessary to reverse to a passing place to allow one to pass.

Roads

The standard of roads is generally good but stretches of major roads may be bumpy and rutted as a result of use by heavy freight traffic. Caravanners in particular should take care to avoid wheels being caught in ruts.

Some roads are narrow, especially in the mountains, and may not have a central yellow line. State roads are shown in red on maps and are asphalted but may not have kerbs and may, therefore, easily become cracked and rutted. Many roads have barriers mounted close to the side of the road.

Secondary roads have a gravel surface that can be tricky when wet and may be in poor condition for some weeks during and after the spring thaw.

Do not assume that roads with an E prefix are necessarily major roads - sections of the E39, for example, are still single-track with passing places. The E6 road is asphalted all the way to the Swedish border in the south and to Kirkenes in the north. You may encounter reverse camber on both left and right-hand bends.

Some roads in the fjord region have many hairpin bends and can be challenging. Roads may narrow to a single carriageway and single-track bridges often appear without any advance warning.

Gradients on main highways are generally moderate, not over 10%, but the inside of hairpin bends may be much steeper than this. There is a gradient of 20% on the E68 from Gudvangen (on the southern tip of the Sognefjord) to Stalheim, but a tunnel under the steepest section of the Stalheim road eliminates this difficult section.

Maps showing roads closed to caravans and those only recommended for use by experienced caravanners, together with rest stops, may be obtained from the Norwegian Tourist Board, Norwegian local road authority offices and from the NAF.

Because of the nature of the country's roads – and the beauty of the scenery – average daily mileage may be less than anticipated. Major repairs to roads and tunnels take place during the summer months and traffic controls may cause delays. Ferries make up an integral part of a number of routes, particularly when travelling north along the coast, which also causes slow progress.

Care should be taken to avoid collisions with elk, deer and reindeer, particularly at dawn and dusk. Accidents involving any kind of animal must be reported to the police.

A number of roads are closed in winter, including the E69 to the North Cape, due to snow conditions; some do not open until late May or early June.

Road Signs and Markings

European highways are prefixed with the letter E and are indicated by signs bearing white letters and figures on a green background, national highways (Riksvei or Stamvei) are indicated by black figures prefixed Rv on a yellow background and local, county roads (Fylkesvei) by black figures on a white background. County road numbers do not generally appear on maps.

Lines in the middle of the carriageway are yellow. Bus, cycle and taxi lanes are marked in white.

Some signs have been introduced, for example a square blue sign showing a car and '2+' in white means that cars carrying more than two people can use bus lanes. Square signs indicate the presence of speed cameras, small rectangular signs indicate the exit numbers on highways and main roads, and a number of triangular signs with a yellow background indicate a temporary danger. Signs advising maximum speeds on bends, obstructions, etc, should be respected.

In addition to international road signs, the following signs may also be seen:

Passing place

Place of intrest

Norwegian	English Translation
All stans førbudt	No stopping allowed
Arbeide pa vegen	Roadworks ahead
Enveiskjøring	One-way traffic
Ikke møte	No passing, single line traffic
Kjør sakte	Drive slowly
Løs grus	Loose chippings
Møteplass	Passing place
Omkjøring	Diversion
Rasteplass	Lay-by

Speed Limits

	Open Road (km/h)	Motorway (km/h)
Car Solo	80	90-100
Car towing caravan/ trailer	80	80
Motorhome under 3500kg	80	90-100
Motorhome 3500-7500kg	80	80

Drivers should pay close attention to speed limits, which are in general significantly lower than in the UK. Fines for exceeding speed limits are high and often have to be paid on the spot. Radar detectors are illegal.

In residential areas the speed limit may be as low as 30 km/h (18 mph). Frequent speed controls are in operation. Ramps and speed control bumps are not always signposted.

Vehicles over 3,500kg are restricted to 80 km/h (50 mph) on motorways and highways, regardless of signs showing higher general limits.

Towing

Drivers of cars and caravans with a combined length of more than 12.4 metres must check from the list of national highways and/or municipal roads may not be allowed on some routes.

You can check this information with the Road User Information Centre (Vegtrafikksentralen), tel: 02030 within Norway or (0047) 91 50 20 30 from abroad, www.vegvesen.no/en/Traffic and click on Truckers' Guide, or from the Norwegian Tourist Board or NAF. For a motorhome the maximum length is 12 metres (12.4 metres for those registered before September 1997).

Any vehicle towing must have extended towing mirrors fitted.

Some secondary roads have a maximum width of less than 2.55 metres. If your caravan is wider than 2.3 metres and more than 50cm wider than your car, white reflectors must be mounted on the front of your car mirrors. More information is available from the Road User Information Centre.

It is understood that the Rv55 from Sogndal to Lom and the Rv63 north from Geiranger are not suitable for caravans exceeding 5 metres in length, or those without an adequate power/weight ratio.

Traffic Jams

Roads in general are rarely busy but the roads in and around the cities of Oslo, Bergen, Kristiansand and Trondheim suffer traffic jams during rush hours and at the beginning and end of the holiday season.

The E6 Oslo-Svinesund road at the border with Sweden and the E18 Oslo-Kristiansand road are generally busy during the June to August holiday period. During the summer you should also expect delays at ferry terminals.

Tunnels

The road network includes approximately 950 tunnels, most of which can be found in the counties of Hordaland and Sogn og Fjordane in western Norway. Most tunnels are illuminated and about half are ventilated. There are emergency telephones at the entrance to tunnels and inside them. Tunnels also have refuges which can be used by motorists in the event of an emergency.

Laersdal Tunnel

The Lærsdal road tunnel links the Rv50 from just east of Aurlandsvangen to the E16 east of Lærdalsoyri, by-passing the ferry link from Gudvangen to Lærsdal. The toll-free 24.5km long tunnel is illuminated and ventilated throughout and has a number of caverns at regular intervals which act as turning points and, it is reported, help dispel any feelings of claustrophobia. An alternative route is to take the Rødnes tunnel and then the Rv53, but this involves a steep climb beyond Øvre Ardal.

Lofoten and Vesterålen Islands

The Lofoten Islands can be reached by ferries from Bodø & Skutvik and the Vesteralen Islands can be reached by road (E10) west of Narvik. The individual islands of the Lofoten and Vesterålen groups are connected to each other by bridge or tunnel and the two groups of islands are linked by the E10 Lofast route from Gullesfjordbotn in Vesterålen to Fiskebøl in Lofoten. This route was formerly only possible by ferry.

Oslo Tunnel

A 3km long toll-free tunnel runs from east to west Oslo.

Violation of Traffic Regulations

The police are empowered to impose and collect on-the-spot fines for infringement of traffic regulations.

Motorways

There are 300km of 4 lane motorways signposted by the prefix A, which are situated around the towns of Bergen and Oslo. In addition there are category B motorways with 2 lanes.

There are normally no emergency telephones on motorways.

Motorway Tolls

There are many toll roads throughout the country and most have an electronic toll system. Vehicles are categorised as follows:

Class 1 – Motorcycles

Class 2 – Car, with or without trailer, with a total weight less than 3,500kg and maximum length of 6m.

Class 3 – Vehicle with or without trailer and a total weight of more than 3,500kg or between 6m and 12.4m in length.

Payment

If you have not registered your credit card under the Visitors' Payment scheme (see below) you would normally pass through tolls in the lanes marked 'Mynt/Coin' or 'Manuell'. You either pay manually or at a coin machine – keep a supply of small change handy as it is understood that the machines do not issue change. Most toll roads have a facility for credit card payment. Drivers of vehicles over 3,500kg must, if there is one, drive through the 'Manuell' lane.

Don't be tempted to pass through unmanned tolls without paying, as checks are made. However, many toll road operators have installed fully automatic toll stations – AutoPASS – where a sign indicates that you should not stop. Drivers without an AutoPASS can stop and pay at a nearby Esso stations (following the 'KR-Service' signs) within three days of being eligible to pay a toll, or they will receive an invoice by post at their home address. This also applies to drivers of foreign-registered vehicles.

Visitors' Payment

Alternatively, and more conveniently, there is now a 'Visitors' Payment' system for which you register and pay NOK 300 (vehicles below 3,500kg) or NOK 1,000 (over 3,500kg) by credit card. You specify how long your account is to be operative (maximum three months) and it is then automatically debited when you pass a pay point. Three months after your 'Visitors' Payment' has expired your account will be credited with any balance remaining. See www.autopass.no (English option) for more information and to open an account.

This system means you can drive through all toll roads in the AutoPASS lane and pay automatically at toll stations and pay points where there is no option for manual payment. You do not need an AutoPASS tag which is designed for residents and long-stay visitors and for which you have to enter into a contract.

City Tolls

Toll ring roads are in place around major cities charging drivers to take their vehicles into city centres (charge applied one-way only). For example, the toll for the use of the Oslo ring road for an outfit under 6 meters and under 3,500kg is NOK32 whilst an outfit between 6.01-12 meters and over 3,500kg is NOK96 depending on the weight and length of your vehicle (2016)

Other Tolls

Because of the mountainous terrain and the numerous fjords and streams, there are many bridges and tunnels where tolls are normally payable. Tunnels may be narrow and unlit and care is needed when suddenly entering an unlit tunnel from bright daylight. Alternative routes to avoid tolls can be full of obstacles which are not marked on a map, e.g. narrow stretches with sharp turns and/or poor road surface, and are best avoided.

Svinesund Bridge

There is a 700 metre long bridge linking Norway and Sweden on the E6 at Svinesund (Sweden) – the busiest border crossing between the two countries. Tolls are NOK20 for vehicles up to 3,500kg and NOK100 for vehicles over 3,500kgs (2017 prices).

Touring

International ferry services operate between Norway and Denmark, Germany, Iceland and Sweden. Routes from Harwich to Denmark and Newcastle to the Netherlands are in operation as gateways to Europe and, in addition, a daily overnight ferry service connects Copenhagen and Oslo.

A green 'i' sign indicates a tourist information office which is open all year with extended opening hours in summer, whereas a red sign means that the office is only open during the summer season.

Norwegians take their school and industrial holidays from mid-June to mid-August; travelling outside this season will ensure that facilities are less crowded and more economically priced. Winter brings the inevitable snowfall with some of the most reliable snow conditions in Europe. The winter sports season is from November to April.

Alta, on the coast north of the Arctic Circle, boasts the most extensive prehistoric rock carvings in Europe and has been declared a UNESCO World Heritage Site. Other World Heritage Sites include Geirangerfjord, Nærøyfjord, Bryggen in Bergen and the wooden buildings in Røros.

City cards are available for Oslo and Bergen, giving unlimited free travel on public transport, free public parking and free or discounted admission to museums and tourist attractions. They can be bought from tourist information centres, hotels and campsites in or near the city, from some kiosks or online at www.visitoslo.com or www.visitbergen.com.

Wine and spirits are only available from special, state-owned shops (vinmonopolet) usually found in larger towns, and are expensive, as are cigarettes. Beer is available from supermarkets. Smoking in bars, restaurants and public places is prohibited. Tipping is not expected in restaurants.

English is widely spoken, often fluently, by virtually everyone under the age of 60.

The Midnight Sun and Northern Lights

The best time to experience the midnight sun is early or high summer. The sun does not sink below the horizon at the North Cape (Nordkapp) from the second week in May to the last week in July.

Midsummer Night's Eve is celebrated all over the country with thousands of bonfires along the fjords.

You can hope to see the Northern Lights (Aurora Borealis) between November and February depending on weather conditions. You need to go north of the Arctic Circle, which crosses Norway, just south of Bodø on the Nordland coast. Occasionally the Northern Lights may be seen in southern Norway, again depending on weather conditions.

North Cape (Nordkapp)

A tunnel links the island of Magerøya, on which the North Cape is situated, to the mainland.

North Cape is open from the beginning of May until the end of September. It is possible to visit in winter; contact the Nordkapp Tourist Office, www.nordkapp.no or tel: (0047) 78 47 70 30. A charge of NOK 270 per adult and NOK 95 per child (2017) is payable to enter the North Cape Hall area. This is a tourist centre where there are exhibitions, displays, restaurants, shops and a post office, as well as an area of hardstanding for parking. This charge covers a stay of up to 48 hours. More information is given in the campsite entry for Nordkapp or on the website www.nordnorge.com. There are no cash machines at North Cape but credit cards are accepted in shops and restaurants, as are euros and sterling.

The true northernmost point of Norway is in fact at Knivskjellodden on a peninsular to the west of North Cape which is marked by a modest monument and a wooden box where you can record your name in a log book. It is possible to walk the 18km round trip from a car park on the E69 to Knivskjellodden but the walk should not be undertaken lightly. Later you can claim a certificate to mark your achievement from the tourist office in Honningsvåg by quoting the reference number of your signed entry in the log book.

The Order of Bluenosed Caravanners

Visitors to the Arctic Circle from anywhere in the world may apply for membership of the Order of Bluenosed Caravanners, which will be recognised by the issue of a certificate by the International Caravanning Association (ICA). For further details contact David Hirst on 01422 372390, or email: david.hirst118@gmail.com and attach a photograph of yourselves and your outfit under any Arctic Circle signpost, together with the date and country of crossing and the names of those who made the crossing. This service is free to members of the ICA (annual membership £20); the fee for non-members is £5. Coloured plastic decals for your outfit, indicating membership of the Order, are also available at a cost of £4. Cheques should be payable to the ICA. See www.icacaravanning.org.

Public Transport

The public transport network is excellent and efficient with bus routes extending to remote villages. For economical travel buy a 24 hour bus pass (campsites often sell them), valid when stamped for the first time. Many train routes run through very scenic countryside and special offers and discounts mean that train travel is reasonably priced. Only Oslo has a metro system. Trams operate in Bergen and Trondheim.

Using domestic public ferry services is often the quickest way of travelling around Norway and from place to place along the coast and within fjords. Most operate from very early in the morning until late at night. Booking is not normally necessary except in the height of the holiday season when there may be long queues to the more popular destinations. However, internal ferries can be expensive in high season and you may wish to plan your route carefully in order to avoid them.

The ultimate ferry journey is the Norwegian steamer trip (hurtigrute) up the coast from Bergen to Kirkenes. A daily service operates in both directions and the steamer stops at about 30 ports on the way. The round trip lasts eleven days.

The scenic round trip from Bergen or Oslo, 'Norway in a Nutshell', takes you through some of the most beautiful scenery in the country. It combines rail, boat and coach travel on the scenic Bergen railway, the breathtaking Flåm Railway, and takes in the Aurlandsfjord, the narrow Naerøyfjord and the steep Stalheimskleiva. Further details are available from the Norwegian Tourist Board.

You can safely hail a taxi off the street or take one from a taxi stand. Most drivers speak English and all taxis are equipped for taking payment by credit card.

Sites in Norway

ALESUND *1B1* (1km N Coastal) *62.47571, 6.15688* **Ålesund Bobilsenter, Storgata 39, 6015 Ålesund (Møre og Romsdal)** Foll coast to N of town cent & m'van sps; well sp. Sm, hdstg, unshd; wc; mv service pnt; shwrs; EHU; some traff noise; motor c'vans only Ccard acc. "No on-site warden; site on water's edge adj sea wall; conv town cent; v nice facs in wonderful location." May-Sep. NOK 200 2014*

ALESUND *1B1* (3km E Urban/Coastal) *62.46986, 6.19839* **Volsdalen Camping, Sjømannsveien, 6008 Ålesund (Møre og Romsdal) [tel 70 12 58 90; fax 70 12 14 94; v.camp@online.no; www.volsdalen camping.no]** Foll Rv136 two Centrum, ignore 1st camping sp (Prinsen), take 2nd site sp Volsdalsberga to exit R, up slip rd. At top turn L over E136 then immed R, site on L. Sm, mkd pitch, hdstg, terr, unshd; htd wc; chem disp; mv service pnt; shwrs NOK10; EHU (10A) NOK30 (no earth); gas; lndry; shop on site & 500m; rest, snacks high ssn; cooking facs; TV rm; 40% statics; dogs; bus 600m; poss cr; Eng spkn; adv bkg; quiet; ccard acc; red long stay. "Stunning location; some pitches o'looking fjord; sm pitches not suitable lge o'fits high ssn; 75% travellers; site unkempt; new san facs being built (2013); rec NH; only site for c'van nr Alesund, so adv bkg strongly advised; town 30 min walk." ♦ 1 May-1 Sep. NOK 250 2014*

⊞ **ALTA** *2G1* (6km S Rural) *69.92904, 23.26136* **Alta River Camping, Steinfossveien 5, 9518 Øvre Alta (Finnmark) [tel 78 43 43 53; fax 78 43 69 02; post@alta-river-camping.no; www.alta-river-camping.no]** Fr E6 (by-passing Alta), take E93 S sp Kautokeino. Site clearly sp on L (opp information board). Med, pt shd; htd wc; chem disp; mv service pnt; sauna; shwrs NOK10; EHU (10-16A) NOK30; lndry; shop; cooking facs; playgrnd; ltd wifi; TV; Eng spkn; adv bkg; quiet; ccard acc; CKE/CCI. "Excel facs; o'looks salmon rv; pitches not mkd and close together, some hdstg; elec point poss no earth; facs dated but clean; elec poss no earth." ♦ NOK 279 2014*

⊞ **ALTA** *2G1* (7km S Rural) *69.92735, 23.27075* **Alta Strand Camping & Apartments, Stenfossveien 29, 9518 Øvre Alta (Finnmark) [tel 78 43 40 22; fax 78 43 42 40; mail@altacamping.no; www.altacamping.no]** Fr E6 (W of Alta) take Rv93 S sp Kautokeino. Three sites adj in 3km on L, clearly sp, Strand is last one. Sm, hdstg, unshd; htd wc; chem disp; mv service pnt; sauna; shwrs inc; fam bthrm; EHU (16A) NOK50 (poss no earth); lndry (inc dryer); shop 5km; snacks; bar; BBQ; cooking facs; rv 500m; playgrnd; wifi; 20% statics; dogs; phone; car wash; twin axles; Eng spkn; adv bkg; ccard acc; CKE/CCI. "Gd for visiting rock carvings; midnight sun visible fr nrby Alta museum; excel." ♦ ltd. NOK 272 2017*

⊞ **ALVDAL** *1C2* (5km NE Rural) *62.13115, 10.56896* **Gjelten Bru Camping, 2560 Alvdal (Hedmark) [tel 62 48 74 44; fax 62 48 70 20; www.nafcamp.com/gjelten-camping]** Fr Rv3 join rd 29 at Alvdal. Cross rv opp general store to site on rv bank. Sm, mkd pitch, pt shd; wc; chem disp; mv service pnt; fam bthrm; shwrs NOK5; EHU (10A) NOK40; lndry (inc dryer); playgrnd; games area; fishing; dogs; Eng spkn; quiet. "V pleasant site; friendly owner." NOK 237 2016*

ANDALSNES *1B1* (3km S Rural) *62.55223, 7.70394* **Åndalsnes Camping & Motell, 6300 Åndalsnes (Møre og Romsdal) [tel 71 22 16 29; fax 71 22 63 60; epost@andalsnes-camping.no; www.andalsnes-camping.com]** Foll E136 to o'skirts of Åndalsnes. Foll sp Ålesund x-ing rv bdge twd W & L immed. Lge, pt shd; wc; chem disp; mv service pnt; shwrs NOK15; EHU (10-16A) NOK40 (check earth); lndry; shop; rest, snacks; fishing; boating; wifi; TV; ccard acc; red CKE/CCI. "Excel facs; rvside, excel mountain scenery; nr Troll Rd & Wall; nice site; grnd can be soft; poss long lead req (poss no earth); gd cent site." ♦ 1 May-30 Sep. NOK 242 2014*

"That's changed – Should I let The Club know?"

If you find something on site that's different from the site entry, fill in a report and let us know. See camc.com/europereport.

ANDALSNES *1B1* (11km S Rural) *62.4940, 7.75846* **Trollveggen Camping, Horgheimseidet, 6300 Åndalsnes (Møre og Romsdal) [tel 71 22 37 00; fax 71 22 16 31; post@trollveggen.com; www.troll veggen.com]** Sp on W side of E136, dir Dombås. Sm, mkd pitch, terr, pt shd; htd wc; chem disp; mv service pnt; fam bthrm; shwrs NOK25; EHU (16A) NOK40; lndry (inc dryer); kiosk; rest 5km; BBQ; cooking facs; playgrnd; fishing; golf 10km; bike hire; wifi; statics; dogs; Eng spkn; adv bkg; quiet; ccard acc. "Friendly, family-run site; excel touring base; outstanding scenery; at foot of Trollveggen wall - shd fr late afternoon; ideal site for walking in Romsal; on Trollsteig classic rte." ♦ ltd. 10 May-19 Sep. NOK 258 2014*

ANDALSNES *1B1* (23km NW Rural Coastal) *62.58720, 7.53004* **Saltkjelsnes Camping, N-6350 Eidsbygda [tel 71 22 39 00; fax 71 22 12 00; camping@saltkjelsnes.no; www.saltkjelsnes.no]** FV64 twds Molde, site on L sp Eidsbyga. Sm, pt sl, terr, pt shd; htd wc; chem disp; mv service pnt; shwrs; EHU (10a) 40 NOK; lndry; shop 10km; BBQ; cooking facs; wifi; boat hire; fishing; 60% statics; dogs; twin axles; poss cr; Eng spkn; quiet. "Lovely location; site small & space ltd, but 1st class facs; Rodven Stavkirke 10km; vg." 1 Apr-1 Oct. NOK 287 2015*

AURLAND see Flåm *1B2*

BALESTRAND *1B2* (1km S Coastal) *61.20220, 6.53140* **Sjøtun Camping, 6899 Balestrand (Sogn og Fjordane) [tel/fax 57 69 12 23; camping@sjotun.com; www.sjotun.com]** Fr Dragsvik ferry or fr W on by-pass; foll int'l site sp. Sm, pt sl, unshd; htd wc; chem disp (wc); mv service pnt; shwrs inc; EHU (16A) NOK25; lndry; shop, rest, snacks 1km; BBQ; cooking facs; shgl beach 1km; few statics; dogs; phone; Eng spkn; adv bkg; quiet; red long stay; CKE/CCI. "Neat, well-kept site with gd view of Sognefjord; poss diff if wet due grass pitches." 1 Jun-28 Feb & 15 Apr-1 Oct. NOK 317 2014*

BARDU see Setermoen *2F2*

BERGEN *1A3* (21km E Rural) *60.37381, 5.45768* **Lone Camping, Hardangerveien 697, 5268 Haukeland (Horda-Rogaland) [tel 55 39 29 60; fax 55 39 29 79; booking@lonecamping.no; www.lonecamping.no]** Fr N on E39 until junc with E16. foll sp Voss to rndabt junc with Rv580 sp Nesttun. Foll Rv580 S for approx 5km, site sp on L. Fr S on E39 until Nesttun, foll Rv580 N sp Indre Arna for approx 6km, site sp on R. Recep is sm bureau adj g'ge or, if unmanned, in g'ge. Do NOT go into Bergen city cent. Site is 20km by rd fr Bergen. Lge, pt sl, pt shd, some hdstg; wc; chem disp; mv service pnt; shwrs NOK10 (no earth); EHU (16A) NOK40; gas; lndry; shop; supmkt adj; snacks; playgrnd; lake sw, fishing & boating; wifi; TV rm; some statics; phone; bus to Bergen; site clsd 5 Nov-19 Dec & New Year; poss v cr; Eng spkn; quiet; red 3+ days; ccard acc; CKE/CCI. "Well-organised; helpful staff; peaceful lakeside setting; superb views; lakeside pitches diff when wet; bus at camp ent for Bergen (35 mins)." 2 Jan-20 Dec. NOK 294 2014*

BERGEN *1A3* (17km SE Rural) *60.35220, 5.43520* **Bratland Camping, Bratlandsveien 6, 5268 Haukeland (Hordaland) [tel 55 10 13 38 & 92 61 52 00 (mob); fax 55 10 53 60; post@bratlandcamping.no; www.bratlandcamping.no]** Fr N on E39 until junc with E16, foll sp Voss to rndabt junc with Rv580 sp Nesttun. Foll Rv580 S for approx 4km; site sp on L. Fr Voss on E16, emerge fr tunnel to rndabt, turn L onto Rv580. Then as above. Site 16km by rd fr Bergen. Sm, some hdstg, unshd; wc; chem disp; mv service pnt; shwrs NOK10; EHU (10A) NOK40; lndry (inc dryer); shop; gd cooking facs; wifi; TV rm; 10% statics; bus to Bergen at site ent; poss cr; Eng spkn; rd noise; ccard acc; CKE/CCI. "Clean, family-run site; gd, modern san facs; v helpful, friendly owners; conv Bergen, nrby stave church & Grieg's home; great loc." ♦ 1 May-15 Sep. NOK 267 2016*

BERGEN *1A3* (6km SSE Urban) *60.35405, 5.35962* **Bergenshallen, Vilhelm Bjerknes Vei 24, 5081 Bergen [tel 47 55 30 88 50; www.visitnorway.com]** Head SW on E16/E39. Exit onto E39 twrds Stavanger/Rv580, take exit. At rndabt take 3rd exit onto Mindeallé. Turn R to stay on Mindeallé, go thro 1 rndabt, cont onto Rv582. Thro 1 rndabt then at next rndabt take 2nd exit onto Fv252. Turn R onto Hagerups vei, cont onto Vilhelm Bjerknes'vei. Turn L and site is on the R. Sm, hdstg, unshd; own san rec; mv service pnt; EHU (on some pitches); dogs inc; train adj. "28 spaces for MV's only; arrive early; adj to Bergen light Rail - 15 mins to city cent; only fasc are water, emptying toilet & waste disposal; excel location for visiting Bergen; no shwrs or wc." 1 May-31 Aug. NOK 150 2014*

BERLEVAG *2H1* (600m E Coastal) *70.85716, 29.09933* **Berlevåg Pensjonat Camping, Havnagata 8, 9980 Berlevåg (Finnmark) [tel 41 54 42 55; post@berlevag-pensjonat.no; www.berlevag-pensjonat.no]** Leave E6 at Tanabru, foll Rv890 to Berlevåg. Site sp at beg of vill. Sm, unshd; htd wc; chem disp; mv service pnt; shwrs NOK10; EHU (16A) NOK40; lndry (inc dryer); shop 500m; BBQ; cooking facs; playgrnd; beach; library & lounge; wifi; TV rm; phone; Eng spkn; adv bkg; ccard acc; CKE/CCI. "Busy fishing port on edge of Barents Sea; museum, glassworks, WW2 resistance history; v helpful staff as site is also TO; site will open outside Jun-Sep on request if contacted ahead; rec arr early; excel site." ♦ 1 Jun-30 Sep. NOK 237 2016*

BIRISTRAND see Lillehammer *1C2*

BIRTAVARRE *2G1* (700m S Rural) *69.49051, 20.82976* **Camping Birtavarre (TR34), 9147 Birtavarre (Troms) [tel/fax 77 71 77 07; mail@birtavarrecamping.com; www.birtavarrecamping.com]** On E6 Olderdalen to Nordkjsobotn, sp. Or foll sp fr vill. Med, unshd; wc; chem disp; mv service pnt; fam bthrm; shwrs NOK10; EHU NOK45; lndry; shop 1km; snacks; cooking facs; fjord sw; Eng spkn; some rd noise; ccard acc; CKE/CCI."Basic site; OK for NH." 1 May-15 Oct. NOK 195 2014*

BO *1C3* (9km SE Rural) *59.38478, 9.18171* **Teksten Camping AS, Strannavegen 140, 3810 Gvary [tel 35 95 55 96; fax 35 95 54 40; teksten@barnascamping.no; www.barnascamping.no]** On 36 dir Skien. Go thro Gvarv. Site sp on L. 700m fr main rd by rv. Med, mkd pitch, terr, pt shd; htd wc; chem disp; mv service pnt; fam bthrm; lndry; cooking facs; playgrnd; sw adj, sand; games area; games rm; 30% statics; twin axles; poss cr; Eng spkn; adv bkg; quiet; ccard acc; CKE/CCI. "Vg site for children." 1 May-9 Sep. NOK 258 2015*

⊞ **BODO** *2F2* (2km SE Rural) *67.2695, 14.42483* **Camping Bodøsjoen, Båtstøveien 1, 8013 Bodø (Nordland) [tel 75 56 36 80; fax 75 56 46 89; bodocamp@yahoo.no; www.bodocamp.no]** Fr E on Rv80 at Bodø sp, turn L at traff lts by Esso g'ge sp airport & camping. L at next rndabt, foll camping sp. Lge, pt sl, unshd; wc; chem disp; shwrs inc; EHU (10A) NOK20 (no earth); lndry; shop 1km; rest 2km; beach; bus 1km; boat hire; fishing excursions; bus 250m; Eng spkn; aircraft noise; CKE/CCI. "Conv Lofoten ferry; superb views; midnight sun (Jun-Jul); Mt Rønvik 3.2km fr camp." ♦ NOK 252 2014*

⊞ **BODO** *2F2* (28km SE Coastal) *67.23545, 14.62125* **Saltstraumen Camping, Knapplund, 8056 Saltstraumen (Nordland) [tel 75 58 75 60; fax 75 58 75 40; saltstraumen@pluscamp.no; www. saltstraumen-camping.no]** Fr Bodø take Rv80 for 19km; turn S onto rte 17 at Løding; site sp in Saltstraumen. Med, hdstg, unshd; htd wc; chem disp; mv service pnt; fam bthrm; shwrs inc; EHU (16A) NOK30; gas; lndry (inc dryer); shop adj; rest adj; BBQ; cooking facs; playgrnd; fishing; bike hire; boating; wifi; TV; phone; 50% statics; dogs; bus 300m; twin axles; poss cr; Eng spkn; adv bkg; quiet; ccard acc; CKE/CCI. "5 min walk to Mælstrom, the 'angler's paradise'; v busy high ssn - rec arr early; site a bit tired." ♦ ltd. NOK 272 2017*

BOSBERG see Trondheim *2E3*

BOVERDALEN see Lom *1C2*

⊞ **BREMSNES** *1B1* (6km W Coastal) *63.08043, 7.59535* **Skjerneset Brygge Camping, Ekkilsøy, 6530 Averøy (Møre og Romsdal) [tel 71 51 18 94; fax 71 51 18 15; info@skjerneset.com; www.skjerneset. com]** Foll sp to Ekkilsøya Island on Rv64 (off Averøy Island). Site on R over bdge. Sm, some hdstg, pt shd; htd wc; chem disp; mv service pnt; shwrs inc; EHU (10-16A) NOK30; lndry; sm shop; cooking facs; boat hire; fishing; sat TV; apartments to rent; quiet. "Charming, clean, peaceful site adj working harbour; beautiful outlook; basic san facs; waterside pitches - unfenced deep water in places; museum adj." NOK 200 2015*

BRIKSDALSBRE see Olden *1B2*

⊞ **BRONNOYSUND** *2E3* (14km SW Coastal) *65.39340, 12.09920* **Torghatten Camping, 8900 Torghatten (Nordland) [tel 75 02 54 95; post@ torghatten.net; www.rv17.no/torghatten-camping/]** Fr Rv17 onto Rv76 to Brønnøysund, foll sp Torghatten. Site at base of Torghatten mountain. Sm, pt sl, unshd; wc; chem disp; mv service pnt; shwrs inc; EHU (16A) NOK30; lndry; shop; snacks; bar; playgrnd; sea water pool & beach adj; bus; phone; Eng spkn; quiet. "Take care speed humps in/out Brønnøysund; vg." ♦ ltd. NOK 140 2016*

⊞ **BRUFLAT** *1C2* (10km SE Rural) *60.82932, 9.75050* **Etna Familiecamping, Maslangrudvegen 50, 2890 Etnedal [tel 61 12 17 55 or 94 81 90 56 (mob); info@ etnacamping.no; www.etnacamping.no]** Fr Gjovik, W on 33 past Dokka. Site on R approx 2 km past 251. Downhill to ent. Lge, pt sl, terr, pt shd; htd wc; chem disp, dedicated pnt; mv service pnt; fam bthrm; shwrs; lndry; snacks; pool; games rm; TV rm; 20% statics; twin axles; Eng spkn; adv bkg; quiet; ccard acc; CKE/ CCI. "Relaxing site; sep area for touring; may need long lead, some still 2 pin; vg." ♦ ltd. NOK 276 2015*

BUD *1B1* (1km SE Coastal) *62.9040, 6.92866* **PlusCamp Bud (MR11), 6430 Bud (Møre og Romsdal) [tel 71 26 10 23 or 97 70 05 44 (mob); fax 71 26 11 47; bud@pluscamp.no; www.budcamping. no]** Site on Rv664, sp fr Bud. Med, pt sl, unshd; htd wc; chem disp; mv service pnt; fam bthrm; shwrs NOK10; EHU (16A) NOK40; lndry (inc dryer); shop; snacks; cooking facs; playgrnd; sand beach & sw adj; boat hire; fishing; TV rm; wifi; 50% statics; dogs; Eng spkn; quiet; ccard acc; CKE/CCI. "Waterfront site with beautiful views; 20 min walk to vill shops/rest; gd facs; gd location for start of Atlantic Highway, National Tourist Rte & for cycling; vg site." ♦ 20 Apr-1 Oct. NOK 270 2015*

"I like to fill in the reports as I travel from site to site"

You'll find report forms at the back of this guide, or you can fill them in online at camc.com/europereport.

⊞ **BYGLANDSFJORD** *1B4* (3km N Rural) *58.68895, 7.80322* **Neset Camping, 4741 Byglandsfjord (Aust-Agder) [tel 37 93 40 50; fax 37 93 43 93; post@neset.no; www.neset.no]** N on Rv9 fr Evje, thro Byglandsfjord, site on L. Lge, pt sl, unshd; htd wc; chem disp; mv service pnt; fam bthrm; sauna; shwrs NOK5; EHU (10A) NOK30; gas; lndry (inc dryer); shop; snacks; rest; BBQ; cooking facs; playgrnd; lake sw & beach adj; fishing; windsurfing; boat & bike hire; wifi; TV rm; 40% statics; dogs; Eng spkn; adv bkg; quiet; ccard acc. "Wonderful location on lakeside; elk safaris; walks; ww rafting nrby; check elec earth." ♦ NOK 304 2014*

BYRKJELO *1B2* (250m S Rural) *61.73026, 6.50843* **Byrkjelo Camping & Hytter, 6826 Byrkjelo (Sogn og Fjordane) [tel 91 73 65 97; fax 57 86 71 54; mail@ byrkjelo-camping.no; www.byrkjelo-camping.tefre. com]** Fr S site ent on L as ent town, clearly sp. Sm, some hdstg, pt shd, wc; chem disp; fam bthrm; shwrs NOK5; EHU (10A) NOK30; lndry; shop, snacks adj; rest 500m; cooking facs; playgrnd; htd pool; paddling pool; fishing; cycling; solarium; wifi; 25% statics; phone; Eng spkn; adv bkg; quiet but some rd noise; ccard acc; CKE/CCI. "Horseriding, mountain & glacier walking; excel, well kept site; great facs." ♦ 30 Mar-20 Sep. NOK 190 2014*

NORWAY

DALSGRENDA see Mo i Rana *2F2*

DOMBAS *1C2* (6km S Rural) *62.02991, 9.17586* **Bjørkhol Camping, 2660 Dombås (Oppland) [tel 61 24 13 31; post@bjorkhol.no; www.bjorkhol.no]** Site on E6. Sm, pt sl, pt shd; htd wc; chem disp; mv service pnt; shwrs NOK5; EHU (10A) NOK40 (long lead poss req); lndry; shop; rest, snacks, bar 6km; cooking facs; playgrnd; 10% statics; dogs; phone; Eng spkn; adv bkg; quiet; CKE/CCI. "A well-kept, friendly, family-owned, basic site; excel mountain walking in area." 1 May-1 Sep. NOK 150 2013*

DRAMMEN *1C3* (25km SE Coastal) *59.60003, 10.40383* **Homannsberget Camping, Strømmveien 55, 3060 Svelvik (Vestfold) [tel 33 77 25 63 or 91 30 98 52 (mob); post@homannsberget.no; www.homannsberget.no]** Head SW on E18, take exit 25 twr Svelvik/RV319, at rndabt take 3rd exit onto E134. At next rndabt take 1st exit onto Bjørnsons gate/ Rv282. Turn L onto Havnegata/Rv319. Cont on Rv319, go thro 1 rndabt. Site on the L. Med, mkd pitch, unshd; mv service pnt; shwr NOK5; EHU; lndry (inc dryer); shop; bar; playgrnd; beach adj; games area; wifi; twin axles; poss cr; adv bkg; quiet; ccard acc; CKE/CCI. "Vg site; train stn within 20 mins; site is also a strawberry farm & orchard." 1 May-1 Sep. NOK 245 2014*

EDLAND *1B3* (6km E Rural) *59.72378, 7.69712* **Velemoen Camping, 3895 Edland Vinje i Telemark [tel 35 07 01 09 or 90 89 40 49 (mob); fax 35 07 02 15; velemoen@frisurf.no; www.velemoen.no]** Fr E site on L off E134 bef Edland; Fr W site is on R, 8km after Haukeligrend on Lake Tveitevatnet. Sm, hdstg, pt sl, unshd; wc; fam bthrm; shwrs 10NOK; EHU (16A, no earth); lndry; shops 1km; BBQ; cooking facs; playgrnd; lake sw adj; TV rm; 10% statics; dogs; phone; twin axles; Eng spkn; adv bkg; quiet; red for long stay/LS. "V helpful owner; immac san facs; beautiful lakeside/mountain location; on S side of Hardangervidda National Park; on main E-W rte Oslo-Bergen; excel." ♦ ltd. 15 May-1 Oct. NOK 250 2017*

⊞ **EGERSUND** *1A4* (4km N Rural) *58.4788, 5.9909* **Steinsnes NAF Camping, Jærveien 190, Tengs, 4370 Egersund (Horda-Rogaland) [tel 97 40 09 66; fax 51 49 40 73; post@steinsnescamping.no; www.steinsnescamping.no]** Site located S of Rv44 & on bank of rv; rv bdge at Tengs Bru. Med, mkd pitch, unshd; wc; chem disp; mv service pnt; shwrs NOK5; EHU (4A) NOK35; lndry; shops adj; snacks adj; bar 2km; BBQ; playgrnd; sand beach 8km; horseriding school adj; phone; poss cr; Eng spkn; adv bkg; quiet but some rd noise; ccard acc; CKE/CCI. "Spectacular rapids 1km (salmon leaping in July); on North Sea cycle rte; conv ferry to Denmark or Bergen; vg." ♦ NOK 230 2013*

EIDFJORD *1B3* (7km SE Rural) *60.42563, 7.12318* **Sæbø Camping (HO11), 5784 Øvre-Eidfjord (Hordaland) [tel 53 66 59 27 or 55 10 20 48; scampi@online.no; www.saebocamping.com]** Site N of Rv7 bet Eidfjord & Geilo, 2nd on L after tunnel & bdge; clearly sp. Med, pt shd; htd wc; chem disp; mv service pnt; fam bthrm; shwrs NOK10; EHU (10A) NOK30 (earth fault); lndry (inc dryer); shop; rest, snacks 500m; cooking facs; playgrnd; boating; quiet; CKE/CCI. "Vg; beautiful lakeside setting; adj to excel nature cent with museum/shop/theatre; clean san facs; helpful staff; gd location for walking & cycling." ♦ 1 May-30 Sep. NOK 248 2014*

⊞ **ELVERUM** *1D2* (2km S Rural) *60.86701, 11.55623* **Elverum Camping, Halvdan Gransvei 6, 2407 Elverum (Hedmark) [tel 62 41 67 16; fax 62 41 68 17; booking@elverumcamping.no; www.elverumcamping.no]** Site sp fr Rv20 dir Kongsvinger. Lge, pt shd; htd wc; chem disp; mv service pnt; shwrs inc; EHU (10A) NOK40; lndry; shop, rest, snacks, bar 2km; BBQ; playgrnd; 20% statics; phone; dogs; adv bkg; Eng spkn; quiet. "Vg; museum of forestry adj; rlwy museum at Hamar (30km)." NOK 280 2016*

⊞ **FAGERNES** *1C2* (600m S Rural) *60.98189, 9.23125* **Camping Fagernes, Tyinvegen 23, 2900 Fagernes (Oppland) [tel 61 36 05 10; fax 61 36 07 51; post@fagernes-camping.no; www.fagernes-camping.no]** Site on N side of Fagernes on E16. Lge, some hdg pitch, pt sl, pt shd; htd wc; chem disp; mv service pnt; fam bthrm; shwrs NOK12; EHU (10-16A) NOK30; lndry; shop; rest, snacks; bar; cooking facs; playgrnd; lake sw; activity cent; cycling; skiing; fishing; car wash; TV; 90% statics; dogs; phone; poss cr; Eng spkn; quiet LS; ccard acc; CKE/CCI. "Helpful owner; ltd water pnts; Valdres folk museum park adj highly rec; fjord views; excel new san facs & site refurbished (2015); vg." ♦ NOK 275 2015*

FARSUND *1A4* (6km S Rural) *58.0663, 6.7957* **Lomsesanden Familiecamping, Loshavneveien 228, 4550 Farsund (Vest-Agder) [tel 38 39 09 13; e-vetlan@online.no; www.lomsesanden.no]** Exit E39 at Lyngdal onto Rv43 to Farsund & foll camp sps. (NB Rv465 fr Kvinesdal not suitable for c'vans.) Med, pt shd; wc; chem disp; fam bthrm; shwrs NOK10; EHU (10A) NOK45; lndry; shop; playgrnd; dir access sand beach adj; fishing; TV; 95% statics; dogs; Eng spkn; adv bkg rec; quiet; ccard acc. "Gd site in beautiful location." 1 May-15 Sep. NOK 200 2016*

⊞ **FAUSKE** *2F2* (15km NE Coastal) *67.34618, 15.59533* **Strømhaug Camping, Strømhaugveien 2, 8226 Straumen (Nordland) [tel 75 69 71 06; fax 75 69 76 06; mail@stromhaug.no; www.stromhaug.no]** N fr Fauske on E6, turn off sp Straumen, site sp. Sm, pt sl, pt shd; htd wc; chem disp; mv service pnt; shwrs NOK10; EHU (6-10A) inc; lndry; shop, rest, snacks, bar adj; cooking facs; playgrnd; fishing; boating; TV; Eng spkn; red 7+ days. "Site on rv bank; salmon-fishing in Aug." ♦ NOK 239 2013*

⊞ **FAUSKE** *2F2* (5km S Urban) *67.23988, 15.41961* **Fauske Camping & Motel, Leivset, 8201 Fauske (Nordland) [tel 75 64 84 01; fax 75 64 84 13; fausm@online.no]** Fr S site on R of E6, approx 6km fr exit of Kvenflåg rd tunnel, & 2km bef Finneid town board. Fr N site on L approx 1km after rv bdge. Sm, sl, pt shd; wc; mv service pnt; fam bthrm; shwrs NOK10; EHU (10A) NOK40; lndry; shop 2km; snacks; cooking facs; playgrnd; sw 2km; fishing; cycling; wifi; dogs; poss cr; some Eng spkn; adv bkg; some rd noise; ccard acc. "Vg; phone ahead LS to check open; v close to E6 rd." NOK 267 2016*

⊞ **FJAERLAND** *1B2* (4km N Rural) *61.42758, 6.76211* **Bøyum Camping, 5855 Fjærland (Sogn og Fjordane) [tel 57 69 32 52; post@boyumcamping.no; www.boyumcamping.no]** On Rv5 Sogndal to Skei. Shortly after end of toll tunnel on L, well sp. Sm, hdstg, unshd; htd wc; chem disp; mv service pnt; shwrs NOK10; EHU; lndry (inc dryer); ltd shop; café; snacks; cooking facs; playgrnd; wifi; bike hire; wifi; TV rm; 30% statics; phone; poss cr; Eng spkn; adv bkg; sm rd noise; ccard acc; CKE/CCI. "Adj glacier museum, conv for glacier & fjord trips; beautiful location nr fjord (no views); visit Mundal for 2nd hand books; helpful owner; superb, clean site; vg." ♦ NOK 270 2017*

FLAKK see Trondheim *1C1*

FLAM *1B2* (1km WNW Urban) *60.86296, 7.10985* **Flåm Camping, Nedre Brekkevegen 12, 5743 Flåm (Sogn og Fjordane) [tel 57 63 21 21; camping@flaam-camping.no; www.flaam-camping.no]** Fr Lærdal Tunnel cont on E16 thro 2 more tunnels. At end of 2nd tunnel (Fretheim Tunnel) turn L immed to Sentrum. Turn L at x-rds, site on L. Med, hdstg, pt sl, terr, pt shd; htd wc; chem disp; mv service pnt; serviced pitches; fam bthrm; shwrs NOK10; EHU (10A) inc; lndry (inc dryer); shop; supmkt nrby; rest, snacks & bar 500m; BBQ; cooking facs; playgrnd; bike hire; watersports; boating; fishing; dogs free; no o'fits over 8.5m; phone; poss cr; Eng spkn; quiet but noise fr rd & cruise ships during day; ccard acc; red long stay; CKE/CCI. "Well-kept, friendly, busy, family-run site; excel san facs; conv mountain walks, excel location for Flambana rlwy, Aurlandsvangen 7km - gd shops; gd cycling base; excel." ♦ 1 Mar-31 Oct. NOK 300 2015*

⊞ **FLEKKEFJORD** *1A4* (6km ESE Rural) *58.28868, 6.7173* **Egenes Camping (VA7), 4400 Flekkefjord (Vest-Agder) [tel 38 32 01 48; fax 38 32 01 11; post@egenescamping.no; www.egenes.no]** Located N of E39 dir Seland. Med, mkd pitch, pt shd; htd wc; chem disp; mv service pnt; fam bthrm; shwrs NOK10; EHU (5A) NOK40; lndry; shop; snacks; playgrnd; TV; 75% statics; phone; ccard acc; red CKE/CCI. "Ltd facs LS; overflow car park area with facs for tourers 0.5km; poss cr; lovely situation." ♦ NOK 250 2014*

⊞ **FLORO** *1A2* (2km E Coastal) *61.59420, 5.07244* **Pluscamp Krokane (SF15), Strandgt 30, 6900 Florø (Sogn og Fjordane) [tel 57 75 22 50; fax 57 75 22 60; post@krocamp.no; www.krocamp.no]** On Rv5 Forde to Florø, on ent town turn L at rndabt sp Krokane, then immed R & foll rd to coast. Turn L, pass marina to site, sp. Steep ent/exit. Sm, hdstg, pt sl, pt shd; htd wc; chem disp; mv service pnt; fam bthrm; shwrs NOK10; EHU (10A) NOK30; lndry; shop 2km; rest, snacks, bar 2km; playgrnd; htd, covrd pool 1km; sand beach adj; boat hire; fishing; internet; 80% statics; phone; bus; Eng spkn; quiet; CKE/CCI. "V sm area for tourers; Florø interesting fishing town with boat trips etc." ♦ NOK 130 2016*

FORDE *1A2* (3km E Rural) *61.44940, 5.89008* **Førde Gjestehus & Camping (SF94), Kronborgvegen 44, Havstad, 6800 Førde (Romsdal Sogn og Fjordane) [tel 46 80 60 00; post@fordecamping.no; www.fordecamping.no]** Site is on NE o'skirts Forde. At rndabt on E39at Havstad foll sp 'Hospital', site on R in 1km; well sp. Med, mkd pitch, some hdstg, pt shd; htd wc; chem disp; mv service pnt; shwrs inc; fam bthrm; EHU (16A) inc; lndry; shop; rest; cooking facs; playgrnd; rv sw adj; TV rm; some statics; phone; Eng spkn; adv bkg; quiet; ccard acc; CKE/CCI. "Pleasant, peaceful site." ♦ ltd. 1 Jan-29 Feb & 15 Apr-1 Oct. NOK 304 2013*

FREDRIKSTAD *1C4* (16km SE Coastal) *59.13942, 11.03855* **Bevo Camping, Bevoveien 31, 1634 Gamle Fredrikstad [tel 69 34 92 15; info@bevo.no; www.bevo.no]** Avoid app fr Fredrikstad. Fr E6 junc 4, take RV110 (Fredrikstad) then L on RV111 & L on RV107 (Torsnesveien). Foll signs to campsite. Sm, mkd pitch, pt shd; wc; chem disp; shwrs 10kr; EHU; lndry rm; shop; snacks; sw sand beach adj; poss cr; quiet; CCI. "Isolated site on Oslo Fjord; 15 mins to Gamle Frederikstad by car." 28 Apr-8 Sep. NOK 260 2014*

⊞ **GEILO** *1B3* (2km NE Urban) *60.54251, 8.23495* **Breie Hytter & Camping, Lauvrudvegen 11, 3580 Geilomoen, Geilo [tel 32 09 04 12 or 97 16 46 01 (mob); fax 32 09 10 44; post@breiehytter.no; www.breiehytter.no]** Fr Geilo take RV7 twds Gol & Sundre. Site sp, take R into Lauvrudvegen. Sm, unshd; wc; chem disp; shwr; EHU inc; shop 1.5km; rest 1.5km; bar 1.5km; 30% statics; quiet; CCI. "Vg for long or sh stays; pleasant, well kept site in residential area; helpful owner." NOK 170 2014*

⊞ **GEILO** *1B3* (2km NE Rural) *60.54422, 8.23637* **Øen Turistsenter & Geilo Vandrerhjem, Lienvegen 139, 3580 Geilo [tel 32 08 70 60; fax 32 08 70 66; post@oenturist.no; www.oenturist.no]** Fr Geilo on Rv.7 twds Gol. Turn L onto Lienvegen & site. Med, hdg/gravel pitch, pt sl, pt shd; wc; sauna; shwrs inc; EHU (10A) 30 NOK; lndry (inc dryer); rest; BBQ; cooking facs; wifi; 30% statics; dogs; Eng spkn; quiet, some rd noise; CKE/CCI. "Vg site." NOK 230 2015*

NORWAY

GEIRANGER *1B1* (350m S Rural) *62.09998, 7.20421* **Camping Geiranger, 6216 Geiranger (Møre og Romsdal) [tel/fax 70 26 31 20; post@geirangercamping.no; www.geirangercamping.no]** Site on fjord edge in vill. On Rv63 Eidsdal-Geiranger take lower rd thro vill to site on R & on both sides of rv. Rv63 not suitable for c'vans - steep hill & hairpins, use ferry fr Hellesylt. Lge, pt sl, unshd; wc; chem disp; mv service pnt; shwrs NOK10; ltd EHU (16A) NOK35; lndry (inc dryer); BBQ; cooking facs; playgrnd; wifi; dogs; poss cr; Eng spkn; quiet but noise of waterfall; ccard acc; no adv bkgs; CKE/CCI. "Busy site in superb location, gd touring base, gd boat trips on fjord, facs (inc EHU) ltd if site full; gd facs." ♦ 10 May-20 Sep. NOK 270 2015*

GEIRANGER *1B1* (2km NNW Rural) *62.11548, 7.18437* **Grande Hytteutleige og Camping, 6216 Geiranger (Møre og Romsdal) [tel 70 26 30 68; office@grande-hytteutleige.no; www.grande-hytteutleige.no]** Head N on Rv63, in 2.3km turn L at the foot of zigzags, then 1st R. Site on the L. Sm, pt sl; htd wc; shwr 15 NOK; EHU (16A); lndry; cooking facs; internet; wifi; Eng spkn; quiet; ccard acc. "Friendly staff; conv for Fjord cruise, vg site." May-Oct. NOK 250 2014*

⊞ **GOL** *1C2* (3km S Rural) *60.70023, 9.00416* **Gol Campingsenter (BU17), Heradveien 7, 3550 Gol (Buskerud) [tel 32 07 41 44; fax 32 07 53 96; gol@pluscamp.no; www.golcamp.no]** Ent on R of Rv7 fr Gol twd Nesbyen. Lge, pt sl, unshd; htd wc; chem disp; mv service pnt; fam bthrm; sauna; shwrs inc; EHU (16A) inc; lndry (inc dryer); gas; shop; supmkt 2km; rest, snacks; bar; cooking facs; playgrnd; htd pool; padding pool; rv sw 2km; games area; wifi; TV rm; poss noisy; ccard acc; CKE/CCI. "Excel; lge extn with full facs across main rd - modern & clean." ♦ NOK 245 (4 persons) 2016*

⊞ **GOL** *1C2* (2km SW Rural) *60.69161, 8.91909* **Personbråten Camping, 3550 Gol (Buskerud) [tel 90 78 32 73; leif.personbraten@c2i.net]** Fr Gol to Geilo on Rv7, on L on rvside. Med, pt shd; wc; chem disp (wc); shwrs inc; EHU (10A; lndry; BBQ; cooking facs; playgrnd; fishing; cycling; rv sw 1km; wifi; adv bkg; Eng spkn; CKE/CCI. "On rvside; v pleasant; poss noise fr rd & rv; honesty box if office unmanned; excel NH." NOK 217 2016*

GRANLI see Kongsvinger *1D3*

⊞ **GRIMSBU** *1C2* (N Rural) *62.15546, 10.17198* **Grimsbu Turistsenter, 2582 Grimsbu (Oppland) [tel 62 49 35 29; fax 62 49 35 62; mail@grimsbu.no; www.grimsbu.no]** On Rv29 11km E of Folldal, well sp. Med, pt sl, pt shd; htd wc; chem disp; mv service pnt; sauna; private san facs avail; shwrs NOK10; EHU (16A) NOK30; lndry (inc dryer); shop; rest, snacks; BBQ; cooking facs; playgrnd; lake sw 1.5km; rv fishing; bike & boat hire; fitness rm; wifi; TV rm; Eng spkn; adv bkg; quiet; ccard acc. "Family-run site; beautiful situation." ♦ NOK 243 (CChq acc) 2014*

⊞ **GRIMSTAD** *1B4* (5km NE Coastal) *58.36888, 8.63722* **Moysand Familiecamping, Moy, 4885 Grimstad (Aust-Agder) [tel 90 53 55 93; mail@moysand-familiecamping.no; www.moysand-familiecamping.no]** Exit A18 junc 78 onto Rv420 E twd Fevik. Foll site sp on rd to Riksveien, site 2km after Riksveien. Lge, mkd pitch, pt shd; htd wc; fam bthrm; private san facs avail; shwrs; EHU metered; lndry (inc dryer); shop; supmkt 5km; rest; BBQ; cooking facs; playgrnd; fishing; boat hire; TV; some statics; dogs; adv bkg; quiet. ♦ NOK 190 2016*

⊞ **GRONG** *2E3* (2km S Rural) *64.4604, 644604* **Langnes Camping, 7870 Grong (Nord-Trøndelag) [tel 47 68 83 33; post@langnescamping.no; langnescamping.no]** N on E6 turn off S of bdge over rv on by-pass, site sp. Med, mkd pitch, some hdstg, unshd; htd wc; chem disp; mv service pnt; shwrs NOK10; EHU (10A) NOK35; lndry (inc dryer); snacks; rest 3km; BBQ; cooking facs; playgrnd; rv sw & beach nr; rv fishing; drying rm for skiers; games area; games rm; wifi; TV; some statics; Quick Stop pitches; Eng spkn; adv bkg; quiet. "Helpful staff; pleasant, family-run site; free phone to owner if site clsd; gd facs." ♦ NOK 140 2016*

"We must tell The Club about that great site we found"

Get your site reports in by mid-August and we'll do our best to get your updates into the next edition.

GUDVANGEN *1B2* (1km SW Rural) *60.87206, 6.82873* **Vang Camping, 5747 Gudvangen (Sogn og Fjordane) [tel/fax 57 63 39 26; post@vang-camping.no; www.vang-camping.no]** At S end of of Nærøy Fjord on E16 at edge of vill. Sm, some hdstg, unshd; wc; chem disp/mv service pnt at Shell g'ge 1km; shwrs NOK5; EHU (16A) NOK30 (poss no earth); lndry; shop 1km; rest 1km at ferry; Eng spkn; quiet but some rd noise; no ccard acc; CKE/CCI. "Immac site in beautiful valley with waterfalls; spectacular scenery; cruises on adj fjord; bus to Flam; poor san facs (2015)." 1 May-15 Sep. NOK 225 2015*

HAMALVOLL see Os I Osterdalen *1D1*

HAMMERFEST *2G1* (1km E Urban) *70.65890, 23.71335* **Storvannet Camping, Storvannsveien 103, 9615 Hammerfest (Finnmark) [tel 78 41 10 10; storvannet@yahoo.no]** Descend into & cont thro town. Turn R immed after x-ing rv bdge. Site at top of Storvannet lake nr mouth of Rv Storelva. Sp. Med, some hdstg; pt sl; unshd; htd wc; chem disp; shwrs NOK10; EHU NOK40; lndry (inc dryer); shop 3km; rest 3km; BBQ; cooking facs; sw adj; fishing; dogs; poss cr; Eng spkn; quiet; 10% red +3 days; CKE/CCI. "Vg; by attractive lake; 2km out of town." ♦ 1 Jun-15 Sep. NOK 230 2014*

HAMRESANDEN see Kristiansand *1B4*

HAUGE *1A4* (5km NE Rural) *58.36166, 6.30944* **Bakkaåno Camping, Bakkaveien, Fidje 4380 Hauge i Dalane (Rogaland) [tel 51 47 78 52 or 930 50 219 (mob); visit@bakkaanocamping.no; www.bakkaano camping.no]** Heading E fr Hauge on Rv44, over rv & immed turn L & foll site sp. Site on L, recep on R over golf course at white house. Rd narr. Med, pt shd; wc; chem disp; mv service pnt; shwrs NOK1; EHU (5A) NOK30; shop; cooking facs; sw & fishing adj; 80% statics; Eng spkn; quiet. "Sep area for tourers; friendly, welcoming owners." ♦ ltd. Easter-30 Sep. NOK 220 2013*

HAUKELAND see Bergen *1A3*

HELLESYLT *1B1* (400m S Coastal) *62.08329, 6.87224* **Hellesylt Camping, 6218 Hellesylt (Møre og Romsdal) [tel 90 20 68 85; fax 70 26 52 10; postmottak@hellesyltturistsenter.no; www. hellesyltturistsenter.no]** Site on edge of fjord, sp fr cent of vill dir Geiranger. Sm, unshd; htd wc; chem disp; mv service pnt; shwrs NOK10; EHU (10A) NOK30; lndry (inc dryer); sm shop; supmkt 100m, rest adj; shgl beach; wifi; 40% statics; dogs; Eng spkn; adv bkg; quiet; no ccard acc; CKE/CCI. "Conv ferry to Geiranger; adj fjord surrounded by mountains - great views; gd rest in local hotel; beautiful church nr." ♦ ltd. 15 Apr-30 Sep. NOK 140 2014*

HONNINGSVAG *2H1* (8km NW Coastal) *71.02625, 25.89091* **Nordkapp Camping, 9751 Honningsvåg (Finnmark) [tel 78 47 33 77; post@nordkapp camping.no; www.nordkappcamping.no]** En rte Nordkapp on E69, site clearly sp. Sm, unshd; htd wc; chem disp; mv service pnt; fam bthrm; shwrs NOK5; EHU (16A) NOK40; lndry (inc dryer); BBQ; cooking facs; lake 5km; wifi; 10% statics; dogs NOK10; bus 100m; twin axles; Eng spkn; quiet; ccard acc; red CKE/CCI. "Vg; reindeer on site." ♦ ltd. 1 May-30 Sep. NOK 319 2017*

HORTEN *1C3* (3km S Rural/Coastal) *59.39776, 10.47582* **Rørestrand Camping, Parkveien 34, 3186 Horten (Vestfold) [tel 33 07 33 40; fax 33 07 47 90; booking@rorestrandcamping.no; rorestrandcamping.no]** Fr Horten foll Rv19 for 500m S to rndabt, then foll sp. Sm, sl, unshd; htd wc; chem disp; fam bthrm; shwrs NOK10; EHU (10A) NOK40; lndry (inc dryer); shop; snacks; playgrnd; games area; 90% statics; dogs; phone; poss cr; Eng spkn; quiet; ccard acc; CKE/CCI. "Conv NH en rte Oslo; facs stretched high ssn." ♦ ltd. 1 May-15 Sep. NOK 250 2016*

HOVAG see Kristiansand *1B4*

⊞ **JORPELAND** *1A3* (5km SE Rural) *58.99925, 6.0922* **Preikestolen Camping (RO17), Preikestolvegan 97, 4100 Jørpeland (Horda-Rogaland) [tel 47 48 19 39 50; fax 51 74 80 77; info@preikestolencamping.com; www.preikestolencamping.com]** Fr S exit Rv13 to Preikestolen to R, site sp. Rd narr in places, care needed. Med, hdstg, unshd; wc; chem disp; mv service pnt; shwrs inc; EHU (16A) NOK40; lndry; shop & 10km; rest, snacks; bar; playgrnd; rv sw adj; games area; dogs; phone; bus to Preikestolen parking; poss cr; adv bkg; Eng spkn; quiet; red long stay; ccard acc; CKE/ CCI. "Marvellous views; poss walk to Pulpit Rock but not easy; conv Stavanger by ferry; excel facs, esp shwrs; midge repellent ess; long lead poss needed; poss no earth." ♦ NOK 322 2016*

⊞ **KARASJOK** *2H1* (1km SW Rural) *69.46888, 25.48908* **Camping Karasjok, Kautokeinoveien, 9730 Karasjok (Finnmark) [tel 78 46 61 35; fax 78 46 66 97; karasjokcamping@runbox.no or booking@ karacamp.no]** Sp in town; fr x-rds in town & N of rv bdge take Rv92 W dir Kautokeino, site 900m on L. Sm, pt shd; htd wc; chem disp; mv service pnt 1km; shwrs NOK5; EHU (10A) NOK40; lndry (inc dryer); shops 1km; playgrnd; wifi; Eng spkn; adv bkg; v quiet; ccard acc; CKE/CCI. "Youth hostel & cabins on site; gd, clean site & facs; lge pitches suitable RVs & lge o'fits; sh walk to Sami park & museum." ♦ NOK 211 2014*

⊞ **KAUTOKEINO** *2G1* (2.5km S Rural) *68.99760, 23.03662* **Arctic Motell & Kautokeino Camping, Suomaluodda 16, 9520 Kautokeino (Finnmark) [tel 78 48 54 00; samicamp@me.com; www.kautokeino camping.no]** Well sp fr Rv93. Sm, pt sl, unshd; htd wc; shwrs NOK10; EHU NOK30; lndry; shop; rest; 20% statics; poss cr; Eng spkn; quiet. "No chem disp; Juhls silver gallery worth visit; gd, friendly site." NOK 247 2016*

⊞ **KILBOGHAMN** *2E2* (3km S Coastal) *66.50667, 13.21608* **Hilstad Camping, 8752 Kilboghamn (Nordland) [tel 75 09 71 86; fax 75 09 71 01; post@ polarcamp.com or booking@polarcamp.com; www. polarcamp.com]** N on Rv17 sp to L just bef Kilboghamn ferry. Sm, hdstg, terr, unshd; wc; chem disp; shwrs inc; EHU (10A); lndry; shop; rest, snacks; bar; playgrnd; shgl beach adj; fishing; 40% statics; phone; poss cr; Eng spkn; quiet. "Superb location on Arctic Circle; ltd san facs in high ssn; fishing/boat trips arranged." NOK 235 2014*

⊞ **KINSARVIK** *1B3* (500m SW Rural/Coastal) *60.37426, 6.71866* **Kinsarvik Camping, RV13, 5780 Kinsarvik (Hordaland) [tel 53 66 32 90; evald@ kinsarvikcamping.no; www.kinsarvikcamping.no]** Fr SW edge of vill on rv. At Esso g'ge foll sp uphill fr cent of Kinsarvik. Sm, pt shd; wc; chem disp, mv service pnt at Esso g'ge; fam bthrm; shwrs NOK10; EHU (10A) NOK30 (poss no earth); lndry; sm shop 400m; snacks; cooking facs; playgrnd; fishing; TV; 80% statics; bus 400m; quiet; CKE/CCI. "Wonderful views over Hardanger Fjord." NOK 284 2013*

KIRKENES *2H1* (92km SSW Rural) *69.21283, 29.15560* **Ovre Pasvik Camping, Vaggetem, 9925 Svanvik [tel 95 91 13 05; atle.randa@pasvik camping.no; www.pasvikcamping.no]** On the R of Rte 885. Sp fr rd. Sm, hdstg, pt sl, pt shd; wc; sauna; shwrs NOK10; EHU; lndry; BBQ; cooking facs; wifi; 50% statics; dogs; Eng spkn; CKE/CCI. "Clean facs, dated & basic; gd for birdwatching; fishing; canoeing; gd." Mid Apr-Mid Oct. NOK 250 2016*

⊞ **KONGSBERG** *1C3* (7km N Rural) *59.71683, 9.61133* **Pikerfoss Camping, Svendsplassveien 2, 3614 Kongsberg (Buskerud) [tel 32 72 49 78 or 91 19 07 41; mail@pikerfoss.no or erikfred@online.no; www.pikerfoss.no]** Fr E134 in Kongsberg turn N bef x-ring rv & go N bet rv (on L) & rlwy line (on R) on Bærvergrendveien. Site on R just after x-ing rlwy line. Sm, mkd pitch, pt shd; htd wc; chem disp; shwrs inc; EHU (10A) NOK30; lndry; shop, rest, snacks, bar 6km; playgrnd; 75% statics; Eng spkn; quiet; ccard acc. "Modern, clean facs; lge pitches; facs stretched high ssn; excel." NOK 160 2014*

KONGSVINGER *1D3* (10km S Rural) *60.11786, 12.05208* **Sigernessjøen Familiecamping, Strenelsrud Gård, Arko-Vegen, 2210 Granli (Hedmark) [tel 40 60 11 22; post@sigernescamp.no; www.sigernescamp.no]** On N side of Rv2 Kongsvinger to Swedish border, well sp. Med, pt sl, pt shd; htd wc; chem disp; fam bthrm; shwrs inc; EHU (10A) NOK40; lndry (inc dryer); playgrnd; lake sw adj; golf adj; wifi; 30% statics; Eng spkn; quiet. "Gd." 1 May-30 Sep. NOK 250 2016*

KRISTIANSAND *1B4* (12km NE Coastal) *58.19011, 8.08283* **Hamresanden Camping, Hamresandveien 3, 4656 Hamresanden (Vest-Agder) [tel 38 14 42 80; fax 38 14 42 81; info@hamresanden.com; www.hamresanden.com]** Fr E18 foll sp Kjevik airport then Hamresanden & site. Lge, pt shd; htd wc; chem disp; fam bthrm; shwrs NOK15; EHU (10A) inc; lndry; rest, snacks; bar; cooking facs; playgrnd; htd pool; waterslides; sand beach & sw adj; watersports; tennis; boat & bike hire; games area; TV; 10% statics; dogs; bus; poss cr; Eng spkn; noise fr airport; ccard acc. ♦ 1 May-30 Sep. NOK 295 2014*

KRISTIANSAND *1B4* (2.7km E Coastal) *58.14701, 8.0303* **Camping Roligheden, Framnesveien, 4632 Kristiansand (Vest-Agder) [tel 38 09 67 22; fax 38 09 11 17; roligheden@roligheden.no; www.roligheden.no]** Sp fr E18 on N side of town. Lge, pt sl, pt shd; wc; chem disp; mv service pnt; shwrs NOK40; EHU (25A) NOK40; lndry; supmkt 400m; rest adj; playgrnd; sand beach adj; 5% statics; bus; poss cr; Eng spkn; quiet; ccard acc; red CKE/CCI. "Conv for ferry & exploring Kristiansand & district; 40 min walk to town; poss travellers; NH/sh stay only; site v run down; lovely coastal walks." 31 May-1 Sep. NOK 300 2014*

⊞ **KRISTIANSAND** *1B4* (12km E Rural) *58.12187, 8.06568* **Kristiansand Feriesenter, Dvergsnesveien 571, 4639 Kristiansand (Vest-Agder) [tel 38 04 19 80; fax 38 04 19 81; post@kristiansandferiesenter.no; www.dvergsnestangen.no]** Turn S off E18 jnc 91, 6km E of Kristiansand after Varoddbrua onto Rv401, cont for 5.5km foll sps to site. Rd narr last 3km. Lge, mkd pitch, sl, shd; htd wc; chem disp; mv service pnt; fam bthrm; shwrs NOK12 pre paid; EHU (16A) inc; lndry; shop; snacks; cooking facs; playgrnd; sw in fjord but rocky; fishing; boat hire; TV; phone; poss cr; quiet; ccard acc; CKE/CCI. "Gd NH; conv for ferry (20 mins); beautiful location; helpful, friendly staff." ♦ NOK 417 2014*

⊞ **KRISTIANSAND** *1B4* (23km E Coastal) *58.12551, 8.2310* **Skottevik Feriesenter (AA1), Hæstadsvingen, 4770 Høvåg (Aust-Agder) [tel 37 26 90 30; fax 37 26 90 33; post@skottevik.no; www.skottevik.no]** Fr Kristiansand, take E18 E, turn onto Rv401 twd Høvåg; site sp. Lge, pt shd; wc; chem disp; mv service pnt; private bathrms avail; shwrs NOK10; EHU (10A) NOK45; gas; lndry; shop; snacks & bar high ssn; rest 3km; playgrnd; htd pool; paddling pool; beach; 9-hole golf course; wifi; entmnt; poss cr; Eng spkn; adv bkg; quiet; ccard acc; CKE/CCI. "Beautiful area." ♦ NOK 205 2013*

⊞ **KRISTIANSUND** *1B1* (3km N Rural) *63.12543, 7.74106* **Atlanten Motel & Camping, Dalaveien 22, 6501 Kristiansund (Møre og Romsdal) [tel 71 67 11 04; fax 71 67 24 05; resepsjonen@atlanten.no; www.atlanten.no]** Fr Atlantic Rd (Atlanterhavsveien) & Bremsnes-Kristiansund ferry, foll sp on leaving ferry 5km to site. Med, terr, hdstg, pt shd; htd wc; chem disp; mv service pnt; fam bthrm; shwrs inc; EHU (6A) NOK40; lndry; shops; BBQ; cooking facs; playgrnd; pool 300m; shgl beach 2km; dogs; phone; Eng spkn; adv bkg; quiet; ccard acc; CKE/CCI. "Conv Kristiansund & fjords; boat trips to Grip Is with Stave Church; site clsd 20-31 Dec." ♦ NOK 170 2014*

KROKELVDALEN see Tromsø *2F1*

KROKSTRANDA *2F2* (300m SE Rural) *66.46233, 15.09344* **Krokstrand Camping, Saltfjellveien 1573, 8630 Krokstranda (Nordland) [tel/fax 75 16 60 74; toverakvaag@msn.com]** Nr Krokstrand bdge on E6, 18km S of Artic Circle & approx 50km N of Mo i Rana. Med, pt sl, pt shd; htd wc; chem disp; mv service pnt; fam bthrm; shwrs NOK5-10; EHU (10A) NOK30; lndry (inc dryer); shop; rest; snacks bar; cooking facs; playgrnd; fishing; 20% statics; phone; train; Eng spkn; adv bkg; ccard acc; quiet; CKE/CCI. "Conv Polar Circle Cent; gd." 1 Jun-1 Sep. NOK 280 2014*

KVANNDAL see Granvin *1B2*

KVISVIKA *1B1* (8km NE Coastal) *63.10910, 8.07875* **Magnillen Camping, 6674 Kvisvika (Møre og Romsdal) [tel 71 53 25 59; jarl-mo@online.no; www.magnillen.no]** Fr W turn L off E39 approx 5km after Vettafjellet (N); thro Kvisvika & after another 9km turn L into site; sp. Sm, unshd; wc; chem disp; mv service pnt; serviced pitches; shwrs NOK10; EHU (10A) NOK30; gas; lndry; shop 8km; snacks; BBQ; playgrnd; lake sw & sand beach adj; boat hire; 50% statics; Eng spkn; adv bkg; quiet; ccard acc; red long stay; CKE/CCI. "Site adj sm harbour; gd views." ♦ ltd. NOK 170 2016*

⊞ **LAERDALSOYRI** *1B2* (26km E Rural) *61.06725, 7.82170* **Borgund Hyttesenter and Camping, 6888 Borgund in Laerdal [tel 57 66 81 71 or 90 62 08 59 (mob); ovoldum@alb.no; hyttesenter.com]** Site on L of E16 just aft Borgunds Tunnel. Well sp in adv aft rd to Borgund Stave Church. Sm, open, hdstg, unshd; wc; chem disp; mv service pnt; shwrs NOK10-5mins; EHU (16A) no earth; lndry; snacks; BBQ; cooking facs; playgrnd; bike hire; wifi; tv rm; 10% statics; dogs; phone; bus 500m; Eng spkn; adv bkg; rd noise; red LS/long stay. "Gd for Borgund Stave Church, Laerdal tunnel, Glacier ctr & historic rtes; gd." ♦ ltd. NOK 220 2017*

LAERDALSOYRI *1B2* (800m NW Rural/Coastal) *61.10056, 7.47031* **Lærdal Ferie & Fritidspark, Grandavegen 5, 6886 Lærdal (Sogn og Fjordane) [tel 57 66 66 95; fax 57 66 87 81; info@laerdalferiepark.com; www.laerdalferiepark.com]** Site on N side of Lærdal off Rv5/E16 adj Sognefjord. Med, unshd; htd wc; chem disp; mv service pnt; fam bthrm; shwrs NOK5; EHU NOK40 (poss no earth); lndry (inc dryer); shop; supmkt 400m; rest high ssn; snacks; bar; BBQ; cooking facs; playgrnd; shgl beach adj; boat & bike hire; tennis; games area; games rm; golf 12km; wifi; TV rm; dogs; phone; Eng spkn; quiet; ccard acc; red long stay/CKE/CCI. "Modern, clean, gd value site; excel san & cooking facs; lovely location adj fjord ferry terminal & nr attractive vill; gd touring base; friendly, helpful owners - will open on request outside dates shown; nice site next to Fjord." ♦ 27 Mar-25 Oct. NOK 291 (CChq acc) 2014*

LANGFJORDBOTN *2G1* (1km S Rural) *70.02781, 22.2817* **Altafjord Camping, 9545 Langfjordbotn (Finnmark) [tel/fax 78 43 80 00; booking@altafjord-camping.no; www.altafjord-camping.no]** On E6, 600m S of exit to Bognelv, site adj to fjord across E6, sp. Dist by rd fr Alta 80km. Med, hdstg, terr, unshd; htd wc; serviced pitches; chem disp; sauna; shwrs NOK5; EHU (16A); gas; lndry; shops adj; cooking facs; sand & shgl beach; fjord sw & fishing; bike hire; TV rm; wifi; 50% statics; dogs; phone; poss cr; Eng spkn; no adv bkg; quiet; ccard acc. "Friendly owner; excel views; boat hire; mountaineering." 1 Jun-1 Sep. NOK 271 2016*

⊞ **LARVIK** *1C4* (1km S Urban) *59.04902, 10.03330* **Larvic Bobilparkering, Tollerudden, Larvik (Vestfold) [www.bobilplassen.no]** Fr E18 exit at Rv303 twd Larvik. At rndabt take 1st exit onto Strandpromenaden. Sm, hdstg, unshd; EHU (3A); BBQ; 0% statics; dogs; quiet. "Gd; parking lot for m'vans; NH only; 8 mkd pitches, honesty box for payment." NOK 137 2016*

⊞ **LARVIK** *1C4* (37km SSW Coastal) *59.00872, 9.70290* **Rognstranda Camping, Rognsveien 146, 3960 Stathelle (Vestfold) [tel 35 97 39 11 or 92 04 56 61 (mob); post@rognstrandacamping.no; www.rognstrandacamping.no]** Fr Larvik head SW on E18 for 34km. Turn L onto Tangvallveien, R onto Rognsveien. After 1.4km turn L. Then take 2nd L and 1st R. Site on L. Lge, pt sl, unshd; htd wc; mv service pnt; shwr; EHU (2 pin); lndry (inc dryer); shop; sandy beach adj; twin axles; poss cr; Eng spkn; adv bkg; CKE/CCI. "Coastal walks; v clean modern facs; 2 areas for sh stay; site popular with MH for NH; vg." NOK 320 2014*

⊞ **LILLEHAMMER** *1C2* (10km S Urban) *61.10275, 10.46278* **Camping Lillehammer, Dampsagveien 47, 2609 Lillehammer (Oppland) [tel 61 25 33 33; fax 61 25 33 65; resepsjon@lillehammer-camping.no; www.lillehammer-camping.no]** Exit E6 at Lillehammer Sentrum. Turn 1st R at 1st rndabt, foll rd around Strandtorget shopping cent, cont approx 1.5km along lakeside rd. Med, mkd pitch, some hdstg, unshd; wc; chem disp; mv service pnt; fam bthrm; shwrs NOK10; EHU (10A) inc (check earth); gas; lndry (inc dryer); shop 2km; playgrnd; pool 2km; internet; TV rm; statics; dogs; phone; poss cr; Eng spkn; adv bkg; quiet; ccard acc; red CKE/CCI. "Excel san facs, site adj Lake Mjøsa; gd views, conv town & skiing areas; site adj to c'van cent, spare parts etc; facs need updating." ♦ NOK 300 2016*

LOFOTEN AND VESTERALEN ISLANDS Campsites in towns in the Lofoten and Vesteralen Islands are listed together at the end of the Norwegian site entry pages.

LOM *1C2* (70m E Rural) *61.83812, 8.56969* **Camping Nordal Turistsenter, 2686 Lom (Oppland) [tel 61 21 93 00; fax 61 21 93 01; booking@nordalturistsenter.no; www.nordalturistsenter.no]** In cent Lom at x-rds R of Rv15. Ent by rndabt bet Esso stn & recep. Site at foot of Sognefjell Pass. Med, pt shd; htd wc; chem disp; mv service pnt; fam bthrm; sauna; shwrs inc; EHU (10A) (no earth); lndry; shop adj; rest; snacks adj; bar; cooking facs; playgrnd; TV rm; some statics; dogs; Eng spkn; adv bkg; ccard acc; CKE/CCI. "Split level site; bottom level quiet; top level adj to recep - often noisy due to rd noise & w/end coach parties; gd, modern san facs; mosquitoes troublesome in hot weather; busy tourist area; pleasant site; nice vill." 15 May-30 Sep. NOK 356 2015*

NORWAY

LOM *1C2* (14km NW Rural) *61.87923, 8.33326* **Storøya Camping, Rv15, 2690 Skjåk (Oppland) [tel 61 21 43 51; post@storoyacamping.com; www.storoyacamping.com]** Site clearly sp N of Rv15. Sm, pt shd; htd wc; shwrs; EHU (10A); some statics; quiet. "Friendly, little site with basic facs; excel san facs (2014)." 15 May-15 Sep. NOK 200 2014*

LUNDE *1C3* (750m W Rural) *59.29844, 9.09041* **Telemark Kanalcamping, Slusevegen 21, 3825 Lunde [tel 91 57 54 21; post@kanalcamping.no; www.kanalcamping.no]** Fr Rv 359 foll sp to Lunde slues. Site on L 1km fr cent of Lunde. Med, open plan, hdstg, sl, unshd; wc; chem disp; mv service pnt; fam bthrm; shwr 10 NOK; EHU (16A); BBQ; lake adj; boat hire; wifi; dogs; bus/train 1km; twin axles; Eng spkn; adv bkg; CKE/CCI. "Site on Telemark canal; lovely position; gd cycling/walking; site & san facs being developed, current san facs adequate (2015); vg." ♦ ltd. Mar-Sep. NOK 210 2015*

LUSTER see Skjolden *1B2*

MALMEFJORDEN see Molde *1B1*

MALVIK *1D1* (2km E Rural) *63.43243, 10.70778* **Storsand Gård Camping (ST68), 7563 Malvik (Sør-Trøndelag) [tel 73 97 63 60; fax 73 97 73 46; post@storsandcamping.no; www.storsandcamping.no]** On N side of E6 N, site sp. Rec use E6 toll rd fr S, 2nd exit after tunnel. Many lge speed humps on local rd Rv950, care needed. Lge, unshd; wc; chem disp; shwrs NOK10; EHU (16A); lndry; shop; cooking facs; playgrnd; shgl beach; fishing; games area; TV; some statics; phone; poss cr; rlwy noise. ♦ ltd. 15 May-1 Sep. NOK 364 2015*

⊞ **MALVIK** *1D1* (2km W Coastal) *63.44064, 10.63978* **Vikhammer Camping, Vikhammerløkka 4, 7560 Vikhammer [tel 73 97 61 64; vikcampi@online.no; www.vikhammer.no]** E fr Trondheim on E6. Immed bef toll plaza take ramp sp Vikhammer/Ransheim & turn R, then foll sp Vikhammer. After approx 6km at traff lts cont strt on Rv950 to rndabt & take 3rd exit sp motel & site. Fr N exit E6 after airport sp Hell, then Malvik/Hommelvik. Then take Rv950 to site. NB Many lge speed humps on Rv950, care req. Sm, terr, unshd; htd wc; chem disp; mv service pnt; shwrs inc; EHU (16A) NOK30; shop 1km; rest; bar; BBQ; wifi; 75% statics; dogs; phone; bus adj; Eng spkn; adv bkg; rd & rlwy noise; ccard acc; CKE/CCI. "Insuffiicient san facs; site muddy after rain; migrant workers in statics." ♦ NOK 258 2014*

MANDAL *1B4* (3.5km N Rural) *58.04213, 7.49436* **Sandnes Camping, Holumsveien 133, 4516 Mandal (Vest-Agder) [tel 38 26 51 51 or 98 88 73 66; sandnescamping@online.no; www.sandnescamping.com]** On E39 Kristiansand to Stavanger. Turn N onto Rv455, site on R 1.4km. Med, some hdstg, pt shd; htd wc; chem disp; mv service pnt; fam bthrm; shwrs NOK10; EHU (16A) NOK40 (poss rev pol); lndry; shop, rest, snacks, bar in Mandal; cooking facs; BBQ; sand beach 2.5km; rv sw & beach nr; fishing; boating; 5% statics; dogs; wifi NOK20; phone; Eng spkn; adv bkg; quiet; CKE/CCI. "Excel, well-kept site; friendly, helpful owners; superb scenery; nature trails thro adj pine forest; Mandal pretty town with longest sandy beach in Norway, conv Kristiansand ferry & Lindesnes, Norway's most S point." ♦ 1 May-1 Sep. NOK 260 2014*

MAURANGER see Odda *1A3*

⊞ **MAURVANGEN** *1C2* (100m SW Rural) *61.48838, 8.84176* **Maurvangen Hyttegrend Camping, Besseggen Fjellpark, 2680 Maurvangen VÅGÅ (Oppland) [tel 61 23 89 22; fax 61 23 89 58; post@maurvangen.no; www.maurvangen.no]** At rv bdge turn off Rv51. Foll sp. Med, pt hdstg, pt sl, pt shd; wc; mv service pnt; chem disp; fam bthrm; shwrs NOK15; EHU (10A) inc; lndry; shop; rest, snacks; BBQ; cooking facs; playgrnd; lake sw 5km; fishing; cycling; wifi; TV; phone; Eng spkn; adv bkg; quiet; CKE/CCI. "White water rafting; gd views; rd 51 poss clsd Nov to mid-May; gd hill-walking cent; lovely site." ♦ NOK 300 2016*

MELHUS *1C1* (8km NW Coastal) *63.32635, 10.21564* **Øysand Camping (ST38), Øysandan, 7224 Melhus (Sør-Trøndelag) [tel 72 87 24 15 or 92 08 71 74 (mob); fax 72 85 22 81; post@oysandcamping.no; www.oysandcamping.no]** Fr Melhus, N on E6; then L (W) onto E39; site sp. Med, mkd pitch, unshd; wc; chem disp (wc); shwrs NOK15; EHU (10A) NOK50; lndry; shop; rest, snacks; bar; BBQ; cooking facs; playgrnd; lake sw, fishing, boating & beach adj; games area; wifi; statics; dogs; phone; poss cr; Eng spkn; noise fr daytrippers; ccard acc; red long stay; CKE/CCI. "Fair site with gd views; facs stretched if full; next to Fjord; beach open to day trippers; barrier clsd at night." ♦ ltd. 1 May-1 Sep. NOK 240 2014*

MEVIK see Ornes *2E2*

MO I RANA *2F2* (17km SW Rural) *66.23307, 13.89178* **Yttervik Camping, Sørlandsveien 874, 8617 Dalsgrenda (Nordland) [tel 75 16 45 65 or 90 98 73 55 (mob); fax 75 16 92 57; ranjas@online.no; www.yttervikcamping.no]** Sp S of Mo i Rana, on W side of E6, cross sm bdge over rlwy, diff for long o'fits. Sm, mkd pitch, hdstg, unshd; htd wc; chem disp; shwrs NOK5; EHU (16A) NOK40 (no earth); lndry; sm shop; rest; playgrnd; fishing; 50% statics; dogs; poss cr; Eng spkn; adv bkg; quiet; ccard acc; CKE/CCI. "Pleasant location on edge fjord; friendly owners; clean, well-run site; gd new facs (2015); rd works on E6, easier access to site in 2017." 1 Jun-15 Sep. NOK 248 2016*

⊞ **MOLDE** *1B1* (4km E Rural) *62.74258, 7.2333* **Camping Kviltorp, Fannestrandveien 140, 6400 Molde (Møre og Romsdal) [tel 71 21 17 42 or 47 90 14 83 05 (mob); fax 71 21 10 19; kviltorp.camping@online.no; www.kviltorpcamping.no]** On app fr S, Rv64 (toll) turn L onto E39/Rv62, site on L, sp. Nr airport. Med, pt sl, pt shd; htd wc; fam bthrm; shwrs NOK10; EHU (10A) NOK35; gas; lndry; shop & adj; rest, snacks; playgrnd; pool 3km; fjord sw adj; fishing; boating; solarium; TV; phone; Eng spkn; aircraft & rd noise; ccard acc; CKE/CCI. "Conv Molde; adj Romsdal Fjord (some pitches avail on fjord-side); wonderful mountain views; excel, clean facs; poor security - site open to rd on 1 side; helpful owners; gd site; cycle track into Molde." ♦ NOK 260 2015*

⊞ **MOSJOEN** *2E3* (2km E Rural) *65.83453, 13.21971* **Mosjøen Camping & Hotel, Kippermoen, 8657 Mosjøen (Nordland) [tel 75 17 79 00; fax 77 17 79 01; mosjoen-camping@hotmail.com; www.mosjoencamping.no]** E6 by-passes town, well sp on W side of E6 by rndabt. Fr S only mkd by flag 500m bef rndabt at start Mosjøen bypass. Med, hdstg, terr, unshd; htd wc; chem disp (wc); mv service pnt; shwrs inc; fam bthrm; EHU (16A) NOK40; lndry (inc dryer); shop 1km; rest, snacks; bar; playgrnd; pool; bowling alley; games rm; entmnt; wifi; TV rm; 40% statics; dogs; phone; twin axles; poss cr; Eng spkn; adv bkg; rd noise; ccard acc; CKE/CCI. "Clean, v basic san facs; gd site; gd kitchen facs and san facs, friendly staff; lge spmkt nrby; pizza rest; lively local ctr; gd." ♦ ltd. NOK 298 2017*

NARVIK *2F2* (2km NE Rural) *68.4506, 17.45851* **Camping Narvik, Rombaksveien 75, 8517 Narvik (Nordland) [tel 76 94 58 10; fax 76 94 14 20; narvikcamping@narvikcamping.com; www.narvikcamping.com]** Sp on E6, site by rd. Med, terr, unshd; wc; chem disp; fam bthrm; sauna; shwrs NOK20; EHU (6-10A) inc (no earth); lndry; shop; rest; BBQ; TV; phone; poss cr; Eng spkn; adv bkg; rd/rlwy noise; ccard acc; red CKE/CCI. "Facs 'tired' & stretched high ssn (may need to share electrics) & poss unkempt; no privacy in shwrs; walk/cycle to town, 20 mins; 3-level site, chem disp 3rd level only; poor NH/sh stay only." ♦ 1 Mar-30 Sep. NOK 211 2014*

NESTTUN see Bergen *1A3*

NORDKAPP *2H1* **See also Skarsvåg.**

⊞ **NORDKAPP** *2H1* (100m S Rural/Coastal) *71.16795, 25.78174* **Nordkapphallen Carpark, 9764 Nordkapp (Finnmark) [tel 78 47 68 60; fax 78 47 68 61; nordkapphallen@rica.no; www.rica.no]** N on E69. Hdstg, pt sl, unshd; wc (0100-1100); own san; rest; bar; shop; 1 Nov-1 Apr private vehicles not permitted - buses in convoy (daily) only. "Max stay 48 hrs; no other o'night or site charges; price inc visit to Nordkapp Cent; no facs; very exposed gravel surface; excel for viewing midnight sun." NOK 260 (per person) 2016*

NORDKJOSBOTN *2G1* (200m S Rural) *69.21623, 19.55530* **Bjørnebo Camping, Sentrumsveien 10, 9040 Nordkjosbotn (Troms) [tel 77 72 81 61]** Fr junc of E6 & E8 (Tromsø) 200m S turn L twd Nordkjosbotn, site 200m on L. Sm, pt shd; htd wc; chem disp; fam bthrm; shwrs NOK10; EHU (16A) NOK30; lndry; shop adj; snacks; bar; playgrnd; TV; dogs; phone; Eng spkn. "Conv for day trip to Tromsø; friendly owners." ♦ 5 Jun-15 Aug. NOK 200 2014*

NOTODDEN *1C3* (1km W Rural) *59.55850, 9.24878* **Notodden Bobilcamp, Nesøya 11, 3674 Notodden [tel 47 41 39 57 01; www.notoddencamping.com]** 1km W of Notodden on the E134. Sm, hdstg, pt shd, wc; chemp disp; mv service pnt; shwrs; bus/tram 1km. "City run stop over; low charge for all facs except electric; no one on site, owner calls in evening." NOK 150 2014*

⊞ **ODDA** *1A3* (2km S Rural) *60.0533, 6.5426* **Odda Camping, Jordalsveien 29, 5750 Odda (Hordaland) [tel 94 14 12 79; fax 53 64 12 92; post@oddacamping.no; www.oddacamping.no]** Sp on Rv13; adj sports complex, nr lakeside. Med, pt shd; htd wc; mv service pnt; private san facs avail; shwrs NOK10; EHU (16A) NOK40; lndry (with dryer); shop 1km; rest 1km; BBQ; lake fishing; watersports; bike hire; games area; dogs; Eng spkn; quiet. "Beautiful area; nr Hardanger Fjord; watersports with canoes for hire; owner owns a guesthouse where you can use wifi & organise trips." ♦ NOK 150 2016*

OLDEN *1B2* (22km S Rural) *61.66513, 6.81600* **Camping Melkevoll Bretun, Oldedalen, 6792 Briksdalsbre (Sogn og Fjordane) [tel 57 87 38 64; fax 57 87 38 90; post@melkevoll.no; www.melkevoll.no]** Take rte to Briksdal glacier to end of rd. Med, hdg pitch, terr, unshd; htd wc; chem disp; mv service pnt; fam bthrm; sauna; shwrs NOK10; EHU (25A) NOK30; lndry; shop; snacks; cooking facs; playgrnd; internet; phone; Eng spkn; quiet; ccard acc. "Walks to glacier; excel views glaciers some pitches; excel." 15 Apr-15 Oct. NOK 170 2013*

⊞ **OPPDAL** *1C1* (2.6km NE Rural) *62.60649, 9.73028* **Solly Camping, Gorsetråket, 7340 Oppdal (Sør-Trøndelag) [tel 72 42 44 16; anug@online.no]** Site sp on E6. Sm, pt shd; wc; chem disp 10km; mv service pnt; shwrs inc; EHU (10A) inc; lndry; shop 2km; rest, snacks, bar 2km; BBQ; sm playgrnd; htd pool 2km; games area 1km; internet; TV; dogs; bus nr; train 2km; poss cr; Eng spkn; adv bkg; quiet; CKE/CCI. "Nr Dovrefjell National Park; rv rafting nrby; gd walking & cycle paths; ski area in winter; very pleasant site; gd NH." NOK 150 2013*

NORWAY

⊞ **OPPDAL** *1C1* (13km SW Rural) *62.49886, 9.58853* **Magalaupe Camping, 7340 Oppdal (Sør-Trøndelag) [tel/fax 72 42 46 84 or 99 25 99 93 (mob); anja.moene@gmail.com; www.magalaupe.no]** On W side of E6 Dombås to Trondheim rd, sp on side of Rv Driva. Med, pt sl, unshd; htd wc; chem disp; mv service pnt; sauna; shwrs NOK10; EHU (10-16A) NOK20; lndry; shop; supmkt 11km; snacks; bar; cooking facs; playgrnd; fishing; bike hire; TV rm; some statics; dogs; Eng spkn; quiet. "Sh walk to waterfalls; musk oxen safaries run by owner; excel; facs satisfactory; quiet site." NOK 158 2015*

⊞ **OPPDAL** *1C1* (12km W Rural) *62.61640, 9.47845* **Trollheimsporten Turistsenter Bobil Plass, Festa, 7340 Oppdal [tel 47 48464241 or 41339130; turist@oppdal.com; campingoppdal.no]** In Oppal on E6 take turning onto Rte 70. Site on R of Rte 70 in about 15km. Sm, hdstg, pt sl; wc; chem disp; mv service pnt; shwrs NOK10; EHU; lndry; café; bar; TV; 50% statics; Eng spkn. "This site is only for MH; vg." NOK 150 2016*

⊞ **ORNES** *2E2* (7km NW Rural) *66.91327, 13.62995* **Reipa Camping, N 8146 Reipa [tel 75 75 57 74 or 95 48 19 53; post@reipacamping.com; www.reipacamping.com]** Head NE on Havneveien twd Chr. Tidemanns vei/Rv17, then turn R onto Havneveien/Fv456. Sm; htd wc; chem disp; mv service pnt; shwrs inc; EHU inc (16A); playgrnd; internet; wifi; dogs; Eng spkn; adv bkg; ccard acc; CKE/CCI. "Gd NH on classic Rv17." NOK 230 2014*

⊞ **OS I OSTERDALEN** *1D1* (2km NE Rural) *62.50430, 11.25938* **Røste Hyttetun & Camping, 2550 Os I Østerdalen (Sør-Trøndelag) [tel 62 49 70 55; post@rostecamping.no; www.rostecamping.no]** Sp on Rv30. Sm; wc; chem disp; shwrs NOK10; EHU NOK40; lndry (inc dryer); cooking facs; playgrnd; fishing 150m; wifi; TV rm; some statics; quiet. NOK 207 2016*

OSLO *1C3* (5km SE Urban) *59.8984, 10.7734* **Ekeberg Camping, Ekebergveien 65, 1181 Oslo [tel 22 19 85 68; fax 22 67 04 36; mail@ekebergcamping.no; www.ekebergcamping.no]** Fr Göteborg to Oslo on E6 leave 2km bef Oslo; sp Ekeberg, foll sp to site. Fr S on E6 just after passing thro Oslo ent toll take slip rd sp Ekeberg; camp sp about 6km, up 10% hill. V lge, sl, unshd; wc; chem disp; mv service pnt; shwrs NOK10; fam bthrm; ltd EHU (6-10A) inc (long lead poss req & poss rev pol); gas; lndry (inc dryer); shop; supmkt 1km; rest 200m; snacks; bar; playgrnd; dogs; internet; bus/tram to city - tickets fr site recep; poss cr; Eng spkn; no adv bkg; ccard acc; CKE/CCI. "Insufficient EHU & leads running across rds; area without hook-ups flatter & quieter; use san facs block taps for fresh water; easy access to Oslo cent & places of interest; avoid site during annual children's football tournament end Jul/beg Aug - queues for pitches & facs very stretched; poss ssn workers on site; recep open 0730-2300; helpful staff." ♦ 1 Jun-1 Sep. NOK 355 (4 persons) 2013*

OSLO *1C3* (5km W Urban) *59.91802, 10.67554* **Sjølyst Marina Campervan Parking, Drammensveien 160, Sjølyst Båtopplag, 0273 Oslo [tel/fax 22 50 91 93; post@bobilparkering.no; www.bobilparkering.no]** Fr E exit E18 at junc after Bygdøy (museums) junc. At rndabt take last exit, go under E18 & into site. Fr W leave E18 at Sjølyst junc, at bottom of slip rd turn R into site. Sm, hdstg, unshd; own san rec; chem disp; mv service pnt; shwrs NOK10; EHU inc; snacks; BBQ; dogs; bus adj; clsd 2300-0700; Eng spkn; quiet. "Gd, basic site, pt of marina; m'vans only - pay at machine; san facs clsd o'night; 30 min walk city cent." ♦ 1 Jun-15 Sep. NOK 300 2016*

⊞ **OSLO** *1C3* (9km NW Urban) *59.9623, 10.6429* **NAF Camping Bogstad, Ankerveien 117, Røa, 0766 Oslo [tel 22 51 08 00; fax 22 51 08 50; bogstad@naf.no; www.bogstadcamping.no]** Fr N on E16 cont to E18 & turn E twd Oslo. After approx 7km exit & proceed N twds Røa and Bogstad. Site sp adj Oslo golf club. V lge, some mkd pitch, pt sl, pt shd; htd wc; chem disp; mv service pnt; shwrs NOK10 (swipe card fr recep); EHU (10A) NOK50 (long lead poss req); lndry (inc dryer); shop adj; snacks; lake nr; 25% statics; dogs; poss very cr; Eng spkn; adv bkg; bus to Oslo 100m; wifi; ccard acc; CKE/CCI. "Beautiful area with walking trails; avoid area of site with statics & many ssn workers (behind recep), far end OK with lake views; modern, clean san facs; helpful staff; recep open 24 hrs; conv Oslo cent; bus stop nrby, bus every 10 mins; 30 mins to cent; gd." ♦ NOK 335 2014*

OVRE EIDFJORD **see Eidfjord** *1B3*

⊞ **OYSTESE** *1A3* (2.4km SSW Coastal) *60.36828, 6.18969* **Hardanger Feriesenter, Hardangerfjordvegen 341, 5600 Norheimsund [tel 92 05 09 55; booking@hardangerferiesenter.no; www.hardanger-resort.com]** Directly at Rv7 in Kvam, app 2.5km E of Norheimsund on the shores of Hardangerfjord. Sm, pt sl, unshd; wc; mv service pnt; shwrs (5 NOK); EHU (10A); lndry (inc dryer); rest; BBQ; cooking facs; beach; 50% statics; dogs; poss cr high ssn; Eng spkn; quiet; CKE/CCI. "Boat hire & pier on site; vg." NOK 250 2015*

⊞ **PORSGRUNN** *1C4* (5km SE Rural) *59.11183, 9.71208* **Camping Olavsberget, Nystrandveien 64, 3944 Porsgrunn (Vestfold) [tel/fax 35 51 12 05]** Leave E18 at Eidanger onto Rv354 N; foll camp sp for 1km; site on L. Fr Porsgrunn foll Rv36 S; just bef E18 junc turn L; foll sp as above. Med, pt sl, unshd; wc; shwrs; EHU (16A) NOK30 (no earth); lndry (inc dryer); sm shop; supmkt 1km; snacks; sand beach adj with diving boards; 60% statics; poss cr; rd noise; no ccard acc; clsd 2300-0700; wifi; Eng spkn; CKE/CCI. "Well-run site; public access to beach thro site; gd walks in wood; visits to Maritime Brevik & mineral mine, Porsgrunn porcelain factory & shop, Telemark Canal inc boat tour." ♦ NOK 200 2014*

RAMFJORDBOTN **see Sakariasjord** *2F1*

⊞ **RANDSVERK** *1C2* (800m NE Rural) *61.73016, 9.08155* **Randsverk Camping, Fjellvegen 1972 Randsverk (Oppland) [tel 61 23 87 45; fax 61 23 93 61; randsverk.kiosk@c2i.net; www.randsverk-camping.no]** Heading S on Rv51, 20km fr junc with Rv15, site on L on ent vill of Randsverk. Med, hdstg, sl, terr, unshd; htd wc; chem disp; mv service pnt; shwrs; EHU (10A) inc (long lead poss req); lndry (inc dryer); shop 26km; rest, snacks; BBQ; cooking facs; playgrnd; wifi; twin axles; Eng spkn; poss cr; quiet. "V scenic rds; excel area for walking or driving excursions; excel san facs; vg site in area." NOK 270 2015*

⊞ **RISOR** *1C4* (18km SW Coastal) *58.69083, 9.16333* **Sørlandet Feriecenter, Sandnes, 4950 Risør [tel 37 15 40 80; sorferie@online.no; www.sorlandet-feriesenter.no]** Fr N take E18 to Sørlandsporten then Rv416 to Risør, then Rv411 to Laget. Foll sp Sørlandet. Fr S exit E18 at Tvedestrand & cont to Laget, then foll site sp. Site is 20km by rd fr Risør. Med, mkd pitch, pt shd; htd wc; chem disp; fam bthrm; private san facs avail; shwrs; EHU inc; lndry (inc dryer); shop; supmkt 1km; rest; bar; cooking facs; playgrnd; sand beach; watersports; boat & bike hire; tennis 1km; fitness rm; games rm; wifi; cab TV; some statics; dogs; adv bkg; Eng spkn; quiet. ♦ NOK 317 (CChq acc) 2014*

⊞ **RISOR** *1C4* (10km W Coastal) *58.72592, 9.07783* **Risør Resort Moen Camping, 4950 Risor [tel 37 15 50 91; fax 37 15 50 92; karen@moen-camping.no; www.moen-camping.no]** Fr E18 S, L onto 416 twds Risor. Site sp on L. Med, unshd; htd wc; fam bthrm; shwrs inc; lndry (inc dryer); snacks; BBQ; cooking facs; playgrnd; sand beach; games area; wifi; TV rm; 90% statics; dogs; poss cr; Eng spkn; ccard acc; CCI. "Well cared for, popular site; EHU & water widely spaced; volleyball; boat hire." NOK 400 2014*

⊞ **RODBERG** *1C3* (6.5km SE Rural) *60.23533, 9.0040* **Fjordgløtt Camping, Vrenne, 3630 Rødberg (Buskerud) [tel 32 74 13 35 or 97 15 96 53 (mob); fax 32 74 16 90; info@fjordglott.net; www.fjordglott.net]** Fr Rødberg on Rv40 dir Kongsberg, take R turn sp Vrenne, cross bdge & foll sp past power stn. Med, mkd pitch, terr, pt shd; htd wc; chem disp; 75% serviced pitches; fam bthrm; sauna; shwrs NOK10; EHU (16A) NOK30; lndry; shop; snacks; playgrnd; lake sw; fishing; 40% statics; phone; Eng spkn; quiet; ccard acc; CKE/CCI. "Lovely views of fjord; excel facs; well kept." ♦ NOK 240 2014*

RODBERG *1C3* (10km W Rural) *60.26602, 8.78878* **Uvdal Resort, N-3632 Uvdal (Buskerud) [tel 32 74 31 08; fax 99 22 82 10; aud@uvdalresort.no; www.uvdalresort.no]** Fr Rodberg, take Rv40 W for about 9km. Site on R. Sm; htd wc; chem disp; mv service pnt; shwr 5nok; EHU (16A) 30nok; lndry (inc dryer); snacks; playgrnd; games area; Eng spkn; ccard acc; CKE/CCI. "Family run; level site by rv; fishing & kayaking; vg site." 1 May-30 Sep. NOK 190 2014*

⊞ **ROLDAL** *1B3* (500m E Rural) *59.83103, 6.82888* **Røldal Hyttegrend & Camping, Kyrkjevegen 49, 5760 Røldal (Hordaland) [tel 53 64 71 33; fax 53 64 39 41; adm@roldal-camping.no; www.roldal-camping.no]** Fr E on E134 turn L on ent vill, site sp. Sm, pt shd; htd wc; chem disp; mv service pnt; fam bthrm; shwrs NOK10; fam bthrm; EHU (10A) NOK30; gas; lndry; shop; snacks; cooking facs; playgrnd; rv sw adj; wifi; TV rm; 20% statics; dogs; phone; Eng spkn; adv bkg; ccard acc; red CKE/CCI. "Gd walking, angling." ♦ ltd. NOK 206 2014*

⊞ **ROLDAL** *1B3* (1km SW Rural) *59.83012, 6.81061* **Seim Camping, 5760 Røldal (Horda-Rogaland) [tel/fax 53 64 73 71 or 97 53 35 17 (mob) or 90 91 90 63 (mob); seim@seimcamp.no; www.seimcamp.no]** App fr SW on E134, site sp at ent town. Turn R off main rd & R again. Med, pt sl, pt shd; htd wc; chem disp; fam bthrm; shwrs NOK5; EHU (20A) NOK40; lndry; shop, rest, snacks, bar 200m; playgrnd; fishing; boating; dogs; Eng spkn; CKE/CCI. "Gd walks; beautiful views; prehistoric burial mounds & museum on site; poss rd noise." ♦ ltd. NOK 193 2014*

ROROS *1D1* (550m S Urban) *62.57078, 11.38295* **Idrettsparken Hotel & Camping, Øra 25, 7374 Røros (Sør-Trøndelag) [tel 72 41 10 89; fax 72 41 23 77; ihotell@online.no; www.idrettsparken.no]** Heading twd Trondheim on Rv30 to Røros cent, turn L at rndabt into Peter Møllersvei, over rlwy line, L again & foll sp to site. Sm, unshd; htd wc; shwrs NOK10; EHU (16A) NOK35; shops & pool nr; quiet. "Tours of museums & mines; nature reserve & nature park nr; no chem disp - use dump point at fire stn on Rv30; fair NH." ♦ ltd. 1 May-30 Sep. NOK 300 2014*

RORVIK *2E3* (2km NE Coastal) *64.8729, 11.2609* **Nesset Camping, Engan, 7900 Rørvik (Nord-Trøndelag) [tel 74 39 06 60]** Fr cent of Rørvik on Rv770, foll sp to site. Med, hdg pitch, hdstg, pt sl, terr, pt shd; htd wc; chem disp; shwrs NOK10; EHU (10A); sw adj; some statics; Eng spkn; quiet. "Many pitches with fjord view; facs stretched high ssn; beware of speed bumps on app rd." May-Sep. NOK 250 2014*

RUNDE ISLAND *1A1* **Sites on Runde Island are listed together at the end of the Norway site entry pages.**

SALTSTRAUMEN see Bodø *2F2*

⊞ **SARPSBORG** *1C3* (10km NW Rural) *59.31800, 10.98049* **Utne Camping, Desideriasvei 43, 1719 Greaker [tel 47 69 14 71 26; fax 47 69 14 74 19; post@utnecamping.no; www.utnecamping.no]** Leave E6 at junc 9 sp Sollikrysset. Take 118 S (Desiderias vei), 2km to site on R. Sm, pt sl, unshd; htd wc; chem disp; shwrs NOK10; EHU (10A) NOK60; lndry (inc dryer); BBQ; playgrnd; games area; wifi; tv rm; dogs; bus adj; twin axles; Eng spkn; adv bkg; quiet (some traff noise); ccard acc; CKE/CCI. "Conv acc fr E6; pleasant open site; excel." NOK 294 2017*

⊞ **SKARNES** *1D3* (10km SW Rural) *60.19910, 11.58054* **Sanngrund Camping, Oslovegen 910, 2100 Skarnes (Hedmark) [tel 62 96 46 60; fax 62 96 46 69; booking@sanngrund.no; www.sanngrund.no]** Fr Skarnes foll Rv2 S; site sp on L. Sm, mkd pitch, pt shd; htd wc; chem disp; mv service pnt; fam bthrm; shwrs inc; EHU inc; lndry; shop 10km; rest, snacks; BBQ; cooking facs; playgrnd; rv sw & fishing adj; TV; 50% statics; poss cr; Eng spkn; rd noise; CKE. "Conv NH to/fr Oslo (approx 70km); pleasant rest; fair site." ♦ ltd. NOK 235 2016*

SKARSVAG *2G1* (1km SW Coastal) *71.1073, 25.81238* **Kirkeporten Camping, 9763 Skarsvåg (Finnmark) [tel 90 96 06 48; fax 78 47 52 47; kipo@kirkeporten.no; www.kirkeporten.no]** Foll E69 fr Honningsvåg for 20km to Skarsvåg junc; site sp at junc & on L after 2km immed bef vill. Sm, hdstg, pt sl, unshd; htd wc; chem disp; mv service pnt; sauna; shwrs inc; EHU (16A) NOK35; lndry (inc dryer); rest, snacks; bar; TV; wifi; poss cr; Eng spkn; adv bkg; quiet; ccard acc; CKE/CCI. "Site on edge sm fishing vill 10km fr N Cape, ringed by mountains; exposed location; claims to be world's most N site; helpful, knowledgeable owner; vg rest; clean facs but stretched if site full; poss reindeer on site; highly rec; arr early; camping area extended & modernised (2016)." ♦ 15 May-15 Sep. NOK 247 2016*

SKIBOTN *2G1* (400m N Coastal) *69.39397, 20.26797* **NAF Camping Skibotn, 9143 Skibotn (Troms) [tel 77 71 52 77]** On W of E6 400m N of town. Sm, pt sl, unshd; wc; chem disp; shwrs NOK10 (10 mins); EHU (10A) NOK25; gas; lndry; cooking facs; fishing; Eng spkn. "NH only, dir access to beach on fjord; poss traff noise fr E6." 1 Jun-31 Aug. NOK 200 2014*

SKIBOTN *2G1* (1km SE Rural) *69.38166, 20.29528* **Olderelv Camping (TR30), 9048 Skibotn (Troms) [tel 77 71 54 44 or 91 13 17 00 (mob); fax 77 71 51 62; firmapost@olderelv.no; www.olderelv.no]** W of E6 1km N of junc at E8. Lge, mkd pitch, hdstg, pt sl, unshd; wc; chem disp; mv service pnt; sauna; fam bthrm; shwrs NOK10; EHU (16A) NOK40; lndry (inc dryer); shop; café; snacks; bar; BBQ; cooking facs; playgrnd; solarium; wifi; 80% statics; dogs free; phone; twin axles; Eng spkn; adv bkg; quiet; ccard acc. "Well-maintained & clean; dryest area of Troms; vg walking; v busy; vg." ♦ 15 May-1 Sep. NOK 292 2017*

SKJAK see Lom *1C2*

SKJOLDEN *1B2* (3km E Rural) *61.48453, 7.6505* **Vassbakken Camping, RV 55, 6876 Skjolden (Romsdal SogneFjord) [tel 57 68 61 88 or 57 68 67 00; fax 57 68 61 85; info@vassbakken.com; www.skjolden.com/vassbakken]** Site on Rv55. Sm, pt shd; wc; chem disp; mv service pnt; fam bthrm; sauna; shwrs NOK10; EHU (10A) NOK30; lndry; sm shop & 3km; rest, snacks; playgrnd; lake sw & fishing adj; wifi; TV; phone; Eng spkn; no adv bkg; ccard acc. "Mountain setting; waterfall ad, gd walking & fishing; ltd facs until June." 1 May-20 Sep. NOK 254 2013*

SOGNDALSFJORA *1B2* (15km NE Rural) *61.30738, 7.21500* **Lyngmo Camping (SF16), Lyngmovegen 12, 6869 Hafslo (Sogn of Fjordane) [tel 57 68 43 66; fax 57 68 39 29; lyngmo@lyngmoinfo.com; www.lyngmoinfo.com]** Fr Rv55 Sogndal-Gaupne turn L at sp Galden. Immed turn R at camping sp & foll gravel rd down to site on lakeside. Sm, pt sl, unshd; wc; chem disp; mv service pnt; fam bthrm; shwrs; EHU; lndry rm; cooking facs; lake sw & fishing; some statics; phone; Eng spkn; quiet; ccard acc; CKE/CCI. "Beautiful location; steep hill to san facs block." 19 Jun-24 Aug. 2014*

⊞ **SOGNDALSFJORA** *1B2* (4.5km SE Coastal) *61.2118, 7.12106* **Camping Kjørnes, 6856 Sogndal (Sogn og Fjordane) [tel 57 67 45 80 or 975 44 156 (mob); fax 57 67 33 26; camping@kjornes.no; www.kjornes.no]** Fr W foll sp in Sogndal for Kaupanger/ Lærdal (Rv5) over bdge. Fr E (Rv55) turn L at T-junc with rd 5 over bdge. Site on R; sharp R turn into narr lane (passing places); site ent on R in approx 500m. Med, hdstg, pt sl, terr, unshd; wc; chem disp; mv service pnt; fam bthrm; shwrs NOK10; EHU (10-16A) NOK40 (no earth); lndry (inc dryer); shops, rest, snacks 3.5km; cooking facs; playgrnd; beach adj; boat launching; fishing; wifi; 20% statics; dogs; phone; bus 500m; twin axles; poss cr; Eng spkn; adv bkg; rd noise; ccard acc; red long stay/ LS; CKE/CCI. "Useful for ferries; stunning location on edge of fjord; superb san facs, the best!; excel site; v highly rec." ♦ ltd. NOK 303 2017*

SOGNDALSFJORA *1B2* (100m S Rural) *61.22490, 7.10218* **Stedje Camping, Kyrkjevegen 2, 6851 Sogndal (Sogn og Fjordane) [tel 57 67 10 12; fax 57 67 11 90; post@scamping.no; www.scamping.no]** W fr Hella to Sogndal, turn L off Rv55 adj Shell petrol stn, site clearly sp, narr ent. Med, sl, pt shd; htd wc; chem disp; mv service pnt; fam bthrm; shwrs NOK10; EHU (16A) NOK40 (check earth); lndry; shop; snacks; playgrnd; lake sw & beach 500m; watersports; solarium; bike hire; wifi; TV; Eng spkn; quiet; CKE/CCI. "1st gd site after Vangsnes-Hella ferry - in orchard; poss poor facs early ssn; poss v diff in wet for lge m'vans; conv visit to 12th C Urnes stave church." ♦ 1 Jun-31 Aug. NOK 140 2014*

SPANGEREID *1A4* (8km S Coastal) *57.99593, 7.09003* **Lindesnes Camping, Lillehavn, 4521 Spangereid (Vest-Agder) [tel 38 25 88 74 or 91 60 22 76 (mob); fax 38 25 88 92; gabrielsen@lindesnescamping.no; www.lindesnescamping.no]** Fr E39 at Vigeland turn S onto Rv460 sp Lindesnes lighthouse (Fyr). Approx 8km after vill of Spangereid turn L sp Lillehavn, site sp. Sm, pt sl, pt shd; htd wc; chem disp; mv service pnt; shwrs NOK10; EHU (16A) NOK40; lndry; BBQ; cooking facs; dogs; phone; poss cr; Eng spkn; adv bkg; quiet; ccard acc; CKE/CCI. "Excel, clean, well-run site; pitches not mkd adv early arr." 1 Apr-30 Sep. NOK 210 2013*

STABBURSNES see Lakselv *2G1*

STAVANGER *1A3* (3.5km SW Rural) *58.9525, 5.71388* **Mosvangen Camping, Henrik Ibsens Gate, 4021 Stavanger (Rogaland) [tel 51 53 29 71; fax 51 87 20 55; info@mosvangencamping.no; www.mosvangen camping.no]** Fr Stavanger foll sp E39/Rv510; site well sp. Fr Sandnes on E39 exit Ullandhaug; foll camp sp. Med, some hdstg, sl, pt shd; wc; chem disp; mv service pnt; shwrs NOK10; EHU (10A) NOK40 (no earth & poss intermittent supply); lndry (inc dryer); kiosk; shop 500m; rest 1km; cooking facs; playgrnd; lake sw adj; sand beach 10km; dogs; phone; bus; poss v cr; Eng spkn; quiet but some rd noise; ccard acc; CKE/CCI. "Excel for wooden city of Stavanger; easy, pleasant walk to town cent; soft grnd in wet weather; facs well used but clean but stretched when site full; helpful manager; excel rustic type of site; bus to cent nr ent." ♦ 1 Apr-1 Oct. NOK 250 2016*

"Satellite navigation makes touring much easier"

Remember most sat navs don't know if you're towing or in a larger vehicle – always use yours alongside maps and site directions.

STAVERN see Larvik *1C4*

⊞ **STEINKJER** *2E3* (14km N Rural) *64.10977, 11.57816* **Follingstua Camping, Haugåshalla 6, 7732 Steinkjer (Nord-Trøndelag) [tel 74 14 71 90; fax 74 14 71 88; post@follingstua.no; www.follingstua.com]** N on E6, site on R, well sp. Sm, mkd pitch, hdstg, terr, unshd; htd wc; chem disp; mv service pnt; fam bthrm; shwrs NOK20; EHU (16A) NOK40; lndry (inc dryer); shop 11km; rest, snacks; bar; BBQ; playgrnd; lake & beach adj; fishing; boating; bike hire; wifi; TV rm; 60% statics; dogs; phone; bus 200m; twin axles; Eng spkn; poss cr; adv bkg; quiet. "Excel san facs down 10 steps; some lakeside pitches; nr Gold Rd tour of local craft & food producers; excel." ♦ ltd. NOK 292 2017*

STOREN *1C1* (1.5km NE Rural) *63.04465, 10.29078* **Vårvolden Camping (ST17), Volløyan 3A, 7290 Støren (Sør-Trøndelag) [tel/fax 72 43 20 24; varvolden.camping@gauldalen.no]** Leave E6 for Støren & foll site sp. Sm, unshd; htd wc; chem disp; mv service pnt; fam bthrm; shwrs; EHU (16A); lndry (inc dryer); shop 500m; rest, snacks 1km; cooking facs; playgrnd; 20% statics; dogs; Eng spkn; CKE/CCI. "Vg." ♦ 15 May-1 Sep. NOK 202 2013*

STORFORSHEI *2F2* (6km N Rural) *66.37946, 14.60366* **Camping Skogly Overnatting, Saltfjellveien 931, Skogly, 8630 Storforshei (Nordland) [tel 97 66 74 68; post@skoglyovernatting.com]** N fr Mo i Rana for 30km, site on L of E6. Sm, hdstg, unshd; htd wc; chem disp (wc); fam bthrm; shwrs inc; EHU NOK40; cooking facs; Eng spkn; quiet. "Excel facs; helpful owner." ♦ ltd. 1 May-20 Sep. NOK 180 2013*

⊞ **STORJORD** *2F2* (1km Rural) *66.81317, 15.40055* **Saltdal Turistsenter, 8255 Storjord (Nordland) [tel 75 68 24 50; fax 75 68 24 51; firmapost@saltdal-turistsenter.no; www.saltdal-turistsenter.no]** Site is 35km S of Rognan by-pass on E6, 700m N of junc of Rv77, adj filling stn. Med, mkd pitch, some hdstg, terr, pt shd; htd wc; chem disp; mv service pnt; shwrs NOK10; EHU (10A) NOK25; lndry; shop; rest, snacks; BBQ; cooking facs; playgrnd; 99% statics; wifi; phone; Eng spkn; adv bkg; quiet; CKE/CCI. "M'way-style service stn & lorry park; tightly packed cabins & statics; 10 pitches only for tourers; excel rv walks fr site; beautiful area; NH only; secure barrier; clean facs, could be stretched if full." ♦ NOK 263 2014*

STRAUMEN see Fauske *2F2*

STRYN *1B2* (10km E Rural) *61.93347, 6.88640* **Mindresunde Camping (SF43), 6783 Stryn (Sogn og Fjordane) [tel 57 87 75 32 or 41 56 63 16 (mob); fax 57 87 75 40; post@mindresunde.no; www.mindresunde.no]** 2nd site on Rv15 on N side of rd. Sm, mkd pitch, pt sl, unshd; htd wc; chem disp; mv service pnt; fam bthrm; shwrs NOK10; EHU inc (earth prob); lndry; shop; snacks; playgrnd; shgl beach; TV; car wash; Eng spkn; adv bkg; little rd noise; CKE/CCI. "Well-kept, pleasant site; many pitches on lake; friendly staff; site yourself; vg views; excel facs; conv Geiranger, Briksdal glacier & Strynefjellet summer ski cent; gd walking." ♦ 1 Apr-1 Nov. NOK 220 2014*

STRYN *1B2* (12km E Rural) *61.9314, 6.92121* **Strynsvatn Camping, Meland, 6783 Stryn (Sogn og Fjordane) [tel 57 87 75 43; fax 57 87 75 65; camping@strynsvatn.no; www.strynsvatn.no]** On Rv15 Lom to Stryn, on L. Sm, terr, unshd; wc; chem disp; mv service pnt; sauna; shwrs NOK10; EHU (10A) inc (poss earth fault); lndry (inc dryer); shop; snacks; playgrnd; lake adj; wifi; TV; 20% statics; Eng spkn; adv bkg; quiet; ccard acc; CKE/CCI. "Superb site; excel facs & v clean, gd views/walking; v friendly owners." ♦ 1 May-30 Sep. NOK 247 2016*

TANA *2H1* (5km SE Rural) *70.1663, 28.2279* **Tana Familiecamping, Skiippagurra, 9845 Tana (Finnmark) [tel 78 92 86 30; fax 78 92 86 31; tana@famcamp.net]** On ent Tana fr W, cross bdge on E6, heading E sp Kirkenes; site on L in approx 4km. Sm, pt sl, unshd; htd wc; chem disp; mv service pnt; sauna; shwrs inc; EHU (16A); lndry (inc dryer); rest; BBQ; playgrnd; Eng spkn; ccard acc; quiet. 20 May-1 Oct. NOK 217 (CChq acc) 2016*

TENNEVOLL *2F2* (5km SW Rural) *68.67881, 17.91421* **Lapphaugen Turiststasjon, General Fleischers Vei 365, 9357 Tennevoll [tel 77 17 71 27; postmaster@lapphaugen.no; www.lapphaugen.no]** On the L of E6 approx 60km N of Narvik. Sm, grassy, hdstg, pt sl, terr, unshd; wc; chem disp; mv service pnt; fam bthrm; shwrs NOK10; EHU; EHU (16A) NOK40; lndry (inc dryer); café; snack; BBQ; cooking facs; playgrnd; wifi; 50% statics; dogs; twin axles; Eng spkn; adv bkg; red LS/long stay. "Gd." ♦ ltd. 12 Feb-16 Dec. NOK 200 2017*

⊞ **TINN AUSTBYGD** *1B3* (8km S Rural) *59.98903, 8.81665* **Sandviken Camping (TE13), 3650 Tinn Austbygd (Telemark) [tel 35 09 81 73; fax 35 09 41 05; post@sandviken-camping.no; www.sandviken-camping.no]** Site is off Rv364 on L after passing thro Tinn Austbygd. Med, pt shd; htd wc; chem disp; mv service pnt; fam bthrm; sauna; shwrs NOK10; EHU (10A) NOK35 (check earth); gas; lndry; shop high ssn; BBQ; cooking facs; playgrnd; lake sw; games rm; games area; boat hire; TV rm; some statics; dogs; phone; poss cr; Eng spkn; CKE/CCI. "Superb, peaceful location at head of Lake Tinnsjø; sh walk thro woods to shops & bank; conv for museum at Rjukan heavy water plant." ♦ NOK 245 2016*

TJOTTA *2E3* (26km N Rural) *65.94692, 12.46255* **Sandnessjøen Camping, Steiro, 8800 Sandnessjøen, Norge [tel 97 56 20 50 or 75 04 54 40; post@ssj.no; www.ssj.no]** Head NW on Rv17 twrds Parkveien. Site is on R. Sm, Pt sl, unshd; htd wc; chem disp; shwrs inc; EHU; lndry (inc dryer); BBQ; cooking facs; dogs; Eng spkn; some aircraft noise; ccard acc. "Excel san facs; fjord views; gd hiking & fishing; excel site." ♦ 1 May-31 Aug. NOK 250 2014*

"There aren't many sites open at this time of year"

If you're travelling outside peak season remember to call ahead to check site opening dates – even if the entry says 'open all year'.

TREUNGEN *1B4* (18km N Rural) *59.15560, 8.50611* **Søftestad Camping, Nissedal, 3855 Treungen (Aust-Agder) [tel 41 92 76 20]** N fr Kristiansand on Rv41 to Treungen, then alongside E edge of Nisser Water to Nissedal, site sp. Sm, shd; wc; chem disp; fam bthrm; shwrs 10nok; EHU (10A) inc; lndry; BBQ; playgrnd; phone; bus adj; Eng spkn; adv bkg; quiet; red long stay; CKE/CCI. "Close to Telemarken heavy water plant; beautiful alt rte N fr Kristiansand - rd suitable for towed c'vans; gorgeous views over lake." ♦ ltd. 1 May-1 Sep. NOK 162 2014*

TROGSTAD *1D3* (6km N Rural) *59.68888, 11.29275* **Olberg Camping, Olberg, 1860 Trøgstad (Østfold) [tel 99 37 45 08; fax 69 82 85 55; froesol@online.no]** Fr Mysen on E18 go N on Rv22 for approx 20km dir Lillestrøm. Site is 2km 2 of Båstad. Sm, hdg pitch, pt shd; htd wc; chem disp; shwrs; fam bthrm; EHU (10-16A) NOK35; lndry (ind dryer); kiosk; snacks; BBQ; playgrnd; pool; beach 3km; fishing; tennis 200m; ice-skating; TV; phone; Eng spkn; adv bkg; quiet; ccard acc; red long stay/CKE/CCI. "Site on lge, working farm with elk safaris; local bread & crafts; farm museum; conv Oslo (40km); v helpful staff; gd for NH or longer." ♦ 1 May-1 Oct. NOK 200 2014*

⊞ **TROMSO** *2F1* (27km NE Coastal) *69.77765, 19.38273* **Skittenelv Camping, Ullstindveien 736, 9022 Krokelvdalen (Troms) [tel 46 85 80 00; fax 77 69 00 50; post@skittenelvcamping.no; www.skittenelvcamping.no]** Fr S end of Tromsø Bdge on E8, foll sps to Kroken & Oldervik. Site on N side of rd Fv53. Med, some hdstg, unshd; htd wc; chem disp; sauna; shwrs NOK10; EHU (10A) NOK50; lndry (inc dryer); shop; snacks; BBQ; playgrnd; htd pool; paddling pool; waterslide; fishing; games rm; wifi; TV; some statics; dogs free; quiet; ccard acc; red CKE/CCI. "Beautiful situation on edge of fjord; arctic sea birds; some facs dated but nice; location o'looking Fjord." ♦ NOK 258 2014*

⊞ **TROMSO** *2F1* (5km E Rural) *69.64735, 19.01505* **Tromsø Camping, 9020 Tromsdalen (Troms) [tel 77 63 80 37; fax 77 63 85 24; post@tromsocamping.no; www.tromsocamping.no]** At rndabt on edge of Tromsø take 2nd exit under E8 bdge. Shortly turn R & foll sp. Do not cross narr bdge but turn R then fork L to site. Sm, unshd; wc; chem disp; shwrs inc; mv service pnt; EHU (10-16A) NOK50; lndry (inc dryer); shops 1.5km; snacks; playgrnd; wifi; dogs; poss cr; Eng spkn; some noise fr stadium; CKE. "V busy site; surrounded by fast rv after rain; poss mkt traders on site; rec visit to Arctic church at midnight; many improvements; excel san facs (2016)." NOK 356 2016*

⊞ **TRONDHEIM** *1C1* (2km SW Urban) *63.42556, 10.38137* **Parking Øya Stadium, 7030 Trondheim** N on E6, foll sp for St Olevs Hospital. Parking is beyond hospital at side of Øya Stadium running track. Sm. "Free parking; gets busy; MV's only; no facs; o'night parking allowed; 10 min easy walk to cent of Trondheim; excel." 2014*

TRONDHEIM *1C1* (14km W Rural) *63.45004, 10.20230* **Flakk Camping (ST19), 7070 Flakk (Sør-Trøndelag) [tel 72 84 39 00; contact@flakk-camping.no; www.flakk-camping.no]** Fr N on E6 to Trondheim cent, then foll sp Fosen onto Rv715 W; site sp & adj Flakk ferry terminal; fr S to Trondheim take Rv707 to site & ferry. Med, pt sl, unshd; wc; chem disp; mv service pnt; fam bthrm; shwrs inc; EHU (10A) NOK40 (check earth); lndry; shop 5km; supmkt 8km; dogs; bus to city; poss cr; Eng spkn; adv bkg; ccard acc; CKE/CCI. "V well-kept site; clean facs; pleasant view over fjord; parts poss muddy after rain; site by ferry terminal (Need to be on R), some ferry noise at night; helpful owner; no earth on elec." ♦ 1 May-1 Sep. NOK 338 2014*

ULSVAG *2F2* (3km NE Coastal) *68.13273, 15.89699* **Sorkil Fjordcamping, Sorkil 8276 [tel 75 77 16 60 or 41 66 08 42 (mob); kontakt@sorkil.no; www.sorkil.no]** Head NE fr Ulsvag on E6, turn R in abt 2.7km onto site. Sm, mkd pitch, pt sl, unshd; htd wc; chem disp; shwr; wc x1; EHU (16A) NOK40; lndry NOK30; lndry rm; BBQ; beach adj; wifi; Eng spkn; quiet. "Lovely site S of ferry; adj Fjord excel for midnight sun and fishing." 1 May-30 Sep. 2014*

UTVIKA *1C3* (500m N Rural) *60.02972, 10.26316* **Utvika Camping (BU14), Utstranda 263, 3531 Utvika (Buskerud) [tel/fax 32 16 06 70; post@utvika.no; www.utvika.no]** Site on loop rd fr E16 N of Nes twd Hønefoss. Site sp but sp opp site ent v sm. Med, mkd pitch, hdstg, pt sl, unshd; wc; chem disp; mv service pnt; fam bthrm; shwrs NOK10; EHU (10A) NOK30; lndry (inc dryer); shop; playgrnd; lake sw adj; wifi; cab TV; 80% statics; twin axles; Eng spkn; adv bkg; quiet; red LS; CKE/CCI. "Conv Oslo (40km) & better than Oslo city sites; busy, friendly site; san facs inadequate when busy." ♦ 1 May-1 Oct. NOK 289 2017*

⊞ **VADSO** *2H1* (18km W Coastal) *70.11935, 29.33155* **Vestre Jakobselv Camping, Lilledalsveien 6, 9801 Vestre Jakobselv (Finnmark) [tel 78 95 60 64; post@vj-camping.no; www.vj-camping.no]** E fr Tana for approx 50km on E6/E75 dir Vadsø, site sp, 1km N of Vestre Jakobselv. Sm, hdstg, pt shd; wc; chem disp; mv service pnt; shwrs inc; EHU (10A) NOK40; lndry; shop 2km; cooking facs; 10% statics; dogs; bus 1km; Eng spkn; quiet; ccard acc; red CKE/CCI. "Conv Vadsø & Vardø - interesting towns." ♦ ltd. NOK 150 2016*

VAGAMO *1C2* (1km S Rural) *61.86950, 9.10291* **Smedsmo Camping, Vågåvegen 80, 2680 Vågåmo (Oppland) [tel 61 23 74 50; fax 61 23 74 14; smedsmo@online.no]** Behind petrol stn on Rv15 twd Lom. Med, hdstg, unshd; wc; chem disp; mv service pnt; fam bthrm; shwrs NOK20; EHU (16A) NOK40; lndry; snacks at g'ge; BBQ; cooking facs; playgrnd; TV; 50% statics; dogs; twin axles; Eng spkn; ccard acc; CKE/CCI. "Gd touring base; site now sep fr g'ge; fair." ♦ ltd. 1 May-30 Sep. NOK 290 2017*

VALLE *1B3* (12km N Rural) *59.2441, 7.4753* **Flateland Camping & Hyttesenter, 4747 Valle (Aust-Agder) [tel 95 00 55 00; flateland.camping@broadpark.no; www.flatelandcamping.no]** On W side of Rv9 to Bykle, 1km N of junc with Rv45 Dalen. Med, pt sl, pt shd; htd wc; chem disp; mv service pnt; shwrs NOK10; EHU (10A) NOK30; lndry (inc dryer); shop 600m; BBQ; cooking facs; playgrnd; rv adj; boat hire; wifi; 20% cabins; dogs; Eng spkn; quiet; ccard acc; CKE/CCI. "Pleasant; site yourself; fee collected pm; water trampolin; rvside walks; climbing; excel site." 1 Jun-1 Sep. NOK 160 2014*

⊞ **VANG** *1B2* (1.7km NW Rural) *61.13032, 8.54352* **Bøflaten Camping, 2975 Vang I Valdres (Sogn og Fjordane) [tel 61 36 74 20; fax 22 29 46 87; info@boflaten.com; www.boflaten.com]** Sp on E16 55km NW of Fagernes. Sm, pt shd; wc; chem disp; shwrs; EHU (10A) NOK40; lndry (inc dryer); supmkt 1.5km; BBQ (charcoal/gas); cooking facs; playgrnd; lake sw & shgl beach adj; games area; wifi; 10% statics; dogs; phone; twin axles; Eng spkn; quiet; ccard acc; CKE/CCI. "Beautiful area; lakeside; useful NH & gd winter sports site; walks nrby; guided excursions; boat, canoe, bike & TV hire; excel." ♦ NOK 237 2016*

⊞ **VANGSNES** *1B2* (N Rural/Coastal) *61.17483, 6.63729* **Solvang Camping & Motel, 6894 Vangsnes (Sogn og Fjordane) [tel 57 69 66 20; fax 57 69 67 55; post@solvangcamping.com; www.solvangcamping.com]** Site at end of peninsula, on S side of Sognefjord on Rv13, immed overlkg ferry terminal. Sm, sl, pt shd; wc; fam bthrm; shwrs inc; EHU NOK30; lndry; shops adj & 300m; rest, snacks; bar; playgrnd; pool; lake sw; fishing; boating; TV; some noise fr ferries. "Wonderful views; useful sh stay/NH for x-ing Sognefjord; delightful." NOK 185 2016*

VANGSNES *1B2* (3km S Rural) *61.14515, 6.62330* **Tveit Camping (SF32), 6894 Vangsnes (Sogn og Fjordane) [tel 57 69 66 00; fax 57 69 66 70; tveitca@online.no; www.tveitcamping.no]** On Rv13; sp. Sm, terr, pt shd; htd wc; chem disp; mv service pnt; fam bthrm; shwrs NOK10; EHU (10A) NOK25; lndry (inc dryer); kiosk; shop, rest, snacks 3.5km; playgrnd; boating; boat & bike hire; wifi; TV; 30% statics; dogs; phone; quiet; red long stay/CKE/CCI. "Sw poss off rocky shore; views of Sognefjord." ♦ 1 May-1 Oct. NOK 192 2016*

⊞ **VASSENDEN** *1A2* (2km SW Rural) *61.48785, 6.08366* **PlusCamp Jølstraholmen, 6847 Vassenden (Sogn og Fjordane) [tel 95 29 78 79; post@jolstraholmen.no; www.jolstraholmen.no]** On R of E39, site is 2km SW of Vassenden at Statoil petrol stn. Med, hdg pitch, terr, pt sl, pt shd; htd wc; mv service pnt; chem disp; fam bthrm; shwrs NOK6; EHU (10-16A) NOK40; lndry (inc dryer); shop; rest, snacks; BBQ; playgrnd; paddling pool; rv & lake sw & fishing; ski lift 500m; cab TV; 70% statics; dogs; Eng spkn; no adv bkg; quiet; ccard acc; red CKE/CCI. "Rv flows thro site; gd facs; friendly site; ltd facs for tourers; NH." ♦ NOK 286 2016*

⊞ **VEGA** *2E3* (6km S Rural) *65.64353, 11.95110* **Vega Camping, 8980 Vega [tel 47 94 35 00 80; post@vegacamping.no; www.vegacamping.no]** Fr Fv90 head NW, take 1st L onto Fv90, turn L twd Fv84, turn R onto Fv84. After 1.6km turn L, then take 2nd L. Site in 450m. Sm, unshd; htd wc; chem disp; shwrs 20NOK; EHU (16A) inc; cooking facs; sw lake; 0% statics; dogs; Eng spkn; quiet; cash only. "Island ideal for cycling/walking; Elder Duck cent; beautiful location; excel site." NOK 230 2014*

⊞ **VESTBY** *1C3* (3km N Rural) *59.62620, 10.73126* **Vestby Gjestegard & Hyttepark, Hytteveien 11, 1540 Vestby [tel 47 64 95 98 00; info@vestbyhyttepark.co; www.vestbyhyttepark.no]** Junc 17 on E6. Foll sp. Site behind Esso stn on W of E6. Sm, hdstg, pt sl, unshd, wc; shwrs inc; lndry rm; snacks; playgrnd; 90% statics; poss cr; End spkn; noisy, rd; ccard acc; CKE/CCI. "Limited touring space, mainly chalets; NH only." NOK 210 2016*

VIKHAMMER see Malvik *1D1*

VIKOYRI *1B2* (180m N Rural) *61.08884, 6.57721* **Vik Camping, 6891 Vikøyri (Sogn og Fjordane) [tel 57 69 51 25; grolilje@hotmail.com]** Sp in cent of Vikøyri dir Ligtvor; 67km N of Voss on Rv13. Sm, unshd; htd wc; chem disp; shwrs; EHU (10A) (no earth); lndry; shop 200m; wifi; dogs; quiet; Eng spkn; CKE/CCI. "Conv for ferry fr Vangsnes, easier access than other sites; gd NH." ♦ 1 May-30 Sep. NOK 178 2016*

VIKSDALEN *1A2* (12km SE Rural) *61.32628, 6.26926* **Hov Camping, Eldalsdalen, 6978 Viksdalen (Sogn og Fjordane) [tel 57 71 79 37 or 911 88 466 (mob); fax 57 71 79 55; ottarhov@c2i.net; www.viksdalen.no/hov-hyttegrend]** Fr Dragsvik N on Rv13, site is approx 9km S of junc with Rv610, sp. Sm, hdstg, unshd; htd wc; fam bthrm; shwrs NOK10; EHU (8-10A)inc; lndry (inc dryer); shop; playgrnd; fishing; bike hire; Eng spkn; quiet; ccard acc; CKE/CCI. "Attractive site with boating on lake; wcs by parking area; all other facs 150m; remote area." ♦ 1 Apr-30 Sep. NOK 180 2013*

VOSS *1A2* (300m S Rural) *60.62476, 6.42235* **Voss Camping, Prestegardsmoen 40, 5700 Voss (Hordaland) [tel/fax 56 51 15 97 or 90 18 11 20; post@vosscamping.no; www.vosscamping.no]** Exit town on E16 & camping sp; by lake nr cent of Voss; app fr W on E16, site visible by lake on R; 2nd turn on R in town to site in 300m. Sm, mkd pitch, hdstg, terr, pt shd; htd wc; chem disp; shwrs NOK10; EHU (10A) NOK45; lndry; shop 500m; snacks; playgrnd; htd pool; watersports; beach/lake adj; boat & bike hire; few statics; phone; poss v cr; Eng spkn; no adv bkg; ccard acc; CKE/CCI. "Excel cent for fjords; cable car stn in walking dist; tourist bureau; most pitches hdstg gravel but narr/sm." 1 Jan-1 Oct. NOK 225 2014*

LOFOTEN ISLANDS

FREDVANG see Ramberg *2E2*

KABELVAG see Svolvær *2F2*

KLEPPSTAD see Svolvær *2F2*

RAMBERG *2E2* (7km W Rural) *68.0975, 13.1619* **Strand & Skærgårdscamping, 8387 Fredvang [tel 76 09 42 33 or 76 09 46 46; fax 76 09 41 12; mail@fredvangcamping.no; www.fredvangcamp.no]** Foll Fredvang sp fr E10; site sp in vill cent. Sm, unshd; htd wc; chem disp; mv service pnt; shwrs NOK10; EHU (16A) NOK25; lndry; kiosk; cooking facs; sand beach adj; boat hire & launching; sat TV; Eng spkn; quiet; CKE/CCI. "View of midnight sun; surrounded by sand beach, sea & mountains; peaceful; gd san facs, tired (unisex), stretched when busy; friendly." 20 May-31 Aug. NOK 240 2016*

SORVAGEN *2E2* (3km N Coastal) *67.90017, 13.04656* **Moskenes Camping, 8392 Sørvågen [tel 99 48 94 05; info@moskenescamping.no; www.moskenescamping.no]** Fr ferry turn L, then immed R opp terminal exit, site up sh unmade rd, sp. Med, hdstg, terr, unshd; htd wc; chem disp; mv service pnt; EHU (16A) NOK10; lndry; shop 2km; snacks 1km; bar (high ssn); wifi; no statics; Eng spkn; quiet. "Excel NH; gd san facs." May-Sep. NOK 248 2016*

SVOLVAER *2F2* (15km W Coastal) *68.20573, 14.42576* **Sandvika Fjord & Sjøhuscamping (N09), Ørsvågveien 45, 8310 Kabelvåg [tel 76 07 81 45; fax 76 07 87 09; post@sandvika-camping.no; www.sandvika-camping.no]** Sp on S of E10; app lane thro 1 other site. Lge, mkd pitch, terr, unshd; wc; chem disp; mv service pnt; fam bthrm; sauna; shwrs NOK10; EHU (16A) NOK35 (poss rev pol); lndry (inc dryer); shop, rest high ssn; snacks; playgrnd; pool; boating; fishing; bike hire; wifi; TV; phone; bus nr; currency exchange; poss cr; Eng spkn; quiet; ccard acc. "Ideal for trip thro Lofoten Islands; conv Svolvær main fishing port; vg; beautiful views; helpful staff; san facs stretched in high ssn." ♦ 15 Apr-30 Sep. NOK 258 2014*

SVOLVAER *2F2* (26km NW Coastal) *68.27619, 14.30207* **Rystad Lofoten Camping, Brennaveien 235, 8313 Kleppstad [tel 47 91658954; kwes_8@hotmail.com; www.rystadcamping.com]** Foll E10 W out of Svolvaer. Just bef bdge to Grimsoya Island turn R, sp to Rystad. Site sp fr this junc, about 2km on L. Sm, pt sl; wc; chem disp; mv service pnt; shwr NOK10; EHU; lndry (inc dryer); BBQ; sea sw adj; wifi; Eng spkn; quiet; CKE/CCI. "Gd for birdwatching; lovely sea views; gd for photographing midnight sun; vg site." 1 May-30 Sep. NOK 220 2016*

RUNDE ISLAND

⊞ **RUNDE** *1A1* (4km NW Rural/Coastal) *62.40416, 5.62525* **Camping Goksøyr, 6096 Runde (Møre og Romsdal) [tel 70 08 59 05 or 924 12 298 (mob); fax 70 08 59 60; camping@goksoyr.no; www.goksoeyr-camping.com]** Take causeway/bdge to Runde Island. Turn R off bdge & foll rd round island, thro tunnel. Rd ends 1km after site. Sm, hdstg, unshd; wc; chem disp; mv service pnt; shwrs NOK10; EHU (16A) NOK30; lndry; shop; snacks; fishing; bike hire; phone; Eng spkn; adv bkg; quiet; CKE/CCI. "Excel birdwatching (inc puffins); site on water's edge; boat trips avail; basic facs poss inadequate when site full; owner helps with pitching; vg." NOK 190 2014*

VESTERALEN ISLANDS

ANDENES *2F1* (3km SW Coastal) *69.30390, 16.06621* **Andenes Camping, Bleiksveien 34, 8480 Andenes [tel 47 41 34 03 88; fax 47 76 11 56 10; camping@whalesafari.no; www.andenescamping.no]** Site on L of Rv82, sp. Sm, some hdstg, unshd; htd wc; chem disp; mv service pnt; shwrs NOK10; EHU (16A) inc (check earth); shop 250m; cooking facs; sand beach adj; Eng spkn; some rd noise; CKE/CCI. "Nice, sandy beaches; conv whale safari, summer ferry to Gryllefjord & Bleiksøya bird cliff; gd for midnight sun; beautiful location; whale trips." 1 Jun-30 Aug. NOK 200200 2014*

⊞ **ANDENES** *2F1* (9.6km SW Coastal) *69.27552, 15.96372* **Midnattsol Camping, Gardsveien 8, 8481 Bleik [tel 47 47 84 32 19; midnattsol.camping@gmail.com; www.midnattsolcamping.com]** Take Rte 82 S. Then turn R onto Rte 976 sp Bleik. Site at side of Rte 976 just bef Bleik. Sm, pt sl, unshd; wc; chem disp; mv service pnt; shwrs (10NOK); EHU; lndry (inc dryer); BBQ; cooking facs; sea adj; wifi; dogs; cr hg ssn; Eng spkn; quiet; CKE/CCI. "Sandy beach; walks; birdwatching; conv for puffin & whale safaris & fishing boat trips; golf & sports grnd adj; lovely site; sea views; friendly owner." NOK 198 2016*

ANDENES *2F1* (21km SW Coastal) *69.20410, 15.84674* **Stave Camping & Hot Pools, Stave 8489 Nordmela [tel 92 60 12 57; info@stavecamping.no; www.stavecamping.no]** Head S on Storgata/Rv82 twds Stadionveien, cont to foll Rv82, turn R onto Fv976, bear L onto Laksebakkveien, cont onto Fv976; site on L. Sm, pt unshd; htd wc; chem disp; shwr 20NOK; EHU (16A) 40NOK; nearest shop 18km; cooking facs; beach adj; wifi; Eng spkn; ccard acc. "Excel for midnight sun, hot tubs 250NOK pn." 17 May-1 Sep. NOK 230 2014*

⊞ **HARSTAD** *2F2* (5km S Coastal) *68.77231, 16.57878* **Harstad Camping, Nessevegen 55, 9411 Harstad [tel 77 07 36 62; postmaster@harstad-camping.no; www.harstad-camping.no]** Sp fr E10/Rv83. Med, pt sl, unshd; wc; chem disp; shwrs NOK10; EHU (16A) inc; shop; snacks 1km; rest 5km; playgrnd; fishing; boating; wifi; quiet; ccard acc; CKE/CCI. "San facs poss stretched high ssn; lovely situation." ♦ NOK 276 (6 persons) 2016*

⊞ **RISOYHAMN** *2F1* (13km S Coastal) *68.88408, 15.60304* **Andøy Friluftssenter & Camping, Buksnesfjord, 8484 Risøyhamn [tel/fax 76 14 88 04; firmapost@andoy-friluftssenter.no; www.andoy-friluftssenter.no]** Exit E10 onto Rv82 sp Sortland; in 31km at bdge to Sortland do not cross bdge but cont N on Rv82 sp Andenes. Site on R in 38km at Buknesfjord. Sm, hdstg, pt sl, unshd; htd wc; chem disp; shwrs inc; EHU (10A) NOK50; lndry; rest, snacks; playgrnd; lake sw; fishing; 50% statics; Eng spkn; adv bkg; quiet; ccard acc; CKE/CCI. "Lake fishing; guided mountain walks; easy access for whale-watching; v clean facs; gourmet meals." ♦ ltd. NOK 250 2016*

⊞ **SORTLAND** *2F2* (2km NW Rural) *68.70286, 15.3919* **Camping Sortland & Motel, Vesterveien 51, 8400 Sortland [tel 76 11 03 00; fax 76 12 25 78; hj.bergseng@sortland-camping.no; www.sortland-camping.no]** Exit E10 onto Rv82 sp Sortland; in 31km turn L over bdge to Sortland, L again at end bdge. Site sp in approx 1km immed past church. Foll rd uphill for 1km, site on R. Med, hdstg, pt shd; wc; chem disp; fam bthrm; shwrs NOK10; EHU (16A) (no earth) NOK30; gas; lndry; shop; snacks; cooking facs; playgrnd; skiing; cycling; walking; fishing; boating; solarium; gym; wifi; TV; phone; poss cr; Eng spkn; quiet; ccard acc; CKE/CCI. "Basic, clean site; helpful staff; gd base to tour islands; facs stretched when full." NOK 250 2016*

STO *2F1* (700m W Coastal) *69.01922, 15.10894* **Stø Bobilcamp, 8438 Stø [tel 97 63 36 48; stobobilcamp@gmail.com; www.stobobilcamp.no]** Site sp fr cent of Stø. Sm, hdstg, unshd; htd wc; chem disp; mv service pnt; shwrs inc; EHU (16A) NOK30; shop; rest; cooking facs; fishing; bike hire; some statics; poss cr; quiet; Eng spkn. "View of midnight sun; 10min walk to whale boat safari; coastal walks, Queen Sonja's walk fr site, v scenic but poss strenuous; facs stretched high ssn; site open to public for parking." ♦ ltd. 1 May-10 Sep. NOK 130233 2016*

A
B
C
D
▲ see map 2
0
50
100 kms
0
50 mls
1
2
3
4
TRONDHEIM
Malvik
KRISTIANSUND
Bremsnes
Kvisvika
Melhus
Bud
Støren
MOLDE
ÅLESUND
Runde
Åndalsnes
Oppdal
Røros
Os I Osterdalen
Hellesylt
Geiranger
Stryn
Dombås
Grimsbu
Alvdal
Olden
Florø
Byrkjelo
Lom
VAGAMO
Vassenden
FØRDE
Viksdalen
FJÆRLAND
Skjolden
Randsverk
Maurvangen
Balestrand
Sogndalsfjøra
Vangsnes
Vikøyri
Lærdalsøyri
Vang
Gudvangen
Flåm
FAGERNES
LILLEHAMMER
VOSS
Bruflat
Elverum
Gol
HAMAR
BERGEN
Øystese
Eidfjord
Kinsarvik
Geilo
Odda
Rodberg
Skarnes
KONGSVING
Røldal
Tinn Austbygd
UTVIKA
OSLO
Edland
Kongsberg
DRAMMEN
NOTODDEN
Trøgstad
Vestby
Bø
Horten
Valle
Lunde
STAVANGER
Jørpeland
SARPSBORG
Porsgrunn
Fredrikstad
SANDNES
Treungen
HALDEN
LARVIK
Risør
Byglandsfjord
Egersund
Hauge
FLEKKEFJORD
Grimstad
Farsund
KRISTIANSAND
Spangereid
Mandal
© Collins Bartholomew Ltd
3
30
20
40
4
2
13
9
42

Map 1

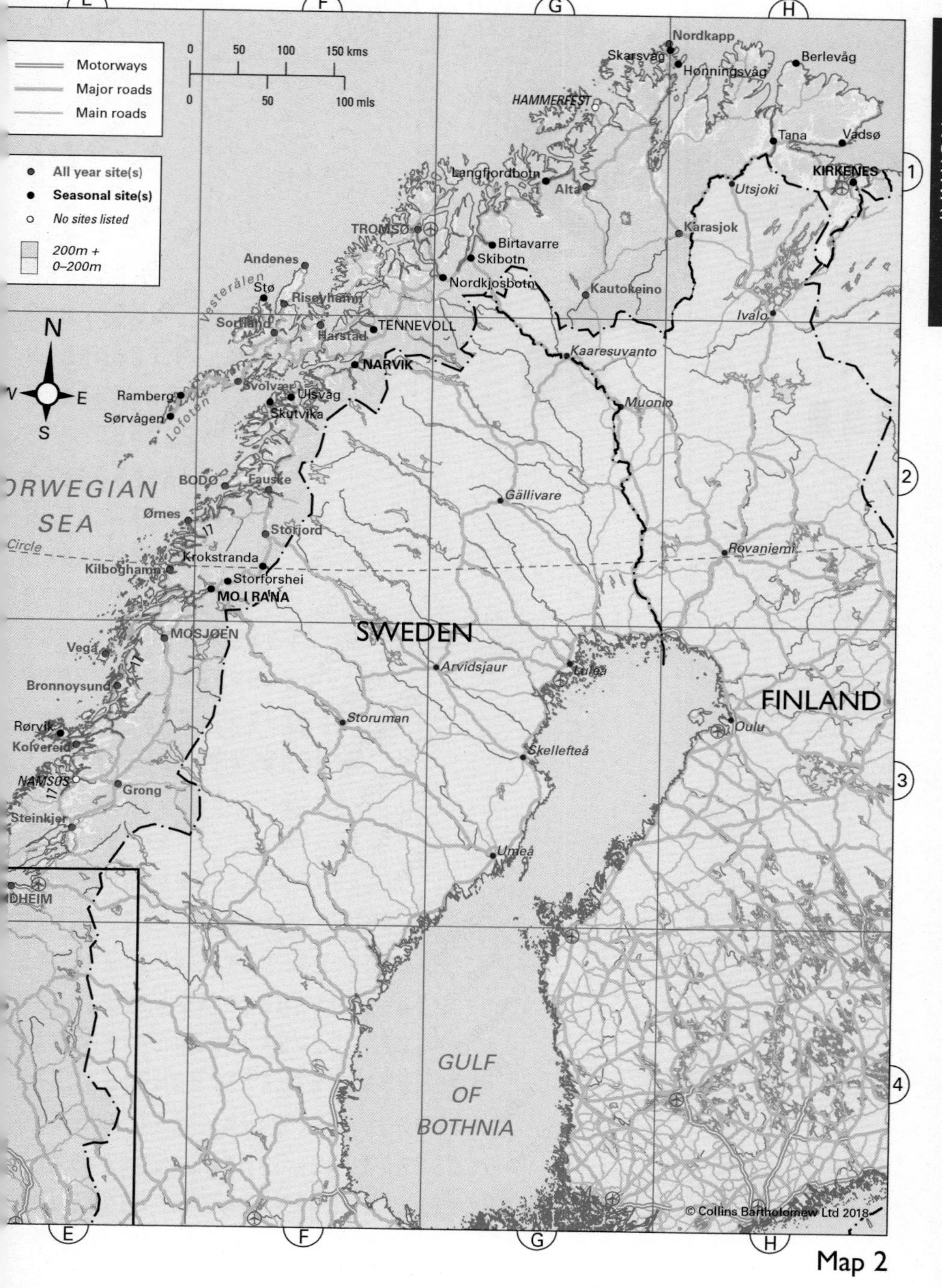
E
F
G
H
Motorways
Major roads
Main roads
0 50 100 150 kms
0 50 100 mls
All year site(s)
Seasonal site(s)
No sites listed
200m +
0–200m
Nordkapp
Skarsvåg
Honningsvåg
Berlevåg
HAMMERFEST
Tana
Vadsø
KIRKENES
Langfjordbotn
Alta
Utsjoki
Karasjok
TROMSØ
Birtavarre
Skibotn
Andenes
Nordkjosbotn
Kautokeino
Stø
Risøyhamn
Vesterålen
Sortland
Harstad
TENNEVOLL
Ivalo
Kaaresuvanto
NARVIK
Ramberg
Svolvær
Ulsvåg
Sørvågen
Skutvika
Lofoten
Muonio
BODØ
Fauske
NORWEGIAN
SEA
Gällivare
Ørnes
Storjord
Circle
Rovaniemi
Krokstranda
Kilboghamn
Storforshei
MO I RANA
MOSJØEN
SWEDEN
Vega
Arvidsjaur
Luleå
Bronnoysund
FINLAND
Storuman
Oulu
Rørvik
Kolvereid
Skellefteå
NAMSOS
Grong
Steinkjer
Umeå
DHEIM
GULF
OF
BOTHNIA
© Collins Bartholomew Ltd 2018
1
2
3
4

Map 2

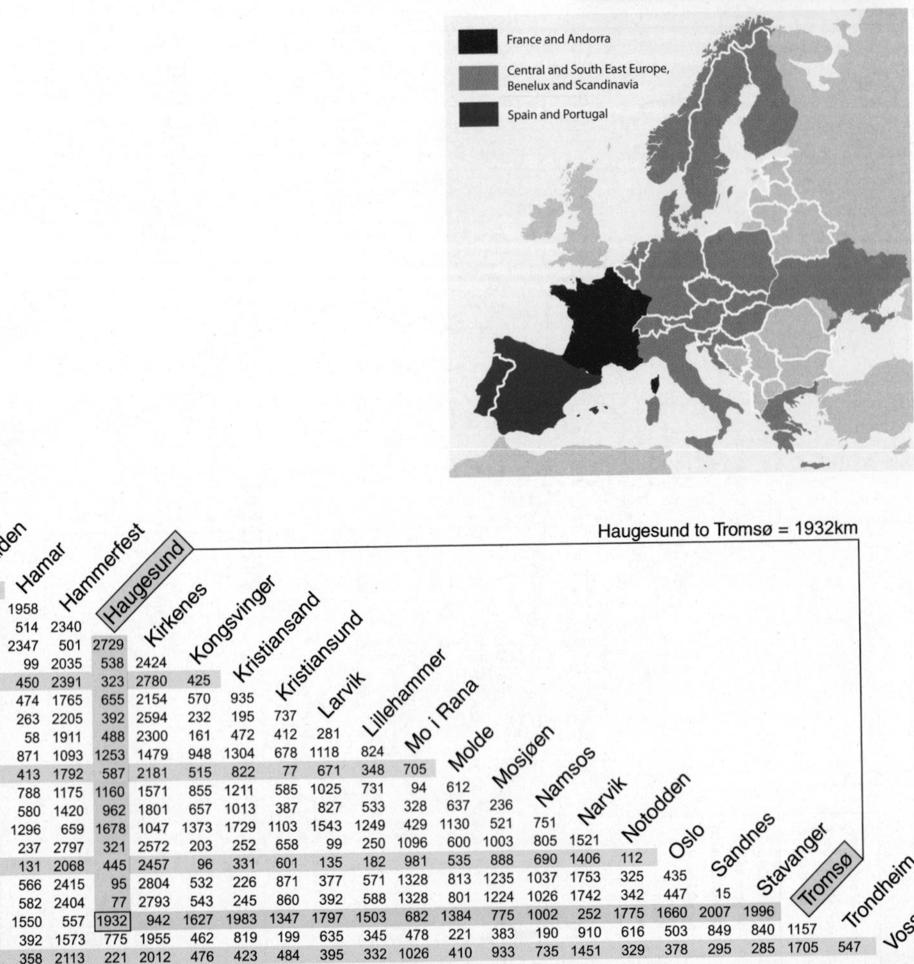

Haugesund to Tromsø = 1932km

	Ålesund	Arendal	Bergen	Bodø	Drammen	Fagernes	Flekkefjord	Førde	Halden	Hamar	Hammerfest	Haugesund	Kirkenes	Kongsvinger	Kristiansand	Kristiansund	Larvik	Lillehammer	Mo i Rana	Molde	Mosjøen	Namsos	Narvik	Notodden	Oslo	Sandnes	Stavanger	Tromsø	Trondheim
Arendal	788																												
Bergen	382	480																											
Bodø	1070	1475	1366																										
Drammen	576	219	447	1366																									
Fagernes	455	421	558	1122	199																								
Flekkefjord	773	189	399	1663	411	578																							
Førde	211	584	177	1256	413	283	498																						
Halden	691	262	589	1317	159	310	449	555																					
Hamar	441	395	481	1112	173	146	564	413	234																				
Hammerfest	1916	2321	2212	966	2113	1968	2509	2102	2163	1958																			
Haugesund	518	362	135	1494	387	401	211	313	495	514	2340																		
Kirkenes	2305	2710	2601	1361	2502	2357	2899	2491	3146	2347	501	2729																	
Kongsvinger	544	357	598	1189	137	225	548	518	169	99	2035	538	2424																
Kristiansand	869	69	486	1545	293	487	117	601	320	450	2391	323	2780	425															
Kristiansund	155	867	561	919	589	460	980	347	661	474	1765	655	2154	570	935														
Larvik	673	131	462	1359	95	292	314	496	138	263	2205	392	2594	232	195	737													
Lillehammer	387	406	454	1056	192	114	588	387	307	58	1911	488	2300	161	472	412	281												
Mo i Rana	829	1234	1125	241	1026	881	1422	1548	1076	871	1093	1253	1479	948	1304	678	1118	824											
Molde	80	745	453	946	546	492	939	276	648	413	1792	587	2181	515	822	77	671	348	705										
Mosjøen	736	1141	1032	337	933	788	1329	922	983	788	1175	1160	1571	855	1211	585	1025	731	94	612									
Namsos	538	943	834	572	735	599	1131	724	785	580	1420	962	1801	657	1013	387	827	533	328	637	236								
Narvik	1254	1659	1550	303	1451	1306	1847	1440	1501	1296	659	1678	1047	1373	1729	1103	1543	1249	429	1130	521	751							
Notodden	635	179	403	1337	67	273	329	429	168	237	2797	321	2572	203	252	658	99	250	1096	600	1003	805	1521						
Oslo	576	265	485	1222	41	190	451	465	120	131	2068	445	2457	96	331	601	135	182	981	535	888	690	1406	112					
Sandnes	693	298	215	1569	394	508	108	390	506	566	2415	95	2804	532	226	871	377	571	1328	813	1235	1037	1753	325	435				
Stavanger	581	317	197	1558	409	524	127	377	517	582	2404	77	2793	543	245	860	392	588	1328	801	1224	1026	1742	342	447	15			
Tromsø	1508	1913	1804	562	1705	1560	2101	1694	1755	1550	557	1932	942	1627	1983	1347	1797	1503	682	1384	775	1002	252	1775	1660	2007	1996		
Trondheim	307	754	645	719	546	410	938	532	598	392	1573	775	1955	462	819	199	635	345	478	221	383	190	910	616	503	849	840	1157	
Voss	350	418	101	1267	335	451	423	178	498	358	2113	221	2012	476	423	484	395	332	1026	410	933	735	1451	329	378	295	285	1705	547

Wroclaw

Welcome to Poland

Poland is a country with a deep sense of history, cultural identity and resilience that has been built over thousands of years. The historic and beautiful centre of Kraków is a must see, while the engaging and fascinating museums of Warsaw are also a fantastic experience.

For those looking for relaxation, the Polish countryside is peaceful and unspoilt. There are many hiking trails scattered around the country taking you alongside rivers, through thick forests and around mountains.

Country highlights

Amber, sometimes called the gold of the Baltic, has been crafted in Poland for centuries. Amber products are still produced and sold with the best place to shop being Cloth Hall in the heart of Kraków.

Poland has been producing vodka since the early Middle Ages, and is the birthplace of this spirit. The vodka distilled in Poland is considered some of the finest in the world and vodka tasting events are held around the country.

Major towns and cities

- Warsaw – Poland's capital and the largest city in the country.
- Kraków – a charming and beautiful place that has retained its historic feel.
- Łódź - the high street is one of the longest in the world.
- Wrocław – a city with plenty of landmarks and wonderful buildings.

Attractions

- Main Square, Kraków – a bustling, medieval market square filled with historic buildings and monuments.
- Białowi¿ea Forest – the remains of a primeval forest, home to European bison, ancient oaks and a magical beauty.
- Wieliczka Salt Mine – discover a fascinating mix of history, art and industry in one of Poland's oldest salt mines.

Find out more

www.poland.travel
Tel: 0048 (0) 22 53 67 070 Polish Tourist Office

Country Information

Population (approx): 38.3 million

Capital: Warsaw (population approx 1.7 million)

Area: 312,685 sq km

Bordered by: Belarus, Czech Republic, Germany, Lithuania, Russia, Slovakia, Ukraine

Terrain: Mostly flat plain with many lakes; mountains along southern border

Climate: Changeable continental climate with cold, often severe winters and hot summers; rainfall spread throughout the year; late spring and early autumn are the best times to visit

Coastline: 440km

Highest Point: Rysy 2,499m

Language: Polish

Local Time: GMT or BST + 1, i.e. 1 hour ahead of the UK all year

Currency: Zloty (PLN) divided into 100 groszy; £1 = PLN 4.76; PLN10 = £2.10 (November 2017)

Emergency numbers: Police 997; Fire brigade 998; Ambulance 999. Call 112 for any service.

Public Holidays 2018: Jan 1, 6; Apr 16, 17; May 1, 3 (Constitution Day); Jun 4, 15; Aug 15; Nov 1, 11 (Independence Day); Dec 25, 26.

School summer holidays run from the last week of June to the end of August.

Camping and Caravanning

There are around 250 organised campsites throughout Poland, with the most attractive areas being the Mazurian lake district and along the coast. Campsites are usually open from the beginning of May or June to the middle or end of September, but the season only really starts towards the end of June. Until then facilities may be very limited and grass may not be cut, etc.

You can download details of approximately 160 sites (including GPS co-ordinates) from the website of the Polish Federation of Camping & Caravanning, www.pfcc.eu.

Campsites are classified into two categories. Category one sites provide larger pitches and better amenities, but it may still be advisable to use your own facilities. There are also some basic sites which are not supervised and are equipped only with drinking water, toilets and washing facilities. Sites may be in need of modernisation but, on the whole, sanitary facilities are clean although they may provide little privacy. Some new sites are being built to higher standards. A site may close earlier than its published date if the weather is bad.

Many sites are not signposted from main roads and may be difficult to find. It is advisable to obtain a large scale atlas or good maps of the areas to be visited and not rely on one map covering the whole of Poland.

Casual/wild camping is not recommended and is prohibited in national parks (except on organised sites) and in sand dunes along the coast.

Cycling

There are several long-distance cycle routes using a combination of roads with light motor traffic, forest trails or tracks along waterways. There are some cycle lanes on main roads where cyclists may not ride two or more abreast.

Electricity and Gas

The current on most campsites is 10 amps. Plugs have two round pins. There are some CEE connections.

It is understood that both propane and butane supplies are widely available, but cylinders are not exchangeable and it may be necessary to refill. The Caravan and Motorhome Club does not recommend this practice and you should aim to take enough gas to last during your stay. Some campsites have kitchens which you may use to conserve your gas supplies.

Entry Formalities

British and Irish passport holders may visit Poland for up to three months without a visa. At campsites reception staff should undertake any required registration formalities with local authorities.

Medical Services

For simple complaints and basic advice consult staff in a pharmacy (apteka). Some English may be spoken. In general, medical facilities are comparatively inexpensive and of a good standard. Medical staff are well qualified. English is not always widely spoken and you may face language difficulties.

You will need a European Health Insurance Card (EHIC) to obtain emergency treatment from doctors, dentists and hospitals contracted to the state health care system, the NFZ. Reimbursements for any charges that you incur can be claimed from the NFZ office in Warsaw. You will have to pay a proportion of the cost of prescriptions, which is not refundable in Poland.

Private health clinics offering a good standard of medical care can also be found in large cities.

Opening Hours

Banks: Mon-Fri 9am-4pm; Sat 9am-1pm.

Museums: Tue-Sun 10am-5pm; closed Mon.

Post Offices: Mon-Fri 8am-6pm; Sat 8am-2pm (on rota basis).

Shops: Mon-Fri 11am-8pm; Sat 9am-2pm/4pm; food shops open and close earlier; supermarkets open until 9pm/10pm.

Safety and Security

Most visits to Poland are trouble free and violent crime is rare, but there is a risk of robbery in tourist areas, particularly near hotels, at main railway stations and on public transport. Passengers are most at risk when boarding and leaving trains or trams. Avoid walking alone at night, particularly in dark or poorly-lit streets or in public parks.

Some tourists have been the target of a scam in which men claiming to be plain clothes police officers ask visitors to show their identity documents and bank cards, and then ask for their PIN(s).

Theft of and from vehicles is common so do not leave vehicle documentation or valuables in your car. Foreign registered cars may be targeted, especially in large, busy supermarket car parks.

Cases have been reported of vehicles with foreign number plates being stopped by gangs posing as police officers, either claiming a routine traffic control or at the scene of fake accidents, particularly in rural and tourist areas. If in doubt, when flagged down keep all doors and windows locked, remain in your vehicle and ask to see identification. The motoring organisation, PZM, advises that any car or document inspection performed outside built-up areas can only be carried out by uniformed police officers and at night these officials must use a police patrol car. Although police officers do not have to be in uniform within built-up areas, they must always present their police identity card. More details are available to motorists at Polish road borders.

An emergency helpline has been set up to assist visitors who have been victims of crime or who require assistance tel: 0800 200300 (freephone) or +48 608 599999 (mobile number). The helpline operates from 1 June to 30 September between 10am and 10pm.

Do not leave drinks or food unattended or accept drinks from strangers. There has been a small number of reports of drinks being spiked and of visitors having their valuables stolen whilst drugged.

British Embassy
UL KAWALERII 12
00-468 WARSZAWA
Tel: (022) 3110000
www.ukinpoland.fco.gov.uk

Irish Embassy
UL MYSIA 5, 00-496 WARSZAWA
Tel: (022) 5642200
www.embassyofireland.pl.

Border Posts

Customs posts are open 24 hours a day throughout the year. Cars crossing the eastern borders, especially to Lithuania and Belarus, are usually intensively scrutinised by the Polish authorities in an effort to combat widespread smuggling of stolen cars. Travellers should ensure all documents are in order.

Borders may be busy at weekends with cross border shoppers, and in particular the crossing from Germany via Frankfurt-on-Oder can be heavily congested on Saturday mornings.

Documents

Driving Licence

The standard pink UK paper driving licence is recognised, but if you hold the old style green UK licence or a Northern Irish licence issued prior to 1991 you are advised to update it to a photocard licence in order to avoid any local difficulties.

Passport

You should carry your passport with you at all times.

Vehicle(s)

You must carry your original vehicle registration certificate (V5C), insurance documentation and MOT certificate (if applicable) at all times. You may be asked for these if you are stopped by the police and, in particular, when crossing borders. If you do not own the vehicle(s) you will need a letter of authority from the owner, together with the vehicle's original documentation.

Money

Cash can easily be obtained from ATMs in banks and shopping centres. ATMs offer an English option.

Major credit cards are widely accepted in hotels, restaurants and shops but you may find that supermarkets do not accept them. Take particular care with credit/debit cards and don't lose sight of them during transactions.

Sterling and euros are readily accepted at exchange bureaux but Scottish and Northern Irish bank notes are not generally recognised and you may have difficulties trying to exchange them.

Carry your credit card issuers'/banks' 24-hour UK contact numbers in case of loss or theft of your cards.

Motoring in Poland

Poland is a major east to west route for heavy vehicles and driving can be hazardous. There are few dual carriageways and even main roads between large towns can be narrow and poorly surfaced. Slow moving agricultural and horse-drawn vehicles are common in rural areas. Street lighting is weak even in major cities.

Local driving standards are poor and speed limits, traffic lights and road signs are often ignored. Drivers rarely indicate before manoeuvring and you may encounter aggressive tailgating, overtaking on blind bends and overtaking on the inside. Take particular care on national holiday weekends when there is a surge in road accidents.

It is not advisable to drive a right hand drive vehicle alone for long distances or to drive long distances at night. At dusk watch out for cyclists riding without lights along the edge of the road or on its shoulder.

Hitchhikers use an up and down motion of the hand to ask for a lift. This may be confused with flagging down.

Accidents

A driver involved in an accident must call the police, obtain an official record of damages and forward it to the insurance company of the Polish driver involved (if applicable), for example, the Polish National Insurance Division (PZU) or the Polish Insurance Association (WARTA). Members of AIT/FIA affiliated clubs, such as The Caravan and Motorhome Club, can obtain help from the touring office ('Autotour') of the Polish motoring organisation, Polski Zwiazek Motorowy (PZM), tel: (022) 8496904 or (022) 8499361.

If people are injured, you must call an ambulance or doctor. By law, it is an offence for a driver not to obtain first aid for accident victims or to leave the scene of an accident. In such circumstances the authorities may withdraw a tourist's passport and driving licence, vehicle registration certificate or even the vehicle itself and the penalties can be a prison sentence and a fine.

Alcohol

There is zero tolerance for drink-driving; the permitted level of alcohol is 20 milligrams in 100 millilitres of blood, which in practice equates to zero. At the request of the police or if an accident has occurred a driver must undergo a blood test which, if positive, may lead to a prison sentence, withdrawal of driving licence and a fine. Penalty points will be notified to the authorities in the motorist's home country.

Breakdown Service

The toll free telephone number for breakdown assistance throughout the country is 981.

The PZM runs a breakdown service covering the entire country 24 hours a day. Members of AIT and FIA affiliated clubs, such as The Caravan and Motorhome Club, should call the PZM Emergency Centre on
(022) 5328433. Staff speak English. Roadside assistance must be paid for in cash.

Essential Equipment

Fire extinguisher

It is compulsory to carry a fire extinguisher on board all vehicles.

First aid kit

It is not compulsory to have a first aid kit but it is recommended.

Lights

Dipped headlights must be used at all times. Bulbs are more likely to fail with constant use and you are recommended to carry spares. In bad visibility use your horn to indicate that you are going to overtake.

Warning Triangles

You must use a warning triangle when a vehicle is stationary on a road in poor visibility (less than 100 metres) and if the vehicle is likely to obstruct traffic. On a normal road the triangle must be placed between 30 and 50 metres behind the vehicle and must be clearly visible to oncoming traffic; on a motorway, it must be placed 100 metres behind the vehicle. Hazard warning lights may be used in addition to, but not instead of, a triangle.

Child Restraint System

Children under the age of 12 years old and under the height of 1.5m must use a suitable restraint system that has been adapted to their size. It is prohibited to place a child in a rear facing seat in the front of the vehicle if the car is equipped with airbags.

Fuel

The usual opening hours for petrol stations are from 8am to 7pm; many on main roads and international routes and in large towns are open 24 hours. Credit cards are widely accepted. LPG (Autogas) is widely available from service stations.

Parking

There are parking meters in many towns and signs display parking restrictions or prohibitions. There are many supervised car parks charging an hourly rate. Illegally parked cars causing an obstruction may be towed away and impounded, in which case the driver will be fined. Wheel clamps are in use.

Sidelights must be used when parking in unlit streets during the hours of darkness.

Priority

Priority should be given to traffic coming from the right at intersections of roads of equal importance, however vehicles on rails always have priority. At roundabouts traffic already on a roundabout has priority.

Give way to buses pulling out from bus stops. Trams have priority over other vehicles at all times. Where there is no central reservation or island you should stop to allow passengers alighting from trams to cross to the pavement.

Roads

All roads are hard surfaced and the majority of them are asphalted. However, actual road surfaces may be poor; even some major roads are constructed of cement or cobbles and heavily rutted. Average journey speed is about 50 km/h (31 mph).

Some roads, notably those running into Warsaw, have a two metre wide strip on the nearside to pull onto in order to allow other vehicles to overtake. Oncoming lorries expect other motorists to pull over when they are overtaking.

Overtake trams on the right unless in a one-way street.

Road Signs and Markings

Road signs and markings conform to international standards. Motorway and national road numbers are indicated in red and white, and local roads by yellow signs with black numbering. Signs on motorways are blue with white lettering and on main roads they are green and white.

The following road signs may be seen:

Polish	English Translation
Rondzie	Roundabout
Wstep szbroniony	No Entry
Wyjscie	Exit

You may also encounter the following:

Crossroads and road junctions may not be marked with white 'stop' lines, and other road markings in general may be well worn and all but invisible, so always take extra care.

Speed Limits

Paid parking between 7am and 6pm

Residential area- predestrians have priority

Toll road

Rutted road

Winding road

Emergency vehicles

	Open Road (km/h)	Motorway (km/h)
Car Solo	90	140
Car towing caravan/trailer	70	80
Motorhome under 3500kg	90	140
Motorhome 3500-7500kg	70	80

In built up areas the speed limit is 50 km/h (31 mph) between 5am and 11pm, and 60 km/h (37 mph) between 11pm and 5am.

For vehicles over 3,500kg all speed limits are the same as for a car and caravan outfit. In residential zones indicated by entry/exit signs, the maximum speed is 20 km/h (13 mph). The use of radar detectors is illegal.

Traffic Lights

Look out for a small, non-illuminated green arrow under traffic lights, which permits a right turn against a red traffic light if the junction is clear.

Violation of Traffic Regulations

Motorists must not cross a road's solid central white line or even allow wheels to run on it. Radar speed traps are frequently in place on blind corners where speed restrictions apply. Police are very keen to enforce traffic regulations with verbal warnings and/or on the spot fines. Fines are heavy and drivers of foreign registered vehicles will be required to pay in cash. Always obtain an official receipt.

Motorways and Tolls

There are approximately 1420km of motorways in Poland. Tolls are levied on sections and vary in price, for example, the A1 Rusocin to Nowe Marzy is PLN 41.80 (2015 prices) for a car towing a caravan weighing under 3500kg.

An electronic toll system is in place for vehicles which weigh over 3,500kg, including motorhomes and car and caravan combinations if the total weight is over 3,500kg. These vehicles will need to be equipped with an electronic device called a viaBOX. Visit www.viatoll.pl/en and select the 'Trucks' option for details of toll costs for motorhomes and car/caravan combinations weighing over 3500kg.

An electronic option is also available for vehicles and car/caravan combinations which weigh under 3500kg - go to the above website and choose the 'Cars' options for details.

There are emergency telephones every 2km along motorways. Recent visitors report that newer stretches of motorway have rest areas with chemical disposal and waste water disposal facilities.

Touring

Poland's climate does not permit the production of wine, the national drinks being varieties of vodka and plum brandy. It is usual to leave a tip of between 10 to 15%.

There are over 9,000 lakes in Poland, mostly in the north. The regions of Western Pomerania, Kaszubia and Mazuria are a paradise for sailing enthusiasts, anglers and nature lovers. In order to protect areas of great natural beauty, national parks and nature reserves have been created, two of the most interesting of which are the Tatra National Park covering the whole of the Polish Tatra mountains, and the Slowinksi National Park with its 'shifting' sand dunes.

There are 14 UNESCO World Heritage sites including the restored historic centres of Warsaw and Kraków, the medieval, walled town of Toruń and Auschwitz Concentration Camp. Other towns worth a visit are Chopin's birthplace at Zelazowa Wola, Wieliczka with its salt mines where statues and a chapel are carved out of salt, and Wrocław.

White and brown signs placed strategically in cities and near sites of interest pinpoint architectural and natural landmarks, places of religious worship, etc. Each sign includes not only information on the name of and distance to a particular attraction, but also a pictogram of the attraction, e.g. Jasna Góra monastery. Themed routes, such as the trail of the wooden churches in the Małopolska Region (south of Kraków), are marked in a similar way.

A Warsaw Tourist Card and a Kraków Tourist Card are available, both valid for up to three days and offering free travel on public transport and free entry to many museums, together with discounts at selected restaurants and shops and on sightseeing and local excursions. Buy the cards from tourist information centres, travel agents or hotels.

The Polish people are generally friendly, helpful and polite. English is becoming increasingly widely spoken in major cities.

Public Transport & Local Travel

For security reasons recent visitors recommend using guarded car parks such as those in Warsaw on the embankment below the Old Town, in the Palace of Culture and near the Tomb of the Unknown Soldier.

Problems have been reported involving overcharging by non-regulated taxi drivers. Use only taxis from official ranks whose vehicles have the name and telephone number of the taxi company on the door and on the roof (beside the occupied/unoccupied light). They also display a rate card in the window of the vehicle. Taxis with a crest but no company name are not officially registered.

There are frequent ferries from Gydnia, Swinoujscie and Gdansk to Denmark, Germany and Sweden. There are no car ferry services on internal waters but passenger services operate along the Baltic Coast, on the Mazurian lakes and on some rivers, for example, between Warsaw and Gdansk.

There is a metro system in Warsaw linking the centre to the north and south of the city. It is possible to buy a daily or weekly tourist pass which is valid for all means of public transport – bus, tram and metro. Buy tickets at newspaper stands and kiosks displaying a sign 'bilety'. Tickets must be punched before travelling at the yellow machines at the entrance to metro stations or on board buses and trams. You will incur an on the spot fine if you are caught travelling without a valid ticket.

Sites in Poland

AUSCHWITZ see Oświęcim *D3*

BAKOW see Kluczbork *C2*

BARANOWO see Poznań *B2*

BIALOWIEZA *B4* (3km W Rural) *52.69395, 23.83088* **Camping U Michała (No. 124), ul Krzyże 11, 17-230 Białowieża [(085) 6812703; info@bialowieza-forest.com; http://bialowieza-forest.com/miejsce/camping-u-michala-bialowieza]** Exit Bielsk Podlaski onto rd 689; cont past Hajnówka for 17m; site on R at end of vill. Sm, mkd pitch, pt shd; wc; chem disp; shwrs inc; EHU (16A); lndry; playgrnd; bike hire; poss cr; quiet. "Gd san facs." ♦ 15 Apr-30 Sep. PLN 50 2016*

BOGACZEWO see Gizycko *A3*

CHMIELNO see Kartuzy *A2*

CZESTOCHOWA *C3* (4km W Urban) *50.81122, 19.09131* **Camping Oleńka (No. 76), ul Oleńki 10, 42-200 Częstochowa [tel/fax (034) 3606066; camping@mosir.pl; www.mosir.pl]** Fr A1/E75 foll sp Jasna Góra monastery, pick up sm white camping sp to site. Lge, pt shd; wc; chem disp; shwrs inc; EHU (20A); lndry; shops nrby; rest; bar; playgrnd; pool 2km; wifi; TV; 20% statics; dogs; phone; Eng spkn; no adv bkg; quiet; ccard acc; red CKE/CCI. "Guided tours; monastery worth visit; gd NH/sh stay nr Jasna Góra & Black Madonna painting; poor security; san facs unclean & poorly maintained." ♦ 1 May-15 Oct. PLN 58 2016*

ELK *A3* (3km SW Urban) *53.81545, 22.35215* **Camping Plaża Miejska (No. 62), ul Parkowa 2, 19-300 Ełk [(087) 6109700; fax 6102723; mosir@elk.com.pl; http://mosir.elk.pl/plaza-miejska/camping/]** Fr town cent on rd 16 take rd 65/669 dir Białystok. After 200m cross rv & immed turn R, site 100m on L. Sm, mkd pitch, hdstg, pt shd; htd wc; shwrs inc; EHU (10A) inc; shop 500m; snacks; bar; cooking facs; lake sw & sand beach 200m; quiet; CKE/CCI. "Gd security; well-maintained, clean site adj town cent & attractive lake; gd touring base lake district." ♦ 1 Jun-1 Sep. PLN 65 2016*

FROMBORK *A3* (1km E Rural/Coastal) *54.35877, 19.69572* **Camping Frombork (No. 12), ul Braniewska, 14-530 Frombork [(0506) 803151; kontakt@campingfrombork.pl; www.campingfrombork.pl]** Fr Frombork on rd 504 dir Braniewo, site on L. Med, pt shd; wc; chem disp & mv service pnt at car wash; shwrs inc; EHU inc; lndry; shop 1km; bar; BBQ; playgrnd; sand beach 2km; games area; dogs; quiet. "Pleasant, basic site; san facs tatty but clean (2009); pleasant countryside." 1 May-30 Sep. PLN 60 2013*

GAJ see Krakow *D3*

GDANSK *A2* (9km E Coastal) *54.37021, 18.72938* **Camping Stogi (No. 218), ul Wydmy 9, 80-656 Gdańsk [(058) 3073915; fax 3042259; jan@camping-gdansk.pl; www.kemping-gdansk.pl]** E fr Gdańsk on rd 7 (E77) for approx 2km, then L foll sp for Stogi. Then foll tram rte no. 8 to Stogi Plaza/Beach. Site is 100m fr tram terminus, well sp. Med, hdstg; wc; chem disp; shwrs inc; EHU (10-16A) PLN11; lndry; shop; snacks; bar; BBQ; playgrnd; sand beach adj; games area; wifi; 75% statics; tram 100m; poss cr & poss noise fr school parties; CKE/CCI. "Basic site, more a holiday camp for school groups; ltd facs LS; close to huge, clean beach; gd security; vg site; sep area for m'vans; san facs upgraded (2013)." 25 Apr-5 Oct. PLN 89 2013*

⊞ **JELENIA GORA** *C2* (2km SE Urban) *50.89638, 15.74266* **Auto-Camping Park (No. 130), ul Sudecka 42, 58-500 Jelenia Góra [tel/fax (075) 7524525; campingpark@interia.pl; www.camping.karkonosz.pl]** In town foll sp to Karpacz on rd 367. Site 100m fr hotel. Well sp. Med, some hdstg, pt terr, pt shd; wc in recep building; shwrs inc; EHU (6-10A) PLN10 (poss rev pol); lndry; shops 100m; rest 200m; snacks; pool, tennis & sports facs 500m; wifi; TV; 20% statics; dogs PLN5; adv bkg; quiet but some rd noise; ccard acc; red CKE/CCI. "Conv Karkanosze mountains & Czech border; well-run, clean, neat site nr hotel with gd, modern facs; 20 min walk to pleasant town; staff friendly, helpful & obliging; conv NH; gd facs." ♦ PLN 53 2015*

KARPACZ *D2* (3km N Rural) *50.80428, 15.76776* **Camping Wiśniowa Polana (No. 142), Miłków 40A, 58-535 Mlłków [tel/fax (0510) 111415; camping-milkow@karkonosz.pl; www.camping-milkow.karkonosz.pl]** Fr Jelenia Góra to Kowary on rte 367, turn R at junc with rte 366 at Kowary, site on E of Miłków by rv. Med, some hdstg, pt shd; wc; chem disp (wc); mv service pnt; shwrs inc; EHU (10A) PLN10; lndry; shop 500m; snacks; bar; BBQ; playgrnd; pool; paddling pool; fishing; games area; internet; dogs PLN5; quiet; red snr citizens/CKE/CCI. "Well-kept, guarded site & facs; v friendly staff; 7km fr chairlift onto mountain ridge; gd walking - map fr recep." ♦ 1 May-30 Sep. PLN 55 2013*

⊞ **KARTUZY** *A2* (9km W Rural) *54.31983, 18.11736* **Camping Tamowa (No. 181), Zawory 47A, 83-333 Chmielno [tel/fax (058) 6842535; camping@tamowa.pl; www.tamowa.pl]** Fr Gdańsk take rd 7 & rd 211 to Kartuzy, cont for approx 4km on 211. Turn L for Chmielno; site sp fr vill on lakesite along narr, bumpy app rd. Med, terr, unshd; wc; chem disp; sauna; shwrs PLN2; EHU (10-16A) inc; shop 1km; snacks; bar; BBQ; playgrnd; lake sw adj; boat & bike hire; little Eng spkn; quiet; CKE/CCI. "Attractive, well-kept site in beautiful location; friendly owner; not suitable lge o'fits; v nice site; shop 0.5m." PLN 54 2012*

KATOWICE *D3* (4km SE Rural) *50.24355, 19.04795* **Camping Dolina Trzech Statow (No. 215), ul Trzech Stawow 23, 40-291 Katowice [tel/fax (032) 2565939 or (032) 2555388; camping@mosir.katowice.pl; camping.mosir.katowice.pl]** Exit A4 at junc Murckowska & foll sp on rd 86 Sosnowiec. In 500m turn R & foll site sp. Med, pt sl, shd; htd wc; shwrs inc; EHU (16A) PLN2.50/kwh; shop 1km; rest adj; snacks; bar; cooking facs; playgrnd; lake; tennis; dogs PLN5; Eng spkn; adv bkg; quiet; ccard acc; red CKE/CCI. "V clean facs but basic & little privacy; vg." ♦
1 May-30 Sep. PLN 45 2016*

KAZIMIERZ DOLNY *C3* (2km N Rural) *51.33106, 21.95879* **Campsite Pielak, Pulawska 82, 24-120 Kazimierz Dolny (Lubelskie) [(069) 1047409]** Site sp on the S824 300m N of the town. Sm, pt sl, pt shd; wc; chem disp; mv service pnt; fam bthrm; shwrs; EHU (16A); lndry; shop (50m); rest & bar (50m); BBQ; cooking facs; pool & beach (50m); kayaking; wifi; dogs; bus adj; twin axles; Eng spkn; quiet; CCI. "V friendly owners, warm welcome; walking dist to town; close to rv; open grassy site; historic town; excel." ♦ ltd.
1 May-30 Oct. PLN 72 2016*

"We must tell The Club about that great site we found"

Get your site reports in by mid-August and we'll do our best to get your updates into the next edition.

⊞ **KLODZKO** *D2* (13km W Urban) *50.41502, 16.51335* **Camping Polanica-Zdroj (No. 169), ul Sportowa 7, 57-320 Polanica-Zdrój [(074) 8681210; fax 8681211; osir.polanica@neostrada.pl; www.osir.polanica.net/pl]** Foll sp fr rd 8/E67. Site is 1km N of Polanica-Zdrój. Med, pt shd; htd wc; shwrs inc; EHU (6A) PLN9.50; shop & 500m; snacks; rest; tennis; many statics adj; dogs PLN5; poss cr; Eng spkn; quiet; ccard acc; CKE/CCI. "Well-run site; clean san facs; helpful warden; easy walk to pleasant spa town - many rests/cafés; wifi free in recep." PLN 49 2014*

KOLOBRZEG *A2* (1km NE Coastal) *54.18131, 15.59566* **Camping Baltic (No. 78), ul 4 Dywizji, 78-100 Kołobrzeg [tel/fax (094) 3524569 or (0606) 411954 (mob); baltic78@post.pl; www.camping.kolobrzeg.pl]** Nr Solny Hotel on NE edge of town over rlwy x-ing; sp fr rndabt in vill. Med, pt shd; wc; chem disp; mv service pnt; shwrs; shops 500m; EHU (10-16A) PLN10; shop, rest adj; snacks; bar; playgrnd; sand beach 800m; TV; dogs PLN3; phone; poss cr; Eng spkn; adv bkg; rd & rlwy noise; ccard acc; red long stay/CKE/CCI. "V helpful staff; easy walk/cycle to town; well kept site with spotless facs; easy walk into town."
♦ 15 Apr-15 Oct. PLN 103 2013*

KRAKOW *D3* (5km N Urban) *50.09454, 19.94127* **Camping Clepardia (No. 103), ul Pachońskiego 28A, 31-223 Kraków [(012) 4159672; fax 6378063; clepardia@gmail.com; www.clepardia.com.pl]** Fr Kraków cent take rd 7/E77 N twds Warsaw for 3km. Turn L onto rd 79 'Opolska' & foll sp 'Domki Kempingowe - Bungalows'. Fr A4/E40 exit onto E462 then S on rd 79 'Pasternik' thro to 'J Conrada & foll sp. Site is nr lge Elea supmkt & Clepardia Basen (sw pools). Med, mkd pitch, pt shd; wc; chem disp; shwrs inc; EHU (6A) PLN12; lndry; supmkt, rest 250m; pool adj; wifi; dogs free; phone; bus 250m; poss cr; Eng spkn; no adv bkg; aircraft noise; CKE/CCI. "Busy site with tightly packed pitches - rec arr bef 1700 high ssn to secure pitch; excel, clean, modern san facs; ltd EHU if site full; muddy in wet weather; friendly, helpful staff; gd security; well maintained." 15 Apr-15 Oct. PLN 94
2017*

KRAKOW *D3* (8km S Urban) *50.01546, 19.92525* **Camping Krakowianka (No. 171), ul Żywiecka Boczna 2, 30-427 Kraków [tel/fax (012) 2681135; hotel@krakowianka.com.pl or hotel@krakowianka.info; www.krakowianka.com.pl]** Exit A4 at Wezel Opatkowice & head N on E77 twd city cent for approx 3km. After passing Carrefour supmkt on R, turn L at next traff lts & foll site sp. Lge, pt shd; wc; chem disp; shwrs; EHU (16A) inc; lndry; supmkt 400m; rest 1.5km; snacks; playgrnd; pool adj; games area; TV; some statics; dogs; wifi; phone; tram; car wash. "Ltd, basic facs; conv tram to town; shwrs in hotel v clean & plenty hot water; gd site; nice snack/bar."
1 May-30 Sep. PLN 50 2013*

⊞ **KRAKOW** *D3* (7km SW Rural) *50.04638, 19.88111* **Camping Smok (No. 46), ul Kamedulska 18, 30-252 Kraków [tel/fax 48 12 429 88 00; info@smok.krakow.pl; www.smok.krakow.pl]** Fr Kraków W ring rd site sp as No 46. Fr S 1st exit immed after x-ing rv onto rd 780 twd Kraków. Med, pt sl, shd; wc; chem disp; mv service pnt; shwrs inc; EHU (5-10A) PLN12; lndry; sm shop; supmkt 4km; rest 1km; playgrnd; lake sw & windsurfing 6km; dogs PLN5; poss v cr; some Eng spkn; adv bkg (rec for upper pitches); quiet but some rd noise; red long stay/CKE/CCI. "On rd to Auschwitz; salt mine at Wieliczka; friendly, well-kept site; spotless san facs; lower field (m'vans) poss muddy after rain - tractor tow avail; poss rallies on site; gd tour base; frequent bus to Krakow connects with trams to cent; cycle rte to cent; gd security; tours with pick-up fr site; excel; v helpful and friendly." PLN 85 2014*

KRETOWINY see Morąg *A3*

LEBA *A2* (2km N Coastal) *54.76150, 17.53833* **Camping Morski (No. 21), ul Turystyczna 3, 84-360 Łeba [tel/fax (059) 8661380; camp21@op.pl; www.camping21.interleba.pl]** N fr Lębork on E214. In Łeba foll sp Camping Raphael & pass rlwy stn on L, over rv bdge twd sea. Site sp. Lge, hdg/mkd pitch, pt shd; htd wc; chem disp; mv service pnt; fam bthrm; shwrs inc; EHU (10A) PLN12; lndry (inc dryer); shop adj; rest; bar; BBQ; cooking facs; playgrnd; sand beach 150m; tennis; wifi; TV; dogs PLN8; phone; poss cr, adv bkg; CKE/CCI. "Nice, well-run site in gd position; modern san facs; pleasant resort; excel; Lacka sand dunes worth a visit." ♦ 1 May-30 Sep. PLN 94 (CChq acc) 2013*

LEBA *A2* (2km NE Urban) *54.76580, 17.57145* **Camping Przymorze Nr. 48, ul. Nadmorska 9, 84-360 Leba [059 866 5016; fax 866 1304; biuro@camping.leba.pl; www.camping.leba.pl]** Take DW214 dir Leba, at rndabt take 1st exit onto aleja swietego Jakuba. Turn R onto Nadmorska & foll sp to camp. Lge, mkd pitch, pt shd; htd wc; chem disp; mv service pnt; shwrs inc; EHU; lndry; shop; rest; BBQ; playgrnd; sandy beach 0.5km; wifi; TV rm; 10% statics; dogs; phone; bus adj; poss cr; Eng spkn; quiet; ccard acc; CCI. "Excel site; shops & rest in walking dist; interesting harbour with fresh fish for sale; windsurfing; lovely sandy beach." ♦ 1 May-30 Sep. PLN 110 2014*

LEGNICA *C2* (13km SE Rural) *51.14216, 16.24006* **Camping Legnickie Pole (No. 234), Ul Henryka Brodatego 7, 59-241 Legnickie Pole [(076) 8582397; fax 8627577; osir.legnica@wp.pl; www.osir.legnica.pl]** Fr A4/E40 fr Görlitz take exit dir Legnickie Pole/Jawor, foll sp to vill & site. Sharp L turn after leaving main rd. Site sp on S o'skirts of Legnica on E65 & fr m'way. Sm, pt shd; wc; shwrs inc; EHU (10A) inc; shop 500m; snacks; bar; playgrnd; dogs PLN8; poss cr; no adv bkg; red rate LS; CKE/CCI. "Helpful, friendly welcome; clean, basic facs (hot water to shwrs only); poss diff after heavy rain; gd NH on way S; pleasant vill." ♦ 1 May-30 Sep. PLN 44 2017*

LUBLIN *C4* (8km S Rural) *51.19186, 22.52725* **Camping Graf Marina (No. 65), ul Krężnicka 6, 20-518 Lublin [tel/fax (081) 7441070 or (0607) 455320; info@graf-marina.pl; grafmarina.obitur.pl]** Take rd 19 S & cross rlwy line; lge parking area after 1.8km then L after 300m (no sp but leads to Zemborzyce); in 5km cross rlwy then L at T-junc; site on R in 5km on lakeside. Med, hdg/mkd pitch, unshd; wc; own san; shwrs inc; EHU (10A); shop 3km; rest; sand beach & lake sw adj; statics; Eng spkn; quiet but rd & rlwy noise; CKE/CCI. "Marina adj; sailing; fishing; site run down (early ssn 2011); sodden after rain." 1 May-30 Sep. PLN 71 2016*

MIELNO *A2* (800m E Coastal) *54.26272, 16.07245* **Camping Rodzinny (No. 105), ul Chrobrego 51, 76-032 Mielno [(094) 3189385; fax 3475008; recepcja@campingrodzinny.pl; www.campingrodzinny.pl]** Fr Koszalin W on rd 11, turn N onto rd 165 to Mielno turn R at rdbt then 1 1/2 km & foll site sp. Site on L thro narr gate bet gardens - easy to miss. Sm, pt shd; htd wc; chem disp; EHU (6A) PLN1.50; lndry; shop; BBQ; cooking facs; playgrnd; sand beach 500m; games rm; internet; some statics; dogs PLN5; poss cr; some Eng spkn; adv bkg; quiet; CKE/CCI. "Easy walk to town; secure, well-kept, family-owned site; gd san facs; Gd site local to beach and shops; friendly owners." ♦ 15 Apr-15 Nov. PLN 88 2013*

"I need an on-site restaurant"

We do our best to make sure site information is correct, but it is always best to check any must-have facilities are still available or will be open during your visit.

MIKOLAJKI *A3* (1.5km SW Rural) *53.7954, 21.56471* **Camping Wagabunda (No. 2), ul Leśna 2, 11-730 Mikołajki [tel/fax (087) 4216018; wagabunda-mikolajki@wagabunda-mikolajki.pl; www.wagabunda-mikolajki.pl]** Exit town by rd 16 dir Mrągowo & site sp to L. Med, pt sl, unshd; wc; shwrs inc; EHU (16A) PLN13; lndry; shop & 1.5km; rest, snacks; shgl beach 2km; lake sw 400m; games area; TV; 50% statics; dogs PLN2.50; phone; poss cr; adv bkg; quiet; no ccard acc; twin-axles extra charge; Eng spkn; red LS/CKE/CCI. "Pleasant site nr nice town; san facs adequate but need update (2011); conv Masurian Lakes & historical sites; vg site; 10 min walk into town." ♦ 1 May-30 Sep. PLN 82 2013*

MORAG *A3* (11km E Rural) *53.90373, 20.02753* **Camping Kretowiny (No. 247), Kretowiny29, 14-300 Morag [(089) 7582440 or (697) 523402 (mob); pensjonat@narie.pl; www.narie.pl]** Fr cent Morąg foll rd 527 S twd Olsztyn but bef exit town, fork L at sp Żabi Róg/Kretowiny. Site sp on Lake Jezioro Narie. Med, hdg pitch, pt shd; wc; chem disp; shwrs; EHU (6A) PLN8; lndry; shop; rest; bar; playgrnd; lake sw; fishing; watersports; tennis; games area; games rm; quiet; CKE/CCI. "On shore of lge, lovely lake with sw, boating, fishing; pleasant, attractive site." ♦ 1 May-30 Sep. PLN 34 2013*

⊞ **MRAGOWO** *A3* (11km N Rural) *53.94278, 21.32001* **Camping Seeblick, Ruska Wieś 1, 11-700 Mrągowo [tel/fax (089) 7413155; marian.seeblick@gmail.com; www.campingpension.de]** Fr Mrągowo N on rd 591 dir Ketrzyn, site sp. Med, terr, pt shd; htd wc; chem disp; shwrs inc; EHU inc; lndry rm; shop 500m; rest; bar; lake sw; boating; tennis; games area; entmnt; quiet. "Gd but ltd san facs; lots for kids to do; shop nrby; little Eng spkn." PLN 50 2012*

⊞ **NIEDZICA** *D3* (3.5km SE Urban) *49.40477, 20.33411* **Camping Polana Sosny (No. 38), Osiedle Na Polanie Sosny, 34-441 Niedzica [tel/fax (018) 2629403; polana.sosny@niedzica.pl; www.niedzica.pl]** Rte 969 fr Nowy Targ. At Dębno turn R & foll sp to border (lake on L). At 11km pass castle & 1st dam on L twds 2nd Dunajec dam. Site sp. Sm, mkd pitch, unshd; htd wc; chem disp; shwrs; fam bthrm; EHU inc; lndryl shop 1.5km; rest adj; snacks; bar; cooking facs; rv adj; watersports; games area; phone; quiet but noise fr dam; adv bkg; quiet; red long stay; CKE/CCI. "Beautiful, well-maintained site in superb location; friendly, helpful staff; clean, modern san facs; excel walks in mountains; 2km to Slovakian border; vg touring base." ♦ PLN 50 2016*

⊞ **OSWIECIM** *D3* (4km S Rural) *50.02262, 19.19891* **Centre for Dialogue & Prayer in Auschwitz, ul Maksymiliana Kolbego 1, 32-600 Oświęcim [(033) 8431000; fax 8431001; biuro@centrum-dialogu.oswiecim.pl; www.centrum-dialogu.oswiecim.pl]** 700m fr Auschwitz 1 museum car park on parallel rd to S, on forecourt of hotel-like building. Sm, hdstg, unshd; wc; shwrs inc; EHU inc; shops 2km; rest; BBQ; phone; Eng spkn; rd noise; CKE/CCI. "Conv Auschwitz museum & Auschwitz-Birkenau (3km); clean, modern, site; gd, clean san facs, similar quality to UK CC sites; friendly, helpful staff; very nice site; excel facs; a gem of a site; highly rec." ♦ PLN 80 2015*

⊞ **OSWIECIM** *D3* (2km W Urban) *50.02895, 19.20054* **Parking Przy Museum Auschwitz, 32-600 Oświęcim** Foll sp to Auschwitz museum fr rd 933. Parking area is on opp side of rd (away fr main car park) by TO. M'vans only. Sm; EHU (6A) PLN7; shop; rest, snacks; bar; internet; water PLN6; dogs; quiet. "NH only permitted; ltd EHU; allow 4 hrs for museum tour; basically a big car park with a few elec points; internet at TO or wifi at pizza rest." PLN 40 2014*

POLANICA ZDROJ see Kłodzko *D2*

⊞ **POZNAN** *B2* (5km E Urban) *52.40343, 16.98399* **Camping Malta (No. 155), ul Krańcowa 98, 61-036 Poznań-Malta [(061) 8766203; fax 8766283; camping@malta.poznan.pl; www.poznan.pl]** Fr A2/E30 Poznań bypass leave at rte 2/11 dir Poznań. Turn R at traff lts onto rte 5/E261 sp Malta, Zoo & camping, site sp. Sm, hdg pitch, pt shd; htd wc; chem disp; shwrs inc; EHU (16A) inc; lndry; shop; snacks; bar; shop 1km; lake adj; many statics; tram to city; Eng spkn; quiet but loud disco across lake at w/end; ccard acc; red CKE/CCI. "Clean tidy site on lake with sports but poss unkempt pitches LS; 6 tram stops to Poznań Sq; vg 24-hr security; helpful staff; site amongst sports facs by lake." ♦ PLN 108 2014*

PRZEWORSK *D4* (1km W Urban) *50.06138, 22.48361* **Camping Pastewnik (No. 221), ul Łańcucka 2, 37-200 Przeworsk [(016) 6492300; fax 6492301; zajazdpastewnik@hot.pl; www.pastewnik.prv.pl]** On N side of N4/E40, sp. Sm, pt shd; wc; shwrs inc; EHU (10A) PLN10; lndry; shop adj; rest, snacks; bar; playgrnd; Eng spkn; rd noise; ccard acc; CKE/CCI. "Conv NH/sh stay with motel & rest; Łańcut Castle & Carriage Museum 25km; elec v dubious, no socket circuit breakers." 1 May-30 Sep. PLN 112 2013*

⊞ **RUCIANE NIDA** *A3* (8km N Rural) *53.68668, 21.54713* **Camping Nad Zatoka (No. 9), Wygryny 52, 12-220 Ruciane Nida [(087) 4231597 or (502) 328111 (mob); fax 4236342; zbigre@orange.pl; www.ter-lid.com.pl]** Fr rte 58 N onto rd 610 NE twds Piecki for 4km. Turn R for Wygryny 2km, foll sp in vill. Sm, pt sl, unshd; wc; chem disp; mv service pnt; shwrs inc; EHU (16A) PLN10; lndry; shop 300m; rest, bar nrby; BBQ; playgrnd; sand beach; lake sw; canoe & bike hire; dogs PLN6; poss cr; quiet. "Private site in field on lakeside; beautiful scenery; vg san facs; excel." PLN 50 2013*

RYDZEWO MILKI see Giżycko *A3*

SANDOMIERZ *C3* (1km E Urban) *50.68010, 21.75502* **Camping Browarny (No. 201), ul Żwirki I Wigury 1, 27-600 Sandomierz [(015) 8332703; fax 8323050; wmajsak@poczta.fm; www.majsak.pl]** Diff app to site off dual c'way. App on rd 77 fr N only. Avoid town ctr, 2.5 tonne weight limit. Sm, pt shd; wc; chem disp; mv service pnt; shwrs inc; EHU (16A) PLN10; lndry; shop in town; rest nr; bar; BBQ; cooking facs; playgrnd; games rm; dogs; wifi; phone; bus adj; poss cr; Eng spkn; adv bkg; some rd noise; CKE/CCI. "Attractive sm town in walking dist; vg site; helpful staff; red for 'vans under 5mtrs." ♦ 1 May-30 Sep. PLN 57 2017*

SOPOT *A2* (2km N Urban) *54.46136, 18.5556* **Camping Kamienny Potok (No. 19), ul Zamkowa Góra 25, 220-474 and 27-468 Sopot [tel/fax (058) 5500445; kempingnr19@wp.pl; www.kemping19.cba.pl]** Fr Gdańsk rte 27 twds Sopot. Site on R just behind Shell petrol stn. Fr N on rte 6/E28 turn S at Gdynia, onto new section of E28, for 7.5km. Turn L onto rte 220 by 'Euromarket' for 5km. Turn R onto rte 27 (S) twd Gdańsk & site nr Shell g'ge on opp c'way. Lge, mkd pitch, pt shd; wc; chem disp; shwrs inc; EHU (2-20A) PLN10; lndry; shop 500m; snacks; bar; playgrnd; internet; TV; phone; poss cr; rd & rlwy noise; ccard acc; red CKE/CCI. "Pleasant site; friendly & helpful staff; frequent trains for Gdansk 250m; modern, clean san facs; gd security; gd walking/cycling track into town; busy site; upgrades in process (2012)." 1 May-30 Sep. PLN 72 2012*

STETTIN see Szczecin *B1*

STRZESZYNEK see Poznań *B2*

SULECIN *B1* (4km S Rural) *52.40911, 15.11761* **Camping Marina (No. 50), Ostrów 76, 69-200 Sulęcin [tel/fax (957) 552294 or (171) 3704553; przemyslaw-gula@wp.pl; www.camping-marina.eu]** Cross border fr Frankfurt-an-Oder & take rd 2 to Torzym (35km). In Torzym turn L onto rd 138 dir Sulęcin; thro Tursk & site in 3km. Med, mkd pitch, pt shd; wc; mv service pnt; shwrs; EHU €2; lndry; supmkt 4km; snacks; bar; playgrnd; lake sw; fishing; bike hire; wifi; TV rm; some statics; dogs €1; adv bkg; quiet; red CKE/CCI. "Gd, modern san facs; gd walking/cycling; pleasant, relaxing site; conv Berlin." ♦ 1 Apr-31 Oct. PLN 63 2013*

SUWALKI *A3* (11km SE Rural) *54.0767, 23.0742* **Kajaki Camping Pokoje, 16-412 Stary Folwark 44, Wigry [(087) 5637789; wigry@wigry.info; www.wigry.info]** Fr Suwalki take 653 dir Sejny. In about 11km turn R in Stary Folwark at PTTK sp. Site on R in approx 100m. Sm, unshd; wc; chem disp; shwrs inc; EHU (10A) inc; lndry; BBQ; lake sw & kayaking nrby; wifi; Eng spkn; quiet. "Nr lake in National Park; kayaking fr site; vg site." 1 May-30 Sep. PLN 40 2016*

SWIECIE *B2* (1km S Urban) *53.40321, 18.45574* **Camping Zamek (No. 54), ul Zamkowa 10, 86-100 Świecie [tel/fax (052) 3311726 or 604 993 070; recepcja@camping-zamek.pl; www.camping-zamek.pl]** S fr Gdańsk on E75 take rd 1 to Chełmno & Świecie. Cross Rv Wisła & L at x-rds in Świecie cent; site sp at traff lts. Med, shd; wc; own san rec; shwrs; EHU (10A); lndry; shop; bar; playgrnd; games area; fishing; 50% statics; dogs; phone; quiet. "Interesting town & churches; helpful staff; in castle grnds (tower visible fr rd); if gate clsd, ring bell on L; new tolet block (2012)." 1 May-15 Sep. PLN 25 2012*

⊞ **SWINOUJSCIE** *A1* (2km N Coastal) *53.91709, 14.25693* **Camping Relax (No. 44), ul Słowackiego 1, 72-600 Świnoujście [(097) 3213912; relax@osir.uznam.net.pl; www.camping-relax.com.pl]** Fr E rd 3/E65 cross rv on free ferry. Fr town cent N for 500m. No vehicle border x-ing fr W. V lge, shd; wc; shwrs inc; EHU (16A) PLN10; lndry; shops 500m; snacks; cooking facs; playgrnd; beach 200m; games rm; wifi; phone; quiet; adv bkg; ccard acc. "Nice town; gd beach; gd walking; site popular with families; red snr citizens." PLN 65 2012*

⊞ **SZCZECIN/STETTIN** *B1* (8km SE Rural) *53.39505, 14.63640* **Marina Camping (No. 25), ul Przestrzenna 23, 70-800 Szczecin-Dabie [tel/fax (091) 4601165; camping.marina@pro.onet.pl; www.campingmarina.pl]** Fr E28/A6 take A10 sp Szczecin. Immed after rlwy bdge turn R sp Dąbie. At traff lts in cent Dąbie turn L, site on R in approx 2km on lake. Med, pt shd; htd wc; mv service pnt; fam bthrm; shwrs; EHU (6A) inc; lndry (inc dryer); shop 2km; supmkt 3km; rest, snacks; bar; lake sw; boat hire; tennis; games area; dog; wifi; bus to Stettin; poss cr; noise fr late arr & early deps; red CKE/CCI. "Pleasant, lakeside site; clean, modern san facs but inadequate if site full; bus tickets fr recep; helpful staff; vg site on lake side." PLN 106 (CChq acc) 2014*

⊞ **TARNOW** *D3* (2km N Rural) *50.02320, 20.98813* **Camping Pod Jabłoniami (No. 202), ul Piłsudskiego 28a, 33-100 Tarnów [(014) 6215124; fax 6522933; recepcja@camping.tarnow.pl; www.camping.tarnow.pl]** E fr Kraków on E40, foll sp to Tarnów 'Centrum'. Turn L by Tesco & foll sp to site. Sm, pt sl, pt shd; wc; chem disp; shwrs inc; EHU (16A) PLN10; lndry; supmkt 2km; rest, bar 1km; BBQ; playgrnd; pool adj; wifi; TV; poss cr; Eng spkn; some rd noise; red CKE/CCI. "Walk to attractive town; vg site." ♦ ltd. PLN 85 2013*

⊞ **TORUN** *B2* (2km S Urban) *53.00138, 18.60472* **Camping Tramp (No. 33), ul Kujawska 14, 87-100 Torún [tel/fax (056) 6547187; tramp@mosir.torun.pl; www.mosir.torun.pl]** Cross bdge S of town & take 1st L at traff lts, site sp in 500m on rvside. Med, shd; wc; chem disp; shwrs; EHU (10A) inc; lndry; shop 500m; rest 1.5km; snacks; bar; games area; wifi; some statics; dogs PLN4.50; continual traff noise & poss noise fr bar; red CKE/CCI. "Noisy, busy site but reasonable; walking dist fr interesting old town across bdge; gd security; NH/sh stay only." ♦ PLN 68 2016*

UCIECHOW *C2* (1km E Rural) *50.75561, 16.69412* **Camping Forteca, ul. Wroclawska 12, 58-211 Uciechów (Dolnoslaskie) [(074) 8323008; info@campingforteca.nl; www.campingforteca.nl]** Fr cent of Dzierzoniów foll rd 384 twds Lagiewniki and Wroclaw for 4km. In cent of Uciechów go ahead at crossrds. After 400m turn R down gravel track sp to rest and parking. Sm, pt sl; wc; chem disp; child/fam bthrm; shwrs; EHU (16A) 15 ZL; rest, bar; BBQ; lake adj; wifi; 10% appartments; dog 5 ZL; twin axle; Eng spkn; adv bkg acc; CKE/CCI. "Pitches surround lake where sw; fishing and boating permitted; new clean toilet block; helpful, friendly family owners; lovely peaceful site LS; open plan, grassy site." 1 Apr-1 Oct. PLN 88 2013*

"Satellite navigation makes touring much easier"

Remember most sat navs don't know if you're towing or in a larger vehicle – always use yours alongside maps and site directions.

USTKA *A2* (1.6km SE Urban) *54.57655, 16.88088* **Camping Morski (No. 101), ul Armii Krajowej 4, Przewloka, 76-270 Ustka [tel/fax (059) 8144789 or 8144426; cam_mor@pro.onet.pl; www.camping-morski.afr.pl]** Fr Koszalin & Sławno to łlupsk on rd 6/E28 turn L to Ustka. Foll main rd which bears R & foll camping sp to R. After 200m turn R at rndabt & camp on L after 300m. Sm, pt shd; wc; shwrs; EHU (6A) inc; lndry; shop 500m; rest adj; snacks; bar; BBQ; playgrnd; beach 1.3km; tennis; dogs; quiet; red long stay/CKE/CCI. "Seaside resort with gd shopping & fishing port; vg for children; gd cycling; gd NH; 30 min walk to town." ♦ 1 May-30 Sep. PLN 60 2013*

WARSZAWA *B3* (13km SE Urban) *52.17798, 21.14727* **Camping Wok (No. 90), ul Odrębna 16, 04-867 Warszawa [(022) 6127951; fax 6166127; wok@campingwok.warszawa.pl; www.campingwok.warszawa.pl]** Fr city cent or fr W on E30, take bdge on E30 over Rv Wisła to E side of rv. Then take rte 801 for approx 8km (dual c'way). At rndabt double back for 600m & take 3rd R into Odrębna. Site 200m on R. Sm, shd; htd wc; chem disp; mv service pnt; fam bthrm; shwrs inc; EHU (10-16A) PLN15; gas; lndry; shop 700m; rest 1km; snacks; bar; BBQ; cooking facs; playgrnd; games area; internet; TV; bus/tram adj; Eng spkn; adv bkg; quiet; ccard acc; red CKE/CCI. "Lovely little site; v secure; spotless, modern san facs; helpful staff."
1 Apr-31 Oct. PLN 85 2012*

WARSZAWA *B3* (4km W Urban) *52.2144, 20.96575* **Majawa Camping (No. 123), ul Bitwy Warszawskiej 19/20, 02-366 Warszawa-Szczęśliwice [(022) 8229121; fax 8237244; biuro@majawa.pl; www.majawa.pl]** Fr W on E30/rd 2 at junc with E67/rd 8 rd goes S thro tunnel under rlwy then strt on under new over-pass. Site on R in 100m. On E67/rd 8 fr Wrocław app concrete monument 3m high in middle of tramway; turn L at traff lts. Hotel Vera on R, site on L. Fr cent of Warsaw, take rd no. 7/8 700m twds Katowice. Not v well sp fr cent of town. Ent & exit diff due v busy rd. Sm, pt shd; wc; chem disp; shwrs inc; EHU (6A) PLN15; lndry rm; shop 300m; rest 100m; BBQ; tennis; some statics; phone; bus 500m; poss cr; Eng spkn; quiet; ccard acc; red CKE/CCI. "Easy access to Warsaw & Royal Castle; gd meals at adj bowling alley or Vera hotel; poss lge rallies on site; friendly; poor condition but well positioned to get into city."
1 May-30 Sep. PLN 152 2014*

WARSZAWA *B3* (17km W Rural) *52.23066, 20.79196* **Campsite Kaputy 222, Sochaczewska 222, 05-850 Kreczki, (Mazowieckie) [(022) 1100061; biuro@camping222.pl; www.camping222.pl]** Head S on SS36, take exit Pescate twd Pescate/Lecco/Malgrate/SS583/Bellagio/Calco, cont strt; at rndabt take 3rd exit via Roma, go thro 1 rndabt; cont onto Via Statale, turn L onto Via Foppaola, site on L. Med, mkd pitch, htd wc; chem disp; mv service pnt; shwr; EHU 15PLN; lndry; bread on site; wifi 10PLN; dogs 5PLN; public transport adj; Eng spkn; quiet; CCI. "Fishing lake on site; NH or visit to Warsaw; excel san facs; clean, spacious site & easy to find." ♦ 15 Apr-31 Oct. PLN 95 2014*

WEGORZEWO *A3* (4km SE Rural) *54.18647, 21.77018* **Camping Rusałka (No. 175), ul Lesna 2, 11-600 Węgorzewo [(087) 4272191; fax 4272049; camp.175@wp.pl; www.cmazur.pl]** Fr rte 63 fr Giżycko to Węgorzewo turn W approx 3km SW of Węgorzewo. Foll sp to site. Lge, pt shd; wc; chem disp (wc); shwrs inc; EHU PLN8; lndry; shops 2km; snacks; bar; playgrnd; lake sw adj; fishing; sailing; many statics; dogs; quiet. "Lovely pt of Lake District; delightful situation; all facs at top of steep hill." 1 May-30 Sep. PLN 48 2012*

WIELICZKA *D3* (1.5km SE Urban) *49.98273, 20.07611* **Motel Camping Wierzynka, ul Wierzynka 9, 32-020 Wieliczka [tel/fax (012) 2783614; motel@nawierzynka.pl; www.nawierzynka.pl]** Site sp fr E40/rte 4 about 2km fr salt mine. Sm, some hdstg, pt sl, pt shd; wc; shwrs; EHU (10A) PLN10 (rev pol); shop 1.5km; rest, snacks; bar; bike hire; wifi; bus to Krakow; train 1km; poss cr; Eng spkn; quiet; ccard acc (fee); CKE/CCI. "10 pitches in pleasant setting; helpful staff; facs basic but clean; shwrs erratic; 2km fr salt mines; vg site, local to salt mines; shwr portacabin, but clean."
1 May-30 Sep. PLN 80 2014*

WROCLAW *C2* (4km NE Urban) *51.11722, 17.09138* **Stadion Olimpijski Camp (No. 117), ul Padarewskiego 35, 51-620 Wrocław [tel/fax (071) 3484651]** Fr A4 into Wrocław foll N8 sp Warszawa thro city. On N8 dir Warszawa, pass McDonalds, at fork in rd take Sienkiewicza to end, then Rozyckiego to stadium, site on R. If poss foll sp 'stadion' to camp; head for lighting towers of sports stadium if seen thro trees. Lge, pt shd; wc; shwrs inc; EHU (16A) PLN7.50; lndry rm; shops, rest adj; snacks; bar; BBQ; playgrnd; pool 700m; 10% statics; dogs; tram nr; phone; poss cr; no adv bkg; poss noise fr stadium; red CKE/CCI. "San facs basic but clean; site in need of modernisation (2010); gd security; v conv for city; run down."
1 May-15 Oct. PLN 75 2016*

⊞ **ZAKOPANE** *D3* (4km NE Rural) *49.32415, 19.98506* **Camping Harenda (No. 160), Oś Harenda 51B, 34-500 Zakopane [tel/fax (018) 2014700; harenda51b@gmail.com; www.harenda.tatrynet.pl]** On main rd to Zakopane fr N, after town sp turn R into petrol stn with McDonalds. Cont to R, pass Cmp Ustep on L then turn L over rv bdge to site in 200m on R. Med, pt sl, pt shd; htd wc; shwrs inc; chem disp; mv service pnt; EHU (10A) PLN10 (long lead req); lndry; shop 100m; rest; BBQ; playgrnd; dogs; wifi; poss cr; Eng spkn; no adv bkg; some train noise & barking dogs; red CKE/CCI. "Gd views Tatra mountains fr site; superb walking; poss rallies on site; poss unkempt LS; laundry done at modest cost; vg rest; rafting (not white water) on Dunajec Rv; Nowy Targ rec; lower site poss muddy in wet weather." PLN 52 2014*

ZAKOPANE *D3* (4km NE Rural) *49.32229, 19.98550* **Camping Ustup (No. 207), ul Ustup K/5, 34-500 Zakopane-Ustup [(0605) 950007; camping.ustup@gmail.com]** Turn R off Kraków-Zakopane rd 47 at petrol stn/McDonalds just after 1st town sp. Turn R again immed (also sp Cmg Harenda), site on L in 200m. Sm, pt sl, unshd; wc; chem disp; fam bthrm; shwrs inc; EHU (10A) inc; shop adj; rest opp; playgrnd; bus to town cent; poss cr; adv bkg; quiet; CKE/CCI. "Ideal cent for Tatra region; mountain views; excel, family-run site; v welcoming, friendly & helpful owner (ltd Eng); vg, clean san facs; grassy pitches; coach tours arranged fr adj g'ge info desk." 1 May-5 Oct. PLN 94 2014*

⊞ **ZAKOPANE** *D3* (3km SE Urban) *49.2830, 19.9690* **Camping Pod Krokwia (No. 97), ul Żeromskiego 26, 34-500 Zakopane [tel/fax (018) 2012256; camp@podkrokwia.pl; www.podkrokwia.pl]** Sp fr town cent. Fr N 2nd exit at 1st rndbt; strt over at 2nd rndbt; turn R at 3rd rndabt, then R in 250m. Site on L. Lge, hdstg, pt sl, shd; wc; chem disp; shwrs inc; EHU (10A) inc; lndry; shop 500m; rest, snacks; bar nr; BBQ; cooking facs; playgrnd; pool, tennis adj; bus to Kraków; ski slopes & cable cars; rafting on rapids; wifi; TV; dogs PLN5; phone; poss cr; Eng spkn; quiet; CKE/CCI. "Lge tent area; few mkd pitches; poss scruffy LS; poor san facs; conv town cent; muddy when set; conv Tatra Mountains; mountain walks; town v touristy; vg loc; ltd facs; free gas stove." PLN 65.4 2012*

⊞ **ZAMOSC** *C4* (1km SW Rural) *50.71919, 23.23908* **Camping Duet (No. 253), ul Królowej Jadwigi 14, 22-400 Zamość [tel/fax (084) 6392499; duet@virgo.com.pl]** Fr Zamość cent W on rd 74, site on R bef Castorama. Sm, pt shd; wc; chem disp (wc); shwrs inc; EHU PLN12; shop opp; rest, snacks; bar; pool 150m; some statics; dogs; poss cr; quiet; CKE/CCI. "Walk to attractive town; fair sh stay/NH." PLN 59 2016*

⊞ **ZGORZELEC** *C1* (1km N Urban) *51.15957, 15.00069* **Camping Zgorzelec, ul Lubańska 1a, 59-900 Zgorzelec [(075) 7752436; ardi@op.pl]** Ent Zgorzelec fr Germany & foll rd sp Zagan. Turn L at traff lts at BP g'ge INTO Lubanska rd sp 351 site on R after 560m, bef downwards hill. Only sp is at camp gate. Sm, pt sl, unshd; wc; EHU inc; CKE/CCI. "Conv NH." PLN 60 2012*

"There aren't many sites open at this time of year"

If you're travelling outside peak season remember to call ahead to check site opening dates – even if the entry says 'open all year'.

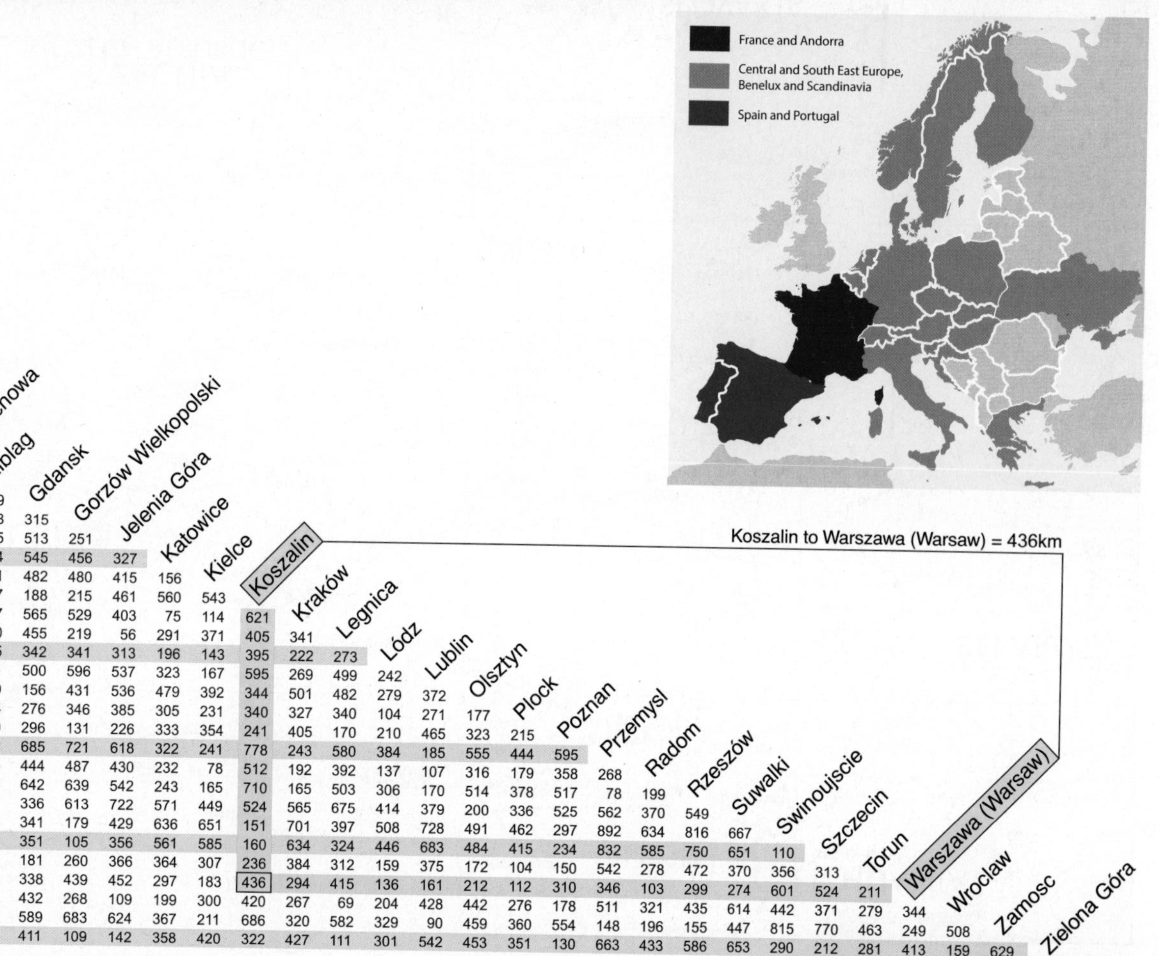

Koszalin to Warszawa (Warsaw) = 436km

	Biala Podlaska	Bialystok	Bielsko-Biala	Bydgoszcz	Czestochowa	Elblag	Gdansk	Gorzów Wielkopolski	Jelenia Góra	Katowice	Kielce	Koszalin	Kraków	Legnica	Lódz	Lublin	Olsztyn	Plock	Poznan	Przemysl	Radom	Rzeszów	Suwalki	Swinoujscie	Szczecin	Torun	Warszawa (Warsaw)	Wroclaw	Zamosc
Bialystok	149																												
Bielsko-Biala	472	543																											
Bydgoszcz	412	392	447																										
Czestochowa	365	410	133	314																									
Elblag	404	320	584	171	451																								
Gdansk	461	379	617	167	473	59																							
Gorzów Wielkopolski	596	603	496	214	415	333	315																						
Jelenia Góra	605	641	348	344	285	515	513	251																					
Katowice	416	485	58	391	75	524	545	456	327																				
Kielce	262	365	207	348	124	461	482	480	415	156																			
Koszalin	596	570	618	198	508	247	188	215	461	560	543																		
Kraków	376	477	86	434	114	567	565	529	403	75	114	621																	
Legnica	567	603	301	288	247	460	455	219	56	291	371	405	341																
Lódz	286	322	252	203	121	325	342	341	313	196	143	395	222	273															
Lublin	127	260	362	421	288	441	500	596	537	323	167	595	269	499	242														
Olsztyn	305	223	537	217	401	99	156	431	536	479	392	344	501	482	279	372													
Plock	267	270	363	150	230	234	276	346	385	305	231	340	327	340	104	271	177												
Poznan	470	488	387	131	289	300	296	131	226	333	354	241	405	170	210	465	323	215											
Przemysl	312	445	319	588	342	622	685	721	618	322	241	778	243	580	384	185	555	444	595										
Radom	184	285	285	322	181	383	444	487	430	232	78	512	192	392	137	107	316	179	358	268									
Rzeszów	297	430	238	513	272	585	642	639	542	243	165	710	165	503	306	170	514	378	517	78	199								
Suwalki	269	117	631	417	497	277	336	613	722	571	449	524	565	675	414	379	200	336	525	562	370	549							
Swinoujscie	730	701	676	312	586	400	341	179	429	636	651	151	701	397	508	728	491	462	297	892	634	816	667						
Szczecin	677	656	603	267	520	374	351	105	356	561	585	160	634	324	446	683	484	415	234	832	585	750	651	110					
Torun	366	347	422	46	290	167	181	260	366	364	307	236	384	312	159	375	172	104	150	542	278	472	370	356	313				
Warszawa (Warsaw)	157	188	355	252	222	280	338	439	452	297	183	436	294	415	136	161	212	112	310	346	103	299	274	601	524	211			
Wroclaw	496	532	230	265	176	436	432	268	109	199	300	420	267	69	204	428	442	276	178	511	321	435	614	442	371	279	344		
Zamosc	180	334	392	514	335	532	589	683	624	367	211	686	320	582	329	90	459	360	554	148	196	155	447	815	770	463	249	508	
Zielona Góra	570	601	387	259	328	430	411	109	142	358	420	322	427	111	301	542	453	351	130	663	433	586	653	290	212	281	413	159	629

BALTIC SEA
BORNHOLM IS
(Denmark)
RUSSIA
LITHUANIA
BELARUS
UKRAINE
GERMANY
CZECHIA
(CZECH REPUBLIC)
SLOVAKIA
Kaliningrad
VILNIUS
Marijampole
Hrodna
Slonim
Brest
Kovel'
Rostock
Greifswald
Sassnitz
ŚWINOUJŚCIE
Pasewalk
BERLIN
Frankfurt an der Oder
Cottbus
Dresden
Görlitz
Liberec
PRAHA
Hradec Králové
Ostrava
Mielno
Kołobrzeg
KOSZALIN
Ustka
Łeba
Kartuzy
Sopot
GDAŃSK
Frombork
Morąg
OLSZTYN
Mrągowo
Mikołajki
Ruciane-Nida
Węgorzewo
SUWAŁKI
Ełk
BIAŁYSTOK
Białowieża
BIAŁA PODLASKA
SZCZECIN
GORZÓW WIELKOPOLSKI
Sulecin
POZNAŃ
BYDGOSZCZ
Świecie
TORUŃ
PŁOCK
WARSZAWA
ZIELONA GÓRA
ŁÓDŹ
RADOM
Kazimierz Dolny
LUBLIN
ZAMOŚĆ
Uciechów
LEGNICA
WROCŁAW
Zgorzelec
JELENIA GÓRA
Karpacz
Kłodzko
CZĘSTOCHOWA
KIELCE
Sandomierz
KATOWICE
Oświęcim
KRAKÓW
Wieliczka
Tarnów
BIELSKO-BIAŁA
RZESZÓW
Przeworsk
Niedzica
Zakopane
A1
A2
A4
A18
N
E
S
W
All year site(s)
Seasonal site(s)
No sites listed
200m +
0–200m
0
50 kms
0
30 mls
Motorways
Major roads
Main roads
© Collins Bartholomew Ltd 2018

transport and a free one hour walking tour of the Old Town. The card can be obtained at tourist information centres, at the central railway station and at hotels.

In general Slovakia does not cater for the physically handicapped. For example, it is normal for cars to park on the pavement and dropped kerbs are perceived as helping drivers to achieve this without damaging tyres or suspension! Public transport invariably requires large steps to be climbed and bus and tram drivers tend to accelerate from stops at great speed, catching passengers by surprise. Access to most buildings is by steps, rather than ramps. However effort is now being taken to make buildings more accessible.

German is the most common second language, English is not widely understood or spoken.

Public Transport

From April to September hydrofoil services operate from Bratislava to Vienna and Budapest.

In Bratislava bus, trolley bus and tram tickets are valid for periods of up to 60 minutes, extending to up to 90 minutes at night and weekends. Buy them from kiosks and yellow ticket machines. Alternatively you can buy tickets valid for one or several city zones for a fixed period, e.g. 24, 48 or 72 hours or for seven days. Ensure that you validate your ticket on boarding the bus or tram.

Passengers aged 70 and over travel free; carry your passport as proof of age. You must buy a ticket for dogs travelling on public transport and they must be muzzled. You must also purchase a ticket for large items of luggage. For more information see www.imhd.zoznam.sk/ba.

Bojnice Castle

Sites in Slovakia

⊞ **BANSKA BYSTRICA** *B2* (11km W Rural) *48.7540, 487540* **Autocamping Tajov, 97634 Tajov [(048) 4197320; ks.rovdyklev@rovdyklev; www.velkydvor.sk/en]** Fr Tajov dir Kordíky. Site well sp 2km NW of Tajov. Sm, pt sl, unshd; htd wc; chem disp; shwrs inc; EHU (6-10A) inc; shop; snacks; bar; rest 300m; playgrnd; wifi; TV; statics; bus; quiet; red CKE/CCI. "Lovely setting in wooded valley; friendly welcome." € 16.00 2016*

BRATISLAVA *C1* (9km NE Urban) *48.18801, 17.18488* **Autocamping Zlaté Piesky, Senecká Cesta 12, 82104 Bratislava [tel/fax (02) 44257373 or 44450592; kempi@netax.sk; www.intercamp.sk]** Exit D1/E75 junc sp Zlaté Piesky. Site on S side of rd 61 (E75) at NE edge of Bratislava. Look for pedestrian bdge over rd to tram terminus, ent thro adj traff lts. If x-ing Bratislava foll sp for Žilina. In summer a 2nd, quieter, drier site is opened. For 1st site turn L when ent leisure complex; for 2nd site carry strt on then turn R. Med, shd; wc; shwrs inc; EHU (10A) €3 (long lead poss req); shop; supmkt (Tesco) 300m; rest, snacks; bar; playgrnd; sw & pedalos on lake; fishing; tennis; golf 10km; entmnt; dogs €2; phone; tram to city; poss cr; Eng spkn; v noisy fr adj m'way & bar; red CKE/CCI. "Basic site on lge leisure complex; no privacy in shwrs; ltd hot water; muddy in wet; security guard at night & secure rm for bikes etc but reg, major security problems as site grnds open to public; helpful, friendly staff; interesting city." 1 May-15 Oct. € 13.00 2016*

BREZNO *B3* (6km SE Rural) *48.79501, 19.72867* **Camping Sedliacky Dvor, Hliník 7, 97701 Brezno [(048) 911 078 303; info@sedliackydvor.com; www.sedliackydvor.com]** Fr cent of Brezno at traff lts nr Hotel Dumbier take rd 530/72 SE sp Tisovec. In approx 5km cross rlwy line & ent vill of Rohozná. At end of vill turn L after Camping sp. Site in 500m. Sm, pt shd; wc; shwrs; EHU (10A) €3.25; lndry; cooking facs; pool; games area; wifi; dogs €1; Eng spkn; adv bkg; quiet. "Excel site in lovely orchard setting; welcoming Dutch owners; camp fires in evening; excel facs." 15 Apr-31 Oct. € 22.50 2013*

CEROVO *C2* (8km E Rural) *48.25228, 19.21783* **Camping Lazy, Cerovo 163, 96252 Cerovo [(090) 8590837; info@minicamping.eu; www.campinglazy.eu]** S fr Zvolen on rd 66 dir Krupina. S of Krupina turn L onto rd 526 to Bzovik. After church in Bzovik turn R sp Kozí Vrbovok, Trpin & Litava. Cont thro Litava (agricultural co-operative, Družstvo, on R) & cont for approx 5km to T-junc with bus shelter & turn R. Do not foll sp Cerovo on R but cont to forest & look out for sm lane & site sp to R. Sm, pt sl, pt shd; wc; chem disp; shwrs; EHU (4-6A) €2.50; lndry; some statics (equipped tents); dogs free; quiet. "Site on working farm; ideal for nature lovers, hikers, dog owners; pleasant, helpful owners; v clean, modern facs." 1 May-30 Sep. € 16.00 2013*

DEMANOVSKA DOLINA see Liptovský Mikuláš *B3*

⊞ **LEVOCA** *B3* (5km N Rural) *49.04982, 20.58727* **Autocamping Levočská Dolina, 05401 Levoča [tel/fax (053) 4512705 or 4512701; rzlevoca@pobox.sk]** Site on E side of minor rd 533 running N fr E50 at Dolina to Levočská Dolina. Steep ent; ltd access lge o'fits. Med, sl, pt shd; wc; chem disp; shwrs inc; EHU (16A) €3; lndry; shop 3km; rest, snacks; bar; playgrnd; ski lift 2.5km; TV; dogs €1.50; Eng spkn; quiet; CKE/CCI. "Diff in wet weather due v sl grnd; friendly staff; interesting old town; Spišský Hrad castle worth visit; walks in forests around site." € 18.00 2016*

⊞ **LIPTOVSKY MIKULAS** *B3* (11km NW Rural) *49.13608, 19.5125* **Resort Villa Betula (formerly Penzión), 03223 Liptovský Sielnica [(907) 812327; villabetula@villabetula.sk; www.villabetula.sk]** Fr rd 18/E50 exit onto R584 to Liptovský Mikuláš, site on N of lake 6km past Autocamp. Med, unshd; wc; chem disp; sauna; fam bthrm; shwrs inc; EHU (10A) inc; rest; bar; playgrnd; lake sw adj; bike hire; jacuzzi; wifi; dogs €7; phone; Eng spkn; quiet; ccard acc; CKE/CCI. "Family-friendly, gem of a site in wonderful area of lakes, mountains & forest; welcoming, helpful owners; v clean & well-kept; vg rest; site at rear of hotel; excel for long or sh stay." € 26.00 2015*

"That's changed – Should I let The Club know?"

If you find something on site that's different from the site entry, fill in a report and let us know. See camc.com/europereport.

LIPTOVSKY SIELNICA see Liptovský Mikuláš *B3*

LIPTOVSKY TRNOVEC see Liptovský Mikuláš *B3*

NITRIANSKE RUDNO *B2* (1km N Rural) *48.80457, 18.47601* **Autocamping Nitrianske Rudno, 97226 Nitrianske Rudno [(090) 5204739; info@camping-nrudno.sk; www.camping-nrudno.sk]** E fr Bánovce & Dolné Vestenice on rd 50, turn N onto rd 574. Site on shore of Lake Nitrianske Rudno, sp in vill. Med, pt shd; wc; shwrs; EHU €2.50; lndry; snacks; bar; cooking facs; playgrnd; lake sw; watersports; games area; internet; entmnt; some statics; dogs €1; adv bkg; quiet; red CKE/CCI. "Welcoming, helpful owner; pleasant location." 1 Jun-30 Sep. € 13.00 2016*

PREŠOV *B4* (13km W Rural) *49.00386, 21.08145* **Autokemping A Motorest Kemp, Chminianske Nová Ves, District Prešov 082 33 [0517 795190 or 0905 191056 (mob); kemppo@kemppo.sk; www.kemppo.sk]** Fr W on Rte 18/D1/E50, take exit twd Vit'az/ Hrabkov, site on R. Sm pt shd; wc shwrs inc; gas; EHU €4; lndry with campers kitchen; shop, rest, snacks, bar, BBQ; cooking facs; plygrnd; games area; dog €2; twin axles acc; Eng spkn; quiet; ccard acc; CKE/CCI. "Site behind motorest Kemp on Rte 18; recep in rest; 5 chalets for rent on site; fair site." Feb-Dec. € 15.00 2014*

ROZNAVA *B3* (6km E Rural) *48.64920, 20.59796* **Autocamping Krásnohorské, Hradná 475, 04941 Krásnohorské Podhradie [(058) 7325457; fax 7921332]** E fr Rožňava on rd 50/E571 foll sp Krásnohorské Podhradie. Site under shadow of castle. Sm, pt shd; wc; shwrs; mainly huts. "Lovely setting in pine woods; primitive facs but plenty of hot water; conv for cave visits." € 10.00 2012*

TAJOV see Banská Bystrica *B2*

TATRANSKA LOMINICA *B3* (2.6km S Rural) *49.14974, 20.27968* **Camping Rijo (formerly Jupela), Dolny Smokovec, 3705981 Vysoke Tatry [(421) 911 616530; rijocamping@rijocamping.eu; www.rijocamping.eu]** Fr Tatranska Lominca travel W on 537 take L turn twrds Nova Lesna. Foll sp to site. Sm, pt shd; wc; chem disp; shwrs; EHU 16A €3.50; snacks; bar; BBQ; playgrnd; adv bkg. "Beautiful location nr to mountain torrent; conv for walking in Takranska; basic clean san facs; lovely spot; walks and scenice drives." 7 May-16 Sep. € 13.00 2013*

⊞ **TATRANSKA LOMNICA** *B3* (2.5km ESE Rural) *49.15830, 20.30979* **Intercamp Tatranec, 05960 Tatranská Lomnica [(052) 4467092; fax 4467082; hoteltatranec@hoteltatranec.com]** NE fr Poprad on rd 67, after 8km turn L over level x-ing, thro Vel'ká Lomnica twds Tatranská Lomnica on rd 540. Site on L. Lge, pt sl, unshd; wc; chem disp; shwrs inc; EHU (6A) inc; lndry; shop & 4km; rest; bar; playgrnd; wifi; entmnt; Eng spkn; adv bkg; quiet; red CKE/CCI. "Superb views of High Tatras; conv cable car, train etc; excel base for walking & holiday resort; hotel adj; poor, dated facs & ltd privacy." € 18.50 2015*

TERCHOVA *B2* (3km SW Rural) *49.24779, 18.98866* **Autocamp Belá, Nižné Kamence, 01305 Belá [(041) 5695135 or (905) 742514; camp@bela.sk; www.campingbela.eu]** Fr Zilina foll rd 583 twd Terchová. Site on L 3km after vill of Belá. Med, pt shd; wc; chem disp; mv service pnt; shwrs €0.30; EHU (10A) €3; lndry rm; shop; rest, snacks; BBQ; cooking facs; playgrnd; tennis; 10% statics; dogs €1; rd noise. "Delightful rvside site; gd welcome; clean, modern san facs; conv walking in Malá Fatra mountains." 1 May-15 Oct. € 11.50 2016*

TRENCIN *B2* (2km N Urban) *48.90011, 18.04076* **Autocamping Na Ostrove, Ostrov, 91101 Trenčín [(032) 7434013; autocamping.tn@mail.pvt.sk; http://web.viapvt.sk/autocamping.tn]** Fr SW on rd 61/E75 cross rv at Hotel Tatra, 1st L dir Sihot, go under rlwy bdge. 1st L, then immed 1st L again, then R at stadium, cross canal to island, site on L. Sm, unshd; wc; chem disp; shwrs inc; 25% serviced pitches; EHU (10A) €3; lndry; shop in town; snacks; bar; cooking facs; pool 500m; 90% statics; dogs €1.50; poss cr; some Eng spkn; some noise fr rlwy & sports stadium; CKE/CCI. "Popular NH en rte Poland, rec arr early high ssn; on rvside in run down pt of town adj sports stadium; adj delightful town with fairy-tale castle; poss waterlogged in wet; facs old but clean - some lack privacy." 1 May-15 Sep. € 18.00 2013*

ZVOLEN *B2* (6km NW Rural) *48.60611, 19.10175* **Autocamp Kovácová, Kúpeľná ul, 96237 Kovácová [(045) 5445220; recent@recent.sk]** Fr E77/66 dir Banská Bystrica turn at sp Kovácová. In vill foll site sp. Med, pt sl, pt shd; wc; chem disp (wc); shwrs inc; EHU €2.50; lndry rm; shop 500m; snacks; bar; BBQ; cooking facs; htd pool adj; TV rm; 40% statics; Eng spkn; quiet; CKE/CCI. "Clean site but run down (6/09); friendly owner." 30 May-31 Aug. € 9.00 2016*

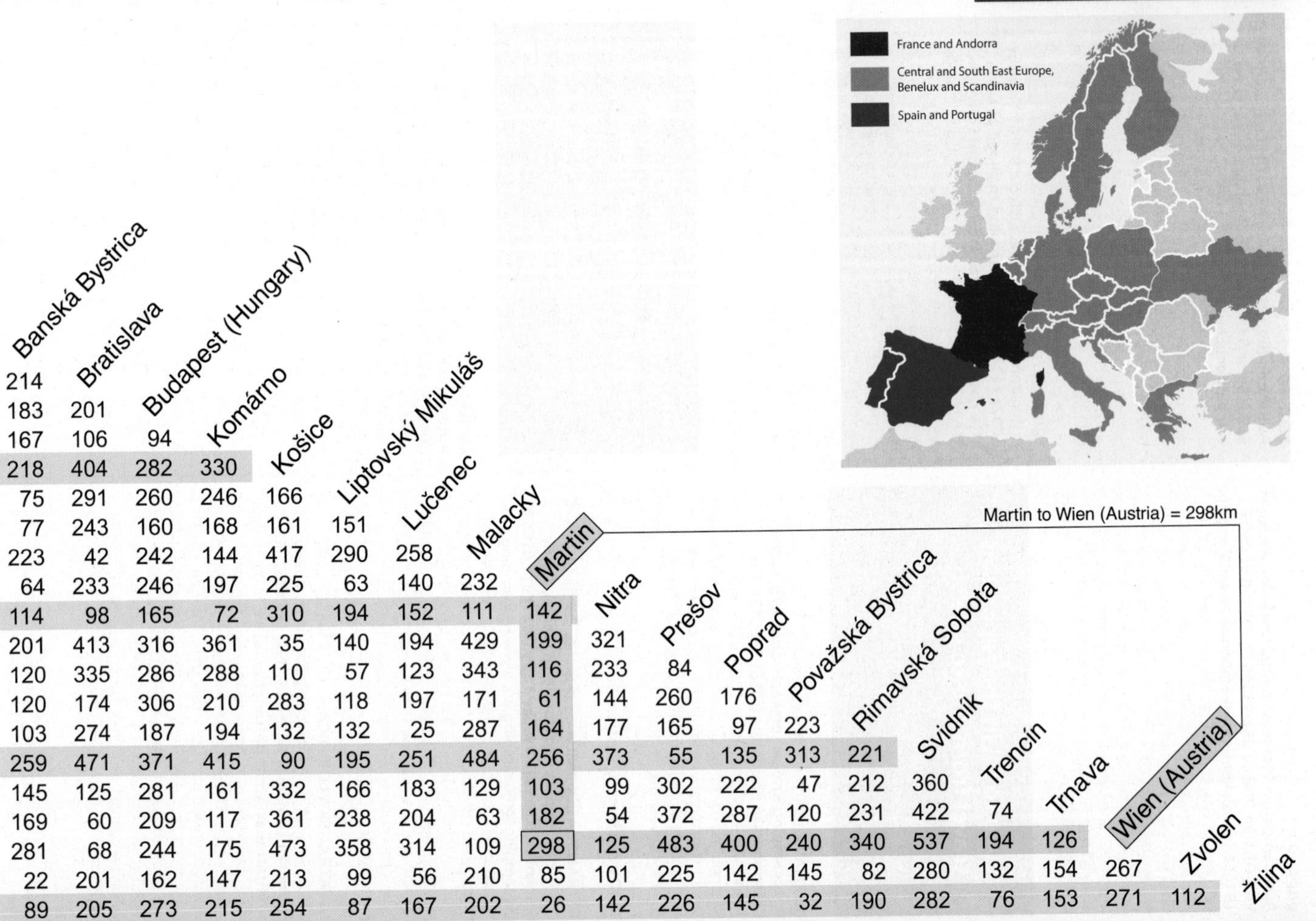

	Banská Bystrica	Bratislava	Budapest (Hungary)	Komárno	Košice	Liptovský Mikuláš	Lučenec	Malacky	Martin	Nitra	Prešov	Poprad	Považská Bystrica	Rimavská Sobota	Svidník	Trencín	Trnava	Wien (Austria)	Zvolen
Bratislava	214																		
Budapest (Hungary)	183	201																	
Komárno	167	106	94																
Košice	218	404	282	330															
Liptovský Mikuláš	75	291	260	246	166														
Lučenec	77	243	160	168	161	151													
Malacky	223	42	242	144	417	290	258												
Martin	64	233	246	197	225	63	140	232											
Nitra	114	98	165	72	310	194	152	111	142										
Prešov	201	413	316	361	35	140	194	429	199	321									
Poprad	120	335	286	288	110	57	123	343	116	233	84								
Považská Bystrica	120	174	306	210	283	118	197	171	61	144	260	176							
Rimavská Sobota	103	274	187	194	132	132	25	287	164	177	165	97	223						
Svidník	259	471	371	415	90	195	251	484	256	373	55	135	313	221					
Trencín	145	125	281	161	332	166	183	129	103	99	302	222	47	212	360				
Trnava	169	60	209	117	361	238	204	63	182	54	372	287	120	231	422	74			
Wien (Austria)	281	68	244	175	473	358	314	109	298	125	483	400	240	340	537	194	126		
Zvolen	22	201	162	147	213	99	56	210	85	101	225	142	145	82	280	132	154	267	
Žilina	89	205	273	215	254	87	167	202	26	142	226	145	32	190	282	76	153	271	112

Martin to Wien (Austria) = 298km

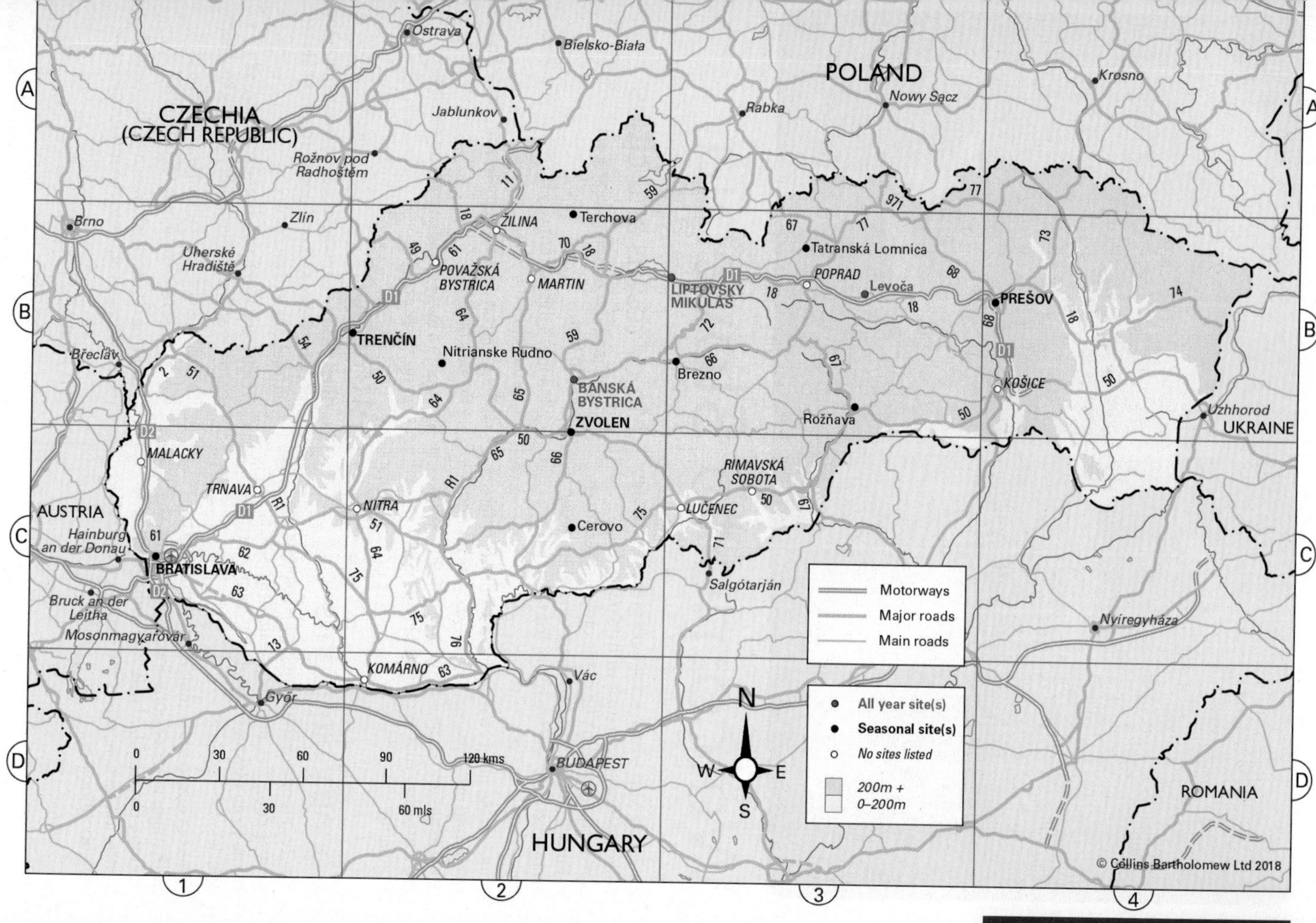
POLAND
CZECHIA
(CZECH REPUBLIC)
AUSTRIA
HUNGARY
UKRAINE
ROMANIA
Ostrava
Bielsko-Biała
Krosno
Nowy Sącz
Rabka
Jablunkov
Rožnov pod Radhoštěm
Brno
Zlín
Uherské Hradiště
Břeclav
ŽILINA
Terchova
POVAŽSKÁ BYSTRICA
MARTIN
LIPTOVSKÝ MIKULÁŠ
Tatranská Lomnica
POPRAD
Levoča
PREŠOV
TRENČÍN
Nitrianske Rudno
Brezno
BANSKÁ BYSTRICA
ZVOLEN
KOŠICE
Rožňava
Uzhhorod
MALACKY
TRNAVA
NITRA
RIMAVSKÁ SOBOTA
LUČENEC
Cerovo
Hainburg an der Donau
BRATISLAVA
Bruck an der Leitha
Mosonmagyaróvár
Salgótarján
Nyíregyháza
KOMÁRNO
Győr
Vác
BUDAPEST
Motorways
Major roads
Main roads
All year site(s)
Seasonal site(s)
No sites listed
200m +
0–200m
N
W
E
S
0
30
60
90
120 kms
60 mls
© Collins Bartholomew Ltd 2018

Lake Zelenci

Welcome to Slovenia

Equipped with an extraordinarily pretty landscape, Slovenia is deeply in tune with its natural surroundings and is one of the greenest countries in Europe. Outdoor pursuits are wholeheartedly embraced here and are top of the list when it comes to attractions.

There is also plenty to see and do for history fans to see and do - this small country boasts around 500 castles and manor houses. Not to be missed are the hilltop castles of Bled, Ljubljana and Predjama.

Country highlights

Slovenia is one of the world's most biologically diverse countries, and despite its small size is home to an estimated total of 45,000 - 120,000 species.

Slovenia is also a key centre for winter sports, with major competitions and events held in the country on a regular basis. Kanin, the highest ski centre in Slovenia, offers the opportunity to ski to neighbouring Italy.

Major towns and cities

- Ljubljana - a charming capital with an old-world feel.
- Maribor - this vibrant city holds many events throughout the year.
- Celje - an ancient settlement with Celtic and Roman origins.
- Kranj - a lively city with a castle and 14th century church.

Attractions

- Bled Castle - a medieval castle overlooking the popular Lake Bled, and one of the most visited attractions in the country.
- Tivoli Park, Ljubljana - home to botanical gardens and a contemporary history museum.
- Škocjan Caves - an extraordinary series of caves renowned as a natural treasure.
- Predjama Castle, Postojna - a gothic castle built 700 years ago into the mouth of a cave.

Find out more

www.slovenia.info
Tel: 0038 (0) 61 58 98 550 Slovenian Tourist Board

Touring

A 10% tip is usual in restaurants and for taxi drivers.

The capital, Ljubljana, is a gem of a city with many Baroque and Art Nouveau influences. The works of the world renowned architect Jože Plecnik are among the finest urban monuments in the city. A Ljubljana Card is available for one, two or three days and offers free travel on city buses, tourist boat trips, the city funicular, guided tours and the tourist train to Ljubljana Castle, plus free admission to museums together with discounts at a wide range of shops, restaurants and bars. You can buy the card at the main bus and railway stations, hotels and tourist information centres or from www.visitljubljana.si.

The largest cave in Europe is situated at Postojna, south west of Ljubljana and is a 'must' for tourists. Also worth visiting are the mountains, rivers and woods of Triglav National Park, which covers the major part of the Julian Alps, together with the oldest town in Slovenia, Ptuj, and the city of Maribor. In Lipica guided tours are available around the stud, home to the world famous Lipizzaner horses.

There is a hydrofoil service between Portorož and Venice from April to November.

Slovenian is the official language although Serbo-Croat is widely spoken. Most Slovenians speak at least one other major European language and many, especially the young, speak English.

Public Transport

There is an extensive bus network in Ljubljana. Buy a yellow 'top-up' Urbana card for a one-off payment of €2 from news-stands, tobacconists, tourist information offices or the central bus station and add credit (between €1 and €50) at the same locations or at the green Urbanomati machines around the city. When boarding a bus simply touch the card to one of the card readers at the front of the bus and €1.20 will be deducted allowing 90 minutes of unlimited travel regardless of how many changes you make. Taxis are generally safe, clean and reliable. Fares are metered. For longer distances ordering a taxi by phone will attract lower rates.

Bled

Sites in Slovenia

ANKARAN see Koper *D1*

BLED *B2 (4km SE Rural) 46.35527, 14.14833* **Camping Šobec, Šobčeva Cesta 25, 4248 Lesce [(04) 5353700; fax 5353701; sobec@siol.net; www.sobec.si]** Exit rte 1 at Lesce, site sp. Lge, pt shd, pt sl; wc; chem disp; mv service pnt; shwrs; EHU (16A) €3.70 (poss long lead req); lndry; shop; rest, snacks; bar; playgrnd; rv pool; many sports & activities; bike hire; internet; TV; wifi; dogs €3.50; bus 2km; Eng spkn; ccard acc; red 7+ days/CKE/CCI. "Excel, tranquil rvside site in wooded area surrounded by rv; friendly, helpful staff; lge pitches; clean san facs; gd rest; gd walking/cycling; real camping atmosphere, plenty of space; def rec; beautiful area; conv NH en-rte to Croatia." ♦ 15 Apr-1 Oct. € 35.00 2017*

BLED *B2 (6km SE Urban) 46.34772, 14.17284* **Camping Radovljica, Kopališka 9, 4240 Radovljica [(04) 5315770; fax 5301229; pkrad@plavalnicklub-radovljica.si]** Exit A1/E61 junc Bled/Bohinj, site in cent of Radovljica bet bus & train stn sp Camping & Sw. Med, pt sl, pt shd; wc; chem disp; shwrs inc; EHU (16A) inc; shop 500m; rest 300m; snacks adj; bar; playgrnd; pool adj; paddling pool; bike hire; fitness rm; wifi; 10% statics; dogs; poss cr; quiet; red long stay. "Vg; security gate; vg, clean san facs; gd NH; friendly staff." 1 Jun-15 Sep. € 38.00 2013*

BLED *B2 (4km SW Rural) 46.36155, 14.08066* **Camping Bled, Kidričeva 10c, SI 4260 Bled [04 5752000; fax 5752002; info@camping-bled.com; www.camping-bled.com]** Fr Ljubljana take E16/A2 & exit dir Bled/Lesce. At rndabt take 2nd exit for Bled & cont along rd 209. In Bled take rd around lake on L (lake on R), site sp - winding rd. Lge, some mkd pitch, pt sl, pt shd; wc; chem disp; mv service pnt; fam bthrm; shwrs inc; EHU (16A) inc (long lead req some pitches - fr recep); gas; lndry (inc dryer); shop, rest adj; snacks; bar; BBQ; playgrnd; shgl beach; lake sw adj; spa cent nrby; fishing; white water rafting; paragliding; horseriding; bike hire; games area; wifi; entmnt; games rm; TV rm; dogs €3; twin-axles acc (rec check in adv); m'van & car wash; dog shwrs; bus to Ljubljana adj; Eng spkn; fairly quiet but some rlwy noise; ccard acc; red long stay/LS/snr citizens/CKE/CCI. "Beautifully situated nr lake; busy, popular, well-run site; well-drained in bad weather altho lower pitches poss muddy; modern, clean san facs, stretched in ssn; helpful, efficient staff; conv Vintgar Gorge, Bled Castle, Lake Bohinj, Dragna Valley; excel walking/cycling around lake; excel rest." ♦ 1 Apr-15 Oct. € 33.00 SBS - X03 2017*

⊞ **BOHINJSKA BISTRICA** *B1 (800m NW Rural) 46.27438, 13.94798* **Camping Danica Bohinj, Triglavska 60, 4264 Bohinjska Bistrica [(04) 5721702; fax 5723330; info@camp-danica.si; www.camp-danica.si]** Site on o'skts of vill clearly sp. Med, pt shd; wc; chem disp; mv service pnt; shwrs; EHU (6A) inc (long lead poss req); gas; lndry; shops 500m; rest, snacks; bar; tennis; entmnt; lake sw 6km; canoe & kayak hire; fly-fishing; wifi; 10% statics; dogs €2; Eng spkn; quiet; ccard acc; red long stay/CCI. "Excel site, spacious, open, attractive site in beautiful valley; gd walking & climbing; gd, clean san facs but poss stretched high ssn; conv bus to Ljubljana & Lake Bohinji." € 38.00 2014*

"I need an on-site restaurant"

We do our best to make sure site information is correct, but it is always best to check any must-have facilities are still available or will be open during your visit.

BOHINJSKO JEZERO see Bohinjska Bistrica *B1*

BOVEC *B1 (1km E Rural) 46.33659, 13.55803* **Autocamp Polovnik, Ledina 8, 5230 Bovec [(05) 3896007; fax 3896006; kamp.polovnik@siol.net; www.kamp-polovnik.com]** Sp on rd 206 down fr Predil Pass (1,156m - 14% gradient) fr Italy - do not turn into vill. Site 200m after turn to Bovec. Sm, pt shd; wc; chem disp; shwrs €0.50; EHU (16A) €2.50 (poss rev pol); lndry (inc dryer); shop adj; rest, snacks; bar; BBQ; tennis; fishing; wifi; poss cr; no adv bkg; quiet; ccard acc; CKE/CCI. "Helpful staff; clean facs; muddy when wet; friendly staff." 1 Apr-15 Oct. € 30.00 2013*

BOVEC *B1 (9km E Rural) 46.33527, 13.64416* **Camping Soča, Soča 8, 5232 Soča [(05) 3889318; fax 3881409; kamp.soca@siol.net]** Sp on S side of rd 206 in national park, nr turning for Lepena approx 3km bef Soča vill. Lge, pt terr, pt shd; htd wc; chem disp; mv service pnt; shwrs inc; EHU (6A) inc; lndry; shop, rest 2km; snacks; bar; BBQ; playrnd; rv & shgl beach adj; TV rm; 50% statics (sep area); dogs €1; poss cr; Eng spkn; quiet; red long stay. "Beautiful situation in rv valley; gd, modern san facs; gd walking, rafting; gd touring base Triglav National Park; excel; braziers and wood avail; walking and cycling tracks fr site." ♦ ltd. 1 Apr-31 Oct. € 35.00 2013*

⊞ **BREZICE** *C3* (5km S Rural) *45.89138, 15.62611* **Camping Terme Čatež, Topliška Cesta 35, 8251 Čatež ob Savi [(07) 4936700; fax 6207804; info@terme-catez.si; www.terme-catez.si]** Exit E70 at Brežice, foll brown sp to Terme Čatež, then site sp. Lge, mkd pitch, pt shd; htd wc; chem disp; mv service pnt; sauna; fam bthrm; shwrs inc; EHU (10A) inc; gas; lndry (inc dryer); supmkt; rest, snacks; bar; BBQ area; playgrnd; thermal water complex, inc 10 outdoor & 3 indoor pools, waterfalls & whirlpools, etc; paddling pool; fishing; golf 7km; boating; canoeing; tennis; fitness studio; games area; bike hire; games rm; wifi; entmnt; TV; 50% statics (sep area); dogs €4; poss cr; wifi; Eng spkn; adv bkg; ccard acc; red LS; CKE/CCI. "Site in lge thermal spa & health resort; many sports, leisure & health facs; shops 2km; select own pitch - best at edge of site; gd family site; conv Zagreb; san facs dated (2013); not value for money." ♦ € 67.00 SBS - X05 2013*

CATEZ OB SAVI see Brežice *C3*

KAMNIK *B2* (1km NE Urban) *46.22724, 14.61902* **Kamp Resnik, Nevlje 1a, 1240 Kamnik [(01) 8317314; fax 8318192; info@kampresnik.com; www.kampresnik.com]** Fr Ljubljana foll rd sp Celje then turn N for Kamnik. Fr Kemnik by-pass (E side of rv) bear R thro 2 sets traff lts, site 200m on L just after sports cent - site ent not obvious, turn bef zebra x-ing opp pub. Fr E on rd 414, site sp. Med, pt shd; wc (some cont); chem disp; mv service pnt; shwrs; EHU (10A) €3; gas; lndry; shops 500m; rest, snacks 100m; bar; playgrnd; pool adj; thermal spa, golf course nr; 5% statics; dogs; bus; Eng spkn; adv bkg; some daytime rd noise; ccard acc; red CKE/CCI. "Conv Ljubljana & Kamnik Alps; friendly staff; pleasant, well-kept; facs upgraded (2016)." 1 May-30 Sep. € 17.00 2016*

"Satellite navigation makes touring much easier"

Remember most sat navs don't know if you're towing or in a larger vehicle - always use yours alongside maps and site directions.

⊞ **KOBARID** *B1* (1km NE Rural) *46.25070, 13.58664* **Kamp Koren, Drežniške Ravne 33, 5222 Kobarid [(05) 3891311; fax 3891310; info@kamp-koren.si; www.kamp-koren.si]** Turn E fr main rd in town, site well sp dir Drežnica. Med, pt shd; htd wc (some cont); chem disp; mv service pnt; shwrs inc; EHU (16A) €4; shop; lndry; snacks; rest 500m; playgrnd; bike hire; canoeing; internet; TV rm; dogs €2; Eng spkn; quiet; ccard acc; red LS/long stay/CKE/CCI. "Vg, clean facs but stretched; friendly, helpful staff; pitches cramped; pleasant location in beautiful rv valley; excel walk to waterfall (3hrs); WW1 museum in town; lge elec lead poss req." ♦ € 30.00 2017*

KOPER *D1* (7km N Coastal) *45.57818, 13.73573* **Camping Adria, Jadranska Zesta 25, 6280 Ankaran [(05) 6637350; fax 6637360; camp@adria-ankaran.si; www.adria-ankaran.si]** Fr A1/E70/E61 onto rd 10 then rd 406 to Ankaran. Or cross Italian border at Lazzaretto & foll sp to site in 3km. Site sp in vill. Lge, mkd pitch, shd; wc; chem disp; mv service pnt; sauna; private san facs avail; shwrs inc; EHU (10A) €3; lndry (inc dryer); shop; supmkt adj; rest, snacks; bar; BBQ; playgrnd; 2 pools (1 Olympic-size); waterslide; beach adj; tennis; bike hire; wifi; entmnt; 60% statics; dogs €4; bus 500m; ccard acc. "Old town of Koper worth a visit; Vinakoper winery rec N of site on dual c'way; poss noisy groups high ssn; insect repellent req; clean san facs but red LS; gd rest; vg." ♦ 14 Apr-14 Oct. € 46.00 2013*

"There aren't many sites open at this time of year"

If you're travelling outside peak season remember to call ahead to check site opening dates - even if the entry says 'open all year'.

⊞ **KRANJSKA GORA** *B1* (14km E Rural) *46.46446, 13.95773* **Camping Kamne, Dovje 9, 4281 Mojstrana [tel/fax (04) 5891105; info@campingkamne.com; www.campingkamne.com]** Sp fr rd 201 bet Jesenice & Kranjska Gora, 2km E of Mojstrana. Do not go thro vill of Dovje. Sm, terr, pt shd; some hdstg; htd wc; chem disp; mv service pnt; shwrs €0.50; EHU (6A) €2.50-3.50; lndry (inc dryer); shop 1km; rest 1.5km; snacks; bar; playgrnd; sm pool; fishing; hiking; tennis; bike hire; TV rm; 10% statics; dogs €2; bus to Kranjska Gora fr site; Eng spkn; quiet but some rd noise; red long stay/CKE/CCI. "Conv Triglav National Park & border; views Mount Triglav; warm welcome; ltd san facs stretched high ssn; friendly helpful staff; gd cycling along old rlwy track." ♦ € 19.00 2013*

⊞ **LENDAVA** *B4* (2km S Rural) *46.55195, 16.45875* **Camping Terme Lendava (Part Naturist), Tomšičeva 2a, 9220 Lendava [(02) 5774400; fax 5774412; info@terme-lendava.si; www.terme-lendava.si]** Site well sp, adj hotel complex. Med, pt shd; htd wc; chem disp; mv service pnt; private bthrms avail; sauna; shwrs inc; EHU (16A) €4; lndry; shop 200m; rest, snacks; bar; no BBQ; playgrnd; 2 pools (1 htd, covrd); naturist pool; paddling pool; waterslide; tennis; games area; bike hire; fitness rm; internet; TV rm; some statics; dogs €3; adv bkg; ccard acc. "Conv Hungarian & Croatian borders; use of spa inc; unisex san facs." € 45.00 2013*

LESCE see Bled *B2*

⊞ **LJUBLJANA** *C2* (5km N Urban) *46.09752, 14.51870* **Ljubljana Resort, Dunajska Cesta 270, 1000 Ljubljana [(01) 5890130; fax 5890129; ljubljana.resort@gpl.si; www.ljubljanaresort.si]** Fr Maribor take A1 twd Ljubljana, at junc Zadobrova take Ljubljana ring rd twd Kranj & exit junc 3 sp Lj - Ježica, Bežigrad. At x-rds turn R twd Črnuče along Dunajska Cesta, turn R 100m bef rlwy x-ing. Fr N (Jesenica/Karawanken tunnel) exit A2/E66 at junc 13 sp Ljubljana Črnuče & foll rd for 3.5km; at rndabt junc with Dunajska Cesta rd turn R (1st exit); site on L in 200m. Lge, hdg/mkd pitch, pt shd; htd wc; chem disp; mv service pnt; shwrs inc; EHU (10A) €4.50; lndry/dishwash area; lndry (inc dryer); shop; supmkt 900m; rest, snacks; bar; BBQ (gas/elec, sep area); playgrnd; htd pool complex adj; whirlpools; paddling pool; naturist sunbathing adj pool; rv fishing; tennis; bike hire; horseriding 500m; archery; fitness club; wifi; entmnt; games rm; some statics; dogs €3; phone; bus to city at site ent (tickets at recep); Eng spkn; some rlwy noise; ccard acc; red LS/CKE/CCI. "Busy site by rv; gd rest; red facs LS; pitches nr hotel poss noisy due late-night functions; some pitches muddy when wet; conv for city; cycle & walking path along Rv Sava; friendly, helpful staff." ♦ € 33.00 SBS - X04 2017*

⊞ **MARIBOR** *B3* (5km SW Urban) *46.5355, 15.60508* **Camping Centre Kekec, Pohorska ulica 35c, 2000 Maribor [040 665 732; info@cck.si or bernard@cck.si; www.cck.si]** Fr S on A1 exit Maribor Jug; foll rd until you see Bauhaus shopping cent on the R, turn L at this x-rd; turn R after approx 400m; turn L after approx 100m; site on L after approx 3km opp the Terano Hotel. Sm, mkd pitch, hdstg, pt sl, terr, unshd; htd wc; chem disp; mv service pnt; fam bthrm; shwrs; EHU (25A) €3; lndry; rest & bar 250m; BBQ; wifi; dogs €1.50; Eng spkn; adv bkg; ccard acc; CKE/CCI. "Rec for larger o'fits as lge pitches avail but care with narr ent rd; v nice site." € 23.00 2017*

MOJSTRANA see Kranjska Gora *B1*

⊞ **NAZARJE** *B2* (7km W Rural) *46.31166, 14.90916* **Camping Menina, Varpolje 105, 3332 Rečica ob Savinji [(0) 40525266; info@campingmenina.com]** Fr rte E57 bet Ljubljana & Celje, turn N twd Nazarje, then dir Ljubno for 3km. Site sp. Med, mkd pitch, some hdstg, shd; wc; chem disp; mv service pnt; shwrs inc; EHU (6-16A) €3; lndry (inc dryer); rest, snacks; bar; playgrnd; lake sw adj; bike hire; wifi; 10% statics; dogs €3; Eng spkn; adv bkg; quiet; red CKE/CCI. "Helpful owners; delightful site in woodland; very ltd facs in winter." € 26.00 2016*

NOVA GORICA *C1* (7km SE Rural) *45.94182, 13.71761* **Camping Lijak - Mladovan Farm, Ozeljan 6A, 5261 Šempas [(05) 3088557; fax 53079619; camp.lijak@volja.net; www.camplijak.com]** Fr Nova Gorica take rd 444 twd Ljubljana/Ajdovščina. Site on L bef turn-off to Ozeljan. Sm, pt shd; htd wc; chem disp; shwrs inc; EHU (10A) €3 (poss long lead req); shop 1km; snacks; BBQ; wifi; some statics; dogs €1; phone; bus; Eng spkn; slight rd noise; red LS. "Farm site in wine-growing area; weekly wine tasting; hang-gliding area, enthusiasts use site; friendly owner; gd san facs." 15 Mar-31 Oct. € 35.50 2013*

PODCETRTEK see Rogaška Slatina *B3*

PORTOROZ *D1* (3km S Coastal) *45.50138, 13.59388* **Camping Lucija, Obala 77, 6320 Portorož [(05) 6906000; fax 6906900; camp.lucija@bernardingroup.si; www.camp-lucija.si]** Fr Koper (N) on rd 111, turn R at traff lts in Lucija. Take next L, then 2nd L into site. Nr Metropol Hotel, site sp. Lge, pt shd; wc; mv service pnt; serviced pitches; shwrs inc; EHU (6-10A) €4.50; lndry; shop; rest; bar; beach adj; bike hire; 60% statics; dogs €5; poss cr; Eng spkn; poss noisy; ccard acc; red CKE/CCI. "Conv Piran old town by bike or bus; sea views; sep area for tourers, extra for beach pitch; sm pitches; vg facs; busy site; gd public beach; noise fr disco opp till 4am." ♦ 11 Mar-2 Nov. € 37.00 2016*

POSTOJNA *C2* (5km NW Rural) *45.80551, 14.20470* **Camping Pivka Jama, Veliki Otok 50, 6230 Postojna [(05) 7203993; fax 7265348; avtokamp.pivka.jama@siol.net; www.camping-postojna.com]** Fr N or S Exit A1/E61 strt over traff lts, R at rdbt then bear L at next, foll sp to caves grotto (Postojnska Jama). Pass caves on R & then foll signs for Predjama Castle. 3km after caves site sp. Narr, winding app rd. Lge, hdstg, pt sl, terr, hdstg, shd; htd wc; chem disp; mv service pnt; shwrs inc; EHU (6A) €3.70 (rev pol); lndry; shop; rest, snacks; bar; cooking facs; playgrnd; pool; paddling pool; tennis; 50% statics; dogs; poss v cr; Eng spkn; adv bkg; quiet but noisy nr sw pool; ccard acc; red LS CKE/CCI. "Gd forest site; gd rest with live Tirolean music; gd san facs, needs updating (2017); used as transit to Croatia, open 24 hrs; caves 4km a must visit (take warm clothing!)." 15 Apr-31 Oct. € 29.00 SBS - X09 2017*

⊞ **PREBOLD** *B3* (200m N Rural) *46.24027, 15.08790* **Camping Dolina, Dolenja Vas 147, 3312 Prebold [(03) 5724378; fax 5742591; camp@dolina.si; www.dolina.si]** On A1/E57 turn R 16km fr Celje sp Prebold & foll sp, site on N edge of vill. Sm, unshd; wc; chem disp; shwrs (inc); EHU (6-10A) €3.30; gas; lndry; shop 400m; rest in hotel 800m; htd pool; bike hire; wifi; dogs €2; poss cr; quiet; red long stay; CKE/CCI. "Gd clean facs but no changing area in shwrs; helpful, friendly owner; conv Savinja valley; gd walking." € 20.00 2016*

PREBOLD *B3* (350m N Rural) *46.23832, 15.09266* **Camping Park, Latkova Vas 227, 3312 Prebold [(03) 7001986; info@campingpark.si; www.campingpark.si]** Fr A1/E57 or rd 5 exit at Prebold. Foll site sp for 400m, cross Rv Savinja & site on L. Sm, shd; htd wc; chem disp; shwrs inc; EHU (6A) inc; lndry; shops 2km; rest; bar; BBQ; games area; some Eng spkn; adv bkg; quiet; 10% red CKE/CCI. "V pleasant, well-kept site but ltd facs; pleasant walks by rv; helpful owners own adj hotel; gd walking & cycling." 1 Apr-31 Oct. € 20.00 2012*

⊞ **PTUJ** *B4* (3km NW Rural) *46.42236, 15.85478* **Autokamp Terme Ptuj, Pot V Toplice 9, 2250 Ptuj [(02) 7494100; fax 7494520; info@terme-ptuj.si; www.terme-ptuj.si]** S fr Maribor on A4 or rd 1/E59; turn L onto rd 2 sp Ptuj (exit junc 2 fr A4); on app Ptuj foll sp Golf/Terme Camping to L off rd 2; site after leisure complex on Rv Drava. Diff to find when app fr SW on rd 432. Med, pt shd; htd wc; chem disp; mv service pnt; sauna; steam rm; shwrs inc; EHU (10A) €4; gas; lndry (inc dryer); shop 2km; rest, snacks, bar; BBQ; playgrnd; htd, covrd pools/spa; waterslide; games area; tennis; fitness rm; bike hire; golf 1km; internet; statics; dogs €4; phone; weekly bus to Vienna; poss cr; Eng spkn; red LS/long stay/snr citizens/CKE/CCI. "Helpful staff; clean san facs, poss stretched high ssn; pitches muddy in wet; superb water park free to campers; lovely area; castle & monastery in Ptuj old town worth a visit; new san facs (2013)." ♦ ltd. € 58.00 2013*

RECICA OB SAVINJI see Mozirje *B3*

ROGASKA SLATINA *B3* (12km S Rural) *46.16499, 15.60495* **Camping Natura Terme Olimia, Zdraviliška Cesta 24, 3254 Podčetrtek [(03) 8297000; fax 5829700; info@terme-olimia.com; www.terme-olimia.com]** Fr Celje take rte E dir Rogaška Slatina. Turn S sp Podčetrtek just bef Rogaška. Site on L (waterchutes) alongside Rv Solta on Croatian border in approx 10km. Sm, unshd; htd wc; chem disp; mv service pnt; sauna; shwrs inc; EHU (10-16A) €3.20; lndry; shop high ssn; rest 800m; snacks; bar; playgrnd; 2 htd pools (1 covrd); paddling pool; waterslide; fitness rm; tennis; bike hire; horseriding 2km; golf 4km; wifi; TV rm; phone; adv bkg; ccard acc; red CKE/CCI. "Aqualuna Thermal Pk adj; vg walking country with wooded hillsides." ♦ 15 Apr-15 Oct. € 32.00 (CChq acc) 2016*

SKOFJA LOKA *B2* (12km E Rural) *46.17455, 14.41720* **Camping Smlednik (Part Naturist), Dragočajna 14a, 1216 Smlednik [(01) 3627002; camp@dm-campsmlednik.si; www.dm-campsmlednik.si]** Fr Ljubljana N on E61 take turning W onto rd 413 sp Zapoge & Zbilje. After Valburg & bef x-ing rv turn R to Dragočajna & site. Lge, terr, pt shd; wc; chem disp; shwrs inc; EHU (6-10A) €3-4; shop; snacks; bar; BBQ; canoeing; tennis; many statics; dogs €1; Eng spkn; quiet; CKE/CCI. "Pleasant rvside location; steep site; sep sm naturist site; shwrs poss only warm as solar powered; ltd facs LS; poss muddy when wet." 1 May-15 Oct. € 24.00 2013*

SOCA see Bovec *B1*

"That's changed – Should I let The Club know?"

If you find something on site that's different from the site entry, fill in a report and let us know. See camc.com/europereport.

VELENJE *B3* (2km NW Rural) *46.36832, 15.08864* **Autocamp Jezero, Cesta Simona Blatnika 26, 3320 Velenje [(03) 5866466; mastodontbar@gmail.com]** Exit A1/E57 at Velenje & cont to 2nd traff lts, then turn R. Turn L at 3rd traff lts & foll site sp. Site on lakeside. Med, mkd pitch, pt shd; wc; chem disp; mv service pnt; shwrs; EHU (10A) inc; lndry; supmkt 2km; rest 300m; snacks; playgrnd; lake sw; watersports; tennis; games area; fitness rm; internet; some statics; dogs €1.50; quiet. "Lovely location but nr coal-powered power stn; poss unkempt LS; Velenje coal mining museum worth visit 1km; san facs need refurb (2015); poor." ♦ 1 May-30 Sep. € 22.00 2015*

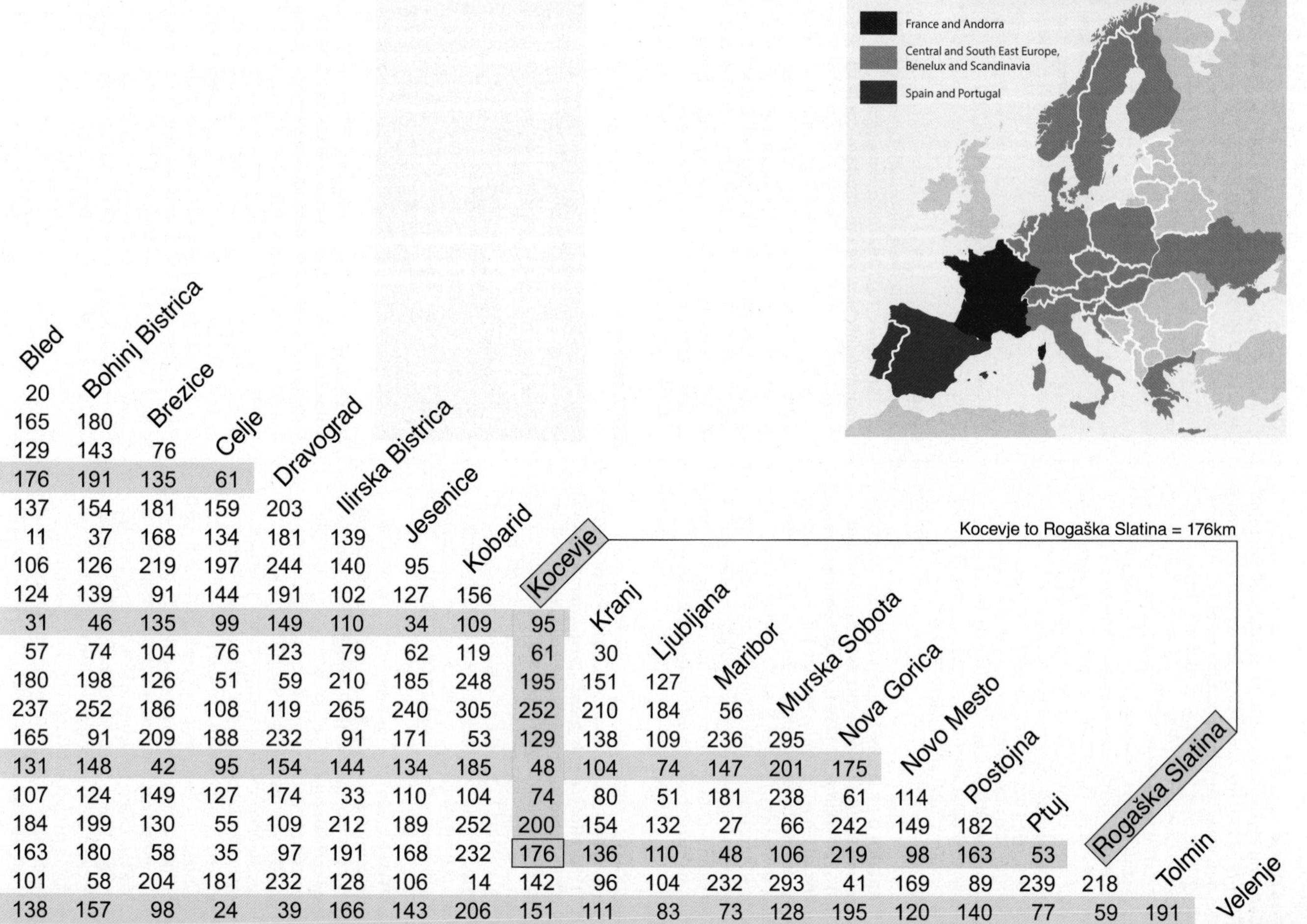

	Bled	Bohinj Bistrica	Brezice	Celje	Dravograd	Ilirska Bistrica	Jesenice	Kobarid	Kocevje	Kranj	Ljubljana	Maribor	Murska Sobota	Nova Gorica	Novo Mesto	Postojna	Ptuj	Rogaška Slatina	Tolmin
Bohinj Bistrica	20																		
Brezice	165	180																	
Celje	129	143	76																
Dravograd	176	191	135	61															
Ilirska Bistrica	137	154	181	159	203														
Jesenice	11	37	168	134	181	139													
Kobarid	106	126	219	197	244	140	95												
Kocevje	124	139	91	144	191	102	127	156											
Kranj	31	46	135	99	149	110	34	109	95										
Ljubljana	57	74	104	76	123	79	62	119	61	30									
Maribor	180	198	126	51	59	210	185	248	195	151	127								
Murska Sobota	237	252	186	108	119	265	240	305	252	210	184	56							
Nova Gorica	165	91	209	188	232	91	171	53	129	138	109	236	295						
Novo Mesto	131	148	42	95	154	144	134	185	48	104	74	147	201	175					
Postojna	107	124	149	127	174	33	110	104	74	80	51	181	238	61	114				
Ptuj	184	199	130	55	109	212	189	252	200	154	132	27	66	242	149	182			
Rogaška Slatina	163	180	58	35	97	191	168	232	176	136	110	48	106	219	98	163	53		
Tolmin	101	58	204	181	232	128	106	14	142	96	104	232	293	41	169	89	239	218	
Velenje	138	157	98	24	39	166	143	206	151	111	83	73	128	195	120	140	77	59	191

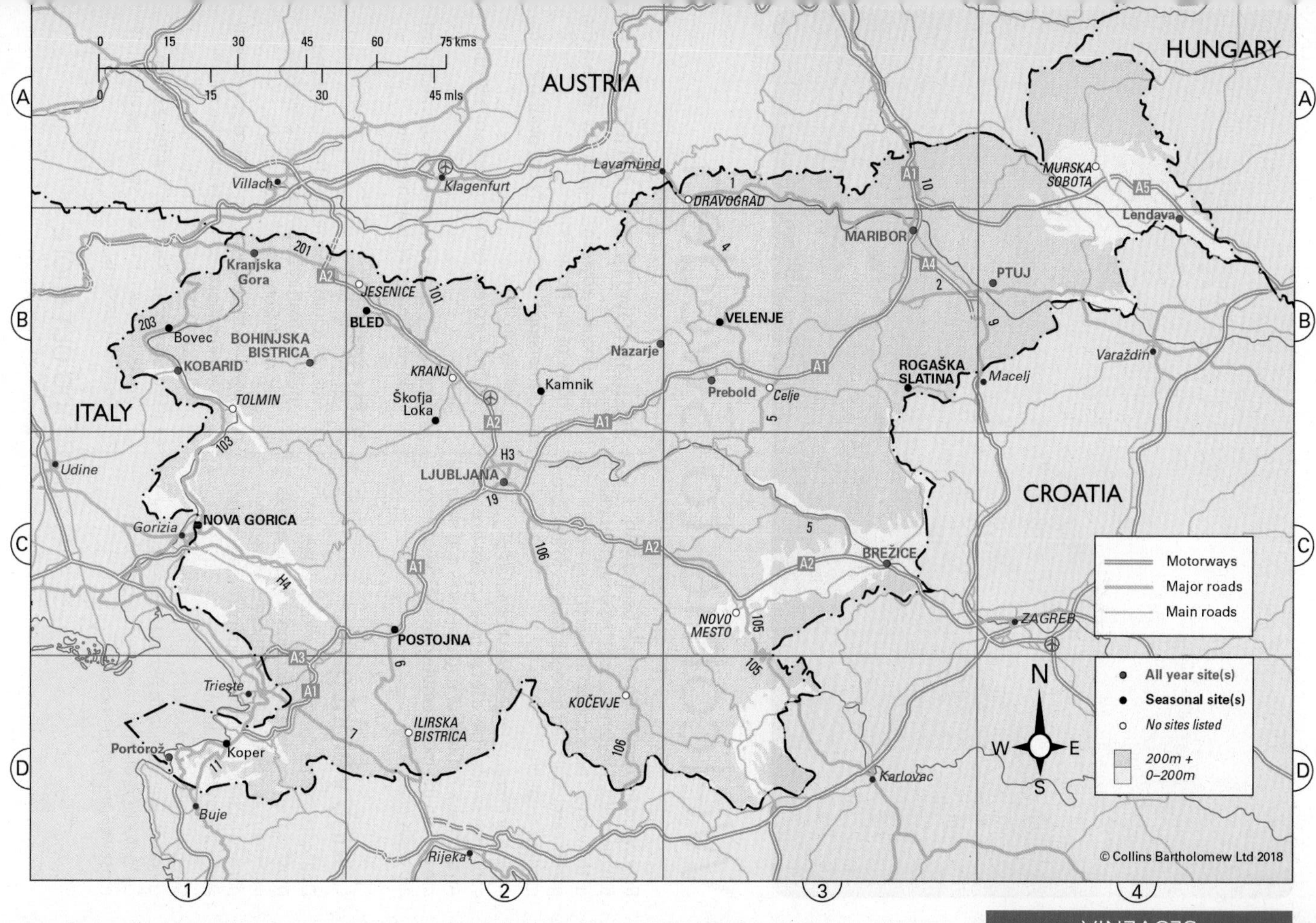
HUNGARY
AUSTRIA
ITALY
CROATIA
Motorways
Major roads
Main roads
All year site(s)
Seasonal site(s)
No sites listed
200m +
0–200m
N
E
S
W
© Collins Bartholomew Ltd 2018
0
15
30
45
60
75 kms
45 mls
Lendava
MURSKA SOBOTA
Varaždin
PTUJ
Macelj
ROGAŠKA SLATINA
MARIBOR
BREŽICE
Karlovac
ZAGREB
Celje
Prebold
VELENJE
DRAVOGRAD
Lavamünd
NOVO MESTO
Nazarje
KOČEVJE
Kamnik
LJUBLJANA
Klagenfurt
KRANJ
Škofja Loka
POSTOJNA
ILIRSKA BISTRICA
Rijeka
BLED
JESENICE
BOHINJSKA BISTRICA
Villach
Kranjska Gora
TOLMIN
NOVA GORICA
Trieste
Koper
Bovec
KOBARID
Gorizia
Buje
Portorož
Udine
A1
A2
A3
A4
A5
H3
H4
A
B
C
D
1
2
3
4

Aurora Borealis in Abisko National Park

Welcome to Sweden

Renowned for combining simple beauty with functionality, Sweden is one of the design capitals of the world. This is shown in everything from gothic cathedrals and baroque palaces to its more modern creations.

As one of Europe's largest, least populated countries Sweden has a lot of green space to enjoy. An extensive network of national parks and trails mean even the most remote parts of the country are easily accessible.

Country highlights

Due to its shorter summers, Sweden makes the most of the long days by packing as many events into them as possible. One of these is a crayfish party, which is a traditional summertime eating and drinking celebration.

Sweden is also celebrated for its rich variety of children's literature, with Astrid Lindgren's Pippi Longstocking, or Pippi Långstrump, one of the most well-known creations.

Major towns and cities

- Stockholm – a dynamic capital city which is the home of the Nobel Prize.
- Gothenburg – this port city has plenty of history on show.
- Malmö – a green city with plenty of beautiful parks.
- Uppsala – this city has ancient roots and boast a dominating cathedral and castle.

Attractions

- Vasa Museum, Stockholm – This fascinating museum features a fantastically preserved shipwreck from the 17th century
- Sigtuna – the oldest town in Sweden, boasting a picturesque medieval centre filled with restaurants, shops and cafés.
- Drottningholm Palace – A residence of the Swedish royal family, this stunning palace has beautiful gardens.

Find out more

www.visitsweden.com
Tel: 0046 (0) 87 89 10 00 Swedish Tourist Office

Country Information

Population (approx): 9.8 million

Capital: Stockholm (population 915,000 approx)

Area: 450,000 sqkm

Bordered by: Finland, Norway

Terrain: Mostly flat or gently rolling lowlands; mountains in the west

Climate: Cold, cloudy winters, sub-arctic in the north; cool/warm summers. The best time to visit is between May and September; August can be hot and wet. Be prepared for occasional sub-zero temperatures and snowfalls, even in summer months

Coastline: 3,218km

Highest Point: Kebnekaise 2,104m

Language: Swedish

Local Time: GMT or BST + 1, i.e. 1 hour ahead of the UK all year

Currency: Krona (SEK) divided into 100 öre; £1 = SEK 11.22, SEK 100 = £8.91 (Novemeber 2017)

Emergency Numbers: Police 112 (or 11414 for non-emergency calls); Fire Brigade 112; Ambulance 112. Operators speak English

Public Holidays 2018: Jan 1, 6; Mar 30; Apr 1, 2; May 1,10,20; Jun 6, 23; Nov 3; Dec 25, 26.

School summer holidays are from early June to the second or third week of August

Camping and Caravanning

Camping and caravanning are very popular, but because summer is short the season is brief - from May to late August/early September, although winter caravanning is increasing in popularity. High season on most sites ends around the middle of August when prices and site office opening hours are reduced or sites close altogether. There are more than 1,000 campsites, about 350 of which remain open during the winter particularly in mountainous regions near to ski resorts. Those that are open all year may offer fewer or no facilities from mid-September to April and advance booking may be required.

In late June and July advance booking is recommended, especially at campsites along the west coast (north and south of Göteborg), on the islands of Öland and Gotland and near other popular tourist areas.

Approximately 500 campsites are members of the SCR (Svenska Campingvärdars Riksfärbund – Swedish Campsite Owners' Association), which are classified from 1 to 5 stars. Visitors wishing to use these sites must have a Camping Key Europe card. You can buy the Camping Key Europe at campsites for around €20 and you will be given a temporary card, or you can order it in advance from www.camping.se/en for 150 SEK (2015 prices). If ordering in advance you should allow at least 3 weeks for delivery.

Most Swedes use electric hook-ups so caravanners using their battery may obtain a pitch which is on a less congested part of the site. Also aim to arrive by mid afternoon to get a better pitch, since many Swedes arrive late. It is reported that hand basins on sites often do not have plugs so it is advisable to carry a flat universal plug when touring.

Many sites have a 'Quick Stop' amenity which provides safe, secure overnight facilities on, or adjacent to, a site. This normally includes the use of sanitary facilities. 'Quick Stop' rates are about two thirds of the regular camping rate if you arrive after 9pm and leave before 9am.

Casual/wild camping is normally permitted (except in National Parks and recreational areas), however for security reasons it is not recommended to spend the night in a vehicle on the roadside or in a public car park. Instead use the 'Quick Stop' amenity at campsites. In any event local parking rules and signposting should always be observed.

Alternatively there are around 150 organised 'ställplatser' mainly intended for motorhomes but generally car and caravan outfits may also use them for an overnight stay at the discretion of the site's manager. For a list of 'ställplatser' see www.campinggladje.se/resa.

Most designated rest areas along highways are owned and managed by the Vågverket (Swedish Roads Administration) which, although not officially ranked as 'ställplatser', offer adequate parking space and various facilities for motorhomes staying overnight. A map showing these rest areas is available at local tourist offices.

Cycling

The network of cycle lanes in Sweden is growing rapidly and many cycle routes are named and signposted. In some cases cycle lanes are combined with foot paths.
See www.svenska-cykelsallskapet.se.

The 'Sverigeleden' cycle trail covers the whole country and connects all major ports and cities. The 190km cycle route along the Göta Canal from Sjötorp on Lake Vänern to Mem on the Baltic coast is relatively flat and hence a very popular route.

The wearing of a safety helmet is compulsory for children up to the age of 15 and is recommended for everyone.

Electricity and Gas

On campsites the current is usually 10 amps or more and round two-pin plugs are used. CEE connections are becoming standard.

Propane (gasol) is the gas most widely obtainable at more than 2,000 Primus dealers; you will need to buy an appropriate adaptor. It is understood that it is possible to sell back your propane cylinder at the end of your holiday and outlets will also exchange the corresponding Norwegian Progas cylinders. Recent visitors report that major distributors will refill cylinders but they must be of a recognised make/type and in perfect condition. The Caravan and Motorhome Club does not recommend the refilling of cylinders.

Butane gas is available from a number of outlets including some petrol stations. It is understood that Campingaz 904 and 907 cylinders are available but recent visitors report that they may be difficult to find, and virtually impossible in the north of the country. For more information on butane suppliers contact the Swedish Campsite Owners' Association (SCR) by email: info@scr.se

Ensure that you are well-equipped with gas if venturing north of central Sweden as it may be difficult to find an exchange point. Many sites have communal kitchen facilities which enable visitors to make great savings on their own gas supply.

Entry Formalities

Holders of valid British and Irish passports may visit Sweden for up to three months without a visa.

Regulations for Pets

In order to protect the countryside and wildlife, dogs are not allowed to run off the lead from 1 March to 20 August and at other times in certain areas.

Dogs travelling directly from the UK and Ireland must be microchipped and have an EU pet passport. For more information please visit www.jordbruksverket.se (english option) and go to the 'Animals' section.

Medical Services

Health care facilities are generally very good and most medical staff speak English. The general practitioner system does not apply; instead visit the nearest hospital clinic (Akutmottagning or Värdcentral) and present your passport and European Health Insurance Card (EHIC). You will be charged a fee for the clinic visit (free for anyone under 20) plus a daily standard charge if it is necessary to stay in hospital. These charges are non-refundable in Sweden.

Prescriptions are dispensed at pharmacies (apotek) which are open during normal shopping hours. Emergency prescriptions can be obtained at hospitals. Dental surgeons or clinics (tandläkare or folktandvård) offer emergency out-of-hours services in major cities but you may have to pay the full cost of treatment.

The use of mosquito repellent is recommended, particularly from mid June to September when mosquitos are most common. Mosquitos are generally more often encountered in the north of Sweden rather than the south.

Visitors to remote areas should consider the relative inaccessibility of the emergency services. In northern Sweden mobile phone coverage does not generally extend beyond main roads and the coast.

Opening Hours

Banks: Mon-Fri 9.30am-3pm or 5pm and until 5.30pm one day a week in larger towns. Many banks do not handle cash after 3pm and some banks will not handle cash at all.

Museums: Check locally, opening hours can vary.

Post Offices: Post offices no longer exist. Mail is dealt with at local shops, kiosks and petrol stations; opening hours vary.

Shops: 8am-8pm every day. Shops generally close early the day before a public holiday.

Safety and Security

Petty crime levels are much lower than in most other European countries but you should take the usual commonsense precautions. Pickpocketing is common in the summer months in major cities where tourists may be targeted for their passports and cash.

In recent years there have been incidents of 'highway robbery' from motorhomes parked on the roadside, especially on the west coast between Malmö and Gothenburg.

Sweden shares with the rest of Europe an underlying threat from terrorism. Attacks could be indiscriminate and against civilian targets in public places, including tourist sites.

British Embassy
SKARPÖGATAN 6-8,115 93 STOCKHOLM
Tel: (08) 6713000
www.ukinsweden.fco.gov.uk/en/

Irish Embassy
Hovslagargatan 5, 111 48 STOCKHOLM
Tel: (08) 54504040
www.dfa.ie/sweden

Customs Regulations

Visitors arriving from an EU country via a non-EU country (e.g. Norway) may bring quantities of tobacco and alcohol obtained in EU countries, plus the amounts allowed duty-free from non-EU countries. However, you must be able to produce proof of purchase for goods from EU countries and goods must be for your personal use.

Border Posts

There are approximately 40 Customs posts along the Swedish/Norwegian border. They are situated on all main roads and are normally open Mon to Fri from 8.30am - 4pm/5pm.

Travellers with dutiable goods must cross the land borders during hours when the Customs posts are open. However, travellers without dutiable goods may cross the border outside Customs post opening hours.

The main border posts with Finland are at Haparanda, Övertornea, Pajala and Karesuando.

Documents

Driving Licence

A UK driving licence is only valid when it bears a photograph of the holder, i.e. a photocard licence, or when it is carried together with photographic proof of identity, such as a passport.

Money

Foreign currency may be exchanged in banks and bureaux de change.

Major credit cards are widely used both for major and minor transactions and cash machines (Bankomat or Minuten) are widespread. It is advisable to carry your passport or photocard driving licence if paying with a credit card as you may be asked for photographic proof of identity.

Motoring in Sweden

Accidents

In the case of an accident it is not necessary to call the police unless there are injuries to drivers or passengers and/or vehicles are badly damaged, but drivers are required to give their details to the other persons involved before leaving the accident scene. A driver leaving the scene of an accident without following this procedure may be fined.

If you are involved in an accident with a possible third party claim, you are strongly recommended to report the accident to the national Swedish insurance bureau which will act as claims agent. Contact Trafikförsäkringsforeningen in Stockholm, tel: 08 522 78100, info@ tff.se, www.tff.se.

Accidents involving wild animals (e.g. elk, reindeer, bear, wolf, etc) must be reported to the police immediately by calling 112 or 11414 and the spot where the accident took place must be marked by putting up reflective tape or anything clearly noticeable so that the police can find it easily.

Collisions must be reported even if the animal involved is not injured. After reporting the accident and marking out the place, a driver may leave. Accidents involving smaller animals (badgers, foxes, etc) need not be reported.

Alcohol

Penalties for driving a motor vehicle under the influence of alcohol are extremely severe. The police carry out random breath tests. If the level of alcohol exceeds 20 milligrams in 100 millilitres of blood a fine will be imposed and driving licence withdrawn. This level is considerably lower than that permitted in the UK (80 milligrams) and equates to virtually zero. A level exceeding 100 milligrams is considered to be severe drink driving for which a jail sentence of up to two years may be imposed and licence withdrawn.

Breakdown Service

The motoring organisation, Motormännens Riksförbund (known as the 'M'), does not operate a breakdown service. It does, however, have an agreement with 'AssistanceKåren' (a nationwide road service company) which operates a 24-hour, all-year service and can be contacted free on (020) 912912 or 08 6275757 from a foreign-registered mobile phone. Phone boxes are becoming quite scarce and it is advisable to carry a mobile phone. There are normally no emergency telephones along motorways or dual carriageways. Charges for assistance and towing vary according to day and time and payment by credit card is accepted.

Essential Equipment

Warning Triangle

It is compulsory for foreign registered vehicles to carry a warning triangle. They should be placed as a distance of 50 meters behind the vehicle on ordinary roads and 100 meters on motorways.

Lights

Dipped headlights are compulsory at all times, regardless of weather conditions. Bulbs are more likely to fail with constant use and you are recommended to carry spares. Fog lights may be used when visibility is poor but they must not be used together with dipped headlights.

Vehicles parked or stopped on a poorly lit road at night, including dawn, dusk and bad weather, must have their parking lights switched on.

Child Restraint System

Children under the height of 135cm must be seated in a child restraint or child seat. A child aged 15 or over, or 135cm in height or taller, can use normal seat belts in the car.

Children under the height of 140cm are only allowed in the front seat if the passenger seat airbag has been deactivated.

Winter Driving

The winter months are periods of severe cold and you should be prepared for harsh conditions. The fitting of winter tyres is compulsory for vehicles from 1st December to 31st March in the event of severe winter road conditions, i.e. the road is covered with ice or snow, or if the road is wet and the temperature is around freezing point. Trailers towed by these vehicles must also be equipped with winter tyres. These regulations apply to foreign registered vehicles.

Fuel

Petrol stations are usually open from 7am to 9pm. Near motorways and main roads and in most cities they may remain open until 10pm or even for 24 hours. Outside large towns garages seldom stay open all night but most have self-service pumps (possibly not for diesel) which accept credit cards. In the far north filling stations may be few and far between so keep your tank topped up. Credit cards are accepted.

LPG (known as gasol) is sold at a very limited number of petrol stations mainly located in central and southern Sweden.

Low Emission Zones

There are Low Emission Zones (Miljözen) in Sweden. Please see www.lowemissionzones.eu for the most up-to-date information.

Overtaking

Take care when overtaking long vehicles. A typical long-distance Swedish truck is a six-wheeled unit towing a huge articulated trailer, i.e. a very long load.

Many roads in Sweden have wide shoulders or a climbing lane to the right of the regular lane and these permit drivers of slow moving vehicles or wide vehicles to pull over to allow other traffic to pass. These climbing lanes and shoulders should not be used as another traffic lane.

Parking

Parking meters and other parking restrictions are in use in several large towns. Vehicles must be parked facing the direction of the flow of traffic. Wheel clamps are not in use but illegally parked vehicles may be towed away and, in addition to a parking fine, a release fee will be charged.

In an area signposted 'P' parking is permitted for a maximum of 24 hours, unless otherwise stated.

Priority

Vehicles driving on roads designated and signposted (with a yellow diamond on a black background) as primary roads always have priority. On all other roads, as a general rule, vehicles coming from the right have priority, unless signs indicate otherwise. This rule is sometimes ignored however, especially by vehicles on roads regarded as major roads but not signposted as such.

At most roundabouts signs indicate that traffic already on the roundabout has priority, i.e. from the left.

Give trams priority at all times. Where there is no refuge at a tram stop, you must stop to allow passengers to board and alight from the tram.

Roads

The condition of national and country roads is good although some minor roads may be covered with oil-gravel only. Road surfaces may be damaged following the spring thaw, and some may be closed or have weight restrictions imposed during that period. Gradients are generally slight and there are no roads that need to be avoided for vehicles towing a caravan.

Road repairs tend to be intensive during the short summer season. Information on major roadworks and road conditions on E roads and major national roads can be obtained from www.trafikverket.se.

There is a good road link with Norway in the far north of Sweden. The Kiruna-Narvik road is open all year from Kiruna to the border. It is a wide road with no steep gradients.

There is generally little or no heavy goods traffic on roads during the Christmas, Easter and midsummer holidays or on the days preceding these holidays so good progress can be made.

Road Signs and Markings

Road signs and markings conform to international standards. Warning lines (usually on narrow roads) are broken lines with short intervals which indicate that visibility is limited in one or both directions; they may be crossed when overtaking. Unbroken lines should not be crossed at any time.

National roads (riksvägar) have two-digit numbers and country roads (länsvägar) have three-digit numbers. Roads which have been incorporated into the European road network – E roads – generally have no other national number.

Direction and information signs for motorways and roads which form part of the European road network are green. Signs for national roads and the more important country roads are blue. Signs for local roads are white with black numerals.

The following are some other signs that you may see:

Passing place

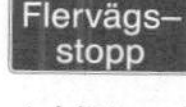

Additional stop sign

Accident

Swedish	English Tanslation
Enkelriktat	One way
Farlig kurva	Dangerous bend
Grusad väg	Loose chippings
Höger	Right
Ingen infart	No entrance
Parkering förbjuden	No parking
Vänster	Left

Speed Limits

	Open Road (km/h)	Motorway (km/h)
Car Solo	60-100	90-120
Car towing caravan/trailer	70-80	80
Motorhome under 3500kg	60-100	90-120
Motorhome 3500-7500kg	70-100	90-120

Speed limits are no longer based on the category of road but on the quality and safety level of the roads themselves. As a result limits may vary from one town to another and along stretches of the same road. It is advisable, therefore, to pay close attention to road signs as speed limits are strictly enforced. If in doubt, or if no speed limit is indicated, you are advised to keep to 70 km/h (44 mph) until you see a speed limit sign.

Outside built-up areas, including expressways, speeds up to 100 km/h (62 mph) may be permitted according to road signs, providing a lower maximum speed is not applicable for certain vehicle categories. Vehicles with trailers must never exceed 80 km/h (49mph). On motorways the maximum permitted speed is 110 or 120 km/h (68 or 74 mph). During the winter a speed limit of 90 km/h (56 mph) is in force on some motorways and dual carriageways. This limit is signposted.

In most residential areas and during certain periods in areas near schools, speed is limited to 30 km/h (18 mph) according to road signs. Periods indicated in black mean Monday to Friday, those in black in brackets mean Saturday and the eves of public holidays, and those indicated in red mean Sunday and public holidays.

Speed limits for motorhomes under 3,500kg and privately registered motorhomes over 3,500kg are the same as for solo cars. Speed cameras are in use on many roads. The use of radar detectors is not permitted.

Traffic Lights

A green arrow indicates that traffic may proceed with caution in the direction of the arrow but pedestrians must be given priority. A flashing amber light indicates that a crossing/turning must be made with caution.

Violation of Traffic Regulations

Police are authorised to impose and collect fines for violation of minor traffic offences which must be paid at a bank, normally within two to three weeks. Offences, which may qualify for a fine include driving without lights in daylight, speeding, lack of a warning triangle or nationality plate (GB or IRL) or a dirty or missing number plate.

If a fine is not paid and the driver is a resident of another EU country, notice of the fine will be forwarded to the authorities in the driver's country of residence.

Jaywalking is not permitted; pedestrians must use official crossings.

Motorways

There are approximately 1,900 kms of motorway and 560 kms of semi-motorway or dual carriageway, all confined to the south of the country and relatively free of heavy traffic by UK standards. There are no service areas or petrol stations on motorways; these are situated near the exits and are indicated on motorway exit signs. Please note that there are no petrol stations close to the 110km long Uppsala to Gälve motorway.

Tolls

Tolls for private vehicles have now been introduced. The Motala by-pass (on road 50m in central Sweden) the toll will be 5 SEK and for the Sundsvall by-pass (on E4 in northern Sweden) the toll will be 9 SEK. Göteborg(E6) 9-22 SEK.

Toll Bridges

The Øresund Bridge links Malmö in Sweden with Copenhagen in Denmark and means that it is possible to drive all the way from mainland Europe by motorway. The crossing is via a 7.8 km bridge to the artificial island of Peberholm and a 4 km tunnel. Tolls (payable in cash, including EUR, SEK or DKK or by credit card) are levied on the Swedish side and are as follows for single journeys (2016 prices subject to change)

Vehicle(s)	Price
Solo car or motorhome up to 6 metres	€ 50
Car + caravan/trailer or motorhome over 6 metres	€ 100

Vehicle length is measured electronically and even a slight overhang over six metres will result in payment of the higher tariff.

Speed limits apply in the tunnel and on the bridge, and during periods of high wind the bridge is closed to caravans. Bicycles are not allowed. Information on the Øresund Bridge can be found on www.oeresundsbron.com.

Svinesund Bridge

There is a 700 metre long bridge linking Sweden and Norway on the E6, at Svinesund. Tolls are SEK24 (NOK20) for light vehicles and SEK120 (NOK100) for vehicles over 3,500kgs (2016).

Touring

Ferry services connect Sweden with Denmark, Estonia, Finland, Germany, Latvia, Lithuania, Norway and Poland; some services only operate in the summer. Full details are available from Visit Sweden, www.visitsweden.com. Scheduled car ferry services also operate between the mainland and the island of Gotland during the summer season.

In the south and centre the touring season lasts from May to September. In the north it is a little shorter, the countryside being particularly beautiful at each end of the season. Campsites are most crowded over the midsummer holiday period and during the Swedish industrial holidays in the last two weeks of July and first week of August. Tourist attractions may close before the end of August or operate on reduced opening hours.

Sweden has 15 UNESCO World Heritage sites and 29 national parks which, together with nature reserves, cover eight percent of the country. Information on national parks and nature reserves is available on www.naturvardsverket.se.

Inland, particularly near lakes, visitors should be armed with spray-on, rub-on and electric plug-in insect repellent devices as mosquitoes and midges are a problem.

Discount cards are available in Stockholm and Gothenburg offering free public transport and free admission to many museums and other attractions, plus free boat and canal sightseeing trips. Buy the cards at tourist information offices, hotels, kiosks, some campsites and online – see www.stockholmtown.com or www.goteborg.com.

Local tourist offices are excellent sources of information and advice; look for the blue and yellow 'i' signs. Information points at lay-bys at the entrance to many towns are good sources of street maps.

A good-value 'dagens rätt' (dish of the day) is available in most restaurants at lunchtime. A service charge is usually included in restaurant bills but an additional small tip is normal if you have received good service.

The most popular alcoholic drink is lager, available in five strengths. Wines, spirits and strong beer are sold only through the state-owned 'Systembolaget' shops, open from Monday to Friday and on Saturday morning, with branches all over the country. Light beer can be bought from grocery shops and supermarkets. The minimum age for buying alcoholic drinks is 20 years at Systembolaget and 18 years in pubs, bars and licensed restaurants.

It is not permitted to smoke in restaurants, pubs or bars or in any place where food and drinks are served.

The Midnight Sun and Northern Lights

The Midnight Sun is visible north of the Arctic Circle from about the end of May until the middle of July.

The Northern Lights (Aurora Borealis) are often visible during the winter from early evening until midnight. They are seen more frequently the further north you travel. The best viewing areas in Sweden are north of the Arctic Circle between September and March.

The Order of Bluenosed Caravanners

Visitors to the Arctic Circle from anywhere in the world may apply for membership of the Order of Bluenosed Caravanners which will be recognised by the issue of a certificate by the International Caravanning Association (ICA).
For more information contact David Hirst on telephone 01422 372390, or email: david.hirst118@gmail.com and attach a photograph of yourselves and your outfit under any Arctic Circle signpost, together with the date and country of crossing and the names of those who made the crossing. This service is free to members of the ICA (annual membership £20); the fee for non-members is £5. Coloured plastic decals for your outfit, indicating membership of the Order, are also available at a cost of £4. Cheques should be payable to the ICA. See www.icacaravanning.org.

Public Transport & Local Travel

Stockholm has an extensive network of underground trains (T-bana), commuter trains, buses and trams. Underground station entrances are marked with a blue 'T' on a white background. You can buy single tickets for one of three zones at the time of your journey, or save money by buying tickets in advance. A discount applies if you are aged 65 or over. Single tickets and prepaid tickets are valid for one hour after beginning your journey. Travel cards offer reduced price public transport throughout the Greater Stockholm area for periods of 1, 3, 7 or 30 days, regardless of zone – see www.sl.se (click on 'Visitor') for details of routes, fares and tickets.

For information on public transport systems in Göteborg and Malmö, see www.vasttrafik.se and www.skanetrafiken.se.

Stockholm is built on an archipelago of islands and island hopping ferries operate all year. You can buy single tickets or an island hopping pass for use on the Waxholmsbolaget and Cinderella fleet of ferries.

Confirm your taxi fare before setting off in the vehicle. Some companies have fixed fares which vary according to the day of the week and time of day. A full price list must be on display. Payment by credit card is generally accepted. It is usual to round up the fare shown on the meter by way of a tip.

Sweden is a country of lakes, rivers and archipelagos and, as a result, there are over 12,000 bridges. Road ferries, which form part of the national road network, make up the majority of other crossings; no bookings are necessary or possible. Most ferries are free of charge and services are frequent and crossings very short.

A congestion charge was introduced in Stockholm in 2007. Drivers of foreign-registered vehicles are exempt from the charge. For more information go to www.visitstockholm.com. In some other towns traffic restrictions may apply during certain periods and these are signposted.

When giving directions Swedes will often refer to distances in 'miles'. A Swedish 'mile' is, in fact, approximately ten kilometres. All road signs are in kilometres so if a Swede tells you it is 3 miles to a town, expect the journey to be around 30km.

Sites in Sweden

⊞ **AHUS** *2F4* (1km NE Urban/Coastal) *55.94118, 14.31286* **First Camp Ahus (formerly Regenbogen), Kolonivägen 59, 29633 Åhus [(044) 248969; ahus@firstcamp.se; firstcamp.se]** Take rd 118 fr Kristianstad SE twd Åhus. Site well sp fr ent to town. Lge, mkd pitch, hdstg, pt shd; htd wc; chem disp; mv service pnt; fam bthrm; sauna; shwrs inc; EHU (10A) SEK29; lndry (inc dryer); shop; rest, bar 500m; BBQ; playgrnd; htd pool 300m; sand beach 150m; some statics; dogs; site clsd 3 Nov-16 Dec; poss cr; Eng spkn; quiet; ccard acc; CKE. "Gd base for walking, cycling, watersports; excel fishing; famous area for artists." ♦ SEK 260 2016*

ALMHULT *2F3* (2km N Rural) *56.56818, 14.13217* **Sjöstugans Camping (G5), Campingvägen, Bökhult, 34394 Älmhult [(0476) 71600; fax 15750; info@sjostugan.com; www.sjostugan.com]** Fr Växjö SW on rd 23, at rndabt turn W to Älmhult. Fr town cent turn N on Ljungbyvägen, site in 1.5km on lakeside, well sp. Med, pt sl, pt shd; htd wc; chem disp; mv service pnt; fam bthrm; sauna; shwrs; EHU (16A) SEK45; lndry (inc dryer); shop 1.5km; rest, snacks; bar; BBQ; cooking facs; playgrnd; lake & sand beach adj; games area; canoe hire; wifi; 25% statics; dogs; bus 500m; twin axles; Eng spkn; adv bkg; quiet; ccard acc; CKE. "Some lakeside pitches; well-kept site; 1st Ikea store opened here in 1958; v helpful staff; excel." ♦ 1 May-30 Sep. SEK 283 2017*

⊞ **AMAL** *2E2* (1km SE Urban) *59.0465, 12.7236* **Örnäs Camping (P2), Gamla Örnäsgatan, 66222 Åmål [(0532) 17097; fax 71624; ornascamping@amal.se; www.amal.se]** Leave rd 45 to Åmål, site sp. Sm, some hdstg, pt sl, terr, pt shd; htd wc; chem disp; mv service pnt; sauna; shwrs SEK5 for 4 min; EHU (10A) inc; lndry (inc dryer); shop, rest 1km; snacks; bar; playgrnd; sand beach/lake adj; fishing; tennis; boat & bike hire; wifi; some statics; dogs; Eng spkn; red 7 days; ccard acc; CCS. "Gd views Lake Vänern." ♦ ltd. SEK 275 2017*

⊞ **ARBOGA** *2G1* (13km S Rural) *59.28134, 15.90509* **Herrfallets Camping (U14), 73293 Arboga [(0589) 40110; fax 40133; reception@herrfallet.se; www.herrfallet.se]** Foll sp fr E20/E18, turn off at Sätra junc twd Arboga, cross rv. Foll sp to Herrfallet/Västermo. Med, mkd pitch, pt shd; htd wc; chem disp; 50% serviced pitches; mv service pnt; fam bthrm; sauna; shwrs SEK10; EHU (10A) SEK40; lndry (inc dryer); shop; rest; bar; BBQ; playgrnd; lake sw & beach; boating; bike hire; wifi; entmnt; dogs; phone; quiet; ccard acc; CKE/CCI. "Lovely spot on edge Lake Hjälmaren." ♦ SEK 270 2016*

ARJANG *2E1* (26km SE Rural) *59.30399, 12.44662* **Camping Grinsby, Grindsbyn 100, Sillerud, 67295 Årjäng [(0573) 42022; fax 40175; campgrinsby@telia.com; www.campgrinsby.se]** On E18 SE fr Årjäng & Sillerud, turn L at site sp. Site in 2km on Stora Bör lake. Med, some hdstg, terr, pt shd; htd wc; chem disp; mv service pnt; fam bthrm; shwrs SEK10; EHU (10A) SEK40; lndry (inc dryer); shop; BBQ; cooking facs; playgrnd; sand beach & lake sw adj; boat & bike hire; games rm; some statics; dogs; phone; Eng spkn; adv bkg; quiet; ccard acc; CKE/CCI. "A 'wilderness' site in beautiful setting; many walking paths; friendly, helpful staff; vg san facs." ♦ ltd. 1 May-3 Sep. SEK 231 2017*

⊞ **ARJEPLOG** *1C2* (1.5km W Rural) *66.05007, 17.86298* **Kraja Camping (BD1), Krajaudden, 93090 Arjeplog [(0961) 31500; fax 31599; kraja@silverresort.se; www.kraja.se]** NW fr Arvidsjaur thro Arjeplog vill to site on R. Lge, unshd; htd wc; chem disp; mv service pnt; fam bthrm; sauna; shwrs inc; EHU (16A) SEK40; lndry (inc dryer); shop; rest; bar; BBQ; cooking facs; playgrnd; htd pool; paddling pool; sand beach; lake sw 4km; fishing; boating; TV; wifi; 90% statics; dogs; bus 500m; twin axles; phone; Eng spkn; adv bkg; poss cr; quiet; CKE. "Gd cent for local Lapp area; hotel on site with full facs; 20 touring pitches; v pleasant & helpful staff; keypad security at night; excel Sami silver museum in town." ♦ SEK 235 2017*

⊞ **ASARNA** *1B3* (9km S Rural) *62.56340, 14.38786* **Kvarnsjö Camp, Kvarnsjö 696, 84031 Åsarna [tel/fax (0682) 22016; info@kvarnsjocamp.com; www.kvarnsjocamp.com]** Fr N on E45 3km after Åsarna turn R onto rd 316 dir Klövsjo. In 8km turn L sp Cmp Kvarnsjö. In 8km cross rlwy, thro vill, site on L in 1km. Fr S 9km after Rätan turn L dir Klövsjo. In 1.5km bear R at Y-junc site in 4km. Sm, hdstg, terr, unshd; wc; chem disp; mv service pnt; sauna; shwrs inc; EHU (10A) SEK40; lndry; shop 16km; dogs; Eng spkn; adv bkg; quiet. CKE/CCI. "CL-type family-run site o'looking woods & mountains; excel walking, fishing; boating, fresh bread/breakfast in high sssn." SEK 200 2017*

ASKIM see Göteborg *2E3*

BARSEBACK *2E4* (1km W Coastal) *55.77030, 12.92621* **Barsebäckstrand Camping (M19), Kustvägen 125, 24657 Barsebäck [(046) 776079; info@barsebackstrand.se; www.barsebackstrand.se]** Fr S exit E6 junc 23 sp 'Center Syd' & foll sp Barsebäck thro vill. Turn L at T-junc, site in 2km, sp. Fr N exit junc 24 & foll coast rd 'Kustvägen' to site in 5km. Med, mkd pitch, terr, unshd; htd wc; chem disp; mv service pnt; shwrs inc; EHU (10A) SEK40; lndry rm; shop 4km; rest, snacks; cooking facs; playgrnd; beach & sw adj; 40% statics; dogs free; poss cr; Eng spkn; adv bkg; quiet; CKE. "Vg site; excel rest." ♦ 26 Apr-1 Sep. SEK 250 2013*

SWEDEN

BERGKVARA *2G4* (1km E Coastal) *56.39043, 16.09061* **Dalskärs Camping (H15), Dalskärvägen11, 385 40 Bergkvara [(0709) 415567; info@dalskarscamping.se; www.dalskarscamping.se]** Exit E22 in Bergkvara twd Dalskärsbadet, site sp. Med, mkd pitch, pt shd; wc; chem disp; mv service pnt; fam bthrm; sauna; shwrs SEK5; EHU SEK40; lndry; shop; rest; bar; htd pool; paddling pool; sand beach adj; boat & bike hire; games area; wifi; some statics; dogs free; phone; Eng spkn; quiet; ccard acc. "Gd family site; san facs adequate; excel rest; scenic location." ♦ 24 Apr-11 Sep. SEK 220 2013*

⊞ **BOCKSJO** *2F2* (5km NW Rural) *58.68058, 14.59911* **Stenkällegårdens Camping i Tiveden, 54695 Stenkällegården [(0505) 60015; fax 60085; stenkallegarden@swipnet.se; www.stenkallegarden.se]** N on rd 49 fr Karlsborg, turn L at Bocksjö, site sp on L in 2km. Pt of rte single track with passing places. Med, mkd pitch, pt sl, terr, pt shd; htd wc; chem disp; mv service pnt; fam bthrm; sauna; shwrs SEK10, EHU (10A) SEK40; lndry (inc dryer); shop; rest; cooking facs; BBQ; playgrnd; lake sw; fishing; boat hire; wifi; TV rm; 30% statics; dogs; site clsd last 2 weeks Apr & 1st 2 weeks Oct; Eng spkn; quiet; ccard acc; CKE. "Gd cycling; mkd walking trails; spacious, sheltered site; clean san facs; skiing on site in winter; Tividen National Park 5km." ♦ SEK 250 2016*

"I like to fill in the reports as I travel from site to site"

You'll find report forms at the back of this guide, or you can fill them in online at camc.com/europereport.

⊞ **BORAS** *2E3* (2.5km N Urban) *57.73885, 12.93608* **Caming Borås Salteman (P11), Campinggatan 25, 50602 Borås [(033) 353280; fax 140582; info@borascamping.com; www.borascamping.com]** Exit N40 fr Göteborg for Borås Centrum; foll sps to Djur Park R42 to Trollhätten thro town; well sp. Med, mkd pitch, pt sl, pt shd; wc; chem disp; mv service pnt; shwrs inc; EHU (10A) SEK30; lndry rm; shop 3km; rest, snacks; cooking facs; playgrnd; pool 500m; boating; wifi; tv rm; 10% statics; dogs; bus 350m; Quickstop o'night facs; twin axles; poss cr; Eng spkn; adv bkg; some rd noise; CKE. "Gd pitches adj rv with paths; gd zoo 500m; gd, clean facs; nr sports stadium/tennis courts." ♦ ltd. SEK 270 2017*

BORENSBERG *2G2* (1.5km S Rural) *58.55663, 15.27911* **Strandbadets Camping, 59030 Borensberg [(0141) 40385; info@strandbadetscamping.se; www.strandbadetscamping.se]** Site sp off rd 36. Med, pt shd; wc; mv service pnt; fam bthrm; shwrs; EHU (10A) SEK40; lndry; shop, rest in vill; snacks; cooking facs; playgrnd; lake sw & beach; fishing; few statics; quiet; CKE. "Gd base for Östergötland & Lake Vättern area; cycle rte along Göta Canal." 22 Apr-11 Sep. SEK 190 2013*

BROMMA see Stockholm *2H2*

DALS LANGED see Bengtsfors *2E2*

⊞ **DOROTEA** *1C3* (500m SW Rural) *64.25850, 16.38833* **Doro Camping, Storgatan 1A, 91731 Dorotea [(0942) 10238; fax 10779; reception@dorocamp.com; www.dorocamping.com]** Site on E side of E45. Med, pt sl, pt shd; wc; chem disp; sauna; fam bthrm; shwrs inc; EHU (10A) SEK50; lndry (inc dryer); shop; snacks; cooking facs; lake sw; playgrnd; fishing; golf; hiking; internet; some statics; site clsd Nov; poss cr; Eng spkn; quiet. ♦ ltd. SEK 218 2016*

⊞ **ED** *2E2* (2km E Rural) *58.89931, 11.93486* **Gröne Backe Camping (P8), Södra Moränvägen 64, 66832 Ed [(0534) 10144; fax 10145; gronebackecamping@telia.com]** App Ed on rd 164/166, site sp on Lake Lilla Le. Med, pt sl, shd; wc; chem disp; sauna; fam bthrm; shwrs SEK5; EHU (10A) SEK40; lndry (inc dryer); shops, rest, snacks 300m; playgrnd; lake sw; bike hire; wifi; quiet; ccard acc; CKE. "Excel for boating." SEK 291 2016*

⊞ **EKSJO** *2F3* (1km E Rural) *57.66766, 14.98923* **Eksjö Camping (F13), Prästängsvägen 5, 57536 Eksjö [(0381) 39500; fax 14096; info@eksjocamping.se; www.eksjocamping.se]** Site sp fr town cent on rd 33 twd Västervik, on lakeside. Med, shd; wc; chem disp; mv service pnt; fam bthrm; shwrs; EHU (10A) SEK45; lndry (inc dryer); shop; rest, snacks; bar; playgrnd; covrd pool 100m; lake sw adj; fishing; boating; bike hire; wifi; 10% statics; dogs; phone; poss cr; no adv bkg; quiet; ccard acc; CKE. "Gd cent glass region; attractive countryside & old town." ♦ SEK 250 2016*

ELDSBERGA see Halmstad *2E3*

⊞ **ENKOPING** *2H1* (6km S Rural) *59.59334, 17.07146* **Bredsand Camping & Stugby, Bredsandsvägen 22, 74948 Enköping [(0171) 80011; bredsand@nordiccamping.se; www.nordiccamping.se]** Fr E18 or rd 55 foll sp to site, well sp on Lake Mälaren. Med, mkd pitch, pt sl, pt shd; htd wc; chem disp; mv service pnt; fam bthrm; shwrs inc; EHU (10A) SEK50; lndry (inc dryer); supmkt 4km; rest, snacks; lake sw & beach adj; 50% statics; dogs; quiet; CKE. "Vg site." SEK 287 2015*

⊞ **FALKOPING** *2F2* (1km W Rural) *58.17595, 13.52726* **Mössebergs Camping & Stugby (R7), Lidgatan 4, 52102 Falköping [(0515) 17349; mossebergscamping@telia.com]** Exit rd 184 at Falköping; foll Int'l Camping sps or sps to Mösseberg; site also sp fr rds 46 & 47 & in town. Site on plateau overlkg town. Med, mkd pitch, pt shd; wc; mv service pnt; fam bthrm; sauna; shwrs SEK5; EHU SEK40; lndry (inc dryer); cooking facs; shops 1km; playgrnd; pool 400m; lake sw 400m; wifi; some statics; dogs; phone; quiet; ccard acc; CKE. ♦ SEK 230 2016*

⊞ **FILIPSTAD** *2F1* (1km N Rural) *59.72035, 14.15899* **Munkeberg Camping (S5), Skillervägen, 68233 Filipstad [tel/fax (0590) 50100; alterschwede@telia.com; www.munkeberg.com]** Fr Karlstad take rd 63 to Filipstad. In town foll sp for rd 246 twd Hagfors, site sp in town. Med, pt sl, pt shd; htd wc; chem disp; shwrs inc; EHU (10A) SEK30; lndry (inc dryer); shop 1km; snacks; playgrnd; lake sw; boating; fishing; wifi; some statics; dogs; adv bkg; quiet; CKE/CCI. "Beautiful lakeside site; gd for touring old mining district." ♦ SEK 208 2016*

FROSON see Östersund *1B3*

⊞ **GADDEDE** *1B2* (400m NE Rural) *64.50400, 14.14900* **Gäddede Camping & Stugby, Sagavägen 9, 83090 Gäddede [(0672) 10035; fax 10511; info@gaddedecamping.com; www.gaddedecamping.se]** On ent Gäddede cent on rd 342, turn R & site in 500m on R, sp. Med, mkd pitch, pt shd; htd wc; chem disp; sauna; shwrs SEK5; EHU (10A) SEK50; lndry; shop 500m; rest 100m; playgrnd; htd pool; paddling pool; canoe hire; fishing; games area; games rm; TV; 10% statics; dogs; poss cr; Eng spkn; adv bkg; quiet; ccard acc; CKE/CCI. "Gd touring base 'Wilderness Way'." ♦ SEK 198 2016*

GAMLEBY *2G2* (1km SE Coastal) *57.88475, 16.41373* **KustCamp Gamleby (formerly Hammarsbadets), Hammarsvägen 10, 59432 Gamleby [(0493) 10221; fax 12686; info@campa.se; www.campa.se]** On E22 Kalmar-Norrköping, foll sp to site 2km off main rd. Med, mkd pitch, terr, pt shd; wc; chem disp; mv service pnt; fam bthrm; sauna; shwrs SEK5; EHU (10A) SEK45; lndry (inc dryer); shop; rest, snacks; bar; playgrnd; pool; sand beach adj; lake sw; boat & bike hire; tennis; wifi; some statics; dogs; phone; Quickstop o'night facs; quiet; ccard acc; CKE/CCI. "Clean, well-kept, relaxing site." 1 May-15 Sep. SEK 312 2016*

⊞ **GESUNDA** *1B4* (2km N Rural) *60.90100, 14.58500* **Sollerö Camping (W60), Levsnäs, 79290 Sollerön [(0250) 22230; fax 22268; info@sollerocamping.se; www.sollerocamping.se]** Fr Gesunda take bdge to Sollerön Island in Lake Siljan. Site immed on R on reaching island; clearly visible fr bdge. Lge, pt sl, pt shd; wc; chem disp; mv service pnt; fam bthrm; sauna; shwrs inc; EHU (10A) SEK30; lndry (inc dryer); shop; snacks; bar; playgrnd; lake sw adj; canoe & boat hire; tennis; wifi; poss cr; adv bkg; quiet; ccard acc; CKE/CCI. "Beautiful outlook to S across lake; gd base for Dalarna folklore area; gd site & facs; every 7th day is free." ♦ SEK 260 2017*

GLOMMEN see Falkenberg *2E3*

⊞ **GOTEBORG** *2E3* (4km E Rural) *57.7053, 12.0286* **Lisebergsbyn Camping Kärralund (O39), Olbersgatan 1, 41655 Göteborg [(031) 840200; fax 840500; lisebergsbyn@liseberg.se; www.liseberg.se]** Exit E6/E20 junc 71 onto rd 40 E & foll sp Lisebergsbyn, site well sp. Lge, pt sl, terr, unshd; wc; chem disp; mv service pnt; fam bthrm; shwrs inc; EHU (16A) inc; gas; lndry (inc dryer); shop (open only once a week LS); supmkt nrby; rest; snacks; bar; BBQ; cooking facs; games area; playgrnd; wifi; TV rm; 25% statics; dogs; phone; tram 400m; twin axles; Eng spkn; poss cr/noisy high ssn; Eng spkn; adv bkg rec; red LS; ccard acc; red LS & Sun-Fri; CKE. "Boat trips arranged; vg, well-run site; LS arr early to obtain barrier key; poss travellers on site; cycle path to Liseberg amusement park & town cent; impressive, organised & professional staff; lovely site; san facs outstanding." ♦ SEK 450 2017*

⊞ **GOTEBORG** *2E3* (7km W) *57.70413, 12.02989* **Lisebergs Ställplats, Olbersgatan 9, 416 55 Göteborg [031 840 200; lisebergsbyn@liseberg.se; www.liseberg.se]** Take Backebogatan to Litteraturgatan. Then E6 and Delsjövägen to Olbersgatan. At rndabt take 1st exit to Olbersgatan, Turn R & R again, site on L. Sm, mkd pitch, hdstg, pt shd; own san rec; chem disp; mv service pnt; EHU (10A) inc; BBQ; playgrnd; wifi; dogs; Eng spkn; adv bkg; ccard acc. "Tram at bottom of hill past main site ent, main site off will help with travel info etc; excel." SEK 240 2016*

GOTHENBURG see Göteborg *2E3*

GRANNA *2F2* (500m NW Rural) *58.02783, 14.45821* **Grännastrandens Familjecamping (F3), Hamnen, 56300 Gränna [(0390) 10706; fax 41260; info@grannacamping.se; www.grannacamping.se]** In cent of Gränna down rd twd Lake Vättern, sp Visingsö Island. Lge, unshd; wc; chem disp; mv service pnt; fam bthrm; shwrs; EHU (10A) metered + conn fee; lndry (inc dryer); shop; rest adj; playgrnd; lake sw & beach; wifi; sat TV; some cottages; dogs; poss v cr; CKE. "Ballooning cent of Sweden; Visingsö Island, Brahehus ruined castle, glass-blowing 3km; vg site; gd location; excel, clean san facs, excel camp kitchen." ♦ 30 Apr-3 Oct. SEK 300 2016*

⊞ **GREBBESTAD** *2E2* (1km S Coastal) *58.6832, 586832* **Grebbestads Familjecamping (O10), Rörvik, 45795 Grebbestad, Sverige [(0525) 61211; fax 14319; info@grebbestadfjorden.com; www.grebbestadfjorden.com]** Exit E6 at Tanumshede sp Grebbestad; foll rd thro vill, past harbour; site on R approx 500m after harbour. Lge, mkd pitch, pt sl, unshd; wc; chem disp; mv service pnt; fam bthrm; sauna; shwrs inc; EHU (10A) SEK50; lndry (inc dryer); sm shop & 500m; snacks; cooking facs; htd pool 1km; sand beach 150m; games area; wifi; mainly statics; phone; dogs; poss cr; Eng spkn; adv bkg; quiet; ccard acc; CKE. "Well-maintained site 500m fr busy fishing/yachting harbour; meadowland; excel mv services; helpful staff; vg facs, lge cr noisy site." ♦ SEK 350 2013*

SWEDEN

⊞ **HALMSTAD** *2E3* (10km S Coastal) *56.59033, 12.94430* **Gullbrannagården Camping (N27), 31031 Eldsberga [tel/fax (035) 42180; mail@gullbrannagarden.se; www.gullbrannagarden.se]** Fr S site sp on E6. Lge, pt sl, pt shd; wc; chem disp; mv service pnt; fam bthrm; shwrs inc; EHU SEK45; lndry; shop; snacks; cooking facs; playgrnd; sand beach 500m; games rm; wifi; entmnt; 60% statics; dogs; poss cr; Eng spkn; adv bkg; quiet. "Christian-run site; church & bible classes; alcohol discouraged; OK for those of like mind." ♦ SEK 290 2016*

HAMBURGSUND *2E2* (1km S Coastal) *58.54075, 11.28240* **Rorviks Camping, Rorviksangen 15 45747 Hamburgsund [05 25 33 573; info@rorvikscamping.se; www.rorvikscamping.se]** Take exit 103 on the E6 (bet Tatum V-Munkedal). Foll 163 W to Kville. Turn L to Hamburgsund, cont S 1km. Campsite on R. Lge, mkd pitch, hdstg, pt shd; wc; chem disp; mv service pnt; fam bthrm; shwr (5kr); EHU (10A) inc; lndry (inc dryer); shop; BBQ; cooking facs; games area; entmnt; 10% statics; dogs; bus 1km; twin axles; Eng spkn; adv bkg; CCI. "Quiet, low key site in a great area; vg." 1 May-31 Aug. SEK 350 2014*

⊞ **HAPARANDA** *1D2* (15km N Rural) *65.9620, 24.0378* **Kukkolaforsen Camping (BD27), Kukkolaforsen 184, 95391 Haparanda [(0922) 31000; info@kukkolaforsen.se; www.kukkolaforsen.se]** On rd 99 on banks of Rv Tornionjoki. Med, pt shd; htd wc; chem disp; fam bthrm; sauna; shwrs inc; EHU (10A) SEK40; lndry; shop; rest, snacks; bar; playgrnd; fishing; bike hire; wifi; TV; statics; phone; adv bkg; ccard acc; CKE. "Friendly staff; rv rapids." SEK 280 2016*

HARNOSAND *1C3* (2.5km NE Coastal) *62.64451, 17.97123* **Sälstens Camping (Y21), Sälsten 22, 87133 Härnösand [tel/fax (0611) 18150; salsten.camping@telia.com]** On Gulf of Bothnia, E of town & on S side of inlet; exit off E4; foll sp for Härnösand town cent, then intn'l camping sp; then site. Sm, mkd pitch, terr, pt shd; htd wc; chem disp; shwrs inc; EHU (10A); lndry (inc dryer); shop; playgrnd; beach; wifi; TV; Eng spkn; quiet; CKE. "Folk museum in town; excel site." ♦ ltd. 15 May-31 Aug. SEK 250 2016*

HEBERG see Falkenberg *2E3*

HEDESUNDA *2G1* (5km SE Rural) *60.35000, 17.02100* **Hedesunda Camping (formerly Sandsnäs), Övägen 68, 81040 Hedesunda [tel/fax (0291) 44123; info@hedesundacamping.se; www.hedesundacamping.se]** Exit rd 67 L at sp Hedesunda. Foll camp sp thro Hedesunda; past church, cont about 4km to Hedesunda Island. Sm, pt shd; htd wc; chem disp; shwrs inc; EHU (6A) SEK30; gas; lndry (inc dryer); shop 3km; rest, snacks; cooking facs; playgrnd; sand beach & lake sw adj; boat hire; fishing; wifi; TV; poss cr at w/end; Eng spkn; quiet; red 16+ days; CKE. "Peaceful, lakeside site; organised activities in ssn; helpful staff." ♦ 1 May-31 Oct. SEK 260 2016*

HEDEVIKEN see Hede *1B3*

⊞ **HELSINGBORG** *2E4* (5km S Coastal) *56.0034, 12.7300* **Campingplatsen Råå Vallar (M3), Kustgatan, 25270 Råå [(042) 182600; fax 107681; raavallar@nordiccamping.se; www.nordiccamping.se]** Exit E6 into Helsingborg onto rd 111 to Råå, foll sp to camp. Lge, pt shd; htd wc; fam bthrm; sauna; shwrs inc; EHU (10A) SEK50; gas; lndry (inc dryer); shop; rest, snacks; bar; playgrnd; pool; paddling pool; sand beach; fishing; sports cent 2km; golf 5km; wifi; some statics; phone; Quickstop o'night facs; poss cr; ccard acc; CKE/CCI. "Excel, secure site with gd facs; friendly, helpful staff; excursions to Copenhagen via Helsingør or Landskrona; town bus excursions to King's Summer Palace daily; boat trips to glass works at Hyllinge." ♦ SEK 410 2016*

HOGANAS *2E4* (8km N Rural) *56.27061, 12.52981* **FirstCamp Mölle (M1), Kullabergsvägen, 26042 Mölle [(042) 347384; fax 347729; molle@firstcamp.se; www.firstcamp.se]** Site is S of Mölle at junc of rds 11 & 111, at foot of Kullaberg. Lge, pt sl, unshd; htd wc; chem disp; mv service pnt; sauna; shwrs inc; EHU (10A) inc; lndry (inc dryer); shop; rest, snacks; bar; cooking facs; playgrnd; beach 1.5km; fishing; games area; walking; golf; wifi; entmnt; 10% statics; dogs; Quickstop o'night facs; Eng spkn; quiet; ccard acc. "Steep slope to san facs; Krapperups Castle & park sh walk fr site; excel outdoor activities." ♦ 1 Apr-30 Sep. SEK 417 2016*

HOVA *2F2* (8.7km NE Coastal) *58.90998, 14.28995* **Otterbergets Bad & Camping, 54891 Hova [050633 127 or 0738064 935; info@otterbergetscamping.com; www.otterbergetscamping.com]** Fr Laxa take E20 rd; site sp approx 4km fr Hova; drive 2 km thro woods to site. Med, mkd pitch, pt shd; wc; chem disp; mv service pnt; fam bthrm; shwrs (metered); EHU (16A) SEK 40; lndry (inc dryer); snacks; BBQ; cooking facs; playgrnd; sauna; beach adj; wifi; 10% statics; dogs; poss cr; Eng spkn; adv bking; quiet; red LS; CCI. "Attractive site with private access to lake; events held such as fishing competition & trade fairs (when site may be busy); v helpful Dutch owners; recep 0800-2200; san facs vg; excel." ♦ 15 Apr-1 Nov. SEK 253 2017*

JOKKMOKK *1C2* (3km SE Rural) *66.59453, 19.89145* **Artic Camp Jokkmokk, Notudden, 96222 Jokkmokk [(0971) 12370; fax 12476; campingcenter@jokkmokk.com; www.jokkmokkcampingcenter.com]** Sp fr rd 45. In Jokkmokk take rd 97 E, site in 3km on N side of rd situated bet rv & rd. Lge, mkd pitch, pt shd; htd wc; chem disp; mv service pnt; sauna; shwrs inc; EHU (10A) SEK40 (poss rev pol); lndry (inc dryer); sm shop & 3km; rest, snacks; bar; playgrnd; 3 htd pools high ssn; waterslide; lake sw adj; fishing; bike hire; internet; some statics; dogs; Eng spkn; adv bkg; ccard acc; quiet; CKE. "Friendly, clean, well-maintained site 5km inside Arctic Circle; gd area for Sami culture; excel playgrnd; lakeside setting, gd pool." ♦ 15 May-15 Sep. SEK 266 2017*

⊞ **JOKKMOKK** *1C2* (3km W Rural) *66.60500, 19.76200* **Skabram Stugby & Camping, Skabram 206, 96299 Jokkmokk [(0971) 10752; info@skabram.se; www.skabram.se]** Site sp fr E45 along rd 97, Storgatan. Sm, pt hdstg, pt shd; htd wc; chem disp; mv service pnt; sauna; shwrs inc; EHU (16A) SEK25; lndry rm; BBQ; cooking facs; lake sw adj; boating; fishing; wifi; 10% statics; dogs; bus 3km; twin axles; Eng spkn; adv bkg; quiet. "Vg; canoe & dog sleigh trips; relaxing site; lovely sm fm type site; v quiet location; gd san facs." ♦ ltd. SEK 185 2017*

⊞ **JONKOPING** *2F3* (2.5km E Urban) *57.7876, 14.2195* **Swecamp Villa Björkhagen (F6), Friggagatan 31, 55454 Jönköping [(036) 122863; fax 126687; info@villabjorkhagen.se; www.villabjorkhagen.se]** Fr N exit E4 junc 99 or fr S exit E4 junc 98a & foll sp Rosenlund/Elmia & site sp nr exhibition cent. Site on Lake Vättern. Lge, mkd pitch, pt sl, pt shd; htd wc; chem disp; mv service pnt; fam bthrm; sauna; shwrs inc; EHU (10A) SEK35; lndry (inc dryer) shop; rest; bar; playgrnd; htd, covrd pool complex, waterslide 300m; lake sw 500m; fishing; bike hire; wifi; entmnt; sat TV; 50% statics; dogs; phone; Quickstop o'night facs; poss v cr; quiet; ccard acc; CKE. "Gd rest; prone to flooding after heavy rain; some facs run down & site untidy (2010); site charges increase considerably during exhibitions & site v full; pitches well mkd; easy walk into town along sea front." ♦ SEK 265 2014*

JONKOPING *2F3* (15km S Rural) *57.66245, 14.18407* **Lovsjöbadens Camping (F7), Hyltena, 55592 Jönköping [(036) 182010; info@lovsjocamping.se; www.lovsjocamping.se]** Exit E4 at Hyltena, site sp on lakeside. Sm, mkd pitch, terr, pt sl; wc; chem disp; fam bthrm; shwrs inc; EHU (10-16A) SEK30; lndry (inc dryer); snacks; BBQ; cooking facs; lake sw; boat & bike hire; games rm; wifi; TV; some statics; dogs; Eng spkn; adv bkg; quiet; ccard acc; CKE. "V friendly owners; vg site by sm lake; busy in high ssn; sm sw beach; rowing boats for hire." ♦ 15 May-15 Sep. SEK 260 2015*

KALMAR *2G3* (2km S Coastal) *56.64975, 16.32705* **Stensö Camping (H12), Stensövägen, 39247 Kalmar [(0480) 88803; fax 420476; info@stensocamping.se; www.stensocamping.se]** Fr E22 foll sp Sjukhus (hosp) then camping sp - this avoids town cent. Fr town cent, site sp. Lge, some mkd pitch, pt sl, shd; wc; chem disp; mv service pnt; fam bthrm; shwrs inc; EHU (10A) SEK40 (check pol); lndry (inc dryer); shop; rest, snacks; bar; cooking facs; playgrnd; pool 1km; sand beach adj; fishing; boating; cycling; wifi; some statics; phone; Quickstop o'night facs; Eng spkn; ccard acc; CKE. "Conv Öland Island (over bdge); glass factories in vicinity; walking dist to town; helpful, friendly staff; new clean san facs (2014); excel." ♦ 27 Mar-30 Sep. SEK 276 2016*

KAPPELLSKAR *2H1* (500m W Rural) *59.72046, 19.05045* **Camping Kapellskär (B9), Riddersholm 985, 76015 Gräddö [(0176) 44233]** Fr Norrtälje take E18 E sp Kapellskär. At ferry sp turn R, site in 1km, sp. Last 700m on unmade rd. Med, mkd pitch, some hdstg, terr, pt shd; htd wc; chem disp; mv service pnt; fam bthrm; shwrs inc; EHU (10A) SEK40; lndry (inc dryer); shop; rest 1.5km; snacks; bar; playgrnd; bike hire; games area; 60% statics; dogs; Eng spkn; adv bkg; quiet; ccard acc; CKE. "Conv for ferry terminal; fair site." 1 May-29 Sep. SEK 272 2015*

KARESUANDO *1D1* (2km SE Rural) *68.43396, 22.51577* **Karesuando Camping, Laestadiusvagen 185, 98016 Karesuando [(0981) 20139; fax 20381; karesuando.camping@hotmail.com; www.karesuando.se/foretag/camping/camping.htm]** Travelling N on E45, in town cont past bdge to Finland onto rd 99 for approx 2km; site on L. App fr Finland, turn L after x-ing bdge; cont on 99 for 2km. Sm, unshd; wc; chem disp; mv service point; sauna; shwrs; EHU (10A) inc; lndry; cafe; snacks; BBQ; playgrnd; rv adj; games area; 50% statics; dogs; twin axles; poss cr; Eng spkn; adv bkg; quiet; CKE/CCI. "Model Sami vill on site; cash point in PO; poss mosquito prob; canoe hire avail; gd view of midnight sun on rv; unmkd pitches, fills up quickly." ♦ ltd. 15 May-15 Sep. SEK 200 2014*

KARLSHAMN *2F4* (3km SE Coastal) *56.15953, 14.89085* **Kolleviks Camping (K7), Kolleviksvägen, 37430 Karlshamn [(0454) 19280; fax 16280; kollevik@karlshamn.se; www.karlshamn.se]** Fr E22 dir Karlshamn & Hamnar (harbour), then site well sp. Med, mkd pitch, pt sl, pt shd; htd wc; chem disp; mv service pnt; fam bthrm; shwrs SEK5; EHU (10A) SEK45; lndry (inc dryer); shop; rest, snacks; playgrnd; pool 1km; sand beach adj; canoeing; 25% statics; Quickstop o'night facs; Eng spkn; adv bkg; quiet; ccard acc; red long stay/LS; CKE. "Helpful owner; attractive location inc harbour; gd base for area; ltd facs LS; well-kept site; facs tired, poss stretched when busy." ♦ 26 Apr-14 Sep. SEK 155 2012*

KARLSKRONA *2G4* (2km NE Coastal) *56.1729, 15.5675* **Dragsö Camping (K10), Dragsövägen 14, 37137 Karlskrona [(0455) 15354; fax 15277; info@dragso.se; www.dragsocamping.se]** Foll app to town cent, taking m'way. At end of m'way foll sp to Dragsö. Site sp - on its own island. Lge, mkd pitch, pt shd; htd wc; mv service pnt; fam bthrm; sauna; shwrs; EHU (10A) inc; lndry (inc dryer); kiosk; supmkt, rest 3km; snacks; bar; playgrnd; beach adj; fishing; boating; bike hire; wifi; entmnt; TV rm; some statics; dogs; Quickstop o'night facs; poss v cr; CKE. "Sea bathing; rocky cliffs; scenic beauty; gd." ♦ 1Apr-10 Oct. SEK 323 2013*

⊞ **KARLSTAD** *2F1* (9km W Rural) *59.36233, 13.35891* **Swecamp Bomstad-Badens (S9), Bomstadsvägen 640, 65346 Karlstad [(054) 535068; fax 535375; info@bomstad-baden.se; www.bomstadbaden.se]** 2km S of E18 on Lake Vänern. Foll sp thro woods. Lge, pt sl, shd; wc; chem disp; mv service pnt; fam bthrm; shwrs SEK10; EHU (10A) SEK50; lndry (inc dryer); shop; supmkt 4km; snacks; bar; BBQ; playgrnd; pool; sand beach; lake sw; fishing; canoeing; bike hire; wifi; entmnt; statics; phone; adv bkg; CKE. "Excel base; beautiful site in trees; gd walks on mkd trails." ♦
SEK 290 2013*

⊞ **KATRINEHOLM** *2G2* (2km S Rural) *58.9696, 16.21035* **Djulö Camping (D6), Djulögatan 51, 64192 Katrineholm [tel/fax (0150) 57242; info@djulocamping.se; www.djulocamping.se]** At Norrköping on E4 cont twd Stockholm for about 3km, turn L onto rd 55 N twd Katrineholm. Camping site sp in 2km. Lge, hdstg, pt sl; wc; mv service pnt; fam bthrm; shwrs SEK1; EHU (10A) SEK35; gas; lndry (inc dryer); shop 2km; rest 2km; snacks; playgrnd; lake sw; boating; fishing; games area; bike hire; wifi; poss cr; adv bkg; quiet; ccard acc; CKE. "On lakeside in lge park; well-run, friendly site." ♦ SEK 291 2016*

⊞ **KIL** *2F1* (7km N Rural) *59.54603, 13.34145* **Frykenbadens Camping (S17), Stubberud, 66591 Kil [(0554) 40940; fax 41010; info@frykenbaden.se; www.frykenbaden.se]** Fr Karlstad take rd 61 to Kil, site clearly sp on lakeside. Lge, pt sl, pt shd; wc; chem disp; mv service pnt; fam bthrm; sauna SEK5; shwrs; EHU (10A) SEK40; lndry (inc dryer); shop; snacks; bar; playgrnd; lake sw; fishing; boat-launching; bike hire; wifi; TV; phone; Quickstop o'night facs; quiet; adv bkg; CKE. "Very clean, spacious waterfront site." ♦
SEK 307 2016*

⊞ **KIRUNA** *1C1* (1.6km NE Urban) *67.8604, 20.2405* **Ripan Hotel & Camping, Campingvägen 5, 98135 Kiruna [(0980) 63000; fax 63040; info@ripan.se; www.ripan.se]** Site sp fr town cent. Med, unshd, mkd pitch, hdstg; htd wc; chem disp; sauna; shwrs inc; EHU (10A) inc; lndry; shop 500m; rest; bar; playgrnd; htd pool; cab TV; wifi; poss cr; quiet; Eng spkn; ccard acc. "No privacy in shwrs; easy walk to town; public footpath thro site (top end) - poss v noisy & disruptive; trips to Kirunavaara Deep Mine fr tourist info office; no security fence." ♦ SEK 323 2016*

KIVIK *2F4* (1.6km N Rural/Coastal) *55.69135, 14.21373* **Kiviks Familjecamping (L35), Väg 9, 27732 Kivik [(0414) 70930; fax 70934; info@kivikscamping.se; www.kivikscamping.se]** On rd 9 o'looking sea, sp. Med, mkd pitch, unshd; wc; chem disp; mv service pnt; fam bthrm; shwrs SEK5; EHU SEK35; lndry (inc dryer); shop; rest; BBQ; cooking facs; playgrnd; shgl/sand beach 1km; entmnt; wifi (recep area); TV rm; phone; 20% statics; dogs; Eng spkn; ccard acc; CKE. "Steam rlwy w/end in summer at Brösarp; cider/apple area; easy walk to town; rev pol certain pitches." ♦
16 Apr-9 Oct. SEK 230 2016*

KOLMARDEN *2G2* (2km SE Coastal) *58.6597, 586597* **First Camp Kolmården (E3), 61834 Kolmården [(011) 398250; fax 397081; kolmarden@firstcamp.se; www.firstcamp.se]** Fr E4 NE fr Norrköping take 1st Kolmården exit sp Kolmården Djur & Naturpark. Site on sea 2km bef Naturpark. Lge, pt terr, pt shd; htd wc; chem disp; mv service pnt; fam bthrm; sauna; shwrs SEK5; EHU (10A); lndry (inc dryer); shop; kiosk; rest, snacks; bar; cooking facs; playgrnd; beach adj; waterslide; boat & bike hire; entmnt; TV rm; wifi; 10% statics; dogs; phone; ccard acc; CKE. "Gd site; nr to Kilmarden zoo & aquarium; well mkd pitches." ♦
17 Apr-30 Sep. SEK 383 2014*

KUNGALV *2E2* (1km SE Rural) *57.86211, 11.99613* **Kungälvs Vandrarhem & Camping (O37), Färjevägen 2, 44231 Kungälv [(0303) 18900; fax (303) 19295; info@kungalvsvandrarhem.se; www.kungalvsvandrarhem.se]** Exit E6 junc 85 or 86 & foll sp Kungälv cent, then sp 'Bohus Fästning'. Site sp. Sm, mkd pitch, some hdstg, shd; htd wc; chem disp; mv service pnt; fam bthrm; shwrs inc; EHU (12A) SEK40; lndry (inc dryer); shop; rest, snacks; bar; gas BBQ; playgrnd; wifi; some statics; dogs; bus adj; Eng spkn; quiet; ccard acc; red long stay; CC1. "Site adj Bonus Fästning (fort) & Kungälv Church (17th C) on rv bank; find pitch & check in at recep 0800-1000 & 1700-1900; door code fr recep for san facs; gd NH." ♦ ltd.
15 Apr-30 Sep. SEK 250 2014*

KUNGSBACKA *2E3* (5km SE Rural) *57.42492, 12.15860* **Silverlyckans Camping, Varbergsvägen 875, 43433 Fjärås [(0300) 541349; www.silverlyckan.eu]** Exit E6/E20 junc 58 dir Åsa. Site in 400m on L. Med, pt sl, unshd; htd wc; chem disp; mv service pnt (refill only); shwrs SEK5; EHU (10A) SEK30; lndry; shop, rest, snacks 3km; cooking facs; playgrnd; htd pool 3km; sand beach 4km; 10% statics; dogs; bus adj; Eng spkn; adv bkg; quiet. "Vg site; rec visit Tjolöholms Slott (castle)." 1 May-15 Sep. SEK 180 2014*

⊞ **KUNGSHAMN** *2E2* (2km NE Coastal) *58.36569, 11.28077* **Swecamp Johannesvik, Wagga Nordgard 1, 45634 Kungshamn [tel/fax (0523) 32387; info@johannesvik.nu; www.johannesvik.nu]** Fr E6 rte 171 to Askum, dir Kungshamn, thro Hovenaset, over bdge. Ent to site on R (sp). Lge, mkd pitch, terr, unshd; htd wc; chem disp; mv service pnt; shwrs; fam bthrm; EHU inc; gas; BBQ; lndry rm; cooking facs; rest, snacks, bar, shop hg ssn only, otherwise 2km; playgrnd; beach adj; shingle; tv rm; dogs; poss cr; quiet; adv bkg; dep req; Eng spkn; red long stay; CKE/CCI. "Barrier card SEK150 dep; shwr card SEK6 (3mins); gd." SEK 381
2017*

KVIDINGE see Klippan *2F4*

LANDSKRONA *2E4* (4km N Rural) *55.90098, 12.8042* **Borstahusens Camping (M5), Campingvägen, 26161 Landskrona [(0418) 10837; fax 22042; bengt@borstahusenscamping.se; www.borstahusenscamping.se]** Exit E6/E20 at 'Landskrona N' & foll sp for Borstahusen 4.5km fr E6/D20. Lge; htd wc; chem disp; shwrs inc; fam bthrm; EHU (10A) SEK40; lndry (inc dryer); shop; snacks 200m; playgrnd; htd pool 2km; tennis; bike hire; game reserve; golf; wifi; TV rm; 75% statics; phone; poss v cr; ccard acc; CKE/CCI. "Gd, pleasant site on edge of Kattegat; sm pitches; boat to Ven Island fr town." ♦ 21 Apr-11 Sep. SEK 320 2015*

⊞ **LIDKOPING** *2F2* (3km N Rural) *58.51375, 13.14008* **Krono Camping (R3), Läckögaten, 53154 Lidköping [(0510) 26804; fax 21135; info@kronocamping.com; www.kronocamping.com]** On Lake Vänern nr Folkparken, on rd to Läckö; at Lidköping ring rd foll int'l camping sp. Lge, pt shd; serviced pitch; wc; chem disp; mv service pnt; fam bthrm; some serviced pitches; shwrs inc; EHU (10A) inc; gas; lndry (inc dryer); shop; rest 300m; playgrnd; htd pool 300m; lake sw 300m; watersports; wifi; cab TV (via el hook-up); quiet; ccard acc; CKE. "V clean, friendly, well-run site; open pinewoods on lakeside; interesting area." ♦ SEK 412 2015*

LIMHAMN see Malmo *2E4*

LJUNGBY *2F3* (1km N Urban) *56.84228, 13.95251* **Ljungby Camping Park, Campingvägen 1, 34122 Ljungby [tel/fax (0372) 10350; reservation@ljungby-semesterby.se; www.ljungby-semesterby.se]** Exit E4 at Ljungby N, site sp. Med, shd; htd wc; chem disp; shwrs inc; EHU (10A) SEK35; lndry (inc dryer); shop; rest (Jun-Aug); playgrnd; htd pool adj; paddling pool; cycling; poss cr in ssn; ccard acc; CKE. "Adv bkg ess high ssn." 1 May-31 Aug. SEK 256 2016*

"I need an on-site restaurant"

We do our best to make sure site information is correct, but it is always best to check any must-have facilities are still available or will be open during your visit.

⊞ **LJUSDAL** *1B3* (3km W Rural) *61.83894, 16.04059* **Ljusdals Camping (X21), Ramsjövägen 56, 82730 Ljusdal [(0651) 12958; info@ljusdalscamping.se; www.ljusdalscamping.se]** Leave Ljusdal on Rv83 dir Ånge, site on R in 3km. Med, pt shd; htd wc; chem disp; mv service pnt; sauna; shwrs inc; EHU (10A) SEK40; lndry (inc dryer); rest, snacks; bar; cooking facs; playgrnd; lake sw & beach adj; games area; bike hire; wifi; entmnt; some statics; dogs; Eng spkn; adv bkg; ccard acc; CKE. ♦ SEK 255 2014*

LOMMA see Malmö *2E4*

⊞ **LULEA** *1D2* (8km W Coastal) *65.59565, 22.07221* **First Camp Luleå (BD18), Arcusvägen 110, 97594 Luleå [(0920) 60300; fax 60315; lulea@firstcamp.se; www.firstcamp.se/lulea]** Exit E4 on R 500m N of Luleälv Rv bdge. Foll sp 'Arcus' (recreation complex). V lge, mkd pitch, pt shd; htd wc; chem disp; mv service pnt; fam bthrm; sauna; shwrs inc; EHU (10A) inc; lndry (inc dryer); shop; rest, snacks; bar; cooking facs; playgrnd; htd pool complex 700m; sand beach adj; tennis 300m; bike hire; wifi; TV; dogs; phone; car wash; Eng spkn; adv bkg; quiet; ccard acc; CKE. "Excel family site; many sports facs; san facs poss stretched high ssn; suitable RVs & twin-axles; adj rlwy museum." ♦ SEK 365 2014*

MALMO *2E4* (11km N Coastal) *55.68873, 13.05756* **Habo-Ljung Camping (M23), Södra Västkustvägen 12, 23434 Lomma [(040) 411210; fax 414310; info@haboljungcamping.se; www.haboljungcamping.se]** Turn off E6 dir Lomma, head N for Bjärred, site on L. Lge, pt shd; htd wc (cont); chem disp; mv service pnt; fam bthrm; shwrs inc; EHU (10A) SEK40; lndry (inc dryer); shop; snacks; BBQ; cooking facs; playgrnd; sand beach adj; entmnt; 5% statics; phone; poss cr; Eng spkn; poss noisy; ccard acc; CKE. "Conv NH; vg; location for wind & kite surfing; 20 min walk along beach to town." ♦ ltd. 15 Apr-15 Sep. SEK 280 2014*

⊞ **MALMO** *2E4* (7km SW Urban) *55.5722, 12.90686* **Malmö Camping & Feriesenter (M8), Strandgatan 101, Sibbarp, 21611 Limhamn [(040) 155165; fax 159777; malmocamping@malmo.se; www.firstcamp.se]** Fr Öresund Bdge take 1st exit & foll sp Limhamn & Sibbarp, then int'l campsite sp. Fr N on E6 round Malmö until last exit bef bdge (sp), then as above. Fr Dragør-Limnhamn ferry turn R on exit dock. Site in 1km on R, nr sea, in park-like setting. V lge, hdg/mkd pitches, pt sl, pt shd; htd wc; chem disp; mv service pnt; fam bthrm; shwrs; EHU (16A) inc (poss rev pol); gas; lndry (inc dryer); shops; rest, snacks; BBQ; cooking facs; playgrnd; pool 400m; sand beach 250m; games area; games rm; windsurfing; bike hire; entmnt; wifi; TV rm; 20% statics; dogs; phone; bus to Malmo; twin axles; poss cr; Eng spkn; no adv bkg; quiet; ccard acc; CKE. "Easy cycle to town cent; facs poss stretched high ssn; v busy city site; well-laid out; conv Öresund Bdge; lovely site; v friendly, helpful staff; gd clean new (2016) san facs blocks." ♦ SEK 395 2017*

⊞ **MALUNG** *2F1* (1km W Rural) *60.68296, 13.70243* **Malungs Camping (W22), Bullsjövägen, 78235 Malung [(0280) 18650; fax 18615; info@malungscamping.se; www.malungscamping.se]** Fr Stöllet take rd 45 to Malung, site sp. Lge, pt shd; htd wc; chem disp; fam bthrm; shwrs inc; EHU (10A) SEK40; lndry (inc dryer); shop; snacks; playgrnd; pool; fishing; boating; bike hire; wifi; TV; car wash; Quickstop o'night facs; quiet; ccard acc; CKE. ♦ SEK 260 2016*

⊞ **MARIESTAD** *2F2* (2km NW Rural) *58.7154, 13.79516* **Ekuddens Camping (R2), 54245 Mariestad [(0501) 10637; fax 18601; andreas.appelgren@mariestad.se or ekudden@nordiccamping.se; www.ekuddenscamping.se]** Fr E20 take turn off twd Mariestad. At 1st rndabt foll ring rd clockwise until site sp on Lake Vänern. Lge, shd; wc; mv service pnt; sauna; shwrs inc; EHU (10A) SEK40; gas; lndry (inc dryer); shop; rest; bar; playgrnd; htd pool; beach; golf 2km; bike hire; dogs; phone; Quickstop o'night facs; ccard acc; CKE. "Gd views fr lakeside pitches; friendly, helpful staff; gd san facs." ♦ SEK 294 2014*

MARKARYD *2F3* (500m N Urban) *56.46475, 13.60066* **Camping Park Sjötorpet (G4), Strandvägen 4, 28531 Markaryd [(0433) 10316; fax 12391; reservation@sjotorpet-roc.se; www.sjotorpet-roc.se]** E4 fr Helsingborg (ferry) site is bet E4 N turn to Markaryd & rd 117, sp. Narr app. Sm, pt sl, pt shd; htd wc; shwrs inc; chem disp; mv service pnt; fam bthrm; EHU (10A) SEK40; lndry (inc dryer); shop; rest, snacks; bar; cooking facs; playgrnd; lake sw; fishing; boating; bike hire; wifi; some statics; dogs; phone; poss cr; Eng spkn; quiet; ccard acc; CKE. "Excel san & cooking facs; well-run site; new owners (2017), helpful." ♦ 1 Apr-31 Oct. SEK 270 2017*

MARSTRAND *2E2* (1.4km NE Coastal) *57.89380, 11.60510* **Marstrands Camping (036), Långedalsvägen 16, 44030 Marstrand [(0303) 60584; fax 60440; info@marstrandcamping.se; www.marstrandscamping.se]** Exit A6 dir Kungsälv/Marstrand & foll rd 168 to Marstrand. Site sp on Koön Island. App rd to site v narr. Med, pt sl, pt shd; htd wc; chem disp; mv service pnt; fam bthrm; shwrs (no privacy & prepaid cards needed); EHU (10A) SEK45; lndry; shop; cooking facs; playgrnd; shgl beach; wifi; TV; 50% statics; dogs; poss v cr; adv bkg; quiet; ccard acc; CKE. "Ferry to Marstrand Island; recep not staffed in LS." ♦ 12 Apr-2 Oct. SEK 350 2017*

MELLBYSTRAND *2E3* (1km N Coastal/Urban) *56.51961, 12.94628* **Marias Camping (N18), Norra Strandvägen 1, 312 60 Mellbystrand [(0430) 28585; fax 27321; info@mariascamping.se; www.mariascamping.se]** 20km N of Båstad, exit junc 41 fr E6 W onto rd 24, site sp off coast rd N. Lge, hdg/mkd pitch, pt shd; htd wc; chem disp (wc); mv service pnt; fam bthrm; shwrs; EHU inc; lndry (inc dryer); shop; rest; snacks; bar; cooking facs; playgrnd; sand beach adj; games rm; internet; TV; dogs; bus 500m; Eng spkn; adv bkg; quiet; CKE. "Vg site beside dunes; beautiful beach." ♦ ltd. 21 Apr-26 Aug. SEK 320 2013*

MELLERUD *2E2* (15km N Rural) *58.81968, 12.41519* **Haverud Camping, Kanalvagen 4, 464 72 Haverud [(0530) 30770; hafrestromsif@telia.com; www.hafrestromsif.se]** Signposted in Haverund. Sm, mkd pitch, hdstg, terr, unshd; wc; shwrs inc; EHU; lndry; rest, snacks adj; playgrnd; sw adj lake; Eng spkn; quiet; CKE/CCI. "Self pitch on arr, fees collected am or pay at visitors ctr at canal; gd." ♦ ltd. 25 Apr-14 Sep. SEK 220 2017*

⊞ **MELLERUD** *2E2* (4km SE Coastal) *58.68933, 12.51711* **Mellerud SweCamp Vita Sandar (P13), 46421 Mellerud [(0530) 12260; fax 12934; mail@vitasandarscamping.se; www.vitasandarscamping.se]** Fr S on rd 45 take Dalslandsgatan Rd on R & foll sp. Fr N turn L twd Sunnanåhamn, Vita Sandar. Med, pt shd; htd wc; chem disp; mv service pnt; sauna; shwrs SEK5; fam bthrm; EHU (10A) SEK50; lndry (inc dryer); shop; rest, snacks; bar; cooking facs; playgrnd; htd pool; waterslides; sand beach & lake sw; boat & bike hire; fishing; tennis; games area; wifi; TV rm; 20% statics; dogs; Quickstop o'night facs; poss cr; quiet; ccard acc; red LS; CKE/CCI. "Pleasant family site in pine trees; excel sw." ♦ SEK 420 2013*

MOLLE see Höganäs *2E4*

MOLNDAL see Göteborg *2E3*

NOSSEBRO *2E2* (500m N Urban) *58.19195, 12.72161* **Nossebrobadets Camping (R22), Marknadsgatan 4, 46530 Nossebro [(0512) 57043; fax 57042; info@nossebrobadet.se; www.nossebrobadet.se]** N fr Alingsås on E20; exit N to Nossebro, site in 16km. Clearly sp. Sm, pt sl, unshd; wc; mv service pnt; sauna; shwrs; EHU inc; lndry (inc dryer); shop 500m; playgrnd; 2 pools (1 covrd); fishing; boat hire; sports grnd adj; bike hire; some statics; dogs; quiet. "Vg NH; stream thro site." ♦ 25 Apr-31 Aug. SEK 200 2013*

⊞ **NYNASHAMN** *2H2* (1km NW Coastal) *58.90717, 17.93805* **Nicksta Camping (B8), Nickstabadsvägen 17, 14943 Nynäshamn [(08) 52012780; fax 52015317; info@nickstacamping.se; www.nickstacamping.se]** Fr Stockholm on Rv 73 to Nynäshamn. Foll site sp, turning R at ICA supmkt, then immed L (sp poss cov'rd by hedge.) Med, pt sl, pt shd; htd wc; chem disp; mv service pnt; fam bthrm; shwrs inc; EHU (10A) SEK50; lndry (inc dryer); shop 700m; snacks; cooking facs; playgrnd; beach adj; waterslide; games area; bike hire; wifi; some statics; dogs; train 600m; site clsd mid-Dec to mid-Jan; Quickstop o'night facs; Eng spkn; CKE. "Gd site; ferries to Gotland & Poland." ♦ SEK 343 2016*

OLAND ISLAND Campsites in towns on Öland Island are listed together at the end of the Swedish site entry pages.

OREBRO *2G2* (3km S Rural) *59.2554, 15.18955* **Gustavsviks Camping (T2), Sommarrovägen, 70229 Örebro [(019) 196950; fax 196961; camping@gustavsvik.com; www.gustavsvik.com]** Foll sp fr E18/E20 & rd 51 to site. V lge, mkd pitch, pt sl, pt shd; htd wc; chem disp; some serviced pitches; mv service pnt; fam bthrm; shwrs inc; EHU (10A) SEK80 inc sat TV (poss rev pol); gas; lndry (inc dryer); shop; kiosk; rest, snacks; bar; BBQ; cooking facs; playgrnd; 2 pools (1 htd, covrd); waterslide; paddling pool; lake sw & beach adj; golf nr; gym; solarium; wifi; entmnt; cab TV; 10% statics; dogs; phone; bus; Eng spkn; quiet; ccard acc; CKE. "Excel family site; excel facs; gentle stroll to town; very highly rec; beautiful site." ♦ 15 Apr-6 Nov. SEK 240 2016*

⊞ **ORSA** *1B4* (1km W Rural) *61.12090, 14.59890* **Orsa Camping (W3), Timmervägen 1, 79421 Orsa [(0250) 46200; fax 46260; info@orsacamping.se; www.orsacamping.se]** Sp fr town cent & fr rd 45. V lge, pt shd; htd wc; shwrs inc; fam bthrm; sauna; EHU (10A) SEK50; mv service pnt; lndry (inc dryer); shops 500m; rest; bar; cooking facs; playgrnd; 4 htd pools high ssn; waterslide; sand beach & lake sw; fishing; canoe & bike hire; tennis; wifi; entmnt; sat TV; 5% statics; phone; quiet; CKE. "Excel countryside; bear reserve 15km; gd general facs but ltd LS." ♦ SEK 375 (CChq acc) 2016*

"Satellite navigation makes touring much easier"

Remember most sat navs don't know if you're towing or in a larger vehicle – always use yours alongside maps and site directions.

OSKARSHAMN *2G3* (3km SE Coastal) *57.2517, 16.49206* **Gunnarsö Camping (H7), Östersjövägen 103, 57263 Oskarshamn [tel/fax (0491) 77220; gunnarso@oskarshamn.se; www.oskarshamn.se]** Fr E22 dir Oskarshamn, site sp on Kalmar Sound. Med, pt shd; htd wc; chem disp; mv service pnt; fam bthrm; sauna; shwrs SEK5; EHU (10A) SEK35; lndry (inc dryer); shop; snacks; playgrnd; 2 pools; watersports; wifi; TV; 40% statics; dogs; phone; adv bkg; quiet; ccard acc; CKE. "Beautiful location; many pitches with gd views; gd walking/cycling." ♦ 1 May-15 Sep. SEK 332 2016*

⊞ **OSTERSUND** *1B3* (3km SE Rural) *63.15955, 14.6731* **Östersunds Camping (Z11), Krondikesvägen 95, 83146 Östersund [(063) 144615; fax 144323; ostersundscamping@ostersund.se; www.ostersundscamping.se]** At Odensala on lakeside, well sp fr E14. Lge, mkd pitch, hdstg, pt sl, pt shd; htd wc; chem disp; mv service pnt; fam bthrm; sauna; shwrs inc; EHU (10A) SEK50 (poss rev pol); lndry (inc dryer); shop 1km; rest; bar; cooking facs; playgrnd; pool; paddling pool; tennis; wifi; cab TV; 80% statics; dogs; phone; bus; poss cr; quiet; ccard acc; CKE."Gd NH; very helpful staff." ♦ SEK 190 2016*

⊞ **PAJALA** *1D1* (1.5km SE Rural) *67.20381, 23.4084* **Pajala Camping (BD8), Tannavägen 65, 98431 Pajala [tel/fax (0978) 74180 or (0702) 107448; pajalacamping@gmail.com; www.pajalacamping.se]** Site sp fr rd 99. Med, mkd pitch, hdstg, pt shd; htd wc; chem disp; mv service pnt; fam bthrm; sauna; shwrs inc; EHU (10A) SEK30; lndry (inc dryer); shop; snacks; cooking facs; playgrnd; tennis; bike hire; wifi; TV rm; dogs; bus 1.5km; Eng spkn; adv bkg; quiet; ccard acc; red long stay; CKE. "Clean, well-presented site; delightful owner; salmon-fishing in rv in ssn (mid-Jun approx)." ♦ SEK 190 2016*

RAMVIK *1C3* (1km S Rural) *62.79911, 17.86931* **Snibbens Camping (Y19), Snibben 139, 87016 Ramvik [tel/fax (0612) 40505; info@snibbenscamping.com; www.snibbenscamping.com]** Fr S on E4, 23km N of Härnösand; after high bdge sighted take slip rd dir Kramfors; site sp in 2.5km on L just bef Ramvik. Med, mkd pitch, pt sl, pt shd; htd wc; chem disp; mv service pnt; fam bthrm; shwrs inc; EHU (16A) SEK20; lndry (inc dryer); shop 1km; rest, snacks; bar; cooking facs; playgrnd; lake sw & beach adj; fishing; boat hire; wifi; TV rm; some statics; bus; poss cr; Eng spkn; quiet; ccard acc; CKE. "Helpful owners; delightful site with lakeside setting; v peaceful even when busy; spotless facs & lovely camp kitchen with seating areas inside & out; conv Höga Kusten suspension bdge; delightful site in beautiful surroundings." ♦ 6 May-11 Sep. SEK 212 2013*

RATTVIK *1B4* (1km W Rural) *60.88891, 15.10881* **Siljansbadets Camping (W8), Långbryggevägen 4, 79532 Rättvik [(0248) 56118; fax 51689; camp@siljansbadet.com; www.siljansbadet.com]** Fr S on rd 70 thro Rättvik. Immed outside town turn L at rndabt, site sp on Lake Siljan. Height restriction 3.5m. V lge, mkd pitch, pt shd; wc; chem disp; mv service pnt; fam bthrm; shwrs inc; EHU (16A) SEK50; lndry (inc dryer); shop & rest 500m; bar; BBQ; cooking facs; playgrnd; lake sw & sand beach; boat hire; games area; wifi; TV rm; 15% statics; dogs; bus/train; twin axles; poss cr; Eng spkn; quiet; ccard acc. "Lovely scenic lakeside location; conv town cent; excel san facs; excel site." ♦ 26 Apr-6 Oct. SEK 355 2017*

RYD see Urshult *2F3*

⊞ **SAFFLE** *2F2* (6km S Rural) *59.08326, 12.88616* **Duse Udde Camping (S11), 66180 Säffle [(0533) 42000; fax 42002; duseudde@krokstad.se; www.duseudde.se]** Site sp fr rd 45. Med, pt sl, shd; wc; mv service pnt; fam bthrm; sauna; shwrs SEK10; EHU (10A) SEK50; lndry (inc dryer); shop; rest high ssn; snacks; bar; playgrnd; watersports; pool 6km; beach; lake sw; bike hire; wifi; entmnt; bus; 20% statics; phone; dogs; Quickstop o'night facs; quiet; ccard acc; red long stay; CKE. "Place to relax; useful base for Värmland area with nature walks." ♦ SEK 180 2016*

SANDARNE see Söderhamn *1C4*

SARNA *1B3* (1km S Rural) *61.69281, 13.14696* **Särna Camping (W32), Särnavägen 6, 79090 Särna [(0253) 10851; fax 32055; camping@sarnacamping.se; www.sarnacamping.se]** Turn R off rd 70 opp fire stn. Med, terr, pt shd; wc; chem disp; mv service pnt; sauna; shwrs SEK5; EHU (10A) SEK35; lndry (inc dryer); shop, rest, snacks 200m; playgrnd; shgl beach; bike hire; wifi; poss cr; adv bkg; quiet. "Beautiful setting o'looking lake; pleasant town." ♦ 19 May-30 Sep. SEK 245 2016*

⊞ **SIMRISHAMN** *2F4* (2km N Coastal) *55.57021, 14.33611* **Tobisviks Camping (L14), Tobisvägen, 27294 Simrishamn [(0414) 412778; info@tobisvikscamping.se; http://tobisvikscamping.se]** By sea at N app to town. Lge, pt shd; wc; chem disp; mv service pnt; shwrs SEK1/min; EHU (10A) SEK50; lndry (inc dryer); shop 400m; rest 2km; htd pool; watersports; TV; phone; ccard acc; CKE. SEK 210 2016*

SKANOR *2E4* (2km SE Coastal) *55.39750, 12.86555* **Calsterbo Camping & Resort (formerly Ljungens Camping), Strandbadsvägen, 23942 Falsterbo [(040) 6024020 or (414) 401180; info@falsterboresort.se; falsterboresort.se]** Fr E6/E22 exit to W sp Höllviken onto rd 100. Foll sp Skanör/Falsterbo. Site sp on L at rndabt at ent to town, dir Falsterbo. Lge, mkd pitch, some hdstg, pt shd; htd wc; chem disp; mv service pnt; fam bthrm; shwrs SEK5; EHU (10A) SEK40; lndry (inc dryer); shop; snacks high ssn; BBQ; cooking facs; playgrnd; sand beach 200m; wifi; TV; 50% statics; dogs; bus; Eng spkn; no adv bkg; aircraft noise (under flight path Copenhagen airport) ccard acc; CKE. "Conv Viking Vill museum; nature reserve adj; gd birdwatching, cycling; vg; new management, new recep & ongoing work on facs (2017)." ♦ 29 Apr-28 Sep. SEK 290 2017*

SKARHOLMEN see Stockholm *2H2*

⊞ **SKELLEFTEA** *1C2* (1.5km N Rural) *64.76156, 20.97513* **Skellefteå Camping (AC18), Mossgaten, 93170 Skellefteå [(0910) 735500; fax 701890; skellefteacamping@skelleftea.se; www.skelleftea.se/skellefteacamping]** Turn W off E4; well sp behind g'ge. Also sp as Camping Stugby. Lge, mkd pitch, pt sl, unshd; htd wc; chem disp; mv service pnt; sauna; shwrs inc; EHU (10A) SEK60; lndry (inc dryer); shop; rest, snacks 100m; bar 1km; BBQ; cooking facs; playgrnd; htd pool; waterslide; sand beach 5km; fishing; tennis 150m; bike hire; games area; wifi; TV rm; 10% statics; dogs; phone; poss cr; Eng spkn; quiet; ccard acc; CKE. "Friendly, clean site in pine trees on sheltered inlet; lge pitches suitable RVs & twin-axles; Nordanå Cultural Cent & Bonnstan Church Vill in walking dist; if site clsd book in at Statoil stn 500m S on E4 at rndabt. Exc san facs, lgr camp kitchen, helpful staff, lge supmkt nrby." ♦ SEK 330 2017*

SKELLEFTEA *1C2* (7km NE Coastal) *64.77681, 21.11993* **Bovikens Havsbad Camping (AC60), 93140 Skellefteå [tel/fax (0910) 54000; cecilia@bovikenshavsbad.se; www.bovikenscamping.se]** Site sp off E4, site in 5km. Med, mkd pitch, pt shd; wc; chem disp; fam bthrm; shwrs inc; EHU; lndry (inc dryer); snacks; playgrnd; sand beach adj; tennis nr; TV rm; some statics; dogs; poss cr; Eng spkn; adv bkg; quiet; ccard acc; CKE. "Gd family site by secluded beach; friendly owner; excel birdwatching; avoid shwr cubicles with elec heaters nr floor level; v nice!" ♦ 16 May-14 Sep. SEK 360 2014*

SODERALA see Söderhamn *1C4*

⊞ **SODERHAMN** *1C4* (10km SE Coastal) *61.24843, 17.19506* **Stenö Havsbad Camping (X9), Stenövägen, 82022 Sandarne [(0270) 60000; steno@nordiccamping.se; www.nordiccamping.se]** Exit E4 at sp Bollnäs-Sandarne (S of Söderhamn turn), foll sp Sandarne at Östansjö, turn L at camping sp. Lge, shd; wc; chem disp; fam bthrm; mv service pnt; shwrs inc; EHU (10A) SEK50; lndry (inc dryer); shop; rest, snacks; bar; cooking facs; playgrnd; pool 12km; sand beach; games area; wifi; TV rm; some statics; phone; bus; poss cr; adv bkg; quiet; ccard acc; CKE. "Adj nature reserve." ♦ SEK 307 2016*

SODERKOPING *2G2* (1km N Rural) *58.49163, 16.30618* **Skeppsdockans Camping (E34), Dockan 1, 61421 Söderköping [(0121) 21630; korskullenscamp@hotmail.com; www.soderkopingscamping.se]** On E22 immed N of canal bdge. Sm, mkd pitch, unshd; htd wc; chem disp; shwrs inc; EHU SEK40; lndry (inc dryer); rest & shops 1km; cooking facs; canal sw; bike hire; TV; Eng spkn; quiet; ccard acc; CKE. "On side of Gota Canal; peaceful." ♦ 30 Apr-2 Oct. SEK 220 2016*

SOLLENTUNA see Stockholm *2H2*

SOLLERON see Gesunda *1B4*

⊞ **SORSELE** *1C2* (400m W Rural) *65.53428, 17.52663* **Sorsele Camping (AC21), Fritidsvägen, Näset, 92070 Sorsele [(0952) 10124; fax 10625; info@lapplandskatan.nu; www.lapplandskatan.nu]** N on rd 45/363 fr Storuman to Arvidsjaur. In Sorsele vill turn W for 500m; site sp. Med, unshd; htd wc; chem disp; fam bthrm; shwrs; EHU (16A) SEK35; lndry (inc dryer); shop 200m; playgrnd; pool; beach; canoeing; fishing; hiking; bike hire; wifi; TV; some statics; dogs; phone; poss cr; quiet; ccard acc; CKE. "Nature reserve; interesting ancient Lapp vill; friendly, welcoming; attractive site." ♦ SEK 183 2014*

STENKALLEGARDEN see Bocksjö *2F2*

⊞ **STOCKHOLM** *2H2* (15km N Rural) *59.43821, 17.99223* **Rösjöbadens Camping (B1), Lomvägen 100, 19256 Sollentuna [(08) 962184; fax 929195; info@rosjobaden.se; www.rosjobaden.se]** Take E18 m'way N fr Stockholm, sp Norrtälje. Pass Morby Centrum on L after 7km. Take Sollentuna exit, turn L & foll Sollentuna rd 265/262 for approx 5km. At 2nd set of traff lts with pylons adj, turn R on sm rd, clear sp to site. Lge, pt sl, pt shd; wc; chem disp; mv service pnt; fam bthrm; shwrs inc; EHU (16A); lndry (inc dryer); shops; snacks; BBQ; cooking facs; playgrnd; fishing; boating; lake sw fr pontoons; sat TV; 90% statics; dogs; bus 150m; twin axles; Quickstop o'night facs; Eng spkn; adv bkg; quiet; CKE. "Conv Morby Centrum, lge shopping cent, petrol, metro to city; pleasant walks in woods & lakeside; san facs adequate; staff uninterested; site run as a residential site; fair." ♦ ltd. SEK 330 2017*

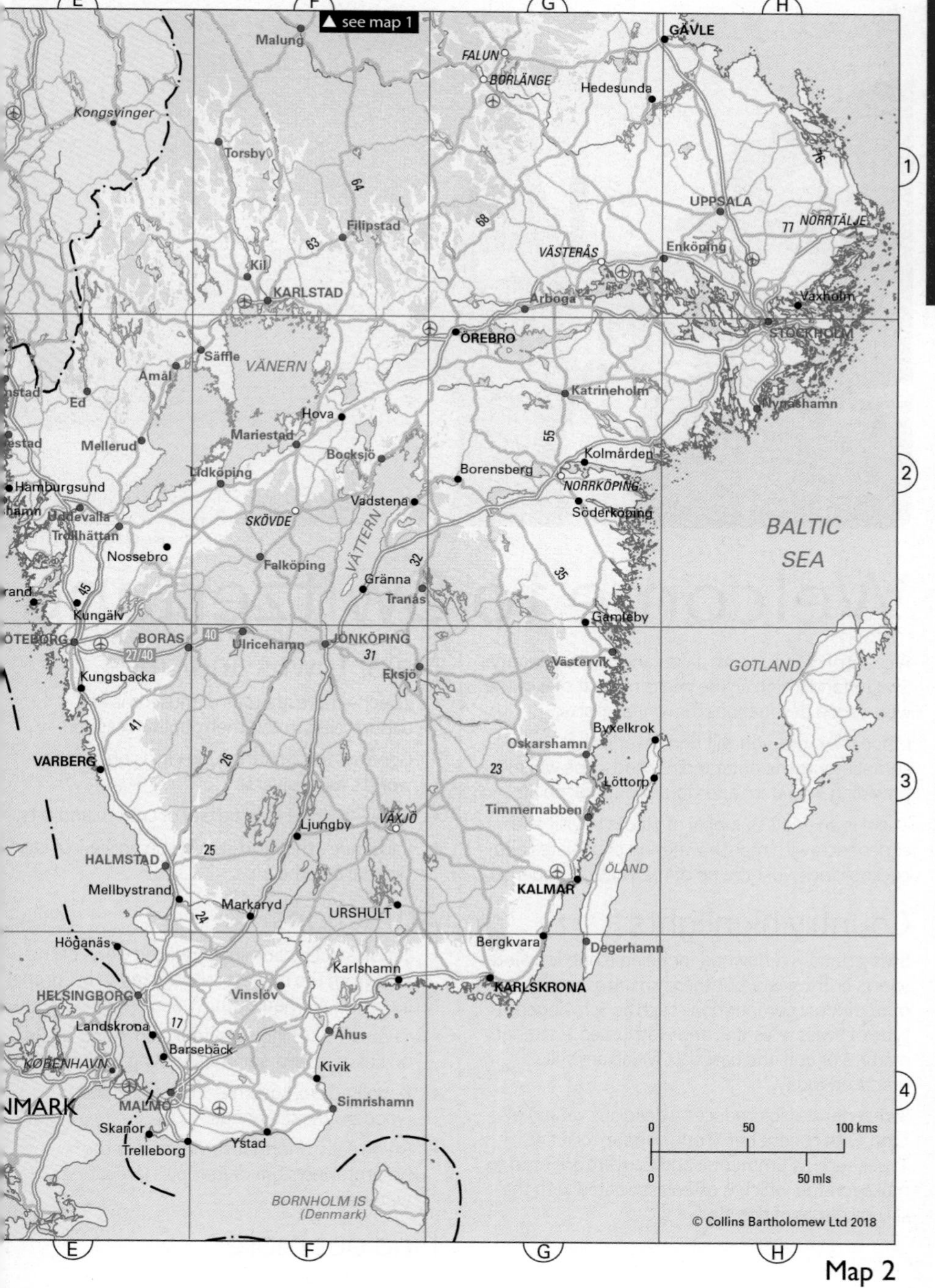

see map 1
Malung
FALUN
GÄVLE
BORLÄNGE
Hedesunda
Kongsvinger
Torsby
UPPSALA
NORRTÄLJE
Filipstad
VÄSTERÅS
Enköping
Kil
KARLSTAD
Arboga
Vaxholm
ÖREBRO
STOCKHOLM
Säffle
VÄNERN
Åmål
Ed
Katrineholm
Nynäshamn
Hova
Mariestad
Mellerud
Bocksjö
Kolmården
Borensberg
Lidköping
Hamburgsund
NORRKÖPING
Vadstena
Söderköping
Uddevalla
SKÖVDE
Trollhättan
BALTIC SEA
Nossebro
Falköping
VÄTTERN
Gränna
Tranås
Kungälv
Gamleby
BORAS
Ulricehamn
JÖNKÖPING
Västervik
Kungsbacka
Eksjö
GOTLAND
Byxelkrok
Oskarshamn
VARBERG
Löttorp
Timmernabben
Ljungby
VÄXJÖ
HALMSTAD
ÖLAND
KALMAR
Mellbystrand
Markaryd
URSHULT
Höganäs
Bergkvara
Degerhamn
Karlshamn
KARLSKRONA
HELSINGBORG
Vinslöv
Landskrona
Åhus
Barsebäck
KØBENHAVN
Kivik
MALMÖ
Simrishamn
Skanör
Trelleborg
Ystad
BORNHOLM IS (Denmark)
0 50 100 kms
0 50 mls

Map 2

Oberhofen Castle in Thun lake

Welcome to Switzerland

A country of mountains, lakes and natural beauty, Switzerland's high alpine peaks make it one of the world's top destinations for winter sports.

Inside the cities, you will find a world that compliments the outstanding landscape while providing a modern and vibrant outlook on life.

There is an endless supply of places to visit and experience, with mouth-watering chocolates and cuckoo clocks just the tip of the cultural iceberg.

Country highlights

Switzerland is renowned for being a hub for winter sports enthusiasts, but there are also a variety of traditional competitions such as Schwingen, a type of Swiss wrestling and Hornussen, a strange mixture of golf and baseball, which are still practiced today.

Switzerland also produces a delicious variety of food, with cheese being one of its specialities. Types such as Emmental and Gruyère are used to make fondue, which is often associated with the skiing culture of the Alps.

Major towns and cities

- Zürich – there are tons of museums and cultural sites in this metropolitan capital.
- Geneva – this breathtaking city is one of the world's most diverse.
- Basel – a world-leading city of culture and arts.
- Lausanne – this city has a stunning view of Lake Geneva and the Alps.

Attractions

- Jungfraujoch – admire unrivalled views of the Alps from the highest railway station in Europe, located 3,43 metres above sea level.
- Château de Chillon, Veytaux – an island castle on Lake Geneva, set in a stunning backdrop.
- Kapellbrücke, Lucerne – Europe's oldest wooden covered bridge.
- Rhine Falls, Shaffhausen – discover the breathtaking sight of Europe's largest waterfall.

Find out more

www.myswitzerland.com
Tel: 0041 (0) 80 01 00 20 029 Swiss Tourist Office

Country Information

Population: 8.1 million

Capital: Bern (population 128,848)

Area: 41,285 sq km

Bordered by: Austria, France, Germany, Italy, Liechtenstein

Terrain: Mostly mountainous; Alps in the south, Jura in the north-west; central plateau of rolling hills, plains and large lakes

Climate: Temperate climate varying with altitude; cold, cloudy, rainy or snowy winters; cool to warm summers with occasional showers

Highest Point: Dufourspitze 4,634m

Languages: French, German, Italian, Romansch

Local Time: GMT or BST + 1, i.e. 1 hour ahead of the UK all year

Currency: Swiss Franc (CHF) divided into 100 centimes; £1 = CHF 1.32, CHF 10 = £7.57 (November 2017)

Emergency numbers: Police 117; Fire brigade 118; Ambulance 144 or 112 for any service

Public Holidays 2018: Jan 1, 2; Mar 30; Apr 30; May 10, 20, 21, 31; Aug 1, (National Day); Sept 16; Nov 1; Dec 25, 26

School summer holidays vary by canton but are approximately from early July to mid/end August.

Camping and Caravanning

There are approximately 340 campsites available to touring caravanners, with around 100 sites remaining open in winter. Some sites may be nearly full with statics, with only a small area for tourers.

There are 27 Touring Club Suisse (TCS) sites and affiliated sites classified into five categories according to amenities available. All TCS campsites have a service station with facilities for emptying sanitary tanks. For further information and current rates see www.reise-tcs ch. The Swiss Camp Sites Association (VSC/ACS) produces a camping and road map covering approximately 180 sites, including charges and classification. See www.swisscamps.ch.

To download a guide to more than 40 campsites, including those open in winter, in the Bernese Oberland region of Switzerland see www.camping-bo.ch

The Swiss are environmentally conscious with only limited scope for removing waste. Recycling is vigorously promoted and it is normal to have to put rubbish in special plastic bags obtainable from campsites. A 'rubbish charge' or 'entsorgungstaxe' of approximately CHF 3 per person per day is commonly charged.

A visitors' tax, varying according to the area, is levied in addition to the site charges.

The rules on casual/wild camping differ from canton to canton. It may be tolerated in some areas with the permission of the landowner or local police, or in motorway service areas, but local laws – particularly on hygiene – must not be contravened. For reasons of security the Caravan and Motorhome Club recommends that overnight stops should always be at recognised campsites.

Cycling

Switzerland has 9,000 km of cycle trails, including nine national cycle routes, which have been planned to suit all categories of cyclist from families to sports cyclists. Maps of cycle routes are available from www.schweizmobil.ch. Routes are marked by red and white signs. The problem of strenuous uphill gradients can be overcome by using trails routed near railway lines. Most trains will transport bicycles and often bicycles are available for hire at stations. Switzerland Tourism can provide more information.

Children under the age of 6 may only cycle on the road if accompanied by a person over 16 years of age.

Transportation of Bicycles

Bicycles may be carried on the roof of a car providing they are attached to an adequate roof rack and providing the total height does not exceed 4 metres. Bicycles carried on special carriers at the rear of a vehicle can exceed the width of the vehicle by 20 cm on each side, but the total width must not exceed 2 metres. The rear lights and number plate must remain visible and the driver's view must not be obstructed.

Electricity and Gas

Usually current on campsites varies between 4 and 16 amps. Plugs have two or, more usually, three round pins. Some campsites have CEE connections. Some may lend or hire out adaptors

– but do not rely on it – and it may be advisable to purchase an appropriate adaptor cable with a Swiss 3-pin plug. Adaptors are readily available in local supermarkets.

The full range of Campingaz cylinders is available from large supermarkets.

Entry Formalities

Holders of valid British or Irish passports may enter Switzerland without a visa for a period of up to 3 months.

Medical Services

There are reciprocal emergency health care arrangements with Switzerland for EU citizens. A European Health Insurance Card (EHIC) will enable you to get reduced cost for emergency treatment in a public hospital but you will be required to pay the full cost of treatment and apply afterwards for a refund from the Department for Work & Pensions on your return to the UK. Ensure that any doctor you visit is registered with the national Swiss Health Insurance Scheme. Dental treatment is not covered.

You will have to pay 50% of the costs of any medically-required ambulance transport within Switzerland and/or Liechtenstein, including air ambulance. There is a fixed charge for in-patient treatment in a public hospital.

If you are planning to participate in sports activities, such as skiing and mountaineering, your personal holiday insurance should be extended to cover these activities and should also include cover for mountain rescue and helicopter rescue costs.

Opening Hours

Banks: Mon-Fri 8.30am-4.30pm (some close for lunch; late opening once a week to 5.30pm/6pm in some towns).

Museums: Check locally as times vary.

Post Offices: Mon-Fri 7.30am-12pm & 13.45pm-6pm (no lunch break in main towns); Sat 7.30am-11am.

Shops: Mon-Fri 8am/8.30am-6.30pm/7pm (closed lunch time) & Sat 8am-4pm/7pm (sometimes lunch time closing); shops close early on the eve of a public holiday. Food shops may be closed on religious and public holidays.

Safety and Security

Most visits to Switzerland and Liechtenstein are trouble-free and the crime rate is low. However, petty theft is on the increase and you should be alert to pickpockets, confidence tricksters and thieves in city centres, railway stations and other public places.

You should be aware of the risks involved in the more hazardous sports activities and take note of weather forecasts and conditions, which can change rapidly in the mountains. You should be well-equipped; do not undertake the activity alone, study the itinerary and inform someone of your plans. Off-piste skiers should follow the advice given by local authorities and guides; to ignore such advice could put yourselves and other mountain users in danger.

Switzerland and Liechtenstein share with the rest of Europe an underlying threat from terrorism. Attacks could be indiscriminate and against civilian targets in public places, including tourist sites.

British Embassy

THUNSTRASSE 50, CH-3005 BERN
Tel: 031 3597700
www.ukinswitzerland.fco.gov.uk/en

Irish Embassy

KIRCHENFELDSTRASSE 68, CH-3000 BERN 6
Tel: 031 3521442
www.embassyofireland.ch

Customs Regulations

Alcohol and Tobacco

Switzerland is not a member of the EU and visitors aged 17 years and over may import the following items duty-free:

200 cigarettes or 50 cigars or
250 g tobacco

2 litres of alcoholic drink up to 15% proof
1 litre of alcoholic drink over 15% proof

All goods are duty free up to a total combined value of CHF300, including alcohol and tobacco products.

Caravans and Motorhomes

Caravans registered outside Switzerland may be imported without formality up to a height of 4 metres, width of 2.55 metres and length of 12 metres (including towbar). The total length of car + caravan/trailer must not exceed 18.75 metres.

Food

From EU countries you may import per person 1 kg of meat and/or meat products (excluding game).

Refund of VAT on Export

A foreign visitor who buys goods in Switzerland in a 'Tax-Back SA' or 'Global Refund Schweiz AG' shop may obtain a VAT refund (7.6%) on condition that the value of the goods is at least CHF 300 including VAT. Visitors should complete a form in the shop and produce it, together with the goods purchased, at Customs on leaving Switzerland. See www.globalrefund.com for more information.

Documents

Vehicle(s)

Carry your original vehicle registration certificate (V5C), MOT certificate (if applicable) and insurance documentation at all times. Recent visitors report that drivers may be asked to produce proof of vehicle ownership at the border and failure to do so may mean that entry into Switzerland is refused. If you are driving a vehicle which does not belong to you, you should be in possession of a letter of authorisation from the owner.

Money

Prices in shops are often displayed in both Swiss francs and euros. Major credit cards are widely accepted, although you may find small supermarkets and restaurants do not accept them. Recent visitors report that some retail outlets may accept only one kind of credit card (MasterCard or VISA), not both, and it may be advisable to carry one of each. You may occasionally find that a surcharge is imposed for the use of credit cards.

Carry your credit card issuers'/banks' 24-hour UK contact numbers in case of loss or theft of your cards.

Motoring in Switzerland

Accidents

In the case of accidents involving property damage only, when drivers decide not to call the police, a European Accident Statement must be completed.

In the case of injury or of damage to the road, road signs, lights etc, the police must be called.

Alcohol

The maximum permitted level of alcohol is 50 milligrams in 100 millilitres of blood, i.e. lower than that permitted in the UK (80 milligrams). A lower limit of 10 milligrams in 100 millilitres applies for new drivers of up to three years. A blood test may be required after an accident, and if found positive, the penalty is either a fine or a prison sentence, plus withdrawal of permission to drive in Switzerland for at least two months. Police carry out random breath tests.

Breakdown Service

The motoring and leisure organisation Touring Club Suisse (TCS) operates a 24-hour breakdown service, 'Patrouille TCS'. To call for help throughout Switzerland and Liechtenstein, dial 140. On motorways use emergency phones and ask for TCS.

Members of clubs affiliated to the AIT, such as Tthe Caravan and Motorhome Club, who can show a current membership card will be charged reduced rates for breakdown assistance and towing, according to the time of day and/or the distance towed. Payment by credit card is accepted.

Essential Equipment

Lights

Dipped headlights are compulsory at all times, even during the day. Bulbs are more likely to fail with constant use and you are recommended to carry spares.

Nationality Plate (GB or IRL Stickers)

Strictly-speaking, it is necessary to display a conventional nationality plate or sticker when driving outside EU member states, even when vehicle number plates incorporate the GB or IRL Euro-symbol. However, the Swiss authorities have adopted a commonsense approach and confirm that it is not necessary to display a separate GB or IRL sticker if your number plates display the GB or IRL Euro-symbol. If your number plates do not incorporate this symbol then you will need a separate sticker.

Warning Triangles

All vehicles must be equipped with a warning triangle which has to be within easy reach and not in the boot.

Child Restraint System

Vehicles registered outside of Switzerland that are temporarily imported into the country, have to comply with the country of registration with regards to safety belt equipment and child restraint regulations. All children up to 12 years of age must be placed in an approved UN ECE 44.03 regulation child restraint, unless they measure more than 150cm and are over seven years old.

Winter Driving

Alpine winters often make driving more difficult. You should equip your vehicle(s) with winter tyres and snow chains and check road conditions prior to departure.
A sign depicting a wheel and chains indicates where snow chains are required for the mountain road ahead.

Snow chains are compulsory in areas where indicated by the appropriate road sign. They must be fitted on at least two drive wheels.

Fuel

Prices of petrol vary according to the brand and region, being slightly cheaper in self-service stations. Credit cards are generally accepted.

On motorways, where prices are slightly higher, some service stations are open 24 hours and others are open from 6am to 10pm or 11pm only, but petrol is available outside these hours from automatic pumps where payment can be made by means of bank notes or credit cards.

There are 47 outlets (December 2017) selling LPG (GPL) – see www.jaquet-ge.ch for a list of outlets and a map showing their location.

Mountain Roads and Tunnels

One of the most attractive features of Switzerland for motorists is the network of finely engineered mountain passes, ranging from easy main road routes to high passes that may be open only from June to October. In the Alps most roads over passes have been modernised; only the Umbrail Pass, which is not recommended for caravans, is not completely tarred. Passes have a good roadside telephone service for calling aid quickly in the event of trouble.

A blue rectangular sign depicting a yellow horn indicates a mountain postal road and the same sign with a red diagonal stripe indicates the end of the postal road. On such roads, vehicles belonging to the postal services have priority.

During certain hours, one-way traffic only is permitted on certain mountain roads. The hours during which traffic may proceed in either or both directions are posted at each end of the road. The TCS road map of Switzerland, scale 1:300,000, indicates this type of road.

Speed must always be moderate on mountain passes, very steep roads and roads with numerous bends. Drivers must not travel at a speed which would prevent them from stopping within the distance they can see ahead.

When it is difficult to pass oncoming vehicles, the heavier vehicle has priority.

Slow-moving vehicles are required by law to use the lay-bys provided on alpine roads to allow the free flow of faster traffic. This is the case where a car towing a caravan causes a queue of vehicles capable of a higher speed.

Parking

Parking in cities is difficult and it is worth using the numerous Park & Ride schemes which operate around major towns and cities. Illegal parking of any kind is much less tolerated in Switzerland than in any of its neighbours and fines are common for even minor violations.

Pay and display car parks and parking meters are used throughout the country and permitted parking time varies from 15 minutes to 2 hours. Feeding meters is not allowed. Wheel clamps are not used, but vehicles causing an obstruction may be removed to a car pound.

You may park in a 'blue zone' for limited periods free of charge providing you display a parking disc in your vehicle. These are available from petrol stations, kiosks, restaurants and police stations. Parking in a marked red zone is free for up to 15 hours with a red parking disc obtainable from police stations, tourist offices, etc.

Parking on pavements is not allowed. Do not park where there is a sign 'Stationierungsverbot' or 'Interdiction de Stationner'. Continuous or broken yellow lines and crosses at the side of the road and any other yellow markings also indicate that parking is prohibited.

Priority

In general, traffic (including bicycles) coming from the right has priority at intersections but drivers approaching a roundabout must give way to all traffic already on the roundabout, i.e. from the left, unless otherwise indicated by signs. However, vehicles on main roads – indicated by a yellow diamond with a white border or a white triangle with a red border and an arrow pointing upwards – have priority over traffic entering from secondary roads.

Please be aware sometimes pedestrians have right of way and will expect vehicles to stop for them.

Roads

Switzerland has some 72,000 kilometres of well-surfaced roads, from motorways to local municipal roads, all well-signposted. Four-wheel drive vehicles must not be driven off road without the permission of the local authority.

During daylight hours outside built-up areas you must sound your horn before sharp bends where visibility is limited. After dark this warning must be given by flashing your headlights.

Dial the following numbers for information:

162: Weather information

163: Road conditions, mountain passes, access to tunnels and traffic news

187: In winter, avalanche bulletins; in summer, wind forecasts for Swiss lakes

It is also possible to obtain updated information on road conditions via teletext in larger motorway service areas.

Motorway Tax

To be able to use national roads (motorways and semi-motorways) in Switzerland, motor vehicles and trailers up to a total weight of 3,500kg must have a vehicle sticker (vignette). The ticket is valid for 14 months from 1st December every year and costs CHF40 (2015). An additional fee is charged for caravans and trailers. The sticker allows multiple re-entry into Switzerland during the period of validity.

If you enter a motorway or semi-motorway without a sticker you will be fined CHF200 and also the cost of the sticker. The stickers can be bought from custom offices, petrol stations or TCS offices in Switzerland or alternatively they can be purchased from the UK before travelling by calling the Swiss Travel Centre on 0207 420 4934.

Heavy Vehicle Tax

Vehicles (including motorhomes) over 3,500kg must pay a heavy vehicle tax on entry into Switzerland which is applicable for all roads. This charge applies for every day you are in Switzerland and your vehicle is on the road. For a 10-day pass (valid for a year) you self-select the days that your vehicle is on the road and, therefore, you are not penalised if your motorhome is parked at a campsite and not driven on a public road. This heavy vehicle tax applies to any Swiss road and replaces the need for a motorway vignette.

This particular tax is only payable at the border on entry into Switzerland and if there is any doubt about the exact weight of your vehicle it will be weighed. An inspection may be carried out at any time and is likely at the exit border. Failure to pay the tax can result in an immediate fine.

Road Signs and Markings

Road signs and markings conform to international standards.

White lettering on a green background indicates motorways, whereas state and provincial main roads outside built-up areas have white lettering on a blue background. This is the reverse of the colouring used in France and Germany and may initially cause confusion when driving from one country to the other. Road signs on secondary roads are white with black lettering.

The following are some road signs which you may encounter:

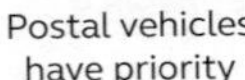

Postal vehicles have priority

Parking disc compulsory

Slow lane

One-way street with a two-way cycle lane

Speed Limits

	Open Road (km/h)	Motorway (km/h)
Car Solo	80-100	120
Car towing caravan/ trailer	80	80
Motorhome under 3500kg	80-100	120
Motorhome 3500-7500kg	80	80

The fundamental rule, which applies to all motor vehicles and bicycles, is that you must always have the speed of your vehicle under control and must adapt your speed to the conditions of the road, traffic and visibility. On minor secondary roads without speed limit signs speed should be reduced to 50 km/h (31 mph) where the road enters a built-up area. The speed limit in residential areas is 30 km/h (18 mph). Speeding fines are severe.

When travelling solo the speed limit on dual carriageways is 100 km/h (62 mph) and on motorways, 120 km/h (74 mph) unless otherwise indicated by signs. On motorways with at least three lanes in the same direction, the left outside lane may only be used by vehicles which can exceed 80 km/h (50 mph).

Motorhomes with a laden weight of under 3,500 kg are not subject to any special regulations. Those over 3,500 kg may not exceed 80 km/h (50 mph) on motorways.

In road tunnels with two lanes in each direction, speed is limited to 100 km/h (62 mph); in the St Gotthard tunnel and San Bernardino tunnels the limit is 80 km/h (50 mph).

It is illegal to transport or use radar detection devices. If your GPS navigation system has a function to identify the location of fixed speed cameras, this must be deactivated.

Traffic Jams

Traffic congestion occurs near tunnels in particular, during the busy summer months, at the St Gotthard tunnel on Friday afternoons and Saturday mornings. When congestion is severe and in order to prevent motorists coming to a standstill in the tunnel, traffic police stop vehicles before the tunnel entrance and direct them through in groups.

Other bottlenecks occur on the roads around Luzern (A2) and Bern (A1, A6 and A12), the border crossing at Chiasso (A2), the A9 around Lausanne and between Vevey and Chexbres, and the A13 BellinzonaSargans, mainly before the San Bernardino tunnel.

Traffic Lights

Outside peak rush hours traffic lights flashing amber mean proceed with caution.

Violation of Traffic Regulations

The police may impose and collect on-the-spot fines for minor infringements. In the case of more serious violations, they may require a deposit equal to the estimated amount of the fine. Fines for serious offences are set according to the income of the offender. Drivers of foreign-registered vehicles may be asked for a cash deposit against the value of the fine.

Motorways

There are 1,700 km of motorways and dual carriageways. To use these roads motor vehicles and trailers up to a total weight of 3,500kg must display a vignette. Motorists using roads to avoid motorways and dual carriageways may find it necessary to detour through small villages, often with poor signposting. In addition, due to a diversion, you may be re-routed onto roads where the motorway vignette is required.

If you have visited Switzerland before, make sure you remove your old sticker from your windscreen.

There are emergency telephones along the motorways.

Touring

The peak season for winter sports is from December to the end of April in all major resorts. February and March are the months with the most hours of winter sunshine and good snow for skiing. Summer skiing is also possible in a few resorts. Information on snow conditions, including avalanche bulletins, is available in English from www.slf.ch.

Besides being famous for watches, chocolate and cheese, the Swiss have a fine reputation as restaurateurs, but eating out can be expensive. Local beers are light but pleasant and some very drinkable wines are produced.

There are a number of UNESCO World Heritage Sites in Switzerland including the three castles of Bellinzona, Bern Old Town, the Monastery of St John at Müstair, the Jungfrau, the Aletsch Glacier and the Bietschhoorn region.

Liechtenstein is a principality of 160 sq km sharing borders with Switzerland and Austria. The capital, Vaduz, has a population of approximately 5,500 and German is the official language. The official currency is the Swiss franc. There are no passport or Customs controls on the border between Switzerland and Liechtenstein.

Public Transport & Local Travel

Some towns are inaccessible by road, e.g. Zermatt and Wengen, and can only be reached by train or tram.

The Swiss integrated transport system is well known for its efficiency, convenience and punctuality. Co-ordinated timetables ensure fast, trouble-free interchange from one means of transport to another. Yellow post buses take travellers off the beaten track to the remotest regions. As far as railways are concerned, in addition to efficient inter-city travel, there is an extensive network of mountain railways, including aerial cableways, funiculars and ski-lifts.

Half-fare tickets are available for attractions such as cable cars, railways and lake steamers.

In addition, Switzerland Tourism offers a public transport map and a number of other useful publications. See www.swisstravelsystem.com.

All visitors to campsites and hotels in Interlaken are issued with a pass allowing free bus and train travel in the area.

A ferry operates on Lake Constance (Bodensee) between Romanshorn and Friedrichshafen (Germany) saving a 70km drive. The crossing takes 40 minutes. Telephone 071 4667888 for more information; www.bodensee-schiffe.ch. A frequent ferry service also operates between Konstanz and Meersburg on the main route between Zürich, Ulm, Augsburg and Munich (Germany); information is available on a German telephone number, 0049 7531 8030; www.stadtwerke.konstanz.de. The crossing takes 20 minutes. Principal internal ferry services are on Lake Lucerne between Beckenried and Gersau, www.autofaehre.ch, and on Lake Zürich between Horgen and Meilen, www.faehre.ch. All these services transport cars and caravans.

Sites in Switzerland

AARBURG *A2* (1km SW Rural) *47.31601, 7.89488* **Camping Wiggerspitz, Hofmattstrasse 40, 4663 Aarburg [062 7915810; fax 7915811; info@camping-aarburg.ch; www.camping-aarburg.ch]** Exit A1/A2/E35 junc 46 sp Rothrist/Olten, foll sp to site. Med, mkd pitch, pt shd; htd wc; chem disp; mv service pnt; shwrs CHF1; EHU (6A) CHF3 (rev pol), long lead req; gas; lndry; shop; rest 500m; snacks; bar; BBQ; htd pool adj; 25% statics; dogs CHF1; phone; rlwy noise; red CKE/CCI. "Conv Luzern, Zürich, Bern; picturesque, walled town; excel, clean site; friendly warden; excel san facs; site is popular so rec adv bkg." 1 May-15 Sep. CHF 29.00 2015*

AESCHI see Spiez *C2*

AGNO see Lugano *D3*

AIGLE *C2* (1km N Rural) *46.32385, 6.96206* **Camping de la Piscine, Ave des Glariers 1, 1860 Aigle [tel/fax 024 4662660]** Turn W off N9 (Aigle-Lausanne) at N edge of Aigle, site sp. Foll rd for 400m, site past pool on L. Med, pt shd; wc; chem disp; mv service pnt; shwrs inc; EHU (4A) CHF3.50 (adaptor avail); gas; lndry; sm shop; snacks; bar; playgrnd; pool; tennis; fishing; bike hire; some statics; dogs CHF4; poss cr; Eng spkn; adv bkg; quiet but a little rlwy noise; ccard acc; red CKE/CCI. "V helpful owner; vg, well-maintained site; pleasant town & gd touring base; outlook on to vineyards; easy flat walk into town, about 10 mins." 6 Apr-30 Sep. CHF 35.00 2013*

⊞ **ALTDORF** *B3* (2km N Rural) *46.89256, 8.62800* **Remo-Camp Moosbad, Flüelerstrsse 122, 6460 Altdorf [041 8708541; fax 8708161]** Exit A2 at Altdorf junc 36. Foll sp Altdorf to rndabt & turn R. Site 200m on L adj cable car & sports cent. Sm, pt shd; wc; chem disp; mv service pnt; shwrs CHF1; EHU (10A) CHF3 (adaptor loan); lndry (inc dryer); shop & 200m; rest; bar; BBQ; public pool, waterslide & rest adj; 80% statics; dogs €1; phone; poss cr; Eng spkn; some rd & rlwy noise; ccard not acc; CKE/CCI. "Ideal windsurfing; useful NH en rte Italy; friendly welcome; excel san facs; excel rest; superb views; gd base for train trip over St Gotthard pass; plenty to see & do in Altdorf; bus & cable car combos avail." CHF 35.00 2016*

ANDEER see Thusis *C4*

ANDELFINGEN *A3* (1km NE Rural) *47.59698, 8.68376* **TCS Camping Rässenwies, Alte Steinerstrasse 1, 8451 Kleinandelfingen [079 2383535; raessenwies@tcs-ccz.ch; www.tcs-ccz.ch]** On N4 Schaffhausen-Winterthur rd, site well sp in Kleinandelfingen, on Rv Thur. Sm, unshd; wc; shwrs; EHU CHF3.50; gas; lndry; shop pool 1km; fishing; dogs CHF3.50; quiet. "Beautiful area; v friendly." 20 Mar-4 Oct. CHF 43.00 2013*

BASEL *A2* (10km S Urban) *47.49963, 7.60283* **Camping Waldhort, Heideweg 16, 4153 Basel-Reinach [061 7116429; fax 7139835; info@camping-waldhort.ch; www.camping-waldhort.ch]** Fr Basel foll m'way sp to Delémont & exit m'way at Reinach-Nord exit; at top of slip rd, turn R & L at 1st traff lts (about 300m). Site on L in approx 1km at curve in rd with tramway on R, sp. Basel best app off German m'way rather than French. Lge, mkd pitch, pt shd; wc; chem disp; mv service pnt; fam bthrm; shwrs inc; EHU (6A) inc; gas; lndry; shop; rest 500m; snacks; playgrnd; pool; paddling pool; 50% statics; dogs CHF3; tram 500m (tickets fr recep); poss cr; Eng spkn; adv bkg; m'way noise; ccard acc; 10% red CKE/CCI. "Rec arr early in high ssn; helpful staff; gd sized pitches; m'van pitches sm; excel san facs; gates clsd 2200-0700; site muddy when wet; excel art museums in Basel." ♦ 1 Mar-29 Oct. CHF 47.00 2013*

VALLORBE *B1 (700m SW Urban) 46.71055, 6.37472* **Camping Pré Sous Ville, 10 Rue des Fontaines, 1337 Vallorbe [021 8432309; yvan.favre@vallorbe.com]** Foll camping sp in town. Med, mkd pitch, pt shd; wc; chem disp; mv service pnt; shwrs inc; EHU (10A) CHF5; gas; lndry; rest, snacks adj; bar; playgrnd; htd pool adj; fishing; tennis; games area; 20% statics; dogs; Eng spkn; quiet; red CKE/CCI. "Gd, clean facs; gd size pitches; site yourself if warden absent; conv for Vallée de Joux, Lake Geneva & Jura; views down valley." ♦ 15 Apr-15 Oct. CHF 37.00 2016*

VESENAZ see Genève *C1*

VETROZ see Sion *C2*

> **"There aren't many sites open at this time of year"**
>
> If you're travelling outside peak season remember to call ahead to check site opening dates – even if the entry says 'open all year'.

⊞ **VILLENEUVE** *C1 (5km W Rural) 46.39333, 6.89527* **Camping Les Grangettes, Rue des Grangettes, 1845 Noville [021 9601503; fax 9602030; noville@treyvaud.com; www.les-grangettes.ch]** Fr N9 Montreux-Aigle rd, take Villeneuve exit, at end slip rd turn N twds Villeneuve. At 1st traff lts turn L to Noville, turn R by PO, site sp. Narr app rd. Med, mkd pitch, unshd; htd wc; chem disp; mv service pnt; shwrs; EHU (10A) CHF4; lndry; shop on site & 3km; rest, snacks; bar; pool 3km; lake sw; fishing; boating; 80% statics; dogs CHF3; phone; sep car park; Eng spkn; quiet. "Beautifully situated on SE corner Lake Geneva o'looking Montreux; sep tourer area; poss noisy in high ssn." ♦ CHF 50.00 2014*

VILLENEUVE *C1 (12km W Rural) 46.38666, 6.86055* **Camping Rive-Bleue, Bouveret-Plage, 1897 Le Bouveret [024 4812161; fax 4812108; info@camping-rive-bleue.ch; www.camping-rive-bleue.ch]** Fr Montreux foll sp to Evian to S side of Lake Geneva. Turn R after sp 'Bienvenue Bouveret'. Foll camp sp to Aqua Park. Site on R approx 1km fr main rd. Lge, mkd pitch, pt shd; wc; chem disp; mv service pnt; shwrs inc; EHU (10A) CHF4.20 (adaptor avail - check earth); gas; lndry; rest & snacks adj; shop; playgrnd; pool adj; waterslide; lake sw; watersports; tennis; 20% statics; dogs CHF2.60; wifi; sep car park; Eng spkn; adv bkg; quiet; CKE/CCI. "Well-maintained, well-ordered, completely flat site in lovely setting on lake; friendly staff; water/waste pnts scarce; vg facs but red LS; 15 mins walk to vill with supmkt; conv ferries around Lake Geneva; cars must be parked in sep public car park; gd cyling area; free bicycles for 4 hrs fr vill; 1st class san block." 1 Apr-12 Oct. CHF 43.00 2014*

VIRA GAMBAROGNO see Locarno *C3*

VISP *C2 (1.6km NW Rural) 46.29730, 7.87269* **Camping Schwimmbad Mühleye, 3930 Visp [027 9462084; fax 9463469; info@camping-visp.ch; www.camping-visp.ch]** Exit main rd E2 at W end of town bet Esso petrol stn & rv bdge at Camping sp. Site nr pool. Lge, pt shd; wc; chem disp; shwrs; EHU (13A) CHF3.50; gas; lndry; shops 500m; snacks; bar; playgrnd; lge pool adj; tennis; fishing; 20% statics; dogs CHF2; Eng spkn; some noise fr rlwy & sometimes rifle range; red long stay/LS/CKE/CCI. "Gd for Zermatt & Matterhorn; recep at sw pool ent; gd value espec LS; suitable lge o'fits." 10 Mar-31 Oct. CHF 35.00 2015*

VITZNAU *B3 (500m SE Rural) 47.00683, 8.48621* **Camping Vitznau, Altdorfstrasse, 6354 Vitznau [041 3971280; fax 3972457; info@camping-vitznau.ch; www.camping-vitznau.ch]** On E edge of Vitznau, sp. Fr Küssnacht twd Brunnen turn L at RC church with tall clock tower. Lge, terr, hdstg, pt shd; wc; chem disp; mv service pnt; shwrs inc; EHU (16A) CHF4 (adaptors on loan); gas; lndry; shop & 500m; bar; pool; lake sw & beach 500m; tennis; 40% statics; dogs CHF5; Quickstop o'night facs CHF20; poss cr; Eng spkn; adv bkg rec; quiet; card acc; red LS; ccard acc; red long stay; CKE/CCI. "Excel, v clean, family-run site; friendly owner will help with pitching; max c'van length 7m high ssn; sm pitches; some site rds tight & steep; recep closes 1830 hrs; fine views lakes & mountains; many activities inc walking; gd dog-walking; conv ferry terminal, cable cars & mountain rlwy (tickets avail on site); gd saving by using 'tell-pass'; lake steamer to Luzern 500m; gd pool, sm shop." ♦ ltd. 1 Apr-1 Oct. CHF 54.00 SBS - S05 2016*

WABERN see Bern *B2*

WAGENHAUSEN see Schaffhausen *A3*

WILDERSWIL see Interlaken *C2*

⊞ **WINTERTHUR** *A3 (3km N Rural) 47.51965, 8.71655* **Camping am Schützenweiher, Eichliwaldstrasse 4, 8400 Winterthur [tel/fax 052 2125260; camping platz@win.ch; www.camping-winterthur.info]** Fr A1/E60 exit Winterthur-Ohringen dir Winterthur, turn R & foll site sp, site adj police stn in about 200m. Sm, shd; htd wc; chem disp; shwrs CHF1; EHU CHF3; gas; lndry; shops adj; rest; playgrnd; pool 3km; 8% statics; dogs CHF4; phone; poss cr; Eng spkn; some m'way noise; red CKE/CCI. "Helpful owner; office open 1900-2000 to register & pay; find own pitch outside these hrs; sm pitches; NH only." CHF 37.00 2016*

YVONAND see Yverdon *B1*

ZERMATT *D2* (6km N Rural) *46.06450, 7.77500* **Camping Alphubel, 3929 Täsch (Wallis) [027 9673635; welcome@campingtaesch.ch; www.campingtaesch.ch]** Turn down R-hand slip rd over level x-ing & bdge after rlwy stn in Täsch, & foll sp to site. S bend bdge poss diff for lge o'fits at app. Med, unshd; htd wc; chem disp; mv service pnt; shwrs inc; EHU (10A) CHF5 (long lead poss req); lndry; shops 200m; rest adj; htd pool 1km; tennis; fishing; dogs CHF2; recep clsd 1200-1400; poss cr; Eng spkn; no adv bkg; quiet but rlwy noise; ccard not acc. "Conv for frequent train to Zermatt fr vill; superb scenery & walking; helpful owner; vg, modern san facs; excel." 8 May-14 Oct. CHF 49.00 2013*

ZURICH *A3* (4km S Rural) *47.33633, 8.54167* **Camping Seebucht, Seestrasse 559, 8038 Zürich-Wollishofen [044 4821612; fax 4821660; 2008@camping-zurich.ch; www.camping-zurich.ch]** Fr city foll rd 3 (twd Chur) on S side of lake; foll camping sp. Lge, hdstg, pt shd; wc; chem disp; mv service pnt; shwrs CHF2; EHU (6A) CHF5; gas; lndry; shop; rest, snacks; bar; BBQ; playgrnd; pool 3km; lake sw; watersports; fishing; tennis; 80% statics; dogs CHF5; bus; poss cr & noisy; Eng spkn; rd & rlwy noise. "Parking in Zürich v diff, use bus; sm area for tourers; conv NH, v sm pitches." ♦ 1 May-30 Sep. CHF 39.00 2012*

⊞ **ZWEISIMMEN** *C2* (1km N Rural) *46.56338, 7.37691* **Camping Fankhauser, Ey Gässli 2, 3770 Zweisimmen [033 7221356; fax 7221351; info@camping-fankhauser.ch; www.camping-fankhauser.ch]** N6 exit Spiez, then foll sp Zweisimmen. On o'skts of town turn L at camping sp immed bef Agip petrol stn, site on L immed after rlwy x-ing. Med, pt sl; htd wc; chem disp; mv service pnt; shwrs CHF0.50; EHU (10A) CHF3.50 or metered; lndry; shop 1km; rest, snacks, bar 1km; BBQ; playgrnd; pool 800m; fishing; golf; 90% statics; dogs free; phone; Eng spkn; adv bkg; some rlwy noise & glider tow planes at w/end; CKE/CCI. "Gd NH." CHF 28.00 2016*

"That's changed – Should I let The Club know?"

If you find something on site that's different from the site entry, fill in a report and let us know. See camc.com/europereport.

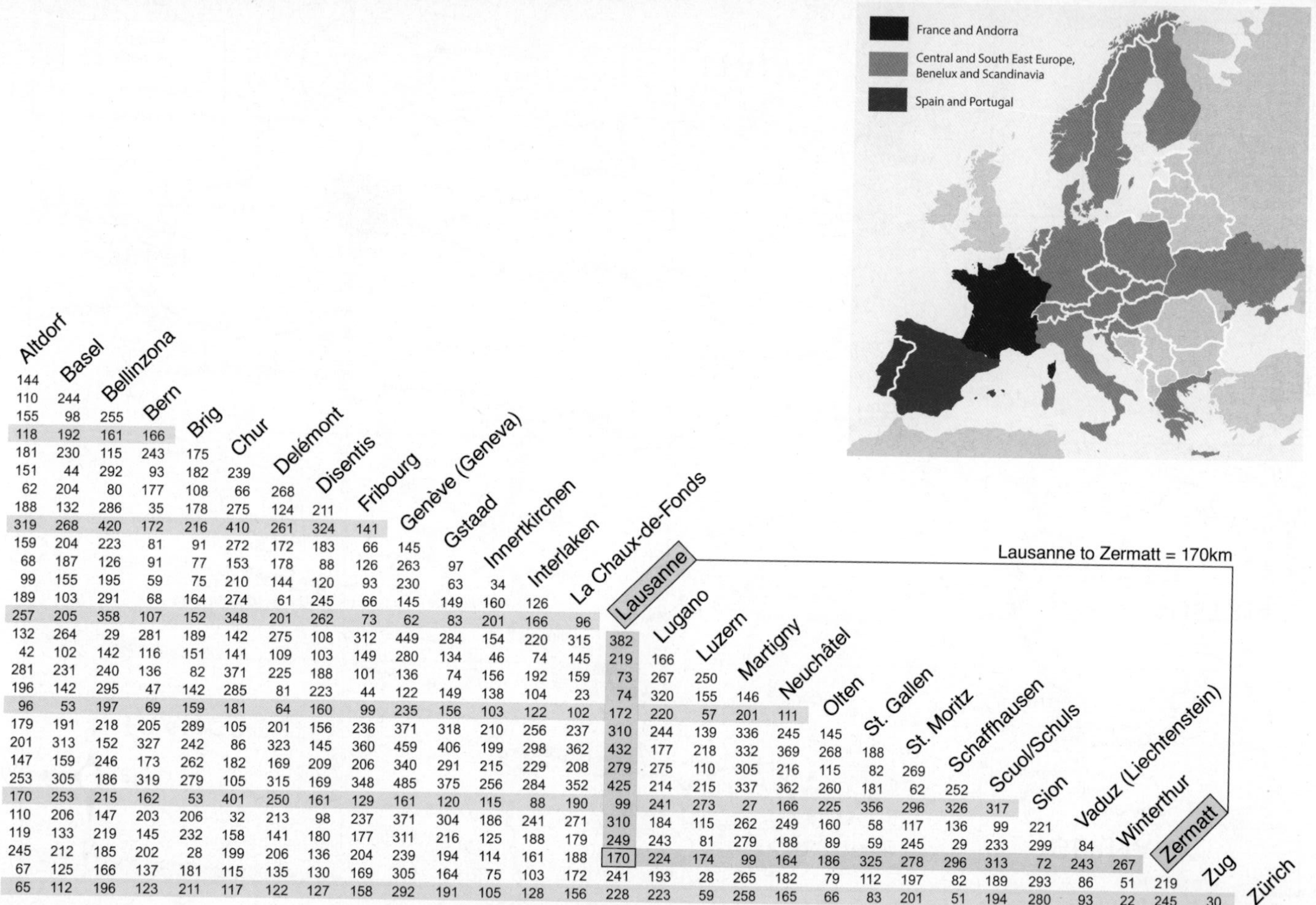

	Altdorf	Basel	Bellinzona	Bern	Brig	Chur	Delémont	Disentis	Fribourg	Genève (Geneva)	Gstaad	Innertkirchen	Interlaken	La Chaux-de-Fonds	Lausanne	Lugano	Luzern	Martigny	Neuchâtel	Olten	St. Gallen	St. Moritz	Schaffhausen	Scuol/Schuls	Sion	Vaduz (Liechtenstein)	Winterthur	Zermatt	Zug
Basel	144																												
Bellinzona	110	244																											
Bern	155	98	255																										
Brig	118	192	161	166																									
Chur	181	230	115	243	175																								
Delémont	151	44	292	93	182	239																							
Disentis	62	204	80	177	108	66	268																						
Fribourg	188	132	286	35	178	275	124	211																					
Genève (Geneva)	319	268	420	172	216	410	261	324	141																				
Gstaad	159	204	223	81	91	272	172	183	66	145																			
Innertkirchen	68	187	126	91	77	153	178	88	126	263	97																		
Interlaken	99	155	195	59	75	210	144	120	93	230	63	34																	
La Chaux-de-Fonds	189	103	291	68	164	274	61	245	66	145	149	160	126																
Lausanne	257	205	358	107	152	348	201	262	73	62	83	201	166	96															
Lugano	132	264	29	281	189	142	275	108	312	449	284	154	220	315	382														
Luzern	42	102	142	116	151	141	109	103	149	280	134	46	74	145	219	166													
Martigny	281	231	240	136	82	371	225	188	101	136	74	156	192	159	73	267	250												
Neuchâtel	196	142	295	47	142	285	81	223	44	122	149	138	104	23	74	320	155	146											
Olten	96	53	197	69	159	181	64	160	99	235	156	103	122	102	172	220	57	201	111										
St. Gallen	179	191	218	205	289	105	201	156	236	371	318	210	256	237	310	244	139	336	245	145									
St. Moritz	201	313	152	327	242	86	323	145	360	459	406	199	298	362	432	177	218	332	369	268	188								
Schaffhausen	147	159	246	173	262	182	169	209	206	340	291	215	229	208	279	275	110	305	216	115	82	269							
Scuol/Schuls	253	305	186	319	279	105	315	169	348	485	375	256	284	352	425	214	215	337	362	260	181	62	252						
Sion	170	253	215	162	53	401	250	161	129	161	120	115	88	190	99	241	273	27	166	225	356	296	326	317					
Vaduz (Liechtenstein)	110	206	147	203	206	32	213	98	237	371	304	186	241	271	310	184	115	262	249	160	58	117	136	99	221				
Winterthur	119	133	219	145	232	158	141	180	177	311	216	125	188	179	249	243	81	279	188	89	59	245	29	233	299	84			
Zermatt	245	212	185	202	28	199	206	136	204	239	194	114	161	188	170	224	174	99	164	186	325	278	296	313	72	243	267		
Zug	67	125	166	137	181	115	135	130	169	305	164	75	103	172	241	193	28	265	182	79	112	197	82	189	293	86	51	219	
Zürich	65	112	196	123	211	117	122	127	158	292	191	105	128	156	228	223	59	258	165	66	83	201	51	194	280	93	22	245	30

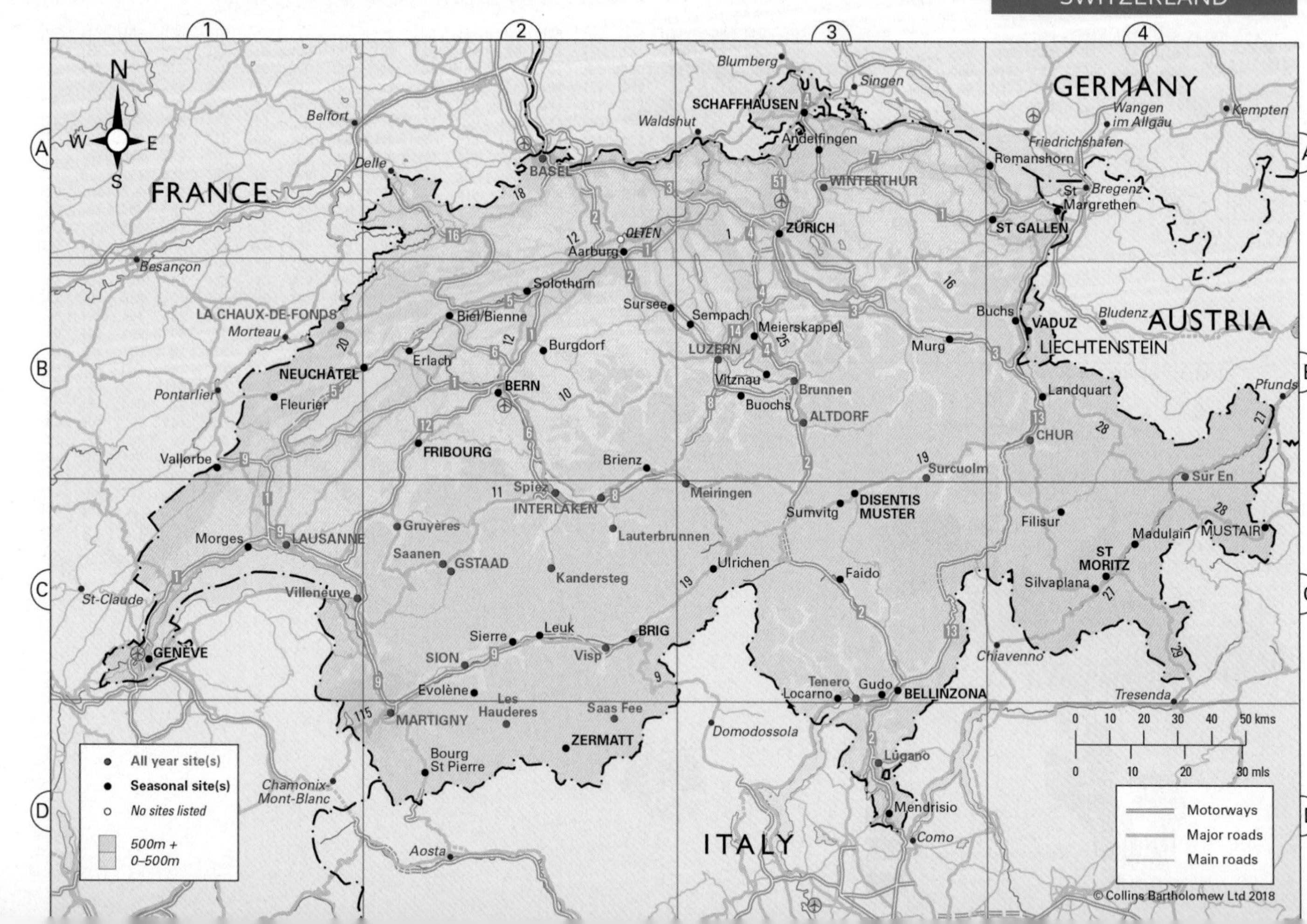

GERMANY
AUSTRIA
LIECHTENSTEIN
FRANCE
ITALY
N
E
S
W
A
B
C
D
1
2
3
4
Kempten
Wangen im Allgäu
Friedrichshafen
Romanshorn
Bregenz
St Margrethen
ST GALLEN
VADUZ
Buchs
Bludenz
Landquart
CHUR
Pfunds
Sur En
MUSTAIR
Madulain
ST MORITZ
Silvaplana
Filisur
Tresenda
Chiavenno
Singen
Blumberg
SCHAFFHAUSEN
Andelfingen
WINTERTHUR
ZÜRICH
Murg
Surcuolm
DISENTIS MUSTER
Sumvitg
Faido
BELLINZONA
Gudo
Tenero
Locarno
Lugano
Mendrisio
Como
Domodossola
Waldshut
Meierskappel
Brunnen
ALTDORF
Buchs
Vitznau
Sempach
LUZERN
Meiringen
Ulrichen
Lauterbrunnen
BRIG
Visp
Saas Fee
ZERMATT
Sursee
OLTEN
Aarburg
Burgdorf
Solothurn
Brienz
INTERLAKEN
Spiez
Kandersteg
Leuk
BASEL
Biel/Bienne
BERN
FRIBOURG
Erlach
Gruyères
Saanen
GSTAAD
Sierre
SION
Evolène
Les Hauderes
MARTIGNY
Bourg St Pierre
Aosta
Delle
Belfort
LA CHAUX-DE-FONDS
NEUCHÂTEL
Fleurier
Morteau
LAUSANNE
Villeneuve
Morges
Vallorbe
Pontarlier
Besançon
GENÈVE
St-Claude
Chamonix-Mont-Blanc
0
10
20
30
40
50 kms
30 mls
Motorways
Major roads
Main roads
© Collins Bartholomew Ltd 2018
All year site(s)
Seasonal site(s)
No sites listed
500m +
0–500m

Site Report Form

If campsite is already listed, complete only those sections of the form where changes apply or alternatively use the Abbreviated Site Report form on the following pages.

Sites not reported on for 5 years may be deleted from the guide

Year of guide used	20 18	Is site listed?	Listed on page no...........	Unlisted (circled)	Date of visit	14-15 / 6 / 18

A – CAMPSITE NAME AND LOCATION

Country	Italy	Name of town/village site listed under *(see Sites Location Maps)*	CORVARA *		
Distance & direction from centre of town site is listed under *(in a straight line)*	2 km	eg N, NE, S, SW: W	Urban	Rural: ✓	Coastal
Site open all year?	Y / N	Period site is open *(if not all year)*	......../........ to ..../........		
Site name	C. Colfosco			Naturist site	Y / N (N circled)
Site address					
Telephone		Fax			
E-mail		Website			

B – CAMPSITE CHARGES

Charge for outfit + 2 adults in local currency	PRICE		EL PNTS inc in this price?	Y / N	Amps.........

C – DIRECTIONS

Brief, specific directions to site (in km) *To convert miles to kilometres multiply by 8 and divide by 5 or use Conversion Table in guide*	Leave A22 (m'way from Brenner) at Bressanone exit. Follow E66/S49 E. At San Lorenzo, ~~turn S~~ on S244 for 28km to Corvara. In town turn R, dir Passo Gardena. Site on L in 2km sp.
GPS	Latitude 46.550697 (eg 12.34567) Longitude 11.859960 (eg 1.23456 or -1.23456)

D – CAMPSITE DESCRIPTION

SITE size ie number of pitches	Small Max 50	SM	Medium 51-150	MED	Large 151-500	LGE	Very large 500+	V LGE	Unchanged

PITCH size	eg small, medium, large, very large, various	Unchanged

Pitch features if **NOT** open-plan/grassy	Hedged	HDG PITCH	Marked or numbered	MKD PITCH	Hardstanding or gravel	HDSTG (circled)	Unchanged
If site is **NOT** level, is it	Part sloping	PT SL	Sloping	SL	Terraced	TERR	Unchanged
Is site shaded?	Shaded	SHD	Part shaded	PT SHD	Unshaded	UNSHD (circled)	Unchanged

E – CAMPSITE FACILITIES

WC	Heated	HTD WC	Continental	CONT	Own San recommended	OWN SAN REC
Chemical disposal point	CHEM DISP (circled)	Dedicated point	✓	WC only		
Motorhome waste discharge and water refill point		MV SERVICE PNT	✓			
Child / baby facilities (bathroom)	CHILD / BABY FACS ✓	Family bathroom		FAM BTHRM		
Hot shower(s)	SHWR(S) (circled)	Inc in site fee?	Y (circled) / N	Price..................*(if not inc)*		
ELECTRIC HOOK UP *if not included in price above*	EL PNTS metered	Price..............................		Amps..............................		
Supplies of bottled gas	GAS	On site	Y / N	Or in .... Kms		
Launderette / Washing Machine	LNDTTE (circled)	Inc dryer Y (circled) / N		LNDRY RM *(if no washing machine)*		

You can also complete forms online: camc.com/europereport

CUT ALONG DOTTED LINE

F – FOOD & DRINK

MINI MKT

Shop(s) / supermarket	SHOP(S) / SUPMKT	On site		or	.... kms
Bread / milk delivered	TRADSMN ✓				
Restaurant / cafeteria	REST ✓	On site		or	.... kms
Snack bar / take-away	SNACKS	On site		or	.... kms
Bar	BAR ✓	On site		or	.... kms
Barbecue allowed	BBQ ✓	Charcoal	Gas	Elec	Sep area
Cooking facilities	COOKING FACS				

G – LEISURE FACILITIES

Playground	PLAYGRND					
Swimming pool	POOL	On site		or ....km	Heated	Covered
Beach	BEACH	Adj		or ....km	Sand	Shingle
Alternative swimming *(lake)*	SW	Adj		or ....km	Sand	Shingle
Games /sports area / Games room	GAMES AREA	GAMES ROOM				
Entertainment in high season	ENTMNT					
Internet use by visitors	INTERNET	Wifi Internet		WIFI ✓		
Television room	TV RM	Satellite / Cable to pitches		TV CAB / SAT		

H – OTHER INFORMATION

% Static caravans / mobile homes / chalets / cottages / fixed tents on site				............% STATICS
Dogs allowed	DOGS	Y / N	Price per night .... *(if allowed)*	
Phone	PHONE	On site	Adj	
Bus / tram / train	BUS / TRAM / TRAIN	Adj	or .... km	
Twin axles caravans allowed?	TWIN AXLES Y / N	Possibly crowded in high season		POSS CR
English spoken	ENG SPKN ✓			
Advance bookings accepted	ADV BKG ✓	Y / N		
Noise levels on site in season	NOISY / QUIET ✓	If noisy, why?		
Credit card accepted	CCARD ACC	Reduction low season		RED LOW SSN
Camping Key Europe or Camping Card International accepted in lieu of passport	CKE/CCI	INF card required *(If naturist site)*		Y / N
Facilities for disabled	Full wheelchair facilities	♦	Limited disabled facilities	♦ ltd

I – ADDITIONAL REMARKS AND/OR ITEMS OF INTEREST

Tourist attractions, unusual features or other facilities, eg waterslide, tennis, cycle hire, watersports, horseriding, separate car park, walking distance to shops etc * new dot needed on map for Corvara SSW of Bruneck. 5000ft – cool nights!	YOUR OPINION OF THE SITE: EXCEL VERY GOOD ✓ GOOD FAIR / POOR NIGHT HALT ONLY
Your comments & opinions may be used in future editions of the guide, if you do not wish them to be used please tick	

J – MEMBER DETAILS

ARE YOU A:	Caravanner		Motorhomer	✓	Trailer-tenter?	
NAME:			MEMBERSHIP NO:			
			POST CODE:			
DO YOU NEED MORE BLANK SITE REPORT FORMS?			YES		NO	

Please use a separate form for each campsite and do not send receipts. Owing to the large number of site reports received, it is not possible to enter into correspondence. Please return completed form to:

The Editor, Overseas Touring Guides, East Grinstead House
East Grinstead, West Sussex RH19 1UA

Please note that due to changes in the rules regarding freepost we are no longer able to provide a freepost address for the return of Site Report Forms. You can still supply your site reports free online by visiting camc.com/europereport. We apologise for any inconvenience this may cause.

Site Report Form

If campsite is already listed, complete only those sections of the form where changes apply or alternatively use the Abbreviated Site Report form on the following pages.

Sites not reported on for 5 years may be deleted from the guide

Year of guide used	20.........	Is site listed?	Listed on page no...........	Unlisted	Date of visit	......../......../........

A – CAMPSITE NAME AND LOCATION

Country		Name of town/village site listed under *(see Sites Location Maps)*			
Distance & direction from centre of town site is listed under *(in a straight line)*	..................km	eg N, NE, S, SW	Urban	Rural	Coastal
Site open all year?	Y / N	Period site is open *(if not all year)*	................./................. to ..../.................		
Site name				Naturist site	Y / N
Site address					
Telephone		Fax			
E-mail		Website			

B – CAMPSITE CHARGES

Charge for outfit + 2 adults in local currency	PRICE		EL PNTS inc in this price?	Y / N	Amps ....

C – DIRECTIONS

Brief, specific directions to site (in km) *To convert miles to kilometres multiply by 8 and divide by 5 or use Conversion Table in guide*	
GPS	Latitude..*(eg 12.34567)* Longitude..*(eg 1.23456 or -1.23456)*

D – CAMPSITE DESCRIPTION

SITE size ie number of pitches	Small Max 50	SM	Medium 51-150	MED	Large 151-500	LGE	Very large 500+	V LGE	Unchanged

PITCH size	*eg small, medium, large, very large, various*	Unchanged

Pitch features if **NOT** open-plan/grassy	Hedged	HDG PITCH	Marked or numbered	MKD PITCH	Hardstanding or gravel	HDSTG	Unchanged
If site is **NOT** level, is it	Part sloping	PT SL	Sloping	SL	Terraced	TERR	Unchanged
Is site shaded?	Shaded	SHD	Part shaded	PT SHD	Unshaded	UNSHD	Unchanged

E – CAMPSITE FACILITIES

WC	Heated	HTD WC	Continental	CONT	Own San recommended	OWN SAN REC

Chemical disposal point	CHEM DISP	Dedicated point		WC only	
Motorhome waste discharge and water refill point		MV SERVICE PNT			
Child / baby facilities (bathroom)	CHILD / BABY FACS	Family bathroom		FAM BTHRM	
Hot shower(s)	SHWR(S)	Inc in site fee?	Y / N	Price..................*(if not inc)*	
ELECTRIC HOOK UP *if not included in price above*	EL PNTS	Price....................................		Amps....................................	
Supplies of bottled gas	GAS	On site	Y / N	Or in .... Kms	
Launderette / Washing Machine	LNDTTE	Inc dryer Y / N		LNDRY RM *(if no washing machine)*	

You can also complete forms online: camc.com/europereport

CUT ALONG DOTTED LINE

F – FOOD & DRINK

Shop(s) / supermarket	SHOP(S) / SUPMKT	On site		or	.... kms
Bread / milk delivered	TRADSMN				
Restaurant / cafeteria	REST	On site		or	.... kms
Snack bar / take-away	SNACKS	On site		or	.... kms
Bar	BAR	On site		or	.... kms
Barbecue allowed	BBQ	Charcoal	Gas	Elec	Sep area
Cooking facilities	COOKING FACS				

G – LEISURE FACILITIES

Playground	PLAYGRND					
Swimming pool	POOL	On site		or ....km	Heated	Covered
Beach	BEACH	Adj		or ....km	Sand	Shingle
Alternative swimming *(lake)*	SW	Adj		or ....km	Sand	Shingle
Games /sports area / Games room	GAMES AREA	GAMES ROOM				
Entertainment in high season	ENTMNT					
Internet use by visitors	INTERNET	Wifi Internet		WIFI		
Television room	TV RM	Satellite / Cable to pitches		TV CAB / SAT		

H – OTHER INFORMATION

% Static caravans / mobile homes / chalets / cottages / fixed tents on site				.............% STATICS
Dogs allowed	DOGS	Y / N	Price per night .... *(if allowed)*	
Phone	PHONE	On site	Adj	
Bus / tram / train	BUS / TRAM / TRAIN	Adj	or .... km	
Twin axles caravans allowed?	TWIN AXLES Y / N	Possibly crowded in high season		POSS CR
English spoken	ENG SPKN			
Advance bookings accepted	ADV BKG	Y / N		
Noise levels on site in season	NOISY / QUIET	If noisy, why?		
Credit card accepted	CCARD ACC	Reduction low season		RED LOW SSN
Camping Key Europe or Camping Card International accepted in lieu of passport	CKE/CCI	INF card required *(If naturist site)*		Y / N
Facilities for disabled	Full wheelchair facilities	♦	Limited disabled facilities	♦ ltd

I – ADDITIONAL REMARKS AND/OR ITEMS OF INTEREST

Tourist attractions, unusual features or other facilities, eg waterslide, tennis, cycle hire, watersports, horseriding, separate car park, walking distance to shops etc	YOUR OPINION OF THE SITE:
Cycle tracks, mountain walks from site.	EXCEL
	VERY GOOD (circled)
	GOOD
	FAIR / POOR
	NIGHT HALT ONLY

Your comments & opinions may be used in future editions of the guide, if you do not wish them to be used please tick ....

J – MEMBER DETAILS

ARE YOU A:	Caravanner		Motorhomer		Trailer-tenter?	
NAME:			MEMBERSHIP NO:			
			POST CODE:			
DO YOU NEED MORE BLANK SITE REPORT FORMS?			YES		NO	

Please use a separate form for each campsite and do not send receipts. Owing to the large number of site reports received, it is not possible to enter into correspondence. Please return completed form to:

The Editor, Overseas Touring Guides, East Grinstead House
East Grinstead, West Sussex RH19 1UA

Please note that due to changes in the rules regarding freepost we are no longer able to provide a freepost address for the return of Site Report Forms. You can still supply your site reports free online by visiting camc.com/europereport. We apologise for any inconvenience this may cause.

Abbreviated Site Report Form

Use this abbreviated Site Report Form if you have visited a number of sites and there are no changes (or only small changes) to their entries in the guide. If reporting on a new site, or reporting several changes, please use the full version of the report form. **If advising prices,** these should be for an outfit, and 2 adults for one night's stay. **Please indicate high or low season prices and whether electricity is included.**

Remember, if you don't tell us about sites you have visited, they may eventually be deleted from the guide. ✓ 16/7/18

Year of guide used	20 18	Page No.	129	Name of town/village site listed under	ROCHEFORT
Site Name	Communal Les Roches			Date of visit	23/5/18
GPS	Latitude.....(eg 12.34567)	Longitude.....(eg 1.23456 or -1.23456)			

Site is in: Andorra / Austria / (Belgium) / Croatia / Czech Republic / Denmark / Finland / France / Germany / Greece / Hungary / Italy / Luxembourg / Netherlands / Norway / Poland / Portugal / Slovakia / Slovenia / Spain / Sweden / Switzerland

Comments: As described. ACSI site

Charge for outfit + 2 adults in local currency	High Season	Low Season	Elec inc in price?	(Y) / N	.....amps
		€13.50	Price of elec (if not inc)		.....amps

Year of guide used	20 18	Page No.	253	Name of town/village site listed under	NENNIG
Site Name	Dreiländereck			Date of visit	24-25/5/18
GPS	Latitude.....(eg 12.34567)	Longitude.....(eg 1.23456 or -1.23456)			

Site is in: Andorra / Austria / Belgium / Croatia / Czech Republic / Denmark / Finland / France / (Germany) / Greece / Hungary / Italy / Luxembourg / Netherlands / Norway / Poland / Portugal / Slovakia / Slovenia / Spain / Sweden / Switzerland

Comments: As described. ✓ 16/7/18

Charge for outfit + 2 adults in local currency	High Season	Low Season	Elec inc in price?	(Y) / N	.....amps
		€ 18.30	Price of elec (if not inc)		.....amps

Year of guide used	20 18	Page No.	238	Name of town/village site listed under	Illertissen
Site Name	Camping Illertissen			Date of visit	26-27/5/18
GPS	Latitude.....(eg 12.34567)	Longitude.....(eg 1.23456 or -1.23456)			

Site is in: Andorra / Austria / Belgium / Croatia / Czech Republic / Denmark / Finland / France / (Germany) / Greece / Hungary / Italy / Luxembourg / Netherlands / Norway / Poland / Portugal / Slovakia / Slovenia / Spain / Sweden / Switzerland

Comments: As described. ACSI site. ✓ 16/7/18

Charge for car, caravan & 2 adults in local currency	High Season	Low Season	Elec inc in price?	(Y) / N	.....amps
		€ 19.00	Price of elec (if not inc)		.....amps

Please fill in your details and send to the address on the reverse of this form.
You can also complete forms online: camc.com/europereport

✂ CUT ALONG DOTTED LINE

Year of guide used	20 18	Page No.	98	Name of town/village site listed under	GRÄN
Site Name	Comfort Camping Grän			Date of visit	28-31 / 5 / 18
GPS	Latitude...........(eg 12.34567)	Longitude...........(eg 1.23456 or -1.23456)			

Site is in: Andorra / (Austria) / Belgium / Croatia / Czech Republic / Denmark / Finland / France / Germany / Greece / Hungary / Italy / Luxembourg / Netherlands / Norway / Poland / Portugal / Slovakia / Slovenia / Spain / Sweden / Switzerland

Comments: As described. ACSI site 16/7/18 ✓

Charge for outfit + 2 adults in local currency	High Season	Low Season €23-90	Elec inc in price?	(Y) / N	............amps
			Price of elec (if not inc)		............amps

Year of guide used	20 18	Page No.	105	Name of town/village site listed under	OETZ
Site Name	Ötztal Arena Camp Krismer			Date of visit	1-3 / 6 / 18
GPS	Latitude...........(eg 12.34567)	Longitude...........(eg 1.23456 or -1.23456)			

Site is in: Andorra / (Austria) / Belgium / Croatia / Czech Republic / Denmark / Finland / France / Germany / Greece / Hungary / Italy / Luxembourg / Netherlands / Norway / Poland / Portugal / Slovakia / Slovenia / Spain / Sweden / Switzerland

Comments: As described. 19/7/18 ✓ €22.50?

Charge for outfit + 2 adults in local currency	High Season	Low Season €	Elec inc in price?	(Y) / N	............amps
			Price of elec (if not inc)		............amps

Year of guide used	20 18	Page No.	352	Name of town/village site listed under	SAN VALENTINO ALLA MUTA
Site Name	Camping Thöni			Date of visit	4-5 / 6 / 18
GPS	Latitude...........(eg 12.34567)	Longitude...........(eg 1.23456 or -1.23456)			

Site is in: Andorra / Austria / Belgium / Croatia / Czech Republic / Denmark / Finland / France / Germany / Greece / Hungary / (Italy) / Luxembourg / Netherlands / Norway / Poland / Portugal / Slovakia / Slovenia / Spain / Sweden / Switzerland

Comments: As described. 19/7/18 ✓

Charge for outfit + 2 adults in local currency	High Season	Low Season €23-80	Elec inc in price?	(Y) / N	............amps
			Price of elec (if not inc)		............amps

Your comments & opinions may be used in future editions of the guide, if you do not wish them to be used please tick ....

Name ....

Membership No. ....

Post Code ....

Are you a Caravanner / Motorhomer / Trailer-Tenter?

Do you need more blank Site Report forms? YES / NO

Please return completed forms to:
The Editor – Overseas Touring Guides
East Grinstead House
East Grinstead
West Sussex
RH19 1FH
Please note that due to changes in the rules regarding freepost we are no longer able to provide a freepost address for the return of Site Report Forms. You can still supply your site reports free online by visiting camc.com/europereport. We apologise for any inconvenience this may cause.

You can also complete forms online: camc.com/europereport

Abbreviated Site Report Form

Use this abbreviated Site Report Form if you have visited a number of sites and there are no changes (or only small changes) to their entries in the guide. If reporting on a new site, or reporting several changes, please use the full version of the report form. **If advising prices,** these should be for an outfit, and 2 adults for one night's stay. **Please indicate high or low season prices and whether electricity is included.**

Remember, if you don't tell us about sites you have visited, they may eventually be deleted from the guide.

Year of guide used	20 18	Page No.	341	Name of town/village site listed under	MERANO / MERAN
Site Name	C. Hermitage			Date of visit	6-7 / 6 / 18
GPS	Latitude..........(eg 12.34567) Longitude..........(eg 1.23456 or -1.23456)				
Site is in: Andorra / Austria / Belgium / Croatia / Czech Republic / Denmark / Finland / France / Germany / Greece / Hungary / Italy (circled) / Luxembourg / Netherlands / Norway / Poland / Portugal / Slovakia / Slovenia / Spain / Sweden / Switzerland					
Comments: As described. ACSI site 19/7/18 ✓					
Charge for outfit + 2 adults in local currency	High Season	Low Season €24.70	Elec inc in price?	Y (circled) / N	............amps
			Price of elec (if not inc)		............amps

Year of guide used	20 18	Page No.	349	Name of town/village site listed under	PREDAZZO
Site Name	C. Valle Verde			Date of visit	8-10 / 6 / 18
GPS	Latitude..........(eg 12.34567) Longitude..........(eg 1.23456 or -1.23456)				
Site is in: Andorra / Austria / Belgium / Croatia / Czech Republic / Denmark / Finland / France / Germany / Greece / Hungary / Italy (circled) / Luxembourg / Netherlands / Norway / Poland / Portugal / Slovakia / Slovenia / Spain / Sweden / Switzerland					
Comments: Fr Predazzo take SS50 E. Many attractions only open late June. Otherwise as described. ACSI site 19/7/18 ✓					
Charge for outfit + 2 adults in local currency	High Season	Low Season €21.00	Elec inc in price?	Y (circled) / N	............amps
			Price of elec (if not inc)		............amps

Year of guide used	20 18	Page No.	348	Name of town/village site listed under	POZZA DI FASSA
Site Name	C. Catinaccio Rosengarten			Date of visit	11-13 / 6 / 18
GPS	Latitude..........(eg 12.34567) Longitude..........(eg 1.23456 or -1.23456)				
Site is in: Andorra / Austria / Belgium / Croatia / Czech Republic / Denmark / Finland / France / Germany / Greece / Hungary / Italy (circled) / Luxembourg / Netherlands / Norway / Poland / Portugal / Slovakia / Slovenia / Spain / Sweden / Switzerland					
Comments: Free taxi to cable car still offered (2018) As described 19/7/18 ✓					
Charge for car, caravan & 2 adults in local currency	High Season	Low Season €23-30	Elec inc in price?	Y (circled) / N	............amps
			Price of elec (if not inc)		............amps

Please fill in your details and send to the address on the reverse of this form.

You can also complete forms online: camc.com/europereport

CUT ALONG DOTTED LINE

Year of guide used	20 18	Page No.	108	Name of town/village site listed under	SEEFELD IN TIROL
Site Name	Camping Alpin			Date of visit	16-17 / 6 / 18
GPS	Latitude.....(eg 12.34567) Longitude.....(eg 1.23456 or -1.23456)				
Site is in: Andorra / (Austria) / Belgium / Croatia / Czech Republic / Denmark / Finland / France / Germany / Greece / Hungary / Italy / Luxembourg / Netherlands / Norway / Poland / Portugal / Slovakia / Slovenia / Spain / Sweden / Switzerland					
Comments: free courtesy bus to town & funicular. ACSI price given ✓ 19/7/18					
Charge for outfit + 2 adults in local currency	High Season	Low Season €24.55	Elec inc in price?	Y / (N)	.....amps
			Price of elec (if not inc)	0.80/kWh	.....amps

Year of guide used	20 18	Page No.	246	Name of town/village site listed under	LINDAU (BODENSEE)
Site Name	Park-Camping			Date of visit	18-19 / 6 / 18
GPS	Latitude.....(eg 12.34567) Longitude.....(eg 1.23456 or -1.23456)				
Site is in: Andorra / Austria / Belgium / Croatia / Czech Republic / Denmark / Finland / France / (Germany) / Greece / Hungary / Italy / Luxembourg / Netherlands / Norway / Poland / Portugal / Slovakia / Slovenia / Spain / Sweden / Switzerland					
Comments: NB Korridor scheme round Bregenz abolished. Pfänder tunnel now complete and only Austrian m'way vignette required. Cycle routes from campsite ✓ 19/7/18					
Charge for outfit + 2 adults in local currency	High Season	Low Season €36-00	Elec inc in price?	(Y) / N	10 amps
			Price of elec (if not inc)		.....amps

Year of guide used	20 18	Page No.	270	Name of town/village site listed under	ÜBERLINGEN
Site Name	Camping Nell, Überlingen-Nussdorf			Date of visit	20-21 / 6 / 18
GPS	Latitude.....(eg 12.34567) Longitude.....(eg 1.23456 or -1.23456)				
Site is in: Andorra / Austria / Belgium / Croatia / Czech Republic / Denmark / Finland / France / (Germany) / Greece / Hungary / Italy / Luxembourg / Netherlands / Norway / Poland / Portugal / Slovakia / Slovenia / Spain / Sweden / Switzerland					
Comments: ✓ 19/7/18					
Charge for outfit + 2 adults in local currency	High Season	Low Season €23.50	Elec inc in price?	Y / (N)	.....amps
			Price of elec (if not inc)	0.50/kWh	.....amps

Your comments & opinions may be used in future editions of the guide, if you do not wish them to be used please tick ....

Name .....

Membership No. .....

Post Code .....

Are you a Caravanner / Motorhomer / Trailer-Tenter?

Do you need more blank Site Report forms? YES / NO

Please return completed forms to:
The Editor – Overseas Touring Guides
East Grinstead House
East Grinstead
West Sussex
RH19 1FH
Please note that due to changes in the rules regarding freepost we are no longer able to provide a freepost address for the return of Site Report Forms. You can still supply your site reports free online by visiting camc.com/europereport.
We apologise for any inconvenience this may cause.

You can also complete forms online: camc.com/europereport

Index

Index

M

N

O

P

R

R cont'd

S

T

V

W